Production and Operations Management

An Applied Modern Approach

Joseph S. Martinich
University of Missouri-St. Louis

John Wiley & Sons, Inc.
New York • Chichester • Brisbane • Toronto • Singapore • Weinheim

Acquisitions Editor Beth Lang Golub
Senior Developmental Editor Nancy Perry
Marketing Manager Leslie Hines
Production Manager Charlotte Hyland
Outside Production Management Suzanne Ingrao of Ingrao Associates
Senior Designer Laura Nicholls
Manufacturing Manager Mark Cirillo
Photo Editor Hilary Newman
Senior Illustration Coordinator Anna Melhorn

Cover Photos by: (top) Paul Chesley/Tony Stone Images, New York, Inc.
(center) Mark Joseph/Tony Stone Images, New York, Inc.
(bottom) Charles Thatcher/Tony Stone Images, New York, Inc.

This book was set in 10/12 pt Noverese by Ruttle, Shaw, and Wetherill and printed and bound by Von Hoffmann Press. The cover was printed by Phoenix Color.

Recognizing the importance of preserving what has been written, it is a policy of John Wiley & Sons, Inc. to have books of enduring value published in the United States printed on acid-free paper, and we exert our best efforts to that end.

Library of Congress Cataloging in Publication Data

Martinich, Joseph Stanislaus, 1950–
Production and operations management : an applied modern approach / by Joseph S. Martinich.
p. cm.
includes bibliographical references and index.
ISBN 0–471–54632–1 (cloth : alk. paper)
1. Production management. 2. Industrial engineering. I. Title.
TS155.M3345 1997
658.5—dc20 96–28170
CIP

Printed in the United States of America

10 9 8 7 6 5 4 3 2 1

ABOUT THE AUTHOR

To Vicki: My wife and pipeline to computer technology

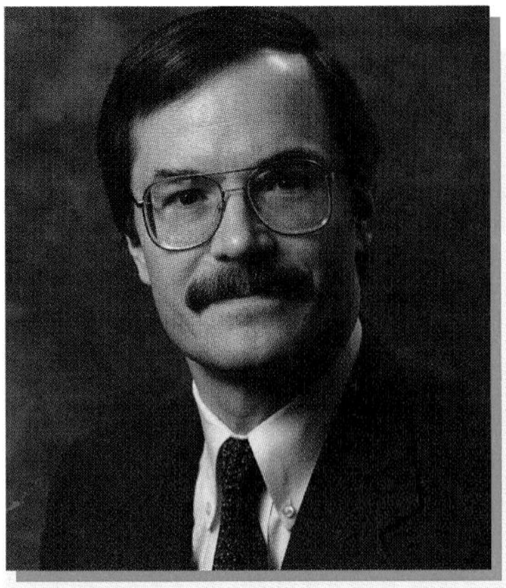

Joseph S. Martinich is Professor of Operations Management at the University of Missouri-St. Louis. He holds a B.S. degree in Industrial Engineering from Northwestern University; an M.A. in Economics from California State University-Fullerton; and a Ph.D. in Industrial Engineering and Management Sciences from Northwestern University. He has worked and/or consulted for companies in the steel, oil and chemical, paperboard and packaging, retail, business services, and publishing industries, as well as for governmental and not-for-profit organizations. He has held visiting and adjunct faculty positions at the John M. Olin School of Business Administration of Washington University (St. Louis), the Engineering Management Department of the University of Missouri-Rolla, and the Industrial Engineering Department of California State Polytechnic University-Pomona.

Dr. Martinich is the co-author (with Arthur P. Hurter) of the book *Facility Location and the Theory of Production* (Kluwer Academic), and he is the author of nearly 20 scholarly articles and reviews. His work has appeared in leading journals, such as *Decision Sciences*, *European Journal of Operational Research*, *Naval Research Logistics*, *American Economic Review*, *Journal of Regional Science*, and *Technological Forecasting and Social Change*. His early research focused on the interrelationship between production technology, process selection, and facility location decisions, and the effects of uncertainty and government intervention on these decisions. His current research includes the environmental aspects of operations management, and the application of Lean Production methods to service systems, not-for-profit organizations, and small businesses.

PREFACE

No one undertakes a five-year writing project without compelling personal reasons. In my case I had taught production and operations management for 12 years to over a thousand students, 98% of whom were not operations management majors but rather were majoring in accounting, marketing, finance, MIS, and several other fields. Few students had any idea what operations management was, and their quantitative skills were quite varied, with many of them exhibiting severe math anxiety. These factors presented several special challenges in teaching this course: how to demonstrate the relevance of operations management to this wide variety of non-majors; how to teach the thought processes and analytical reasoning required in operations management in a mathematically accessible and interesting way that reduces math anxiety; how to eliminate artificial separations between quantitative and qualitative/behavioral material; and how to make the discussion and examples realistic, and familiarize students with the richness and importance of operations, without overwhelming them.

Over the years, I prepared in-class notes, transparencies, and exercises that addressed these issues in the course, but I found no textbook that adequately assisted the students (and me) in doing so. Many students encouraged me to turn my notes into a book because they found them more readable and interesting than the text. Little did I know that this "conversion" of notes would take five years of my life, but I believe the result has been a book that will help instructors teach, and students learn, about the extent, substance, and excitement of operations management.

GOALS AND CORRESPONDING FEATURES

In writing this book I had the following goals:

1. ***To demonstrate the importance of operations management to non-majors.*** Anyone seeking a supervisory or managerial career in marketing, accounting, finance, engineering, MIS, medicine, law, and most other professions, will find that a large part of their jobs will be devoted to operational issues.
   - Opening each chapter is an **On the Job** box, which briefly describes the featured person's operations management activities. Many of the people profiled work outside the operations function of their companies; they include accounting managers, financial officers, customer service and sales personnel, purchasing managers, engineers, and entrepreneurs. Few had extensive formal training in operations management, but most have found that their formal exposure to operations management, though limited, has been invaluable.
   - **Over 200 companies** are used to illustrate the applicability and importance of operations management to a wide variety of organizations, as well as a variety of jobs.
   - Each chapter contains an **In Good Company** box, which describes how the profiled organization has addressed the operations management issues in that chapter to improve its performance.
2. ***To familiarize students with real production systems.*** Although many of my students hold part- or full-time jobs, most of them are familiar with very few production systems and frequently with only a small part of their own companies, such as the accounts receivable department. Accountants, sales representatives, and computer systems analysts who understand the general nature and activities of production systems are better able to work with and communicate with customers, suppliers, and co-workers and be more effective in their jobs.
   - **Chapter 3,** therefore, provides **tours of four production systems.** These tours, which include both manufacturing and service operations, describe the main activities involved in producing the compa-

nies' products, whether it be a roll of linerboard or a title insurance policy. More importantly, the chapter identifies operational problems and issues important to the success of the company. These discussions preview and motivate the topics to be covered in the remainder of the book.

- The end-of-chapter **Cases** and some in-text **examples** have also been designed to provide descriptions of real production systems or parts of systems.

3. ***To make the topics realistic and applicable.*** Because of their work experiences, students want to see how the topic applies to their jobs. They have also encountered the ambiguities, "messiness," and unanticipated consequences of real situations, so they will not accept tools that work only in idealized worlds.
   - I have used real examples extensively to show how companies and workers are confronting P/OM issues and problems. Over 100 photos make the people, companies, and situations more tangible.
   - Many of the illustrative examples are a bit longer and "messier" than the "toy" problems commonly used in texts. Typically, a single example will grow in complexity and realism as the discussion progresses and additional factors are introduced. For example, Chapter 7 first presents the rationale, thought-process, and mechanics of a standard heuristic for designing a single repetitive flow process (assembly line). Unlike many P/OM texts, however, this chapter then discusses methods for improving the design, including switching heuristics and nonquantitative considerations involving staffing, technology, and task synergies. More advanced topics, such as the use of parallel work-stations, parallel production lines, and the effects of randomness and variation on the production system, are presented for instructors who wish to cover the topic in greater depth. Without being smothered in mathematical calculations, students can see the complexity of operational problems and possible approaches to resolving them and become familiar with available tools.
   - The end-of-chapter **Cases** provide detailed and realistic examples of how quantitative and qualitative aspects of P/OM must be integrated to solve real problems and bring together the topics of the chapter and related chapters. With two exceptions (Walt Disney World and Southwest Airlines), the companies used are fictitious, but the problems underlying most of the cases are a synthesis of actual situations from my experiences and those of colleagues or from written reports. The cases are quite different from those in other books in that they tell a story of the problem and how it was solved. They demonstrate the problems that occur in implementation; the unexpected events that can occur; and how behavioral and quantitative tools can be combined to obtain better solutions than either one alone can achieve. Although the cases are not designed for "solution," discussion questions are provided with each one.

4. ***To provide a state-of-the art treatment of topics.*** In the past 20 years, businesses have radically changed the way they design and produce goods and services; they have redesigned jobs and work systems, quality management systems, and material management and inventory systems, and they have changed the technologies they use at a dizzying pace. Terms such as *lean production*, *just-in-time production*, *electronic data interchange*, *total quality management*, *concurrent engineering*, and *cellular production* have entered the vernacular of the business press.
   - These approaches and methodologies are not simply tacked onto this book as a separate "new methods" section resembling a glossary. They are discussed extensively throughout the book in an integrated fashion. For example, not only is Chapter 11 devoted entirely to *quality management*, total quality management principles and techniques are woven into the chapters on operations strategy, product design, process design, job design, and lean production.
   - Entire chapters or substantial sections, not just brief abstracts, are devoted to topics such as *lean and just-in-time production*, *cellular production*, and *vendor relations*.
   - Attention to the *ecological implications* of operations decisions has been increasing, and not

simply because of environmental regulations. Several chapters contain sections that point out, and illustrate with real examples, the opportunities that exist for companies to increase profits by designing products and production processes and managing operations in an environmentally sound manner.

5. ***To emphasize the strategic role of operations in organizations.*** The major changes occurring in business have involved fundamental changes in strategy. Companies such as Hewlett-Packard, Southwest Airlines, Walt Disney, Wal-Mart, Toyota, and Chrysler have become successful not simply because they have marketed their products well, but because they have developed production systems that allow them to excel in various ways: introducing new products more quickly, producing products of higher quality or at lower cost than competitors, or being more responsive and flexible in the timeliness of delivery and variety of products produced.
   - Chapter 2, therefore, provides an extensive discussion of the *role of operations in the development and execution of an organization's strategy.* The need for compatibility between the marketing strategy, such as one based on providing customized products, and the operations strategy and production system is emphasized. Numerous real-world examples and numerical illustrations are used to show how companies can, and have, exploited operational strengths.
   - Subsequent chapters dealing with *system design issues* reinforce and expand the discussion of operations strategy, such as how capacity and facility location decisions can be used to enhance competitive position.
6. ***To make the quantitative models and tools accessible.*** The proliferation of computers and model-based software has made the use of quantitative models and methods in operations management *more* wide-spread and important rather than less so. However, the form and level of knowledge students need regarding quantitative methods has changed. Every student needs to develop the ability to analyze a situation or problem, identify what information is known, structure the problem, identify what is to be determined, and select a method for finding the solution.
   - When presenting quantitative material I have tried to focus on the thought-process of how to approach various types of problems, and *when* and *why* the approach presented is appropriate in practice.
   - To a large extent, I have avoided presenting quantitative material in a fashion where assumptions and formulas are stated, followed by a "toy" numerical example where the student simply substitutes numbers for variables. Because my illustrative examples explain *the rationale of the approach and the reasons* for each step, the mathematical steps are more intuitive, less magical, and more likely to be comprehended and retained by students.
   - **Solved Problems** are provided at the end of all chapters that contain quantitative material. The solutions for these problems are explained in detail, providing further reinforcement and practice for students.

ORGANIZATION OF THE BOOK

The general organization of the book is consistent with most P/OM courses. It begins with *general background information* on operations management, strategy, and production processes. It then discusses issues related to the *design* of production systems.. The final part focuses on shorter-term operations *planning* and *control* decisions. Three features of the organization of the book should also assist instruction.

Topics are integrated and reinforced. Topics such as quality management and lean production permeate so many aspects of operations that it is artificial to segment totally their coverage from other operations management topics. For example, mistake-proofing of jobs (*poka yoke*) is a common tool used in quality management, but not to include it in the job design chapter would be to omit an important job design principle. For this reason, many popular topics are covered in more than one place in the book. Typically, one chapter will provide detailed discussion of the topic, but it will be discussed within other relevant chapters as well. This approach allows instructors to omit chapters from the course and still be able to cover desired topics.

Quantitative and qualitative topics are integrated. To perform good operational planning and to solve operational problems, a manager must utilize a wide set of skills and knowledge. A theme of this book is that quantitative methods are *tools* to be used as part of the decision-making process, not an end in themselves. Too often operations management topics and problems are divided into mutually exclusive categories—quantitative or qualitative—where one and only one approach is presented. I have organized the book by general topics or problems and have included whatever knowledge or skills are helpful or appropriate. For example, Chapter 9 not only presents mathematical models of queueing systems, it also considers "qualitative" issues, such as the relative advantages of single waiting lines and express servers, the psychology of waiting, and selection of appropriate performance measures.

The book is flexible and usable by a wide audience. Material in this book has been used at four universities in both undergraduate and graduate business courses and in a senior level engineering management course with success. The topics covered in introductory P/OM courses vary considerably from school to school and instructor to instructor. Therefore, this book contains all the standard P/OM topics, from which an instructor can customize his or her course. Further, almost all chapters are sufficiently self-contained so any set of chapters can be combined for a course.

Instructors should find this text very flexible with respect to the degree of mathematical content desired in the course. By choosing to include or omit individual chapter sections, **Chapter Supplements**, or **Tutorials**, instructors can use this book for courses ranging from those with quite modest to very substantial mathematical emphasis. The core of the book only assumes students have prerequisite knowledge of college algebra and basic probability and statistics. For those schools that wish to introduce management science tools, such as linear programming or simulation, as part of the P/OM course, three **Tutorials** provide in-depth introductions with special focus on how these tools can be used for operations management. At those schools where students have more advanced mathematical preparation, such as a prerequisite management science course, the tutorials can either be omitted or sections of them can be used to illustrate the application of these tools to P/OM topics.

OTHER FEATURES

In addition to the features mentioned earlier—**On the Job** and **In Good Company** profiles, **End-of-Chapter Cases**, **Plant Tours**, and **Solved Problems**—the book contains several other features that support the learning process:

- ***Chapter Summaries.*** The most important issues discussed in the chapter are presented in one- or two-sentence statements at the end of each chapter. These reinforce key ideas and provide a quick reference for the main ideas.
- ***Highlighted Formulas and Key Formulas Section.*** The most important and frequently needed formulas and equations are highlighted with color in the body of the chapter. They are then printed together at the end of the chapter for easy reference when students are solving numerical problems.
- ***Highlighted Key Terms and Key Terms Section.*** Key terms are highlighted in bold where they are first defined and then are listed at the end of each chapter with the page number cited where their definition was given.
- ***End-of-Chapter Problems.*** The book contains approximately 250 end-of-chapter problems. I have intentionally tried to provide a set of problems with a wide range of difficulty from the very direct and simple to relatively complex mini-cases requiring considerable analysis and possibly the use of computer software. (The most difficult ones are designated by an asterisk *.) To a large extent, the problems have been constructed in pairs; problems 1 and 2 address the same topic, and so on. In general, even-numbered problems will only use data from other even-numbered problems and similarly for odd-numbered problems. The answers to almost all odd-numbered problems are given at the end of the book.
- ***Discussion and Review Questions.*** Over 270 questions are provided at the end of the chapters. These not only help students review the important topics, but many require students to relate the topics to their own experiences and to draw upon several topics together to answer the questions.

SUPPLEMENTARY MATERIALS

Instructor's Guide. The Instructor's Guide was written by the author to make sure it was compatible with the themes and style of the text. For each chapter, the Guide contains: (1) a list of learning objectives, (2) possible in-class exercises to motivate or illustrate the chapter topic, (3) suggested examples or additional comments instructors can use to illustrate topics, (4) solutions to all end-of-chapter problems, (5) answers to review and discussion questions where there is a dominant answer (for many questions, especially those requiring students to use their own experiences no single answer exists), and (6) possible answers to the case questions.

PowerPoint Presentation. These PowerPoint lecture slides contain a combination of key concepts, images, and examples from the text. Developed by Lance Matheson of Virginia Tech, the slides are divided into a thorough presentation file for each chapter, and consist of over 600 instructional images. Designed according to the organization of the material in the text, this series of electronic transparencies can be used for classroom presentation to reinforce P/OM concepts visually and graphically.

Computer Software. Software developed by Y. Chang (developer of QSOM™ Prentice Hall) is available with the book. However, the book is designed so it can be used with any of the standard operations management or management science packages.

Test Bank. Including objective questions and problems, as well as short-answer and essay questions, the Test Bank has been designed to meet the varying testing needs of instructors.

Computerized Test Bank. The entire Test Bank is also available in a computerized form, allowing instructors to create and modify exams. It is available in a Windows format for IBM and IBM compatibles.

Video Tapes. The Wiley/Nightly Business Report Video contains segments from the highly respected Nightly Business Report that have been selected for their applicability to P/OM concepts, their discussion of various companies and industries, and for their reinforcement of key concepts in the text. Each segment is approximately 3-5 minutes long and can be used to introduce topics to students and provide a real-world context for related concepts. Additionally, a selection of plant tour videos are available, related to companies and industries in the text.

Software Animated Simulations. This selection of software simulations of key concepts from the text are designed for use in classroom presentation. The simulations, including queuing and JIT scheduling, allow instructors to demonstrate the effects of key parameters.

Supplement CD-ROM. This CD-ROM contains all of the supplements for this text (excluding video) in computerized form, allowing instructors to print, edit, and project the material as needed. Instructors may print out any of the material for their own use or for distribution to students. Also included on the CD-ROM are the Software Animated Simulations, the PowerPoint Presentations, and the text illustrations. Available for IMB or IBM compatibles.

ACKNOWLEDGMENTS

This book is the result of hard work by many people. First, I would like to thank the hundreds of students who used parts of this book in class and provided helpful feedback. I would especially like to thank Carolyne Weigel Schriefer, my research assistant for this book. I am also grateful to Professor L. S. Hiraoka's P/OM students at Kean College of New Jersey, who told us what pedagogical elements were most useful to them as they studied and who evaluated the proposed design of the text. Second, I would like to thank the following faculty reviewers who reviewed various drafts very conscientiously and provided superb comments to improve the style and content of the text.

John Buzacott	York University
Barbara Flynn	Iowa State University
Frank Forst	Loyola University of Chicago
Gregory Frazier	University of Oregon
Manton Gibbs	Indiana University of Pennsylvania
S. K. Goyal	Concordia University, Montreal
Jeff Heyl	DePaul University

Tim Ireland	Oklahoma State University
Thomas Johnson	University of Southern Florida
V. Kannan	Michigan State University
Gary Kern	University of Notre Dame
Jerzy Kyparisis	Florida International University
Hon-Shiang Lau	Oklahoma State University
Phillip Lederer	University of Rochester
Lewis Litteral	University of Richmond
Timothy Lowe	University of Iowa
James Luxhoj	Rutgers University
Lance Matheson	Virginia Polytechnic Institute
George Monahan	University of Illinois-Urbana-Champaign
C. Carl Pegels	SUNY-Buffalo
Fred Raafat	San Diego State University
Farhad Raiszadeh	University of Tennessee-Chattanooga
Jeffrey Ringuest	Boston College
Dan Rinks	Louisiana State University
Rudolph Russell	University of South Carolina
Joseph Sarkis	University of Texas-Arlington
Todd Schultz	Augusta College
Ramesh Soni	Indiana University of Pennsylvania
Ashok Srinivasan	Purdue University
John Steelquist	Chaminade University

Third, I would like to thank those people at Wiley who believed in this project and helped to produce a book of which I can be proud: Beth Lang Golub, Nancy Perry, Leslie Hines, Francine Banner, David Kear, Charlotte Hyland, Anna Melhorn, Laura Nicholls, and Hilary Newman. Many thanks also go to Suzanne Ingrao for her work in producing the book. I would like to give special thanks to Elisa Adams, my development editor. Throughout the process she gave me direct and constructive comments and helped me to keep up my spirits and to maintain at least a modicum of sanity. Fourth, I would like to thank those people featured in the "On the Job" profiles, those who helped with the plant tours, and those people and companies who provided photos and reviewed narratives used in the book. Finally, this is a "first edition" book, so I hope instructors will be patient with any deficiencies they find. Many difficult trade-offs and decisions had to be made about what topics to include and how to present them. The collective experiences and wisdom of my P/OM colleagues is far beyond my own knowledge. So I seek your suggestions, advice, and even critical comments that will help me to make future editions better. I want to practice continuous improvement and make the second edition even better than the first. Please feel free to e-mail me at martinic@umslvma.umsl.edu.

CONTENTS

PART 1 An Introduction to Operations and Strategy

Chapter 1 Production Systems and Operations Management 5

1.1 P/OM'S VALUE TO YOU 6
On the Job: Carol R. Caruthers, Price Waterhouse LLP 6

1.2 PRODUCTION SYSTEMS AND THE FUNCTIONAL UNITS OF ORGANIZATIONS 7
Production of Goods and Services 7
Functional Units of the Organization 9

1.3 WHAT IS OPERATIONS MANAGEMENT? 10
Operations as a Strategic Weapon: Reaching the Goals 11
In Good Company: Quality Drives the Gap 12
Responsibilities and Challenges Facing Operations Managers 13
Skills and Knowledge Needed to Be a Successful Operations Manager 16

1.4 THE HISTORY OF OPERATIONS MANAGEMENT 18
The Industrial Revolution 18
Scientific Management 20
The Human Relations Movement 23
Operations Research/Management Science (OR/MS) 24
Computers in Operations Management 24
The Japanese Production System 25
Operations Management Today 27

1.5 OPERATIONS MANAGEMENT, PRODUCTIVITY, AND COMPETITIVENESS 28

1.6 OPERATIONS MANAGEMENT IS FOR EVERYONE 29

Chapter 2 Operations Strategy 34

2.1 STEERING THE SHIP 35
On the Job: Bob Anastasi, CTI-Cryogenics 35

2.2 THE ORGANIZATION'S STRATEGY 36
Goals 36
Market and Competitive Analysis 37
Selecting Products, Markets, and Order-Winning Dimensions 37
Philosophy and Policies 38
The Business Unit Strategy 38

2.3 OPERATIONS AS A COMPETITIVE WEAPON 38

2.4 DEVELOPING AN OPERATIONS STRATEGY 40

2.5 OPERATIONALIZING GOALS AND MEASURING PERFORMANCE 41
Measuring Productivity 42
Cost Measures and Accounting Practices 44
Goal-Based Measures of Performance 45

2.6 GUIDING OPERATIONS DECISIONS: OPERATIONS SUBSTRATEGIES 47
Technology Strategy: Capabilities and Expertise 47
Capacity Strategy 49
Facility Location Strategy 51
Process Strategy 53
Quality Strategy 56
Human Resources Strategy 56
Information in Operations Strategy 57

2.7 PRODUCTION COST STRUCTURE AND THE OPERATIONS AND MARKETING STRATEGIES 58
Leverage and Capacity Utilization 58
Using Experience Effects and Economies of Scale Strategically 60
In Good Company: Hewlett-Packard's Strategy Takes Aim at Its Competitors 63

2.8 REVISING AND UPDATING THE OPERATIONS STRATEGY 63
Walt Disney World, Orlando, Florida: An Operations Strategy Case 68

CHAPTER 3 TOURS OF OPERATIONS 71

3.1 ONE SIZE DOES NOT FIT ALL 72

3.2 JEFFERSON SMURFIT CORPORATION: PAPERBOARD MANUFACTURING 72
Products 73
Pulp Preparation 74
The Fourdrinier Machine 75
Winding, Cutting, and Shipping 76
Major Operational Issues 76

3.3 STANDARD REGISTER COMPANY: PRODUCTION OF BUSINESS FORMS 79
Order Receipt and Production Scheduling 81
Printing 82
Collating and Finishing 83
Packing and Shipping 84
Major Operational Issues 84

3.4 UNITED PARCEL SERVICE (UPS): LOCAL, NATIONAL, AND WORLDWIDE DELIVERY 87
The Delivery Network and a Typical Delivery Cycle 87
The Facility 89
Sorting 89
Loading 90
Major Operational Issues 90

3.5 APPROVED STATEWIDE TITLE AGENCY: PROCESSING TITLE INSURANCE 91
Customers and Products 92
The Production Process 93
Major Operational Issues 94

PART 2 DESIGNING PRODUCTION SYSTEMS 98

CHAPTER 4 FORECASTING 101

4.1 GOOD DECISIONS BEGIN WITH GOOD FORECASTS 102
On the Job: Jayne Rosselli, Garden Valley Ranch 102

What Is Forecasting? 102
Importance of Demand Forecasting 103
In Good Company: Compaq Bets on Forecasts—and Wins Big 104

4.2 FORECASTING METHODS 105
The Role of Time 105
Quantitative versus Qualitative Methods 106

4.3 QUALITATIVE FORECASTING METHODS 106
When to Use Qualitative Methods 107
How to Improve Qualitative Forecasting 107

4.4 QUANTITATIVE FORECASTING METHODS 110
Background and Strategy of Quantitative Forecasting 110
Steps in Modeling 111
Time Series and Causal Models 113

4.5 CONSTANT PROCESSES AND THE CUMULATIVE AVERAGE 115

4.6 QUASI-CONSTANT PROCESSES 117
Simple Moving Average 118
Weighted Moving Average 119
Simple Exponential Smoothing 120

4.7 COMPARING ALTERNATIVE MODELS 122
Verifying Model Assumptions 122
Evaluating Forecast Accuracy 123

4.8 LINEAR TREND PROCESSES 126
Linear Regression for Trend Processes 127
Moving Linear Regression 129
Double Exponential Smoothing 130

4.9 SEASONAL PROCESSES 132
Constant or Quasi-Constant Processes with Seasonality 133
Linear Trend Processes with Seasonality 137

4.10 CAUSAL MODELS 141
Selecting an Independent Variable 141
Estimating the Relationship and Forecasting 142
Practical Hints for Using Causal Models 144

4.11 ADVANCED MODELS 144

4.12 IMPLEMENTATION AND USE OF FORECASTING SYSTEMS 145
Model Evaluation and Testing 145
Combining Forecasting Methods 145
Monitoring Forecasts: Tracking Signals and Adaptive Models 146
Buildup and Breakdown Models 148

Reynolds and Hill College: A Forecasting Case 162

TUTORIAL 1 OPTIMIZATION MODELS, LINEAR PROGRAMMING, AND HEURISTICS 166

T1.1 MATHEMATICAL MODELS AND OPERATIONS DECISION MAKING 167

T1.2 CONSTRAINED OPTIMIZATION MODELS 167

T1.3 ADVANTAGES AND PITFALLS OF USING OPTIMIZATION MODELS 170

T1.4 CHARACTERISTICS AND ASSUMPTIONS OF LINEAR PROGRAMMING MODELS 172

T1.5 FORMULATING LINEAR PROGRAMS 173
Steps in Problem Formulation 173
Feed Mix or Diet Problem 173
Blending Problem 175
Multiperiod Planning 177

T1.6 THE GEOMETRY OF LINEAR PROGRAMS 179
Graphical Solution 180
Multiple Optima, Infeasible Problems, and Unbounded Problems 182

T1.7 THE SIMPLEX ALGORITHM 182
Preparing the Problem for Solution 183
The Algebraic Foundations of the Algorithm 184
The Initial Simplex Tableau 185
The Simplex Pivot and the Second Tableau 186
The Third Tableau 187
The Fourth Tableau 187
General Comments About the Algorithm 188

T1.8 USING ARTIFICIAL VARIABLES 188
The Big-M Method 189
The Two-Phase Method 190

T1.9 INFEASIBLE PROBLEMS, MULTIPLE OPTIMA, UNBOUNDEDNESS, AND DEGENERACY 191

T1.10 COMPUTER SOLUTION OF LINEAR PROGRAMS 191
Problem Input 191
Computer Output 191
Sensitivity Analysis 191

T1.11 USING LINEAR PROGRAMMING MODELS FOR DECISION MAKING 193
Healthy Pet Food Revisited 193
Solar Oil Company Revisited: Updating Production Decisions 195

T1.12 INTEGER AND MIXED-INTEGER PROGRAMS 195

T1.13 HEURISTIC METHODS IN OPERATIONS 197
Characteristics 197
Advantages of Heuristics 197

Chapter 5 Product Design and Operations 211

5.1 THE PRODUCT DESIGN REVOLUTION 212
On the Job: Dee Ambrosia, Standard Register Company 212

5.2 PRODUCT DEVELOPMENT 213

5.3 THE PRODUCT DESIGN PROCESS 214
Designing for Production 215
Concurrent Design and Engineering 215
Team Design 217
Working with Customers and Suppliers 217

5.4 BASIC PRINCIPLES OF DESIGNING PRODUCTS FOR PRODUCTION 219
Minimize the Number of Parts Used 220
Use Common Components 221
Use Standard Components 221
Simplify the Assembly Process 222
Use Modularity to Obtain Product Variety 225
Make Product Specifications and Tolerances Reasonable 226
Design for Robustness 227

5.5 PRODUCT DESIGN TOOLS 228
Quality Function Deployment 228
Value Analysis 231
The Taguchi Method 232
Computer-Aided Design 234
Design for Manufacturability and Design for Assembly 235
In Good Company: Boeing's Design Takes Off 236
Prototyping 237

5.6 PRODUCT DESIGN FOR SERVICES 237

5.7 PRODUCTION DOCUMENTS 238

5.8 ENVIRONMENTALLY SENSITIVE DESIGN 240

Fibre-Pack: A Product Design Case 244

Chapter 5 Supplement Product Reliability 247

5s.1 COMPUTING PRODUCT RELIABILITY 247

5s.2 INCREASING RELIABILITY USING REDUNDANT (BACKUP) COMPONENTS 247

Chapter 6 Capacity Planning and Facility Location 250

6.1 THE IMPORTANCE OF CAPACITY AND LOCATION DECISIONS 251
On the Job: Sandy Boyd, Espresso Roma 251

6.2 MEASURING CAPACITY 252
Factors That Determine Capacity 253

6.3 CAPACITY STRATEGY 255
The Organization of Production and Facility Focus 255
Capacity Expansion Strategies 257
Demand Strategies 260

6.4 CAPACITY PLANNING AND EVALUATION METHODS 262
Forecasting Demand and Capacity Requirements 262
Break-Even Analysis 263
Decision Analysis 265

6.5 FACILITY LOCATION 266

6.6 LOCATION DECISION STAGES AND FACTORS AFFECTING FACILITY LOCATION 266
The Regional Decision 267
The Local Decision 268
The Site Decision 270
Public Service Facilities 270
Retail/Competitive Service Facilities 271

6.7 A SCORING RULE FOR LOCATION DECISION MAKING 272
In Good Company: Mercedes Benz Finds a Home in Alabama 274

6.8 MATHEMATICAL MODELS FOR FACILITY LOCATION PLANNING 275
Adding Capacity at an Existing or New Facility 278
Locating Several Facilities Simultaneously: Fixed-Charge Problem 278
Public Service Facility Location Models 280
Planar Location: Median and Center of Gravity Models 282

6.9 LOCATING FACILITIES GLOBALLY 285
Why Have Foreign Operations? 285
A Checklist for Evaluating Foreign Sites 286
Shenandoah Valley Trauma Centers: A Facility Location Case 295

CHAPTER 6 SUPPLEMENT
SOLVING TRANSPORTATION PROBLEMS 298

6s.1 INTRODUCTION 298
6s.2 PREPARING THE PROBLEM AND THE TRANSPORTATION TABLEAU 298
6s.3 OBTAINING AN INITIAL FEASIBLE SOLUTION 299
Northwest Corner Method 300
Vogel's Approximation Method 300
6s.4 THE STEPPING STONE METHOD 301
Checking for Optimality 301
Obtaining an Improved Solution 302
6s.5 THE MODIFIED DISTRIBUTION METHOD 303
6s.6 SPECIAL SITUATIONS 304
Maximization Problems 304
Total Supply Not Equal to Total Demand 304
Degeneracy 305

TUTORIAL 2 DECISION ANALYSIS 312

T2.1 UNCERTAINTY AND RISK IN DECISION MAKING 313
T2.2 STATIC DECISIONS 313
Decision Criteria 313
T2.3 SEQUENTIAL DECISIONS AND DECISION TREES 315
Constructing a Decision Tree 315
Folding Back the Tree and Computing the Expected Payoff 315
Expected Value of Perfect Information 318

CHAPTER 7 SELECTING THE PROCESS STRUCTURE AND TECHNOLOGY 325

7.1 THERE'S MORE THAN ONE WAY TO MAKE THAT PRODUCT 326
On the Job: Marvin D. Dixon, Nabisco Foods, Inc. 326
7.2 A COMMON CLASSIFICATION OF PRODUCTION PROCESS STRUCTURES 327
7.3 FLOW PROCESSES 328
Continuous Flow Processes 329
Repetitive or Discrete Flow Processes 330
Disconnected or Batch Flow Processes 331
Advantages and Disadvantages of Flow Processes 331
7.4 JOB-SHOP PROCESSES 332
7.5 CELLULAR PROCESSES 335
7.6 PROJECT PROCESSES 340
7.7 MODERN PRODUCTION TECHNOLOGIES 340
Group Technology 341
Process Automation 342
Computer-Aided Design/Computer-Assisted Manufacturing 344
Flexible Manufacturing Systems 344
Computer-Integrated Manufacturing 346
Bar Coding and Optical Scanning 346
Electronic Data Interchange 347
Process Technology and the Environment 348
In Good Company: Waste Turns to Energy for Anheuser-Busch 349
7.8 METHODS FOR EVALUATING PROCESS AND TECHNOLOGY ALTERNATIVES 349
Product Variety and Volume 350
The Product-Process Matrix 350
Analyzing Costs and Risk: Crossover Analysis 352
Capital Investment Analysis: Net Present Value 355
7.9 SERVICE SYSTEMS STRUCTURE 356
The Service Package and Intended Customers 357
Customer Contact Intensity 358
Service System Design and Strategy 360

7.10 CUSTOMIZING THE PRODUCTION PROCESS 360
Southwest Airlines: A Process Structure and Technology Case 366

CHAPTER 8 PROCESS DESIGN AND FACILITY LAYOUT 369

8.1 GOING WITH THE FLOW IN PROCESS DESIGN AND LAYOUT 370
On the Job: Chuck Wise, U.S. Precision Lens 370

8.2 DESIGN OF REPETITIVE PROCESSES: LINE BALANCING AND PRODUCT LAYOUT 371
Decomposing the Process Into Tasks 372
Criteria for Evaluating Work Station Design 372
Cycle Time, Production Rate, and Efficiency 373
A Work Station–Minimizing Heuristic 374
Improving Line Design to Increase Balance and Output 377
Parallel Work Stations 380
Parallel Production Lines 381
Mixed Model Production 382
Continuous and Batch Flow Processes 383
Spatial Configuration 384
The Effects of Randomness on Line Design 385

8.3 DESIGN OF FUNCTIONAL LAYOUTS 387
Procedure for Designing Functional Layouts 388
Structured Analytical Layout Tools 391
Craft 394

8.4 DESIGN OF CELLULAR PROCESSES 397
Cell Composition and Type 397
Production Flow Analysis 398
Trade-offs and Considerations in the Detailed Design 400
Spatial Configuration 402
In Good Company: Hybrids Bloom at Sony Corporation 403

8.5 DESIGN OF SERVICE SYSTEMS 404
The Process Flow Diagram and the Process Chart 404
The Service Blueprint 406

8.6 LAYOUT OF SOME SERVICE FACILITIES 408
Warehouse and Storage Layout 408
Retail Facilities Layout 410
Pesti-Chemical: A Process Design and Capacity Expansion Case 422

CHAPTER 9 WAITING LINES 426

9.1 QUEUEING THEORY 427
On the Job: Deb Holler, Great Western Bank 427

9.2 CHARACTERISTICS OF QUEUEING SYSTEMS 429
Customer Characteristics 430
Service Characteristics 432
System Configuration 433

9.3 NOTATION, TERMINOLOGY, AND THE EXPLODING QUEUE PROPERTY 434
Measures of System Performance 435
Capacity Utilization and the Exploding Queue Property 436
The Kendall-Lee Notation for Queueing Systems 437

9.4 SINGLE-SERVER SYSTEMS WITH EXPONENTIAL SERVICE TIMES (M/M/1 SYSTEMS) 437

9.5 MULTISERVER SYSTEMS WITH EXPONENTIAL SERVICE TIMES (M/M/S SYSTEMS) 441
Benefits of Pooling Servers Into One System 445
The Number of Queues for Multiserver Systems 446

9.6 SINGLE-SERVER SYSTEMS WITH GENERAL OR CONSTANT SERVICE TIMES (M/G/1 AND M/D/1 SYSTEMS) 448

9.7 THE ROLE OF VARIANCE IN QUEUEING SYSTEMS 450
Slower Servers Are Sometimes More Efficient 451
Pacing of Customer Arrivals Reduces Waiting 451
Exploiting Customer Heterogeneity to Improve Service 452
Other Issues Regarding Designated Servers 454

9.8 M/M/S SYSTEMS WITH A FINITE CUSTOMER POPULATION 455

9.9 SERIAL AND NETWORK QUEUEING SYSTEMS 458
Queueing Networks 461

9.10 BEHAVIORAL AND OTHER CONSIDERATIONS IN QUEUEING 462
Nonlinear Waiting Costs and the Psychology of Queueing 462
In Good Company: L. L. Bean Lines It Up 463
Additional Suggestions for Improving Queueing Systems 466

Interstate Rail and Trucking Company: A Case Study in Applying Queueing Theory 477

TUTORIAL 3 SIMULATION ANALYSIS FOR OPERATIONS MANAGEMENT 481

T3.1 A FLEXIBLE AND WIDELY USED TOOL 482

T3.2 TYPES OF SIMULATION MODELS 482
Continuous versus Discrete Event Models 482
Stochastic versus Deterministic Models 482
Examples 483

T3.3 STEPS IN SIMULATION MODELING AND ANALYSIS 485

T3.4 METHODS FOR SIMULATING TIME 487
Fixed-Time Incrementing 487
Next-Event Incrementing 487

T3.5 GENERATING RANDOM PHENOMENA 487
Generating Random Observations from a Discrete Probability Distribution 489
Generating Random Observations from a Continuous Probability Distribution 490
Generating Observations from a Continuous Uniform [a,b] Distribution 491
Generating Random Observations from an Exponential Distribution 492
Generating Observations from a Normal Distribution 493

T3.6 SAMPLE SIMULATIONS 494
A Random Production Line Simulation 494
A Queueing Simulation 496

T3.7 EVALUATING SIMULATION OUTPUT 499

T3.8 SIMULATION AND COMPUTER SOFTWARE 501

CHAPTER 10 JOB DESIGN, WORK METHODS, AND ORGANIZATION 508

10.1 PEOPLE MAKE THE DIFFERENCE 509
On the Job: Richard Kowalewski, Roots Canada 509

10.2 JOB DESIGN 509
Job Content 510
Responsibility for Quality and Process Improvement 513
In Good Company: John Deere Overhauls Jobs . . . and Pay . . . and Productivity 514
Automation and the Human–Machine Interface 514

10.3 METHODS ANALYSIS AND IMPROVEMENT 515
Methods Analysis 516
Some Simple Principles of Job Design 523
Work Aids and Ergonomics 524
Training 528

10.4 WORK STANDARDS 529

10.5 WORK OBSERVATION AND MEASUREMENT 530
Motion and Time Study 530
Using Time-Study Data to Compute Standard Times 532
Elemental Standard-Time Data 532
Micro-Motion and Predetermined Motion-Time Data 533
Work Sampling 533

10.6 THE WORK ENVIRONMENT 536
Environmental Factors Affecting Worker Performance 536
Safety and Health 537

10.7 THE ORGANIZATION OF WORK 538
Sociotechnical Systems and Autonomous Work Groups 539
Job Flexibility in Time and Location 540
Compensation and Incentives 542
Unions 543

Ferro-Stamping Inc.: A Job Redesign Case 548

CHAPTER 10 SUPPLEMENT
LEARNING AND EXPERIENCE CURVES 552

10s.1 LEARNING EFFECTS 552
10s.2 THE RATE OF LEARNING AND LEARNING CURVES 552
10s.3 DERIVING A LEARNING CURVE 553
Choice of Production Units 556
Forgetting 556
10s.4 EXPERIENCE CURVES 556

CHAPTER 11 THE QUALITY MANAGEMENT SYSTEM 560

11.1 THE NEW PHILOSOPHY OF QUALITY 561
On the Job: Valerie Mayer, ADT 561
11.2 WHAT IS PRODUCT QUALITY? 563
The Dimensions of Quality 563
In Good Company: UPS Delivers Relationships 565
11.3 THE QUALITY COST AUDIT 565
Quality Cost Categories 566
Typical and Desirable Cost Distributions 567
Obtaining Quality Cost Data 569
Two Examples of Quality Cost Audits and Scorecards 570
11.4 ACHIEVING AND ENHANCING PRODUCT QUALITY 574
11.5 DESIGN QUALITY 574
Identifying Customer Preferences 575
Incorporating Customer Preferences Into the Product 575
11.6 QUALITY CONFORMANCE 576
Product Design and Quality Conformance 576
Process Design and Quality Conformance 577
Production Operations and Quality Conformance 580
11.7 STATISTICAL QUALITY CONTROL 581
Statistical Process Control 582
SPC by Variables 583
SPC by Attributes 593
Defect Tracking and Cause–Effect Analysis 594
11.8 SERVICE QUALITY 597
11.9 TOTAL QUALITY MANAGEMENT 598
History of TQM 598
The Principles of TQM 599
Why TQM Programs Fail and Succeed 601
11.10 PROSPECTS FOR PRODUCT QUALITY 604
The Baldrige Awards 604
ISO 90000 Standards and Certification 605
Digicomp Computer: A Quality Management Case 611

CHAPTER 11 SUPPLEMENT
ACCEPTANCE SAMPLING 615

11s.1 THE PURPOSE OF ACCEPTANCE SAMPLING 615
11s.2 TYPES OF ACCEPTANCE SAMPLING PLANS 615
Selecting a Plan 615
11s.3 OPERATING CURVES 616
Computing α and β for a Typical Sampling Plan 616
11s.4 DERIVING A SAMPLING PLAN 617
11s.5 THE ROLE OF ACCEPTANCE SAMPLING 618

PART 3 SCHEDULING, OPERATING, AND CONTROLLING THE PRODUCTION SYSTEM 620

CHAPTER 12 AGGREGATE PLANNING 622

12.1 LINKING LONG-TERM AND SHORT-TERM PLANNING 623
On the Job: Randy Sanderson, Famous-Barr Stores 623

12.2 AGGREGATE UNITS OF PRODUCTION AND RESOURCES 625

12.3 THE AGGREGATE PLANNING PROCESS AND VARIABLES: CONTROLLING SUPPLY 626
Forecasting 627
Identifying the Planning Variables 627
Implementing an Aggregate Plan: The Rolling Horizon 627

12.4 SIMPLE PLANNING HEURISTICS 628
The Chase Demand Strategy 630
The Level Workforce Strategy 631

12.5 USING LINEAR PROGRAMMING FOR AGGREGATE PLANNING 633
A Linear Programming Model 633
Refinements and Variations of the Model 636
Dynamic Planning and Implementing the Linear Program 638

12.6 DISAGGREGATING THE AGGREGATE PLAN 639
Factors in Disaggregation 640
The Master Production Schedule 641

12.7 DEMAND INFLUENCING TACTICS TO REDUCE COST 642
Advertising, Pricing, and Product Promotion 644
Countercyclic But Similar Products 644
In Good Company: Polaris Industries Has All Seasons Covered 645
Reservation Systems 645

Force-Master: An Aggregate Planning Case 652

CHAPTER 13 INVENTORY PLANNING AND MANAGING MATERIALS WITH INDEPENDENT DEMANDS 658

13.1 CLASSICAL INVENTORY ANALYSIS IN A JUST-IN-TIME WORLD 659
On the Job: Gil Burford, Chrysler Corporation 660

13.2 REASONS FOR HOLDING INVENTORIES 661
Economic Efficiency 661
Quick Customer Response 662
Risk Reduction and Safety 662
Exploiting or Protecting Against Unusual Events 663
Types of Inventories 663

13.3 INVENTORY-RELATED COSTS 664
Holding Costs 664
Ordering or Setup Costs 664
Shortage or Stockout Costs 665
Hidden Costs 665

13.4 CHARACTERISTICS OF INVENTORY MODELS 665
Independent versus Dependent Demand 665
Inventory Review Policies 666
Continuous versus One-Period Decisions 666

13.5 THE BASIC ECONOMIC ORDER QUANTITY MODEL 667
Computing the Reorder Point 667
Computing the Optimal Order Quantity 668
Validity of the Assumptions and Model Robustness 671

13.6 THE EOQ MODEL WITH QUANTITY DISCOUNTS 672

13.7 THE ECONOMIC PRODUCTION LOT-SIZE MODEL 676

13.8 SAFETY STOCK POLICIES 678
Selecting the Reorder Point Based On Service Level 679
Selecting the Reorder Point Using Cost Analysis 683

13.9 PERIODIC REVIEW POLICIES 684
In Good Company: Fine-Tuning Inventory Control at Syntex Agribusiness 685

13.10 ONE-PERIOD MODELS 687
Optimal Order Quantity: Continuous Demand Distribution 688
Optimal Order Quantity: Discrete Demand Distribution 689
Computing the Expected Profit 691
The Evaluation Criterion 692
Flexible Spending Accounts: A Personal Financial Application 692

13.11 IMPLEMENTING INVENTORY MANAGEMENT SYSTEMS 693
ABC Classification of Items and the Pareto Principle 694
Data Requirements 695
The Two-Bin System 698
Purchasing Policies and Sole versus Multiple Sourcing 698
Materials and the Environment 699

Mediserve, Inc.: An Inventory Management Case 709

CHAPTER 14 MANAGING MATERIALS WITH DEPENDENT DEMANDS 715

14.1 DEPENDENT DEMAND AND IRREGULAR PRODUCTION PATTERNS 716
On the Job: Satish C. Nayak, Union Electric Company 717

14.2 STRUCTURE AND PRINCIPLES OF MRP 719

14.3 MRP INPUTS 720
The Master Schedule File 720
The Bill-of-Materials File 721
The Inventory Records File 724

14.4 MRP LOGIC AND MECHANICS 724
Exploding the Product 725
Developing the Material Requirements Plans 725
Consolidating Requirements 727

14.5 MRP OUTPUTS 728

14.6 LOT SIZING IN MRP 729
Economic Order Quantity 729
Part-Period Balancing 730
The Wagner-Whitin Optimization Algorithm 732

14.7 CAPACITY REQUIREMENTS PLANNING 733

14.8 UPDATING THE MRP SYSTEM AND SYSTEM NERVOUSNESS 735
Net-Change Systems 735
Regenerative Systems 735
Time Fences 736
Rolling Horizon 736

14.9 UNCERTAINTY AND SAFETY STOCK 736

14.10 MRP II: MANUFACTURING RESOURCES PLANNING 737

14.11 BENEFITS, LIMITATIONS, AND IMPLEMENTATION OF MRP 737
Benefits 738
Limitations and Implementation Problems 738
Computer-Based Systems 740
In Good Company: Tubetronics 740

Waste Overhaul, Inc.: An MRP Case 747

CHAPTER 15 JUST-IN-TIME, LEAN, AND SYNCHRONOUS PRODUCTION SYSTEMS 750

15.1 THE JUST-IN-TIME REVOLUTION 751
On the Job: Bruce Hamilton, United Electric Controls 752

15.2 AN IDEAL PRODUCTION SYSTEM AND JIT PRODUCTION 753
An Ideal World for Production 753

15.3 THE PRINCIPLES OF LITTLE JIT: JIT SCHEDULING 756

Speculative versus Assured Production: Push versus Pull Systems 756
Large versus Small Lot Sizes 757
Comparing JIT and Classical Scheduling 757
Quick Response as a Substitute for Inventories 759

15.4 THE MECHANICS OF JIT PRODUCTION 760
The Number and Size of Kanbans 761

15.5 THE INGREDIENTS OF BIG JIT: APPROACHING THE IDEAL SYSTEM 762
Quick Setups: Single-Minute Exchange of Dies 762
Reliable Delivery of Materials 767
Reducing Machine Breakdowns: Total Productive Maintenance 769
Quality and JIT Production 772
Continuous Improvement 774
JIT and Employee Morale 775

15.6 IMPLEMENTING JIT PRODUCTION 775
When to Use JIT Scheduling 775
When Not to Use JIT: JIT versus MRP 777
Guidelines for JIT Implementation 777
JIT in Service and Hybrid Industries 779
In Good Company: Federal-Mogul Corporation Gives JIT a Second Chance 780

15.7 SYNCHRONOUS PRODUCTION AND THE THEORY OF CONSTRAINTS 781
Some Principles of Synchronous Production 782
The Drum-Buffer-Rope Mechanism 783
JIT, Synchronous Production, and MRP 784
UKAX: A Case of Lean Production 789

CHAPTER 16 OPERATIONS AND PERSONNEL SCHEDULING 797

16.1 EVERY MANAGER'S CHALLENGE 798
On the Job: Diane Conboy, Brigham-Women's Hospital 798

16.2 SCHEDULING PRODUCTION FOR CONTINUOUS AND REPETITIVE FLOW PROCESSES 799
Coordinating Production Lot Sizes with Cyclic Production Schedules 799

16.3 SCHEDULING BATCH PRODUCTION SYSTEMS 803
Approaches to Job Sequencing 803
Criteria for Evaluating Schedules 803
Sequencing Rules for the One-Stage Problem 804
Two-Stage and Three-Stage Flow Processes 807
Dynamic Dispatching Rules and Multistage Systems 810

16.4 OPTIMIZED PRODUCTION TECHNOLOGY 814

16.5 ASSIGNMENT PROBLEMS 815
Hungarian Method 815
Unbalanced Assignment Problems 818

16.6 SCHEDULING SERVICE OPERATIONS 819
Pricing and Promotion 819
Appointment and Reservation Systems 819

16.7 PERSONNEL SCHEDULING 821
In Good Company: Smooth Sailing in Hampton Roads 824

16.8 IMPLEMENTING PRODUCTION AND PERSONNEL SCHEDULING 825
Home Helper Discount: A Scheduling Case 834

CHAPTER 17 PROJECT PLANNING AND SCHEDULING 838

17.1 PRODUCING UNIQUE PRODUCTS 839
On the Job: Mike Sargenti, Service Construction Company 839

17.2 THE CHARACTERISTICS OF A PROJECT AND THE ROLE OF THE PROJECT MANAGER 840
Project Environments 841
Challenges of the Project Manager 841
Benefits of Project Work 841

17.3 DATA COLLECTION AND ANALYSIS 841
Dividing the Project into Tasks 842
Identifying Precedence Relationships 842
Estimating Task Times 842
Data Collection as an Iterative Process 843

17.4 PROJECT SCHEDULING: GANTT CHARTS 844

17.5 NETWORK-BASED PROJECT SCHEDULING METHODS: PERT/CPM 845
In Good Company: Software Charms the Viper at Chrysler Corporation 847
Activity-on-Arc Convention 847
Activity-on-Node Convention 849
Which Convention to Use 849

17.6 COMPUTING THE PROJECT COMPLETION TIME AND CRITICAL PATH 849
The Two-Pass Method 849
Finding the Critical Path 853

17.7 IMPROVING THE PROJECT SCHEDULE: TIME–COST TRADE-OFFS 853
Crashing 854
Optimizing the Time–Cost Trade-offs 856

17.8 PROBABILISTIC TASK TIME ESTIMATES 856
Probability Distribution for Task Times 857
Deriving the Probability Distribution for Project Completion Time 858
Answering Probabilistic Questions 860
Validity of Assumptions and Simulation 861

17.9 MONITORING PROJECTS USING PERT/CPM 862

17.10 IMPLEMENTATION AND USE OF PROJECT SCHEDULING METHODS 864
Flood Relief Concert: A Project Planning Case 873

APPENDIX A: STANDARD NORMAL DISTRIBUTION A1

APPENDIX B: ANSWERS TO SELECTED PROBLEMS A2

PHOTO CREDITS PC-1

COMPANY INDEX CI-1

NAME INDEX NI-1

SUBJECT INDEX SI-1

STUDENT TO STUDENT

Hello!

I am a business student with an emphasis in accounting, and I hope to get a job as a staff accountant in a large firm. I took a required production/operations management course. I was pleasently surprised at how interesting and exciting this course was. I had expected a rather dry description of production systems but soon realized that operations management is about how all types of companies can effectively manage and improve the way they conduct their business. This course has introduced me to the management tools that can help me become more organized and efficient in my duties as a staff accountant.

If you are like me, you've probably never seen the inside of a manufacturing plant. You will find the plant tours in Chapter 3 very helpful in describing the components of a production system as well as introducing the issues and problems that are relevant to operations management. In each chapter, Dr. Martinich gives you many examples of how actual service and manufacturing companies deal with the basic operations topics of process design, queueing, and scheduling. For instance, the "In Good Company" box describes how a company has applied the concepts discussed in the chapter to solve its specific problems and improve its performance.

This course can be difficult because much of the material is quantitative in nature. Dr. Martinich explains the reasons behind the quantitative models and makes the necessary math more intuitive and easier to understand. Further, to illustrate how real problems are solved, Dr. Martinich combines the quantitative solutions with the qualitative factors that are important to operations. The interplay between quantitative and qualitative factors is presented in the fun and interesting cases at the end of each chapter.

Recently, you have probably read many newspaper and business magazine articles on lean and just-in-time production, electronic data interchange, total quality management, and environmentally responsible companies. This text will give you more background in these and many other current topics as it describes how businesses are using this information to remain competitive. The "On the Job" boxes demonstrate how today's POM professionals and those in various other professions are using the principles of operations management on a daily basis to solve problems and improve the quality of their work.

Good luck, and I hope you enjoy this course as much as I did!

Carolyne Weigel Schriefer
University of Missouri–St. Louis

PRODUCTION AND OPERATIONS MANAGEMENT

PART ONE

An Introduction to Operations and Strategy

Chapter 1: Production Systems and Operations Management

Chapter 2: Operations Strategy

Chapter 3: Tours of Operations

We open this book with a puzzle using an "On the Job" profile to demonstrate for you the broad applicability of the concepts you will learn from it. Throughout this book the "On the Job" and "In Good Company" profiles, the examples, and the cases will illustrate how operations management issues occur in a wide range of organizations, and are an integral part of most managerial jobs, from accountants to engineers to customer service representatives.

The first part of this book provides an introduction to operations management by defining what production systems are and by outlining the responsibilities and problems encountered by the people who manage them. It then describes the strategic importance of operations and how operations should fit with the overall strategy of an organization. We finish our introduction by "touring" four actual production systems and looking carefully at some of the operational issues their managers must face. These three chapters show the wide range of production systems that exist, the ways in which they function, the variety of problems their managers address every day, and the crucial role operations play in the success of organizations.

CHAPTER 1

PRODUCTION SYSTEMS AND OPERATIONS MANAGEMENT

1.1 P/OM'S VALUE TO YOU
On the Job: Carol R. Caruthers, Price Waterhouse LLP

1.2 PRODUCTION SYSTEMS AND THE FUNCTIONAL UNITS OF ORGANIZATIONS
Production of Goods and Services
Functional Units of the Organization

1.3 WHAT IS OPERATIONS MANAGEMENT?
Operations as a Strategic Weapon: Reaching the Goals
In Good Company: Quality Drives the Gap
Responsibilities and Challenges Facing Operations Managers
Skills and Knowledge Needed to Be a Successful Operations Manager

1.4 THE HISTORY OF OPERATIONS MANAGEMENT
The Industrial Revolution
Scientific Management
The Human Relations Movement
Operations Research/Management Science (OR/MS)
Computers in Operations Management
The Japanese Production System
Operations Management Today

1.5 OPERATIONS MANAGEMENT, PRODUCTIVITY, AND COMPETITIVENESS

1.6 OPERATIONS MANAGEMENT IS FOR EVERYONE

1.1 P/OM's Value to You

As a manager for one of the largest companies in its field, Carol Caruthers has a wide range of responsibilities. She must monitor existing work for her customers and assign new work to her staff as it is received. Because of the technical nature of the work, Carol devotes considerable time to making sure her unit has the human resources, training, equipment, and technology needed to provide customers with high-quality products in a timely manner. While managing these day-to-day operations, Carol devotes much of her time to strategic issues: evaluating new tools and technologies, designing new products, restructuring the production process, forecasting sales and staffing needs throughout the country, and designing jobs so that her staff can progress to positions of leadership. Overlaying all of these activities is constant attention to high quality in the products delivered to customers and the work done for the company. What do you think Carol's job title is? See the On the Job box for the answer.

Anyone entering a new course of study should quite naturally ask: "How will this course be of value to me?" Production and operations management (P/OM) may seem foreign to you if you do not plan a career in production. Even students in professional fields such as engineering and business do not often envision themselves as being directly involved in producing products; rather, they anticipate having responsibilities in accounting, finance, marketing, information systems, product design, or human resources management. Yet each of these activities is closely involved with the production and distribution of goods and services, and the more managers know about the system that produces the firm's products, the better able they are to design, market, finance, or manage the activities of the organization. In many ways, managers of these other functions are also managers of operations, and the problems they face are the same as those encountered in the production of the organization's primary products.

On the Job

Carol R. Caruthers, Price Waterhouse LLP

With a concentration in accounting, Carol Caruthers' MBA has served her well in her career at Price Waterhouse LLP. But as National Director, Personal Financial Services, for a Big Six accounting firm, Carol finds her other training valuable too. "I apply what I learned in operations management and management sciences extensively," she says. "It has shaped the way I analyze problems and how I go about solving them."

In addition to delivering personal financial planning and tax services to her own clients, as a national director of a practice unit Carol supervises a decentralized staff and regularly advises her staff's clients in special circumstances requiring concentrated research. Her operations responsibilities include evaluating new tools and technologies, designing new service products, structuring the service delivery process, forecasting staffing needs, and assuring high-quality service for Price Waterhouse customers. These extensive responsibilities give Carol plenty of opportunities to exercise her education in operations management.

This chapter provides a partial answer to the questions "What is production/operations management?" and "Why should I take this course?" It begins by defining production systems and then describes the primary functions of organizations and the way they are related to the operations function. Section 1.3 then defines and describes operations management. Operations management is so broad in scope that the field can best be defined by examples of the responsibilities of operations managers, the types of problems and issues that occur, the principles and goals guiding the manager's decisions and actions, and the skills needed to perform the job well. This discussion also provides an outline for the contents of the book and introduces some of our central themes, such as strategy-driven decision making and knowledge of the organization's real goals. To appreciate the substance of operations management as a discipline and profession, it is helpful to know the historical roots of the field, so Section 1.4 presents a brief history of operations management. During the past decade the business literature has focused increasingly on the importance of operations in achieving international competitiveness. Section 1.5 provides a perspective on the importance of operations in today's world. The chapter concludes by making explicit how managers and staff in other professions, such as accounting or law, can benefit from a knowledge of operations management, and how operations management principles and methods can be of value in everyday personal decisions.

Welcome to operations management. The journey should be fruitful even if the waters are sometimes challenging to navigate.

1.2 PRODUCTION SYSTEMS AND THE FUNCTIONAL UNITS OF ORGANIZATIONS

Most organizations, including not-for-profit organizations, can be described as **production systems**. These organizations transform or convert a set of *inputs*, such as materials, labor, and equipment, into one or more *outputs*, such as automobiles, computers, legal services, health care services, or electricity (see Figure 1.1). The outputs of a production system are normally called **products**; these products may be tangible goods, intangible services, or a combination.

PRODUCTION OF GOODS AND SERVICES

Goods are tangible items that can be touched or held. Production systems that produce goods are often referred to as **manufacturing systems**, and the production of goods is called *manufacturing*. Some common examples of manufactured goods are chemicals, automobiles, steel, computers, airplanes, beverages, packaged food, and

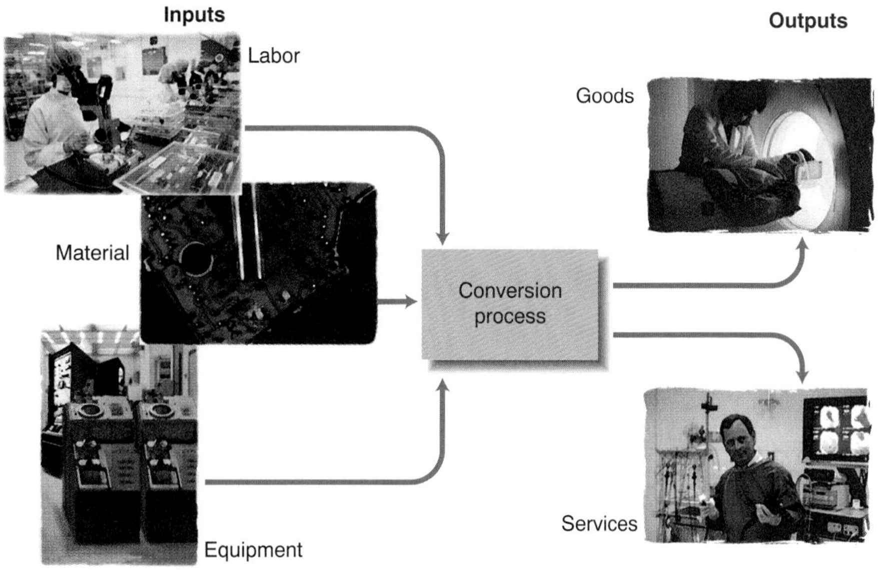

FIGURE 1.1 Production system.

TABLE 1.1 EXAMPLES OF COMBINATION PRODUCTS

Product	Tangible Component	Service Component
Restaurant meal	Prepared food	Delivery to table, cleaning of dishes, ambience
Producer-financed airplane	Airplane	Financial services (loan)
Turnkey computer system/network	Computers, software	Installation, training, maintenance
Home remodeling	New room	Design consultation

Circuit boards are tangible "goods" that are used in almost all electronic devices. Their manufacture has become one of the largest industries worldwide.

furniture. **Services** are intangible products that satisfy some need of a consumer, including the enhancement of a good. Production systems that produce services are referred to as **service systems**. Health care services, legal assistance, financial services, accounting services, educational instruction, and personal transportation are examples of service products; they enhance the consumer's life in some way and serve a useful function, but they cannot be touched or stored. Some services enhance goods, such as cargo transportation, which makes a good available at a more desirable location; warehousing services, which makes a good available at a more desirable time; or technical assistance and support, which helps the consumer utilize a good, such as a computer, more fully and efficiently.

Products can also be a combination of goods and services. Restaurants produce the tangible product of a meal, along with the intangible services of delivery, cleaning of dishes, and a pleasant environment. Table 1.1 lists some products that are combinations of goods and services.

The principles and methods discussed in this book apply broadly to managing systems that produce goods, services, or a combination. However, there are some important differences between the production of goods and the production of services:

1. Systems that produce tangible goods usually rely more heavily on raw material inputs than do service systems.
2. Goods usually can be stored for later use and transported over space before use, whereas services usually cannot.

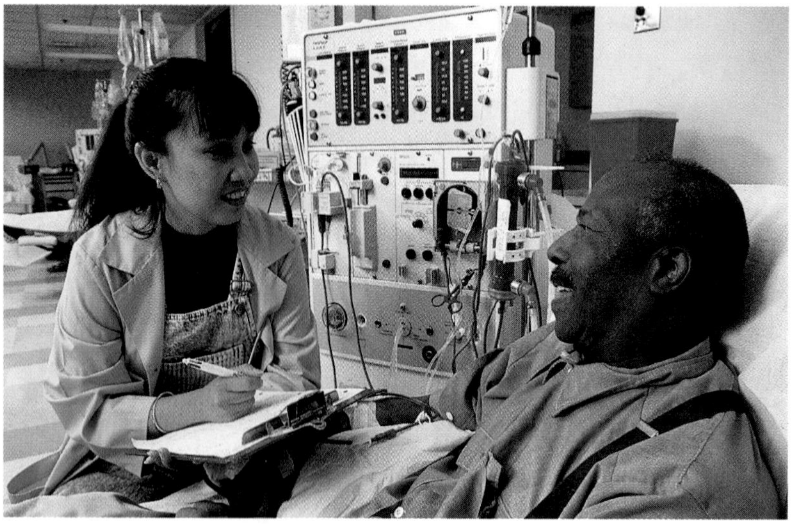

Health care is an essential service with extensive job opportunities. Operations management is becoming increasingly important in the health care industry.

Construction contractors provide both services (design advice, financing) and tangible goods (buildings) to their customers.

3. Consumers of goods have little, if any, direct involvement with the production of the goods. In contrast, most services require close involvement of the consumer with the production process, and in many cases actual physical contact is essential. (For example, most health care services require the patient to participate personally with doctors, nurses, and technicians; a doctor cannot give a physical examination or remove a tumor without the patient's participation. Similarly, air transportation requires the customer to be on the airplane to obtain the service.)
4. As a result of items 2 and 3, the production of goods can be separated from the consumer in space and time more easily than can the production of services.

The construction and management of all types of production systems involve issues of product, process, and facility design; capacity and location planning; quality assurance; job design; personnel and production scheduling; materials and inventory management; and maintenance. However, the form, frequency, and relative importance of these operational issues will differ according to whether the primary products of the production system are goods, services, or a combination.

FUNCTIONAL UNITS OF THE ORGANIZATION

The activities of business organizations are usually divided into several functions, each with its own personnel and responsibilities. The three primary functions are the marketing, financial, and operations functions. The **marketing function** serves to identify and/or create demand for the organization's products. The **financial function**, which includes accounting activities, provides the financial resources necessary to produce, market, and distribute the organization's products. This includes monitoring the financial condition, profitability, and performance characteristics of the organization and providing financial information for decision making.

This book is a study of the third primary function: the **operations** (or **production**) **function**, which is responsible for producing the products and distributing them to customers. More than half of all workers in the United States are directly involved in the operations function of organizations, and over three-fourths of a typical organization's material and equipment costs are incurred by the operations function. These facts imply that relatively small cost savings in operations, of say 1–2%, can produce a 5–20% increase in net profit.

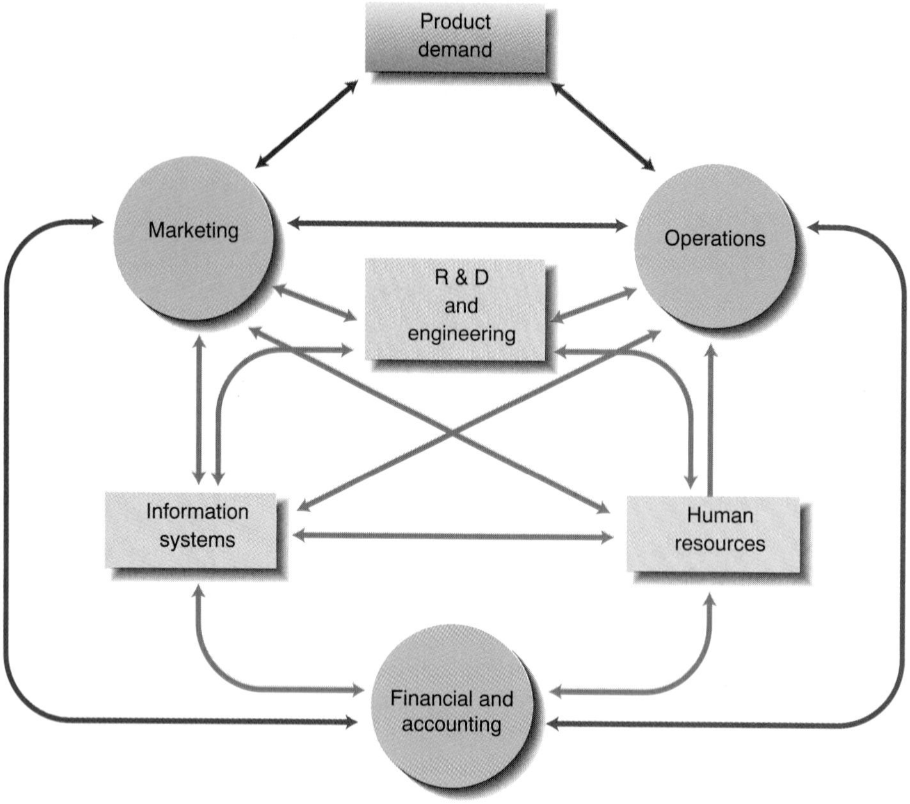

FIGURE 1.2 Functional divisions of an organization.

As illustrated in Figure 1.2, the three primary functions are not independent; in fact, there is considerable interaction among them. The demand for products drives the operations function. Requirements for facilities, equipment, human resources, and materials drive the financial function. Accounting and financial policies influence operations decisions, and the operations function directly affects future product demand and availability of financial resources.

Most organizations have additional supporting functions as well. For example, many organizations have an information systems function that gathers, organizes, and distributes information to the other functional units. The research and development and engineering functions provide technical assistance in the design of both the products and the production processes that make the products. The human resources function assists with the recruitment, training, evaluation, and compensation of personnel. All these functions interact constantly with the operations function.

1.3 WHAT IS OPERATIONS MANAGEMENT?

Operations management is a discipline and profession that studies (and practices) the *process* of planning, designing, and operating production systems and subsystems to achieve the goals of the organization.

Four aspects of this definition are worth noting.

1. Operations management deals with the *process*. A person need not hold the job title "operations manager" or "production manager" in order to be an operations manager. Production schedulers, quality assurance supervisors, materials managers, department supervisors, and store managers are primarily operations managers; furthermore, those who manage any personnel, equipment, or materials perform operations management tasks, although they may not be primarily operations managers.
2. The term *management* should be interpreted broadly to include designing the system and performing all activities necessary to operate the system, including directing personnel and acquiring materials and equipment.
3. The word *subsystems* is included to highlight the fact that one does not need to manage the production of the organization's final products to be an operations manager. Organizations have many subsystems that provide products to other parts of the production system. For example, the cost accounting department for an auto manufacturer provides products (reports and various accounting information) to other units of the company, even though its products do not go into the final product, automobiles. However, the cost accounting department is a production subsystem, and the manager of the department is an operations manager, even though the manager is part of the accounting function and has the title "cost accounting manager."
4. The definition does not say that the goal of operations management is to minimize costs. Most organizations have more than one goal, and although efficiency, productivity, and cost reduction are important considerations, cost minimization is usually not a principal goal. The primary goals of most businesses are to earn a steady (and growing) stream of profits and to maintain long-term demand for their products so as to stay in existence. The decisions made by operations managers influence the revenue component of the profit equation as well as the cost, and they affect the long-term demand for the organization's products. Therefore, operations decisions should be made with these ultimate goals in mind, not simply cost. (For example, Mercedes Benz has a higher cost per automobile than Hyundai, but we should not conclude from this that Hyundai's production system is necessarily superior to that of Mercedes Benz.) Similarly, not-for-profit organizations commonly have as their goal to deliver cost-effective levels and types of services. Providing the lowest-cost education or health care may not be desirable for the organization or society.

The remainder of this section describes operations management by expanding on these four aspects and identifying the skills needed to be an effective operations manager.

OPERATIONS AS A STRATEGIC WEAPON: REACHING THE GOALS

During the 1980s, the catch word of business was *productivity*. Books were written, conferences organized, research centers created, and speeches delivered, all centering on this term. Many definitions of **productivity** have been proposed (some of which will be presented in Chapter 2), but they all deal with using resources more efficiently, thereby reducing the unit cost of production. Everything else being equal, it is inarguably better to use fewer inputs to produce output. But focusing excessively on cost reduction can lead to poor decisions that are contrary to the goals and well-being of the organization. Instead, operations decisions should be made and implemented so as to achieve the broader goals of the organization, such as profitability and growth, or, for not-for-profit organizations, better public service.

Every organization should have a **strategy** that reflects its mission and defines its organizational goals, policies, and performance measures precisely. The strategy should describe what general products the organization will produce, how it will compete most directly for customers, and how performance will be measured. It should identify where effort should be concentrated and what competitive advantages the organization will exploit. A well-designed strategy should help the organization coordinate its organizational components and provide direction so that all actions contribute to the goals (see "In Good Company: Quality Drives the Gap").

Each functional unit—marketing, finance, operations, and so on—should have its own strategy, which is designed to support the organization's strategy and to enhance the ability of the organization to achieve its goals. Many businesses historically viewed their strategy solely in terms of marketing: deciding what products to make and what markets to serve. The operations function was considered to have a minimal strategic role; it was supposed to produce and deliver the products specified by the marketing function at minimum cost. More recently, thanks to the work of Wickham Skinner, Robert Hayes, Steven Wheelwright, Terry Hill, and others, the importance of a proactive operations strategy has been recognized. Decisions about operations can enhance the organization's ability to compete for customers with respect to price, quality, responsiveness and reliability of delivery, product customization, and flexibility. In fact, unless the operations strategy is consistent with the organization's strategy, even good operational performance can harm the organization. For example, if a company markets a product based on quick delivery and product customization, but the operations function is focusing on product standardization and low cost, then the product may not sell even if the operations function is successful at keeping unit costs low.

IN GOOD COMPANY

Quality Drives the Gap

Created in 1969 primarily as a jeans supplier, The Gap chain of clothing stores really took off in 1984 with a big boost in quality, and it is now the No. 2 clothing brand in the United States. The Gap achieved much of its success by being operations driven. It features its own designs and tightly controls the quality of the materials and manufacturing that go into them. The Gap has also developed an outstanding distribution system whereby stores in major cities, such as New York City, are supplied with new merchandise daily. The Gap's focus on operations extends to the retail stores themselves; maintenance, including painting, is done weekly, and every detail of product displays is closely monitored.

Source: Russell Mitchell, "The Gap," *Business Week*, March 9, 1992, pp. 58–64.

Recognizing the importance of the organization's goals and strategy has changed operational decision making. For example, equipment and production processes can now be selected and economically justified primarily because they reduce product delivery time or increase the range of products that can be produced, thereby improving the firm's ability to attract and retain customers, rather than because they reduce the cost of making existing products. Evaluating alternatives with respect to strategic goals, and not simply cost, must become a part of all operations decision making. Because organizational goals and strategy increasingly influence operations management, we begin our substantive coverage of operations management with a detailed discussion of operations strategy in Chapter 2. Attention to strategic considerations of operations decisions is an integral part of this book.

RESPONSIBILITIES AND CHALLENGES FACING OPERATIONS MANAGERS

The range of challenges and responsibilities that can confront managers of operations is enormous (see Table 1.2). Few operations managers are likely to encounter all, or even a majority, of the problems discussed here, but one or more of them may come within the domain of almost every manager. The responsibilities of operations managers can be divided into those that primarily involve designing the production system or subsystems and those that involve scheduling, operating, and controlling the system. In this book we present the design issues first because these establish the parameters within which operating decisions must be made. This is not to imply that design issues are more common or are faced more often by operations managers; in fact, the opposite is true. Products, facilities, processes, and support systems are designed or redesigned infrequently, and they are usually part of the responsibilities of upper-level managers. In contrast, shorter-term operational problems, such as scheduling personnel and equipment and managing materials, occur every day and are likely to be within the realm of more managers, especially lower-level managers.

Many of the specific areas of responsibility for operations managers are summarized below. We discuss them in detail in subsequent chapters.

Product Design

At the heart of all operational decisions is the product itself. The design characteristics of the product will affect the way the production system should be designed and operated. For example, the materials used in a product will affect what types of machining must be performed, whether or not production equipment must be adjusted and new tools and fixtures required, and how well employees can assemble the product. Similarly, the variety of items offered by a restaurant and its willingness to customize orders will affect the food preparation process, the equipment, materials, and personnel required, and the cost of preparation.

TABLE 1.2 RESPONSIBILITIES OF AN OPERATIONS MANAGER

Design and Planning	*Operation and Control*
Product design	Aggregate/intermediate-term planning
Capacity planning	Materials management and inventory control
Process design and choice of technologies	Maintenance
Facility location	Scheduling personnel, equipment, jobs
Facility design and layout	Distribution and logistics
Job design and work organization	
Product quality assurance	

By considering production implications while the product is being designed, firms can make a higher-quality product at lower cost. For this reason, many organizations now include personnel from operations as part of the product design team. Chapter 5 discusses the product design process and explains how it is intimately related to the design and operation of the production process.

Capacity Planning and Process Design

Important strategic issues for retailers are the size of their stores (capacity) and the variety of the goods they sell.

Two fundamental design issues are how to produce the firm's products and how much production capacity to have. The design of the production process is crucial to supporting the marketing strategy of the organization. For example, a company that intends to compete primarily through low price can often utilize an inflexible but efficient production process, whereas a company that plans to offer customized products needs production flexibility. The design of the production process requires decisions to be made regarding the arrangement of individual production activities, the division of work and specialization of labor, and the choice of equipment and technology.

Closely related to the production method is the production capacity desired. Some of the capacity decisions facing operations managers are of great strategic importance, such as deciding how many television sets a new factory should be able to produce per year, how many airplanes to have in a commercial fleet, or how much floor space a grocery store should have. Other capacity decisions are tactical, such as how many photocopiers to have in a building or how many customer service representatives to have answering customer calls. These issues are discussed in Chapters 6 to 9.

Facility Location and Layout

Many operations management problems have important spatial aspects. The decisions on where to locate a factory, restaurant, police station, or school have long-term strategic significance because they determine how much it will cost to make products and how well customers can be served. Decisions about the internal design of facilities range from determining the layout of a complete manufacturing process to choosing where to display certain products in a retail store, how to arrange different items in a warehouse, where to locate a computer lab on a university campus, or where to locate a photocopier in a building. Chapters 6 and 8 discuss approaches to solving these facility location and layout problems.

Job Design and Work Organization

The choice of a production process directly affects the number and skill level of personnel required. Some major issues facing managers are the design of jobs, the development and use of work standards, the organization of work, and the role of personnel in producing high-quality products. For example, a constant issue in job design is how many tasks and responsibilities a job should include. There are both advantages and disadvantages to having jobs with a small number of well-defined tasks versus jobs having many tasks. Trade-offs must be made based on the characteristics of the available workforce and the types of products made. Chapter 10 discusses issues of job design and work organization, along with the overall role of human resources in the production process.

Product Quality

An organization's philosophy about quality should be an explicit component of its strategy. The way quality is viewed will influence both the design and the operation of the production system. For example, some companies compete primarily with respect to price. They often establish a minimum acceptable product quality and then try to minimize the production cost while achieving it. Other companies compete primarily in terms of product quality. They focus on achieving the highest-quality product in the market while keeping cost within some limit. Regardless of the strategy chosen, achieving product quality requires more than hiring quality control inspectors. It means integrating a quality assurance system into the design and operating procedures of the entire production system.

The final quality of a product and the cost of achieving that quality are directly affected by the design of the product, the type of equipment used, the way the equipment is maintained, the quality and training of the workers, the quality and handling of raw materials, and the procedures for testing and evaluating the product. For this reason, we discuss product quality issues in several chapters that have direct relevance to product quality, such as product design and job design. In addition, Chapter 11 provides a complete framework for establishing a total quality management system and the operational practices supporting it.

Coordinating Production Resources and Demand

Managers can execute short-term operations more efficiently when intermediate-term plans have been made several months in advance to match production resources with anticipated product demand. These intermediate-term plans coordinate personnel decisions, such as hiring, training, layoffs, and overtime, with production scheduling, inventory decisions, and subcontracting. Chapter 12 presents methods to improve the intermediate-term planning of production resources, and it suggests ways to influence product demand to match production capabilities more profitably.

Managing Materials and Inventories

In the short term, operations managers devote much of their energy to inventory and materials management, and scheduling operations and personnel. Important questions to consider are what to buy, from whom to buy, when to buy, and how much to buy. For example, should a company buy one month's supply of paper every month or one year's supply once a year? Should a company increase the amount it purchases from a supplier to take advantage of a quantity discount? Should a company use only one supplier for an item or several suppliers? How much in-process inventories should be kept at each stage of the production process? These questions are discussed in Chapters 13 and 14.

Many companies are beginning to design and use production systems based on the **just-in-time production** principle, in which materials are acquired or produced "just in time" for use at the next production stage. This system uses scheduling and lot-sizing procedures to keep inventories to a minimum without harming the efficiency of the production process or reducing customer service. These production systems often include many other features, such as improved work methods, maintenance procedures, and quality assurance methods, and they have produced many other benefits, including higher product quality, simplified production scheduling, and improved employee morale. Chapter 15 discusses these systems in detail and illustrates their advantages and disadvantages.

Scheduling Personnel, Equipment, and Work

For most managers the scheduling of personnel, machines, production jobs, and projects is a never-ending task. The following examples are typical of the problems encountered.

1. A bank has customer demands that vary considerably from day to day and over the course of a day. How many full-time and part-time workers should the bank em-

ploy, what days should each one work, when they should start work, how many hours should they work, and when should their meal breaks be scheduled?

2. A manufacturer that makes products to customer specifications uses 12 separate types of operations. Each product requires between one and eight of these operations. At any given time there are dozens of customer orders at various stages of completion. What rule(s) should be used to determine which job should be run at each operation (or machine)? How can jobs be sequenced to reduce inventories and shorten production times?
3. A company's sales department is moving to a larger building. The existing office must be vacated no later than December 10. What tasks, such as ordering new phone lines and moving computers, have to be done, who should do them, and when must each task be started so that the move is accomplished by the deadline without interrupting ongoing sales activities?

In each of these situations a manager must make trade-offs among costs, customer service, and quality while allocating scarce production resources, such as people and machines, over time. However, each situation has unique features for which distinct decision models can be utilized. Chapters 16 and 17 discuss a wide range of scheduling problems, such as those mentioned above, which occur regularly in production systems.

SKILLS AND KNOWLEDGE NEEDED TO BE A SUCCESSFUL OPERATIONS MANAGER

Operations management is concerned with the *process* of how to design, plan, and operate production systems. Clearly, to be an effective operations manager, it is important to be sensitive to the physical and psychological characteristics of employees and to interact well with people on a personal basis. In addition, three other skills are important: (1) general knowledge of production processes, (2) knowledge and understanding of operations management principles, and (3) working knowledge of decision-making tools and techniques to help solve problems that occur in managing operations. This book contains numerous discussions and illustrations of how and where behavioral and psychological issues need to be considered and integrated with analytical tools to solve operational problems. But it is not intended to provide an introduction to managerial psychology or organizational behavior. Instead, attention is devoted primarily to the other three skills.

Knowledge of Production Processes

Production systems are made up of interwoven subsystems, so decisions made by one manager or department often affect other departments or subsystems. Consequently, to identify, understand, and solve operational problems effectively, it is important for managers to understand the entire production system. For example, changing a material ordering policy in one department may influence machine operations in another department. Furthermore, knowing how products are made, where bottlenecks exist in the system, and what the demand patterns are for different products can help in support functions, such as designing more accurate accounting systems, more useful information systems, and more effective and profitable pricing and promotion strategies.

Few students have much familiarity with production processes, so Chapter 3 provides detailed descriptions (called *plant tours*) of four production systems: two manufacturing and two service systems. In addition, many of the examples and end-of-chapter cases provide short descriptions of actual production processes, which should expand your familiarity with the range of operations that exist.

Production Principles

Through analysis and experience, a variety of principles have been developed to solve many of the problems an operations manager is likely to encounter. Each chapter presents principles and tools to solve a specific type of operational problem, the reasoning supporting these principles and tools, and examples of their application. The detailed cases at the end of the chapters play a crucial role in synthesizing the principles and methods and illustrating their use in practice. You should read these cases even if they are not assigned.

Analytical Tools

Many decisions can be made using personal experience and simple decision rules. However, production systems and their accompanying problems have become increasingly complex, so these simple rules and experience often are inadequate. During the past 50 years, many tools and techniques have been developed that can be very useful for solving operational problems. The advent of the computer has been especially significant in implementing these techniques in practice and changing the way many operational decisions are made.

Analytical tools developed for specific P/OM problems, such as statistical process control, learning curves, and scheduling heuristics, have been incorporated directly into the applicable chapters or included in chapter supplements. Five categories of decision aids—forecasting methods, queueing analysis, optimization models and linear programming, decision analysis, and simulation—are so important and broadly applicable that they have been treated differently. Forecasting and queueing analysis (the study of waiting lines) are such integral aspects of operations management that separate chapters have been devoted to them. Linear programming (and optimization models), decision analysis, and simulation are even more widely applicable business and engineering tools. They are often major topics in introductory quantitative methods or management science courses, which some students may have already completed. So these topics are contained in separate Tutorials, which can be omitted without loss of continuity in the other chapters. However, even if you are familiar with one or more of these tools from other courses, reading these chapters should be helpful because they include practical advice and illustrations for using these methods in operational decisions.

These methods have extensive applicability to operations management practice (examples are given in Table 1.3), and they are becoming more common components of managers' expected set of tools. Although most chapters can be read and understood without an in-depth knowledge of these tools, their use in solving operations management problems is illustrated throughout the book.

Despite the frequent backlash against "numbers people" and the use of quantitative methods in business, analytical decision-making methods and mathematical models can be valuable tools for production and operations management. Wickham Skinner, a noted Harvard professor of manufacturing strategy, has stated that analytical and mathematical operations management tools "cannot be thrown away, and indeed, they must be used more than ever." But their use must be guided by better understanding of the organization's production system, goals, and strategy. Skinner emphasizes that these tools have tremendous potential benefits because "they are designed to integrate, to consider systems as a whole," and they can solve more complex problems. He also notes that there is a shortage of managers who have this knowledge and can apply it.[1]

One of the goals of this book is to prepare you to use analytical methods, where appropriate, and to illustrate how they can be used in many areas of management.

---

[1]Wickham, Skinner *Manufacturing in the Corporate Strategy*, Wiley, New York, 1978, pp. 7, 16–17.

TABLE 1.3 ANALYTICAL TOOLS USED IN OPERATIONS MANAGEMENT

Tools	Examples of Applications
Forecasting methods	Predicting product demand Predicting credit card payments Predicting material prices
Optimization models	
Linear programming	Scheduling production Scheduling personnel Formulating products (material blending)
Integer programming	Locating facilities Scheduling machines
Heuristics	Scheduling jobs Designing facilities Designing production processes
Queueing analysis	Planning capacity Configuring and designing processes
Decision analysis	Planning capacity Locating facilities Selecting new products
Simulation	Designing facilities and processes Scheduling operations Managing inventories

1.4 THE HISTORY OF OPERATIONS MANAGEMENT

Production systems have existed since the earliest days of civilization, as evidenced by the pyramids of Egypt, the Great Wall of China, and the archaeological remains of many once thriving cities of Asia, North Africa, Europe, and the Americas. Decisions about the design of products, location of facilities, scheduling of personnel, and acquisition of materials clearly had to be made. Some of the modern principles of operations management were known and utilized in ancient societies. For example, specialization of labor was quite common in ancient Greece.

With relatively few exceptions, until the eighteenth century most goods were produced by artisans working either alone or as part of a small shop. Specialization of labor was sometimes employed, but the general scale of operations was usually small and labor intensive. The typical production facility had a handful of apprentice workers overseen by the owner-master craftsman. Its technology was embodied in minds and hands rather than equipment. Product design and the production process were united in the person of the owner; quality control, personnel scheduling, and materials management were done from experience using simple rules; markets were small, and distribution was uncomplicated.

THE INDUSTRIAL REVOLUTION

Modern operations management began in the **Industrial Revolution**. In eighteenth-century England, technological advances created monumental changes in the way products were produced, the scale of operations, the size of markets, and the organizational structure of personnel. The first major technological innovations appeared in the textile industry. Between 1733 and 1785 the inventions of the flying shuttle, the spin-

Building the Great Wall of China necessitated solving numerous operations problems, such as material acquisition and transport, personnel training and scheduling, facility location, and the organization of work.

ning jenny, the water frame, the mule spinner, and the power loom revolutionized the industry.

The innovations in spinning and weaving were important because they represented a significant step toward replacing human labor with other sources of power (mainly water and mule power), and they embodied skill and technology in machines rather than people. The machines made it possible for unskilled workers to make cloth of better quality than skilled weavers could make by hand. However, three other developments were necessary for the Industrial Revolution to become widespread: (1) invention of the steam engine, (2) mass production of interchangeable parts, and (3) creation of machine tools.

James Watt received his first patent for the steam engine in 1769, and the first industrial applications occurred around 1785. In 1793 Eli Whitney used the steam engine in his cotton gin, which removed the seeds from cotton. Soon afterward, the steam engine was used to create the first train (by Richard Trevithick in 1802) and the first steamboat (by Robert Fulton in 1807). This began a long stream of applications whereby human and animal power were replaced by engine power.

Whitney's more significant contributions were the establishment of the first factory utilizing interchangeable parts made on machines and his development of early metalworking tools. In 1798 he signed a contract with the U.S. Congress to make 10,000 identical muskets at the comparatively low price of $13.40 each. Until the opening of Whitney's factory, components for most products were made individually to fit each item. For example, the components of one musket were crafted to fit that specific musket, and they could not be used for a different musket even of the same type. Although **interchangeable parts** had appeared repeatedly throughout the previous five centuries, these were usually for simple assemblies and the components were still made by hand. Whitney's plan was to make the parts using machines. To achieve the required accuracy and consistency, he had to improve existing metalworking tools and invent new ones.

At about this time, the machine tool industry began to develop in England and America. Until then wooden parts had been commonly used for machines because they could be shaped with greater precision than metal parts, but they did not withstand wear. In 1797 Henry Maudley developed the power-driven lead-screw tool hold for lathes. This improved the precision of parts made on lathes. Soon other metalworking tools were developed that made larger-scale production of metal machines and tools possible.

The Industrial Revolution was in full swing in England by 1825. Factories utilizing steam-powered machines were common in many industries. Production of goods increased substantially, and prices generally decreased as a result of the greater productivity. As with most revolutions, changes brought problems. Workers were displaced by machines (which led to the Luddite Rebellion of 1812, in which English workers smashed textile equipment and murdered factory owners.)[2] Wages remained low, factories were drab and unhealthy, working days of 14–16 hours were common, and women and children (many as young as 10 years old) were used almost exclusively as labor in several industries (such as textiles). These conditions were so oppressive and so widespread that the British Parliament passed a steady stream of laws providing for greater rights and protection for workers.

The Industrial Revolution spread to the United States soon after the American Revolutionary War. Industrialization developed quickly in the United States for two reasons. First, the U.S. economy was expanding because of the attraction of free land in the West. This created a constant shortage of labor, especially skilled craftsmen. Second, there was a general openness to new ideas; the lack of an existing industrial base meant that there was no established way of doing things. Mechanization made it possible to produce more goods with less labor and less skilled labor.Industrialization and mechanization changed the scale and organization of production. Planning and coordination of labor and materials, designing jobs, training workers, and distribution of goods became major problems. Operations became so large that company owners were no longer able to oversee closely all the aspects of their companies. Capital requirements became much larger, so new forms of ownership were created: multimember partnerships and public stock ownership. The production process was broken down into discrete components so that specialized machines could be designed to perform each step of the process and workers could become more efficient at performing a small set of tasks—**specialization of labor**. Each of these components had to be supervised and coordinated with the other components of the organization. A class of professional managers to design, plan, and supervise the operations of the company was soon needed.

SCIENTIFIC MANAGEMENT

Charles Babbage, a prominent mathematician and engineer (who is best known today for designing the predecessor of the digital computer, called a *difference engine*) was one of the first to propose using scientific methods to solve business problems and improve production processes. In 1832 Babbage wrote *On the Economy of Machines and Manufactures*, in which he recommended the use of time study, wage incentive plans, research and development to improve products and processes, and economic analysis for selecting the location of facilities. But these recommendations went relatively unnoticed, and the study of operations management evolved slowly until the end of the nineteenth century.

[2]A brief discussion of the Luddite rebellion can be found in Alan Robinson, *Continuous Improvement in Operations*, Productivity Press, Cambridge, MA, 1991, pp. xxii–xxiv.

As the management class grew, interest in how to manage operations increased. During the second half of the nineteenth century, scientific discoveries in astronomy, chemistry, physics, and biology led to the belief that the world was governed by natural laws. The structure of scientific inquiry formed the foundation of what was later called **scientific management.** The basis for scientific management was the belief that there were laws governing production systems, just as there were laws for natural systems. If those laws could be identified, they could be used to find the best way to perform any job and the best way to make a product. The scientific laws of natural systems were discovered through observation and experimentation. Proponents of scientific management believed the same approach would work for discovering the laws of production systems. Throughout the 1870s and 1880s, considerable research focused on the management of shop operations, and books devoted to shop management such as Frederic Smith's *Workshop Management* (1878) and Henry Metcalfe's *Cost of Manufactures* (1885) began to appear.

These activities provided the groundwork for the most important person in the development of scientific management, Frederick W. Taylor (1856–1915), who is often referred to as the father of scientific management. Taylor's primary contributions were not in developing specific scientific management techniques. Rather, he applied existing methods in imaginative and dramatic ways, synthesized and verified these ideas to produce an overall philosophy of management, developed tools to help execute his philosophy, and then, most important, zealously promoted these ideas through his writing and public appearances.[3]

Taylor's philosophy was based on four principles:

1. There are basic scientific laws that govern work. Using scientific methods, management can determine what these laws are and use them to design the best way to do any task.
2. Every person is different, and these differences can be exploited in managing production by matching the right person to the right task and by training workers to develop and utilize their skills fully. This matching and training should be done scientifically through observation and experimentation.
3. Employee self-interest should be utilized to improve productivity. If management explains to workers the logic behind the job design and provides them with appropriate incentives, then it will be in the employees' best interests to perform their tasks as designed. Consequently, Taylor developed wage incentive plans that rewarded workers for producing more than some (scientifically determined) standard and punished those who produced less than the standard.
4. There should be separation of responsibilities between floor workers and managers. Taylor recommended the creation of staff groups that specialize in developing production processes, designing jobs and work methods, establishing wage incentive programs, selecting and training workers, and planning and coordinating activities. These staff groups and the line managers would then teach the floor workers what to do and how and when to do it. This idea was widely adopted, and these staff workers became what were known as **industrial engineers** (Taylor is also known as the father of industrial engineering.) Taylor developed several tools, such as production standards, production control systems to maintain appropri-

[3]Taylor's main ideas are presented in his book *The Principles of Scientific Management* (1911). A detailed biography of Taylor and his work is contained in Frank Barkley Copley, *Frederick W. Taylor: Father of Scientific Management*, American Society of Mechanical Engineers, New York, 1923.

ate production procedures and standards, and production and routing documents to assist in this planning and coordination.

One of Taylor's best-known studies illustrates his creativity and dramatic flair. Taylor observed workers loading pig iron onto rail cars. He determined that they were using the wrong motions, working too hard, and becoming overly tired and unproductive. Taylor selected one of the workers, to whom he gave the alias Schmidt, and offered him \$1.85 per day (instead of the \$1.15 he had been making) if he would follow Taylor's directions on how to lift, carry, and put down the pigs (blocks) of iron and take frequent short rests. Following Taylor's direction, Schmidt loaded 47 tons of iron in one day (versus the average of 12.5 tons before the change). Workers willing to follow this approach had their pay increased, and the cost per ton to the company decreased substantially.

Taylor described this and other experiments in speeches and books and attracted considerable attention to scientific management. However, his anti-union feelings and his statements likening workers to oxen led to congressional hearings to investigate complaints from unions regarding scientific management. In fact, legislation outlawing some scientific management methods on federal jobs was passed.

Although Taylor brought national attention to scientific management, a large number of his contemporaries and disciples, such as Frank and Lillian Gilbreth and Henry Gantt, were responsible for spreading its principles throughout industry. The contributions of the Gilbreths are especially noteworthy. The foundations of the Japanese production system described below, especially continuous improvement and elimination of waste, were widely taught by the Gilbreths in the first decades of the twentieth century. Rather than blaming workers and unions for inefficiency, the Gilbreths supported unions and held management responsible for the problems.

Frank Gilbreth began his career as a bricklayer, and throughout his life he had great empathy for workers. Gilbreth carefully studied the different ways bricklayers laid bricks to determine the best way. In addition, he developed equipment and tools to make the work physically easier; his philosophy was "work smarter, not harder." At the age of 27 he started his own construction business, which specialized in high-quality "speed building." Gilbreth's bricklayers laid five times more bricks than the industry average in a day, and they were paid considerably more. Gilbreth's approach of treating workers with respect and rewarding them for their greater productivity caused them to appreciate the improvements he suggested rather than resent them.

Lillian Gilbreth was also very active in the scientific management movement. She was one of the first people to study the environmental and psychological aspects of work. A noted teacher, author, and lecturer, she introduced scientific management methods throughout the world. The Gilbreths also took scientific management out of factories and applied it to many service operations, such as in hospitals and offices and in designing work methods and tools for the disabled. Lillian Gilbreth even wrote a book on how to apply scientific management to "home-making." The Gilbreths also had a flair for the humorous. Frank was known for stopping and observing people doing work almost anywhere and then showing them how to do it better. The Gilbreths are best known to the general public as the subjects of the humorous and informative book and movie *Cheaper by the Dozen*, which describes how they used scientific management to raise their 12 children.[4]

---

[4]The principal ideas of the Gilbreths are contained in William Spriegel and Clark Myers, *The Writings of the Gilbreths*, Irwin, Homewood IL, 1953. *Cheaper by the Dozen*, by Frank B. Gilbreth and Ernestine Gilbreth Carey, remains a humorous and instructive classic. *Time Out for Happiness*, by Frank B. Gilbreth (1970), provides additional biographical material on the Gilbreths, especially on Lillian's professional life.

The Rouge River Ford Motor plant, which produced the Model-T Ford, made its own components, and it contained the first large scale moving assembly line. It can be considered the first Just-In-Time production system.

Some of the fruits of scientific management could be seen in 1913, when Henry Ford constructed the first moving assembly line. With Ford's new production process each automobile chassis moved along a line mechanically. Each worker on the line had only a small amount of work to perform before the chassis moved to the next work station. The results were astounding; labor input for final assembly per auto decreased from 12.5 to 1.5 person-hours, the amount of skill required was much less than when a single individual assembled the entire auto, and the price of autos plummeted, making them affordable to the average person. Equally important aspects of the system were the emphasis on product simplification, component standardization, inventory control, and material management. Ford's production line can be considered the first large-scale just-in-time production system. (Taiichi Ohno, a codeveloper of the Toyota production system, credits Henry Ford with many of the features of the Toyota system.)

Coordination of production and simplification were applied to other parts of the system, such as production of the raw steel and manufacture of the automobile parts. The system operated with little raw material, in-process, and final product inventories. Ford claimed that iron ore arriving at his docks left his plant as a finished car in approximately two days.

THE HUMAN RELATIONS MOVEMENT

The purpose of scientific management was to design jobs better, train workers, and provide financial incentives to increase worker productivity. The social and psychological aspects of work other than financial self-interest were not considered significant. In the 1920s, a field of psychology developed based on the idea that other factors, such as work environment, social group pressure, and employee–management relations, had an important effect on productivity. The studies that initiated this movement were begun in 1927 at the Hawthorne plant of Western Electric Company; they are now called the **Hawthorne Studies**.

The Hawthorne studies consisted of several experiments that ran for over 10 years. In one group of experiments, called the *illumination experiments*, two groups of workers were selected and put in separate rooms. The test group had the level of illumination increased, while the control group worked under normal illumination. The researchers found that the productivity of both groups increased substantially. The tests were repeated several times, with the test group put under different levels of illumination, including very poor light. In each case the productivity of both groups increased. After a few years the researchers finally concluded that the workers were responding to the attention they received, not the illumination; by being selected and put in separate rooms, the workers considered themselves special and worked harder. Other experiments supported their results.[5]

Further experiments seemed to show that close friendships and group incentive pay could increase productivity, while negative peer pressure could inhibit workers from producing above the informally accepted group norm. There has been considerable criticism of the Hawthorne Studies, and of the interpretation of the data and the conclusions, but they remain noteworthy because they started a stream of research on social psychology and worker performance.

[5]The original report of the Hawthorne experiments is presented in *Management and the Worker* (Harvard University Press, Cambridge, MA, 1947) by F. J. Roethlisberger and W. J. Dickson, the principal researchers on the experiments. Also see *Hawthorne Revisited* by Henry Landsberger, Cornell University Press, Ithaca, NY, 1958.

OPERATIONS RESEARCH/ MANAGEMENT SCIENCE (OR/MS)

Mathematical models and analysis were used sporadically during the nineteenth and early twentieth centuries to solve operational problems. For example, Max Weber constructed mathematical models in the nineteenth century to evaluate location decisions, Ford Harris derived the basic economic order quantity equation in 1913, A. K. Erlang constructed models of queues and stochastic systems in the 1930s, and Walter Shewhart developed statistical quality control tools in the 1920s and 1930s. However, it is only in the past 50 years that mathematical analysis has been used extensively to solve business problems.

During World War II the British government created interdisciplinary teams of scientists to perform research on military operations, such as shipping logistics, search and detection (including the development of radar), and aircraft design and vulnerability. This work was designated "operational research." The U.S. and Canadian governments created similar "operations research" teams to study their own military operations. Much of this early **operations research** work utilized mathematical models and analysis in the solution of problems. This work was so successful that after the war similar approaches were applied to solving operational problems in business and government. (This industrial work was sometimes called **management science**. The terms operations research and managment science are often used interchangeably nowadays, so we will use the shorthand OR/MS when referring to either.)

In its early years, OR/MS represented a new methodology for operations management rather than a different field. This was reflected by the fact that most of the early university programs in OR/MS originated in industrial engineering departments. The types of problems regularly studied were personnel and production scheduling, vehicle routing and logistics, facility location, capacity planning and facility design, queueing, inventory planning, and statistical quality control; all these are mainstream problems in managing operations. For this reason, a working knowledge of OR/MS principles and techniques is essential for any modern manager of operations. When the mathematical models and solution techniques proved valuable for solving operational problems, they were then applied to other areas of business and government, especially finance, engineering, marketing, and accounting. Subsequently OR/MS was recognized as a separate discipline, one that dealt with methodologies rather than specific problem areas.

COMPUTERS IN OPERATIONS MANAGEMENT

The development of digital computers coincided with the growth of OR/MS. After World War II the magnitude and complexity of organizations grew rapidly. OR/MS models and solution methods lent themselves to large-scale operational problems, but only if rapid computational capabilities were available; digital computers provided them. Without digital computers the use of OR/MS methods, which are now widely used in industry, would have been stifled.

Computers rapidly gained wide use for many other operations management functions. One early use of computers was in machine control and automation. Beginning with the Industrial Revolution, using machines to replace human labor was central to improving productivity and product quality. But even with automation, people were required to monitor and adjust the machines and coordinate the material flows into and out of the machines. Computers have now taken over these tasks for some equipment. Computers are used to control machine movements; to monitor tool settings, equipment or material temperatures, and fluid flow rates; and to make continuous adjustments to rollers, valves, or heaters. Today a dozen people in an air-conditioned computer control room can run a modern steel hot-rolling mill, producing more steel than 25 years ago when several hundred people were required to operate a lower-capacity mill with lower product quality, working under more uncomfortable and dangerous conditions. Computers are now used to control and coordinate material movements among several machines and to change tool settings for the machines continuously (these are called *flexible manufacturing systems* or FMSs). *Computer-aided Design* (CAD) helps to speed up product development, standardize the parts used in products, and make it easier to transfer tool movement information to computer control equipment. Computers have revolutionized many service operations as well, such as optical scanning of products, point-of-sale computers, and automatic bank tellers.

One of the most important uses of computers in operations management is in providing better information flow. Taylor developed production documents that greatly improved information flow in factories, but information still moved slowly and was not always accurate. Computers are now used to maintain customer information, production records, inventory information, and payroll and personnel data. This information can be maintained and updated quickly and shared instantaneously with those who need it, such as department heads, machine operators, production schedulers, and materials managers. Production jobs and materials can be tracked throughout the production process, and information can be transferred easily from department to department and to customers.

THE JAPANESE PRODUCTION SYSTEM

During the 1970s, Japanese companies became significant players in the world economy, especially in products such as steel, automobiles, housewares, and consumer electronics. During the 1980s, they came to dominate many industries. The robustness of the Japanese economy is especially amazing in light of Japan's devastated condition at the end of World War II. This success has caused operations managers throughout the world to study how Japanese companies were able to develop this production dominance. The answer, now commonly called the **Japanese production system**, is a synthesis and enhancement of relatively old ideas imported from the United States.

A little-known fact is that the major components of the Japanese production system were introduced to Japan soon after World War II through a series of management training programs provided by the U.S. government: the **Civil Communication Section (CCS)** seminars, the **Training Within Industry (TWI)** courses, and the **Management Training Program (MTP)**. The material for these seminars and training sessions was developed during World War II to help U.S. companies gear up for the demands put on them during the war. They were very successful in the United States, but apparently their influence diminished after the war. In contrast, Japanese companies adopted

The principles of Japanese or "Lean" Production Systems are an integral part of the operations at Saturn's Spring Hill, Tennessee, plant.

these methods and continued to improve them. They invited American production experts such as Joseph Juran and W. Edwards Deming to help them.[6]

The Japanese production system is based on three principles or goals:

1. ***Quality comes first.*** A large proportion of the CCS seminars was devoted to the management of quality. One section of the 1949 course manual contains the statement: "The primary objective of the company is to put the quality of the product ahead of all other consideration."[7] High Japanese product quality is based on several features: (a) designing products for better quality, (b) holding everyone responsible for product quality rather than using inspectors, (c) making the product correct the first time to avoid rework and rejects, and (d) utilizing statistical quality control methods where appropriate.
2. ***Improve the product and process continuously.*** Most advances in process technology are the result of many small improvements over time. The Japanese production system encourages workers and supervisors to suggest improvements that reduce cost and increase quality. In contrast to scientific management, which had experts study the production system and make changes that workers were ordered to carry out, the Japanese system relies on production workers, who are closest to the system, to make suggestions. This low-level engineering enhances worker satisfaction and utilizes firsthand expertise. This approach was used by U.S. companies, such as Lincoln Electric and Procter and Gamble, before World War II, but it was another idea that did not spread in the United States the way it did in Japan. Quality circles and suggestion systems are two specific programs used to promote continuous improvement.
3. ***Eliminate all forms of waste.*** The Japanese production system focuses on identifying all forms of waste and eliminating them. Any activity or material that costs money but does not add value to the product is eliminated. It is this idea that led to inventory reduction methods such as just-in-time production. Inventories usually do not add value to the product but they cost money, so any reduction in inventories that does not jeopardize on-time delivery is beneficial. Similarly, quality defects are a form of waste and must be eliminated. This idea is the motivation behind the quality policy of making things right the first time.

The way Japanese companies such as Toyota implement these principles is as important as the principles themselves. First, there is total organizational commitment and involvement. Everyone is responsible for product quality, process improvement, and reduction of waste. These are not assigned to separate quality control or process engineering departments. Second, because they have greater responsibility, workers require more education and training; Japanese companies devote considerable resources to training. Third, Japanese companies still utilize classical scientific management principles of experimentation and measurement to see whether or not alternative methods are better. Industrial engineering is an integral component of most Japanese manufacturing companies.

In summary, the Japanese production system is based on U.S. ideas that have been synthesized and improved by the Japanese. For the most part, the benefits of this pro-

---

[6]Alan Robinson's article "Origins of the Modern Japanese Management Style," in Alan Robinson (ed.), *Continuous Improvement in Operations* (Productivity Press, Cambridge, MA, 1991), provides a good discussion of post–World War II management assistance to Japan. Also see Kenneth Hopper, "Creating Japan's New Industrial Management: The Americans as Teachers," *Human Resource Management*, Summer 1982, pp. 13–34.

[7]Ibid., p. 23.

duction system have little to do with cultural differences; they are available to any company or country willing to base its production on these basic principles.

OPERATIONS MANAGEMENT TODAY

An interesting aspect of operations management is that most of the vital problems a century ago are still important today. The basic principles and strategies for solving them have existed for many years, but we now have better tools and information to execute them. However, some new challenges face operations managers today.

The Service Economy

Since 1960, service industries such as health care, banking, insurance, travel and entertainment, government services, and retailing have grown rapidly in the United States compared to manufacturing. Although service-sector jobs now greatly outnumber those in manufacturing, an interesting fact is that manufacturing made up a larger percentage of U.S. gross national product (GNP) in 1995 than it did in 1955! The big difference in employment growth has been due mostly to a large difference in productivity improvement: productivity has increased far more in manufacturing than in services. This disparity points out the need for more effort to improve service operations.

Service operations face almost all the problems encountered in manufacturing systems. So it is no surprise that applications of operations management to service systems have become more common. This is the reason the field of production management has been renamed *production/operations management* or simply *operations management*. What *is* surprising is that its principles have not been used even more. A characteristic of service organizations that has limited the application of operations management methods is that the operations function is often diffused throughout the organization. In manufacturing, by contrast, one organizational group can handle most of the activities involved in making the primary goods. Therefore, operations management expertise can be concentrated within this "production" group. In contrast, in service organizations, sales, marketing, customer service, and operations responsibilities are often intermingled because the customer frequently is in direct contact with the service production system. For example, the manager of a department in a large retail store is not only responsible for sales, customer service, and marketing (developing product displays, promotions, and pricing) but is also responsible for purchasing supplies, managing inventories, purchasing equipment, and scheduling employees. These are all areas in which a knowledge of operations management can be valuable. Thus, the shift to a service economy has made it more important for all business professionals to have a knowledge of operations management.

Environmental Awareness

A new challenge facing operations managers is to make production systems environmentally compatible yet efficient. There are many opportunities for doing this, such as reducing production of harmful by-products, recycling waste materials and energy, reducing packaging, using closed water systems for cooling and waste discharge, and even scheduling employee work hours to reduce traffic and air pollution. Many companies have found that using environmentally sound production methods is not only socially responsible but also economically beneficial. For example, Herman Miller, Inc., saves over $3 million a year by reducing the packaging it uses to ship products, selling recyclable materials, and using a waste-to-energy plant.[8]

---

[8] David Woodruff, "Herman Miller: How Green Is My Factory," *Business Week*, Sept. 16, 1991, pp. 54–56.

1.5 OPERATIONS MANAGEMENT, PRODUCTIVITY, AND COMPETITIVENESS

At the organizational level it is easy to see why high productivity and well-run operations are important. Those companies that provide the best values for their customers will prosper. The best value is determined by what customers receive in terms of product function, quality, and timeliness relative to the price they pay. So, when a company reduces its cost of operations, or adds more function or quality to its products at the same cost, it improves its competitive position. The best salespeople in the world cannot sell poor-value products over the long term; customers will eventually learn. Nor can financial restructuring and accounting manipulations turn a poorly operating company into a healthy one; these actions can only give short-term cash infusions. The ultimate survival of an organization depends on what it produces, how well it produces it, and how well it markets what it produces.

Good operations and productivity are important to the health of countries as well as of individual organizations. Many measures are used to evaluate the economic strength and health of nations: per capita GNP, average income per worker, unemployment rate, and per capita manufacturing output. Regardless of the measure chosen, those countries that are economically healthiest and best able to care for their citizens are the ones that compete well in the international marketplace. The ability to compete depends on how much value can be added to products relative to the cost of adding that value. Those countries that can produce more value with less labor can afford to pay their workers more.

During the 1960s and 1970s, productivity increased at higher rates in Japan and Western Europe than in the United States. This was a major reason for the greater relative increase in the standard of living of those countries and the decline in the value of the U.S. dollar relative to the Japanese yen and most Western European currencies. Countries that devalue their currencies effectively discount the prices of goods made in those countries and decrease the real wages of their workers. Although a decline in the value of the dollar makes U.S. products more price competitive, the long-term consequence is lower real wages and profits.

The good news for the United States is that its companies are learning their lesson. In recent years, U.S. manufacturing companies such as Xerox, Cummins Engine, General Electric, Ford, and Motorola have substantially increased product quality while reducing production costs. For example, Motorola reduced its defect rate by over 99% in five years while generating annual cost savings of over $600 million.[9] Overall, manufacturing productivity in the United States increased at an average annual rate of 3.5% from 1980 to 1990 compared to only 2.3% in the 1970s. This increased productivity, coupled with low wage increases and changes in foreign exchange rates, caused the cost of labor in dollars per unit of manufacturing output in the United States to increase from 1982 to 1993 by only 16% (see Figure 1.3). In contrast, during the same period the per unit labor cost increased by 124% in Japan and 101% in Germany! One consequence is that U. S. exports of manufactured goods (in constant dollars) have more than doubled in the past 10 years. Although exchange rates played a major role in this improved competitiveness, the relative improvement in the productivity rate has been important. In fact, despite the impression given by the popular press, *absolute* productivity in the

[9]G. Christian Hill, and Ken Yamada, "Motorola Illustrates How an Aged Giant Can Remain Vibrant," *Wall Street Journal*, Dec. 9, 1992,

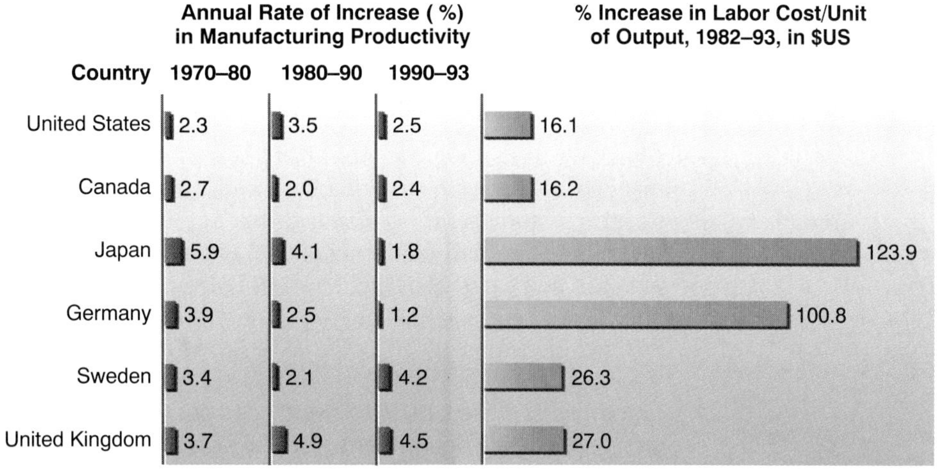

FIGURE 1.3 Relative growth in manufacturing productivity and labor cost/unit of output in U.S. dollars for selected countries. Source: Monthly Labor Review, U.S. Dept. of Labor, Bureau of Labor Statistics, April, 1991, p. 86 and April, 1995, p. 132.

United States (in contrast to productivity *growth*) has been estimated (even by Japanese sources) to be as much as 50% higher than in Japan.[10]

However, while growth in manufacturing productivity in the United States has increased in recent years, growth in service productivity has lagged behind.[11] This is troubling because the opportunities for improving productivity in the service sector are many. Unfortunately, most managers in service companies have almost no training in operations management. Referring to quality and productivity improvements in office work, Curt W. Reimann, who runs the Malcolm Baldrige National Quality Award program, stated, "I don't think most people have fully realized the potential there yet."[12] The material covered in this book should help make those entering the service sector more aware of opportunities for productivity improvement and more capable of implementing changes.

1.6 OPERATIONS MANAGEMENT IS FOR EVERYONE

Operations management is a *process* and a way of thinking, not simply a profession. Knowledge about the production systems, the thought process, and the decision-making tools presented in this book should be of professional value to anyone who man-

[10]For discussions of relative national productivities, see Everette Gardner, Jr., and John Ivancevich, "Productivity in the U.S. and Japan: A Reexamination," *Interfaces* November–December, 1994, pp. 66–73; and Christopher Farrell, "Is the Japanese Dynamo Losing Juice?" *Business Week*, June 27, 1994, p. 44.

[11]There has been much debate about how to measure service productivity, and many researchers claim that service productivity growth has been underestimated. See Alfred Malabre, Jr., and Lindley Clark, Jr., "Many Fields, Like Insurance, Just Defy Measurement: Outsourcing Clouds the Data," *Wall Street Journal*, Aug. 12, 1992, ; and Richard McKenzie, "The Myth of the Decline in Production Jobs," *St. Louis Post-Dispatch*, Mar. 18, 1986, .

[12]Aaron Bernstein, "Quality Is Becoming Job One in the Office, Too," *Business Week*, Apr. 29, 1991, p. 52.

ages people, materials, or machines. The "On the Job" inserts in this book show how managers of various functions in many types of organizations use operations management. The following examples provide a small glimpse of how operations management can be used in nontraditional ways in various business settings.

1. Chuck Wise (see "On the Job" in Chapter 8), while head of Corning Inc.'s tax unit, decided to apply the productivity and quality improvement methods used in Corning's manufacturing plants to his accounting operation. Using product and process design and quality management principles (described in Chapters 5, 8, and 11), he began by asking himself, "Who is the customer for our product?" The answer, which is usually not easy to determine for many office operations, was the Internal Revenue Service. So he asked the IRS to rate the product his department was supplying. For years Corning had spent hundreds of person-hours each year preparing its tax return, which included thousands of accounts that detailed the expenses of each department. The IRS said they did not need these details, and in fact, trying to reconcile them added to their work. So the Tax Department at Corning changed its product design and stopped preparing the detailed expense accounts. This saved Corning over 400 person-hours a year and allowed the IRS to reduce its auditing time from 18 to 15 months.[13]
2. A multinational oil company wished to buy another company. To obtain special tax benefits, the purchase had to be completed before the end of the calendar year. Unfortunately, the legal process was very long, and the purchase deadline loomed. The head of the legal department asked an in-house consultant to analyze the merger time schedule. By using a project scheduling technique called PERT/CPM, which will be covered in Chapter 17, the consultant was able to pinpoint the bottleneck in the process. The bottleneck was then eliminated and the purchase completed on time.

A knowledge of operations management can be valuable at a personal level as well. Although you need not make your household a scientific management laboratory, as Lillian Gilbreth did, you can use operations management principles and methods to be more efficient and effective in your personal life. For example, the inventory methods presented in Chapter 13 can be used to make better decisions at the grocery store about whether or not to take advantage of a quantity discount, and the job design techniques described in Chapter 10 can help make house painting, yard work, and other household chores more efficient and less tiring.

These personal decisions do not merit in-depth study, but they can be improved by using even simple versions of the analyses presented in this book. Some personal decisions, however, such as buying a house, leasing a car, and purchasing insurance involve large amounts of money and considerable risk, and they merit serious analytical study. Operations management methods can sometimes help with these more significant personal decisions, as the following example illustrates.

U.S. tax law allows employers to create accounts for employees called *flexible spending accounts*. With these accounts employees are allowed to set aside, before taxes, a specified amount of their pay for health care and child care expenses incurred during the year. This is a substantial benefit for most employees and can reduce taxes by thousands of dollars a year. The only complication is that employees must declare before the year starts how much money will be put in each account; this amount cannot be changed during the year. If qualifying expenses during the year are less than the

[13]Ibid., p. 53.

amount the employee put in, the funds remaining in the account are forfeited. If qualifying expenses are greater than the amount put in the account, the employee must pay the difference from after-tax dollars, thereby missing an opportunity to reduce taxes further. The question facing the employee each year is how much to put in each account.

Donald Rosenfield has shown how this problem can be solved using the one-period inventory model presented in Chapter 13. This result has been presented to employees at many organizations and has probably allowed employees to save millions of dollars in taxes by helping them select their contributions more effectively.[14]

Operations management is certainly not a cure for all the ills of the world. But it can be rewarding, both professionally and personally, if you constantly look for ways to apply the concepts and techniques to everyday decisions.

SUMMARY

- **Production systems** convert inputs into useful outputs, called **products.**
- Tangible products are called **goods**; they are produced by **manufacturing systems.**
- Intangible products are called **services**; they are produced by **service systems.**
- Some products are a combination of goods and services.
- The production of goods differs from the production of services in the following ways:
  - Production of goods requires more material inputs than production of services.
  - Goods normally can be stored for future use, whereas services cannot.
  - Consumers must often participate or be in contact with service delivery systems but not with manufacturing systems.
- Organizations need a good **strategy** to survive and succeed, and operations should play an important role in that strategy.
- **Operations management** involves the process of planning, designing, and operating production systems and subsystems.
- Most managers have operations management responsibilities; these include product design, capacity planning, process design, facility location, facility design and layout, quality assurance, materials management and inventory control, scheduling, and maintenance planning
- Operations managers need analytical tools to be most effective.
- The **Japanese Production System** is based on three principles:
  - Quality comes first.
  - Improve product and process quality continuously.
  - Eliminate all forms of waste.
- Business productivity is crucial to the health of the nation as well as the survival of individual organizations.
- Operations management principles and tools can be useful in almost any job and in our everyday lives.

KEY TERMS

Civil Communication Section (CCS) **25**
financial function **9**
goods **7**
Hawthorne Studies **23**
Human Relations Movement **23**
industrial engineers **21**
Industrial Revolution **18**
interchangeable parts **19**
Japanese production system **25**
management science **24**
Management Training Program (MTP) **25**
manufacturing systems **7**
marketing function **9**
operations (or production) function **9**
operations management **10**
operations research **24**
production systems **7**
productivity **11**

[14]Donald B. Rosenfield, "Optimal Management of Tax-Sheltered Employee Reimbursement Programs," *Interfaces*, Vol. 16, No. 3, 1986, pp. 68–72.

products **7**
scientific management **21**
services **8**
service systems **8**
specialization of labor **20**
strategy **12**
Training Within Industry (TWI) **25**

DISCUSSION AND REVIEW QUESTIONS

1. List two products, not mentioned in the chapter, of the following types:
   (a) goods.
   (b) services.
   (c) combination of a good and a service.

   Explain why each product fits into the selected category.
2. Discuss the major differences between the production of goods and the production of services.
3. Select a product/production process with which you are familiar. (a) List the most important inputs for making the product. (b) Describe in some detail how the production process converts these inputs into the product.
4. Select a production process with which you are familiar. Identify and describe two specific operations management problems (e.g., inventory management) that are important for that process. Be precise and specify in detail why these problems are especially important for the selected process.
5. List and discuss what you think are the two most common/important operations management problems encountered by people in the following jobs:
   (a) A high school principal.
   (b) Manager of a restaurant.
   (c) Manager of the auditing department for a public accounting firm.
   (d) Manager of a full-service branch bank.
   (e) Regional sales manager for a manufacturer of men's and women's clothing.
6. The eighteenth-century innovations in spinning and weaving had two significant components: (1) replacement of human labor with other sources of power and (2) embodiment of skill or technology in machines rather than people. (a) How and why would these two components improve general economic conditions? (b) Identify two modern production innovations and explain how they exhibit these two components.
7. What were the major differences between scientific management, as taught by Frederick Taylor, and that espoused by the Gilbreths?
8. Other than for cash registers, list two different ways computers were used in operations to serve you as a customer in the past week.
9. What are the three basic principles of Japanese manufacturing systems? Why do you think it took so long for American companies to adopt these principles in their production systems?
10. Rather than working so hard to increase productivity to be internationally competitive, why should not countries simply impose import restrictions? How would import restrictions hurt the country imposing them? Under what conditions might such restrictions be appropriate?
11. Think of a job you held or at which you currently work. Give one detailed example of an operations management responsibility you had in that job.
12. Describe how an organization not mentioned in this chapter has changed some aspect of its operations to reduce environmental damage.
13. Give an example of how you might be able to use the knowledge gained in this course in your everyday life.

SELECTED READINGS

BERNSTEIN, AARON. "Quality Is Becoming Job One in the Office, Too," *Business Week*, Apr. 29, 1991, pp. 52–56.

CLARK, KIM, and ROBERT HAYES. "Recapturing America's Heritage," *California Management Review*, Summer 1988, pp. 9–33.

COPLEY, FRANK B. *Frederick W. Taylor: Father of Scientific Management*, American Society of Mechanical Engineers, New York, 1923.

ERLENKOTTER, DONALD. "Ford Whitman Harris and the Economic Order Quantity Model," *Operations Research*, Vol. 38, 1990, pp. 937–946.

HAYES, ROBERT H., and STEVEN C. WHEELWRIGHT. *Restoring Our Competitive Edge: Competing Through Manufacturing*, Wiley, New York, 1984.

HOPPER, KENNETH. "Creating Japan's New Industrial Management: The Americans as Teachers," *Human Resource Management*, Summer 1982, pp. 13–34.

LANDSBERGER, HENRY. *Hawthorne Revisited*, Cornell University Press, Ithaca, NY, 1958.

ROBINSON, ALAN. "Origins of the Modern Japanese Management Style," in Alan Robinson (ed.), *Continuous Improvement in Operations*, Productivity Press, Cambridge, MA, 1991.

ROETHLISBERGER, F. J., and W. J. DICKSON. *Management and the Worker*, Harvard University Press, Cambridge, MA, 1947.

ROSENFIELD, DONALD B. "Optimal Management of Tax-Sheltered Employee Reimbursement Programs," *Interfaces*, Vol. 16, No. 3, 1986, pp. 68–72.

SKINNER, WICKHAM. *Manufacturing in the Corporate Strategy*, Wiley, New York, 1978.

SPRIEGEL, WILLIAM, and CLARK MYERS. *The Writings of the Gilbreths*, Richard D. Irwin, Homewood, IL, 1953.

TAYLOR, FREDERICK W. *The Principles of Scientific Management*, Harper and Bros., New York, 1911.

WOODRUFF, DAVID. "Herman Miller: How Green Is My Factory," *Business Week*, Sept. 16, 1991, pp. 54–56.

YOST, EDNA. *Frank and Lillian Gilbreth, Partners for Life*, Rutgers University Press, New Brunswick, NJ, 1949.

CHAPTER 2

OPERATIONS STRATEGY

2.1 STEERING THE SHIP
On the Job: Bob Anastasi, CTI-Cryogenics

2.2 THE ORGANIZATION'S STRATEGY
Goals
Market and Competitive Analysis
Selecting Products, Markets, and Order-Winning Dimensions
Philosophy and Policies
The Business Unit Strategy

2.3 OPERATIONS AS A COMPETITIVE WEAPON

2.4 DEVELOPING AN OPERATIONS STRATEGY

2.5 OPERATIONALIZING GOALS AND MEASURING PERFORMANCE
Measuring Productivity
Cost Measures and Accounting Practices
Goal-Based Measures of Performance

2.6 GUIDING OPERATIONS DECISIONS: OPERATIONS SUBSTRATEGIES
Technology Strategy: Capabilities and Expertise
Capacity Strategy
Facility Location Strategy
Process Strategy
Quality Strategy
Human Resources Strategy
Information in Operations Strategy

2.7 PRODUCTION COST STRUCTURE AND THE OPERATIONS AND MARKETING STRATEGIES
Leverage and Capacity Utilization
Using Experience Effects and Economies of Scale Strategically
In Good Company: Hewlett-Packard's Strategy Takes Aim at Its Competitors

2.8 REVISING AND UPDATING THE OPERATIONS STRATEGY

Walt Disney World, Orlando, Florida: An Operations Strategy Case

2.1 Steering the Ship

Without a set of long-term goals and a plan for achieving them, an organization is like a crew on a rudderless ship without a map or compass. An organization's **strategy** is the map, compass, and rudder for the organization. It tells members of the organization where it wants to go and how to get there, and it provides a mechanism for steering the organization. The members are the engine and crew for the ship; they provide the power to move it, and they control the rudder. But without a strategy, even good employees are unable to find their way to the organization's goals.

A central theme of this book is that operational decisions should be consistent with and promote the organization's overall goals. CTI-Cryogenics, a producer of cryogenic vacuum pumps used in semiconductor manufacturing equipment, has built its reputation on supplying customers with the products they want when they need them. To support this time-focused and customer-driven strategy, Bob Anastasi, the subject of this chapter's On the Job box, has helped to make that company's production system extremely flexible and responsive.

This chapter provides a preview of the role of operations in the organization's strategy and achievement of its goals. We first describe the components of an organization's overall strategy and how the **operations strategy** fits within it. We then discuss the major components of an operations strategy and explain how operations can be used as a competitive weapon by the organization. It is rare to find a successful organization that does not have a strong operations strategy; the In Good Company box (Hewlett-Packard's Strategy Takes Aim at Its Competitors) and end-of-chapter case (Walt Disney World, Orlando: An Operations Strategy Case) provide two examples of successful strategies. In contrast, *postmortem* studies of unsuccessful organizations frequently conclude that a poor or nonexistent operations strategy was instrumental in the organization's demise.

On the Job

Bob Anastasi: CTI-Cryogenics

Competing in the cryogenic vacuum pump industry presents not only technological challenges but strategic ones as well. As vice-president of operations at CTI-Cryogenics, a division of Helix Technology Corporation, Bob Anastasi has met the challenge and helped his company become an industry leader by developing a strategy that is both time focused and customer driven.

To provide customers with ever-changing state-of-the-art products when they want them, Bob has guided development of a production system that is highly flexible and responsive. The production process, technology, job designs, and material flow all focus on service and time. The system, which can produce CTI's full line of products each day in lot sizes as small as a single unit, is driven by a just-in-time mechanism; each day it makes what it sells. There is no stockroom because components arrive and are used in the production process the same day. The system's flexibility also allows CTI to introduce new products quickly to take advantage of the company's superiority in cryogenic technology.

"In addition to evaluating new production processes and technologies," Bob says, "I am constantly confronting the issue of which steps of the production chain CTI should perform itself and which ones it should outsource to suppliers." Bob's training in mechanical engineering and operations research has provided him with the technical and financial tools necessary to make these decisions.

2.2 THE ORGANIZATION'S STRATEGY

An organization strategy is multifaceted, and its development requires several distinct steps, which are summarized in Table 2.1. The **organization strategy** guides the creation of individual business unit strategies when separate business units exist and the strategies of the individual business functions: operations, marketing, and financial.

It is important to recognize that there is no one best strategy for all firms. Companies within the same industry often have very different strategies, yet each may perform very well (or poorly). Certainly for some products and markets some strategies work well and others do not, but studies indicate that it is important to have a clear strategy that utilizes the organization's strengths and to execute it as planned. For example, Sony and Hewlett-Packard have followed the strategy of being leaders in product innovation, while Matsushita and Texas Instruments have focused on process innovation, becoming low-cost, high-quality producers of large market products. Yet each has been successful within the scientific and consumer electronics industry.

Let us look carefully at how an organization builds a strategy, following the steps presented in Table 2.1.

GOALS

A good strategy begins with an explicit statement of the organization's goals (called a **mission statement**) and the criteria to be used to evaluate their achievement. Organizations may have several goals, but usually one or two are dominant. For-profit companies strive to maximize shareholder value. A closely related goal is to achieve a high (and growing) profit level over the long term to ensure survival. This might be measured by average annual growth in earnings over the last five years or by average return on equity over a similar period. A secondary goal might be to achieve security and stability (as measured by variance in profit measures or the debt/equity ratio).

Nonprofit organizations need explicit statements of goals even more than for-profit companies because their goals are often less apparent and may be more difficult to measure. For example, a symphony orchestra may establish as goals (1) to be recognized as a leading orchestra in the country (or the world), (2) to maintain a sound financial condition, and (3) to perform for as wide an audience as possible. These might be measured by (1) annual rankings in periodicals, Grammy nominations and awards, or recordings on major record labels, (2) net reserves, endowments, or the latest operating surplus/deficit, and (3) the number of people attending concerts in its home city, on tour, or from special demographic groups, such as children.

TABLE 2.1 STEPS IN DEVELOPING AN ORGANIZATION STRATEGY

1. Establish organizational goals
2. Analyze:
   a. Market characteristics
   b. Competition
   c. Competitive Strengths and Weaknesses
3. Identify and select:
   a. Products
   b. Geographic Markets
   c. Order-winning Dimensions
4. Specify policy constraints and guidelines

MARKET AND COMPETITIVE ANALYSIS

An organization will be most successful when it provides products of better value to its customers than its competitors do. This requires that the organization gather information about the intended customers: the features they are looking for in products, the amount they are willing to pay, and the product choices they made in the past and why they made those choices. To understand these product choices, the organization must also gather information about competing products and the characteristics of the companies that provide them. For example, one company may have a history of providing low-priced but low-quality products, while another competitor is known for its product innovation. Determining these characteristics can help a company identify product opportunities that are not being used by other companies.

Although identifying product and market opportunities is important, success requires that the organization be capable of exploiting these opportunities. For example, a chemical company may recognize that there is customer demand for specialty chemicals that can be produced and delivered within 48 hours. But if the company does not have the facilities or technical expertise to do so, it cannot exploit this opportunity. Therefore, an important step in developing a strategy is for the organization to determine its strengths and weaknesses relative to those of competitors. Like an athlete, an organization is usually most successful when it utilizes its strengths to the fullest and stays away from those activities where its weaknesses would be a serious liability. Self-assessment, combined with the market and competitive analysis, may identify components of the organization that need to be strengthened to take advantage of opportunities. So, in addition to exploiting existing strengths, an organization's strategy may mandate creating new strengths or enhancing existing ones.

SELECTING PRODUCTS, MARKETS, AND ORDER-WINNING DIMENSIONS

Its market and competitive analysis should provide the organization with the information necessary to decide which products it will produce; the markets in which to compete; and the dimensions, such as price or quality, in which it plans to excel to compete successfully. The product/market plan should specify which products the firm will produce and/or which customers it will serve, and, where appropriate, which products it will not produce and which customers it will not serve. A computer manufacturer, for example, may decide that it will concentrate on products for the commercial work station market but will not serve the personal computer market.

No matter how well a company selects its products and markets, a requirement for earning a profit is to sell the products. Customers consider many factors when buying a product, such as price, quality, utility, availability, and promptness of delivery. They compare how well a product and a supplier perform on these and other dimensions relative to competing products and suppliers. It is difficult for a company to be superior to its competitors in every dimension (lowest price, highest quality, most innovative). So, successful companies try to excel in one or two of these dimensions, called **order-winning dimensions**, and perform adequately in the other dimensions. Organizations that do not establish and exploit their competitive advantages often spread their efforts too thin and lack focus; they do not distinguish their products in any dimension; and they tend to be unsuccessful.

The most common order-winning dimensions are price, quality (including service), delivery (speed and reliability), flexibility (product variety and customization, volume changes), and innovation (uniqueness of products and speed of product development). These are selected based on the company's competitive advantages, including its financial resources, geographical distribution of facilities, technological or product development capabilities, proprietary processes, and human resources. A company such as

Corning has superior engineering personnel and production methods that allow it to produce glass products that other companies cannot produce; it uses this expertise to produce unique products that have no close substitutes. By contrast, a company such as steel maker Nucor, has an excellent work force and specially designed equipment that allow it to produce standard steel products at lower cost than competitors; therefore, Nucor competes by using price as its primary order-winning dimension.

PHILOSOPHY AND POLICIES

Along with a specification of products, markets, and order-winning dimensions, a strategic plan should contain any policy constraints within which the organization will operate. These may result from company philosophy or ethical principles or from beliefs about fundamental ingredients for achieving long-term goals; for example, there will be no layoffs, or the company will only stay in markets in which it is one of the two largest competitors.

THE BUSINESS UNIT STRATEGY

Large organizations are often divided into separate operating divisions, subsidiary companies, or product line groups that operate as relatively autonomous business units, controlling their own marketing, production, and financial functions. The business units of a company that produces thousands of products and competes in many different geographical markets do not face the same product opportunities and competitive challenges. So, each should have its own business strategy. The business unit strategies should be developed in the same way as the organization strategy, and they will have much in common with that of the parent organization, especially its goals. But differences in competitive strengths and weaknesses, as well as market conditions, may cause business units to have different strategies with respect to the type and size of their product portfolios and the order-winning dimensions they utilize. (When we refer to the *organization strategy*, we mean the business unit strategy when such units exist in the organization.)

2.3 OPERATIONS AS A COMPETITIVE WEAPON

In conjunction with developing the organization's strategy, each functional unit within the organization should establish a strategic plan that supports the organization's strategy and works to achieve its goals. Historically, the organization strategies of most companies focused on the marketing function—which products to make, which markets to penetrate, and along which dimensions to compete most intensively. However, most aspects of the marketing function affect the operations function to some degree. Every time a product is introduced or revised, or the ways the product will be promoted are changed, the production system feels the effect. This is especially true for services, where frequently the service system *is* the product.

It is now recognized that the operations (production) function plays an essential role in achieving the organization's goals and should be an integral part of the organization's strategy. The marketing strategy should not simply flow into or dictate the operations strategy. The operations strategy needs to be proactive instead of reactive; the characteristics and competitive advantages of the operations function should influence which new products to make, which markets to serve, and especially along which dimensions the company can compete most effectively. Much of the success of Wal-Mart can be attributed to the fact that its founder, Sam Walton, was called "obsessed with

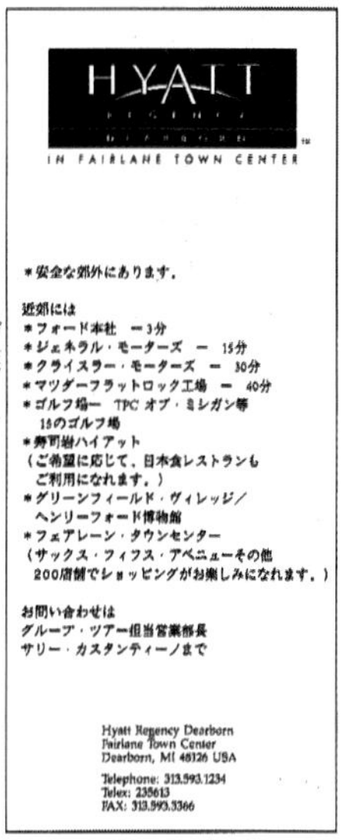

HYATT
IN FAIRLANE TOWN CENTER
*安全な郊外にあります。
近郊には
*フォード本社 ー3分
*ジェネラル・モーターズ ー 15分
*クライスラー・モーターズ ー 30分
*マツダーフラットロック工場 ー 40分
*ゴルフ場ー TPC オブ・ミシガン等
15のゴルフ場
*寿司树ハイアット
(ご希望に応じて、日本食レストランも
ご利用になれます。)
*グリーンフィールド・ヴィレッジ/
ヘンリーフォード博物館
*フェアレーン・タウンセンター
(サックス・フィフス・アベニューその他
200店舗でショッピングがお楽しみになれます。)
お問い合わせは
グループ・ツアー担当営業部長
サリー・カスタンティーノまで
Hyatt Regency Dearborn
Fairlane Town Center
Dearborn, MI 48126 USA
Telephone: 313.593.1234
Telex: 235613
FAX: 313.593.3366

The Hyatt Regency Hotels in Detroit and Dearborn, Michigan, distinguish themselves from competitors by having Japanese speaking employees and providing brochures in Japanese. This helps them compete for the business of Japanese auto executives.

operations." The following examples show how operational strengths can be used effectively as competitive weapons.

1. ***Product/Process Expertise.*** A company can have special expertise in making certain products. For example, Sharp Corporporation has prospered in consumer electronics thanks to its dominance in producing liquid crystal displays. Similarly, the Detroit Hyatt Regency Hotel has Japanese-speaking employees to assist Japanese customers, a service few other U.S. hotels offer.

2. ***Quick Delivery.*** A company can have a production process and capacity that allows it to produce a product and satisfy a customer's request quickly. Among many familiar examples are one-hour eyeglass manufacturing, one-hour photo developing, and same-day dry-cleaning and shoe repair.

3. ***Short Product Cycle.*** Research has shown that the first company to enter a market gains a significant market share advantage over subsequent competitors. A McKinsey and Company study showed that a delay of six months in bringing a product to market can cost a company one-third of the product's *lifetime* profit potential.[1] The speed of product introduction is greatly dependent on the production system; those companies that can put new products into production quickly obtain this advantage. Hewlett-Packard, which is this chapter's In Good Company feature, has dominated the laser printer industry because it was the first in the market, and it has continued to bring out new products quickly before its competitors can catch up.

4. ***Production Flexibility.*** Some companies specialize in having highly flexible and rapidly responsive operations. Celestica, Inc., a Canadian computer component manufacturer, uses equipment that is not bolted to the floor so that production lines can be reconfigured within hours or days to make new and different products. This flexibility has allowed Celestica to expand from making a few products for only one customer (IBM) to making hundreds of products for over 40 different companies. Likewise, Dell Computer established itself initially by using a build-to-order production system that promised delivery of customized personal computers within five days of ordering.

5. ***Low-Cost Process.*** A company with an especially efficient production system or access to a low-cost resource may be able to make standard products at lower cost than its competitors. For example, steel companies such as Nucor have competed successfully on price against larger integrated steel producers by using processes called *mini-mills*. Mini-mills gain their price advantage by processing scrap steel rather than producing primary steel from iron ore and by producing a limited set of commodity products. In the service sector, Southwest Airlines has become an industry leader by developing the lowest-cost passenger airline system in the United States.

6. ***Convenience and Location.*** Facility location can provide substantial competitive advantage, especially when it is interwoven with the marketing strategy. For example, American Express Corporation competes primarily based on location convenience. It has more offices located throughout the world to replace lost or stolen travelers checks and to provide other travel services than its competitors. This convenience allows American Express to charge higher fees for many of its services.

---

[1]See Joseph T. Vesey, "The New Competitors: They Think in Terms of 'Speed-to-Market'," *Academy of Management Executive*, Vol. 5, No. 2, 1991, pp. 23–33.

7. **Product Variety and Facility Size.** In some industries, the variety of products offered and the size of operations can provide a competitive advantage. Grocery stores and "superstore" retailers increasingly compete by having larger stores that carry a larger inventory of products and offer additional services, such as video rental and banking services.
8. **Quality.** A company that can produce a product of higher quality than its competitors can increase its sales volume while commanding a higher price. Toyota Motors and McDonald's are two examples of companies that have used quality as a competitive weapon. Both companies initially used low price as their primary order-winning dimension, and they developed production processes that allowed them to be low-cost producers. But each company worked hard on its production processes to develop a reputation for high quality as well. Toyota is able to outsell competitors consistently while being priced higher because of its higher perceived quality. One component of product quality, especially for restaurants, is product consistency. McDonald's Restaurants has been especially successful at achieving consistency with respect to food quality, quick service, and cleanliness of facilities.

2.4 DEVELOPING AN OPERATIONS STRATEGY

The organization strategy and the operations strategy should be developed together because the selection of products, markets, and order-winning dimensions may be driven by operational factors. The operations strategy should identify the goals of the operations function (these are sometimes called the *strategic production tasks*). These goals represent the things the operations function must do well so that, when combined with the efforts of the other functions, the organization will excel in its order-winning dimensions and achieve its overall goals (Figure 2.1).

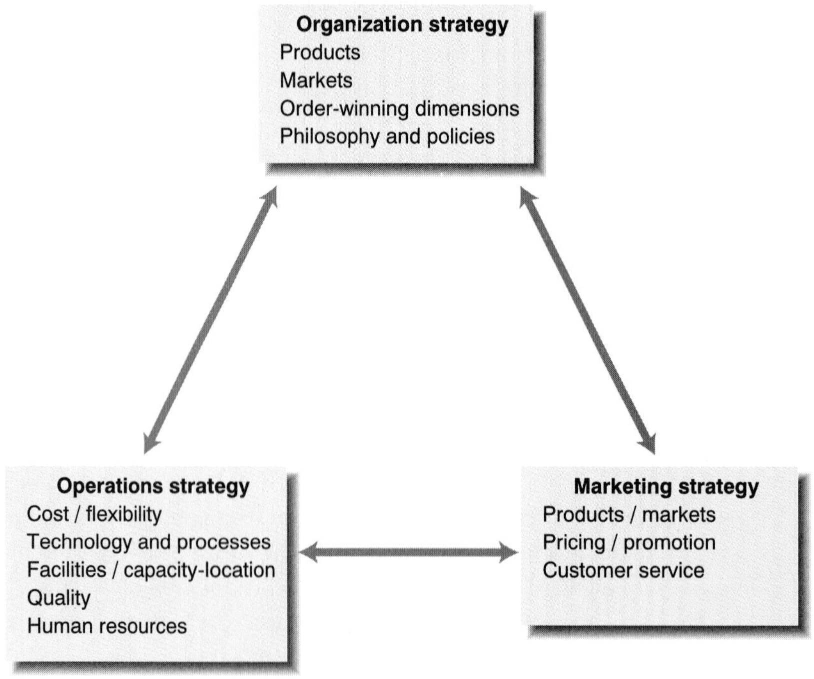

FIGURE 2.1 Relationships among organization, operations, and marketing strategies.

Barnes and Nobel uses its large facilities and book selection to compete for customers.

Just as the organization's strategic plan should guide the strategies and policies of the functional units, the operations strategy should guide decisions related to the design, planning, and operation of the production system. Consequently, the operations strategy should include explicit substrategies or plans for those aspects of operations that play an important role. For example, a retail company such as Barnes and Noble, which competes in terms of the large selection of books carried, should have explicit substrategies for facility capacity and design and inventory management. The Walt Disney World case at the end of the chapter shows how almost every aspect of operations can be used to support a company's strategy, but most organizations can compete very effectively by emphasizing one or two operational strengths in their strategies.

Regardless of the specific strategy devised, the operations strategy should be consistent with the marketing strategy. To illustrate, suppose the operations strategy focuses on minimizing production costs, but the marketing strategy emphasizes product customization and quick response. Decisions made by the operations function, such as to specialize production processes and utilize long production runs, may achieve the operations goal of reducing cost, but they run counter to the way the products are being marketed. This will almost certainly lead to disaster.

The following sections describe the components of an operations strategy, and they further illustrate how operations can be used to gain strategic advantages.

2.5 OPERATIONALIZING GOALS AND MEASURING PERFORMANCE

The operations strategy should identify those activities that the operations function must perform for the organization to achieve its goals. Therefore, the operations strategy should include goals that address *effectiveness* (doing the right things) as well as *efficiency* (doing things right). Unfortunately, many organizations limit their operational goals to short-term measures of productivity and cost. Perhaps they have made the assumption that any reduction in cost or any increase in a productivity measure will help achieve the organization's goals. But this is frequently not true. Limiting the operations goals to cost minimization and efficiency ignores many order-winning dimensions that affect sales and revenue, such as quality, product variety, and quick response. Although being efficient and keeping costs low can improve profits, cost minimization is not the same as profit maximization, and achieving the former could sacrifice the latter.

Even when appropriate operations goals are specified, such as providing consistently on-time delivery or having the best product quality in the industry, they must be translated into tangible performance measures, and these measures must be used in the evaluation and reward system. When top management evaluates the performance of operations departments and employees only in terms of cost or productivity measures, the likely consequence is that employees concentrate on making their performance look good relative to those measures, ignoring the other goals. This would be bad enough if the cost and productivity measures accurately evaluated achievement of at least a cost goal, but in many cases they do not even do that. In fact, they can create incentives for employees to choose options that increase total cost and decrease real productivity. A case in point is given by Example 1 in Chapter 9. In that case the loading dock productivity for a company, as measured by trucks loaded per worker, is maximized by having a small loading crew. But the result is that trucks and their drivers wait much longer to have trucks loaded and unloaded, which decreases real productivity, increases total cost, and decreases profit.

Because of their widespread use, we discuss measures of productivity and cost first. We then present some other operational goals and measures.

MEASURING PRODUCTIVITY

Productivity can be defined as the amount of output produced divided by the amount of input used. The greater the amount of output produced from a fixed quantity of inputs, the higher the productivity. Similarly, the smaller the quantity of inputs required to produce a fixed amount of outputs, the higher the productivity. At a conceptual level this is an easy idea to grasp; however, at a practical level, measuring and comparing productivities can present problems, as the following cases illustrate.

1. When there are several inputs and outputs, it can be difficult to combine them into common units of measure. For example, is a system that produces 1000 12-ounce beverage bottles and 2000 16-ounce bottles per hour more productive than one that produces 1500 12-ounce bottles and 1200 20-ounce bottles?
2. How should we compare the productivity of systems that make similar products of different quality? If a production process yields an automobile, it makes a difference whether the output is a Toyota Tercel or an Infiniti Q45.
3. For many services, such as legal cases, the product is unique for each customer. Does a change in the production process that allows a lawyer to resolve 10% more cases than in the previous year mean that there has been a 10% increase in productivity? Unless the characteristics and mix of cases were similar in the two years, this is difficult to determine.

Output/Labor Ratio

Because of these problems productivity is measured in various ways, depending on the circumstances. One measure is the **output/labor ratio**:

output/labor ratio = units of output produced/person-hours of labor used

At a macro level this ratio has been used to compare different production systems that make commodity-type products when the raw material inputs are essentially the same for all producers. For example, the productivity of different steel-making processes and the productivity of the steel industries in different countries are often measured by the ratio of tons of steel produced per person-hour (or its reciprocal: person-hours per ton of steel). The output/labor ratio is also the measure used by the U.S. Bureau of Labor Statistics to measure and compare national productivities, such as in Figure 1.3.

The output/labor ratio is most useful in operations management for evaluating the performance of individual machines or departments over time or for comparing the performance of individuals performing the same tasks. For example, the productivity of a bottling operation might be measured by the number of bottles filled per person-hour (assuming all bottles are of the same volume). This ratio could be used (1) to determine whether a change in a work method has improved the efficiency of an operation over time, (2) to compare the productivity of workers on different shifts, or (3) to compare the performance of different managers who supervise the same department or machines.

The output/labor ratio can be a meaningful measure in certain circumstances, but frequently it does *not* measure the contribution to or achievement of the organization's goals. Furthermore, if it is the primary or sole measure used to evaluate and compensate managers or workers, it can be counterproductive. The following actual situation demonstrates just one of the many pitfalls of this measure and how a seemingly good concept can fail in practice.

EXAMPLE 1

A production machine requires one operator and either one or two people to remove and pack the product as it comes out of the machine. With one packer, 8000 units per hour can be produced; with two packers, the machine speed can be increased to 10,500 units per hour. Using the output/labor ratio as a measure of performance (and the basis for reward), the manager of this machine has an incentive to use one packer instead of two because the output per person-hour is (8000/2) = 4000 with one packer and (10,500/3) = 3500 with two packers. Yet in many situations this may be a less *profitable* approach than using two packers: (1) the extra capacity of 2500 units per operating hour may eliminate the need for additional production facilities or may reduce the amount of overtime required; (2) if the operation is at capacity, the second packer may make it possible to fill an order at a profitable level that could not otherwise be accepted in the short term; or (3) the faster rate may allow quicker delivery, which can justify a price premium.

Value-Based Productivity Measures

When a variety of products is produced and the quality and mix change over time, outputs need to be converted to a common measure. This can be done using the **output value/labor ratio**:

output value/labor ratio =
monetary value of output produced/person-hours of labor used

An obvious problem with this, and with any measure that uses labor as the only input, is that it omits other important production inputs, such as equipment and raw materials, and it ignores production labor that has been used by suppliers of components. For example, a company can increase its output value/labor ratio by using higher-quality materials, which may generate higher revenue, or by transferring component production to other companies to reduce its own labor input. However, these actions may not increase profit in every case.

One way to handle this is to use **value-added** rather than the total value of the output as the output measure:

value-added = monetary value of output – cost of inputs excluding labor

The **value-added/labor ratio** then measures how much additional value is created by the company's workers, not those of its suppliers. One problem with productivity measures that use monetary values of output is that productivity can change simply due to short-term changes in prices even though nothing has changed in the production process. (This is illustrated in problem 5 at the end of the chapter.) For operations management purposes, this is not desirable because we want to measure the performance of the production system, not the marketing effectiveness.

These and other common productivity measures are also defective in that they use the amount (or value) of output *produced* rather than the amount *shipped*. These are often quite different, and because productivity is measured in terms of what is produced, production departments will often intentionally produce more than is needed, or they will produce the wrong mix of products because it may make their productivity appear better. For example, they will produce more of a product that is already on the production line, even though it is not needed, because it will avoid the downtime needed to change over to production of a product the company needs to ship. Ultimately this is detrimental to the company, but the production department looks good in terms of productivity.

Although productivity measures have some benefit, they seem to be most appropriate for comparisons among homogeneous situations. These situations tend to occur at the macroeconomic and microeconomic extremes: comparing two economies or an entire industry in two countries, or comparing two machines or departments making the same product in the same company. Productivity measures tend not to be useful, and may even be counterproductive, at the company, division, and possibly department level.

A major danger in using productivity measures at the division or company level is that they can often be improved by shrinking operations. Stephen Roach of Morgan Stanley warns against shrinking an organization simply to increase productivity: "It's a recipe for total capitulation of market share." In the short term the productivity measures may look good, but long-term profitability is doomed. Instead Roach recommends improving the organization of work and adopting better technologies.[2] These actions create long-term productivity increases that are healthier not only for the company but for the economy as a whole.

COST MEASURES AND ACCOUNTING PRACTICES

Standard productivity measures are very narrow measures of performance. To make informed product and operations decisions, it is necessary to have good information about the cost and profitability of various products and processes. Many organizations address this need by creating *profit centers* or *cost centers* within the operations function. An important practical issue is how the profit and costs will be computed for internal business units, especially how indirect costs and revenues will be allocated.

The historical purpose of cost accounting was to identify and classify the costs incurred by an organization and to assign or allocate those costs to the organizational units and the products responsible for them. In theory this should help the organization to determine what it costs to make each product, what it costs to serve each customer, and whether or not each unit of operation is performing profitably. But in fact there are two major deficiencies with classical methods. First, the allocation of fixed and indirect costs among cost or profit centers is usually not valid or accurate. Second, in managing operations and making other business decisions, it is the *incremental* (or marginal) costs and revenues that are important. Traditional cost accounting misrepresents the true production cost structure by converting fixed overhead and indirect costs into variable costs and reporting historical average costs as incremental costs.

Many of the costs incurred by an organization are not easy to assign to specific cost centers and products. For example, all departments in a company may benefit from research and development, corporate finance, personnel, accounting, information systems, engineering services, and public relations, but in ways that vary considerably from department to department. Similarly, indirect labor costs, such as the costs of division and department managers, support services, utilities, and taxes, are not caused by any one product or machine but are incurred by an entire facility or department, regardless of its level of operation.

---

[2]From Karen Penner, "Slash-and-Burn Cost-Cutting Could Singe the Recovery," *Business Week*, May 6, 1991, p. 73.

When cost accounting was first developed, production systems were simpler and more compartmentalized, with smaller product lines. A large majority of the production costs were in the form of materials and direct labor; indirect labor and other overhead made up a small proportion of total cost. Consequently, it was easier to determine which products and units were primarily responsible for many of the indirect costs, and there was little incentive to refine the allocation scheme more carefully. However, production processes have become more complex and less direct-labor intensive, and product lines are more varied. In manufacturing, direct labor costs are now typically less than 25% of overhead and indirect labor costs. As a result, fewer costs can be clearly assigned to individual products and processes; more of the costs need to be allocated to multiple products and units; and so the allocation scheme needs to reflect more accurately the real generators of costs and contributors of value. Unfortunately, this does not frequently happen.

For accounting simplicity, those costs that cannot be tied directly to a single product are often put into a pool and allocated to all relevant products and cost centers based on some measure of usage, such as direct labor hours, machine operating hours, or units of product processed. For example, if the total overhead cost to be allocated for the year is $1,500,000 and a facility expects to use 60,000 direct labor hours of work during the year, the allocation cost per direct labor hour will be $1,500,000/60,000 direct labor hours = $25/direct labor hour. Then each cost center and product is charged this amount for each direct labor hour it uses.

However, even if this allocation is accurate, using allocated costs in decision making can be dangerous. High allocations of overhead and indirect costs based on direct labor hours leads to misdirected operational effort: managers focus excessively on reducing direct labor hours because a reduction of one direct labor hour may reduce the allocated cost by many times the direct cost. But a reduction of direct labor time will not, in fact, reduce the overhead and indirect costs for the company at all. It simply makes it look as if the department is reducing the overhead cost. Worse yet, some of the actions commonly taken to reduce direct labor hours, such as understaffing or not training workers adequately, are often disruptive and incur higher long-term total costs or hurt revenue.

The deficiencies of using classical cost accounting methods for evaluation and decision making have been recognized by the accounting profession, and these methods are being changed. For example, **activity-based costing** uses production activities as a more direct link (than departments) between indirect/overhead costs and the products made. This normally results in more accurate measures of real operating costs.[3]

GOAL-BASED MEASURES OF PERFORMANCE

After this review of the most common performance measures, you might ask the obvious question: how *should* an organization operationalize its goals through its measures of performance? In practice it is often difficult to measure directly the effects of operations decisions on the organization's overall goals. Operations management is a continual process of making trade-offs, and measures must be used so that the appropriate trade-offs are considered. Various measures of cost, on-time performance, labor productivity, quality, technical capability, and flexibility, which promote and correlate with achievement of the organization's goals, are needed.

[3] All business students, but especially accounting students, should read H. Thomas Johnson and Robert S. Kaplan, *Relevance Lost: The Rise and Fall of Management Accounting*, Boston, Harvard Business School Press, 1991. Also see Peter Drucker's article, "We Need to Measure, Not Count," *Wall Street Journal*, Apr. 13, 1993.

The following principles should be used when selecting performance measures: (1) long-term goals require measures of long-term performance, (2) measures should reflect revenue impacts as well as cost impacts where appropriate, (3) measures should evaluate organizationwide impacts (e.g., if the decisions in one department can affect costs in another department, then the measures must include the effects in both departments), and (4) different measures are needed for different organizational levels.

Direct and objective measures of cost, quality, delivery, and other dimensions are desirable, but indirect and subjective measures, such as safety, employee turnover, technological currency, and production flexibility, can also be of value. Although these characteristics cannot be measured precisely, their effects on long-term profitability and competitiveness are real.

The following are some possible performance measures that operationalize common goals and order-winning dimensions. The existence and formal evaluation of such dimensions is a clear signal to operations decision makers that these factors are important.

1. **Quality.** The consequences of unacceptable product quality are so severe that this dimension must be measured well and weighted heavily in performance appraisals. Poor quality steals capacity, wastes resources, delays deliveries, and aggravates customers. Each operational unit should be evaluated with respect to its quality of work. Measures such as percentage of the product that is unusable at the next stage of production or returned by customers should be closely monitored.
2. **On-Time Delivery.** Short-term costs can sometimes be reduced and productivity increased by *not* meeting delivery due dates. But late deliveries affect future costs and revenues, so performance measures need to include, for example, the percentage of work that was performed by a due date (these may be customer due dates or dates by which the next production stages need the product).
3. **Employee Turnover.** High employee turnover usually leads to high training costs, low productivity, and poor quality. Abnormally high employee turnover can also be a signal that there is a managerial problem and poor morale.
4. **Safety.** Accidents are costly and delay production; many companies use safety measures, such as the number of accidents per person-hour worked, as major factors in decisions about managers' raises.
5. **Technical Capability.** Employees and facilities must be technically current. Subjective evaluation of the firm's ability to introduce new products or quantitative measures of the time needed to introduce new products may be used.
6. **Machine Breakdowns.** Unexpected machine breakdowns lead to high repair costs and cause production disruptions. High breakdown rates can also indicate machines running at excessive speeds, poor maintenance, or both. Using measures of machine availability promotes better maintenance and wise use.

Policies and decisions that produce *real* improvements with respect to these measures can dramatically reduce costs and enhance long-term competitiveness and profitability, and thus the survival, of an organization. Less obvious is the significant role that good operational performance plays in revenue generation. The more competitive a product market is, the more important it is for a company to distinguish itself from its competitors in some order-winning dimension. Thus, an incremental improvement in product quality or on-time delivery may be just enough to separate a company's product from those of its competitors and increase its sales.

2.6 GUIDING OPERATIONS DECISIONS: OPERATIONS SUBSTRATEGIES

The operations strategy of the successful retailer The Gap has been described as "a network of sites shrewdly chosen . . . a carefully tended vision of a Gap store as a clean, well-lighted place where harried consumers can shop easily and quickly. It's a culture that fusses over the most mundane details, from cleaning floors to rounding corners at GapKids stores for safety sake. And it's a high-tech distribution network that keeps 1,200 Gap stores constantly stocked with fresh merchandise."[4] This section describes how various aspects of operations can support the operations strategy and be used as competitive weapons to win customers.

TECHNOLOGY STRATEGY: CAPABILITIES AND EXPERTISE

A company's **technology** can be defined as the equipment, people, and procedures used to produce its products. The choice of technology affects almost every aspect of the production process: the level of personnel skills and training; the equipment; the location, plant characteristics, and scale of operation; and even operational issues such as space requirements, scheduling, tooling, safety, and maintenance. A company's technological capabilities and the ways in which it uses technologies are important strategic issues.

Maintaining Technical Capability

A major handicap for some U.S. managers has been their aversion to technology. Technological illiteracy is a liability not only for operations managers but for all managers. Studies indicate that technology-averse managers lose confidence, their skills become obsolete, and they do not understand technology-dependent issues, including marketing and product design. It is not necessary to be an engineer to be an operations manager, but a basic knowledge of technologies is important. Most necessary is knowing

[4]From Russell Mitchell, "The Gap," *Business Week*, Mar. 9, 1992, pp. 59–60.

GapKids stores are designed for safety and convenient shopping. The Gap Inc. excels in fussing over the operational details.

what questions to ask and understanding how technology fits into the organization's strategy.

Technology aversion is partly to blame for the loss of world competitiveness by some U.S. companies in the 1970s. A basic operations question for every organization is what parts of the production process should be done by the company itself and which parts, if any, should be contracted out (or **outsourced**). There has been a strong tendency for U.S. companies to get rid of difficult production tasks. But the short-term cost savings of this strategy are usually more than outweighed by the long-run disadvantages. Many new products, product improvements, and cost reductions are created by those performing the production process. By not performing the difficult tasks itself, a company loses its production know-how and eliminates a major portion of its product and process development infrastructure. Terry Hill argues that "if the manufacturing task is easy, any company can do it! Therefore, the key to manufacturing success is to resolve the difficult manufacturing issues, for this is where the high profits are found."[5]

This principle has been demonstrated again and again in practice. Bowmar Instruments was the originator of the handheld calculator. In the first two to three years after its introduction, Bowmar dominated the calculator market. But Bowmar was essentially a product designer and assembler of components. It did not make the electronic components that were the heart of the calculator, relying on other companies to produce them. As the market grew, suppliers such as Texas Instruments entered the calculator business themselves, and they were able to produce calculators at lower prices and include new advances in their products more quickly. When Bowmar tried to integrate backward into component manufacturing, it did not have the technological infrastructure to accomplish this fast enough and had to file for bankruptcy protection.

Benefits of Technological Capabilities

There are several advantages of having strong technological expertise. First, product and process innovation are more effective when they are done together. Intimate knowledge of the production technology and process makes it possible to understand how changes in product design can mesh with the current process and how current or new technologies can be applied to products. For example, Corning used its technological expertise in making glass for sunglasses and auto headlights to develop the glass used in liquid crystal displays. Second, proprietary processes are powerful weapons against competitors. By not having to rely on outside suppliers of technology, a company is able to protect proprietary information. Finally, by being involved in the design and manufacture of the equipment and process itself, a company is better able to maintain the production system and modify it when necessary.

Two companies that have used technological capability as a strategic weapon are Hewlett-Packard (H-P) and Walt Disney. H-P Laboratories director, Joel S. Birnbaum, considers H-P's "secret weapon" to be its "unique mix of core technologies that no single rival could match." For example, H-P combined its expertise in computers, computer networking, and test and measurement instruments to win a $63 million contract with Ford Motor Company for diagnostic equipment. This was a combination of strengths no other company was able to match.[6]

Walt Disney may not be perceived as a high-tech company, but it has one of the deepest and broadest technology bases of any service company in the world. Almost all of its animated movies and theme park attractions are conceived and designed by its

---

[5]Terry Hill, *Manufacturing Strategy: Text and Cases*, Richard D. Irwin, Homewood, IL, 1989, p. 140.

[6]From Robert D. Hof, "Hewlett-Packard Digs Deep for a Digital Future," *Business Week*, Oct. 18, 1993, p. 72.

subsidiary, Walt Disney Imagineering. Its theme-parks have outstanding industrial engineering staffs that are known to be world leaders in queueing, facility layout, and people management. Disney has also been quick to adopt technological advances in its hotel chain, such as computerized reservations and billing and guest services, including self check-in and check-out, fax machines, micro-computers, and TV-based guest room shopping. Walt Disney's movie division animation is unrivaled.

Applying Technology Throughout the Organization

The benefits of technological capabilities are not limited to the primary production system. Many companies have used technology to gain a strategic advantage in other operations subsystems, especially in service organizations. The following are a few examples:

1. Many companies have developed computer systems, called **electronic data interchange (EDI)**, that link customers with suppliers. The principal features of EDI systems are that customers can place orders directly in the supplier's order system and can track the orders themselves to have up-to-date information about delivery, and suppliers can track sales or usage of their products by customers and automatically replenish customers' stocks. The reduction in lead time for the customer and better planning for both customer and supplier can reduce costs and increase sales. For example, when Dillard's Department Stores instituted a system called *Quick Response Program*, suppliers were able to track sales of their products at Dillard's stores and restock Dillard's in 60% less time than previously. Companies that have been willing to develop and utilize EDI technology first have gained a clear competitive advantage.
2. Point-of-sale cash registers give retail companies up-to-the-minute information about which products are selling and which are not. This helps companies replenish stocks more quickly, identify and drop products that are not selling well, and keep inventory costs low.
3. Many companies use bar codes and optical scanning technology to track materials flowing through the production system. Manufacturers use it to track work-in-process, airlines use it to track luggage, and retailers use it to track sales and inventories.

Maintaining technological capability is expensive in the short run, but not having it can be fatal in the long run. A technology strategy needs to be coordinated consciously with the overall strategy so that it supports the organization, and it should be intended for long-term survival and prosperity. With a well-done technology strategy, technological capabilities can be used to revitalize and strengthen the entire organization.

CAPACITY STRATEGY

Facilities play an essential role in the production and distribution of products. Because substantial costs and lead time are required to establish, expand, or close facilities, organizations should have a facilities component in their operations strategy. The locations, capacities, and functions of an organization's facilities are interrelated. For example, if a company decides to have one large facility rather than several smaller facilities, the facility will probably be located centrally with respect to its markets, and it may use a production process that exploits its large volume. In addition, the facilities strategy should be closely linked to the marketing strategy. For example, if a retail company plans to compete based on the variety of products stocked, facilities must have the capacity to display and store them.

System Capacity Strategies

In devising a capacity strategy, a company needs to consider both the capacity of the entire system (all facilities) and the capacity of individual facilities. Adding or expanding facilities is expensive and should not be done in a haphazard fashion. A clear strategy should exist for deciding when to do this and how much capacity to add. There are four common capacity expansion strategies:

1. Add capacity before it is needed, thereby maintaining excess capacity to satisfy unexpected surges in demand.
2. Let capacity lag behind demand, thereby maximizing capacity utilization.
3. Try to match capacity to demand over time.
4. Add capacity on a regular basis, regardless of short-term demand fluctuations.

The choice of strategy depends on the cost and demand structure of the product/market and the primary order-winning dimensions of the company. The advantages and disadvantages of these strategies will be discussed in detail in Chapter 6, but the capacity strategy chosen clearly has implications for the company's overall performance. If a company plans to market its products based on a quick response to customer needs, especially changes in customer volume, then a strategy that maintains excess capacity to accommodate these changes is likely to be more effective than one that leaves the company constantly short of capacity.

Frequently the largest companies in an industry will use their system capacity as an order-winning dimension. For example, United, Delta, and American Airlines frequently advertise the large number of routes they serve and their total number of flights each day. The implication is that their large network capacities provide better customer service. System capacity can be an especially effective competitive weapon when there are significant economies of scale in the production system. (A production process or production system is said to exhibit **economies of scale** if the per unit cost decreases as production volume increases, that is, if doubling the output rate increases the total cost by less than a factor of 2.) This is most likely to occur in industries where there are large fixed costs of operation. For example, in the United States, large hospital networks are forming because significant economies of scale can be obtained by sharing expensive equipment, specializing the functions of each facility in the network, and negotiating more advantageous prices from suppliers in exchange for large-volume purchases. The large network of physicians and services is also advantageous in winning medical insurance business from large employers and insurance companies.

Facility Sizing

In addition to overall production capacity, organizations must select the size or capacity of individual facilities. Several factors should be considered:

1. ***Economies of Scale versus Distribution Costs.*** Suppose a company expects to sell 1 million units per year of its product. If the company's production process exhibits economies of scale at the facility level, then from a production cost viewpoint only, it would be more efficient to have one large 1 million units per year facility rather than, say, ten 100,000 units per year facilities. However, suppose the demand was distributed relatively evenly throughout the country. If the smaller plants are constructed and spread throughout the country, each plant would be located closer to its customers, so distribution costs would be lower than with one centralized facility. The most cost-efficient strategy overall would have to include both production costs and distribution costs.
2. ***Lumpiness of Capacity.*** Production capacity can be added to some processes only

in large increments; that is, they are "lumpy." For example, it is not cost effective for a steel company to add only 50,000 tons per year of hot-rolling capacity. It would need to construct an entirely new hot-rolling mill with at least 1 million tons per year capacity.

3. **Product Variety and Customer Service.** For some firms, especially service providers such as grocery stores, toy stores, hospitals, and hotels, large facility capacity can provide better customer service as well as potentially lower costs. In these cases, a larger facility can offer a wider variety of products and services, which can be used as an order-winning dimension. For example, the book retailer Barnes and Noble has decided to compete in terms of product selection as well as price. To offer a larger selection of books, as well as other services such as an in-store cafe, Barnes and Noble has had to construct much larger stores than the typical bookstore. In some cases, facility capacity is the most important weapon a company has. For example, hotels competing for large conventions compete primarily in terms of number of sleeping rooms and meeting rooms. Those with insufficient capacity are quickly eliminated from consideration by potential customers.

FACILITY LOCATION STRATEGY

Where companies locate their facilities directly affects their cost of producing products, the sales they can generate, and even whether they will have access to certain markets. Deciding when and where to open facilities in a coordinated fashion is a major aspect of an organization's strategy.

Market Proximity versus Production Costs

The cost of producing a product varies from location to location because of differences in the availability, quality, and cost of materials; land and labor; and differences in taxes and government incentives. When developing a location strategy, firms must determine how important it is for facilities to be spatially close to their customers versus how important it is to be located where production costs will be low. For some products, especially goods, the location of production facilities has little impact on revenues. For example, most customers do not care whether a toy was made in Chicago, Seattle, or Hong Kong; their criteria for purchasing the toy are the price, quality, and characteristics of the toy and the proximity of the toy store, not the manufacturing plant. Manufacturers of these types of products will locate facilities where they can produce and distribute the product at minimum cost.

For some products, however, spatial proximity to customers has a substantial impact on revenue generation. This is especially true of service companies such as restaurants, grocery stores, repair shops, gasoline stations, and theaters. Willingness to buy the services, and the prices that can be charged, are influenced in part by the spatial convenience of the facility relative to the facilities of competitors. Although production cost is an important consideration, in these cases companies must study the net effect from revenues and costs when selecting a location. A location with a high production cost, such as the Burger King restaurant on the Champs Elysees in Paris, may be highly profitable if it generates large revenues.

Factors to consider include the current and predicted spatial distribution of customers, the interaction among facilities of the same company, and the locations of competitors' facilities. Some companies, such as McDonald's, have been *location leaders*, identifying locations where a growing customer population has no nearby facility providing the product. By being the first to open a facility in that spatial market, the company usually pays less for the required land, obtains the best site in terms of centrality and highway access, and establishes a customer base. Companies using a *follower* strategy wait for a competitor or a complementary company to open a facility, and then they open one nearby. This reduces evaluation and search costs and reduces the risk of locating in an undesirable area.

Dynamic Expansion

If an organization plans to add one facility a year for the next five years, the best location for the first facility is not necessarily the same as it would be if it were the only facility. The timing of their opening also affects when and where additional facilities should be added.

Au Bon Pain, a restaurant chain that serves sandwiches and pastries to people wanting a quick meal, has added new store locations in an unorthodox but successful manner. When it started in Boston, Au Bon Pain identified its market to be primarily *walking* working people and shoppers who wanted a quick meal; it did not expect people to go out of their way to drive to its restaurants. As it added restaurants, rather than placing them far from its existing restaurants so as not to compete with itself, the chain located new restaurants within a few blocks of its existing ones. This unorthodox strategy made it easier to service the restaurants with materials and personnel, and it was based on the company's marketing strategy: because its target market was downtown workers and shoppers who were walking, the geographical market area for each restaurant was very small. Once customers found out about Au Bon Pain, they knew that wherever they were in the downtown area, they were within walking distance of an Au Bon Pain restaurant.[7]

International Location Strategy

Companies throughout the world are becoming more globally oriented. By expanding their focus to other countries, companies are able to increase their markets and increase sales, allowing them to exploit economies of scale more fully. In addition to the obvious situations where physical contact with the customer is necessary, such as in a restaurant, there are other reasons to open foreign production facilities: economic efficiency, diversification and risk reduction, and access to foreign markets.

1. ***Efficiency.*** The costs of labor, materials, land, and equipment, as well as tax rates and government regulations, vary considerably from country to country. These factors can be exploited to produce and distribute products in the least costly manner. For example, low-skill, labor-intensive operations can be performed in countries where labor is least expensive. The most familiar instances are assembly and sewing plants in low-wage countries such as Mexico, Malaysia, and China. Thousands of plants, called *maquiladoras*, have been established in Mexico just across the U.S. border. Materials and components are produced in factories in the United States (or elsewhere), where it is most cost effective, and then shipped to a maquiladora plant for labor-intensive work such as assembly. The product is then sent back to its affiliated plant in the United States for final processing and shipment without incurring an import tariff.

   Another form of efficiency occurs when companies develop different types of expertise at different locations throughout the world. All this specialized expertise can then be used for all their products. For example, when the Otis Elevator division of United Technologies developed a new product, the French division worked on the door systems, the Spanish division did the small-gear components, the

[7] As Au Bon Pain has expanded into suburban areas, it has modified this location strategy.

German division the electronics, the Japanese division the motor drives, and an American plant the systems integration. This globalization of the development process cut the development cycle time in half and saved more than $10 million.[8]

2. ***Diversification and Risk Reduction.*** Fluctuations in exchange rates, inflation rates, labor productivity, and wage rates can substantially change the relative production costs among countries over relatively short periods of time. For example, Figure 1.3 (page 00) shows that from 1982 to 1993 the labor cost per unit of output in U.S. dollars increased by over 100% in Japan and Germany but by only 16% in the United States and Canada. If a company sells its products internationally but produces them only in one country, it runs a high risk that during periods of unfavorable exchange rates and so on, its costs relative to those of competitors producing in other countries may make it unable to compete. (Of course, during periods of favorable exchange rates, it would have an advantage if it can survive the bad times.) By locating production facilities in several countries, especially those where it sells its products, the company can transfer production among facilities to take advantage of these price and exchange rate fluctuations. Many multinational companies, such as Sony, Hewlett-Packard, Toyota, IBM, and Phillips NV, use this strategy.

3. ***Market Access.*** The location of production facilities can affect the firm's ability to sell products in three ways. First, some people have strong feelings about buying products from companies that produce in their own countries. Japanese manufacturers have established plants in the United States and Europe to lessen the public animosity that was developing against imported Japanese products. (It was only later that many of these American and European plants actually became lower-cost production facilities than their Japanese counterparts.) Second, producers of industrial components that are sold to other manufacturers find that physical proximity to customers is helpful. Close proximity makes it easier for them to share information, work jointly on product designs, and deliver components more reliably to customers who use just-in-time production systems.

   Third, there are statutory reasons for locating production facilities in some foreign countries. Some countries have *home content laws* that impose import restrictions or quotas on products produced in foreign countries or outside some specified trading bloc of countries, such as the North American Free Trade Agreement (NAFTA) Group or the European Union (EU). For example, country X may state that if more than 40% (in monetary value) of the parts and assembly of a television set are from outside the country or some trading group of nations, a large import duty is imposed on that television when it is imported into country X.

PROCESS STRATEGY

Two important dimensions of a production system are its flexibility, in terms of the variety and volume of products it can produce, and its efficiency in terms of cost. At one extreme of the production continuum are project processes. **Project processes**, which have maximum flexibility, are designed to make unique products, such as a building, a computer program, a financial audit, or a space shuttle. Project processes are limited in their ability to exploit the production efficiencies of repetitiveness and specialization.

At the other extreme of the continuum are **repetitive** and **continuous flow processes**, which are designed to produce a specific product or narrow range of prod-

[8]From Robert Sanford, "Global Marketplace Is Upon Us," *St. Louis Post- Dispatch*, May 24, 1991.

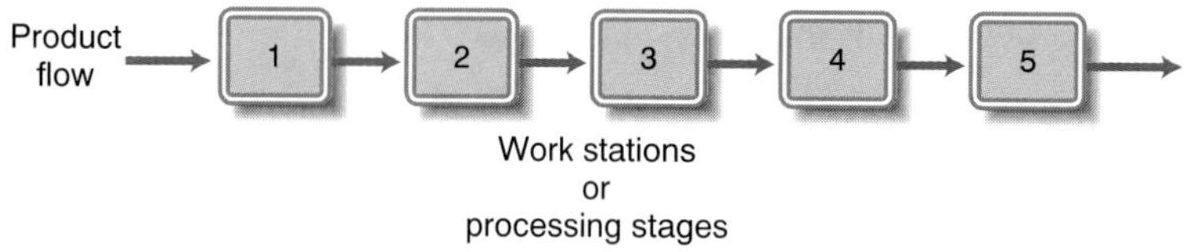

FIGURE 2.2 Product flow in a repetitive or continuous flow process.

ucts in large volume at low cost. These processes tend to be highly automated, usually with specialized equipment and job designs, and all products move continuously or nearly continuously through the system in the same sequence (Figure 2.2). But they have limited flexibility for producing a wide range of products, and they cannot respond quickly to changes in products. Auto assembly, some electronics assembly, computer assembly, and car washes are examples of repetitive processes; paper manufacturing, water processing, and many packaging operations are examples of continuous flow processes.

In the middle of the process continuum are job shops, batch flow processes (also called flow shops), and cellular processes. These are intended to produce a wide variety of low- to medium-volume products. In **job shops**, personnel and equipment are grouped and located by the type of task or function they perform into work units or departments. Each work unit performs one type of task; for example, a group of cutting machines in a factory or an X-ray unit in a hospital might each be a discrete department. Identical products are processed and transported together in batches to utilize the same machine and tool setups. Job shops have considerable flexibility because products can move from work unit to work unit in any sequence, as illustrated in Figure 2.3. These processes are normally used by companies such as machine shops, commercial printers, hospitals, and some retail stores to produce a wide range of products, often to customer specifications. **Batch flow processes** and **cellular processes** combine some of the features of a flow process and a job shop to provide good production efficiency while maintaining production flexibility.

The best type of process and production technologies to use will depend on the variety and volume of products that the system must produce and the order-winning dimensions the company is using to compete. The decision is complicated by the fact

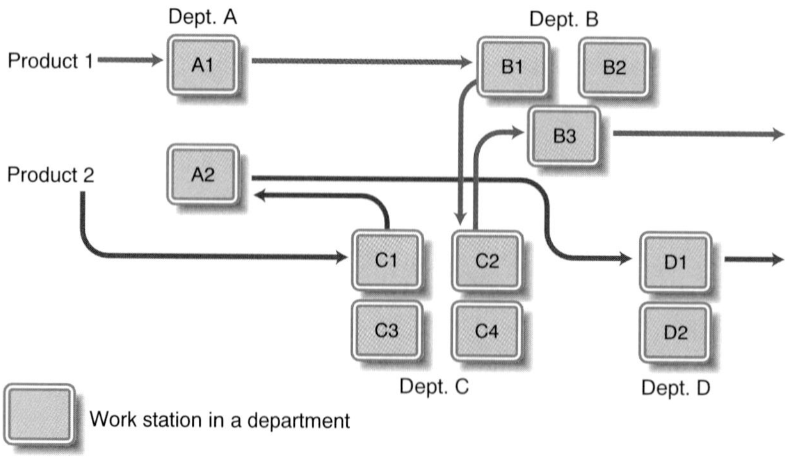

FIGURE 2.3 Product flow in a job shop.

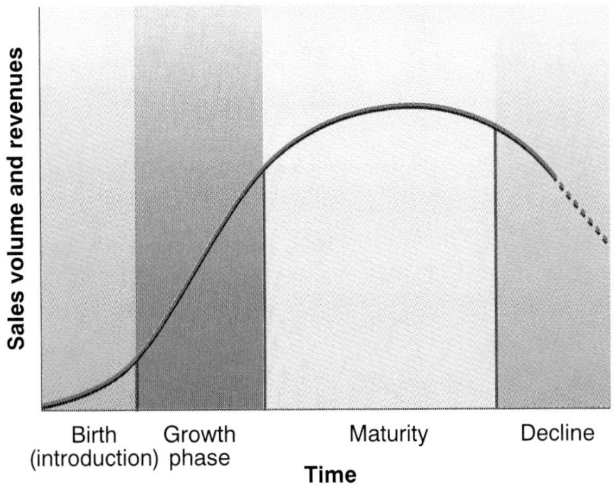

FIGURE 2.4 Product sales during product life cycle.

that a company may change its order-winning dimensions for a product or product line over time.

The Product Life Cycle

Products have lives just like living organisms: they are born, grow, change, mature, and eventually die. Figure 2.4 illustrates how sales volume and revenues change during the **product life cycle**. The lives of products vary considerably, from a few months (stylish clothes, toys), to a few years (computers and automobiles), to several decades (DC-9 airplanes, the Monopoly game, a quarter-pound hamburger at McDonald's).

Throughout its life cycle, both the product and the process used to produce it may evolve and change. The best production process for an organization to use depends on where the product is in its life cycle and on what other products are to be produced by the same process. In the early part of a product's life cycle, volume is low and customer preferences are not fully understood. Flexibility in the production process is important at this stage to accommodate product design changes and to test alternative production methods to determine which will be most cost effective for larger-volume production. In fact, production may occur at a facility designed specifically for producing prototype and low-volume products.

Once the product enters its growth phase, production volume must increase rapidly to accommodate customers. Although some changes can still be made to the product and the production process, at this stage they usually have to be minor so as not to disrupt the production system.[9] The larger volume and stable product design increase the desirability of using more efficient production systems, such as a repetitive flow process, for products at this stage.

After a product has matured, little product modification occurs. The operations focus becomes cost reduction and quality improvement through work methods improvements, changes in materials, use of specialized production equipment, and possibly through reducing the number of varieties or optional features of the product.

---

[9]With sufficient planning, substantial changes to both the product and the production process can still be made at this stage. Automobile manufacturers, for instance, often continue production of a general model of car for several years, but they will make regular changes once or twice each year on a planned basis.

In Chapter 7 we introduce a tool called the product/process matrix, which can help a company select the best type of production process to use according to its portfolio of products and where the products are in their life cycles.

Quality Strategy

Almost every major corporate "revival" reported in the business press involves a greater strategic emphasis on product quality and customer service. Good product quality is not something that will occur on its own; it requires organizational support and a plan for achieving it. Companies that are internationally successful have organizationwide quality programs, often under the name **Total Quality Management (TQM)**, that include the following features.

1. Quality is customer focused and customer driven.
2. There is an organizationwide statement or philosophy with respect to quality.
3. Everyone in the organization is responsible for quality and customer service.
4. Quality improvement is viewed as complementary to efficiency improvement, not as a hindrance.
5. Employees are treated with respect, and are empowered to make suggestions and changes that improve product quality and efficiency.

It is essential to identify clearly the role product quality is to play in the overall strategy, especially how it will be linked with marketing. For example, General Motors established product quality and customer satisfaction as major order-winning dimensions of its Saturn division. When the first delivered Saturns proved to have defects, Saturn workers picked up the autos at the owners' houses, made the repairs, and returned them to minimize inconvenience. Industry opinion was that this action turned a potential catastrophe into a marketing bonus.

How should product quality be measured? In addition to standard measures such as defect rates, direct evaluations by customers should be used. For service industries such as retailing, banking, and product repair, the way customers feel they are treated in terms of courtesy, honesty, and responsiveness can be as important as the efficiency of service.

Once general quality goals have been established, an organizational mechanism has to be put in place to make sure they are achieved. The difficult strategic issues are to select the appropriate trade-offs and the role of product quality for the company, as well as to ensure consistency between the marketing and operations functions. Product quality is intimately related to the production process used, the quality of management, and the training and job design for workers. Thus, these must all be brought together at the strategic level.

HUMAN RESOURCES STRATEGY

Personnel policies that are inconsistent with the technology, facilities, process, and quality strategies can lead to failure. The following examples illustrate the need to coordinate the human resources strategy with other aspects of operations.

1. If a company selects the strategy of being a technology leader, then its human resources strategy must recognize that it needs well-educated workers, that workers may need extensive ongoing training; and that they are likely to demand greater control over their jobs. Hewlett-Packard and Microsoft are two companies noted for personnel policies and work environments that support their technological emphasis.

2. General Electric has adopted a strategy of international growth, with special interest in penetrating Asian, Central American, and South American markets. To support this global strategy, GE has started programs to train and rotate foreign managers among job assignments to develop a more international cadre of management talent.
3. A company's policy on layoffs and use of temporary and part-time workers should support, and be supported by, its decisions with respect to facility location, process and job design, production scheduling, and inventory management. In 1991 both Honda and Toyota temporarily ignored their policies of maintaining low inventories and allowed the finished car inventories at their U.S. plants to increase to record levels rather than halt production and lay off workers.[10] One of their initial reasons for locating in the United States was public relations, which would clearly be hurt if they laid off workers. It also would have hurt morale and encouraged union activity because a major component of both firms' human resources strategies and production systems is job security.

INFORMATION IN OPERATIONS STRATEGY

During the 1980s, companies began to recognize that acquiring and processing better information more quickly could provide a competitive advantage. Ito-Yokado (owner of 7-Eleven Japan and majority owner of the Southland Corporation, which owns U.S. 7-Eleven) has used point-of-sale systems to identify sales patterns more quickly, improve product availability, reduce inventory costs, and schedule operations better. Accurate, timely data also help an organization to provide reliable delivery dates to customers, identify bottlenecks as they change over time, and accurately estimate the consequences of incremental changes in demand.

Good information flow is at the heart of any well-operated production system. The way information flows within an organization has a major effect on how quickly it can produce a product and respond to customer orders. For example, some fast-food restaurants now have computer terminals that immediately transmit to the kitchen orders placed at the counter so that cooking can begin immediately, reducing customer waiting by one or two minutes. Smooth information flow, however, does not necessarily imply a need for sophisticated computer technology. The highly successful just-in-time production system was developed by Toyota without using computers, yet it has effective information flow. However, computer technology has made many production improvements possible. For example, flexible manufacturing systems depend on computer processing for control and transfer of information, and computer-based optical scanning and bar-coding systems have improved our ability to track the flow of materials and orders through production systems.

Designing the information system is a strategic issue because it is integral to the organizational structure: who must communicate with whom, how, and when. Information must flow from marketing and product design to production, purchasing, receiving, and personnel, within departments in production, to shipping, and back to marketing. In addition, people who need information need to receive it in a timely manner. Figure 2.5 shows how information must be distributed throughout the organization to make sure that products are made and distributed correctly and efficiently.

---

[10]See Krystal Miller, "Honda, Seeking to Avert Output Cuts, Stores 2,000 Cars at Ohio Parking Lot," *Wall Street Journal*, Mar. 5, 1991.

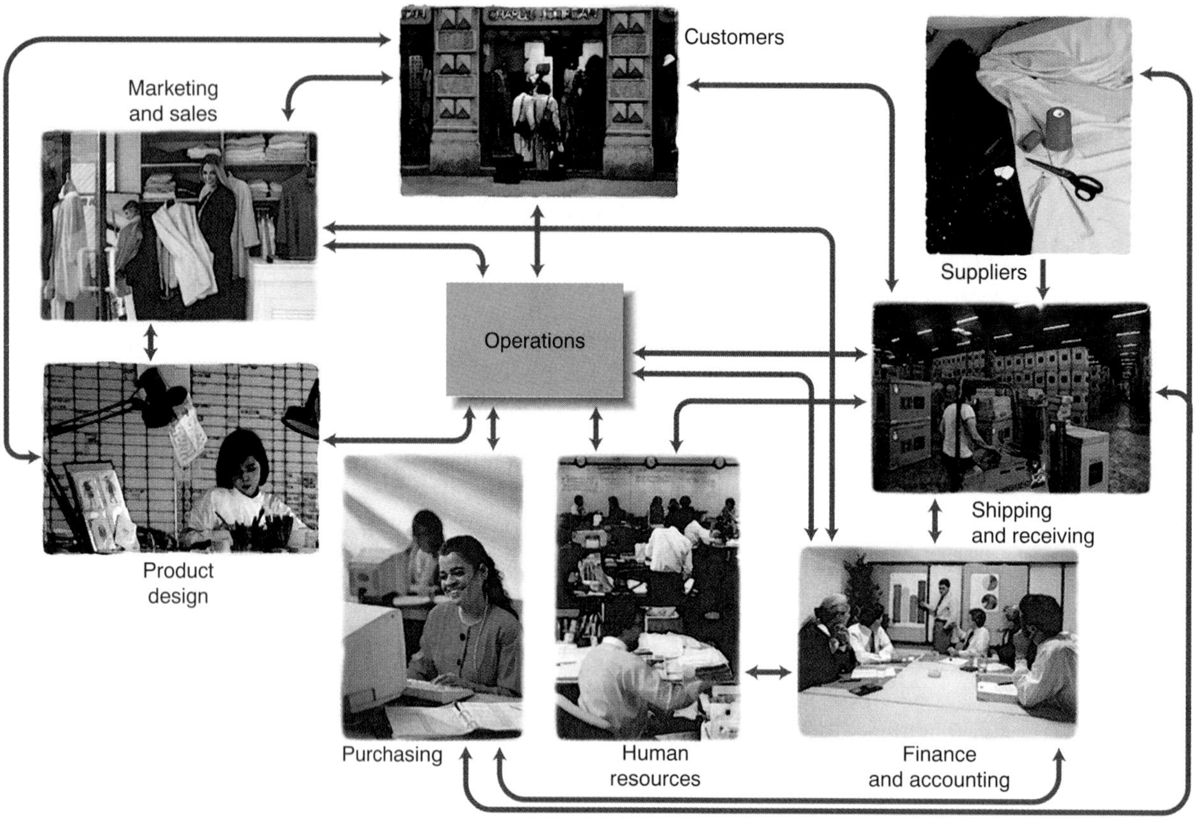

FIGURE 2.5 Information flows in a clothing manufacturing company.

2.7 PRODUCTION COST STRUCTURE AND THE OPERATIONS AND MARKETING STRATEGIES

The interrelationships between the operations and marketing strategies have been emphasized throughout this chapter. But one aspect of operations that has special importance for the organization's marketing and overall strategy is its cost structure. What factors influence the cost of supplying its products? How are these related to scale of operations? How can they be expected to change over time? To what extent can the company affect them? The answers to these questions directly influence the marketing strategy, including pricing, promotion, product offerings, and operating hours.

LEVERAGE AND CAPACITY UTILIZATION

It is common to express the cost structure for an organization as a function of its output level: $C(x)$, where x is the rate of output. This is called the **production cost function** for the organization. A typical production cost function is given in Figure 2.6. Important features of this function are the relative values of the fixed cost component, the marginal costs, and the general shape of the function. If the organization has a large fixed cost of production relative to its incremental cost, it is said to be highly **leveraged**. This means that small increases or decreases in sales volume have a large effect on net profits, as illustrated in Figure 2.7.

If a company has high fixed costs but low marginal costs, it cannot afford to leave large amounts of its capacity unused, and it has an incentive to sell incremental

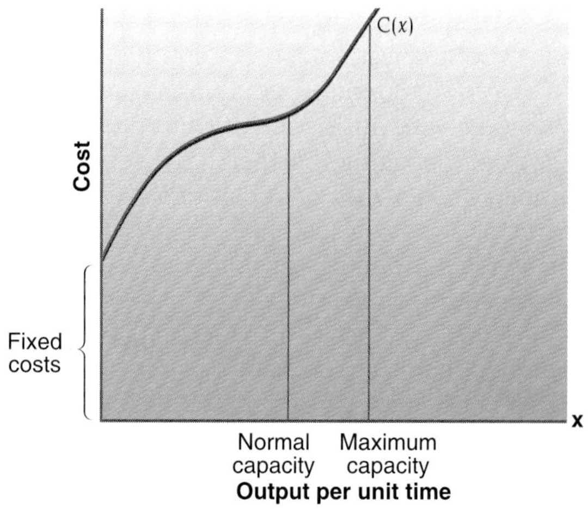

FIGURE 2.6 Typical production cost function.

amounts of its product at a discount to utilize its capacity (assuming this does not hurt normal sales). Especially when demand has seasonal and cyclical patterns, and if the timing of demand can be partially influenced by price, companies can benefit from differential pricing and promotion to increase profits. Many service industries, such as the airline, hotel, restaurant, and long-distance phone industries, have extremely large fixed costs to provide service at peak times, but their marginal costs are relatively low. These industries extensively use seasonal or time-of-day price discounting and promotions, such as coupons and frequent-flier programs, to obtain additional customers. As long as the price is above the marginal cost *and the pricing does not cause a loss of revenue from existing customers*, it can be beneficial to use this strategy.

The cost of operations is a function of several variables, such as materials, different types of labor, machine utilization, facilities, and utilities. The functional relationships between each of these variables, output volume, and total cost are normally not constant with volume. The consequence is that the incremental cost of production can increase and decrease over ranges of production volume, and it can be different for different times of the day or year.

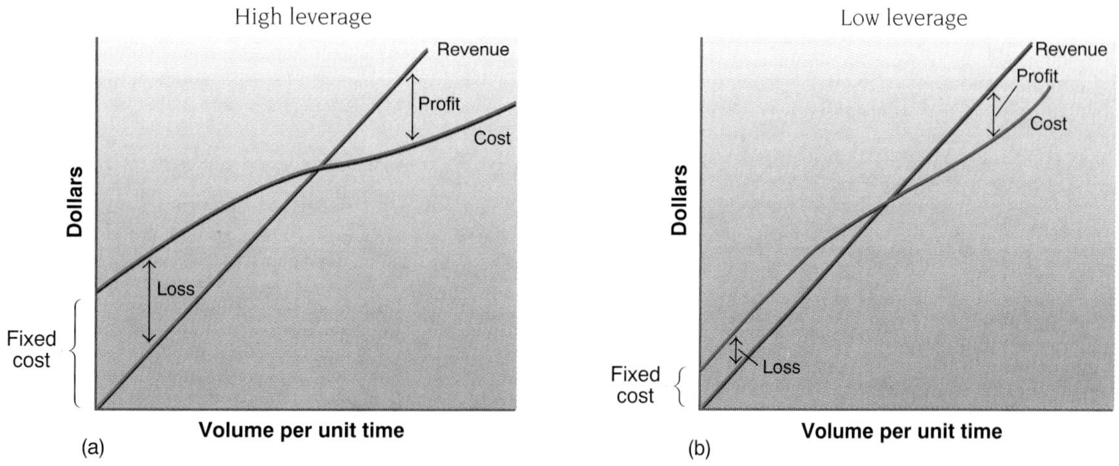

FIGURE 2.7 Cost, revenue, and profit for high-leverage and low-leverage companies.

The specific cost structure for an organization can affect marketing strategy in terms of the company's willingness to accept certain types of business, the potential benefits of price discounting and product promotions, and its optimal service level. The last factor is especially relevant for service organizations. For example, an important but frequently overlooked marketing dimension for service organizations is the business hours it maintains. Grocery stores, department stores, gasoline stations, restaurants, and repair companies can win customers based on what days and hours they are open. Even small incremental revenues can sometimes justify longer operating hours if the incremental cost of staying open is small.

Better utilization of facility capacity and low marginal costs of operation can also justify expanding product offerings. For example, many fast-food restaurants now offer breakfast at low prices because the facility costs are essentially fixed; the only incremental costs are for labor and food, which are relatively small for breakfast items. Similarly, an all-night gasoline station can become a convenience food store with a small incremental investment in facilities and working capital.

USING EXPERIENCE EFFECTS AND ECONOMIES OF SCALE STRATEGICALLY

Two aspects of cost structure that have been exploited strategically are experience effects and economies of scale. Production of most products exhibit what are called **experience effects**: as the *cumulative* number of units made increases, the per unit cost of production decreases. There are several reasons for this. One reason is the worker learning effect. Over 60 years ago, it was shown empirically that as workers made more and more units of a product, they became more skilled and efficient at performing their tasks and made improvements in the tasks. This effect was represented by the **learning curve**, which describes how the labor content (person-hours) required to make a unit of a product decreases as the total number of units made increases. For many years it was believed that the per unit cost reduction was due primarily to worker learning. But worker learning could not explain why per unit cost reductions continued even when there was turnover of employees over time. Further research suggests that many other factors contribute to this cost reduction. Some of these other factors are improvements in the process itself, improved equipment and facilities, better management and information flows, and exploitation of scale economies. The term **experience curve** was drawn from the learning curve to describe these combined effects.

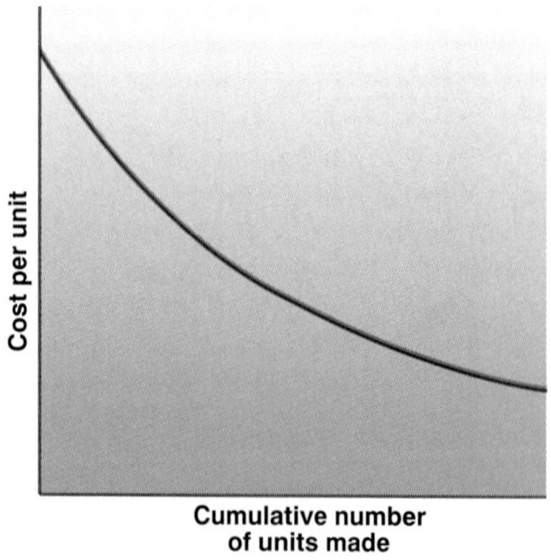

FIGURE 2.8 Experience curve .

The details of deriving and using experience curves are given in the supplement to Chapter 10, but Figure 2.8 illustrates its meaning. Experience curves are defined so that a production process is said to have an X% experience curve if the cost of making the 2Nth unit of the product is X% of the cost of making the Nth unit. For example, if it cost a company $500 to make the first unit of a product, $400 to make the second, $320 to make the fourth, and $256 to make the eighth, we would say that the process exhibits an 80% experience curve ($400 is 80% of $500, $320 is 80% of $400, and so on).

Experience effects obviously have an impact on the costs of production. When a production process exhibits both experience effects and economies of scale (the higher the *rate* of production, the lower the per unit cost), the company with the largest market share has a tremendous competitive advantage. The steeper the experience curve (i.e., the faster cost decreases with cumulative volume) and the more pronounced the economies of scale, the greater the benefits to the volume leader. By using an aggressive pricing strategy, a company can gain a large market share that takes advantage of experience effects and economies of scale.

EXAMPLE 2

Two electronics companies, Eurosound and Sushivox, introduced similar compact disc players that had only minor differences. The production processes of these companies were almost identical: (1) each company incurred a fixed annual cost of $5 million, and (2) the marginal cost of production for the Nth unit of production (measured by 10,000 CD players) could be approximated by a 70% experience curve, whereby it cost $15 million to make the first unit (i.e., the first 10,000 CD players). Sushivox set a price of $1000 for its CD players and emphasized low price in its marketing, whereas Eurosound emphasized high quality, offering a five-year warranty, and set a price of $1600. The first year, Sushivox sold 40,000 players and Eurosound sold 20,000. Their respective profit calculations are given in Table 2.2.

TABLE 2.2 FIRST-YEAR PROFITS

	Eurosound	Sushivox
Sales revenue	$32,000,000	$40,000,000
Fixed cost	5,000,000	5,000,000
Variable cost	25,500,000	41,370,000
Profit	1,500,000	(6,370,000)

The second year, Sushivox dropped its price to $600 and Eurosound lowered its price to $1000. Sales that year were 120,000 for Sushivox and 40,000 for Eurosound. Second-year profits are given in Table 2.3.

TABLE 2.3 SECOND-YEAR PROFITS

	Eurosound	Sushivox
Sales revenue	$40,000,000	$72,000,000
Fixed cost	5,000,000	5,000,000
Variable cost	28,395,000	56,340,000
Profit	6,605,000	10,660,000

At this point Eurosound appeared to be in superb condition, with increasing unit sales, dollar sales, and profit. But now Sushivox had moved much farther down the experience curve and was spreading its fixed costs over a much larger volume, with an average production cost of $511 per unit versus $835 for Eurosound. (Its higher profits and volume would also allow it to invest in better production equipment if it wished.) The product was sufficiently established that customers were becoming more price sensitive, and Sushivox was far enough down the experience curve to drop the price to a level where Eurosound could not be profitable. The third year, Sushivox dropped its price to $450 and Eurosound had to drop its price to $500. Sales were 160,000 for Sushivox and 50,000 for Eurosound. Third-year profits are given in Table 2.4.

TABLE 2.4 THIRD-YEAR PROFITS

	Eurosound	Sushivox
Sales revenue	$25,000,000	$72,000,000
Fixed cost	5,000,000	5,000,000
Variable cost	24,450,000	46,950,000
Profit	(4,450,000)	20,050,000

Even though Eurosound's unit sales were increasing and its per unit production cost was decreasing, it was becoming increasingly unprofitable and was on its way out of business. In contrast, Sushivox could earn increasingly higher profits without raising prices because it had a larger sales volume and lower per unit production costs. Its market dominance also allowed it to raise prices if it wanted to do so.

This example illustrates an aggressive strategy that integrates operations with marketing and pricing, which Japanese companies have used very effectively. They have been willing to be the low-priced seller and sacrifice profits for a few years in order to increase their volume, thereby taking advantage of economies of scale and moving down the experience curve farther and faster than their competitors. Once this advantageous operations position is established, the market leader can price aggressively and earn a large profit while making it impossible for competitors to earn a profit and catch up on the experience curve. Competitors are forced into niche markets or compelled to exit the market entirely. What makes this strategy even more effective is that the fortunes of the companies change so quickly. Competitors often make a healthy and increasing profit in the first few years, so they feel that they are doing the right things, but within one or two years they are driven from the market.

Entire industries are based on exploiting the characteristics of cost functions. The computer service industry is a prime example. More and more companies are outsourcing their data processing and information services to computer service companies such as Electronic Data Systems (EDS), IBM, and Andersen Consulting. Data processing and information systems activities are highly leveraged and exhibit significant learning effects. Developing a payroll, inventory, accounting, or other management system involves large development costs, and usually large fixed equipment costs to operate them, but very low incremental operation costs. Thus a computer service company can develop similar systems for many companies and provide these services for less cost than the

IN GOOD COMPANY

Hewlett-Packard's Strategy Takes Aim at Its Competitors

As with most of its entries into new markets, Hewlett-Packard's arrival in the computer printer business rested on a technological breakthrough in its laboratories—the development of the thermal inkjet. The company's success in the printer market, however, has been the result of a brilliant strategy.

Abandoning its usual low-volume, high-profit profile of products, H-P turned its new laser printers into high-volume products. Getting them to market first, the firm was able to sell millions of printers at premium prices. By the time competitors introduced their own products, H-P had moved far down the learning curve and expanded its production capabilities to exploit economies of scale, so it was able to undercut its rivals' prices. Using its ability to develop products quickly as a competitive advantage, H-P has continually introduced new and better printers for which it can use a premium pricing strategy.

H-P has thus stayed ahead of its competitors with new high-margin products while remaining the price and volume leader in the price-competitive large-volume market. This is a storybook example of using operations as a strategic weapon.

Source: Stephen Yoder, "How H-P Uses Tactics of the Japanese to Beat Them at Their Game," *Wall Street Journal*, Sept. 8, 1994.

customer can achieve by doing these tasks itself, and each additional customer pushes down the service company's per unit cost and further increases its learning.[11]

2.8 REVISING AND UPDATING THE OPERATIONS STRATEGY

A strategy is intended to provide steady, long-term direction. However, strategies for individual products and divisions, as well as for the entire organization, must adapt to the evolution of product life cycles and competitive changes in the environment. In 1982 Compaq Computer entered the market as a producer of IBM-clone personal computers. It won market share based primarily on its lower price for equal or better performance. After establishing a reputation for good quality, Compaq evolved from a technology follower to a technology and performance leader. Compaq brought products to market quickly, usually at the top end in performance. As part of this strategy, Compaq no longer priced its products below IBM; for many products Compaq was even able to

[11]There are many problems with outsourcing computer services, such as losing capabilities in computer technology. See Mary Lacity and Rudy Hirschheim, *Information Systems Outsourcing: Myths, Metaphors, and Realities*, Wiley, New York, 1993, for a detailed discussion.

charge a premium. By 1990 personal computers were taking on the characteristics of a commodity product, with fewer recognized differences in product performance among manufacturers and more price sensitivity by customers. Competitors such as Dell, AST, and Gateway 2000 took market share from Compaq and IBM using low prices and quick delivery. A delay in responding to this market change pushed Compaq into financial trouble and a change of leadership. The company devised a new strategy based on low price and quick delivery of customized computers, which pushed it to the top of the market by 1994.

Changes in an organization or a marketing strategy must be transmitted to the operations function. If a company changes its strategy from being a low-priced mass producer of standardized products to being a technological leader that introduces new product lines frequently, the operations strategy must incorporate this change quickly. A good way to evaluate and revise strategies is to visualize the strategic dimensions of importance using graphs and charts. For example, regularly plotting where products lie on the life cycle curve, drawing pictures that show the positions of competitors with respect to order-winning dimensions, or using product/process matrices to match product and process characteristics can be helpful. Business strategy books provide other structured methods for evaluating an organization's current condition and that of its competitive environment. A fact of life is that the world is changing more rapidly than ever before, and this process is unlikely to stop. Those organizations that anticipate, prepare for, and adapt to these changes will be more likely to survive. This is how hockey star Wayne Gretsky has summarized his secret to success: "I skate to where the puck is going to be, not where it has been."[12] Organizations must do likewise.

Summary

- An **organization strategy** describes the organization's goals and provides a plan for achieving them.
- The strategy identifies the products a company will produce, the markets in which it will compete, and the **order-winning dimensions** in which it wishes to excel.
- An **operations strategy** should be developed that identifies those things the operations function must do well to help the organization achieve its goals.
- Operational strengths such as technical expertise, production flexibility, capacity, and facility location can be competitive weapons that help companies excel in their order-winning dimensions.
- Performance measures for evaluating business units and personnel are meant to guide employees in making decisions that achieve the organization's goals and not simply reduce costs.
- The operations strategy should guide decisions related to technological capabilities, facilities, processes, quality, and personnel.
- The production cost structure, **experience effects,** and **economies of scale** can play a crucial role in the organization's strategy.
- The marketing and operations strategies must be consistent and complementary.
- Market environments are constantly changing, so a mechanism should exist for reviewing and revising strategies on a regular basis.

Key Terms

activity-based costing **45**
batch flow processes (flow shops) **54**
cellular process **54**
continuous flow processes **53**
economies of scale **50**
electronic data interchange (EDI) **49**
experience curve **60**

[12]From a talk by George M. C. Fisher, chairman and CEO of Motorola, Inc., to the College of Business Administration, University of Texas at Arlington, Sept. 18, 1990.

experience effects 60
job shops 54
learning curve 60
leveraged 58
mission statement 36
operations strategy 35
order-winning dimensions 37
organization strategy 36
output/labor ratio 42
output value/labor ratio 43
outsourced 48
product life cycle 55
production cost function 58
productivity 42
project processes 53
repetitive flow processes 53
strategy 35
technology 47
Total Quality Management (TQM) 56
value-added 43
value-added/labor ratio 43

SOLVED PROBLEMS

Problem 1: Hydroflow Corp. manufactured 20,000 pumps during a year. The pumps sell for $50 each, and the company spent $10 per pump in materials and it used 8000 person-hrs of labor to make the pumps. Compute the company's (a) output/labor ratio, (b) output value/labor ratio, and (c) value added/labor ratio.

Solution:

(a) output/labor ratio = 20,000 pumps/8000 person-hours of labor
= 2.5 pumps per person-hour

(b) output value/labor ratio = (20,000 pumps × $50 per pump)/8000 person-hours
= $125 per person-hour

(c) value-added = (output value − material costs) = $1,000,000 − $200,000
= $800,000

value-added/labor ratio = $800,000/8000 person-hours
= $100 per person-hour

Problem 2: The Coating Department of a manufacturer has five coating machines, each of which is expected to operate for 1500 hours during the year. The department has been allocated $225,000 of overhead and indirect costs, which is to be assigned to products based on the hours of coating machine time used. (a) Compute the allocated overhead/indirect cost per machine hour. (b) Suppose the company coats 10,000 units of a product using 20 hours of coating machine time. Compute the allocated overhead/indirect cost per unit of product.

Solution:

(a The company expects to use 5 machines × 1500 hours per machine = 7500 machine-hours during the year. The allocated overhead/indirect cost per machine-hour is then

$225,000/7500 machine-hours = $30 per machine-hour

(b) The 10,000 units use 20 hours of machine time, so the allocated overhead/indirect cost is 20 machine-hours × $30 per machine-hour = $600. The allocated cost per unit is then ($600/10,000 units) = $0.06 per unit.

DISCUSSION AND REVIEW QUESTIONS

1. Explain what is meant by order-winning dimensions. Explain their role in an organization's strategy.

2. Select a not-for-profit organization, state its order-winning dimension(s), and explain how it uses them to compete.

3. Name two organizations not mentioned in the chapter, one a producer of goods and the other a provider of services, that have strong technological capabilities in their fields. Give a specific example of how each of them has used this technological capability to gain a strategic advantage.

4. Name an organization not mentioned in the chapter that uses quick delivery/response as its primary order-winning dimension. Explain.
5. Name an organization not mentioned in the chapter that competes primarily using product innovation and short product cycles (i.e., first to market). Explain.
6. Name an organization not mentioned in the chapter that competes primarily using production flexibility (e.g., variety of products or responsiveness to volume changes). Explain.
7. Name two organizations not mentioned in the chapter that use low-cost production/operations to compete; one should be a producer of goods, the other a producer of services. Explain.
8. Name an organization not mentioned in the chapter that uses location as a competitive weapon. Explain.
9. Name an organization not mentioned in the chapter that has used its production capacity strategy to compete.
10. What is wrong with using "minimize the cost of labor" as the primary goal of operations?
11. In what situations are standard productivity measures useful in evaluating operations and guiding operations decision making?
12. What are the deficiencies and problems in using standard productivity measures for guiding operations decision making?
13. Why are classical cost accounting measures not always appropriate for measuring operations performance? Give a specific example of how such measures can promote poor decisions.
14. Think of a job you currently hold or held in the past. Give one example of how better technological knowledge/capability in that position would have improved operations.
15. What is the product life cycle, and how can it affect strategic operations decisions?
16. Explain the relationship between economies of scale and the experience curve.
17. What strategic operational benefits would a service company, such as a retailer or fast-food restaurant operator, obtain from having international facilities?
18. What are the major quality dimensions for the following companies. How would you measure them? (a) Wal-Mart, (b) United Airlines, (c) McDonald's, (d) Sony, (e) AT&T.
19. Why is a human resources strategy necessary? How does it affect the operations strategy?

PROBLEMS

1. Suppose a company manufactures 60 million aluminum cans in a year and uses 24,000 person-hours of labor to make them. The cans sell for \$27.50 per thousand, and the raw materials to make the cans cost \$15.00 per thousand. Compute the company's (a) output/labor ratio, (b) output value/labor ratio, and (c) value-added/labor ratio.
2. Suppose that in Solved Problem 1 Hydroflow Corporation changed its production process and outsourced some of the manufacturing, so that it could now make 20,000 pumps using only 6000 person-hours of labor, but the cost of materials increased to \$20 per pump. (a) Compute the company's output/labor ratio, output value/labor ratio, and value-added/labor ratio. (b) Has Hydroflow become more productive? Can we determine this from the given information?
3. The Finishing Department of a manufacturer has been allocated \$150,000 of overhead and indirect costs. The department is to allocate these costs to individual products based on the person-hours of direct labor used to make the products. The department expects to use 12,000 person-hours of direct labor this year. (a) Compute the allocated overhead/indirect cost per direct-labor hour. (b) Suppose the department supervisor is able to improve efficiency so that all the expected work is accomplished using only 11,000 direct-labor hours. How much money does the company save in overhead and indirect costs?
4. Suppose a company's production cost function could be expressed as follows: annual production cost = $\$500{,}000 + \$2x + \$1{,}000\sqrt{x}$, where x is the number of units of product made annually. (a) Graph production cost as a function of annual production volume. (b) Does this company's production process exhibit economies of scale or diseconomies of scale? Explain. (c) Does this production cost function suggest that there are experience effects?
5. On page 42, the example was given of two production systems: one produced 1000 12-ounce beverage bottles and 2000 16-ounce bottles per hour, while the other produced 1500 12-ounce bottles and 1200 20-ounce bottles. (a) Suppose the company sold the 12-ounce bottles for \$20 per thousand, the 16-ounce bottles for \$25 per thousand, and the 20-ounce bottles for \$32 per thousand. Compute the revenue per hour generated by each system. Which system is

more productive? (b) Suppose the manager of the first system makes improvements so that it can now produce 1000 12-ounce bottles and 2100 16-ounce bottles, but because of market factors the prices it charges for the 12-, 16-, and 20-ounce bottles are now $23, $26, and $36, respectively. Compute the revenue generated by each system. Has the second system become more productive? Has the first system become less productive relative to the second system? If so, should the manager of the second system receive a larger bonus than the manager of the first system? Explain.

6.* Consider a production department that performs one general type of processing on two machines. The department makes three different products on the machines: A, B, and C. Any product can be run on either machine, but the machines are not equally efficient for each product. The production rates by product and machine are as follows:

		Machine		
		1	2	
	A	.01	.015	
Product	B	.01	.0125	Machine Time (hr) per Unit
	C	.015	.010	

Each machine-hour utilizes four hours of direct labor. Each machine has 2000 hours of time available per year. The fixed overhead costs of the department are $600,000/year. This is made up of the costs of equipment (depreciation, maintenance), supervisors, budgeted support services such as quality control and engineering, and unassigned labor time for machine operators due to training, downtime, and lack of work available.

The production volume of the three products in 1995 was 50,000 for A, 150,000 for B, and 175,000 for C. In 1995 products A and B ran only on machine 1 and product C ran only on machine 2, so the direct-labor hours used for this production were 2000 for A (50,000 units × 0.01 machine-hours per unit × 4 direct-labor hours per machine), 6000 for B, and 7000 for C. The direct-labor cost is $20 per hour. Overhead is allocated to products based on direct labor hours, so each hour of direct labor is allocated $600,000/15,000 direct-labor hours = $40/hour.

(a) Using the above overhead allocation, the cost per unit for product A in 1995 was [($20 + $40)/hour × 2000 hours] / 50,000 units = $2.40/unit.

Compute the cost per unit for products B and C in 1995.

(b) Suppose in 1996 the production volumes are expected to be 60,000, 150,000, and 165,000 for A, B, and C, respectively. Because machine 1 was operating at capacity in 1995, the increase in volume for product A means that some production of A or B will have to be transferred to machine 2 in 1996. The least costly action is to move 10,000 units of product B to machine 2. The direct-labor hours will be 2400, 6100, and 6600, respectively, for the three products. Assuming all costs stay the same, the overhead allocation rate per direct-labor hour will now be $600,000/15,100 hours = $39.735/hour.

Compute the per unit costs for the three products in 1996, assuming the expected volumes and costs are correct.

(c) Why have the *per unit* costs in 1996 changed for each product? Have the productivities for producing the products changed? Explain.

(d) Suppose the three products all sold for $5.00 per unit. The company has decided to reduce its product line to two products. The vice-president for marketing has suggested that the product with the lowest profit per unit be the one eliminated. Is this a good criterion to use? Suppose the expected demand for each product is 20% above the predicted sales in 1996; which product should be eliminated to maximize profit? Explain why.

CASE

Walt Disney World, Orlando, Florida: An Operations Strategy Case

Walt Disney World, Orlando, provides a good example of how operations strategy and marketing strategy can combine for overall success. In 1955 Walt Disney opened Disneyland in Anaheim, California. The park was extremely successful, not only at serving the people of Southern California, but also as a national tourist attraction. All around Disneyland hotels, motels, restaurants, and souvenir stands opened. Although Disneyland earned a good profit from ticket sales and concessions, a large part of the tourists' spending for hotels, meals, and souvenirs went to these other companies. Walt Disney learned from this when he decided to open another theme park, Walt Disney World.

Disney began planning Walt Disney World (WDW) in the mid-1960s, and it opened in Florida in 1971. WDW was to be a substantially enhanced version of Disneyland that would retain the successful features of Disneyland but provide a complete family vacation in which children and adults could be entertained and educated in a safe, clean environment. This product definition was an order of magnitude larger than that of Disneyland; the Magic Kingdom theme park would be the initial focus to attract customers, but it would be only a small piece of the overall product and operations. Walt Disney was intent on making sure that Walt Disney, Inc., rather than others provided and benefited from all of the auxiliary activities of the theme park.

Marketing Strategy

The marketing strategy for WDW was simple. It would be a total family vacation experience, with activities that adults and children could enjoy both together and separately. The primary order-winning dimensions were to be product uniqueness, variety, and quality, but not price. There would be a wide variety of activities such as the Magic Kingdom, golf, boating, and water sports. There would also be educational activities such as EPCOT (the Experimental Prototype Community of Tomorrow) and wildlife preserves. This variety would allow visitors to customize their vacations. An important part of the experience was that visitors could totally eliminate the normal hassles of family vacations (other than the cost) by staying on the WDW grounds at a Disney hotel. Visitors could go from the Orlando airport to WDW and never leave Walt Disney World until they left for home. To make the product complete, every aspect of the visitors' experiences would be pleasant; quality assurance was paramount.

Operations Strategy

The product that WDW is selling is its facilities and their operation. The magnitude and complexity of the system made strategic planning essential, and Walt Disney, Inc., has done it well.

Facility Location

A crucial component of the strategy for WDW was selecting a location. Several factors were important:

1. A large site was necessary so that WDW could grow and contain all the support activities and facilities needed.
2. WDW had to be in a warm climate where it could be used year round.
3. It should not compete with Disneyland.
4. Walt Disney, Inc., had to have complete legal independence in terms of development so that it would not continually have to seek zoning or construction approvals.
5. The park had to be in an area experiencing population growth and had to be attractive to both U.S. and international visitors.

These factors combined to make the central part of Florida ideal. Disney was able to purchase a large undeveloped area near Orlando and obtain almost complete legal independence in terms of development. By being on the East Coast, the location did not compete with Disneyland. It was also in one of the fastest-growing areas of the country and was readily accessible to foreign tourists from Central and South America and Europe. Its proximity to baseball training camps, established beach resorts, and the Cape Canaveral Space Center enhanced its desirability for visitors who wanted to combine their visits to these attractions with a day or two at WDW.

Capacity

Walt Disney, Inc., bought a much larger site than it thought it would ever use to give it maximum development flexibility. It has followed a plan of steady capacity expansion over time, ignoring short-term fluctuations in tourism. It has been willing to turn away customers during peak periods rather than accelerate expansion in the short term. There are many different components of capacity within the WDW complex. Disney has added major attractions approximately every 10 years: after the opening of the Magic Kingdom in 1971, EPCOT was opened in

Walt Disney World, Orlando, Florida, has used product uniqueness and product quality as its order-winning dimensions. All aspects of its operations have been used to support its strategy to make it the world's theme-park leader.

1982, the Disney-MGM Studios was opened in 1990, and the new Disney's Wild Animal Kingdom is scheduled to open in 1998. Within each of these major attractions, one or two new rides or exhibits are added or enhanced each year. Hotel capacity has been added at a steady rate in line with long-term demand and in a way that broadens the customer base. Hotel facilities range from high-priced luxury facilities to lower-price cabins and camping areas. Some hotels are designed for families with children and others for adults. Although Disney has added capacity at a steady pace, it has lagged the additions so as not to incur high facilities costs until the demand could support it; consequently, Disney hotels have occupancy rates above 90% much of the year.

Facility Design and Layout

The WDW complex and the attractions and facilities within it are spatially designed to provide visitor convenience while encouraging visitors to spend money. Distinct activities are separated so that adults can isolate themselves from children if they wish, yet all the facilities are linked together by monorail, boats, buses, or walking paths so that people can travel between facilities quickly. In the family hotels, electronic game rooms are on the main floor, with fast-food restaurants nearby, so that children can be easily entertained with minimum parental supervision (as long as the kids have a fist full of money). In the Magic Kingdom, EPCOT, and MGM Studios, restaurants are well distributed so that any desire for food or drink is quickly satisfied. Golf courses, wild-life areas (Discovery Island), and lakes perform triple duty as sources of entertainment, sight and sound buffers between activities, and aesthetic scenery for guests.

Process and Technology

Disney has always been a company that desired self-reliance. As such, it has established and maintained a strong technological competence in those areas considered essential to its operations: product development, equipment design and maintenance, and industrial engineering. Walt Disney Imagineering designs and supervises the development and construction of all rides and exhibits. This intimate involvement provides the technical foundation for it to maintain them well and to make improvements over time. The industrial engineering capability of Walt Disney, Inc., is as good as that of any service company in the world. The largest operational problems facing amusement park operators are moving people through the system efficiently and minimizing aggravation from waiting in line. Disney is a leader in designing and managing waiting lines, as well as maximizing the number of people using rides and exhibits without creating a feeling of being hurried.

Personnel and Quality

Most companies claim that their greatest resource is their personnel; unfortunately, not all of them act on their claim. At Disney personnel are the heart of operations. All the attractions in the world will not make for a pleasant vacation experience if they are operated poorly and the personnel are discourteous and unfriendly. WDW needs a wide variety of people for its operations, from engineers and artists to nurses, cooks, ride operators, and performers. The guiding theme of its personnel strategy is to hire the most talented people possible, train them well, and indoctrinate them with the understanding that each of them *is* WDW. Employees not only must be competent in their jobs, they must be friendly and helpful. WDW does not compete heavily on price; those who visit WDW are usually willing to pay a substantial premium for quality, and it can only be delivered by competent, trained, and friendly personnel.

One dimension of quality that Disney stresses at all of its attractions is safe, clean surroundings. People are working constantly to make sure there is no litter on the ground and that bathrooms are clean. Unruly behavior is not tolerated at all; employees are in instant contact with security workers who ensure that no disturbances occur.

Information

Coordinating all the different aspects of WDW is a complicated undertaking. An integral part of the overall strategy is an information network that keeps all the players informed. For example, within the major attractions, most employees have access to radios or phones so that problems (machine breakdown, excessive lines requiring more workers, a sick visitor) can be reported immediately and assistance provided. Hotels and restaurants are electronically connected so that guests can make reservations for meals or nightclub shows and arrange for airline tickets and child care. Providing helpful information to customers is a distinctive and effective aspect of WDW's information strategy. At the Magic Kingdom, most rides have signs that indicate the expected waiting time to get on the ride so that parents can plan their activities, and a special TV channel provides information about WDW attractions on hotel guests' television sets.

Each of these strategic features—location, capacity, layout, technology, personnel, and information—enhances the quality of the product and promote sales. Strength in one dimension enhances the strength in other dimensions, just as a deficiency in one area could weaken another.

Walt Disney World Case Study Questions

1. Suppose competing attractions, such as Sea World and Universal Studios, lower their prices of admission. How should WDW respond?
2. How can WDW utilize customer information better to increase its volume of business?
3. What weaknesses or limitations do you see in the WDW strategy?
4.* In contrast to its success at WDW, Walt Disney, Inc.'s, EuroDisney facility outside Paris has been a financial failure. Identify and explain the strategic mistakes Disney made in opening that facility.

Selected Readings

ATKINSON, ANTHONY, et al. *Management Accounting*, Prentice-Hall, Englewood Cliffs, NJ, 1995.

DRUCKER, PETER. "We Need to Measure, Not Count," *Wall Street Journal*, Apr. 13, 1993.

GARVIN, DAVID A. *Operations Strategy*, Prentice-Hall,1992. Englewood Cliffs, NJ.

GHEMAWAT, P. "Building Strategy on the Experience Curve," *Harvard Business Review*, March–April 1985, pp. 143–149.

HAMMONDS, KEITH H. "Corning's Class Act," *Business Week*, May 13, 1991, pp. 68-76.

HAYES, ROBERT H., GARY P. PISANO, and DAVID M. UPTON. *Strategic Operations: Competing Through Capabilities*, The Free Press, New York, 1996.

HAYES, ROBERT H., and STEVEN C. WHEELWRIGHT. *Restoring Our Competitive Edge: Competing Through Manufacturing*, Wiley, New York, 1984.

HILL, TERRY. *Manufacturing Strategy: Text and Cases* (2nd ed.), Richard D. Irwin, Homewood, IL,1993.

JOHNSON, H. THOMAS, and ROBERT S. KAPLAN. *Relevance Lost: The Rise and Fall of Management Accounting*, Harvard Business School Press, Boston, 1991.

KNOWLTON, CHRISTOPHER. "How Disney Keeps the Magic Going," *Forbes*, Dec. 4,1989, pp. 112–122.

MERZ, C. M., and A. HARDY. "ABC Puts Accountants on Design Team at HP," *Management Accounting*, September. 1993, pp. 22–27.

MILLER, JEFFREY G., and ALEDA V. ROTH. "A Taxonomy of Manufacturing Strategies," *Management Science*, Vol. 40, 1994, pp. 285–304,.

SKINNER, WICKHAM. *Manufacturing in the Corporate Strategy*, Wiley, New York, 1978.

SKINNER, WICKHAM. "The Productivity Paradox," *Harvard Business Review*, July–August 1986, pp. 55–59.

THOMPSON, ARTHUR A., JR., and A. J. STRICKLAND III. *Strategic Management: Concepts and Cases* (7th ed.), Richard D. Irwin, Homewood, IL, 1993.

VESEY, JOSEPH T. "The New Competitors: They Think in Terms of 'Speed-to-Market'," *Academy of Management Executive*, Vol. 5, No. 2, 1991, pp. 23–33.

CHAPTER 3

TOURS OF OPERATIONS

3.1 ONE SIZE DOES NOT FIT ALL

3.2 JEFFERSON SMURFIT CORPORATION: PAPERBOARD MANUFACTURING
- Products
- Pulp Preparation
- The Fourdrinier Machine
- Winding, Cutting, and Shipping
- Major Operational Issues

3.3 STANDARD REGISTER COMPANY: PRODUCTION OF BUSINESS FORMS
- Order Receipt and Production Scheduling
- Printing
- Collating and Finishing
- Packing and Shipping
- Major Operational Issues

3.4 UNITED PARCEL SERVICE (UPS): LOCAL, NATIONAL, AND WORLDWIDE DELIVERY
- The Delivery Network and a Typical Delivery Cycle
- The Facility
- Sorting
- Loading
- Major Operational Issues

3.5 APPROVED STATEWIDE TITLE AGENCY: PROCESSING TITLE INSURANCE
- Customers and Products
- The Production Process
- Major Operational Issues

3.1 ONE SIZE DOES NOT FIT ALL

Unlike some socks or pantyhose that are made so that "one size fits all," one production process does not fit all products and companies. Each company has its own unique production processes in order to match its own set of products, desired output rates, and production locations. Despite these differences, there are many similarities among companies in the structure of their processes, their technologies, and their work methods. One secret of good operations management is to understand the similarities and differences among production processes, the reasons for them, and the advantages and disadvantages of each. Frequently ideas and technologies from one industry can be successfully transferred to another very different industry, such as optical scanning technology, which has spread from the retail industry to other service and manufacturing industries.

In this chapter we "walk" through the actual production systems of four different firms. Two of them are classical manufacturing systems that produce goods, and two are service operations. These companies, which are leaders in their industries, were selected to illustrate the wide range of activities required to produce common goods and services, and to illuminate the wide range of issues and problems encountered in operations management.

As you take these plant tours, you should look for the similarities and differences among the processes. You should especially think about the following questions:

1. What role do product quality, technology, and forecasting play in each system?
2. What are the most important operational issues, such as job design, inventory management, or scheduling, that each company must resolve?
3. How does each company's product mix and market size affect the structure and scale of its production process?
4. What are the differences between the two systems that manufacture goods and the two systems that provide services?

Let us begin our tours in Alton, Illinois.

3.2 JEFFERSON SMURFIT CORPORATION: PAPERBOARD MANUFACTURING[1]

Jefferson Smurfit Corporation is a major producer of paperboard, packaging, and newsprint and the largest collector and recycler of waste paper in the United States. Jefferson Smurfit (whose primary shareholder is Jefferson Smurfit Group PLC of Dublin, Ireland) operates approximately 150 mills and converting plants in Canada, the United States, Mexico, and Puerto Rico. One of its major product lines is corrugated shipping containers, which made up approximately 40% of its 1994 sales of $3 billion.

Corrugated containers are the boxes companies use to ship their products, such as packages of breakfast cereal or computers, to stores. A typical corrugated container is made up of two layers of brown linerboard with one piece of "corrugating medium" board fluted in an accordion shape between them, as shown in Figure 3.1. Heavy-duty containers can have double or triple layers of fluting and liner material.

---

[1]The author would like to thank Bill Wandmacker, Dell Brooks, and Cecil Longwisch of Jefferson Smurfit for their assistance in preparing this plant tour.

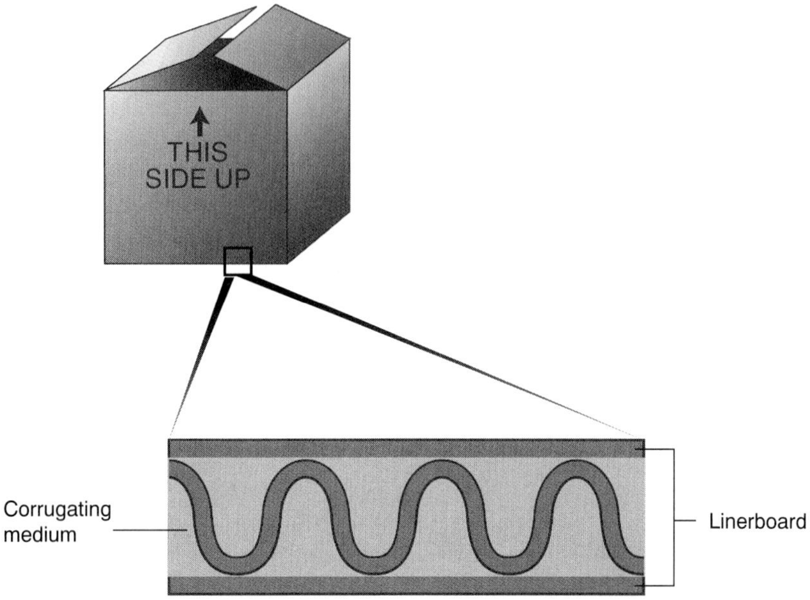

FIGURE 3.1 Corrugated paperboard.

Jefferson Smurfit produces linerboard and corrugating medium at paperboard mills, which it sells to its own container converting plants and to those of other companies. Linerboard and corrugating medium are types of paperboard, which is essentially extra-thick paper made to have special properties with respect to strength, water resistance, and absorption (for glue). Paperboard and paper are made using essentially the same process, invented over 150 years ago by Nicholas-Louis Robert and patented by the Fourdrinier brothers. Called the **Fourdrinier process**, it makes paperboard on an endless wire screen or *fabric*. This is a **continuous flow process** because it transforms mushy pulp into a roll of dry paper through a series of continuously operating, tightly connected, synchronized processing stages. Although tremendous improvements have increased both the productivity and the quality of products, the basic process has remained the same.

The following description of paper and paperboard manufacturing is based on a tour of Jefferson Smurfit's Alton, Illinois, corrugating medium mill. The mill has two paperboard machines producing a total of 635 tons of corrugating medium per day, and it employs approximately 250 people. The corrugating medium is made entirely from recycled postconsumer waste.

PRODUCTS

The Alton mill, like most paperboard mills, makes a very narrow range of products: 26- to 33-pound corrugating medium (the types are defined by their weight per 1000 square feet of product). One machine produces 250–275 tons per day with a maximum reel width of 151 inches, and the other machine produces 360–390 tons per day with a maximum reel width of 192 inches. Typically the paperboard is produced to approximately the maximum width and then cut into two or three narrower rolls according to customer orders.

When the Alton mill first began making 100% recycled paperboard in the 1970s, it had trouble finding customers because many firms preferred paperboard made from virgin wood fibers, which has a cleaner look and was perceived to be of better quality. However, with customers' increased desire to use recycled materials, the Alton mill's products are now in high demand. With improvements in the papermaking process, it is now recognized that except for slight differences in color, which are not important for corrugating medium, the quality of the product made from recycled paper is as good as that of products made from virgin wood fibers.

PULP PREPARATION

The paperboard-making process begins by creating pulp made up of approximately 4% fiber and 96% water. The two primary sources of fiber for paper and paperboard are wood and recycled waste paper (although some high-quality papers are still made from cotton fibers). At the Alton mill 85–100% of the fiber comes from recycled corrugated containers, and the remaining 0–15% comes from recycled mixed waste papers (the mixture of corrugated containers and mixed waste paper depends on the relative prices of the wastes).

All the waste paper is brought in by railcar and truck and unloaded by forklift trucks. It is fed into hydrapulpers, which add water and mix the result like giant food blenders. As the paper is mixed it breaks down into fibers, and large impurities such as Styrofoam, metal, and plastic are removed. The rate at which waste is fed into the hydrapulpers is controlled by computers that monitor the composition of the pulp. The pulp is then removed and sent through two cleaners, a centrifugal cleaner and a screen cleaner, to remove smaller impurities. (See Figure 3.2 for an illustration of the entire process.) Even small pieces of plastic or metal can stop production by causing the paper to break; they can also damage the carrying fabrics, which are costly to replace.

The pulp then moves through a series of operations in which chemicals are added to control acidity, fibers are cut to smaller and more uniform size, and starch is added to promote bonding among the fibers to increase strength. After each operation the pulp passes through storage chests so that the rate of flow can be controlled.

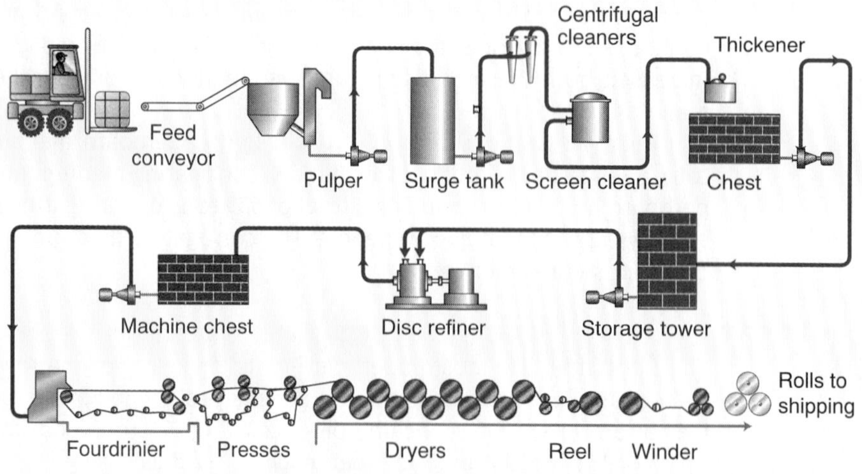

FIGURE 3.2 Flow diagram of the production process at Jefferson Smurfit's Alton mill.

THE FOURDRINIER MACHINE

When the pulp has been cleaned and refined, more water is added to transform the thick slurry into a watery mixture made up of less than 1% fiber and over 99% water. The pulp is then pumped into a "headbox" that stretches the width of the Fourdrinier machine. Pulp from the headbox is spread very precisely onto a continuously moving screen belt called a *forming fabric* (the amount of pulp is determined by the grade of paperboard to be made). The fabric, which is several hundred feet long, is made of a fine plastic mesh similar to the material in a screen door. It is carried by rollers in a continuous loop (at a rate of approximately 1650 feet per minute or 19 miles per hour) between the headbox and the second section of the machine, made up of presses. As the pulp is carried by the fabric from the headbox to the presses, water drains from the pulp through its mesh and falls into a collection tank under the machine for reuse. At the end of the forming fabric section the pulp, which is now 27% fiber and 73% water, has gained some firmness and begins to look like paperboard. The paperboard is then transferred to a continuously moving felt belt or *blanket*, which carries it through a series of presses that press out additional water.

When the paperboard leaves the presses, it is transferred to rollers that carry it through a series of steam dryers. Paperboard must dry evenly across the width of the roll; otherwise, the sheet may break or the quality of the paper may be affected. To achieve uniform drying, the machine has sensors that measure the moisture of the paperboard across the width of the machine. A computer uses this information to control both the temperature of the dryers and water sprays (as well as to control a steambox in the Fourdrinier section of the machine) in order to equalize the moisture across the width of the paperboard while it is drying.

This is the front ("wet") end of a paper machine. The headbox distributes pulp on the forming fabric which is moving nearly 20 miles per hour. Water drains from the pulp on this fabric into a tank below. The continuous sheet of paper then moves into the drying section of the machine.

A worker operates the rewinder/slitter, which cuts large paper reels of up to 13 tons into sizes requested by the customer.

WINDING, CUTTING, AND SHIPPING

When the paperboard leaves the dryers, it passes onto a reel that winds it into rolls that can weigh up to 12 tons. At the end of a reel the paperboard is cut "on the fly," and the continuous sheet begins winding onto a second reel spool so that the paper machine does not stop running. The finished roll is then transferred to a slitter and rewinder, where it is cut into two or three narrower widths.[2]

While the paperboard is prepared for slitting, samples across the entire width are tested for weight, strength, and absorption. If the paperboard is found to be defective, it is sent to a separate area to be repulped. In addition to checking the final quality, computers monitor quality throughout the process (mainly by checking moisture content). Statistical process control (which is discussed in Chapter 11) is used to adjust the process before serious quality problems occur.

Acceptable paperboard is then transported to the shipping area, where the rolls are wrapped, labeled, and loaded onto trucks. Unless a customer asks Jefferson Smurfit to hold the paperboard for a few days, the order is generally shipped within 30 minutes after it comes off the paperboard machines, because a large number of customers are served according to a just-in-time arrangement. This not only minimizes paperboard inventories for its customers, it makes Jefferson Smurfit's end-product inventories very small compared to its scale of operations.

MAJOR OPERATIONAL ISSUES

In some respects, Jefferson Smurfit's Alton mill is relatively simple to manage compared to other types of manufacturing plants. For example, the narrow product line makes product changeovers infrequent and comparatively simple. Furthermore, the highly automated process, which operates 24 hours a day, seven days a week, makes staffing and scheduling relatively easy. Normally only six production workers are needed on each machine: two at the front (or "wet") end, one at the back (or "dry") end, and three at the slitter/winder unit. Once a crew is established, it works a fixed sched-

[2]Each roll off the Fourdrinier machine is actually rewound into two rolls of each cut width of paperboard. In other words, a 10-ton, 192-inch-wide roll off the paperboard machine that is cut to widths of 50, 60, and 80 inches would produce *six* rolls of paper: two rolls of 50-inch, two of 60-inch, and two of 80-inch paperboard, with 2 inches of trim waste.

This paper machine is longer than a football field, yet it is operated by only three workers with the assistance of computers.

ule; the number of workers does not have to be changed frequently according to changes in product mix or demand patterns, as happens in other industries. Although these aspects of operations are relatively simple, many other operational issues are complex and crucial for the Alton mill.

Process Design and Technology

The modern paperboard manufacturing process is highly automated and capital intensive; a paper machine alone costs over $200 million. Because the process requires the paper to be transferred continuously from stage to stage, each roller, fabric, and felt must be perfectly synchronized to keep the paper from breaking. What especially complicates synchronization is that as paper dries it contracts, and it must be stretched evenly to maintain quality without breaking. This is done by having each successive section of the machine run a little faster than the previous section. The process must be designed not only to provide this speed differential but also to make it easy to adjust as needed.

The drying process must also be uniform across the width of the paper, so the moisture and drying rate of the paper must be monitored carefully and the water sprays and drying temperatures adjusted to ensure quality and productivity. A major change in recent years is the extent to which automation and computerization are used to monitor and adjust the operation. A machine longer than a football field is essentially being operated by only three workers.

Materials Handling and Inventory Management

Although very few employees are required to operate the paperboard machines themselves, a substantial part of the work force is involved in handling materials. Each day approximately 700 tons of waste paper must be received and transported to the pulpers to produce 635 tons of corrugating medium. These 635 tons of paperboard, in the form of several hundred multiton rolls, must be loaded onto trucks for shipment or temporarily stored. As part of the manufacturing process, other materials, such as lime, must be transported and loaded into processing units, and waste materials must be removed from the pulp cleaning operations. Of course, handling and transporting the pulp itself through the pulping and cleaning process into the headbox presents many problems, such as controlling the rate of flow, minimizing spills, and keeping the facility reasonably clean. Finally, approximately 400 tons of pulverized coal are unloaded from railcars and loaded into boilers each day. The boilers produce steam to drive the paperboard machines and dry the paperboard.

Because a huge amount of material passes through the production process and because that material is a primary production cost, good inventory management is essential. Jefferson Smurfit's Alton plant has been extremely successful at keeping all types of inventory to a minimum. The financial penalty for unexpectedly shutting down a capital-intensive process, such as a paperboard mill, is quite high, so companies in these industries typically maintain large raw material inventories, as much as several months' worth in some cases. Jefferson Smurfit, however, typically operates with only a one-week supply of waste paper without encountering shutdowns due to material shortages. Furthermore, because of the continuous nature of the process, there are essentially no in-process inventories, and as mentioned earlier, most of the product is shipped within 30 minutes of completion, so the final product inventories are minimal as well. This is an outstanding example of good inventory management for any industry.

Environmental Challenges

Paperboard production has historically been a highly polluting process because it requires large amounts of energy, and because it consumes and contaminates large quantities of water. The Alton mill has made tremendous strides in reducing its effects on the environment. By converting to low-sulfur coal and installing emission control equipment, it has reduced its sulfur emissions by over 75%. The Alton mill, which uses its own water wells as its source of fresh water, has an advanced tertiary (three levels of cleaning) treatment system to purify its waste water, making the treated water cleaner than that in the Mississippi River, into which it is discharged. Through conservation efforts and by reusing water before treatment, the mill has reduced its water usage from 2.1 million to 1.4 million gallons per day. As a business built on environmental awareness, collecting and using recycled paper in production, Jefferson Smurfit has an acute sensitivity to environmental issues.

Production Planning and Scheduling

Paperboard manufacturing has some distinct production planning problems. For example, Jefferson Smurfit may have open orders for thousands of rolls of paperboard of different widths and different due dates for delivery. What it must do is to group orders so that when a roll of paperboard is slit into smaller rolls, the amount of excess trim waste is minimized. For example, cutting a 192-inch roll into two rolls of 82-inch widths leaves 28 inches of trim waste, whereas cutting it into three rolls with widths of 51, 62, and 78 inches leaves only 1 inch of waste.

A second problem is determining the mix of scrap paper to use as input to the process. Although it is desirable to use 100% corrugated container waste, when the relative cost of corrugated waste gets too high, it becomes cost effective to use some mixed waste, even if it has lower fiber yields and more contaminants to remove. Both the trim problem (called the **cutting-stock problem**) and the selection of the best mix of scrap inputs (called the **blending problem**) can be solved using the optimization methods presented in Tutorial 1.

Product Quality

Among the major accomplishments of the paper and paperboard industries has been their ability to improve product quality while simultaneously increasing productivity. Electronic sensors can measure differences in drying more accurately than previously used manual methods (which required tapping the moist paper with a stick and listening for differences in the sound emitted). This information can be processed immediately by computers, and the water sprays and temperature controls of the machine can be adjusted. The Alton mill also uses statistical process control to track deviations in the paperboard from the desired thickness and strength. Problems with the process can be detected and corrected *before* defective product is made rather than afterward.

Poor quality can also affect the cost of production in several ways. The first and most obvious result is that paperboard of unacceptable quality must be repulped, wasting precious production capacity, which could postpone deliveries. Second, uneven drying or contaminants in the pulp can break the paper in the machine, causing a shutdown. Depending on the seriousness of the break and whether equipment is damaged, it can take anywhere from five minutes to several hours to get the machine operating again. Third, contaminants in the pulp, such as metal or plastic clips, can damage the forming fabric or felt blankets, which can cost up to $45,000 to replace.

Maintenance

By now it should be clear that shutdowns of the process are avoided as much as possible. However, the wear and tear on the rollers, felts, and blankets from operating 24 hours a day, seven days a week is considerable. To prevent breakdowns, the mill shuts down each machine one day a month for approximately 10 hours to perform preventive maintenance. During this period, rollers, fabrics, felt blankets, and other parts are replaced as needed, thereby reducing more costly and disruptive breakdowns.

Although Jefferson Smurfit makes products to customers' specifications in terms of roll width and paperboard weight and strength, the range of products is actually quite small. Changing from product to product requires minimal adjustments in most cases, and this can often be done without stopping the process. Our next tour is of a production process that makes thousands of different products every year, each requiring substantial setup time on a variety of machines.

3.3 STANDARD REGISTER COMPANY: PRODUCTION OF BUSINESS FORMS[3]

Standard Register Company is a diversified producer of business forms, document processing equipment and services, and electronic systems products. The company is headquartered in Dayton, Ohio, and had sales of over $750 million in 1994. One of its primary business lines is the production of paper business forms, such as patient admission data forms for hospitals, student application forms for universities, job applications, order forms, cash receipts, and financial documents including bank drafts. Most of these forms are customized, such as the one shown in Figure 3.3, although some of them are stock forms that can be purchased in business supply stores. Probably at least once a week you come into contact with a form manufactured by Standard Register. For example, if you recently had a pizza delivered to your house, the order and delivery tag on the box may have been printed by Standard Register.

The Forms Division of Standard Register has 11 manufacturing plants in the United States. The following description is based on a tour of the Kirksville, Missouri, plant, which is one of the largest and most complex production facilities in the division.

[3]The author would like to thank Peter Redding, Bob Herrick, David Sevits, and Dee Ambrosia of Standard Register for their assistance in preparing this plant tour.

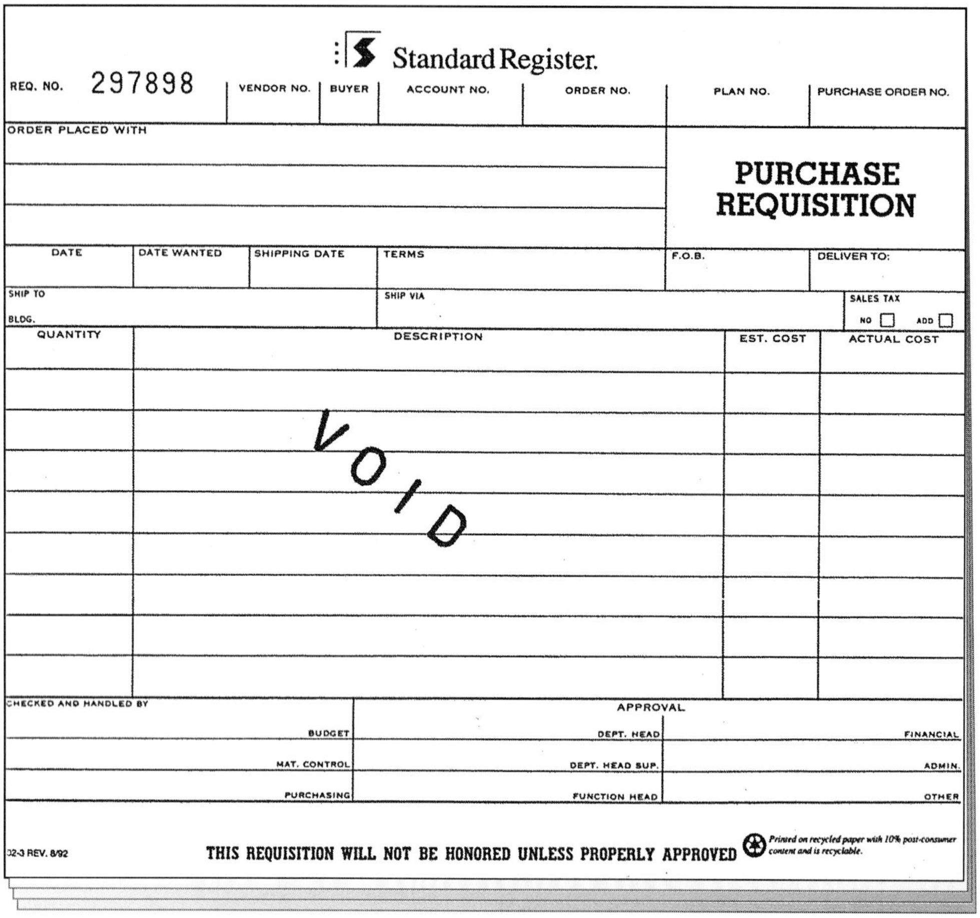

Standard Register.

REQ. NO. 297898 | VENDOR NO. | BUYER | ACCOUNT NO. | ORDER NO. | PLAN NO. | PURCHASE ORDER NO.

ORDER PLACED WITH

PURCHASE REQUISITION

DATE | DATE WANTED | SHIPPING DATE | TERMS | F.O.B. | DELIVER TO:

SHIP TO | SHIP VIA | SALES TAX NO ☐ ADD ☐

BLDG.

QUANTITY	DESCRIPTION	EST. COST	ACTUAL COST
	VOID		

CHECKED AND HANDLED BY | APPROVAL

BUDGET | DEPT. HEAD | FINANCIAL

MAT. CONTROL | DEPT. HEAD SUP. | ADMIN.

PURCHASING | FUNCTION HEAD | OTHER

02-3 REV. 8/92

THIS REQUISITION WILL NOT BE HONORED UNLESS PROPERLY APPROVED

Printed on recycled paper with 10% post-consumer content and is recyclable.

FIGURE 3.3 A typical business form made by Standard Register.

Thousands of different products are made by Standard Register, a typical product being a three- or four-layer (multisheet) business form, possibly with carbon paper between the layers. The different layers of the form are normally different colors to make separation and distribution of the various copies easier. For example, in a three-layer order form, the white copy might go into a master file, the pink copy to production as a work order, and the yellow copy to a customer as confirmation of the order. We will follow a typical product through the production system, from the time the order is submitted until it is loaded onto a truck for shipment.

The production process of Standard Register has the structure of what is called a **job shop process**, in which people and machines that perform a specific activity, such as printing, cutting, or binding, are grouped together in a department. Products are processed in batches (entire orders) in a department before being sent on to the next department, rather than items flowing continuously or one at a time from department to department. In contrast to the paperboard manufacturing process, job shops have considerable flexibility in that each product can take a unique route through the system. The number and type of production activities performed, and the sequence in which they are performed, can differ from product to product.

ORDER RECEIPT AND PRODUCTION SCHEDULING

The process begins with a sales representative working with the customer to design or redesign the business form to make it cost effective, functional, and attractive. Personnel from the plant often participate in the design process, providing information on how changes in design would affect the production cost and quality of the product.

Once a design for the form has been established and a purchase contract issued by the customer, the order is transmitted by the sales representative to the Sales Support Department at the manufacturing plant. (See Figure 3.4 for an illustration of the entire production process.) To an increasing degree, these orders are being transmitted electronically for greater speed and accuracy. If the order is an original order (first-time product), it includes a design of the form to be made. If it is a repeat order, Standard Register has the design and a sample of the form on file. For every product, a history file (a large envelope) is established and maintained. This file includes a record of any

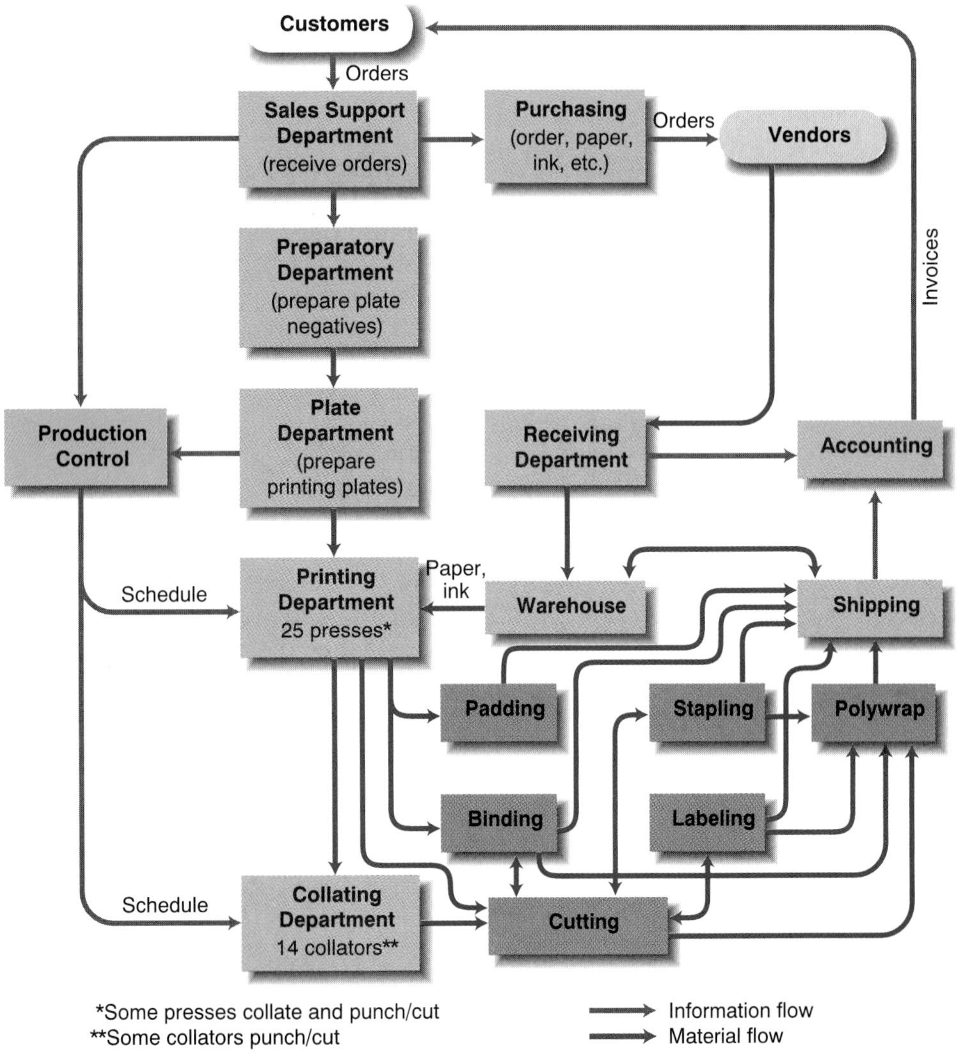

FIGURE 3.4 Flow diagram of the production process at Standard Register's Kirksville plant.

changes in the design, and especially a history of production or other problems that have occurred and how they were solved, so that any experiences gained in making the product better will be utilized in reorders. On repeat orders no new purchase contract is necessary, so the customer does not have to fill out company addresses, product specifications, or delivery locations. The customer simply provides the due date, order quantity, and any changes from the previous order. Standard Register then puts the new order number on the history file and writes any changes on a history log. This process eliminates considerable paperwork for the customer and for Standard Register, and it reduces the chances of transcription errors.

The Sales Support Department is organized into teams, each of which handles certain sales districts or major national accounts. If someone is sick or on vacation, other members of the team will be familiar with the customer and its products. Each order is assigned to a sales support order coordinator. This person checks the new or existing design to make sure that there are no problems or ambiguities. If there are questions, the order coordinator contacts the sales representative or the customer to discuss them. The order coordinator reviews the product history and notes any special problems or actions that the production personnel should know. These are written on the job ticket that travels with the job through production.

The order coordinator then determines what materials will be needed in production: the amount and type of paper, ink, shipping cartons, labels, carbon paper, and so on. The coordinator checks the company inventory records, and if the materials are available she puts a "hold" on them and assigns them to the order. If materials are not available, she notifies the Purchasing Department and purchase orders are issued for them. The order coordinator then computes the amount of production time (printing, collating) that will be needed and checks the current production schedules and machine load charts to determine when the job can be scheduled and on which machines, so that delivery can be made by the customer's due date. There are 25 printing presses, each with different capabilities in terms of the number of colors and the width of paper that can be printed; 14 collating machines (which put several sheets of forms and possibly carbon paper together); and several machines for binding, cutting, labeling, and other finishing operations. The order coordinators use conversion charts for each machine to help them compute the amount of time required to process jobs with various characteristics.

Working backward, the order coordinator determines when the last process has to be started, the second last process started, and so on, to ensure on-time delivery. She then tries to schedule each machine to begin no later than these dates. The coordinator, however, must make sure that all the necessary materials will be available before the press begins printing the job. Therefore, another part of the job is to monitor orders each day to make sure that the materials are received when needed and to expedite them when they are not. Every day, sales support order coordinators receive a report on the status of every job in the plant so that they can monitor the jobs moving through the production system without having to go into the plant and track down their location in the production process. (They can also use a computer terminal to obtain nearly the real-time status of any job.)

PRINTING

When a new order leaves Sales Support it goes to the Preparatory Department to begin the process of converting the product design into printing plates for the printing presses. This is done using what is essentially a computer-aided design (CAD) system. The product design is copied into the CAD system and converted to digitized computer code, which is used to transform the design into a photographic positive of the printing. (In fact, the product designs are often digitized by the customer or the Standard Register sales office and sent to the manufacturing plant.) The positive is then used to prepare a photographic negative for each color to be printed. At each step the positives and negatives are checked for accuracy to ensure quality. (On repeat orders the photographic negatives and possibly old printing plates already exist, which eliminates these steps.)

The negatives are sent to the Plate Department, where a machine uses them to "burn" the image of the form onto an aluminum printing plate. The printing plates, which are thin and flexible, will bend around the printing cylinders on the presses. Each color to be printed on the form requires its own printing plate to go on its own printing cylinder. The Preparatory Department, which makes several hundred plates a day, will normally produce the plates for a job within one day of receiving the negatives.

When the plates are ready, the Production Control Department takes over the job; it monitors receipt of raw materials, performs the final scheduling, and tracks the job through the production system while working closely with Sales Support. Once all the materials and printing plates for a job are available, the Production Control Department takes the tentative schedule of jobs and forms a final schedule for each machine. In creating a final schedule of jobs, Production Control takes into account the similarity of jobs, so jobs that use the same inks or papers are scheduled consecutively, whenever possible, to reduce changeover time from job to job.

Rolls of paper for several jobs are lined up in front of each printing press so press operators are not delayed in their work.

Production Control issues job tickets to each press; the job tickets for the next several jobs are always posted by each machine. The material handler for the department goes from press to press and checks the job tickets. Using a computer, he identifies the warehouse location of the paper for each job, which he locates and transports to the appropriate press and lines it up by the feed (or unwind) end. He then clearly marks the order number on the rolls of paper to eliminate errors. The paper for the next several jobs will always be in place so that press operators do not have to wait for paper.

The machine operators then use the information on the job ticket to set up the press: installing the printing plates and inks, connecting any auxiliary units such as a numbering unit, and threading the paper through the rollers. Color coding is used to identify "hot" jobs (rush orders) and special or large dollar volume orders, which require the quality assurance technician to approve the setup before production starts.

Each press is different, and a typical press may perform several functions. In addition to printing from one to four colors on the paper, it may have a numbering unit that prints sequential numbers or bar codes on the forms, a unit that punches holes or notches in the forms, and a perforator that cuts perforation scores to make the forms fold or tear easily (some can even print and collate). As the paper progresses through the press, a different color ink is applied by a plate at each printing stand. It then may go through numbering, punching, and scoring units. The product coming out the back of the press may be printed rolls, connected but folded sheets, or cut sheets. The items that are not to be shipped directly to customers are packed by the operators and put in work-in-process storage until they can be processed at the next production stage.

COLLATING AND FINISHING

After leaving the press, most products proceed to a collating machine that puts 2 or more (up to 14) rolls of printed forms together, possibly with carbon paper between the layers (the forms may use carbonless paper that have a coating on the paper itself, so it prints when pressure is applied). The collator aligns multiple layers of forms, and glues or crimps them together with notches so that they stay together. The collator may then cut them into individual forms, or they may be sent to a separate cutter.

A collator combines several colors of paper (and for this job carbon paper) into a multipage form.

After collating (or directly after the printing), some products undergo additional processing. For example, some go to a padding machine that puts a rubberized glue on the forms and turns them into pads; others may be stapled into books of forms. The order of operations can vary from product to product. Some forms are padded or stapled and then cut; occasionally they are cut and then padded or stapled. Other machines perform finishing operations as well, such as a labeling machine that puts labels on forms. The variety of finishing operations, the fact that not all forms are collated, and the highly variable demands put on the different finishing operations make balancing the work flow, staffing, and scheduling major challenges. Therefore, workers who can do a variety of jobs are invaluable.

PACKING AND SHIPPING

When the forms are completed they are packed in corrugated cartons, possibly after being wrapped in polyethylene. Labels are put on the cartons, and then the packaged products are placed on conveyers that carry them to the loading dock area. The cartons are put on pallets, wrapped with polyethylene, and banded to keep out moisture, to keep cartons from shifting, and to protect them from damage.

The Shipping Department then moves the pallets to the warehouse for storage until the order is shipped, or the order is loaded directly onto a truck for shipment. Most orders are of less than truckload size, so the Shipping Department tries to combine deliveries to the same general area on one truck for greater efficiency.

When the order is shipped, the completed job ticket is sent to the Accounting Department to be checked for accuracy. Then a bill is sent to the customer.

MAJOR OPERATIONAL ISSUES

A number of aspects of Standard Register's manufacturing system merit special attention.

Personnel and Job Design

At the Kirksville plant, employees are encouraged to learn new skills and jobs and to move up in the company. Most employees are given **cross-training** to do several different jobs, not only in their own departments but in other departments as well. For example, not only can press operators set up and run several different presses, but some can work in order entry or platemaking if necessary. To encourage cross-training, the Kirksville plant is developing a pay system that rewards such versatility, along with other key performance measures such as team work and quality. This versatility is extremely valuable to the company because in a job shop with such a wide variety of products, there are several processes that do not always have enough work to support an entire person, such as ink mixing or carton making. Being able to move workers to other departments or work stations where they are needed greatly increases flexibility and efficiency. In addition, employees are better able to see the big picture of the production system, which helps them to avoid mistakes caused by job myopia. They are also more qualified to think of improvements in the system.

The employees benefit from cross-training as well. First, cross-training has made it possible for Standard Register to avoid layoffs for several years, even during economic downturns. Second, it makes the work more interesting and varied. The most telling measure of success is that of the 220 employees at the plant in mid-1994, approximately two-thirds had been working there for at least 20 years—an incredible record in any industry.

Product Quality

Standard Register uses a **total quality management** system that devotes considerable attention to working with customers. From product design through final shipment and billing, the company works with its customers to determine what they want, how they want it, and how well they think they are being served. Standard Register employees visit customers' facilities to help them solve problems and utilize the forms more efficiently, and customers are invited to Standard Register's plants to observe their products being produced.

Although there are numerous quality checks in the production system, an important aspect of the system is that the responsibility for product quality rests entirely with the machine operators. They can seek help from supervisors and quality control personnel, but ultimately they are responsible. However, several aids built into the system make quality control easier. The product history file keeps a record of quality problems and solutions, so operators have the benefit of experience and learning on previous runs of the product; this avoids repeat mistakes. The job ticket given to the operator has a setup checklist that reminds the operator to check the quality of each aspect of the setup as it is completed. The job ticket also includes any special information

At Standard Register machine operators are responsible for the quality of their work. Here a printer operator checks the printing quality of a job.

needed to set up and run the job correctly, especially warnings of potential problems. Sample copies of the product or the product design are readily available so that the operator can compare the product with the samples whenever necessary. And, of course, quality control personnel are available to answer questions and check the quality of the work.

Because primary responsibility rests with the production personnel, the quality control staff at Standard Register is very small. However, one of its most important responsibilities (in addition to establishing quality standards and production procedures) is to investigate all problems and complaints systematically and to provide a written resolution. This way mistakes do not slip through the cracks or get waved off as something that will be looked at later. Historical data on quality performance and the sources of problems play an important role in continuously improving product quality.

Inventory System

Standard Register uses a large volume and variety of paper, so the acquisition and storage of paper is an important operational issue. Paper inventory levels are checked daily, and if the levels fall below a designated reorder point, an order is placed. Data are maintained on paper usage by type so that requirements can be forecast, and reorder points and order quantities can be adjusted when appropriate.

Under increasing pressure to reduce order lead times, Standard Register has begun utilizing an electronic data interchange (EDI) system whenever possible. EDI allows Standard Register to place orders and schedule production with some of its paper suppliers directly through computer transmission. This saves the time needed to create a purchase order, send it to a supplier's sales rep, then transmit it to the supplier's plant and schedule the order. Along with other improvements, EDI has allowed Standard Register to reduce the lead time it can offer its customers from six weeks to less than two.

Environmental Concerns

Standard Register has found that environmentally wise operations are also profitable. Printing has historically been an industry with environmental problems, mainly the discharge of toxins from the pigments and solvents in inks. Standard Register replaced environmentally damaging inks with soybean-based inks that greatly reduce air and water pollution. These inks cost no more than toxic inks, they perform as well, and customers prefer them. In fact, the Kirksville plant received a quality award from the Missouri Soybean Producers Association for products produced with soy-based inks.

Companies working with paper products have historically been active participants in recycling paper. Standard Register produces considerable paper scrap; for example, as much as 20 tons of punch holes alone may be produced in one month. These and other paper scraps are recycled. The aluminum and silver from the platemaking process and from used printing plates are recycled as well.

Technological Improvements

Technological and process improvements are continually being made at the plant. One of the most important is the extensive use of bar coding and optical scanning. Bar codes are placed on all job documents and materials, and scanning wands in each department and at each machine are used to record automatically materials and documents that pass through an operation. By scanning a job ticket and typing a few key strokes, an employee can record data on production times, downtime, maintenance, and material waste in a central database. This system has not only improved the company's ability to monitor the status of jobs within the production system, it has also provided faster and more accurate information on the costs of producing a job, machine performance, and maintenance problems. The chance of mistakenly charging materials or processing for one job to another job has been greatly reduced. This system required extensive training, but the payoff has been worth it.

Our first two plant tours were of systems that manufacture goods we encounter every day. The next two plant tours are of service production systems. The first company, United Parcel Service, provides worldwide parcel delivery services. The second company, Approved Statewide Title Agency, provides title insurance for a local market.

3.4 UNITED PARCEL SERVICE (UPS): LOCAL, NATIONAL, AND WORLDWIDE DELIVERY[4]

UPS is probably one of the most familiar companies in the United States. In 1994 over 3 billion parcels and documents were shipped by this company (nearly 12 million per day), generating revenue of over $19 billion. UPS, with over 315,000 employees, is one of the largest employers of college students in the United States. In addition to having the largest fleet of ground trucks in the world (130,000 vehicles), UPS has one of the largest air fleets of any company, owning or chartering over 400 planes.

UPS is a pure service company that provides transportation services to over 1 million regular customers (shippers who receive daily pickup service) plus tens of millions of occasional customers. Its service enhances the value of goods by moving them from shipper to recipient. Although its main product is parcel and document delivery, the range of services is quite large, including overnight air delivery, worldwide delivery, parcel pickup, hazardous material shipment, and parcel tracking. UPS also provides logistics consulting, warehousing of materials such as spare parts for customers that can be shipped immediately on notification, and even consolidating and repackaging of products (e.g., it may receive computer components from various supply sources, consolidate them into one shipment, and send them to the manufacturer's customers).

The magnitude and range of production systems used by UPS are too large to discuss in just a few pages, so here we will look only at the processing of a typical ground delivery package and the operations of a parcel handling (hub) facility.

THE DELIVERY NETWORK AND A TYPICAL DELIVERY CYCLE

UPS was the developer of the now widely used "hub-and-spoke" delivery system. UPS has over 60 ground delivery hubs located throughout the United States. These hubs serve as primary sorting facilities for a region of the country and as exchange points for packages moving long distances by land. Each hub region is divided into subregions (typically 10–20), each of which is served by an *operating center* (connected to the hub by spokes), as shown in Figure 3.5. The *operating centers* are the home bases for the well-known brown delivery trucks called *package cars*, which provide all pickup and delivery service within the subregion. (The hub typically acts as an operating center itself with its own fleet of package cars.)

The delivery system then operates as shown in Figure 3.6. During the afternoon, the package car drivers of an operating center pick up packages from their customers and return them to the operating center. The packages are loaded into large trailer trucks,

[4]The author would like to thank Chris Brown, Burke Workman, and Gary Aldrich of United Parcel Service for their assistance in preparing this plant tour.

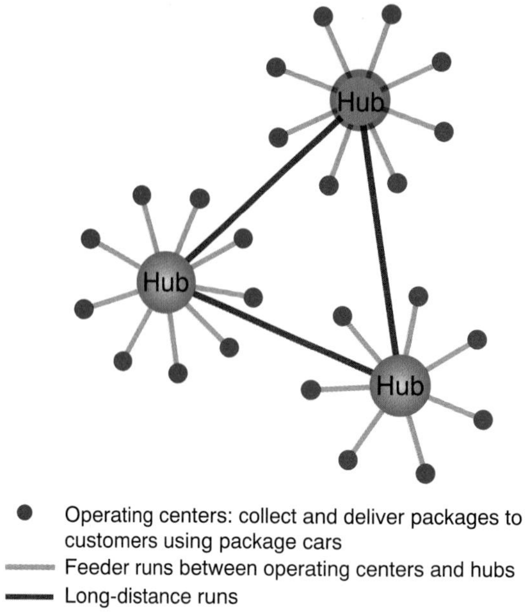

FIGURE 3.5 The hub-and-spoke network used by UPS.

called *feeders*, that haul the packages to their affiliated hub. At the hub the packages are sorted according to destination. The sorted packages are then loaded back into the feeder trucks, some destined for the operating centers within the hub region and some destined for other hubs around the country. Between 2:00 A.M. and 6:00 A.M. the feeder trucks arrive back at the operating centers (or hubs), where they are unloaded, sorted, and reloaded into package cars. That morning the drivers deliver the packages to the

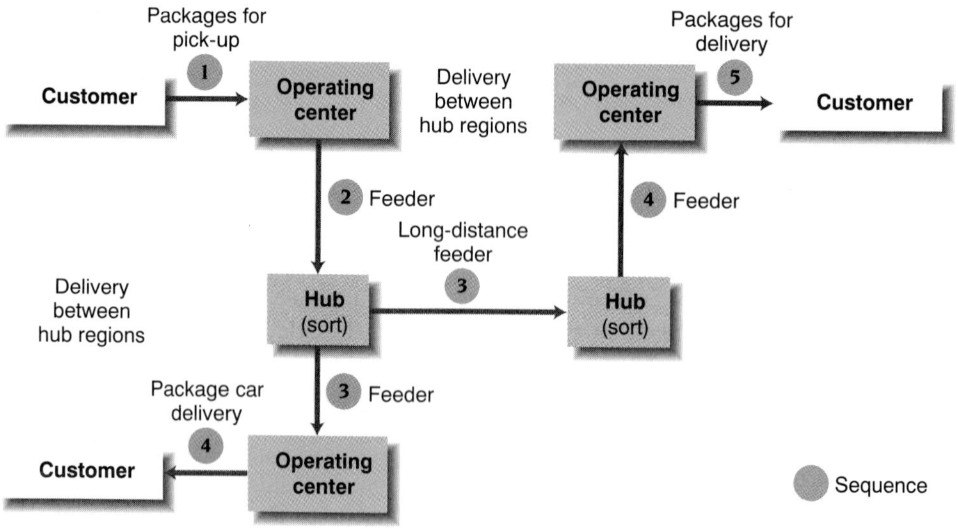

FIGURE 3.6 The UPS delivery cycle.

customers in their zones (each operating center area is divided into delivery/pickup zones). In the afternoon the drivers repeat the process, picking up packages from the customers in their zones. Therefore, deliveries within the same hub region will normally occur within one day, and deliveries between hub regions within a day's drive will normally occur within two days. The UPS air delivery system works the same way, but the hubs are located at airports.

THE FACILITY

The success of this system depends on the efficiency of the hub operations. Trucks must be unloaded, packages sorted, and trucks reloaded in a very short period of time, with peak activities occurring between 6 P.M. and 2 A.M. The Earth City (St. Louis, Missouri, area) hub is typical of many hubs. In addition to acting as a hub, it serves as an operating center, housing over 250 package cars. The facility contains 25 miles of conveyers, has interior parking spots for 225 package cars, has 206 loading docks for feeder trucks (51 used for unloading and 155 for loading), and employs approximately 800 people, of whom 650 are part-time, many of them college students. The facility will typically sort 44,000 parcels per hour with a capacity of over 50,000 per hour.

As an operating center as well as a hub, the Earth City facility sends out approximately 250 package car drivers every morning to deliver packages that had been loaded that morning. In the afternoon (from 2:30 P.M. to 7:00 P.M.) the drivers redrive their routes and pick up packages from their customers. The cars return to the processing center to be unloaded; each car has a designated parking location. Parcels are unloaded from the package cars and put on conveyers to be carried to a sorting area. In addition to its own cars, the Earth City hub receives parcels from feeders (trailer trucks) from the other operating centers in its region and from other hubs around the country. These trucks are unloaded at one of the 51 unloading docks around the outside of the facility. Packages from these trucks are also unloaded onto conveyers that carry them to the sorting area. (The number of trucks coming into and leaving the dock area is so large that a separate yard control center manages the truck movements into and out of the docks to optimize utilization of the area and trucks and to prevent accidents.)

SORTING

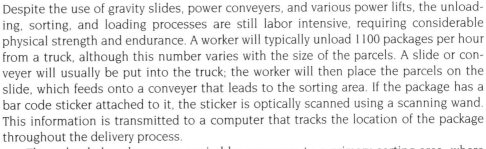

Despite the use of gravity slides, power conveyers, and various power lifts, the unloading, sorting, and loading processes are still labor intensive, requiring considerable physical strength and endurance. A worker will typically unload 1100 packages per hour from a truck, although this number varies with the size of the parcels. A slide or conveyer will usually be put into the truck; the worker will then place the parcels on the slide, which feeds onto a conveyer that leads to the sorting area. If the package has a bar code sticker attached to it, the sticker is optically scanned using a scanning wand. This information is transmitted to a computer that tracks the location of the package throughout the delivery process.

Every day hundreds of workers sort packages by destination among miles of automated conveyors.

The unloaded packages are carried by conveyers to a primary sorting area, where they are sorted according to zip codes (which correspond to hub or operating center locations) and moved by hand onto other conveyers that send the packages to the appropriate loading docks. For destinations in certain zip codes, the packages are routed to a secondary sorting area for additional sorting. (This is usually for areas where zip codes are split between operating centers and special knowledge is needed for sorting.) Small packages destined for the same operating center or customer are packaged together in a plastic bag as early in the process as possible so that they can be handled as a unit rather than each one sorted individually.

LOADING

Packages for customers within the hub's operating center area (which will be delivered by one of the hub's package cars) are sent by conveyer to the package car loading area. Packages travel on conveyers past the package cars. Loaders located near the cars remove from the conveyer parcels that are assigned to their cars and place them in holding cages. They then load the parcels into the package cars according to size and in order of delivery. Within the package cars there are two sets of shelves on each sidewall so that parcels can be loaded in three layers (floor, first shelf, and top shelf according to the planned delivery sequence, with the heaviest items on the floor).

Feeder trucks are loaded the "UPS way" to achieve maximum space utilization.

Parcels going to other operating centers or hubs are either (1) put on the general conveyer system that leads parcels past feeder trucks, where they must be identified, picked off the conveyer, and loaded manually into feeders, or (2) for high-volume routes, put on special conveyers that take parcels directly to a designated feeder truck for loading (they do not have to be identified and removed from a moving conveyer). Packages are loaded onto the feeder truck by either one or two loaders. Loading feeders, which is typically done as packages arrive from the conveyer, is a task that is constantly being studied by UPS. A truck that is efficiently loaded can carry as much as 30% more packages than an average truck.

MAJOR OPERATIONAL ISSUES

Process Design and Facility Layout

Despite the variety of services offered, the UPS ground delivery system produces one general product, package delivery service, and it is provided in the same way for all packages. Because of the high volume and uniform method of processing, UPS has designed the production systems at its hubs to be similar to those of an automobile assembly line. In these systems, called **repetitive flow processes**, each unit of production (each package, in this case) undergoes the same processing in the same sequence, and the units are processed one at a time. The facility is arranged to promote smooth flow of packages through the facility, and the docks are arranged to minimize the traffic congestion of arriving, departing, and moving trucks.

Routing, Truck Assignments, and Service Region Design

For packages being shipped within the same hub region the logistics are relatively simple: the packages are picked up by a package car, taken to the hub for sorting, and then sent to another operating center in the region and delivered. However, for packages moving between hubs, a key issue is how to route the packages to their destination. Efficiency dictates that UPS try to ship feeder trucks that are as full as possible. Although there are preferred routings for packages, these are regularly modified to utilize available truck space. So a package from St. Louis to Philadelphia may go via Pittsburgh one day and via Cleveland the next day, depending on which trucks have space available. Interhub loads are monitored and forecast daily, and shipments are coordinated among the hubs. So the St. Louis hub would coordinate with the Cleveland hub to make sure that Cleveland could ship the packages to Philadelphia without undue delay. UPS has been quite successful matching loads to trucks, as evidenced by the fact that fewer than 2% of the feeders are sent less than 50% full and over 63% are at least 90% full.

At the delivery level, key operational issues are the configuration of operating center areas within hub regions, delivery zones within operating center subregions, and delivery routes within zones. These decisions must take into account the current and anticipated shipping patterns and volumes of customers. Hub regions, operating centers, and delivery zones are continually being revised and reconfigured to improve the efficiency and quality of service.

Job Design and Training

UPS has been a leader in studying and developing work methods for almost every job in the company. Using motion and time studies and experimenting with alternative work methods, UPS has developed detailed written work methods for each job. As part of this process, work standards have been established, such as for the number of packages that can be loaded or sorted by a worker each hour. These standards serve several purposes, including staffing, scheduling, and monitoring employee performance. They are not, however, used to determine pay; if an employee's performance is well below the work standard, the supervisor will work with the employee to improve work methods.

Because many of the jobs at UPS require lifting, bending, and reaching, teaching employees the correct and safe way to perform these tasks is an important part of training. Work aids such as tables, lifts, conveyers, and slides are used wherever possible to reduce exertion, and color-coded labels and zip code charts are used to reduce the chance of sorting errors. An important part of the loading job is learning to load trucks the "UPS way" so as to maximize the load carried by the truck.

Scheduling

Perhaps the major operational problem confronting UPS is scheduling. Trucks bringing packages to the hub must arrive early enough to be unloaded and sorted so that they can be reloaded and sent out in time to arrive at their destinations the next morning. During the course of a few hours, hundreds of trucks must be unloaded and reloaded; feeder trucks must be assigned to an unloading dock and then moved to a loading dock. All the trucks cannot be unloaded or loaded at the same time, so loading and unloading crews must be coordinated to move among the trucks efficiently.

To assist in scheduling loading crews and sorting crews, the movement and loading/unloading of trucks, and the assignment of packages to feeders (routing), UPS forecasts daily shipments and uses computer simulation to test loading schedules. Even small improvements in loading and sorting efficiency can translate into millions of dollars of savings for a large operation.

UPS has established itself as a world leader in the package delivery industry by solving many of these operations problems. It has used specialization of labor very well, and its large size has allowed it to maintain an industrial engineering staff that is continually working to improve operations and serve its customers better. At a small company, such as the next stop on our tour, workers often must be multitalented. Managers may have to wear the hats of supervisor, purchasing manager, facility designer, and personnel director all at the same time.

3.5 APPROVED STATEWIDE TITLE AGENCY: PROCESSING TITLE INSURANCE[5]

Almost all buyers of residential real estate purchase title insurance; in fact, almost all mortgage lenders require it. When a person purchases a home or other real property, he or she is given a title to it. A *title* can be defined as a bundle of rights associated with the

[5]The author would like to thank Arthur Smialek, Jr., of Approved Statewide Title Agency for his assistance in preparing this plant tour.

property. Before the purchase can be completed and a title issued, the issuer of the insurance or its agent does a *title search*, which is an examination of public records to determine exactly what those property rights are. For example, the title search would determine that the person selling the property actually owns the property, that there are no outstanding taxes or assessments on the property to be paid, that there are no legal judgments or liens against the property, and that there are no heirs of previous owners with claims to the property. (If there are outstanding taxes, liens, or claims against the property, the prospective buyer may be obligated to pay the claims or else the property may be confiscated and auctioned by the government to pay them.) In addition, the title search should determine whether the rights include mineral and water rights, whether there are restrictions on the use of the property, and whether easements have been granted to other parties.

The purpose of a title search and title insurance is to make the prospective buyer fully aware of the property rights and to protect the buyer (and the lender) from claims against the title. The title insurance company provides a legal description of the property and rights; makes a search of public records to guarantee ownership by the seller, identifying any encumbrances on the title; and then issues an insurance policy to the buyer (and the mortgage lender in most cases) protecting the buyer against any undisclosed claims or ownership disputes. If a claim arises, the insurance company defends the buyer's title in court and pays for any losses in the event that the defense is unsuccessful. (New title insurance is also required by lenders when an owner refinances the mortgage to protect the company against claims against the property that may have originated while the property was owned by the current owner. This is a major source of business for title insurance companies.)

Approved Statewide Title Agency (ASTA) has seven offices and approximately 60 employees serving six counties in northeastern Ohio. The agency's primary products are title search, title insurance, and escrow services for real estate buyers and lenders. ASTA acts as an agent for major insurance underwriters. That is, ASTA handles the entire title search process, except that when the title insurance policy is issued, the risk (the responsibility for defending the title and paying judgments) is transferred to a large insurance underwriter (in exchange for a fee). In addition to title insurance, ASTA provides other information services for realtors, such as legal descriptions of properties and property tax information (called *legals and taxes*), and recent selling prices of comparable properties in the area of the target property (called *comps*). The legals and taxes are free; comps are provided at a nominal cost to realtors as a way to promote insurance business rather than as profit-making services themselves. The following sections describe the production process of ASTA's main office in Cleveland, Ohio, which performs title searches, issues title insurance policies, and provides legals and taxes, comps, and other services for realtors and lenders. Although it is the largest of ASTA's offices, it employs only 15–20 people, approximately half of whom are stationed outside the office.

CUSTOMERS AND PRODUCTS

The customer relationship in the title insurance industry is a complicated one because the supplier of the insurance, such as ASTA, is usually not selected by the person receiving and paying for the insurance, the property buyer. Few people have a "family" title insurance company the way they have a family doctor, lawyer, or auto mechanic. Title insurance is a service with which few people are familiar, and most people will use it only a few times in their lives. In fact, most people have never heard of title insurance until they buy their first home. They will normally use the title insurance company recommended by a realtor (often the seller's realtor) or by their lender, and it is the realtor or lender that normally places the order with the title insurance company and handles all communication with it; the property buyer rarely comes into contact with the title insurance company. Title insurance companies, therefore, focus on providing quick, high-quality, and complete (one-stop shopping) services to realtors and lenders. This is the reason ASTA and other title insurance companies provide low-profit auxiliary services, such as legals and taxes and comps, to realtors in order to obtain customers for their primary products.

THE PRODUCTION PROCESS

The production process, which is illustrated in Figure 3.7, begins when a realtor or lender calls the service department at ASTA. There are two main product streams: support services (legals and taxes and comps) and title insurance. If the request is for a legal description of a property, property tax information, or comparable property price information, the request goes to a person specifically assigned to prepare these as part of her job. Using a computer she searches a database of county property records to obtain some of the desired information, and she contacts an examiner at the county courthouse to obtain the rest. She then organizes and prints a report for the customer, usually within hours of the request, thereby providing same-day service. (This way a realtor who is contacted by a prospective seller can call on the seller the same day with

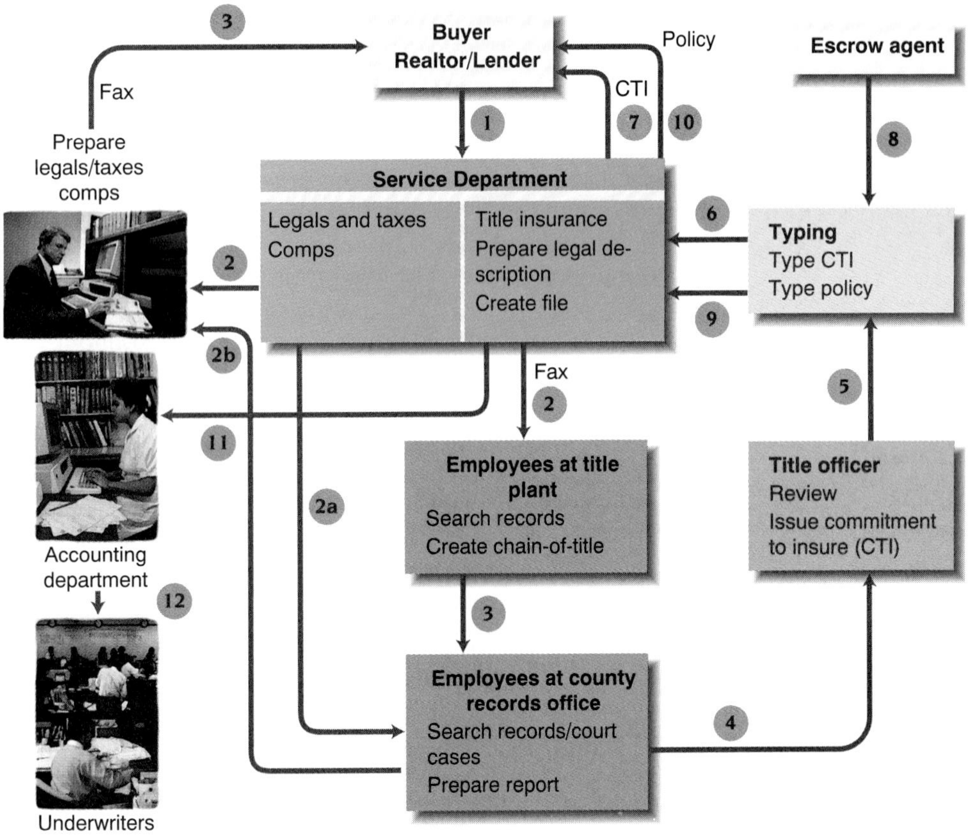

FIGURE 3.7 Flow diagram of ASTA's production process.

this information, impressing the seller and increasing the probability that the seller will select that realtor to sell the house.)

Requests for title insurance are often initiated by the lender after the mortgage has been approved. On receiving the request, an employee in ASTA's service department creates both a paper file and a computer file for the policy and a legal description of the property if one has not already been prepared. The legal description is then sent by fax to employees who are off site at a title plant. A *title plant* is a for-profit facility that has a copies of all legal documents related to properties filed with the county. The title plant arranges the records in an easy-to-search form. Employees of ASTA search the records and prepare a *chain-of-title*, which is a chronological list of all documents related to the property.

The chain-of-title is then sent to ASTA employees stationed at the County Administration Building. These employees examine the actual county documents, and court cases related to them, to determine the resolution and status of any claims against the property. They then write a summary report and send it to the title officer at the title office (the St. Louis office in this case). The title officer reviews the information and, if it is complete, prepares a *commitment to insure*. The commitment to insure, which includes a history of all previous liens and their resolution, is a promise to insure the property subject to any qualifying conditions, such as that the insurance will be valid when a $100 subdivision assessment is paid. The commitment is typed by the typing department and a copy sent to the lender by fax to speed to purchase process; an official copy is also sent by mail. The file is then returned to storage in the service department.

Ownership of the property is transferred by an escrow agent. The *escrow agent* acts as an unbiased third party to make sure that both parties to the sale fulfill the sales contract. In simple terms, the buyer (or the lender on the buyer's behalf) gives the required funds to the escrow agent, the seller gives the deed to the agent, and the escrow agent verifies that all other requirements have been satisfied (house inspection performed, house insurance purchased). The escrow agent then transfers the money to the seller's mortgage holder and the seller, instructs the title agent to record the deed and loan documents with the county, and transfers the deed to the buyer (or mortgage holder). Once the deed and loan documents have been filed with the county, ASTA is notified and the typing department prepares title insurance policies and sends them to the service department. The service department sends the policies to the property buyer and lender, and the transaction is recorded by ASTA's accounting department. Every month ASTA sends a list of the policies it has assigned to its major underwriters so that they have a record of whom they are insuring.

MAJOR OPERATIONAL ISSUES

ASTA competes in a highly cyclical and seasonal service industry that requires the speedy preparation of accurate information. This presents several operational challenges.

Forecasting, Staffing, and Scheduling

The demand for title insurance and auxiliary services is closely correlated with the rate at which homes are purchased and mortgages are refinanced, which is highly variable. It is not unusual for the demand for title insurance—which depends on changes in interest rates, the business cycle, and the time of year—to double or triple, or to decrease by 50–75%, over the course of a few months. These large swings in demand make staffing and scheduling quite difficult. Title insurance companies such as ASTA tend to be quite small, with two or three people assigned to perform each of the major tasks.

Eliminating one person, such as a document examiner at the county records office, can reduce processing capacity by 33–50%. Many of these jobs are quite skilled and require months of training, so ASTA cannot simply hire and fire people from month to month and still provide fast, accurate service.

The challenge facing ASTA's management is to forecast the demand pattern and decide how to use overtime work, reduced work weeks, temporary hiring and layoffs, and permanent hiring and layoffs to remain solvent in the short run while maintaining long-term health and viability. One approach ASTA has used to give it more flexibility is to cross-train some of its workers so that they can be moved around as needed. This allows ASTA to split workers between departments to reduce the "lumpiness" of production capacity, and it provides backup when employees are sick.

Technology

ASTA has revolutionized its process technology in the past few years. All the information it uses, such as legal descriptions of property, tax records, and sales prices of comparable homes, used to be obtained by searching paper records at various sites. Much of this information is now available in computer databases that can be searched and matched, prepared in report form (along with maps if necessary), and sent to the customer within hours or even minutes. In the past, information and documents had to be physically transported among ASTA's office, the title plant, the county records office, and customers. Now much of it can be transmitted by computer or fax within minutes. During a two-year period in the early 1990s, ASTA went from having few computers to being almost totally computerized. The conversion was expensive and risky, but ASTA's management decided to make the conversion during a period of low demand. It used the slack time to install and test the equipment and software and to train employees without disrupting operations. Soon interest rates dropped and demand increased rapidly, which provided additional cash, allowing ASTA to hire a management information systems director as well. This investment has paid off; ASTA's management believes that without this conversion, the company may not have survived. Instead it has continued to grow.

Quality

Quality is important for all companies, but mistakes by a title company almost surely turn into costs. Not identifying an outstanding claim, or providing an inaccurate property description or list of property rights and restrictions, will ultimately lead to a claim against the insurance policy. Although the claim is legally the responsibility of the un-

ASTA employee searches data base for legal documents related to a property.

derwriter, if ASTA made too many mistakes that generated claims, the underwriters would either increase the fees they charge ASTA to underwrite insurance policies, or would simply not underwrite policies, effectively putting ASTA out of business. In addition, even when property owners collect on insured claims, they are often displeased by the inconvenience of having had to file a claim. In fact, one of ASTA's competitive advantages is its low error rate, which allows it to obtain favorable underwriting rates and gives it a good image among realtors and lenders.

The four plant tours presented here have not only illustrated the variety of production processes that exist in practice, they have also introduced a visual tool that is invaluable in operations management: **flow diagrams** (or **flow charts**). For each company we presented a production flow diagram, such as Figures 3.2 and 3.4, that showed how products, materials, or information flow through the production process. There is no better way to understand the steps of a production process and to identify ways to simplify and improve it than to construct such a diagram. We will use flow diagrams throughout the remainder of the book to analyze the design of production processes, the layout of facilities, and the jobs performed by workers. In your current and future jobs, you should construct flow diagrams for yourself to see how your job fits into the production subsystem of your department and how your department's work fits into the overall production process. The enlightenment gained from this exercise can help you to make fundamental improvements in your company, such as those made by Chuck Wise (see Chapter 1), which can propel your career upward.

SUMMARY

- Jefferson Smurfit's Alton plant produces a narrow set of products in large volume, so it is able to use a cost-efficient but inflexible **continuous flow process**. All its products are made the same way; the only major differences among the products are roll width and paperboard weight (thickness).
- Standard Register uses a **job shop process** to provide it with flexibility in the variety of products it produces. As with most job shop operations, production scheduling and quality control are major operations management issues for Standard Register.
- In its parcel sorting and loading operation, UPS utilizes **repetitive flow processes** similar to those of an automobile assembly line because all parcels are sorted in the same general way. The labor intensity of the system and the need to deliver parcels on time require UPS to devote considerable attention to scheduling, job design, and truck routing.
- Although ASTA provides a limited set of services, each customer request must be processed separately and each one is unique because each property has its own history and requires a customized search of records and analysis. ASTA's small size and highly variable customer demand make staffing, training, and personnel scheduling major managerial issues.
- **Flow diagrams** are figures that show the movement of products, materials, or information through a production system or subsystem.

KEY TERMS

blending problem **78**
continuous flow process **73**
cross-training **84**
cutting-stock problem **78**
flow diagrams (flow charts) **96**
Fourdrinier process **73**
job shop process **80**
repetitive flow processes **90**
total quality management **85**

Discussion and Review

1. Jefferson Smurfit's Alton plant can produce hundreds of different products in terms of roll width and paperboard weight, so why does the plant tour say that it produces a narrow product line? How does this affect its production process?
2. Why is a machine breakdown at Jefferson Smurfit more serious than a breakdown at a company such as Standard Register?
3. What actions have been taken at Jefferson Smurfit's Alton plant to reduce its effect on the environment? Identify another industry that could take similar actions.
4. Because every product it produces is different and since new products are produced every day, what steps does Standard Register take to ensure product quality?
5. Why is optical scanning and computerized material tracking likely to be of greater benefit to Standard Register than to Jefferson Smurfit?
6. Why does it make sense for UPS to use mostly part-time workers in its sorting operation, whereas it does not make sense for the other three companies toured?
7. Why is cross-training so important at ASTA? Why would it be of less value at UPS?
8. Explain how ASTA's same-day service in providing legals and taxes and comps supports its marketing function (i.e., helps sales).
9. Which of the following are major operations management issues for Jefferson Smurfit and Standard Register but not for UPS and ASTA: quality management, job training, inventory management, and maintenance? Explain.
10. How has each company used technology to improve its operations?
11. How are demand forecasts used in each of the four companies? For which companies do you think demand forecasting is most important? Why?

PART TWO

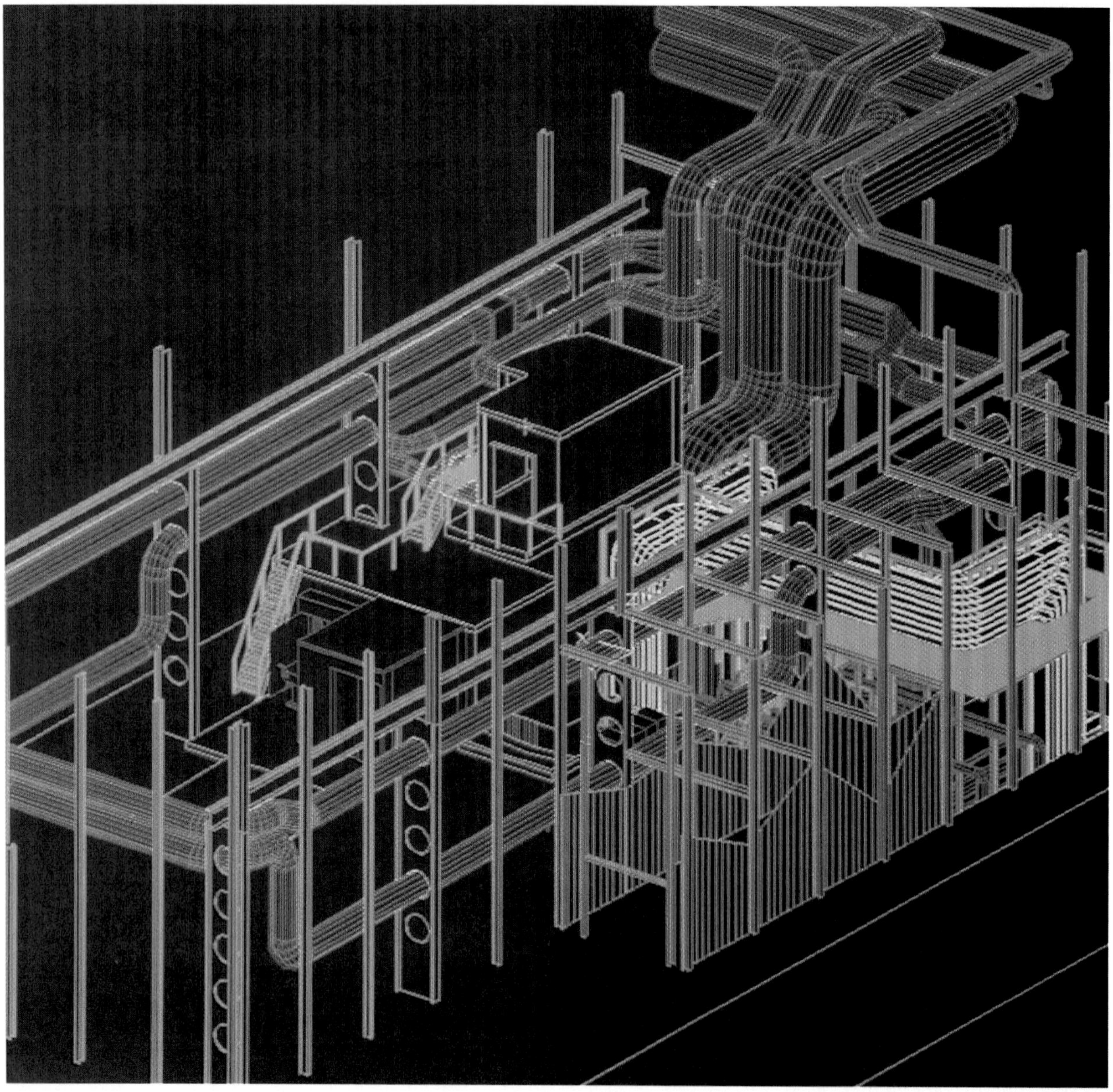

DESIGNING PRODUCTION SYSTEMS

Chapter 4	Forecasting
Tutorial 1	Optimization Models and Linear Programming
Chapter 5	Product Design and Operations
Chapter 6	Capacity Planning and Facility Location
Tutorial 2	Decision Analysis
Chapter 7	Selecting the Process Structure and Technology
Chapter 8	Process Design and Facility Layout
Chapter 9	Waiting Lines
Tutorial 3	Simulation Analysis for Operations Management
Chapter 10	Job Design, Work Methods, and Organization
Chapter 11	The Quality Management System

Like a healthy heart, a well-designed production system establishes an operating environment in which everything else works better. This part describes how such a system can be achieved. A key ingredient for designing and operating production systems well is reliable forecasting, so we begin Part 2 with an introduction to forecasting methods, especially common statistical models. We then turn to major operational design issues. We first discuss how to design products to enhance their quality and to make them easier and less expensive to produce in less time. We then move on to the design of the production system, facilities, and individual production processes. Some of the key design issues are determining the number, size, and location of facilities, the technologies to use, the structure of the production process, the division of work, the spatial configuration of the process, and the effects of randomness and variation on the system.

People are the glue that holds production systems together, so this part discusses the role of humans in the production process and the design of jobs. Quality must be designed into the product and its assurance must be built into the overall production system. For these reasons we include quality assurance in this part as a strategic design issue.

Designing and evaluating production systems is not easy, but analytical tools, such as linear programming, decision analysis, and simulation can help. This part includes three tutorials on these topics. Even those who have covered these topics previously should find the tutorials valuable because they illustrate how these tools can be used specifically in operations management.

CHAPTER 4

FORECASTING

4.1 GOOD DECISIONS BEGIN WITH GOOD FORECASTS
On the Job: Jayne Rosselli, Garden Valley Ranch
What Is Forecasting?
Importance of Demand Forecasting
In Good Company: Compaq Bets on Forecasts—and Wins Big

4.2 FORECASTING METHODS
The Role of Time
Quantitative versus Qualitative Methods

4.3 QUALITATIVE FORECASTING METHODS
When to Use Qualitative Methods
How to Improve Qualitative Forecasting

4.4 QUANTITATIVE FORECASTING METHODS
Background and Strategy of Quantitative Forecasting
Steps in Modeling
Time Series and Causal Models

4.5 CONSTANT PROCESSES AND THE CUMULATIVE AVERAGE

4.6 QUASI-CONSTANT PROCESSES
Simple Moving Average
Weighted Moving Average
Simple Exponential Smoothing

4.7 COMPARING ALTERNATIVE MODELS
Verifying Model Assumptions
Evaluating Forecast Accuracy

4.8 LINEAR TREND PROCESSES
Linear Regression for Trend Processes
Moving Linear Regression
Double Exponential Smoothing

4.9 SEASONAL PROCESSES
Constant or Quasi-Constant Processes with Seasonality
Linear Trend Processes with Seasonality

4.10 CAUSAL MODELS
Selecting an Independent Variable
Estimating the Relationship and Forecasting
Practical Hints for Using Causal Models

4.11 ADVANCED MODELS

4.12 IMPLEMENTATION AND USE OF FORECASTING SYSTEMS
Model Evaluation and Testing
Combining Forecasting Methods
Monitoring Forecasts: Tracking Signals and Adaptive Models
Buildup and Breakdown Models

Reynolds and Hill College: A Forecasting Case

4.1 GOOD DECISIONS BEGIN WITH GOOD FORECASTS

The demand for flowers varies greatly from month to month, and varieties and colors go in and out of fashion quickly. Therefore, the success of flower producers, such as Garden Valley Ranch, depends greatly on accurately predicting customers' demands. Jayne Rosselli (featured in On the Job below) uses these forecasts to determine the number and types of plants Garden Valley Ranch should purchase and plant each year, to be harvested and sold later. Every day managers throughout the world must schedule personnel and production, place orders for materials, and decide whether to introduce new products, expand production capacity, or open new facilities. In making these decisions, managers such as Jayne Rosselli must consider what the future business environment will be: product demands, prices, transport rates, availability of raw materials and labor, and government regulations. Although we seldom know for sure what will happen in the future, there are techniques that can help us to predict specific aspects of the future and to understand the amount of uncertainty that exists. The better our ability to predict the future, the better our decisions are likely to be.

ON THE JOB

JAYNE ROSSELLI, GARDEN VALLEY RANCH

Garden Valley Ranch specializes in supplying its customers with hand-selected and hand-processed fresh roses, grown outdoors in its beautiful Petaluma, California, location. As managing partner, Jayne Rosselli phones customers every morning for orders and then supervises the selection, processing, packing, and shipping of each day's yield of over 500 ten-stem bunches, most of them destined for the wholesale flower market 3000 miles away in New York City.

Varieties and colors go in and out of fashion, says Jayne, and in order to have on hand today the roses that buyers will want tomorrow, the ranch must forecast demand for color and quantity months in advance. Jayne orders plants each summer from her own suppliers, who deliver in December. The roses go into the ground in January and are ready to harvest in the spring. "You really have to understand your customer," Jayne says, "why they use your product and what they do with it. Here, we ask our customers often. When you know as much as possible about your customers, and who their customers are, it isn't so difficult to predict their future needs."

WHAT IS FORECASTING?

Forecasting is the art and science of predicting future events. Early humans forecast the availability of food before deciding where to hunt on a particular day, and the Romans forecast the strength of armies (and potential booty) before deciding whether or not to invade a region. Today farmers forecast weather conditions before deciding whether or not to plant on a particular day, and students forecast the difficulty of courses before deciding on their schedules for a semester.

Although accurate forecasting has always been important for managing organizations, it has become even more so in recent years. As markets and organizations have become larger and more complex, and as change occurs more rapidly, the time frame for making decisions has decreased and the consequences of making poor decisions have become more severe. As a result, the forecasting process must become more systematic and accurate and, to whatever extent possible, more automated.

People in business and government are most often interested in predicting the numerical value of some characteristic of their work environment, such as the level of demand for a product, the prime interest rate, or the gross national product during some future time period. Of course, sometimes they are interested in forecasting a specific event, such as whether a competitor will enter a market or whether a new tax will be enacted. The purpose of making forecasts (however they are obtained) is to use them, either explicitly or implicitly, as inputs into some decision-making process.

IMPORTANCE OF DEMAND FORECASTING

Demand forecasts drive many aspects of an organization, from planning facilities, personnel, production, and materials acquisition to marketing and distribution (see Figure 4.1). Inaccurate demand forecasts can lead to over- or understaffing of operations, product shortages, excess inventories, and late deliveries. By contrast, accurate demand forecasts can lead to timely introduction of products, opening of facilities, and adjustments in staffing and inventory levels. Accurate forecasts can help companies increase their profits by millions of dollars, whereas inaccurate forecasts can produce equally large losses, as demonstrated by Compaq Computer, featured in this chapter's In Good Company box.

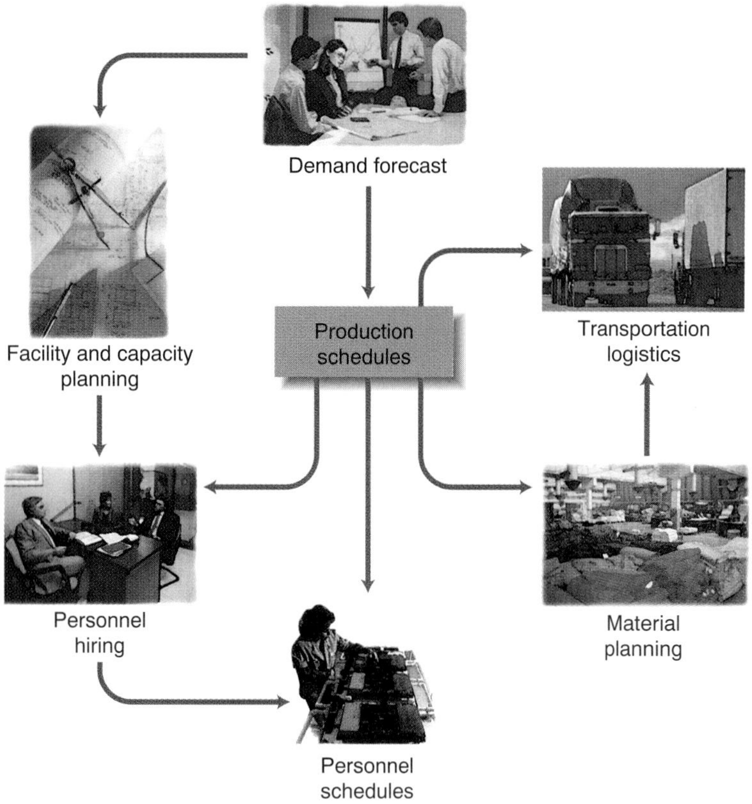

FIGURE 4.1 The role of demand forecasts in operations.

IN GOOD COMPANY

Compaq Bets on Forecasts—and Wins Big

The dynamic and competitive nature of the personal computer industry has been well characterized by Kevin L. Bohren, marketing vice-president of Compaq Computer Corporation's Desktop Division: "It used to be every new product had six months of uniqueness. Now, it's a long weekend." Compaq Computer Corporation, the market leader in personal computers, understands that in such a dynamic market demand forecasting is challenging but crucial. In 1993 Compaq underestimated customer demand and ran short of computers during the crucial Christmas holiday season, which cost it over $50 million in sales. However, Compaq nearly doubled its product inventories going into the 1994 holiday season based on forecasts of strong demands; this risk paid off, resulting in hundreds of millions of dollars of additional sales.

Compaq has developed a sophisticated forecasting and decision model to predict the effects of prices and competitors' behavior on demand. This model led Compaq to slow its release of Pentium-based computers early in 1995 and to increase production of its 486-based computers instead. This flew in the face of industry practice, whereby companies typically release their new products as soon as possible. But the model indicated that immediate demand for the Pentiums would be lower than others were predicting, while a substantial demand for 486 machines still existed. The forecast was correct, and Compaq estimated that its decision produced an additional $50 million in profit in the first quarter of 1995.

Primary Sources: Gary Williams, "At Compaq, a Desktop Crystal Ball," *Business Week*, Mar. 20, 1995, pp. 96–97; and Peter Burrows, "Yes, Compaq, There Is a Santa Claus," *Business Week*, Jan. 30, 1995, p. 6.

Organizations forecast many phenomena other than product demands, such as interest rates, market share, and prices. But because of the importance of demand forecasts, in this chapter our discussion will focus on forecasting product demands. Product demands also exhibit most of the characteristics that are likely to arise when forecasting other variables, so the same methods used to forecast demands can be used to forecast these other variables as well.

This chapter presents general procedures and specific techniques for forecasting. They are *tools*; they will not eliminate uncertainty completely, and in some cases they will not be appropriate. But in most cases these methods can provide considerable help in predicting future events and making informed decisions.

4.2 FORECASTING METHODS

Many methods have been used to make forecasts of future phenomena. The extent to which one method will be superior to another depends on the specific circumstances. For example, one model may be useful for forecasting the weekly demand for donuts at a donut shop but terrible for forecasting yearly sales of nuclear power plants. Before choosing a general forecasting method, it is important to answer the following questions:

1. What is the purpose of the forecasts? For what decisions will they be used?
2. What lead time is necessary for the forecasts to be of value?
3. What specific entity (variable) is to be forecast?
4. What do we know about the entity being forecast? What factors affect or are related to it?
5. What data or information about the entity are available?

Depending on the answers to these questions, a manager may choose a less accurate method that produces more timely forecasts, or may decide to forecast individual components of a variable and then combine them rather than forecasting the variable directly. There are techniques to help in these and other cases.

THE ROLE OF TIME

The time horizons for forecasts can be quite varied, and they are usually a function of the purpose of the forecasts and the types of decisions for which they will be used. For example, for strategic planning, such as deciding whether to introduce a new product or expand production capabilities, a company would be interested in the long-term demand (2–10 years ahead) for that product. In contrast, for making daily personnel schedules or purchasing decisions, forecasts of short-term demand (a few days to a few months ahead) are of interest.

As a standard convention, forecasts are usually classified into one of three forecasting time horizons: short-term, intermediate-term, and long-term.

1. ***Short-Term Forecasts.*** Short-term forecasts usually look no more than three months ahead. These forecasts are used for tactical decision making, such as job sequencing and production scheduling, machine assignments, personnel scheduling, purchasing and inventory planning, and maintenance planning. As such, these forecasts tend to be for narrow or specific entities, such as demand for a specific good or service. Because of the narrow focus and the short time intervals between forecasts, short-term forecasts are usually obtained using simple statistical methods.
2. ***Intermediate-Term Forecasts.*** Intermediate-term forecasts have a time frame of three months to two years, with 3–12 months being the most common period. From an operational viewpoint, these forecasts are most commonly used for aggregate production planning, including decisions that alter shorter-term capacity such as subcontracting and overtime. Some personnel planning (such as deciding to hire new workers, in contrast to actual employee scheduling) and logistical planning decisions also use these forecasts. Intermediate-term forecasts are usually made for aggregate entities, such as all the products of some type or made by some facility, rather than for individual products. Moderately complex statistical models are normally used to make these forecasts.

3. **Long-Term Forecasts.** Long-term forecasts usually have a time frame of two to five years. Their most common use is for planning the introduction of new products and major capital expenditures, such as new facilities or capacity expansion. Long-term forecasts are usually made for aggregate entities or even macroeconomic phenomena, such as industrywide sales or gross national product. These forecasts are typically made using either complex mathematical models or qualitative methods.

QUANTITATIVE VERSUS QUALITATIVE METHODS

Forecasting methods are classified as quantitative or qualitative. The difference between the two is the process by which forecasts are generated, not the results. **Quantitative forecasting methods** use mathematical models to represent relationships among relevant variables based on historical data and/or known relationships. The models are then used in conjunction with historical data to forecast demands (or some other quantity). These methods are sometimes referred to as **objective forecasting methods** because the underlying assumptions of the forecasting model and the data used can be stated precisely, independent of the user. Thus, if two individuals use the same model and same data, they should get the same forecasts.

In contrast, **qualitative forecasting methods** rely on one or more individuals to generate forecasts without using mathematical models alone; for example, a sales manager may predict future sales for the division based on informal discussions with some customers. Qualitative forecasting incorporates the forecaster's experiences, intuition, values, and personal biases into the forecast. These are considered **subjective forecasting methods** because there is no way to determine exactly what information is being used by the forecaster and how. Such forecasts are specific to the forecaster and cannot be duplicated by others. For example, if two individuals attempt to predict the market penetration of a new product, their forecasts will probably be somewhat different because they are drawing on different experiences and are likely to weight the importance of those experiences differently.

Although it may appear that quantitative models should be more consistent and accurate because of their inherent "objectivity," in practice the results depend on the circumstances. Quantitative forecasting methods generally assume that the environment in which the forecast is being made is relatively stable, so that the economic/technical/social relationships that held in the past will be the same in the future. For short-term or intermediate-term forecasts this is usually the case, so quantitative methods are frequently used for these forecasts. However, over longer time horizons or in unstable circumstances, such as when the possibility of a war, trade embargo, change of government, or major technological innovation exists, fundamental environmental conditions and relationships may change. In these circumstances, qualitative forecasting methodologies can often be superior to quantitative methods because they are better able to anticipate and evaluate the possible consequences of such structural changes.

We now explore these two types of methods in greater detail.

4.3 QUALITATIVE FORECASTING METHODS

Quantitative forecasting methods assume that the quantity to be forecast will be affected in the future by the same things that affected it in the past and in the same way. Quantitative models therefore require a substantial amount of reliable, consistent historical data to provide good forecasts. However, in many circumstances these conditions are not satisfied, so qualitative methods should be used.

WHEN TO USE QUALITATIVE METHODS

In general, we should consider using qualitative forecasting techniques when one or more of the following conditions exist:

1. *Little or no historical data on the phenomenon to be forecast exist.* For example, forecasting the demand for a new product presents a problem; by definition there are no historical data of previous demand.
2. *The relevant environment is likely to be unstable during the forecast horizon.* If major shocks to the system are likely to occur during the forecast horizon, historical relationships are likely to change. For example, the oil embargo of 1973, the integration of the European Union in 1992, and the North American Free Trade Agreement of 1994 created major changes in worldwide business operations. Price and demand forecasts based on previous conditions can be grossly inaccurate.
3. *The forecast has a long time horizon, such as more than three to five years.* The longer the time horizon, the more likely that structural changes in the environment, such as changes in technology, competition, or government regulations, will occur. Quantitative models may not be able to capture these changes.

HOW TO IMPROVE QUALITATIVE FORECASTING

The primary drawback of using qualitative forecasting methods is that they rely primarily on the information gathering and processing capabilities of the person making the forecast and cannot be independently duplicated. (Another person might obtain the same forecast, but it is impossible to duplicate the *process* unless the first person is using a well-defined decision rule.) In spite of this subjectivity, qualitative forecasts can be improved over time by using the following methodological enhancements.

Standardize the Process

Decision makers who are called on to perform qualitative forecasting often have to make similar forecasts again and again. For example, a district sales manager may have to make monthly or quarterly sales projections on a regular basis. In these cases, it is useful for the sales manager to analyze how he goes about making the forecast: what data does he use, and how does he combine them to obtain the forecast? By identifying these things, the sales manager can make sure that the same types of data are gathered each time and processed similarly. This does not prevent the sales manager from changing the forecasting method, but when he does, he will be more cognizant of the fact that a change in method is occurring.

To illustrate standardization, suppose the sales manager obtains his forecast by asking 10 customers about their purchasing plans during the next three months. Standardization of the process might involve making sure that the same customers are surveyed each month, that the same questions are asked, and preferably that the same person from each company is contacted. By having the same information base for each period, the forecaster is better able to understand and refine his method and obtain more accurate and consistent forecasts.

Monitor Forecasts

Most people are not very good forecasters unless they have received some training. One of the best ways to improve qualitative forecasting is to monitor the performance of the forecaster(s). Each time a forecast is made, it should be compared later with the actual outcome to determine its accuracy. By monitoring performance, the forecaster (or a user of the forecast) can adjust initial forecasts to correct for bias. For example, if a person finds that she consistently overestimates projected sales, she can modify her method or simply adjust her initial forecasts to eliminate the bias and improve her accuracy. Sometimes these biases may be subtle and require careful analysis of the monitored results. For example, some macroeconomic forecasters are known to be overly optimistic in their forecasts during strong periods in the business cycle and overly pessimistic during bad periods. Thus, they do not consistently overestimate or underestimate; instead they need to consider the current economic conditions when adjusting or correcting their forecasts.

Monitoring has proved to be an effective mechanism for improving meteorological forecasting in the United States. It is now common for meteorologists to forecast the probability of rain occurring in 10% increments. Over the long term, if it rains only 30% of the time when the forecaster has predicted a 50% chance of rain, the meteorologist can adjust her forecasts accordingly. Experience with weather forecasters indicates that such correction is possible and improves forecasting accuracy.[1]

Create Incentives for Accuracy

When the manager of a major league baseball team predicts at the beginning of the season that his team will contend for the championship, there may be more driving this prediction than hope and enthusiasm; the manager has an incentive to mispredict. He is trying to encourage people to buy tickets to games and to buy them as early as possible. Predicting a successful season is more likely to accomplish this than making a possibly more accurate prediction of finishing near the bottom of the league. The same phenomenon occurs throughout business and government. People are often put in situations where it is beneficial to them to make a biased forecast. For example, a district sales manager may be asked to forecast sales within his district during the next year. If this forecast is then used to establish his sales quota, and if the manager's bonus is based on the amount by which actual sales exceed the quota, the manager is likely to give a lower prediction of sales than he otherwise would.

To whatever extent possible, incentives to be inaccurate should be removed and incentives to be accurate adopted. One strategy is to separate the forecaster from the person who will be directly affected by the forecast. For example, an economic planner may be asked to make demand forecasts (possibly using input from sales personnel) rather than the sales managers. The forecaster would be rewarded based on the accuracy of the forecast, while the sales manager would be rewarded based on sales relative to previous years and the forecast value.

Use Group Methodologies

It is frequently better to utilize the knowledge of several experts to make a forecast rather than relying on a single person. One advantage of group methods is that a wider range of experiences and knowledge can be extracted. This is especially useful when forecasting the likelihood and consequences of technological innovations or political upheavals. As an example, in 1979 many experts in the U.S. oil and gas industry were predicting modest increases in the price of oil. But an oil company representative stationed in Iran used his personal knowledge of the conditions in that country to predict

[1]See A. H. Murphy and H. Daan, "Impacts of Feedback and Experience on the Quality of Subjective Probability Forecasts: Comparison of Results from the First and Second Years of the Zierikzee Experiment," *Monthly Weather Review*, Vol. 112, 1984, pp. 413–428.

the imminent overthrow of the Shah and the resulting reduction in the supply of oil from Iran, which would cause a substantial increase in the price of oil. Such crucial information is likely to be obtained only if a broad cross section of experts is consulted.

A second reason for using several experts to forecast is to balance out different biases. The *Wall Street Journal* and Robert Eggert's *Blue Chip Report* (a monthly economic newsletter) regularly survey groups of economists and ask them to forecast the values of major economic measures such as interest rates and gross national product growth. A study by the National Bureau of Economic Research showed that over an 11-year period the average of the economists' forecasts in the *Blue Chip Report* was more accurate than the forecasts of three-quarters of the individual experts. Furthermore, the average forecasts were rarely far off the actual values, whereas individual forecasters often were.[2] One reason for the success of the *Blue Chip Report's* accuracy is that Robert Eggert closely monitors the performance of individual forecasters, and those who are consistently way out of line are replaced.

The knowledge and opinions of several people can be utilized and combined in several ways to develop a forecast. The following are some of the most commonly used methods.

1. ***Group Averaging.*** This method simply involves taking individual forecasts and averaging them. There are several advantages to this approach. First, it is easy. Second, members of the group do not have to be organized as a group; in fact, they do not even have to know they are part of a group forecast. For example, many companies subscribe to multiple forecasting services, such as Chase Econometrics or Wharton Econometrics, and then average the forecasts from these services with the forecasts of one or more in-house economists (this allows qualitative and quantitative forecasts to be combined). Third, the weights given to each individual can be varied based on past performance.

   The primary drawback of this method is that there is no interaction among the forecasters. There is no sharing of knowledge or explanation of their reasoning. For example, if a group member shares knowledge about a new technology, the group may be able to deduce its effects on the company better than any one group member could do alone.

2. ***Group Consensus.*** With this method, members meet as a group. Each member gives a forecast and then explains how he or she arrived at it, especially communicating any special information that might not be known to others in the group, such as a potential new use for a product. The members can then discuss the forecasts and supporting information. The ultimate goal is to agree on one forecast—the **consensus forecast**.

   There are several drawbacks to this method. First, there may be sufficiently strong differences of opinion that no consensus forecast results. The second drawback, which is sometimes the cause of the first, is that in face-to-face meetings individuals will sometimes disagree with each other, and refuse to alter their initial forecasts, because of personality differences or turf battles. Third, members of subordinate rank may not be willing to express opinions that disagree with those of higher rank, especially direct superiors. In some cases the people of lower

[2]See, "If One Economist Goofs, Will 46 Do Any Better? Robert Eggert Thinks So, and He May Be Right," *Wall Street Journal*, April 6, 1983, for a discussion of Eggert's approach and its verification by the National Bureau of Economic Research. Also see J. Scott Armstrong, *Long-Range Forecasting: From Crystal Balls to Computers* (Wiley, New York, 1985), for many examples of how combined forecasts outperform individuals.

rank may possess the best knowledge, but they may not express their opinions freely in this setting.

3. ***Delphi Method.*** This method was developed specifically to achieve the benefits of group information exchange while alleviating the problem of personality conflicts. Normally the group leader or decision maker will ask several experts to provide a forecast, supporting arguments, and the information used to arrive at the forecast. This information is compiled and summarized and then reported to each expert in writing without revealing the identities of the experts. Using this information, new forecasts and supporting arguments are requested. This process is repeated until one or more consensus forecasts are obtained.

   This method allows each expert to benefit from the experience and knowledge of the other experts, but by not meeting face to face or even knowing the identity of the other group members, personality and turf conflicts are reduced and lower-ranking employees may be more willing to give honest opinions. One drawback of this method is that it is slower and more costly than the other two. However, advances in telecommunications have reduced the time required and enhanced its appeal.

4.4 QUANTITATIVE FORECASTING METHODS[3]

Qualitative forecasting methods have considerable value in certain situations. But for most operational decisions, the forecasting environment is sufficiently stable and enough data are available to allow quantitative forecasting methods to be used. Quantitative models can be difficult to develop, but once developed, they are easy to apply and automate. Many different people can use the models to generate the forecasts they require without knowing all the inner workings of the model and without having years of experience in dealing with the forecast phenomenon. Quantitative models also provide continuity as personnel change, so forecasts of the same phenomenon will be generated the same way over time rather than changing with the personnel.

BACKGROUND AND STRATEGY OF QUANTITATIVE FORECASTING

Quantitative forecasting is an iterative process in which we study and analyze relevant data, develop a model, evaluate the model versus actual data, and then either adopt, refine, or revise the form of the model. We repeat this process as many times as are needed to obtain an acceptable model. The better one is at choosing an initial forecasting model, the simpler the task of eventually identifying a good model. If social science relationships were as deterministic as most physical relationships (in which E always equals mc^2), the task of choosing an initial model would be much easier. Unfortunately, the phenomena in which business forecasters are most interested are not so well behaved.

Even the most stable product demands, such as for bread, exhibit some randomness. Statistically, we explain this by saying that the phenomenon we wish to forecast is a random variable. A **random variable** Y_t, such as the demand for a particular soap during some month t, is a quantity whose value we do not know in advance of some event (month t being completed). The actual demand for our soap product during month t (the value Y_t takes on) is likely to be a function of how long the product has

[3]Students may want to review random variables, probability distributions, and linear regression methods from their introductory statistics course before proceeding.

been on the market, the demand in previous months, the price of that soap and of competing soaps, the amount spent on advertising, and the number of competitors. It could also be affected by unpredictable changes in competitors' products, changes in weather, or even news stories indicating that some soaps are better than others. The values of Y_t for successive time periods are being generated by an extremely complicated process that we will never know exactly. So how can we accurately forecast the future values of Y_t?

The strategy we use in quantitative forecasting is the following:

1. We observe the actual values Y_t takes on over time (we will designate these actual historical values as $y_1, \ldots, y_T$) and possibly the values of other variables that may be related to Y_t.
2. From these actual values (called **time series data**) we select a function, $f(.)$, that we believe approximately describes the real process.
3. We then act as if the real process has the form

   $$Y_t = f(.) + \varepsilon_t$$

   where ε_t is a random component that is assumed to be a normally distributed random variable (bell-shaped curve) with a mean value of zero. (For simplicity we will assume here that the random component is *added* to $f(.)$, but in practice we sometimes assume that it multiplies $f(.)$.)
4. Because the random component cannot be predicted and has an average value of zero, we ignore it in making our forecast (except for estimating the possible error of our forecast). If the function $f(.)$ approximates the actual generating process closely, we can simply compute its value and use it to forecast future values of Y_t. We will designate our *forecast* of the value Y_t will take on at time t as F_t; so $F_t = f(.)$.

The arguments of the function $f(.)$ (the variables used in computing its value) may be previous values of Y_t, measures of time, or values of other physically different variables. For example, Y_t may have the form

$$Y_t = f(t, Y_{t-1}, P_t) + \varepsilon_t$$

which indicates that we believe Y_t is a function of time t, the previous value of Y_t, and some physically different variable, say the product's price at time t, P_t. The essence of statistical forecasting is to identify which **independent** (or **predictor**) **variables** may be related to the variable we wish to forecast, called the **dependent variable**, and to determine a specific function $f(.)$ that describes the relationship. Our goal is to use as simple a function as possible, while producing accurate forecasts.

STEPS IN MODELING

Once we have determined the entity we wish to forecast, the purpose or use of the forecasts, and the time horizon for the forecasts, the primary steps in developing and using quantitative forecasting models are as follows.

1. ***Graph the relevant data.*** Appropriate graphs can help the forecaster develop intuition about the phenomenon being modeled. For example, graphs such as Figure 4.2 can help determine whether demand is increasing or decreasing over time and whether changes in demand appear linear or nonlinear. These graphs will also help to determine whether there are peculiarities in the data that need investigation. If the data exhibit patterns that are different from those the forecaster ex-

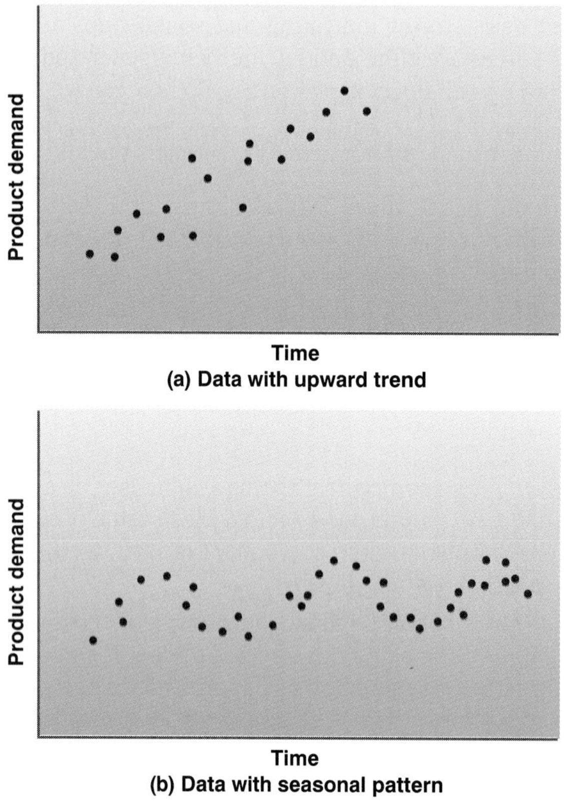

FIGURE 4.2 Typical graphs of demand data.

pected, this might be a signal to check the data collection and data entry procedure for errors or to learn the reasons for the discrepancy.

More important, graphing the data should help make the forecaster more efficient in selecting appropriate forms for the function $f(.)$. For example, if the data exhibit a linear trend over time, such as in Figure 4.2a, the forecaster would probably begin by assuming that the values of Y_t are being generated by a linear trend process: $Y_t = a + bt + \varepsilon_t$, where a and b are constants, t is time, and ε_t is a random component. Similarly, seasonal patterns such as in Figure 4.2b can often be identified visually in graphs of the raw data, and then these patterns can be incorporated into the function $f(.)$.

2. ***Select a general form of the function.*** After analyzing the plotted data, we conjecture (guess) a general form for the function $f(.)$. For example, we may conjecture that the underlying process is a "constant process" that can be represented by $Y_t = a + \varepsilon_t$, where a is a constant and ε_t is a normally distributed random component.
3. ***Estimate the parameters of the function.*** In any general family of functions there is an infinite number of unique functions. In this step we use historical data to es-

timate the specific function that best fits the data. **Parameters** are the constants that appear within each function that make it unique. For example, in step 2 we may conjecture that the real process can be described by a constant process of the form $Y_t = a + \varepsilon_t$; in step 3 we narrow this down by determining the numerical value for the parameter a that best fits the data.

4. ***Evaluate the quality of the model.*** Several different functional forms or estimation procedures may produce reasonable approximations of the actual process. In this step we use measures of forecast accuracy to compare one model with other possible models. This is done by comparing the performance of the different models with actual historical values for some common period of time. In addition, the model should be checked to verify that its parameters are statistically significant (meaningful) and that the underlying assumptions of the model (e.g., the error terms are normally distributed around zero) are satisfied.
5. ***Select and implement the best model.*** Based on step 4, the best model is selected and used for forecasting. Which model is best may depend on factors such as the model's simplicity, forecast stability, timeliness, and cost, not just its accuracy. Although with quantitative forecasting we want to find a function that approximates the true underlying process, we also want a model that is simple, timely, and inexpensive to use while still producing consistently accurate forecasts. For example, we may be able to determine that $Y_t = X_{t-1} + Z_{t-1}/W_{t-2} + \varepsilon_t$ is a good representation of the underlying process. But if it is extremely expensive or impossible to obtain the values of X_{t-1}, Z_{t-1}, or W_{t-2} early enough to make a meaningful forecast for Y_t, then this is a poor *forecasting* model even though it is a good *explanatory* model.

No matter how good a model appears to be during the analysis, any new forecasting model should be monitored for several periods to make sure it performs as well as expected.

TIME SERIES AND CAUSAL MODELS

Statistical forecasting models are usually divided into two categories, time series and causal, according to the general form of the function used to describe the process. **Time series models** forecast the future values of the dependent variable, such as the demand for steel bars, using only previous values of that variable. **Causal models** (also called **associative models**) assume that the value of the dependent variable is a function of, or is related to, the values of other variables that are knowable in a timely fashion.

In time series forecasting we try to decompose the process we are forecasting into its components. Each component is then represented by some mathematical term in the function $f(.)$. The following five components are the most common (see Figure 4.3):

1. A **permanent component** (P), which describes the long-run average level of the process, or the "basis level" of the process at some point in time if there is a trend.
2. A **trend component** (T), which describes any long-term upward or downward movement in the process over time. This might be due to changes in population or income levels. An important special case occurs when the trend is linear. In this case the value of the process increases or decreases, on average, the same amount each time period.
3. A **seasonal component** (S), which describes any *regular* fluctuations above or below the basic process (such as daily, weekly, monthly, or quarterly effects). For

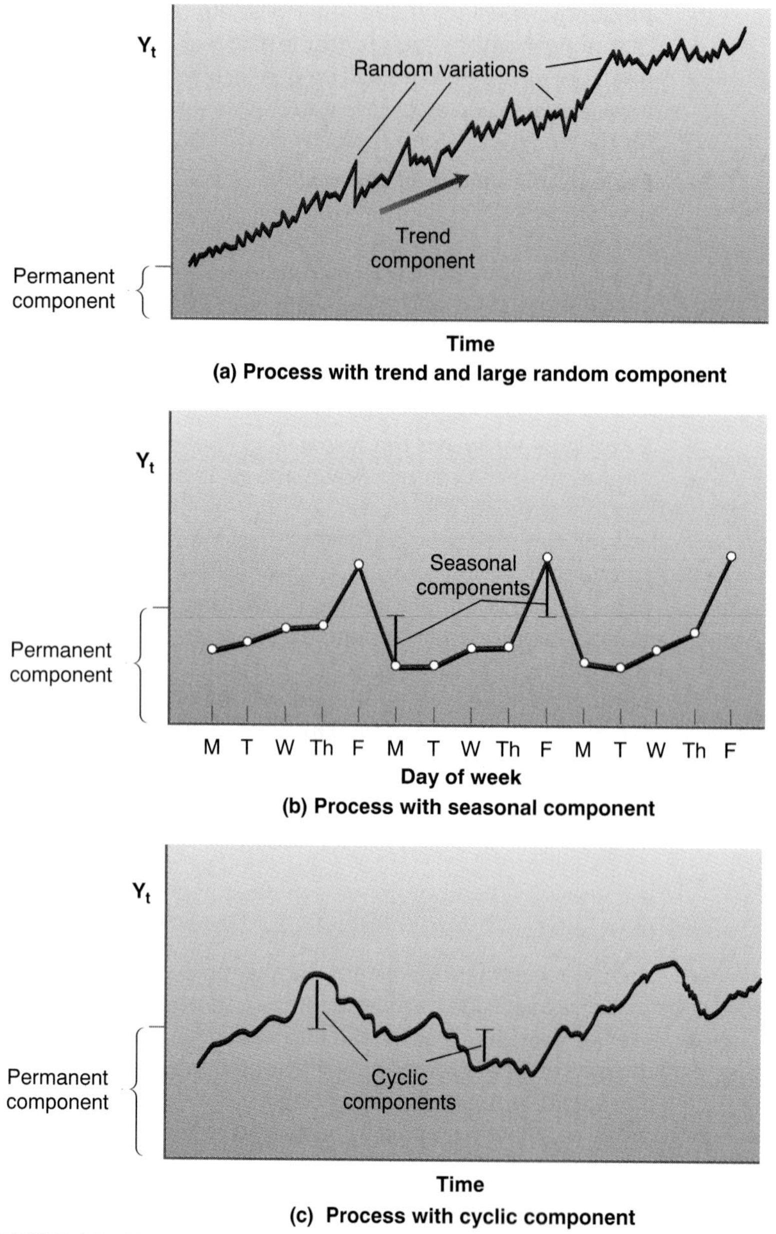

FIGURE 4.3 Time series components.

example, an electric utility company may experience systematically higher demand in the summer because of high air conditioner usage and in the winter due to furnace or electric heater usage, and low demand in the fall and spring due to moderate temperatures.

4. A **cyclic component** (C), which describes patterns in the data that occur as a function of the business cycle; these tend to vary irregularly and have a periodicity of several years.

5. A **random component** (ε_t), which represents random blips that follow no regular pattern; we usually assume that they come from a normal probability distribution with a mean value of zero.

Normally time series models do not include all five components. For example, rarely is a cyclic component included because sufficient data are usually not available, and the irregularity of the effects makes it almost impossible to represent this component. The components that are included can be combined in various ways. For example, a model might have the form

$$Y_t = (P + T) + S + \varepsilon_t$$

In other circumstances the process may combine some components additively and others multiplicatively, such as

$$Y_t = (P + T) \times S + \varepsilon_t$$

In practice, a small number of general functional forms are used for time series modeling. Although very simple, these models frequently provide sufficiently accurate forecasts to be useful, especially for making short-term or intermediate-term forecasts. We will consider the most common functional forms here.

4.5 CONSTANT PROCESSES AND THE CUMULATIVE AVERAGE

Suppose the historical data for a random variable Y_t look like those in Figure 4.4. There is no discernible trend, seasonal pattern, or cyclic pattern; instead, it appears that these data could have been generated by a process that has only a permanent and a random component of the form

$$Y_t = a + \varepsilon_t \tag{4.1}$$

where a is a constant (a model parameter) and ε_t is a normally distributed random variable with a mean value of zero. The process described by equation (4.1) is called a **constant process**. That is, the data points in Figure 4.4 appear to be the result of taking a

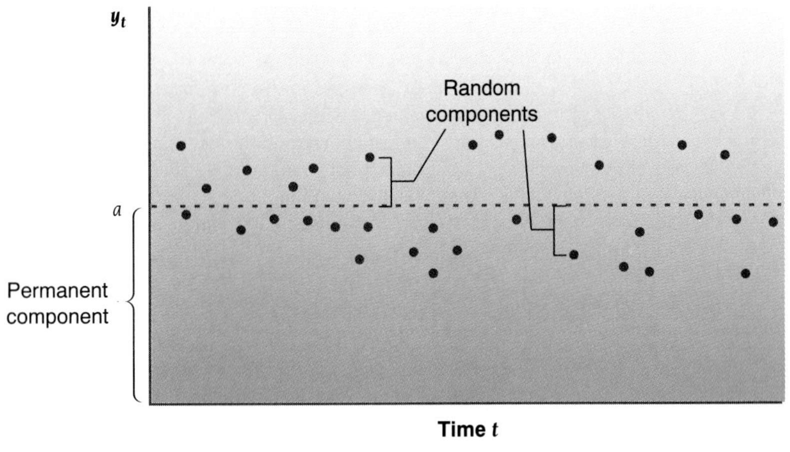

FIGURE 4.4 A constant process.

constant a and then adding a randomly generated value ε_t to it. (This process is typical of the demand for a mature, stable product.) Because the random component is not predictable and averages zero over the long run, if we believe that equation (4.1) accurately describes the process we wish to predict, then our best forecast for any future value of Y_t would be $F_t = a$.

Our problem is then to determine the value of a that most accurately describes the underlying process generating values of Y_t.[4] If we believe the process is truly constant over time, with deviations from a being caused by unpredictable factors that average out to zero over the long run, an intuitive approach to estimate the value of a is to simply average all the previous observations, $y_1, \ldots, y_T$, that we have. (Remember, we are using uppercase Y_t to indicate the random process itself and lowercase y_t to indicate the values Y_t took on at some previous time t; i.e., y_t is a data point.) Because we use all the available data, this average is called the **cumulative average (CA)**:

$$\text{CA} = \Big(\sum_{t=1}^{T} y_t\Big)/T$$

If we believe the process is truly constant over time, we can use CA as our estimator for a, so our **cumulative average forecasting model** is $F_t = \text{CA}$. Our best forecast *now* (time T) for the next period *and any future periods* is CA.[5] The following example illustrates this approach.

EXAMPLE 1

At the end of each week, the owner of the Meersburg Grocery Store wishes to forecast demand for bread at his store during the following week. He believes weekly demand is relatively constant over the long term, so he plans to use a cumulative average to forecast. Weekly sales for the past nine weeks, along with the forecasts that *would have resulted* from using a cumulative average, are given in Table 4.1.

Assuming that sales were equal to demand, we can treat the sales data as a time series of demands. (We must be careful here; if demand exceeded available bread sup-

[4] To be precise, because the value we derive for a (or any model parameter) is simply an estimate of the real value, we call it an *estimate* of the parameter, and the formula we use to compute the estimate is called an *estimator* of the parameter. To distinguish between the real value and an estimate of the parameter value, an estimate (or estimator) is sometimes given a different designation, such as $\hat{a}$. For simplicity, here we will treat the parameters and our estimates of them as being the same.

[5] In addition to being an intuitive approach for forecasting a constant process, the cumulative average is what is called the *least squares estimator* for the parameter a. This means that the sum of the squared deviations between our observations $y_1, \ldots, y_T$ and the value a

$$\sum_{t=1}^{T} (y_t - a)^2$$

is minimized when a is replaced with CA. This implies that if we had used the value of CA, computed at time T, as our forecast for the periods $1, \ldots, T$, the sum of the squared errors resulting would have been minimized.

TABLE 4.1 FORECASTS FOR MEERSBURG BAKERY USING THE CUMULATIVE AVERAGE

	Week t	y_t Actual Sales (Loaves)	F_t Forecast	
Historical data	1	110	—	
	2	102	110.00 =	(110)/1
	3	108	106.00	(110 + 102)/2
	4	121	106.67	(110 + 102 + 108)/3
	5	112	110.25	(110 + 102 + 108 + 121)/4
	6	105	110.60	(110 + 102 + 108 + 121 + 112)/5
	7	114	109.67	(110 + 102 + 108 + 121 + 112 + 105)/6
	8	106	110.29	(110 + 102 + 108 + . . . + 105 + 114)/7
	9	115	109.75	(110 + 102 + 108 + . . . + 114 + 106)/8
Forecasts of future periods	10	—	110.33	(110 + 102 + 108 + . . . + 106 + 115)/9
	11	—	110.33	(110 + 102 + 108 + . . . + 106 + 115)/9

plies during any given week, then sales would understate the actual demand.) Using a cumulative average at the end of week 9, the forecast for week 10 would be

$$F_{10} = (110 + 102 + 108 + 121 + 112 + 105 + 114 + 106 + 115)/9 = 110.33$$

If we believe the demand for bread is really a constant (but random) process, it follows that *at the end of week* 9 our forecasts for weeks 11, 12, and so on should also be 110.33. (Notice that in Table 4.1 we are assuming that forecasts for week $t + 1$ can be computed as soon as week t is complete. This is a reasonable assumption here because at the end of a week we are likely to know how much bread we sold.) At the end of each week, as more data become available, we would revise our forecasts.

4.6 QUASI-CONSTANT PROCESSES

In many situations the phenomenon being forecast does not appear to be coming from a completely constant process when the historical data are considered over a long period of time, but over shorter time intervals the process looks relatively constant, such as in Figure 4.5. Another way of viewing this is to say that the underlying process has the general form of a constant process, but the parameter a seems to wander slowly, following no particular pattern. At two widely separated points in time the values of a might be quite different, but in any local time period a is relatively constant. This process is sometimes called a **quasi-constant process**. In this case, using a cumulative average to estimate a and forecast the process can lead to substantial errors. For example, if the value of a is slowly decreasing over time, then the old data used in computing the cumulative average will cause the forecasts to overestimate the future values of the process. Thus, for a quasi-constant process it makes sense either to use only recent data or to give heavier weight to more recent data, rather than equally weighting all available data.

Quasi-constant processes are common in practice—for example, the average monthly short-term interest rate or the weekly demand for milk. The most commonly

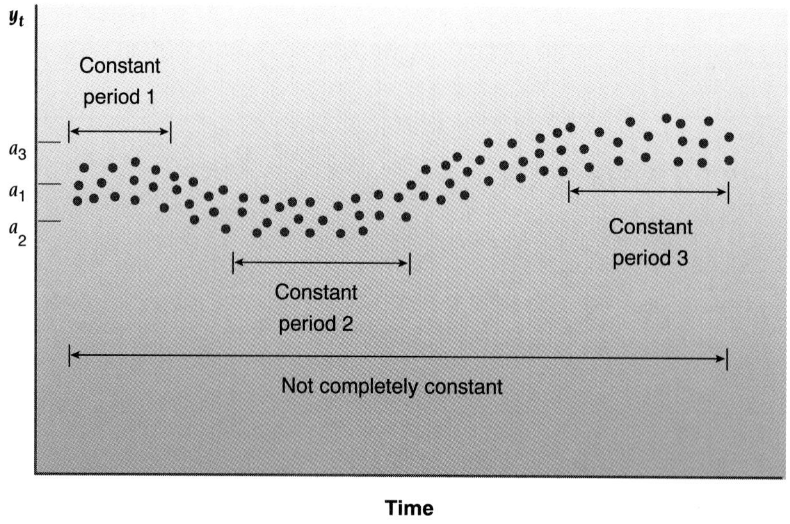

FIGURE 4.5 A quasi-constant process.

used methods for forecasting future values of quasi-constant processes are **moving averages,** whereby only the most recent data are used, and **weighted averages**, whereby recent data receive larger weight than older data. The three most common versions of these methods are the simple moving average, the weighted moving average, and simple exponential smoothing.

SIMPLE MOVING AVERAGE

If we believe the process of interest is quasi-constant, then we want to estimate the *current* value of a, rather than the long-term average of a. In this case an intuitive method for estimating a is given by

$$\text{SMA(N)} = \left[y_T + y_{T-1} + \ldots + y_{T-N+1}\right]/N \qquad (4.2)$$

The expression in equation (4.2) is the average of the N most recent data points and is called the **N-period simple moving average (SMA(N))**.[6] The number of periods averaged, N, can be any positive integer. The N-period simple moving average forecast for a period is then $F_t = \text{SMA(N)}$.

The smaller the value of N, the more responsive the moving average is to changes in the underlying parameter, a; the larger the value of N, the more stable our estimates of a and therefore the more stable our forecasts will be over time. The best value of N to use will depend on the specific situation. In practice, we would probably try several different values of N to see which one produced the most accurate forecasts. Values of N

[6]Just as CA is the least squares estimator of a for periods 1 through T, SMA(N) is the least squares estimator of a for the N most recent data points; that is, the value of a given by equation (4.2) minimizes

$$\sum_{t=T-N+1}^{T} (y_t - a)^2$$

between 3 and 10 are most common, although much larger values are sometimes used, especially for daily data.

EXAMPLE 2

Table 4.2 contains the forecasts that would have occurred for Meersburg Grocery in Example 1 using a simple moving average with $N = 3$.

At the end of week 9, the forecast for week 10 (and all subsequent weeks) would be

$$F_{10} = (114 + 106 + 115)/3 = 111.67$$

TABLE 4.2 FORECASTS FOR MEERSBURG BAKERY USING THE SMA(3) MODEL

Week t	y_t Actual Sales (Loaves)	F_t Forecast	
1	110	—	
2	102	—	
3	108	—	
4	121	106.67 =	(110 + 102 + 108)/3
5	112	110.33	(102 + 108 + 121)/3
6	105	113.67	(108 + 121 + 112)/3
7	114	112.67	(121 + 112 + 105)/3
8	106	110.33	(112 + 105 + 114)/3
9	115	108.33	(105 + 114 + 106)/3
10	—	111.67	(114 + 106 + 115)/3
11	—	111.67	(114 + 106 + 115)/3

WEIGHTED MOVING AVERAGE

The simple moving average approach gives the same weight to each of the N most recent data points. The argument can be made that if the parameter a is really changing over time, then the most recent data should receive a higher weight than older data. One approach is to assign differential weights, such as 0.4, 0.3, 0.2, and 0.1, to the data. Our estimate for a would then be

$$a = 0.4y_T + 0.3y_{T-1} + 0.2y_{T-2} + 0.1y_{T-3}$$

Notice that the weights we used sum to 1.0. In general, we define an **N-period weighted moving average (WMA(N))** as

$$\text{WMA(N)} = w_1 y_T + w_2 y_{T-1} + \ldots + w_N y_{T-N+1} \tag{4.3}$$

Weights are assigned to only the N most recent data points; the weight w_1 is assigned to the most recent data point, w_2 to the second most recent, and so on. The weights must sum to 1 and satisfy the condition

$$w_1 > w_2 > \ldots > w_N > 0$$

that is, the weights get smaller for older data.

Any set of weights that satisfies these conditions can be used to compute a weighted moving average. However, it is most common to choose a weighting scheme that differentiates the weights in some regular fashion. One example of this method is the **sum-of-digits weights**. In this method we first specify the number of data points, N, we wish to include. Next, we compute the sum of all integers from 1 through N (call this sum S); then $w_1 = N/S$, $w_2 = (N-1)/S, \ldots, w_N = 1/S$. For example, if $N = 5$, then $S = 1 + 2 + 3 + 4 + 5 = 15$, and the weights are $w_1 = 5/15$, $w_2 = 4/15, \ldots, w_5 = 1/15$. Each weight is $1/S$ less than the previous weight, and the weights sum to 1. Our forecast at time T for any future period would then be WMA(N) computed at time T. In practice, different values for N, and thus different weights, would be tested to determine which provides the best forecasts for a given variable.

EXAMPLE 3

Table 4.3 contains the weighted moving average forecasts for Meersburg Grocery if we use the sum-of-digits weighting scheme with $N = 4$. At the end of week 9, the forecast for period 10 (and any future week) would be

$$F_{10} = (0.4)(115) + (0.3)(106) + (0.2)(114) + (0.1)(105) = 111.1$$

TABLE 4.3 FORECASTS FOR MEERSBURG BAKERY USING THE WMA(4) MODEL

Week t	y_t Actual Sales (Loaves)	F_t Forecast	
1	110	—	
2	102	—	
3	108	—	
4	121	—	
5	112	112.2 =	0.4(121) + 0.3(108) + 0.2(102) + 0.1(110)
6	105	112.9	0.4(112) + 0.3(121) + 0.2(108) + 0.1(102)
7	114	110.6	0.4(105) + 0.3(112) + 0.2(121) + 0.1(108)
8	106	111.6	0.4(114) + 0.3(105) + 0.2(112) + 0.1(121)
9	115	108.8	0.4(106) + 0.3(114) + 0.2(105) + 0.1(112)
10	—	111.1	0.4(115) + 0.3(106) + 0.2(114) + 0.1(105)
11	—	111.1	0.4(115) + 0.3(106) + 0.2(114) + 0.1(105)

One risk with using a weighted moving average is that the one or two most recent time periods can have an extremely large effect on the forecast. This causes weighted moving average models to produce somewhat more responsive but less stable forecasts than simple moving average models for the same value of N.

SIMPLE EXPONENTIAL SMOOTHING

Although they are simple and intuitive, the simple moving average and weighted moving average methods have drawbacks. One drawback is that in order to estimate the value of a, we must store the N most recent data points. Historically, this created practical problems when using large values of N because models of this sort are often used in automated inventory/purchasing systems where forecasts for hundreds or thousands of items may be made daily or weekly. Second, because only a few data points are weighted, short-term, random blips in the data can distort the forecasts and make the series of forecasts unstable.

An alternative to these methods that solves both problems is **simple exponential smoothing (SES)**, one of the most widely used forecasting methods in operations management. Simple exponential smoothing uses an iterative equation to revise its forecast (estimate of a) for each period based on the accuracy of its most recent forecast. Specifically, suppose that F_T is our forecast for period T (our estimate of a) made at the end of period $T - 1$. Once observation y_T is known, we revise our estimate of a, and thus our forecast for period $T + 1$, as follows:

$$F_{T+1} = a = F_T + \alpha(y_T - F_T) \tag{4.4}$$

where α is called a **smoothing constant** with $0 \leq \alpha \leq 1$ and $y_T - F_T$ is the forecasting error in period T. In other words, the forecast for any period is just the forecast for the previous period adjusted by a fraction of the forecasting error in the previous period. If the previous forecast exceeded the actual value, then the new forecast is adjusted downward by α times the error, and if the previous forecast was less than the actual value, then the forecast is adjusted upward by α times the error. Notice that only three values must be stored: the most recent forecast, F_T, the most recent data point, y_T, and the smoothing constant, α.

The constant α smoothes out the error adjustment so that the forecast does not react too much to random fluctuations. The larger the value of α, the more the forecasts react to variations in the y_t values and the less stable the forecasts. In the extreme case of $\alpha = 1$, the exponential smoothing model reduces to $F_{T+1} = y_T$, which is sometimes called the **naive model**; the forecast for the next time period is equal to the actual value in the previous time period. Each value of α will give a different set of forecasts and therefore represents a different forecasting model. In practice, values of α in the range 0.05 to 0.30 are most commonly used.

In addition to its minimal data storage requirements, for normal values of α simple exponential smoothing tends to produce more stable forecasts than the simple or weighted moving average. This is partly because the forecasts from simple exponential smoothing are actually weighted averages of all previous data, not just the most recent data. Solved problem 4 at the end of this chapter shows that the simple exponential smoothing forecast for any period is actually the weighted average of all previous observations with weights $w_1 = \alpha$, $w_2 = \alpha(1 - \alpha)$, $w_3 = \alpha(1 - \alpha)^2$,. . . . The weights decrease exponentially with age, where the weight for any data point is $(1 - \alpha)$ as large as the one for the next most recent data point. (For example, if $\alpha = 0.3$, $w_1 = 0.3$, $w_2 = 0.3(1 - 0.3) = 0.21$, $w_3 = 0.3(1 - 0.3)^2 = 0.147$, and so on.)

Because SES is an iterative process, in addition to specifying a value for the smoothing constant, α, we must provide an initial forecast for some earlier point in time. It is common practice to do either of the following:

1. Set the initial forecast equal to the actual value at the initial time period (i.e., $F_1 = y_1$) or
2. Set the initial forecast equal to the *average* of some initial actual values (e.g., $F_1 = [y_1 + y_2 + y_3]/3$).

EXAMPLE 4

Table 4.4 gives the forecasts that would be generated for Meersburg Grocery by an exponential smoothing model using $\alpha = 0.2$ and an initial forecast for week 1 of $F_1 = y_1 = 110$.

The forecast for week 10 would be

$$F_{10} = 109.7 + 0.2(115 - 109.7) = 110.8$$

TABLE 4.4 FORECASTS FOR MEERSBURG BAKERY USING THE SES MODEL

Week t	y_t Actual Sales (Loaves)	F_t Forecast	
1	110	110	
2	102	110.0	= 110.0 + 0.2(110 − 110)
3	108	108.4	110.0 + 0.2(102 − 110.0)
4	121	108.3	108.4 + 0.2(108 − 108.4)
5	112	110.8	108.3 + 0.2(121 − 108.3)
6	105	111.0	110.8 + 0.2(112 − 110.8)
7	114	109.8	111.0 + 0.2(105 − 111.0)
8	106	110.6	109.8 + 0.2(114 − 109.8)
9	115	109.7	110.6 + 0.2(106 − 110.6)
10	—	110.8	109.7 + 0.2(115 − 109.7)
11	—	110.8	109.7 + 0.2(115 − 109.7)

4.7 COMPARING ALTERNATIVE MODELS

For any set of historical data, several models can be reasonable candidates to represent the underlying process. For example, if we feel relatively confident that the underlying process is quasi-constant, we could use a simple moving average, a weighted moving average, or an exponential smoothing model. Furthermore, within each of these categories there is a different model represented by each value of N, each choice of weights w_i, and each value of α, respectively. A key issue is to determine, for any specific situation, which of the models under consideration is best. To evaluate alternative models we should validate the assumptions and compare the forecast accuracy of each model.

VERIFYING MODEL ASSUMPTIONS

The first step is to verify whether the underlying assumptions for the models are satisfied; if they are seriously violated, we should be reluctant to use the model. For example, most statistical forecasting models assume that the resulting forecasting errors should look as if they are from a normal distribution with a mean of zero. In other words, the model should overpredict and underpredict about equally, with smaller errors being much more common than larger errors. In practice, we would plot the errors for each model and verify that they do in fact appear to be coming from such a distribution. We would also compute the **mean error (ME)** or **bias**, defined as

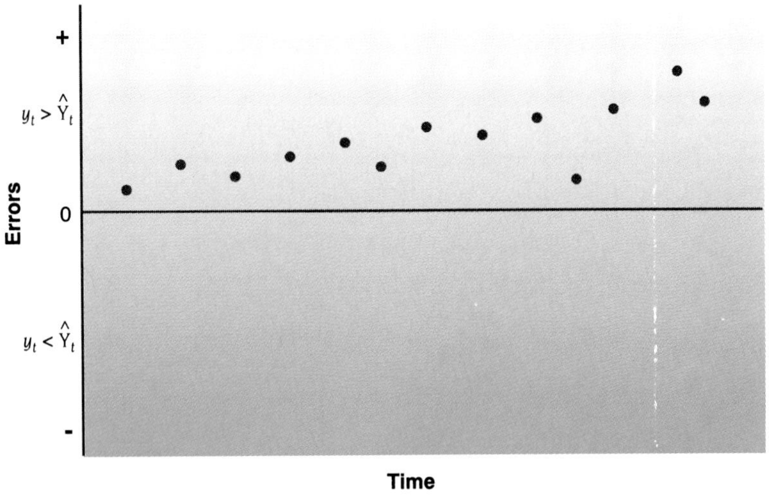

FIGURE 4.6 Forecasting errors when a simple moving average model is used to forecast a trend process.

$$\mathrm{ME} = \sum_{i=1}^{K} \left(y_i - F_i \right) / K$$

where $y_i - F_i$ is the forecast error in period i and K is the number of time periods over which the evaluation is being conducted (it may be less than the number of data points available). If the mean error is too far from zero, we would conclude that the model has an unacceptable bias.[7]

Plotting model errors not only helps verify model assumptions, it also helps determine whether there is a seasonal pattern or a significant bias in the errors. This information can be used to construct a better model. For example, suppose Figure 4.6 was a plot of the errors for a simple moving average model we were testing. The errors are clearly biased, with the model consistently underpredicting future values. This suggests that the underlying process is *not* quasi-constant, which a simple moving average model assumes, but actually has an upward trend. The simple moving average model is inappropriate; instead, a linear trend model should be considered.

When appropriate, we should also verify that any model parameter estimates are statistically significant. This is especially important for more complex models, such as linear trend processes and causal models. (Tests of statistical significance for the models presented in this chapter can be found in most forecasting texts.)

EVALUATING FORECAST ACCURACY

Once the model assumptions have been verified, we evaluate the relative accuracy of the model forecasts. Three measures of accuracy are often used: the **mean squared**

[7]We can determine whether the errors approximate a normal distribution by using a chi-squared goodness-of-fit test; this can be found in most elementary statistics texts.

error (MSE), the **mean absolute deviation (MAD)**, and the **mean absolute percentage error (MAPE)**.

$$\text{MSE} = \left[\sum_{i=1}^{K} (y_i - F_i)^2\right] \Big/ K$$

$$\text{MAD} = \left[\sum_{i=1}^{K} |y_i - F_i|\right] \Big/ K$$

$$\text{MAPE} = 100 \times \left[\sum_{i=1}^{K} |y_i - F_i|/y_i\right] \Big/ K$$

where the summations are taken over a common set of K data points. The K data points should be chosen so that a forecast can be obtained for each of the methods being compared. If a model requires time to "stabilize" after some initial starting point (e.g., in exponential smoothing an initial forecast is chosen rather than computed by the model), enough data must be left out of the comparison to allow this stabilization for all the models.

The mean squared error is the most commonly used criterion for evaluating models for two reasons. First, it penalizes large forecasting errors more than proportionately. Most users of forecasts prefer a model that produces consistently moderate errors to one that produces some small errors and some very large errors. Second, the mean squared error (when multiplied by an appropriate constant) can be used to estimate the variance of the random error component, ε_t. This quantity can then be used to test the statistical significance of various model parameters and to construct confidence intervals for forecasts.

The mean absolute deviation and mean absolute percentage error are most useful for presenting results to other decision makers. These measures provide a better intuitive feel for how much error is likely to occur when using a forecast from the model. In most situations the three measures will be consistent in the sense that the model with the lowest mean squared error will also have the lowest mean absolute deviation and mean absolute percentage error. This makes selection of the model simple. However, occasionally one model may be better with respect to one criterion but worse on another. In that case, experience and statistical knowledge become important in deciding which model is better.

To illustrate the use of these measures, consider the data for the Meersburg Grocery example. Suppose we have narrowed our choice of forecasting models to a simple moving average with $N = 3$, a weighted moving average with weights 4/10, 3/10, 2/10, and 1/10, and a simple exponential smoothing model with $\alpha = 0.2$. Table 4.5 combines the forecasts from Tables 4.2–4.4 and includes the errors and squared errors that would have occurred if each of these models had been used to forecast the time series values.

There are not enough forecasting errors to verify whether or not the errors are normally distributed with a mean of zero, but at least it appears that both positive and negative errors are occurring with each model and that the mean errors are small, so there is no consistent bias in the models. To compare the accuracy of the models, we now compute the MSE, MAD, and MAPE for each model over a common set of data. We chose weeks 6–9 for this comparison because this period allows all forecasting models

TABLE 4.5 ERRORS FOR THREE FORECASTING MODELS

	Week	Actual Sales (Loaves)	SMA(3)			WMA(4)			SES (α = 0.2)		
			Forecast	Error	Error^2	Forecast	Error	Error^2	Forecast	Error	Error^2
	1	110	—	—	—	—	—	—	110,0	—	—
	2	102	—	—	—	—	—	—	110.0	−8.0	64.0
	3	108	—	—	—	—	—	—	108.4	−0.4	0.2
	4	121	106.7	+14.3	204.5	—	—	—	108.3	+12.7	161.3
	5	112	110.3	+ 1.7	2.9	112.2	−0.2	0.0	110.8	+ 1.2	1.4
Evaluation period	6	105	113.7	−8.7	75.7	112.9	−7.9	62.4	111.0	−6.0	36.0
	7	114	112.7	+ 1.3	1.7	110.6	+ 3.4	11.6	109.8	+ 4.2	17.6
	8	106	110.3	−4.3	18.5	111.6	−5.6	31.4	110.6	−4.6	21.2
	9	115	108.3	+ 6.7	44.9	108.8	+ 6.2	38.4	109.7	+ 5.3	28.1

to have made at least one forecast before the comparison period in order to stabilize. The results are given in Table 4.6.

On all three measures the weighted moving average model produces the least accurate forecasts. The simple exponential smoothing and simple moving average models are relatively similar with respect to the mean absolute deviation and mean absolute percentage error, but the exponential smoothing model is clearly superior with respect to the mean squared error. This suggests that although the average errors for the two models are approximately the same, the SMA(3) has more large and small errors, whereas the SES model has more errors of moderate size. We would probably select the exponential smoothing model for this reason (of course, in practice we would rarely make a decision based on errors from only four time periods).

It is important to make the comparison using the same time periods for each model rather than using all periods for which forecasts could be made. The reason is that the process may have behaved unusually during a period included in the evaluation of one model but not in another model. The model evaluation that includes the unusual period would be penalized by an abnormally large error that the other models would not face. For example, in the Meersburg Grocery example, demand in week 4 is unusually large. If week 4 were included in the error evaluation for the SMA(3) and simple exponential smoothing models, because forecasts exist, they would appear worse than the WMA(4) model, which had no forecast for this period.

The same general evaluation procedure would be used when comparing other types of quantitative models. That is, first, model assumptions are checked and then measures of accuracy are calculated. When models of different complexity are being considered—for example, a model without seasonality versus one that includes seasonality—the additional complexity needs to be weighed against the improved accuracy. A somewhat less accurate model may be preferable if it is easier and cheaper to use and understand.

We now proceed to models for more complex processes.

TABLE 4.6 COMPARING THE ACCURACY OF THREE FORECASTING MODELS

	SMA(3)	WMA(4)	SES α = 0.2
MSE	35.20	35.95	25.73
MAD	5.25	5.78	5.03
MAPE	4.83%	5.30%	4.59%

4.8 LINEAR TREND PROCESSES

Table 4.7 contains the number of emergency room patients treated each month at Metro Hospital during the past year. Suppose we use the cumulative average and SMA(4) models to forecast future numbers of monthly patients. Table 4.8 contains the forecasts that would be obtained and the resulting errors.

The cumulative average consistently underpredicts future values; 10 of the 11 errors are positive, and the mean absolute deviation is 42.1. The SMA(4) model performs somewhat better, with a mean absolute deviation of 25.1, but still the errors are consistently positive and do not appear to be from a normal distribution around zero. The errors not only indicate that the data do not appear to have come from a constant or quasi-constant process, they also suggest a better model. Because the models underpredict, this suggests that there is an upward trend of some sort in the time series. If we

TABLE 4.7 EMERGENCY ROOM PATIENTS DATA FOR METRO HOSPITAL

t	Month	Patients
1	January	328
2	February	310
3	March	355
4	April	362
5	May	375
6	June	380
7	July	408
8	August	415
9	September	417
10	October	412
11	November	429
12	December	434

TABLE 4.8 FORECASTS FOR METRO HOSPITAL USING THE CUMULATIVE AVERAGE AND SMA(4) MODELS

			Cum. Aver.		SMA(4)	
t	Month	Patients	Forecast	Error	Forecast	Error
1	January	328	—	—	—	—
2	February	310	328.0	−18.0	—	—
3	March	355	319.0	+36.0	—	—
4	April	362	331.0	+31.0	—	—
5	May	375	338.8	+36.2	338.8	+36.2
6	June	380	346.0	+34.0	350.5	+29.5
7	July	408	351.7	+56.3	68.0	+40.0
8	August	415	359.7	+55.3	381.3	+33.7
9	September	417	366.6	+50.4	394.5	+22.5
10	October	412	372.2	+39.8	405.0	+ 7.0
11	November	429	376.2	+52.8	413.0	+16.0
12	December	434	381.0	+53.0	418.3	+15.7
				MAD = 42.1		MAD = 25.1

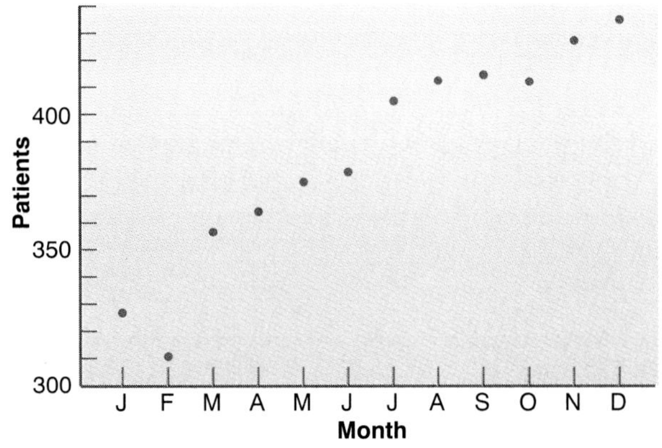

FIGURE 4.7 Graph of Metro Hospital emergency room patients.

plot the data, as done in Figure 4.7, we see a definite upward trend over time. Therefore, it is reasonable to conjecture that our model should contain a trend component.

The simplest model with a trend component is a **linear trend model**:

$$Y_t = a + bt + \varepsilon_t \tag{4.5}$$

where a and b are constants and t measures time on some scale. The name *linear trend* comes from the fact that in equation (4.5) the value of Y_t is a linear function of time. (Notice that a is the expected value of Y_0, the expected value of Y_t at the time origin, $t = 0$. In this sense a can be thought of as the permanent or basis component and bt as the trend component.) If we believe that data, such as number of emergency room patients, can be described by a linear trend model, the next step is to determine which values of a and b best describe the process. We can then use the model

$$F_t = a + bt$$

to forecast the future values of Y_t because the errors are assumed to average zero.

LINEAR REGRESSION FOR TREND PROCESSES

From elementary statistics we know that if a random variable Y is a linear function of some variable X—that is, $Y = a + bX$—then for a given set of n paired observations of the variables $(x_1,y_1), \ldots, (x_n,y_n)$, the least squares estimators for a and b are

$$b = \frac{n(\Sigma\, x_i y_i) - (\Sigma\, x_i)\,(\Sigma\, y_i)}{n(\Sigma\, x_i^2) - (\Sigma\, x_i)^2} \tag{4.6}$$

$$a = [(\Sigma\, y_i)/n] - b[(\Sigma\, x_i)/n] \tag{4.7}$$

So for the linear trend process in equation (4.5) we can treat time t as the variable X and Y_t as the variable Y.

EXAMPLE 5

To forecast the number of emergency room patients at Metro Hospital each month, we can pair up each time observation (x_i) with the number of patients in month i (y_i). The data in Table 4.7 can then be written as 12 paired observations (x_i, y_i): (1,328), (2,310), . . . , (12,434). These are rewritten in Table 4.9, along with the values x_i^2 and $x_i y_i$, to make it easier to compute equations (4.6) and (4.7).

TABLE 4.9 COMPUTATIONS FOR METRO HOSPITAL LINEAR REGRESSION

x_i Time Period	y_i Patients	x_i^2	$x_i y_i$
1	328	1	328
2	310	4	620
3	355	9	1,065
4	362	16	1,448
5	375	25	1,875
6	380	36	2,280
7	408	49	2,856
8	415	64	3,320
9	417	81	3,753
10	412	100	4,120
11	429	121	4,719
12	434	144	5,208
78	4625	650	31,592

Substituting the data from Table 4.9 into equations (4.6) and (4.7) gives

$$b = \frac{12(31{,}592) - (78)(4625)}{12(650) - (78)^2} = \frac{18{,}354}{1716} = 10.7$$

$$a = (4625 / 12) - 10.7(78 / 12) = 315.9$$

We conclude that the number of emergency room patients requiring treatment each month can be predicted by the linear function

$$F_t = 315.9 + 10.7t \tag{4.8}$$

To determine what the forecast *would have been* in period 6, we simply replace t in equation (4.8) with the value 6, so

$$F_6 = 315.9 + 10.7(6) = 380.1$$

Table 4.10 lists the forecasts and the errors that would have resulted from the model given by equation (4.8).[8] The errors in Table 4.10 are well distributed around zero. This

[8]Notice that equation (4.8) and thus the forecasts in Table 4.10 are computed using all 12 months of data. This is a different convention than that used for the earlier models, where forecasts for a time period were computed using only data available before that period. Although using all the historical data available at time T to make retrospective forecasts of earlier periods is common in practice for trend models, it is preferable to use only previous data to forecast future values because those are the only values that would have been known at the time of the forecasts. This is discussed in Section 4.12.

TABLE 4.10 FORECASTS FOR METRO HOSPITAL USING THE LINEAR TREND REGRESSION MODEL

t	Month	y_t Patients	F_t Forecast	Error
1	January	328	326.6	+ 1.42
2	February	310	337.3	– 27.3
3	March	355	348.0	+ 7.0
4	April	362	358.7	+ 3.3
5	May	375	369.4	+ 5.6
6	June	380	380.1	– 0.1
7	July	408	390.8	+ 17.2
8	August	415	401.5	+ 13.5
9	September	417	412.2	+ 4.8
10	October	412	422.9	– 10.9
11	November	429	433.6	– 4.6
12	December	434	444.3	– 10.3
				MAD = 8.8

would lead us to believe that the linear trend model satisfies the assumptions concerning forecasting errors, and it appears to be a reasonably good approximation for the actual process.

The forecast for period 13 (January of the subsequent year) would be computed by substituting $t = 13$ into equation (4.8):

$$F_{13} = 315.9 + 10.7\,(13) = 455.0$$

A forecast for any other future period could be made by performing the same type of substitution. For example, the forecast for March (period 15) would be

$$F_{15} = 315.9 + 10.7\,(15) = 476.4$$

Even if equation (4.8) is a reasonably good predictor of patient demand, one must recognize that the forecasts obtained will rarely equal the number of patients who actually appear. There will always be some error. The magnitude of error that can be expected can be represented using confidence intervals. The theory and procedures underlying confidence intervals are provided in most introductory statistics texts and will not be presented here. However, a major qualitative result is that as one makes forecasts farther into the future, the greater the uncertainty and average magnitude of error; one cannot be as confident about a forecast for demand three months from now as about demand one month from now.

MOVING LINEAR REGRESSION

If the underlying process we are forecasting is a stable linear trend (i.e., the parameters a and b are not changing over time), then after each time period we should add the new observation for Y_t to our data set, recompute equations (4.6) and (4.7) to obtain a revised version of model (4.8), and then substitute the appropriate value for t into the model to get the forecasts. Because a and b are stable, the more data we use, the more accurate our estimates should be.

However, just as constant processes are not always totally constant over the long term, linear trend processes do not always retain the same shape (slope and intercept) over the long term. Therefore, in practice it is common to reestimate the parameters a and b, using a *moving* estimation approach. The simplest way is to use simple linear regression but use only the N most recent paired observations in equations (4.6) and (4.7) (this is called **moving linear regression** and is comparable to using a simple moving average for quasi-constant processes). Each time a new observation is obtained, that observation is added to the data set and the oldest observation (now $N+1$ periods old) is deleted. This way, if a and b are changing over time, the oldest data do not bias the model.

DOUBLE EXPONENTIAL SMOOTHING

A popular alternative to moving linear regression is an extension of simple exponential smoothing called **double exponential smoothing (DES)** or **trend-adjusted moving average**. We will use Holt's method of DES here. With double exponential smoothing, each period we compute new estimates of the slope and intercept parameters using a smoothing method similar to that for simple exponential smoothing. Holt's method uses two smoothing constants: α to smooth the intercept and β to smooth the slope.

There is an important difference in convention between linear regression and Holt's method with respect to the time origin and intercept. In regression the assumed time origin is at time zero, so the parameter a is the intercept of the line $a + bt$ at time zero. In Holt's method the time origin moves with t. To differentiate the estimators from DES and linear regression, we will use different notation. I_t will estimate the mean value of the process (the intercept) at the most recent time period, t; and S_t will be the estimator of b at time t. (Notice that $I_t - tS_t$ is then an estimator for a.) At time t the one-period-ahead forecast is then

$$F_{t+1} = I_t + S_t$$

(More generally, at time t the k-period-ahead forecast is $F_{t+k} = I_t + kS_t$.) I_t and S_t are computed as follows:

$$\begin{aligned} I_t &= (I_{t-1} + S_{t-1}) + \alpha\left[y_t - (I_{t-1} + S_{t-1})\right] \\ &= F_t + \alpha\left[y_t - F_t\right] \end{aligned} \tag{4.9}$$

= forecast for period t + α[actual value in t – forecast for t]

$$S_t = S_{t-1} + \beta\left[(I_t - I_{t-1}) - S_{t-1}\right] \tag{4.10}$$

= slope estimate for period t + β [actual slope in t – slope estimate for t]

The term $I_{t-1} + S_{t-1}$ in equation (4.9) is the one-period-ahead forecast for period t made using the estimators at time $t-1$. Equation (4.9) revises I_t to equal I_{t-1} adjusted by α times the error in period t, so it is essentially identical to the simple exponential smoothing equation. The term $I_t - I_{t-1}$ in equation (4.10) is the actual change in the process between time $t-1$ and t attributed to the trend (notice that equation (4.9) must be solved before equation (4.10)). Equation (4.10) sets the value of S_t equal to the previously estimated slope, S_{t-1}, adjusted by β times the error in the slope estimation.

EXAMPLE 6

Suppose that in the Metro Hospital example $\alpha = 0.2$, $\beta = 0.1$, $I_0 = 316$, and $S_0 = 10.5$. Then for

Period 1:

$$F_1 = I_0 + S_0$$
$$= 316.0 + 10.5 = 326.5$$

$$I_1 = (I_0 + S_0) + \alpha\left[y_1 - (I_0 + S_0)\right]$$
$$= 326.5 + 0.2\,(328 - 326.5) = 326.8$$

$$S_1 = S_0 + \beta\left[(I_1 - I_0) - S_0\right]$$
$$= 10.5 + 0.1\,[(326.8 - 316) - 10.5] = 10.5$$

Period 2:

$$F_2 = 326.8 + 10.5 = 337.3$$
$$I_2 = 337.3 + 0.2\,(310 - 337.3) = 331.9$$
$$S_t = 10.5 + 0.1\left[(331.9 - 326.8) - 10.5\right] = 10.0$$

Period 3:

$$F_3 = 331.9 + 10.0 = 341.9$$
$$I_3 = 341.9 + 0.2\,(355 - 341.9) = 344.5$$
$$S_3 = 10.0 + 0.1\left[(344.5 - 331.9) - 10.0\right] = 10.3$$

Table 4.11 gives the values for I_t, S_t, and the forecasts that would result from this model. To make forecasts for future periods, we compute

$$I_{12} = 445.5 + 0.2(434 - 445.5) = 443.2$$
$$S_{12} = 10.7 + 0.1\left[(443.2 - 434.8) - 10.7\right] = 10.5$$

Then $F_{13} = 443.2 + 10.5 = 453.7$. If we wanted to make a forecast for period 15, then $F_{12+3} = 443.2 + 3(10.5) = 474.7$.

TABLE 4.11 FORECASTS FOR METRO HOSPITAL USING DOUBLE EXPONENTIAL SMOOTHING

t	Patients	I_{t-1}	S_{t-1}	$F_t = I_{t-1} + S_{t-1}$	Error
1	328	316.0	10.5	326.5	+ 1.5
2	310	326.8	10.5	337.3	−27.3
3	355	331.9	10.0	341.9	+13.1
4	362	344.5	10.3	354.8	+ 7.2
5	375	356.2	10.4	366.6	+ 8.4
6	380	368.3	10.6	378.9	+ 1.1
7	408	379.1	10.6	389.7	+18.3
8	415	393.4	11.0	404.4	+10.6
9	417	406.5	11.2	417.7	−0.7
10	412	417.6	11.2	428.8	−16.8
11	429	425.4	10.9	436.3	−7.3
12	434	434.8	10.7	445.5	−11.5
					MAD = 10.3

Two technical issues of double exponential smoothing are the choice of the smoothing constants and the choice of initial values for I_t and S_t. Usually α and β are set to values less than 0.2, and $\beta \le \alpha$. The initial values of I_t and S_t can be obtained by using linear regression on some initial set of data.

4.9 SEASONAL PROCESSES

Many real phenomena exhibit seasonal patterns that may be associated with a calendar quarter, calendar month, week, or even day. For example, in the United States sales of turkeys are high in November and December because of Thanksgiving and Christmas. Similarly the demands for lawn fertilizers and skiing lessons have clear seasonal patterns. Sometimes, however, the seasonal patterns are less obvious. Credit card payments to retail companies have daily seasonal effects. Each day of the week has its own pattern (substantial receipts occur on Mondays because of the weekend mail), and other special days have patterns, such as the day after a holiday or after Social Security checks are issued. If we can identify these seasonal patterns, we can incorporate them into our forecasting models to improve our forecasts.

Forecasting phenomena that exhibit seasonality does not require completely different models. Instead we can use models based on simple processes, such as a quasi-constant process, and then overlay them with seasonal components. The seasonal components represent a systematic deviation from the average or long-term pattern of the process.

Seasonality is usually incorporated into forecasting models in one of two ways: additively or multiplicatively. In an **additive seasonal model** we represent the seasonal components as *quantities* that are added to or subtracted from the basic process according to the season. The assumption is that even if the long-term trend of the process is increasing or decreasing, the magnitudes of the seasonal effects stay the same. In a **multiplicative seasonal model** the seasonal components are *proportions* or *percentages* that multiply the basic process according to the season. If there is an upward trend in the process, the magnitudes of the seasonal effects will increase proportionately with the process. The multiplicative form of seasonality is used more widely in practice, so we will only present that case here.

Both credit card usage and credit card payments exhibit seasonal patterns according to the day of the week, day of the month, and month of the year.

CONSTANT OR QUASI-CONSTANT PROCESSES WITH SEASONALITY

The first step in constructing a seasonal model (after graphing the data and conjecturing that we have a seasonal process) is to estimate the values of the **seasonal factors** or **seasonal indices** in the model; we will denote the seasonal factor for season s by c_s. We then use the seasonal factors to remove the seasonal effects from the actual data; this is called **deseasonalizing** the data. We then treat the deseasonalized data as if they were a separate time series, and we construct a model that we believe would predict future values of the deseasonalized process. The total model is obtained by combining the seasonal factors with the model for the deseasonalized process.

We now illustrate the mechanics of this procedure for a constant or quasi-constant process with multiplicative seasonal variations.

EXAMPLE 7

Peggy Cutter is the manager of teller operations for a branch of Imperial Commerce Bank. She is responsible for daily scheduling and staffing of bank tellers. The number of tellers required depends on the number of customer transactions. Peggy has collected data on the number of transactions each day for the past three weeks (see Table 4.12).

When Peggy plotted the data, they appeared to be randomly scattered around the mean value of 485.2 transactions per day. So she decided to test a cumulative average forecasting method. The forecasts and errors from using a cumulative average are given in Table 4.12. Although the errors were scattered around zero, they were unacceptably large on average. When she plotted the errors in Figure 4.8, she saw a strong pattern: The errors for Mondays and Fridays were always positive and the errors for Tuesdays, Wednesdays, and Thursdays were always negative. This made her think that there may

TABLE 4.12 FORECASTS FOR IMPERIAL COMMERCE BANK USING THE CUMULATIVE AVERAGE

Week	Day	y_t Actual Trans.	F_t Cum. Ave	Errors	Error^2
1	Mon	624	—	—	—
	Tue	325	624.0	−299.0	89,401
	Wed	401	474.5	− 73.5	5,402
	Thu	423	450.0	− 27.0	729
	Fri	679	443.3	+235.7	55,554
2	Mon	598	490.4	+107.6	11,577
	Tue	342	508.3	−166.3	27,657
	Wed	417	484.6	− 67.6	4,570
	Thu	358	476.1	−118.1	13,948
	Fri	642	463.0	+179.0	32,041
3	Mon	671	480.9	+190.1	36,138
	Tue	380	498.2	−118.8	13,971
	Wed	426	488.3	− 62.3	3,881
	Thu	372	483.5	−111.5	12,432
	Fri	620	475.6	+144.4	20,851
				MAD = 135.7	MSE = 23,440

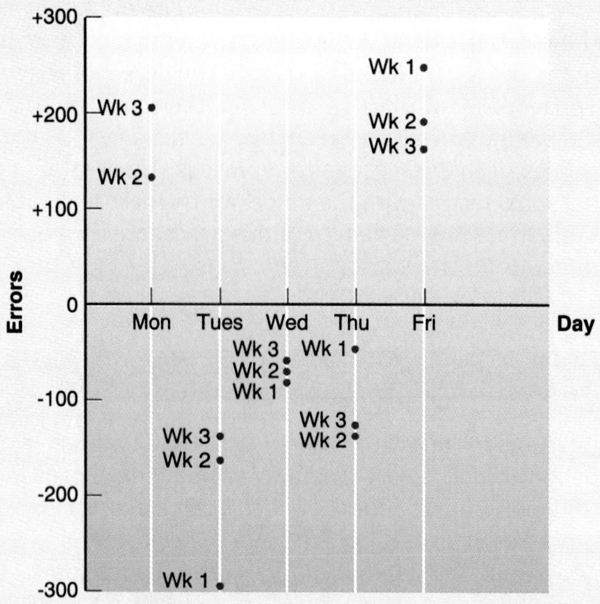

FIGURE 4.8 Errors from the cumulative average by day of the week.

TABLE 4.13 DESEASONALIZING DATA FOR IMPERIAL COMMERCE BANK

t	Wk	Day	(1) Actual	(2) Centered Moving Ave.	(3) Seasonal Ratio	(4) Deseasonalized Data
1	1	Mon	624			488 = 624/1.278
2	1	Tue	325			443
3	1	Wed	401	490.4	0.818 = 401/490.4	472
4	1	Thu	423	485.2	0.872	529
5	1	Fri	679	488.6	1.390	508
6	2	Mon	598	491.8	1.216	468
7	2	Tue	342	478.8	0.714	466
8	2	Wed	417	471.4	0.885	491
9	2	Thu	358	486.0	0.737	448
10	2	Fri	642	493.6	1.301	480
11	3	Mon	671	495.4	1.354	525
12	3	Tue	380	498.2	0.763	518
13	3	Wed	426	493.8	0.863	501
14	3	Thu	372			465
15	3	Fri	620			463

$c_1 = (1.216 + 1.354)/2 = 1.2850 \times [5/5.0288] \rightarrow 1.278$

$c_2 = (0.714 + 0.763)/2 = 0.7385 \times [5/5.0288] \rightarrow 0.734$

$c_3 = (0.818 + 0.885 + 0.863)/3 = 0.8553 \times [5/5.0288] \rightarrow 0.850$

$c_4 = (0.872 + 0.737)/2 = 0.8045 \times [5/5.0288] \rightarrow 0.800$

$c_5 = (1.390 + 1.301)/2 = 1.3455 \times [5/5.0288] \rightarrow 1.338$

Total 5.0288 5.000

be a seasonal component in the process. Specifically, she conjectured that the number of daily transactions was a constant process with multiplicative seasonality:

$$Y_t = a\,c_s + \varepsilon_t \tag{4.11}$$

where a permanent component, a, is multiplied by a seasonal factor, c_s, depending on the day of the week, and ε_t is a random component.

There are several ways to estimate the seasonal factors c_s and then to deseasonalize the data. The procedure we present here is one that can be used without change for more complicated seasonal processes, such as linear trends with seasonality. The procedure for estimating the parameters in equation (4.11) is given below. The computations for deseasonalizing the data are shown in Table 4.13, and the forecasts from the model are presented in Table 4.14.

Steps for Constructing Constant Process Model with Multiplicative Seasonality

1. Compute a series of N-period moving averages, where N is the number of seasons (five in this example). Each moving average will contain exactly one observation from each season. This moving average, which we will call the **centered moving average (CMA)**, is associated with the midpoint of the time periods being averaged. So the centered moving average of periods 1–5 is 490.4 and is associated with time 3. The centered moving average for periods 2–6 is 485.2 and is associ-

TABLE 4.14 FORECASTS FOR IMPERIAL COMMERCE BANK ASSUMING A CONSTANT PROCESS WITHMULTIPLICATIVE SEASONALITY

t	Wk	Day	(1) y_t Actual	(2) Dy_t Deseason. Data	(3) Deseason. Cum. Ave.	×	(4) c_s Season. Factor	=	(5) F_t Forecast	Error	Error^2
1	1	Mon	624	488	—		—		—	—	—
2	1	Tue	325	443	488		0.734		358	−33	1089
3	1	Wed	401	472	466		0.850		396	+ 5	25
4	1	Thu	423	529	468		0.800		374	+ 49	2401
5	1	Fri	679	508	483		1.338		646	+ 33	1089
6	2	Mon	598	468	488		1.278		623	−25	625
7	2	Tue	342	466	485		0.734		356	−14	196
8	2	Wed	417	491	482		0.850		410	+ 7	49
9	2	Thu	358	448	483		0.800		386	−28	784
10	2	Fri	642	480	479		1.338		641	+ 1	1
11	3	Mon	671	525	479		1.278		612	+ 59	3481
12	3	Tue	380	518	483		0.734		355	+ 25	625
13	3	Wed	426	501	486		0.850		413	+ 13	169
14	3	Thu	372	465	487		0.800		390	−18	324
15	3	Fri	620	463	486		1.338		650	−30	900
16	4	Mon	—	—	484		1.278		619	—	—
17	4	Tue	—	—	484		0.734		355	—	—
					For periods 2–15				MAD = 24.3		MSE = 840

ated with time 4. (If the number of seasons is even, each moving average corresponds to a point in time midway between the time periods. We then average successive pairs of moving averages to obtain a centered moving average centered at a real time period. The example in the next subsection illustrates this case.)

2. For each time period for which a centered moving average exists, we compute the ratio of the *actual* time series value divided by the centered moving average at that point, that is, the values in column (3) = column (1)/column (2).
3. The ratios in column (3) can be viewed as observations for the actual seasonal factors, c_s (with some randomness thrown in). We use these to estimate c_s for each season by averaging all ratios corresponding to that season. The estimators should average 1.00 (i.e., the seasonal factors should sum to N, the number of seasons); otherwise, there will be a bias in the model. If the sum of the c_s values does not equal N, we scale the estimators by multiplying them all by $N/(\Sigma c_s)$ so that they sum to N. For example, $\Sigma c_s = 5.0288$, so our estimate of c_1 is $c_1 = [(1.216 + 1.354)/2] \times [5.0/5.0288] = 1.278$. The values for c_s are calculated at the bottom of Table 4.13.[9]
4. The seasonal factors, c_s, are then used to remove the seasonal effects from the original data. This is done by dividing the original time series values in column (1) by the appropriate c_s; this gives the deseasonalized data in column (4) of Table 4.13.
5. The deseasonalized data in column (4) are now treated as a separate time series. If we graphed it, we would see that it looks like a constant or quasi-constant process: $Y_t = a + \varepsilon_t$. We then estimate the value of the constant a for the deseasonalized data exactly as we would for any constant or quasi-constant process. For illustration and comparison with Peggy Cutter's first model, we have used a cumulative average to estimate a each period.
6. The forecasts generated by our seasonal model, which are given in column (5) of Table 4.14, are obtained by taking the value of a computed for that period (the forecast for the deseasonalized data) in column (3) and multiplying it by the appropriate seasonal factor estimator, c_s, in column (4). For example, the cumulative average of the deseasonalized data for the first six periods is 485. Because period 7 is a Tuesday, the (retrospective) forecast for period 7 is

$$F_7 = (485)\ (0.734) = 356$$

The forecast for a future period, such as time 16, would be

$$F_{16} = (484)\ (1.278) = 619$$

where 484 is the cumulative average of the deseasonalized data for the first 15 time periods and 1.278 is the seasonal factor for Mondays.

[9] If the sum of the c_s values is within 1% of N, rescaling of the seasonal factors is sometimes omitted because the resulting bias is so small.

Not only are the magnitudes of the errors smaller for the seasonal model than for the pure cumulative average model, but the error *pattern* is better; the errors look normally scattered around zero, and there is no pattern by day of the week.

Two details of the procedure and example require further comment. First, in step 1 the moving averages are computed the same way as the simple moving averages in Section 4.6, but they are being used for a very different purpose. In Section 4.6 we computed the simple moving average for some periods, say 1–5, to obtain an estimate of the parameter a for a quasi-constant process, and then we used this estimate as a *forecast* of the future values of the process. In step 1 we intentionally average one observation from each season around a center point to get the average value of the process at that point with the seasonal effects balanced out. We then use deviations between the actual data points and these centered moving averages to measure the amount of variation due to seasonality. Second, we could have used a simple moving average or simple exponential smoothing to forecast the deseasonalized data, instead of the cumulative average, and the procedure would have been the same.

LINEAR TREND PROCESSES WITH SEASONALITY

The same method used in the previous example can be used for other seasonal processes, such as a linear trend process with seasonality. The data are deseasonalized in the same way. Then the deseasonalized data are treated as a separate time series, and a model is constructed to estimate the deseasonalized process. The following example illustrates this fact. It also shows how to center the moving averages when there is an even number of seasons.

EXAMPLE 8

James Shortroad, manager of manufacturing for Antietam Carpet Company, wanted to forecast future quarterly demand for a type of carpet so that he could plan fiber acquisition, personnel hiring, and training programs during the next 6–12 months. Table 4.15 lists the number of square yards of carpet sold on a quarterly basis during the past three years.

James knew that sales of this type of carpet had been increasing over time, so he first used equations (4.6) and (4.7) to construct a linear trend model for sales:

$$b = \frac{12(18{,}510) - (78)(2580)}{12(650) - (78)^2} = \frac{20{,}880}{1716} = 12.2$$

$$a = (2580 / 12) - 12.2(78 / 12) = 135.7$$

Thus, the resulting model was

$$F_t = 135.7 + 12.2t \tag{4.12}$$

Table 4.16 gives the forecasts and the errors that would have occurred using this model. Figure 4.9 graphs the data and the trend line in equation (4.12).

TABLE 4.15 CARPET SOLD BY ANTIETAM CARPET COMPANY (thousands of square yards)

Year	Qt 1	Qt 2	Qt 3	Qt 4
1	160	170	140	150
2	230	240	180	200
3	310	310	230	260

TABLE 4.16 FORECASTS FOR ANTIETAM CARPET USING THE LINEAR TREND MODEL

t	Yr	Quarter	y_t Actual	F_t Forecast	Error	Error^2
1	1	1	160	147.9	+12.1	146.4
2	1	2	170	160.1	+ 9.9	98.0
3	1	3	140	172.3	−32.3	1043.3
4	1	4	150	184.5	−34.5	1190.3
5	2	1	230	196.7	+33.3	1108.9
6	2	2	240	208.9	+31.1	967.2
7	2	3	180	221.1	−41.1	1689.2
8	2	4	200	233.3	−33.3	1108.9
9	3	1	310	245.5	+64.5	4160.3
10	3	2	310	257.7	+52.3	2735.3
11	3	3	230	269.9	−39.9	1592.0
12	3	4	260	282.1	−22.1	488.4
					MAD = 33.9	MSE = 1360.7

James inspected the errors in Table 4.16 and found that the errors for the first and second quarters of each year were consistently positive, while the errors for the third and fourth quarters of each year were consistently negative. This confirmed his suspicion that there was some seasonality in carpet sales. So he decided to test a **linear trend model with multiplicative seasonality**:

$$Y_t = [a + bt]c_s + \varepsilon_t \tag{4.13}$$

where the c_s terms are the seasonal factors associated with season (quarter) s. The steps required to construct the model are the same as those in the previous subsection. The computations for Antietam are given in Table 4.17.

Steps for Constructing a Linear Trend Model with Multiplicative Seasonality

1. We compute a series of four-period moving averages (because there are four seasons) and associate each with the midpoint of the time periods averaged. So the average of periods 1–4 is 155.0, and it is associated with the point in time 2.5. Because the number of seasons is even, each moving average corresponds to a time

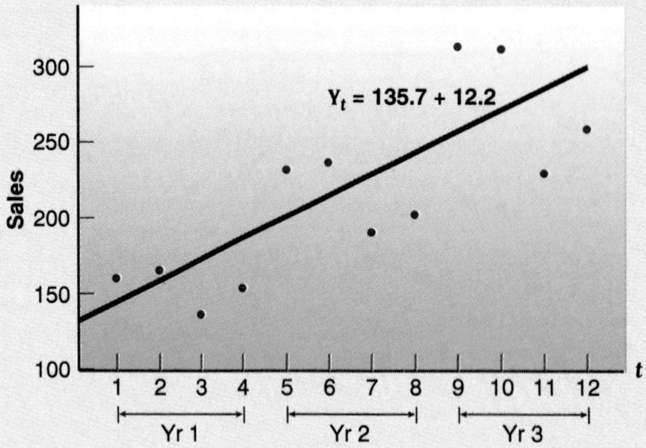

FIGURE 4.9 Data and trend line for Antietam Carpet.

TABLE 4.17 DESEASONALIZING ANTIETAM CARPET SALES

t	Yr	Quarter	(1) Actual	(2) Moving Average	(3) Centered M.A.	(4) Seasonal Ratio	(5) Deseasonalized Data
1	1	1	160				134 = 160 / 1.191
2	1	2	170	155.0			147
3	1	3	140	172.5	163.75	0.855	169
4	1	4	150	190.0	181.25	0.828	182
5	2	1	230	200.0	195.00	1.179	193
6	2	2	240	212.5	206.25	1.164	208
7	2	3	180	232.5	222.50	0.809	217
8	2	4	200	250.0	241.25	0.829	242
9	3	1	310	262.5	256.25	1.210	260
10	3	2	310	277.5	270.00	1.148	269
11	3	3	230				277
12	3	4	260				315

$c_1 = (1.179 + 1.210)/2 = 1.195\ [4/4.011] \rightarrow 1.191$
$c_2 = (1.164 + 1.148)/2 = 1.156\ [4/4.011] \rightarrow 1.153$
$c_3 = (0.855 + 0.809)/2 = 0.832\ [4/4.011] \rightarrow 0.830$
$c_4 = (0.828 + 0.829)/2 = 0.828\ [4/4.011] \rightarrow 0.826$
Total 4.011 4.000

midway between time periods. We average successive pairs of moving averages to obtain centered moving averages centered at actual time periods (e.g., we average the moving averages associated with times 2.5 and 3.5 to obtain the centered moving average at time 3: (155.0 + 172.5)/2 = 163.75).

2. For each time period with a centered moving average, we compute the ratio of the actual time series value divided by the centered moving average at that point: column (4) = column(1)/column (3).
3. For each season, we average the corresponding ratios in column (4) to obtain an estimate for the seasonal factors, c_s. Because the sum of the seasonal factors equals 4.011 rather than 4, we scale the seasonal factors by multiplying them by (4/4.011).
4. We divide the original data in column (1) by the appropriate seasonal factor estimates, c_s, to obtain the deseasonalized data in column (5).
5. We use equations (4.6) and (4.7) to obtain estimates of a and b, using linear regression on the deseasonalized data:

$$b = \frac{12(19{,}188) - (78)(2613)}{12(650) - (78)^2} = 15.4$$

$$a = [(2613)/12] - 15.4(78/12) = 117.6$$

The linear trend forecasting model with multiplicative seasonality is then given by

$$F_t = [117.6 + 15.4\,t]\, c_s \tag{4.14}$$

where the c_s values are given in Table 4.17. So, for example,

$$F_6 = [117.6 + 15.4(6)] \times [1.153] = 242$$

TABLE 4.18 FORECASTS USING THE LINEAR TREND WITH THE MULTIPLICATIVE SEASONALITY MODEL

t	Yr	Quarter	y_t Actual	F_t Forecast	Error	Error^2
1	1	1	160	158	+ 2	4
2	1	2	170	171	−1	1
3	1	3	140	136	+ 4	16
4	1	4	150	148	+ 2	4
5	2	1	230	232	−2	4
6	2	2	240	242	−2	4
7	2	3	180	187	−7	49
8	2	4	200	199	+ 1	1
9	3	1	310	305	+ 5	25
10	3	2	310	313	−3	9
11	3	3	230	238	−8	64
12	3	4	260	250	+10	100
					MAD = 3.9	MSE = 23.4

The forecasts and errors resulting from equation (4.14) are given in Table 4.18. Not only are the mean absolute deviation and mean squared error for the seasonal model significantly smaller than for the pure linear trend model, the errors appear to be randomly scattered around zero and exhibit no seasonal pattern.

In practice, seasonal effects are not always as strong or distinct as they were in the preceding two examples. But when seasonal patterns can be identified in the time series data, explicitly incorporating seasonality into the forecasting model will normally improve the forecasts substantially. However, there are some special considerations and warnings to keep in mind when constructing models with seasonality. First, the data requirements for seasonal models are greater than for models without seasonality. To obtain reasonably good estimates of the seasonal factors, you should probably have at least 4, and preferably 5–10 observations of each season. Second, seasonal models are more complex than nonseasonal models, and they contain many more parameters to estimate. This fact alone means that they should fit or explain past data better than simpler models; therefore, the mean absolute deviation and mean squared error for the seasonal model should be much smaller than those for simpler models; otherwise, it is not worthwhile to use the seasonal model. How much smaller the mean absolute deviation and mean squared error should be compared to a simpler model to justify its use can be determined precisely by comparing the standard error of estimate for each model. (This is beyond the scope of this book, but the appropriate formulas can be found in most forecasting textbooks.)

Finally, if you believe there is seasonality in the variable you are forecasting, but your seasonal model does not produce significantly more accurate forecasts than the model without seasonality, you may be incorporating seasonality in the wrong way. For example, you may be assuming that the seasonality is multiplicative, but in fact it may be better modeled as additive. The form of seasonality can make an especially big difference in the accuracy of forecasting models with trends.

Just as there are smoothing methods to obtain forecasts for quasi-constant and linear trend processes, P. R. Winters developed a smoothing method for seasonal processes. This method is beyond the scope of this book, but it can be found in any forecasting text.

4.10 CAUSAL MODELS

Time series models are usually effective for short- to intermediate-term forecasting. However, in many cases the previous values for a variable provide no useful information about the future values for the variable. Then it is sometimes possible to identify other independent (or predictor) variables that are probabilistically related to the dependent variable we are trying to forecast. If timely information regarding the independent variable(s) is available, it can be used to obtain forecasts for the dependent variable. This approach is referred to as **causal** or **associative forecasting** because it assumes that the values taken on by the independent variables have a causal influence on the values taken on by the dependent variable. In practice, we do not care whether the independent variable influences the dependent variable; we only care that the variables are related in such a way that knowing the value of the independent variable will help us forecast the future value of the dependent variable. That is, we are not attempting to *explain* the phenomenon, only *forecast* it. For example, the independent and dependent variables may both be affected by a third (possibly unknown) variable, but the independent variable shows its effects first. By observing changes in the value of the independent variable, we can predict changes in the value of the dependent variable.

In this section we will focus on the simplest of the causal models: models with a linear relationship between a single independent variable and the dependent variable. Specifically we will assume that

$$Y = a + bX + \varepsilon$$

where Y is the dependent variable associated with some time period, X is an independent variable associated with some (possibly different) time period, and ε is a normally distributed random variable with a mean of zero. These models are called **simple linear causal models**.

SELECTING AN INDEPENDENT VARIABLE

The first step in causal modeling is to identify an independent variable related to the dependent variable to be forecast. It is essential that the forecaster learn as much as possible about the dependent variable and its environment in order to propose some variables that are likely to be related to it. For example, the number of students who are likely to enroll in the third grade in a school district next fall is related to the number of students who were enrolled in the second grade this past year. It is also related to the net migration of families into the school district during the past year. Similarly, the number of refrigerators demanded during a year may be related to the number of marriages, housing starts, employment rate, or gross national product during various time periods.

Once a possible independent variable is identified, the next step is to pair actual observations of it, x_i, with observations, y_i, of the dependent variable and plot them. Note that two physically different variables may be related, but there may be a time lag in the relationship; that is, the value of the dependent variable may be related to the value of the independent variable at an earlier period. Table 4.19 lists new auto sales

TABLE 4.19 AUTO AND OIL FILTER SALES

Quarter	New Car Sales (000,000)	Oil Filter Sales (000,000)
1	2.45	10.10
2	2.70	9.75
3	2.20	10.10
4	2.85	10.90
5	3.10	8.70
6	2.90	11.70
7	3.20	12.50
8	2.50	11.50
9	2.75	13.00

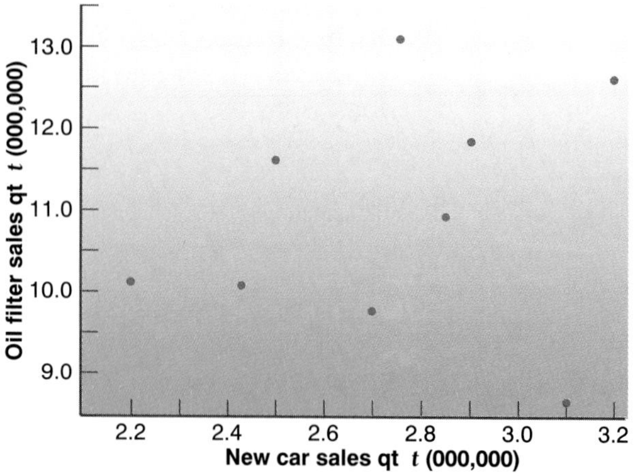

FIGURE 4.10 Oil filter sales versus new auto sales with no time lag.

and oil filter sales on a quarterly basis. If we pair the data so that x_i is the new car sales during quarter t and y_i is the oil filter sales during quarter t, we get the pattern shown in Figure 4.10. There is no apparent relationship between the x_i and y_i values. In contrast, if we let x_i be new car sales during quarter $t - 2$ and y_i be oil filter sales during quarter t, we get the pattern shown in Figure 4.11. (In Figure 4.10 there are nine pairs, one for each time period; in Figure 4.11 there are only seven pairs because of the two-period lag.)

From Figure 4.10 one might conclude that new car sales and oil filter sales are unrelated, whereas Figure 4.11 suggests a strong linear relationship between the two variables. Therefore, it is a good idea to plot possible independent and dependent variables using several time lags.

ESTIMATING THE RELATIONSHIP AND FORECASTING

Once the data have been plotted in various ways, we select an independent variable that has a discernible relationship with the dependent variable and conjecture the form of the relationship. For now we will assume that the relationship is linear.

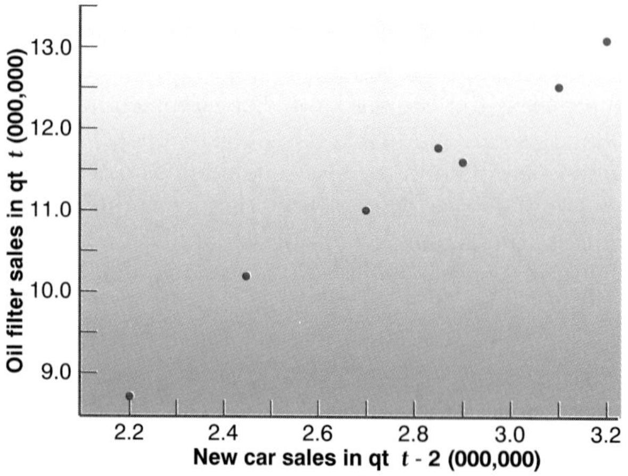

FIGURE 4.11 Oil filter sales versus new auto sales with two-quarter lag.

EXAMPLE 9

Suppose we are interested in forecasting oil filter sales on a quarterly basis using the data in Table 4.19. From Figure 4.11 we conjecture that oil filter sales during period t (OF_t) are a linear function of new car sales during period $t - 2$ (NC_{t-2}):

$$OF_t = a + b\, NC_{t-2}$$

The next question is, what are the best values for a and b based on the data? Just as we did in Section 4.8, we can use equations (4.6) and (4.7) to obtain the values of a and b that best describe the relationship between the variables Y and X, where $Y = OF_t$ and $X = NC_{t-2}$. Because of the two-period lag there are seven pairs of data (x_i, y_i), which are given in Table 4.20.

TABLE 4.20 COMPUTATIONS FOR THE LINEAR CAUSAL MODEL OF OIL FILTER SALES

i	NC_{t-2} x_i	OF_t y_i	x_i^2	$x_i y_i$
1	2.45	10.10	6.00	24.75
2	2.70	10.90	7.29	29.43
3	2.20	8.70	4.84	19.14
4	2.85	11.70	8.12	33.35
5	3.10	12.50	9.61	38.75
6	2.90	11.50	8.41	33.35
7	3.20	13.00	10.24	41.60
	19.40	78.40	54.51	220.37

Substituting the appropriate values from Table 4.20 into equations (4.6) and (4.7) gives

$$b = \frac{7(220.37) - (19.40)(78.40)}{7(54.51) - (19.40)^2} = 4.15$$

$$a = [(78.40/7] - 4.15\,[(19.40)/7] = -\,0.30$$

So the estimated relationship is

$$OF_t = -\,0.30 + 4.15\, NC_{t-2}$$

Table 4.21 lists the forecasts and errors that would have occurred if this relationship had been used to forecast the oil filter sales in periods 3–9.

TABLE 4.21 FORECASTS OF OIL FILTER SALES USING LINEAR CAUSAL MODEL

Quarter	y_t Actual	F_t Forecast		Error	Error^2
3	10.10	9.87	= −0.30 + 4.15(2.45)	+0.23	0.05
4	10.90	10.91	= −0.30 + 4.15(2.70)	−0.01	0.00
5	8.70	8.83	= −0.30 + 4.15(2.20)	−0.13	0.02
6	11.70	11.53	= −0.30 + 4.15(2.85)	+0.17	0.03
7	12.50	12.57	= −0.30 + 4.15(3.10)	−0.07	0.00
8	11.50	11.74	= −0.30 + 4.15(2.90)	−0.24	0.05
9	13.00	12.98	= −0.30 + 4.15(3.20)	+0.02	0.00
				MAD = 0.12	MSE = 0.02

The mean absolute deviation and mean squared error for this model are extremely small, and the mean absolute percentage error is approximately 1%. Not only does this model fit the data well, but it has the property that the information needed to make a forecast for quarter 10 is available at the end of quarter 8:

$$OF_{10} = -0.30 + 4.15\,(2.50) = 10.08$$

PRACTICAL HINTS FOR USING CAUSAL MODELS

When working with causal models in practice, it is important to keep in mind the ultimate purpose of the exercise: *to construct a model that produces accurate and timely forecasts*. We may be able to identify strong relationships among variables, but if we cannot obtain observations for the independent variables in a sufficiently timely manner to forecast the dependent variable, this is of little value for forecasting. In the previous example, even if we found oil filter sales in quarter t to be perfectly related to new car sales in quarter t, we could not use this information to forecast oil filter sales in period $t + 1$ because we would not know new car sales for period $t + 1$ until after period $t + 1$ occurs, in which case we no longer need the forecast. So, when constructing causal models, we usually *prefer* to have a **time lag** between the independent and dependent variables. An exception to this is if there exists a good forecasting method for the independent variable, so that a forecast value for the independent variable could be used to forecast the dependent variable. In this case, the independent variable should be the *forecast* value of the independent variable, not the actual value, because that is what will be used to drive the model. A second exception occurs when the value of the independent variable is controllable. For example, suppose the independent variable is "number of TV commercials for our product in period t" and the dependent variable is "sales in period t." Because our company selects the amount of advertising it will do in advance, we will know the number of commercials it will have on TV during period t before period t occurs, so a time lag would not be necessary.

The need for timeliness implies that we sometimes use less accurate models because they provide usable forecasts. For example, a few years ago the author determined that the spot price for a major commodity at time t, P_t, was related to the inventories of that commodity at major storage sites around the world at time t, I_t. Unfortunately, it took almost six months before accurate inventory data were available for any point in time; that is, one would not know the inventories on January 31 of a year until approximately July 31. So if on February 1 we wanted to forecast average prices during February, we would have to wait until August 1 to make the forecast, which would be useless. An alternative was to use inventory data from only a few sites that were available within two to three months. The relationship between P_t and I_{t-3} was much weaker than that between P_t and I_t, but it was strong enough to assist in forecasting P_t, and the forecasts could be timely.

4.11 ADVANCED MODELS

The previous models are the most elementary models used for forecasting. They were presented to provide a general feel for statistical forecasting. Even so, many of these models are sufficiently robust to be used widely. However, it is not uncommon to encounter situations where these simple models do not produce good forecasts. Time series models that include nonlinear trends and causal models that contain more than one independent variable are common in practice, especially for making intermediate- to long-term forecasts. In addition, there are cases where forecasting errors are not independent from period to period; instead, successive errors are correlated and can be used to improve subsequent forecasts. Models that use these relationships are called **ARIMA (autoregressive/integrated/moving average) models**. Box and Jenkins have developed a method for identifying and constructing such models. These advanced models are beyond the scope of this book, but detailed discussions of them can be found in standard forecasting books, such as the one by Makridakis, Wheelwright, and McGee (see Selected Readings).

4.12 IMPLEMENTATION AND USE OF FORECASTING SYSTEMS

Forecasting is used to predict a wide variety of phenomena: demands, prices, populations, enrollments, interest rates, cash flows, and corporate profits. Whatever the phenomenon being forecast, how well the forecasting model will perform in practice and the amount of benefit it will provide depend on how the model is structured, how well it has been evaluated and tested, and how it is used and monitored in practice.

MODEL EVALUATION AND TESTING

For any forecasting model, accuracy and reliability are crucial. Even when a model fits the historical data well (in the sense that if the model had been used in earlier periods, it would have produced relatively small, unbiased errors), this does not guarantee that the model will predict *future* values of the phenomenon very well. However, although this risk always exists, there are certain precautions we can take to improve the likelihood that the selected forecasting method will perform well.

If there are sufficient data, one precaution is to perform a "holdout" evaluation of the models. With this procedure we divide the available data into two sets; we use the first set, containing the oldest data, to estimate parameters and perform an initial evaluation of the goodness of each model. We then use the models to make forecasts for the second set of data, the **holdout data**. Forecasts for these holdout data are made only using data that would have been available before the forecast was made; that is, we act as if the holdout data are future observations. By comparing the forecast accuracy of the models against the holdout data, we get a better idea not only of which model best explains the past, but also of which model is likely to predict the future most accurately. Although there is no fixed rule, we usually use one-half to three-fourths of the data for initial parameter estimation and model screening and the remaining one-fourth to one-half as our holdout data.

Whenever possible, a second precaution is not to implement a specific model until we have had a chance to observe its real forecasting performance for at least a few time periods (in some circumstances, such as with quarterly or yearly forecasting models, this may not be feasible). If the first few real forecasts the model generates are reasonably accurate, this should improve our confidence in the appropriateness of the model.

COMBINING FORECASTING METHODS

Not only can qualitative forecasting be improved by combining several forecasts, quantitative forecasting can be improved in the same way. Makridakis and Winkler found that if no one model describes the process well, combining several different simple models, usually by averaging their forecasts, often produces more accurate forecasts over the long run than does a more complicated model. They also found that as the number of methods averaged was increased, the mean absolute percentage error and the variance of the errors decreased. An obvious benefit from combining forecasts is that if any one of the models is poor, its influence is diminished.[10]

MONITORING FORECASTS: TRACKING SIGNALS AND ADAPTIVE MODELS

One reason for using quantitative forecasting models is to be able to automate the forecasting process. Even if a mathematical model were no more accurate than a qualitative procedure, the ability to make forecasts with a model is worthwhile because it frees up human time for other productive work, and forecasts from a model can be computerized and integrated with other operational systems. For example, companies that purchase thousands of distinct items from suppliers often use automated decision rules to decide when to order each item and how much to order. These decision rules, however, require forecasts of future use or sales. Automated forecasting systems can be constructed to collect actual usage data regularly to make forecasts and to update inventory records; the forecasts are then used in computerized decision rules to determine whether or not to place an order. By automating the forecasting and integrating it with the purchasing system, the work of dozens of people can be done by a computer in a more accurate and timely fashion.

Because it is easy to automate forecasting models, there is a tendency to do so and then to ignore them until a disaster occurs. This can be dangerous because even forecasting models that initially produce accurate forecasts can go out of kilter if the underlying process changes. Therefore, it is a good idea to build an automatic monitoring mechanism into any automated forecasting system.

Tracking Signal

One automatic monitoring mechanism that keeps track of a model's forecasting accuracy is the **tracking signal (TS)**, defined as the ratio of cumulative forecasting errors (not the *absolute value* of errors) to the mean absolute deviation:

$$TS = \Sigma\,(y_i - F_i)/\text{MAD}$$

where the summation is over a specified set of periods and the MAD is recomputed every period. After each period TS is computed. As long as the errors remain relatively small and unbiased, the absolute value of TS will remain small and the model is left to operate without intervention. By contrast, if |TS| exceeds some specified limit (usually in the range 3–8), a warning is generated. A person can then investigate the problem in depth to determine whether or not the forecasting model needs to be modified or replaced.

EXAMPLE 10

Table 4.22 gives a series of actual data points, forecasts from a model, and the resulting value of TS. The first five periods are used to obtain an initial estimate of the MAD and to test the accuracy of the model. The MAD for these first five periods is 4.0. For each subsequent period, we compute the error and the cumulative errors from period 6 on. For example, for period 8 the error is $(y_8 - F_8) = (133 - 136) = -3$. The cumulative error

[10]See S. Makridakis and R. L. Winkler "Averages of Forecasts," *Management Science*, Vol. 29, 1983, pp. 987–996.

TABLE 4.22 FORECASTING ERRORS AND TRACKING SIGNAL

Period	y_i Actual	F_i Forecast	$(y_i - F_i)$ Error	Sum of Errors Periods 6→	MAD Periods 1 →	TS
1	129	136	−7	—	—	—
2	141	136	+ 5	—	—	—
3	136	139	−3	—	—	—
4	132	136	−4	—	—	—
5	135	134	+1	—	4.00	—
6	140	138	+2	+2	3.67	+0.54
7	134	137	−3	−1	3.57	−0.28
8	133	136	−3	−4	3.50	−1.14
9	130	136	−6	−10	3.78	−2.65
10	128	133	−5	−15	4.30	−3.49
11	127	131	−4	−19	3.91	−4.86

from periods 6–8 is −4, and the MAD for periods 1–8 is 3.50, so the tracking signal value is TS = −4/3.50 = −1.14. As long as |TS| is less than some limit, say 4.0, the model is considered to be functioning well.

A major problem with the tracking signal is that because it uses the cumulative error, there are situations where the forecasting model can become inaccurate and the tracking signal will not catch it. One case is where the absolute magnitude of the errors gets large, but as long as the errors are both positive and negative and cancel out each other, the cumulative error and thus |TS| stay small. For example, in Table 4.22, if the errors in periods 6–11 had been +9, −12, +15, −13, +12, and −12, the tracking signal would not indicate a problem even though the forecasts are very inaccurate. A second problem occurs when errors cycle, several positive then several negative, but the magnitudes are sufficiently small so that |TS| does not trigger a warning. In practice, we would like to identify these conditions, but the tracking signal often will not catch them.

An approach that is becoming popular for identifying the first case, where the magnitude of errors is abnormally large, is to use a **tracking control chart**. With this approach, if the absolute magnitude of the error in a period is greater than some limit, usually $3\sqrt{MSE}$, a warning is signaled.

Adaptive Models and Focus Forecasting

An alternative to immediate human intervention is to build into the system an adaptive mechanism. Based on the model's performance, the adaptive mechanism either maintains the existing model, modifies the model, or gives a warning asking for human intervention. One type of adaptive model is called focus forecasting. **Focus forecasting** uses several different models (e.g., cumulative average, exponential smoothing) to forecast each period. The model that gives the best forecast in one period (or several consecutive periods) is the one used to compute the actual forecast for the next period. If another model then becomes more accurate, that model is used in subsequent periods until it is replaced. This approach works well if, when a model becomes preferable to alternatives, it remains that way for several consecutive time periods. However, if in every period a different model is most accurate, we would always be using a model other than the best one for that period.

BUILDUP AND BREAKDOWN MODELS

In some situations, it is more effective to forecast the variable(s) of interest indirectly using a two-step process rather than creating a model that forecasts the variable directly. Specifically, if the variable of interest, such as the sales of a company, is one component of a more aggregate variable, industrywide sales, it may be easier and more accurate to forecast the aggregate variable and then break it down into its components, one of which is our variable of interest. This approach is called a **breakdown** or **decomposition method**. Similarly, in some cases our variable of interest may be made up of several component variables, and it may be better to develop forecasts for the components and then combine them to get the forecast for the desired variable. This is called a **buildup** or **composition method**.

There are at least two reasons for using one of these approaches. First, in some cases accurate forecasting models may already exist for some more aggregate variable or for the components of the variable we want to forecast; we can then use that information to forecast the desired variable. Second, there are times when we want forecasts of several related components (e.g., sales for different divisions in a company), and these forecasts must be consistent with some overall forecast.

To illustrate when a buildup approach might be used, suppose the U.S. Department of Transportation (USDOT) has decided that it needs to forecast the number of traffic accidents expected each year. Suppose further that each state already makes a statewide forecast of accidents, that these forecasts are relatively accurate, and that the errors appear to be uncorrelated from state to state. Then the USDOT may decide to make its forecast by simply summing the statewide forecasts. Not only would this be easy and inexpensive for the USDOT, but there would automatically be consistency between the states and the national government because the national forecast would equal the sum of the statewide forecasts.

To illustrate when a breakdown system might be used, suppose a company in a rapidly growing industry would like to forecast its sales, and accurate forecasts of total industry sales are readily available. The company may find it easier and more accurate to construct a model of the company's *market share* over time, use a forecasting service to obtain the industry forecast, and then multiply this by its predicted market share to forecast the company's sales. This approach can be more accurate than a direct forecast of a company's sales when sales have been changing over time due to changes in both total market size and the company's market share. For example, suppose an industry has been growing 20% per year and the firm's market share has been growing 10% per year. If the firm forecast its sales based only on its own previous sales, it may predict a 30% increase next year. However, suppose the company's market share has grown rapidly to the point where it dominates the market, so its market share model predicts no further sales gains due to market share growth. Then the company would predict sales growth of 20% in line with the market as a whole.

Breakdown and buildup systems allow the integration of various forecasting methods. For example, in the case above, an extremely complex causal model might be appropriate for forecasting industrywide demand, and then a simple decomposition rule can be used to forecast one company's market share. If we restricted ourselves to a direct approach, causal relationships between one company's sales and other variables might be difficult to identify. There are no simple rules for determining when to try a buildup or breakdown approach; however, knowing that such approaches exist expands our bag of tools. The case at the end of the chapter illustrates how a buildup approach can not only improve forecast accuracy, but can also help one understand the dynamics underlying the variable being forecast.

SUMMARY

- To make good decisions in a dynamic environment, it is essential to have some idea about the future decision environment.
- **Forecasting** is the art and science of predicting future events.
- Before developing a forecasting procedure, one must consider the following issues: the purpose or use of the forecast, what specific variables should be forecast, what lead time is necessary to make the forecast usable, and what data are available.
- **Quantitative forecasting methods** assume that the environment is stable, and that relationships that affected the variable to be forecast in the past will continue to affect it in the future in the same way.
- **Qualitative forecasting methods** are most appropriate in those cases where mathematical models are not suitable, such as where data are not available or the environment is highly unstable and changing.
- Qualitative forecasting can be improved by standardizing the process, monitoring performance, using groups, and providing appropriate incentives.
- **Time series models** forecast the future values of a variable using only previous values of that variable.
- **Causal models** forecast the future values of a variable using the values of other physically different variables.
- **Seasonal models** include components that describe deviations from the underlying process that occur on a regular basis, normally related to calendar events.
- A **tracking signal** monitors the performance of a forecasting model and automatically indicates whether the model needs to be revised.
- The characteristics and uses of the different forecasting methods and models are summarized in Table 4.23.

TABLE 4.23 CHARACTERISTICS OF FORECASTING METHODS

Method	When to Use	Normal Time Horizon	Computational Complexity	Cost
Qualitative				
Individual prediction	Little data Unstable environ.	Intermediate	Low	Low
Group methods Delphi	Little data	Long-term	Low	Moderate/high
Quantitative Models—Time Series				
Cumul. ave.	Constant process	Short	Low	Low
Simple/weighted moving ave.	Quasi-constant process	Short	Low	Low
Simple expon. smoothing	Quasi-constant process	Short	Low	Low
Linear (trend) regression	Linear trend process	Intermediate	Moderate	Moderate
Double exponential smoothing	Linear trend process	Intermediate	Low	Moderate
Seasonality models	Seasonal process	Short/interm.	Moderate	High
Quantitative Models—Causal				
Linear regression	Linear association	Interm./long	Moderate	Moderate

Key Terms

additive seasonal model **132**
ARIMA (autoregressive/integrated/moving average) models **145**
breakdown (decomposition) method **148**
buildup (composition) method **148**
causal models (associative models) **113**
centered moving average (CMA) **135**
consensus forecast **109**
constant process **115**
cumulative average (CA) **116**
cumulative average forecasting model **116**
cyclic component **114**
Delphi method **110**
dependent variable **111**
deseasonalizing **133**
double exponential smoothing (DES) (trend-adjusted moving average) **130**
focus forecasting **147**
forecasting **102**
group averaging **109**
group consensus **109**
holdout data **145**
independent (predictor) variables **111**
linear trend model **127**
linear trend model with multiplicative seasonality **138**
mean absolute deviation (MAD) **124**
mean absolute percentage error (MAPE) **124**
mean error (ME) (bias) **122**
mean squared error (MSE) **123**
moving averages **118**
moving linear regression **130**
multiplicative seasonal model **132**
N-period simple moving average (SMA(N)) **118**
N-period weighted moving average (WMA(N)) **119**
naive model **121**
qualitative forecasting (subjective forecasting) methods **106**
quantitative forecasting (objective forecasting) methods **106**
quasi-constant process **117**
parameters **113**
permanent component **113**
random component **115**
random variable **110**
seasonal component **113**
seasonal factors (seasonal indices) **133**
simple exponential smoothing (SES) **121**
simple linear causal models **141**
smoothing constant **121**
sum-of-digits weights **120**
time lag **114**
time series data **111**
time series models **113**
tracking control chart **147**
tracking signal (TS) **146**
trend component **113**
weighted averages **118**

Key Formulas

Cumulative Average: $CA = (\sum_{t=1}^{T} y_t)/T$

Simple Moving Average:

$$SMA(N) = \left[y_T + y_{T-1} + \ldots + y_{T-N+1}\right]/N$$

Weighted Moving Average:

$$WMA(N) = w_1 y_T + w_2 y_{T-1} + \ldots + w_N y_{T-N+1}$$

Simple Exponential Smoothing Forecast:

$$F_{T+1} = F_T + \alpha(y_T - F_T)$$

Mean Error: $ME = \sum_{i=1}^{K} (y_i - F_i)/K$

Mean Squared Error: $MSE = \left[\sum_{i=1}^{K} (y_i - F_i)^2\right]/K$

Mean Absolute Deviation: $MAD = \left[\sum_{i=1}^{K} |y_i - F_i|\right]/K$

Mean Absolute Percentage Error:

$$MAPE = 100 \times \left[\sum_{i=1}^{K} |y_i - F_i|/y_i\right]/K$$

Linear Regression Coefficients:

$$b = \frac{n(\sum x_i y_i) - (\sum x_i)(\sum y_i)}{n(\sum x_i^2) - (\sum x_i)^2}$$

$$a = \left[(\sum y_i)/n\right] - b\left[(\sum x_i)/n\right]$$

Double Exponential Smoothing Equations:

$$F_{t+1} = I_t + S_t$$

where $I_t = F_t + \alpha[y_t - F_t]$

$$S_t = S_{t-1} + \beta\left[(I_t - I_{t-1}) - S_{t-1}\right]$$

Tracking Signal: $TS = \Sigma(y_i - F_i)/MAD$

SOLVED PROBLEMS

Problem 1: Agri-Chem Corporation would like to forecast monthly sales of one of its products. Sales for the past 12 months are as follows:

Month	Sales
Jan	522
Feb	576
Mar	511
Apr	539
May	547
Jun	505
Jul	544
Aug	509
Sep	563
Oct	551
Nov	538
Dec	560

(a) Graph the sales for this product over time.

(b) Compute the forecasts that would have been produced by

(i) a cumulative average and

(ii) a simple moving average with N = 5.

(c) Compute the mean absolute deviation and mean squared error for each model during the last six months.

(d) For the better of the two models, compute a forecast for the next month (January).

Solution:

(a) A graph of sales is given in Figure 4.12.

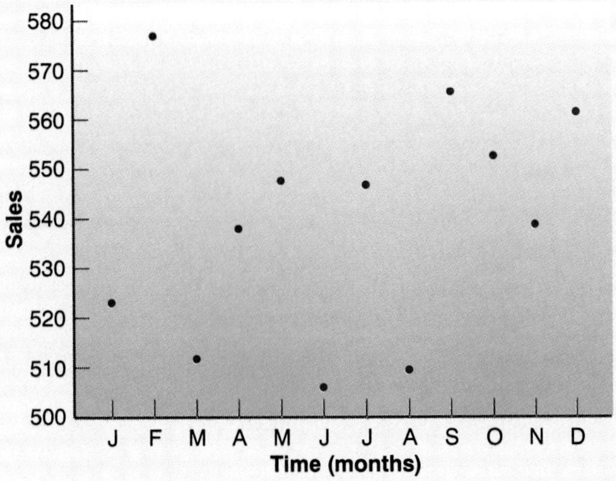

FIGURE 4.12 Agri-Chem sales.

(b)

		Cumulative Average			SMA(5)		
Month	y_t Sales	F_t Forecast	Errors	Errors^2	F_t Forecast	Errors	Errors^2
Jan	522	—	—	—	—	—	—
Feb	576	522	+ 54	2916			
Mar	511	549	− 38	1444	—	—	
Apr	539	536	+ 3	9	—	—	—
May	547	537	+ 10	100	—	—	—
Jun	505	539	− 34	1156	539	− 34	1156
Jul	544	533	+ 11	121	536	+ 8	64
Aug	509	535	− 26	676	529	− 20	400
Sep	563	532	+ 31	961	529	+ 34	1156
Oct	551	535	+ 16	256	534	+ 17	289
Nov	538	537	+ 1	1	534	+ 4	16
Dec	560	537	+23	529	541	+ 19	361

Some sample computations: The forecast for July using the cumulative average is $F_7 = (522 + 576 + \ldots + 547 + 505)/6 = 533$. The forecast for November using the SMA(5) model is $F_5 = (505 + 544 + 509 + 563 + 551)/5 = 534$.

(c) Comparing the accuracy of the two models during periods 7–12, we get:

	Cum. Ave.	SMA(5)
MAD	18	17
MSE	424	381

The two models are very close in accuracy, but the SMA(5) is slightly better.

(d) For the SMA(5) model, $F_{13} = (509 + 563 + 551 + 538 + 560)/5 = 544$.

Problem 2: Quaker Brand Foods uses oats in some of its cereal products. The price of oats is volatile, so Quaker would like to forecast the average weekly price. The average prices per bushel for the past eight weeks are as follows:

Week	Average Price/Bushel ($)
1	1.16
2	1.21
3	1.22
4	1.25
5	1.23
6	1.19
7	1.20
8	1.17

(a) Using a weighted moving average with N = 3 and weights of 3/6, 2/6, and 1/6, compute the forecasts that would have occurred during the past 5 weeks.

(b) Compute the forecasts that would have occurred using a simple exponential smoothing model with $\alpha = 0.30$ and an initial forecast for week 1 of $1.18.

(c) Compute and compare the mean absolute deviation and mean absolute percentage error for each model during weeks 5–8.

(d) For the better of the two models, compute a forecast for week 9.

Solution: (a) and (b) The forecasts and errors for the two models are given below. For example, the forecast for week 6 using the WMA(3) model is $F_6 = 3/6(1.23) + 2/6(1.25) + 1/6(1.22) = 1.23$. For the SES model, $F_6 = 1.21 + 0.3(1.23 - 1.21) = 1.22$.

Week	y_t Price/Bushel	WMA(3) F_t Forecast	WMA(3) Errors	WMA(3) % Errors	SES α = 0.3 F_t Forecast	SES α = 0.3 Errors	SES α = 0.3 % Errors
1	1.16	—	—	—	1.18	−0.02	1.7%
2	1.21	—	—	—	1.17	+0.04	3.3%
3	1.22	—	—	—	1.18	+0.04	3.3%
4	1.25	1.21	+0.04	3.2%	1.19	+0.06	4.8%
5	1.23	1.23	0	0%	1.21	+0.02	1.6%
6	1.19	1.23	−0.04	3.4%	1.22	−0.03	2.5%
7	1.20	1.21	−0.01	0.8%	1.21	−0.01	0.8%
8	1.17	1.20	−0.03	2.6%	1.21	−0.04	3.4%

(c) Comparing the accuracy of the two models during weeks 5–8:

	WMA(3)	SES
MAD	0.020	0.025
MAPE	1.7%	2.1%

The WMA(3) model is slightly more accurate.

(d) The forecast for week 9 is $F_9 = (3/6)(1.17) + (2/6)(1.20) + (1/6)(1.19) = 1.18$.

Problem 3: The manager of a hotel is considering expanding his hotel. Below are the number of nights the hotel was at least 95% booked during each of the last seven years.

	Year 1	2	3	4	5	6	7
Nights Booked	16	21	24	28	32	34	39

(a) Compute the least squares regression equation that expresses the number of nights that are 95% booked each year as a linear function of time.

(b Compute the forecasting errors that would have resulted from the model.

(c) Compute the forecasts for years 8 and 9 using this model.

Solution: (a) The data are rewritten below, with the x_i values being the time periods and the y_i values being the number of nights that are 95% booked.

Year x_i	Nights Booked y_i	x_i^2	$x_i y_i$
1	16	1	16
2	21	4	42
3	24	9	72
4	28	16	112
5	32	25	160
6	34	36	204
7	39	49	273
28	194	140	879

Substituting this information into equations (4.6) and (4.7), we get

$$b = [7(879) - (28)(194)] / [7(140) - (28)^2] = 3.7$$

$$a = [194/7] - 3.7[28/7] = 12.9$$

Our model is then

$$F_t = 12.9 + 3.7t$$

(b) The resulting forecasts and errors are as follows:

Year	y_t Nights Booked	F_t Forecast	Error
1	16	16.6	−0.6
2	21	20.3	+0.7
3	24	24.0	0
4	28	27.7	+0.3
5	32	31.4	+0.6
6	34	35.1	−1.1
7	39	38.8	+0.2

(c) The forecasts for years 8 and 9 will be

$$F_8 = 12.9 + 3.7(8) = 42.5$$

$$F_9 = 12.9 + 3.7(9) = 46.2$$

Problem 4: Show that simple exponential smoothing is actually a weighted average of all previous data.

Solution: The iterative equation $F_{T+1} = F_T + \alpha(y_T - F_T)$ can be rewritten as

$$F_{T+1} = \alpha y_T + (1 - \alpha)F_T \tag{4.15}$$

Then successively substituting the expression $F_{t+1} = \alpha y_t + (1 - \alpha)F_t$ into equation (4.15) for every t, yields

$$\begin{aligned} F_{T+1} &= \alpha y_T + (1-\alpha)\left[\alpha y_{T-1} + (1-\alpha)F_{T-1}\right] \\ &= \alpha y_T + \alpha(1-\alpha)y_{T-1} + (1-\alpha)^2\left[\alpha y_{T-2} + (1-\alpha)F_{T-2}\right] \\ &\;\;\vdots \\ &= \alpha\left[\sum_{k=0}^{T-1} (1-\alpha)^k y_{T-k}\right] + (1-\alpha)^T F_0 \end{aligned} \tag{4.16}$$

where F_0 is some initial forecast used to initiate the process. In equation (4.16) $w_1 = \alpha$, $w_2 = \alpha(1 - \alpha)$, $w_3 = \alpha(1 - \alpha)^2$, ... The weights decrease exponentially with age, where the weight for any data point is $(1 - \alpha)$ as large as the one for the next most recent data point.

Problem 5: Hans Gumph, the operations vice president for Dynamo Machine Works, would like to forecast future quarterly demand for drill presses. The number of drill presses sold on a quarterly basis during the past three years is as follows:

	Presses Sold			
Year	Qt 1	Qt 2	Qt 3	Qt 4
1	120	150	190	180
2	220	240	300	270
3	330	340	410	370

Hans believes there may be some seasonality in the underlying process.

(a) Construct a linear trend model with multiplicative seasonality for Hans.

(b) Compute the forecasts, errors, mean absolute deviation, and mean squared error for the model.

(c) From these results, would you conclude that seasonality exists?

Solution: (a) Using the procedure used in Section 4.9 for Antietam Carpet, Table 4.24 gives the deseasonalized data. We then use equations (4.6) and (4.7) to estimate the trend line for the *deseasonalized data*:

$$b = \frac{12(23{,}950) - (78)(3127)}{12(650) - (78)^2} = 25.35$$

$$a = [(3127)/12] - 25.35(78/12) = 95.81$$

The linear trend model with multiplicative seasonality is then given by

$$F_t = [95.81 + 25.35t]c_s$$

where the c_s values are given in Table 4.24.

TABLE 4.24 DESEASONALIZING THE DYNAMO MACHINE DATA FOR THE MULTIPLICATIVE MODEL

t	Yr	Quarter	(1) Actual	(2) Moving Average	(3) Centered M.A.	(4) Seasonal Ratio	(5) Deseasonalized Data
1	1	1	120				119.2 = 120/1.007
2	1	2	150	160.0			154.0
3	1	3	190	185.0	172.50	1.101	172.1
4	1	4	180	207.5	196.25	0.917	196.9
5	2	1	220	235.0	221.25	0.994	218.5
6	2	2	240	257.5	246.25	0.975	246.4
7	2	3	300	285.0	271.25	1.106	271.7
8	2	4	270	310.0	297.50	0.909	295.4
9	3	1	330	337.5	323.75	1.019	327.7
10	3	2	340	362.5	350.00	0.971	349.1
11	3	3	410				371.4
12	3	4	370				404.8

$c_1 = (0.994 + 1.019)/2 = 1.006 \times [4/3.995] \rightarrow 1.007$

$c_2 = (0.975 + 0.971)/2 = 0.973 \times [4/3.995] \rightarrow 0.974$

$c_3 = (1.101 + 1.106)/2 = 1.103 \times [4/3.995] \rightarrow 1.104$

$c_4 = (0.917 + 0.909)/2 = 0.913 \times [4/3.995] \rightarrow 0.914$

Total 3.995 3.999

(b) The forecasts and errors resulting from this model are given in Table 4.25.

(c) The errors in Table 4.25 are small in value and randomly scattered around zero, so the seasonal model appears to approximate the process well.

TABLE 4.25 FORECASTS AND ERRORS FOR DYNAMO MACHINE USING MULTIPLICATIVE SEASONALITY

t	Yr	Quarter	y_t Actual	F_t Forecast	Error	Error^2
1	1	1	120	122	−2	4
2	1	2	150	143	+7	49
3	1	3	190	190	0	0
4	1	4	180	180	0	0
5	2	1	220	224	−4	16
6	2	2	240	241	−1	1
7	2	3	300	302	−2	4
8	2	4	270	273	−3	9
9	3	1	330	326	+4	16
10	3	2	340	340	0	0
11	3	3	410	414	−4	16
12	3	4	370	366	+4	16
					MAD = 2.58	MSE = 10.92

Problem 6: American Electric Company believes that the amount of electricity usage in its service area during the summer is related to the average daily temperature in the region (defined as the average of the daily high temperature and daily low temperature). The following table gives the average daily temperature for 10 days and the amount of electricity used in the region that day.

(a) Construct a linear causal model that expresses electricity usage in a day as a function of the average temperature that day.

(b) Suppose the forecasted high and low temperatures for the next two days are 88°F and 70°F for day 1 and 90°F and 72°F for day 2. Forecast the expected electricity usage each day.

(c) Is there a potential problem with using the temperature forecasts in this model? How should it be corrected?

Day	x_i Average Temperature	y_i Usage (000 kwh)
1	81	65
2	84	69
3	85	71
4	78	62
5	75	59
6	76	62
7	81	67
8	80	66
9	85	72
10	83	68

Solution: (a) Letting x_i be the average daily temperature during day t and letting y_i be the electricity usage during day t, $\Sigma x_i = 808$, $\Sigma y_i = 661$, $\Sigma x_i^2 = 65{,}402$, and $\Sigma x_i y_i = 53{,}540$. Then

$$b = [10(53{,}540) - (808)(661)] / [10(65{,}402) - (808)2] = 1312/1156 = 1.1$$

$$a = (661/10) - 1.1(808/10) = -22.8$$

So (Electricity Usage)$_t$ = −22.8 + 1.1(Average Temperature)$_t$.

(b) The forecast average temperatures for the next two days are (88 + 70)/2 = 79 and (90 + 72)/2 = 81. So the forecast electricity usage will be

Day 1: electricity usage = −22.8 + 1.1(79) = 64.1 thousand kwh

Day 2: electricity usage = −22.8 + 1.1(81) = 66.3 thousand kwh

(c) The model in part (a) was developed using *actual* average temperatures as the independent variable. In part (b) we used the *forecast* of the average temperature to forecast electricity usage. To be correct, if we plan to substitute the temperature forecasts into our model to make our electricity forecasts, the independent variable should be the *forecast* of the average temperature, and the parameters a and b should be computed using historical temperature forecasts.

Problem 7: Use Holt's double exponential smoothing method to compute demand forecasts for periods 2–7 for the following data. Use $\alpha = 0.2$, $\beta = 0.2$, $I_1 = 108$, $S_1 = 0$.

Period	Demand
1	108
2	110
3	106
4	108
5	108
6	105

Solution: The forecast for period 2 is $F_2 = I_1 + S_1 = 108 + 0 = 108$.

We then compute I_2 and S_2 using equations (4S.1) and (4S.2) :

$$I_2 = (I_1 + S_1) + \alpha[y_2 - (I_1 + S_1)]$$
$$= (108 + 0) + 0.2[110 - (108 + 0)] = 108.4$$

$$S_2 = S_1 + \beta[(I_2 - I_1) - S_1]$$
$$= 0 + 0.2[(108.4 - 108) - 0] = +0.08$$

Our forecast for period 3 would then be $F_3 = I_2 + S_2 = 108.4 + 0.08 = 108.48$. Repeating this process produces the following values for I_t, S_t, and forecasts F_t:

t	I_t	S_t	F_t
2	108.40	+0.08	108.00
3	107.98	−0.02	108.48
4	107.97	−0.02	107.96
5	107.96	−0.02	107.95
6	107.35	−0.14	107.94
7	—	—	107.21

Discussion and Review Questions

1. Under what conditions is a qualitative forecasting approach likely to be preferred to a quantitative approach?
2. What is the fundamental assumption underlying quantitative forecasting models?
3. Name and discuss three ways in which qualitative forecasting can be improved.
4. Explain why combining forecasts from several people or models should produce forecasts that have less variability of errors than forecasts produced by individual people or models.
5. What is the most important step in constructing a quantitative model? Why?
6. What is the difference between the mean squared

error and the mean absolute deviation? What are the pros and cons of using each for comparing alternative models?

7. Why do time series models rarely include cyclic components?
8. Why would simple exponential smoothing usually not be a good method for long-term price forecasts?
9. Suppose a time series has high variation in values (e.g., the values range from 50 to 175). There is no clear trend to the data (the average for the first one-third, second one-third, and third one-third of the data are approximately the same). Does this high variation imply that the process is quasi-constant rather than constant? Why or why not?
10. To get the initial forecast for simple exponential smoothing, what would be the advantage of using the average of the actual values in the first three periods rather than setting the first forecast equal to the first actual observation?
11. After constructing a model and computing retrospective forecasts for the data, why should we plot the errors? As long as the mean error, mean absolute deviation, mean absolute percentage error, and mean squared error are reasonably small, what would a plot of the errors tell us? How would we use this information?
12. Suppose, in the Meersburg example, we did not know the sales in week t until one week later (t + 1); how would this change our forecasting if we used a cumulative average?
13. Give an example not mentioned in the chapter of a situation in which one might use a buildup forecasting model and an example of one in which one might use a breakdown model.

PROBLEMS

1. The actual quarterly sales and the forecasts made by the sales manager for a company are as follows:

	Yr 1				Yr 2				Yr 3			
Qt	1	2	3	4	1	2	3	4	1	2	3	4
Forecast	60	70	60	65	70	73	75	70	67	65	63	70
Actual	65	63	67	68	71	72	68	67	65	64	70	75

Evaluate the forecasting performance of the manager; compute her mean error, mean absolute deviation, mean squared error, and mean absolute percentage error. Are there any patterns in the errors that she can use to improve her forecasting?

2. Below are the demand forecasts from three individuals and the actual values that occurred.

Period	Forecaster 1	Forecaster 2	Forecaster 3	Actual
1	45	55	48	52
2	50	60	55	62
3	55	60	52	54
4	50	58	47	53
5	45	55	53	54
6	47	53	50	46

(a) For each forecaster, compute the mean absolute deviation and mean squared error. (b) For each period compute the average of the three forecasts, and compute the mean absolute deviation and mean squared error that would have occurred if this average had been used as the forecast. (c) Compare the results of the individual forecasters with the result obtained by using the average of the three forecasts computed in part (b).

3. Fast-Mart buys donuts from a supplier every morning, which it then sells during the day. It buys the donuts for $0.25 each and sells them for $0.49 each. Any donut not sold during the day must be thrown away. Below are the actual *demands* (not sales) for donuts each day during a seven-day period, along with the demand forecasts made by two employees of Fast-Mart. Suppose that each day the number of donuts bought by Fast-Mart from its supplier equals the demand *forecast* for that day. (a) Compute the net profit Fast-Mart would have made during those seven days if it had used the forecasts from person 1. (Note that Fast-Mart cannot sell more donuts in a day than the amount it bought from its supplier.) (b) Repeat part (a) using the forecasts from person 2. (c) How much extra profit per day would be earned on average by using the forecasts of person 2 rather than those of person 1?

Day	Actual Demand	Person 1 Forecast	Person 2 Forecast
	165	150	170
2	190	170	185
3	145	160	155
4	210	190	225
5	200	175	190
6	170	190	180
7	120	140	135

4. The Techright Computer Hypermart has collected data on the number of computers it sold during the

past 15 months. (a) Plot the data against time. (b) What type of process appears to describe the data? Why?

Year 1												Year 2		
Jan	Feb	Mar	Apr	May	Jun	Jul	Aug	Sep	Oct	Nov	Dec	Jan	Feb	Mar
320	404	397	415	361	440	348	328	351	426	439	601	340	427	454

5. For the Techright data in problem 4, compute the forecasts for April of year 2 using (a) a cumulative average, (b) a simple moving average with $N = 5$, and (c) a weighted moving average with weights 1/2, 1/3, and 1/6.

6. Magnum Auto Dealership has collected quarterly sales data for the past 10 quarters. (a) Compute the forecasts that would have occurred in quarters 6–10 using a cumulative average. (b) Compute the forecasts that would have occurred in quarters 6–10 using a simple moving average with $N = 4$. (c) Compute the mean absolute deviation and mean squared error for each model for these five quarters; which model is better and why?

Period	1	2	3	4	5	6	7	8	9	10
Sales	275	320	302	175	408	302	295	226	340	327

7. The numbers of parcels shipped from the St. Louis Post Office during each of the past eight weeks are given below. (a) Compute the forecasts that would have occurred during weeks 5–8 using an SMA(3) model. (b) Compute the forecasts that would have occurred during weeks 5–8 using the cumulative average. (c) For each model, compute the mean absolute deviation and mean squared error; which model is more accurate during this time interval?

Week	Parcels
1	6,349
2	9,639
3	6,786
4	10,432
5	7,403
6	8,107
7	11,365
8	8,490

8. A company has collected weekly sales data for the past 12 weeks. (a) Compute the forecasts that would have occurred for weeks 5–12 using a weighted moving average with weights of 4/10, 3/10, 2/10, and 1/10. (b) Compute the forecasts that would have occurred for weeks 5–12 using simple exponential smoothing with $\alpha = 0.25$, and let the forecast for week 4, F_4, be the average of actual sales in weeks 1–3. (c) Compute the mean absolute deviation and mean squared error for each model and determine which model is better. Explain.

Week	1	2	3	4	5	6	7	8	9	10	11	12
Sales	32	29	34	36	38	36	34	31	33	29	32	33

9. Daily attendance at a movie theater for the past six Fridays is given below. (a) Let the forecast for week 3 equal the average actual attendance for the first two weeks. Compute the forecasts for weeks 4, 5, and 6 that would have resulted from using simple exponential smoothing with $\alpha = 0.25$. (b) Compute the mean absolute deviation, mean absolute percentage error, and mean squared error for weeks 4–6. (c) Use this model to forecast theater attendance on Friday of the seventh week.

Week	Attendance
1	1165
2	1328
3	1290
4	1389
5	1436
6	1297

10. Using the data in problem 8, compute the forecasts that would have occurred in weeks 7–12 using (a) a simple moving average with $N = 2$, and (b) a simple moving average with $N = 5$. (c) For which model do the forecasts change more rapidly? Why does this make sense?

11. A company has collected sales data for the past nine months. Compute the forecasts that would have occurred in months 6–9 using simple exponential smoothing with a smoothing constant of (a) $\alpha = 0.3$ and (b) $\alpha = 0.1$. In each case, let the forecast for month 5 be $F_5 = 43.75$.

Month	1	2	3	4	5	6	7	8	9
Sales	48	42	47	38	37	44	52	44	51

12. The cost per standardized long distance phone call has been decreasing over time. Using the following data for the last 8 years: (a) use linear regression to compute an expression for cost as a linear function of time and (b) use that equation to predict the standardized cost for year 10.

Year	1	2	3	4	5	6	7	8
Standardized Cost	3.25	3.05	2.98	2.93	2.91	2.58	2.44	2.37

13. To plan staffing for the credit department, Jane Dinar, the department manager of a discount store, would like to predict the number of credit transactions the company will have to process next year. The number of credit card transactions processed has been increasing over time. Using the following data for the past 10 years: (a) compute the linear regression equation expressing the number of credit card transactions as a function of time, and (b) use that equation to predict the number of credit card transactions in each of the next two years.

Year	1	2	3	4	5	6	7	8	9	10
No. of Trans. (000)	32	36	39	40	47	46	49	55	52	58

14. The manager of the Burger Prince Restaurant would like to predict the demand for hamburger patties each day. She has collected data for three weeks.

	Week 1	Week 2	Week 3
Sunday	345	380	360
Monday	820	750	780
Tuesday	800	805	740
Wednesday	770	650	805
Thursday	690	745	790
Friday	620	660	580
Saturday	450	410	460

(a) Construct a constant process with multiplicative daily seasonality model using these data. Use the cumulative average to estimate the parameter a in the deseasonalized process. (b) Forecast the hamburger patty demand for Sunday, Monday, and Tuesday of week 4 using the model in part (a).

15. Wilson's Creek National Battlefield Park (WCNBP) evaluated its past attendance patterns and determined that during the summer months the number of visitors each day is approximately a quasi-constant process with multiplicative daily seasonality: Attendance $= a \times c_s + \varepsilon_t$. WCNBP uses a 10-day moving average of the *deseasonalized data* to estimate the parameter a. Below are the actual attendance values for the past 10 days. Suppose the seasonal factors for Sunday through Saturday are 1.39, 0.87, 0.74, 0.63, 0.81, 1.22, and 1.34, respectively. Forecast the attendance for Sunday and Monday of week 76. (Note: You must deseasonalize the data first to estimate the parameter a.)

Week	Day	Attendance
74	Thu	2581
74	Fri	3662
74	Sat	3909
75	Sun	4277
75	Mon	2748
75	Tue	2353
75	Wed	1997
75	Thu	2485
75	Fri	3642
75	Sat	4104

16. The National Museum of Art in London would like to predict attendance at the museum in order to schedule personnel and to purchase food and materials more cost effectively. The museum staff have collected the following quarterly attendance data for the past 12 quarters:

Year	1				2				3			
Quarter	1	2	3	4	1	2	3	4	1	2	3	4
Attendance (0000)	59	94	128	68	64	97	126	75	65	101	138	77

(a) Construct a linear trend model with multiplicative seasonality to predict future quarterly attendance.
(b) Use the model in part (a) to predict attendance for quarters 1 and 2 of year 4.

17. The University of Missouri–St. Louis has determined that its full-time equivalent enrollment each semester (fall, winter, summer) can be approximated by the following linear trend model with multiplicative seasonality:

$$(\text{Enrollment})_t = (8423 + 72t)\, c_s + \varepsilon_t$$

Assuming that the seasonal factors are 1.17, 1.08, and 0.75, forecast the university's enrollment for the fall, winter, and summer semesters of year 6 (i.e., $t =$ 16, 17, and 18, respectively).

18. Carbon Steel Corporation (CSC) believes that demand for its steel products is closely related to sales of automobiles in North America. CSC has collected quarterly data on automobile sales and its steel sales for the past three years.

Year	1				2				3			
Quarter	1	2	3	4	1	2	3	4	1	2	3	4
Auto Sales (00,000)	12	17	24	21	14	21	29	21	15	20	24	19
CSC Sales (0000 tons)	52	31	40	63	52	35	51	73	54	39	49	60

(a) Plot CSC's quarterly sales as a function of auto sales in the *previous* quarter. (b) Use linear regression to express CSC's quarterly sales as a linear function of auto sales in the previous quarter. (c) CSC expects auto sales for the first quarter of year 4 to be 1,400,000 vehicles. Use the equation in part (b) to predict CSC's sales in quarter 1 of year 4.

19. Ninja-Ninja, Inc., wants to forecast its quarterly sales. Ninja-Ninja believes that its sales in a quarter are a function of its total advertising expenditures in the *preceding two quarters combined*. (a) Use the following data for the past eight quarters to construct a forecasting model that expresses quarterly sales as a linear function of advertising expenditures in the previous two quarters combined. (b) Use the model in part (a) to forecast sales in quarter 1 of year 3.

Yr	Qt	Advertising Expenditures	Sales Volume
1	1	12	30
	2	10	32
	3	10	34
	4	14	29
2	1	15	37
	2	16	45
	3	15	46
	4	20	47

20. The St. Louis Police Department believes that auto thefts in a quarter are related to the number of autos sold in the preceding *year* (four quarters). They have the following data for the past two years:

Yr	Qt	Auto Sales (000)	Auto Thefts (00)
1	1	15	19
	2	17	18
	3	18	24
	4	19	20
2	1	18	29
	2	15	35
	3	16	34
	4	23	32

(a) Construct the least squares regression equation that expresses quarterly auto *thefts* as a linear function of *total* auto sales in the preceding *year* (four quarters combined). (b) Use the model in part (a) to forecast auto thefts in the first quarter of year 3.

21. Using the data from problem 13, forecast the number of credit card transactions for years 10 and 11 using Holt's method of double exponential smoothing. Use $\alpha = 0.2$ and $\beta = 0.1$, and let $I_9 = 50$ and $S_9 = 2.5$.

22. Using the data in problem 12, use Holt's double exponential smoothing method to forecast the cost per standardized call for years 8 and 9; let $\alpha = 0.25$ and $\beta = 0.2$, and let $I_7 = 2.40$ and $S_7 = -0.12$.

23.* Peete, Widget, and Wickell (PWW) is a local accounting firm specializing in small business accounting. Melvin Peete, managing partner of PWW, would like to predict the demand for PWW's services next year so that he can make hiring plans for new accountants. Melvin believes that PWW's demand is closely related to the number of new business licenses issued in the county. On the 15th of every month the county announces how many new business licenses were issued in the previous month. Melvin has combined the monthly data with PWW's billing hours for the past eight years.

Year	New Licenses	PWW Billing Hours
1987	247	44,000
1988	310	41,500
1989	325	52,200
1990	270	53,100
1991	235	48,700
1992	280	46,000
1993	350	52,000
1994	300	58,000

(a) Construct a model that expresses billing hours in a year as a linear function of new business licenses issued in that year. Does there appear to be a meaningful linear relationship? Forecast the billing hours for 1995. Is there a problem?

(b) William Widget noted that most small businesses do not consult accountants until their business has been open for 6–12 months. So he thinks that billing hours in a year are more likely related to the number of new business licenses issued in the previous year. Construct a linear model that expresses this relationship. Forecast the billing hours for 1995.

(c) Using the model in part (b), Melvin Peete would like to make a forecast for each year at the end of the preceding December. But on December 31 Melvin will only know the number of business licenses issued in the first 11 months of the year. What should he do in order to make an accurate forecast? (Note: He must make the forecast for the following year by December 31.)

CASE

Reynolds and Hill College: A Forecasting Case

The president of Reynolds and Hill College (RHC), a small liberal arts school, has decided that he needs more accurate forecasts of private contributions to the college to better plan its program development and budgeting. A primary source of contributions is alumni. In 1990 the college began to forecast annual alumni contributions using a linear trend model. Relevant data for the last 11 years and the forecasts using the linear trend model for the past 4 years are given in Table 4.26.

The college has been unhappy with the linear trend model because it has consistently underpredicted contributions. Although the college is happy to receive the extra contributions, it has not undertaken new programs in a timely manner because it did not expect to have the necessary resources. Brenda Farrell, the vice-president of budgeting, decided to construct a better method for forecasting.

To get a fair comparison of various models, she decided to act as if she had been using each model since 1990 and compare the errors that would have resulted using each model from 1991 to 1994. Only data that would have been available at the time of the forecast would be used to estimate model parameters and make forecasts.

Linear Trend Model

Brenda began her analysis by reviewing how the college obtained its forecasts for the past four years using the linear trend model. Using only the first seven years' worth of data, the least squares regression trend line was

$$\text{Alumni Contributions}_t = AC_t = 11.95 + 16.82t$$

where $t = 1$ corresponds to the year 1984. So the forecast for 1991 ($t = 8$) was

$$AC_8 = 11.95 + 16.82(8) = 146.51$$

The forecasts for the next three years were derived as follows (remember that for $t = 9$ the first eight years of data were used to estimate a and b; for $t = 10$ the first nine years of data were used; etc.):

$$AC_9 = 8.98 + 17.81(9) = 169.27$$
$$AC_{10} = 5.25 + 18.93(10) = 194.55$$
$$AC_{11} = 1.83 + 19.86\,(11) = 220.29$$

Growth Rate Model

By plotting the alumni contributions against time, Brenda saw that the upward trend was nonlinear, with the slope increasing over time; this explained why the linear trend model underpredicted. Brenda tried to construct a nonlinear trend model, but she found it hard to fit the data well. The forecasts were only slightly more accurate than those obtained with the linear trend model, and the nonlinear trend model did not provide any insight into the contribution process itself.

A simpler alternative was to construct a "growth rate" model in which the value of alumni contributions grew as a percentage of its previous value (i.e., alumni contributions increased by a constant *rate* not a constant *quantity*). This could be treated as a linear causal model in which the dependent variable was alumni contributions in year t and the independent variable was alumni contributions in year $t - 1$:

$$AC_t = a + bAC_{t-1}$$

In other words, AC_{t-1} was the independent variable X and AC_t was the dependent variable Y. Brenda paired observations so that the x_i values were the contributions in period $t - 1$ and the y_i values were the contributions in period t, as shown in Table 4.27. After each year, new estimates for the parameters a and b were computed, and thus new regression equations were constructed. The resulting regression equaltions and forecasts for 1991–1994 were as follows:

$$AC_7 = 5.43 + 1.16\,AC_6 = 163.67$$
$$AC_8 = 7.83 + 1.12\,AC_7 = 185.18$$
$$AC_9 = 6.94 + 1.13\,AC_8 = 217.23$$
$$AC_{10} = 8.29 + 1.11\,AC_9 = 243.05$$

The forecasts from this model were more accurate than those obtained from the linear trend model and exhibited no clear bias for overpredicting or underpredicting. In addition, the model was extremely simple and easy to use. However, Brenda was concerned that this model might not be able to predict the effects of slowly decreasing student enrollments and an aging population of alumni. Nor did the model give any insight into how to increase contributions.

Buildup of Linear Models

Brenda decided to construct a model that decomposed the alumni contributing process into more fundamental behavioral components. First, she asked, "What factors directly influence annual alumni contributions?" The two most obvious factors were (1) the number of alumni contributing, and (2) the average amount each alumnus con-

TABLE 4.26 ALUMNI CONTRIBUTIONS AND LINEAR TREND FORECASTS

Year	Number of Alumni Living	Number of Alumni Contributing	Amount Contributed by Alumni ($000)	Linear Trend Forecast	Error
1984	13,515	1419	36.90		
1985	13,811	1527	43.17		
1986	14,070	1695	59.10		
1987	14,361	1874	74.11		
1988	14,654	2061	91.88		
1989	15,002	2245	113.05		
1990	15,189	2459	136.41		
1991	15,470	2635	158.35	146.51	+11.84
1992	15,790	2841	186.10	169.27	+16.83
1993	16,101	3062	211.50	194.55	+16.95
1994	16,431	3280	248.75	220.29	+28.46

tributed. Total annual alumni contributions are by definition the product of these two quantities. If she could predict each of these quantities accurately, she might be able to get a more accurate overall model and obtain a better understanding of the underlying process, which might be helpful in other decision-making areas. (For example, should the college focus on getting more alumni to contribute or on getting currently contributing alumni to increase their contributions?)

The next step was to study the relevant data (see Table 4.28). For example, contributions per contributing alumnus (last column of the table) were increasing linearly over time. Thus, a linear trend model might be a good way to forecast this *component*. The number of contributing alumni was also increasing over time but not linearly. Brenda did not want to construct a nonlinear model to predict the number of contributing alumni each year, so she considered decomposing the process further. Specifically, the number of contributing alumni depends on two things: the *number of living alumni* in the pool of potential donors and the *fraction of alumni contributing*. Brenda found that the number of living alumni had been increasing at a relatively linear rate (of approximately 300 per year) and the fraction of alumni contributing was increasing linearly (at a rate of approximately 0.01 per year). So the nonlinear form for contributing alumni appeared to result from taking the product of two linearly increasing subcomponents. Therefore, she speculated that it would be easier to work with linear models of the subcomponents than with a nonlinear but more aggregate component: contributing alumni.

With this approach, Brenda constructed three simple linear trend models to forecast each component: (1) the number of living alumni, L_t; (2) the fraction of alumni who contribute, F_t; and (3) the average contribution per alumni contributor, C_t. The total annual alumni contributions would then be $AC_t = L_t \times F_t \times C_t$.

TABLE 4.27 FORECASTS OF ALUMNI CONTRIBUTIONS USING THE GROWTH RATE MODEL

Year	x_i Contributions in Year $t-1$	y_i Contributions in Year t	Forecast Causal Growth Model	Error
1985	36.90	43.17		
1986	43.17	59.10		
1987	59.10	74.11		
1988	74.11	91.88		
1989	91.88	113.05		
1990	113.05	136.41		
1991	136.41	158.35	163.67	−5.32
1992	158.35	186.10	185.18	+0.92
1993	186.10	211.50	217.23	−5.73
1994	211.50	248.75	243.05	+5.70

TABLE 4.28 DATA FOR BUILDUP MODEL

Year	t	L_t Number Living	Number Contributing	F_t Fraction Contributing	C_t Contribution per Contributor
1984	1	13,515	1419	0.105	26.00
1985	2	13,811	1527	0.111	28.27
1986	3	14,070	1695	0.120	34.87
1987	4	14,361	1874	0.130	39.55
1988	5	14,654	2061	0.141	44.58
1989	6	15,002	2245	0.150	50.36
1990	7	15,189	2459	0.162	54.81
1991	8	15,470	2635	0.170	60.09
1992	9	15,790	2841	0.180	65.51
1993	10	16,101	3062	0.190	69.08
1994	11	16,431	3280	0.200	75.84

Then, using equations (4.6) and (4.7), the linear trend models for living alumni, fraction contributing, and contribution per contributor, are as follows for 1991–94.

$$L_8 = 13{,}231 + 285.3t = 15{,}513$$
$$L_9 = 13{,}241 + 281.7t = 15{,}776$$
$$L_{10} = 13{,}238 + 282.6t = 16{,}064$$
$$L_{11} = 13{,}231 + 284.6t = 16{,}362$$

$$F_8 = 0.091 + 0.010t = 0.171$$
$$F_9 = 0.091 + 0.010t = 0.181$$
$$F_{10} = 0.091 + 0.010t = 0.191$$
$$F_{11} = 0.091 + 0.010t = 0.201$$ [11]

$$C_8 = 19.74 + 5.01t = 59.82$$
$$C_9 = 19.68 + 5.03t = 64.95$$
$$C_{10} = 19.54 + 5.07t = 70.24$$
$$C_{11} = 19.76 + 5.01t = 74.87$$

To obtain a forecast for alumni contributions in year t, we take the product of L_t, F_t, and C_t. The forecasts for AC_t and the resulting errors are given in Table 4.29.

$$AC_8 = 15{,}513 \times 0.171 \times 59.82 = 158{,}686$$
$$AC_9 = 15{,}776 \times 0.181 \times 64.95 = 185{,}462$$
$$AC_{10} = 16{,}064 \times 0.191 \times 70.24 = 215{,}512$$
$$AC_{11} = 16{,}362 \times 0.201 \times 74.87 = 246{,}230$$

This model is more accurate in its hypothetical forecasts than the linear growth model. In addition, it provides some insight into the reason alumni contributions have been growing in absolute amounts, but at a decreasing percentage rate. The number of alumni has been growing by approximately 300 each year (so the percentage growth rate of alumni is decreasing over time), the fraction of alumni contributing has been increasing by 0.01 each year, and the average contribution has been increasing by $5 per year.

Which model the college should use depends on various factors. Both the growth rate and buildup models are quite accurate; the difference in accuracy of a few thousand dollars each year is probably not crucial. The linear causal growth model is simpler because it involves only data for one variable, alumni contributions, and requires only one linear regression estimation each year. The buildup model is slightly more accurate, but it requires estimating three regression equations and doing more data collection and analysis. However, because the buildup model appears to represent the fundamental contribution process more precisely, if fundamental changes to the environment occurred, this model would probably be better able to predict the consequences. For example, if the number of living alumni is expected to de-

[11] The parameter estimates in these four equations change slightly each period, but not within the first three decimal places, so the models look identical.

TABLE 4.29 BUILDUP MODEL FORECASTS

Year	y_i Contributions in Year t	Buildup Model Forecasts	Error
1984	36.90		
1985	43.17		
1986	59.10		
1987	74.11		
1988	91.88		
1989	113.05		
1990	136.41		
1991	158.35	158.69	−0.34
1992	186.10	185.46	−0.36
1993	211.50	215.51	−4.01
1994	248.75	246.23	+2.52

crease due to more alumni reaching old age and dying or enrollments decreasing, the effect on contributions is likely to be predictable. In contrast, the linear causal model assumes that the general growth pattern will not change dramatically; all underlying relationships will stay approximately the same. Clearly, this assumption would be violated if the alumni pool stops growing. As a result, the linear causal model would consistently overpredict in future periods.

A second major advantage of the buildup model is the insight into the alumni contribution process that could be used for other decision making. For example, by understanding the different components affecting total contributions, the college might be better able to design and modify its fund-raising strategy. For example, suppose that in the past the college followed the policy of sending a letter each year to previous contributors asking them to increase their contribution by $10. This letter, and the stated increment, may explain why the average contribution has increased by a relatively constant dollar amount rather than by a percentage amount. The college might modify its solicitation letter. Also, as time passes, it will be harder to increase the fraction of alumni who contribute because this variable has a practical limit. Suppose it is extremely rare for a college to receive contributions from more than 25% of its alumni. The buildup model might then suggest that as this limit is reached, it might be more effective to transfer some fund-raising efforts from trying to increase the fraction of alumni contributing to increasing the donations from alumni already contributing.

QUESTIONS

1. Suppose the growth in the number of living alumni began to slow down. How should Brenda Farrell change her model/procedure for forecasting annual alumni contributions?
2. The nonlinear trend model $AC_t = 9.6t^{1.35}$ predicts contributions (in $000) from 1991 to 1994 almost as accurately as the buildup model described in the case. (The forecasts for the four years would be 159.02, 186.42, 214.92, and 244.43, with errors of −0.67, −0.32, −3.42, and +4.32.) What disadvantages might there be in using this model for forecasting during the next 5–10 years?
3. How might the alumni contribution process change during the next 5–10 years? How might the forecasting model be modified to accommodate these changes?

SELECTED READINGS

ARMSTRONG, J. SCOTT. "Forecasting by Extrapolation: Conclusions from Twenty-Five Years of Research," *Interfaces* 14, 1984, pp. 52–66.

ARMSTRONG, J. SCOTT. *Long-Range Forecasting: From Crystal Ball to Computer* (2nd ed.), Wiley, New York, 1985.

BOWERMAN, B. L. *Forecasting and Time Series* (3rd ed.), Duxbury, Belmont, CA, 1993.

BOX, G. E. P., et al. *Time Series Analysis, Forecasting, and Control* (3rd ed.), Prentice-Hall, Englewood Cliffs, NJ, 1994.

BROWN, R. G. *Smoothing, Forecasting, and Prediction of Discrete Time Series*, Prentice-Hall, Englewood Cliffs, NJ, 1962.

CHAMBERS, J. C., S. K. MULLICK, and D. D. SMITH, "How to Choose the Right Forecasting Technique," *Harvard Business Review*, Vol. 65, 1971, pp. 45–74.

DELURGIO, STEPHEN A., and CARL D. BHAME. *Forecasting Systems for Operations Management*, Business One Irwin, Homewood, Il, 1991.

DRAPER, N. R., and H. SMITH. *Applied Regression Analysis* (2nd ed.), Wiley, New York, 1981.

MAKRIDAKIS, S., S. C. WHEELWRIGHT, and V. E. MCGEE. *Forecasting: Methods and Applications* (2nd ed.), Wiley, New York, 1983.

MAKRIDAKIS, S., and R. L. WINKLER. "Averages of Forecasts," *Management Science*, Vol. 29, 1983, pp. 987–996.

MALABRE, ALFRED L., JR. "If One Economist Goofs, Will 46 Do Any Better? Robert Eggert Thinks So, and He May Be Right," *Wall Street Journal*, Apr. 6, 1983.

MURPHY, A. H., and H. DAAN. "Impacts of Feedback and Experience on the Quality of Subjective Probability Forecasts: Comparison of Results from the First and Second Years of the Zierikzee Experiment," *Monthly Weather Review*, Vol. 112, 1984, pp. 413–428.

SANDERS, NADA R., and KARL B. MANRODT. "Forecasting Practices in U.S. Corporations: Survey Results," *Interfaces*, Vol. 24, No. 2, 1994, pp. 92–100.

SMITH, BERNARD T. *Focus Forecasting: Computer Techniques for Inventory Control*, CBI Publishing, Boston, 1984.

TRIGG, D. W. "Monitoring a Forecasting System," *Operational Research Quarterly*, Vol. 15, 1964, pp. 271–274.

WINTERS, P. R. "Forecasting Sales by Exponentially Weighted Moving Averages," *Management Science*, Vol. 6, 1960, pp. 324–342.

TUTORIAL 1

OPTIMIZATION MODELS, LINEAR PROGRAMMING, AND HEURISTICS

T1.1 MATHEMATICAL MODELS AND OPERATIONS DECISION MAKING

T1.2 CONSTRAINED OPTIMIZATION MODELS

T1.3 ADVANTAGES AND PITFALLS OF USING OPTIMIZATION MODELS

T1.4 CHARACTERISTICS AND ASSUMPTIONS OF LINEAR PROGRAMMING MODELS

T1.5 FORMULATING LINEAR PROGRAMS
- Steps in Problem Formulation
- Feed Mix or Diet Problem
- Blending Problem
- Multiperiod Planning

T1.6 THE GEOMETRY OF LINEAR PROGRAMS
- Graphical Solution
- Multiple Optima, Infeasible Problems, and Unbounded Problems

T1.7 THE SIMPLEX ALGORITHM
- Preparing the Problem for Solution
- The Algebraic Foundations of the Algorithm
- The Initial Simplex Tableau
- The Simplex Pivot and the Second Tableau
- The Third Tableau
- The Fourth Tableau
- General Comments About the Algorithm

T1.8 USING ARTIFICIAL VARIABLES
- The Big-M Method
- The Two-Phase Method

T1.9 INFEASIBLE PROBLEMS, MULTIPLE OPTIMA, UNBOUNDEDNESS, AND DEGENERACY

T1.10 COMPUTER SOLUTION OF LINEAR PROGRAMS
- Problem Input
- Computer Output
- Sensitivity Analysis

T1.11 USING LINEAR PROGRAMMING MODELS FOR DECISION MAKING
- Healthy Pet Food Revisited
- Solar Oil Company Revisited: Updating Production Decisions

T1.12 INTEGER AND MIXED-INTEGER PROGRAMS

T1.13 HEURISTIC METHODS IN OPERATIONS
- Characteristics
- Advantages of Heuristics

T1.1 MATHEMATICAL MODELS AND OPERATIONS DECISION MAKING

Advances in business and engineering research and computer technology have greatly expanded managers' use of analytical tools in operations decision making. The use of mathematical models has become especially wide-spread. A **model** is a representation of reality that captures the essential features of an object, system, or problem without being cluttered by unimportant details. Most of us are familiar with models; we have all seen plastic or wood models of airplanes, buildings, or the earth (a globe). In these types of models, the plastic or wood is said to be the "medium" of the model because the representation is embodied or contained in the medium. For the models in this tutorial the medium is mathematics; that is, we represent the important aspects of a system or problem in mathematical form using variables, parameters, and functions. By analyzing and manipulating the model, we can learn how the real system will behave under various conditions, and we can determine the best system design or action to take to achieve our goals.

Using mathematical models is cheaper, faster, and safer than constructing and manipulating a real system. For example, suppose we wanted to determine what mixture of recycled scrap paper should be used to produce some type of paperboard at minimum cost. One approach is to experiment with a few combinations, check to see if the quality is acceptable, and then perform a separate cost computation. Because not all combinations are checked, the optimum combination will probably not be found. Alternatively, we can use the types of models presented in this tutorial to evaluate all possible mixtures (an infinite number actually) to find the one that satisfies the product specifications at the lowest cost. This can be done more quickly and inexpensively than using the trial-and-error approach.

Many problems in operations management, such as the location of facilities, routing and scheduling of vehicles, scheduling of personnel, machines, and jobs, and the management of inventories, can be structured as constrained optimization models. **Constrained optimization models** are mathematical models designed to find the best solution with respect to some evaluation criterion from a set of alternative solutions, which are defined by a set of mathematical constraints—mathematical inequalities or equalities. There are several types of constrained optimization models, but *linear programs* are especially popular because many real problems satisfy the model assumptions, and methods exist that find the best solution relatively easily. Consequently most of this tutorial is devoted to linear programs. The use of *integer programs* for operations management has been increasing rapidly, so these are briefly discussed as well. Some P/OM problems that can be structured as optimization problems cannot be solved efficiently to obtain the optimal solution. In these cases empirically tested rules of thumb, called *heuristics*, are used to find good though not necessarily optimum solutions. Heuristics are briefly presented here and used throughout the book.

T1.2 CONSTRAINED OPTIMIZATION MODELS

Constrained optimization models contain three major components: decision variables, an objective function, and constraints.

1. ***Decision Variables.*** **Decision variables** are physical quantities controlled by the decision maker that are represented by mathematical symbols. For example, the decision variable x_j might represent the number of pounds of product j that a company will produce during some month. Decision variables can take on any of a set of possible values (hence the name *variable*); however, the decision maker's goal is to find the best values for them. Selecting the best numerical values for the variables is what constitutes making a decision or solving the model.
2. ***Objective Function.*** The **objective function** defines the criterion for evaluating the goodness or badness of a solution. Specifically, it is a mathematical function of the decision variables that converts a **solution** (defined as a set of numerical values for the decision variables) into a numerical evaluation of that solution. For example, the objective function may measure the profit or cost that occurs as a function of the amounts of various products produced (variables). The objective function must also specify a direction of optimization, either to maximize or minimize, to indicate whether the function is measuring something desirable (profit) or undesirable (cost). Other possible objectives might be to maximize utility, minimize the number of student bus-miles traveled, minimize the average waiting time of customers, or maximize the probability that a system functions correctly. For many real-life problems, several criteria could be used to evaluate alternatives. The objective function states which one the decision maker wishes to use. An optimal solution *for the model* is then the best solution *as measured by that criterion*; the solution is not necessarily optimal in a universal sense.

3. ***Constraints.*** The **constraints** are a set of functional equalities or inequalities that represent physical, economic, technological, legal, ethical, or other restrictions on what numerical values can be assigned to the decision variables. The constraints might ensure that no more input is used than that which is available, or they might ensure that no more pollution is generated in some period of time than is allowed by law. The constraints can also be used for definitional or "conservation of mass" purposes, such as defining the number of employees at the start of period $t + 1$ as equal to the number of employees at the start of period t, plus those added during period t, minus those leaving the organization during period t. Thus, in constrained optimization models we want to find the values for the decision variables that maximize or minimize an objective function but that also satisfy all constraints.

The objective function and the constraints contain numerical constants. These constants, which may represent prices, demands, technological coefficients, or limits on resources, describe the assumed environment for the model; they are called parameters or coefficients. The values of the parameters are fixed as part of the model, whereas the values taken on by the decision variables are controllable by the decision maker and determined by solving the model.

The following example illustrates how an operational problem can be represented and analyzed using a constrained optimization model.

EXAMPLE 1

The Healthy Pet Food Company manufactures two types of dog food: Meaties and Yummies. Each package of Meaties contains 2 pounds of cereal and 3 pounds of meat; each package of Yummies contains 3 pounds of cereal and 1.5 pounds of meat. Healthy believes it can sell as much of each dog food as it can make at the following prices: \$2.80 per package for Meaties and \$2.00 per package for Yummies. Healthy's production is limited, however, in several ways. First, Healthy can buy only up to 400,000 pounds of cereal each month at \$0.20 per pound, and it can buy only up to 300,000 pounds of meat each month at \$0.50 per pound. In addition, a special piece of machinery is required to make Meaties, and this machine has a capacity of 90,000 packages per month (there is no comparable limit on Yummies). The variable cost of blending and packing the dog food is \$0.25 per package for Meaties and \$0.20 per package for Yummies. This information is summarized in Table T1.1.

Suppose you are the manager of the Dogfood Division of the Healthy Pet Food Company. Your salary is based on the profit of the division, so you have an incentive to maximize its profit. How should you operate the division to maximize its profit and your salary?

The Decision Variables We first have to identify those things over which we have control: the decision variables. In this problem we have direct control over two quantities:

1. The number of packages of Meaties to make each month.
2. The number of packages of Yummies to make each month.

TABLE T1.1 HEALTHY PET FOOD DATA

	Meaties	Yummies
Sale price per package	\$2.80	\$2.00
Raw materials per package		
Cereal	2.0 lb	3.0 lb
Meat	3.0 lb	1.5 lb
Variable cost—blending and packing	\$0.25/pack	\$0.20/pack

	Cost /lb	Available/month
Cereal	\$0.20	400,000 lb
Meat	\$0.50	300,000 lb
Production capacity for Meaties		90,000 packs/month

Within the model these two quantities will appear repeatedly, so we would like to represent them in a simple fashion; we will designate these variables by the symbols M and Y:

M = number of packages of Meaties to make each month
Y = number of packages of Yummies to make each month

Notice that the amount of meat to use each month and the amount of cereal to use each month are not good choices for the variables. First, we control these only indirectly through our choice of M and Y. More important, using these as variables could lead to ambiguous production plans. If we determined how much cereal and meat to use in production, this would not tell us *how* to use it—how much of each dog food to make. In contrast, once we have determined the values for M and Y, we know exactly what to produce and how much meat and cereal will be used.

The Objective Function Any pair of numerical values for the variables M and Y constitutes a production plan. For example, $M = 10{,}000$ and $Y = 20{,}000$ means that we should make 10,000 packages of Meaties and 20,000 packages of Yummies each month. But how do we know whether or not this is a good production plan? To determine this, we need to specify a criterion for evaluation—an objective function. The most appropriate objective function is to maximize monthly profit (actually, the contribution to profit; fixed costs are ignored because any plan that maximizes revenue minus variable costs will maximize profit as well). The profit earned by Healthy is a direct function of the amount of each dogfood made and sold, the decision variables. Monthly profit, designated as z, can be written as follows:

z = (profit per pack of Meaties) × (number of packs of Meaties made and sold per month)
+ (profit per pack of Yummies) × (number of packs of Yummies made and sold per month)

The profit per package for each dogfood can be computed as follows:

		Meaties	Yummies
	Selling price	\$2.80	\$2.00
Minus			
	Meat	\$1.50	\$0.75
	Cereal	\$0.40	\$0.60
	Blending and packing	\$0.25	\$0.20
	Profit per package	\$0.65	\$0.45

We can then write monthly profit as

$$z = 0.65\,M + 0.45\,Y$$

The Constraints If we want to make z as large as possible, why do we not just make M and Y equal to infinity and earn an infinite profit? The reason is that there are limits on the availability of meat and cereal and on production capacity for Meaties. (In reality there is also a limit on demand, but we are ignoring that here for simplicity. The issue of demand is discussed in Section T1.11.) We want to maximize z, but subject to satisfying the stated *constraints*. To solve the problem, we need to express these constraints in the form of mathematical equalities or inequalities containing the decision variables.

We begin with the constraint on the availability of cereal:

(The number of lb. of cereal used in production each month) $\leq$ 400,000 lb.

The left-hand side (l.h.s.) of the constraint is directly determined by the number of packages of Meaties and Yummies made. Specifically, the l.h.s. is

(lb. of cereal per pack of Meaties) × (packs of Meaties made and sold per month)
+ (lb. of cereal per pack of Yummies) × (packs of Yummies made and sold per month)

Substituting the cereal content for each product and the decision variables into this expression, we can write the constraint as

$$2\,M + 3\,Y \leq 400{,}000$$

Using similar reasoning, the restriction on the availability of meat can be expressed as

$$3\,M + 1.5\,Y \leq 300{,}000$$

In addition to these constraints, the number of packages of Meaties produced each month cannot exceed 90,000; that is,

$$M \leq 90{,}000$$

Finally, negative production levels do not make sense, so we require that $M \geq 0$ and $Y \geq 0$. Putting all these pieces together gives the following constrained optimization model:

$$\begin{aligned} \text{Maximize } z = \$0.65\,M + \$0.45\,Y & \\ \text{Subject to} \quad 2\,M + 3\,Y &\leq 400{,}000 \\ 3\,M + 1.5\,Y &\leq 300{,}000 \\ M &\leq 90{,}000 \\ M, Y &\geq 0 \end{aligned}$$

This type of model is called a **linear programming model** or a **linear program** because the objective function is linear and the functions in all the constraints (the left-hand sides) are linear.[1] Linear programs can be solved easily using methods discussed later in this tutorial. The optimum for the Healthy Pet Food problem is $M = 50{,}000$, $Y = 100{,}000$, and $z = \$77{,}500$; that is, Healthy should make 50,000 packages of Meaties and 100,000 packages of Yummies each month, and it will earn a monthly profit of $77,500. Before discussing the characteristics and uses of linear programs in detail, we consider the advantages and disadvantages of optimization models in general.

TI.3 ADVANTAGES AND PITFALLS OF USING OPTIMIZATION MODELS

It is reasonable to ask what we gain from using optimization models. The main benefit is that they allow us to evaluate possible solutions in a quick, safe, and inexpensive way without actually constructing and experimenting with them. Optimization models also provide the following additional benefits.

1. ***Structures the thought process.*** Constructing an optimization model of a problem forces a decision maker to think through the problem in a concise, organized fashion. For example, to construct a constrained optimization model, the decision maker must determine what factors he or she controls, that is, what are the decision variables. Then the decision maker needs to specify precisely how the possible solutions will be evaluated, that is, what criteria will be used in the evaluation. Finally, the decision maker must describe the decision environment; this includes any political, legal, technological, or financial restrictions on actions, as well as estimates of (future) prices, demands, and availabilities. Many decision makers find that formulating such a model (sometimes with the help of an analyst) is so informative in itself that either the best action to take becomes obvious or the set of feasible actions is reduced to a manageable number. Thus, modeling acts as a way of organizing and clarifying.
2. ***Increases objectivity.*** Mathematical models make the decision process more objective in the sense that our assumptions and criteria are clearly specified. Al-

[1] A linear function is one made up of a sum of terms that have the form of a constant times a variable (the constants can be zero or negative). No variable is raised to a power other than 1, such as x_1^2; no variables multiply or divide each other, such as x_1/x_3; and no nonlinear transformations of the variables occurs, such as $\log x_1$.

though models reflect the experiences and biases of those who construct them, these biases can be identified by an outside observer. Explicit use of a model can sometimes help to resolve disagreements and obtain agreement on a solution. By using a model as a point of reference, the parties can focus their discussion and disagreements on its assumptions and components. Once the model is agreed on, people tend to be more willing to live by the results.

3. ***Makes complex problems more tractable.*** Many of the most important and interesting problems in managing an organization are large and complex and deal with subtle, but significant, interrelationships among organizational units. Without a model, the human mind is simply unable to grasp and evaluate all the important aspects of the problem effectively. For example, in determining the optimal amounts of various products to ship from spatially dispersed warehouses to spatially dispersed customers and the routes that should be taken, the human mind cannot make the billions of simultaneous trade-offs that are necessary, so the decision maker normally resorts to simple rules of thumb, which in some cases can be far from optimal. Similarly, actions of one part of the organization (the scheduling or staffing of a loading dock) can affect the performance of other units (the transportation department). Unless these interrelationships are appropriately captured, the actions selected may be optimal for the individual units but suboptimal for the organization as a whole. Optimization models make it easier to solve complex organizationwide decisions.
4. ***Makes problems amenable to mathematical and computer solution.*** By representing a real problem in the form of a mathematical model, we can often take advantage of mathematical solution and analysis techniques and computers in a way that would not otherwise be possible. Algorithms developed and refined over the past 45 years use the power of both applied mathematics and computers to solve problems that have been formulated as optimization models.
5. ***Facilitates "what if" analysis.*** Mathematical models not only make it relatively easy to find the optimal solution for a specific model and scenario, they make "what if" analysis both orderly and convenient. With "what if" analysis we recognize that the prices, demands, and product availabilities assumed in constructing the model are simply forecasts and may not be realized in practice. Therefore, we also want to know how the optimal solution would change as the values of these parameters vary from the originally assumed values; that is, we want to know how sensitive the optimal solution is to the assumptions of the model. (For this reason, "what if" analysis is also called *sensitivity or parametric analysis.*) With optimization models we can add, delete or modify constraints, and modify or completely change the objective function, and determine the new optimum quickly, sometimes even without re-solving the model.

Pitfalls In spite of their many advantages, mathematical models are not a panacea. They contain pitfalls, and poor decisions can result from their use. By their nature, mathematical models tend to be complex. Consequently, inexperienced modelers will often mismodel the real problem: important decision variables or relationships may be omitted or the model or methodology may be inappropriate for the situation. The actual formulation or construction of the model is the most crucial step of the process: *the optimal solution to the wrong problem is of no value!*

A second pitfall is failure to understand the role of modeling in the decision-making process. The optimal solution for a model is not necessarily the optimal solution for the real problem underlying the model. Mathematical models are tools that can help make a good decision; however, they are not the only factor that should go into making the final decision. In some situations the real-world problem is so well structured and the criterion for evaluating the goodness of possible solutions is so clear that the optimal solution for the model representing the problem can be directly implemented as the solution for the problem itself, sometimes without human intervention. For example, inventory control, product shipping, and production scheduling problems are often so well defined that relevant data can be put into a computer-based model and purchase orders, shipping schedules, shipping routes, and production schedules can be generated and implemented without human intervention. However, for many other problems, mathematical models are intended only to capture part of the problem. The model may evaluate the solutions only with respect to one or a few quantifiable criteria; nonquantifiable criteria or other nonquantifiable factors may be omitted and need to be treated separately.

One way to protect against the misuse of mathematical models is to perform a full diagnostic check of the model before it is implemented. This check may include a trial period of operation in which the analyst solves the model under a variety of assumed decision environments and checks the solutions for their reasonableness. If the model represents an existing system, it is often possible to compare the solutions from the model with those obtained without the model.

The bottom line for evaluating a model is whether or not it helps a decision maker identify and implement solutions that are better than those that would have been obtained and implemented without the model. Further, the model should increase the decision maker's confidence in the decision and the willingness to implement it.

T1.4 CHARACTERISTICS AND ASSUMPTIONS OF LINEAR PROGRAMMING MODELS

Linear programs are constrained optimization models that satisfy three requirements:

1. The decision variables must be continuous; they can take on any value (including fractional values) within some restricted range.
2. The objective function must be a linear function.
3. The left-hand sides of the constraints must be linear functions.

Thus, linear programs can be written in the following form:

$$\text{Maximize or minimize } z = c_1x_1 + c_2x_2 + \ldots + c_nx_n$$

$$\begin{aligned}
\text{Subject to} \quad & a_{11}x_1 + a_{12}x_2 + \ldots + a_{1n}x_n \;\begin{smallmatrix}\le\\=\\\ge\end{smallmatrix}\; b_1 \\
& a_{21}x_1 + a_{22}x_2 + \ldots + a_{2n}x_n \;\begin{smallmatrix}\le\\=\\\ge\end{smallmatrix}\; b_2 \\
& \qquad \vdots \\
& a_{m1}x_1 + a_{m2}x_2 + \ldots + a_{mn}x_n \;\begin{smallmatrix}\le\\=\\\ge\end{smallmatrix}\; b_m
\end{aligned}$$

where the x_j values are decision variables and the c_j, a_{ij}, and b_i values are constants, called **parameters** or **coefficients**, that are given or specified by the problem assumptions. In addition, most linear programs also have the requirement that all the decision variables be nonnegative.

Linear programs implicitly assume that certain properties of the underlying problem hold. Before delving into linear programming in detail, let us summarize these implicit assumptions.

1. ***Proportionality.*** With linear programs we assume that the contribution of individual variables in the objective function and constraints is proportional to their value. That is, if we double the value of a variable, we double the contribution *of that variable* to the objective function and each constraint in which the variable appears; the contribution *per unit* of the variable is constant. For example, suppose the variable x_j is the number of units of product j produced and c_j is the cost per unit to produce product j. If doubling the amount of product j produced doubles its cost, the per unit cost is constant and the proportionality assumption is satisfied. If the cost per unit decreases as output increases (as in the case of economies of scale), then the proportionality assumption is violated.
2. ***Additivity.*** Additivity means that the total value of the objective function and each constraint function can be obtained by adding up the individual contributions from each variable; *there are no additional synergistic or antisynergistic* effects. Synergistic or antisynergistic relationships are not especially common, but in those cases where they do occur, they can be important and must be identified or a highly inappropriate model (and solution) could result.
3. ***Divisibility.*** The decision variables in linear programs are allowed to take on any real numerical values within some range specified by the constraints. This assumption means the variables are not restricted to taking on integer values. In most problems this assumption is not very restrictive; either the model solution can be rounded off without significant loss of quality in the solution or the variables make sense as fractional values. For example, if a variable represents the number of automobiles assembled per hour, then a variable value of 34.25 per hour means that the units should be produced at a *rate* of one every (60/34.25) = 1.75 minutes. When fractional values would *not* make a sensible solution, such as the number of flights an airline should have each day between two cities, the problem should be formulated and solved as an integer program where integrality is handled explicitly. This type of problem is discussed in Section T1.12.
4. ***Certainty.*** The assumption of certainty is not a restriction but rather a warning about the interpretation of the solution. We assume that the parameter values in the model are known with certainty or are at least treated that way. The optimal solution we obtain is optimal for the specific problem we formulated. If the parameter values turn out to be wrong, then the resulting solution may in fact not be optimal at all.

   But normally we do not know the values of these parameters with certainty; they may represent forecasts of future prices, demands, or supplies. In fact, identifying the effects of such uncertainty is one of the main benefits of using linear programming models. We can easily modify and re-solve our model to determine how sensitive the optimum is to our assumptions.

In practice, the assumptions of proportionality and additivity require the greatest care and are most likely to be unwittingly violated by the modeler. With experience, we should be able to recognize when integrality of the variables is essential and must be modeled explicitly.

T1.5 FORMULATING LINEAR PROGRAMS

This section presents simple examples of real managerial problems that can be formulated as linear programs. (How to solve and interpret the solutions will be discussed later.) Each example has a name describing the type of problem, but in real life, problems are seldom as pure and clean as these examples. Therefore, we recommend against trying to memorize and match the problems illustrated here with real problems you may encounter. In practice, problems may contain a mixture of features from several of the categories illustrated here. You should focus on why and how various physical relationships can be best represented in model form.

Model formulation is the most important and usually the most difficult aspect of solving a real problem. Solving a model that does not accurately represent the real problem is useless. There is no simple way to formulate optimization problems, but the following suggestions obtained from years of actual experience may help.

STEPS IN PROBLEM FORMULATION

1. ***Identify and define the decision variables for the problem.*** Sometimes it is difficult to specify exactly what the decision maker controls. One trick that can help is to assume that the decision maker is going to leave town for a year and must leave the *implementation of the solution* to an assistant. The decision variables are those quantities that the decision maker would have to tell the assistant so that the solution could be implemented without ambiguity and without requiring the assistant to make any decision.

   It is important to define the variables completely and precisely. All units of measure need to be stated explicitly, including time units if appropriate. For example, if the variables represent quantities of a product to be produced, these should be defined in terms of tons per hour, units per day, barrels per month, or some other appropriate units. The more complete and precise the definitions of the variables, the easier it is to formulate the rest of the model.

2. ***Define the objective function.*** That is, determine the criterion for evaluating alternative solutions. The objective function will normally be the sum of terms made up of a variable multiplied by some appropriate coefficient (parameter). For example, the coefficients might be profit per unit of production, distance traveled per unit transported, or cost per person hired. If the decision variables are well defined and the objective function can be stated in words precisely, it is usually easy to determine the appropriate coefficients for the variables in the objective function.

3. ***Identify and express mathematically all of the relevant constraints.*** It is often beneficial to express each constraint in words before trying to put it into mathematical form. The written constraint can then be decomposed into its fundamental components, again in words. It is then easy to substitute the appropriate numerical coefficients and variable names for the written terms. A common mistake is to use variables in the constraints that have not been defined in the problem. This is not valid, and this mistake is frequently caused by not defining the original variables precisely enough. The formulation process is iterative, however, and sometimes, while writing the objective function or constraints, we may recognize the need to define additional variables or redefine some existing variables. This is perfectly acceptable as long as all the variables used in the objective and constraint functions have been defined and "tied together" where needed. For example, if one of the variables is the total production of the company and five other variables represent the production at the company's five plants, then there must be a constraint that forces total production to equal the sum of the production at the plants.

We now illustrate the formulation process for typical operations problems.

FEED MIX OR DIET PROBLEM

One of the first problems ever solved using linear programming is the **feed mix problem**, which is illustrated below.

EXAMPLE 2

International Wool Company operates a large farm on which sheep are raised. The manager of the farm has determined that for the sheep to grow in the desired fashion, they should receive at least minimum amounts of four nutrients (the nutrients are nontoxic, so the sheep can consume more than the minimum without harm). The manager is considering three different grains to feed

TABLE T1.2 INTERNATIONAL WOOL DATA

		Grain			Minimum
		1	2	3	Daily Req.
Nutrient	A	20	30	70	110
	B	10	10	0	18
	C	50	30	0	90
	D	6	2.5	10	14
Cost (¢/lb)		41	36	96	

the sheep. Table T1.2 lists the number of units of each nutrient in each pound of grain, along with the minimum daily requirements of each nutrient for each sheep and the cost of each grain. The manager believes that as long as a sheep receives the minimum daily amount of each nutrient, it will be healthy and will produce a standard amount of wool. The manager also wishes to raise the sheep at minimum cost.

The quantities that the manager controls are the amounts of each grain to feed each sheep per day. So we define

x_j = No. of lb of grain j (= 1, 2, 3) to feed each sheep per day

Notice that the units of measure are completely specified. In addition, the variables are expressed on a per sheep basis; if we minimize the cost per sheep, we minimize the cost for any group of sheep.

The daily feed cost per sheep will be the sum of the terms:

(cost/lb of grain j) × (lb. of grain j fed to each sheep per day)

That is, the objective function is to

$$\text{Minimize } z = 41\,x_1 + 36\,x_2 + 96\,x_3$$

Why cannot the manager simply make all the variables equal to zero? This would keep costs at zero, but he would have a flock of dead sheep. In other words, there are minimum nutrient constraints that must be satisfied. The values of the variables must be chosen so that

No. of units of nutrient A consumed each day by each sheep ≥ 110.

Expressing this in terms of the variables yields

$$20\,x_1 + 30\,x_2 + 70\,x_3 \geq 110$$

The constraints for the other nutrients are then

$$\begin{aligned} 10\,x_1 + 10\,x_2 \quad & \geq 18 \\ 50\,x_1 + 30\,x_2 \quad & \geq 90 \\ 6\,x_1 + 2.5\,x_2 + 10\,x_3 & \geq 14, \end{aligned}$$

and finally

$$\text{all } x_j\text{'s} \geq 0$$

The optimal solution to this problem (obtained using a computer package) is $x_1 = 0.595$, $x_2 = 2.008$, $x_3 = 0.541$, and $z = 148.6$ cents.

It is common practice to take a model initially utilized for one application and apply it to other situations. Many models in the physical and life sciences have been applied to problems in the social sciences. The feed mix problem is a good example of a case where one might use the same basic structure of a model in different applications. For example, a golf course manager can use it to select the best mix of fertilizers to provide the grass with the desired amounts of active chemicals (nitrogen, phosphorus, potash). The manager's problem is structurally the same as that faced by the manager of International Wool.

Although the basic structure of one model may be appropriate for another application, frequently the model needs to be modified to accommodate the unique features of the new situation. For example, suppose the U.S. Army decided to use the feed mix model to select a cost-minimizing diet for its soldiers that satisfies minimum nutritional requirements. The basic feed mix problem makes several subtle assumptions that do not necessarily hold for humans. First, issues of taste have been ignored; we assumed that the sheep will eat whatever grain mixture we feed them. Humans, however, have varying tastes that must be considered; some foods may not taste good together in the same meal. Second, not all soldiers are of the same size or have the same appetite. Third, the basic feed mix model is a static model: the optimal feed mix today is the same as that of tomorrow and the next 500 days unless relative prices or some other parameters change. We do not want to feed people the same meal day after day. Most of these modifications can be incorporated into a new form of the feed mix model. For example, a 28-day menu cycle could be constructed where x_{ij} could be the amount of food i eaten on day j of the cycle. Then constraints could restrict how much of or how often certain foods could be eaten. The resulting model is a more complex optimization model that includes integer variables, but it will be more useful because it better represents reality.

BLENDING PROBLEM

In the Healthy Pet Food example, called a **product mix problem**, the company was trying to determine *how much* of various products to make. The mixture of *inputs* used in each product was fixed. In many industries such as the oil, chemical, paper, metals, and food processing industries, a company controls not only how much of a product to make but also the mix of inputs to use in making it; this problem is called a **blending problem**.

EXAMPLE 3

Solar Oil Company is a gasoline refiner and wholesaler. It sells two products to gas stations: regular and premium gasoline. It makes these two final products by blending together four raw gasolines and adding some chemical additives (the amount and cost of the additives per barrel are assumed to be independent of the mixture). Each gasoline has an octane rating that reflects its energy content. Table T1.3 lists the octane, purchase price per barrel, and availability at that price per day. This table also gives the required minimum octane for each final gasoline, the net selling price per barrel (removing the cost of the additives), and the expected daily demand for gas at that price (Solar can sell all the gas it produces up to that amount).

The blending of gasoline is approximately a linear operation in terms of volume and octane: if x barrels of 80 octane gasoline are blended with y barrels of 90 octane gasoline, this will produce $x + y$ barrels of gasoline with an octane of $[80\,x + 90\,y] / [x + y]$. In other words, there is no

TABLE T1.3 SOLAR OIL DATA

		Octane	Cost ($/b)	Avail./Day
Raw gasolines	1	86	17.00	20,000
	2	88	18.00	15,000
	3	92	20.50	15,000
	4	96	23.00	10,000
		Octane	Price ($/b)	Max. demand/day
Products	Regular	89	19.50	35,000
	Premium	93	22.00	23,000

significant volume gain or loss, and the octane of the mixture is a weighted average of the octanes of the inputs.

The manager of Solar Oil's operation is interested in maximizing the company's profit. The first question is, what quantities does the manager control? What can the manager manipulate to influence profit? It would be incomplete simply to say that the manager controls the amount of each final gasoline to make. The manager controls, and must determine, *how* to make each final gas and *how much* to make. This can be expressed by letting

x_{ij} = No. of barrels of raw gas i (=1, . . . , 4) used per day to make final gas j (= R, P)

be the decision variables.

Each barrel of raw gas i that is blended into final gas j and then sold generates a profit equal to its selling price minus its cost. The objective function is the sum of all terms of the form

(profit per barrel of raw gas i blended into gas j) × (No. of barrels of raw gas i blended into gas j per day)

Substituting for these gives

$$\text{Maximize } z = 2.5\,x_{1R} + 1.5\,x_{2R} - x_{3R} - 3.5\,x_{4R} + 5.0\,x_{1P} + 4.0\,x_{2P} + 1.5\,x_{3P} - x_{4P}$$

Notice that the coefficients for some of the variables are negative; for example, Solar loses $1.00 on each barrel of raw gas 4 that is blended into premium. Does this imply that the optimal value for these variables must be zero and that they can be dropped from the problem? No! In blending operations, it is common for some low-cost materials to be combined with high-cost materials. Although it appears that we are losing money on the high-cost materials, they make the low-cost materials more valuable, and in most cases the final product cannot be made without them. For example, tungsten steel combines low-cost iron ore or scrap (worth $100/ton) with tungsten (costing thousands of dollars per ton) to make steel that might sell for $500 per ton. The manufacturer loses money on the tungsten (on a per ton basis) but is more than compensated by the enhanced value of the iron ore. Therefore, we should not omit variables from the problem unless we can prove without doubt, in advance, that their optimum values will be zero. It is safer to leave the variables in the problem; if their optimal value is zero, this will be determined when the problem is solved.

The next step is to identify the constraints. The availability constraint for each raw gasoline is

barrels of raw gas i used/day $\leq$ barrels of raw gas i available/day

The number of barrels of raw gas i used each day is the amount used to make regular gasoline x_{iR} plus the amount used each day to make premium gasoline x_{iP}. The availability constraints can then be written as follows:

$$x_{1R} + x_{1P} \leq 20{,}000$$
$$x_{2R} + x_{2P} \leq 15{,}000$$
$$x_{3R} + x_{3P} \leq 15{,}000$$
$$x_{4R} + x_{4P} \leq 10{,}000$$

The demand constraints put an upper limit on how much regular and premium gasoline can be sold. The total amount made of each is the sum of the raw gasolines allocated to making each gasoline each day. In other words,

$$x_{1R} + x_{2R} + x_{3R} + x_{4R} \leq 35{,}000$$
$$x_{1P} + x_{2P} + x_{3P} + x_{4P} \leq 23{,}000$$

If the model formulation were left at this stage, the optimal solution would be to mix the lowest-cost gasolines into the final products, regardless of octane. Therefore, we need to include constraints that guarantee that the variables will take on values that produce final gasolines with at least the minimum specified octane ratings. The octane rating of the regular gasoline that is produced will be a weighted average of the octanes of the raw gasolines used to make regular; that is,

octane of regular = [86(barrels of raw gas 1 used/day to make regular)
+ 88(barrels of raw gas 2 used/day to make regular)
+ . . . + 96(barrels of raw gas 4 used/day to make regular)]
/[total barrels of raw gases blended into regular gas/day]

which should be at least 89. Substituting the appropriate variable names for these quantities produces the constraint

$$[86\ x_{1R} + 88\ x_{2R} + 92\ x_{3R} + 96\ x_{4R}] / [x_{1R} + x_{2R} + x_{3R} + x_{4R}] \geq 89$$

Multiplying both sides by $(x_{1R} + \ldots + x_{4R})$ and then gathering terms so that variables appear only once and all are on the left-hand side yields

$$-3\ x_{1R} - x_{2R} + 3\ x_{3R} + 7\ x_{4R} \geq 0$$

Using the same approach to guarantee an octane of 93 for premium gas produces the constraint

$$-7\ x_{1P} - 5\ x_{2P} - x_{3P} + 3\ x_{4P} \geq 0$$

Finally, all variables should be nonnegative in value.

The optimal solution to this linear program is $x_{1R} = 11{,}428.57$, $x_{2R} = 9107.14$, $x_{3R} = 14{,}464.29$, $x_{4R} = 0$, $x_{1P} = 0$, $x_{2P} = 5892.86$, $x_{3P} = 535.71$, $x_{4P} = 10{,}000$, and $z = \$42{,}142.86$/day.

In this example, fractional amounts of raw gasoline input are perfectly reasonable; fluids can be finely measured, and the solution represents a flow *rate*. However, even for a simple problem of this sort, the optimal solution is far from obvious even to an intelligent production manager or petroleum engineer. With linear programming the daily profit might be 3–5% better than that achieved using an intelligent seat-of-the-pants approach. A 3% savings represents approximately \$350,000 to \$400,000 per year—not bad for using a simple model. Furthermore, as raw material prices change, which may happen almost daily, the optimal blend and output levels can be quickly revised.

MULTIPERIOD PLANNING

Linear programming is used extensively for planning and scheduling of operations. One important form of planning is called **aggregate planning**, which concentrates on scheduling production, personnel, and inventory levels during intermediate-term planning horizons such as 3–12 months. The following example is a simple version of this type of planning; Chapter 12 provides a more extensive presentation.

EXAMPLE 4

Basel Tool and Die Company (BTD) makes large industrial pipe wrenches in one of its factories. The marketing department has estimated the demands for this product during the next six months to be as follows:

Month	Demand
January	370
February	430
March	380
April	450
May	520
June	440

With the current labor force, BTD believes it can make approximately 420 pipe wrenches per month at a cost of $40 per wrench using regular-time production. An additional 80 wrenches per month can be made using overtime production, but the cost per wrench for overtime production is $45 per wrench. Wrenches can be made in one month and held in inventory for later shipment at a cost of $3 per month per wrench. The monthly demand for wrenches must be satisfied every month. At the end of December (beginning of January) BTD has 10 wrenches in inventory. BTD wants to plan its production, including overtime, and inventory for the next six months so as to maximize profit. Assuming that the revenue for these wrenches is fixed (or at least not controllable by the production manager), the production manager can maximize profit by minimizing the total costs incurred in producing and delivering the wrenches.

The quantities that the decision maker controls are (1) the number of wrenches to make each month using regular-time production, (2) the number of wrenches to make each month using overtime production, and indirectly (3) the number of wrenches to keep in inventory at the end of each month. So we can define our decision variables as follows (to keep a clear time convention, we will assume that wrenches are made during a month; at the end of the month, wrenches are shipped to customers; any wrench not shipped incurs a holding cost for that month):

R_t = number of wrenches made during month t using regular-time production
O_t = number of wrenches made during month t using overtime production
I_t = number of wrenches in inventory at the end of month t

where for each variable, $t = 1, \ldots, 6$. Notice that for wrenches kept in inventory there is no need to keep track of when they were made.

The objective is to choose the values of the variables to minimize the total cost incurred during the next six months.[2] The total cost is made up of the production cost of making the wrenches, during both regular time and overtime, and the inventory cost. The objective can then be written as follows:

$$\text{minimize } z = \sum_{t=1}^{6} (40\, R_t + 45\, O_t + 3\, I_t)$$

The easiest constraints to represent are those limiting the amount of regular-time and overtime production each month:

$$R_t \leq 420 \quad \text{for } t = 1, \ldots, 6$$

and

$$O_t \leq 80 \quad \text{for } t = 1, \ldots, 6$$

In addition, we need constraints guaranteeing that demand is satisfied each month. At this point the model becomes tricky, and experience is helpful. We might think it would be sufficient to add

[2]If the time value of money were important in the problem, the present value of the costs for each month would be used.

a constraint for each month stating that beginning inventory for that month plus total production must be at least as large as the demand for that month; for example,

$$10 + R_1 + O_1 \geq 370$$
$$I_1 + R_2 + O_2 \geq 430$$

and so forth. However, if we were to solve the problem as it stands, the optimal solution would be to let $R_1 = 360$, all other R_t values and all O_t values equal zero, $I_1 = 430$, $I_2 = 380$, $I_3 = 450$, $I_4 = 520$, $I_5 = 440$, and $I_6 = 0$. This means we should satisfy the demands in the last five months using inventories (because inventories are cheap but producing wrenches is expensive). However, this makes no physical sense because inventories are the result of excess production. This problem occurs because there are no constraints *defining* what the relationship must be among inventories, production, and demand. Therefore, we need constraints that define inventories as follows:

(wrenches in inventory at beginning of month t) + (wrenches made during month t)
= (wrenches shipped at end of month t) + (wrenches in inventory at end of month t)

Converting these to mathematical form, we get the constraints

$$\begin{array}{llll} 10 + R_1 + O_1 & = 370 + I_1 & \text{or} & R_1 + O_1 - I_1 = 360 \\ I_1 + R_2 + O_2 & = 430 + I_2 & \text{or} & R_2 + O_2 + I_1 - I_2 = 430 \\ I_2 + R_3 + O_3 & = 380 + I_3 & \text{or} & R_3 + O_3 + I_2 - I_3 = 380 \\ I_3 + R_4 + O_4 & = 450 + I_4 & \text{or} & R_4 + O_4 + I_3 - I_4 = 450 \\ I_4 + R_5 + O_5 & = 520 + I_5 & \text{or} & R_5 + O_5 + I_4 - I_5 = 520 \\ I_5 + R_6 + O_6 & = 440 + I_6 & \text{or} & R_6 + O_6 + I_5 - I_6 = 440 \end{array}$$

If the inventory variables are restricted to being nonnegative and these constraints are satisfied, then the previous demand constraints are satisfied as well. These inventory definition constraints perform double duty: they not only define inventories, they also guarantee that demand will be satisfied, so separate demand constraints are not needed.

Finally, we require all variables to be nonnegative. The optimal solution for the problem is $R_1 = 370$, $R_2 = \ldots = R_6 = 420$, $O_1 = O_2 = O_3 = 0$, $O_4 = 10$, $O_5 = 80$, $O_6 = 20$, $I_1 = 10$, $I_2 = 0$, $I_3 = 40$, $I_4 = 20$, $I_5 = I_6 = 0$.

T1.6 THE GEOMETRY OF LINEAR PROGRAMS

The characteristic that makes linear programs easy to solve is their simple geometric structure. To clarify our discussion of the geometry and solution methods, we begin by defining some terminology. A **solution** for a linear program is *any* set of numerical values for the variables. These values need not be the best values and do not even have to satisfy the constraints or make sense. For example, in the Healthy Pet Food problem, $M = 25$ and $Y = -800$ is a solution, but it does not satisfy the constraints, nor does it make physical sense. A **feasible solution** is a solution that satisfies *all* of the constraints. The **feasible set** or **feasible region** is the set of all feasible solutions. Finally, an **optimal solution** is a feasible solution that produces the best objective function value possible. Figure T1.1 illustrates the relationships among these types of solutions.

We will use the Healthy Pet Food example from Section T1.2 to illustrate the geometry of linear programs and to show how two-variable problems can be solved graphically. The linear programming formulation for the Healthy Pet Food problem was

$$\text{Maximize } z = 0.65\,M + 0.45\,Y$$

$$\begin{array}{lrl} \text{Subject to} & 2\,M + 3\,Y & \leq 400{,}000 \\ & 3\,M + 1.5\,Y & \leq 300{,}000 \\ & M & \leq 90{,}000 \\ & M, Y & \geq 0 \end{array}$$

where M is the number of packages of Meaties made and sold per month and Y is the number of packages of Yummies made and sold per month. Suppose we construct a coordinate system with M measured on the horizontal axis and Y measured on the vertical axis, as shown in Fig-

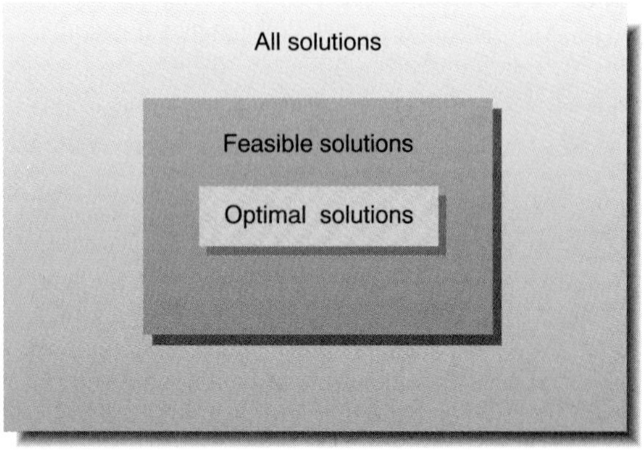

FIGURE T1.1 Relationship among solutions.

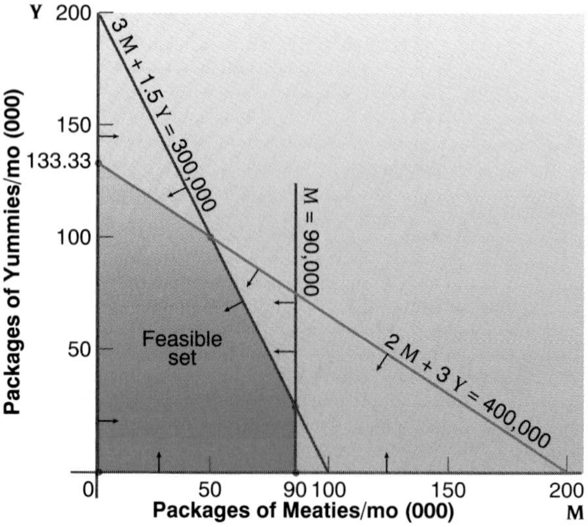

FIGURE T1.2 Graphical representation of the Healthy Pet Food problem.

ure T1.2. Each point in the M–Y plane corresponds to a product mix or production plan; the coordinate values for each point represent conceivable, though not necessarily physically possible, values for the variables. Furthermore, every possible product mix can be represented by a point in the M–Y plane. The best solution is the point that makes the objective function as large as possible yet satisfies all the constraints.

GRAPHICAL SOLUTION

We begin the solution process by finding the feasible set (the points or product mixes that satisfy all of the constraints). The geometric representation of a linear inequality is the set of points that lie on and on one side of the line obtained by replacing the inequality sign with an equality sign.

The constraint $M \geq 0$ restricts us to the points on or to the right of the vertical axis (the line $M = 0$). The constraint $Y \geq 0$ restricts us to the points on or above the horizontal axis. Therefore, only points in the upper right quadrant of Figure T1.2 are feasible. Next, we consider the constraint $2\ M + 3\ Y \leq 400{,}000$. To find the points that satisfy this inequality, we construct the line $2\ M + 3\ Y = 400{,}000$ by finding two points that lie on the line and then constructing a line through these points. The easiest points to find on the line are the ones that lie on the two axes. We first set M equal to zero and solve for Y; this yields the point ($M = 0$, Y = 133,333.33). We then set Y equal to zero and solve for M; this yields the point ($M = 200{,}000$, $Y = 0$). This line is plotted on Figure T1.2). We now determine on which side of this line the points satisfy the constraint. If one point satisfies the constraint, then all points on the same side of the line satisfy the constraint; if one point does not satisfy the constraint, then no point on that side of the line satisfies the constraint but all the points on the opposite side of the line do satisfy the constraint. It makes sense to select a simple point with which to work, such as ($M = 0$, $Y = 0$). This point satisfies the constraint $2\ M + 3\ Y \leq 400{,}000$, so all points to the lower left of the line do also. The points to the upper right of the line represent product mixes that require more than 400,000 pounds of cereal each month and can be eliminated from consideration.

We can do the same thing for the meat constraint: $3\ M + 1.5\ Y \leq 300{,}000$. We find two points on the line $3M + 1.5\ Y = 300{,}000$. We first set $M = 0$ and solve for Y, and then set $Y = 0$ and solve for M, yielding the points ($M = 0$, $Y = 200{,}000$) and ($M = 100{,}000$, $Y = 0$). Checking a point on one side of the line shows that the points on or to the lower left of the line are the ones that satisfy the constraint.

Finally, the constraint $M \leq 90{,}000$ is satisfied by the points that lie on or to the left of the vertical line $M = 90{,}000$. The feasible set is the set of points in the five-sided shaded area in Figure T1.2. The feasible set for a linear program will always have a shape like the one in this problem, with edges that are straight lines and corners where the edges meet. The corners of the feasible set are called **extreme points**. Notice that each extreme point is formed by the intersection of two or more constraints.

The optimal solution can be deduced using lines called **objective function contours**. A **contour** line is simply a line of constant value with respect to some attribute. In the case of Healthy Pet Food, all the points on a given contour line will generate the same level of profit. To construct a contour, we fix the value of the objective function

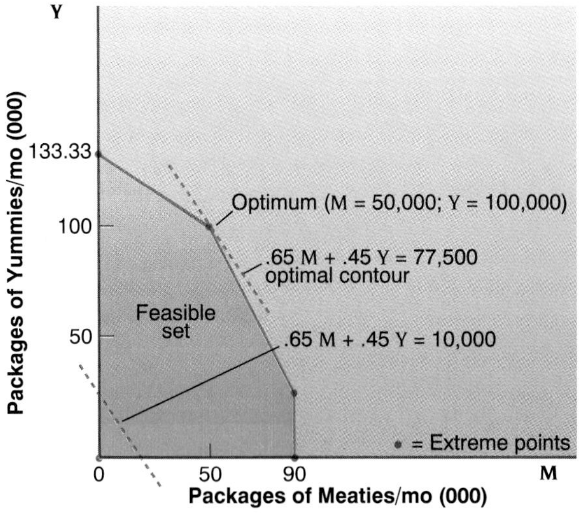

FIGURE T1.3 Graphical solution of the Healthy Pet Food problem.

equal to some constant, say \$10,000: $0.65\ M + 0.45\ Y = 10{,}000$. This contour line is plotted on Figure T1.3. This line passes through the feasible set; every point in the feasible set that lies on this contour represents a product mix that is both feasible and generates a profit of \$10,000 per month.

Because a profit of \$10,000 is clearly achievable, we can try to increase this to, say, \$20,000. A new contour line is formed that is parallel to the first contour but higher up. This line also passes through the feasible set, so an infinite number of feasible solutions will generate a profit of \$20,000 per month. (The contour lines are parallel because their slopes are determined only by the coefficients of the variables, 0.65 and 0.45; the intercepts of the contours are determined by the constants chosen for profit level.) We can continue this process until we find the contour line associated with the highest profit that still passes through at least one feasible point.

Intuitively we would guess that this optimal contour will pass through an extreme point of the feasible set. In fact, this can be proved to hold in general.

Fundamental Theorem of Linear Programming: If a finite optimal solution exists, then at least one extreme point is optimal.

This theorem implies that we can simply "slide" the contours up or down until we find the outermost extreme point(s) that either maximize(s) or minimize(s) the objective function. In the case of Healthy Pet Food the highest profit contour is $0.65\ M + 0.45\ Y = \$77{,}500$ and the optimum is $M = 50{,}000$, $Y = 100{,}000$. This means Healthy should produce and sell 50,000 packages of Meaties and 100,000 packages of Yummies each month; the contribution to profit will be \$77,500 per month.

To find the *exact* coordinate values for the optimum from the graph:

1. We identify the (two) constraints that intersect to form the extreme point through which the optimal contour passes,
2. We solve simultaneously the equations corresponding to the constraints to find the point that lies on both lines (the extreme point).

In this example the optimal extreme point was formed by the intersection of the lines $2\ M + 3\ Y = 400{,}000$ and $3\ M + 1.5\ Y = 300{,}000$.

To solve equations simultaneously, we use the following property: We can (1) multiply any constraint by a nonzero constant or (2) add or subtract a multiple of any equation to or from any other equation, without changing the set of solutions that solve the equations simultaneously.

Therefore, to solve the equations

$$\begin{aligned} 2\ M + \quad 3\ Y &= 400{,}000 \\ 3\ M + 1.5\ Y &= 300{,}000 \end{aligned}$$

simultaneously, we can subtract two times the second equation from the first equation, leaving

$$\begin{aligned} -4\ M \qquad\quad &= -200{,}000 \\ 3\ M + 1.5\ Y &= \ \ 300{,}000 \end{aligned}$$

The first equation is easily solved: $M = 50{,}000$. Substituting this value into the second equation gives $3(50{,}000) + 1.5\ Y = 300{,}000$, or $Y = 100{,}000$. This method can be used for any set of linear equations as long as the number of variables and equations is equal.[3]

Minimization problems can be solved in the same way, except that we find the contour with the smallest value that still touches a feasible point.

In practice, we do not use this sliding contour approach because it is impractical and inefficient for large problems. The simplex method, discussed in the next section, instead moves from one extreme point to another in an efficient way so that the objective function values of successive extreme points never get worse, and it can determine when it has found an optimum.

[3]This statement assumes that there are no redundant (linearly dependent) equations. Redundant equations can be written as linear combinations of other equations in the set.

MULTIPLE OPTIMA, INFEASIBLE PROBLEMS, AND UNBOUNDED PROBLEMS

Three conditions or qualifications should be noticed in the fundamental theorem of linear programming. First, the theorem does not say that *only* extreme points can be optimal. Second, it applies only if a feasible solution exists. Third, the optimum must be finite.

Multiple Optima If a finite optimum exists for the problem, there will be an extreme point that is optimal, but it may not be unique. Two or more adjacent extreme points (they share a common edge) may tie for the best solution. In this case not only are the extreme points optimal, but all the points on the edge connecting them are optimal as well. Geometrically this means that the optimal contour line lies on or passes through the entire edge connecting the extreme points. This would have occurred in the Healthy Pet Food example if the objective function had been to maximize $z = 0.30\,M + 0.45\,Y$. Then the optimal profit contour would be $0.30\,M + 0.45\,Y = \$60{,}000$, which passes through the extreme points ($M = 0$, $Y = 133{,}333.33$) and ($M = 50{,}000$, $Y = 100{,}000$). Every product mix on the line segment connecting these extreme points is optimal, such as $M = 20{,}000$, $Y = 120{,}000$).

Infeasible Problem In real life we often face situations where it is impossible to satisfy all the restrictions confronting us. For example, suppose Healthy Pet Food wanted to supply at least 160,000 packages of dog food each month; that is, $M + Y \geq 160{,}000$. No points satisfy the original constraints and $M + Y \geq 160{,}000$ simultaneously. Identifying this situation is useful because we can then identify which constraints might be relaxed to obtain a feasible solution and what the consequences of relaxing the constraints will be.

Unbounded Problem Sometimes a linear program may have an unbounded solution. In this situation the objective function can achieve a value of positive infinity for a maximization problem or negative infinity for a minimization problem. For example, consider the problem

$$\begin{aligned} \text{Maximize } z = A + 2\,B & \\ \text{Subject to } \quad A \qquad & \leq 10 \\ 2\,A + \quad B & \geq 5 \\ A,\, B \quad & \geq 0 \end{aligned}$$

As long as A is kept less than or equal to 10, B can be increased without limit and the objective function increases without limit: there is no finite optimum. Notice that unboundedness refers to the objective function value, not the constraint set. It is true that for the objective function to be unbounded the feasible region must be unbounded in some direction; however, an unbounded feasible set does *not* imply that there is no finite optimum. To see this, we simply have to change the objective of the preceding example to minimize $A + 2\,B$. The feasible set is unaffected, and therefore still unbounded in some direction, but the optimal solution is ($A = 2.5$, $B = 0$, $z = 2.5$).

Although infeasible problems can occur in practice, an unbounded problem generally indicates that the modeler forgot or misrepresented one or more constraints, such as a limit on demand for a product or the supply of a resource. When an unbounded problem is encountered, the modeler should study the situation to see what limitations exist that are not being explicitly stated in the constraints.

T1.7 THE SIMPLEX ALGORITHM

In 1949 George Dantzig developed an efficient procedure for solving linear programs called the **simplex method** or **simplex algorithm** (an algorithm is simply a repetitive procedure for solving a problem). This is the most widely used method in instructional and commercial computer packages. A method developed by Narendra Karmarkar in 1984 is gaining popularity, but since it requires more sophisticated mathematics, it is not presented here.

The fundamental theorem of linear programming reduces to a finite value the number of feasible solutions that need to be evaluated. One solution strategy might be to identify the coordinates of every extreme point and then evaluate the objective function at each. The one that produces the best objective function value would be the optimum. In practice, this approach is not efficient because the number of extreme points can become very large for real problems with hundreds or thousands of variables and constraints. The graphical solution method presented in Section T1.6 is also not practical for problems with more than two variables.

The simplex algorithm begins by identifying an initial extreme point of the feasible set (sometimes preliminary computations must be performed to find an initial extreme point). The algorithm then looks along each edge intersecting at the extreme point and computes the net effect on the objective function if we were to move along that edge. If the objective function value does not improve by moving along at least one of these edges, it can be proved that the extreme point is optimal. If movement along one or more of the edges would improve the objective function value, we move along one of these edges until we reach a new extreme point. We then repeat the previous steps: we check along each edge intersecting at the extreme point, and then either stop or slide along another edge that improves the objective function value.

This algorithm has many desirable features in practice.

1. It only moves from one extreme point to a better (or equally good) extreme point, thereby skipping large

numbers of suboptimal extreme points without explicitly identifying them. Consequently, it usually only has to check a small subset of the extreme points to find an optimum.

2. When it finds an optimum, it can identify this fact and stop. This characteristic is significant. For certain optimization models, such as integer programs, we can develop procedures that often find optimal or near-optimal solutions quickly, but it takes an enormous effort to verify that the solution is optimal or within some tolerance of the optimum.
3. The algorithm will detect whether the problem is infeasible, is unbounded, or has multiple optima.
4. The algorithm uses very simple mathematics (mainly row operations) that are easy to implement on a computer.

PREPARING THE PROBLEM FOR SOLUTION

To use the simplex algorithm, we must write the problem in what is called **canonical form**. Four conditions must be satisfied for the problem to be in canonical form.

1. The right-hand sides of all functional constraints (the constraints other than nonnegativity on the variables) must be nonnegative. (Zero is an acceptable right-hand-side value.)
2. All constraints must be written as equalities.
3. All variables must have a ≥ 0 restriction.
4. Every functional constraint must contain a variable that appears *only* in that constraint and not in any other constraint; (that is, the variable has a zero coefficient in all other functional constraints), and it must have a +1 coefficient in the constraint in which it appears.

Rarely is a linear programming model in canonical form when it is first formulated, so it must be rewritten in an equivalent form that satisfies these four conditions. The following shows how this conversion can be accomplished.

Nonnegative Right-Hand Sides Suppose a constraint has a negative right-hand side, such as the following:

$$3\,x_1 + 4\,x_2 - 2\,x_3 \leq -6$$

The right-hand side can be made nonnegative by multiplying through the entire constraint by −1, so that the constraint becomes

$$-3\,x_1 - 4\,x_2 + 2\,x_3 \geq 6$$

Notice that the direction of the inequality reverses when the constraint is multiplied by a negative constant.

All Constraints Must Be Equalities Any inequality constraint can be rewritten as an equivalent equality constraint by introducing a nonnegative variable called a **slack variable**. We first consider $\leq$ constraints such as the following:

$$3\,x_1 + 4\,x_2 \leq 12 \qquad \text{(T1.1)}$$

If we define a new variable, s_1, as $s_1 = 12 - (3\,x_1 + 4\,x_2)$, then this constraint can be written as

$$3\,x_1 + 4\,x_2 + s_1 = 12 \qquad \text{(T1.2)}$$

where

$$s_1 \geq 0$$

Any values of x_1 and x_2 that satisfy (T1.1) will also satisfy (T1.2) for some *nonnegative* value of s_1. Similarly, any values for x_1 and x_2 that satisfy (T1.2) using some nonnegative value for s_1 will also satisfy (T1.1). For example, $x_1 = 2$ and $x_2 = 1$ satisfies (T1.1), and these values along with $s_1 = 2$ satisfy (T1.2). For any solution, the variable s_1 measures the "slack" that exists in the constraint. That is, s_1 measures by how much a solution satisfies a constraint.

We use a similar approach to convert $\geq$ constraints into equalities; for example, consider

$$2\,x_1 + 4\,x_2 \geq 10$$

If we define a new variable, s_2, so that $s_2 = (2\,x_1 + 4\,x_2) - 10$, then we can rewrite the constraint as

$$2\,x_1 + 4\,x_2 - s_2 = 10$$
$$s_2 \geq 0$$

In summary, for $\leq$ constraints we *add* a nonnegative slack variable to the left-hand side of the constraint, and for $\geq$ constraints we *subtract* a nonnegative slack variable from the left-hand side of the constraint.

Notice that the slack variables have physical meaning; for example, they may measure how much of an available resource is not used for a given solution or how much of a nutrient an animal receives above some minimum required amount. The slack variables in each constraint measure something different; therefore, each one should have a different designation. A standard convention is to use the notation s_i for a slack variable that has been incorporated into constraint *i*.

All Variables Must Be Nonnegative Almost all linear programming computer packages automatically convert right-hand-side constants into nonnegative values and change constraints into equalities. But they assume all variables are nonnegative. If they are not, the problem must be rewritten so that all variables are nonnegative. For all the linear programs in this book, only nonnegative values for the variables will make sense. In other applications of linear programming, problems may be in a form such that some variables may either be unrestricted in sign or may actually be nonpositive. The interested reader should consult an operations research or linear programming text concerning ways to redefine these variables so that they are nonnegative.

Each Constraint Must Have a Unique Variable with a +1 Coefficient If we take the Healthy Pet Food problem and perform the necessary steps to satisfy the previous three conditions, we get the following:

Maximize $z = 0.65\,M + 0.45\,Y$

$$\begin{aligned} \text{Subject to} \quad & 2\,M + 3\,Y + s_1 = 400{,}000 \\ & 3\,M + 1.5\,Y + s_2 = 300{,}000 \qquad \text{(T1.3)} \\ & M + s_3 = 90{,}000 \\ & \text{All variables} \geq 0 \end{aligned}$$

We now have to check each constraint to see if there is a variable that appears *only* in that constraint and has a coefficient of +1. In the first constraint s_1 satisfies this requirement; in the second constraint s_2 satisfies it; and in the third constraint s_3 satisfies it. Therefore, this problem is now in canonical form and ready to solve.

Notice that if, for example, the second constraint had been $3\,M + 1.5\,Y \geq 300{,}000$, we would have *subtracted* a slack variable from the left-hand side of the constraint: $3\,M + 1.5\,Y - s_2 = 300{,}000$. Although s_2 would appear only in the second constraint, it would have a −1 coefficient there, which does not satisfy the requirement. Multiplying this constraint throughout by −1 will not resolve this difficulty because it will make the right-hand side of the constraint negative. We will see later how we can handle this situation.

THE ALGEBRAIC FOUNDATIONS OF THE ALGORITHM

In the initial formulation the number of constraints may exceed the number of variables, but once the problem is in canonical form the number of variables, say k, should always be at least as large as the number of functional constraints, m. In the Healthy Pet Food problem, $k = 5$ and $m = 3$. Because the number of variables exceeds the number of equations (constraints), there is an infinite number of solutions that satisfy these equations. We can find a solution to these equations by setting the values of k-m of the variables (two in this case) equal to zero and then solving the m equations simultaneously to obtain the values of the remaining m (three) variables. Any solution obtained using this procedure is called a **basic solution.** In a basic solution the k-m variables *set* equal to zero are called the **nonbasic variables** for that solution; the remaining m variables, the values of which are obtained by solving the m equations, are called the **basic variables** for that solution. Notice that basic variables *can* equal zero; nonbasic variables *must* equal zero. The set of basic variables for a basic solution is called the **basis** for that solution; the basic variables are said to be "in the basis" and the nonbasic variables are "not in the basis."

Suppose that after we put the Healthy Pet Food problem into canonical form, we chose M and Y as our nonbasic variables and set them equal to zero. The functional constraints (T1.3) then reduce to

$$\begin{aligned} s_1 &= 400{,}000 \\ s_2 &= 300{,}000 \\ s_3 &= 90{,}000 \end{aligned}$$

This system of equations is trivial to solve. This is not an accident. Once the problem is written in canonical form, there is a basic solution ready to jump out at us. The variable in each constraint that is unique to that constraint and has a coefficient of +1 will be the basic variable *for that constraint*. Not only are there exactly m basic variables, there is also a one-to-one correspondence between each constraint and the basic variables. Any variable that is not basic is nonbasic and is *set* equal to zero. This reduces the m equations to a form in which each equation has only one (basic) variable in it; therefore, that variable must equal the value on the right-hand side.

Basic solutions represent the points where constraints intersect. Not all basic solutions are feasible; if a basic solution is also feasible, it is called a **basic feasible solution**. Basic feasible solutions are the algebraic representation of extreme points (the corners of the feasible set), and we know from the fundamental theorem of linear programming that if a finite optimum exists, an extreme point will be optimal.

The basic feasible solution, $M = 0$, $Y = 0$, $s_1 = 400{,}000$, $s_2 = 300{,}000$, $s_3 = 90{,}000$ (formed by the intersection of the constraint lines $M = 0$ and $Y = 0$), has an objective function value of zero. We now want to determine whether this is the optimal solution. We do this by looking along each constraint that intersects at this extreme point; if the objective function would improve by moving along one of the edges, the current solution is not optimal. If there is no edge along which the objective function improves, the current solution must be optimal.

Moving along an edge is accomplished algebraically by increasing the value of one of the nonbasic variables while keeping all other nonbasic variables equal to zero and then adjusting the values of the basic variables to maintain feasibility. For example, suppose we increase the value of M from 0 to 1, keep $Y = 0$, and adjust the values of the remaining variables. If M increases by one unit, then s_1 must decrease by two units to 399,998 to keep the first equation satisfied; s_2 must decrease by three units to 299,997, and s_3 must decrease by one unit to 89,999. Geometrically we have slid one unit along the M axis (the edge of the $Y \geq 0$ constraint), as illustrated in Figure T1.4. Notice that this solution is *not* a basic solution; a basic solution would have at least two variables equal to zero and would represent a point where constraints intersect.

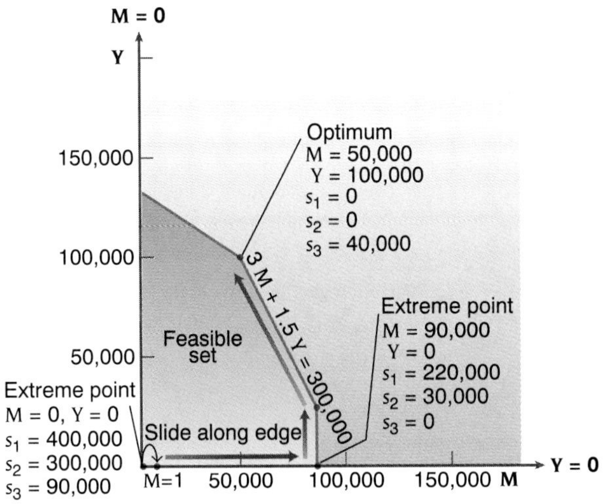

FIGURE T1.4 Geometry of a simplex pivot.

The objective function value has increased by 0.65 by moving one unit along this edge. In fact, each unit we move in this direction causes the objective function to increase by 0.65. Therefore, we want to increase M as much as possible, but as M increases the previous basic variables all decrease. At some point one of them will be forced to zero. Specifically, for every unit M increases, s_1 must decrease by two units; because s_1 begins at 400,000, this means that M can increase by 200,000 units before s_1 hits zero. Similarly, M can increase by 100,000 units before s_2 is forced to zero, and M can increase by 90,000 before s_3 reaches zero. Therefore, the most we can increase M before one of the basic variables is forced to zero is 90,000 units. If M is increased beyond this point, s_3 would become negative and the solution would no longer be feasible.

By increasing M to 90,000, keeping $Y = 0$, and adjusting the other variables, we obtain a new (adjacent) basic feasible solution: $M = 90{,}000$, $Y = 0$, $s_1 = 220{,}000$, $s_2 = 30{,}000$, and $s_3 = 0$, where Y and s_3 are now the nonbasic variables (see Figure T1.4).

THE INITIAL SIMPLEX TABLEAU

The simplex algorithm formalizes the preceding procedure. To use the simplex algorithm, we write the problem in a more efficient form using what are called **simplex tableaus** or **simplex tables**. In a simplex tableau we omit the variable names and work only with the relevant coefficients. Table T1.4 gives the initial simplex tableau for the Healthy Pet Food problem.

In the simplex tableau a column is assigned to each variable. We can then write down the coefficients that apply to each variable by putting the coefficients in the appropriate columns. This avoids the need to write the variable names repeatedly. The top row of numbers is called the *objective function* or *c_j row*. The objective function coefficients for each variable are written in this row, including coefficients that are zero. The next (three) rows contain the coefficients of the constraints. The elements in these rows are called the *a_{ij} values*, where the subscript i designates the number of the constraint and the j identifies which variable it is multiplying. For example, $a_{21} = 3$ is the coefficient in the second constraint and it multiplies the first variable, M. The rightmost column is called the *right-hand side* or *b column*; the element in the ith row of this column will be called b_i. In the second column from the left we list the current basic variable for each constraint. The basic variable for the ith constraint will have a coefficient of +1 in that constraint and a coefficient of 0 in every other constraint. The leftmost column, called the *c_B column*, lists the objective function coefficients for the basic variables. The element in the ith row of this column will be designated c_{Bi}.

TABLE T1.4 FIRST HEALTHY PET FOOD TABLEAU

c_B	Basic Var.	M 0.65	Y 0.45	s_1 0	s_2 0	s_3 0	b	Ratio	
0	s_1	2	3	1	0	0	400,000	(400,000/2) = 200,000	
0	s_2	3	1.5	0	1	0	300,000	(300,000/3) = 100,000	
0	s_3	[1]	0	0	0	1	90,000	(90,000/1) = 90,000	←pivot row
	z_j	0	0	0	0	0	0		
	$c_j - z_j$	0.65	0.45	0	0	0			
		↑ pivot column							

The last two rows of the tableau are used to determine whether the current basic feasible solution is optimal, and if not, which variable should enter the basis. The second row from the bottom is called the *z_j row*. For the jth variable

$$z_j = \sum_{i=1}^{m} a_{ij} c_{Bi}$$

This means that to compute z_j for the jth variable, we go *down* the jth variable column and the c_B column, performing pairwise multiplication and then summing the terms. For example, in Table T1.4 $z_1 = (2 \times 0) + (3 \times 0) + (1 \times 0) = 0$. We perform this operation for every variable *and for the right-hand side values*: $(400{,}000 \times 0) + (300{,}000 \times 0) + (90{,}000 \times 0) = 0$. The z_j in the b column is the objective function value for the basic solution in the tableau. We will explain the physical meaning of the z_j values shortly.

The bottom row is called the *$c_j - z_j$ row*, and it represents exactly that: we subtract the z_j row from the c_j row. (There is no value in the b column because there is no b column value in the c_j row.)

Meaning of z_j and $c_j - z_j$ The algorithm moves from one basic solution to another by

1. increasing the value of a nonbasic variable,
2. keeping the other nonbasic variables equal to zero, and
3. adjusting the values of the basic variables to satisfy the functional constraints.

When this is done, two forces affect the objective function value. There is the direct effect of the nonbasic variable that is being increased in value. The per unit or marginal effect of increasing the jth variable is the objective function coefficient for this variable, c_j. When the basic variables are adjusted to maintain feasibility, however, this adjustment affects the objective function as well. This adjustment effect, often called the **opportunity cost**, is measured by z_j, and it represents the penalty that results from adjusting these basic variables. The net marginal effect on the objective function is $c_j - z_j$. If the $c_j - z_j$ for some nonbasic variable is *positive* in sign, increasing that variable (and adjusting the other variables to remain feasible) would result in a net *increase* in the objective function value.

THE SIMPLEX PIVOT AND THE SECOND TABLEAU

Once the problem is set up in the initial tableau, the algorithm uses the following four-step procedure:

1. ***Check the current basic solution for optimality.*** For a maximization problem, if all the $c_j - z_j$ values are zero or negative, increasing the value of any variable would *not* increase the objective function value. Therefore, the current solution is optimal, and we can stop. For a minimization problem, we stop when all of the $c_j - z_j$ values are zero or positive; this means that increasing the value of any variable would not decrease the objective function value. (Notice that the $c_j - z_j$ values for the basic variables in a tableau will always equal zero.)
2. ***Select the entering variable.*** In Table T1.4 the $c_j - z_j$ values for both M and Y are strictly positive. This means that by bringing either of these variables into the basis we would increase the value of the objective function. There is no way to know in advance which variable will ultimately lead us to the optimum most quickly. A simple rule that works well is to select the variable that has the most positive $c_j - z_j$, if we are maximizing, or the most negative $c_j - z_j$ if we are minimizing. In our example, we would select M to come into the basis (this is called the **entering variable**); the M column is called the **pivot column**.
3. ***Identify the leaving variable.*** As shown above, as we increase the value of M while keeping Y fixed at zero, the other basic variables must change in value to satisfy the constraints. As M increases s_1, s_2, and s_3 all decrease in value. Variable s_3 reaches zero first and leaves the basis. The leaving variable can be determined by using a **ratio test**. For every constraint row i we compute the ratio b_i/a_{is}, *if* $a_{is} > 0$, where column s is the pivot column. That is, we divide the right-hand side of each constraint by the element in the pivot column of the same row, but *only if* the denominator, a_{is}, is *strictly positive* in value. This ratio computes how much the entering variable can increase in value before the basic variable in that constraint is forced down to zero. The variable that will leave the basis (called the **leaving variable**) is the basic variable in the row with the *smallest* ratio; this row is called the **pivot row**. (We require $a_{is} > 0$ because if a_{is} were 0 or negative, as the entering variable increases in value the basic variable in that constraint either stays the same or increases in value; therefore, it could not be driven out of the basis by the entering variable.)

   In Table T1.4 the ratios for the three constraints are $[400{,}000 / 2] = 200{,}000$, $[300{,}000 / 3] = 100{,}000$, and $[90{,}000 / 1] = 90{,}000$. The smallest ratio is for the third constraint, so M will enter the basis as the basic variable *for the third constraint* and force s_3 out of the basis.
4. ***Perform pivot operations to obtain the new canonical form.*** The intersection of the pivot row and pivot column is called the **pivot element**. We now want to rewrite the constraints so that they are mathematically equivalent but also so that the new basic variable, M, appears in only the third constraint and has

TABLE T1.5 SECOND HEALTHY PET FOOD TABLEAU

c_B	Basic Var.	M 0.65	Y 0.45	s_1 0	s_2 0	s_3 0	b	Ratio
0	s_1	0	3	1	0	−2	220,000	(220,000/3) = 73,333
0	s_2	0	[1.5]	0	1	−3	30,000	(30,000/1.5) = 20,000 ←pivot row
0.65	M	1	0	0	0	1	90,000	No ratio
	z_j	0.65	0	0	0	0.65	58,500	
	$c_j - z_j$	0	0.45	0	0	−0.65		
			↑ pivot column					

a coefficient of +1. In other words, we want the M column (the pivot column) to contain a +1 in the pivot element and 0 in every other constraint row. We can do this by using the *row operations* introduced in Section T1.6. The problem does not change if we

a. multiply any equation by a nonzero constant or

b. add or subtract a multiple of any equation to or from any other equation.

We first divide the entire pivot row by the value of the pivot element. In Table T1.4 the pivot element is already equal to 1, so the pivot row does not change; it is just rewritten in Table T1.5. If the pivot element had been 4, we would have divided the entire pivot row (except the two leftmost columns) by 4. The new form of the pivot row will always be a multiple of the current pivot row, so a multiple of this new form of the pivot row can be added to or subtracted from the other rows.

To obtain a zero in the M column of the first constraint, we multiply the pivot row (third row) by 2 and subtract from the first constraint row:

$$\begin{array}{l} |2\ \ 3\ \ 1\ \ 0\ \ 0\ \ 400{,}000| \\ -\,2 \times |1\ \ 0\ \ 0\ \ 0\ \ 1\ \ \ 90{,}000| = |0\ \ 3\ \ 1\ \ 0\ -2\ \ \ 220{,}000|; \end{array}$$

The new form of the first constraint is given in Table T1.5. To obtain a zero in the M column of the second constraint, we multiply the pivot row by 3 and subtract from the second constraint row:

$$\begin{array}{l} |3\ \ 1.5\ \ 0\ \ 1\ \ 0\ \ 300{,}000| \\ -\,3 \times |1\ \ 0\ \ 0\ \ 0\ \ 1\ \ \ 90{,}000| = |0\ \ 1.5\ \ 0\ \ \ 1\ \ -3\ \ \ 30{,}000| \end{array}$$

The result is shown in Table T1.5. Notice that we *always use the pivot row to operate on the other rows*. If we add or subtract multiples of a row other than the pivot row to or from a row, the columns for the other basic variables can become messed up (they will not contain all zeroes except for a +1 in the row for which the variable is basic). Also, notice that because the new form of the pivot row will always have a 1 in the pivot element, we can create a 0 in the pivot column for any other constraint just by multiplying the *new form* of the pivot row by the element in the pivot column of the other row and subtracting the result from that row.

At this point, we can determine the basic solution for the tableau in Table T1.5. Y and s_3 are not in the basis, so they are set equal to zero; then s_1 = 220,000, s_2 = 30,000, and M = 90,000. We then compute the z_j and $c_j - z_j$ elements for each column. For example, $z_2 = (3 \times 0) + (1.5 \times 0) + (0 \times 0.65) = 0$. Notice that the z_j on the right-hand side equals the objective function value, 58,500. We will call this term z from now on.

THE THIRD TABLEAU

The solution in Table T1.5 is not optimal because $c_2 - z_2 = 0.45 > 0$. Therefore, we select Y as our entering variable. The leaving variable is determined by performing the ratio test (dividing the right-hand side values by the a_{ij} values in the Y column). In this case, the second constraint has the smallest ratio (row 3 has no ratio because $a_{32} = 0$), so variable s_2 will leave the basis.

To obtain the new tableau, we divide the pivot row by the pivot element, 1.5, and write the result in Table T1.6. The third row already has a zero in the pivot column, so we just rewrite that constraint. To obtain a zero in the pivot column of the first constraint row, we can multiply the new form of the pivot row in Table T1.6 by 3 and subtract from the first constraint row in Table T1.5. The new tableau is given in Table T1.6. The basic solution in Table T1.6 is M = 90,000, Y = 20,000, s_1 = 160,000, s_2 = 0, s_3 = 0, and z = \$67,500.

THE FOURTH TABLEAU

The solution in Table T1.6 is not optimal because $z_5 = 0.25 > 0$, so we should bring s_3 back into the basis. Notice, first, that a variable can leave the basis and return to it later (but not with the same other basic variables). Second,

TABLE T1.6 THIRD HEALTHY PET FOOD TABLEAU

		M	Y	s_1	s_2	s_3		
c_B	Basic Var.	0.65	0.45	0	0	0	b	Ratio
0	s_1	0	0	1	−2	[4]	160,000	(160,000/4) = 40,000 ←pivot row
0.45	Y	0	1	0	2/3	−2	20,000	No ratio
0.65	M	1	0	0	0	1	90,000	(90,000/1) = 90,000
	z_j	0.65	0.45	0	0.30	−0.25	67,500	
	$c_j - z_j$	0	0	0	−0.30	0.25		
						↑ pivot column		

even though the direct benefit of increasing the value of s_3 is zero, this tableau illustrates that the objective function will increase due to the adjustment of the other basic variables, which is measured by z_5.

By performing the ratio test, we find that s_1 will leave the basis. The new tableau is given in Table T1.7. The resulting basic solution is $M = 50{,}000$, $Y = 100{,}000$, $s_1 = 0$, $s_2 = 0$, $s_3 = 40{,}000$, and $z = \$77{,}500$. This solution is optimal because all of the $c_j - z_j$ values are less than or equal to zero.

GENERAL COMMENTS ABOUT THE ALGORITHM

1. The right-hand sides of the constraints in each tableau should *always* be nonnegative. A negative number on the right-hand side can have two causes: (a) the pivot row was chosen incorrectly (a row other than the one with the smallest ratio was used) or (b) an arithmetic error was made.
2. The $c_j - z_j$ values for the basic variables should always be zero.
3. The objective function value should never get worse in going from one tableau to the next. In fact, it should improve by the product of $c_j - z_j$ for the entering variable and the entering variable's value in the new tableau. For example, in Table T1.6 $c_5 - z_5 = +0.25$, so for each unit s_3 is increased, the objective function should increase by +0.25. Going from the solution in Table T1.6 to the one in Table T1.7, s_3 increased by 40,000 units, so the objective function should increase by 40,000 × \$0.25 = \$10,000, which is exactly what happened.

T1.8 USING ARTIFICIAL VARIABLES

In the Healthy Pet Food problem all of the constraints were ≤ constraints. This means that as soon as slack variables were added to the left-hand side, they satisfied the canonical condition for the constraints and became the initial basic variables. If a linear program has = or ≥ constraints this will not occur, so there is no basic variable readily at hand for an initial basis. For example, consider the problem

Maximize $z = 20A + 6B + 9C$

Subject to
$$4A + 3B + C \le 24$$
$$2A + 4B + 12C \ge 30$$
$$2A + 3B + C = 10$$
All variables ≥ 0

After adding the appropriate slack variables, the problem is

TABLE T1.7 FOURTH HEALTHY PET FOOD TABLEAU

		M	Y	s_1	s_2	s_3	
c_B	Basic Var.	0.65	0.45	0	0	0	b
0	s_3	0	0	1/4	−1/2	1	40,000
0.45	Y	0	1	1/2	−1/3	0	100,000
0.65	M	1	0	−1/4	1/2	0	50,000
	z_j	0.65	0.45	0.0625	0.175	0	77,500
	$c_j - z_j$	0	0	−0.0625	−0.175	0	

Maximize $z = 20A + 6B + 9C$

Subject to
$$4A + 3B + C + s_1 = 24$$
$$2A + 4B + 12C - s_2 = 30$$
$$2A + 3B + C = 10$$
All variables ≥ 0

The variable s_1 appears only in the first constraint and has a coefficient of +1, so it can be the basic variable for the first constraint. Although s_2 appears only in the second constraint, it has a coefficient of −1; therefore, there is no variable in the second constraint that can act as a basic variable (multiplying the second constraint by −1 would make the right-hand side coefficient negative). The third constraint also has no unique variable ready to be basic.

In this case we can create a basic but infeasible solution by adding two new nonnegative variables, A_2 and A_3, to the left-hand side of the second and third constraints. These are called **artificial variables**. (We will use the notation A_i where it is added to the ith constraint.) This gives the new form of the problem, which is in canonical form.

Maximize $z = 20A + 6B + 9C$

Subject to
$$4A + 3B + C + s_1 = 24$$
$$2A + 4B + 12C - s_2 + A_2 = 30$$
$$2A + 3B + C + A_3 = 10$$
All variables ≥ 0

The artificial variables are put into the problem for only one purpose: *to act as basic variables to get the algorithm started*. If an artificial variable is in the problem, it *must* be a basic variable. In the current canonical form the basic variables are s_1, A_2, and A_3, and the corresponding basic solution is $A = B = C = s_2 = 0$, $s_1 = 24$, $A_2 = 30$, and $A_3 = 10$. This is, in fact, a basic solution that occurs at the intersection of the constraint boundaries: $A = 0$, $B = 0$, $C = 0$. But this solution is infeasible because these lines intersect outside the feasible set.

By modifying the objective function to "encourage" the artificial variables to leave the basis, we can use the simplex algorithm to move from an *infeasible* to a *feasible* basic solution. The algorithm then proceeds exactly as in the previous section. There are two ways to modify the problem. The first, called the Big-M *method*, is intuitively simple and will be demonstrated here.

THE BIG-M METHOD

In the **Big-M method** we make the objective function coefficients for the artificial variables either −infinity for maximization problems or +infinity for minimization problems. (The name Big-M comes from the fact that the letter M is used to represent some large number that replaces infinity.) This way, if any artificial variable takes on any positive value, the objective function explodes to −infinity for a maximization problem or to +infinity for a minimization problem. In either case, this method encourages the algorithm to drive the artificial variables to zero by kicking them out of the basis. Rather than use −infinity, in our example we will let M = -1000. The first tableau is then Table T1.8.

Variable C has the most positive $c_j - z_j$, so C will enter the basis. The second row has the smallest ratio, so the basic variable in that row, A_2, will leave the basis. Performing the pivot yields Table T1.9. Notice that the A_2 column has been deleted in Table T1.9. As soon as an artificial variable leaves the basis, it can be dropped from the problem. (Do not do this with other types of variables!) The resulting solution is not optimal so, variable B enters the basis and replaces A_3, giving Table T1.10. Variable A then enters the basis and B leaves, giving Table T1.11.

The optimal solution is then $A = 45/11 = 4.091$, $B = 0$, $C = 20/11 = 1.818$, $s_1 = 64/11 = 5.818$, $s_2 = 0$, and $z = 1080/11 = 98.181$. Although the artificial variables will usually leave the basis quickly, they are not always the first variables to leave, as they were in this example.

TABLE T1.8 FIRST TABLEAU: BIG-M METHOD

c_B	Basic Var.	A 20	B 6	C 9	s_1 0	s_2 0	A_2 −1000	A_3 −1000	b	Ratio	
0	s_1	4	3	1	1	0	0	0	24	(24/1) = 24	
−1,000	A_2	2	4	[12]	0	−1	1	0	30	(30/12) = 2.5	←pivot row
−1,000	A_3	2	3	1	0	0	0	1	10	(10/1) = 10	
	z_j	−4,000	−7,000	−13,000	0	1,000	−1,000	−1,000	−4,000		
	$c_j - z_j$	4,020	7,006	13,009	0	−1,000	0	0			
				↑ pivot column							

TABLE T1.9 SECOND TABLEAU: BIG-M METHOD

c_B	Basic Var.	A 20	B 6	C 9	s_1 0	s_2 0	A_2 −1000	A_3 −1000	b	Ratio	
0	s_1	23/6	8/3	0	1	1/12	—	0	21.5	[21.5/(8/3)] = 8.06	
9	C	1/6	1/3	1	0	−1/12	—	0	2.5	[2.5/(1/3)] = 7.5	
−1000	A_3	11/6	[8/3]	0	0	1/12	—	1	7.5	[7.5(8/3)] = 2.81	←pivot row
	z_j	−1831.8	−2663.7	9	0	−84.1	—	−1000	−7477.5		
	$c_j - z_j$	1851.8	2669.7	0	0	84.1	—	0			
			↑ pivot column								

TABLE T1.10 THIRD TABLEAU: BIG-M METHOD

c_B	Basic Var.	A 20	B 6	C 9	s_1 0	s_2 0	A_2 −1000	A_3 −1000	b	Ratio	
0	s_1	2	0	0	1	0	—	—	14	[14/2] = 7	
9	C	−1/16	0	1	0	−3/32	—	—	25/16	no ratio	
6	B	[11/16]	1	0	0	1/32	—	—	45/16	[45/11] = 4.09	←pivot row
	z_j	57/16	6	9	0	−21/32	—	—	495/16		
	$c_j - z_j$	263/16	0	0	0	21/32	—	—			
		↑ pivot column									

TABLE T1.11 OPTIMAL TABLEAU: BIG-M METHOD

c_B	Basic Var.	A 20	B 6	C 9	s_1 0	s_2 0	A_2 −1000	A_3 −1000	b
0	s_1	0	−32/11	0	1	−1/11	—	—	64/11
9	C	0	1/11	1	0	−1/11	—	—	20/11
20	A	1	16/11	0	0	1/22	—	—	45/11
	z_j	20	329/11	9	0	1/11	—	—	1080/11
	$c_j - z_j$	0	−263/11	0	0	−1/11	—	—	

THE TWO-PHASE METHOD

For the Big-M method to work well, the value of M must be several orders of magnitude larger than the other objective function coefficients. But this large difference in coefficient magnitude can cause numerical instability and roundoff problems in computer programs. An alternative that is used more widely in practice, the two-phase method, accomplishes the same thing but is numerically more stable. The **two-phase method** divides the solution process into two phases. In phase 1 we want to move from the initial basic *infeasible* solution to some basic *feasible* solution; in phase 2 we want to move to the best basic feasible solution. The goal of phase 1 is accomplished by replacing the original objective function with the objective of *minimizing* the sum of the artificial variables. In other words, the c_j values for all variables are 0 except for the artificial variables, which have c_j values of 1. This is the phase 1 objective function *regardless of whether the original objective is to maximize or minimize*. This objective function causes the artificial variables to go to zero by leaving the basis. As soon as all of the artificial variables are out of the basis, phase 2 begins. In phase 2 the original objective function for the problem is used, and solution proceeds as before.

T1.9 INFEASIBLE PROBLEMS, MULTIPLE OPTIMA, UNBOUNDEDNESS, AND DEGENERACY

One good feature of the simplex algorithm is that it identifies infeasible problems, multiple optima, and unboundedness if they exist.

Infeasible Problem If for some tableau the $c_j - z_j$ values satisfy the optimality conditions but at least one artificial variable is still positive (in the basis), then the problem has no feasible solution.

Multiple Optima If the problem has more than one optimum, this will be signaled by the final tableau. In the optimal tableau, if $c_j - z_j$ for a *nonbasic* variable is zero, that variable could be brought into the basis and the objective function would not change in value, so this new solution would also be optimal.

Unbounded Problem If for any tableau $c_j - z_j$ indicates that a nonbasic variable should be brought into the basis, but no ratios can be computed for the constraints because every constraint coefficient in the pivot column is either zero or negative, the problem is unbounded. Increasing the value of the entering variable would improve the objective function value without limit.

Degeneracy The right-hand sides of a tableau should *never* be negative, but they can be zero. When a right-hand side is zero, a basic variable equals zero; this is called a **degenerate solution**. You should treat the zero just like any other number; it can be used as the numerator in the ratio test. The significance of degeneracy is discussed in detail in linear programming texts. Geometrically, degeneracy simply means that the extreme point represented by the basic solution was formed by the intersection of more constraints than were needed, so the same extreme point can be expressed algebraically by several basic solutions.

T1.10 COMPUTER SOLUTION OF LINEAR PROGRAMS

Once a linear program has been formulated, it can be solved using a computer-based solution method. Most commercial and instructional linear programming computer packages use methods based on the simplex algorithm or Karmarkar's method. Many computer packages are available, such as MPSX, LINDO, CPLEX, and OSL on mainframes and LINDO and MathPro on personal computers. Multipurpose instructional programs, such as QSB, QSOM, MSIS, and XXX (the last two are available with this book), contain linear programming modules to solve small problems.

Although each package is slightly different, the input information required and the output provided by typical instructional packages are similar.

PROBLEM INPUT

Most linear programming packages request the following information to set up the problem:

1. Whether the user wants to enter a new problem, read an existing problem from a diskette, modify the current problem in memory, or solve a problem.
2. An identifying name for the problem so that it can be stored on disk or diskette and reused or modified at a future time.
3. Whether the problem involves maximization or minimization.
4. The number of variables in the problem.
5. The names of the variables or whether the user wants to use default names, usually $X1$, $X2$, and so on.
6. The number of constraints in the problem (excluding nonnegativity constraints on the variables).
7. The objective function and constraint coefficients. These can be entered as a data matrix (e.g., from a LOTUS spreadsheet), or a problem template of the objective function and constraints will be displayed with the variables listed and spaces provided for the user to enter the coefficients.

COMPUTER OUTPUT

Most packages offer several output options: to display the optimum, the optimum with sensitivity analysis (discussed below), the initial simplex tableau and the optimum, and so forth. A sample computer output for the Healthy Pet Food problem is given in Figure T1.5. Part (a) of the figure lists the optimal values for the variables in the column labeled "solution": M = 50,000, Y = 100,000, S1 = 0, S2 = 0, S3 = 40,000. The slack variables are added to the problem automatically by the computer package, and their optimal values are listed. At the bottom of Figure T1.5a is the objective function value: $77,500.

SENSITIVITY ANALYSIS

An important use of linear programs is to determine how sensitive the optimal solution is to parameter values in the problem. For example, how would the optimum

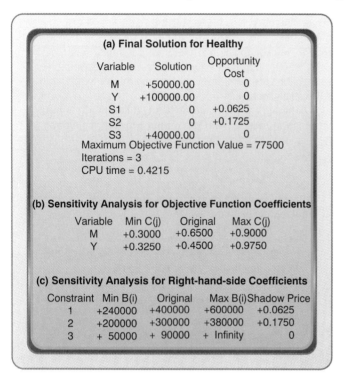

(a) Final Solution for Healthy

Variable	Solution	Opportunity Cost
M	+50000.00	0
Y	+100000.00	0
S1	0	+0.0625
S2	0	+0.1725
S3	+40000.00	0

Maximum Objective Function Value = 77500
Iterations = 3
CPU time = 0.4215

(b) Sensitivity Analysis for Objective Function Coefficients

Variable	Min C(j)	Original	Max C(j)
M	+0.3000	+0.6500	+0.9000
Y	+0.3250	+0.4500	+0.9750

(c) Sensitivity Analysis for Right-hand-side Coefficients

Constraint	Min B(i)	Original	Max B(i)	Shadow Price
1	+240000	+400000	+600000	+0.0625
2	+200000	+300000	+380000	+0.1750
3	+ 50000	+ 90000	+ Infinity	0

FIGURE T1.5 Computer solution for Healthy Pet Food.

change if a price or the availability of a resource were changed? This type of analysis is referred to as **sensitivity analysis** or **parametric analysis**. We will now describe the sensitivity analysis information typically provided by linear programming computer packages. Any introductory operations research or linear programming text will describe how this information is derived mathematically.

Changes in Objective Function Coefficients If an objective function coefficient is changed, this does not affect the feasible set of solutions for the problem. The only effect is on the slope of the objective function contours. As long as the objective function coefficient is changed within some range of values, the same solution will remain optimal. Figure T1.5b, labeled "Sensitivity Analysis for Objective Function Coefficients," lists the range over which each objective function coefficient can vary without the optimal values for the variables changing.

In Figure T1.5b the notation C(j) refers to the objective function coefficient for the jth variable. The values in the column labeled "Original" are the original objective function coefficients in the problem: 0.65 for M and 0.45 for Y. In the M row, the values 0.30 in the "Min C(j)" column and 0.90 in the "Max C(j)" column mean that *as long as all the other data in the problem are held constant*, the solution M = 50,000 and Y = 100,000 would be optimal for any value of C(1) from a minimum of 0.30 to a maximum of 0.90. (Identifying the limits within which C(j) can vary without affecting the optimal solution is called objective function **ranging**.) For example, suppose the profit per package for Meaties was changed from $0.65 to $0.85. The "ranging" information in Figure T1.5b implies that M = 50,000 and Y = 100,000 would still be the optimal solution; however, the optimal amount of profit *would* change (to $87,500).

Similarly, Figure T1.5b indicates that the optimal values of M and Y do not change as long as the objective function coefficient for Y is between 0.325 (Min C(j)) and 0.975 (Max C(j)) and *all other coefficients are at their original values*. One limitation of this analysis is that the range of coefficient values for which the solution remains optimal is valid only when *one* coefficient is modified. If two or more coefficients are changed simultaneously, the ranges given in Figure T1.5b do *not* tell us what would happen. In this case, we would change the coefficient values and re-solve the problem.

Dual Prices and Changes in the Right-Hand-Side Coefficients Suppose the right-hand side of a constraint was changed. For example, in the Healthy Pet Food problem, suppose Healthy could buy up to 400,001 pounds of cereal each month (at $0.20 per pound) instead of 400,000 pounds. Will this change the optimal solution, and if so, how? The information in Figure T1.5 can partially answer these questions. For each constraint there exists what is called the **shadow price** or **dual price**. These are listed in Figure T1.5c for each constraint. The dual price for constraint 1 is 0.0625, and the dual prices for constraints 2 and 3 are 0.1750 and 0, respectively. (Note that the dual prices are also given in Figure T1.5a as the "opportunity costs" for the corresponding slack variables.)

Each constraint has a dual price. The dual price for a constraint is the marginal change in the optimal objective function value that would occur if the right-hand side of that constraint were altered. For example, dual price 0.0625 for constraint 1 implies that if one additional pound of cereal were available (at $0.20 per pound), the optimum production plan could be modified to produce $0.0625 more profit. Similarly, the dual price of $0.175 means that if an additional pound of meat were available (at $0.50 per pound), the optimum could be modified to produce $0.175 more profit. It must be emphasized that these dual prices are valid *only if one right-hand side is modified*; if two or more changes are made simultaneously, these prices may or may not be valid.

Figure T1.5c also gives the *range* of right-hand side values over which the dual prices will be valid. For example, B(1) is the right-hand-side coefficient of the first straint. The table says that *keeping everything else the same*, each additional pound of cereal would increase profit by $0.0625 until the right-hand side equals 600,000 (in the

"Max B(i)" column). Similarly, a reduction in cereal would reduce the profit by $0.0625 per pound until the right-hand side reaches 240,000 lbs (Min B(i)). If the amount of available cereal is changed enough to be outside these limits, new dual prices would apply. This analysis is sometimes called *right-hand-side ranging*.

T1.11 USING LINEAR PROGRAMMING MODELS FOR DECISION MAKING

The formulations in Section T1.5 give the impression that using linear programming is a clean, simple process; we recognize a problem that fits the linear programming framework, model it, solve it, and then we are done. In practice, using linear programming and other optimization models is not so straightforward, nor is it static. Specifically, our goal in using models is to obtain usable solutions that are better than those we would have obtained without the models (whether the solution is mathematically optimal or not), to use the models to revise and update our decisions in a timely fashion, and to increase our confidence in our decisions. We will use the Healthy Pet Food and Solar Oil Company examples to illustrate how we might use the models in practice and to see what benefits we can obtain.

HEALTHY PET FOOD REVISITED

The Healthy Pet Food example was presented as if every aspect of the problem were known with certainty, and a number of simplifying assumptions were made. We now reconsider the situation to illustrate more completely how linear programming models can be used. (See Table T1.1 on page 168 for the original problem data.)

The linear programming formulation for this problem is as follows:

Maximize $z = \$0.65\,M + \$0.45\,Y$

Subject to	$2\,M + 3\,Y \leq 400{,}000$	(cereal constraint)
	$3\,M + 1.5\,Y \leq 300{,}000$	(meat constraint)
	$M \leq 90{,}000$	(Meaties capacity)
	$M, Y \geq 0$	

and the optimal solution is $M = 50{,}000$, $Y = 100{,}000$, and $z = \$77{,}500$ per month. This solution would cause Healthy to use all 400,000 pounds of cereal and all 300,000 pounds of meat available each month at $0.20 and $0.50 per pound, respectively.

Uncertainty Regarding Price and Cost Data In the original problem we assumed that the data given in Table T1.1 were known for sure. In fact, there is considerable uncertainty about the price and cost estimates. For example, suppose that after seeing the preceding solution the vice-president of marketing says, "If we're only going to produce 50,000 packages of Meaties each month, we could charge $3 a package; demand for Meaties would still be at least 50,000 packages per month at that price." Suppose we increased the price of Meaties by $0.20 to $3 per package. How does this change the optimal production plan and Healthy's profits?

The only thing in the problem that changes is the profit per package for Meaties, which increases from $0.65 to $0.85; so we want to

Maximize $z = \$0.85\,M + \$0.45\,Y$

Using the objective function sensitivity analysis information in Figure T1.5 or re-solving the problem with the new objective function, we can determine that the optimal production plan is still $M = 50{,}000$, $Y = 100{,}000$, but the monthly profit increases to $87,500. So with the available resources, the change in the relative profit margins for the two dog foods is not enough to change the optimal product mix, but the profit will increase. The same analysis would apply if we believe that the previously assumed material or packaging costs may not be correct.

This analysis could be performed using a variety of scenarios for product and raw material prices. It would show us if, and how, the optimal product mix will change depending on the actual values of the parameters.

Pricing Additional Resources Returning to the original problem, suppose someone offered to sell us additional cereal or meat, but at a higher price than we are currently paying. The obvious questions are these:

1. What should we be willing to pay for the additional resources?
2. How much of each resource should we buy at various prices?
3. How should the additional resources be used? That is, how should we modify our product mix to utilize the additional resources?

We can answer these questions using the dual prices discussed in the previous section. The dual price for the cereal constraint is $0.0625. This means that Healthy could buy another pound of cereal at the original price of $0.20 per pound and then, by revising its production, could earn another $0.0625. Therefore, Healthy should be willing to pay up to $0.20 + $0.0625 = $0.2625 per pound for additional cereal. (Healthy would obtain the additional profit by increasing its production of Yummies to 100,000.50 and decreasing its production of Meaties to

49,999.75 so as not to use more than 300,000 pounds of meat.)

So Healthy should buy at least one additional pound of cereal as long as its price is less than $0.2625 per pound, but should it buy more? The upper limit on B(1) in Figure T1.5c is 600,000, so the answer is that Healthy should be willing to buy up to an additional 200,000 pounds of cereal (with no additional meat). Once it buys 200,000 additional pounds of cereal, its optimum production plan is to make 200,000 packages of Yummies and no Meaties. Additional cereal, even at $0.01 per pound, would not help Healthy *unless it were able to obtain additional meat as well.*

When only one resource is modified at a time, the dual price and right-hand side ranging information for the original model could be used to determine what price to pay for an additional resource and how much to buy. The new optimum solution, however, is not immediately clear and it requires some additional arithmetic. If two or more resources are being modified simultaneously, the model usually needs to be modified and the problem re-solved. With existing computer packages, such modifying and re-solving are easy.

Evaluating the Effects of Additional Constraints Optimization models are also used to evaluate the consequences of constraints. Consider the original Healthy Pet Food problem again. Suppose a shortage of transportation vehicles has developed, and Healthy's shipper has informed Healthy that it can only ship 135,000 packages of dog food each month, a 10% reduction from Healthy's current optimum level. What should Healthy do, and how much does this restriction cost Healthy each month?

A typical response is to reduce production of all products by 10%, that is, make 45,000 packages of Meaties and 90,000 packages of Yummies. This generates a monthly profit of $69,750, a 10% reduction. This, in fact, is *not* the appropriate response under the circumstances. By adding the constraint $M + Y \leq 135{,}000$ to the original model and solving, we get the solution that $M = 65{,}000$, $Y = 70{,}000$, and $z = \$73{,}750$. So even though total production must be cut by 10%, it is best to *increase* the production of Meaties. The total profit decreases by less than 5%. This suggests that Healthy should only be willing to pay up to $3750 per month for additional monthly shipping capacity of 15,000 packages, not $7750. This result is counterintuitive for many decision makers, but as we can see, the difference in profit between the optimum plan and the across-the-board reduction is substantial.

Incorporating Product Demand Functions into the Model Linear programs dealing with product mix and resource allocation decisions typically assume that prices are fixed by some outside force (e.g., the free market) and that the company's decisions will not influence these prices. In some cases, however, companies control the prices of their outputs and inputs, either directly or indirectly through the amount they produce or purchase. For example, if the company lowers the price of its product, it believes that it can sell more. In these cases, the company is interested both in determining its optimal production or resource allocation strategy and in determining the optimal price(s) for some product(s). When the underlying demand functions, which describe the relationships between product price and demand, exhibit the right properties, linear programming models can be used to solve the price and volume problems simultaneously.

Suppose Healthy believes the amount of each dog food it can sell depends on the price it sets. To keep things simple, we will assume that over reasonable ranges of production the demand functions for Meaties and Yummies can be described by Table T1.12.

One way to solve the problem is to construct nine models, one for each combination of product prices. Each model would have objective function coefficients based on the assumed product prices, and the upper limits on product demand would vary with the price. After solving all nine problems, we would find that the optimum solution is to set the price of Meaties at $3.10 per package and the price of Yummies at $2.00 per package, producing

TABLE T1.12 HEALTHY PET FOOD DEMAND FUNCTION

Meaties	
If price/package is	Market demand/month
$ 3.10	35,000
$ 2.80	60,000
$ 2.60	100,000
Yummies	
If price/package is	Market demand/month
$ 2.25	50,000
$ 2.00	100,000
$ 1.75	140,000

35,000 packages of Meaties and 100,000 packages of Yummies each month; this generates a monthly profit of $78,250. (You might want to solve these problems yourself to verify this result.)

A more direct but mathematically more sophisticated approach is to formulate this as a "0/1 mixed integer problem." Such problems are discussed in Section T1.12. The advantage of the mixed integer model is that one does not have to solve a separate problem for every combination of prices. Such enumeration can become prohibitive with a large number of inputs and outputs and several possible prices.

SOLAR OIL COMPANY REVISITED: UPDATING PRODUCTION DECISIONS

We will use the Solar Oil Company example to illustrate how linear programs can be used to adjust to raw material price changes. (See Table T1.3 on page 175 for the original data.)

The optimal solution for Solar is $x_{1R} = 11{,}428.57$, $x_{2R} = 9107.14$, $x_{3R} = 14{,}464.29$, $x_{4R} = 0$, $x_{1P} = 0$, $x_{2P} = 5892.86$, $x_{3P} = 535.71$, $x_{4P} = 10{,}000$, and $z = \$42{,}142.86$ per day. This means Solar should produce 35,000 barrels of regular gasoline and 16,428.57 barrels of premium gasoline each day.

Now suppose the price of raw gasoline 2 increases by $0.50 to $18.50 per barrel. The only changes to the model are that the objective function coefficients for x_{2R} and x_{2P} must be revised. The new objective function is

$$\text{Max } z = 2.5\, x_{1R} + x_{2R} - x_{3R} - 3.5\, x_{4R} + 5.0\, x_{1P} + 3.5\, x_{2P} + 1.5\, x_{3P} - x_{4P}$$

The optimal solution becomes $x_{1R} = 18{,}500$, $x_{2R} = 0$, $x_{3R} = 15{,}000$, $x_{4R} = 1500$, $x_{1P} = 1500$, $x_{2P} = 3000$, $x_{3P} = 0$, $x_{4P} = 8500$, and $z = \$35{,}500$. With this new solution Solar still should produce 35,000 barrels of regular per day, but it should change its input mix and cut back its production of premium to 13,000 barrels per day. If Solar simply kept its original blend and production plan, the daily profit would be $34,642.86. By adjusting its plan, Solar can obtain $857.14 (or approximately 2.5%) more profit per day.

In many industries the prices of both raw materials and outputs can change almost daily (oil and gas, chemicals, paper, and metals are prime examples). Over the course of a year, a company that is able to adjust its product blend (without hurting product quality) to account for these changes can significantly improve its profit. In practice, of course, Solar would probably use a multiperiod model that allowed it to build up and work down inventories. This makes the problem larger and a bit more complicated, but its use as a dynamic decision aid is essentially the same.

T1.12 INTEGER AND MIXED-INTEGER PROGRAMS

Many operational problems contain decision variables that only make sense if they are integer-valued. In such cases rounding-off the optimum continuous solution may not give an optimum integer-valued solution. This is especially true when the decision variables represent yes/no type decisions; that is, where the decision variables can only equal 1 (yes, take some action) or 0 (no, do not take that action). Constrained optimization models that require all the variables to take on integer values are called **integer programs**. If some of the variables must be integer-valued and some may be continuous, these problems are called **mixed-integer programs**.

Integer and mixed-integer programs are common in problems involving the location of facilities, scheduling or assignment of personnel, sequencing of work, and routing of vehicles. For example, in location problems the variables usually represent whether or not to locate facilities at some possible sites or whether to assign a customer to a given facility. In scheduling problems the variables may represent whether or not a person, crew, or vehicle is assigned to a task or route. The following is a simple illustration of an integer program.

EXAMPLE 5

Lafayette Industries produces customized products for its customers. It currently has 12 completed jobs ready for shipment to the West Coast. One truck is leaving today, one tomorrow, and a third in two days. The jobs to be shipped have more total volume and weight than can be sent by two truckloads. The profit Lafayette will earn on each job is related to when the product is shipped. These values, along with the volume and weight of each job, are listed in Table T1.13. Jobs must be shipped intact; that is, part of a job cannot be shipped on one truck and the rest of it shipped on another. The maximum cargo volume of each truck is 1500 cubic feet, and the max-

TABLE T1.13 LAFAYETTE INDUSTRIES DATA

Job	Volume (cu. ft.)	Weight (000 lbs.)	Profit ($00) if shipped Today	Tomorrow	Next Day
1	350	6	20	20	18
2	300	9	23	21	20
3	160	4	16	15	12
4	400	15	35	33	33
5	470	10	39	38	36
6	250	8	19	19	18
7	400	9	22	20	20
8	650	18	40	36	34
9	620	7	42	40	39
10	270	5	17	16	15
11	180	5	12	12	11
12	210	11	17	15	14

imum cargo weight is 40,000 pounds. The shipping manager of Lafayette wants to determine the assignment of jobs to trucks to maximize the company's profit.

This problem can be formulated as a 0/1 integer program (all variables can take on the values of 0 or 1). The decision variables specify on which truck each job should be shipped. Thus, we define the variables:

$$x_{ij} = 1 \text{ if job } i \text{ is shipped on truck } j, \quad \text{where } i = 1, \ldots, 12 \text{ and } j = 1, 2, 3$$
$$= 0 \text{ otherwise}$$

Then the objective function of maximizing total profit from the 12 jobs can be written as

$$\text{maximize } z = 20\, x_{11} + 20\, x_{12} + 18\, x_{13} + 23\, x_{21} + \ldots + 15\, x_{12,2} + 14\, x_{12,3}$$

To ensure that every job is shipped once and only once, for each job i there would be a constraint:

$$x_{i1} + x_{i2} + x_{i3} = 1 \quad \text{for i} = 1, \ldots, 12$$

In addition, the volume and weight limits for each truck j cannot be exceeded:

$$350\, x_{1j} + 300\, x_{2j} + \ldots + 210\, x_{12j} \leq 1500 \quad \text{for j} = 1, 2, 3$$
$$6\, x_{1j} + 9\, x_{2j} + \ldots + 11\, x_{12j} \leq 40 \quad \text{for j} = 1, 2, 3$$

The optimal solution for this problem is to ship jobs 2, 3, 8, and 10 today, jobs 1, 5, 6, 11, and 12 tomorrow, and jobs 4, 7, and 9 the next day; the profit will be $29,200.

Although integer programs can be very useful, they are much more difficult to solve than linear programs. It might appear that integer programs, especially 0/1 integer programs, should be easier to solve than linear programs because they have a finite number of possible solutions (in contrast to linear programs, which normally have an infinite number of possible solutions). But the simplex method *implicitly* evaluates the infinite number of possible solutions by *explicitly* evaluating relatively few extreme points. For integer programs the number of possible solutions may be finite, but this finite number can be very large, and the number of solutions that must be evaluated explicitly before finding and verifying an optimum is usually many times greater than for linear programs. For example, the Lafayette model has 36 decision variables, each of which can take on the value of 0 or 1. The total number of ways 0s and 1s can be assigned to the variables is $2^{36} > 68{,}700{,}000{,}000$. Many of these are infeasible because they violate the constraints, but there are still several million solutions that are feasible and must be evaluated.

Fortunately, improved solution techniques developed during the past 30 years have made wide application of integer programming practical in operations management. Problems with hundreds or thousands of integer variables are now solved routinely.

T1.13 HEURISTIC METHODS IN OPERATIONS

Many operations problems can be described verbally or formulated mathematically as optimization problems, yet there is no practical way to obtain the optimal solution in a reasonable amount of time, either because the problem is too large or the relationships are too complex. In these cases, solution methods called *heuristics* are often used. A **heuristic** is a rule of thumb or set of steps that produces a solution to a problem. The solution is not guaranteed to be optimal, but if the heuristic is well designed and tested, over the long term the solutions produced should be better than those that would be obtained without the heuristic. Many good heuristics exist for operational problems that can be expressed as integer programs, such as routing, scheduling, sequencing, and facility and process design problems.

CHARACTERISTICS

The heuristics commonly used in operations management have the following characteristics:

1. They are *iterative*: they repeat the same steps over and over.
2. They are usually "greedy" or "myopic." This means that at each step the heuristic makes a decision or selects an action based on the decision's immediate or "local" effect rather than its overall effect on the solution.

Heuristics are normally based on one of two possible strategies: improvement or construction. An **improvement heuristic** begins with a feasible solution to the problem and then iteratively uses rules and procedures to find a better solution. When it cannot find a better solution, it stops. A **construction heuristic** constructs a final solution from scratch. At each iteration another piece of the solution is determined (e.g., the value of one more decision variable). When a complete solution has been constructed, the heuristic stops. Of course, a heuristic can have two components: one that constructs a solution and one that tries to improve it. Following are examples of improvement and construction heuristics.

Vehicle Routing A school district must pick up students at hundreds of bus stops throughout the district and take them to their respective schools. The district needs to determine the number of buses it will need, which bus to assign to each stop, and the routes the buses should take, subject to getting the students to school and satisfying restrictions on bus capacity, driving time, and routing (such as whether a bus can transport students to two or three schools). For even modest-size problems this integer program becomes enormous.

An improvement heuristic called the *Clarke-Wright heuristic*[4] has been used to solve many versions of this problem (notice that this problem structure applies to any vehicles that visit stops, such as delivery and collection vehicles). The heuristic begins by assigning a separate bus to each bus stop. It then uses a decision rule to decide whether or not it is economical to merge two bus routes into one (and eliminate one of the buses). It continues to merge routes until no more improvements can be found.

Production Line Balancing Production lines are made up of interconnected work stations. Each product passes through the same work stations in the same sequence. At each work station, one or more tasks are performed on the product. The production rate of the line is governed by how the tasks are distributed among the work stations: the work station with the most work per unit controls the speed of the line. Ideally, a company would like the workload evenly distributed among the work stations. The design problem is to decide how many work stations to have and which tasks to assign to each. This problem is difficult for realistic problems because (1) task times are "lumpy," that is, tasks require discrete amounts of time and cannot be subdivided into infinitely small pieces and (2) there is some flexibility of the sequencing of tasks. For even modest sized problems this cannot be solved with optimization techniques; construction heuristics must be used. These heuristics assign one task at a time to a work station using various decision rules. When all tasks have been assigned, a feasible design has been obtained. Sometimes an improvement heuristic is then used to search for better designs.

ADVANTAGES OF HEURISTICS

Heuristics have several desirable features:

1. They are simple and easy to understand because they are usually based on some intuitive ideas concerning the problem.
2. They solve problems quickly. Because they are based on simple rules and use a myopic evaluation at each step, little computation is needed.
3. They can be combined with optimization techniques. It is common to break a large problem into pieces,

[4]See G. Clarke and J. W . Wright, "Scheduling of Vehicles from a Central Depot to a Number of Delivery Points," *Operations Research*, Vol. 11, 1963, pp. 568–581.

solve the smaller subproblems with an optimization algorithm, and then use a heuristic to combine the subproblem solutions (and then possibly repeat this procedure).

Development of heuristics involves more than developing good rules of thumb. A representative sample of problems should be tested empirically to gauge the quality of the solutions (how close they are to the optimum objective function value) and how long it takes to obtain the solutions.

SUMMARY

- A **model** is a representation of reality that captures the essential features of an object, a system, or a problem without being cluttered by unimportant details.
- **Constrained optimization models** help to find the best alternative from a set of alternatives defined by a set of mathematical equalities or inequalities.
- Constrained optimization models allow a person to evaluate alternative solutions without having to construct or experiment on a real production system. In addition, they do the following:
  - Help to structure the thought process.
  - Increase objectivity.
  - Make complex problems more tractable.
  - Make problems amenable to mathematical and computer solution.
  - Facilitate "what if" analysis.
- Constrained optimization models are used for many types of operations decisions, including aggregate planning, personnel scheduling, product design and blending, job-shop scheduling, and location and logistical problems.
- **Decision variables** are quantities the decision maker controls.
- An **objective function** measures the goodness or badness of an alternative.
- A **linear programming model** is a type of constrained optimization model that contains only linear functions, and the decision variables are continuous.
- **Sensitivity (parametric) analysis** is the process of evaluating the effects of changes in the model's **parameters** on the **optimal solution**.
- **Integer programs** are optimization models in which the decision variables can only take on integer values. **Mixed-integer programs** are optimization models in which some variables can take on continuous values (fractional) and others can only take on integer values.
- A **heuristic** is a rule of thumb or set of steps that produces a solution to a problem. Heuristics are used to solve complex problems for which efficient optimization methods are not available. Heuristics do not necessarily find the optimal solution.

KEY TERMS

additivity **172**
aggregate planning **177**
artificial variables **189**
basic feasible solution **184**
basic solution **184**
basic variables **184**
basis **184**
Big-M method **189**
blending problem **175**
canonical form **183**
certainty **172**
constrained optimization models **167**
constraints **168**
construction heuristic **197**
contour **180**
decision variables **167**
degenerate solution **191**
divisibility **172**
dual (shadow) price **192**
entering variable **186**
extreme points **180**
feasible set (region) **179**
feasible solution **179**
feed mix problem **173**
heuristic **197**
improvement heuristic **197**
infeasible problem **182**
infeasible solution **190**
integer programs (mixed integer programs) **195**
leaving variable **186**
linear programming model (linear program) **170**
model **167**
multiple optima **182**
nonbasic variables **184**
objective function **167**
objective function contours **180**
opportunity cost **186**
optimal solution **179**
parameters (coefficients) **198**

pivot element **186**
pivot row and pivot column **186**
product mix problem **175**
proportionality **172**
ranging **192**
ratio test **186**
sensitivity (parametric) analysis **192**
simplex method (algorithm) **182**
simplex tableaus (tables) **185**
slack variable **183**
solution **167**
two-phase method **190**
unbounded problem **182**

SOLVED PROBLEMS

Problem 1: Suppose a company manufactures two products, A and B, using three inputs, labor, material R, and material S. To make one unit of product A requires 6 pounds of R, 7.5 pounds of S, and 9 person-hours of labor; to make one unit of product B requires 12 pounds of R, 4.5 pounds of S, and 6 person-hours of labor. The demands for the products are such that the company can sell as much of each product as it can produce and earn a profit of \$3 per unit of A and \$4 per unit of B. However, only 900 pounds of R, 675 pounds of S, and 1200 person-hours of labor are available to the company each day.

(a) Formulate the company's problem as a linear program to maximize profit.

(b) Graph the feasible region for this problem.

(c) Solve the problem graphically by finding the best extreme point.

Solution: (a) The decision maker controls the amount of each product to make each day. So we can define the decision variables as

x_j = No. of units of product j (= A, B) to make each day.

The company's objective is to maximize the profit per day. We want to express "profit per day" as a function of the decision variables so that no matter what numerical values the decision variables take on, the function will compute the daily profit. Total profit per day is equal to

(profit/unit of A made) × (units of A made/day)
+ (profit/unit of B made) × (units of B made/day).

Substituting the appropriate numerical values and variables for these quantities gives an objective function:

$$\text{Maximize } z = 3\,x_A + 4\,x_B$$

The firm wants to maximize this objective function but subject to satisfying constraints on the availability of the inputs. The first restriction is that

No. of person-hours used per day $\leq$ 1200

The number of person-hours used per day is equal to

(person-hours used/unit of A) × (units of A made/day)
+ (person-hours used/unit of B) × (units of B made/day)

Substituting in the appropriate coefficients and variable names yields the constraint

$$9\,x_A + 6\,x_B \leq 1200$$

Repeating this for the raw material restrictions yields the constraints

$$6\,x_A + 12\,x_B \le 900$$
$$7.5\,x_A + 4.5\,x_B \le 675$$

Finally, the variables must be nonnegative:

$$x_A,\ x_B \ge 0$$

Putting all of this together gives the linear programming model:

$$\text{Maximize } z = 3\,x_A + 4\,x_B$$

$$\begin{aligned} \text{Subject to}\quad 9\,x_A + 6\,x_B &\le 1200 \\ 6\,x_A + 12\,x_B &\le 900 \\ 7.5\,x_A + 4.5\,x_B &\le 675 \\ x_A,\ x_B &\ge 0 \end{aligned}$$

(b) The nonnegativity constraints, $x_A \ge 0$ and $x_B \ge 0$, restrict the feasible solutions to the upper-right-hand quadrant of Figure T1.6. We then plot the inequality $9\,x_A + 6\,x_B \le 1200$ by graphing its boundary line, $9\,x_A + 6\,x_B = 1200$, and finding the side that satisfies the constraint. We first set $x_A = 0$ and solve for x_B, which gives $x_B = 200$, and then set $x_B = 0$ and solve for x_A, which gives $x_A = 133.33$. The point $x_A = 0$, $x_B = 0$ satisfies the inequality, so all the points on

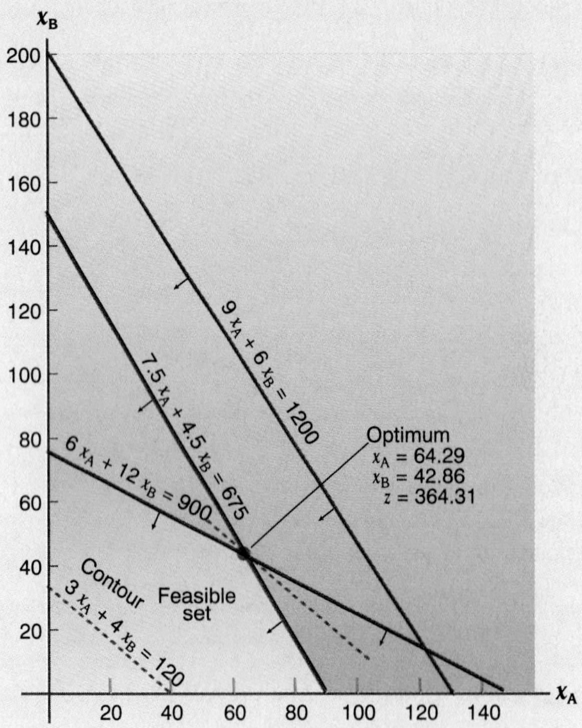

FIGURE T1.6 Graphical solution of solved problem 1.

the same side of the line satisfy this inequality. Repeating this procedure for the other constraints gives the feasible set in Figure T1.6. Notice that the first constraint is redundant; that is, it does not eliminate any solutions that are not already eliminated by the other constraints. It can be eliminated from the problem without changing the feasible set. The feasible set is the four-sided shaded region.

(c) Figure T1.6 shows objective function contours graphed for various profit levels (dotted lines). The contour with the highest value intersects the extreme point formed by the intersection of the second and third constraints. To obtain the coordinates of this point, we solve the two constraint equations simultaneously:

$$\left.\begin{aligned} 6\,x_A + 12\,x_B &= 900 \\ 7.5\,x_A + 4.5\,x_B &= 675 \end{aligned}\right\} \rightarrow x_A = 64.29, \quad x_B = 42.86$$

The objective function value for the highest contour is then $z = 3(64.29) + 4(42.86) = 364.31$.

Problem 2: Chip Green is the head groundskeeper at Birdie Valley Golf Club. For the mix of grass for the golf course, Chip has decided that the best fertilizer would be a 10-8-12 mixture. (Fertilizer is defined by three values—*a*, *b*, and *c*—where *a* is the percentage of nitrogen, *b* is the percentage of phosphorus, and *c* is the percentage of potash in the fertilizer. The remaining material is inert matter.) Chip can buy a 10-8-12 mix of fertilizer for \$21.75 per 100 pounds. But there are other fertilizers on the market at a variety of prices. The chemical content and prices are given below. Chip would like to determine whether or not he could buy several fertilizers and mix them together to obtain a 10-8-12 mixture at a lower cost than \$21.75 per 100 pounds. Recognizing that it might be impossible to obtain an exact 10-8-12 mix from the fertilizers, Chip is willing to accept chemical percentages of at least the target amounts, but no more than 0.5% above them (so the nitrogen level should be between 10% and 10.5%).

(a) Formulate Chip's problem as a linear program;

(b) Solve this problem using a computer package.

Fertilizer	% Ni % Ph % Po	Cost/100 lb
1	10-8-12	\$21.75
2	8-11-15	\$23.50
3	12-7-12	\$22.00
4	10-10-10	\$19.50
5	15-10-6	\$18.50

Solution: (a) Chip is interested in the *mix* of fertilizers to use, so we can define the variables

x_j = lb of fertilizer j in each lb of mixture

The objective is to minimize the cost per pound of fertilizer:

$$\text{Minimize } z = 0.2175\,x_1 + 0.2350\,x_2 + 0.2200\,x_3 + 0.1950\,x_4 + 0.1850\,x_5$$

The main constraints are those that ensure the desired percentage of nitrogen, phosphorus, and potash.

$$\begin{aligned}
10\,x_1 + 8\,x_2 + 12\,x_3 + 10\,x_4 + 15\,x_5 &\geq 10 \\
10\,x_1 + 8\,x_2 + 12\,x_3 + 10\,x_4 + 15\,x_5 &\leq 10.5 \\
8\,x_1 + 11\,x_2 + 7\,x_3 + 10\,x_4 + 10\,x_5 &\geq 8 \\
8\,x_1 + 11\,x_2 + 7\,x_3 + 10\,x_4 + 10\,x_5 &\leq 8.5 \\
12\,x_1 + 15\,x_2 + 12\,x_3 + 10\,x_4 + 6\,x_5 &\geq 12 \\
12\,x_1 + 15\,x_2 + 12\,x_3 + 10\,x_4 + 6\,x_5 &\leq 12.5
\end{aligned}$$

Because the variables are defined as the amount of each type of fertilizer in 1 pound of mixture, we need a constraint that ensures that the mixture adds up to exactly 1 pound:

$$x_1 + x_2 + x_3 + x_4 + x_5 = 1$$

Also, all variables must be nonnegative.

(b) The optimal solution for this problem is $x_1 = 0.225$, $x_2 = 0.15$, $x_3 = 0.40$, $x_4 = 0.225$, $x_5 = 0$, and $z = \$0.21605$. So, by mixing the 10-8-12 fertilizer with three other fertilizers, Chip can reduce the cost. The actual mixture has a chemical content of 10.5-8.5-12.

Problem 3: Solve the following linear program using the simplex method.

$$\text{Minimize } z = 30\,x_1 + 10\,x_2$$

$$\begin{aligned} \text{Subject to} \quad 2\,x_1 + 4\,x_2 &\le 80 \\ x_1 + x_2 &\le 25 \\ 8\,x_1 + 6\,x_2 &\ge 120 \\ x_1, x_2 &\ge 0 \end{aligned}$$

Solution: We first must put the problem in canonical form. All the right-hand sides are nonnegative. To change the constraints into equalities, we (1) add a slack variable s_1 to the first constraint, (2) add a slack variable s_2 to the second constraint, and (3) *subtract* a slack variable s_3 from the third constraint. Variables s_1 and s_2 will be the initial basic variables for constraints 1 and 2, but constraint 3 does not have a basic variable (one that appears only in constraint 3 and with a +1 coefficient), so we add an artificial variable, A_3, to constraint 3.

We now construct the tableau shown in Table T1.14. Because we are minimizing, we assign the artificial variable A_3 a large positive objective function coefficient, say +1000. For the initial solution we compute the z_j and $c_j - z_j$ values for each column. Because we are minimizing the objective function, we select the variable with the most *negative* $c_j - z_j$ value to enter the basis; this is variable x_1. We now perform the ratio test by dividing each of the right-hand-side constants by the corresponding values in the pivot column (the x_1 column). The row with the smallest ratio is the one for constraint 3, so x_1 will enter the basis and A_3 will leave the basis.

We now perform the pivoting operations. We divide constraint 3 by the pivot element, 8. We take 2 times the new form of constraint 3 and subtract it from constraint 1 to give a zero value in the pivot column of constraint 1. Similarly, we subtract 1 times the new form of constraint 3 from constraint 2. The resulting tableau is given in Table T1.15. In this table the $c_j - z_j$ value for x_2 is most negative (it is the only one that is negative), so we bring x_2 into the basis. Constraints 1 and 3 tie for the lowest ratio, so we arbitrarily select constraint 1 as the pivot row (actually, there are

TABLE T1.14 FIRST TABLEAU: PROBLEM 3

		x_1	x_2	s_1	s_2	s_3	A_3			
C_B	Basic Var.	30	10	0	0	0	1,000	b	Ratio	
0	s_1	2	4	1	0	0	0	80	(80/2) = 40	
0	s_2	1	1	0	1	0	0	25	(25/1) = 25	
1,000	A_3	[8]	6	0	0	−1	1	120	(120/8) = 15	←pivot row
	z_j	8,000	6,000	0	0	−1,000	1,000	120,000		
	$c_j - z_j$	−7,970	−5,990	0	0	1,000	0			
		↑ pivot column								

TABLE T1.15 SECOND TABLEAU: PROBLEM 3

C_B	Basic Var.	x_1 30	x_2 10	s_1 0	s_2 0	s_3 0	A_3 1,000	b	Ratio
0	s_1	0	5/2	1	0	1/2	—	50	(50/2.5) = 20 ←pivot row
0	s_2	0	1/4	0	1	1/8	—	10	(10/0.25) = 40
30	x_1	1	3/4	0	0	−1/8	—	15	(15/0.75) = 20
	z_j	30	90/4	0	0	−30/8	—	450	
	$c_j - z_j$	0	−50/4	0	0	30/8	—		

↑ pivot column

tie-breaking rules, but they are beyond the scope of this book). Performing the pivot operations gives the tableau in Table T1.16. No $c_j - z_j$ value is positive in this table, so the solution there is optimal. To get the solution, we set the nonbasic variables, s_1 and s_3, equal to zero and the basic variables equal to the values in the "b" column: $x_1 = 0$, $x_2 = 20$, and $s_2 = 5$, and the objective function value is $z = 200$. (Notice that this is a degenerate solution because a basic variable equals zero.)

TABLE T1.16 THIRD TABLEAU: PROBLEM 3

C_B	Basic Var.	x_1 30	x_2 10	s_1 0	s_2 0	s_3 0	A_3 1,000	b
10	x_2	0	1	2/5	0	1/10	—	20
0	s_2	0	0	−1/10	1	1/10	—	5
30	x_1	1	0	−3/10	0	−2/10	—	0
	z_j	30	10	−5	0	−5	—	200
	$c_j - z_j$	0	0	5	0	5	—	

DISCUSSION AND REVIEW QUESTIONS

1. What are the three primary components of a constrained optimization model?
2. Explain the difference between a parameter and a decision variable.
3. What are the primary assumptions underlying linear programming models?
4. If most parameters represent estimates that are not known with certainty, how can constrained optimization models be of any value for decision making?
5. What does it mean when a problem has an unbounded solution? If you formulated a real problem and the solution was unbounded, what does this imply about your model?
6. What does it mean to perform sensitivity or "what if" analysis?
7. Explain the meaning of dual prices. Why would one want to know the value of a dual price, and how might it be used?
8. What is the difference between a linear programming model and an integer programming model? Under what conditions could a linear program be used to approximate an integer program?
9. What is a heuristic? Why would someone use it to solve a problem that could be formulated as a constrained optimization model?

PROBLEMS

1. Deutchlander Machine Company (DMC) makes two types of printing presses: a four-color litho and a two-color litho. Demand for both products is booming and exceeds DMC's ability to satisfy it. Most raw

materials are plentiful, but production is limited by three factors: a shortage of steel rollers, gear cutting capacity, and roller polishing capacity. Each four-color press requires 16 rollers, and each two-color press requires 8 rollers. The four-color presses require 30 hours of gear cutting and 8 hours of polishing time, and the two-color presses require 12 hours of gear cutting and 3 hours of polishing time. DMC is able to buy 100 rollers per week, and it has 160 hours of gear cutting time and 40 hours of polishing time available per week.

To avoid harming long-term sales, DMC does not want to raise prices. At current prices DMC will earn a profit of DM24,000 on each four-color press made and DM10,000 on each two-color press made. So as not to abandon either product market, DMC also wants to produce at least two units of each press each week. (a) Formulate DMC's problem as a linear program to maximize its profit. (b) Solve the problem (either graphically, using the simplex method, or using a computer) and explain in words DMC's optimal solution.

2. Robertville Furniture Company (RFC) makes two types of dressers: the Classic and the Modern. RFC sells the Classic for $310 and the Modern for $350. At these prices RFC believes it can sell up to 20 Classic and 25 Modern dressers per week. Each type of dresser is made of oak and covered with a pecan veneer. The wood requirements for each dresser are given in the table below. Oak costs $1.50 per board foot, and pecan veneer costs $2 per square foot. The dressers must go through two manufacturing departments: cutting and veneering. The machine hours required for each dresser are also given below. RFC has only 40 hours of production time available each week in each department, and it can obtain up to 2000 board feet of oak and 1500 square feet of pecan veneer each week. The cost of operating each manufacturing department is essentially fixed, so RFC would like to maximize its contribution to overhead (revenue minus variable costs). (a) Formulate RFC's problem as a linear program, defining your variables clearly. (b) Solve the problem (graphically, using the simplex method, or using a computer) and state what RFC should do (i.e., explain RFC's optimal solution in words). (c) What resource is limiting RFC's production?

	Oak/Dresser (Board Ft)	Pecan/Dresser (Sq Ft)	Cutting Time (Hr/Dresser)	Veneering Time (Hr/Dresser)
Classic	90	50	1.20	1.00
Modern	100	60	0.90	1.20

3. Western Pulp (WP) produces recycled paperboard for box manufacturers by combining four grades of recycled paper stock. Each grade of stock has a different strength, color, and texture. The strength, color, and texture of the paperboard are approximately a weighted average of those characteristics of the paper inputs. The table below gives the characteristics of the paper stocks and their cost per ton. WP has received an order for 500 tons of paperboard with a strength rating of at least 7, a color of at least 5, and texture of at least 6. WP would like to determine the least costly mix required to produce this paperboard. (a) Formulate the problem as a linear program. (b) Solve this problem on a computer and explain the optimal solution.

Paper Grade	Strength	Color	Texture	Cost/Ton
1	8	9	8	$150
2	6	7	5	$110
3	5	5	6	$ 90
4	3	4	5	$ 50

4. Volcano Potato Company (VPC) grows potatoes, processes them, and then sells three potato products: fresh potatoes, frozen french fried potatoes, and frozen hash ball potatoes (shredded and then reconstituted balls of potatoes with a soft consistency). During the next two months, VPC expects to harvest 8 million pounds of potatoes. VPC would like to determine how much of each product should be made from the potatoes. Potatoes are graded according to quality on a 0–5 scale. VPC divides its potatoes into three grades: A, B, and C. Grade A potatoes have an average quality rating of 4.5; grade B potatoes have an average quality rating of 2.5, and grade C potatoes have a quality rating below 1 and are not used for any products. From historical data and estimates based on the current growing season's weather VPC believes the distribution of potato quality will be:

Grade	A	B	C
% of Harvest	50	40	10

Fresh potatoes earn a profit of $0.40 per pound after processing costs, but only grade A potatoes can be sold as fresh potatoes. Frozen french fried potatoes earn $0.32 per pound after processing costs, but the potatoes used must have an average quality rating of at least 3.5. Hash balls earn $0.25 per pound after processing costs, but the potatoes used must have an average quality rating of at least 3.0. Assume that these ratings are linear in the sense that the quality rating of a mixture equals the weighted average of the inputs. VPC believes it can sell as much french fried and hash ball potatoes as it can make, but it believes the total demand for its fresh potatoes during the next two months is 2.5 million pounds. (a) Formulate a linear programming model to determine the best use for the potatoes so as to maximize VPC's profit. (b) Solve the problem using a computer and explain the answer in words. (c)* Suppose VPC could buy additional grade A potatoes at $0.35 per pound; how much should it buy? Explain.

5. Manfred Leaks manages a large discount store. His biggest problem has been scheduling cashiers so that he has an adequate number without having too many. The store is open from 9 A.M. to 9 P.M. every day of the week. Based on historical data, he found that the customer patterns for Monday to Thursday are essentially the same, but those for Friday, Saturday, and Sunday are all different. He divided the day into three four-hour segments and estimated how many cashiers were needed for each time period for each day of the week. These are given in the following table.

Day of Week	Mon–Thur	Fri	Sat	Sun
9 A.M. to 1 P.M.	6	3	10	4
1 P.M. to 5 P.M.	5	8	14	12
5 P.M. to 9 P.M.	8	4	7	6

Employees must work continuous eight-hour shifts beginning at 9 A.M. or 1 P.M., and their weekly schedules must be made up of five consecutive days of work with two consecutive days off (and they work the same hours each workday). Manfred would like to devise weekly schedules that will minimize the total number of cashiers needed, but the schedules must be such that the minimum cashier requirements in the table are satisfied. (a) Formulate Manfred's problem as a linear program; be sure to define the variables precisely. (Hint: there are 14 possible schedules; there will be one variable corresponding to each schedule.) (b) Solve the problem using a computer. (c) Is the assumption of divisibility satisfied? Will your answer to this question be true in general? Explain.

6. Checker Credit Service provides credit information to its customers throughout the country twenty-four hours a day. Rosalind Hanks is the manager of phone services. She supervises credit reps who answer customers' calls. From historical data she has estimated that the following number of credit reps are needed during various times of the day.

Time Period	No. of Reps Needed
Midnight to 4 A.M.	3
4 A.M. to 8 A.M.	6
8 A.M. to noon	13
Noon to 4 P.M.	15
4 P.M. to 8 P.M.	12
8 P.M. to midnight	9

Employees work shifts of eight consecutive hours, and shifts can start at the beginning of any of the six periods shown in the table. Ms. Hanks has complete freedom in deciding the *number* of days each employee works each week, so she is interested only in knowing how many employees should start work at the beginning of each time period to minimize the total number of employees needed each day. (a) Formulate her problem as a linear program. (Hint: there will be six decision variables.) (b) Solve the problem using a computer. (c) Is the divisibility assumption satisfied? (d)* Suppose full-time employees were paid $8 per hour, and suppose part-time employees could be hired to work four-hour shifts for $5 per hour. But part-time employees are only half as efficient as full-time employees (i.e., Checker needs two part-time employees to do the work of one full-time employee). Formulate and solve the new problem.

7. Ronald Stimpson is regional sales manager for an industrial products company. His region contains four sales districts. He supervises 10 sales representatives and controls an advertising budget of $800,000 per year. Mr. Stimpson believes that sales in a district are related to the amount of advertising and the number of sales reps assigned to the district. Based on historical data, his estimates of incremental annual sales per dollar of advertising and sales per sales rep for each district are given in the following table. Mr. Stimpson would like to determine how to allocate sales reps and the advertising budget among the four districts to maximize sales. To maintain a reasonable presence in each market, however, each district must be assigned at least one sales rep, and at least $50,000 must be spent on advertising in each market.

District	1	2	3	4
$ sales/$ advertising	7	12	10	11
$ sales (0000)/sales rep	38	25	36	41

(a) Formulate a linear programming model to help Mr. Stimpson solve his problem. (b) Solve the problem using a computer.

8.* Great Plains Advertising Company (GPAC) has a $150,000 advertising budget to advertise an automobile firm. GPAC is considering advertising in newspapers and on television. The more GPAC advertises in a particular medium, the less effective additional ads are in reaching new customers. The following table lists the number of new customers reached by each ad. Each newspaper ad costs $1500, and each television ad costs $10,000. At most 30 newspaper ads and 15 television ads can be placed. Also, GPAC would like to use at least as many newspaper ads as television ads. Formulate a linear program that will maximize the number of new customers contacted subject to the previous restrictions. (Hint: You need six variables, not two.)

	No. of Ads	New Customers/Ad.
Newspaper	1–10	900
	11–20	600
	21–30	300
Television	1–5	10000
	6–10	5000
	11–15	2000

9. The demand for a company's product during the next four months is given below. It costs the company \$9 per unit to produce the product using regular-time labor and \$12 per unit to produce the product using overtime labor. A maximum of 500 units can be made each month using regular-time labor. There is no limit on overtime production. Excess units produced can be stored at a cost of \$2 per unit per month. (a) Formulate this company's problem as a linear program to minimize its total production and storage costs during the next four months and to satisfy demand (there are no initial inventories). (b) Solve the problem using a computer.

Month	Demand
1	450
2	575
3	490
4	530

10. Tavisbond Manufacturing Company makes high-grade pipe for the oil and chemical industries. Tavisbond must plan its production for the next seven months: March to September. The forecast demands (in thousands of feet) for its pipe are as follows:

Mar	Apr	May	June	July	Aug	Sept
40	60	70	80	90	100	80

Tavisbond can make 75,000 feet of pipe per month using regular-time production at a cost of \$1.25 per foot. Tavisbond can make an additional 15,000 feet of pipe each month using overtime production at a cost of \$1.50 per foot. Any pipe made in one month and sold in a subsequent month incurs an inventory holding cost of \$0.15 per foot per month. Tavisbond expects to end February with 5000 feet of pipe in inventory and would like to end September with 10,000 feet of pipe in inventory. (a) Formulate Tavisbond's problem as a linear program to minimize its total cost during the next seven months and to ensure that it delivers the predicted amounts of pipe on time. (b) Solve the problem using a computer.

11. Metallica Manufacturing Company has seen the demand for two new types of metal alloys explode in recent months. The alloys, which are made by mixing copper, nickel, and aluminum, do not require an exact formulation of components but must satisfy the following general specifications:

Alloy A	Alloy B
At least 40% copper	No more than 35% copper
At least 10% nickel	At least 40% nickel
No more than 25% nickel	No more than 30% aluminum
Aluminum content must be exactly twice that of nickel	

Copper costs \$2 per pound, nickel \$3 per pound, and aluminum \$1.50 per pound. Metallica has a limit of 2000 pounds of copper, 3000 pounds of nickel, and 4000 pounds of aluminum available each day. Assume that the company can sell as much of each alloy as it makes at a price of \$5 per pound for alloy A and \$6 per pound for alloy B. (a) Formulate the company's problem as a linear program to maximize profit. (b) Solve the problem using a computer.

12. Wilson Creek Farm has 200 acres of land available for planting. The owner is considering planting three crops: corn, soybeans, and wheat. The production yield, water requirements, and labor requirements for a salable crop are given below. The owner expects to have only 35,000 gallons of water available per week to use for the crops, and during the growing season he will only have 8000 person-hours of labor available. The expected profit per bushel of each crop is \$1.00 for corn, \$1.60 for soybeans, and \$3.00 for wheat. The owner can use any mix of crops (i.e., he can plant the same crop on all 200 acres or he can plant all three crops in different proportions). (a) Formulate the problem as a linear program to find the profit-maximizing planting strategy. (b) Solve the problem using a computer.

Crop	Bushels/Acre Produced	Water Required (Gal/Acre/Week)	Person–Hours Labor Required/Acre
Corn	300	200	35
Soybeans	200	150	40
Wheat	80	125	30

13. A manufacturing company has three manufacturing plants located throughout the country. The company supplies four major wholesalers distributed throughout the country with a product made at these three plants. The manufacturing cost is \$12 per unit at plant A, \$10 per unit at plant B, and \$11 per unit at plant C. The shipping cost between each plant and each wholesaler is given below. The units demanded by each wholesaler are also listed below, along with the production capacity at each manufacturing plant. The company wishes to satisfy the demands of each wholesaler at minimum total cost (production plus shipping). However, no plant should be operating at less than 60% of its capacity. (a) Formulate a linear program to solve the company's problem. (b) Solve the problem using a computer.

	Manufacturing Plant	Wholesaler 1	2	3	4	Capacity
Transport cost per unit shipped	A	7	10	16	5	300
	B	10	4	8	12	400
	C	11	8	10	9	500
	Demand	150	300	350	250	

14. AMCHEM Chemical Company produces three products: A, B, and C. Each product requires labor to produce it, and production of each product creates pollutants. By law the firm is not allowed to produce more than the following pollutants per day: 200 pounds of sulfur dioxide, 300 pounds of carbon monoxide, 150 pounds of hydrogen sulfide, and 50 pounds of benzene. The total number of person-hours of labor available per day is 6000. In addition, the total output per day of products A and B combined cannot be more than the output of product C. Each pound of product A generates a profit of $5, each pound of B generates $7, and each pound of C generates $4. Pollutant and labor rates per hundred pounds of product are given below. (a) Formulate this problem as a linear program to maximize daily profit. (b) Solve the problem using a computer.

		A	B	C
Pounds of Pollutants/ 100 Lb of Product	Sulf diox	.10	.05	.20
	Carb mon	.18	.04	.03
	Hyd sulf	.25	.15	.02
	Benzene	.01	.06	.04
Pers-Hr/ 100 Lb of product	Labor	3.0	2.0	4.5

15. International Fiber Company (IFC) makes newsprint for newspapers. IFC has three paper mills, A, B, and C, spread throughout the country. The cost of producing newsprint varies from mill to mill. IFC estimates that the marginal production cost for each ton of newsprint is $210 at mill A, $225 at B, and $220 at C. IFC supplies five primary geographical markets from these three mills. The monthly demand at each market, the per ton shipping cost between each mill and each market, and the monthly production capacity of each mill are as follows:

	Mill	Market 1	2	3	4	5	Capacity (Tons/Month)
Shipping Cost/Ton	A	20	25	30	15	35	1200
	B	30	20	32	28	19	1500
	C	25	18	28	23	31	900
Monthly demand		600	1000	500	800	500	

IFC would like to satisfy all market demands at minimum total cost (production plus transportation). Formulate a linear program to solve IFC's problem. (Hint: let x_{ij} = tons of newsprint made at mill i and sent to market j each month, a total of 15 variables.)

16.* Enviroclean Waste Disposal Company collects toxic wastes from commercial and industrial sites and transports them to one of its three treatment centers, where the materials are either incinerated, chemically treated to reduce their toxicity, or stored in an approved manner. Each treatment center has a limited capacity: centers A and B can process 50 tons per day, and center C can process 75 tons per day. Enviroclean serves six general districts. The round-trip travel and collection times from the six regions to the treatment centers and the predicted daily volumes of waste generated in each district are given in the following table.

District	Treatment Center* A	B	C	Daily Vol. (Tons/Day)
1	1.2	1.1	3.2	20
2	0.5	1.3	2.5	30
3	1.0	0.4	1.9	45
4	1.5	1.6	1.4	25
5	2.4	1.5	1.6	20
6	2.6	1.9	0.5	25

*Round-trip travel plus collection times in hours.

Each district is served by several trucks because each truck can handle approximately 5 tons of wastes per load. Trucks are stationed at each treatment center and then they go to a district to collect wastes and return to the center. The cost of collection is approximately proportional to the travel plus collection time because drivers are paid on a per-hour basis and do not work 8-hr days. (a) Enviroclean would like to determine how much of each district's wastes should be collected and sent to each treatment center to minimize collection cost. Formulate this problem as a linear program. (b) Solve the problem using a computer. (c) Does the fact that each truck can carry 5 tons of waste violate the divisibility assumption? Does it make the formulation and solution in (a) and (b) invalid? Explain.

17.* The demand for Emca Inc.'s product during the next four months is given below. The product is made up of two components, A and B. Emca can either manufacture the components itself or subcontract to another company. If Emca manufactures the components, each component must go through two production departments: fabricating and finishing. Component A requires two hours of fabricating time and four hours of finishing time; component B requires three hours of fabricating time and two hours of finishing time. Each department has 550 hours of time available each month for production. Emca has determined that it costs $200 per unit of A that is made and $240 per unit of B. Emca believes that its production capacity is insufficient to satisfy the demand, so it has arranged to buy some units of A and B from a subcontractor for $220 per unit of A and $255 per unit of B. Any units of the components can be held in inventory at a cost of $8 per month. (a) Formulate Emca's planning problem as a linear program to minimize its cost during the next four months while delivering the amount demanded each month. (b) Solve the problem using a computer.

Month	Demand
1	90
2	85
3	95
4	100

18.* (The previous examples all dealt with the problems faced by private firms. The following is a simplified version of an actual public sector problem.) The Appleville School District has two high schools, each of which has a capacity of 4000 students. Approximately one-third of the high school students in the district are members of racial minorities. The district can be divided into four distinct communities. The number of students in each community expected to attend a public high school next year and the distance from the center of each community to each high school are listed in Table T1.17.

Historically the two high schools have been racially unbalanced, with school A having a disproportionately high enrollment of minority students and school B having a disproportionately high enrollment of majority students. To satisfy a court agreement to achieve better racial balance between the schools, each high school must have at least 24% and no more than 44% of its enrollment made up of minority students (the overall minority enrollment in the district is 34%). The school district would like to determine how many students of each type (majority and minority) should be sent from each community to each high school to minimize total student bus miles traveled. (a) Formulate this problem as a linear program. (Hint: let

x_{ij} = number of majority students from community i assigned to H.S. j

and

y_{ij} = number of minority students from community i assigned to H.S. j

where $i = 1, 2, 3, 4$ and j = A, B.)
(b) Solve this problem using a computer.

19. Solve the following linear program graphically.

$$\begin{aligned} \text{Minimize } z = 10A + 7.5B \\ \text{Subject to} \quad 4A + 2B &\geq 10 \\ -3A + 2B &\leq 3 \\ A + B &\leq 3 \\ A, B &\geq 0 \end{aligned}$$

TABLE T1.17 APPLEVILLE SCHOOL DISTRICT DATA

Community	No. of Majority Students	No. of Minority Students	Miles to H.S. A	Miles to H.S. B
1	1900	250	3.4	1.5
2	1700	400	2.4	2.2
3	800	650	1.1	2.9
4	550	1250	1.7	2.8
Total	4950	2550		

20. Solve the following linear program graphically.

$$\begin{aligned} \text{Maximize } z &= x_1 + 2x_2 \\ \text{Subject to } \quad & 6x_1 + 3x_2 \le 15 \\ & 2x_1 - x_2 \ge 4 \\ & x_1, x_2 \ge 0 \end{aligned}$$

21. Solve the following linear program graphically.

$$\begin{aligned} \text{Minimize } z &= 4A + B \\ \text{Subject to } \quad & 3A + 2B \ge 12 \\ & 2A - 6B \le -18 \\ & A - B \le 2 \\ & A, B \ge 0 \end{aligned}$$

22. Solve the following linear program using the simplex algorithm.

$$\begin{aligned} \text{Maximize } z &= 2A + 4B + 3C \\ \text{Subject to } \quad & 3A + 4B + 2C \le 60 \\ & 2A + B + 2C \le 40 \\ & A + 3B + 2C \le 80 \\ & A, B, C \ge 0 \end{aligned}$$

23. Solve the following linear program using the simplex algorithm.

$$\begin{aligned} \text{Maximize } z &= 5.0X + 8.0Y \\ \text{Subject to } \quad & 2.5X + 5.0Y \le 50 \\ & 2.0X + 1.0Y \le 20 \\ & 7.5X + 2.0Y \le 60 \\ & X, Y \ge 0 \end{aligned}$$

24. Solve the following linear program using the simplex algorithm.

$$\begin{aligned} \text{Maximize } z &= 15x_1 + 25x_2 + 10x_3 \\ \text{Subject to } \quad & -6x_2 + 3x_3 \ge 12 \\ & x_1 + 4x_2 + 2x_3 = 10 \\ & \text{All } x_j\text{'s} \ge 0 \end{aligned}$$

25. Solve the following linear program using the simplex algorithm.

$$\begin{aligned} \text{Minimize } z &= 3A + 4B + C \\ \text{Subject to } \quad & 2A + B + C \ge 20 \\ & A + B + 5C = 15 \\ & A, B, C \ge 0 \end{aligned}$$

26. Solve the following linear program using the simplex algorithm.

$$\begin{aligned} \text{Maximize } z &= 4x_1 + 2x_2 - 2x_3 \\ \text{Subject to } \quad & 3x_1 + 6x_2 - 3x_3 \le 90 \\ & 3x_1 + x_2 + x_3 \le 180 \\ & x_1 - x_2 + x_3 = 60 \\ & \text{All } x_j\text{'s} \ge 0 \end{aligned}$$

27. (Integer Programming) A company has five repair crews that it can send to customer locations to repair equipment. Each crew has different skills and experience; therefore, their costs for service calls differ from job to job. The company has received calls from five customers requiring service crews. The manager of the company's service department has made the following estimates of how much it will cost to provide the required service for each customer for each service crew.

		Customer				
		A	B	C	D	E
	1	8	7	5	4	11
	2	6	9	6	8	10
Service Crew	3	10	6	7	9	12
	4	11	10	10	11	13
	5	7	8	8	6	11

Each crew can serve only one customer. The company wants to minimize the total cost of servicing the customers, and each customer must be serviced. Formulate this problem as a 0/1 integer program.

28. (Integer Program) The demand for tickets on Gateway Airlines has grown so much that it intends to buy several new airplanes. There are four types of aircraft from which to choose: the DC-20, the Boeing 797, the Lockheed Bi-Star, and the Eurostar 10. The cost, capacity, and required maintenance time per month for each type of plane are shown in the table below. Gateway wishes to buy the new planes at minimum total cost subject to capacity, maintenance, and training requirements. The new planes must be able to carry a combined total of at least 3400 passengers and have a combined total maintenance requirement of no more than 240 hours per month. In addition, because it is so difficult for workers to become familiar with several different types of planes, Gateway does not want to buy more than two different types of planes. The decision on which planes to buy is further complicated by the fact that there are only five Bi-Stars and seven Eurostars available for purchase. Formulate this problem as a mixed integer program.

	Cost ($mill)	Capacity (People)	Maintenance (Hr/Month)
DC-20	52	305	22
Boeing 797	78	385	27
Bi-Star	60	280	15
Eurostar 10	54	265	17

SELECTED READING

EPPEN, G. D., F. J. GOULD, and C. P SCHMIDT. *Introductory Management Science* (4th ed.), Prentice-Hall, Englewood Cliffs, N.J., 1993.

HILLIER, FREDERICK S., and GERALD J. LIEBERMAN. *Introduction to Operations Research* (4th ed.), Holden-Day, Oakland, Calif., 1986.

MARKLAND, ROBERT. *Topics in Management Science* (3rd ed.), Wiley, New York, 1989.

RAVINDRAN, A., DON. T. PHILIPS, and JAMES J. SOLBERG. *Operations Research: Principles and Practice* (2nd ed.), Wiley, New York, 1986.

WINSTON, WAYNE L. *Operations Research: Applications and Algorithms* (2nd ed.), PWS-Kent, Boston, 1991.

CHAPTER 5

PRODUCT DESIGN AND OPERATIONS

5.1 THE PRODUCT DESIGN REVOLUTION
On the Job: Dee Ambrosia, Standard Register Company

5.2 PRODUCT DEVELOPMENT

5.3 THE PRODUCT DESIGN PROCESS
Designing for Production
Concurrent Design and Engineering
Team Design
Working with Customers and Suppliers

5.4 BASIC PRINCIPLES OF DESIGNING PRODUCTS FOR PRODUCTION
Minimize the Number of Parts Used
Use Common Components
Use Standard Components
Simplify the Assembly Process
Use Modularity to Obtain Product Variety
Make Product Specifications and Tolerances Reasonable
Design for Robustness

5.5 PRODUCT DESIGN TOOLS
Quality Function Deployment
Value Analysis
The Taguchi Method
Computer-Aided Design
Design for Manufacturability and Design for Assembly
Prototyping
In Good Company: Boeing's Design Takes Off

5.6 PRODUCT DESIGN FOR SERVICES

5.7 PRODUCTION DOCUMENTS

5.8 ENVIRONMENTALLY SENSITIVE DESIGN

Fibre-Pack: A Product Design Case

5.1 THE PRODUCT DESIGN REVOLUTION

The ultimate focus of every production system is the product it yields. In recent years the business press has reported on dozens of companies, such as General Electric, Ford, Xerox, Marriott, IBM, Taco Bell, Motorola, Hewlett-Packard, 3M, and Cincinnati Milacron, that have dramatically reduced their costs, improved their quality, and shortened their product development time, primarily by using new product design philosophies and techniques. In many cases, improvements in the product design process have reduced production costs by 20–40%, cut product development time by more than half, and improved quality by a factor of 10 or more. The common features underlying these improvements are greater attention during product design to how the product will be made, concurrent design of the product and the production process, and the use of multidisciplinary product design teams that include personnel from operations, engineering, marketing, and purchasing, as well as from customers and suppliers. One person who has been a part of this new design approach is Dee Ambrosia, a Customer/Sales Support Coordinator for Standard Register Company. Dee, the focus of this chapter's "On the Job" feature, helped redesign a customer's delivery route form to improve employee safety.

This chapter is based on the successful methods reported by companies like Standard Register. It begins with an overview of product development and the phases of the product development process. Next, it discusses the product design process and the benefits of these new approaches. Section 5.4 presents fundamental principles of design that make products more reliable and less costly to produce, and Section 5.5 describes some tools and techniques that can help implement these principles. The design of service products includes several unique considerations that are different from those of manufactured products; these issues are introduced in Section 5.6 and discussed further in Chapter 8. Section 5.7 explains the types of production documents

ON THE JOB

DEE AMBROSIA, STANDARD REGISTER COMPANY

When delivery truck drivers think about their safety on the job, they probably don't think about their route forms, which list the addresses of their deliveries. But improving the layout of such a form made it easier for one firm's drivers to read the addresses and improved their safety.

Dee Ambrosia, who helped redesign the form, is a Customer/Sales Support Coordinator for Standard Register Company, a major producer of business forms. Helping customers redesign forms is just one part of Dee's responsibilities. She and her fellow coordinators are a crucial link between customers and Standard Register's production process. Dee receives purchase orders from customers, checks the customer information, and verifies the correctness of the design drawing. She then evaluates the specifications of the form, including type of paper, color of ink, style of lettering, and physical layout. Next, she works with other employees to procure all the raw materials needed to produce the order, from printing plates, inks, and paper to shipping cartons. After computing the production time required for the order, Dee prepares a preliminary production schedule for the order on the printing presses, collators, and other machines so that delivery will occur by the due date. Each day Dee monitors reports that track the progress of each order through the plant, speeding any jobs that fall behind schedule.

needed to convert a product design into an operating production system. The design of a product is crucial in determining the extent to which a product will be compatible with the environment. Section 5.8 briefly describes how attention to environmental impacts during product design can often reduce production costs while making a product more environmentally friendly.

5.2 PRODUCT DEVELOPMENT

Product development begins with identification of a consumer need or desire and a way to satisfy it with a good or service. It is difficult to characterize exactly what causes new product needs and desires, but socioeconomic and technological changes are two primary forces. For example, the increasing number of two-worker families has expanded the need for products such as cleaning services, extended child care, convenience foods, and general-purpose errand services. Increasing incomes, especially for teenagers, have created the demand for entertainment products such as videocassette players, movie rental services, and all-music television stations. Technological changes (often in conjunction with socioeconomic changes) have been the basis for new products such as personal computers, facsimile machines, and cellular telephones.

Once an idea has been formulated, product development progresses through the following stages.

1. ***Identification and Evaluation of the Market.*** Many product ideas that satisfy legitimate consumer needs never become products because the market for the product is too small or too difficult to identify and serve relative to the expected costs of product development and production. Measuring market potential at this stage can be difficult because the product exists only as an idea, with a rough description of its design features. Determining the market size necessary to support the product is also difficult because very little may be known about the cost to produce and distribute the product; therefore, the likely selling price and profit margins are rough estimates. Usually market surveys, focus groups, and interviews are used at this stage, not only to determine the existence of a market but also to develop preliminary information about which features of the product are most attractive to likely customers and what price structure would be most effective.
2. ***Development of a Detailed Product Design and Prototyping.*** If a market for the product is believed to exist, the next step is to develop a detailed product design. The desired functional features of the product must be specified clearly. Based on the desired features, preliminary production specifications and process designs can be developed; that is, a plan should be developed of *how to make the product* so as to have the desired functions. At this stage, the active involvement of a person knowledgeable about operations becomes important.

   The detailed design phase is iterative; the initial product design is evaluated with respect to various criteria, such as achievement of functional customer requirements and product specifications, expected quality and reliability of the product, producibility and cost of the product, and the impact on production of the company's other products. After this review, the product design and the planned production process are almost always modified. A method that has been used successfully at this stage is prototyping. A **prototype** is a physical mockup (or a graphical representation or computer simulation) of the product. By using prototypes, personnel from marketing, operations, and design can speak the same language and evaluate the product before large-scale production begins. In addition, customers can play with the prototype or react to a demonstration of the product and provide useful information.

At this stage, preliminary development of production documents that specify the components needed to produce the product, the sequencing of production tasks, and drawings of the product and its major components can help to guide the design process. In addition to prototyping, techniques and tools such as value analysis and computer-aided-design, which are discussed later, can be valuable at this stage.

3. ***Ramp-Up of Production.*** Once a working design is available, the product can be produced in small quantities. Additional design changes may occur either to improve the quality of the product or to reduce the cost of production. Additional market testing can be performed with an operational product (this may involve providing the product to small groups of test customers or actually promoting and selling the product in a test market). Based on feedback from this market testing, a decision is made either to terminate the product or to increase, or "ramp up," the rate of production, usually after incorporating modifications in response to test customers' comments.
4. ***Product Modification and Redesign.*** Product and process design is an ongoing activity. After the product has been on the market for a while, feedback from customers and changes in technology and competing products should motivate changes in the product's design. In addition, experience with producing the product, especially at higher volumes, should lead to changes in design that lower the cost of production and improve the product's quality.

5.3 THE PRODUCT DESIGN PROCESS

Historically, many companies have used what is called an *over-the-wall* design process. A group of product designers worked on the design until they were satisfied. Then they "threw the design over the wall" to the production people, who were expected to make the product. The product designers focused almost entirely on the product's characteristics from a functional, aesthetic, and marketing viewpoint, with little concern for how much it would cost to make the product or even whether it *could* be made. As a result, it was common for the production department to send the design back to the product designers for changes, either because they could not make the product (or make it well) or because the cost of production was prohibitive. The product designers often resisted these changes, and because they occurred after the fact, the changes that were made were often compensations for fundamental flaws in the design rather than corrections of the underlying problems. The consequences of this process were slow product development and introduction, high cost, and poor product quality.

In recent years, many companies have reduced production costs, decreased product development time, and improved product quality by changing their product design processes. The product design processes of these companies have four common elements:

1. A philosophy of designing for production.
2. Concurrent design of the product and the production process.
3. Use of multidisciplinary teams.
4. Collaboration with suppliers and customers.

DESIGNING FOR PRODUCTION

Designing for production is a philosophy by which the designer thinks about how the product will be made (or the service delivered) as the product is being designed so that potential production problems caused by the design can be resolved early in the design process. The basic premise of this philosophy is that the ultimate cost and quality of the product and the time to bring the product to market are primarily determined by how well the product is designed with respect to its producibility. (Studies have shown that 70–95% of the final product cost and much of its quality are determined by its design.[1])

An important aspect of designing for production is to simplify the design and standardize the parts and processes used. As detailed product designs are developed and prototypes constructed, preliminary production documents are designed to identify the types of parts needed and the machining, processing, material handling, and assembly required. For example, by selecting one type of fastener (a clip) rather than another (a screw) or by changing the shape or orientation of a component, a designer can simplify machining or assembly or use a standard part rather than a specially made one. Making these decisions *before* a final product design is established is cheaper and less time-consuming than trying to make them after production begins. For example, to avoid costly equipment modifications, Chrysler designers worked with operations personnel to make sure that a new car model would not be too high to fit in paint-dipping tanks, and Taco Bell designed many of its menu items specifically for preparation in the smaller kitchens it now uses in redesigned restaurants.

Many companies have reported substantial cost and quality benefits from paying attention to production during product design. For example, New York Air Brake reported 30–50% reductions in parts and costs, and Ford saved $1.2 billion in one year alone.[2]

CONCURRENT DESIGN AND ENGINEERING

One way to ensure that product design is compatible with and promotes efficient, high-quality production is to design and test the production process while the product is being designed; this method is called **concurrent design** or **concurrent engineering (CE)**. As the product is being designed, engineers and production personnel develop the actual production system or a prototype system (either in physical or computer-simulated form) to determine how the product will be made. They also evaluate how well the design characteristics fit the company's proposed and existing production equipment, methods, capabilities, and product mix.

In some cases, actual prototypes of the product are made to test machining, processing, and assembly. Even fast-food restaurants such as McDonald's, Pizza Hut, and Taco Bell concurrently test new menu items or services (such as fax orders or food delivery) at test-site restaurants to determine if they mesh with the existing operations and facilities.

For complex products that require numerous components and several types of processing, making physical prototype production systems may be impractical. When this happens, computer programs can be used to design and simulate the proposed production system before the actual system is constructed. This makes it possible to predict the effects of eliminating or changing parts, changing machining or processing op-

---

[1]Richard Walleigh, "Product Design for Low-Cost Manufacturing," *The Journal of Business Strategy*, July–August 1989, pp. 37–41.

[2]Otis Port and Wendy Zellner, "Pssst! Want a Secret for Making Superproducts?" *Business Week*, Oct. 2, 1989, pp. 106–110.

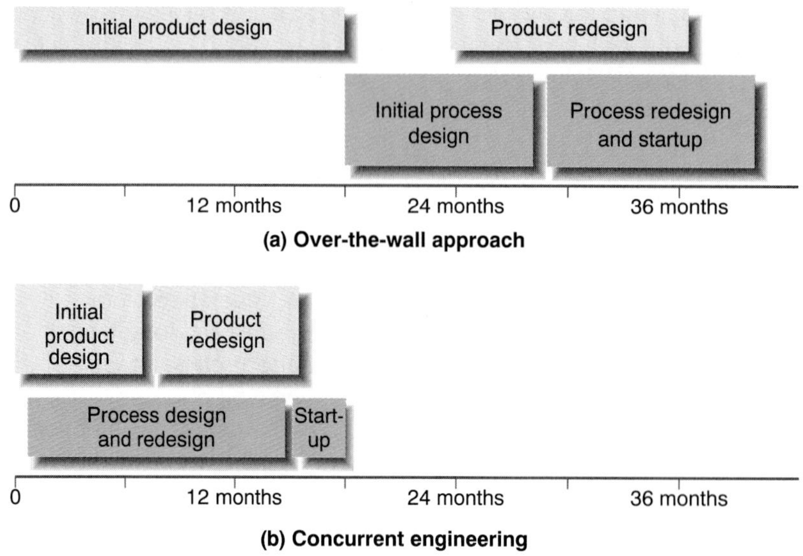

FIGURE 5.1 Product development time.

erations, and evaluating the impact of the new product on existing products made at the facility. Boeing Company, which is profiled in this chapter's "In Good Company" feature, used such computer programs to design its 777 (which contains over 130,000 engineered parts and 3 million rivets, screws, and fasteners) and its production process simultaneously.

One obvious benefit of CE is that it reduces product development and introduction time substantially, as illustrated in Figure 5.1. With an over-the-wall design approach, designers may spend 18 months designing the product and then pass it to the process engineering and operations personnel. The process design and ramp-up of production may take another 18 months or more, much of which is spent sending the product back to the product designers for modifications to make the product producible. CE reduces this development time in two ways. First, process design and testing begin soon after product design begins. In Figure 5.1, process design may begin 1 month rather than 18 months after the start of product design. Second, testing the production process while the product is in its early stages makes design modifications easier. In addition, normal start-up problems and after-the-fact product redesigns are reduced, so the total process design and start-up time can be cut substantially. A variety of companies, such as Allen-Bradley, Honeywell, and Motorola, have reported reductions in product cycle time of 50–95% using CE.

In addition to the time savings, CE produces higher-quality products at much lower cost. Fundamental design problems can be identified and resolved earlier, and product simplification is easier. For example, Cincinnati Milacron, a major machine tool manufacturer, reported that it uses 30–40% fewer parts and produces products at 36% less cost than earlier because of CE. CE also helped Boeing reduce the number of engineering changes, reworks, and errors on its 777 model by over 50%.[3]

[3]See Christopher Farrell and Zachary Schiller, "Stuck: How Companies Cope When They Can't Raise Prices," *Business Week*, Nov. 15, 1993, pp. 146–155; and John Holusha, "Can Boeing's New Baby Fly Financially?" *New York Times*, Mar. 27, 1994.

Chrysler Corp. used input from its assembly workers to improve the design of its Neon model of autos.

TEAM DESIGN

Although in theory design for production can be performed by individual product designers, this concept and CE imply that operations personnel should be involved in the product design at an early stage. Increasingly, companies are including personnel from operations, marketing, sales, engineering, and purchasing on product design teams. A purchasing agent can guide the design so that it uses standard or common parts whenever possible. An engineer can evaluate whether the design could be changed to require simpler machining processes or less expensive tooling. Operations personnel can determine how the product will fit within existing processes, how easily it can be assembled, and whether design changes will reduce production costs. For example, manufacturing engineers on the Boeing 777 design team changed a bend in the fuselage that had been in all its previous planes and solved a 30-year manufacturing nightmare.

Shop floor workers are even included in product design or redesign teams. For example, Chrysler included union production workers on the design teams for its Neon automobile, with the goal of making it easier to build, with fewer defects. At one point 90 production workers helped to assemble the first production prototype; then they made suggestions on how to redesign it to improve production. During the design process, production workers suggested over 4000 design changes, many of which were implemented.[4]

WORKING WITH CUSTOMERS AND SUPPLIERS

The use of multidisciplinary product design teams is becoming widespread, and companies that have included customers and suppliers on these teams report significant benefits. The following discussion presents some of these benefits.

Customer Involvement

For a product to be successful it must satisfy the needs of customers, not just those of its designers. The best way to find out what features customers want in a product, and how easy it is to use, is to ask them. For many years, computer software companies have used "beta sites" (test customers) to evaluate new software and suggest changes. Now companies such as Boeing, Fisher-Price, and Marriott regularly include customers in the design process itself.

[4]David Woodruff, "Chrysler's Neon," *Business Week*, May 3, 1993, pp. 116–126.

Business travelers helped Marriott Corp. design and test its Courtyard Hotels to make them fit customers' needs better. For example, all Courtyards have small but functional restaurants specializing in providing breakfast, which business travelers requested, rather than larger three-meal restaurants.

1. Boeing included representatives of its major customers on its 777 design teams. A suggestion from United Airlines' engineers that Boeing divide the longest wing flap on the 777 in half has simplified repair.
2. Fisher-Price uses children and parents to test prototype products and to suggest new products or improvements to existing ones.
3. Marriott actively involved potential customers (business travelers) in the design of its Courtyard Hotel chain. Customers were asked which features of a hotel they most liked and disliked, and which features they would like that hotels do not offer. Hotel prototypes were then tested by actual customers, and their feedback was used to modify the design and amenities of the Courtyard Hotels.

Collaboration with customers produces better-quality products that are more in tune with customers' wishes and reduces costs as well. An unorthodox example of this process occurred when Chuck Wise, the former head of Corning, Inc.'s, tax department (see Chapter 1 and the "On the Job" segment in Chapter 8), decided to reevaluate his department's product—the tax returns and documentation sent to the Internal Revenue Service (IRS). During his meetings with IRS representatives, he found that Corning provided more documents and information than the IRS wanted or needed, all of which had to be checked. Using this feedback from its customer, the IRS, Corning's tax department was able to simplify its product, streamline its operations, reduce costs, and provide a tax return that the IRS could audit more easily and quickly.

Supplier Involvement

Equipment and material suppliers can identify potential problems and recommend improvement before the product design is finalized. In many cases, the supplier can direct a customer to use components that are similar or identical to those the supplier makes for other customers or that use the same tools or processing. Leif Soderberg gives an example comparing two customers of an unnamed supplier of electrical components.[5] One customer provided the supplier with a detailed design of a proprietary subassembly and wanted it produced exactly as designed. The supplier won the order with a bid price of $75 per unit with a profit margin of 12%. A different customer asked the supplier to assign two of its engineers to help the customer develop a subassembly similar to that of the first customer. The supplier's engineers suggested changes that allowed it to use mostly standard parts in producing the subassembly. They signed an agreement to sell the subassemblies for $25 each and had a profit margin of 40%. Such savings are not uncommon. A study by the consulting firm A. T. Kearney, Inc., found that involving

[5]Leif Soderberg, "America's Engineering Gap," *Wall Street Journal*, Jan. 30, 1989.

suppliers in the product development process can cut the costs of purchased parts and services by 30%.[6]

In addition to cost benefits, supplier–customer cooperation can improve the quality of the product. For example, Rockwell International, one of Honda's suppliers, redesigned the Accord's rear cargo area to add more space. This saved Honda money and provided a better car to Honda's customers.

5.4 BASIC PRINCIPLES OF DESIGNING PRODUCTS FOR PRODUCTION[7]

Attention to production, CE, and team design are important in obtaining compatibility between the product and the production process. But this is not enough. Those involved in product design need design principles and tools to guide their thinking and to help them evaluate alternative product designs. Academically trained product designers learn these principles in design school, but many people now getting involved in product design, such as Dee Ambrosia (see the "On The Job" feature), come from professions where they receive no such training. This section presents some of the most important design principles that have emerged from studying successful products and companies, and Section 5.5 briefly describes popular design tools that are available to help implement them.

The overriding principle of product design is "Make it simple!" Simplicity of design facilitates both production and consumption. Simple designs often require fewer parts, simpler tooling and machining, and less and simpler assembly—all of which promote lower production cost, easier use, and greater product reliability. Good design does not necessarily mean using the newest or most exotic technology; rather, it utilizes the most appropriate technology to accomplish the purpose of the product as easily, cheaply, and reliably as possible. This idea underlies the Canon Camera slogan, "It's so advanced, it's simple," and the statement by Daniel Ling, IBM's manager of human factors, "[Product] complexity is actually a sign of technological immaturity."[8]

Simplicity of design and simplification of the production process can be promoted by using the principles summarized in Table 5.1.

TABLE 5.1 DESIGN PRINCIPLES TO SIMPLIFY PRODUCTS AND PROCESSES

1. Minimize the number of parts.
2. Use common components and processes.
3. Use standard components and tools.
4. Simplify assembly
   - Easy-to-use fasteners
   - Attention to orientation and accessibility during assembly
   - Attention to testing
   - Foolproof operations and assembly
5. Use modularity to obtain variety.
6. Make product specifications and tolerances reasonable.
7. Design products to be robust.

---

[6]Neal Templin and Jeff Cole, "Manufacturers Use Suppliers to Help Them Develop New Products," *Wall Street Journal*, Dec. 19, 1994.

[7]This section is based partially on the good discussions of design principles and examples in Walleigh, op. cit., and Daniel E. Whitney, "Manufacturing by Design," *Harvard Business Review*, July–August 1988, pp.83–91.

[8]Bruce Nussbaum and Robert Neff, "I Can't Work This Thing," *Business Week*, Apr. 29, 1991, pp. 58–66.

MINIMIZE THE NUMBER OF PARTS USED

Numerous companies have reported substantial cost savings by reducing the number of separate components used in their products.[9]

1. General Electric reduced the number of parts used to make a circuit breaker box from 28,000 to 1275.
2. Keithley Instruments reduced the number of fasteners that assembly workers had to screw in or bolt from 36 to 2.
3. GM's 1995 Chevy Lumina had 900 fewer parts than its predecessor.
4. Cincinnati Milacron cut the number of parts in its Model T-10 Machining Center from 2542 to 709 and cut assembly time from 1800 to 700 hours compared to the model it replaced.
5. Compaq Computer reduced the number of parts in its Prolinea Model Computer from 171 to 86 and cut assembly time in half.
6. Northern Telecom reduced the number of parts in one of its telephones from 325 to 156 and assembly time from 23 to 9 minutes.
7. McDonnell Douglas Corporation reduced the number of parts in its F18 Hornet airplane from 13,181 to 8808. One module was reduced from 44 parts to just 6 and its assembly time was cut from 50 to 5 hours.

Through improved product design, Northern Telecom Ltd. was able to reduce the number of parts in its telephones by over 50% and the assembly time by over 60%.

The cost and quality benefits of parts reduction are summarized succinctly by consultant/designer Vincent Altamuro:

> "The component piece parts that you eliminate are parts that you don't have to design, you don't have to assign a parts number to, you don't have to buy, you don't have to count and inventory, you don't have to assign shelf space for it, it cannot fail inspection, you don't have to have a bowl feeder to feed it, you don't have to have a robot or person assemble it, and it can't break—so you are home free."[10]

Although reducing the number of parts is almost always desirable, there are times when additional parts may be beneficial. When Honda was redesigning its 1994 Accord, Japanese designers planned to eliminate a bracket on top of the engine. But manufacturing engineers on the design team pointed out that the bracket was used in the Marysville, Ohio, plant to transport the engine through the assembly process. By leaving the bracket on, Honda saved thousands of dollars in assembly costs. In this case, attention to the production system helped to override appropriately the design principle of minimizing the number of parts.[11]

Parts reduction can be aided by using systematic design evaluation techniques such as value analysis and design for assembly, which are discussed in the next section. These methods take the designer through a product part by part, evaluating the need for and functionality of each part. Parts can sometimes be eliminated either because their function is unnecessary or because they can be combined with another part.

---

[9] The following examples are taken from Timothy D. Schellhardt and Carol Hymowitz, "U.S. Manufacturers Gird for Competition," *Wall Street Journal*, May 2, 1989; P. Thomas O'Boyle, "Reborn Ohio Industry Is Clean, High-Tech and Shock-Absorbent," *Wall Street Journal*, Aug. 17, 1990; David Woodruff, "Can a Tune-Up Make Chevy a Contender?" *Business Week*, July 25, 1994, pp. 70–71; Schiller and Farrell, op. cit.; Scott McCartney, "Compaq Borrows Wal-Mart's Idea to Boost Production," *Wall Street Journal*, June 17, 1994; Tim Warner, "Computers as a Competitive Burden," *Technology Review*, March–April, 1988, pp. 22–24; William Flannery, "Assembly System May Set Standard for Lowest Cost," *St. Louis Post-Dispatch*, Oct. 3, 1994.

[10] George Melloan, "Robots Talk Back to Product Designers," *Wall Street Journal*, May 26, 1987.

[11] Karen Lowry Miller, "A Car Is Born," *Business Week*, Sept. 13, 1993, pp. 64–72.

USE COMMON COMPONENTS

One way for a company to reduce the total number of components is to use **common components**—components that are common across several products or used in several processes. For example, if a company makes 100 different electric appliances that all require electric motors, it should not use 100 different motors. Instead, the company may be able to use only 5 or 10 motors for all 100 appliances. If a new product is designed using unique components, extra costs are incurred because the company must design, make (or buy), and stock the new components; it may also need to develop new jigs, tools, fixtures, and machinery to produce and assemble them. By contrast, common components can be made or purchased in larger quantities than unique components, which will normally reduce costs further.

Most major auto manufacturers now utilize 50% or more common components for their automobile models. For example, the U.S. and European versions of the Ford Mondeo now share 75% common components, a stark contrast to earlier Ford models. Toyota Motors reported savings of $660 million by redesigning its cars to share more common components.[12]

This principle can be applied to the design of service products and systems as well. For example, unlike many airlines that use several models of airplanes, Southwest Airlines uses only Boeing 737s. As a result, Southwest pilots and mechanics need to be trained on only one type of plane, replacement parts inventories (a large expense for airlines) must be maintained for only one type of plane, and cleaning and turnaround procedures can be standardized for quicker service.

Using common components also improves quality in at least three ways. First, parts produced in larger quantities generally have more consistent quality (the larger volume may justify the use of better production processes). Second, there is less chance of using the wrong part in assembly when there are fewer different types of parts. Third, assembly tools and methods do not have to be changed for different product runs. The use of common equipment or materials in services also tends to increase worker proficiency, which can improve quality and reliability. For example, using only one type of computer or one type of business form for several different services can reduce the chance of mistakes.

USE STANDARD COMPONENTS

Components unique to one company's products, especially those that have unusual dimensions or unusual physical properties, have to be specially made and often cost several times more than **standard** (off-the-shelf) **components**. In addition to their obvious cost advantage, standard components sometimes provide better product quality and performance at lower price than customized components. For example, suppose a designer calculates that a new product requires at least a 0.65-hp motor. Usually, the higher the horsepower of a motor the more it costs, so the designer may design the product to contain a 0.65-hp motor. In fact, using a standard 0.75-hp motor is cheaper. It also provides better performance and more reliability because less strain will be put on the motor.

Identifying where standard components can be used is one way in which suppliers can be quite helpful. Dana Corporation, a major supplier of parts to the auto industry, has a database of 18,000 U-joint parts for axles. Dana can design new U-joints for customers cheaply and quickly (prototypes can be built within hours) using off-the-shelf parts.

---

[12]See Richard Melcher, "Meet Ford's Brave New 'World Car'," *Business Week*, Jan. 18, 1993, p. 46, and William Spindle, "Toyota Retooled," *Business Week*, Apr. 4, 1994, pp. 54–57.

The use of standard components to reduce costs has been increasing among all companies, including small manufacturers. For example, an integral part of a cost-reduction program at Quad-Tech, a $10 million per year manufacturer of engineering test equipment, was redesigning its products to use more standard components.[13]

SIMPLIFY THE ASSEMBLY PROCESS

Regardless of whether the product is assembled using automated or manual processes, the simpler the process the less expensive and more reliable the product will be. In order for automated assembly equipment such as robots to be used, assembly processes must be very simple (robots do not see well and have very limited dexterity and sense of touch). Many companies, such as IBM, have discovered that simplifying the product design to accommodate automated assembly has made manual assembly so fast and reliable that, ironically, it is sometimes less expensive to use than automated assembly.

Parts reduction and assembly simplification can often be aided by preparing preliminary production documents, such as assembly drawings and assembly charts, early in the product design process. An **assembly drawing**, presented in Figure 5.2 for a gear transfer unit, shows the product exploded component by component. When a product is visualized, we can see how parts can be eliminated or assembly steps simplified. For example, rather than having separate flange pieces connected to the base plate by bolts, as shown in Figure 5.2 the base plate can be machined to include the flange pieces, thereby eliminating 10 parts (2 flanges, 4 bolts, and 4 nuts) and all the assembly

[13]Laurel Touby, "The Big Squeeze on Small Businesses," *Business Week*, July 19, 1993, pp. 66–67.

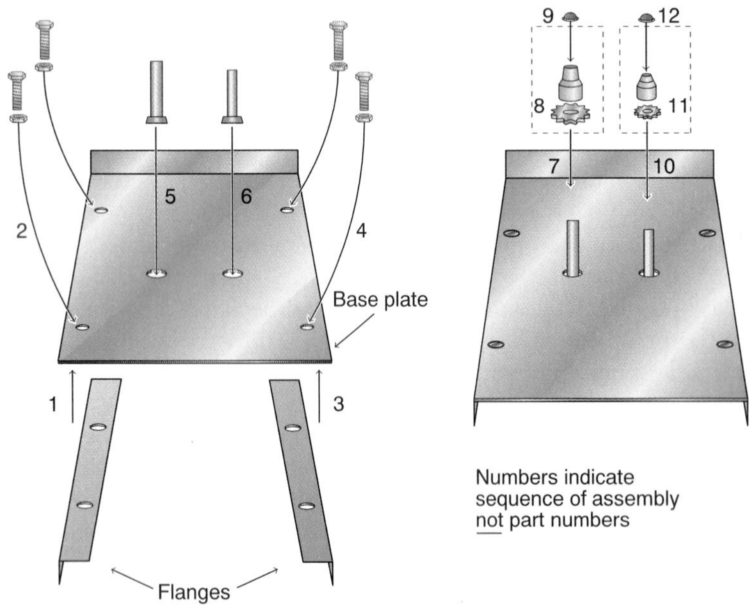

FIGURE 5.2 Assembly drawing of original gear transfer unit.

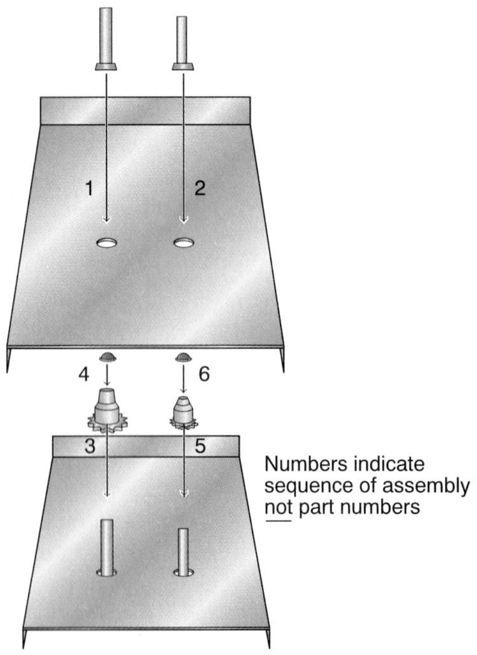

FIGURE 5.3 Assembly drawing of revised gear transfer unit.

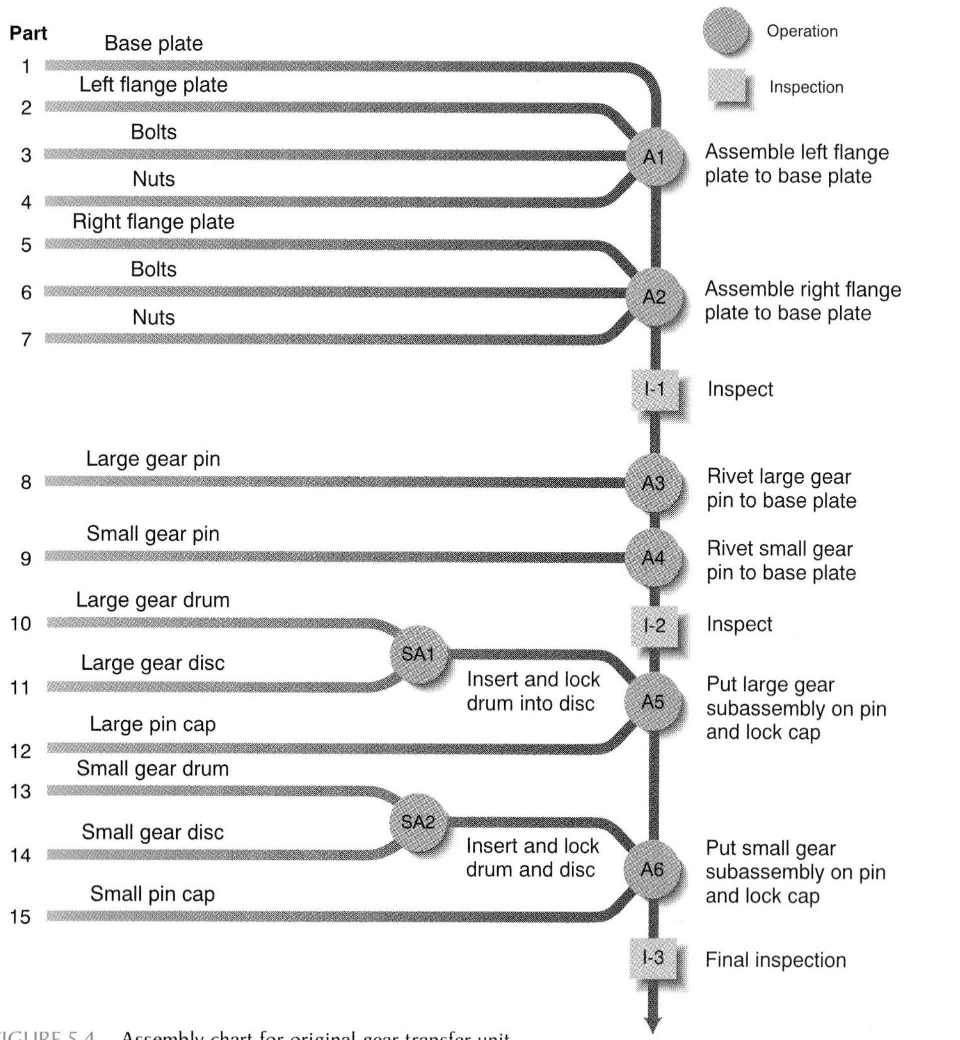

FIGURE 5.4 Assembly chart for original gear transfer unit.

required. Similarly, the gears can be made as one piece rather than as a drum and disc that must be connected. Figure 5.3 shows an assembly drawing for a revised version of the gear transfer unit. An assembly chart is a schematic diagram of how, and in what sequence, the components of the product will be assembled. Most products can be made in hundreds or thousands of different ways in terms of which parts will be combined into subassemblies and then combined in a final assembly, as well as the sequencing of assembly tasks. An assembly chart makes it easier to visualize these alternatives. Figures 5.4 and 5.5 are assembly charts for the two versions of the gear transfer unit.

Computer software exists to simulate the production process so that a designer can evaluate the assembly consequences of making a change in the product design. Changes in product design can be evaluated to see whether they make the assembly sequence easier, whether lubrication points or fasteners will be more accessible during assembly, and whether quality tests can be performed efficiently.

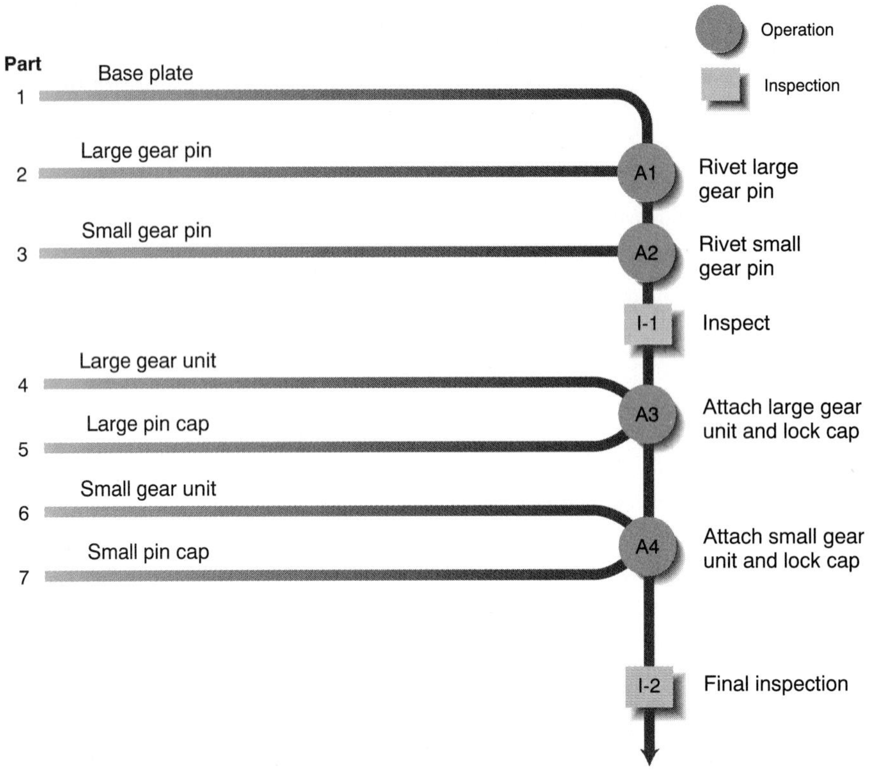

FIGURE 5.5 Assembly chart for revised gear transfer unit.

In some cases, by using more expensive components, assembly can be simplified enough to reduce the total production cost. For example, Chrysler decided to replace one part of a car with a part that cost 30% more; this reduced assembly time enough so that the total cost decreased and the quality of the product increased.[14]

Four product design characteristics especially influence the ease and quality of assembly: the fasteners used, the orientation and accessibility of components, product testing, and mistake-proofing of assembly.

1. ***Fasteners.*** Much assembly labor involves fastening one component to another using bolts, screws, or snaps. The type, shape, and size of the fastener will affect the cost and quality of the fastening task. A few years ago, Volkswagen decided to use screws with cone-shaped tips, even though they were 18% more expensive than normal screws, because they go into holes more easily, especially when the parts being fastened are not well aligned. The change simplified assembly so much that fastening could be done by robots, which substantially reduced costs. These screws became so popular throughout the auto industry that within two years the price of cone-shaped screws had dropped to that of ordinary flat-tipped screws.[15]
2. ***Orientation and Accessibility in Assembly.*** Anyone who has assembled toys, household appliances, or furniture knows that the sequence of assembly and the orientation of components when tasks are performed are crucial. A simple task,

[14]Kathleen Kerwin, "Can Jack Smith Fix GM?" *Business Week*, Nov. 1, 1993, pp. 126–131.

[15]From Whitney, op. cit.

such as fastening a bolt and nut, becomes extremely difficult and time-consuming if there are other components in the way or if several components have to be aligned and held together. The same is true in the manufacturing of products. Paying attention to whether or not tasks will be obstructed can save considerable effort. Unfortunately, in some products and processes, an earlier assembly step has to be undone in order to perform a subsequent step.

If a product has to be repositioned frequently, assembly becomes more difficult and time-consuming. Through careful planning and design, it is often possible to have all parts added from the same side of the product or added in a "stacking" fashion so that it can be assembled or transported without excessive handling. Similarly, if parts have to be connected from difficult angles, productivity and quality suffer. Nissan changed the bolts on its engine mounts, gas tanks, and radios so that they were tightened from above rather than below, thereby making them more accessible and *using* rather than *fighting against* gravity during assembly.

3. **Design for Testing.** Most products of reasonable complexity require testing after assembly. The costs of testing can be reduced and the quality of the product improved by designing the components and assembly sequence so that testing can be performed easily at one or more stages before final assembly. Detecting and correcting defects early in the process avoids the cost and wasted capacity of performing additional assembly on a defective product. In addition, early testing usually makes diagnosis of a problem easier than testing the final product. Testing should occur where it will provide the most information. For example, performing a test between two tasks that have almost no chance of creating a defect is a waste of effort; instead, a test might be performed after a high-risk activity.
4. **Mistake-Proof Assembly.** A final aspect of simplifying assembly is to design the product so that it is difficult or impossible to assemble it incorrectly, that is, **mistake-proofing** it. For example, bolts intended to go in one hole can be designed not to fit in other holes by using different shapes or by putting special notching on fasteners or in holes. This practice may violate the principle of using standard or common parts, so some trade-off in relative costs and benefits must be made. Alternatively, all the fasteners used at one step of the process can be identical so that no wrong fastener can be used. Color-coding, letter-coding, and position-marking of parts can also reduce errors and speed up assembly. Wires, plugs, and outlets that need to be connected can be coded so that the red wire attaches to the red connector, and so on. For example, Nissan marks panels to show where brake tubes and fuel hoses should be attached to avoid mistakes.

USE MODULARITY TO OBTAIN PRODUCT VARIETY

In order to satisfy a wide array of customers, firms sometimes provide a variety of model options for a product. Variety can be expensive if each model has many unique parts or requires different processing or costly production changeovers. An efficient way to provide product variety at low cost is to use **modularity**. This is done by dividing the product into generic parts or modules and then determining which variations of each module would be desirable from a marketing and manufacturing viewpoint. For example, suppose a product is made up of five modules. If there are three varieties of each module, the company can make $3^5 = 243$ different models of the product using only 10 more components (modules) than would be needed to make one model of the product (three versions of 5 modules = 15 total modules minus 5 needed for any single model). Thus, the product can be customized for the customer at little additional material cost.

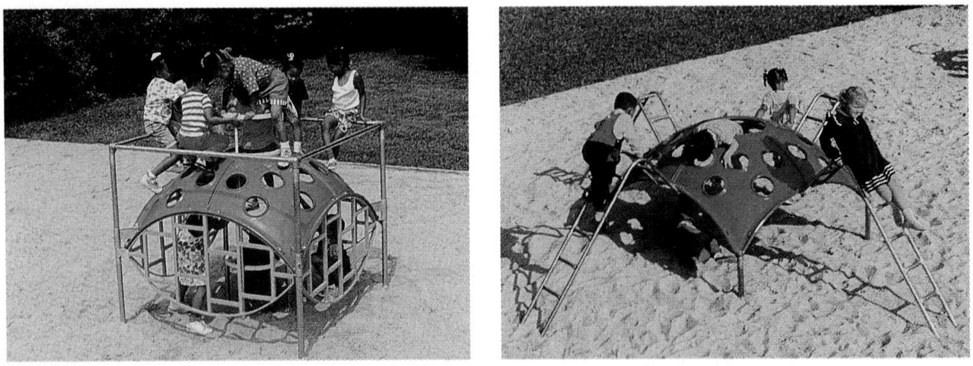

PCA Industries uses common components and modular design to produce hundreds of different playground products from a small number of basic parts. The "Jr. Squirrel House" (left) and "Charlotte the Spider" (right) use the same four-panel blue-body module, heavy-duty aluminum supports, and fasteners.

Modular design can be advantageous in two other ways. First, if alternative versions of a module are packaged exactly the same way and connected to the rest of the product the same way, other components of the product do not have to be specially designed for each version of the module, and the assembly processes for different models of the product can be identical. If two alternative versions of the same module have naturally different shapes and sizes, they can be encased in the same housing to make them interchangeable in the assembly process. For example, computer manufacturers use a variety of hard drives and central processing units. Even though their working elements are different, they are housed in the same-shaped housings with the same connecting mechanism to make assembly identical for all versions. This approach is especially helpful in automated or robotic operations; the robot does not need to adjust to different shapes or be reprogrammed; as long as the correct component is there, the processing is the same for alternative modules. A second benefit of modularity is that combining several functions into a single module simplifies testing, especially if the modules are enclosed in identical housings.

MAKE PRODUCT SPECIFICATIONS AND TOLERANCES REASONABLE

Normally, the more demanding the specifications for a component the more it will cost. Therefore, the physical properties specified for products and their components should not be far more demanding than needed to make the product function well even under extreme usage conditions. For example, the material used in a classroom desk does not have to withstand the same forces and have the same strength-to-weight ratio as the metal used on an airplane wing. Thus we would not use the same physical specifications for the two. Although this principle is obvious in such an extreme case, it is not uncommon for designers to specify unnecessarily demanding requirements for some components that increase the cost without enhancing product quality. This principle extends to product packaging. Compaq Computer saved $6 a box in packaging by changing from packaging "that could survive a fall down the Himalayas" to a more reasonable one.[16]

[16]Michael Allen, "Bottom Fishing: Developing New Line of Low-Priced PCs Shakes Up Compaq," *Wall Street Journal*, June 15, 1992.

A second consideration is to make the product specifications and tolerances compatible with and achievable by the production process. For example, if a manufacturing process is technologically capable of producing components to only ± 0.01 inch accuracy, components requiring a ± 0.001-inch tolerance specification can be obtained only by performing 100% inspection, sorting, and reworking those that fall outside the tolerance range; this can be prohibitively expensive. Either the product must be redesigned, the tolerances reevaluated, or the production equipment and process changed.

DESIGN FOR ROBUSTNESS

Even the best production systems will experience variations in materials, wear and tear on equipment, and worker fatigue. These and other factors will cause variations in product attributes such as the weight, length, strength, or alignment of the product, which can reduce product quality. In recent years, a procedure called **robust design** has been introduced in an attempt to design products in a way that (1) reduces the normal variation in product attributes that will occur during production and (2) makes product performance less sensitive to the variations that do occur.

1. ***Reducing Attribute Variations.*** One popular approach for reducing variations in product attributes is called the *Taguchi method* (named after Genichi Taguchi, its developer). This method, which is explained in detail in Section 5.5, uses physical experiments to determine which product and process characteristics most affect the attribute variations of a product. Based on the experiments, the designer selects product features and production methods that minimize these variations.
2. ***Reducing Quality Effects of Attribute Variations.*** A second aspect of robust design involves accommodating attribute variations, such as in the length or thickness of a component, in a way that minimizes their effects on product performance and quality.

An example utilizing both aspects of robust design is illustrated in Figure 5.6. One subassembly of a product required connecting two curved tubes. There were two important factors in product quality: (1) the tubes had to be connected securely and (2) the total length of the fastened tubes had to be exactly 36 inches. The original design (shown in Figure 5.6a) used a metal sleeve with two bolts and nuts to connect two 18-inch tubes. The holes in the sleeve and tubes did not always align perfectly, which made

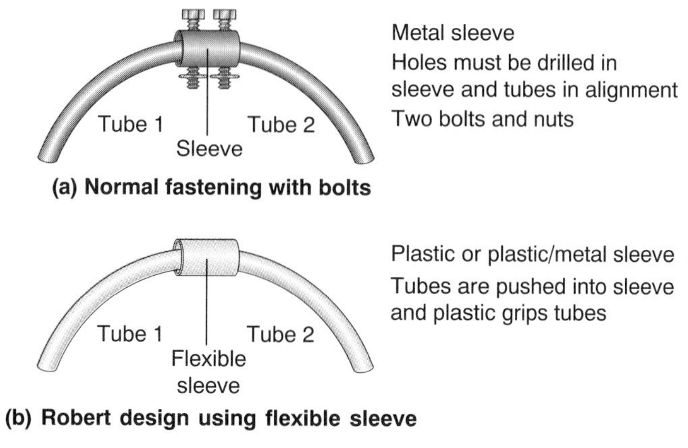

FIGURE 5.6 Two fastening designs.

it difficult to connect them and caused inconsistency in the total length of the tubes. Even when the holes were drilled exactly the specified distance from the ends of the tubes and perfectly matched the holes in the sleeve, variations in tube length caused variations in total length. For example, if one tube was 18.01 inches long and the other was 18.02 inches long, the total length of the tubes would be at least 36.03 inches long (and frequently longer due to variations in hole locations).

A revised robust design (shown in Figure 5.6b) used a flexible metal sleeve with a plastic liner. The tubes were pushed into the sleeve, and the plastic gripped the tubes tightly. The flexible sleeve totally eliminated the variations due to drilling and aligning the holes for the bolts. The flexible sleeve design also accommodated variations in tube length easily. The target length for each tube was reduced to 17.98 inches, with a target 0.04-inch gap between the tubes within the sleeve. If the tubes were a bit longer than the target values, they were simply pushed closer together in the sleeve. If they were shorter than the target values, a slightly larger gap was left in the sleeve. The total length of the tubes was used as the guide. This made quality relatively insensitive to variations in individual tube lengths.

In addition to improving the quality of the product, the robust design significantly reduced costs because (1) holes no longer had to be drilled in the tubes and the sleeve, thereby eliminating a costly operation, (2) the cost of the bolts and nuts was saved, and (3) sliding the tubes into the flexible sleeve was simpler and faster than aligning the holes and tightening two bolts.

5.5 PRODUCT DESIGN TOOLS

Several tools and methods have been developed to help product designers make products of higher quality at lower cost. The following six tools are examples.

QUALITY FUNCTION DEPLOYMENT

An important aspect of product design is to identify customers' preferences with respect to product features and to convert them into appropriate technical or design attributes. Professor Yoji Akao developed a structured method for doing this called **quality function deployment (QFD)**. The method is based on completing a series of matrices and then combining them into a comprehensive table referred to as the **house of quality**.

The basic **QFD relationship matrix** relates the customer's requirements to the technical attributes of the product. The list of customer requirements is obtained by asking customers what specific features or types of performance are important to them. These requirements are usually quite tangible, although not always directly quantifiable. Figure 5.7 is a QFD relationship matrix for a laptop portable computer. It lists eight customer requirements, ranging from portability features (size and weight) and battery charging to computational performance and durability. (Cost is an important criterion for almost all products, but it is normally treated separately from this analysis.) Not all the requirements are equally important, so next to the customer requirements the average relative importance is specified (again based on customer interviews). Various ranking schemes can be used; here customers were asked to rate the requirements from 0 to 5, with 5 being the most important. The importance ratings in Figure 5.7 are the average ratings of responding customers rounded to the nearest 0.5.

Product designers/engineers then identify which technical attributes of laptop computers affect customer requirements; these are the columns of Figure 5.7. To keep

Customer Requirements	Importance	Case material	Battery type/size	Screen type/size	RAM capacity	Hard drive type/size	Keyboard type/size
		Technical attributes					
Light weight	4.5	●	○	●	●	●	●
Small size (fit in briefcase)	3.0		○	●	▲	●	○
Long operation between recharging	3.5		○				
Large keys on keyboard	2.0						○
Short time to recharge	1.5		○				
Readable screen	3.0			○			
Durable (unbreakable)	2.0	○	●			●	●
Fast processor/large memory capacity	4.0				○	○	
Attribute importance		31.5	118.5	49.5	52.5	64.5	64.5

Relationship codes ○ Strong=9 ● Medium=3 ▲ Weak=1

FIGURE 5.7 QFD relationship matrix for a laptop computer.

the size of Figure 5.7 manageable for illustrative purposes, we combined some attributes, such as battery type and size, and limited the number of technical attributes to six; more than these actually exist. The body of the relationship matrix is then completed by company designers to show the magnitude of the relationships between customer requirements and technical attributes. (In Figure 5.7 the strength of the relationship is on a 0–9 scale, with no relationship being 0, a weak relationship being 1, medium being 3, and strong being 9. This is the convention Akao uses.) Notice that a single technical attribute may affect several customer requirements, and it may affect them in opposite directions. For example, large battery capacity and size will increase the operating time until recharging, but it will also increase the weight and size of the computer. A technical attribute that affects several customer requirements is even more important because of the trade-offs that must be made, such as among weight, cost, and performance. (The positive and negative effects do not cancel each other out.) A customer requirement that is addressed by no technical attribute should motivate serious thinking about how it can be incorporated into the product.

Across the bottom of the table is an "Attribute Importance" rating for each technical attribute. This is computed by multiplying the importance rating of each customer requirement by the relationship rating for the attribute and customer requirement and then summing down the column. For example, the Attribute Importance rating for the attribute "hard-drive type/size" is $(4.5 \times 3) + (3.0 \times 3) + (2.0 \times 3) + (4.0 \times 9) = 64.5$. During product design, those attributes with the largest Attribute Importance ratings would normally receive the greatest attention.

The QFD relationship matrix can be expanded in various ways, one of which is to perform an explicit competitive analysis in terms of both customer requirements and technical attributes. This requires that the company first identify the most important

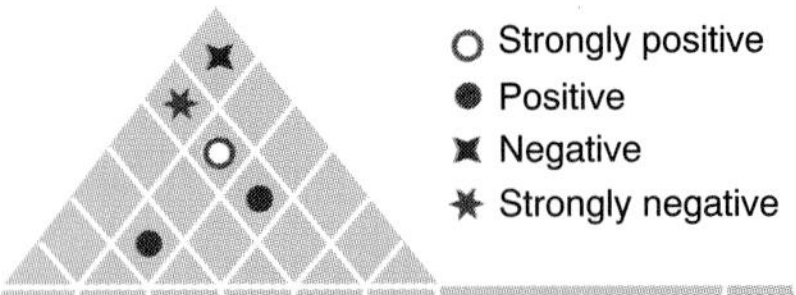

Customer Requirements	Importance	Case material	Battery type/size	Screen type/size	RAM capacity	Hard drive type/size	Keyboard drive type/size	Customer evaluation: Us	Competitor 1	Competitor 2	Competitor 3	Target (best product)	Ratio=Target/US
Light weight	4.5	●	O	●	●	●	●	3	3	4	2	4	1.3
Small size	3.0		O	●	▲	●	O	3	4	5	3	5	1.7
Long operation between recharging	3.5							5	4	3	3	5	1.0
Large keys on keyboard	2.0						O	2	5	3	4	5	2.5
Short time to recharge	1.5		O					2	2	3	3	3	1.5
Readable screen	3.0			O				3	4	2	1	4	1.3
Durable (unbreakable)	2.0	O	●			●	●	2	3	4	5	5	2.5
Fast processor/large memory capacity	4.0				O	O		4	3	4	4	4	1.0
Measurable performance: Us		3	3	3	4	3	2						
Comp 1		4	4	4	3	4	5						
Comp 2		3	4	2	3	3	3						
Comp 3		3	2	1	4	3	3						
Raw importance		31.5	118.5	49.5	52.5	64.5	64.5	Total 381					
% importance		8.3	31.1	13.0	13.8	16.9	16.9	100					

O Strong=9
● Medium=3
▲ Weak=1

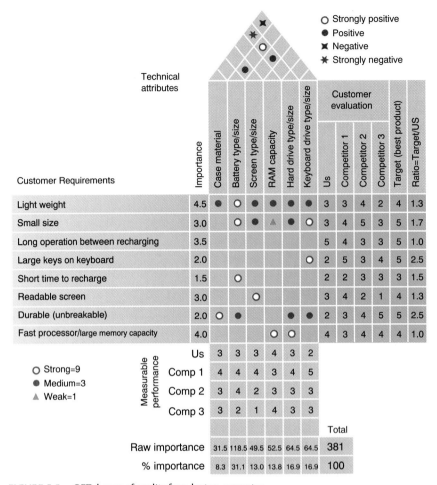

FIGURE 5.8 QFD house of quality for a laptop computer.

competing products and then evaluate how well each product, including its own, performs with respect to each customer requirement. (This is shown on the right side of Figure 5.8 in the "Customer Evaluation" columns, where ratings go from 1 for poor to 5 for excellent.) It is better to obtain these assessments directly from customers rather than asking the company designers to evaluate each product's performance. The second dimension of the competitive analysis requires the company literally to tear apart, or *reverse engineer*, each product to determine the form or value of each product's technical attributes. This technical attribute evaluation is shown near the bottom of Figure 5.8, labeled "Measurable Performance."

A secondary matrix of information that can be helpful in designing some products is a trade-off table that compares the technical attributes themselves. Sometimes improving one attribute will also improve another, or improving one attribute may harm another. For example, the size or type of battery may be correlated with the size or type of hard disk used. The trade-off matrix is normally configured as a half-matrix and acts as the "roof" of the house of quality, as shown in Figure 5.8.

From all this information the designers can develop preliminary target values for the proposed product with respect to each customer requirement and each technical attribute. The competitor values for each customer requirement and technical attribute act as benchmarks for the design. Of course, the anticipated product performance based on target requirement values will not always be realized, so the design process must be iterative, with some method for verifying the performance of the design.

QFD helps to identify not only the features customers want in products, but also helps to identify those features that customers do not value highly and can be eliminated. For example, Chrysler used QFD in developing the Neon and found that customers did not want power windows; therefore, much less expensive crank-type windows were used.

VALUE ANALYSIS

Value analysis (or **value engineering**) is a design methodology developed by Lawrence Miles in the late 1940s that focuses on the function of the product, rather than on its structure or form, and tries to maximize the economic value of a product or component relative to its cost. The principles of value analysis predate and encompass many of the design principles presented in Sections 5.3 and 5.4. Three important aspects of value analysis are (1) the use of multidisciplinary teams, (2) a systematic procedure for evaluating product functionality and value, and (3) a focus on product simplification.

Value analysis normally begins by analyzing the product as a whole, then each subassembly, and finally each component if necessary. A series of questions are used to guide the process at each step.

The first step is to specify the function of the product and to identify those product characteristics and dimensions that are of value to customers. Typical questions might be:

What is the product or component?

What is its function? What does it do? Why do we need to do it?

What characteristics are of value to the customer? How will the customer use the product?

It is helpful to define the function of a product or component using two-word statements made up of an active verb and a noun. For example, to the question "What is the product or component supposed to do?" the answers might be: control current (electrical device), heat fluid (heating element in machine), transfer funds (bank check), cure illness (medical procedure), or perform computations (computer). This type of answer reveals the core of the product.

The second step in the analysis is to determine how each product characteristic or component contributes to its value (functionality) and to determine what each component costs. Typical questions might be:

How does this component contribute to functionality? How does it increase the product's value?

What does it cost?

The final step is the creative phase of value analysis, in which we redesign the product or component to reduce its cost or improve its value. During this phase, team members focus especially on simplifying the design and evaluating the appropriateness of the product specifications, using the following questions:

Can this be done another way? Can it be done more cheaply?

Is the item overengineered? Does it do more than necessary?

Can the item's function be combined with that of another component? How much does it cost to do this?

Can a standard or existing component be used?

Can a different material be used?

Can this product be made easier to assemble?

The answers to these questions represent design alternatives that can be compared and evaluated in terms of their value and cost.

Value engineering played an important role in Honda's design of its 1994 Accord. Each part had to pass careful examination by a value engineering team. Not until the part passed this evaluation (answering questions such as: Why this shape? Why this material?) could a designer sketch a prototype part.

One of the best sources on value analysis is still Miles's book, *Techniques of Value Analysis and Engineering*.

THE TAGUCHI METHOD

The **Taguchi method** is one of the most popular tools used in robust design. Taguchi's approach is based on three principles:

1. When the value of a product attribute, such as shape or length, deviates from its target value, the cost to society (consumers and producers) in terms of lower quality increases more than linearly (increases at an increasing rate), as shown in Figure 5.9.
2. The design features of the product and the production process together determine the amount of variation in the product attributes.
3. Using experimentation, those product and process characteristics that affect product attributes can be determined, and by manipulating these characteristics, products can be designed to reduce the attribute variations that result from normal production variations.

To illustrate Taguchi's approach, consider the production of metal sheets that require a very smooth, uniform, 0.005-inch coating of plastic. The production process involves passing the metal sheets through a bath of liquid plastic and then through an

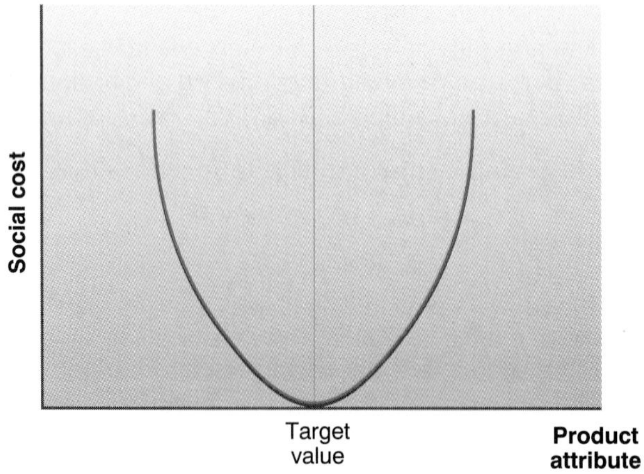

FIGURE 5.9 Cost of deviations from target value.

oven to dry. The type of metal and plastic used (product design features) and the temperature of the plastic, time of "bathing," and drying temperature and time (process design features) will all affect the thickness, uniformity, and smoothness of the coating. With Taguchi's approach we experiment with different product and process design characteristics to determine which combination will produce the least variation in product quality (deviations from the attribute target) under *normal* production conditions.

Suppose we consider the effects of two product design features, the type of plastic used and the surface quality of the metal. Figure 5.10a shows the relationship between various types of plastics, categorized by their viscosity, and the smoothness and uniformity rating (SUR) of the coating under fixed bathing and drying conditions for a fixed metal surface quality. Figure 5.10b shows the relationship between the metal surface quality and the SUR of the coating for a fixed plastic viscosity and fixed bathing and drying conditions. In Figure 5.10a the normal distributions on the horizontal axis around plastic types P_1 and P_2 show the inherent variation in viscosity for the two types

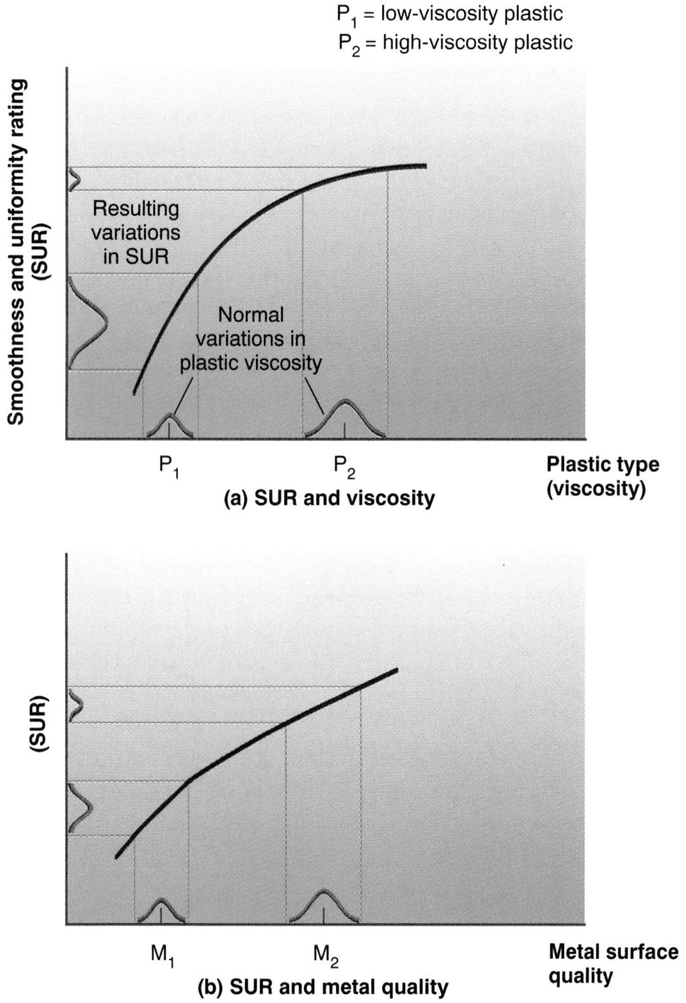

FIGURE 5.10 Relationship between SUR and product characteristics.

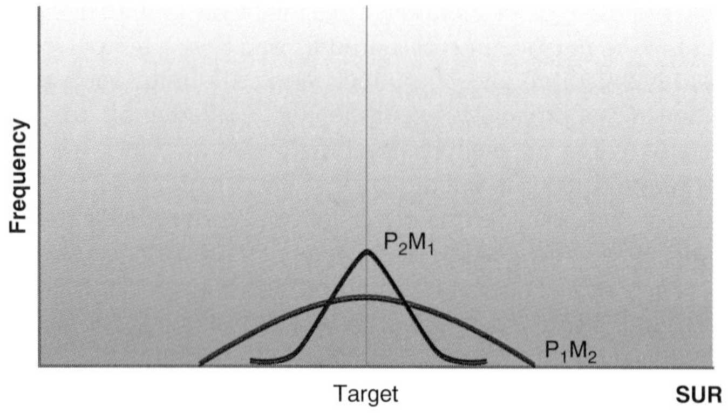

FIGURE 5.11 Frequency distribution of SUR for two product designs: (P_2M_1) and (P_1M_2).

of plastic. The resulting *variation* in smoothness and uniformity is shown on the vertical axis. Notice that the SUR is highly sensitive to low-viscosity plastics but relatively insensitive to high-viscosity plastics. Figure 5.10b demonstrates the same information for two types of metal surfaces, M_1 and M_2.

Suppose the desired *target* level of coating smoothness and uniformity can be obtained by using the plastic/metal combination (P_1M_2) or (P_2M_1). In this case, product design (P_2M_1) produces less *variation* in smoothness and uniformity because (1) the SUR is very sensitive to plastic viscosity at lower levels but relatively insensitive to viscosity at higher levels and (2) the sensitivity of SUR to metal surface quality is relatively constant for high- and low-quality surfaces. This result is especially surprising to the casual observer because the inherent variation in viscosity itself is much higher for the high-viscosity plastic, P_2, than for the low-viscosity plastic, P_1. Figure 5.11 provides a frequency distribution of the resulting SUR for the two designs, (P_2M_1) and (P_1M_2).

This Taguchi analysis can be extended to studying the relationship between process characteristics such as belt speed (drying time) or drying temperature and SUR. For example, low-temperature, low-speed drying may produce less variation in coating smoothness and uniformity than high-temperature, high-speed drying.

The apparent difficulty with this method is that if there are several product and process design features, each with several possible alternative "levels" or "settings," the number of experiments is prohibitively large. One of Taguchi's contributions is that he suggested statistical experimental design techniques to extract a maximum of information about several design features with a minimum of experimentation.

COMPUTER-AIDED DESIGN

An increasingly popular tool for product design is **computer-aided design (CAD)**. CAD systems are computer programs, or integrated packages of work station hardware and software, that allow the user to draw and easily modify product designs on a computer screen. Advanced CAD systems provide designers with at least three major benefits.

1. ***Graphics Capabilities.*** CAD systems allow the designer to view a product from different perspectives, including three-dimensional rotations, and various cross-sections. The designer can also make proportional changes in scale, or change the angle of an arc with a click of a computer mouse, rather than having to redraw the entire product.

Computer-Aided Design (CAD) systems allow a designer to see designs in three dimensions and to perform structural stress, aerodynamic stability, and other engineering tests automatically.

2. **Design Storage and Retrieval.** Some CAD systems can store the design characteristics of existing products and components. Then, for example, if a company needs a gear for a new product, the designer can enter the relevant information about the gear, such as its diameter, tooth pattern, and required hardness, into the CAD system. The CAD system determines whether the company is already using an identical or sufficiently similar gear, in which case a new one is unnecessary. If not, a gear that has similar properties may exist. The designer can then use the design of this similar gear as a starting point for the new gear. This capability not only promotes the use of common components but also reduces design time.
3. **Automatic Evaluation of Specifications.** One of the most time-consuming aspects of design for highly technical products is calculating whether or not product specifications, such as strength, heat resistance, or aerodynamic drag, are satisfied. These calculations can be programmed into some CAD systems, so that whenever the designer changes the design (by altering the shape or material to be used), these performance characteristics are recalculated automatically and compared to the product requirements. (This is sometimes called **computer-aided engineering** or **CAE**.)

The overall benefits of CAD systems can be substantial. The features described above reduce development time and cost, and they improve product quality because more design options can be evaluated in greater detail more quickly. For example, Motorola used three-dimensional CAD to produce its award-winning MicroTac pocket-sized cellular telephone two years ahead of the competition. It is not uncommon for CAD systems to reduce product cycle times by 10–50%.

Even greater time and cost reductions have resulted from recent advances whereby CAD-generated designs are converted automatically into software programs for computerized production machines. These are called **computer-aided design/computer-assisted manufacturing (CAD/CAM)** systems. This automatic conversion eliminates the costly and time-consuming step of having a person convert design drawings into a computer program for computer-controlled production equipment, such as robots or machine tools. CAD and CAD/CAM systems are not used by large automotive or electronics companies alone. Feature Enterprises, the largest maker of wedding jewelry in the United States, reported that its CAD/CAM system reduced the time required to design and make jewelry from five months to one week.[17]

DESIGN FOR MANUFACTURABILITY AND DESIGN FOR ASSEMBLY

Design for manufacturability (DFM) and **Design for assembly (DFA)** are structured methodologies that guide the designer through the design stages. (Because of their similarity in form and approach, we will use the designation DFM/A and treat them as one methodology here.) DFM/A uses catalogs of information, guidelines, checklists, charts, tables, diagrams, and graphs to help the designer develop a design plan, decompose products into components and assemblies, evaluate the production costs of product designs, and ultimately simplify and improve the product design. The methodology focuses especially on the machining, handling, and assembly implications of design dimensions, clearances, shape, and orientation. This methodology is now available, and most widely used, in the form of interactive computer software. The most widely used DFM/A methodology and software is that developed by Geoffry Boothroyd and Peter Dewhurst.

[17]William, Symonds "Pushing Design to Dizzying Speed," *Business Week*, Oct. 21, 1991, pp. 64–68.

In order to design the product well, it is important to know early in the process whether or not the product will be assembled manually, using special-purpose automated assembly, or by multipurpose automated methods, such as robots. Boothroyd and Dewhurst have developed assembly method charts to help determine the best general assembly method, based on expected production volume and product characteristics. Once a general method, such as manual assembly, is selected, DFM/A provides a systematic analysis of the assembly process. Using tables and worksheets provided by the DFM/A system, along with assembly drawings, the designer can estimate how long it will take to perform each assembly step. DFM/A is especially helpful for evaluating and improving the joining techniques required to connect parts, and it suggests ways to eliminate parts (parts reduction and joining simplification are a special focus of DFM/A). Some DFM/A systems now include expert system modules that utilize the experiences and knowledge of expert designers. A more recent extension of DFM/A, developed by Boothroyd and Dewhurst, is a system called **design for service (DFS)**, which helps designers make their products easier to service by locating those components most likely to need servicing on the outer layers of the product.

IN GOOD COMPANY

Boeing's Design Takes Off

In its effort to survive the worst airline slump in the history of aviation, Boeing Company has changed the way it tackles every facet of its business, especially the way it designs and builds airplanes. In a revolutionary move, the once secretive firm worked side by side with its customers, such as United Airlines and All Nippon Airlines, in designing its new 777 passenger airplane. These customers helped Boeing design the 777 to satisfy one of their requests for flexibility: the ability to reconfigure the airplane's interior, including galleys and piping, within hours.

Boeing implemented many other changes in its design process for the 777. It used multidisciplinary teams that included suppliers, customers, and pilots, as well as its own employees from manufacturing, purchasing, and marketing. The company designed the manufacturing process and the airplane concurrently, using sophisticated computer simulations to evaluate the manufacturing implications of any product design change. Boeing estimates that its concurrent and collaborative design process reduced the number of design changes, reworks, and errors by 50%, and when the first 777 came off the assembly line, its parts fit together so perfectly that its nose-to-tail measurement was less than 23/1000 of an inch from design goals—an unprecedented degree of accuracy. This collaboration has helped suppliers produce key parts in half the normal cycle time. This design process has since been adopted by Boeing for all of its products.

Primary Sources: Neal Templin and Jeff Cole, "Manufacturers Use Suppliers to Help Them Develop New Products," *Wall Street Journal*, Dec. 19, 1994, Dori J. Yang and Andrea Rothman, "Reinventing Boeing," *Business Week*, Mar. 1, 1993, pp. 60–67.

Numerous companies have adopted DFM/A in their product design process. IBM used it to reduce assembly time for its Proprinter computer printers from 30 to 3 minutes, and Texas Instruments reported reductions in the number of parts, metal fabrication time, number of assembly steps, and assembly time of 70–85% by using DFA.[18]

PROTOTYPING

An important tool for facilitating customer collaboration is prototyping. Prototypes are physical or graphical representations of the proposed product. Whether a compact disc player or a hotel, prototypes allow customers to obtain a better sense of the product and its use, and it helps engineers and operations personnel design the production system. Companies such as 3M, Sony, Xerox, and Black & Decker use prototypes extensively to improve creativity and communication in the design process. For example, Sony used prototypes in developing its Walkman series of radios. At first, customers had trouble conceiving of the idea of a small portable radio with headphones; many thought it was a crazy idea. But when they had a chance to try out prototype versions, most of them were impressed with the product and provided useful feedback.

Rapid prototyping that allows several prototype cycles can lead to faster product development than a single prototype cycle because it reduces product and production debugging. Traditionally, the drawback to prototyping in some industries was the inability to make three-dimensional metal or ceramic prototypes quickly. However, new technologies such as *CAD casting* can convert computer designs into molds that can be used to make prototypes quickly.

5.6 PRODUCT DESIGN FOR SERVICES

For many services, the design of the service product and the design of the service system are inseparable. Changing the design of the services offered will require changes in the production system. For example, when United Parcel Service began to offer package tracking services, whereby a customer could determine exactly where its shipments were at any time, UPS had to place bar codes on packages and have optical scanning capabilities at every handling point in the delivery system. It also required the installation of computers and data transmission equipment on all trucks and required changes in the jobs of material handlers.

The general design principles and procedures, such as simplicity, CE, and prototyping, apply to designing service products as well as goods. However, there are additional considerations of special importance when designing service products.

1. ***To What Extent Will the Customer Be Involved in the Process?*** For example, will a retail operation be primarily self-service (Kmart and Wal-Mart)? Will a financial institution allow customers to execute their own transactions using automatic teller machines or telephones (Citibank or Charles Schwab)? Normally, greater customer involvement is incorporated into the product either to reduce costs or to provide greater convenience to the customer by, for instance, eliminating the need to wait for a salesperson. However, in some cases, systems can be designed to provide better service at lower prices by having *less* customer involvement. For example, Gasoline Heaven, a service station in Commack, New York has *no* self-service pumps. The owner found that most people were much too slow at pump-

[18]Port and Zellner, op. cit.

Citibank was a leader in providing automatic teller machines for customers. By "serving themselves," customers could avoid waiting in line and receive faster service.

ing their gas and paying their bills. By having well-trained attendants pump gasoline at all the pumps, he is able to achieve greater utilization of his facilities and sell more gasoline. As a result, he can provide a full-service product while still charging self-service prices.

2. ***How Quickly Will Service Be Provided?*** Human queueing systems (waiting lines) are an important aspect of product quality for services. The intended speed of service will affect staffing, job design, scheduling, and facility layout. Some retail stores, such as Ikea Furniture, keep costs down by having a minimum number of service and checkout personnel. This sometimes causes long lines and substantial customer waiting, but Goran Carstedt, president of Ikea's North American operations, summarizes Ikea's strategy: "Our customers understand our philosophy, which calls for each of us to do a little in order to save a lot. They value our low prices."[19] In contrast, Citibank has created an automated self-service branch to deliver quick service. Marvin Cooper of Citibank explains the facility's design as follows: "The branch is built for speed—an easy in, easy out."[20]
3. ***How Standardized or Customized Will the Service Be?*** For example, freight rail service is usually highly standardized: trains are scheduled to run between specific locations, and if customers want to ship or receive materials, they must be ready at those times. Some U.S. rail carriers now provide customized train routes and schedules for large customers. This requires the companies to divide their fleets and have more flexible scheduling and routing in their rail systems.
4. ***What Variety of Services Will Be Offered?*** If a fast-food restaurant will provide only carry-out service, there is no need for seating space in the facility or extra service personnel to clean the tables. Similarly, a full-service brokerage house needs to have a much more extensive operation (a securities research staff) than a discount brokerage house that only executes trades.
5. ***What Geographical Area Will Be Served?*** For example, Eastern Connection, Inc., is an overnight parcel delivery service. It serves only the northeastern U.S. corridor from Portland, Maine, to Washington, D.C. So, in contrast to its national and international competitors, such as UPS and Federal Express, Eastern's limited service area allows it to make all shipments using trucks rather than needing an air fleet. Another example is provided by American Express Corporation, which sells its products based on quick worldwide replacement of lost or stolen traveler's checks and credit cards. This product characteristic requires a large international network of American Express offices and agents with a telecommunications system linking them.

5.7 PRODUCTION DOCUMENTS

Once a product has been designed, the months or years of thought and evaluation contained in the design must be transferred to the operations function so that the design can be transformed into a salable product. The design information is transferred to operations and converted into a usable form using *production documents*—drawings, tables,

[19]Jeffrey A. Trachtenberg, "Ikea Furniture Chain Pleases with Its Prices, Not With Its Service," *Wall Street Journal*, Sept. 17, 1991.

[20]Ellen Memmelaar, "At Citibank, Waiting Is Easiest Part," *American Banker*, Apr. 4, 1990.

lists, and narratives that assist operations employees in producing the product. Following are some of the more important and common production documents.

1. **Engineering or Design Drawings.** **Engineering drawings** are detailed line drawings of the product and each component. These drawings normally show the physical dimensions of the product and its components, the specification tolerances (e.g., the item must be 11.00 inches long ± 0.01 inch), and the materials to be used. These drawings also show how the product and its components should look when correctly produced.
2. **Bill of Materials.** The **bill of materials** is a list of all the components needed to produce the product. For each component there is a physical description, an identification number, and a required quantity listed (Figure 5.12).
3. **Assembly Drawing.** The **assembly drawing**, which was illustrated in Figures 5.2 and 5.3, may be the most important document for an assembly operation (especially for parents putting together toys). An assembly drawing is a drawing of the product, exploded component by component. The drawing shows how each component of the product fits together in relation to the other components; it therefore demonstrates how one would assemble the components to make the final product.
4. **Assembly Chart.** The **assembly chart**, illustrated in Figures 5.4 and 5.5, is a schematic diagram that shows the sequence in which components are assembled, how and where in the production process subassemblies are made, how and when the subassemblies are put together to make the final product, and where in the production process supporting activities such as inspecting and packaging occur.
5. **Route Sheet.** The **route sheet** is an operation-based rather than component-based listing of the production process. The route sheet lists each operation that must be performed, any materials needed in the operation, and any equipment used in the operation. Route sheets usually include labor standards (how long the operation should take), and they may include operational instructions. A route sheet is also called a **process sheet**, and it is sometimes combined with other production documents such as work orders.

Part no.	Description	Assembly level	Quantity	Source
P1000	Base plate	1	1	Manufactured
P1101	Left flange	1	1	Manufactured
P1102	Right flange	1	1	Manufactured
F0500	$1 \times 1/4$-in. bolt	1	4	Purchased
F0805	$1/4$-in. nut	1	4	Purchased
F1200	$1\,3/4$-in. gear pin	1	1	Purchased
F1205	$1\,1/4$-in. gear pin	1	1	Purchased
G0500	Large gear drum	2	1	Manufactured
G0600	Small gear drum	2	1	Manufactured
G1000	Large gear disk	2	1	Manufactured
G1100	Small gear disk	2	1	Manufactured
F2000	Large pin cap	1	1	Purchased
F2005	Small pin cap	1	1	Purchased

FIGURE 5.12 Bill of materials for gear transfer unit.

Many other documents, such as job instructions, load charts, and work orders, are used to control the operation of the production process. Some of these will be discussed in a later chapter dealing with the scheduling and control of operations.

Production documents were originally developed for manufacturing operations, but comparable documentation is now commonly used for the production of many services. For example, a **service blueprint**, which is the service equivalent of an assembly chart, shows each step in a service process. Service production documents are discussed in detail in Chapter 8.

Increasingly, companies are creating, storing, and transmitting production documents in electronic form. Thus, the documents do not have to be transmitted physically from person to person or place to place, and several people can use the same document at once (through their computers). In addition, when the document is changed, everyone will have the updated version; there will not be two or three different versions of the document in the system, which can lead to confusion and production problems.

5.8 ENVIRONMENTALLY SENSITIVE DESIGN

During the past three decades, there has been mounting pressure for companies to be more environmentally sensitive in terms of the products they produce and the processes they use. Many companies have acted grudgingly, changing their products and processes only to comply with environmental regulations and to avoid legal penalties. Other companies have responded enthusiastically, seeing environmentally sound behavior as socially responsible and profitable. For example, one company replaced a five-layer finish on its products with a three-layer finish. The new finish eliminated the use of cadmium, a toxic heavy metal, and a cyanide bath solution for plating the cadmium. This not only ended the use and disposal of two highly toxic materials, it also reduced operating costs by 25%.

Much of the public focus on environmentalism has been on pollution emissions and wastes from manufacturing facilities and on material recycling efforts. Consequently, many companies have concentrated their environmental efforts on changing their production processes to reduce toxic emissions and by-products and on increasing their participation in recycling programs. Both of these efforts are commendable and frequently profitable policies. But the extent to which emissions and wastes can be reduced and the ease with which products can be recycled are often greatly affected by product design. In addition, recycling and detoxifying materials is a corrective action; good product design can reduce the amount and toxicity of materials consumed in the first place.

Evaluating the environmental friendliness of a product is not easy because the production and use of the product affect the environment in many ways. Furthermore, the product cannot be evaluated in one dimension alone, such as the amount of recycled materials used. A fair evaluation must consider how much environmental damage or burden occurs in the production of the raw materials, in the production of the product itself, during use of the product, and during disposal. In other words, we must evaluate the total effect on the environment during the product's entire life cycle. For example, in some cases it is both more cost effective and environmentally sound to make a durable and reusable product that uses more resources in its production than a product that consumes less resources but can be used only once.

There are several ways in which products can be designed to be less environmentally damaging and less costly to produce. The following are approaches that offer the greatest opportunity.

1. ***Reduce the Amount of Materials Used.*** Whenever less materials are used to make a product, the environment will benefit (assuming it does not reduce the product's life). For example, McDonald's restaurants reduced their paper napkin weight by 21%, with no effect on customer use. However, a similar attempt to reduce the gauge of plastic straws was unsuccessful because customers complained that they were too flimsy.[21]
2. ***Substitute for Harmful Materials.*** Advances in materials science and chemistry have made it possible to replace toxic materials that previously had no adequate substitutes. For example, we saw in Chapter 3 that Standard Register Company replaced its old inks, which used toxic pigments and solvents, with environmentally friendly soybean-based inks.
3. ***Use Recycled Materials.*** All the recycling efforts in the world will not help the environment unless companies use the recycled materials in their products. In some cases, such as aluminum cans, the cost of using recycled materials is less than that of the alternatives. In other cases, recycled materials may cost more, so a company must determine whether other benefits can accrue from using recycled materials. For example, many companies use recycling as a marketing tool by printing on their packaging the amount of recycled material it contains.
4. ***Make Products Durable or Recyclable.*** By using more resources, a product can sometimes be made more durable and reusable. Over the life of the product, this can result in lower costs for the customer and less damage to the environment than a less material-intensive product that is used only once. For example, recognizing that spent laser printer cartridges were a disposal problem, one producer of cartridges redesigned its product by coating the machine's drum with silicone and used a toner that continuously cleaned the drum. This made the cartridges refillable and reduced the operating cost by two-thirds compared to other printer cartridges.

Designing environmentally sound products can be good business, and more companies are using this practice as a marketing tool. In fact, many companies strongly favor suppliers that make environmentally sound products. However, companies that try to be environmentally responsible are not always rewarded for their efforts. For example, some customers perceive products made from recycled material to be of lower quality than those made from virgin materials. Also, some companies have made false claims regarding the environmental friendliness of their products, which has led some consumers to be skeptical of even legitimate claims. Therefore, companies should be sensitive to the perceptions of their customers when they use environmental friendliness as a marketing tool.

---

[21]Waste Reduction Task Force, *Final Report*, Environmental Defense Fund and McDonald's Corporation, 1991.

SUMMARY

- The four steps in product development are to (1) identify and evaluate the market for the product, (2) develop a detailed product design and prototype, (3) ramp up production, and (4) modify and redesign the product based on customer feedback and market changes.
- Successful companies exhibit four common features in their product design process: (1) they consider production implications during product design, (2) they design the product and the production process concurrently, (3) they use multidisciplinary design teams, and (4) they include customers and suppliers in the design process.
- The overriding principle in product design is simplicity: Make it simple.
- Products can be simplified by:
  - Minimizing the number of parts used.
  - Using common parts and processes for several products.
  - Using standard components and tools.
  - Simplifying assembly.
  - Using modularity to achieve product variety and simplify assembly.
  - Making product specifications and tolerances reasonable.
  - Designing products to be robust.
- **Quality function deployment (QFD)** is a tool to help identify customers' preferences and to select the best technical attributes to include in products to satisfy those preferences.
- **Value analysis, design for manufacturability (DFM) design for assembly (DFA)**, and **computer-aided design (CAD)** can help reduce the number of parts used and increase the use of common and standard parts.
- **Robust design** is a procedure intended to reduce (1) the amount of variation in a product's attributes and (2) the effect on quality resulting from attribute variations.
- The design of service products requires special attention to features such as customer involvement and speed of service.
- The environmental friendliness of products can be greatly enhanced by devoting greater attention to environmental impacts during product design.

KEY TERMS

assembly chart **239**
assembly drawing **222**
bill of materials **239**
common components **221**
computer-aided design (CAD) **234**
computer-aided design/computer-assisted manufacturing (CAD/CAM) **235**
computed-aided engineering (CAE) **235**
concurrent design (concurrent engineering) (CE) **215**
design for assembly (DFA) **235**
design for manufacturability (DFM) **235**
design for service (DFS) **236**
engineering drawings **239**
house of quality **228**
mistake-proofing **225**
modularity **225**
prototype **213**
quality function deployment (QFD) **228**
QFD relationship matrix **228**
robust design **227**
route sheet (process sheet) **239**
service blueprint **240**
standard components **221**
Taguchi method **232**
value analysis (value engineering) **231**

DISCUSSION AND REVIEW QUESTIONS

1. How can the use of prototyping in product design both improve product quality and lower product cost? Give specific examples and explain.
2. What four elements of product design are now commonly used to improve the design?
3. If CE and the use of multidisciplinary design teams are such good ideas, why do you think they were not widely used until recently? What organizational barriers may have prevented their use? How could these barriers be eliminated?

4. Give a specific example of how a supplier could aid the product design of its customer.
5. What are the benefits of using QFD? What advantage does it have over simply using focus groups or questionnaires?
6. Is product simplification in conflict with advancing product technology? Explain why or why not.
7. Reducing the number of parts in a product will normally reduce costs, but why will it also improve quality?
8. Give a specific example, not mentioned in the book, of how common components could be used for some familiar products made by the same company.
9. How can a product be designed to mistake-proof its production (assembly)?
10. How does the use of modular components simplify products and reduce the production costs?
11. What are the two main aspects of robust design? Should not robustness be irrelevant if the product is designed well? Explain why or why not?
12. Give a specific example, not mentioned in the book, of how product simplification principles have been used in the design of a common service product.
13. What is the major drawback of using the Taguchi method?
14. Explain why the following statement is not true: "CAD is simply a fancy way of producing product drawings."
15. What does DFM/A provide that a smart designer could not do personally?
16. What is the role of production documents (a) during the product design stage and (b) during the production stage? Give a specific example of a production document and how it would be used in both stages.
17. Describe three ways in which products can be designed or redesigned to be more environmentally compatible.
18.* (*Project*) Select a specific product with which you are familiar. Use QFD to construct a house-of-quality table. Customer preference data should be obtained from interviews with your friends or other people who use the product. At a minimum, the analysis should include a relationship matrix and a competitive analysis.

CASE

Fibre-Pack: A Product Design Case

Fibre-Pack, Ltd., is an international paperboard and packaging producer. One of its product lines is cardboard folding cartons for products such as breakfast cereal, laundry detergent, and frozen foods. Most of Fibre-Pack's cartons are made to order because they are printed with the customer's product information and must fit the size and requirements of the product to be put into the cartons. A customer usually gives general specifications to Fibre-Pack, which then works with the customer to design a specific carton. The design specifications include size dimensions, type and thickness of paperboard used, coatings, type of printing, type of folding, and type of glue used. The final cost of the carton is determined primarily by three things: the cost for paperboard, the labor and machine costs of printing and cutting, and the labor and machine costs of folding and gluing the cartons. (If the carton is to be coated with wax, this is a fourth major cost.)

Fibre-Pack was approached by a new customer, Napthal International Ltd. (NIL), which wanted to purchase 100,000 cartons to be released in four shipments of 25,000 each over the next six months. NIL asked for a bid from Fibre-Pack on this order; the general product specifications are given in Table 5.2.

NIL provided Fibre-Pack with one of the cartons it currently uses as a starting point and benchmark for its bid. The characteristics of the current carton are given in Table 5.3; a drawing of the carton before folding and gluing is given in Figure 5.13; a drawing of the carton after it is filled with product by NIL is given in Figure 5.14.

The product designer for Fibre-Pack, who was attempting to be cost conscious, initially recommended using a lower-quality, relatively thin paperboard and a box size of 12 × 9 × 3 inches. The new design would have lowered the burst strength to 100 pounds and the puncture rating to 6.0 and would have used a blank size of 450 square inches, so less paperboard and cheaper paperboard would be used while still satisfying the customer's specifications.

When this design was sent to the folding and gluing department supervisor, she said that because of the flimsy paperboard, the cartons would have to be folded and glued at a slower speed to prevent jamming. She also said that the larger the box height, the fewer cartons that could be produced for any given machine speed. She recommended using a heavier (and stronger) paperboard

TABLE 5.2 CUSTOMER SPECIFICATIONS

Dimensions	
Height	11–13 in.
Width	8–10 in.
Thickness	2.5–3.5 in.
Total volume	≥ 324 cu. in.
Burst strength	≥ 100 lbs
Puncture rating	≥ 6
Printing	
Colors	2
Quality	rotogravure or lithograph

TABLE 5.3 CURRENT PRODUCT CHARACTERISTICS

Height	11.5 in.
Width	9.5 in.
Thickness	3.0 in.
Total volume (height × width × thickness)	327.75 cu. in.
Blank size (height + 2 × thickness) (2 × width + 2 × thickness + 1 in.)	455.00 sq. in.
Burst strength	105 lb
Puncture rating	6.2
Paperboard stock	grade C 80% recycled fiber
Printing and cutting	on two-color rotogravure
Folded and glued	on a Foldlock 200 line

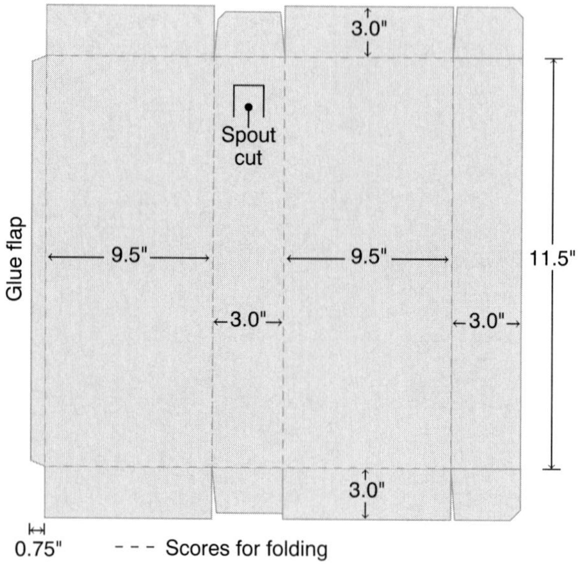

FIGURE 5.13 Design drawing of NIL's current carton.

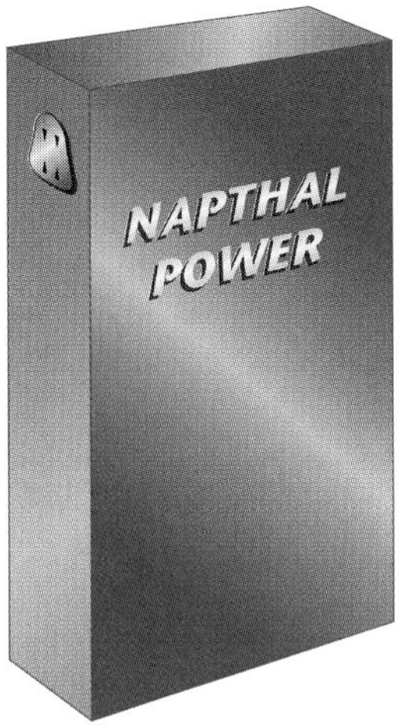

FIGURE 5.14 NIL's current carton when filled.

and reducing the box height as much as possible. The printing department supervisor felt that a heavier paperboard might make printing a little slower, although he agreed that it might reduce the likelihood of breaks and jams, which could increase the net efficiency of the printing and cutting.

Because of the folding and gluing supervisor's insistence, the designer came up with a new design with a box size of 11 × 9.25 × 3.25 inches that used a stronger paperboard. (The new design characteristics are summarized in Table 5.4.) The material costs were increased over those of the original design, but production experiments showed that the labor cost and machine time dropped substantially, so that the overall cost was lower. After testing the cartons in its filling process, the customer considered the new design to be superior in quality to the current design in three ways. First, the customer was able to fill the cartons faster, with less spillage and waste than the current cartons because the new cartons had a larger fill area of 30.06 square inches (width × thickness) than the 28.5 square inches of the current cartons. The customer had not thought of this issue before, so it was not in the specifications. Second, the new carton had a slightly larger volume, so the product had more room to settle and compact after filling and did not have to be filled as full. Third, the stronger paperboard dramatically reduced the number of carton breakages during filling by the customer. NIL subsequently transferred the carton business for their other products to Fibre-Pak because of the lower-cost, higher-quality cartons.

TABLE 5.4 NEW PRODUCT CHARACTERISTICS

Height	11.00 in.
Width	9.25 in.
Thickness	3.25 in.
Total volume	330.69 cu. in.
Blank size	455.00 sq. in.
(height + 2 × thickness)(2 × width + 2 × thickness + 1 in.)	
Burst Strength	115 lb
Puncture rating	6.7
Paperboard stock: grade B 80% recycled fiber	
Printing and cutting: on two-color rotogravure	
Folded and glued: on a Foldlock 200 line	

This example is typical. Even product designers who are attempting to be cost and operations conscious can benefit from the knowledge of a person who works in operations daily. Seemingly minor changes in product dimensions, fabrication, and materials can have enormous effects on the ultimate cost and quality of the product.

QUESTIONS

1. Suppose approximately 20% of the cost of a carton is the cost of paperboard, and suppose the thin paperboard the Fibre-Pak designer originally recommended is 10% less expensive (on a surface area, not weight, basis) than the heavier paperboard ultimately used. Taking into account the smaller blank size of the 12 × 9 × 3 inch design, approximately how much less expensive would the paperboard be for the original design compared to the final design as a percentage of total carton cost?
2. Suppose folding and gluing accounts for approximately 30% of a carton's cost. How much faster (more productive) would the folding and gluing have to be for the final design than for the original design in order to compensate for the extra paperboard cost computed in question 1?
3. What specific environmental factors should Fibre-Pak and NIL consider while redesigning NIL's carton? How would these be affected by the carton design?

Selected Readings

Akao, Yoji, and Tetsuichi Asaka (Eds.). *Quality Function Deployment: Integrating Customers Into Product Design*, Productivity Press, Cambridge, MA, 1990.

Andreasen, M. M., S. Kahler, and T. Lund (with K. G. Swift). *Design for Assembly* (2nd ed.), IFS Publications, Bedford, U.K., 1988.

Anonymous. "The Challenge of Going Green," *Harvard Business Review*, July–August 1994, pp. 37–50.

Bacon, Glenn, Sarah Beckman, David Mowery, and Edith Wilson. "Managing Product Definition in High-Technology Industries: A Pilot Study," *California Management Review*, Vol. 36, Spring 1994, pp. 32–56.

Boothroyd, G., Peter Dewhurst, and Winston Knight. *Product Design for Manufacture and Assembly*, Marcel Dekker, New York, 1994.

Erevelles, Winston F. *Design for Assemblability/Design for Manufacturability: An Assessment of Its Need, Usage Level, and Effectiveness*, M.S. thesis, University of Missouri–Rolla, 1990.

Keoleian, Gregory, and Dan Menerey. *Life Cycle Design Guidance Manual: Environmental Requirements and the Product System*, U.S. Environmental Protection Agency, Cincinnati, OH, 1993.

Miles, Lawrence D. *Techniques of Value Analysis and Engineering* (2nd ed.), McGraw-Hill, New York, 1972.

Miller, Karen Lowry. "Overhaul in Japan," *Business Week*, Dec. 21, 1992, pp. 80–86.

———. "A Car Is Born," *Business Week*, Sept. 13, 1993, pp. 64–72.

Nussbaum, Bruce, and Robert Neff. "I Can't Work This Thing," *Business Week*, Apr. 29, 1991, pp. 58–66.

Phadke, M. S. *Quality Engineering Using Robust Design*, Prentice-Hall, Englewood Cliffs, NJ, 1989.

Port, Otis, and Wendy Zellner. "Pssst! Want a Secret for Making Superproducts?" *Business Week*, Oct. 2, 1989, pp. 106–110.

Rosenthal, Stephen R. *Effective Product Design and Development: How to Cut Lead Time and Increase Customer Satisfaction*, Business One Irwin, Homewood, IL, 1992.

Schrage, Michael. "Notes on Collaboration," *Wall Street Journal*, June 19, 1995.

Smith, Emily. "How to Manufacture It So It'll Be Easier to Fix," *Business Week*, Feb. 14, 1994, p. 119.

Symond, William. "Pushing Design to Dizzying Speed," *Business Week*, Oct. 21, 1991, pp. 64–68.

Templin, Neal, and Jeff Cole. "Manufacturers Use Suppliers to Help Them Develop New Products," *Wall Street Journal*, Dec. 19, 1994.

Walleigh, Richard. "Product Design for Low-Cost Manufacturing," *The Journal of Business Strategy*, July–August, 1989, pp. 37–41.

Whitney, Daniel E. "Manufacturing by Design," *Harvard Business Review*, July–August 1988, pp. 83–91.

Woodruff, David. "Chrysler's Neon," *Business Week*, May 3, 1993, pp. 116–126.

CHAPTER 5 SUPPLEMENT

PRODUCT RELIABILITY

5s.1 COMPUTING PRODUCT RELIABILITY

5s.2 INCREASING RELIABILITY USING REDUNDANT (BACKUP) COMPONENTS

For most manufactured goods, an important measure of product quality is the probability that the product will perform at an acceptable level for at least some specified period of time. This is called the **reliability** of the product. Although reliability is certainly affected by whether or not components are made and assembled correctly, it can be consciously increased or decreased through product design.

5s.1 COMPUTING PRODUCT RELIABILITY

The reliability of a product depends on the number, reliability, and configuration of its individual components. Suppose a product is made up of three components, A, B, and C, and all three components must operate correctly for the product to operate correctly. Suppose the probabilities of components A, B, and C operating correctly for some specified period of time T are 0.95, 0.80, and 0.90, respectively. If the reliabilities of the components are independent of each other (in other words, the failure of one component does not affect the probability of another component's failing), then the probability the product works correctly for at least T time is $0.95 \times 0.80 \times 0.90 = 0.684$, as shown in Figure 5S.1.

The reliability of the entire product will be less than that of the individual components, and as the number of components increases, the reliability of the product will decrease accordingly. Even if the reliability of the individual components is high, if there are many of them the chance that *at least one* will fail within T time can be significant. For example, suppose a product is made up of 25 components and each has a 0.99 probability of functioning correctly for T time. If each component must operate correctly for the product to operate correctly, then the probability that the product will operate correctly for T time is $(0.99)^{25} = 0.78$: a 22% chance of failure. Think of how many products are made up of hundreds, thousands, or even millions of components. The reliability of individual components has to be extremely high for those products to operate correctly.

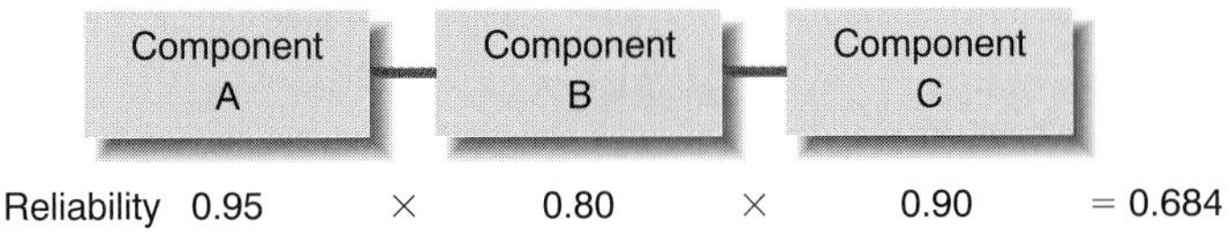

FIGURE 5S.1 Reliability of a three-component product.

Despite our best efforts, few components will ever be 100% reliable. So an important design issue, especially when designing critical equipment such as airplanes, automobiles, medical devices, and spacecraft, is how to increase product reliability in a cost-effective way. We have already discussed one strategy: simplify the product design, especially by reducing the number of parts. For example, if the 25-component product mentioned above could be reduced to 10 components, the product's reliability would increase to $(0.99)^{10} = 0.90$. Of course, parts reduction is often achieved by combining the functions of several parts into one component. In that case, the probability that the multifunction component operates correctly may be less than that of any individual part, but the reduction in reliability is often small and usually the multifunction component will be more reliable than the original parts combined. For example, suppose we could replace the original 25 parts with 10 more complex components that each has a reliability of 0.98. This would produce a product reliability of $(0.98)^{10} = 0.82$, which is greater than that of the original design.

5s.2 INCREASING RELIABILITY USING REDUNDANT (BACKUP) COMPONENTS

A second approach that is used in especially critical equipment is to use **redundant** or **backup components**.

Returning to our original three-component example, Figure 5S.2 shows the original product, except now there are two units of component B in parallel. If either unit operates correctly, then function B is accomplished. Alternatively, we can say that B has a backup unit. Function B will fail to be accomplished only if *both* units of B fail; the probability of this occurring is Prob(B_1 fails) × Prob(B_2 fails) = (1 − 0.80) × (1 − 0.80) = 0.04. So the probability that function B will be accomplished (at least one unit of B operates for T time) is 1 − 0.04 = 0.96, and the probability that the product will function for T time is 0.90 × 0.96 × 0.90 = 0.778.

Redundant components add cost and complexity to a product, so we want to add such components in the most cost-effective way possible. If only one component can have a redundant unit, the greatest improvement in reliability will be achieved by assigning the redundant unit to the component with the lowest reliability. However, differences in cost sometimes make it advantageous to back up more reliable components instead.

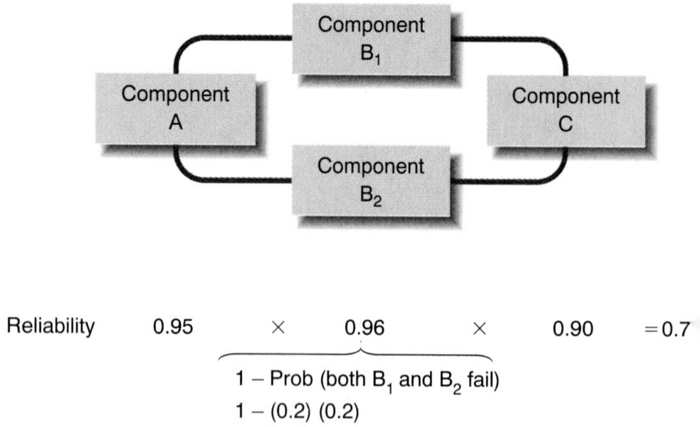

FIGURE 5S.2 Reliability of a three-component product with redundancy.

KEY TERMS

redundant (backup) components 247
reliability 247

SOLVED PROBLEM

Problem 1. Neutron Electronics makes a radio transmitter with five major components, designated A through E. The cost and reliability of each component are as follows:

Component	Reliability	Cost/Unit
A	0.98	$ 3.50
B	0.99	$ 7.00
C	0.97	$12.00
D	0.95	$ 4.00
E	0.97	$ 5.00

(a) If each component must operate correctly for the product to operate correctly, compute the reliability of a transmitter made using one unit of each component.

(b) Suppose Neutron is willing to increase the cost of the transmitter by up to $7.50 in order to increase the reliability of the transmitter. Which component(s) should have backup units to maximize reliability?

Solution

(a) The reliability of the transmitter will be the product of the reliabilities of the individual components: 0.98 × 0.99 × 0.97 × 0.95 × 0.97 = 0.87.

(b) There are six possible designs for the transmitter that will include redundant components and cost no more than $7.50. The cost and reliabilities for each design are as follows:

Redundant Components	Extra Cost	Reliability
1 A	\$3.50	$[1-(0.02)(0.02)] \times 0.99 \times 0.97 \times 0.95 \times 0.97 = 0.884$
2 A's	\$7.00	$[1-(0.2)(0.2)(0.2)] \times 0.99 \times 0.97 \times 0.95 \times 0.97 = 0.885$
1 B	\$7.00	$0.98 \times [1-(0.01)(0.01)] \times 0.97 \times 0.95 \times 0.97 = 0.876$
1 D	\$4.00	$0.98 \times 0.99 \times 0.97 \times [1-(0.05)(0.05)] \times 0.97 = 0.911$
1 A and 1 D	\$7.50	$[1-(0.02)(0.02)] \times 0.99 \times 0.97 \times [1-(0.05)(0.05)] \times 0.97 = 0.929$
1 E	\$5.00	$0.98 \times 0.99 \times 0.97 \times 0.95 \times [1-(0.03)(0.03)] = 0.893$

The best design is to have two units of A and D (one backup of each).

PROBLEMS

1. Harris Machine Company makes a hydraulic pump composed of four components. The reliabilities of the individual components are 0.99, 0.95, 0.98, and 0.995, respectively. If all four components must function correctly for the pump to function correctly, compute the reliability of the pump.

2. A computer software company has a four-person team developing a new software system. Three members of the team are each responsible for developing one of the program modules. The fourth person is assigned to integrate the three modules. The probability that the three team members will program their individual modules correctly is 0.97. The probability that the fourth person will integrate the modules correctly is 0.95. Compute the probability that the entire program will operate correctly.

3. An auto parts manufacturer makes a fuel injection system composed of six components, designated A through F. Components A, B, and C each have a 50,000-mile reliability (will not fail for at least 50,000 miles) of 0.98, and components D, E, and F each have a reliability of 0.96. (a) Compute the reliability of the fuel injection system. (b) A new design for the fuel injection system would combine the functions of components B, C, and D into one component; this new multifunction component would have a reliability of only 0.95. Compute the reliability of the new design, which now has only four components. Does this new design result in a more reliable product?

4. A manufacturer of complex electronic systems makes a product containing 20 different components. Each component has a 0.99 reliability. (a) Compute the reliability of the product. (b) Suppose the company redesigned the product by combining component functions. The new design is made up of six components with a reliability of 0.99 and five components with a reliability of 0.98. Compute the reliability of the new product design. Should the company use the new design?

5. A company makes a product using four components, A, B, C, and D. The reliability of the components are 0.995, 0.99, 0.98, and 0.975, respectively. (a) Compute the reliability of the product. (b) Suppose the company redesigned the product to include a second unit of component C to back up the first unit in case it failed. Compute the reliability of the product with this redundant component. (c) If the company could add two redundant units to the product, which components should have them? Explain why.

6.* A company makes a product that contains three components with reliabilities of 0.99, 0.98, and 0.99. (a) Compute the reliability of the product. (b) The company is considering adding a redundant unit for each component in the product to increase reliability. However, an additional component that controls the redundant units (it signals the redundant units to operate if the primary units fail) would have to be added, and this has a reliability of 0.97. (Even if the three primary units operate correctly, the backup control component must operate correctly for the product to function.) Compute the probability of the redesigned product. (c) Which design should the company use?

7. A company makes a product using four components with the following costs and reliabilities.

Component	Cost	Reliability
A	\$25	0.995
B	\$40	0.990
C	\$80	0.980
D	\$60	0.975

The company has \$250 to spend on components for the product. Determine the design that will produce the most reliable product; that is, determine how many of each component should be included. There must be at least one unit of each of the four components.

CHAPTER 6

Capacity Planning and Facility Location

6.1 THE IMPORTANCE OF CAPACITY AND LOCATION DECISIONS
On the Job: Sandy Boyd, Espresso Roma

6.2 MEASURING CAPACITY
Factors That Determine Capacity

6.3 CAPACITY STRATEGY
The Organization of Production and Facility Focus
Capacity Expansion Strategies
Demand Strategies

6.4 CAPACITY PLANNING AND EVALUATION METHODS
Forecasting Demand and Capacity Requirements
Break-Even Analysis
Decision Analysis

6.5 FACILITY LOCATION

6.6 LOCATION DECISION STAGES AND FACTORS AFFECTING FACILITY LOCATION
The Regional Decision
The Local Decision
The Site Decision
Public Service Facilities
Retail/Competitive Service Facilities

6.7 A SCORING RULE FOR LOCATION DECISION MAKING
In Good Company: Mercedes Benz Finds a Home in Alabama

6.8 MATHEMATICAL MODELS FOR FACILITY LOCATION PLANNING
Adding Capacity at an Existing or New Facility
Locating Several Facilities Simultaneously: Fixed-Charge Problem
Public Service Facility Location Models
Planar Location: Median and Center of Gravity Models

6.9 LOCATING FACILITIES GLOBALLY
Why Have Foreign Operations?
A Checklist for Evaluating Foreign Sites

Shenandoah Valley Trauma Centers: A Facility Location Case

6.1 The Importance of Capacity and Location Decisions

Selecting the amount of production capacity to have and the locations of facilities are important strategic decisions for any organization. These decisions establish the parameters within which the organization must operate in the short to intermediate term. For example, if a company builds a manufacturing plant that is too small for the demand, it will lose potential sales or have to incur high overtime or subcontracting costs to meet the demand. If a paper company builds a mill in a sparsely populated forest area to use trees as its source of pulp, the location may make alternative production technologies, such as those using recycled paper, less viable for the mill in the future.

Capacity and location decisions are important for several reasons. First, the designed capacity for a process or facility and the location of that facility will fix the production technology and cost structure. Large-capacity facilities often use large, specialized, high-speed equipment and specialized labor; consequently, they normally have relatively high fixed costs and lower marginal costs of production than do facilities designed to produce smaller output levels. Similarly, a manufacturing facility that is located in a less developed country to utilize low-cost labor will probably use a labor-intensive process and have a different cost structure than one located in the United States that may be more capital intensive but has higher labor productivity.

Second, capacity and location decisions require large financial investments and long planning lead times and are not easily reversible in the short term. (We cannot easily move a $1 billion auto plant to a new location quickly.) Third, the amount of capacity available and the locations of facilities affect the company's ability to serve customers quickly and conveniently. For example, Sandy Boyd (the subject of this chapter's "On the Job" profile) has found that selecting the right location for his company's coffeehouses—in areas where there is plenty of parking and foot traffic—is crucial to their success. For these reasons, considerable analysis and study are warranted before making capacity and location decisions.

On the Job

Sandy Boyd, Espresso Roma

Sandy Boyd was still a mechanical engineering student at Berkeley when he and a partner opened a coffeehouse near the campus, trying to fill a gap in the market for a comfortable place to have coffee, linger, and even study a bit. Fourteen years later he is president of Espresso Roma, a chain of 25 successful coffeehouses in university towns all over California and the Rocky Mountain states. Each shop has its own ambience, thanks to Sandy's location strategy—part art, part science.

Coffeehouses are even more popular now, but Sandy still succeeds by looking for university towns like San Diego, La Jolla, Santa Barbara, and Davis, where a good location is likely to be a corner property near energetic and compatible businesses like Kinko's Copies, and where there is plenty of parking and foot traffic. Once a potential spot is located, Sandy will spend a couple of days in the neighborhood getting an idea of whether the location will draw customers who create the right ambience. The location has to "feel right," and Sandy follows instincts he's developed through successes and failures.

With his original customers entering their 30s, Sandy may be looking at shopping center locations rather than campuses in seeking out new sites. While "the instinct is still there," he says, he plans to rely more heavily on demographics in selecting these sites.

The key capacity issues facing a company are *how much* capacity to have, *when* to add (or eliminate) it, *what type* of capacity to add, and *where*. Capacity and location decisions are clearly interrelated, so they are introduced together in this chapter. The chapter first focuses on long-term capacity planning and strategy, especially at the company and facility level. (Short-term adjustments to capacity and the capacity of individual processes are discussed in later chapters.) The chapter then presents methods for selecting facility locations, including models that explicitly integrate capacity and location decisions.

6.2 MEASURING CAPACITY

Capacity is the rate at which output can be produced by an operating unit—a machine, process, facility, or company. It is expressed in terms of the number of units of output produced per unit time, such as the number of automobiles that can be assembled per year or the number of students who can be taught per semester. Capacity information is important for planning and scheduling because it tells us how much customer demand we can satisfy and how we might schedule production to satisfy fluctuating demand.

Although the concept of production capacity seems simple, there are various ways to measure capacity according to how output is defined and the assumed operating conditions. The first problem in measuring capacity is defining output. If the production unit produces a single product or narrow range of similar products, then the appropriate measure of output is usually straightforward. For example, if an assembly plant assembles only one type of computer, the capacity might be expressed as the number of computers that can be assembled per month. A theater might measure capacity as the number of customers it can serve per day.

The complication occurs when the process or facility produces two or more products that have different output rates. For example, suppose a facility produces laptop computers and desktop computers; laptops can be produced at twice the rate of desktops. Then capacity expressed in terms of the total number of units produced would make no sense without specifying a product mix. For example, the plant could make 100,000 laptop computers and 150,000 desktop computers per year (250,000 total units) *or* 300,000 laptop computers and 50,000 desktop computers per year (350,000 total units). In these cases we sometimes use measures of inputs or processing capability, such as the number of machine hours, hours of assembly time, or number of operating rooms available for use.

The second issue in measuring capacity is the conditions under which the system is assumed to operate. The **design capacity** is the maximum rate at which the process can operate on a continual basis under *ideal* conditions. In the short term, output rates above the design capacity can be achieved by increasing the speeds of machines, working overtime, or temporarily deferring maintenance. Although companies may operate their facilities above the design capacity for short periods of time to satisfy surges in demand, it is usually not cost effective (nor safe) to operate at those levels for extended periods due to machine wear and worker fatigue. The **effective capacity** is the rate of production that can be achieved for extended periods under *normal* conditions, taking into account the product mix, maintenance, scheduling methods, employee training, and rest periods.

Due to fluctuations in demand, unexpected production disruptions, and an intentional desire to reserve excess capacity for emergencies, the *actual* production rate will be less than the effective capacity over the long term. The extent to which production capacity is actually being used is measured by two ratios: **capacity utilization** and **capacity efficiency**:

capacity utilization = actual output/design capacity

capacity efficiency = actual output/effective capacity

A common mistake of many managers is to focus excessively on high capacity efficiency. This factor may be more of an indication of high product demand, which keeps the production system busy, than a sign of efficient operation. In fact, extremely high capacity efficiency may restrict a company's ability to respond quickly to changes in the market. A more fruitful focus for operations managers is capacity utilization, especially the difference between effective capacity and design capacity. This difference represents losses in production capabilities due to personnel deficiencies, poor scheduling, maintenance problems, poor quality, and other factors, and it identifies opportunities for increasing effective capacity at little or no cost.

FACTORS THAT DETERMINE CAPACITY

Ultimately, the output from a production facility or system is not determined simply by the physical size of the facility, the sizes or types of machines, or the number of employees working. Production capacity, especially effective capacity, is affected by the design of the products and processes, the training of employees, the management of quality, and many other factors. The most important factors affecting production capacity are discussed below; ways that they can be used to enhance productivity are discussed in subsequent chapters.

1. ***Process Design.*** In multistage production processes the maximum rate of output that can be achieved is governed by the slowest (lowest-capacity) stage. For example, to make golf clubs, the individual components of the club—the head, shaft, and grip—must first be manufactured. The shaft must then be joined to the head, the grip glued to the shaft, and the club tested for weight, balance, and alignment. The process design in Figure 6.1a has all assembly and testing performed at one stage, which is the slowest stage of production. Figure 6.1b shows that by separating the assembly of the head and shaft from the gluing of the grip and testing, the capacity increases from 210 to 360 clubs per day.
2. ***Product Design.*** Chapter 5 explained how products can be designed to make them easier to produce. With exactly the same personnel and equipment, the capacity for making a product that is well designed for production will be greater than for a poorly designed one.
3. ***Product Variety.*** The fewer types of products made by a production unit and the more similar they are, the more specialized equipment and jobs can be, and the less time lost on product changeovers and machine set-ups. Chapter 7 shows that processes that need to produce a wide variety of products must be structured in a fundamentally different way than those that produce a single type of product. This structure and product variety will reduce production capacity in exchange for greater flexibility.
4. ***Product Quality.*** The way products are made, tested, and inspected will affect the rate at which products of acceptable quality can be produced. In some cases, work methods, testing, and inspections intended to improve quality can reduce production capacity; in other cases, these methods and the resulting reduction in product defects can actually increase effective capacity.

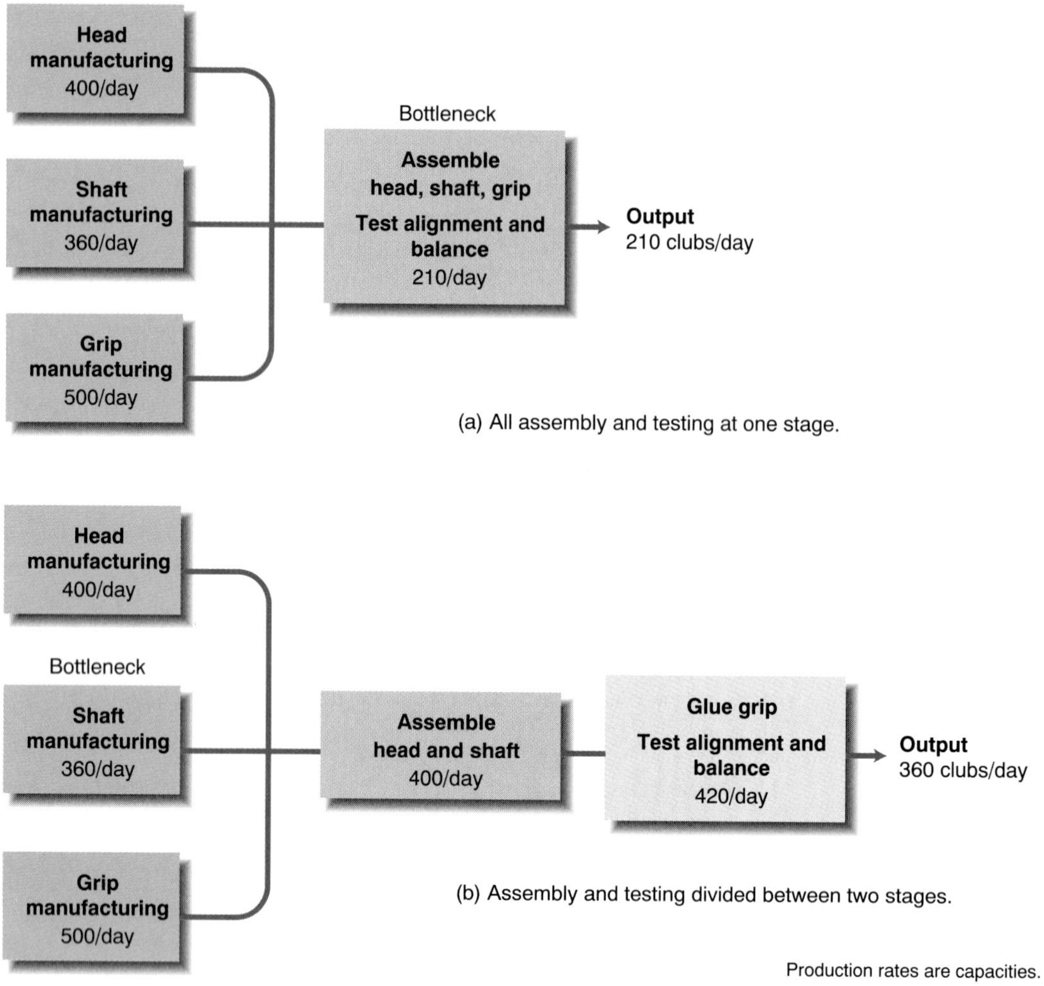

FIGURE 6.1 Golf club production.

5. ***Production Scheduling.*** Scheduling that keeps product flows well balanced and synchronized and unproductive time minimized will utilize machines and personnel better and result in greater effective capacity.
6. ***Materials Management.*** Shortages of materials can cause work stoppages, while excess inventories can cause congestion and wasted time searching for materials. Procedures that keep all processes stocked with just enough materials enhance productivity and capacity.
7. ***Maintenance.*** Equipment breakdowns and defects due to machine wear are two majors sources of lost production. Chapter 15 provides ways in which equipment can be maintained better and downtime reduced at almost no cost.
8. ***Job Design and Personnel Management.*** The amount of output a production system actually produces is greatly determined by the personnel operating the system. Inadequate training, poor job design, overwork, and absenteeism all lead to lost production. Chapter 10 presents ways in which work can be organized and

jobs designed to increase productivity and product quality while simultaneously improving employee morale.

6.3 CAPACITY STRATEGY

The primary purpose of capacity planning is to match the company's production capability with customer demand in the most profitable way. This planning should take into account not only facility, production, and distribution costs, but also lost sales due to the inability to supply on time and any revenue gains due to quick response. Too many companies concentrate their capacity analysis on facility costs; not enough attention is given to the extra costs of capacity shortages and the effects of product availability and responsiveness on sales revenue.

In addition, the capacity strategy should consider the demand pattern as well as supply capabilities. Frequently, we can reduce facility and production costs by producing together products that have countercyclic demand patterns, by altering the time pattern of demand, or by sharing facilities with other companies.

THE ORGANIZATION OF PRODUCTION AND FACILITY FOCUS

A fundamental aspect of capacity decisions is whether facilities are organized around products (the production process for a product or product line is self-contained in a facility), processes (each facility is responsible for one process, such as fabrication or final assembly), or markets (the facility is responsible for supplying a geographic area, which may require production of several products). Consequently, capacity planning not only addresses the amount of output from facilities, but also determines which products and processes are assigned to each facility. When a company evaluates its capacity, it must determine whether it needs to add capacity for producing a specific product, a specific process that will be used in making several products, or a facility at a specific location to serve a geographic region.

The best organization of facilities will be dictated by the economics of production and distribution and by the portfolio of products and geographical markets served by the company.

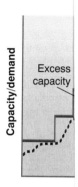

1. ***Product-Organized Facilities.*** Organizing facilities by product type is usually most desirable when there is sufficient demand to justify a dedicated facility and when the components and processing steps to make the product are different from those of the company's other products. For example, Procter and Gamble performs all, or nearly all, of the process of making and packaging powdered detergents, cosmetics, and paper products at facilities dedicated to those products, rather than trying to make them all at the same facility.
2. ***Process-Organized Facilities.*** If all products made by the company use similar components and undergo similar processing, and if there are economies of scale in production, then organizing facilities according to process stages is often best. This is true in the automobile industry, where most companies have facilities dedicated to engine manufacturing, body fabrication, and assembly. They typically do not produce all the parts and assemble the automobiles at one plant. Furthermore, auto companies do not produce 20 different automobile models at each plant to serve a local geographic region. Rather, they may have one or two final assembly sites for each model and then serve the entire continent or world market from those plants.

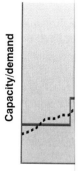

Oil refining capacity can only be added in large increments. This makes the timing of capacity expansion especially important; the risks of product shortages must be balanced with the costs of underutilized capacity.

2. *Demand trailing*—maximize capacity utilization by letting capacity lag behind demand.
3. *Demand matching*—try to match closely capacity to demand over time.
4. *Steady expansion*—add capacity on a regular basis according to long-term needs, regardless of short- to intermediate-term demand fluctuations.

The best expansion strategy will depend on the cost structure and lumpiness of capacity, the product demand pattern, and the primary order-winning dimensions the company has chosen to distinguish itself. The advantages and disadvantages of each strategy are summarized in Table 6.1.

1. ***Demand Leading Strategy.*** By maintaining excess capacity, this strategy allows the company to respond quickly to unexpected increases in demand, and it provides fast delivery to customers without overtime costs or production disruptions. In rapidly growing or highly cyclical markets, companies that have excess capacity can often gain market share by satisfying the demand by customers of competitors that are capacity constrained. For example, in 1990 and again in 1993, Compaq Computer introduced new computer models for which demand outstripped production capacity. Many potential customers bought competing models from other manufacturers who had computers available. In 1994, before it introduced several new lines of computers, Compaq added substantial production capacity in order to meet any unexpectedly large demand, even at the risk of leaving some capacity unutilized.[2]

   The importance of product availability for customer decisions (the willingness or ability of customers to postpone purchases) will influence the viability of a demand leading strategy. For example, a hotel is more likely to lose a sale due to capacity shortage than a producer of furniture because hotel customers probably have a more immediate need and substitutes exist, whereas furniture customers usually have a longer time frame.

   A demand leading strategy can also be used aggressively to keep competitors from expanding. If a company adds capacity when there is no industry shortage, it makes addition of capacity by competitors more difficult for them to justify.

   The principal disadvantage of this strategy is that excess capacity can be very expensive. It is most appropriate in industries that do not require expensive equipment and buildings and least appropriate in those that are equipment intensive. For example, gasoline refining, paper manufacturing, and automobile production need expensive, special-purpose equipment and facilities that require high levels of utilization to be profitable. Rarely does a company in these industries use a demand leading, excess capacity strategy.

2. ***Demand Trailing Strategy.*** At the opposite extreme is maximizing utilization of existing capacity by not adding capacity until demand is expected to exceed current capacity over the long term. This approach usually assumes (a) that a company can increase short-term capacity using overtime work, or possibly subcontracting, and/or (b) that customers will tolerate some delay in delivery. This strategy keeps capital equipment cost per unit low, but overtime and subcontracting costs can be substantial, and there is a high risk of losing sales by not being sufficiently responsive to customer demand.

[2]Peter Burrows, "Compaq Stretches for the Crown," *Business Week*, July 11, 1994, pp. 140–142.

TABLE 6.1 ADVANTAGES AND DISADVANTAGES OF CAPACITY EXPANSION STRATEGIES

1. *Demand Leading (Excess Capacity) Strategy*
   - Advantages
     - Can accommodate new or unexpected demand
     - Can provide quick response and delivery to customers
     - Low overtime and subcontracting costs
   - Disadvantages
     - High cost of unused capacity
2. *Demand Trailing (Maximum Capacity Utilization) Strategy*
   - Advantages
     - Minimizes facility and equipment costs
   - Disadvantages
     - Cannot accommodate new or unexpected demand
     - At peak times, response and delivery to customers are slow
     - High overtime and/or subcontracting costs
     - Often forced to add capacity during peak of business cycle, when costs of expansion are high
3. *Demand Matching Strategy*
   - Advantages
     - Balances capacity and other costs
     - Provides reliable service with ability to respond to unexpected demand
   - Disadvantages
     - Must be able to predict demand well or demand must be relatively constant
4. *Steady Expansion Strategy*
   - Advantages
     - Do not have to outguess competitors
     - Price risk from adding capacity during peak demand periods is reduced
   - Disadvantages
     - Excess capacity can result if long-term demand falls short of expectations

3. ***Demand Matching Strategy.*** The intermediate approach of trying to match capacity to demand is most effective when demand can be accurately predicted, growth in demand occurs at a relatively steady rate, and there is no substantial lumpiness in capacity additions. When these conditions exist, this strategy will usually minimize the combined costs of facility underutilization, lost sales due to shortages, and inventories.
4. ***Steady Expansion Strategy.*** A major disadvantage of the demand trailing and demand matching strategies is that capacity is often not added until the upswing or peak of a business cycle, which is the same time competitors are adding capacity, so the prices for extra capacity are usually high and the lead time for adding it is long. In addition, the capacity often does not become available until the business cycle has turned down, so the company added capacity at a high price but could not use it when needed. A strategy that is similar to dollar cost averaging in stock investing[3] is to add capacity at regular time intervals based on *long-term* rather than shorter-term demand fluctuations. Thus, the company will buy some capacity at low prices during weak periods of the business cycle, becoming available when

[3]Dollar cost averaging is an investment approach whereby the same amount of money is invested in a stock or mutual fund on a regular basis, such as every month, regardless of whether the price of the investment is high or low.

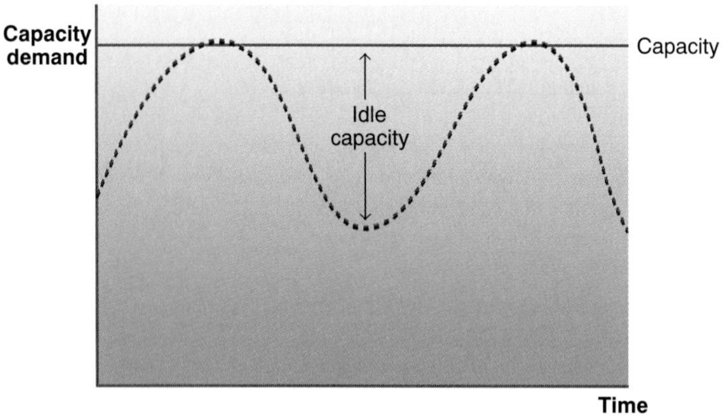

FIGURE 6.3 Fluctuating demand and unused capacity.

demand increases. This strategy also tends to keep technology more current than does a less regular expansion strategy. Although it had to change its strategy in the 1990s due to competitive pressures, Delta Airlines used this strategy quite successfully during the 1970s and 1980s. "By hewing to a disciplined regimen of buying new planes during good times and bad, Delta maintains one of the youngest, most fuel-efficient fleets in the industry. By selling its used planes at a premium, it earned $500 million in capital gains over the past decade, which helped pay for expansion."[4]

DEMAND STRATEGIES

Regardless of the capacity expansion strategy used, a company will almost always benefit if it can satisfy the same total demand using less investment in capacity. A primary cause of underutilized capacity is short-term fluctuations in demand. Some products are highly seasonal, so that demand is very large during certain months of the year, days of the week, or even times of the day. As illustrated in Figure 6.3, if the capacity of the production system is designed to meet the maximum demand rates, a substantial amount of the capacity is unused during low-demand periods. Short-term strategies for controlling demand to match better with capacity are presented in Chapters 12 and 16; here we present strategic actions that can reduce a company's investment in production capacity without harming its ability to satisfy customer demand.

Development of Countercyclic but Similar Products

One of the best strategies for smoothing the production load placed on a facility is to produce similar but **countercyclic products**, whereby the peak demand periods for one product are the low demand periods for the other product. The classic examples of this pattern are companies such as Toro, which produces both lawn mowers and snow blowers. The machining operations and components of these products are very similar, so the two products can be made at the same production facility by the same workers. The sales patterns for the two products, however, are almost exactly opposite each other, as shown in Figure 6.4. Rather than having a lawn mower manufacturing plant that goes underutilized much of the year, the company can make snow blowers at the same facil-

[4]Chuck Hawkins, Pete Engardio, and Wendy Zellner, "If Delta's Going to Make a Move, It's Now or Never," *Business Week*, June 3, 1991, pp. 94–98.

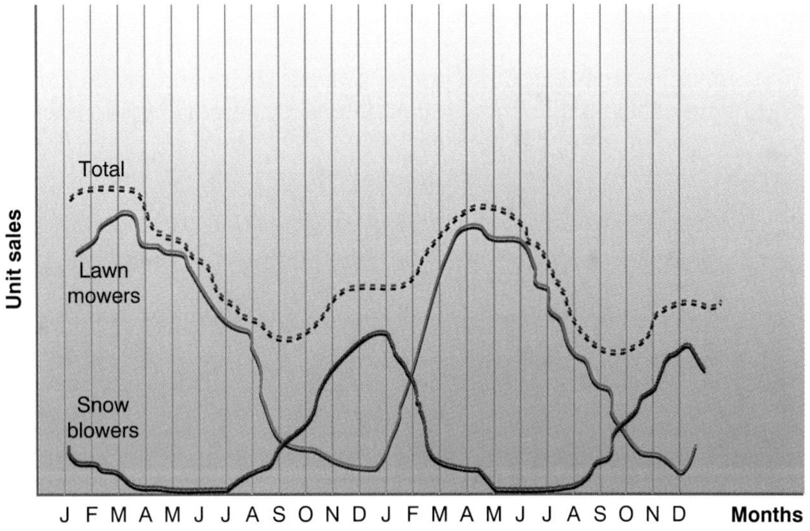

FIGURE 6.4 Wholesale sales of lawn mowers and snow blowers.

ity with no addition to capacity. This strategy also allows the manufacturer to maintain a stable work force and simply modify its mix of products during the year.

Other companies have diversified their product lines in order to produce countercyclic products using the same facilities and personnel, such as a major producer of golf carts and snowmobiles, as well as home building companies (with peak demand during the spring, summer, and fall) that do interior remodeling (with peak demand during the winter). Many service companies have been especially effective in developing countercyclic services, such as ski resorts that become golf and tennis camps during the summer, and retail stores that specialize in garden supplies during most of the year and holiday supplies during November and December.

Differential Pricing and Product Promotion

A typical long-distance telephone company may handle 20 times more calls per hour during a weekday morning than during a weekend evening. For competitive as well as regulatory reasons, the company must have enough capacity to handle all calls even during peak periods. Phone companies incur large fixed costs of capacity (satellites, microwave transmitters and receivers, computers, operations and maintenance staff), yet they have very small marginal costs of production. If the peak demand put on the system were reduced by 10%, tens or hundreds of millions of dollars in capacity costs could be saved. Because some phone usage is discretionary in terms of its timing, long-distance phone companies use differential pricing to encourage customers to call at off-peak times. The savings in capacity costs more than make up for the 50% or larger price discounts offered for off-peak calling.

Service industries with large fixed capacity costs, such as airlines and hotels, have been especially heavy users of differential pricing between seasons, and even between days of the week, to encourage people to move discretionary travel from peak periods to less busy times. In these industries, offering substantial discounts during off-peak periods not only smooths demand but can actually increase total demand. Differential pricing increases demand in off-peak periods, while the company still operates at capacity during peaks; and during peak periods, fewer customers must be turned away due to a shortage of capacity, which increases goodwill.

To a lesser extent, manufacturers also use differential pricing strategies to save on capacity costs. For example, demand for soft drinks is often 20–30% higher during summer months than during other seasons. By offering coupons or price promotions that are usable only during March and April, beverage companies try to push summer demand into off-peak periods.

Capacity Sharing

Suppose five small companies in an industrial park would all like to have a high-speed color copier. Such a machine would produce better products at lower cost than their current copiers. None of the companies has a sufficient volume of work to afford a high-speed color machine, but together they do. So they could buy the copier and share it; they split the capacity cost and receive the full cost and quality benefits of the machine. For example, eight northern Virginia community service organizations share office space, technology, and equipment that none of them could afford individually.

6.4 CAPACITY PLANNING AND EVALUATION METHODS

A major consideration in capacity decisions is the uncertainty of future demand patterns. Therefore, tools that can incorporate this uncertainty in the decision process can be quite valuable. This section introduces two types of tools: break-even analysis and decision analysis. These methods are applicable not only to capacity decisions but also to many other strategic decisions, such as new product introductions, facility locations, and choices of technology where there is considerable uncertainty in demands, prices, or other consequences of actions. Decision analysis, which is briefly presented here, is discussed in greater depth in Tutorial 2.

FORECASTING DEMAND AND CAPACITY REQUIREMENTS

Regardless of the decision methods used, the first step in capacity planning is forecasting product demands. Although there will always be uncertainty regarding future demands, the more accurate the forecasts the more likely the correct decision will be made, and the more confidence the decision maker will have in the decision.

Computing Capacity Requirements

If a new facility or process is intended to produce more than one product, then the demand forecasts for the products have to be converted into comparable production capacity measures.

EXAMPLE 1

Suppose a new facility will be designed to do all the welding for three products: A, B, and C. The per unit welding time for each product (using one welding line) is 20, 40, and 50 seconds, respectively. Suppose the forecast annual demands for the three products are 450,000 for A, 360,000 for B, and 240,000 for C. The total welding line time required per year is then

(450,000 units) × (20 sec/unit) + (360,000 units) × (40 sec/unit) +
(240,000 units) × (50 sec/unit) = 35,400,000 sec or 590,000 min

The company believes that a welding line working two shifts per day, five days a week, could operate approximately 220,000 minutes per year. Therefore, the new facility would need

(590,000 welding min/year)/(220,000 welding min/year/line) = 2.68 → 3 welding lines in the new facility

Dynamic Capacity and Experience Effects

Even without explicit expansion, facilities and processes increase their capacities over time. As a company increases its cumulative production of a product (not its production *rate*), it becomes more efficient at production: the person-hours and machine-hours required to make each unit and the total cost per unit (in constant dollars) decrease. This phenomenon, called **experience effects**, was introduced in Chapter 2, and is discussed in detail in the Supplement to Chapter 10. For many years, it was believed that the per unit cost reduction and capacity expansion over time are due primarily to worker learning: Workers become more skilled at their tasks. But worker learning could not explain why per unit cost reductions and productivity increases continue even when there is employee turnover over time. Further research suggests that many other factors contribute to experience effects, such as improvements in work methods, scheduling, equipment, management and information flows, and product design.

One consequence of learning and experience effects is that for a given facility, the capacity can increase over time without expanding the facility or buying more machines. These changes over time need to be included in the capacity plans of the company.

BREAK-EVEN ANALYSIS

The desired capacity for a process or facility will often dictate the type and size of equipment to be used, the size of the facility, the number and skill level of workers that will be needed, and even the types of raw materials that can be used. These factors determine the *production cost function*, that is, how production cost is related to the output rate. Large-capacity processes normally utilize larger and more expensive equipment and larger facilities than do small-capacity processes, so the fixed costs of production (for amortization of equipment and facilities) are larger. But for large-capacity processes, the incremental cost of producing additional units is smaller than for small-capacity processes. A process designed to produce 10 million units per year may be extremely efficient and have a very small per unit production cost if it produces 9 million units of product per year, but it may be a financial disaster (because of large fixed costs) if actual production and sales are only 1 million units per year. In the latter case, however, a process designed to produce 1 million units per year may be quite profitable even though it may have a higher marginal production cost than the larger-capacity process.

One criterion we use in deciding whether to add capacity is whether or not the additional capacity will be profitable: Will the additional revenue generated by the new production capacity exceed the additional expected costs? This question can be answered using **break-even analysis**, which determines the level of output at which additional revenue equals the additional cost of adding capacity.

We begin by constructing a cost function, which estimates the cost of the new process (or facility or expansion) as a function of its output per unit time. The cost function will typically have the form shown in Figure 6.5. A fixed cost per unit time (repre-

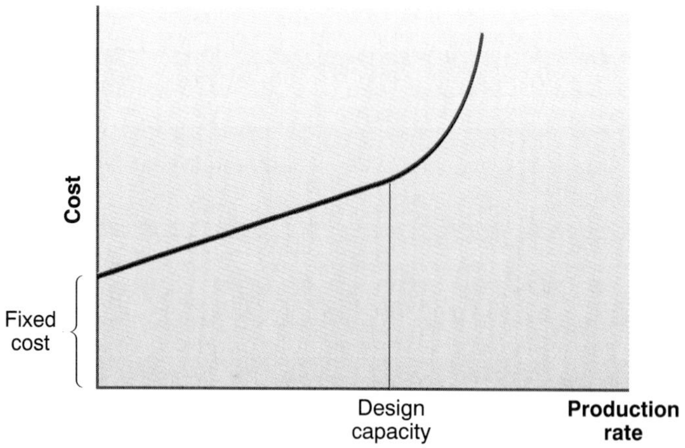

FIGURE 6.5 Typical production cost function.

senting overhead, not the cost of building the facility) is incurred regardless of the production level; then, up to the design capacity, the incremental cost is relatively constant (the cost function is linear). Above the design capacity, incremental costs increase. For simplicity, and because we are most interested in analyzing output levels below the design capacity, we will assume that the cost function is of the form

$$\text{production cost} = \text{fixed cost} + (\text{variable cost} \times \text{output rate})$$
$$= FC + (VC \times Q)$$

Suppose each unit of product made or processed (if the capacity is for one processing stage) generates p dollars of revenue. Then if Q additional units of product are made by the new capacity per unit time, the revenue function is

$$\text{revenue} = p \times Q$$

(To make sense, p clearly should be greater than the variable cost, VC.) One thing we want to know is how large Q would have to be for the additional capacity to become profitable. We answer this question using the following example.

EXAMPLE 2

Piper Industries is considering opening a new manufacturing plant to produce shoes. The new facility will have a capacity of 200,000 pairs of shoes per year and an annual cost function of

$$\text{cost} = \$2{,}500{,}000 + \$12\,Q$$

Piper expects to sell the shoes for \$27 per unit, so annual revenue will be

$$\text{annual revenue} = \$27\,Q$$

The two functions are graphed in Figure 6.6. At low levels of production, costs exceed revenue and Piper loses money on the new facility. As output increases, the revenue curve eventually crosses the cost curve from below, and above that output level the new

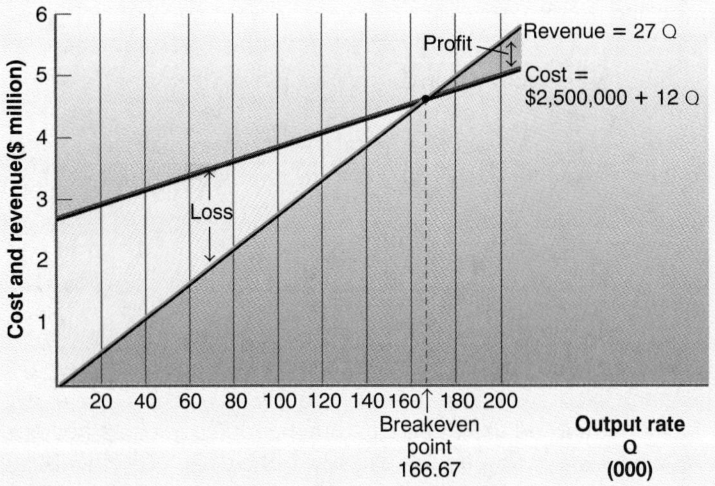

FIGURE 6.6 Piper Industries' cost and revenue curves.

capacity is profitable. The point at which revenue and cost are equal is the **break-even point**. The break-even point can be found by setting the revenue and cost functions equal and solving for the output level Q that makes the two equal:

$$\$27\ Q = \$2{,}500{,}000 + \$12\ Q \rightarrow \$15\ Q = \$2{,}500{,}000 \rightarrow Q = 166{,}667$$

Unless the new facility produces more than 166,667 units per year, it will lose money.

The company can now estimate its expected profits using its forecast sales. The sales forecast may be a single number, a sales range (such as a confidence interval), or a set of sales scenarios. For example, suppose Piper predicts the sales for the facility to be 160,000 pairs of shoes in the first year and to grow by 10,000 units each year after that. The break-even analysis tells us that if the forecasts are accurate, in the first year the additional capacity would be unprofitable (a loss of $100,000) but in subsequent years it would become profitable, so adding the capacity would probably be wise.

Future uncertainty can also be evaluated with break-even analysis. Suppose rather than using a specific sales forecast, Piper believes that its long-term sales depend on the occurrence of certain economic events. Piper believes there is a 20% chance that annual sales will average 150,000 pairs of shoes, a 30% chance of 170,000, a 30% chance of 180,000, and a 20% chance of 200,000. From the break-even analysis, we can see that Piper has a 20% chance of losing money with the new plant and an 80% chance of it being profitable.

DECISION ANALYSIS

In some cases, we may want an even more explicit inclusion of uncertainty in our analysis than with break-even analysis. **Decision analysis** is a set of techniques that evaluates alternative actions by explicitly considering the probabilities and consequences of different future outcomes. Sometimes a company may have the opportunity to take an action now or postpone it until a later time, possibly gathering more information and allowing more of the future to unfold. The questions are then: Should we act now (add capacity)? If so, which action should we take (how much capacity should we add and possibly where)? If not, should we gather information, and how much should we be willing to pay for it? Depending on the information gathered and what transpires in the meantime, what should we do at the next decision point? The tool used to answer these questions is called a *decision tree*.

Tutorial 2 explains decision analysis and decision trees using capacity expansion examples. The techniques, however, are readily applicable to many other operations problems.

6.5 FACILITY LOCATION

Most facility location decisions have their own unique characteristics. For manufacturing facilities the locations of raw materials, labor, and markets are clearly important. For service facilities that require direct customer contact, such as hospitals, hairdressers, and theaters, physical proximity to customers is crucial. For manufacturing facilities, being near competitors may be desirable, whereas for others such as some service facilities, it may not. Some facilities, such as toxic waste dumps or nuclear reactors, have noxious properties, so we do not want them too close to populated areas.

Because of the wide variety of facilities and their unique characteristics, it is often necessary to utilize a variety of analytical evaluation methods. Most location decisions are made in stages, which we will discuss below; at some stages we may use mathematical models to assist our decision making, while at others we may use simple tables and scoring rules. Although it is sometimes difficult to categorize facilities precisely, there are several general types of facilities that have different features and require different analyses: manufacturing, warehouse or distribution, retail, and public service facilities and administrative offices. Before looking at some of these types in detail, we will study the general decision process and identify those aspects of location decision making that are common to most facilities.

6.6 THE LOCATION DECISION STAGES AND FACTORS AFFECTING FACILITY LOCATION

Facility location decisions are commonly made in three stages. At each stage a set of location alternatives is identified, and then an evaluation procedure is used to reduce the set of options. The stages often form a geographic and informational hierarchy and consider, in turn, regional, local, and site decisions (as illustrated in Figure 6.7). At the first stage, location alternatives represent general geographic regions, and the data on each alternative are usually in an aggregated form. After the number of alternatives has been reduced, local alternatives within the remaining regions are identified and evaluated using more precise, detailed data. After further pruning of alternatives, individual site alternatives within the remaining local alternatives are evaluated using detailed site information.

The factors that are most important for evaluating alternatives vary from stage to stage. We will describe each of the decision stages and explain why and how certain factors come into play. We initially focus on general location factors, although they are probably most applicable to manufacturing facilities. Factors that are especially important for public service facilities and retail/competitive facilities are discussed at the end of this section.

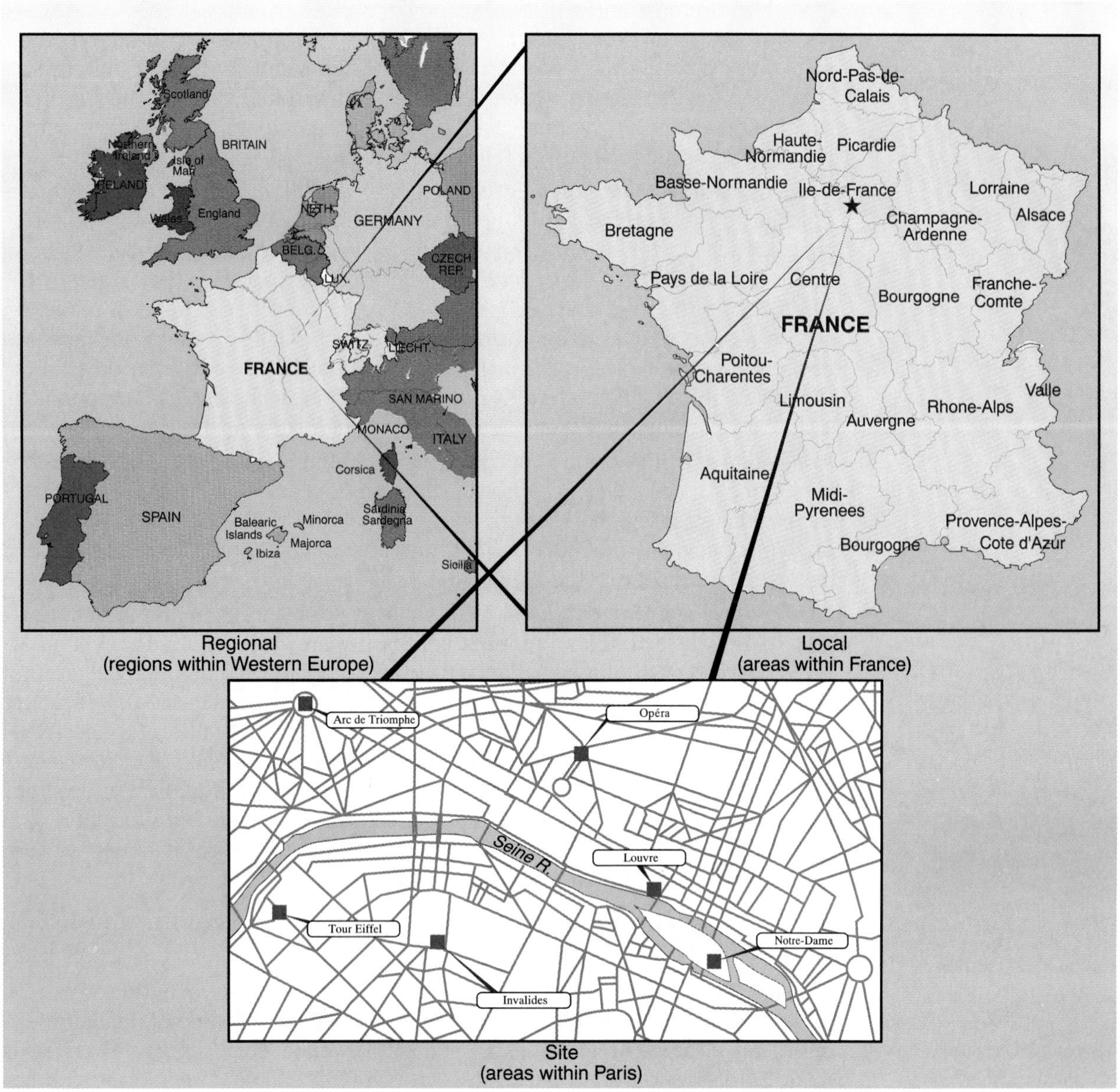

FIGURE 6.7 The location decision stages.

THE REGIONAL DECISION

The first stage of the decision process is usually to make a *regional* decision. Depending on the facility, a region may be a country, a part of a country, a state or province within a country, or a metropolitan area. For example, a firm that is planning to open a facility may decide that it wants to locate either in the northeastern part of the United States or in Western Europe. A state government locating a prison may consider the regions to be regions within the state, such as the northeast or southeast.

At this stage, economic, market, and legal factors tend to be dominant. The following are specific factors of potential importance.

1. ***Market Proximity.*** Manufacturing facilities can usually be located away from ultimate consumers, although close proximity allows shorter and more predictable

lead times for customers (if the customers are industrial customers who use a just-in-time production system, proximity may be crucial). In addition, there sometimes are advantages to locating within the same country as the ultimate consumers or to locating within a special trading bloc, such as the European Union. For service operations, close proximity to customers is usually essential unless services are provided by telecommunication.

2. **Proximity to Raw Materials.** For manufacturing facilities, proximity to raw materials and other material inputs is extremely important to reduce transportation cost and delivery time. *Proximity* may mean being close to a low-cost delivery point rather than to the actual physical sources of the raw materials. For example, the Gulf Coast of the United States is a good location for oil and chemical refineries, not only because there are substantial oil deposits in Texas and Louisiana, but also because oil can be inexpensively imported to this region from other countries. Proximity to raw material sources tends to be relatively less important for service facilities because they are usually less material intensive.
3. **Availability of Utilities.** In some parts of the United States and the world, electric generating capacity, clean water, and other utilities are in short supply. Residential consumers often take for granted the availability of electricity, sewers, and so on, but commercial and industrial facilities are not guaranteed these services and in some cases must provide their own if insufficient capacity exists.
4. **Labor Supply and Unionization.** Companies need to know whether or not the region has a satisfactory pool of labor possessing the skills required and at an acceptable wage rate. Information about the average wage and productivity rates for general categories of workers is easy to obtain for each state in the United States and for many other countries. This level of detail is usually sufficient for decisions at the regional stage. The extent of unionization and the general labor–management environment for each region are also likely to be important. For example, labor–management relationships and the power of unions are quite different in various parts of the United States, and are even more different in countries such as Japan, Germany, Italy, and France.

Some key issues that had to be resolved before the Moscow McDonald's restaurant could be opened were the availability of high quality food (beef, chicken, and potatoes), and the convertibility of the Russian Ruble. It took 10 years to resolve these, but the Moscow McDonald's has been highly successful.

International location decisions have additional factors that can be important, such as the following.

5. **National Taxes.** The tax structure varies considerably from country to country, not only in the level of taxation but also in the form. The United States relies primarily on income (profit) taxes to generate revenue from companies, whereas many European countries use a value-added tax. The form of taxation sometimes favors companies in certain industries.
6. **Legal Restrictions.** Some companies opened facilities abroad assuming that they could import production inputs, but were later confronted with import restrictions or home content laws that prevented them from doing so. In many cases this presented a dilemma because there were no domestic suppliers of the needed inputs.

   Some countries also have restrictions on withdrawing profits or withdrawing them in currency. This may mean that the company has to use bartering or other arrangements to move capital out of the country in which profits were generated.

THE LOCAL DECISION

Once a general region has been identified, many areas or locales within that region may be reasonable alternatives. The local decision usually involves selecting among cities, metropolitan areas, or county-sized areas. For example, at the regional level a company may have decided to locate within the midwestern United States. Within this region possible local alternatives might be the Chicago, St. Louis, or Milwaukee area. At this point additional location factors become relevant.

1. ***Taxes.*** Within the same region taxes can vary considerably, especially within metropolitan regions that cross state boundaries, such as New York, Chicago, Boston, and St. Louis. For example, the difference in the top corporate and personal income tax rates between New York City and Connecticut is approximately 5%. Even within the same state, property and payroll taxes can differ substantially. One factor that has encouraged companies to locate in suburban areas rather than central cities in recent years is that many large cities have imposed personal income taxes and employee "head taxes," thereby increasing the gross wages firms must pay.
2. ***Economic Incentives.*** Local governments commonly entice firms to locate within their jurisdiction by providing financial incentives. These can take the form of direct financial assistance such as free land, low-cost loans, or tax abatements. Sometimes less direct incentives are even more valuable, such as constructing or improving roads, providing for employee training, or modifying zoning restrictions.
3. ***Attractiveness of the Community.*** The quality of housing, rate of crime, quality of schools, cultural institutions, and professional athletic teams influence facility location decisions mainly through their effect on the willingness of employees to relocate and the ability to recruit experienced, skilled labor.
4. ***Compatible Industry.*** There are good reasons why certain parts of the country have high concentrations of facilities in the same industry. For example, Chicago/northwestern Indiana has a high concentration of steel mills; Detroit and St. Louis, auto manufacturers; and Boston and the San Francisco peninsula, computer hardware and software firms. When a manufacturer wants to open a production facility, being close to competitors is often advantageous for several reasons: (a) a supply of labor with the needed skills probably already exists, as well as an infrastructure for training employees (trade schools, community colleges, universities); (b) suppliers of needed materials and services are available; and (c) the community accepts the industry (this is important if the industry has some unpleasant features such as pollution).
5. ***Transportation Network.*** If materials and products must be shipped using a specific mode of transport, one locale may be preferable to another. For example, a facility that needs access to railroads and barges might prefer a locale on a river near a railroad line. In 1993 when Mercedes-Benz was evaluating possible plant sites in the United States, transportation costs were a major concern.[5]
6. ***Government Policy and Attitude.*** Local and state governments can either help or hinder the construction of facilities. Most companies do not want to locate in areas where they are not wanted. According to Mercedes-Benz, the deciding factor in selecting Alabama for its new plant was the zeal and dedication to the project of state officials.
7. ***Environmental Regulations.*** Although most environmental laws are made at the national level, restrictions for each metropolitan area are based on the environmental history of that area. The environmental restrictions in Los Angeles are not

---

[5]David Woodruff and John Templeman, "Why Mercedes Is Alabama Bound," *Business Week*, Oct. 11, 1993, pp. 138–139.

the same as those in Salt Lake City or Knoxville. To open a facility in some cities, a company must essentially buy the "pollution rights" of another company in the area, such as by paying for the installation of pollution equipment on another company's facility so that there is no net addition of pollution to the air and water systems.

THE SITE DECISION

The final stage in the decision process is to identify and select specific facility sites. Recently, it has become common for the second and third stages to be merged, especially when locating large facilities, because in many cases there is only one suitable site within a specific locale. As an inducement, the government sometimes does much of the location analysis at the local level to identify and acquire a site that is then offered to a firm.

The important factors at the site level are often described by very detailed information that can be expensive and time-consuming to obtain. However, this information is often crucial. Some of the important factors at this stage are refinements of more aggregate factors considered at earlier stages. For example, availability of electric generating capacity may be an important issue at stages 1 and 2, whereas access to the electric power grid may be important at stage 3. Similarly, an area may have a generally good transportation system, but a specific site may require substantial investment to connect with the highway or railway network. In addition to access to the utility and transport networks, the following factors are often important.

1. **Space for Expansion.** The importance of space for expansion cannot be overstated. Roger Schmenner[6] found that companies' most common reason for moving their facilities was lack of room for expansion. When companies establish facilities, they want to keep their investment to a minimum, so many of them will not purchase more space than they are likely to need in the foreseeable future; this is especially true of smaller companies. The consequence is that if the company is successful, it quickly outgrows its facilities. Some local governments have responded by buying land in large parcels (say, 50 acres) and leasing it in small sections, holding some in reserve for resident firms' future needs. This is a good strategy for economic development because it secures the successful companies that an area wants; they do not want to lose the growing companies and keep only the stagnant ones.
2. ***Proximity to Other Industry.*** One benefit of office and industrial parks is that several facilities can share equipment and services and obtain lower prices on some services. Several small companies grouped together can share the expense of a photocopier, for example, or a small printing company may find it profitable to open a store near several firms, whereas it would not be profitable to serve only one or two companies. Similarly, refuse collection, parcel delivery, and other services can be supplied more cheaply to a collection of facilities than to one or two. Groups of industrial facilities also tend to attract other support service providers such as accountants, lawyers, and engineers.

PUBLIC SERVICE FACILITIES

Facilities that provide public services, such as police and fire stations, hospitals, schools, post offices, and fire alarm boxes, are often influenced by factors other than those mentioned above. Although cost considerations are important, the most impor-

[6]See Roger W. Schmenner, *Making Business Location Decisions*, Prentice- Hall, Englewood Cliffs, NJ, 1982.

tant factor for these facilities is proximity or access to users. The measure of closeness will vary from case to case. For a fire or police station, response time is more relevant than actual distance, so traffic congestion and road quality also need to be considered.

A second factor for public facilities is their potentially negative aspects. Although the services of schools, fire stations, and hospitals are desirable, most people do not want to be located too close to them. Being a mile from a fire station or hospital, for instance, provides good access without the noise of sirens all night. Public officials must be sensitive to this consideration when locating facilities. Toxic waste disposal facilities, waste incinerators, and nuclear power plants raise even more serious issues, and many specialized books and articles are now available on these topics.

RETAIL/ COMPETITIVE SERVICE FACILITIES

A study of successful service companies indicated that location was often the most important factor in their success.[7] In contrast to manufacturing facilities, most companies that provide services prefer not to be near competitors' facilities. If customers must come to the service facility (retail store, bowling alley) and no competing facilities are nearby, the company has a spatial monopoly, which guarantees it most or all the business within that area.

In practice, however, it is difficult to create a spatial monopoly for many products. Most service companies try to locate where they perceive a substantial concentration of customers. But competitors are aware of this customer concentration as well, so several competing facilities may locate near each other. If a spatial monopoly cannot be obtained, the next best thing may be to locate *close to* competitors to take advantage of **agglomeration effects**. Several similar facilities located near each other create a larger market area: people are willing to travel farther to a location where there are alternative providers of the product they want. This is the reason several fast-food restaurants or department stores may be located together. A 25% share of a large market may be more profitable than a 100% share of a small market.

Shops in large malls benefit from agglomeration effects (grouping many similar companies together). Well-designed malls should also include complementary shops so customers can combine shopping trips, and they should be easily accessible with plenty of parking space.

Several other factors can be important, especially at the site selection stage, when locating service facilities.

1. ***Complementary* Businesses.** Many consumers try to combine purchasing trips to save time, going to the dry cleaners, grocery store, pharmacy, and bank in one trip. It is often beneficial to locate a facility near others that are likely to increase customer traffic but do not compete directly. This is especially true if the other facilities provide complementary products. For example, a pharmacy near a medical office complex is likely to get customers who need to fill a prescription or purchase other medical supplies right after visiting the physician. Well-designed, well-managed shopping centers try to obtain a good balance of tenants that complement each other, with enough concentration of products to generate agglomeration benefits.
2. ***Access.*** It is common to have a gas station on each of the four corners of a busy traffic intersection, yet the sales volume of the stations may differ by 100% or more. Why? Usually it is due not to the difference in product brand, but to the relative accessibility of the stations based on traffic patterns. For example, as shown in Figure 6.8, if most of the traffic moving north on Main Street turns right at the intersection, people are more likely to use the gas station on the southeast corner of the intersection because they can pull into the station easily and leave easily by making two right turns. Similarly, northbound traffic turning left is more likely to

[7] See Richard Gibson, "Location, Luck, Service Can Make a Store Top Star," *Wall Street Journal*, Feb. 1, 1993.

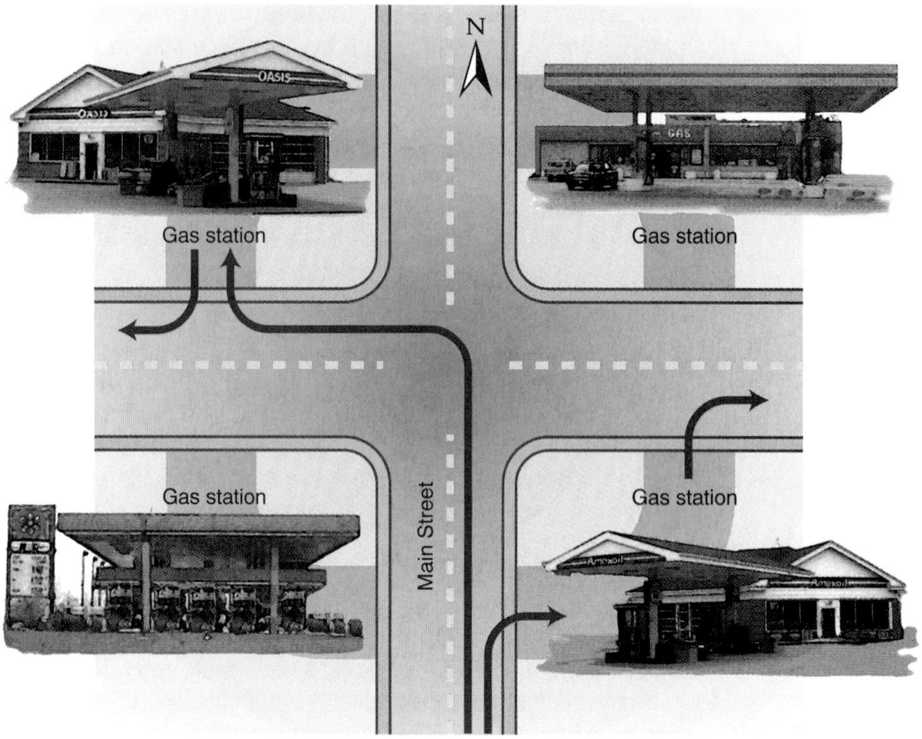

FIGURE 6.8 Traffic flow and accessibility.

use the station on the northwest corner rather than the southwest corner to avoid left turns through traffic. The ability to get into and out of a facility quickly and safely applies to many service facilities, and can be affected by parking as well as traffic characteristics.

3. ***Exposure.*** Many facilities rely heavily on visibility to inform customers of their existence. Therefore, facilities need to be located so that they can be seen easily. Even if a facility is located near many customers or in a shopping center passed by a large amount of traffic, lack of visibility can be disastrous.

These factors do not represent a complete list. Many others can be important, especially when we take a broader view of facility location decisions. For example, installing emergency telephones on a college campus, locating microwave transmission towers, or positioning mobile service facilities or response teams involves factors such as response times, topography of the land, and lines of sight. However, the same general decision process can be used to evaluate and select among alternatives.

6.7 A SCORING RULE FOR LOCATION DECISION MAKING

At each stage of the decision process several location alternatives must be evaluated, and those that seem to be inferior are eliminated from consideration. Two evaluation mechanisms are commonly used in location analysis: scoring rules and optimization models. When cost and/or revenue generation potential or other naturally quantifiable factors (person-miles traveled) are dominant, optimization models can be developed to help decision makers evaluate and select the best location. Optimization models, however, are often very narrow in focus and do not incorporate factors that are not easily convertible into numerical terms.

We will study some common location optimization models in the next section, but we begin here by studying a simple evaluation procedure called the **linear scoring rule (LSR)**, which includes appraisals of qualitative factors.

1. We first identify the factors important for screening or selecting among alternative locations (whether regions, locales, or sites). When selecting factors, there is a constant trade-off between simplicity and completeness. We do not want to omit factors that may be important, yet we do not want to include factors that have a very small effect on our decision. In addition, the only factors important for selecting among alternatives are those on which the alternatives differ. Even if a factor, such as availability of labor, is important, it can be dropped from the analysis if all the alternatives are equally good with respect to it.
2. To each factor we assign a weight proportional to its importance in the decision. Thus, a factor with a weight of 0.20 is considered to be twice as important in the decision as a factor with a weight of 0.10. Normally, we select weights so that they sum to 1.00.
3. We rate each alternative with respect to each factor. Usually the rating is done on a 0–10 or 0–100 scale. When rating alternatives, it is important to choose a scale that is "ratio meaningful," so that a rating of 8 is twice as good as a rating of 4.[8] Sometimes this means *not using* available quantitative measures. For example, if we are rating two sites with respect to the factor "space for expansion," a 50-acre site may *not* be twice as valuable to us as a 25-acre site. If all we ever expect to need (even when planning for expansion) are 15 acres of land, then a 25-acre site and a 50-acre site might both be rated the same.
4. The overall rating for each location alternative is obtained by multiplying the rating on each factor by the factor weight and summing these values.

EXAMPLE 3

Suppose a company wants to evaluate three alternatives, A, B, and C, and will use a 0–10 scale to rate each alternative against each factor. Table 6.2 presents the relevant factors, weights, and ratings.

TABLE 6.2 LOCATION FACTORS AND WEIGHTS

Evaluation Factors	Factor Weights	Location Alternatives A	B	C
Space for expansion	0.2	10	8	5
Proximity to customers	0.3	5	7	10
Access to highways	0.1	4	6	10
Prox. to compatible industry	0.2	8	10	6
Local taxes	0.1	10	6	3
Local labor supply	0.1	6	9	10
Weighted total		7.1	7.8	7.5

[8]Ordinal ratings, which simply rank the alternatives in order with respect to the factor, such as 10 for the best, 9 for the second best, and so on, should *not* be used. Weighted averages of ordinal ratings are meaningless.

From this analysis it would *not* be appropriate to conclude immediately that alternative B is best. First, a difference of 0.3 in the weighted score is not large. Second, the purpose of scoring rules is not only to select or screen alternatives, but also to help the decision maker better understand the options available and the factors that are important. After computing the total weighted score for each alternative, we would study why one alternative scored higher than the others. That is, we would identify the strengths and weaknesses of each alternative. We would then reappraise the ratings each alternative received for each factor, reappraise the weights assigned to each factor, and recompute the weighted score for each alternative. Note that this is not meant to be a form of cheating. The evaluation process is iterative because we learn more about our decision as we gather data and evaluate options. Once we become confident about our choice of factors, their weights, and the ratings, we feel more confident about our final selection of an alternative.

As part of this evaluation process we can also perform simple sensitivity analysis. For example, if there is disagreement or uncertainty regarding the weights for some factors, it is easy to evaluate whether or not, or over what range, the weights can be altered without changing the rankings of the alternatives. For example, if someone feels that "space for expansion" should be the most important factor in Example 3 and receive a weight of 0.3 and "proximity to customers" a weight of 0.2, the weighted scores for the three alternatives become 7.6, 7.9, and 7.0; B is still the best. This type of sensitivity analysis can identify where more precise data or evaluations might be needed.

IN GOOD COMPANY

Mercedes Benz Finds a Home in Alabama

Long secure in its position as a leading maker of luxury cars, the German automaker Mercedes Benz had fallen into some extravagent habits that were beginning to cost it money in the early 1990s. Combined with its cost disadvantage compared to U.S. and Japanese car makers, such wasteful factors as having some of the largest and least efficient production facilities in the world motivated Mercedes to consider locating its newest, $300 million factory in the United States. But in which state?

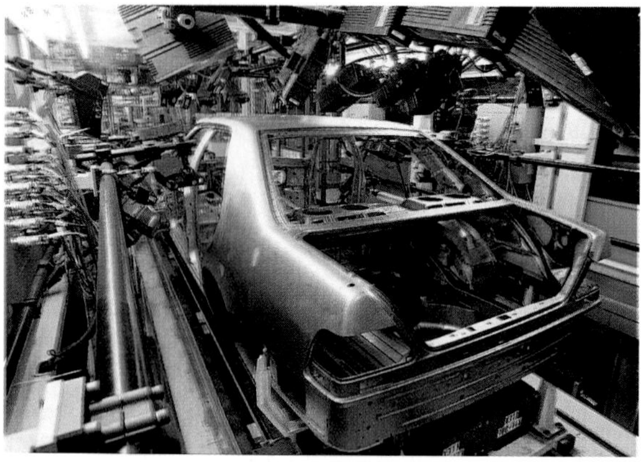

Alabama was ultimately selected from a field of 35 states. With its ready access to the Atlantic Ocean and the Gulf of Mexico, Alabama offered Mercedes a solution to one of its biggest concerns: transportation costs for the new cars, at least half of which were destined for export. Another factor was labor: Mercedes needed to hire about 1500 people, and the availability of workers both young and more experienced, skilled and semi-skilled was a plus, as was Alabama's low unionization rate. Ironically, even Alabama's landscape played a role in beating out North Carolina and South Carolina in the final round. The state's wooded countryside reminded Mercedes officials of home.

Source: David Woodruff and John Templeman, "Why Mercedes Is Alabama Bound," *Business Week*, Oct. 11, 1993, pp. 138–139.

In practice, dozens of factors may be important for a given decision. Many state governments and public utility companies provide workbooks for people performing site location studies. These workbooks list hundreds of possible factors and provide a convenient table, similar to Table 6.2, for performing the analysis. They can help companies avoid overlooking important factors, and they provide a guide for acquiring data.

LSRs rely on some strong assumptions. Although these assumptions do not have to be satisfied perfectly for the method to be useful, they need to be reasonably fulfilled for the results to have validity. First, we assume that location factors are *compensatory*; that is, a good score on one factor can compensate for a poor score on another. This implies that the alternatives are at least acceptable in every dimension. If an alternative is unacceptably poor in some dimension (e.g., the site is too small to build a facility), we would not include that alternative in the scoring rule. Second, the factor weights and ratings must be ratio meaningful. A factor assigned a weight of $2w$ must be twice as important as one assigned a weight of w, and this 2:1 ratio applies over the entire range of assessment levels. Similarly, a location alternative receiving a factor assessment score of $2x$ is considered to be twice as good with respect to that factor as an alternative receiving a score of x on that factor.

The LSR is an attractive decision tool because it can incorporate a wide range of factors into a decision using very simple mathematics. This combination of robustness and simplicity makes the LSR applicable to many other business decisions, such as which person to hire for a job or which type of computer to buy. The quality of the decision, however, will depend on the appropriateness of the decision factors, the factor weights used, and the accuracy of the factor assessments for the alternatives.

6.8 MATHEMATICAL MODELS FOR FACILITY LOCATION PLANNING

Although scoring rules are commonly used in facility location decisions, in many cases either all of the location alternatives are acceptable with respect to the qualitative factors, or one factor, such as cost, is dominant, so that the evaluation is reduced to one criterion. When alternative locations can be evaluated using a single quantitative criterion, such as cost, response time, person-miles traveled, or number of persons within some specified distance of a facility, optimization models can be formulated and solved. The most common location models are **0/1 integer programs**, whereby some or all of the decision variables in the problem take on only the values 1 (locate a facility at some site) or 0 (do not locate a facility at that site). (See Tutorial 1 for a discussion of integer programs.) Before introducing these more complicated integer programs, we begin with a simple model based on a type of linear program called a *transportation problem*.

EXAMPLE 4

Terminal Industries (TI) currently produces a product at three manufacturing plants in Phoenix, Atlanta, and Cleveland. Demand has been growing steadily, and TI either has to expand the capacity of an existing facility or add another facility somewhere else. The company ships its product to five major distributors located in Chicago, Denver, Los Angeles, Dallas, and Philadelphia. At each plant the production cost is made up of a fixed annual overhead cost to keep the plant open plus a constant cost for each unit of production. The product is shipped from the plants to the distributors in standard

TABLE 6.3 DATA FOR TERMINAL INDUSTRIES

	Per Unit Transport Costs							
	Distributors					Annual Fixed Cost	Per Unit Production Cost	Annual Capacity (000)
Existing Plants	Chi	Den	LA	Dal	Phi			
Atlanta	8	12	18	10	7	$500,000	$20	150
Cleveland	4	11	20	12	6	$600,000	$22	180
Phoenix	15	7	8	9	20	$750,000	$18	170
Expected annual demand (000)	120	80	150	100	130			

carload quantities so that the transportation cost per unit of product is constant on any route, but this cost varies with the route based on distance. Table 6.3 lists the plant capacities, annual fixed costs, per unit production costs, per unit transportation costs between each plant and distributor, and expected annual distributor demands.

Annual demand is expected to increase to 580,000 units during the next three to five years, but the current production capacity is only 500,000 units. Suppose the possible options available to the company are the following:

1. Expand and redesign the Atlanta plant. The new annual capacity would be 250,000 units; the annual fixed cost would be $800,000 and the per unit production cost would drop to $19.
2. Expand and redesign the Phoenix plant. The new annual capacity would be 270,000 units; the annual fixed cost would be $1,200,000 and the per unit production cost would remain at $18.
3. Construct a new plant in Tucson.
4. Construct a new plant in Fresno.

Each of the new plants would have an annual capacity of 120,000 units. The plant at Tuscon would have an annual fixed cost of $800,000 and a per unit production cost of $16. The plant at Fresno would have an annual fixed cost of $900,000 and a per unit production cost of $16. The per unit transportation costs between Tuscon and Fresno and the distributors are as follows:

	Distributors				
Potential Plants	Chi	Den	LA	Dal	Phi
Tucson	16	9	9	10	21
Fresno	18	10	4	13	22

We are assuming that each alternative is acceptable with respect to other factors, so we simply want to find the one with the lowest total cost. To compare the alternatives, we first need to determine the optimal production and distribution patterns for each alternative and find which total annual cost is lower. For each alternative, the minimum total annual cost of production and distribution (excluding fixed costs) can be determined by solving a type of linear program called a **transportation problem**. Suppose a company produces a product at M different factories and ships the product to N different customers. Suppose S_i is the production capacity of factory i, D_j is the product demand of customer j, and c_{ij} is the cost per unit to *produce* the product at factory i and *send* it to customer j. If we define x_{ij} as the number of units of product made at factory i

and sent to customer j, the minimum cost production and distribution plan *for that set of facilities* can be obtained by solving the linear program:

$$\text{minimize } z = \sum_{i=1}^{M} \sum_{j=1}^{N} c_{ij} x_{ij}$$

$$\text{subject to} \quad \sum_{j=1}^{N} x_{ij} \le S_i \quad \text{for each factory } i$$

$$\sum_{i=1}^{M} x_{ij} = D_j \quad \text{for every customer } j$$

So, for alternative 1 (expanding the capacity at Atlanta), the optimal production and shipping plan would be obtained by solving the transportation problem using the cost coefficients, capacities, and demands in Table 6.4. The transportation problem for alternative 2 would be identical, except that the capacity of the Atlanta plant would be 150,000, the capacity of the Phoenix plant would be 270,000, and the production cost at Atlanta would be $1 more per unit. The transportation problems for alternatives 3 and 4 would be similar, except that they would have four sources of supply (either Tucson or Fresno being the fourth).

TABLE 6.4 TRANSPORTATION PROBLEM DATA FOR ALTERNATIVE I

	Per Unit Costs for Production and Transportation					
	Chi	Den	LA	Dal	Phi	Capacity (000)
Atlanta	27	31	37	29	26	250
Cleveland	26	33	42	34	28	180
Phoenix	33	25	26	27	38	170
Expected annual demand (000)	120	80	150	100	130	

Methods for solving transportation problems that are faster than the general simplex method are given in the supplement to this chapter. When we solve the transportation problem for each alternative, we obtain the production and shipping plan that minimizes the combined production and transportation cost *for that alternative.* To obtain the *total cost* for each alternative, we must add the fixed cost for that alternative. The costs for each alternative are given in Table 6.5.

TABLE 6.5 ANNUAL COSTS OF THE FOUR LOCATION/CAPACITY ALTERNATIVES

Alternative	Fixed Cost[a]	Production + Transportation Cost[b]	Total
1. Expand Atlanta	$2,150,000	$15,740,000	$17,890,000
2. Expand Phoenix	$2,300,000	$15,650,000	$17,950,000
3. New Tucson	$2,650,000	$15,250,000	$17,900,000
4. New Fresno	$2,750,000	$14,650,000	$17,400,000

[a]Obtained by adding all fixed costs.
[b]Obtained by solving transportation problems.

The optimal solution is to open a new plant in Fresno with a capacity of 120,000 units per year. The optimal production and distribution plan (obtained by solving the transportation problem for alternative 4) is as follows:

Produce	at	and	Send	to
150,000	Atlanta		40,000	Dallas
			110,000	Philadelphia
140,000	Cleveland		120,000	Chicago
			20,000	Philadelphia
170,000	Phoenix		80,000	Denver
			30,000	Los Angeles
			60,000	Dallas
120,000	Fresno		120,000	Los Angeles

ADDING CAPACITY AT AN EXISTING OR NEW FACILITY

In practice, the actual models used can be much more precise and more complicated. Example 4 treated the annual demand as being constant during the planning horizon. In fact, a dynamic version of this problem can be constructed wherein customer demands, plant capacities, and expected costs vary from year to year, allowing us to determine *when* capacity should be expanded as well as *where*.

LOCATING SEVERAL FACILITIES SIMULTANEOUSLY: FIXED-CHARGE PROBLEM

Sometimes we want to select the locations and capacities of several facilities simultaneously. To make our discussion more precise, we will use a specific example.

EXAMPLE 5

Rama Manufacturing has decided to introduce a new line of products. The company wants to open one or more production facilities to serve six geographic markets. It has narrowed the set of possible sites to five, and two different plant capacities are possible at a site: either 150,000 or 300,000 units per year. The fixed cost of the smaller plant size is $1,500,000 per year (including amortization of initial costs), and the per unit production cost is $20; the fixed cost of the larger plant size is $2,800,000 per year, and the per unit production cost is $19. For simplicity we assume that these costs are the same, regardless of plant location (in practice each site could have different costs). The per unit transportation costs and annual demands at each market are listed in Table 6.6.

Rama Manufacturing wants to determine the following:

1. The number of plants to open.
2. The locations of the plants that are opened.
3. The capacity at each plant that is opened.
4. The number of units to produce at each plant and ship to each market in order to minimize the total cost of supplying the six markets with product.

TABLE 6.6 TRANSPORT COSTS AND DEMANDS FOR RAMA MANUFACTURING

Per Unit Transport Costs

	Markets					
Potential Sites	Bos	Chi	Den	LA	Dal	Phi
Atlanta	11	8	12	18	10	7
Cleveland	9	4	11	20	12	6
Hartford	3	12	19	27	16	5
Oakland	25	19	9	6	13	21
Phoenix	26	15	7	8	9	20
Expected annual Demand (000)	70	120	80	150	100	130

This problem can be formulated as a 0/1 mixed-integer program. The number, location, and capacity of the facilities can be determined by defining 10 variables, $y_1, \ldots, y_{10}$ such that the y_i variables can only take on the values 0 or 1. The meanings of the variables are the following:

y_1 = 1 if a 150,000 units/year plant is opened in Atlanta
= 0 if a 150,000 units/year plant is *not* opened in Atlanta

y_2 = 1 if a 300,000 units/year plant is opened in Atlanta
= 0 if a 300,000 units/year plant is *not* opened in Atlanta

y_3 = 1 if a 150,000 units/year plant is opened in Cleveland
= 0 if a 150,000 units/year plant is *not* opened in Cleveland

and so forth.

When the problem is solved, the y_i variables that equal 1 will specify how many plants to have, where they should be located, and what their capacities should be.

A second set of variables, x_{ij}, will represent the production and shipping quantities:

x_{ij} = number of units produced at each facility i (location and size) and sent to market j where $i = 1, \ldots, 10$ and $j = 1, \ldots, 6$ – a total of 60 variables.

The total annual cost resulting from a solution can be expressed as

$$\$1{,}500{,}000\,(y_1 + y_3 + \ldots + y_9) + \$2{,}800{,}000\,(y_2 + y_4 + \ldots + y_{10}) + \sum_{i=1}^{10} \sum_{j=1}^{6} c_{ij}x_{ij}$$

where c_{ij} is the per unit cost to produce the product at facility i and transport it to market j. For example, c_{35} is the cost to make one unit of product at a 150,000 unit per year plant in Cleveland and ship it to Dallas, which would be \$20 for production plus \$12 for shipping, so c_{35} = \$32. The variable production and shipping costs are captured by the $c_{ij}x_{ij}$ terms. If a plant of a certain size at a certain location is constructed, such as a 300,000 unit per year plant at Hartford, then y_6 will equal 1 and the term \$2,800,000 y_6 will add the fixed cost to the total. If $y_6 = 0$, so that a 300,000 unit per year plant is *not* opened in Hartford, no fixed cost for that plant is included in the total cost.

There are two primary sets of constraints: (1) demand constraints that guarantee that each market's demand is satisfied and (2) capacity constraints that limit how much can be supplied from each facility. For each market j the demand constraints can be written as

$$\sum_{i=1}^{10} x_{ij} = D_j$$

where Dj is the annual demand by market j.

For each potential facility i (location/capacity pair), the number of units produced and shipped out of that facility cannot exceed its capacity of S_i if facility i is opened and cannot exceed zero if facility i is not opened. We do not know in advance where we will open facilities and how large their capacities will be (that is what we are trying to determine), so for each facility i we can write this capacity constraint as

$$\sum_{j=1}^{6} x_{ij} \leq S_i y_i$$

If a facility i is opened, then y_i will equal 1 and the capacity will be S_i; if no facility i is opened, then y_i equals 0 and the right-hand side of the constraint becomes 0, which prevents us from shipping any product from facility i.

This type of problem is called a **fixed-charge location problem** because in the objective function there is a fixed charge to open a facility and a constant marginal cost for producing and shipping product. Even modest sized versions of this problem were very difficult to solve until 30 years ago. Now large versions of it can be solved easily using integer programming methods. Solution methods for this problem are beyond the scope of this book, but many student computer packages can solve small versions.

The optimal solution for this problem (obtained using an integer programming computer package) is to build three facilities: a 150,000 unit per year facility in Cleveland, a 300,000 unit per year facility in Hartford, and a 300,00 unit per year facility in Phoenix. The Cleveland plant should ship 120,000 units per year to Chicago and 30,000 units per year to Dallas; the Hartford plant should ship 70,000 units per year to Boston and 130,000 units per year to Philadelphia; and the Phoenix plant should ship 80,000 units per year to Denver, 150,000 units per year to Los Angeles, and 70,000 units per year to Dallas. The total annual cost of this solution is \$23,690,000 (\$7,100,000 fixed cost and \$16,590,000 variable cost).

PUBLIC SERVICE FACILITY LOCATION MODELS

The sites for public service facilities are usually chosen to maximize customer service, subject to a budget constraint, rather than to minimize cost. In this section we present the **p-center model**, which is just one of many models used in public facility location.

Suppose there are customers located at N spatially distinct population centers. The government is considering opening as many as p facilities to serve these customers (the value of p is usually determined by a budget constraint). The government has identified M possible sites for the facilities, and the distance (or time or cost) for customers at location j to be served by a facility at site i is designated d_{ij}.

The government has decided that it would like to select the locations for the facilities to *minimize the maximum distance* (*time or cost*) for any customer. This criterion is sometimes viewed as being more equitable than others because it evaluates the quality of an alternative according to the distance traveled by the worst-off person rather than the

The locations of fire stations are crucial in determining the response time to fires, and thus the quality of service received by the public.

average distance for all customers. As a practical matter, the facility locations that minimize *average* travel distance or cost tend to be close to most people, but some people may be very far away from a serving facility; the difference in service between the best off and worst off is often large. In contrast, the facility locations that minimize the maximum distance anyone must travel tend to have more people approximately the same distance from their serving facility and no one is extremely far away.

The government's problem can be formulated as the following 0/1 mixed-integer program:

Let y_i = 1 if a facility is opened at site i
= 0 if a facility is not opened at site i

Let x_{ij} = 1 if people at location j are assigned to the facility at site i
= 0 otherwise

Let w = the maximum distance between any customer and the serving (closest) facility

The government's problem can then be written as

minimize $z = w$

$$\text{subject to} \quad \sum_{i=1}^{M} y_i \le p \tag{6.1}$$

$$\sum_{i=1}^{M} x_{ij} = 1 \quad \text{for every customer } j = 1, \ldots, N \tag{6.2}$$

$$\sum_{j=1}^{N} x_{ij} \le N y_i \quad \text{for every site } i = 1, \ldots, M \tag{6.3}$$

$$\sum_{i=1}^{M} d_{ij} x_{ij} \le w \quad \text{for every customer } j = 1, \ldots, N \tag{6.4}$$

Constraint (6.1) restricts the number of facilities opened to p. Constraints (6.2) ensure that every customer is assigned to exactly one facility. Constraints (6.3) prevent any customers from being assigned to a site at which no facility is opened ($y_i = 0$). If a facility is opened at site i, then this constraint allows all N customers to be assigned to that site.[9] Constraints (6.4) tie the variable w to the y_i and x_{ij} variables. For each j this constraint computes how far customer j is from the closest facility. The objective function is trying to reduce the value of w as much as possible; the constraint for the customer(s) who must travel the farthest to a facility is the one that determines how small w can be.

If $M = 20$ and $N = 100$, then there are 20 y_i variables and $20 \times 100 = 2000$ x_{ij} variables, for a total of 2020 0/1 variables in the problem. The number of ways of assigning 0s and 1s to these variables is 2^{2020}. (Many of these solutions are not feasible, but the number of feasible ones is still greater than the number of atoms in the universe.) Although the number of possible solutions is finite, it is impossible to check every one explicitly. However, in recent years, solution methods have been developed that make it possible to solve large problems (say, $M = N = 100$) on a personal computer within a few minutes.

A slightly different problem occurs when the government would like to locate facilities so that everyone is within a specified distance (travel time) of a facility. For example, these might be emergency facilities, such as fire or ambulance services, or radio transmitters. The government then wishes to accomplish this using the fewest facilities possible. A customer location is considered to be "covered" by a facility if it is within the specified distance. This problem is called the **covering problem**, and it can be solved by solving a series of p-center problems.

PLANAR LOCATION: MEDIAN AND CENTER OF GRAVITY MODELS

The previous models select the best facility locations from a finite set of potential sites. In some situations we may want to allow a facility, at least in our initial analysis, to be located anywhere, as in the following example.

EXAMPLE 6

Nancy Ross started an appliance repair business three years ago using her garage as a repair shop. Whenever she received a service call, she would drive to the customer's house or business and either repair the appliance on site or bring it back to her shop. Her business has grown so much that she has hired two employees, and she has decided to move her operations out of the garage and open up a separate service and repair shop. She would like to choose a location that minimizes the total (or average) travel time for her service calls.

From historical records she has determined that her customers are unevenly distributed throughout the metropolitan area. To make her problem more manageable, Nancy grouped the customers in the same general area into six regions. For each region she computed the number of trips she expects to make per month. She also deter-

[9] An alternative way of expressing these restrictions is that $x_{ij} \le y_i$ for all $i = 1, \ldots, M$ and $j = 1, \ldots, N$. This version requires $M \times N$ constraints whereas (6.3) uses only M constraints. The surprising fact is that some solution methods are more effective when the constraints are expressed in this alternative form.

TABLE 6.7 CUSTOMER DATA FOR NANCY ROSS

Customer Center i	Round Trips per Month	x Coordinate	y Coordinate
1	30	1	1
2	50	2	5
3	20	3	3
4	60	3	6
5	30	5	2
6	40	7	4

mined the center of each customer region using two-dimensional coordinates. These are listed in Table 6.7 and illustrated in Figure 6.9.

Median Problem

Assuming travel time is proportional to distance, Nancy's problem is to select the coordinates (x,y) of the new repair shop that minimize the total travel distance per month. Suppose we let $d_i(x,y)$ be the travel distance from customer location i to any location (x,y) and let w_i be the number of round trips from the repair shop to customer region i. Then Nancy's problem is to select x and y so as to

$$\text{minimize } z = \sum_{i=1}^{6} w_i d_i(x,y)$$

If the road patterns are such that Nancy could drive between points in a relatively straight line in any direction, the shortest distance between two points (x_i,y_i) and (x_j,y_j)

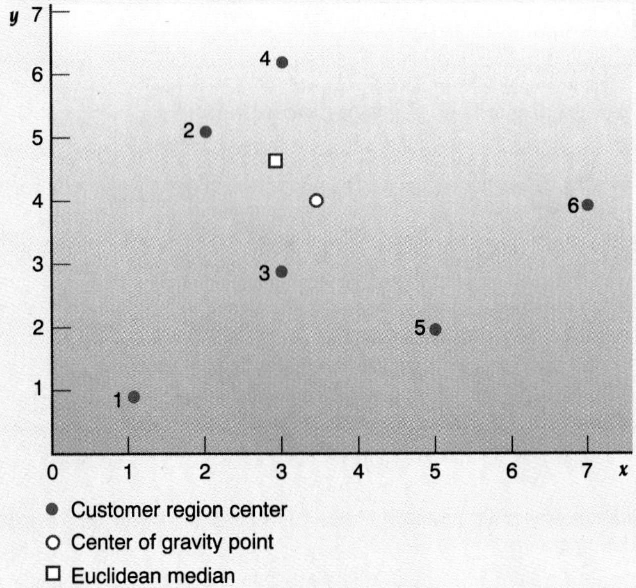

FIGURE 6.9 Customer locations for Nancy Ross.

is the Euclidean distance: $\left[(x_i - x_j)^2 + (y_i - y_j)^2\right]^{1/2}$. Nancy's problem would then be to choose x and y to

$$\text{minimize } z = \sum_{i=1}^{6} w_i \sqrt{(x_i - x)^2 + (y_i - y)^2}$$

This problem is called the **median problem** or the **Steiner-Weber** problem.[10] This problem has an extremely long history, dating back to the seventeenth century. For three customer locations it was solved in 1640 by the mathematician Toricelli, but for more than three customer locations it remained essentially unsolved until well into the twentieth century. This probem may appear easy to solve, but the nonlinearity of the Euclidean distance function and the fact that the objective function is not differentiable at the customer locations (x_i,y_i), made it unsolvable until Weiszfeld developed an algorithm in 1936.

Because of its difficulty and the often long, iterative process required to solve the median problem, some people use an alternative model, the center of gravity model, to approximate it.

Center of Gravity Model

The **center of gravity location model** is equivalent to a problem in mechanics.[11] A key assumption of this model is that the cost or time of travel is proportional to the *square* of the distance, *not to the distance itself*. In this case, Nancy's problem is to choose x and y to

$$\text{minimize } z = \sum_{i=1}^{6} w_i\left[(x_i - x)^2 + (y_i - y)^2\right]$$

The desirable feature of this model is that the optimal location is simply

$$x = \left[\Sigma w_i x_i\right] / \left[\Sigma w_i\right]$$
$$y = \left[\Sigma w_i y_i\right] / \left[\Sigma w_i\right]$$

For Nancy's problem, the center of gravity location is

$$x = [30(1) + 50(2) + 20(3) + 60(3) + 30(5) + 40(7)]/[30 + 50 + 20 + 60 + 30 + 40]$$
$$= 3.48$$

$$y = [30(1) + 50(5) + 20(3) + 60(6) + 30(2) + 40(4)]/[30 + 50 + 20 + 60 + 30 + 40]$$
$$= 4.00$$

It is important to remember that this solution does *not* minimize the total travel cost if cost is proportional to distance (because it is based on cost being proportional to the *squared* distance). It simply approximates the point that does. In fact, the true Euclidean median point (using Weiszfeld' algorithm) is $x = 2.95$ and $y = 4.65$.

---

[10] The term *median* is somewhat misleading because this location minimizes the mean distance traveled, but the name has become standard.

[11] The problem is to find the point about which a system of objects with masses of w_i has the least moment of inertia.

Using Planar Models

Models in which the facility is allowed to be located anywhere in the plane are normally used to obtain an approximate location for the facility that is central to the customers. Once this has been done, a search for actual sites around this location would be performed. In some cases, we might even use another model to evaluate some finite set of sites.

The mathematical models presented in this chapter are just a few of the hundreds that have been used in practice. Another set of location models are *spatial competition* models, which estimate how market share would be distributed among a set of competing facilities. Because of the wide array of models available, it is important to make sure that the assumptions of the model used are reasonably well satisfied for the problem being solved and that the model will answer the questions of interest.

6.9 LOCATING FACILITIES GLOBALLY

In the past 25 years multinational production has increased dramatically, and recent political and economic changes throughout the world, such as the North American Free Trade Agreement (NAFTA) and the General Agreement on Trade and Tariffs (GATT), will further promote this trend. Almost every major company in the United States, Western Europe, and Japan has substantial foreign operations. Fundamental to carrying on foreign business is having facilities from which to operate: production sites, sales offices, or warehouse and distribution centers. The factors used to select the location of a foreign facility are similar to those for any facility, with the addition of some special factors and strategic issues. This section discusses some of the more elementary considerations.

WHY HAVE FOREIGN OPERATIONS?

The question at the heart of this section is, Why should a company have foreign operations? There are at least five major reasons.

1. ***Cost Advantages***—The costs of production inputs vary considerably from one country to another; it may be cheaper to produce the product in a foreign country. For example, it is often advantageous to produce labor-intensive products in countries with low wage rates, assuming productivity and product quality are satisfactory. This is a driving force in the proliferation of U.S. companies opening *maquilidora* assembly plants in Mexico. The problem with low-cost labor, however, is that the productivity and quality of work may be so much lower that the effective cost of the product is higher, as companies such as Zenith and Suzuki have discovered.[12]

   Transportation costs, tariffs, and exchange rate fluctuations can also make foreign facilities more cost effective. The weakening of the U.S. dollar relative to the Japanese yen and the German mark in the 1980's was a major reason for Japanese and German companies increasing their manufacturing presence in the United States.

2. ***Scale Economies***—Sometimes even modest amounts of sales from foreign countries allow companies to achieve economies of scale in production, financing, and

[12]See John J. Dowdy, "Going South? Not So Fast!" *Wall Street Journal*, Nov. 11, 1993, and Judith Valente and Carlta Vitzhum, "With Boom Gone Bust, Spain's Social Agenda Still Haunts Economy," *Wall Street Journal*, June 13, 1994.

marketing and to be able to use large facilities that specialize in one stage of the production process. A firm can thus lower its selling price relative to competitors. This strategy has been utilized by many Japanese firms to obtain worldwide dominance in certain products, such as electronics and automobiles.

3. ***Diversification and Risk Reduction***—Fluctuations in exchange rates, inflation rates, labor productivity, and wage rates can substantially change the relative production costs among countries over relatively short perids of time; high-cost producers can quickly become low-cost producers and vice versa. By producing products in several countries, especially those where it sells its products, a company can transfer production among facilities to take advantage of price and exchange rate fluctuations. In addition, as production costs in individual countries fluctuate dramatically, total production costs for the company's portfolio of plants will be relatively stable because it will contain a mix of production from high-, low-, and moderate-cost countries.
4. ***Government Policies and Foreign Cultural Preferences***—Many governments, even in developed countries, strongly encourage production of essential products within the country. NAFTA and the European Union impose high import tariffs on products not substantially produced within the member countries (for some products, at least 75% of the value must be added within the member countries to avoid a tariff). Some less developed countries, such as India and China, require local manufacturing by most foreign companies selling products there, and they restrict the importation of foreign materials used in the production process. Even when there are no government requirements, consumers often prefer to buy locally produced products, although the facilities may be owned by a foreign company. This is partly due to a desire to support local workers but also because locally produced products often can be tailored to suit local tastes better. For example, even though Adam Opel is owned by General Motors, Opel cars have features designed to appeal to European consumers. Finally, for some products, official standards are set by the government or by an industry group. These differ among countries, making it advantageous to produce in the local market.
5. ***Information and Technology Exchange***—Some countries have developed special expertise. Product ideas and process improvements that are developed in one country can be transferred to another. Even countries that are not known for being technologically or economically advanced can provide important technology transfer. For example, many Western companies are interested in developing operations in Hungary and Russia because these countries have excelled in some branches of science, medicine, and engineering.

A CHECKLIST FOR EVALUATING FOREIGN SITES

Many issues arise in selecting sites for foreign facilities that do not arise in domestic location decisions. Answering the following set of questions can be helpful in selecting the factors that should be used to assess location alternatives.

1. Foreign government policies
   (a) Is foreign ownership of production facilities allowed? Must they be jointly owned?
   (b) Are there import restrictions on the materials used in the production process? Are there export restrictions?
   (c) What currency restrictions exist? Are there restrictions on removing profits from the country?

(d) What tariff regulations exist for exporting the product to other countries? Is the country part of a special trading group (e.g., the European Union)? What are the benefits or restrictions?
(e) Are there special product standards or government approvals that must be satisfied?
(f) What regulations exist regarding the role and authority of labor unions? Are they entitled to sit on corporate boards?
(g) Are there regulations limiting the use of expatriate employees from the nation of the parent company?

2. Foreign customer preferences
(a) Do local consumers have unique product preferences?
(b) Are there cultural preferences for domestically produced goods?
(c) Do the products' names, slogans, and so on have the intended meaning in the local language?
(d) Are there product characteristics that need to be changed to conform to local customs and competing products?

3. Differences in skill and cultural aspects of employees
(a) How well educated and skilled is the local labor force?
(b) Is there a historical affection for or animosity toward the nation of the parent company or the company itself?
(c) What are the standard work practices? Work day? Work week? Vacations? Are these consistent with the operations of the intended facility?
(d) Are there special religious traditions that may affect work methods?
(e) Is there a need for multilingual workers?

4. Foreign resources
(a) Do suppliers of necessary materials and services exist in the foreign country?
(b) Are there special business conventions that must be followed or distribution channels that must be used?

SUMMARY

- Capacity and location decisions establish the parameters within which the company must operate in the short to intermediate term, and they determine the cost structure of production and distribution.
- Capacity planning must answer questions of how much capacity to add, when to add it, what type to add, and where to locate it.
- The **design capacity** is the maximum sustainable output rate under ideal conditions, whereas the **effective capacity** is the sustainable output rate under normal conditions.
- Production capacity is affected by many factors, such as product design, product mix, scheduling, and maintenance, as well as the design of the facility or process itself.
- Capacity strategies need to consider the pattern of demand as well as production capabilities.
- Four strategies for capacity expansion are to lead demand, trail demand, match demand, or expand at a steady pace.
- Two tools for evaluating capacity options are **break-even analysis** and **decision analysis**.
- Facility location decisions are normally made using a three-stage process, which first evaluates potential regions, then locales, and finally sites.
- A **linear scoring rule (LSR)** is a simple way to combine information about several location factors to screen or select from location alternatives.

- Optimization models can be helpful for location decisions when there is a dominant criterion of interest, such as cost or travel time.
- The **fixed-charge location problem** is especially helpful in simultaneously determining the capacities and locations of several facilities.
- The **center of gravity location model** is used primarily to approximate the planar location that minimizes travel distance to customers.
- International facility location decisions must consider many unique evaluation factors, including labor productivity, home content laws, and convertibility of currencies.

KEY TERMS

agglomeration effects **271**
break-even analysis **263**
break-even point **265**
capacity **252**
capacity efficiency **253**
capacity utilization **253**
center of gravity location model **284**
countercyclic products **260**
covering problem **282**
decision analysis **265**
design capacity **252**
diseconomies of scope **256**
effective capacity **252**
experience effects **263**
fixed-charge location problem **280**
focused facility **256**
linear scoring rule (LSR) **273**
median problem (Steiner-Weber problem) **284**
0/1 integer programs **275**
p-center model **280**
plant-within-a-plant (PWP) **256**
transportation problem **276**

KEY FORMULAS

Center of gravity location:

$$x = \underset{i}{\left[\Sigma w_i x_i\right]} \Big/ \left[\Sigma w_i\right]$$

$$y = \underset{i}{\left[\Sigma w_i y_i\right]} \Big/ \left[\Sigma w_i\right]$$

where (x_i, y_i) are the coordinates of customer location i and w_i is the weight at i.

SOLVED PROBLEMS

Problem 1. The State of Missouri requires all motor vehicles to undergo pollution testing every year. The testing is performed using exhaust analysis equipment. The amount of time needed to test a vehicle varies with the type of vehicle. Automobiles require 6 minutes, buses 10 minutes, and trucks 12 minutes. The state must decide how many testing units to have in its St. Louis test center. The test center will be open 6 days a week, 10 hours a day. The state believes that the number of vehicles using the center weekly will be 10,000 automobiles, 200 buses, and 2000 trucks. Compute the minimum number of exhaust analysis units the center needs.

Solution

The test center will be open 60 hours per week, so 3600 minutes of time would be available on each analysis unit. The total time required will be

$$10{,}000(6 \text{ min}) + 200(10 \text{ min}) + 2000(12 \text{ min}) = 86{,}000 \text{ min}$$

So the minimum number of units required would be

$$86{,}000 \text{ min}/3600 \text{ min per unit} = 23.89 \rightarrow 24 \text{ units}$$

This assumes that no units break and that demand is even throughout the year; more than 24 units would probably be needed to accommodate these factors.

Problem 2. Washington Packaging plans to open a new plastic film plant. The company must choose between two possible plant capacities. A 4000-ton per year plant would have an annual fixed cost of \$3,000,000 and a variable production cost of \$1500 per ton. A 6000-ton per year plant would have an annual fixed cost of \$4,200,000 and a variable production cost of \$1250 per ton. Washington expects to sell the plastic film for \$3000 per ton. Compute the break-even point for each capacity plant.

Solution

Setting the production cost functions and revenue function equal and solving for output, the break-even points are as follows:

4000-ton plant:

$$\$3000\,Q = \$3{,}000{,}000 + \$1500\,Q \rightarrow \$1500\,Q = \$3{,}000{,}000 \rightarrow Q = 2000 \text{ tons}$$

6000-ton plant:

$$\$3000\,Q = \$4{,}200{,}000 + \$1250\,Q \rightarrow \$1750\,Q = \$4{,}200{,}000 \rightarrow Q = 2400 \text{ tons}$$

So the larger plant has a higher break-even point (not surprisingly). The smaller plant would break even by operating at only 50% of capacity, and the larger plant would break even by operating at 40% of capacity.

Problem 3. Valence International plans to open a sales and distribution center in Europe to serve the European market. It has narrowed its regional options to three: (1) the United Kingdom/Ireland, (2) Belgium/Netherlands, and (3) Poland. Valence considers six factors to be important in the decision. These factors, their relative weights, and Valence's assessment of each option with respect to each factor are given below. Use a linear scoring rule to evaluate each option.

			Option	
Location Factor	Weight	UK/Ireland	Belg./Neth.	Poland
Access to Western Europe	0.3	8	10	5
Access to Eastern Europe	0.1	4	7	10
Operating cost	0.2	7	5	10
Distribution cost	0.2	6	10	8
Taxes/regulations	0.1	9	6	10
Government cooperation	0.1	10	7	8

Solution

The weighted score for each option is as follows:

UK/Ireland: $0.3(8) + 0.1(4) + 0.2(7) + 0.2(6) + 0.1(9) + 0.1(10) = 7.3$
Belg./Neth. $0.3(10) + 0.1(7) + 0.2(5) + 0.2(10) + 0.1(6) + 0.1(7) = 8.0$
Poland $0.3(5) + 0.1(10) + 0.2(10) + 0.2(8) + 0.1(10) + 0.1(8) = 7.9$

Poland and Belgium/Netherlands are almost identical, so further study would probably be narrowed to these two options.

Problem 4. Mount Hale Hospital plans to open a new hospital to serve five communities. Considerable open space among the communities is available for construction, and travel in the area is relatively direct, so the hospital has decided to use the center of gravity location as a starting point in selecting a location. Compute the center of gravity location.

Community	Population	coordinates x	y
A	2,000	2	5
B	5,000	6	10
C	6,000	1	1
D	4,000	12	0
E	3,000	0	7
Total	20,000		

Solution

Using the center of gravity formula, we get

$$x = [2(2000) + 6(5000) + 1(6000) + 12(4000) + 0(3000)]/[20000] = 4.40$$
$$y = [5(2000) + 10(5000) + 1(6000) + 0(4000) + 7(3000)]/[20000] = 4.35$$

Problem 5. A manufacturing company currently supplies five major customer locations from a single plant. The annual fixed cost of keeping the plant open is $200,000, and the marginal production cost is $6 per unit of output. The firm is considering opening one or more additional plants and possibly closing the existing plant. The firm has identified two possible sites for the new plant(s). The annual fixed cost for any new plant is expected to be $300,000, but the marginal production cost will be only $4 per unit of output. The annual capacities of the current plant and the proposed plants are each 70,000 units. The per unit transport costs from the existing plant and each of the proposed sites to the five customers, and the expected annual demand by each customer, are given below.

	Customers 1	2	3	4	5	
Existing plant	7	9	10	5	6	
Proposed site A	5	8	11	8	6	Transport
Proposed site B	6	10	7	5	5	Cost/Unit
Annual demand (000)	25	30	15	10	20	

Determine where the new plant(s) should be opened, whether the current plant should be closed, and how much should be produced at each plant and sent to each customer to minimize the annual expected cost.

Solution

Because annual demand is 100,000 units, at least two plants must be open. There are four possible solutions: EA, EB, AB, and EAB, where E stands for keeping the existing plant open. For each solution we solve a transportation problem (using the methods presented in the chapter supplement) in which the cost coefficients are the transport plus production costs. Then we add the fixed costs. For example, for the option of keeping the existing plant open and opening a new plant at A, the costs, demands, and capacities would be as follows:

	Customers 1	2	3	4	5	Capacity (000)
Existing plant	13	15	16	11	12	70
Proposed site A	9	12	15	12	10	70
Annual demand (000)	25	30	15	10	20	

The minimum total costs for each option (obtained using the methods in the chapter supplement or a transportation problem computer program) are

	(production + transport cost)	+	fixed cost	=	total cost
EA:	$1,145,000	+	$500,000	=	$1,645,000
EB:	$1,135,000	+	$500,000	=	$1,635,000
AB:	$1,020,000	+	$600,000	=	$1,620,000
EAB:	$1,020,000	+	$800,000	=	$1,820,000

The optimum solution is to close the existing plant and open new plants at A and B. The optimum production and shipping plan would be to make 55,000 units at A and send 25,000 to customer 1 and 30,000 to 2; make 45,000 units at B and send 15,000 units to customer 3, 10,000 to 4, and 20,000 to 5.

DISCUSSION AND REVIEW QUESTIONS

1. What is the difference between the design capacity and the effective capacity of a process?
2. How can changing the design of a product increase the production capacity of a process?
3. What is the difference between product-organized and market-organized facilities?
4. Does the concept of market-organized facilities conflict with that of focused facilities? How can a facility that produces many different products be focused? What could the focus be, and how would this lead to better performance?
5. What are the advantages of using a "steady expansion" capacity strategy?
6. Give an example of a specific company that produces countercyclic products in order to utilize its capacity better; clearly identify the products and explain how they utilize the same production facilities.
7. Suppose a company is considering two alternative levels of capacity expansion. Is the one with the lower break-even point the better alternative? Why or why not? Explain.
8. What are the advantages and disadvantages of using a linear scoring rule to make location decisions?
9. What is the advantage of making facility location decisions in multiple stages (i.e., a regional, then a local, then a site decision)?
10. Select a specific manufacturing company. Identify the factors that would be most important to that company if it wanted to select a location for a new plant. Explain why they are important.
11. Select a specific company whose main product is a service. Suppose that company wanted to open a new facility. Identify the factors that would be most important in the company's location decision and explain why.
12. When would it be more beneficial to use an optimization model than an LSR to select a facility location?
13. Select a specific manufacturing company that sells its products nationally or internationally. What factors would be most important in deciding where to locate its world headquarters? Explain.
14. Select a not-for-profit organization that provides a service. Suppose that organization wanted to open a new facility. Identify the factors that would be most important in its location decision and explain why.
15. Suppose your city wanted to open a public outpatient clinic to serve poor residents. This clinic will not accept emergency cases. It is intended to serve the general nonacute medical needs of the community. You have been hired as a consultant to the city to help it determine where to locate the facility and how large it should be. What specific information would you need to make your recommendations? Assume that you have obtained this information; how would you use it? What mathematical tools might be useful and why?
16. Does the center of gravity location minimize the average travel cost for customers? Explain.

PROBLEMS

1. Canada Wet bottles two sizes of beverage containers in its plant: 12 ounce and 16 ounce. A bottling line can fill 400 12-ounce bottles or 300 16-ounce bottles per hour. If Canada Wet needs to produce 8000 12-ounce bottles and 5000 16-ounce bottles per day, how many bottling lines does it need (assume a bottling line will operate 21 hours per day)?

2. Victoria Furniture makes three types (A, B, and C) of wooden tables. Each type requires machining on a lathe. The lathe times are 8, 6, and 5 minutes per table type, respectively. Victoria needs to produce 12,000 type A, 16,000 type B, and 20,000 type C tables per year. Assuming the company will operate its lathes 420 minutes per day, 250 days per year, compute the minimum number of lathes it will need.

3. Metal Casting Products (MCP) plans to replace its existing metal casting facility with a new one. MCP is considering two possible capacities for the new facility: 300,000 or 450,000 units per year. The 300,000-unit plant would have an annual fixed cost of \$5,000,000 and a per unit production cost of \$45; the 450,000-unit plant would have an annual fixed cost of \$7,000,000 and a per unit cost of \$38. MCP sells its cast products for an average price of \$70 per unit. (a) Compute the break-even point for each capacity alternative. (b) Suppose MCP projects its sales to be 180,000 units next year, and it expects them to grow by 6–8% each year for the next 5–10 years. Which capacity option would you recommend? Explain why.

4. Outland Steel Company plans to build a new hot-strip rolling mill. The mill can be efficiently designed to produce at two possible annual capacities: 4 million or 6.5 million tons per year. The annual fixed cost for the 4-million-ton mill would be \$50,000,000, with a variable production cost of \$16 per ton. The 6.5-million-ton mill would have an annual fixed cost of \$75,000,000 and a production cost of \$14 per ton. Outland estimates that hot rolling contributes \$34 per ton to the value of the steel it produces. (a) Compute the break-even point for each capacity. (b) If Outland expects sales for hot-rolled steel to increase from 3.6 million to 4 million tons per year during the next five years, which capacity mill would you recommend? Explain why.

5. John Anderson is a recent college graduate. He has started his own computer software company, which he expects to grow rapidly during the next few years. John wants to locate his company in an area that is pleasant to live in, attracts good employees at reasonable salaries, and provides easy access to some major markets. He has narrowed his location alternatives to four areas: Southern California, Northern California, New England, and Florida. John has selected five factors he considers to be important, and he has rated each location against each factor using a 0–10 scale. (a) Use an LSR to evaluate the four alternatives. (b) From this evaluation, what would you recommend John do?

Factor	Weight	So. Cal.	No. Cal.	New Eng.	Florida
Sailing/swimming	0.25	10	7	5	9
Good weather	0.20	10	8	6	9
Housing cost	0.15	5	6	7	10
Affordable labor	0.25	7	7	8	10
Close to markets	0.15	9	7	10	7

6. The Midwest Environmental Consortium (MEC) must select a disposal site for low-level radioactive wastes. It has identified three possible sites (A, B, and C). The MEC has selected five important location factors and assessed each location relative to them, as given below. (a) Use an LSR to evaluate the three locations. (b) What would you recommend MEC do?

Factor	Weight	A	B	C
Sparse population	0.25	6	7	10
Geological structure	0.30	10	8	7
Highway access	0.15	5	8	10
Proximity to waste generators	0.20	7	10	6
Operating cost	0.10	9	10	7

7. The Archaeological Field Project (AFP) is working on an archaeological dig over a 6-square-mile desert area. The 40 workers are divided into four teams of various sizes, each working at a separate location of the site. The AFP must select a central location for their camp. The coordinates of the four work locations and the team sizes are listed below. Find the center of gravity location for these locations using team size as the customer weights.

Location	Team Size	Coordinates x	y
1	12	3	8
2	7	7	1
3	13	2	5
4	8	0	6

8. The city of Springfield has decided to open a community center. The city has been divided into six population centers, with the population of each and the coordinates of their centers listed below. The City

Council has decided that the community center should be near the population center of gravity for the city; compute that point.

Pop. Center	Population	Coordinates x	y
1	1300	6	−4
2	5600	2	9
3	4100	0	5
4	3600	10	2
5	1500	4	4
6	2700	8	1

9. (Computer desirable) Greenery Nurseries Company (GNC) currently raises shrubs and flowers at two greenhouses. It supplies flowers to five major plant and flower distributors. Because demand has been increasing, GNC plans to open a new greenhouse. The variable production cost would be the same at any location, but the fixed annual facilities costs would differ slightly. The annual fixed costs would be $40,000 at location A and $45,000 at location B. Table 6.8 lists the capacities of the existing and proposed greenhouses, the demands by each distributor, and the transport costs between each greenhouse location and distributor. Determine where the new greenhouse should be located and the number of truckloads of product to send from each greenhouse to each distributor to minimize the total annual cost.

10. (Computer desirable) The Washington Heights School District (WHSD) has a steadily increasing high school student population. The school board has decided that it must either expand an existing school or open a new one. There are three possible sites under consideration for a new high school. The district has been divided into eight regions for planning purposes. The annual per student costs to transport students from each region to each school location are given in Table 6.9, along with the projected student populations in each region.

If a new school is opened, it will have a capacity of 1200 students and will cost approximately $650,000 per year, in addition to instructional costs. If schools A or B are expanded, they will be expanded by a capacity of 1000 students, and the extra annual cost, in addition to instructional costs, will be approximately $625,000.

(a) Evaluate WHSD's options and determine the best alternative from a purely economic standpoint. (Hint: you must solve a transportation problem for each option or use a fixed-charge model.) (b) What other factors might be important? Do they change which alternative is best in (a) or do they increase its desirability?

TABLE 6.8 DATA FOR GREENERY NURSERIES COMPANY

	Distributors 1	2	3	4	5	Annual Capacity (Truckloads)	
Existing greenhouse 1	24	18	30	14	40	800	Transport Cost ($ per Truckload)
Existing greenhouse 2	29	33	40	23	21	700	
Proposed site A	18	32	23	24	26	800	
Proposed site B	17	26	18	30	23	800	
Annual demand (truckloads)	500	600	300	200	400		

TABLE 6.9 WASHINGTON HEIGHTS SCHOOL DISTRICT DATA

Schools/Sites	Region 1	2	3	4	5	6	7	8	Capacity	
Existing school A	35	25	39	68	59	32	11	27	1600	Annual Transport Cost per Student
Existing school B	75	54	37	12	25	26	41	79	1400	
Proposed site C	56	42	29	28	18	12	22	53	1200	
Proposed site D	28	12	26	47	61	44	52	39	1200	
Proposed site E	43	22	23	42	43	23	25	16	1200	
No. of HS students	400	600	400	650	300	500	650	450		

TABLE 6.10 CONVENIENCE PHARMACY DISTANCE DATA

		Pharmacy							
		A	B	C	D	E	F	G	H
Pharmacy	A	—	12	17	12	22	9	20	18
	B	12	—	26	17	10	18	15	13
	C	17	26	—	20	13	16	12	15
	D	12	17	20	—	8	23	18	7
	E	22	10	13	8	—	14	6	25
	F	9	18	16	23	14	—	32	21
	G	20	15	12	18	6	32	—	13
	H	18	13	15	7	25	21	13	—

11. (p-center problem) Convenience Pharmacy has eight pharmacies in the metropolitan area. These pharmacies are well situated in the middle of population centers. Convenience has decided that it wants to keep one or two of its pharmacies open 24 hours a day. The owner has decided that in order to give good service to all customers, he wants to keep open the pharmacy or pharmacies that would minimize the *maximum distance* between any of his pharmacies and the 24-hour pharmacies. The distances between the pharmacies are given in Table 6.10. (a) Find the one-center location, that is, the pharmacy location that minimizes the maximum distance between any pharmacy and the one open 24 hours. (Hint: start by finding the largest value in each column of Table 6.10.) (b)* Suppose only locations B, C, D, E, and F could be kept open 24 hours. From these five, find the two-center location, that is, the two locations that together would minimize the maximum distance from any of the eight pharmacies to the two 24-hour pharmacies.

12.* (Fixed-charge problem: computer required) Effer-Bubble Beverage Company (EBC) has decided to enter the European beverage market. Rather than open facilities in a piecemeal fashion, the company has decided to develop an overall location strategy for its bottling plants. EBC will produce soft drinks and put them in aluminum or glass containers at one or more bottling plants. It will then ship its products to central wholesaler distribution points throughout Europe. EBC is considering five possible bottling sites, and it will distribute its product to nine distribution points. The cost to open and operate a bottling plant is approximately $4,500,000 per year plus $2.40 per case. The capacity of a plant will be 25,000,000 cases per year. The costs per thousand cases to ship beverages from each potential plant site to each distribution point are given in Table 6.11. (a) Formulate a fixed-charge model that will determine how many plants EBC should have, where they should be located, and how much should be produced at each plant and sent to each distribution point to minimize the total annual cost (be sure to define your variables clearly). (b) Solve the problem, using a computer to determine these values. Explain in words what the company should do.

TABLE 6.11 EFFER-BUBBLE BEVERAGE COMPANY DATA

	Distribution Points									
Plant Sites	1	2	3	4	5	6	7	8	9	
A	214	85	240	318	220	195	245	358	310	
B	308	205	122	180	315	247	210	273	383	Shipping Cost per
C	230	195	250	308	143	90	137	260	215	Thousand Cases ($)
D	331	270	198	220	285	190	67	125	326	
E	364	272	320	395	210	184	238	300	172	
Demand (000 cases/yr)	4500	3000	4500	2800	3600	6500	5600	8000	5000	

CASE

Shenandoah Valley Trauma Centers: A Facility Location Case

A federal government study of health care needs indicated that a rural area of the Shenandoah Valley was in dire need of ambulance service and trauma care facilities. The Shenandoah Valley Development Council (SVDC) was offered a federal grant to study where to open trauma centers to serve the specified rural area. The facilities would be small, but they would provide quick treatment to stabilize patients, who might later be transported to larger hospitals. They would also house an ambulance and crew and act as a 24-hour per day command center to handle emergency calls.

During its initial meetings, the SVDC determined that crucial factors in selecting trauma center locations were (1) response time (time from the trauma center to the patients) and (2) cost. Although the federal government was funding the study, it would not totally fund the construction and operation of the centers; part of the cost would have to be borne by the state and local governments (towns and counties). SVDC believed that the trauma center locations would have to provide reasonably equitable service to residents throughout the region in order to gain the financial and political support of a large proportion of the population.

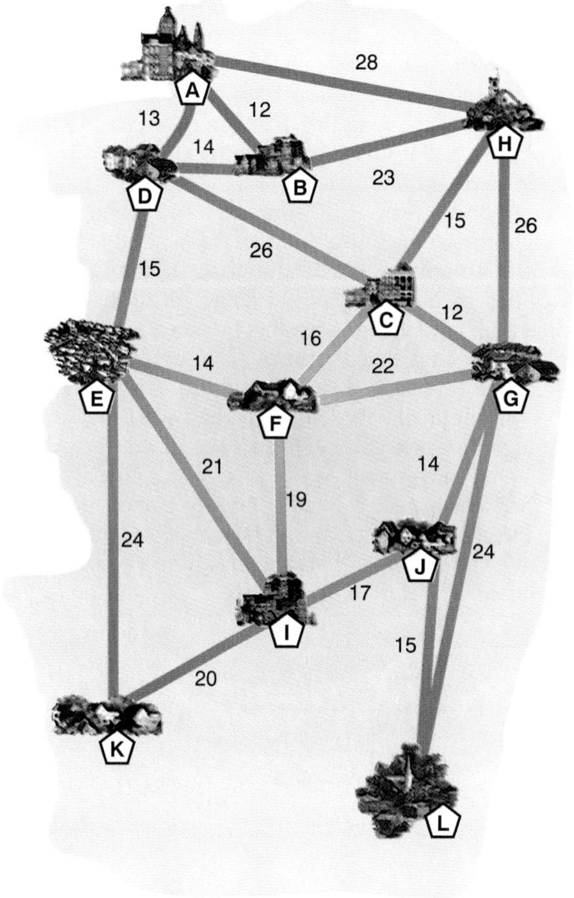

FIGURE 6.10 Shenandoah Valley Region: response times between towns.

Data Collection

The SVDC began by collecting demographic and historical medical emergency data for the area. It found that over 95% of the population lived within 1 mile of the 12 towns in the region, and less than 1% lived more than 5 miles from one of the towns. Therefore, in evaluating service, SVDC decided to measure it in terms of the travel time from the trauma centers to the 12 towns. The configuration of the 12 towns and the estimated travel times among them are given in Figure 6.10.

Siting Criteria and Initial Screening of Location

The trauma centers would treat a wide range of emergency patients: those who could be treated and released (broken bone, sprain, food poisoning), those who were in critical condition and would be stabilized and then moved to a major hospital in a large city, and those whose condition was less critical and would be transferred to one of the two small community hospitals in the towns of Cooper and Edmond. Patients could be held as long as 24–48 hours at the trauma center before transfer to another hospital. Because many emergency calls first come to a police or sheriff's department and the trauma center would need various support services, the SVDC decided that the trauma centers should be located in towns with police or sheriffs' offices that are open 24 hours per day. This reduced the number of possible sites to nine towns: Branton, Cooper, Dixon, Edmond, Freeburg, Granton, Illeron, Jacksonville, and Koenigsberg.

Response Time Evaluation

Although there would be advantages to having a trauma center connected to an existing hospital, the SVDC felt that it was crucial to minimize the response time for an emergency. It was even more crucial that the people in all the towns feel that they were being treated fairly in terms of response time; otherwise, there would be insufficient support to pay for the new trauma centers. Strong objection by even one town was believed to be enough to jeopardize the entire project or limit the number of trauma centers to only one. Therefore, the SVDC decided to determine which sites would minimize the *maximum* response time to any town. The Council believed that this would give them a good starting point from which to choose final sites, and it would provide equitable treatment that could be defended publicly.

To do this, the SVDC staff constructed and solved a series of p-center models (see Section 6.8), with $p = 1, 2, 3,$ and 4. (p-center models determine the best location for p facilities to minimize the maximum distance or travel time from any customer to one of the facilities.) The estimated response times between each pair of towns, given in Table 6.12, were used in the analysis.

The optimal solutions for every value of p from 1 through 4 are given below. The solution for the one-center problem can be obtained easily by finding the largest response time in each column of Table 6.12 and then selecting the column (location) with the smallest value. For $p > 1$, sophisticated algorithms are usually needed to find the optimum.

p	Best Sites to Open	Maximum Response Time (min)
1	(F)	46
2	(E, G)	28
3	(B, I, J)	23
4	(C, D, J, K)	17

If only one trauma center is established, it should be located in Freeburg (F); Leeburg (L) would be the most remote location, 46 minutes away. If two trauma centers are established, they should be located in Edmond (E) and Granton (G), and the most remote communities (Andersonville and Branton) would be 28 minutes away. Additional trauma centers would reduce the maximum response time by five or six minutes each.

Recommendation

When the SVDC held public hearings on their results, it was clear that Leeburg and Andersonville strongly objected to having only one center located in Freeburg because response times to these towns would be 46 and 42 minutes, respectively. Several other towns were also mildly opposed to this alternative because they would have response times of over 30 minutes. After further discussion, consensus was reached that the two-center solution, which would have a maximum response time of 28 minutes, would be supported by all the towns. This alternative also had the advantage that one of the trauma centers would be located at the community hospital in Edmond. Additional trauma centers were not supported because of the cost relative to the incremental reduction in response times. Therefore, the SVDC prepared a recommendation to the federal government to construct two trauma centers, one in Edmond and one in Granton.

The federal government approved the SVDC plan and promised partial funding for the two centers. Funding for the first center was provided immediately, but funding for the second center would not be available for two years. Because of the desirability of the Edmond site, that center was constructed first, and the center at Granton was built two years later. (Notice that if the SVDC had decided to construct only one trauma center now, but expects to

TABLE 6.12 ESTIMATED RESPONSE TIMES BETWEEN TOWNS (MIN)

		Town*											
		A	B	C	D	E	F	G	H	I	J	K	L
Town*	A	—	12	28	13	28	42	40	28	49	58	52	64
	B	12	—	16	14	29	32	28	23	50	42	53	52
	C	28	16	—	26	30	16	12	15	35	26	55	36
	D	13	14	26	—	15	29	38	37	36	52	39	62
	E	28	29	30	15	—	14	36	45	21	38	24	53
	F	42	32	16	29	14	—	22	31	19	36	39	46
	G	40	28	12	38	36	22	—	26	31	14	51	24
	H	28	23	15	37	45	31	26	—	50	40	70	50
	I	49	50	35	36	21	19	31	50	—	17	20	32
	J	58	42	26	52	38	36	14	40	17	—	37	15
	K	52	53	55	39	24	39	51	70	20	37	—	52
	L	64	52	36	62	53	46	24	50	32	15	52	—

*Towns are designated by the first letter in their names.

construct another one in a few years, it should *not* construct the first one at the one-center optimum, Freeburg. Even though this is the one-center optimum, it would be optimal for only a short time. If a second trauma center is opened, the best two-center solution possible *that contains* F is (C, F), which has a maximum response time of 39 minutes rather than 28 minutes.)

QUESTIONS

1. Suppose it was determined that any response time greater than 20 minutes was useless because there was little chance of saving a critically ill or injured patient. How would you change SVDC's analysis?
2. Suppose it were possible to open the trauma centers on roads between the towns rather than in the towns. Would this make it possible to reduce the maximum response time (for a given number of trauma centers)? Explain why or why not.
3. Suppose the federal government decided to provide funding to any set of six or more towns that group together to open their own trauma center. Would this be better than opening two centers for all 12 towns? What is likely to happen?

SELECTED READINGS

FRANCIS, RICHARD L., JOHN WHITE, and L. MCGINNISS. *Facility Layout and Location: An Analytical Approach* (2nd ed.), Prentice-Hall, Englewood Cliffs, NJ, 1991.

HURTER, ARTHUR P., and JOSEPH S. MARTINICH. *Facility Location and the Theory of Production*, Kluwer, Boston, 1989.

KEENEY, RALPH. *Siting Energy Facilities*, Academic Press, New York, 1980.

LOVE, ROBERT, JAMES MORRIS, and GEORGE WESOLOWSKY. *Facilities Location: Models and Methods*, North-Holland, New York, 1988.

MENASE, DANIEL. *Capacity Planning: A Practical Approach*, Prentice-Hall, Englewood Cliffs, NJ, 1993.

MIRCHANDANI, PITU, and RICHARD FRANCIS (eds.). *Discrete Location Theory*, Wiley, New York, 1990.

SCHMENNER, ROGER W. *Making Business Location Decisions*, Prentice-Hall, Englewood Cliffs, NJ, 1982.

WEBBER, MICHAEL J. *Industrial Location*, Sage, Beverly Hills, CA, 1984.

SOLVING TRANSPORTATION PROBLEMS

6s.1 INTRODUCTION
6s.2 PREPARING THE PROBLEM AND THE TRANSPORTATION TABLEAU
6s.3 OBTAINING AN INITIAL FEASIBLE SOLUTION
Northwest Corner Method
Vogel's Approximation Method
6s.4 THE STEPPING STONE METHOD
Checking for Optimality
Obtaining an Improved Solution
6s.5 THE MODIFIED DISTRIBUTION METHOD
6s.6 SPECIAL SITUATIONS
Maximization Problems
Total Supply Not Equal to Total Demand
Degeneracy

6s.1 INTRODUCTION

Transportation problems are linear programs that have a special structure: their constraints can be divided into two sets, supply and demand. (See Tutorial 1 for a discussion of linear programs.) When a problem has this transportation structure, it can be solved using specialized versions of the simplex method that are more efficient than the general simplex method. This supplement presents two of these methods, the *stepping stone method* and the *modified distribution* (MODI) *method*.

6s.2 PREPARING THE PROBLEM AND THE TRANSPORTATION TABLEAU

When a problem is formulated as a transportation problem, two types of entities are implied: points of supply (sources) and points of demand (destinations). Each source i has a supply capacity S_i, and each destination j has a specified demand D_j. The cost to supply a unit of product from source i to destination j is c_{ij}. The problem is to determine how much of the demand at each destination j should be supplied by each source i to minimize the cost. If we define the variables, x_{ij}, to be the number of units of product supplied or transported from source i to destination j, the transportation problem has the form

$$\text{minimize } z = \sum_{i=1}^{M} \sum_{j=1}^{N} c_{ij}x_{ij}$$

$$\text{subject to} \quad \sum_{j=1}^{N} x_{ij} \leq S_i \quad \text{for every source, } i = 1, \ldots, M$$

$$\sum_{i=1}^{M} x_{ij} = D_j \quad \text{for every destination, } j = 1, \ldots, N$$

where M is the number of sources and N is the number of destinations.

To use the stepping stone or MODI method, the problem must be written so that the *total supply* capacity *equals* the *total demand* by all destinations. If this is not the case in the original formulation, a **dummy source** or **dummy destination** can be added to the problem with a capacity or demand that makes up the difference. The variables represented by shipments *from* a dummy source identify which excess demands are not satisfied, and shipments *to* a dummy destination identify where excess

TABLE 6S.1 ZESTY BEVERAGE CO. DATA

	Plant	Market 1	2	3	4	Monthly Capacity*
Shipping cost per 1000 cases	A	2	4	1	3	300
	B	8	2	6	5	300
	C	6	1	4	2	200
Monthly demand*		200	200	300	100	

*Capacity and demand are in thousands of cases.

supply capacity is unused. If total supply equals total demand, then the supply constraints can be written as equalities.

One computational advantage of transportation algorithms is that the problem data can be written and manipulated using a more compact form of tableau (table) than the simplex method. In the general simplex algorithm each variable requires its own column in the tableau, whereas with a transportation problem all the information needed for a variable can be kept in a single cell. In fact, the table used to provide the problem data can be converted easily into the transportation tableau used for solution.

To focus the discussion, consider Zesty Beverage Company (ZBC), which has three bottling plants where it makes Zesty Cola. ZBC supplies four major markets from these plants. The monthly capacities, customer demands, and shipping cost per 1000 cases between each plant and each market are listed in Table 6S.1. The production cost per 1000 cases at each plant is approximately the same, so the company wishes to minimize total transportation cost.

These data can be used to construct a **transportation tableau**, as shown in Figure 6S.1, which is the platform for solving the problem. The intersection of each supply row and demand column forms a square called a **cell**. Each cell corresponds to shipments between the supply source in that row and the market in that column. In the upper right-hand corner of the cell the per unit cost of supplying the customer from that source (the objective function coefficient, c_{ij}) is written. For example, in row B and column 3, the cost $c_{B3} = 6$ is posted. In the main portion of each cell we list the actual shipments between the supply source and the customer; these are the values of the variables x_{ij}. Each supply constraint (called a *row constraint*) corresponds to a row in the tableau; the right-hand sides of the constraints are in the rightmost column. Each demand constraint (*column constraint*) corresponds to a column of the tableau; the right-hand sides of the demand constraints are in the bottom row.

Plant	Market 1	2	3	4	Capacity
A	2	4	1	3	300
B	8	2	6	5	300
C	6	1	4	2	200
Demand	200	200	300	100	

FIGURE 6S.1 Transportation tableau for Zesty Beverage Company.

6s.3 OBTAINING AN INITIAL FEASIBLE SOLUTION

The stepping stone and MODI methods are variations of the simplex method that use computational shortcuts for some of the steps. The general steps of the simplex and transportation methods, however, are essentially the same. The first step is to obtain an initial feasible solution for the problem. It can be proved that if there are M sources and N customers (including any dummy source or dummy customer), then there exists an optimal solution with no more than $M + N - 1$ positive shipments (variables).[1] Both the stepping stone and MODI methods require that there be *exactly* $M + N - 1$ elements in the tableau *explicitly* assigned shipments (some may be assigned shipments of zero). These cells will be called **basic cells** for that solution. Those cells that are not explicitly assigned shipments are called **nonbasic cells** (their shipments are automatically zero).

[1]A solution of this form is called a *basic feasible solution*, and the $M + N - 1$ variables (shipments) explicitly designated as possibly being positive are called the *basic variables* for the solution. See Tutorial 1 for more precise definitions of basic variables and basic feasible solutions.

Initial feasible solutions are obtained using heuristics (simple rules of thumb). The most common heuristics for constructing an initial solution all use the same general iterative scheme.

1. Select a cell (variable) and allocate as large a shipment to that cell as possible without violating a row or column constraint. This process will cause a row or column constraint to be satisfied.
2. Eliminate *one* row or column constraint (and the cells in that row or column) that was satisfied. If all constraints have been satisfied and $M + N - 1$ cells have been assigned explicit shipments, the solution is complete; if not, go to step 1.

The primary difference among heuristics is the way they select the next cell to be allocated shipments in step 1. Two methods are presented here in detail.

NORTHWEST CORNER METHOD

The **northwest (NW) corner method** begins by selecting the cell in the upper-left-hand (northwest) corner of the tableau. This cell is assigned as large a shipment as possible. If the column constraint is satisfied, it is eliminated, and the next cell is selected by moving right to the next column; if the row constraint is satisfied, it is eliminated, and the next cell is selected by moving down to the next row. Figure 6S.2 shows the initial solution that results from the NW corner method.

Notice that there are exactly $M + N - 1 = 6$ cells that contain explicit shipments (corresponding to the variables x_{A1}, x_{A2}, x_{B2}, x_{B3}, x_{C3}, and x_{C4}). The cells that are left blank correspond to zero shipments. The objective function value of this solution is computed separately by multiplying the positive shipments by their objective function coefficients, c_{ij}: $z = (200 \times 2) + (100 \times 4) + \ldots + (100 \times 2) = 2800$.

The NW corner method ignores the objective function coefficients in selecting cells to be allocated shipments. This method would construct the same solution regardless of the objective function. For this reason, the NW corner method is not very good. The better the initial solution, the faster we are likely to find the optimum. The next method, which explicitly considers the objective function coefficients, typically produces very good initial solutions.

Plant	Market 1	Market 2	Market 3	Market 4	Capacity
A	2 200 →	4 100	1	3	300
B	8	↓ 2 100 →	6 200	5	300
C	6	1	↓ 4 100 →	2 100	200
Demand	200	200	300	100	

FIGURE 6S.2 Initial solution—NW corner method.

VOGEL'S APPROXIMATION METHOD

An intuitive approach for selecting cells at step 1 to be assigned shipments is to choose the remaining cell with the smallest cost, c_{ij}. This approach, called the **matrix minimum method**, attempts to serve customers from the lowest-cost source.[2] W. R. Vogel, however, recognized that supplying a customer from the lowest-cost source might force some other customer to be supplied from a very-high-cost source. He therefore suggested that basic cells be selected based on "penalty costs" computed for each row and column. The penalty cost for a row or column is the difference between the smallest c_{ij} and the second smallest c_{ij} in that row or column. For a column, this is the penalty incurred by supplying a customer from the second-lowest-cost source rather than the lowest-cost source. For a row, this is the penalty for supplying the second-lowest-cost customer from that source rather than supplying the lowest-cost customer. The process for **Vogel's approximation method (VAM)** is as follows.

1. Compute the penalty for each row and column.
2. Select the row or column with the largest penalty.
3. Select the cell in that row or column that has the smallest c_{ij} (that has not been deleted).
4. Make the value of that cell as large as possible.
5. Delete one row or column that was satisfied. If all constraints have been satisfied and there are $M + N - 1$ basic cells, stop. If not, go back to step 1 and recompute the penalties without the deleted rows and columns.

The solution generated by VAM is given in Figure 6S.3. The largest penalty initially (with a value of 4) is for column 1. The smallest c_{ij} in that column is for cell A1. So A1 is assigned a shipment of 200 and column 1 is deleted. The column penalties for columns 2–4 do not change, but the penalties for rows A–C can change. There is now a tie for largest penalty between row B and column 3 (both with penalties of 3). The tie can be broken arbitrarily. Suppose we choose column 3. Then the cell in this column with the smallest cost, c_{ij}, is A3; its value is set equal to 100. The row A constraint is satisfied, so it is deleted and

[2]A detailed discussion of the matrix minimum method for obtaining an initial solution can be found in most introductory operations research and management science texts.

Plant	Market 1	2	3	4	Capacity	Penalty
A	2 **200**	4	1 **100**	3	300	~~1~~ 2
B	8	2 **200**	6 **100**	5	300	~~3~~ ~~3~~ 4
C	6	1	4 **100**	2 **100**	200	~~1~~ ~~1~~ 3
Demand	200	200	300	100		
Penalty	4	~~1~~ 1	~~3~~ 2	~~1~~ 3		

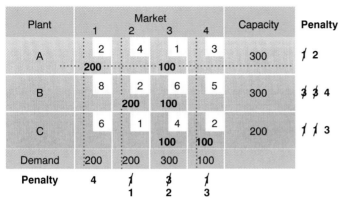

FIGURE 6S.3 Initial solution—VAM.

the column penalties are recomputed. Row B and column 4 are now tied for largest, with a penalty of 3. Suppose we select column 4. Then cell C4 is set equal to 100 and column 4 is deleted. The penalties for rows B and C are recomputed, and row B now has the largest penalty. The cell in row B with the smallest c_{ij} is B2, which is set equal to 200, and column 2 is deleted. Now only one column remains and the remaining cells can be filled in only one way to obtain a feasible solution with $M + N - 1$ basic cells.

The values of the basic cells (variables) are $x_{A1} = 200$, $x_{A3} = 100$, $x_{B2} = 200$, $x_{B3} = 100$, $x_{C3} = 100$, and $x_{C4} = 100$; the nonbasic variables equal zero, and $z = 2100$.

6s.4 THE STEPPING STONE METHOD

The preceding methods only produce an *initial* solution; they do *not* guarantee an optimum one. A separate method must be used to find the optimum. The **stepping stone method** follows the same steps as the simplex method for general linear programs.

CHECKING FOR OPTIMALITY

We first check to see if the initial (or current) solution is optimal. We do this by determining for each *nonbasic* cell how the total cost (the objective function) would change if the shipments corresponding to the nonbasic cell were increased by one unit and the basic cells were adjusted in value to remain feasible. If there is no nonbasic cell whose increased value would reduce costs, then the current solution must be optimal.

To illustrate the procedure for doing this, we will use the NW corner solution in Figure 6S.2 as our initial solution. Consider cell B1, which is blank and therefore nonbasic. If we increase B1 by one unit (ship one unit from B to 1), then cell A1 must decrease by one unit to keep the column 1 constraint satisfied. But if A1 decreases by one unit, then A2 must increase by one to keep the row A constraint satisfied. But then B2 must decrease by one to keep the column 2 constraint satisfied. The new solution is feasible, and the total cost has changed as follows:

B1 increases by 1 → cost increases by 8
A1 decreases by 1 → cost decreases by 2
A2 increases by 1 → cost increases by 4
B2 decreases by 1 → cost decreases by 2

Net effect = +8 − 2 + 4 − 2 = +8

In other words, increasing shipments from source B to market 1 would *increase* the cost by $8 for each unit shipped. So it would be unwise to make B1 a basic cell and increase its value. A simpler and more mechanical way to compute the net effect on the total cost of making a nonbasic cell basic is to construct **circuits**. For each nonbasic variable, a circuit can be constructed that satisfies the follows conditions:

Circuits

1. A circuit is a path that begins and ends at the same nonbasic cell.
2. A circuit can only move horizontally or vertically in the tableau; it cannot move diagonally.
3. A circuit can change direction only at a basic cell, but it does not *have* to do so; it can pass through a basic cell.
4. A circuit can cross itself at a 90° angle, but it cannot backtrack over itself.

As long as you have the right number of basic cells in the solution, a circuit will exist for each nonbasic cell. The circuit may be complicated, including crossing over itself,

Plant	Market 1	2	3	4	Capacity
A	2 200	4 100	1	3	300
B	8	2 100	6 200	5	300
C	6	1	4 100	2 100	200
Demand	200	200	300	100	

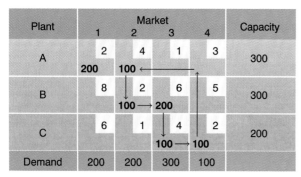

FIGURE 6S.4 Circuit for cell A4.

but one will exist. Figure 6S.4 illustrates a circuit for the nonbasic cell A4.

Once a circuit is constructed for a nonbasic cell, the cell in each *corner* of the circuit is assigned either a + or a – sign as follows. The nonbasic cell where the circuit begins is assigned a +; then, moving around the circuit in either direction, the signs alternate for each corner. The net change in total cost for the nonbasic cell is computed by summing the c_{ij} values at the corners of the circuit, but with the + and – signs included. This is done for cell A3 in Figure 6S.5: +1 – 4 + 2 – 6 = –7. The net changes in cost for the nonbasic cells are the following:

Cell	Net Effect
A3	–7
A4	–3
B1	+8
B4	+1
C1	+8
C2	+1

The net effects on the total cost of increasing the values of A3 and A4 are both negative. If we increase shipments in either of these cells and adjust the basic cells to remain feasible, the objective function will decrease, so the current solution (in Figures 6S.4 and 6S.5) is not optimal.

Plant	Market 1	2	3	4	Capacity
A	2 200	– 4 100	+ 1	3	300
B	8	+ 2 100	– 6 200	5	300
C	6	1	4 100	2 100	200
Demand	200	200	300	100	

FIGURE 6S.5 Net change in cost for nonbasic cell A3.

OBTAINING AN IMPROVED SOLUTION

To obtain an improved solution, we perform the following steps.

1. ***Select the Entering Cell.*** We select the nonbasic cell that causes the largest per unit reduction in cost (the one with the most negative net effect) as the **entering cell**. In this case, the entering cell is A3 because it has a net effect of –7. We now increase the value in cell A3 (the shipments from source A to market 3) as much as possible. The total cost will decrease by 7 for each unit A3 increases.
2. ***Select the Leaving Cell.*** We reconstruct the circuit for the entering cell (A3 in this case) that was used to compute that cell's net effect on cost. A + sign in a cell of the circuit indicates that the shipments assigned to that cell must *increase* by one unit for each unit the entering cell increases in value in order to maintain a feasible solution. Similarly, a – sign in a cell indicates that the shipments in that cell must *decrease* by one unit for each unit the entering cell increases in value. So, if the entering cell increases in value by 50 units, then each cell in its circuit with a + sign would have to increase by 50 and each cell with a – sign would have to decrease by 50. Because every unit by which we increase A3 reduces the total cost by 7, we want to increase the value of the entering cell as much as possible; what stops us is that the value of some basic cell eventually is driven down to zero, and it becomes a nonbasic cell. This will be the cell with the smallest allocation (not the smallest c_{ij}) that contains a – sign. In Figure 6S.5, A2 and B3 both have – signs in the circuit for the entering cell A3. Because A2 = 100 < B3 = 200, A2 will hit zero first and become the **leaving cell** (it is no longer a basic cell). The value of the leaving cell determines how much the entering cell can increase; it can increase by the value of the leaving cell.
3. ***Obtain the New Solution (the Transportation Pivot).*** The transportation tableau now has to be rewritten with the new solution. This is done by increasing the value of every cell in the circuit with a + sign by the value of the leaving cell and decreasing every cell in the circuit with a – sign by the same amount. It is important to note that some cells in the circuit may not have signs because they are not corners; these cells do not change in value. The tableau for the new solution is given in Figure 6S.6. The new solution is x_{A1} = 200, x_{A3} = 100, x_{B2} = 200, x_{B3} = 100, x_{C3} = 100, x_{C4} =

Plant	Market 1	2	3	4	Capacity
A	2 **200**	4	1 **100**	3	300
B	8	2 **200**	6 **100**	5	300
C	6	1	4 **100**	2 **100**	200
Demand	200	200	300	100	

FIGURE 6S.6 Solution after first pivot.

100, all other variables equal zero, and $z = 2100$. This is a decrease of 700 from the previous solution, which is the net effect on cost of cell A3 times the increase of 100 units in cell A3.

For the new solution, we now construct and evaluate circuits for each nonbasic cell to determine the effect on the total cost of increasing the value of each nonbasic cell. If any of them are negative, we repeat the pivoting process to obtain a better solution. If none of them are negative, the current solution is optimal. The net effects on total cost are as follows:

Cell	Net Effect
A2	+7
A4	+4
B1	+1
B4	+1
C1	+1
C2	+1

All of these are nonnegative, so the current solution is optimal.

6s.5 THE MODIFIED DISTRIBUTION METHOD

The stepping stone method requires that a circuit be constructed for each nonbasic cell in order to compute the cell's effect on the objective function. This is extremely cumbersome. The **modified distribution (MODI) method** is identical to the stepping stone method except that it computes the net effects of nonbasic cells on total cost without constructing circuits. For each row i we compute a **row index** u_i, and for each column j we compute a **column index** v_j. For each *basic cell* the equality $c_{ij} = u_i + v_j$ must be satisfied. We can deduce the values of the row and column indices from these equalities. We can then compute the net effects on total cost for the nonbasic cells using the following procedure.

Computing and Using the u_i and v_j Index Values

1. Select a row or column and assign it an index value of 0. (Any row or column can be chosen, although selecting the one with the most basic cells in it provides slight computational benefits.) The index values are written along the right and bottom edges of the tableau, as shown in Figure 6S.7 for the NW corner solution from Figure 6S.2.
2. Within the selected row or column, say row r, there will be at least one basic cell, say in column s. Then the column index v_s must be $v_s = c_{rs} - u_r$.
3. There should now be at least one basic cell for which a row or column index has been computed but for which the other column or row index has not. The latter index can be computed using $u_i = c_{ij} - v_j$ or $v_j = c_{ij} - u_i$. We repeat this until all indices have been computed.

Plant	Market 1	2	3	4	Capacity	u_i
A	2 **200**	4 **100**	1	3	300	0
B	8	2 **100**	6 **200**	5	300	−2
C	6	1	4 **100**	2 **100**	200	−4
Demand	200	200	300	100		
v_j	+2	+4	+8	+6		

FIGURE 6S.7 MODI indices for the initial solution.

4. For every *nonbasic cell*, *ij*, the net effect on the objective function of increasing the *ij* cell by one unit will be $c_{ij} - u_i - v_j$.

We now perform this process for the NW corner solution in Figure 6S.2; the resulting index values are listed in Figure 6S.7.

Computing the Indices

1. We arbitrarily choose row A and set $u_A = 0$.
2. We choose a basic cell in row A, A1. We solve $v_1 = c_{A1} - u_A = 2 - 0 = +2$.
3. We choose basic cell A2 and solve $v_2 = c_{A2} - u_A = 4 - 0 = +4$.
4. We choose basic cell B2 and solve $u_B = c_{B2} - v_2 = 2 - 4 = -2$.
5. We choose basic cell B3 and solve $v_3 = c_{B3} - u_B = 6 - (-2) = +8$.
6. We choose basic cell C3 and solve $u_C = c_{C3} - v_3 = 4 - 8 = -4$.
7. We choose basic cell C4 and solve $v_4 = c_{C4} - u_C = 2 - (-4) = +6$.

We can now use these u_i and v_j values to compute the net effect on the objective function for each *nonbasic* cell:

Cell	Net Effect
A3	$c_{A3} - u_A - v_3 = 1 - 0 - 8 = -7$
A4	$c_{A4} - u_A - v_4 = 3 - 0 - 6 = -3$
B1	$c_{B1} - u_B - v_1 = 8 - (-2) - 2 = +8$
B4	$c_{B4} - u_B - v_4 = 5 - (-2) - 6 = +1$
C1	$c_{C1} - u_C - v_1 = 6 - (-4) - 2 = +8$
C2	$c_{C2} - u_C - v_2 = 1 - (-4) - 4 = +1$

Once the net effects have been computed, the algorithm proceeds the same way as the stepping stone method. Notice that a circuit must be constructed for the entering cell, but only for that cell. After the pivot is completed, new row and column indices must be computed to obtain the new net effects. The next solution and the MODI indices for it are shown in Figure 6S.8.

6S.6 SPECIAL SITUATIONS

The preceding discussion assumed that we wanted to minimize the cost and that total supply equaled total demand. The following section describes what do when other special, though not uncommon, situations occur.

MAXIMIZATION PROBLEMS

Transportation problems can be maximization problems. In that case the solution methods are the same except for the following obvious reversals.

1. In the VAM initialization heuristic, the row and column penalties are computed by taking the difference between the two *largest* c_{ij} values in the row or column rather than the two smallest.
2. In the stepping stone and MODI solution algorithms, the stopping rule for an optimal solution is that the net effect on the objective function for all nonbasic cells must be *nonpositive*. The rule for selecting the entering cell is to select the one with the most *positive* net effect on the objective function rather than the most negative effect.

TOTAL SUPPLY NOT EQUAL TO TOTAL DEMAND

If total supply capacity is greater than total demand, then a dummy customer column is added to the tableau with a demand equal to the difference between total supply and total demand. The variables in this column represent the number of units of "product" shipped from each source to

Plant	Market 1	2	3	4	Capacity	u_i
A	2 / 200	4	1 / 100	3	300	0
B	8	2 / 200	6 / 100	5	300	+5
C	6	1	4 / 100	2 / 100	200	+3
Demand	200	200	300	100		
v_j	+2	−3	+1	−1		

FIGURE 6S.8 MODI indices for the next solution.

the dummy customer—in other words, the amount of capacity at each source that is not used. The c_{ij} values in this case would therefore equal zero, unless there were some cost of unused capacity that we wanted to include in the model. Once this column is added, it is treated like any of the other columns. If total demand exceeded total supply, a dummy source row would be added with a capacity equal to the difference between total demand and total supply. Again, the c_{ij} values in that row would equal zero unless there were a cost of not satisfying the demands of a customer.

DEGENERACY

A **degenerate solution** is one in which one or more of the basic cells has a value of zero. Despite the name, there is nothing wrong with degenerate solutions. These solutions can occur at any time in the solution process. If in the initialization process a row and a column constraint are simultaneously satisfied, a degenerate solution will result. During the pivoting process, if two basic variables are driven to zero simultaneously, degeneracy will result. The important points to remember are these:

1. There must always be $M + N - 1$ basic cells.
2. Only one basic cell can become nonbasic on a pivot. If two basic cells reach zero together, one becomes nonbasic and its cell is blank; the other reaches zero but remains basic. This is designated by writing a zero in the cell.
3. A zero in a basic cell should be treated like any other number in a basic cell; it can be used as a corner of a circuit.

SUMMARY

- **Transportation problems** are linear programs that contain only two sets of constraints: one on supply and the other on demand.
- **Basic cells** have explicit shipments allocated to them; these shipments may be zero. **Nonbasic cells** have no shipments explicitly allocated to them, so their value must be zero.
- The **northwest (NW) corner method** and **Vogel's approximation method (VAM)** are procedures for obtaining an *initial* feasible solution; they do not necessarily produce optimal solutions.
- The **stepping stone method** and the **modified distribution (MODI) method** are procedures that begin with an initial feasible solution and then find an optimal solution.
- A **dummy source** or **dummy destination** is one that is added to the problem to make total supply and total demand equal.
- A **degenerate solution** is simply a solution that has one or more of its basic cells equal to zero. There is nothing wrong with a degenerate solution.

KEY TERMS

basic cells **299**
cell **299**
circuits **301**
column index **303**
degenerate solution **305**
dummy source (destination) **298**
entering cell **302**
leaving cell **302**
matrix minimum method **300**
modified distribution (MODI) method **303**
nonbasic cells **299**
northwest (NW) corner method **300**
row index **303**
stepping stone method **301**
transportation problems **298**
transportation tableau **299**
Vogel's approximation method (VAM) **300**

SOLVED PROBLEMS

Problem 1. Angular Corporation is a wholesaler with three warehouses. It has received orders for a product from three different customers. The per unit cost of supplying each customer from each warehouse is given below, along with the demand of each customer and the available product supply at each warehouse. Construct an initial solution for the problem using (a) the NW corner method and (b) the VAM.

Warehouses	Customers 1	2	3	Available Supply
A	4	8	6	350
B	5	5	8	250
C	6	3	2	100
Demand	300	200	200	

Solution

(a) The NW corner solution is given in Figure 6S.9. We first allocate 300 units to cell A1. Because the column 1 constraint is satisfied, we move horizontally to cell A2 and allocate the largest shipment possible, 50. This satisfies the row A constraint, so we move vertically to cell B2 and continue this process.

(b) The VAM solution is given in Figure 6S.10. We first compute the penalties for each row and column by subtracting the lowest-cost cell from the second-lowest-cost cell in the row or column. The largest penalty is in column 3. So we select cell C3, which is the lowest-cost cell in column 3, and allocate 100 units to it. We delete row C and recompute the column penalties. The largest penalty is now in column 2, so we select cell B2 because that has the lowest-cost coefficient in column 2 that has not yet been deleted. We allocate 200 units to cell B2, delete column 2, and recompute the row penalties. Now row B has the largest penalty,

Warehouses	Customers 1	2	3	Supply	
A	4 300 →	8 50	6	350	
B	5	5 ↓ 150 →	8 100	250	z=3350
C	6	3	2 ↓ 100	100	
Demand	300	200	200		

FIGURE 6S.9 NW solution for solved problem I.

Warehouses	Customers 1	2	3	Supply	Penalty	
A	4 250	8	6 100	350	~~2~~ 2	
B	5 50	5 200	8	250	~~0~~ 3	z=3050
C	6	3	2 100	100	~~1~~	
Demand	300	200	200			
Penalty	~~1~~ 1	~~2~~ 3	~~4~~ 2			

FIGURE 6S.10 VAM solution for solved problem I.

so we choose cell B1 and allocate 50 units. We then delete row B, which leaves only row A. We fill in the remaining cells to achieve a feasible solution.

Problem 2. Beginning with the NW corner solution, solve problem 1 using the stepping stone method.

Solution

Using the solution in Figure 6S.9, we first construct a circuit for each nonbasic cell in order to calculate the effect on total cost of increasing the nonbasic cell in value. The circuits, with corresponding + and – signs, are given for cells A3 and C1 in Figure 6S.11. The net effect on total cost of increasing shipments in cell C1 is then $+6-4+8-5+8-2=+11$. The net effects for the nonbasic cells are:

Cell	Net Effect
A3	–5
B1	+4
C1	+11
C2	+4

The only cell that reduces cost is A3, so we make A3 our entering cell. The cell in the A3 circuit with a – sign that has the smallest shipments is A2, with 50. So we increase the shipments in cells A3 and B2 by 50 and reduce the shipments in cells A2 and B3 by 50, and cell A2 becomes nonbasic. The new solution is shown in Figure 6S.12.

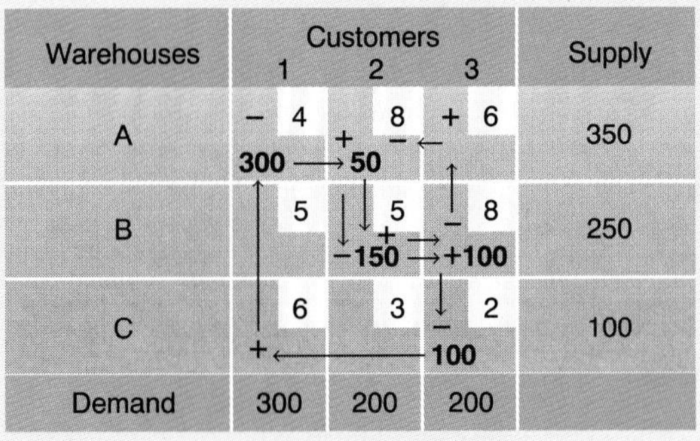

Warehouses
Customers
1 2 3
Supply
A
– 4
8
+ 6
+ –
300 50
350
B
5
5
8
+ –
–150 +100
250
C
6
3
2
+ 100
100
Demand
300 200 200

FIGURE 6S.11 Circuits for cells A3 and C1.

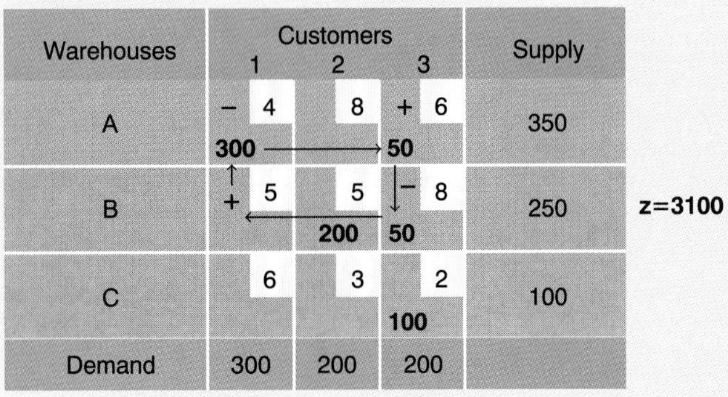

FIGURE 6S.12 Solution after the first iteration.

We now construct new circuits for each nonbasic cell. Their net effects are as follows:

Cell	Net Effect
A2	+5
B1	−1
C1	+6
C2	+4

Making cell B1 basic and increasing its value will reduce the total cost, so we reconstruct its circuit, which is shown in Figure 6S.12. The cell in the circuit with a − sign that has the smallest shipments is cell B3, with 50. So we increase the shipments in cells B1 and A3 by 50 and reduce the shipments in cells A1 and B3 by 50, with B3 becoming nonbasic. The new solution is presented in Figure 6S.13.

We now construct circuits for each of the nonbasic cells and compute their net effect on cost as follows:

Cells	Net Effect
A2	+4
B3	+1
C1	+6
C2	+3

All the net effects are nonnegative, so the solution in Figure 6S.13 is optimal: Angular should ship 250 units from A to 1, 100 units from A to 3, 50 units from B to 1, 200 units from B to 2, and 100 units from C to 3. The total cost would be $z = 3050$.

Problem 3. Dynamet Corporation produces its primary product at three factories, which supply the company's three warehouses. It costs the company $12 per unit to produce the product at factory A, $13 per unit at B, and $14 per unit at C. The per unit transportation costs between each factory and warehouse, along with the monthly requirements of each warehouse and monthly production capacity of each factory, are as follows:

Factory	Warehouses 1	2	3	Monthly Capacity
A	5	4	2	500
B	4	6	5	200
C	4	2	6	200
Monthly demand	300	300	200	

Warehouses	Customers 1	2	3	Supply
A	4 250	8	6 100	350
B	5 50	5 200	8	250
C	6	3	2 100	100
Demand	300	200	200	

z=3050

FIGURE 6S.13 Solution after the second iteration.

Factory	Warehouse 1	2	3	Dummy	Capacity	Penalty
A	17 200	16 100	14 200	0	500	~~14~~ ~~2~~ 1
B	17 100	19	18	0 100	200	~~17~~ ~~1~~ 2
C	18	16 200	20	0	200	~~16~~ ~~2~~ 2
Demand	300	300	200	100		
Penalty	~~0~~ 0	~~0~~ 3	4	0		

z=12,700

FIGURE 6S.14 VAM solution for solved problem 3.

Dynamet wants to determine how much to produce at each factory and ship to each warehouse to minimize its monthly cost. (a) Use the VAM to obtain an initial solution to this problem. (b) Use the MODI method to find the optimum solution.

Solution.

(a) First, we note that total supply is 900 but total demand is only 800. So we must add a dummy warehouse with a monthly demand of 100. We then construct the transportation tableau in Figure 6S.14. The costs in the tableau are the sum of the production and transportation costs; the costs in the dummy column are zero because these represent units that are not produced (unused capacity). We now compute the penalties in each row and column by subtracting the lowest cost from the second lowest cost in that row or column. The largest penalty is +17 for row B. So we select the cell in that row with the smallest cost coefficient, cell B-Dummy, and allocate the maximum shipments possible, 100. We then delete the column and recompute the row penalties. The largest penalty is now in column 3. The cell with the smallest cost coefficient is cell A3, and we allocate 200 units. We then delete column 3 and continue this process. The solution is given in Figure 6S.14.[3]

(b) Beginning with this solution, we now compute the u_i and v_j indices for each row and column. We set $u_A = 0$. Then $v_1 = c_{A1} - u_A = 17 - 0 = 17$; $v_2 = c_{A2} - u_A = 16 - 0 = 16$; $v_3 = c_{A3} - u_A = 14 - 0 = 14$. Continuing this process, we get the u_i and v_j values listed in Figure 6S.15. For each non-

[3]An alternative approach for getting an initial VAM solution for unbalanced problems can be found in S. K. Goyal, "Improving VAM for Unbalanced Transportation Problems," *Journal of the Operational Research Society*, Vol. 35, No. 12, 1984, pp. 1113–1114.

Factory	Warehouse 1	2	3	Dummy	Capacity	u_i
A	17 200	16 100	14 200	0	300	0
B	17 100	19	18	0 100	300	0
C	18	16 200	20	0	200	0
Demand	200	200	300	100		
v_j	+17	+16	+14	0		

FIGURE 6S.15 MODI indices and optimal solution.

basic cell, we now compute the net effect on the objective function of increasing its value. This is $c_{ij} - u_i - v_j$ for each cell ij:

Cell	Net Effect
A-Dummy	0 − 0 − 0 = 0
B2	19 − 0 − 16 = +3
B3	18 − 0 − 14 = +4
C1	18 − 0 − 17 = +1
C3	20 − 0 − 14 = +6
C-Dummy	0 − 0 − 0 = 0

All of these are nonnegative, so this is an optimal solution. (There are alternative optima, however, because the A-Dummy and C-Dummy cells could be made basic with no change in the objective function value.) The objective function value for this solution is

$$200(17) + 100(16) + 200(14) + 100(17) + 100(0) + 200(16) = 12{,}700$$

PROBLEMS

1. A company has three manufacturing plants (in Norfolk, Lexington, and Milwaukee) that produce a product that is then shipped to one of four distribution centers. The three plants can produce 12, 17, and 11 truckloads of product each week, respectively. Each distribution center needs 10 truckloads of product each week. The shipping costs per truckload between the plants and centers are given below. The company would like to determine the amount of product to produce and send from each plant to each distribution center to minimize costs. (a) Construct the NW corner solution. (b) Construct the VAM solution.

	Distribution Center			
Plant	A	B	C	D
Norfolk	80	130	40	70
Lexington	110	140	60	100
Milwaukee	60	120	80	90

2. Stone's River Rock Company crushes rock at three quarries. It then ships the rock to four distribution sites for sale. Quarries A and B can crush 300 tons of rock per day, and quarry C can crush 400 tons per day. The costs per ton to crush and transport rock between each quarry and each distribution center are given here, along with the daily demand at the centers.

	Distribution Center			
Quarry	1	2	3	4
A	12	9	13	12
B	8	14	7	11
C	14	10	13	10
Daily demand	200	350	150	300

Stone's River would like to determine the production and distribution plan that will minimize cost. (a) Construct the NW corner solution. (b) Construct the VAM solution.

3. Find the optimal solution to problem 1 using the stepping stone method. Use the VAM solution as the initial solution.

4. Find the optimal solution to problem 2 using the stepping stone method. Use the VAM solution as the initial solution.

5. North Port Corporation needs to supply three of its customers from the three warehouses it operates. The cost to supply each customer from each warehouse is given below, along with the customer demands and the supplies available at each warehouse. (a) Set up this problem as a transportation problem and find an initial feasible solution using VAM. (b) Beginning with the VAM solution, solve this problem using the MODI method.

	Customer			
Warehouse	1	2	3	Supplies
A	22	34	19	180
B	24	32	18	250
C	21	36	21	320
Demand	250	300	200	

6. A company supplies four customers from four manufacturing plants. The monthly customer demands, monthly production capacities, and the per unit costs to supply each customer from each plant are given below. (a) Construct an initial solution using

VAM. (b) Beginning with this solution, find the optimum using the MODI method.

Plant	Customer 1	2	3	4	Capacity (000)
A	8	6	11	10	20
B	6	3	3	6	10
C	5	1	2	7	40
D	2	4	9	4	30
Demand	25	25	20	30	

7. Wexford Corporation produces a chemical that is in very high demand. Orders for the next three months from its four major customers total 1,100,000 gallons. Wexford produces the chemical at three manufacturing plants, but the total capacity during the next three months is only 1,000,000 gallons. The customer demands, plant capacities, and *profit per unit* of supplying the chemical to each customer from each plant are given below. Wexford wants to determine the production and distribution plan that will *maximize profit* (including finding which customer(s) does not receive all it wants). (a) Construct the VAM solution. (b) Beginning with this solution, find the optimum solution using either the stepping stone or MODI method.

Plant	Customer 1	2	3	4	Capacity (000)
A	12	9	8	9	300
B	14	10	11	6	450
C	15	11	16	8	250
Demand (000)	200	400	200	300	

8.* For the Terminal Industries example (page 275), we had to solve four separate transportation problems to determine where to add capacity. For expansion alternative 1 (adding capacity in Atlanta): (a) construct the VAM solution; (b) find the optimum production and shipping plan using the stepping stone or MODI method. (The data are given in Table 6.4 on page 277.)

Selected Readings

Eppen, G. D., F. J. Gould, and C. P. Schmidt. *Introductory Management Science* (4th ed.), Prentice-Hall, Englewood Cliffs, NJ, 1993.

Markland, Robert. *Topics in Management Science* (3rd ed.), Wiley, New York, 1989.

Ravindran, A., Don. T. Philips, and James J. Solberg. *Operations Research: Principles and Practice* (2nd ed.), Wiley, New York, 1986.

Winston, Wayne L. *Operations Research: Applications and Algorithms* (2nd ed.), PWS-Kent, Boston, 1991.

TUTORIAL 2

DECISION ANALYSIS

T2.1 UNCERTAINTY AND RISK IN DECISION MAKING

T2.2 STATIC DECISIONS
Decision Criteria

T2.3 SEQUENTIAL DECISIONS AND DECISION TREES
Constructing a Decision Tree
Folding Back the Tree and Computing the Expected Payoff
Expected Value of Perfect Information

T2.1 UNCERTAINTY AND RISK IN DECISION MAKING

Most of the models in this book assume that the decision maker knows the necessary parameters with a high degree of certainty. For short- to intermediate-term decisions, where forecasting methods can be quite accurate, this is appropriate. But for some decisions, especially those that have significant long-term impact and are based on predicting what will happen several years into the future, there may be considerable uncertainty regarding the future. In these cases it can be helpful to include uncertainty explicitly in our decision making. In addition, some strategic decisions do not involve making a single decision at one point in time. Instead the decision maker may have to make a series of interrelated decisions over time, where additional information is revealed or obtained between successive decision points.

Many decision-making tools have been developed specifically for solving problems involving uncertainty and sequential decisions. These tools form an important component of a discipline called **decision analysis** or **decision theory**. This tutorial briefly illustrates some of the simpler methods of decision analysis. It should become readily apparent that these methods are applicable to a wide array of problems discussed in this book, such as product design and introduction, capacity planning, technology selection, and facility location. First, we present decision criteria and methods for one-time decisions involving uncertainty. Then we discuss the use of decision trees to make sequential decisions under uncertainty.

T2.2 STATIC DECISIONS

Many decisions have the following structure. We have two or more alternative actions from which to choose. The payoffs or consequences of the alternatives depend on the outcome of some future random event (or states of nature). We do not know exactly what will happen in the future, but we can identify the future outcomes that are possible and the payoffs that would result from each alternative for each outcome. For example, suppose a company wants to construct a facility to produce a new product, but it must decide how large the capacity should be: 200,000, 400,000, or 600,000 units per year. For each capacity alternative the profitability of the plant will depend on the future demand for the product. Suppose the company believes there are three possible demand levels (low, moderate, and high), and it can estimate the profit (or loss) that would result from each capacity/demand level combination. We can then construct the **payoff table**, Table T2.1.

The next step in the decision process is to convert this information into a measure of the desirability of each alternative. To do this, we need to specify our criteria for evaluation.

DECISION CRITERIA

If we know what the future demand will be, the choice is simple: we would choose the capacity that maximizes our profit. For example, if we *know* the future demand will be moderate, we would select a 400,000 unit per year plant because it has the highest payoff of the three alternatives for this level of demand. However, suppose we do not know what the future demand will be. Should we choose the one that has the highest possible payoff? Should we choose the one with the highest guaranteed payoff? What if the probability of future demand being high is 0.99? Does this affect our choice?

The key issue underlying all of these questions is: what criterion should we use to select the best alternative? In other words, how do we measure the goodness of an alternative? Several decision criteria have been proposed. The most appropriate one to use depends on whether or not we have probability estimates of the future events occurring and on our willingness to take risks.

Decision Making Under Uncertainty

A distinction that is sometimes made in decision theory is between situations when we have probability estimates of future events occurring versus those cases when we simply know what could occur, but we have no idea of the probability of each outcome occurring. The first situation is called **decision making under risk** and the second is called **decision making under uncertainty**. Four criteria are commonly proposed for decisions under uncertainty:

TABLE T2.1 PAYOFF TABLE

Capacity	Possible Future Demand			
Alternative	Low	Moderate	High	
200,000/yr	$4.0	$4.5	$ 4.5	Present Values in $ Millions
400,000/yr	$1.5	$7.0	$ 7.5	
600,000/yr	($2.0)	$5.0	$12.0	

Maximax: Determine the *best possible* payoff for each alternative; then select the alternative with the largest one. This is a very optimistic, aggressive criterion because it only considers the best outcome that can occur, not the bad outcomes.

Maximin: Determine the *worst* possible payoff that can occur for each alternative; then select the one with the best "worst" payoff. This is a pessimistic, conservative criterion because it only looks at the worst thing that can happen with each alternative and tries to minimize the bad that can result.

Laplace: Select the alternative that has the best *average* payoff. This criterion treats all future outcomes as being equally likely.

Minimax regret: Compute the **regret** for each payoff, which is the difference between that payoff and the payoff that would have occurred if we had chosen the best alternative for that outcome (the best payoff in that outcome column). For each alternative, determine the largest regret value. Then select the alternative that has the smallest maximum regret. This criterion is for people who tend to second-guess their actions and regret not having made the best choice for the outcome that ultimately occurs.

The optimal alternatives for the payoff table in Table T2.1 using the first three criteria are given in Table T2.2.

The regret values for this example are given in Table T2.3. From this table we see that the 400,000 unit per year capacity has the smallest maximum regret: no matter what level of future demand occurs, the payoff from this alternative will never be more than $4.5 million less than the payoff from the best alternative *for that future demand level*.

When the payoffs are expressed as costs, the maximax and maximin criteria become the **minimin** and **minimax** criteria. In other words, in the former case, we find the smallest cost for each alternative and then choose the alternative with the smallest of these. In the latter case, we find the largest cost for each alternative and then choose the alternative with the smallest "largest" cost.

Decision Making Under Risk

In some cases we not only know what future outcomes could occur, we can also estimate the probabilities of their occurrence. Normally it would make sense to use a decision criterion that includes this additional information. For example, if we believed there was a 0.90 probability that future demand would be low and a 0.01 probability that it would be high, we would certainly have a good reason not to build a large plant.

The most common objective for decision making under risk is to select the alternative that maximizes the **expected payoff** (this is also called the **expected monetary value** if the payoffs are in monetary units). With this objective, for each alternative we compute

$$\text{expected payoff (EP)} = \sum_i \text{prob(outcome } i \text{ occurs)} \times \text{payoff if outcome } i \text{ occurs}$$

Suppose in the preceding example the probabilities of low, moderate, and high future demands occurring are

TABLE T2.2 OPTIMAL SOLUTIONS FOR THE MAXIMAX, MAXIMIN, AND LAPLACE CRITERIA

Capacity Alternative	Best Payoff	Worst Payoff	Average Payoff
200,000/yr	$4.5	$4.0†	$4.33
400,000/yr	$7.5	$1.5	$5.50‡
600,000/yr	$12.0*	($2.0)	$5.00

*Maximax optimum.
†Maximin optimum.
‡Laplace optimum.

TABLE T2.3 REGRET VALUES

Capacity Alternative	Possible Future Demand			Maximum Regret
	Low	Moderate	High	
200,000/yr	0	$2.5	$7.5	$7.5
400,000/yr	$2.5	0	$4.5	$4.5*
600,000/yr	$6.0	$2.0	0	$6.0

*Minimax regret optimum.

0.30, 0.50, and 0.20. Then the expected payoff of each alternative would be

EP(200,000 unit plant) = (0.3)($4.0) + (0.5)($4.5) + (0.2)($4.5) = $4.35

EP(400,000 unit plant) = (0.3)($1.5) + (0.5)($7.0) + (0.2)($7.5) = $5.45

EP(600,000 unit plant) = (0.3)(−$2.0) + (0.5)($5.0) − (0.2)($12.0) = $4.30

So the best alternative in terms of expected payoff is the medium-sized plant.

It is important to recognize that using expected payoff as the decision criterion is based on some assumptions regarding the decision maker's attitudes toward risk. Specifically, this criterion implies that the decision maker is risk neutral. In simple terms, a person is **risk neutral** if she is indifferent between receiving $1000 for certain and facing a gamble with an expected payoff of $1000, such as one with a 0.5 chance of losing $3000 and a 0.5 chance of winning $5000. Most people are not risk neutral with respect to large risks. Rather, they are **risk averse**, which means they would be willing to give up some expected payoff in exchange for less risk. For example, suppose a person holds shares of stock in a company, and he believes that soon the company will either go bankrupt, in which case the stock will be worth nothing, or it will be acquired by another company, in which case the stock will be worth $10,000. Suppose the person owning the stock believes that each outcome is equally likely. The expected value of keeping the stock is 0.5($10,000) + 0.5(0) = $5000. A risk-neutral person would not be willing to sell the stock right now for less than $5000, but a risk-averse person would be willing to take $4999 (or even less) now in exchange for this gamble.

If we are going to face many small risks over time, then we can afford to be risk neutral because the bad and good outcomes are likely to balance out. But when we face just one risk and it has major consequences, we tend to be risk averse. Risk aversion can be incorporated into the evaluation of alternatives, but it is beyond the scope of this book. You should consult the selected readings at the end of this tutorial for information on this subject.

T2.3 SEQUENTIAL DECISIONS AND DECISION TREES

In some situations a decision maker does not simply have to make a single decision at one point in time, such as placing or not placing an order for materials. Rather, she must plan a strategy made up of two or more sequential decisions whereby later decisions depend on what alternative was selected earlier and what random events have transpired in the meantime. The complexity of these sequential decisions makes special tools necessary. The most common tool is the decision tree. A **decision tree** is a line drawing that represents decision points and random events as squares and circles, respectively, and alternative actions and outcomes as line segments. A decision tree helps us to compute the expected payoffs for all contingent decisions. To make the discussion clearer, we will explain decision trees in terms of a specific decision.

Pseudo Corporation has developed a unique new product. Because of its uniqueness, Pseudo does not know how well it will sell. Based on some surveys and focus groups, Pseudo estimates there is a 10% chance that the product will sell extremely well and be a big success; a 60% chance that it will sell moderately well and make a modest profit; and a 30% chance that it will have almost no sales and be a flop. If Pseudo immediately introduces the product nationwide, it estimates that the lifetime present value of profits (losses) from the product will be $20 million if sales are high, $6 million if sales are moderate, and a loss of $5 million if sales are low.

An alternative to introducing the product nationwide immediately is to introduce it in a test market first. If sales do not look promising it can be discontinued, and if sales look promising it can then be introduced nationwide. The delay in introducing the product nationwide, however, will hurt lifetime sales and profits. If the product is introduced in a test market, the profit from the *test market only* will be $1 million if sales *in the test market* are high, $0.2 million if test market sales are moderate, and a loss of $0.5 million if test market sales are low. If the product is introduced nationwide after test marketing, the additional profit will be $15 million if nationwide sales are high, $5 million if they are moderate, and a loss of $5 million if they are low.

Although the test market will help in estimating nationwide sales, the test is not perfect. If test market sales are low, there is a 90% chance that nationwide sales will be low and a 10% chance that they will be moderate. If test market sales are moderate, there is a 5% chance that nationwide sales will be high, a 5% chance that they will be low, and a 90% chance that they will be moderate. If test market sales are high, there is a 70% chance that nationwide sales will be high and a 30% chance that they will be moderate.

Pseudo Corporation must decide whether or not to introduce the product to a test market or introduce it nationwide now. If it uses a test market, then it must later decide whether to introduce it nationwide or discontinue it.

CONSTRUCTING A DECISION TREE

To construct a decision tree, we represent decision points by squares (called **decision nodes**), with a line (tree

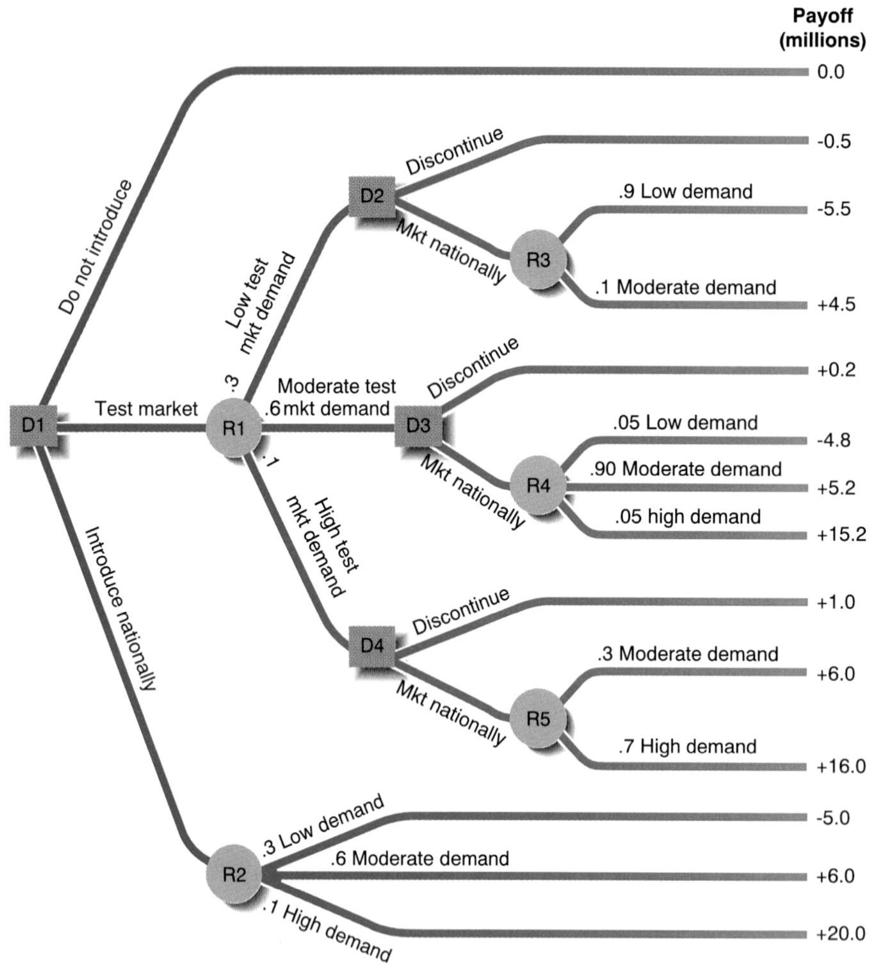

FIGURE T2.1 Pseudo Corporation's decision tree.

branch) coming out of the square for each possible alternative. So initially Pseudo Corporation must decide whether or not to introduce the product in a test market, introduce it nationwide, or not introduce it at all. This is shown as the leftmost square of the decision tree in Figure T2.1. There are three lines emanating from this square, one for each alternative action. For the two alternatives that introduce the product, the next next thing that will happen is a random event, designated by a circle (called an **event node** or **random event node**). In the case of nationwide introduction, either low, moderate, or high demand will occur and the corresponding payoffs will result; each is represented by a line, with the probability of each outcome indicated on the branch. For the test market alternative the random event has three possible outcomes: low, moderate, and high demand *in the test market*. After this random event occurs, Pseudo will have to make another decision on either introducing the product nationally or discontinuing it. These decision points are represented by decision nodes (squares) with two alternative branches exiting them. On each "market nationally" branch (alternative) there will then be another event node (circle) representing the random nationwide sales. For ease of analysis, the *total profits* from the test and national markets are combined and listed at the rightmost end of each branch.

FOLDING BACK THE TREE AND COMPUTING THE EXPECTED PAYOFF

At this point, we can now "fold back" the tree from right to left to determine the expected value of each contingent strategy. (This is shown in Figure T2.2.) For each *event* node we compute the expected value of being at that node; that is, we multiply the payoff at the end of each outcome branch by the probability of that outcome occur-

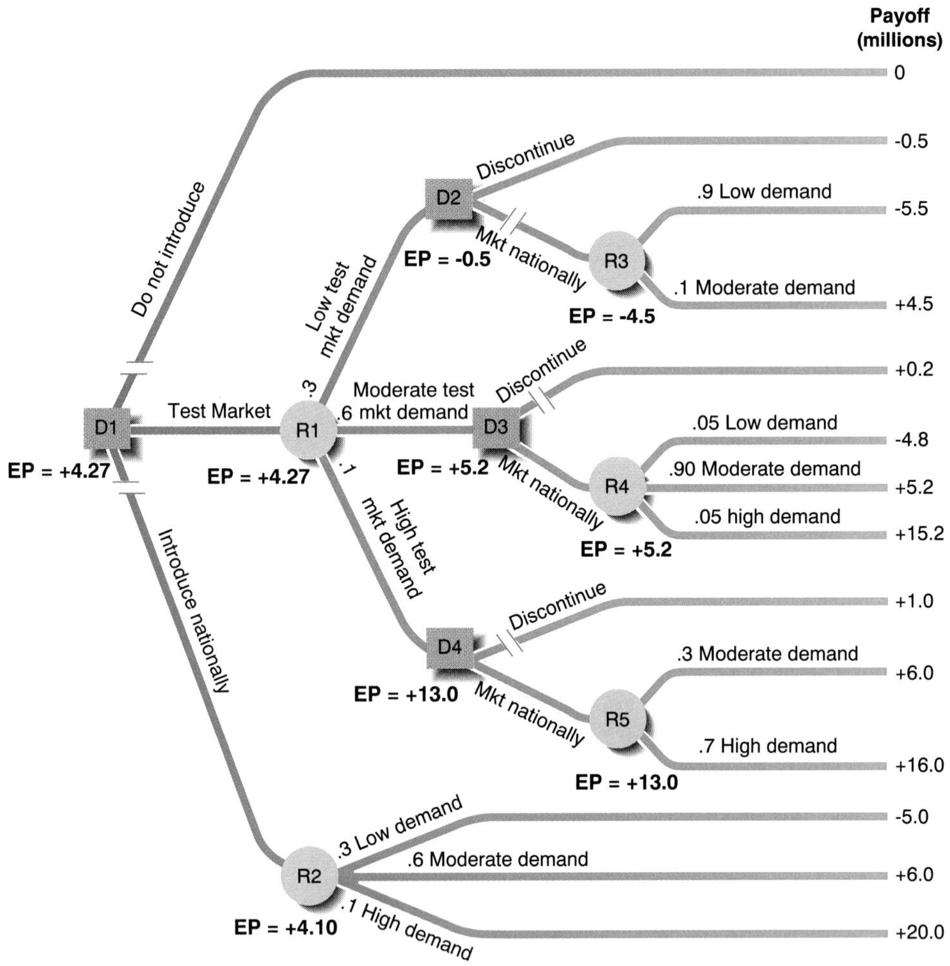

FIGURE T2.2 Pseudo Corporation's decision tree folded back.

ring and then sum these quantities. So for random event node R2 the expected payoff is (0.3)(−$5 million) + (0.6)($6 million) + (0.1)($20 million) = $4.10 million. For random event R3 the expected value is (0.9)(−$5.5 million) + (0.1)($4.5 million) = −$4.5 million. So if the test market has low sales and Pseudo introduces the product nationally anyway, the expected value of the payoffs will be a $4.5 million loss. The expected payoffs for events R4 and R5 are $5.2 million and $13.0 million, respectively.

For each *decision* node we now select the alternative exiting that node that has the best expected payoff. For example, at decision node D2 we would have seen the low sales in the test market. We can now discontinue the product and incur a net loss of $0.5 million or we can introduce the product nationally and have an expected loss of $4.5 million. Clearly, at that point, we would choose to discontinue the product. We put a double hatch (slash) through the "market nationally" alternative exiting D2 to indicate that we do not choose that alternative. The expected payoff of being at D2 is then −$0.5 million. Similarly, at decision points D3 and D4 we would select the "market nationally" alternative and cross out the "discontinue" alternative.

We have now folded the tree back to random event nodes R1 and R2; we have computed the expected value of R2 but need to do the same for R1. The expected value of being at R1 will be (0.3)(−$0.5 million) + (0.6)($5.2 million) + (0.1)($13.0 million) = $4.27 million. We now fold the tree back to the first decision node, D1. At D1 we have three options: do not introduce the product, with an expected payoff of 0; test market the product, with an expected payoff of $4.27 million; or introduce the product nationally, with an expected payoff of $4.10 million. The best alternative is to test market, so we hatch out the other two branches. Our overall strategy is as follows: introduce the product in a test market; if test market sales are low, we discontinue the product, if sales are moderate or high, we introduce the product nationally.

In this case, test marketing the product raises our expected payoff by $0.17 million compared to introducing the product nationally immediately. However, this is not always the case. For example, if the profit we received from introducing the product nationally immediately and having moderate sales had been $6.5 million rather than $6.0 million, the expected value of immediate national introduction would have been $4.40 million, and it would not have paid to test market the product. Although immediate national introduction would have a larger expected payoff, notice that it also would have much greater risk. With immediate national introduction there is a 30% chance of losing $5 million, whereas with the test marketing strategy there is only a 3% chance of losing *more than* $0.5 million (this occurs only if test market sales are moderate and national sales are low, which has a 0.60 × 0.05 = 0.03 probability of occurring).

EXPECTED VALUE OF PERFECT INFORMATION

This example has a common structure for strategic decisions. We have the option of making a binding decision now, or we can gather additional information, usually at some cost, to make the decision later. In this example, even with the lost sales from postponing national introduction, the information gathered by test marketing was worth $170,000 more in expected profit. An important concept in sequential decision making is the **expected value of perfect information (EVPI)**. The EVPI is the maximum amount of money we should be willing to pay someone who could tell us the outcome of some future random event in advance *with complete certainty*.

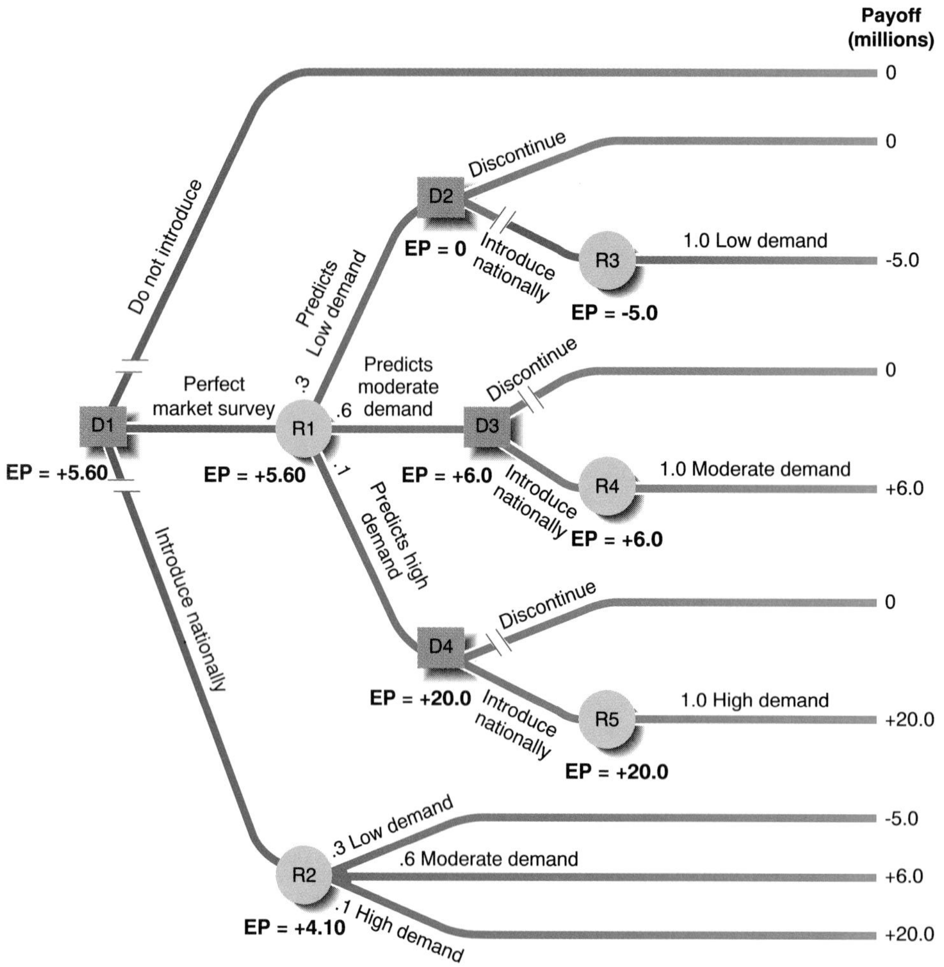

FIGURE T2.3 Pseudo Corporation's decision tree with perfect information test.

In the previous example, suppose someone told us at the beginning of the decision process that he could perform a market survey very quickly, so that it would not postpone introduction of the product. The market survey is perfect in the sense that it will tell us whether or not future sales will be low, moderate, or high. In this case we would have the decision tree in Figure T2.3. If we perform the survey, there is a 30% chance that it will predict low sales, a 60% chance that it will predict moderate sales, and a 10% chance that it will predict high sales. If low sales are predicted, we obviously will not introduce the product; if moderate or high sales are predicted, we will introduce the product nationally. The expected payoff is \$5.60 million. This is \$1.50 million more than we gain by not having the information and simply introducing the product nationally, so we should be willing to pay up to \$1.50 million for this perfect information. (If another alternative was to test market the product, as in Figure T2.2, then the EVPI would be \$5.60 – \$4.27 million = \$1.33 million because the EVPI is the difference between what we would earn with perfect information versus what we would earn from the best alternative strategy available.)

Rarely will we ever be able to obtain perfect information in advance. The EVPI is useful, however, in establishing an upper bound on what we should be willing to pay for *any* information, especially less than perfect information. Frequently, decision makers have the opportunity to obtain additional information that will help them improve their probability estimates of what will happen, but if the cost is greater than the EVPI, then clearly this less than perfect information is not worth acquiring.

SUMMARY

- A **payoff table** lists the payoffs that would result from every random outcome for each decision alternative.
- **Decision making under risk** refers to making decisions when we have probability estimates of future outcomes occurring, whereas **decision making under uncertainty** refers to making decisions when such probability estimates do not exist.
- The **maximax (minimin), maximin (minimax), Laplace,** and **minimax regret** are decision criteria for decision making under uncertainty.
- **Expected payoff** is a criterion for evaluating alternatives for decision making under risk. It is the expected value of possible payoffs for an alternative.
- A **decision tree** is a diagram to help make sequential decisions.
- The **expected value of perfect information (EVPI)** is the difference in expected payoff between knowing with certainty which future outcome will occur and the best alternative available without perfect knowledge of the future.

KEY TERMS

decision analysis (theory) **313**
decision making under risk **313**
decision making under uncertainty **313**
decision nodes **315**
decision tree **315**
event node (random event node) **316**
expected payoff (expected monetary value) **314**
expected value of perfect information (EVPI) **318**
Laplace **314**
maximax (minimin) **314**
maximin (minimax) **314**
minimax regret **314**
payoff table **313**
regret **314**
risk averse **315**
risk neutral **315**

SOLVED PROBLEMS

Problem 1. Internat Corporation wants to open a new manufacturing facility to serve the world market. Internat has narrowed the set of possible locations to four countries: the United States, Ireland, Spain, and Japan. The annual profit that would result from building the plant at each location depends on the relative exchange rates of the currencies in these countries. Internat's economists have identified three possible exchange rate scenarios, and they have estimated the profits that would result (in U.S. dollars) for each scenario and each plant site:

Plant Location	Exchange Rate Scenario 1	2	3	
U.S.	22	13	7	
Ireland	18	16	15	Annual Profits
Spain	12	19	13	in $ Millions
Japan	5	12	25	

(a) Determine the optimal plant location using the following decision criteria: (i) maximax, (ii) maximin, (iii) Laplace, (iv) minimax regret.

(b) If the economists estimated the probabilities of the scenarios occurring to be 0.3, 0.5, and 0.2, respectively, determine the location that maximizes expected profit.

Solution

(a) The following table lists the maximum, minimum, and Laplace (equally weighted average) payoff for each location, where an asterisk indicates the optimum for that criterion.

Plant Location	Exchange Rate Scenario 1	2	3	Maximum Payoff	Minimum Payoff	Laplace Payoff
U.S.	22	13	7	22*	7	14.0
Ireland	18	16	15	18	15*	16.3*
Spain	12	19	13	19	12	14.7
Japan	5	12	25	25	5	14.0

This indicates that the United States is the maximax optimum, and Ireland is both the maximin and Laplace optimum.

The regrets for each payoff are as follows:

Plant Location	Exchange Rate Scenario 1	2	3	Maximum Regret (in $ Millions)
U.S.	0	6	18	18
Ireland	4	3	10	10*
Spain	10	0	12	12
Japan	17	7	0	17

Ireland is also the minimax regret optimum.

(b) The expected payoffs for the four locations are as follows:

$$\text{U.S.:}\quad 0.3(22) + 0.5(13) + 0.2(7) = 14.5$$

$$\text{Ireland:}\quad 0.3(18) + 0.5(16) + 0.2(15) = 16.4$$

$$\text{Spain:}\quad 0.3(12) + 0.5(19) + 0.2(13) = 15.7$$

$$\text{Japan:}\quad 0.3(5) + 0.5(12) + 0.2(25) = 12.5$$

Ireland is the optimum with respect to expected payoff as well.

Problem 2. Fresh Concepts Corporation (FCC) has a new product idea. FCC executives believe there is a 20% chance that sales will be large, a 55% chance that sales will be moderate, and a 25% chance that sales will be low. Because the idea is risky, FCC is not sure whether to produce and sell the product itself or license it to another company and collect a royalty on all sales. If FCC produces the product itself, executives believe the present value of future profits will be $26 million if it is very successful, $10 million if it is moderately successful, and a loss of $6 million if it is unsuccessful. FCC can license the product for three years to another company and receive a royalty, which will be $8 million, $3 million, or $0, according to sales. After three years, FCC could renew the license and receive another $8 million, $3 million, or $0 with certainty. (It is assumed the same level of sales will continue into the future.) Alternatively, FCC could take over production and earn an additional $11 million (of present value) if sales are high and $4 million if they are moderate.

(a) Determine the strategy for FCC that maximizes the expected payoff and compute the expected payoff that would result.

(b) Suppose that for $2 million FCC could determine in advance, with complete accuracy, what the sales will be. Should FCC buy this information? Explain.

(c) Returning to the options in part (a), suppose that if FCC loses more than $3 million, it will go bankrupt and close down. What strategy would you recommend for FCC? Why?

Solution

(a) Figure T2.4 gives the folded-back decision tree for FCC. The expected payoff from simply producing the product immediately is the best strategy, and it has an expected payoff of $9.2 million.

(b) If FCC buys the perfect information, there is a 20% chance that sales would be high, in which case FCC would produce the product and make $26 million. Similarly, there is a 55% chance that sales would be moderate, so FCC would produce the product immediately and make

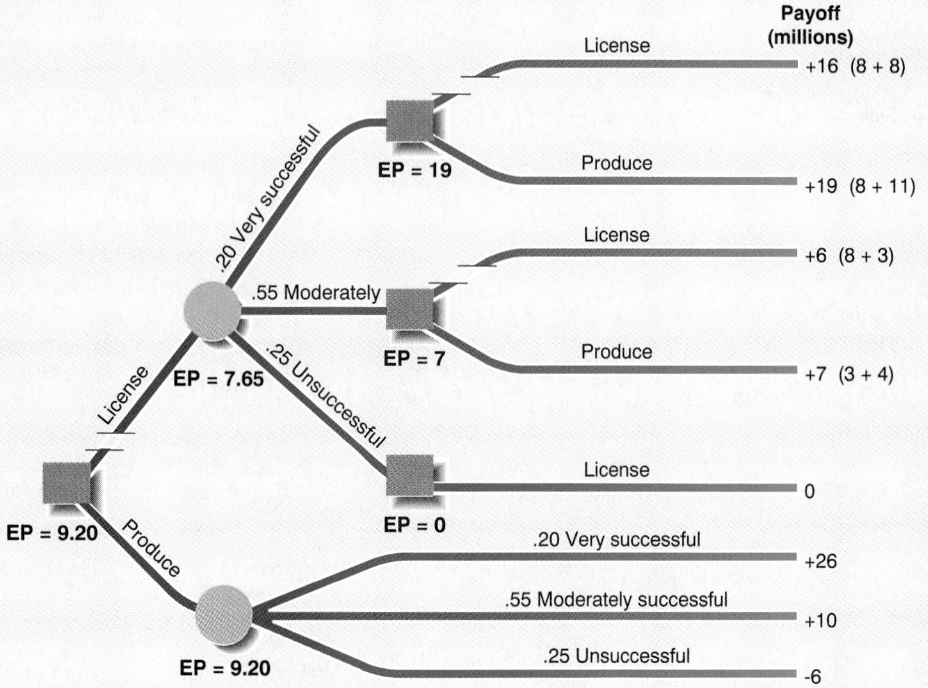

FIGURE T2.4 FCC's decision tree.

$10 million. If sales were low, FCC would not produce the product and no profit would be made or lost. The expected payoff from perfect information would then be

$$0.20(\$26 \text{ million}) + 0.55(\$10 \text{ million}) + 0.25(\$0 \text{ million}) = \$10.7 \text{ million}$$

This is only $1.5 million more than FCC could get from not having the perfect information and producing the product itself; therefore, FCC should not buy the information for $2 million.

(c) By producing the product immediately, FCC runs a 25% chance of losing $6 million and going bankrupt. Even though the expected payoff is $1.55 million less, FCC would probably be better off licensing the product now, and then taking over production in three years if sales are moderate or high. In this case there is no chance of a loss.

PROBLEMS

1. The City of St. Louis is considering an expansion of its airport. There are two expansion plans. The first would accommodate a 25% increase in passenger volume, and the second would accommodate a 50% increase. The return to the city during the next 20 years (chosen by the city as the time frame for evaluating options) depends on how much traffic volume increases. Four scenarios are considered possible: (1) the existing major carrier stops operating, in which case volume will decrease and no expansion is necessary; (2) volume remains stable; (3) volume increases moderately; and (4) volume increases substantially. The expected payoffs for each option under each scenario are as follows:

Expansion Option	Traffic Volume Scenario 1	2	3	4	
No expansion	−0.4	0	0.5	0.5	Net Payoffs
25% expansion	−1.3	−0.9	2.0	2.5	
50% expansion	−1.9	−1.5	1.3	3.0	

(a) Determine the best alternative for each of the following criteria: (i) maximax, (ii) maximin, (iii) Laplace, and (iv) minimax regret. (b) Suppose the probabilities of the scenarios occurring are 0.3, 0.1, 0.3, and 0.3, respectively. Determine the alternative that maximizes the expected payoff.

2. Sharon Long, who is about to graduate with a degree in health service administration, has received job offers from four companies. She has decided to evaluate the jobs based on what she believes her salary will be in five years if she accepts that job. Sharon believes that this outcome is at least partially affected by major government legislation. She has identified three possible legislation scenarios that she believes will impact her salary potential. Her salary estimates for each job and legislative outcome are as follows:

Job Offer	Legislation Scenario 1	2	3	
A	42	40	46	Expected Annual Salary in $ Thousands
B	39	44	43	
C	37	42	50	
D	35	43	52	

(a) Determine Sharon's best alternative using the following criteria: (i) maximax, (ii) maximin, (iii) Laplace, and (iv) minimax regret. (b) If Sharon believes the probabilities of the scenarios occurring are 0.25, 0.25, and 0.50, respectively, which alternative has the largest expected salary?

3. A flu epidemic is predicted to hit the United States this winter. The exact strains of flu that will be predominant are not known, but government researchers have identified two vaccines that they think may be successful in fighting the viruses. However, there are risks in administering the vaccine: some people will die from the vaccine itself, while many people who would have died from the flu will be saved. The total number of people who die from the flu or the vaccine will depend on the exact mix of flu viruses that are predominant. Scientists have estimated the number of flu-related deaths (from the flu or the vaccine) for each of four virus scenarios to be as follows:

Vaccine Alternative	Flu Strain Scenario 1	2	3	4	
Use no vaccine	300	800	900	1200	Number of Flu-Related Deaths
Use vaccine 1	350	600	900	950	
Use vaccine 2	400	850	600	1000	
Use 1 and 2	450	650	650	800	

Notice that the payoffs are deaths, so the lower the value the better. (a) Determine the best *minimin* alternative. (b) Determine the best *minimax* alternative. (c) Determine the best minimax regret alternative. (d) If the probabilities of the four scenarios occurring were 0.3, 0.3, 0.2, and 0.2, which alternative would minimize the expected number of deaths? (e) If you were responsible for this decision, which criterion would you use? Why?

4. Roll-Tech Corporation (RTC) wants to begin producing and selling one of its products in Eastern Europe. Because of the nature of the production process, manufacturing plants can only be built with a capacity of 100,000 units per year, at a cost of $5 million, or 250,000 units per year, at a cost of $10 million. RTC is uncertain about the demand for the product in Eastern Europe, but it estimates that annual demand will be either 50,000, 150,000, or 250,000 units, with probabilities of 0.2, 0.6, and 0.2, respectively. If a 100,000-unit plant is built, the expected lifetime profits (not counting the $5 million construction cost) will be $2 million, $8 million, or $8 million, according to whether demand is 50,000, 150,000, or 250,000 units per year. With a 250,000-unit plant the lifetime profits (not counting the $10 million construction cost) will be $1 million, $12 million, or $20 million for the three demand outcomes. (a) Construct a decision tree for RTC and determine which plant capacity will maximize expected lifetime profits, including construction costs. (b) Suppose that for $1.2 million RTC could perform a market survey that would perfectly predict the actual demand before RTC had to decide on a capacity. Should RTC do this? If so, what sequence of contingent actions should it take? (In other words, what actions should it take depending on the market survey results? Not building any capacity is an acceptable action.) Explain.

5.* Max Crunch is a linebacker for the Cleveland Browns football team. Max has decided that he wants to play football for only three more years, after which he will retire. Max's contract is about to expire, at which time he will become a free agent. Max has been offered a three-year contract with another team for $1.5 million per year; Max will receive the money even if he gets injured or is cut from the team. The Browns have offered Max a one-year contract for $2 million. At the end of the contract, he will again become a free agent, eligible to sign with any team. Max believes that if he has a good year with the Browns he will be offered a two-year contract worth $1.2 million per year, with both years guaranteed, or he could accept a one-year contract for $1.5 million. If Max has a great year, he believes he will be offered a two-year guaranteed contract at $2 million per year, or he could accept a one-year contract for $2.5 million. However, if Max has a bad year or gets hurt, he believes his football career will be over and he will retire at the end of the year. Max believes there is a 50% chance that he will have a good year, a 25% chance that he will have a great year, and a 25% chance that he will get hurt or have a bad year. If he has either a good or a great year this year, Max believes there is a 20% chance that he will have a great year in the second year, a 60% chance that he will have a good year, and a 20% chance of getting hurt or having a bad year. If he has a good second year, he believes he will be offered a $1.2 million contract for his final season. If he has a great second year, he will be offered $2 million for his final season. If he gets hurt or has a bad second season, his career will be over. (a) Construct a decision tree showing Max's options. (Ignore the time-value of money; assume all payoffs are in current dollars.) (b) Fold back the tree and determine Max's best contract strategy, including all contingencies, and compute his expected three-year payoff from this strategy.

6.* Sailjet Corporation plans to introduce a new product. The company can produce up to 50,000 units of the product each year on its existing equipment. There would be no additional cost to the company for using this option except the marginal costs of labor, material, and maintenance of $10 per unit. An alternative is to buy a new machine that would cost $1 million initially and $8 per unit for labor, materials, and so on. This machine could produce up to 200,000 units per year of the product. A third option is to subcontract with another company to produce any necessary production at a cost of $14 per unit. The selling price of the product in any case will be $15 per unit.

(a) The demand during the next five years is random. The marketing department has estimated that there is a 25% chance that annual demand will be 40,000 units, a 60% chance that it will be 80,000 units, and a 15% chance that it will be 160,000 units. Assume that the company must make its decision now for the next five years. Compute the expected value of the profit during the next five years for each of the following alternatives: (i) Don't buy a new machine; handle excess demand using subcontracting, and (ii) Buy the new machine. Which alternative is better? (Hint: If the company does not buy the new machine and the demand ends up being 80,000 units per year, its total profit during the five years will be $1,400,000 or $280,000 per year.)

(b) Suppose that after one year the company knew the demand and could then buy the new machine if it had not already done so. Construct a decision tree showing the company's alternatives and possible outcomes during the five-year period. Determine the optimal strategy (the one that maximizes the expected five-year profit); clearly state what the company should do now and one year from now with all contingencies, and compute the expected five-year profit from this strategy.

SELECTED READINGS

BUNN, DEREK W. *Applied Decision Analysis*, McGraw-Hill, New York, 1984.

MARKLAND, ROBERT. *Topics in Management Science*, 3rd ed., Wiley, New York, 1989.

RAIFFA, HOWARD. *Decision Analysis*, Addison-Wesley, Reading, MA, 1968.

WINSTON, WAYNE L. *Operations Research: Applications and Algorithms*, 2nd ed., PWS-Kent, Boston, 1991.

CHAPTER 7

SELECTING THE PROCESS STRUCTURE AND TECHNOLOGY

7.1 THERE'S MORE THAN ONE WAY TO MAKE THAT PRODUCT
On the Job: Marvin D. Dixon, Nabisco Foods, Inc.

7.2 A COMMON CLASSIFICATION OF PRODUCTION PROCESS STRUCTURES

7.3 FLOW PROCESSES
Continuous Flow Processes
Repetitive or Discrete Flow Processes
Disconnected or Batch Flow Processes
Advantages and Disadvantages of Flow Processes

7.4 JOB-SHOP PROCESSES

7.5 CELLULAR PROCESSES

7.6 PROJECT PROCESSES

7.7 MODERN PRODUCTION TECHNOLOGIES
Group Technology
Process Automation
Computer-Aided Design/Computer-Assisted Manufacturing
Flexible Manufacturing Systems
Computer-Integrated Manufacturing
Bar Coding and Optical Scanning
Electronic Data Interchange
Process Technology and the Environment
In Good Company: Waste Turns to Energy for Anheuser-Busch

7.8 METHODS FOR EVALUATING PROCESS AND TECHNOLOGY ALTERNATIVES
Product Variety and Volume
The Product-Process Matrix
Analyzing Costs and Risk: Crossover Analysis
Capital Investment Analysis: Net Present Value

7.9 SERVICE SYSTEMS STRUCTURE
The Service Package and Intended Customers
Customer Contact Intensity
Service System Design and Strategy

7.10 CUSTOMIZING THE PRODUCTION PROCESS

Southwest Airlines: A Process Structure and Technology Case

7.1 There's More Than One Way to Make That Product

Large commercial bakeries make bread using facilities and mass production methods designed only to make bread. Each group of workers performs one activity, such as mixing the ingredients; then this mixture is passed to the next group of workers, who knead the dough. Still another group handles the baking. The bread is made in large batches, and the process is highly automated and equipment intensive. At small neighborhood bakeries, bread is made in much smaller quantities using a labor-intensive process. One worker may do all the mixing, kneading, and baking and then go off to make completely different products, such as pies, cakes, and cookies. Both production processes make bread, but the volume of production, the equipment, the layout of the facility, the flow of material, the training and skills of the workers, and their responsibilities differ considerably in these two production systems.

Is one method better than the other? In fact, the best production method for a product will vary from company to company, and even within the same company, multiple production methods may be used for good reasons. The designer of a production process needs to consider factors such as the expected scale of operations, the variety of products to be made, the technical requirements of the product, the type of equipment to be used, the relative roles of people and machines, and the amount of flexibility needed in the system. These factors create trade-offs that process designers should evaluate with respect to their impacts on cost, quality, responsiveness, product variety, and flexibility.

Production processes and technologies are not only the domain of production designers and engineers. Marvin Dixon (this chapter's "On the Job" profile) has found that knowledge of Nabisco Foods' production methods and technologies is essential for him to provide the technical assistance and documentation required to register Nabisco's products worldwide.

On the Job

Marvin D. Dixon, Nabisco Foods, Inc.

As Manager, International Technical Services—BioAnalytical and Information Sciences for Nabisco Foods, Inc., Marvin Dixon acts as liaison between Nabisco's U.S. operations and Nabisco International, helping Nabisco's U.S. products to enter foreign markets and Nabisco International's products to enter U.S. markets. One of Marvin's primary responsibilities is to provide Nabisco's global operations with the technical guidance and documentation required for worldwide product registrations. In addition, he coordinates technical assistance to ensure product improvements.

To provide the product registration information and technical assistance necessary, Marvin must be knowledgeable about the methods and technologies used to manufacture all Nabisco products. Therefore, he often visits production facilities around the world and meets with personnel there to understand their needs for technical assistance and support.

An important aspect of Marvin's job is the ability to work and communicate with a wide variety of people from many nations and different professions. His work has taken him to Canada, Mexico, Central and South America, Europe, and Australia. In addition to his several degrees in food sciences and technology, Marvin's previous positions in the food industry involving product development, quality management, product manufacturing, technology transfer, evaluating production processes and facilities of co-packers (contract food manufacturers), and project management prepared him well for his current multifaceted job.

Large commercial bakeries such as the one shown here use more automated and specialized production methods to make bread than do small neighborhood bakeries that make a wide variety of products in small quantities.

This chapter begins a three-chapter discussion of production process design. In this chapter we classify general production process structures according to the flow of materials or customers through the process. We identify conditions under which each structure is likely to be most beneficial, and we explain the advantages and disadvantages of each. An integral part of process design is choosing the technologies to use. In Section 7.7 we provide a brief description of several common technologies used in manufacturing and service industries, such as flexible manufacturing systems, group technology, robotics, computer-integrated manufacturing, optical scanning, and electronic data interchange. With the many options available, methods for evaluating alternatives are essential. Section 7.8 discusses criteria that should be considered when evaluating investments in processes and technologies. Standard analytical techniques, such as the product-process matrix, crossover analysis, and present value analysis are described. Section 7.9 explains how to match the structure of service systems with the characteristics of the service products produced. The chapter concludes with a discussion of the need for companies to customize production processes to match their own requirements.

7.2 A COMMON CLASSIFICATION OF PRODUCTION PROCESS STRUCTURES

Although there is a continuum of production process structures, as shown in Figure 7.1, we often classify processes based on their physical configuration, material and product flow, flexibility, and volume expectation. For presentation purposes, we will classify the process structures into the following four categories:

1. Flow processes.
2. Job-shop processes.
3. Cellular processes.
4. Project processes.

We describe each structure below. Keep in mind that a production system may be made up of several subsystems, each of which may have a different process structure. For example, automobiles are designed using a project process, many of its compo-

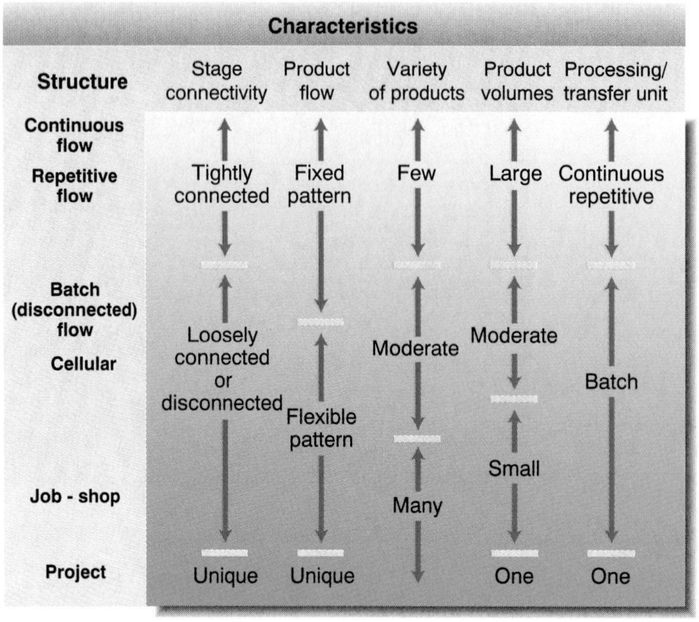

FIGURE 7.1 Continuum of process structures.

nents are produced using job-shop or cellular processes, and final assembly is performed using a repetitive flow process.

The selection of a process structure is determined by many factors. Four of the most important are these:

1. The expected volume and demand pattern for the products.
2. The number of different products to be made by the system and the types of processing each requires.
3. The customer order type, which defines whether the product is **made to stock** (the product's characteristics are set by the producer, and the product is normally made in advance of orders), or **made to order** (the product is made on receiving a customer's order, and its characteristics may be specified by the customer).
4. The physical characteristics of the products and the specific technologies required to produce them (e.g., making steel requires working with large volumes of metal that must be processed at high temperatures).

The following sections explain how these factors should be incorporated into the choice of a process structure.

7.3 FLOW PROCESSES

If all the products to be made by a production system require the same type of processing in the same sequence, it is usually most efficient to structure the process according to the "flow" of the products or sequence of tasks that must be performed to make them. A production process with this type of structure is called a **flow process.** In a flow process the overall production process is decomposed into tasks or operations

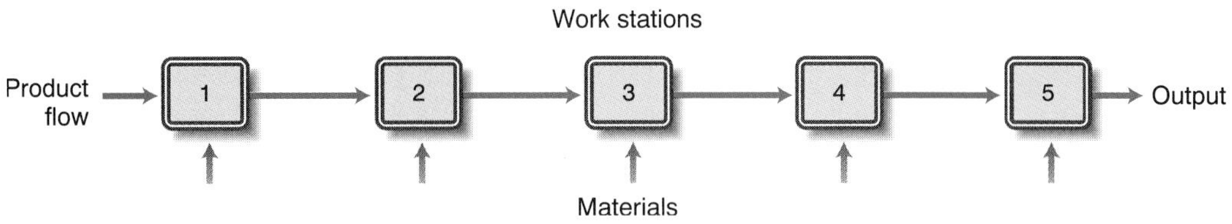

FIGURE 7.2 Flow process structure.

that must be performed. The tasks are assigned to be performed at distinct **work stations** (composed of one or more workers and/or supporting equipment), which are arranged sequentially, as in Figure 7.2. Each unit of product (or each customer, in the case of some services) moves through the work stations in sequence, with the appropriate tasks performed in order. Because all products undergo the same processing at a given stage and materials flow in the same direction, equipment, tools, jobs, and material handling can be specialized for greater efficiency.

The transformation processes for making paper, assembling automobiles, and manufacturing books all have flow structures, but there are two inherent differences among them: (1) the degree of interconnectedness of the work stations and (2) the number of units of product processed and transferred between work stations at one time. Paper is made using a *continuous flow process*; automobiles are commonly assembled using a *repetitive* or *discrete flow process*; and books are manufactured using a *disconnected* or *batch flow process*.

CONTINUOUS FLOW PROCESSES

Continuous flow processes are primarily used in *process industries*, such as paper, chemicals, bulk foods, petroleum, metals, and water. Continuous flow processes are designed to produce large volumes of a small variety of uniform products, such as paper, which require the same processing activities to be performed in a strict sequence. The processing is usually subject to very strict specifications, such as the amount or temperature of materials blended or the speed at which processing must occur. **Continuous flow processes** have a highly interconnected structure whereby material literally moves continuously through the system and the transformation of the product occurs continu-

Hot-strip rolling converts steel slabs into steel coils and sheets of smaller gauge (thickness) using a continuous flow process. With advances in technology a handfull of workers in air-conditioned control booths now operate multi-million ton per year hot-strip mills, which used to require hundreds of workers.

ously, rather than through a sequence of discrete tasks (drilling or assembling a part). Frequently, this is true because the product itself is physically continuous, such as paper, chemicals, or grains, rather than being in discrete units, such as autos or soccer balls. For example, the plant tour of Jefferson Smurfit in Chapter 3 showed that the manufacture of paperboard involves performing five continuous activities: (1) paper fibers (pulp) are prepared by pulping recycled waste paper, which is added to fiber pools; (2) fibers are applied continuously to a moving felt or mesh; (3) water is drained from the pulp as it moves along the mesh; (4) the partially dewatered pulp is transferred to another moving felt that carries it over drying rollers to dry the paper; (5) the paper is rolled and cut. Each of these activities is performed continuously on a physically continuous product.

Continuous flow processes can also be used to produce discrete products or to perform some aspects of the production process for discrete products. Products such as beverages, detergent, and candy are put into cans, boxes, and bags using continuous filling and packaging processes.

The decision to use a continuous flow process is usually apparent because it is dictated by the product or technology. For example, paperboard can only be made efficiently in large volumes using a continuous flow process. By their nature, continuous flow processes tend to be very capital intensive, as well as highly automated and computerized. Although they require large initial costs for equipment and setup, the direct labor costs and per unit production costs are relatively low.

REPETITIVE OR DISCRETE FLOW PROCESSES

Repetitive or **discrete flow processes** are similar to continuous processes in that work stations are tightly connected, and they are organized around the sequence of activities required to produce one general type of product, such as videocassette players, computers, automobiles, cafeteria-style meals, or medical examinations for the army. The flow of the product is not necessarily continuous, but usually units of product are processed and transferred between work stations one at a time in a synchronized manner, hence the name *repetitive*. These processes differ from continuous processes in that the products themselves are physically discrete (a car or toy) and the work required to make them can be divided into discrete tasks (e.g., insert and tighten a bolt). Because the tasks are performed in the same sequence for all products, the traditional spatial layout of repetitive processes involves a line of work stations (as in Figure 7.2); hence these are often called *line processes*. Of course, they do not have to be arranged in a line for the product to flow or the tasks to be performed in a fixed sequence; in fact, Chapter 8 will illustrate the advantages of other spatial arrangements.

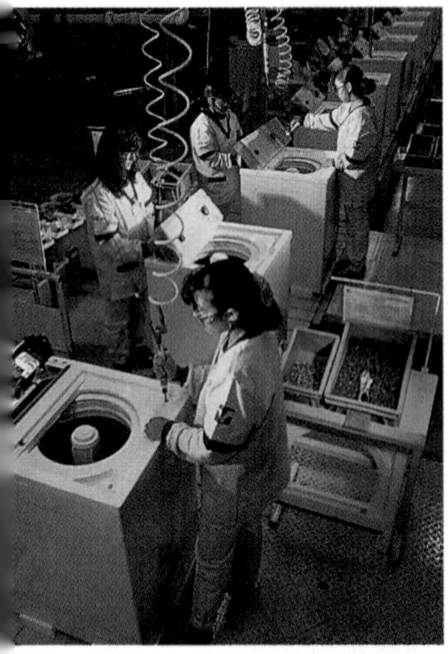

At this Whirlpool washer assembly plant a repetitive flow process is efficient because it produces a large volume of a narrow range of products.

A common version of a repetitive process is an assembly line, such as an automobile assembly line, where the workers or machines at each work station add components to a product moving along the line. A cafeteria restaurant with a fixed line of food is an example of a repetitive service process: at each work station customers can serve themselves or be served by a worker. Although patrons can customize their meals, all customers are "processed" in the same sequence.

As in a continuous flow process, the narrow range of products made in large quantities and the fixed sequence of production tasks facilitate the use of specialized equipment and jobs and greater automation. The primary problems confronted in designing repetitive processes are decomposing the required tasks into appropriate units, assigning and combining the tasks into balanced and compatible workloads at each work station, accommodating some product variety, and adjusting to variation in processing times and production uncertainties, such as machine failures or defective components.

DISCONNECTED OR BATCH FLOW PROCESSES

A book manufacturer (who prints and binds books, not necessarily a publisher, who organizes the writing, printing, and sale of the books) makes all books by performing the same operations in the same sequence (plate making, printing, cutting, folding, stitching, binding). For this reason, it makes sense to structure the production system as a flow process. However, a book manufacturer may produce hundreds of different titles in a year, each with a different production volume (2000 copies of one title and 25,000 of another). At a given stage there may be different machines that can perform similar but not identical operations (a two-color press versus a four-color press); the time required to modify (set up) a machine to go from processing one book title to another may be substantial; and the processing times required to perform different operations, such as printing the pages versus binding the book, can be quite different. For these reasons, it is not efficient to have a system with tightly connected work stations that process and transfer one book at a time, as with an assembly line. Instead, it is more efficient to process a large batch of one title at one stage of the process and then send the entire batch to the next stage for processing. The variation in processing times and batch sizes, and the possibly lengthy setup times between product batches, will cause some products to wait in inventory between stages for a while. Processes that are organized and operated in this fashion are called **batch** or **disconnected flow processes**.

Commercial printing companies often use a batch flow production process. Most products require the same processing steps, but each job is unique and requires its own set-up of equipment, and may require some customized features.

Batch flow processes allow a company to take advantage of the common flow of materials and the ability to use special equipment and jobs at each work station (or department); they also provide the flexibility to produce a variety of products in different volumes. Furthermore, these processes accommodate situations in which different stages of production cannot be synchronized because one stage can be done more quickly than another. Clothing, toys, and specialty chemicals are often made using batch flow processes. In addition, some universities process student applications and banks process home mortgages using batch flow systems.

ADVANTAGES AND DISADVANTAGES OF FLOW PROCESSES

The tightly connected configuration, continuous or repetitive transfer of product, narrow product line, and often automated nature of continuous and repetitive flow processes have several advantages over other production structures. Batch flow processes share some, but not all, of these advantages while not suffering the corresponding disadvantages to as great an extent. The following are the primary advantages and disadvantages of *continuous and repetitive flow processes*.

Advantages

1. *Equipment can be specialized* to perform a narrow range of functions very efficiently.
2. *Jobs can be specialized*, so workers can benefit from repetition of a narrow range of tasks performed at any given work station. Less skilled and lower-wage workers can be used to perform the narrow range of tasks at one work station, or workers cross-trained to work at several work stations can benefit from the repetition while working at a given work station.
3. *Material handling can be simplified* using efficient but inflexible, fixed location material-handling methods, such as conveyers, pipes, and gravity slides.
4. *Work-in-process* (WIP) *inventories are small* because products move between work stations with little or no waiting and storage time in between.
5. *Space utilization is efficient* because there is no need to store in-process inventories, and material handling is performed using conveyors, pipes, or slides, so the wide aisles required by fork lifts and other mobile machines can be reduced or eliminated.

6. *Quality conformance is easier to achieve* because with the narrow range of products (a) workers know the quality requirements and how to achieve them, (b) product changeovers and equipment setups, which are major causes of quality problems, are infrequent, and (c) repetition improves worker skill, so there is less likelihood of errors (assuming jobs are designed to avoid worker boredom, fatigue, or resentment).
7. *Production scheduling and coordination are relatively easy* because there are few separate work orders and only work at the first work station has to be scheduled; work at the other work stations automatically follows in the same sequence.
8. *Costs are easy to monitor* because all products undergo the same processing and use the same resources in consistent amounts.

Disadvantages

1. The primary disadvantage is that *continuous and repetitive flow processes are inflexible*. Only products that require the same processing in the same sequence can be made by the process. In addition, once the process has been established, it is expensive to modify its physical configuration to accommodate new products that require different types of processing or a different sequencing of processing stages. Even changing to new models of the same products, such as an automobile, may require months for the changeover.

   Flow processes are also relatively inflexible in terms of volume changes. For some processes, especially continuous ones, processing must occur at some designed rate for the product to be made correctly. For example, chemicals must be blended or coatings applied to metals at some fixed rate or the chemical reaction or bonding will not occur. If the production system is operated at less than capacity, it may have to be shut down and restarted, which is expensive.
2. *Initial costs are high* because of the specialized equipment used and the substantial work required to design, set up, and balance the workload at each work station.
3. *Work can become tedious and boring* for workers unless jobs are well designed and workers are allowed some flexibility through job rotation and cross-training. Boredom leads to decreased productivity, more frequent mistakes, and quality problems.
4. *The production system is extremely vulnerable* to unplanned work stoppages due to machine breakdowns, defective components, or worker errors. If one part of the production process stops, the entire system must usually stop within seconds or minutes.

Batch flow processes exhibit many of the same advantages, except that equipment and jobs cannot be as specialized, material flow must be more flexible, interstage inventories are necessary (even if small), and greater storage and transport space is needed than for continuous and repetitive processes. However, the disadvantages are less severe because batch processes are more flexible in both product variety and production volumes, work tends to be less tedious, and the system is less vulnerable to shutdowns because some work stations can operate while others are stopped if there are interstage inventories.

7.4 JOB-SHOP PROCESSES

Suppose an organization makes several different products that require different types of processing and the processing for different products is performed in different sequences. For example, Standard Register, which makes thousands of different business

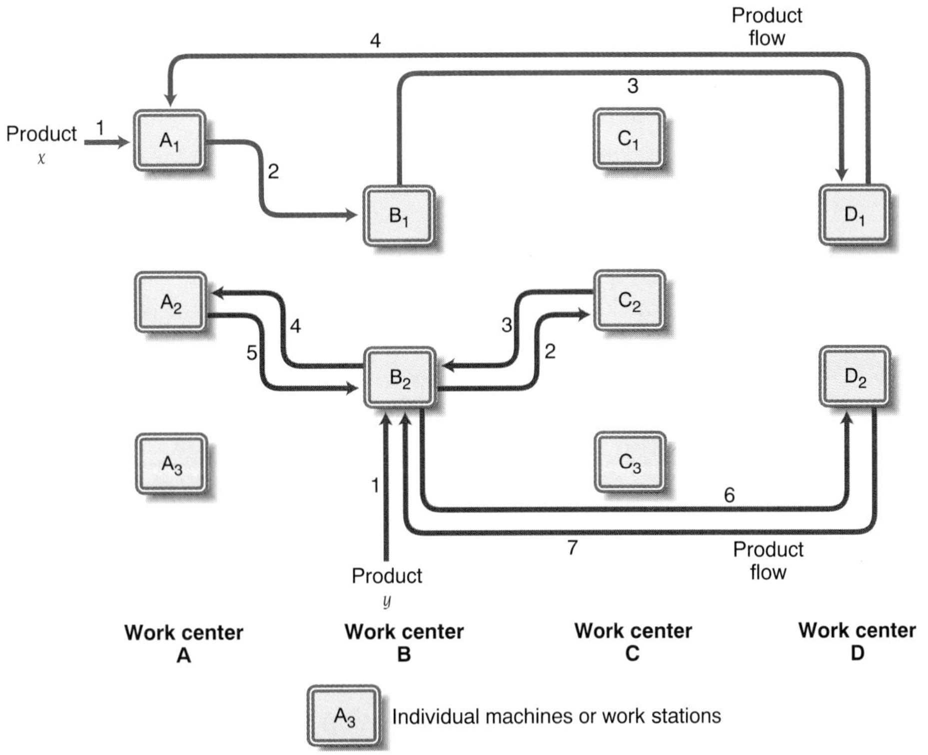

FIGURE 7.3 Job-shop structure and product flow.

forms within the same plant (see Chapter 3), may produce one order of business forms by printing five rolls of paper on one press, then sending it to a collator, then to a cutter, and then to a stapler; the order for a different form may require two rolls of paper to be printed and cut on a combination press/cutter, sent to a padder for gluing, and then sent to another cutter. If the production system were arranged as a strict flow process based on the processing of one product, it would be very expensive to change the configuration of the work stations or to have products "hop" among work stations. Furthermore, the variety of products produced makes the use of specialized machines designed for a specific product impractical.

Instead, when a wide variety of products must be made, especially made-to-order products, production process flexibility is essential. In this case, it may be easier to arrange the system so that similar *types* of processing are performed in the same general area or department using general-purpose equipment, and the spatial layout and material-handling systems can be designed to move products throughout the system in various ways. This type of process, which is illustrated in Figure 7.3, is called a **job-shop process**.[1]

[1]These processes are also sometimes called *intermittent processes*. The term *intermittent* is used because processing at each stage operates intermittently, producing a batch of a product, then stopping for a changeover and operating again. For this reason, batch flow processes are also sometimes categorized as intermittent processes.

Job-shop systems are divided into work centers or departments (like batch flow systems) that are organized around common activities: all the personnel and equipment in a work center are devoted to the same general processing, such as painting, printing, taking blood samples, or teaching mathematics. Products (or customers, in the case of services) can move among the work centers in any sequence, which provides maximum flexibility. Job shops are designed for flexibility so that they can produce small quantities of a wide variety of products, including products that are customized for each customer. Goods that are commonly made using job-shop processes include customized printed products, machined parts from machine shops, furniture, and custom-made pharmaceuticals and chemicals. Colleges, department stores, and hospitals typically use job-shop systems to deliver educational, retail sales, and medical care services.

Advantages of Job-Shop Processes

The advantages and disadvantages of job-shop processes are the opposite of those for continuous and repetitive flow processes. The primary advantage of a job shop is its production flexibility. Any product requiring the types of processing that are available in the work centers can be produced. The number of work centers required, the order in which they are visited, and the amount of time required in each work center can be different for each product. For example, suppose a company had four work centers, A, B, C, and D, such as in Figure 7.3. One of its products (labeled x) may follow the processing sequence A → B → D → A, while another one (labeled y) might have the sequence of B → C → B → A → B → D → B.

The ability to accommodate different processing times and lot sizes is an especially crucial aspect of flexibility. With a job shop, one product may be produced in lots of 10 units, and each unit may require 5 minutes of processing in department A and then 10 minutes in B, whereas another product may be produced in lots of 500 units and each unit requires 10 minutes of processing in department A, 5 minutes in B, and then another 5 minutes in A. This variation would bring a tightly connected flow process to a standstill, but it can be handled readily within a job-shop process. In some job shops there is a dominant flow pattern, such as where almost all jobs require the same processing in the same sequence but perhaps 5% do not. In these cases the job shop can be arranged and operated primarily as a batch flow process, but with some additional flexibility in material handling and scheduling to accommodate odd jobs.

The other major advantages of job shops are low initial costs for general-purpose equipment and greater worker satisfaction because of the variety of work performed.

Disadvantages of Job-Shop Processes

The flexibility and lower capital costs for job-shop processes are not free; the following are some corresponding disadvantages.

1. General-purpose equipment is usually less efficient at processing materials.
2. More skilled, higher-paid employees are needed to set up and operate general-purpose equipment and to modify work methods to make a variety of products.
3. Less efficient but more flexible material-handling methods, such as fork lifts and hand trucks, are required.
4. Work-in-process inventories are needed to keep the work centers operating during equipment setups, as well as to provide the scheduling flexibility needed to coordinate the variety of products and job processing times.
5. The large in-process inventories and flexible material-handling systems require more space than do flow processes.

6. Quality conformance is difficult because workers must be familiar with a wider range of quality requirements, they perform more product changeovers, and they cannot spend as much time refining their work methods for any one product.
7. The variability in process sequencing, lot sizes, and processing times, as well as possible uncertainty about order receipts and due dates, make scheduling and coordinating jobs and equipment very complex. These factors, along with the large in-process inventories, result in long throughput times.
8. The variety of products and their processing requirements make it difficult to assign costs to each product, so it is more difficult to determine the profitability of individual products.

With all these disadvantages, we might wonder why job-shop processes are used. There are at least two answers. First, in many situations the variety of products or the volume of products produced may make the use of a flow process impractical. This is especially true for companies that are competing through product customization. Second, the startup costs of making new products in small quantities are normally much less with a job-shop process than a flow process. In fact, many companies will spawn new products in a job-shop production environment. If sales increase beyond some point, the company may then create a flow process system dedicated to that product. Matching the production process to the portfolio of products made by a company is an important aspect of the process selection decision. Section 7.8 describes the product-process matrix, which can help match the production process and product portfolio, in addition to other analytical tools that are useful in selecting production processes.

7.5 CELLULAR PROCESSES

Organizations often capture some of the efficiencies of flow processes and the flexibility of job-shop processes by creating hybrids of the two, called cellular processes. A **cellular process** can be thought of as a mixture of mini flow processes, called **work cells** (or **cells**), and a job-shop operation. The work cells may perform only two or three activities in a spatially connected flow process, or they may perform several activities connected in sequence.

Cellular processes are most commonly used as substitutes for job-shop processes that need increased productivity. Increasingly, however, they are being used in place of

These manufacturing cells are able to weave their own fabric from glass fibres.

flow processes to obtain greater flexibility. They are also becoming a popular way to organize service operations. For example, The Medical Center of Beaver, Pennsylvania, used to be arranged as a job shop, as are almost all hospitals; each department was separate, and patients had to shuttle among the departments. The Center has converted to a cellular design where "patient centers" have X-ray, pharmacy, and laboratory services within the unit. Both efficiency and patient satisfaction have improved. Banc One Mortgage converted in the opposite direction. Banc One, which once processed mortgages using a desk-to-desk batch flow process, converted to a cellular system whereby teams work together on all aspects of a mortgage simultaneously. This has knocked weeks off the approval time for a mortgage.[2]

To create a cellular process, an organization divides its products into families or groups of products that require similar processing steps in the same sequence. A work cell is then created to perform these steps in the designated sequence for all the products in the family. The output of the cell may be a finished product or a semifinished product that must be sent elsewhere for further processing. Some products will not be appropriate for any cell, and many products cannot be made entirely at a single cell, so there will normally be a "remainder" job-shop subsystem (cell) that can do all the processing steps in any sequence. Standard Register, the producer of business forms, is typical of companies that have converted to work cells. Originally, printing, collating, cutting, and numbering were performed as distinct operations in a job-shop arrangement. Now some printing presses have been converted to work cells that can print, cut, number, and collate together as a continuous flow cell.

The following example illustrates the benefits of cellular processes.

EXAMPLE 1

Suppose a company makes 200 different products. In producing them, the company performs five distinct activities, designated A, B, C, D, and E. Some products are made using three processing steps, while others require as many as nine (the same activity may be repeated several times). Figure 7.4 shows the current production process, which is arranged as a job shop.

Table 7.1 lists the number of products that undergo various sequences of processing. Several sequences occur repeatedly, which suggests the use of work cells. For example, Figure 7.5 gives one possible configuration of a cellular process using the same number of machines. The new configuration has two cells: a two-machine A → B cell and a three-machine B → C → D cell. The remaining machines are kept as a job-shop configuration. The products in families 1, 4, 6, 7, and 8 (140 products) can all be run on the first work cell, and the products in families 3, 7, and 8 can be run on the second work cell.

Some of the benefits of using these cells can be seen by comparing the routing of products in family 8, using the job-shop versus the cellular process. Figure 7.4 shows that with the job-shop process, products in family 8 would have to be loaded onto D, run on D, removed from D, and transported to a storage area, where they would wait until there was time to run on E. Then they would have to be loaded onto E, run on E,

[2]See Stephen Baker, "How One Medical Center Is Healing Itself," *Business Week*, Feb. 21, 1994, p. 106; and John Verity, and Gary McWilliams, "Is It Time to Junk the Way You Use Computers?" *Business Week*, July 22, 1991, pp. 66–69.

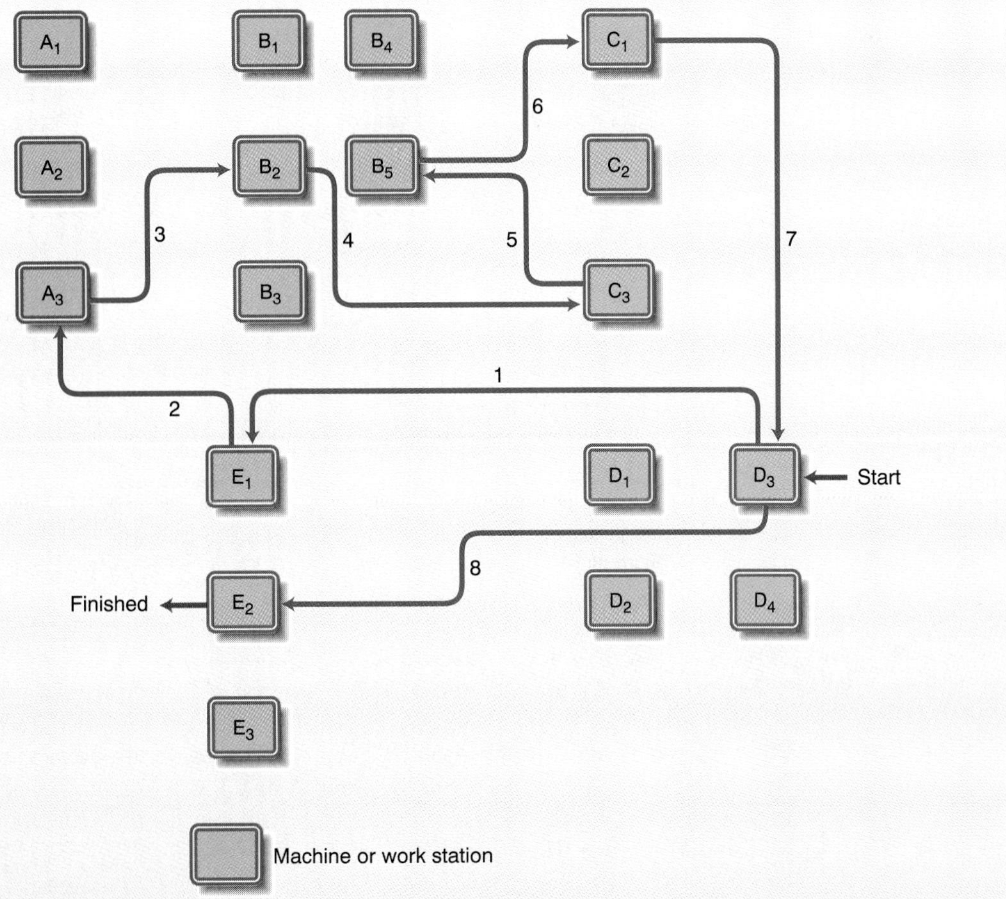

FIGURE 7.4 Flow of Family 8 products through a job-shop process.

removed from E, transported to another storage area to wait until they could be put on A, and so on. At each stage, the products would have to be handled at least twice (and probably three or four times) and stored. The amount of time spent in the system is substantial.

TABLE 7.1 DATA ON PRODUCT FAMILIES

Product Family	Sequence of Activities	No of. Products
1	A → B → D	20
2	A → C → B → E	15
3	B → C → D → E	25
4	C → A → B → D	30
5	A → C → D → E	20
6	C → B → D → A → B → E	40
7	B → A → B → C → D → A	30
8	D → E → A → B → C → B → C → D → E	20

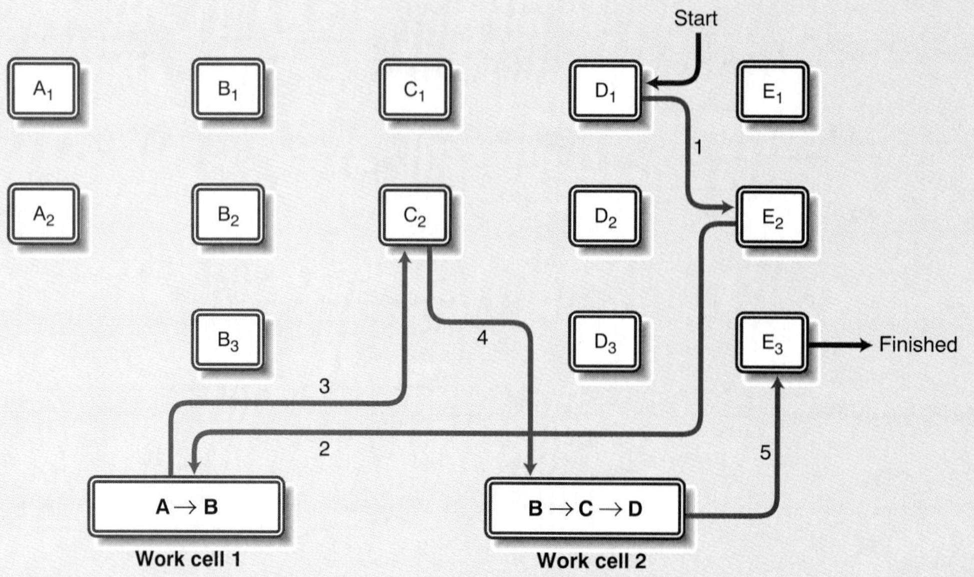

FIGURE 7.5 Flow of Family 8 products through a cellular process.

In contrast, Figure 7.5 shows that with the cellular process, the products go through machines D and E, as above, but then they are loaded onto the A → B cell. They are processed through A and B as a flow process. The extra material handling, transporting, storing, and waiting between A and B are eliminated, saving both time and money. The products then go to storage, are sent to a C machine, run, removed, and sent to storage. They then go to the B → C → D cell. Again the products would be processed through B, C, and D as a flow process, thereby eliminating the extra handling, transporting, and storage between stages B and C and between C and D.

Advantages of Cellular Processes

Companies can benefit by converting even a small proportion of their job-shop work to work cells. When companies can convert a majority of their work to a cellular form, the savings can be enormous. Table 7.2 gives the average benefits reported by 32 companies that converted from a job-shop to a cellular process. The benefits of cellular production as compared with job shops are as follows:

1. *Material handling and transport are reduced* because the work stations (machines) are spatially close and often are operated as repetitive flow processes.
2. *Setup times are reduced* because jobs processed at the same cell often have similar characteristics that require less changeover from job to job.
3. *Throughput time is reduced* because the wait between production stages, the wait for transport, and the transport time are reduced. There is also less waiting time while machines are being set up between jobs.
4. *In-process inventories are smaller* because of more efficient scheduling and reduced setup time disruptions. Also, the shorter throughput times reduce the amount of safety stock needed.

TABLE 7.2 REPORTED BENEFITS FROM 32 COMPANIES IMPLEMENTING CELLULAR MANUFACTURING

Benefit	Mean Percentage Improvement
Reduction in material handling	39.3
Reduction in setup time	32.0
Reduction in throughput time	45.6
Reduction in work-in-process inventories	41.4
Reduction in finished inventories	29.2
Reduction in space needs	31.0
Increase in equipment utilization	23.3
Reduction in number of fixtures	33.1
Reduction in pieces of equipment required to manufacture cell parts	19.5
Reduction in labor cost	26.2
Improvement in labor satisfaction	34.4
Improvement in part quality	29.6

Source: Adapted from Urban Wemmerlov and Nancy L. Hyer, "Cellular Manufacturing in the U.S. Industry: A Survey of Users," International Journal of Production Research, Vol. 27, 1989, pp. 1511–1530.

5. *Less space is needed* because the machines in cells are located close together and less in-process inventory must be stored.
6. Although some investment in equipment is often required, *total equipment costs often decrease* because the increase in efficiency and machine utilization means that less total equipment is needed to produce the same amount of output. In addition, the similarity of products running within cells reduces the number of fixtures and tools needed in production.
7. *Workers enjoy more satisfaction* because they have greater job variety than workers in either flow processes or job shops, since their work often involves several machines and tasks. The workers are also responsible for production of complete products or major portions of products, rather than just one small aspect of the product, and they often work in teams that are assigned to a cell or group of cells.
8. *Quality improves* because of greater job satisfaction, simpler machine setups, and similarity of products within cells, which produce fewer mistakes.

Disadvantages of Cellular Processes

With all these advantages and the fact that cellular processes contain almost all the flexibility of a job shop, the obvious question is, why don't more companies use a cellular approach? The answer is that successful implementation of a cellular production system requires a considerable amount of work and expertise to characterize and classify products and then design the appropriate work cells and remaining job-shop process. (Methods for doing this are discussed in Chapter 8.) The magnitude of the task, however, should not stop organizations from converting their job-shop processes to cellular systems. Despite these problems, many companies have successfully introduced cellular processes, even if on a small scale. A 1994 survey indicated that three-fourths of all large manufacturers and almost 40% of manufacturers with fewer than 100 employees use some cellular manufacturing.[3]

7.6 PROJECT PROCESSES

Some organizations specialize in producing one-of-a-kind products such as construction projects (buildings, highways), computer software, or consulting services. Although such an organization is likely to utilize similar skills and equipment for all the products it makes, the *process* itself often has to be customized: unique skills and equipment may be required and/or combined in new ways. For example, a construction company may use iron workers, cement workers, carpenters, and electricians, as well as cranes and bulldozers, on most jobs, but how they are used, the number used, and the sequence in which they are used will vary from job to job. This type of production process is called a **project process**. The dominant operations management issues for such processes are (1) how to coordinate the wide variety of resources that are needed for the current project, as well as for other projects of the organization, and (2) how to complete the project on schedule and within budget.

The main advantage of a project approach is its flexibility to customize the product. The main disadvantage is the expense. Project processes usually cannot exploit economies of scale, productivity gains from learning, and the general efficiencies of repetitiveness to the same extent that other processes can. However, there is rarely a choice regarding the use of a project approach; the project process is dictated by the product itself. When each product is unique and requires a unique combination of activities, a project process is mandated.

Because the most challenging operational aspects of projects involve scheduling and resource allocation, discussion of project management and scheduling is postponed until Chapter 17.

7.7 MODERN PRODUCTION TECHNOLOGIES

The strategic benefits of technological competence are indicated in a Battelle Laboratories study, which found that the one common factor among firms earning more than a 50% return on investment was a significant technological advantage over competitors.[4] Technological competence can occur in both product development and production methods. In the past few decades, several forms of machine and information technology have revolutionized production processes. Terms such as *flexible manufacturing systems* (FMS), *computer-integrated-manufacturing* (CIM), and *robotics* fill the newspapers. The choice of production technology is integral to the structure and design of production systems. Consequently, managers need to be familiar with the technological tools that are available. This section briefly discusses several of these technologies, including some that are used extensively in service systems.

Although advanced technologies have produced stunning results, it should be kept in mind that successful production processes entail more than simply choosing a par-

---

[3]See Stephanie N. Mehta,"Cell Manufacturing Gains Acceptance at Smaller Plants," *Wall Street Journal*, Sept. 15, 1994.

[4]Cited in Jack R. Meredith, *The Management of Operations: A Conceptual Emphasis* (4th ed.), Wiley, New York, 1992, p. 260.

ticular type of expensive, sophisticated equipment. New technologies will be most effective and efficient if the production system is redesigned and simplified first to use them well, and if they are supported by an appropriate organizational structure, information systems, and personnel training. As in product design, simplification is often the key. Good technologies should simplify the process in some way, either in material handling, in scheduling, or in the human tasks that must be performed.

GROUP TECHNOLOGY

Group technology (GT) is an old concept based on the principle that if we group into families parts or products that have similar characteristics or require similar processing, their similarities can be exploited in many areas of production, including product design, process design and layout, and scheduling. Figure 7.6 shows how a collection of parts might be organized into families according to the type of machining required to make them. The parts in the first family have rounded shapes and require processing on a turning lathe. The parts in the second family all require some type of bending or forming. The parts in the third family are solids with linear shapes that are made by casting or straight-edge cutting tools.

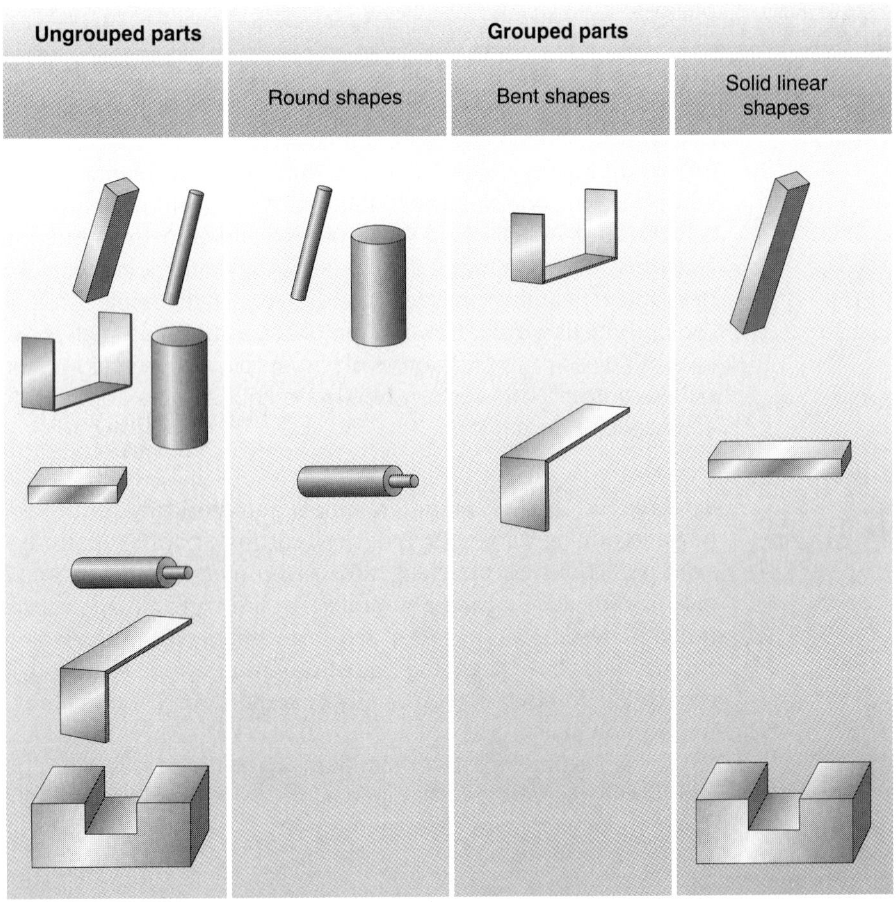

FIGURE 7.6 Grouping parts into families. (Adapted from Jack Meredith, *The Management of Operations*, (4th Ed), Wiley, New York, p. 264)

The GT principle is the basis for many other technologies, such as computer-aided-design (CAD) and cellular manufacturing. To implement GT, a company assigns each part or product a numerical code that describes its characteristics (its shape, size, and the type of material), as well as the type of processing it must undergo (casting, polishing, painting). Depending on its ultimate uses, the GT description can be relatively detailed. This information can then be used in a CAD system, so when a new part (or product) is being designed, existing parts with similar characteristics can be identified and used either as substitutes for the new part or as starting points for a modified part. One use of GT was illustrated in Section 7.5; GT is the basis for cellular production. Products that require similar processing are put in the same family and processed within work cells rather than using a job-shop process.

Finally, GT can be used for scheduling jobs. Jobs within the same family not only require the same type of processing on the same machines, but the machine setups are usually very similar, they often use the same fixtures and components, and they require the same human tasks and quality checks. So even within a job-shop process, and certainly within a cellular process, similar jobs should be scheduled to run successively whenever possible. This reduces the amount of time spent on setups, and it makes the human activities more efficient and higher in quality. For example, in Chapter 3 we saw that Standard Register tries to run sequentially those forms that require the same inks to reduce the time-consuming process of cleaning and changing inks in its printing presses.

PROCESS AUTOMATION

Automation has been instrumental in the productivity gains of recent decades. **Automation** is defined as a set of procedures and machinery that make it possible to perform traditionally human activities automatically. Manufacturing tasks that have been automated include welding, drilling, bending, and painting, as well as process control activities such as checking temperatures and adjusting equipment. In addition, service activities such as entering data, printing bills and documents, keeping track of inventories, and scheduling production are increasingly being automated. Mikio Kitano, Toyota's production guru, however, emphasizes that automation works best when it takes over mindless or unpleasant work; an automated process is not as flexible as a multi-skilled worker.[5] This section briefly describes some common forms of manufacturing and service automation.

Numerically-Controlled Machines

In the 1950s, the first preprogrammed, automatically controlled machine tools for cutting and drilling were built. A desired cutting or drilling pattern was encoded as numerical instructions on punched cards or on magnetic tapes, and the machine tool then moved and cut or moved and drilled according to the instructions. The machines were called **numerically controlled (NC) machines**. With the advance of digital computers, NC machines have been able to perform more varied and more complex tasks. They are now called **computer numerically controlled (CNC) machines** or just **computer-controlled machines**.

CNC machines perform standard machining tasks more quickly than humans. In addition, they require less supervision, are more flexible in changing tasks, and produce products of more consistent quality.

[5]Karen Lowry Miller, "The Factory Guru Tinkering with Toyota," *Business Week*, May 17, 1993, pp. 95–97.

Machining Centers

Advanced versions of CNC machines can automatically select and change tools; these machines are called **machining centers** because they can perform several tasks. Machining centers are often designed with two work tables so that as the machine is processing work on one table, the next part and tool can be prepared on the second table. As soon as the first part is complete, the first table moves away and the second slides into place. This "parallel processing" enhances the machining center's productivity.

Robots

Robots are reprogrammable machines that can perform multiple tasks, especially those requiring complex, three-dimensional movement, manipulation, and, with some robots, tactile sensing and vision. The two most dominant characteristics of robots are their reprogrammable nature (and thus their flexibility) and the variety of movements and manipulations they can perform. Originally, industrial robots were limited to performing very simple tasks such as welding and painting. But over time, more sophisticated versions have been developed that can perform more complex tasks, such as loading and unloading machines, assembling simple products or components, and manipulating drills and other tools to perform several tasks in a variety of positions. Robots are increasingly being used outside of factories. For example, Kajima Corporation is using robots to help construction workers install precast concrete wall panels, and both the University of Wisconsin–Madison and the University of California San Diego Medical Centers are using robots to dispense and/or deliver prescriptions.[6]

Simple industrial robots (see Figure 7.7) are made of three main components: a base, a manipulator, and a gripper. The **base** is a heavy metal cylinder designed to hold the robot in a stable position. The **manipulator** or **arm** is a metal extension with usually two or three "joints" that allow the arm to swivel, stretch, or rotate. Its movements are equivalent to those of a human arm and wrist, except that it can rotate 360° in any direction. The **gripper** can be a hand-like device or pincers for grabbing, a suction device, or an installed tool such as a welding torch. More advanced robots now contain vision systems and mobility systems such as wheels or rollers. These enhancements allow the robots to perform more complicated tasks and to move from place to place.

Although initially developed in the United States, robots are most numerous in Japan, where in 1994 there were over 100,000 in use, compared to the 20,000–25,000 in

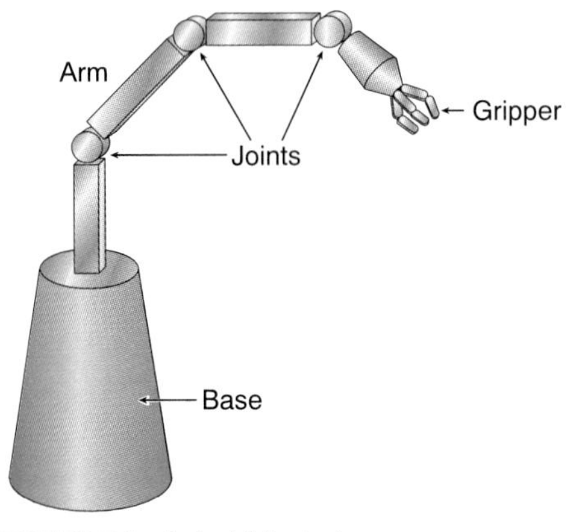

FIGURE 7.7 Industrial robot.

[6]Jim Carlton, "U.S. Contractors Trail Japan in R&D," *Wall Street Journal*, Aug. 6, 1991, and "Business Bulletin," *Wall Street Journal*, Nov. 4, 1993.

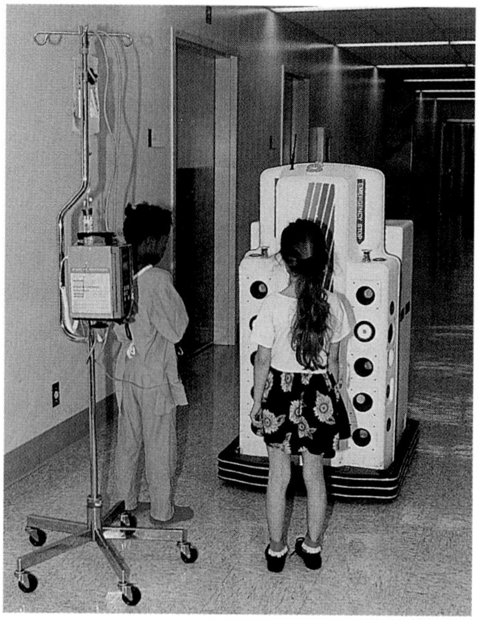

In addition to manufacturing applications such as inserting memory chips (left photo), robots are increasingly being used in service systems, such as the robot used by University of California, San Diego Medical Centers (right) to deliver and dispense prescriptions.

the United States. Not all operations are suited for robots. Even advanced robots are unable to perform many human activities, especially those that require complex spatial judgment, adaptation, and fine manipulation. Even when IBM simplified assembly operations enough to use robots, it found that humans could perform the simplified assembly faster.[7] However, there are clearly many situations in which robots are superior to humans, such as in jobs that involve monotonous or hazardous work. For example, robots are extensively used in the automobile industry for spray painting and welding.

The major drawback of robots is that they are expensive, often costing several hundred thousand dollars, and their setup cost is considerable, although their operating cost is low and they can be used around the clock. A second drawback is that although they are flexible compared to other forms of automation, they are still not as flexible and adaptable as humans (nor can they play on the company softball or bowling team).

COMPUTER-AIDED DESIGN/COMPUTER-ASSISTED MANUFACTURING

Chapter 5 described CAD systems and their benefits in designing products. These systems are now often integrated with computer-controlled machines to create **computer-aided design/computer-assisted manufacturing (CAD/CAM)** systems. The key feature of CAD/CAM systems is that once a product or part design has been completed on the CAD system, it can be automatically encoded as machine instructions for computer-controlled machines. This saves the considerable time and cost of hand-programming the machines, and it reduces the chance of errors.

FLEXIBLE MANUFACTURING SYSTEMS

Flexible Manufacturing Systems (FMS) are self-contained systems of computer-controlled machines, a tool-changing system, and a material-handling system. An FMS is essentially an automated job shop or flexible work cell that can process many differ-

[7]Richard Walleigh, "Product Design for Low-Cost Manufacturing," *The Journal of Business Strategy*, July–August 1989, pp. 37–41.

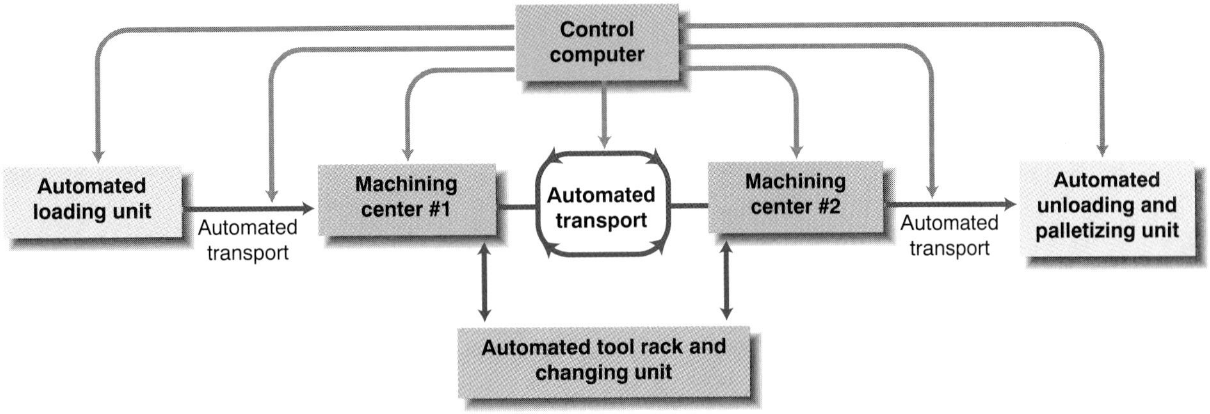

FIGURE 7.8 Typical FMS.

ent parts. FMS have been most successful in making machined parts such as gears, motor parts and casings, electrical components, and handles, although they have also been used in making textiles and assembling products. FMS vary widely in their complexity and capabilities. The simplest FMS is an **FMS module**, which is typically a CNC machine with an automatic tool changer, a tool rack to hold a variety of tools, and an automatic loading and unloading mechanism. The most common FMS is one that has (1) an automated loading system to load materials and parts, (2) two or more machining centers that can change tools automatically, (3) a tool storage and changing system, (4) a material-handling system that moves materials to and from the system and among the machines, (5) an unloading and stacking system, and (6) a computer that controls the movement of materials, the changing of tools, and the movement and operation of the machines (see Figure 7.8).

More complex FMS may include other types of processing equipment as well, such as robots, cleaning equipment, and monitoring equipment, all of which are controlled by the central computer. FMS modules or cells can be connected and coordinated to create complex, flexible production systems that make entire products.

A full FMS (in contrast to a module) has many of the advantages of a work cell, but with the flexibility of a job-shop operation. To see this, consider a company that makes products using three machine-based operations: A, B and C (e.g., drilling, cutting, and grinding). Each product may require several passes through each machine, but each pass may require different drill pieces, cutting blades, and grinders arranged in different positions. For example, one product may require the activity sequence

$$A \rightarrow C \rightarrow B \rightarrow C \rightarrow A \rightarrow C \rightarrow B \rightarrow C$$

whereas another product might require the sequence:

$$B \rightarrow C \rightarrow A \rightarrow B \rightarrow C \rightarrow A \rightarrow C$$

If these products were made using a job-shop process, between each operation the product would be moved and stored and the machines would have to undergo a setup. Because of the cost of setups and material handling, the product would be made in batches.

In contrast, an FMS containing the three types of machines would produce the first product in a repetitive manner unit by unit by shuttling it from A to C to B and so on. While the product was being processed by one machine, the necessary tools would be selected and positioned at the other machines for the next step. The second product would also be made in a repetitive manner, but it would be moved through the machines of the FMS in a different sequence. In effect, the FMS is a flexible work cell; each product undergoes continuous processing without having to move from department to department, but each product can be processed in a unique sequence with unique machine settings. Therefore, the cost and time reductions due to better material handling, minimal in-process waiting, and quicker machine setups are obtained, yet flexibility is maintained. Most important, products can be made in much smaller quantities at lower cost, and firms can respond to demand fluctuations more quickly.

Despite these advantages, North American companies have been slow to adopt FMS technology. Admittedly, FMS are expensive, often costing millions of dollars, and they require considerable expertise and planning to implement successfully. However, when used correctly, the benefits can be substantial. As their name implies, their major benefit is flexibility. For example, Allen-Bradley Corporation, a manufacturer that makes over 300,000 different parts for its products, has an assembly FMS that can switch among 400 distinct products without stopping. Failure to value fully the benefits of greater flexibility and quality has been a major reason for the slow adoption of FMS technology. Methods for evaluating capital investments in production processes and technologies are discussed in Section 7.8.

COMPUTER-INTEGRATED MANUFACTURING

Many organizations utilize the technologies described above. The next step in the technological progression is to tie all the database systems and all the manufacturing equipment and subsystems together into a single integrated system. Such systems are called **computer-integrated manufacturing (CIM)** systems. In theory, a complete CIM system would control and coordinate every phase of production, from initial order receipt to shipment and billing. Specifically, a CIM would take product design information from a CAD system and customer order information and use these to create bills of materials, purchase orders, work instructions, tooling requirements, and machine instructions for CNC machines and other equipment. The system would then develop schedules for production equipment, and coordinate the release and flow of orders and materials throughout the manufacturing facility. As the product moved through the facility it would be tracked and monitored, and information about quality, material yields, machine breakdowns, and tool wear would be gathered and stored for future analysis. An integral part of the CIM system would be the purchasing and inventory control system, which would keep track of all raw material, in-process, and final product inventories and issue purchase orders and product releases automatically. The product releases would automatically trigger shipping and billing documents to be sent to the customer.

CIM systems that do most of these tasks are rare, but some companies, such as Allied Signal, Motorola, Sony, Tektronix, Texas Instruments, and Toshiba, have greatly integrated their design, sales, scheduling, manufacturing, purchasing, and accounting systems.

BAR CODING AND OPTICAL SCANNING

One form of technology that has been applied widely in service systems as well as manufacturing is optical scanning. We are all familiar with the **universal product code (UPC)** that appears on most products we purchase in the grocery store. Each product is assigned a numerical code (which is obtained from a central clearinghouse) that is represented using a series of bars. These bars can then be read using an **optical scanner**,

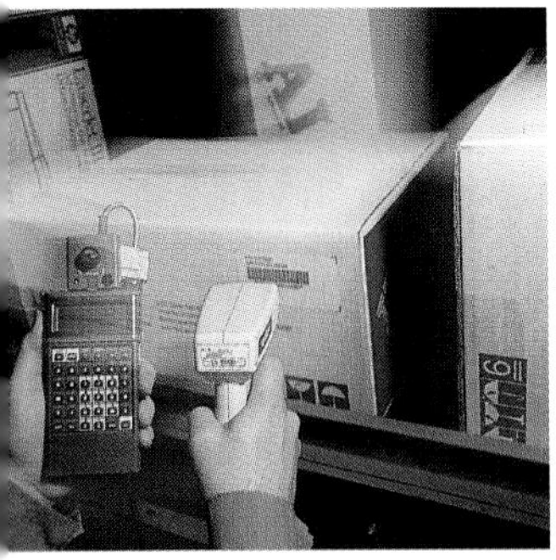

Bar-coding and optical scanning technology has revolutionized material handling processes, including retail and wholesale operations. By scanning shipping and receiving documents and packages the location and quantity of materials can be stored in a computer almost simultaneously.

which bounces beams of light off the code, identifies the number and width of the bars, and converts them into a numerical code. This **bar code**, which is then fed into a computer, can be used to execute a series of transactions, such as assigning a price on a grocery bill, adjusting the inventory level of that product in the store, and tallying information about how many units of that product have been purchased during some period of time. Retail companies have found ever-increasing uses for this information, and it has become a competitive weapon for many. For example, 7-Eleven Japan has been a leader in using this technology to identify products that tend to be purchased together or determine whether sales are being influenced by special marketing promotions. If a large number of customers purchase the products using check cashing cards, credit cards, or debit cards, a store can determine the demographics of purchasers by matching cardholder information with their purchase records.

Bar codes and optical scanning are used extensively for material tracking. Hand-held machines can print bar codes on cards, or on adhesive-backed tickets or labels, which can be attached to packages, parts, boxes, or work orders. The bar codes can then be read at any time with a hand-held wand and the information fed into a computer, so that every box, package, part, or order can be tracked. Airlines use bar codes to track luggage, UPS and Federal Express use them to track packages, and factories use them to track orders, parts, and materials. Bar coding and optical scanning have become essential ingredients for tracking materials and job orders in CIM systems and just-in-time production systems.

In addition to improving tracking and data gathering, bar coding and optical scanning can save labor and reduce the errors of data entry. For example, bar-coded library books that are optically scanned at checkout and at return avoid the time-consuming process of hand-entering the book data into a computer. Bar coding also eliminates the chance of mistyping a call number.

ELECTRONIC DATA INTERCHANGE

Electronic data interchange (EDI) is a computerized system whereby customers and suppliers, and departments within the same company, can share and transmit information electronically in real time. For example, suppliers of a retail store can check the sales and inventories of the products they sell to the store daily, and then automatically release an order to restock rather than waiting for the retailer to issue a purchase order, which may take several days to initiate and transmit. This rapid response lowers the amount of inventory that the retailer needs to keep on hand. For example, Dillard's Department Stores has used an EDI system to reduce its average restocking time by over 60%.[8]

EDI systems can serve other purposes as well. With some systems, customers can track their own orders within their supplier's production system. If an order is running ahead of or behind schedule, the customer can act accordingly. Similarly, suppliers use EDI to track the sales and product usage rates, as well as the inventories, of their customers in order to adjust their own production schedules quickly. If a supplier notices that the sales of customer A have been higher than normal and the sales of customer B have been lower, the supplier may modify its production schedule and run a job for customer A ahead of B, or the supplier may modify the batch sizes for the orders. Even railroad companies, such as Union Pacific, have established EDI systems so that customers can automatically track their shipments' locations throughout the country without having to talk with a customer service representative.

[8]Carol Hymowitz and Thomas O'Boyle, "A Way That Works: Two Disparate Firms Find Keys to Success in Troubled Industries," *Wall Street Journal*, May 29, 1991.

The major feature of EDI is real-time, paperless transfer of information. This allows companies to reduce inventories and to execute more efficient production and shipping schedules. In addition, there can be significant data entry and paperwork processing savings. Rather than receiving paper documents from a customer or supplier and then reentering the data into its own computer system, a company can enter the same data by electronic transfer (*downloading* data). In many cases, hard-copy documents such as purchase orders or information requests can be eliminated entirely. Companies such as Wal-Mart and GE now insist that suppliers use EDI. Wal-Mart claims that EDI is crucial to its strategy of keeping inventories and prices low, and GE has eliminated over 4 million paper transactions a year using EDI.[9]

PROCESS TECHNOLOGY AND THE ENVIRONMENT

Chapter 5 discussed ways in which better choice of materials in product design can lead to products that are less expensive to make, easier to reuse, and less harmful to the environment. But the environmental impact of a product is not dictated by its design alone; it is also determined by the processes and technologies used to produce it. By devoting attention to the environmental impacts and costs, one can more easily identify financial opportunities in the selection of production methods and technologies. In most cases, production efficiency is the friend of the environment rather than its enemy. The following are four ways in which companies have reduced the environmental impacts of their production processes while increasing their profits.

1. ***Reduce Material Usage.*** Although recycling materials is commendable, a better environmental approach is to use no more materials than are necessary. Almost every organization can find areas where it is wasting materials, which does double damage: waste requires more materials to be made, and it creates more waste to dispose of. Excess trim wastes when producing paper, steel, and aluminum, excess use of solvents to clean machines, and the discarding of partially used containers of materials all present opportunities to reduce material usage. For example, the Boston Park Plaza hotel has installed pump dispensers in its bathrooms to eliminate the packaging and waste of discarding partially used bars and bottles of soap, shampoo, and creams. This eliminates 2,000,000 one-ounce plastic containers a year.[10]
2. ***Reduce Production of Toxic Wastes.*** According to Edgar Woolard, chairman of DuPont Company, "When you make a lot of waste you know you don't have control of your operation." DuPont recognized this when, by reducing the amount of one input used at a chemical plant, it reduced plant waste by two-thirds and saved $1 million per year.[11] Reducing the generation of waste at its source is almost always easier and more cost effective than trying to dispose of or process the waste after it is generated.
3. ***Reclaim and Reuse Toxic By-products.*** When wastes are generated by a process, reclaiming and reusing them can be profitable. For example, in its production of nylon fibers, Monsanto Corporation has been capturing toxic solvents before they

[9]William Symonds, "Getting Rid of Paper Is Just the Beginning," *Business Week*, Dec. 21, 1992, pp. 88–89

[10]See, Tedd Saunders, *The Bottom Line of Green Is Black*, HarperCollins, San Francisco, 1993, for this and many more examples of environmentally sensitive processes.

[11]Scott McMurray, "Chemical Firms Find That It Pays to Reduce Pollution at Source," *Wall Street Journal*, June 11, 1991.

IN GOOD COMPANY

Waste Turns to Energy for Anheuser-Busch

By 1997, methane gas made by treating waste water will be helping to power six of Anheuser-Busch's breweries. Anaerobic bacteria are added to brewery waste water containing remnants of corn, rice, hops, and yeasts. The bacteria convert the waste into methane gas, which is sent to the brewery boilers, providing 15% of the brewery's energy. In addition to saving $30 million a year in energy and treatment costs, the process generates 80% less carbon dioxide than the regular treatment process and produces less than half of the solid waste that must be sent to landfills. By 1994 three Anheuser-Busch breweries were already using this process, and installation is underway on three more.

Source: Jim Gallagher, "This Bug's for Anheuser-Busch in Waste-to-Energy System," St. *Louis Post-Dispatch*, July 27, 1994.

escape up the smokestack and then recycles them into the production process. This has reduced toxic air emissions by 90% and saved millions of dollars.[12]

4. ***Increase Energy Efficiency.*** Anheuser-Busch, which is featured in this chapter's "In Good Company" profile, has used a creative technology at its breweries to eliminate toxic waste and improve energy efficiency. Waste water that is laced with corn, rice, hops, and yeast remnants is treated with bacteria that eat the wastes and generate gas that is then burned to power the brewery. Anheuser-Busch estimates that this saves the company $30 million per year in energy and waste treatment costs. A less dramatic way to be more energy efficient is to use more energy-efficient (fluorescent) lighting and high-efficiency motors. Ben and Jerry's Ice Cream reported saving $250,000 a year with these simple measures.[13]

Although it is a last step, recycling paper, and reusing containers, pallets, and other nontoxic materials can save considerable money and reduce the waste stream. Advanced technologies are sometimes necessary, but frequently simple solutions that require little or no investment in equipment can produce meaningful savings.

7.8 METHODS FOR EVALUATING PROCESS AND TECHNOLOGY ALTERNATIVES

Choosing the right production structure and technologies requires consideration of many factors, some of the most important being the volume and variety of products to be made, trade-offs between cost and flexibility, compatibility with the organization's

[12]Ibid.

[13]See Jim Gallagher, "This Bug's for Anheuser-Busch in Waste-to-Energy System," St. *Louis Post-Dispatch*, July 27, 1994, and Saunders, pp. 23–27.

product portfolio, the company's order-winning dimensions, and the relative costs and risks. This section presents methods for analyzing and incorporating these factors into the selection of process structures and technologies.

PRODUCT VARIETY AND VOLUME

Normally, the larger the variety of products to be made by the process and the more the products differ, the more flexible the process must be, and so the more advantageous it is to use a job-shop process. By contrast, the larger the volume of individual products to be made and the fewer varieties of products to be made, the more advantageous it will be to use a flow process.

The variety and volume of products to be made and sold are partially affected by whether the company sells products that are made to stock or made to order. Because made-to-stock items are intended to serve many customers, they are normally produced in larger volumes. Usually the more made-to-order products the company produces, the greater the product variety and the more flexibility its process needs.

The same general ideas apply to service operations as well. Although services cannot be made to stock and stored in inventory, the more standardized the service and the larger the volume, the more likely a flow process (or at least a highly structured process) will be used. For example, processing voters during an election requires performing a standardized service for each voter (checking eligibility, issuing a ballot), so a well-designed flow process is usually most efficient. By contrast, the service required by a customer at a grocery store is made to order, so the production process requires considerable flexibility and would normally be designed as a job shop. Each customer can decide which aisles to visit and in which order, whether or not to go to the bakery, meat counter, deli counter, pharmacy, florist, or movie rental booth.

THE PRODUCT-PROCESS MATRIX

One problem in selecting a production structure is that an organization may use different structures for different sets of products, and the best structure may evolve over time as new products are introduced and existing ones mature and die. As a product passes through different stages of its life cycle, the relative importance of the order-winning dimensions the company wants to emphasize and the demands put on the production system will change. Early in a product's life cycle, its design may undergo frequent changes, demand may be relatively low, and the price may be relatively unimportant. The production process needed for a product at this stage is quite different than for a mature product, which may have a standardized design, is being produced in large volume, and must be priced competitively. To be competitive, organizations must adapt their production systems to changes in individual products over their life cycles and to the overall *mix* of products produced by the process. The best process to use is not necessarily determined by which *single* product will be made, but rather by which *mix* of products will be made.

A helpful framework for studying the relationships between the production process and the product mix and life cycle stages is the **product-process matrix**,[14] shown in Figure 7.9. The horizontal dimension measures production volume, number of products or product varieties, and degree of product standardization. (These may correspond to the stages through which a product progresses over its life cycle.) The vertical dimension represents the process structures, which implicitly specify interconnectedness,

[14]See Robert H. Hayes and Steven C. Wheelwright, *Restoring Our Competitive Edge: Competing Through Manufacturing*, Wiley, New york, 1984, pp. 208–227, for a detailed discussion of the product-process matrix.

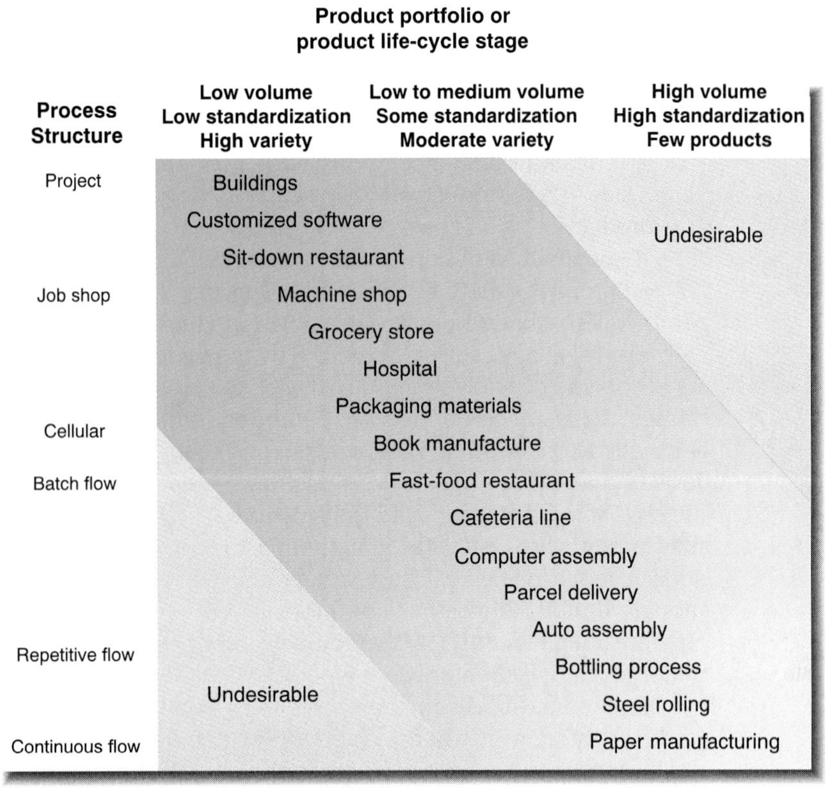

FIGURE 7.9 Product-process matrix.

specialization/flexibility, automation, and throughput volume. A product-process matrix can be used at the company, division, product line, or facility level.

At a general level, companies should match their products and processes so that their product/process position is near the diagonal of the matrix. For example, if a company such as a custom-furniture manufacturer produces many different products in low volumes, it should normally use a job-shop process that has considerable flexibility; it does not need (or desire) a high-volume, specialized process. By contrast, a company that makes a large volume of one or a few similar items, such as office chairs or school desks, would benefit from a highly connected, specially tailored flow process. Companies within the same industry can successfully operate at different points on the matrix as long as they are near the diagonal. For example, fast-food restaurants such as McDonald's have traditionally been near the lower right corner of the matrix (although they have been moving slightly left in recent years), whereas conventional sit-down restaurants are close to the upper left corner. The incompatible strategies represented by points far off the diagonal are usually disastrous.

Strategic Benefits of the Product-Process Matrix

The product-process matrix can help an organization to view its marketing and operations strategies in a unified way. If a company's or division's position is off the diagonal, this highlights a possible inconsistency of strategy. Suppose a company establishes a dominant market position for a product and uses a highly automated flow process to produce it at low cost. Competitors are unable to compete in terms of price, so they try to gain market share by using more product options or customizing the product by using a job-shop process. To counter the loss of market share, the first company may try to expand the number of options and customize products. But this pushes the company directly left on the matrix. It is then using a specialized, high-throughput flow process to make a wider variety of lower-volume items. Its product and process do not match, and its marketing and operations strategies are inconsistent. The company should either reduce the product variety or establish a separate process to make the low-volume products.

The opposite situation can occur as well. A company that has competed successfully on product variety and customization may begin to lose market share to a competitor who has developed an inflexible but efficient production system that competes on price. This has occurred in the U.S. commercial airline industry. The major air carriers all operated relatively high-cost, flexible systems that offered a variety of seating classes, routes, meals, and so on. Southwest Airlines decided to offer a very narrow set of products (one seating class, no assigned seats, no meals, limited route structure); it devised a low-cost, inflexible production system and competed on price. Companies such as United, American, and Delta Airlines tried to compete on price by reducing frills and cutting wages but still maintaining their same production system. This did not work; it reduced their product variety and customization without lowering the costs enough. United Airlines has now established a separate inflexible, low-cost system (a separate airline identity) similar to Southwest's production system to compete in a narrow product market on price.

The product-process matrix also helps companies in choosing technologies and products. By knowing where it is on the matrix, by knowing its competitive advantages, and by knowing where products are in their life cycles, a company can decide more easily whether to add products, drop products, expand capacity, create a specialized process, or increase process flexibility. The matrix is especially helpful in avoiding product proliferation by clearly showing that as products are added, the impact on the production process must be considered.

ANALYZING COSTS AND RISK: CROSSOVER ANALYSIS

The cost structure for a production process will be influenced not only by the general production structure, but also by the designed capacity of the process and the specific technology used. A simple yet informative type of analysis used to evaluate alternative processes and technologies is **crossover analysis**. (Crossover analysis is similar to break-even analysis, which was discussed in Chapter 6.)

Crossover analysis begins by constructing a cost function for each process (or capacity) alternative; this function estimates the cost of production as a function of the production rate (units per year). The cost function contains a fixed cost component and a variable cost component, which may or may not change with production volume. Processes or facilities that are designed to produce large volumes and that are equipment intensive will normally have a relatively large fixed cost but a relatively low variable cost of production. In contrast, processes and facilities that are designed to produce smaller volumes and are labor intensive will normally have a smaller fixed cost of operation but a larger variable cost.

Once these functions have been developed, the expected level or range of product demand can be forecast over the relevant planning horizon. For the likely demand levels, these functions can then be used to determine which alternative is least costly. A good way to determine and illustrate over what range of output levels each alternative is best is to graph the cost functions and identify at which points, called **crossover points**, two alternatives have the same cost, as shown in Figure 7.10. At crossover

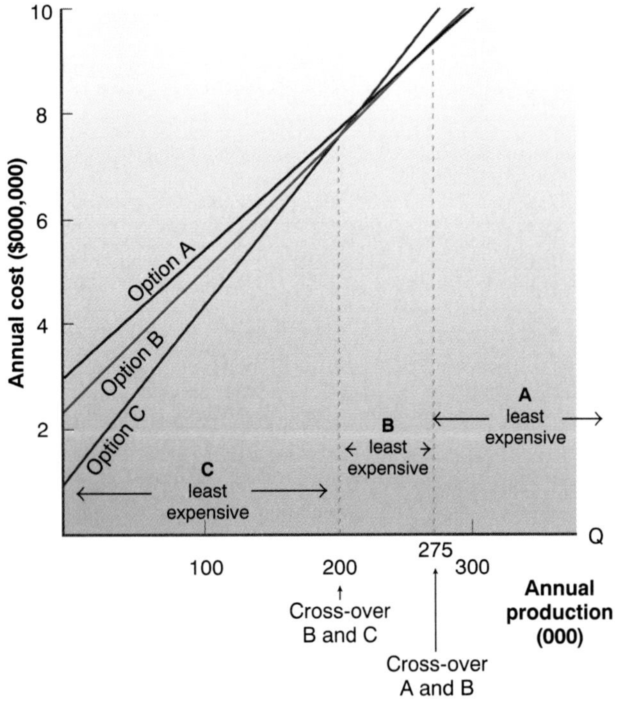

FIGURE 7.10 Cost functions and crossover analysis.

points, one alternative is cheaper at lower volumes and the other alternative is cheaper at higher volumes. These ideas are illustrated by the following example.

EXAMPLE 2

For the past five years, Hydroworks, Inc., has produced a line of faucets. This product is one of several made by the company at its current production facility, but the facility is reaching capacity due to sales growth. The company has decided to construct a new production facility, to open in 1997, with a new process and equipment that will be dedicated, at least initially, to making faucets. The company is considering three options. Option A would be a facility that has an annual capacity of 400,000 faucets per year, and it would use a flow process designed specifically to make faucets. This facility is estimated to have an annual fixed cost of $2,750,000 and a variable cost of $25 per faucet. Option B is a facility that would use a mixture of FMS production cells, some specialized work cells, and a small job-shop processing capability. This facility would have a capacity of 320,000 faucets per year, and it would have enough flexibility that a wider range of faucets and a few other types of fixtures could be made using it. This facility is estimated to have an annual fixed cost of $2,200,000 and a variable cost of $27 per faucet. Option C would use primarily a job-shop process, but it would contain a few work cells for common combinations of activities. This facility could be used to make most of the plumbing products the company offers, not just faucets, and it would have a capacity of approximately 250,000 faucets per year, depending on the mix of products.

The estimated fixed cost is $1,000,000 per year, with a variable cost of $33 per faucet. The company's faucet sales over the past five years are as follows:

Year	Unit Sales
1991	152,000
1992	171,000
1993	186,000
1994	202,000
1995	213,000

The company would like to evaluate its alternatives.

The annual cost functions for the three options are graphed in Figure 7.10. For annual output levels below 200,000 faucets per year, option C is the lowest-cost option. For annual output levels between 200,000 and 275,000 units, option B is cheapest. Finally, for annual output levels above 275,000 units, option A is cheapest. How did we identify these crossover points? Graphically, we could see that option C is the lowest-cost option for low volumes until its curve crosses that of option B. To determine the specific production volume at which options B and C have the same cost, we simply set their two cost functions equal and solve for the unknown volume:

$$\text{annual cost of C} = \$1{,}000{,}000 + \$33\,Q = \$2{,}200{,}000 + \$27\,Q = \text{annual cost of B}$$
$$\rightarrow \$6\,Q = \$1{,}200{,}000$$
$$\rightarrow \quad Q = 200{,}000 \text{ faucets per year}$$

where Q is the annual production volume. Similarly, option B is the lowest-cost option for Q greater than 200,000 until its cost curve crosses that for option A. At that point, the costs of A and B are the same. To determine that volume, we set the cost functions of A and B equal and solve for the production volume:

$$\$2{,}200{,}000 + \$27\,Q = \$2{,}750{,}000 + \$25Q \rightarrow 2Q = 550{,}000 \rightarrow Q = 275{,}000$$

The next step is to forecast the future sales of faucets. Sales appear to be increasing by approximately 15,000 per year (although growth may be slowing somewhat; it is difficult to determine with so little data). Assuming sales will increase yearly at this rate, predicted sales for 1997 and beyond are as follows:

Year	Predicted Sales
1997	243,000
1998	258,000
1999	273,000
2000	288,000
2001	303,000
2002	318,000

We can conclude that under almost any scenario, faucet sales will exceed 200,000 per year, so option C can be eliminated from consideration for both cost and capacity reasons. If sales grow as predicted, during its first three years option B would be less costly than option A. But by the fourth year B would be more expensive than A, and by the sixth year a facility using B would be bumping up against its capacity. If sales of faucets did not increase as rapidly as predicted, then option B would be less costly than option A for a longer period. In addition, if sales growth stops or even declines, option B has more flexibility than option A to produce other products. By contrast, if sales increase faster than predicted, option A would be less costly than option B within the first two or three years.

Because it would probably be uneconomical to use process B initially and then change to A within a few years, one of these two options must be chosen. Crossover analysis allows a convenient form of sensitivity analysis. For example, we can compute how much additional cost or savings would be incurred if option B were chosen and sales were higher or lower than expected. (The probabilities of each scenario could be included in the analysis explicitly using *decision analysis*, which was described in Tutorial 2.) In addition to cost, factors such as the expected useful life, capacity, and flexibility of each facility/process option should be considered before making a final decision. Although crossover analysis will not always provide a clear-cut answer to the process or technology selection question, it frequently can narrow the set of options and clarify the relative financial benefits and risks of the remaining options.

CAPITAL INVESTMENT ANALYSIS: NET PRESENT VALUE

Alternative processes and technologies create different cash outflows and inflows of benefits over time. A common method for evaluating equipment and technology investments is called **present value analysis**. Present value analysis is based on the principle that the same nominal amount of money is worth less in the future than it is now (ignoring inflation) because, by having the money now, we can invest it and earn a real rate of return. Therefore, to evaluate investments that create positive and negative cash flows over time, we must discount future cash flows according to how far in the future they occur. If we believe that we can earn a rate of return of r per year on money[15] then any cash flow n years in the future should be discounted by a factor $[1/(1+r)^n] = (1+r)^{-n}$. The **net present value (NPV)** of an investment is the sum of all cash flows that have been discounted to their equivalent value at some point in time (the present). Investments are undertaken only if the time-discounted value of future benefits exceeds the time-discounted value of investments, that is, if the net present value is positive.

EXAMPLE 3

Suppose a company is considering the purchase of a flexible manufacturing system for \$15 million. It believes that the FMS will reduce costs, increase product quality, and increase the variety of products it makes, so that it will increase profits by \$4.5 million a year for the next three years and by \$4 million a year for the two years after that. Assuming all cash flows occur at the beginning of each year and using a discount rate of $r = 0.12 = 12\%$, the net present value of the investment is

$$\begin{aligned} NPV &= -\$15{,}000{,}000 + (1+0.12)^{-1}(\$4{,}500{,}000) + (1+0.12)^{-2}(\$4{,}500{,}000) + (1+0.12)^{-3} \\ &\quad (\$4{,}500{,}000) + (1+0.12)^{-4}(\$4{,}000{,}000) + (1+0.12)^{-5}(\$4{,}000{,}000) \\ &= -\$15{,}000{,}000 + \$15{,}621{,}000 = +\$621{,}000 \end{aligned}$$

[15]The discount rate r should reflect the rate of return we believe we could earn from alternative investments (the opportunity cost of capital).

The present value of the future benefits exceeds the initial cost, so the net present value of the investment is positive and the project should be undertaken. (In-depth discussions of present value analysis, including tax and depreciation considerations, can be found in the books referred to in the Selected Readings at the end of the chapter.)

Although net present value analysis is theoretically sound, its implementation in practice has received considerable criticism, and it has been blamed for the reluctance of U.S. industries to adopt many technologies. For capital investments that produce new products the incremental benefit is usually clear; it is the additional net revenue generated, which could be forecast. However, for investments in new technologies or processes that make existing products, a common mistake has been to take a narrow view of benefits. Specifically, equipment investment analyses frequently consider the only monetary benefits to be the reduction of production costs for existing products. The baseline for comparison is what the costs will be after adopting the technology versus what they currently are, *assuming the same volume and mix of products*. However, many new technologies are not intended primarily to reduce costs, but rather to make the organization more efficient and competitive in other dimensions, such as product quality, greater product variety or customization capability, shorter product development times, and shorter lead times. These improvements provide tangible monetary benefits by increasing sales or *retaining* sales that might be lost if the investment were not made. This latter issue is most troublesome for companies. The basis for comparison should be what the cash flows would be *without* the investment; if sales would be lost without the investment, then the investment in technology is producing a net inflow relative to this benchmark. In reference specifically to a new, flexible assembly system, Donald Smith of the University of Michigan points out, "Unless we broaden our frame of reference for looking at savings on this equipment, it will be difficult using American accounting techniques to justify the cost of this system."[16]

Another recent change is to treat the investment in new technologies explicitly as a multidimensional decision. That is, if the benefits are not all easily convertible to monetary terms, it may be better to calculate the benefits for each alternative explicitly in terms of quality, flexibility, and so forth, as well as in traditional monetary terms. This multidimensional representation of alternatives sometimes makes the investment decision clear. For example, the direct monetary return on the investment may be only slightly below the desired level, but it may have a large array of other benefits. (A linear scoring rule, as described in Chapter 6 for location decisions, could be used to combine these qualitative factors.)

7.9 SERVICE SYSTEMS STRUCTURE

Despite the similarities between manufacturing and service systems, services differ from manufactured goods in several ways that affect the production system. When selecting the structure of a service system, we should take into account (1) the product package—the type and variety of services and the mix of goods and services to be pro-

[16]Paul C. Judge, "Nissan's Flexible, 'Thinking' Line for Auto Body Assembly," *New York Times*, Aug. 25, 1991.

vided, (2) the form and intensity of customer/server contact and the extent to which activities can be separated from the customer, and (3) the organization's order-winning dimensions and strategy.

THE SERVICE PACKAGE AND INTENDED CUSTOMERS

Design of the service system should begin with a focus on the services to be provided. Most service organizations do not provide a single homogeneous service. Instead, they provide a package of services to their customers, or a combination of goods and services, with the exact mix and form determined by the customers' needs. For example, modern grocery stores not only sell grocery retailing services but also provide other services, such as check cashing and videotape rental. In addition, some grocery stores perform a small amount of manufacturing by processing their own meats or making their own bakery goods. The variety and type of services that the production system needs to provide will affect the structure the service system should take. A system that is intended to provide a narrow range of standard services, such as air transport, can use a mass production, semi–flow process form, whereas a general law firm will need greater flexibility and customization and will use a job-shop or project type process. In recent years, service companies such as Hyatt Legal Services, H&R Block Tax Services, and Southwest Airlines have become successful by providing a very narrow, standardized set of services using an efficient, mass-production service system.

The Manufacturing/ Service Mix

Services such as hair styling, medical care, telephone service, banking, and transportation tend to be provided by pure service systems; little or no manufacturing of goods is involved. In contrast, restaurants, bakeries, hardware stores, and photographic supply stores often produce or manufacture some goods, such as making food or keys or developing photographs, along with providing services. The mix of manufacturing and service activities performed in the same system will affect the skills and training of personnel, the types of facilities and equipment needed, and the general sequencing of activities.

Integrating manufacturing with service production is always a delicate matter. For example, bringing a manufacturing activity, such as developing photographs, into a system originally designed to provide only retail sale services can necessitate major changes to facilities, material control systems, staffing, training, and safety. Such integration is usually most justifiable when strategic marketing reasons exist for performing both manufacturing and service activities.

Site of Services

An important aspect of the service package is the location where the service occurs; specifically, is the service facilities based or field based? **Facilities-based services** are those for which the customer must go to the facility, such as a grocery store or an airport. **Field-based services** are services provided at the customer's location, such as furnace repair. Normally, field-based service systems must be more flexible. Service personnel do not have easy access to the personnel, equipment, and materials at a base facility, so they must be more self-sufficient in terms of their skills, equipment, and materials. Facilities-based services, such as hotels and retailing services, often produce more standardized services; consequently, the service system can be designed to exploit this standardization by using labor specialization and greater automation. In some cases, whether the service will be facilities based or field based is dictated by the technical or physical aspects of the service, such as hotel lodging. In other cases, the same general service can be either field based or facilities based, depending on the organization's strategy. For example, most physicians will treat patients only at their office or in a hospital, but an increasing number are beginning to make house calls (again).

Immediacy of Services

If a company such as a post office offers to provide services on demand, it must have sufficient capacity and flexibility to accommodate substantial variations in demand and in the range of services requested. By not offering service on demand, but rather having customers request services that are provided later (possibly only a few hours or days later), the service provider can utilize a more inflexible system with capacity below that required during peak demand periods. For example, a mutual fund gathers requests to buy or sell the fund during the day and then executes all transactions together overnight using an automated flow process.

CUSTOMER CONTACT INTENSITY

A characteristic that significantly influences the form of the service system is the **customer contact intensity** in regard to the production system. For service products that involve a high degree of customer contact, such as medical care, hair styling, or legal services, the product *is* the service system and the quality of the product *is* the quality of the service system. Consequently, concurrent design of the service package and the service system is not only desirable but essential.

The intensity of customer contact depends on (1) the amount of time the customer is in contact with the service system and its personnel and (2) the form of contact, including the extent to which the customer performs or participates in the service production. Some services, such as medical and educational services, require intense customer involvement or participation and hence exhibit high customer contact intensity. Services such as passenger airline travel require the customer to be in contact with the service system (the plane, the airport) for most of the time the service is provided, but this contact is passive (sitting on a plane) and participation in the service is minimal, hopefully (unless you are a pilot), so customer contact intensity is low to medium.

In some cases, customers can perform part or all of the service using automated voice and computer systems, yet the intensity of contact is low. For example, with Charles Schwab Brokerage, a customer can check stock prices, place orders, and check account information by phone without talking to a person; the customer does all the work. Even though customer participation in the service is high, the structured nature of the system keeps the intensity of the contact low.

Customer contact intensity is important because usually, the lower the intensity or the more structured and controlled the customer contact can be made, the easier it is to use automated and standardized service systems (such as automated voice systems), which are less expensive and often provide better customer service. Services that require minimal customer contact, such as processing medical insurance claims or

TABLE 7.3 INTENSITY OF CUSTOMER CONTACT FOR SELECTED SERVICES

High Customer Contact
Medical Services, Elementary Education, Financial/Tax Consulting

Moderate Customer Contact
Passenger Airlines, Hotels, Sit-down Restaurants, Legal Services, In-bank Financial Services

Low Customer Contact
Mutual Fund, Mail-Order Retail, Postal Service, Fast-food Restaurants

Customer contact intensity

Service mix Product standardization	Low → Medium	Medium → High
High standardization Low variety	**(Airlines, hotels, discount brokers, sporting events, insurance claim processing)** Services separated from customers Flow or cellular process High potential for automation Specialized labor Capital intensive Operations and sales responsibilities separated	**(Retailing, elementary education, hair styling)** Job-shop or cellular process Limited opportunity for automation Multiskilled labor Labor intensive Operations and sales responsibilities mixed
Medium standardization Medium variety … Low standardization High variety	**(Repair shop, landscaping, medical/scientific testing)** Some services separated from customers Job-shop or cellular process Modest potential for automation Multiskilled labor Operations and sales responsibilities somewhat separate	**(Hospitals, financial/tax/legal consulting)** Job-shop or project process Limited opportunity for automation Multiskilled and highly skilled labor Diagnostic and decision-making skills Labor intensive Operations and sales responsibilities mixed

FIGURE 7.11 Service-process matrix.

clearing bank checks, can be separated from the disruptions of customer contacts and performed using mass production methods. Table 7.3 lists various services according to their approximate customer contact intensity.

The Service-Process Matrix

A tool to show the relationship between the degree of customer contact, the degree of product standardization, and the characteristics of the service system is the **service-process matrix**, which is illustrated in Figure 7.11. The horizontal axis measures the intensity of customer/server contact, and the vertical axis measures the standardization and variety of services provided.[17] Within each quadrant of the matrix, common service system design characteristics are listed. Placing a service package in the matrix suggests the degree to which we can decouple activities from the customer, the most likely form of service system to use, the appropriate level of capital or labor intensity, and the degree to which operations and sales functions are likely to be interconnected. The characteristics listed in the service/process matrix should be taken as guidelines, not firm design rules. For example, the labor or capital intensity and the potential for automation will often depend on product-specific factors.

[17] *Product variety* refers to the variety of services, not the variety of facilitating goods involved in the process. For example, a large retail store may sell thousands of very different goods, but the retailing service is highly standardized.

SERVICE SYSTEM DESIGN AND STRATEGY

The service system must not only produce the variety of services desired, it must support the company's strategy and order-winning dimensions. Because of the close relationship between service products and the service production system, the design of the service system should include an in-depth strategic analysis. A service system designed to be efficient and low in cost by limiting customer contact and service customization may be a dismal failure if the organization's strategy and marketing efforts are based on service that is quick, personable, and customized. For example, in an attempt to minimize costs, IBM Credit Corporation once used a batch flow process to arrange financing for customer purchases; the process was slow, requiring six days to approve a loan application. Since the key customer dimension was approval time, IBM changed the system to one-person cells, reducing approval time to four hours and reducing costs as well.[18]

Similarly, an organization that provides personalized and customized service with a flexible system may be unsuccessful if it tries to compete in terms of price. For example, deep-discount securities brokers that compete on price keep their services very simple and standardized and have minimal customer contact—usually only by phone and mail. The same system, even though it may be efficient and low in cost, would not be successful for a full-service securities firm that provides complete financial planning and management services that are customized for each client.

Although there are operational advantages to providing a narrow range of services, operational and strategic benefits can accrue from some degree of service mix. For example, one problem with designing service systems is capacity management and the associated staffing and scheduling of personnel. Some services require enough capacity to handle peaks in demand, but it is expensive to staff for the peaks and have idle capacity at other times. By providing a mix of *related* services, only some of which require real-time (immediate) activity, organizations can provide a wider range of services with greater efficiency. For example, many specialty retail stores (bookstores, stamp and coin shops, souvenir shops) operate a mail-order service using the same facility and personnel. While customers are in the store and need real-time service, the workers serve them. During periods when the employees are not busy with store customers, they process mail orders, which do not require immediate handling. Banks use this approach to provide mail services at little additional cost by using tellers to process mail transactions during their idle periods.

7.10 CUSTOMIZING THE PRODUCTION PROCESS

There is no simple formula for deciding whether or not to use a flow, job-shop, or cellular process or what types of technology to adopt. In fact, the categories of processes are fuzzy, and most production systems are a mixture of process types. Nevertheless, production systems can be designed better by keeping in mind the characteristics, advantages, and disadvantages of each structure.

Especially important is to make sure that the production process is compatible with the organization's products and markets, strategy, and order-winning dimensions; that it is kept as simple as possible; and that each component of the system has a purpose and contributes value to the product. For as obvious as this may seem, too many organizations have production systems that are copied from other organizations and

[18] Michael Hammer and James Champy, *Reengineering the Corporation: A Manifesto for Revolution*, HarperBusiness, San Francisco, 1993.

designed for someone else's product mix, strategy, and order-winning dimensions. Alternatively, the systems have evolved in a piecemeal fashion over time and have lost coherence, compatibility, and focus. The case at the end of the chapter explains how Southwest Airlines revolutionized the passenger airline industry by narrowing its service mix and creating a service system unlike any before it, designed specifically for its products. Airline companies that tried to compete on price and on-time service while using systems designed for a different service mix found their efforts useless. Completely new production systems, more in line with those of Southwest, were required.

SUMMARY

- The four main production structures are the **flow process**, the **job-shop process**, the **cellular process**, and the **project process**.
- **Continuous flow processes** and **repetitive (discrete) flow processes** process each product using the same operations in the same sequence. Work stations are tightly connected and synchronized so that production and transfer of the products can be continuous or one unit at a time. They are most effective in producing large volumes of a narrow variety of products.
- **Batch (disconnected) flow processes** also process products in the same sequence of operations, but production is performed in batches and work stations are not connected.
- Flow processes tend to be efficient because they allow specialization of equipment and jobs, but they lack flexibility.
- Job-shop processes are designed for flexibility so that products can be processed in unique sequences. As a result, they are less efficient for large-volume production than flow processes.
- Cellular processes are a combination of mini flow processes and a job shop. They take advantage of the similarity among products, but they still maintain considerable flexibility.
- **Automation** is the set of procedures and machinery that makes it possible to perform traditionally human activities automatically.
- **Flexible manufacturing systems (FMS)** are self-contained systems of processing and material-handling equipment. They operate as automated work cells or job shops.
- **Computer-integrated manufacturing (CIM)** ties together the sales, product design, purchasing, manufacturing, shipping, and billing subsystems of an organization into one integrated system.
- The **product-process matrix** helps a company match its production structure to its product portfolio and product characteristics.
- **Crossover analysis** identifies the output ranges over which different process design options have the lowest cost.
- **Net present value (NPV)** is a method for incorporating the different values of cash flows over time into investment decisions.
- The best service system structure depends on the service package, customer contact intensity, and organization strategy.

KEY TERMS

automation **342**
bar coding **347**
base **343**
batch (disconnected) flow processes **331**
cellular process **335**
computer-aided design/computer-assisted manufacturing (CAD/CAM) **344**
computer-integrated manufacturing (CIM) **346**
computer-numerically controlled (CNC) machines (computed-controlled machines) **342**
continuous flow process **329**
crossover analysis **352**
crossover points **352**
customer contact intensity **358**
electronic data interchange (EDI) **347**
facilities-based services **357**
field-based services **357**
flexible manufacturing systems (FMS) **344**
flow process **328**
FMS module **345**
gripper **343**

group technology (GT) **341**
job-shop process **333**
machining centers **343**
made to order **328**
made to stock **328**
manipulator (arm) **343**
net present value (NPV) **355**
numerically controlled (NC) machines **342**
optical scanner **346**
present value analysis **355**
product-process matrix **350**
project process **340**
repetitive (discrete) flow processes **330**
robots **343**
service-process matrix **359**
universal product code (UPC) **346**
work cells **335**
work stations **329**

SOLVED PROBLEMS

Problem 1. Suppose a company must select one of three alternative production methods. The annual cost functions for the three methods are as follows:

Process A: \$2,000,000 + 24 Q
Process B: \$3,200,000 + 20 Q
Process C: \$5,000,000 + 15 Q

Over what range of annual production levels would process A be least costly? Process B? Process C?

Solution Figure 7.12 contains the graphs of the three cost functions. To find the crossover point for processes A and B, we set their cost functions equal and solve for production volume:

$$\$2{,}000{,}000 + \$24\ Q = \$3{,}200{,}000 + \$20\ Q \rightarrow \$4\ Q = \$1{,}200{,}000 \rightarrow Q = 300{,}000$$

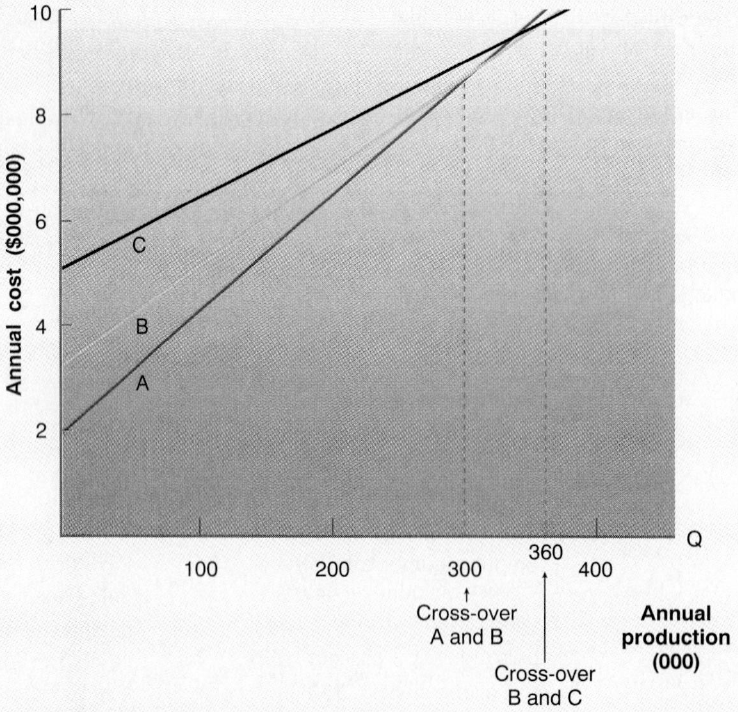

FIGURE 7.12 Cost functions for solved problem 1.

The crossover between B and C is given by

$$\$3{,}200{,}000 + \$20\ Q = \$5{,}000{,}000 + \$15\ Q \rightarrow \$5\ Q = \$1{,}800{,}000 \rightarrow Q = 360{,}000$$

So process A is least costly for a volume of less than 300,000 units per year; B is least costly for volumes between 300,000 and 360,000 per year; and C is least costly for volumes greater than 360,000 per year.

Problem 2. Suppose a new robotic assembly system will cost $4,000,000 initially but will reduce costs and increase quality enough to produce net benefits of $2,000,000, $1,800,000, $1,500,000, and $1,000,000 during the following four years. Using a discount rate of $r = 0.15$, compute the net present value of the investment.

Solution The net present value will be

$$\begin{aligned} NPV &= -\$4{,}000{,}000 + (1.15)^{-1}(\$2{,}000{,}000) + (1.15)^{-2}(\$1{,}800{,}000) + (1.15)^{-3}(\$1{,}500{,}000) + \\ &\quad (1.15)^{-4}(\$1{,}000{,}000) \\ &= -\$4{,}000{,}000 + \$4{,}660{,}000 = +\ \$\ 660{,}000 \end{aligned}$$

So it is worthwhile to invest in the robotic system.

DISCUSSION AND REVIEW QUESTIONS

1. Define a flow process. When would an organization find a flow process structure most appropriate for its production?
2. What are the primary advantages and disadvantages of continuous and repetitive flow processes?
3. Define a job-shop process. When would an organization find a job-shop structure most appropriate for its production?
4. What are the primary advantages and disadvantages of a job-shop process?
5. What is the difference between a batch flow system and a job shop?
6. Define a cellular process. Under what conditions would it be reasonable for an organization to convert from a job-shop production system to a cellular system?
7. What are the primary advantages and disadvantages of a cellular production system?
8. What are the two main differences between a batch flow system and a repetitive flow system?
9. What is a project production process, and when should it be used?
10. Name one product, not mentioned in the chapter, that is commonly made using each of the following: (a) a continuous flow process, (b) a repetitive flow process, (c) a batch flow process, (d) a job-shop process, and (e) a project process.
11. Name a company or industry that usually makes its products using a job-shop process but would probably benefit from using a cellular process instead. Explain why.
12. Give an example of a service that is often provided using a flow process.
13. Give an example of a service that is often provided using a job-shop process.
14. Give an example of a service that is often provided using a cellular process.
15. Explain how converting a job-shop process into a cellular process could reduce throughput time and average in-process inventory.
16. What is meant by group technology? How can it be used to improve the design and operation of a production process?
17. What makes a robot different from other forms of machine automation, such as a numerically controlled drill press?
18. What features of a flexible manufacturing system make it flexible?
19. Give an example of how automation in a service delivery system has affected you personally.
20. What is the purpose of the product-process matrix? How can it help in making process selection decisions?
21. Why should companies not make technology selection decisions based only on a present value analysis? How can a present value analysis be made more useful in technology selection decisions?

22. What factors are especially important in the design of a service production system? How do they affect the design?

23. Give an example of a service where some of the production can be separated from the customer to improve efficiency.

PROBLEMS

1. Acme manufacturing has been producing and selling a product for eight years. The sales data for the past eight years are given below. Acme expects sales to continue their historical growth for several years.

Year	Sales (000)
1	42
2	48
3	52
4	57
5	60
6	68
7	75
8	80

The plant in which Acme is currently producing the product is going to be closed because of its outmoded methods. A new plant is to be constructed this year. The company is considering two different production processes: A and B. Using process A, Acme estimates that its annual costs will be $300,000 plus $5 per unit produced. Using process B, Acme estimates that the cost will be $500,000 plus $3 per unit. (a) Compute the crossover point and identify the range of output levels over which each process has the lowest cost. (b) Assuming that both processes would have a capacity of 120,000 units per year, which process should Acme use? Explain.

2. A company that manufactures hand shovels for gardening is considering three possible production processes. Process A is highly automated, process B uses a moderate amount of automation, and process C is primarily manual. The company has estimated the annual cost functions for each process as follows:

For A: annual cost = $200,000 + $ 5.50 Q
For B: annual cost = $120,000 + $ 6.75 Q
For C: annual cost = $ 50,000 + $ 8.25 Q

where Q is the annual number of hand shovels produced. (a) Graph the three cost functions. (b) Compute the two crossover points and show over what production levels each process would be least expensive.

3. The University of Missouri is considering a new domestic long-distance phone contract. The university has received bids from three companies. The annual cost for each will be a combination of a fixed monthly fee plus a per minute charge for calls, regardless of the destination, as follows:

Contract	Fixed Fee	Per Minute Charge
1	$2500	$0.12
2	$3200	$0.10
3	$6500	$0.06

(a) Compute the crossover points and identify over what range of minutes per month each contract is least expensive. (b) If the university expects to use 40,000–50,000 minutes per month of calls, which option is best?

4.* Arborcraft, Inc. (AI), makes a modest variety of wood furniture. AI currently makes five types of desks, designated A–E, in an old facility. The historical sales for AI over the past seven years are as follows:

Year	Sales of Desk by Product Type					Total
	A	B	C	D	E	
1	1200	1150	900	—	—	3250
2	1250	1200	1000	—	250	3700
3	1300	1350	1150	—	400	4200
4	1300	1400	1250	—	550	4500
5	1250	1400	1300	200	700	4850
6	1200	1350	1350	400	850	5150
7	1150	1250	1400	650	900	5350

AI is constructing a new facility for making desks and must choose between two production processes. The first process is highly automated and uses specialized equipment. The fixed annual cost of this process (for equipment, supervision, etc.) will be $2,500,000. The variable cost (for materials, labor, etc.) will be $200 per desk. There are 6000 hours available on the production "line" each year, and it takes approximately 30 minutes to produce a desk. Product changeovers, however, will be very time-consuming; each changeover will require 100 hours of time (during which no production can occur). Consequently, AI plans to make only four runs of each product each year (i.e., run 25% of the annual demand for A, then for B, C, D, and E; then repeat this cycle). This would keep the number of changeovers down to 20 per year (4 per year for five products).

The second process is less automated, containing both cellular and job-shop components and using more general-purpose tools and equipment. This process requires more direct labor and produces only one desk every 40 minutes, but it is much easier to change over from one product to another, requiring only 10 hours of setup time. This process would also have 6000 hours of time available. The annual fixed cost will be $1,300,000, and the variable cost per desk will be $360. (a) For each process compute the maximum annual output of desks (capacity), assuming four runs of each product per year. (b) For each process, write the equation that expresses total annual cost as a function of annual output. (c) Al considers the recent slowdown in sales to be temporary and believes that during the next five years the historical pattern will return: sales of mature desk types will plateau or decrease, new desk types will be added every two or three years, and in total, sales should grow at the rate of about 300–400 per year. If these assumptions are correct, *based purely upon cost,* which process should Al use? Explain why. (d) What factors other than cost should be considered in the decision and why? Would these change or strengthen your selection in (c)?

5. Tartan Corporation is considering the purchase of a new photocopier. The copier would cost $26,000, but it would reduce copying costs by $8000 per year during the next five years, which is the estimated life of the copier. Compute the net present value of this investment using a discount rate of 12%. Should Tartan buy the copier?

6. Sympac Corporation is considering a major renovation of its metal-working department. It would cost $4,000,000 immediately and another $2,000,000 in two years. However, Sympac estimates the following annual benefits from cost savings and revenue enhancements (investment costs are listed separately to show the relative timing of payments and benefits):

Year	Investment	Benefits
0	$4,000,000	0
1	0	$1,600,000
2	$2,000,000	$1,400,000
3	0	$1,400,000
4	0	$1,300,000
5	0	$1,200,000
6	0	$1,200,000

Compute the net present value of the renovation project using a discount rate of 10%. Should Sympac undertake the renovation? Explain.

7.* Mastodon Corporation is evaluating whether to purchase a flexible manufacturing system. The following table compares the net revenue (sales minus variable costs) during the next five years if it buys the FMS versus keeping the current system.

	Net Annual Revenues	
Year	With FMS	With Current System
0	$18,000,000	$18,000,000
1	$19,500,000	$17,000,000
2	$20,000,000	$17,000,000
3	$20,500,000	$17,000,000
4	$20,500,000	$17,000,000
5	$20,000,000	$17,000,000

If it will cost $7,500,000 in year zero to buy and install the FMS, compute the net present value of the investment using a discount rate of 15%. Should Mastodon buy the FMS?

8. Construct a product-process matrix and locate the production processes of the following companies on it: (a) Domino's Pizza, (b) Burger King Restaurant, (c) Denny's Restaurant, (d) a five-star (very high quality sit-down) restaurant.

CASE

Southwest Airlines: A Process Structure and Technology Case

Southwest Airlines was the seventh largest passenger airline in the United States in 1993, and one of the few airlines that has remained profitable and has even grown in recent years. Its success is based on providing a very limited product and using a simple, focused strategy emphasizing high quality and low price. Southwest is not as well known as other airlines because it does not serve the entire United States and has no international routes. It flies primarily short- to intermediate-range routes, usually 250–750 miles, and provides only one class of service, coach. (Passengers can travel between almost any two cities served by Southwest using two flights.) In contrast to its major competitors, Southwest has also not ventured into other areas of travel and leisure, such as operating hotel or auto rental divisions.

All of Southwest's operational subsystems are designed to support its order-winning dimensions of price and service quality, as defined by the availability of flights, on-time performance, and a minimum of service failures, such as lost baggage and general service complaints. This narrow product focus has made it possible for Southwest to construct its overall service process as a collection of simple, usually low-tech subsystems that use standardized materials and procedures. Let us see how each subsystem works.

Southwest Airlines has simplified its check-in and boarding procedures by having only one class of service, first-come, first-served seating, and reusable boarding passes.

1. ***Ticketing.*** With only one class of service, no reserved seating, and a simple pricing scheme, reservation agents require less training and can process ticket reservations more quickly than other airline agents. The fare structure is so simple that tickets are sold through vending machines at some airports.
2. ***Check-in and Boarding.*** There is no reserved seating on Southwest's planes; it is first-come, first-served at the airport gate. This avoids the time-consuming problems of passengers not getting the seats they reserved. Passengers know the rules and adjust their expectations; if they want a good seat, they get to the gate early. With this policy, Southwest saves the time and expense of tracking and issuing personalized boarding passes; it uses reusable plastic ones instead.
3. ***In-Flight Operations.*** One of the most important features of Southwest's production system is that it uses only one type of aircraft, the Boeing 737. This plane was designed specifically for efficient short-distance flights. Pilots, flight attendants, and mechanics have to be trained, parts stocked, and service equipment and job procedures designed for only one type of plane.

   Because almost all flights are one to two hours long, there is no need for hot foods or for any food even resembling a meal. Only peanuts and beverages are served on most flights, with cookies added for longer ones. Not only does this eliminate the material expense of full meals, but storage and food preparation space is eliminated. Further, flight attendants do not have to spend time preparing food, so fewer attendants (only those required for safety) are needed.

   There are several operational benefits of having only one class of service: (1) more seats can be put on each plane; (2) the cost and complexity of the amenities expected in first-class seats, such as a separate set of foods and magazines, can be eliminated; (3) training and job requirements of flight attendants are reduced; and (4) fewer flight attendants are required.

   With reduced responsibilities, the flight attendants often have free time to do some of the goofy things that have become a Southwest trademark. They will frequently sing songs and tell jokes to entertain passengers, especially if the flight is late.

4. ***Flight Turnaround.*** Southwest is known for having the fastest turnaround of flights in the industry (turnaround time is the interval between the time a plane

arrives at a destination and the time it is ready to leave on the next flight). By turning around planes in 20 minutes or less (compared with 45 minutes or more for many competitors), Southwest is able to fly more flights per day per airplane, utilize its planes better, and spread its fixed costs over more passengers. In addition, with its rapid turnaround, Southwest can offer more flights each day, which provides better customer convenience. For example, two planes assigned to a pair of cities can provide 10 or more flights per day rather than the 6–8 of competitors.

The fast turnaround is due to several factors. (1) Because no meals are served on flights, little food must be brought on board and little garbage has to be removed. Interior clean-up is also minimal. (2) Baggage handling is relatively light because a large proportion of business commuters carry their own baggage onto the plane. (3) Refueling is fast because of the shortness of the flights (little fuel is consumed) and the standardization of the aircraft. (4) All the employees in the turnaround process follow well-designed, standardized procedures, minimizing errors. They work concurrently, and responsibilities are assigned so that all workers need approximately the same amount of time to complete their tasks. Yet employees can help with other jobs when necessary to stay on schedule; it is not uncommon for pilots to vacuum the floors.

5. ***Maintenance.*** By using only one type of aircraft, Southwest is able to keep its maintenance costs low. Mechanics need to know only one type of aircraft (although there are different versions of it), fewer parts have to be kept in inventory, and substantial learning occurs in working with only one aircraft.

Other aspects of Southwest's operations support its overall strategy. Two of the more important ones are its scheduling and route configuration and its airport selection. In the gate operations of most airlines, gates are often under-utilized, either because there is no plane at the gate or because a plane is waiting for turnaround to begin or passengers to board. In contrast, Southwest has the highest utilization rate of gates in the industry. This is due not only to the fast turnaround of planes, but also to the design of their flight schedule and operations at each airport. Although each city is different, Southwest typically has two gates at an airport and serves four to six cities. Flights between that airport and each city are scheduled every hour or every other hour. The arrivals and departures, however, are staggered every 20–30 minutes so that turnaround crews can move from plane to plane as they arrive. At each gate, a plane is scheduled to arrive from a city at, say 8:30 and then return to that city at 9:00. This approach keeps the turnaround crews and the gates almost fully utilized without delaying flights. The system must be working, as Southwest consistently ranks at the top of the industry in on-time performance and fewest customer complaints.

The use of secondary airports has been part of Southwest's strategy for a long time. By using airports such as Love Field in Dallas, Midway Airport in Chicago, and airports in Oakland and Burbank, California, Southwest pays lower landing fees, encounters less congestion, and in many cases is closer to the center of the city than by using the primary airports such as O'Hare.

The central themes in Southwest's service system design are keeping the product mix narrow, focusing on price and service quality, and keeping the system as simple and standardized as possible. What is especially interesting is that some basic design decisions, such as the choice of aircraft or having only one class of service, have beneficial effects in several areas.

QUESTIONS

1. Compare Southwest Airlines with other passenger airlines. What are the major differences between their operations?
2. Identify two specific operations methods used by Southwest Airlines that could easily be adopted by other airlines (without major investment).
3. Identify two specific operations methods used by Southwest Airlines that could be adopted by other service producers outside the airline industry. Describe the companies that could adopt them and how these methods would improve the companies.

SELECTED READINGS

GROOVER, MIKELL P. *Automation, Production Systems, and Computer-Aided Manufacturing*, Prentice-Hall, Englewood Cliffs, NJ, 1987.

HAMMER, MICHAEL and JAMES CHAMPY. *Reengineering the Corporation: A Manifesto for Business Revolution*, HarperBusiness, San Francisco, 1993.

HAYES, ROBERT H., and STEVEN C. WHEELWRIGHT. *Restoring Our Competitive Edge: Competing Through Manufacturing*, Wiley, New York, 1984.

KUSIAK, ANDREW. "Flexible Manufacturing Systems: A Structural Approach," *International Journal of Production Research*, Vol. 23, 1985, pp. 1057–1073.

MCMURRAY, SCOTT. "Chemical Firms Find That It Pays to Reduce Pollution at Source," *Wall Street Journal*, June 11, 1991.

MEHTA, STEPHANIE N. "Cell Manufacturing Gains Acceptance at Smaller Plants," *Wall Street Journal*, Sept. 15, 1994.

MEREDITH, JACK R. *The Management of Operations* (4th ed.), Wiley, 1992.

MILLER, KAREN LOWRY. "The Factory Guru Tinkering with Toyota," *Business Week*, May 17, 1993, pp. 95–97.

O'BRIEN, B. "Southwest Airlines Is a Rare Carrier: It Still Makes Money," *Wall Street Journal*, Oct. 26, 1992.

PARSAEI, H. R., and A. MITAL (eds.). *Economics of Advanced Manufacturing Systems*, Chapman and Hall, New York, 1992.

SAUNDERS, TEDD. *The Bottom Line of Green Is Black*, HarperCollins, San Francisco, 1993.

STEUDEL, HAROLD J., and PAUL DESRUELLE. *Manufacturing in the Nineties*, Van Nostrand Reinhold, New York, 1992.

ZAHRAN, I. N., A. S. ELMAGHRABY, and M. A . SHALABI. "Justification of Cellular Manufacturing Systems," in H. R. Parsaei, and A. Mital (eds.), *Economics of Advanced Manufacturing Systems*, Chapman and Hall, New York, 1992, pp. 73–90.

CHAPTER 8

PROCESS DESIGN AND FACILITY LAYOUT

8.1 GOING WITH THE FLOW IN PROCESS DESIGN AND LAYOUT
On the Job: Chuck Wise, U.S. Precision Lens

8.2 DESIGN OF REPETITIVE PROCESSES: LINE BALANCING AND PRODUCT LAYOUT
Decomposing the Process Into Tasks
Criteria for Evaluating Work Station Design
Cycle Time, Production Rate, and Efficiency
A Work Station–Minimizing Heuristic
Improving Line Design to Increase Balance and Output
Parallel Work Stations
Parallel Production Lines
Mixed Model Production
Continuous and Batch Flow Processes
Spatial Configuration
The Effects of Randomness on Line Design

8.3 DESIGN OF FUNCTIONAL LAYOUTS
Procedure for Designing Functional Layouts
Structured Analytical Layout Tools

8.4 DESIGN OF CELLULAR PROCESSES
Cell Composition and Type
Production Flow Analysis
Trade-offs and Considerations in the Detailed Design
Spatial Configuration
In Good Company: Hybrids Bloom at Sony Corporation

8.5 DESIGN OF SERVICE SYSTEMS
The Process Flow Diagram and the Process Chart
The Service Blueprint

8.6 LAYOUT OF SOME SERVICE FACILITIES
Warehouse and Storage Layout
Retail Facilities Layout

Pesti-Chemical: A Process Design and Capacity Expansion Case

8.1 Going with the Flow in Process Design and Layout

Once a general production structure and technology have been selected, we need to design and allocate work among work stations, work cells, and functional work centers, and the process normally must be implemented within some physical facility. The detailed process design and the spatial layout of the facility and activities substantially influence the efficiency of the production process. For example, the number of windows a drive-through restaurant has, the way they are configured, and the assignment of tasks among the workers at the windows will affect the speed and efficiency of service. Process design should be an ongoing process that applies to production subsystems (accounting department or paint shop), as well as to the system as a whole. Chuck Wise, the focus of this chapter's "On the Job" feature, has put this philosophy into practice by redesigning his company's financial operations so that each process includes only essential, value-added steps. This chapter presents methods for designing and configuring flow, job-shop, and cellular processes, as well as some common service processes.

The production of most goods and services requires several, possibly thousands, of distinct tasks to be performed by humans or machines. Even for a given production structure such as a repetitive flow process, the number of possible ways to allocate tasks among work stations can be enormous. The best design, in terms of number of work stations, number and types of work cells, level of staffing, and distribution of work will depend on many factors, including the desired output rate, the similarity of products, the decomposability or lumpiness of tasks (how long it takes to perform the production tasks), and the similarity or dissimilarity of tasks. One purpose of this chapter is to present methods that help in the *design and allocation of work* for flow processes and cellular processes.

On the Job

Chuck Wise, U.S. Precision Lens

Chuck Wise is Vice-President and Chief Financial Officer at U.S. Precision Lens, Inc., a subsidiary of Corning, Inc., that manufactures lens assemblies for projection televisions. Although Chuck's educational background and his primary job responsibilities are in accounting and finance, he believes a good understanding of work processes and flows is important for doing his job well. For example, to assign production costs to products properly, his staff must understand the processes used to manufacture the products and the costs of each process. More important, Chuck has found that his knowledge of operations helps him communicate with colleagues throughout a strongly engineering-based organization: "The more each side can understand about areas outside their discipline, the better the communication process."

Chuck has put his knowledge of operations management into practice in his own units. Chapter 1 described how Chuck used quality management and process analysis methods to simplify the preparation of Corning's federal tax returns when he was head of its tax unit. He uses the same methods in his current position to redesign his unit's processes to include only essential, value-added steps: "Process redesign is appropriate whether you are dealing with the payroll process that results in paychecks, the accounts payable process wherein vendors get paid, or the overall accounting process wherein you close your books every month."

Because work is divided among separate work stations, cells, or departments, the spatial configuration of the activities will influence the amount, time, and cost of material handling and transport, as well as the ease of movement by personnel and customers. An inefficient layout of activities not only increases direct material handling and storage costs but can also disrupt the flow of materials and personnel, which slows the production process. Therefore, the second purpose of this chapter is to provide methods and principles to help lay out (configure) activities to minimize material handling and facilitate the smooth flow of materials and people. This is especially important for job-shop processes, which must accommodate considerable flexibility in material and personnel movements.

Facility layout plays an important role in most service operations. Operations with high customer contact must be designed to direct and control the movement of customers in the best manner. The criterion for defining "best" may vary from system to system. In one case, the goal may be to serve customers as quickly as possible, such as in a bank or government office. In another case, the goal may be to expose customers to as many products and create as many purchase signals or opportunities as possible without annoying them, such as in a department store.

This chapter first discusses the detailed design of repetitive flow processes, which focuses on balancing the assignment of work at the work stations. The applicability of repetitive flow principles to continuous and disconnected flow processes is briefly explained as well. Section 8.3 then discusses methods for constructing functional layouts, whereby work is divided into work centers or departments. This is the typical configuration for job shops, but it also applies to cellular systems. In addition, for larger systems, this arrangement may include any combination of subsystems, such as a factory containing a mix of flow, cellular, and job-shop processes within the same facility. Section 8.4 considers methods for designing cellular processes and provides suggestions for arranging cells spatially. Methods for designing (redesigning) service processes are presented in Section 8.5, and factors in the layout of two types of service facilities, warehouses and retail stores, are presented in Section 8.6.

8.2 DESIGN OF REPETITIVE PROCESSES: LINE BALANCING AND PRODUCT LAYOUT

For repetitive flow processes, such as Honda's engine assembly line in Anna, Ohio, tasks are distributed among work stations so engines move from work station to work station in a synchronized manner.

Companies normally use a repetitive flow process when the production of all products requires the same tasks to be performed in the same sequence. As a result, the system can be physically designed so that the tasks are performed at work stations arranged in sequential order according to the flow of the product. This spatial arrangement is called a **product layout** because the physical layout of work stations is based on the sequence of tasks required to make the products. If the workload can be evenly distributed among the work stations, there are several advantages to this process design: (1) products can flow from one work station to the next without in-process inventories, (2) material handling can be unidirectional and specialized, and (3) specialization of equipment and labor can be exploited by assigning a narrow range of compatible tasks to each work station. Repetitive processes work well, however, only if the processing tasks are assigned to work stations appropriately. The two major design decisions are (1) how many work stations to have and (2) what tasks to assign to each one. To make these decisions, we must first decompose the production process into individual tasks that can be assigned to work stations.

DECOMPOSING THE PROCESS INTO TASKS

In designing a repetitive flow process (a production line), we start by decomposing the process into elemental tasks, each of which represents a separate unit of work. That is, a task does not *have* to be performed with another task at any work station (although efficiencies are certainly possible by combining similar tasks).

For each task, it is necessary to estimate how long it would take to perform it. This estimate may be based on experimentation or established work standards (work standards are discussed in Chapter 10). Clearly, these times depend on several factors: the number of people working at the work station, their skill and motivation, and their supporting equipment and resources. The **task times** used in the subsequent analysis assume the use of average workers using reasonable support equipment. Later, we will see how deviations from these averages can be utilized to improve the production process design.

Along with time estimates, the designer must determine the precedence requirements for each task. Although all the products require essentially the same processing in the same sequence, at the design stage there is often some flexibility in the exact sequencing of tasks. For example, when assembling an automobile, it may be possible to attach the front doors before the back doors or vice versa. The **precedence requirements** specify which task must be completed before another task can be started. As a group, precedence requirements describe which tasks must be done sequentially and which could be done concurrently.

CRITERIA FOR EVALUATING WORK STATION DESIGN

Once the task information is available, we can determine how many work stations to have and which tasks to perform at each one. The procedure for creating work stations and assigning tasks to them is called **line balancing**. It is so called because a repetitive process is viewed as a line of work stations, and efficiency is maximized by balancing the workload among them. The line-balancing problem is often expressed in one of two possible forms:

1. Determine the minimum number of work stations needed and allocate tasks to them to produce at least some target rate of output.
2. For a given number of work stations, allocate the tasks to maximize the output rate.

In practice, the line design process usually involves solving these two problems sequentially. First, we try to find the minimum number of work stations, and the associated assignment of tasks, that produce at least the minimum target production rate. Then the design is refined to maximize output for that number of work stations. On the surface, it might appear that these should be simple optimization problems (such as those discussed in Tutorial 1), but for actual problems they are often computationally intractable because of the lumpiness of the task times (the tasks cannot be divided into arbitrarily small units), and the set of constraints needed to represent the precedence relationships is large and not well structured. As a result, it is common to use construction heuristics to obtain preliminary line designs and work station assignments. **Construction heuristics** are iterative rules of thumb that construct (rather than improve) solutions for problems. (See Tutorial 1 for a discussion of heuristics.) The heuristics are usually tested empirically to verify that they produce good solutions, but they are not guaranteed to produce optimal solutions. Once these heuristics have been applied to produce a preliminary design, additional types of analysis are used to refine and improve it.

The heuristics used to design repetitive processes implicitly attempt to maximize system efficiency while explicitly ensuring that at least the target rate of output is produced. To use and understand the heuristics, we must first define measures of performance.

CYCLE TIME, PRODUCTION RATE, AND EFFICIENCY

A fundamental principle of multistage production lines is that the output rate of the line is determined by the slowest work station. Consider the three-work-station production line in Figure 8.1. Each unit of product requires 10 minutes of work at work station 1, 15 minutes at work station 2, and 5 minutes at work station 3. The time between production of successive units of the product (ignoring startup effects) is called the **production cycle time** and will be designated c.[1] When there is no variation in task times, the production cycle time is equal to the longest time the product must spend at any work station. This implies that the

production rate $P = 1/c$.

In Figure 8.1 the cycle time $c = 15$ minutes per unit, and the production rate is $P = 1/(15 \text{ minutes per unit}) = 1/15$ unit per minute or 4 units per hour. Work station 2, which requires the most time, is the limiting work station or bottleneck. The **bottleneck work station** controls the speed of production.

During each 15-minute production cycle, work station 1 is busy for 10 minutes and idle for 5 minutes; work station 3 is busy for 5 minutes and idle for 10 minutes; and work station 2 is busy for 15 minutes and never idle. So, during each 15-minute production cycle, 45 minutes of work time are available at the three work stations combined (three work stations × 15 minutes of cycle time), of which 30 minutes (66.7% of the total) are utilized. The **efficiency** or **% balance** of a line is the percentage of available work station time that is used productively. In general, this can be computed by

$$\text{efficiency (\% balance) of the line} = 100\% \times [T/(N \times c)]$$

where T is the total amount of work time required to make a unit of product (at all work stations) and N is the number of work stations on the production line.

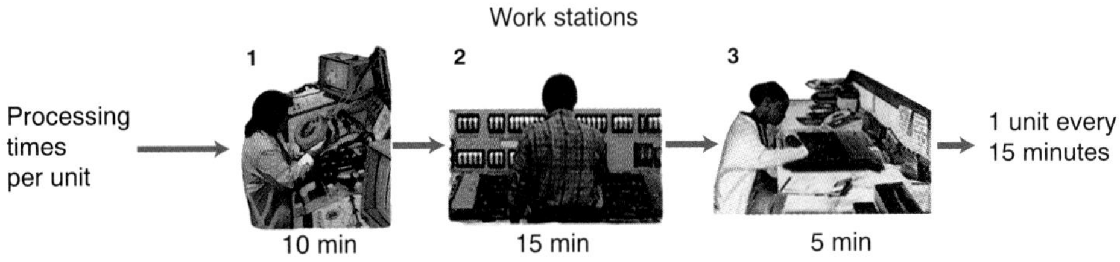

FIGURE 8.1 Unbalanced production line.

[1]In most other contexts, the term *cycle time* refers to the interval between the time an order is received or processing begins and the time the product is shipped. However, in line balancing the term *cycle time* has been assigned this different meaning, and we have retained that usage here.

If the process has a balance of 66.7%, as in Figure 8.1, 33.3% of the available production resources are being wasted due to an unbalanced assignment of work among the work stations. Ideally, we would like 100% balance, which would mean that every work station has exactly the same amount of work time assigned to it. Imbalance in a line design is a serious problem, not only because resources are wasted, but also because the imbalance in the workloads across workers is even more severe. The workers at work station 3 in Figure 8.1 are working only 33% of the time, whereas those at work station 2 are busy 100% of the time.

A WORK STATION–MINIMIZING HEURISTIC

Once the production process has been decomposed into tasks and the estimated task times and precedence relationships have been determined, the next step is to assign tasks to individual work stations. Various heuristics have been devised to help in this process. We will illustrate one of these heuristics using the following example.

EXAMPLE 1

Robert Mikano is the production engineer for Titan Electronic Corp. (TEC). Mikano must design a repetitive production line for assembling computers. Assembly of each computer requires 14 tasks, which are listed in Table 8.1, along with estimated task times and the tasks (called **predecessors**) that must be completed before each task is begun.

TEC wants the assembly line to produce at least 300 computers per day and expects the line to be operating 420 minutes each day. This means that TEC must produce one computer every 84 seconds [(25,200 seconds available each day)/(300 computers to assemble each day)]. Therefore, no more than 84 seconds of work can be assigned to any work station; otherwise, fewer than 300 computers will be produced in a normal work day. In other words, the **maximum cycle time** is 84 seconds. In general,

$$\text{maximum cycle time} = c_{max} = 1/(\text{minimum desired production rate})$$

TABLE 8.1 TASK INFORMATION FOR TITAN ELECTRONICS CORPORATION

Task	Task Time (sec)	Predecessor Tasks
A—Install system chassis	55	—
B—Install internal speaker	30	A
C—Install power supply	50	A
D—Install fan	42	A
E—Install CPU in system board	20	—
F—Install RAM in system board	25	—
G—Install system board in case	45	A, E, F
H—Connect units to power supply	60	B, C, D, G
I—Install video card	36	H
J—Install drive bay chassis	42	H
K—Install options board	30	H
L—Install hard drive	40	J
M—Install floppy drive	36	J
N—Attach panels, cover, fasten	40	I, K, M, N
	Total time, $T = 551$	

In this example,

$$c_{max} = 1/(300 \text{ computers per day})$$
$$= (1/300) \text{ day per computer} = 84 \text{ seconds per computer}$$

A useful exercise is to determine the **theoretical minimum number of work stations** needed to achieve this output rate. If 551 seconds are required to assemble each computer and no work station can perform more than 84 seconds of work on any one computer, then the

$$\text{theoretical minimum number of work stations} = \lceil T/c_{max} \rceil$$
$$= \lceil 551/84 \rceil = \lceil 6.56 \rceil = 7$$

where $\lceil\ \rceil$ means round *up* any fractional value because fractional work stations are not possible. This theoretical minimum number of work stations is derived assuming 100% balance. The minimum number of work stations *actually* possible may be more than this, depending on the precedence relationships and the lumpiness of the task times.

The basic idea in constructing the production line is to assign as much work to each work station as possible without exceeding c_{max}. However, the lumpiness of the task times usually makes it impossible to achieve 100% efficiency.

A simple yet effective heuristic for constructing a repetitive process is the **ranked positional weight technique (RPWT)**. The heuristic is as follows:

1. Construct a diagram of the precedence relationships among the tasks. Arrows are used to show which tasks must precede others; this is done for TEC in Figure 8.2.
2. For each task, add up the task times for that task and *all* tasks that must *follow* it directly and indirectly. This value will be called the **positional weight** for the task. For example, the positional weight for task B is the sum of the task times for tasks

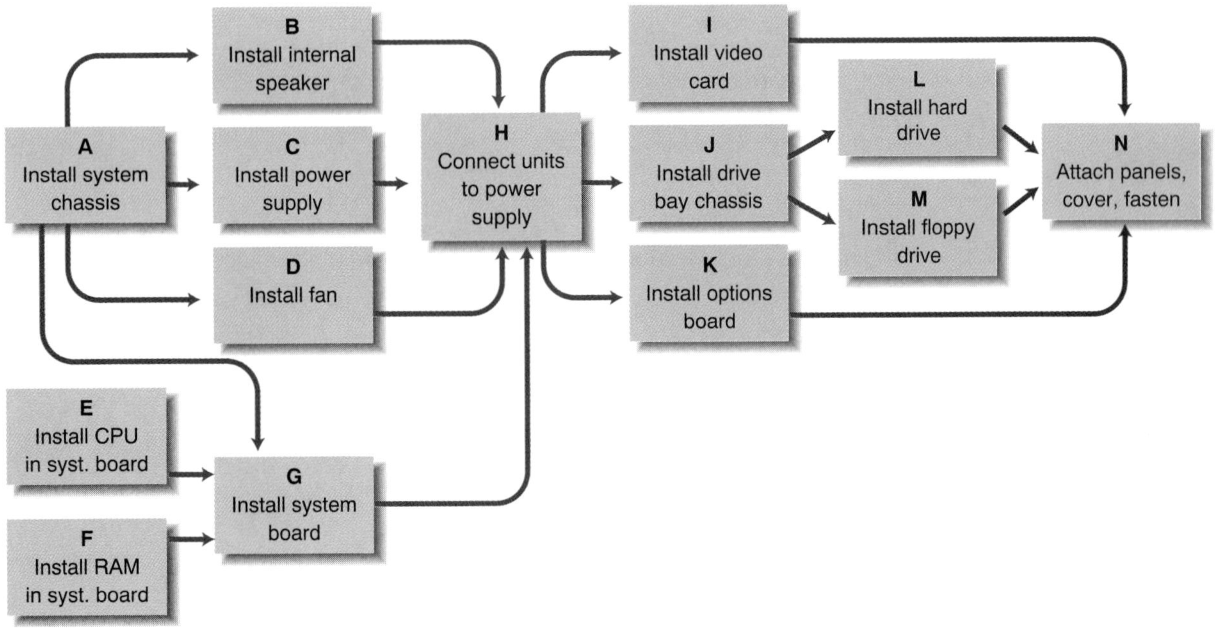

FIGURE 8.2 Precedence diagram for Titan Electronics Corporation.

TABLE 8.2 POSITIONAL WEIGHTS FOR TITAN ELECTRONICS CORPORATION

Task	Task Time (sec)	Positional Weight
A—Install system chassis	55	506
B—Install internal speaker	30	314
C—Install power supply	50	334
D—Install fan	42	326
E—Install CPU in system board	20	349
F—Install RAM in system board	25	354
G—Install system board in case	45	329
H—Connect units to power supply	60	284
I—Install video card	36	76
J—Install drive bay chassis	42	158
K—Install options board	30	70
L—Install hard drive	40	80
M—Install floppy drive	36	76
N—Attach panels, cover, fasten	40	40

B, H, I, J, K, L, M, and N, which is 314 seconds. The positional weights are listed in Table 8.2.

3. Select the task with the largest positional weight and assign it to the first work station.
4. Select the task with the next largest positional weight and assign it to the earliest possible work station that exists, subject to two restrictions:
   (a) the total (task) time assigned to the work station cannot exceed c_{max} and
   (b) all of the task's predecessors must be assigned to that work station or an earlier one. If the task does not satisfy these conditions for an existing work station, create a new work station and assign the task to it.[2]

The rationale for the RPWT is that the positional weight is a measure of the task's importance as a predecessor. Tasks with the largest positional weights have the most subsequent work and tasks depending on them. By assigning these tasks first, we enlarge more quickly the pool of tasks available for assignment to work stations (i.e., those for which all predecessors have been assigned to a work station). This makes it easier to find a task that fits within the limits of the existing work stations.

Applying this heuristic to TEC gives the following:

1. We select task A first because it has the largest positional weight, and we assign it to work station (WS) 1.
2. The next largest positional weight is for task F. It has no predecessors and there is sufficient time available on WS 1, so we assign it to WS 1.
3. The next largest positional weight is for task E. It has no predecessors but there is *not* sufficient time for it at WS 1, so we create a new work station and assign it to WS 2.

[2]In steps 3 and 4, if there is a tie for the next largest positional weight, the tie is broken by selecting the task with the longest task time.

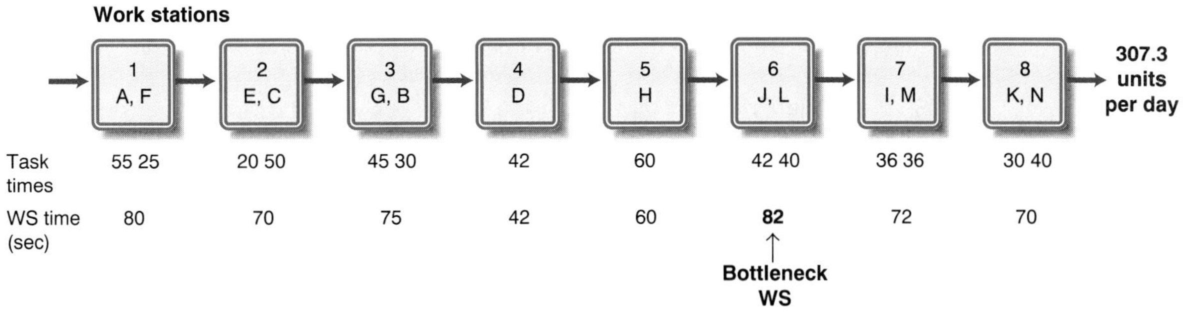

FIGURE 8.3 Production line for Titan Electronics Corporation using RPWT.

4. Continuing this process produces the following assignments in order:

C → WS 2
G → WS 3
D → WS 4
B → WS 3
H → WS 5
J → WS 6
L → WS 6
I → WS 7
M → WS 7
K → WS 8
N → WS 8

The resulting production line is given in Figure 8.3. (Notice that task B was assigned to WS 3 even though some tasks had already been assigned to WS 4. The heuristic always tries to put tasks at the earliest work station possible.)

The longest work station time is 82 seconds, so the *actual* cycle time c = 82 seconds. A computer will be made every 82 seconds, and the actual production rate will be $P = 1/c = 1/(82\text{ sec/unit}) = (1/82)$ unit per second = 307.3 units per day. This is larger than the target production rate because $c < c_{max}$.

The efficiency (% balance) of this line design is

$$\text{efficiency} = [551\text{ sec}/(8\text{ WSs} \times 82\text{ sec})] \times 100\% = 84.0\%$$

Not only is 16.0% of the work station capacity wasted, but the idleness is not evenly distributed: WS 6 is working 100% of the time, whereas the other work stations have 2.5%–48.8% idleness.

IMPROVING LINE DESIGN TO INCREASE BALANCE AND OUTPUT

The design in Figure 8.3 is just a starting point for the production line design. This design can be refined using two approaches: the first utilizes heuristic methods to reassign tasks to improve line balance, and the second uses personnel and technological enhancements. The objective of these refinements is to increase the output and balance of the initial design without increasing the number of work stations.

Improvement Heuristics

Improvement heuristics begin with an initial design, such as the one in Figure 8.3, and then transfer and/or switch tasks among the work stations to reduce the cycle time. The cycle time can be reduced only if the amount of work assigned to a *bottleneck* is reduced. So these heuristics may take a task at a bottleneck work station and transfer it to a non-bottleneck work station or switch it with a less time-consuming task at a nonbottleneck work station. As long as the transfer or switch does not violate the precedence relationships or increase the time of a work station above c, this change will maintain or reduce the cycle time and maintain or increase the output rate.

For example, the following set of switches can improve the design in Figure 8.3:

1. Switch tasks L and K between WS 6 and WS 8 (c drops to 80 seconds; WS 1 and WS 8 become the bottlenecks).
2. Switch tasks M and L between WS 7 and WS 8 (c remains at 80 seconds, but WS 8 is no longer a bottleneck).
3. Switch tasks F and E between WS 1 and WS 2 (c drops to 76; WS 7 and WS 8 become the bottlenecks).

The resulting production line, which is given in Figure 8.4, has a cycle time of 76 seconds and a production rate of 331.6 computers per day. This is 31.6 more than the target, and the efficiency is $[(551 \text{ sec/unit})/(8 \text{ WSs} \times 76 \text{ sec/WS})] \times 100\% = 90.6\%$.

Improvement of the original design is not guaranteed by these heuristics, but 5–10% improvements are not uncommon. Because of the possible improvement, it is not unreasonable to perform the initial heuristic design using a slightly lower target production rate than is really needed. If the design resulting from an improvement heuristic does not produce the target output level, the procedure can be repeated using the real target production rate in the initial heuristic.

Staffing, Job Design, and Technological Improvements

Heuristic methods are very effective at sifting through the potentially billions of alternative configurations and selecting one or a few that have relatively good balance. However, other refinements can be made to the design that heuristics cannot handle easily. This is where human insight, expertise, and experience can be utilized best. The task times used in the heuristics are estimates of average times, assuming a certain type of equipment and staffing at the work station. In addition, the heuristics assume that the task times are constant and independent of each other. In practice, these as-

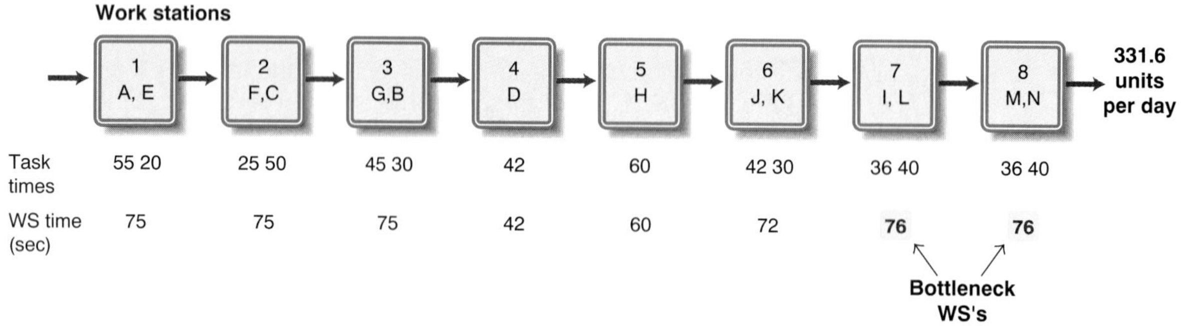

FIGURE 8.4 Revised production line design for Titan Electronics Corporation.

sumptions are rarely true: equipment and staffing are controllable and task times are sometimes affected by what other tasks are performed at the same work station. Rather than creating a problem, this fact presents opportunities for improving the line design.

1. ***Skill Variation.*** Consider the design in Figure 8.4. Based on *average* worker performance, WSs 1, 2, 3, 7, and 8 are working nonstop or almost nonstop, whereas WSs 4 and 5 have considerable idle time (WS 6 has only about 5% idle time). But not all workers are equally skilled, experienced, and quick at every task. This variation can, in fact, be beneficial. We can assign the fastest, most skilled workers to WSs 1, 2, 3, 7, and 8 and the slowest (e.g., newer workers) to WSs 4 and 5. The actual times at WSs 1, 2, 3, 7, and 8 might be reduced to 70–72 seconds, while the times at WSs 4 and 5 might increase to 60–70 seconds. Thus, the cycle time would decrease, output would increase, and there would be less idle time at nonbottleneck WSs.

   Of course, we do not want to punish good workers by putting them at the work stations with the most work and reward the slower workers by putting them at the easier work stations. Instead the job descriptions at the work stations would reflect different levels of required skills and expected output performance. Accordingly, the workers at the more difficult work stations would receive a higher wage than those at the easier work stations. These differentials could form a work ladder whereby new workers start at the easier stations at lower pay and work their way up to the harder, higher-paid work stations.

2. ***Staffing.*** A second way to improve line balance is to change the number of workers at a work station. For example, the original data on task times may have assumed there would be two workers at each work station. Beginning with the design in Figure 8.4, we might want to add additional workers to WSs 1, 2, 3, 7, and 8 (and possibly reduce the number of workers at the other work stations). For example, we may assign one helper to WSs 1–3 who would do simpler work, such as preparing materials for assembly, to free the other workers to do the harder work.

3. ***Support Equipment and Technology.*** The task times used in the initial line design are based on an assumed work station technology and support equipment. In the refinement phase it might be possible to modify the type, number, or speed of support equipment to modify the work station time. For example, better and faster equipment might be used at the bottleneck work stations, whereas slower (perhaps lower-cost) equipment might be substituted at those work stations that will have idle time.

4. ***Checking Task Compatibility.*** The task times were initially assumed to be independent of the other tasks performed at the same work station. In fact, some task times are interrelated. For example, if two tasks require the use of identical tools and equipment or require similar labor skills (such as tasks L and M in Example 1), doing these at the same work station might take less time than performing them at different work stations (and the cost of tools and equipment would be lower). Similarly, some tasks are incompatible and are better not done at the same work station. For example, one task may generate dust, while another requires very clean conditions, or one task might require intense use of arm muscles (lifting or pounding), while another might require intense eye concentration and excellent fine motor skills (threading wires in a small hole). In these cases, the tasks would take more time than average or could not be performed at all if they were assigned to the same work station.

PARALLEL WORK STATIONS

An alternative to having a line operation made up solely of sequential work stations is to have *identical* parallel work stations at *some points* along the line. This structure might be used for several reasons. First, suppose that in the TEC example the required production rate was 480 computers per day, so the maximum cycle time would be 52.5 seconds. Tasks A and H each require more than 52.5 seconds to perform, so there is no way a work station could be constructed to perform these tasks without violating the 52.5-second limit. However, the line design in Figure 8.5 would produce the required 480 computers per day. At stages 1, 3, 4, and 7 there are two identical work stations that would take turns assembling every other computer. This makes the *effective* stage (work station) time half the assigned time. In this example, the parallel work stations could be assigned up to 105 seconds of work and the line would still assemble 480 computers per day. The design in Figure 8.5 has an actual cycle time of 51 seconds. At stage 7, the bottleneck, each of two work stations is assigned 102 seconds of work. During any 102-second period stage 7 will process two computers, so the effective work station time is 51 seconds.

The parallel work stations at stages 1 and 4 were necessary to accommodate tasks A and H. But parallel work stations can also be used to obtain a better mix of tasks. For example, the parallel work stations at stages 3 and 7 were created to achieve better work station utilization (less idle time). This produces a more efficient design than having tasks D, G, I, K, and M at separate work stations, which would have required three extra stages in the production process and one extra work station.

A second reason for using parallel work stations is that more work can be assigned to a single work station, thereby providing greater task variety and job enrichment for workers. For example, in Figure 8.5 the workers at WSs 1a, 1b, 7a, and 7b can perform three tasks instead of one or two, which may make the job more interesting. As a practical matter, it is often best to design fully automated work stations so that they have only one or two tasks to perform, whereas work stations utilizing humans are often better if tasks are varied. Thus, parallel, multitask work stations staffed by humans may be arranged along with single-task, automated work stations.

A final consideration is that some components of a product form natural subassemblies or modules. For example, if in the TEC example several components had to be connected to the system board other than the central processing unit and random access memory, it may be advantageous to put these tasks together at one work station to reduce component handling, repositioning, changing of tools, or holding of compo-

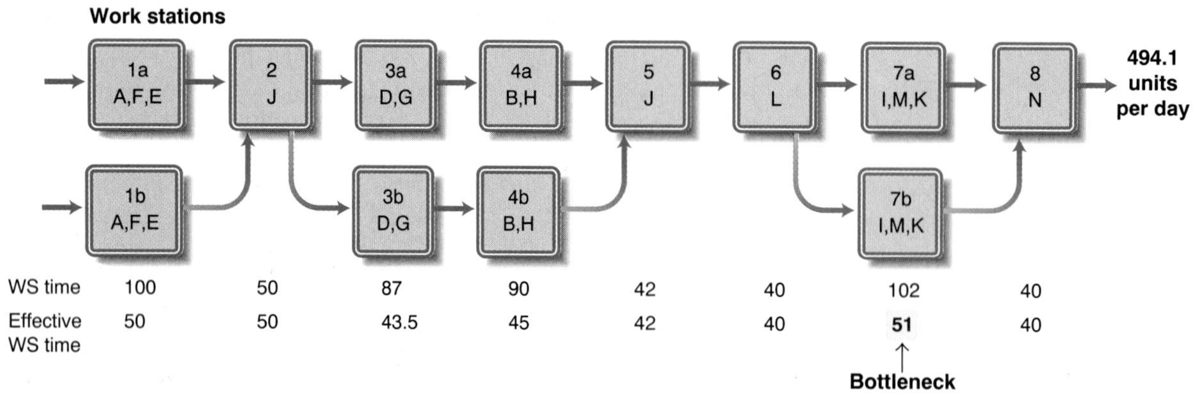

FIGURE 8.5 Production line for Titan Electronics Corporation using parallel work stations.

nents together. The work station might even be pulled off the main assembly line and located so as to feed its output into the main line at the appropriate stage.

PARALLEL PRODUCTION LINES

Especially for very large volume production, a key design issue is whether to have a single, long production line with brief work station times or to have several shorter, lower-volume production lines with longer work station times. Historically, the former approach was more common, but in recent years the latter has gained favor for four reasons.

1. **A Parallel Line System Is Less Vulnerable to Stoppages.** With a single line, any time one work station stops operating, whether due to a machine failure or a quality problem, the entire production system must stop. In contrast, with parallel lines, a stoppage on one line affects only that line.
2. **A Parallel Line System Is Often More Efficient and Flexible.** Most repetitive processes produce more than one product or version of a product. Although the products are similar, changeovers can reduce productivity, and increase the chances of quality problems. With parallel lines the number of versions produced on each line can be reduced, thereby increasing productivity, and the total variety of products that can be made is larger. For example, a single line might make six products, whereas a three-line system could have two of the lines each focus on three of these products and produce an additional three products with the third line.
3. **New Products Can Be Introduced and Existing Product Models Updated More Efficiently with Parallel Lines.** When a new product is introduced on a single line, the entire line often must be stopped. In the U.S. auto industry, historically this meant that production of that model stopped for two to three months. In contrast, parallel lines can be converted one by one, thereby maintaining some production during model changeovers or new product introductions.
4. **Production Jobs Can Be Made More Interesting and Work Teams Used More Effectively with Lower-Volume Parallel Lines.** With parallel lines, more tasks are as-

Parallel production lines allow greater flexibility. Different products can be made on each line at the same time, if desired, or one line can be kept operating while another is shut down for maintenance or product changeover.

signed to each work station than with a single line, so workers at each work station have a wider variety of tasks, which is often more interesting and less fatiguing. It is also easier to implement work teams, cross-training, and job rotation on a small production line than on one large line involving many more workers. (Chapter 10 discusses job design, task variety, work teams, and cross-training in detail.)

These reasons strongly suggest that companies with rapidly increasing sales should consider expanding production capacity by adding production lines rather than creating an entirely new, higher-capacity line. In addition to these benefits, by adding production capacity in smaller increments, it is easier to update production technology continuously without disrupting the existing production system. For companies with sales increasing too slowly to justify adding an entire line, adding parallel work stations at bottlenecks may be more cost effective.

MIXED MODEL PRODUCTION

Repetitive processes are designed assuming that all units produced by the system require approximately the same amount of work at any given work station, even if different products are made. In some cases this is not true, and the differences in processing times at a given work station can create serious disruptions. For example, although an assembly line may assemble only one general model of car (Chrysler Neon or Ford Taurus), the time it takes to install the transmission at a work station can differ by a factor of 2, depending on whether the transmission is automatic or standard. Because almost all the other assembly steps are the same for all models of the automobile, it is not cost effective to have separate production lines for automatic and standard transmission cars (or for cars with expanded versus standard audio packages). One solution is to use parallel work stations. When the product reaches a point where there is substantial difference in work times between models, there could be parallel work stations, one or more specializing in one assembly and the others in another assembly.

An alternative solution is to sequence consecutive products in a way that reduces the effects of these task time differences. For example, suppose assembly of a model of computers is identical for all computers, except that one-third of them require installation of a hard disk and two floppy disk drives, which takes 3 minutes at a disk drive installation work station, and two-thirds require only a hard drive and one floppy drive, which takes 2 minutes. The average time for the disk drive work station is 2.33 minutes per computer: (1/3)(3 min) + (2/3)(2 min). Suppose the production line is designed to have approximately 2.33 minutes of work assigned to each work station. Whenever a three-drive computer reaches the disk drive installation work station, it takes 3 minutes and delays the entire production line. If several three-drive computers were sequenced consecutively, the cycle time would be slowed to 3 minutes per computer, with every work station other than the drive installation one having 0.67 minute of idle time every cycle, as shown in Table 8.3a. When a series of two-drive computers were assembled, the line would then have a 2.33-minute cycle time, with 0.33-minute idleness at the drive installation work station during each cycle. The average cycle time would then be (1/3)(3 min) + (2/3)(2.33) = 2.55 minutes. However, if space were added in front of and following the drive installation work station to hold one computer in inventory, and the computers were sequenced to assemble one three-drive computer and then two two-drive computers, and so on, the cycle time would consistently average 2.33 minutes, as shown in Table 8.3b.

Controlling product sequencing is most effective in smoothing work station time variations when these occur only at one or two work stations. When product differences

TABLE 8.3 CYCLE TIMES IN MIXED MODEL ASSEMBLY OF COMPUTERS

(*a*)

Batches of Three-Drive, Then Two-Drive Computers

Computer	Work Station *k* −1			(Disk Drive Installation) Work Station *k*			Work Station *k* + 1			Cycle
Unit No./Type	Start	Finish	Idle	Start	Finish	Idle	Start	Finish	Idle	Time
1—3D	0	2.33	—	2.33	5.33	—	5.33	7.66	0.67	—
2—3D	2.33	4.66	0.67	5.33	8.33	—	8.33	10.66	0.67	3.00
3—3D	5.33	7.66	0.67	8.33	11.33	—	11.33	13.66	0.67	3.00
4—3D	8.33	10.66	0.67	11.33	14.33	—	14.33	16.66	0.67	3.00
·	·	·	·	·	·		·	·	·	·
·	·	·	·	·	·		·	·	·	·
·	·	·	·	·	·		·	·	·	·
20—3D	56.33	58.66	0.67	59.33	62.33	—	62.33	64.66	0.67	3.00
21—2D	59.33	61.66	0.67	62.33	64.33	0.33	64.66	66.99	—	2.33
22—2D	62.33	64.66	—	64.66	66.66	0.33	66.99	69.32	—	2.33
23—2D	64.66	66.99	—	66.99	68.99	0.33	69.32	71.65	—	2.33
24—2D	66.99	69.32	—	69.32	71.32	0.33	71.65	73.98	—	2.33
·	·	·	·	·	·		·	·	·	·
·	·	·	·	·	·		·	·	·	·
·	·	·	·	·	·		·	·	·	·

(*b*)

Products Sequenced: One Three-Drive, Then Two 2-Drive Computers

Computer	Work Station *k* −1			(Disk Drive Installation) Work Station *k*			Work Station *k* + 1		Cycle
Unit No./Type	Start	Finish	Inven	Start	Finish	Inven	Start	Finish	Time
1—3D	0	2.33	0	2.33	5.33	0	5.33	7.66	—
2—2D	2.33	4.66	1	5.33	7.33	1	7.66	9.99	2.33
3—2D	4.66	6.99	1	7.33	9.33	1	9.99	12.33*	2.34*
4—3D	6.99	9.33*	0	9.33	12.33	0	12.33	14.66	2.33
5—2D	9.33	11.66	1	12.33	14.33	1	14.66	16.99	2.33
6—2D	11.66	13.99	1	14.33	16.33	1	16.99	19.33*	2.34*
7—3D	13.99	16.33*	0	16.33	19.33	0	19.33	21.66	2.33
·	·	·	·	·	·	·	·	·	·
·	·	·	·	·	·	·	·	·	·
·	·	·	·	·	·	·	·	·	·

Work station *k* is the disk drive installation work station
2D = two-drive computer requiring 2 minutes at work station *k*
3D = three-drive computer requiring 3 minutes at work station *k*
All other work stations require 2.33 minutes

*Times are rounded up 0.01 minute to match adjacent stage times.

are so great that work station times vary at several work stations, sequencing alone cannot solve the problem.

CONTINUOUS AND BATCH FLOW PROCESSES

Line balancing most naturally applies to repetitive flow processes, but the same principles apply to continuous and batch flow processes. Processing stages in continuous flow processes are so tightly connected that it is essential for processing times to be the same at each production stage; otherwise, the product cannot flow continuously. In batch flow processing, the unit of production should be thought of as the production batch. The more consistent processing times are from batch to batch and from work station to work station, the more smoothly the process will operate and the less inter-stage inventories will be needed. In some cases, batch sizes may be intentionally modified to obtain more consistent processing times and smoother production flow.

SPATIAL CONFIGURATION

Repetitive (and continuous) flow processes historically have been arranged in a straight line because fixed-position material-handling systems such as conveyers, moving belts, and slides are easier to arrange in this manner—hence the common name **production line** or **line process**. Straight-line spatial configurations, such as the one in Figure 8.6a, have the added advantage that handling of support materials needed for the tasks at each work station is not obstructed and narrow aisles can be used.

In many cases, however, a U-shaped configuration, such as that in Figure 8.6b, is superior to a straight line for the following reasons:

1. Only one loading area is needed to receive raw materials and ship final output. Dock workers can be moved easily between loading outbound and inbound shipments.

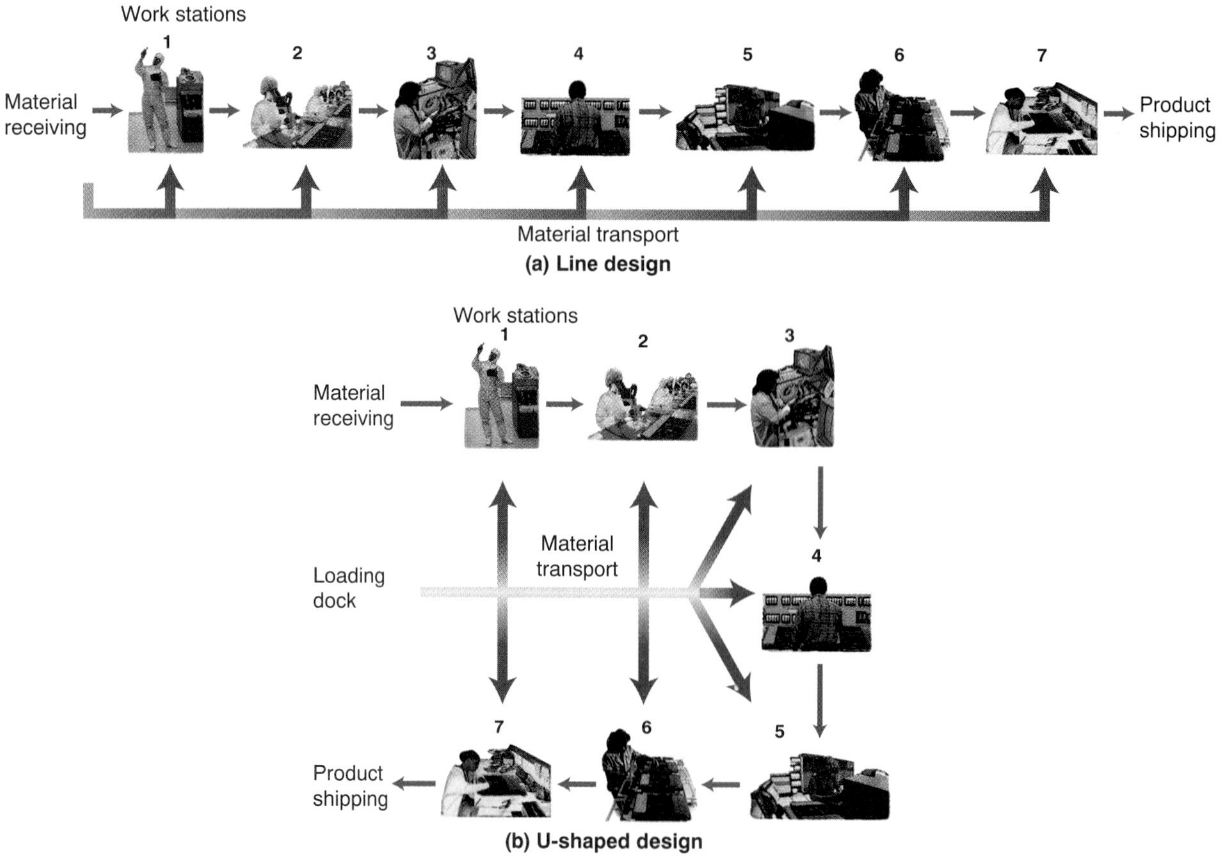

FIGURE 8.6 Spatial configurations of repetitive processes.

2. If materials have to be transported to work stations, such as to be attached to the main product moving along a conveyer system, the distance traveled by material-handling equipment is less with a U shape.
3. Auxiliary workers, such as those preparing materials for work stations, can assist more work stations more easily with the U-shaped design than with a line configuration.
4. A U-shaped configuration provides better visual control of the system because workers can see each other and see more of the process.
5. Less total floor space is needed, and the building shape can be squarer with a U shape. Square buildings are more space efficient than rectangular buildings and cost less to build.[3]

THE EFFECTS OF RANDOMNESS ON LINE DESIGN

The classical principles and heuristics of line balancing are based on the key assumption that at any given work station the same amount of time is required to perform the assigned tasks on every unit of product. In fact, there can be considerable variation in processing times from one unit of output to the next, and this variation can substantially impact the actual output rate.

This can be seen by comparing the two simple production lines in Figure 8.7. The three–work station process in Figure 8.7a was designed so that each work station has exactly three minutes of work assigned to it per unit of product, with no variation from unit to unit. This line, which has 100% balance, will produce 20 units of product each hour, and it requires no buffer inventories between work stations.

The process in Figure 8.7b also has three work stations, and each one has an *average* work time of three minutes, exactly like the process in Figure 8.7a. But the times can vary randomly from unit to unit (and from work station to work station), with a 0.5 probability that the time is two minutes and a 0.5 probability that it is four minutes. To be comparable with the nonrandom case, suppose we operated this line with no buffer in-

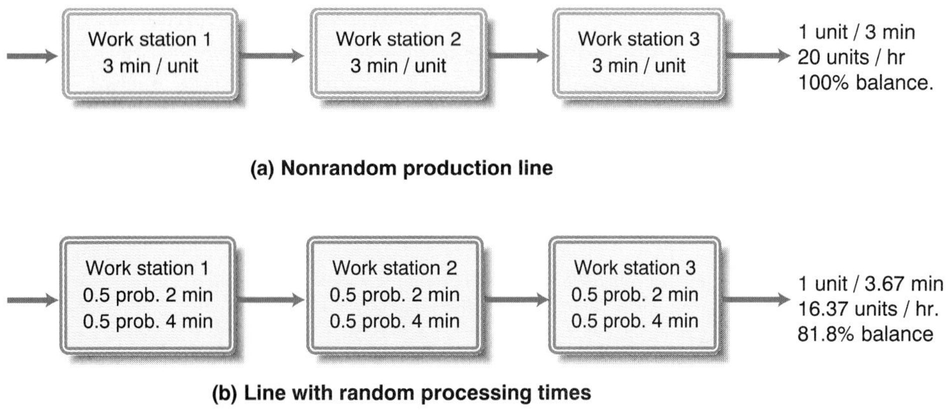

FIGURE 8.7 Effects of random variation on output rate.

[3]A standard engineering and mathematics problem is to find the four-sided shape that has the largest area for a given perimeter, or equivalently, to find the shape with the smallest perimeter for a fixed area. The answer is a square. Because construction costs are closely related to perimeter length, square buildings are normally less expensive to construct than rectangular ones.

TABLE 8.4 SIMULATED STARTING AND ENDING TIMES AT EACH WORK STATION

Time	Work Station 1	Work Station 2	Work Station 3
0–2	Process unit 1	Idle short	Idle short
2–4	Process unit 1	Idle short	Idle short
4–6	Process unit 2	Process unit 1	Idle short
6–8	Idle 2NR	Process unit 1	Idle short
8–10	Process unit 3	Process unit 2	Process unit 1
10–12	Process unit 4	Process unit 3	Process unit 2
12–14	Process unit 4	Idle short, 3NR	Process unit 2
14–16	Process unit 5	Process unit 4	Process unit 3
16–18	Idle 2NR	Process unit 4	Idle short
18–20	Process unit 6	Process unit 5	Process unit 4
20–22	Process unit 6	Process unit 5	Idle short

Notes:
Short = work station idle because there is no input material available.
2NR = work station idle because work station 2 is not ready for input.
3NR = work station idle because work station 3 is not ready for input.

ventories between work stations, so if station k is busy and station $k - 1$ finishes processing a unit, $k - 1$ must stop production until k is ready to accept the unit. Based on a computer simulation of this process, Table 8.4 shows how the process would operate during a typical period of time. (This simulation, including an explanation of how the random work station times are generated, is presented in detail in Tutorial 3.)

Table 8.4 shows that because of the random variations in work times work stations are periodically idle, either because there is no product available to process or because the succeeding work station is busy handling the previous unit and cannot accept the next one. Any idleness results in a loss of production capability that cannot be regained (except possibly by working overtime). This makes the *effective* production rate (the amount that actually can be produced) much less than the 20 units per hour we might expect based on the average work-station time of three minutes. Based on the simulation from which Table 8.4 was extracted, the effective production rate is only 16.37 units per hour (ignoring startup effects). Thus effective work station utilization is only 81.8%; the work stations are idle 18.2% of the time. This loss in capacity is due entirely to the randomness of the processing times.

Causes of Production Randomness

Many factors can cause task times to vary. The following are some of the more common reasons.

1. ***Variation in Materials.*** Even small variations in materials, such as the threading on a bolt or the amount of lubricant on a part, can cause variations in task times.
2. ***Human Variation.*** Because workers are human, fatigue, sneezes, and interruptions can all cause variation in work times.
3. ***Material Shortages.*** When a worker runs out of materials (such as when components are not delivered to the work station on time), the processing time will increase.
4. ***Defects.*** When components are defective, time is spent on corrective actions.
5. ***Mechanical Failures.*** When machines or tools break, considerable delay and variation affect processing times.

6. **Product Differences.** Especially in service systems, each unit of production (each customer) is at least slightly different and may require different task times. Manufacturing systems experience the same problem, though not always to the same degree.
7. **Lot-Size Differences.** In batch flow systems, differences in both product type and batch size can cause variation in processing time.

Design Implications

Some randomness is inherent in all production systems, but the key question is, how should this fact be incorporated into the design of flow processes? The following four suggestions can help designers to make flow processes more efficient and achieve higher effective capacity.

1. **Reduce Randomness.** In general, the more randomness that can be eliminated, the greater the productivity. Randomness can be greatly reduced by using more consistent and higher-quality materials and components, by designing jobs better to eliminate worker fatigue, and by using better preventive maintenance. In fact, reducing production randomness is at the heart of just-in-time and lean production, which are discussed in Chapter 15.
2. **Intentionally Unbalance the Process.** Simulation studies show that when processing times are random, intentionally unbalancing the line can make it run more efficiently. Two successful approaches are (a) to have increasing capacity at each succeeding stage (more capacity in the last stage than the first) or (b) to have the most capacity in the middle stages and less at the beginning and end. Which of these or other designs is best will depend on the amount and location of randomness, the material transfer pattern, and the opportunity for using in-process inventories.
3. **Use Buffer Inventories.** By building in the ability to store unfinished units between work stations, firms can eliminate some work stoppages. Of course, buffer inventories increase inventory and space costs, and in some situations, such as auto assembly, they are not always feasible.
4. **Use Computer Simulation.** The ultimate productivity and responsiveness of a flow process are complicated functions of the task assignments, work station capacities, buffer inventories, and randomness in processing times. Experimenting on an actual production system can be time-consuming and costly, if not impossible. In most cases, computer simulation is an invaluable tool for testing alternative combinations of the above factors.

8.3 DESIGN OF FUNCTIONAL LAYOUTS

Product layouts are efficient when materials and/or people all move through the system in the same sequence. However, job-shop and cellular production processes must be designed for flexibility to accommodate a variety of movement patterns. In these cases, production activities are divided into work centers (or departments) according to the primary activity or process performed, such as drilling, assembling, radiology, or home loan processing. Their spatial configuration can either facilitate or obstruct movement or interactions among the work centers. The spatial configuration of the work centers, called a **functional** (or **process**) **layout**, should be designed to promote efficient, flexible movement among the work centers.

Functional layouts are used not only to configure job-shop and cellular processes, but also to arrange production subsystems within an entire facility. Here some functional work centers may be flow processes such as assembly lines, which use a product layout within the work centers themselves. At the facility level, we may also want to configure work centers that do manufacturing along with those that perform administrative (accounting, personnel) or marketing (sales, advertising) functions.

The importance of good functional layout cannot be overstated. This factor is important in many leading companies, such as 3M, Standard Register, McDonald's, Allen-Bradley, and Walt Disney.

PROCEDURE FOR DESIGNING FUNCTIONAL LAYOUTS

Functional layout design determines the best relative locations of functional work centers. Work centers that interact frequently, with movement of material or people, should be located close together, whereas those that have little interaction can be spatially separated.

The following five-step procedure, which is explained in detail below, is one approach to designing an efficient functional layout.

1. List and describe each functional work center.
2. Obtain a drawing and description of the facility being designed.
3. Identify and estimate the amount of material and personnel flow among work centers.
4. Use structured analytical methods to obtain a good general layout.
5. Evaluate and modify the layout, incorporating details such as machine orientation, storage area location, and equipment access.

Work-Center Description

The first step in the layout process is to identify and describe each work center. The description should include the primary function of the work center (drilling, new accounts, or cashier); its major components, including equipment and number of personnel; and the space required. The description should also include any special access needs (such as access to running water or an elevator) or restrictions (it must be in a "clean" area or away from heat).

Facility Description

For a new facility, the spatial configuration of the work centers and the size and shape of the facility are determined simultaneously. Determining the locations of special structures and fixtures such as elevators, loading docks, and bathrooms becomes part of the layout process. However, in many cases the facility and its characteristics are a given. In these situations, it is necessary to obtain a drawing of the facility being designed (such as the one in Figure 8.8), including shape and dimensions, locations of fixed structures (e.g., elevators, ductwork, pipes), and restrictions on activities, such as weight limits on certain parts of a floor or foundation.

Estimating Work Center Interactions

To minimize transport times and material-handling costs, we would like to place close together those work centers that have the greatest flow of materials and people between them. To estimate the flows between work centers, it is helpful to begin by drawing a **relationship (REL) diagram** such as the one in Figure 8.9.

For manufacturing systems, material flows and transporting costs can be estimated reasonably well using historical routings for products or through work sampling techniques applied to workers or jobs (work sampling is discussed in Chapter 10). The flow

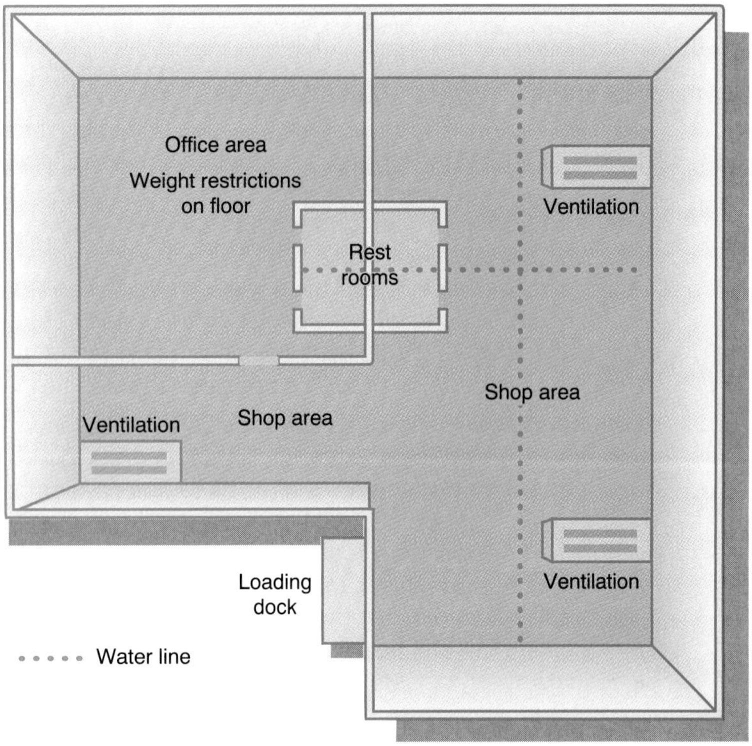

FIGURE 8.8 Drawing of an existing facility.

of people, especially in a service system such as a business office or a university administration building, may be difficult to estimate precisely, although work sampling can be used to obtain rough estimates.

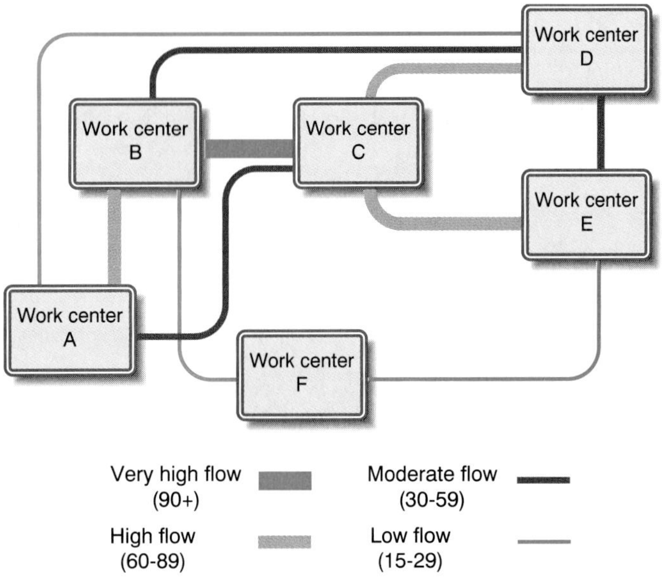

FIGURE 8.9 Relationship flow diagram.

The amounts and/or costs of flows among work centers are usually presented using either a flow matrix, a flow-cost matrix, or a proximity chart.

1. ***Flow Matrix.*** A **flow matrix** is a matrix of the estimated amounts of flow between each pair of work centers. The flow may be materials (expressed as the number of loads transported) or people who move between centers. Each work center corresponds to one row and one column, and the element f_{ij} designates the amount of flow from work center (row) i to work center (column) j. Normally, the direction of flow between work centers is not important, only the total amount, so f_{ij} and f_{ji} can be combined and the flows represented using only the upper right half of a matrix, as illustrated in Table 8.5. In this table $f_{BE} = 30$ means that there are approximately 30 units of flow between work centers B and E each day. This may be pallets of material or trips by employees between the work centers.
2. ***Flow-Cost Matrix.*** A basic assumption of facility layout is that the cost of moving materials or people between work centers is a function of distance traveled. Although more complicated cost functions can be accommodated, often we assume that the per unit cost of material and personnel flows between work centers is proportional to the distance between the centers. So for each type of flow between each pair of departments, i and j, we estimate the cost per unit per unit distance, c_{ij}. Notice, for example, that the cost c_{AD} may be different from the cost c_{BE} because different materials will be transported between A and D than between B and E and different forms of transportation may be used. The cost *per unit distance* for the total flow between work centers i and j, which we will designate C_{ij}, is $C_{ij} = c_{ij}f_{ij}$. (If there are several forms of flow between a pair of work centers, then C_{ij} would be the sum of the costs for all flow types.) The matrix of C_{ij} values is called the **flow-cost matrix**. Table 8.6 is the flow-cost matrix for Table 8.5, where all c_{ij} = \$1 per 100 feet, except that $c_{BC} = c_{DG} = c_{DI}$ = \$2, and $c_{BE} = c_{GH}$ = \$3. So, for example, C_{BE} = \$3 × 30 = \$90 per 100 feet. For every 100 feet of distance separating departments B and E, the company would incur \$90 of flow cost per day.
3. ***Proximity Chart.*** **Proximity charts** (also called **relationship** or **REL charts**) are distinguished from flow and flow-cost matrices by the fact that they describe *qualitatively* the desirability or need for work centers to be close together, rather than providing quantitative measures of flow and cost. These charts are used when it is difficult to measure or estimate precise amounts or costs of flow among work centers. This is common when the primary flows involve people and do not have a direct cost but rather an indirect cost, such as when employees in a corporate head-

TABLE 8.5 FLOW MATRIX

	Work Center									
	A	B	C	D	E	F	G	H	I	
A	—	25	32	0	80	0	30	5	15	
B	—	—	20	10	30	75	0	7	10	
C	—	—	—	0	10	50	45	60	0	
D	—	—	—	—	35	0	25	90	120	Daily Flows Between Work Centers
E	—	—	—	—	—	20	80	0	70	
F	—	—	—	—	—	—	0	150	20	
G	—	—	—	—	—	—	—	50	45	
H	—	—	—	—	—	—	—	—	80	
I	—	—	—	—	—	—	—	—	—	

TABLE 8.6 FLOW-COST MATRIX

	Work Center									
	A	B	C	D	E	F	G	H	I	
A	—	25	32	0	80	0	30	5	15	Daily Cost for Flows Between Work Centers (Dollars per Day per 100 ft)
B	—	—	40	10	90	75	0	7	10	
C	—	—	—	0	10	50	45	60	0	
D	—	—	—	—	35	0	50	90	240	
E	—	—	—	—	—	20	80	0	70	
F	—	—	—	—	—	—	0	150	20	
G	—	—	—	—	—	—	—	150	45	
H	—	—	—	—	—	—	—	—	80	
I	—	—	—	—	—	—	—	—	—	

quarters move among departments (payroll, printing, information systems) to carry out their work.

Proximity charts were popularized by Richard Muther,[4] who expressed them in a form similar to Figure 8.10, but a designer could personalize notation and conventions, such as by representing the data in half-matrix form. Muther uses A, E, I, O, U, and X to designate how important it is that two work centers be close together, either because of the amount of flow between them or because they may share equipment, files, or other resources. Notice that it may be undesirable for some work centers to be near each other—for example, a work center using flammable materials and one using torches or ovens. This situation is denoted by the letter X.

STRUCTURED ANALYTICAL LAYOUT TOOLS

For many years engineers constructed functional layouts manually. Using information from flow-cost matrices or proximity charts, they constructed layouts by first putting close together those work centers with the largest and most costly interactions and

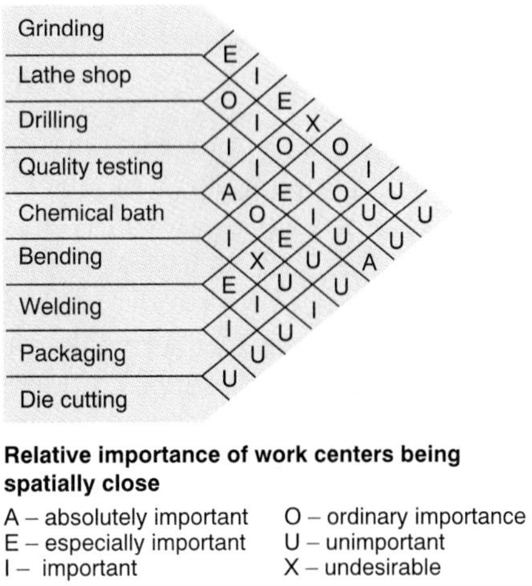

FIGURE 8.10 Proximity chart.

[4]See Richard Muther and John D. Wheeler, *Simplified Systematic Layout Planning*, Management and Industrial Publications, Kansas City, MO, 1962.

then arranging work centers with decreasingly important interactions around them. The designer then attempted to improve the layout incrementally by switching or rearranging the locations of two or three centers, usually those adjacent to each other. For small- to modest-sized layouts this procedure usually produces nearly optimal layouts. But as layouts become larger and more complex, involving say 15 or more work centers, the number of possible configurations and trade-offs among locations increases rapidly, so the human mind cannot explore and evaluate them all. If two or three work centers are initially situated in poor locations, human designers often have trouble identifying this problem and making appropriate reconfigurations. This section describes some simple analytical methods, including computer-based heuristics, that can help construct and improve functional layouts.

A key issue in constructing facility layouts is how to evaluate the goodness of alternative layouts. Suppose we have a flow-cost matrix where C_{ij} is the cost per unit distance of all flows between work centers i and j. For any given layout, let d_{ij} be the distance between work centers i and j.[5] The cost associated with the flow between i and j is $C_{ij}d_{ij}$, and the *total flow cost* (*TFC*) for the flows among all the work centers is

$$TFC = \sum_i \sum_j C_{ij} d_{ij}$$

where the summations are taken over all work center pairs. The TFC provides a concise way to compare specific layouts. Our task is to find the spatial arrangement of the work centers that makes the TFC *as small as possible*. Because the d_{ij} variables are *indirect*, determined by the spatial arrangement of the work centers, normal optimization techniques such as linear or integer programming cannot be used to find the best layout.

Location Assignment Problem

In some cases, the facility layout problem is simply one of assigning work centers to fixed possible locations in the facility.

EXAMPLE 2

Suppose a university wants to determine where to locate six departments within a student services building. The space requirements for the departments are similar and the building has one corridor running down the middle, so the university has decided that there will be three departments on each side of the corridor, as illustrated in Figure 8.11.

Table 8.7 lists the estimated daily flows (movements by students and staff) between each pair of departments. All travel between departments will be measured from the middle of each department, and travelers must use the corridor. (In other words, we will allow only horizontal and vertical movement and there are permanent walls between departments.) So, for example, the distance between the departments assigned to locations 1 and 5 is 300 feet, and the distance between those at locations 3 and 6 is 150 feet.

---

[5]Normally, we measure the distances from the middle of the work centers, but if work centers have a spatial orientation (meaning that there is an entry point and an exit point), then d_{ij} values computed this way may not be accurate.

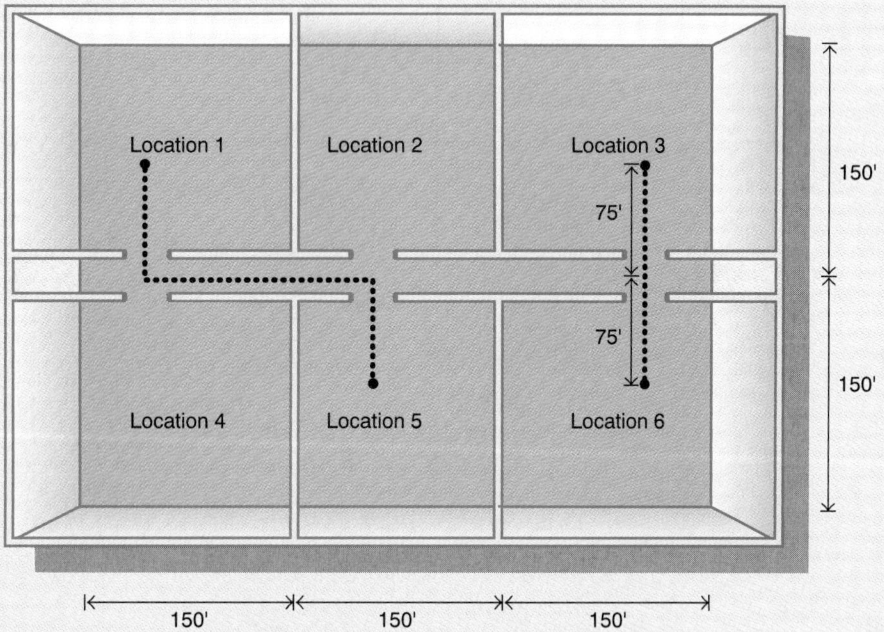

FIGURE 8.11 Available space and configuration in the student services building.

Assuming travel costs per foot are the same for all people, we can let $C_{ij} = c_{ij}$. The university's task is to assign the departments to the six specified locations in a way that minimizes total flow cost:

$$TFC = \sum_{i=A}^{E} \sum_{j>i} c_{ij} d_{ij}$$

We begin by constructing a relationship flow diagram, as shown in Figure 8.9. We see from the figure that C has the largest flows with the largest number of other departments, so in our initial layout we put C in a central location such as location 2. The flow between B and C is the largest (100) and B has substantial flows with other departments, so we put B opposite C in the other central location. Of the remaining four departments, the pair with the largest flow is D and E, so we put them together in loca-

TABLE 8.7 STUDENT SERVICES FLOW MATRIX

	A	B	C	D	E	F	
A. Records	—	60	40	20	20	5	
B. Admissions	—	—	100	30	10	20	Estimated Number of
C. Financial aid	—	—	—	70	80	10	Students/Staff/Visitors
D. Counseling	—	—	—	—	40	10	Moving Between
E. Job placement	—	—	—	—	—	15	Departments per Day
F. Student organizations	—	—	—	—	—	—	

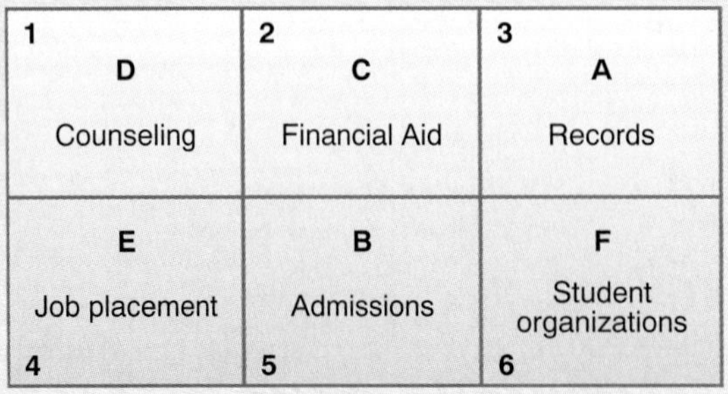

FIGURE 8.12 Layout of student services offices.

tions 1 and 4, and the remaining two departments are initially assigned to locations 3 and 6, giving the layout in Figure 8.12.

The total daily travel with this layout will be

$$c_{AB}d_{AB} + c_{AC}d_{AC} + \ldots + c_{DF}d_{DF} + c_{EF}d_{EF}$$

$$= 60(300 \text{ ft}) + 40(300 \text{ ft}) + \ldots + 10(450 \text{ ft}) + 15(450 \text{ ft}) = 147{,}000 \text{ people-ft}$$

We could then try switching department locations and recomputing the total daily travel to see if another arrangement is better.

Computerized Layout Heuristics

Even when the layout problem only requires assignment of work centers to fixed locations, which is conceptually easy, as the number of work centers grows, fast computers are necessary to evaluate all possible layouts.[6] When the sizes of the departments differ, and their locations and shapes are controllable by the designer, the set of possible layouts explodes, even for modest problems (15–20 work centers). Furthermore, there is no standard optimization technique (i.e., there is no way to handle the variables that describe shape). Despite the superior pattern recognition capabilities of humans, computers are often superior at making spatial trade-offs that involve a large number of simple computations. For this reason, during the last 35 years, several computer-based heuristics have been developed that try to approximate natural search or spatial thought processes. These layout packages fall into two general categories: those based on improvement heuristics and those based upon construction heuristics. Because the former type is more common and simpler to understand, we will look at it first.

CRAFT

The strategies underlying most improvement layout heuristics are similar, so we will look at only one of them. **CRAFT (computerized reallocation of facilities technique)** is one of the oldest and simplest programs. It was developed by Armour and Buffa (1963), and is available for use on microcomputers as well as being part of the IBM Share Network of programs.

Input Data

The input data for CRAFT are as follows:

1. The shape and area of the space available, divided into a grid. Each grid unit represents some specified amount of area (e.g., 500 square feet).

[6]Ignoring the issue of work center shape, if we are simply to assign n work centers to n fixed locations, for $n = 20$ there are 20! or over 2.43×10^{18} unique configurations.

2. A list of all work centers, with the required space of each expressed in terms of grid units. Work centers that must be fixed in a specific location can be designated.
3. A flow or flow-cost matrix for the work centers.
4. An initial layout.

The Heuristic

CRAFT uses the following switching heuristic to improve the current layout.

1. For the current layout the heuristic computes (a) the center point for each work center, (b) the distance, d_{ij}, between the center points for each pair of work centers, and (c) the total flow cost for the layout.
2. For each pair of work centers the heuristic (a) switches the locations of the work centers, (b) recomputes the d_{ij} variables, and (c) computes the total flow cost for the switched layout.
3. The heuristic executes the switch (by rearranging the layout) that produces the largest decrease in total flow cost and goes to step 1. If no switch results in a cost reduction, the heuristic stops.

The Output

Figure 8.13 shows an initial layout and the final layout from CRAFT, using the data in Table 8.5 and department sizes shown in the figure.

CRAFT is not guaranteed to produce an optimal layout (nor are any heuristics), but it will either produce a better layout than the initial one or it will stop quickly. CRAFT also has a reasonable level of flexibility. Work centers can be of different sizes and the

	1	2	3	4	5	6	7	8	9	10
1	A	A	B	B	D	D	F	F	I	I
2	A	A	B	B	D	D	F	F	I	I
3	C	C	E	E	E	E	F	F	I	I
4	C	C	E	E	E	E	G	G	G	G
5	C	C	H	H	H	H	G	G	G	G

Total interdepartmental flow cost – $14,894

(a) Initial layout

	1	2	3	4	5	6	7	8	9	10
1	A	A	B	B	E	E	E	E	I	I
2	A	A	B	B	E	E	G	G	I	I
3	C	C	F	F	F	E	G	G	I	I
4	C	C	F	F	F	E	G	G	D	D
5	C	C	H	H	H	H	G	G	D	D

Total interdepartmental flow cost – $11,768

(b) Final layout

FIGURE 8.13 CRAFT layouts.

Functional layout methods can be used to configure office activities to be efficient, such as this dealing room of Barclays de Zoete in London, England.

location of work centers can be fixed, so structures such as elevators can be incorporated as immovable work centers. Enhanced versions of CRAFT also perform three-way switches in step 2. This increases the chances of finding a good layout, but it also increases the computation time considerably.

One deficiency of CRAFT is that it computes distances between the *middle* of the work centers rather than from actual entry or exit points. As a result, CRAFT is most useful at a macro level of design, where we want work centers located in a reasonably efficient manner with respect to all other work centers. The layout of equipment and work spaces within work centers and the orientation of adjacent work centers are better handled manually, possibly using computer-aided graphics programs similar to CAD packages.

Other Computer Programs

In addition to CRAFT, there are other computerized layout programs. Two popular ones are **CORELAP (computerized relationship layout planning)** and **ALDEP (automated layout design program)**. These programs differ from CRAFT in two ways. First, each is based on **construction heuristics**. That is, they *construct* layouts rather than improve on existing layouts. Second, each uses proximity chart data and tries to maximize some measure of closeness, rather than using flow-cost data and trying to minimize flow cost. ALDEP begins with a pair of work centers that have a closeness rating of "A" (absolutely necessary closeness) and then builds a design by adding one work center at a time according to which has the highest closeness rating. CORELAP uses a similar approach, but it assembles *pairs* of work centers with high closeness ratings first and then connects them. More recently, heuristics that use cluster analytic methods to form substructures of work centers that have dominant flows among them have proven quite effective.

Using Computerized Layout Programs

Do computerized layout programs produce better layouts than those developed solely by humans?[7] The answer seems to be "It depends." Some aspects of layout require superior creative and pattern recognition skills, at which humans excel, while others are computational and experimental and are better suited for computers. One popular approach is to use human designers or a computerized construction heuristic to develop an initial layout. This layout can then be used as the starting point for a computerized improvement heuristic such as CRAFT. The resulting layout can then be evaluated by humans, possibly using CAD-like interactive graphics systems, taking into account the spatial orientation of work centers and equipment, aesthetics, location of storage areas, transportation access, effects on supervision, and safety.

8.4 DESIGN OF CELLULAR PROCESSES

Chapter 7 showed that it can be advantageous for companies that produce many products using a job-shop process to convert some operations into work cells. Products that undergo the same processing in the same sequence can be produced more efficiently in cells, rather than moving to distinct work centers for each type of processing.

The spatial configuration of cellular processes is no more difficult than that of job shops; both are arranged using a functional layout, with the work cells treated as work centers. However, the design of the cells themselves—that is, which operations and machines to have in each cell and how the operations in the cells should be arranged—can be very difficult. For this reason the design of work cells is the primary focus of this section.

CELL COMPOSITION AND TYPE

The **group technology** principle underlying cellular processes is simple: if several products must undergo similar operations, production may be more efficient by grouping these operations into a single work cell. The problem is to determine how many cells to create, which operations to perform in each cell, what product flow should be accommodated in each cell, and ultimately, how each product should be routed through the system.

The two basic types of cells, defined by their layout and production flow, are flow cells and group cells.

Flow Cells

A **flow cell** is a collection of machines or operations arranged as a (tightly connected) flow process: the processing and material flow sequences are the same for all products utilizing the cell. Because of the fixed, one-directional flow, efficient material-handling methods can be used, and work methods can be made simpler and more efficient than at group cells. Figure 8.14 shows a flow cell like one at Standard Register Company that combines printing, sequential numbering, and hole punching.

Group Cells

A **group cell** is a collection of machines or operations that are used or performed together. This cell is flexible; any product that requires these operations to be performed consecutively for production, regardless of the sequence, could be made in the cell. For example, Figure 8.15 shows a group cell in a machine shop made up of a CNC drill, a

---

[7] The issue was debated in the 1970s. The evidence indicates that computed-based layout packages can be very useful, especially when used in conjunction with human evaluation and design.

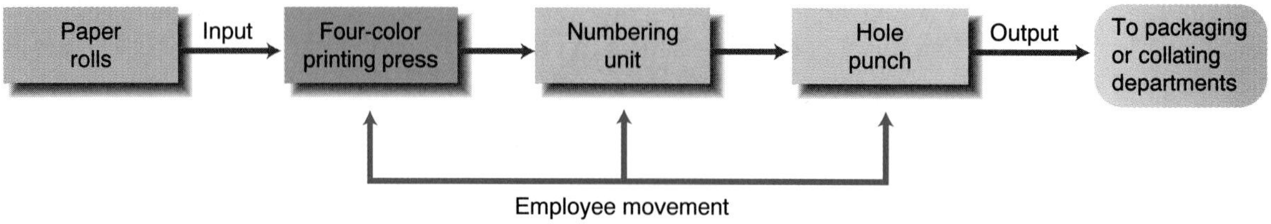

FIGURE 8.14 Flow cell at Standard Register Company.

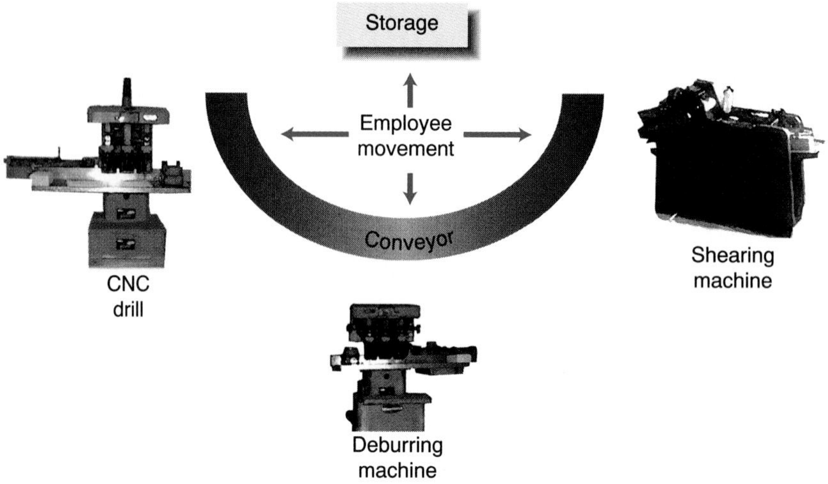

FIGURE 8.15 Machine shop group cell.

shearing machine, and a deburring machine. Products can pass among the machines in any sequence, so one product may require drilling, shearing, and then deburring, while another may require shearing, deburring, drilling, and deburring. Although group cells are not as efficient as flow cells, the close proximity of machines and the processing of similar products make group cells more efficient than performing the same operations at separate work centers. (Notice that a flexible manufacturing system is essentially an automated work cell.)

PRODUCTION FLOW ANALYSIS

The design problem is made especially complicated by the large number of design alternatives and by the many trade-offs that should be considered. The first problem is to determine which operations or machines are shared by a sufficiently large number of products to be candidates for inclusion in a cell. This can be accomplished by performing a **production flow analysis (PFA)**. PFA is a method for analyzing the operations requirements of products and then identifying the types of cells that might best serve groups of products. PFA is a five-step process.

1. ***Data Collection.*** The first step is to determine which set of products and which production operations (machines) should be included in the analysis. For each product we assign a product code to identify its production routing (operation sequence). These data may be obtained from the group technology codes discussed in Chapter 7, if the codes include processing information, or they can be obtained from route sheets (see Chapter 5). When available, lot size, processing time, and annual production data can also be helpful in deciding the number and form of cells.
2. ***Categorizing Products into Packs.*** Once the operations requirements of each product are known, the products are assigned to categories or packs. A **pack** is a set of products or parts that require exactly the same machines or operations for production. (However, the products in the pack may be processed in different sequences. The sequencing issue is resolved later.) For companies producing hundreds or thousands of products or parts, this assignment is usually performed using computerized sorting methods. The number of products in each pack can vary from one to several hundred. Each pack is then assigned an identifying code number.
3. ***Constructing a PFA Chart.*** Once the products are assigned to packs, a PFA chart, such as the one in Figure 8.16, can be constructed. Each column corresponds to a product pack, and each row corresponds to a machine or operation. Each column identifies the operations that must be performed to produce the products in the corresponding pack. For example, the column for pack 01 indicates that all the products in this pack require operations A, D, F, G, H, I, and K.
4. ***Chart Analysis.*** A difficult but crucial step is to analyze the data in the PFA chart to identify reasonable work cells. One approach is to rearrange the columns of the chart so that packs using the same operations are adjacent, as is done in Figure 8.17 for the PFA chart in Figure 8.16. This rearrangement involves an interesting and difficult pattern recognition problem that is beyond the scope of this book

Pack code

Opn or machine code	01	02	03	04	05	06	07	08	09	10	11	12	13	14	15	16
A	X	X		X	X			X				X		X		
B			X	X			X	X	X				X			X
C		X					X			X			X	X		X
D	X	X		X			X	X	X	X	X	X	X			
E		X	X		X	X				X	X			X	X	
F	X		X	X			X				X				X	
G	X	X	X			X	X	X	X	X		X	X		X	X
H	X		X	X			X		X			X	X	X	X	
I	X				X		X	X	X			X	X			X
J					X	X		X		X	X			X		X
K	X	X	X	X	X	X				X	X		X	X	X	X

FIGURE 8.16 PFA chart.

Pack code

Opn or machine code	04	07	10	02	08	16	01	03	15	12	09	13	05	14	06	11
A	X				X		X			X			X	X		
B	X	X			X	X		X			X	X				
C		X	X	X		X						X		X		
D	X	X	X	X			X			X	X	X				X
E			X	X				X	X				X	X	X	X
F	X	X					X	X	X							X
G		X					X	X	X	X	X	X			X	
H	X	X					X	X	X	X	X	X		X		
I		X			X	X	X			X	X	X				
J			X		X	X			X	X	X		X	X	X	X
K	X		X	X		X	X	X	X			X	X	X	X	X

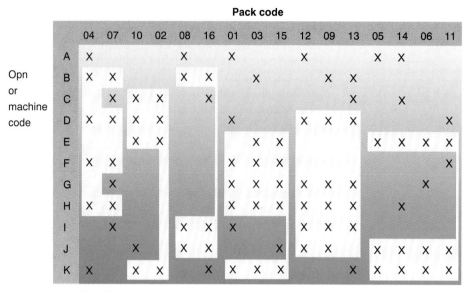

Possible cells and corresponding product packs are enclosed in yellow blocks

FIGURE 8.17 Rearranged PFA chart.

and is the subject of continuing research. In Figure 8.17 dotted lines enclose operations that *may* form logical cells, and the packs that *may* use those cells are identified.

5. ***Detailed Cell Design.*** The blocks in Figure 8.17 provide a starting point for constructing cells. However, to obtain a final cell configuration, many factors and trade-offs must be considered to determine which operations or machines should be in each cell, whether the cells should be group or flow cells, and what the overall mix of cells should be. This step is the most difficult and time-consuming. It requires making tentative designs, evaluating them, and revising them.

TRADE-OFFS AND CONSIDERATIONS IN THE DETAILED DESIGN

Detailed cell design is an iterative process that involves several considerations and trade-offs.

Operations Sequence and Cell Type

Products are normally assigned to packs based on which operations they require, without regard to sequencing. But an important consideration in cell design is precisely the sequence of operations. For a cell to be useful, the operations within it should be performed consecutively. For example, suppose we had a group cell made up of three operations: G, H, and I. A product in pack 09 that had the operation sequence D → B → G → H → I → J could use this cell efficiently because operations G, H, and I are performed consecutively. In contrast, a product in pack 09 with the sequence G → B → H → J → I → D could not use it efficiently because the three operations are not consecutive; the product would be moved into and out of the cell repeatedly, and the process would be no better than a job-shop process.

The operations sequence is also crucial in determining what *type* of cell to construct. Everything else being the same (and assuming sufficient volume is produced), a flow cell is more efficient than a group cell for the same reasons that a flow process is more efficient than a job shop. But this requires that all products processed at the cell undergo the *same operations* in the *same sequence*. For example, suppose the cell described above was a flow cell with the sequence G → H → I. The product with the sequence D → B → G → H → I → J could be processed very efficiently at the flow cell. By contrast, another product in pack 09 with the operation sequence B → G → I → H → J → D could not be processed at that cell. However, if it were a *group* cell, the product could be processed there because G, H, and I are performed consecutively.

The Number of Operations in a Cell

Deciding how many operations to put in a cell is complicated by two conflicting factors:

1. The more operations performed in a flow cell, the greater the gain in efficiency from using it but the fewer the products that could normally be accommodated by the cell.
2. For a group cell, the more operations included the more different products accommodated, but the less efficient it is, on average, to process each product.

For example, any product that requires the sequence –G–H– could be processed at the two-operation *flow cell* G → H. However, a product with the sequence –G–H–K– could not be easily processed at the three-operation *flow cell* G → H → I. In contrast, a four-operation *group cell* G–H–I–K could accommodate products that have sequences, such as –G–I–K– and H–I–G– as well as G–H–I–K, whereas a three-operation cell, such as G–H–K could not accommodate the first two products.

Decomposing the Packs

One issue to keep in mind is that the initial PFA normally assigns products to packs based on what operations must be performed, *regardless* of sequence. To perform the detailed cell design described above, it is necessary to decompose the packs and to look at the operation sequence of products within each pack. Because the products in a pack may use only a small number of the possible operations, it is sometimes possible to perform another, more detailed PFA using individual products or subpacks that take into consideration the *sequence* of operations. From this information the designer can then evaluate more precisely which products could be produced in each possible cell and how well loaded the cell would be based on annual production of the products.

At the detailed design stage, information on processing times and expected production volume for each product is needed. It is not sufficient to know that 10 products could be produced in a cell. If the production volumes for these products are very small, it may not be cost effective to construct a cell for them. If their expected volumes are large, then the cell capacity should be designed accordingly or multiple cells constructed.

Possible Refinements and Comments

In the design of manufacturing systems, units of operation (the rows in Figures 8.16 and 8.17) often correspond to machines such as a turret lathe, waxing machine, welder, or packer. In fact, an important aspect of designing cellular systems is defining the operations. It is reasonable for some operations to involve no machines but instead to be manual activities. In addition, it is not unusual for even large manufacturing systems to utilize only 5 or 10 different types of machines. However, the cost of changing the setup of a machine from one product to the next might be substantial for dissimilar products. Keeping the same general setup from product to product, as well as doing several operations together, may result in considerable cost savings. In this case, the operations

TABLE 8.8 POSSIBLE CELLULAR SYSTEM FOR FIGURE 8.16

Flow Cells	Group Cells	Remainder Job-Shop Cell
1F H → G → F	1G G-H-I-J-K	A, A, B, C, D, E, K
2F K → J	2G B-D-F	
3F C → D → E		

may be defined as specific *setups* for a machine. So several cells may contain the same machines, but each machine might be set up in a different way.

Literally billions of cell configurations are possible for even moderately complex operations. By using PFA, computer heuristics, and experience, a good designer can often narrow these options down to a few alternatives. However, because changing one cell can have a significant impact somewhere else in the system, computer simulation should be used to estimate and evaluate the overall performance of each design alternative. Table 8.8 shows one design that was developed for the data in Figure 8.16. If a product in pack 15 had the operation sequence K → J → H → G → F → E, one possible routing would be to send it to cell 1G to perform operations K and J, and then to cell 1F for operations H, G, and F. Operation E would be performed in the "remainder" job-shop cell.

SPATIAL CONFIGURATION

The layout of the overall cellular system would normally be treated as a functional layout in which each cell and the remainder operations would be treated as work centers. The more pressing spatial issue is the layout of individual cells.

Flow Cells

The same layout principles apply to flow cells as to flow processes. Because of the fixed flow pattern for the products being processed, a fixed transport system such as a conveyer or automated transport device usually connects any machines or work stations. When the flow cell involves only two or three operations or machines, the most efficient configuration may be a linear one like that in Figure 8.14. When the cell involves four or more operations or machines (and sometimes three), a U-shaped configuration, as shown in Figure 8.18, is often superior to a linear arrangement because it allows one or

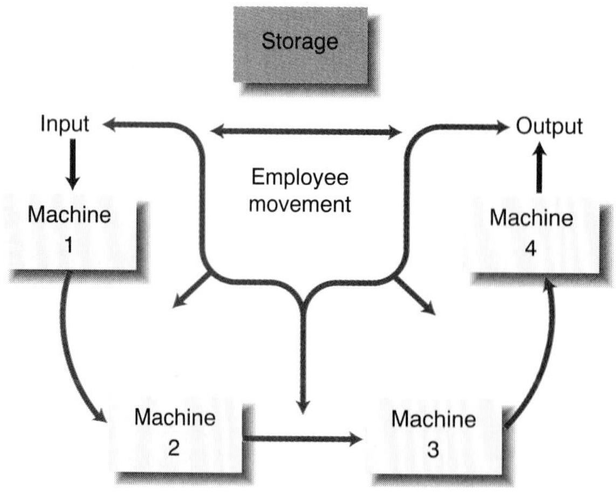

FIGURE 8.18 U-shaped flow cell configuration.

two workers to operate the entire cell with minimal movement. The U-shaped arrangement especially facilitates coprocessing of activities, such as loading input into the first work station and unloading it at the last one. In fact, one of the biggest cost savings of work cells is that they often reduce the total number of workers needed because each machine no longer has a separate worker. In addition, the worker gains job enrichment by having greater and more varied responsibilities.

Group Cells

Because group cells must accommodate a wide variety of routings *within* the cell, they must be configured and connected in a manner that allows free flow of materials and workers. A U-shaped layout satisfies these requirements well. But in contrast to a flow cell, the U-shaped group cell must have flexible material handling, which might be as simple as the worker carrying material between machines, or it might be an automated circular conveyer system or a two-direction conveyer system that allows items to be moved to any location. If the cell involves only two or three machines, it can sometimes be constructed so that the item being processed remains on a work table and the machines "move" to process it. Cells of this type are essentially the same as machining centers or flexible manufacturing cells (see Chapter 7).

IN GOOD COMPANY

Hybrids Bloom at Sony Corporation

In the electronics industry, short product cycles and expanding product varieties have made long assembly lines that produce one product at a time inefficient. An increasing number of companies have been converting their repetitive flow processes to flow process/cellular hybrids to obtain greater production flexibility. Sony Corporation has replaced some of its long assembly lines with several four-person cells. By assigning each cell its own product, Sony is able to make dozens of different products simultaneously. The company has reported many benefits from this change: workers can work at their own pace rather than being controlled by the slowest person on the line; the spatially compact cells reduce material handling; and when one cell has a problem, only that cell stops production, not the entire system. Not only has Sony gained flexibility, it has increased productivity as well.

The cellular structure requires workers to be more skilled at more tasks, so Sony has had to provide greater training. But workers benefit by being able to produce entire products rather than performing one or two monotonous tasks on an assembly line.

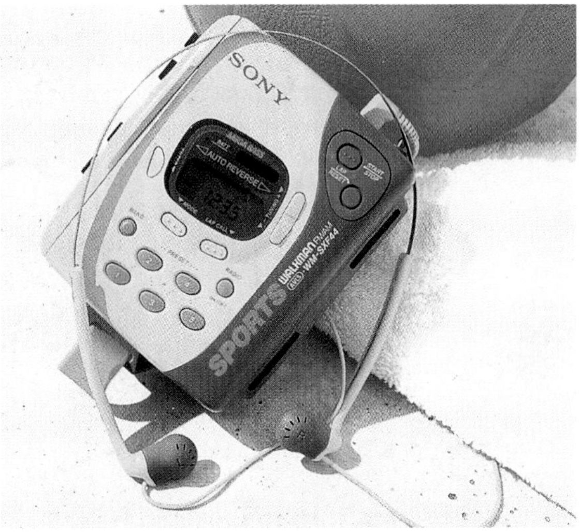

In addition to redesigning work, Sony and other companies have customized the spatial layout of their cells to match the product and the number of workers in the cell. In addition to line and U-shaped cells, cells in the shape of spirals, spiders, Y's, and 6's have been used.

Source: Michael Williams, "Some Plants Tear Out Long Assembly Lines, Switch to Craft Work," *Wall Street Journal*, Oct. 24, 1994.

8.5 DESIGN OF SERVICE SYSTEMS

In theory, the methods for designing service systems should be the same as those for manufacturing systems. But in practice, service system design requires some unique analysis and emphasis on different issues. The best general structure (flow process, job shop, cellular) for a service system is often less obvious initially. Frequently the general structure is not determined until detailed analysis and assignment of tasks is performed. Second, there is often more opportunity for elimination of tasks, concurrent performance of tasks, and flexibility in the decomposition and assignment of tasks than with manufacturing processes. Third, the design must explicitly consider how the system will interact with customers.

A good starting point when designing or redesigning a service process is to perform an operations analysis. An **operations analysis** is a structured study that (1) identifies each task to be performed and the flow of people and materials through the system, and (2) evaluates the tasks and flows to determine ways in which the process can be simplified and improved.

THE PROCESS FLOW DIAGRAM AND THE PROCESS CHART

Two simple tools that can guide an operations analysis are a process flow diagram and a process chart. A **process flow diagram** is an arrow diagram that shows, step by step, the sequence in which a service is performed (or a good is produced) and the corresponding movement of materials, people, or information. Figure 8.19 is a process flow diagram for processing a financial aid application at a university. A **process chart** gives a more detailed breakdown of the process into tasks, and it classifies each activity as being either a processing operation, movement, inspection, delay, or storage, as shown in Figure 8.20. The process flow diagram and process chart can be based on an existing process for a redesign or a tentative design for a new process. Once these documents are developed, they can be used to perform a question-based analysis (similar to value analysis in product design, discussed in Chapter 5). For each activity we ask the questions what, when, where, how, and who:

1. What is being done and why? Could the task be eliminated? What would happen if it were? Could it be combined with another task?

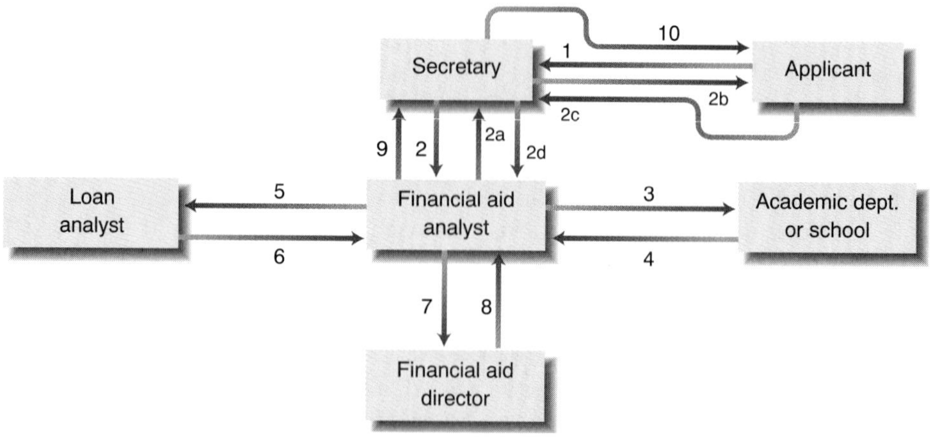

FIGURE 8.19 Process flow diagram for processing financial aid applications.

Activities	Operation ○	Inspection □	Movement ⇨	Delay D	Storage ▷	Time
Secretary receives application: puts in basket	○					1 min
Application waits in basket				D		2 hr
Secretary creates file	○					1 min
Sec. sends application to financial aid analyst			⇨			1 hr
Application waits in queue				D		1 day
Fin. aid (F.A.) analyst checks appl. for completeness		□				10 min
If application not complete						
F.A. analyst sends appl. to sec. to prepare letter to applicant			⇨			1 hr
Application waits in basket				D		4 hr
Sec. prepares and sends letter asking for info.	○					5 min
Wait for applicant to return information				D		10 days
Secretary receives completed application	○					1 min
Application sent to F.A. analyst			⇨			1 hr
Application waits in basket				D		4 hr
F.A. analyst rechecks appl. for completeness		□				5 min
F.A. analyst compute fin. need using formula	○					45 min
F.A. analyst checks eligibility for federal, state, university grants	○					30 min
F.A. analyst sends copy of appl. to school or dept. for dept. grant or employment			⇨			1 day
Application in queue at dept./school				D		3 days
Dept./school evaluates appl.; sends decision to F.A. analyst	○		⇨			1 day
F.A. analyst computes deficiency in fin. aid	○					20 min
F.A. analyst sends application to loan analyst			⇨			1 hr
Wait in basket				D		1 day
Loan analyst evaluates appl.; identifies source and amount of loan	○					30 min
Loan analyst sends report to F.A. analyst			⇨			2 hrs
F.A. analyst prepares total aid package	○					30 min
F.A. analyst sends proposal to F.A. director			⇨			4 hrs
Proposal in basket				D		1 day
F.A. director approves or modifies package and sends to F.A. analyst		□	⇨			10 min
F.A. analyst sends decision to secretary			⇨			1 hr
Wait in basket				D		4 hr
Secretary prepares and sends letter	○					5 min

FIGURE 8.20 Process chart for processing financial aid applications.

2. When in the process is it being done? Must it be done at this time or is there flexibility in the sequencing or timing of the action?
3. Where is the task done? Could it be done elsewhere, and would this change be beneficial?
4. How is the task done? Why is it done this way? Could it be done another way or automated? Are there changes in equipment, tools, or methods that would make it easier to do?

5. Who does the task? Could someone else do it, especially as part of another job? Does the person doing it have the correct skills? Should it be done by someone with higher or lower skills?

This type of analysis not only can lead to the elimination of tasks, reduction in movements, and simplification of work, it can also help to identify opportunities to create work cells or to use more efficient flow processing for some set of activities. This analysis also plays a large role in the design of individual jobs and the organization of workers (which will be discussed in Chapter 10). For example, the information in Figures 8.19 and 8.20 could lead to the creation of a work cell where a loan analyst and a financial aid analyst work together on applications. Interactions and document movements between this cell and the financial aid director (and tasks performed by the director) might be reduced or eliminated.

THE SERVICE BLUEPRINT

Because service operations often involve direct contact with customers, the process should be designed to respond to their needs. One way to improve customer service is to determine which steps in the process slow completion of service and create chances for service mistakes. A **service blueprint**, which is similar to a process flow diagram but with greater detail, is a diagram of the activities performed to provide a service. It (1) includes estimates of the time required for each activity, (2) designates activities that require customer contact, and (3) identifies activities where a service failure may occur. (This is where a mistake or omission is likely to occur and lead to poor customer service.) Figure 8.21 provides a service blueprint for a dry-cleaning store.

A service blueprint provides the following benefits:

1. The visual representation makes it easier to determine which activities are truly necessary, which can be deleted, and which can be modified.
2. Customer contact points are clearly identified. This helps to pinpoint activities that can be performed separately and where opportunities for coprocessing of activities exist.
3. Likely service failure points are identified. This is helpful in developing plans to minimize the chance of a failure and in identifying possible corrective actions if a failure does occur.
4. The service blueprint is an excellent tool for training workers. They can see what activities must be performed and how, where failures are most likely to occur, and how to prevent and correct them.
5. The blueprint is useful for identifying the equipment and materials needed and how the service facilities should be spatially arranged to facilitate the services.
6. Service blueprints can be reconstructed regularly and used to evaluate and improve the service system over time, especially as new technologies become available and the services provided by the system change or expand.

Figure 8.21, which is based on current practice at a dry-cleaning store, can be used to identify ways to improve service. The first thing we might do is to estimate how long a customer remains in the store to obtain various forms of service. For example, a customer who was picking up and dropping off clothes would be in the store approximately 215–260 seconds, depending on the form of payment. If any failures occur, such as not finding garments on the rack, this time could increase substantially.

We can now "walk through" the service blueprint for each type of customer and identify where service time can be reduced and failures eliminated, using the questions

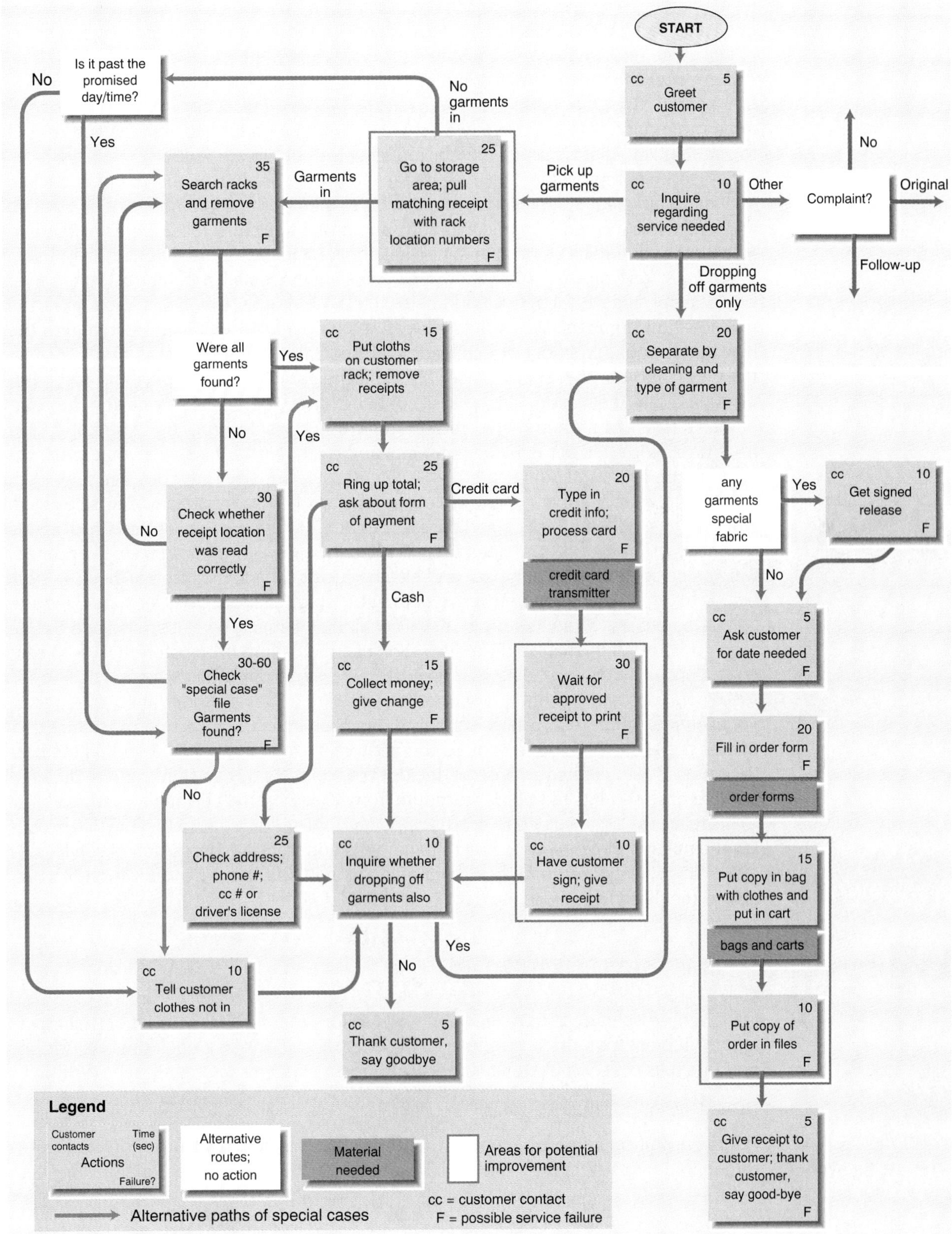

FIGURE 8.21 Service blueprint for a dry-cleaning store.

listed earlier: which activities can be eliminated, combined, automated, or resequenced? Using these questions, we can identify opportunities for improvement, some of which are enclosed by red lines in Figure 8.21. First, in the "dropping off garments" stream, after the order form is completed, there is no reason for the customer to have to wait until the server puts the clothes in the bag and files a copy of the order to receive the receipt. Instead, these two activities could be performed *after* giving a receipt to and thanking the customer, thereby reducing the customer's wait by 25 seconds.

A second improvement can be made at the beginning of the garment pickup stream. Pulling matching receipts to determine whether the garment has been cleaned and where it is located is time-consuming and prone to errors. Because it is a standard activity and requires no customer contact, it could be improved via automation or using a separate flow process subsystem. The store might install a computer; the server would simply type in the receipt numbers, and the computer would display or print the rack location numbers. This would save time compared to manually searching a file box, and it would probably reduce reading errors. The computer records would include the information in the "special case" file, so if the garment is not ready, the computer would indicate the reason. The process could be further automated by having the computer attached to an automated rack system, which would bring the garment to the front desk. With this system, one garment can be brought to the server while other receipt numbers are still being entered (if the customer brings in multiple receipts).

A third area of improvement is in the credit card payment stream. The sales clerk types in the credit information and passes the card through the transmitter, which sends the information to a central computer. The clerk then waits until a receipt is printed, which represents a credit approval, and has the customer sign the receipt. Then the clerk begins to inquire about and process a garment drop-off. Instead, the clerk could inquire about and process a garment drop-off while waiting for credit to be approved and the receipt to be printed. This would reduce the customer's time in the store by 10–40 seconds, depending on whether or not the customer was dropping off garments.

Operations analysis of this sort has been used to improve a wide variety of services. For example, Southwest Airlines used it to establish its load-by-section procedure that boards a plane in half the time of its competitors; Lakeland (Florida) Regional Medical Center used it to cut its turnaround time for routine tests by two-thirds and reduce the number of steps in its radiology procedure from 40 to 8; Aetna Life and Casualty used it to decrease the time needed to process a policy application from 15 to 5 days by reducing the number of people who had to handle the application.[8] The design of service operations is closely related to the design of individual jobs and the organization of workers, so the design of service jobs will be reconsidered in Chapter 10.

8.6 LAYOUT OF SOME SERVICE FACILITIES

Many service operations have unique characteristics that make the layout of their operations different from that of manufacturing operations. This section addresses two important types of service systems: warehouse/storage systems and retail sales facilities.

WAREHOUSE AND STORAGE LAYOUT

Despite significant improvements in material management and inventory reduction throughout industry, there will always be a need for some level of material inventories.

[8]See Keith Hammonds, "The Hospital," *Business Week*, Jan. 17, 1994, pp. 48–61; and Howard Gleckman et. al., "The Technology Payoff," *Business Week*, June 14, 1993, pp. 57–68.

Warehouses should be designed for efficient movement of retrieval vehicles, and products should be arranged so that those items most frequently retrieved together are located near each other to minimize movements.

In fact, the retail and wholesale distribution industries are based entirely on carrying inventories to provide products at more convenient locations and times, and in more affordable quantities, than could be obtained directly from manufacturers. In many industries the cost of material storage and handling is significant, so organizations that can store and retrieve materials most efficiently have a significant competitive advantage.

Configuring a large storage area is a complex operation and is closely tied to the degree of automation to be used. However, three issues are sufficiently important to material storage systems to be worth mentioning briefly.

Three-Dimensional Analysis

Unlike flow process and functional area layouts, which normally require only two-dimensional analysis, material storage facilities often require three-dimensional analysis. For example, when a food wholesaler is designing a warehouse, it must not only decide how long and wide the building should be and how many aisles to have, but also how *high* the storage racks should be and into how many *levels* the racks should be divided. In addition, when stocking the warehouse, it is not sufficient to decide in which aisle to locate an item; one must also consider where in the aisle to place it and how high up (on which shelf). In retail storage the vertical location can affect how well customers can see and retrieve the product.

Product Correlations

Just as the amount of flow between work centers is important in the efficiency of functional layouts, the correlation or "flow" between stored products is important in deciding where to place different items in storage areas. Consider a hardware distributor who stocks 30,000 different products within an automated warehouse. Suppose the distributor receives orders from customers for several different products at a time. A typical order is shown in Figure 8.22. Depending on the size of the order, it may be divided into

Product description	Product #	Qty	Unit Price
1 gal can, Sampson paint, blue	35-1089	20	10.50
1 gal can, Sampson paint, red	35-1091	10	10.50
1 gal can, Sampson paint, white	35-1095	50	9.00
1 gal can, Williams paint, blue	32-0875	15	10.50
3" nylon brush	15-1102	25	2.00
2" nylon brush	15-1100	50	1.50
3" bristle brush	16-0560	10	3.00
8" roller refills	17-1202	20	1.25
4-pack 100 watt lightbulbs	51-0050	75	1.50
4-pack 75 watt lightbulbs	51-0060	25	1.40
12-pack qt 10W-40 oil	73-0100	30	7.00

FIGURE 8.22 Typical order form.

several separate suborders for picking. (*Picking* refers to the process of having a person or machine go through the warehouse and retrieve items from storage to fill the order.) If the items in the order are spread throughout the warehouse, the cost of retrieval is much higher and the effective retrieval capacity of the facility is much lower.

We can reduce travel time and cost by identifying products that are frequently ordered together and storing them close together in the warehouse. For example, a hardware store may order various types of paint and paint brushes together, so it would make sense for the distributor to store these items together. Mathematical techniques such as discriminant analysis and cluster analysis exist for identifying products that are frequently ordered together. The general idea is to compute measures (similar to correlations) that identify pairs or groups of products that are frequently ordered together. This measure can be treated as a measure of flow between product storage areas, and pairs with large values should be located close together if possible.

Product Similarity

Often physically similar products or different brands of the same product are stored together for the following reasons:

1. Different brands of the same product (e.g., different makes and colors of paint) are commonly ordered together.
2. For systems using human order pickers, putting all brands of a product together makes their search easier. If the items are removed by customers themselves, such as in a retail store, grouping similar products together makes it more convenient for customers to search for different brands, sizes, and related products.
3. If some products must be kept warmer or cooler than others, it is less expensive to have one area designed for specific temperatures rather than several.

The general principles listed here apply not only to businesses in retail and wholesale distribution industries. They are equally applicable to organizations that carry large inventories of parts and materials for their own production processes.

RETAIL FACILITIES LAYOUT

The guiding objectives when laying out manufacturing facilities and most service facilities are to minimize cost and to make the flow of materials and people as unobstructed as possible. In retail stores the objective is to encourage customers to buy as much as possible, especially of high-profit items. To encourage and facilitate purchases the store operator must make trade-offs between two often conflicting design considerations: the ease with which customers can move and find desired items versus the retailer's desire to expose the customer to as many products as possible to increase the chance of additional purchases.

Aisle Configuration

In retail store layout, one solution is to design the store and allocate products to locations to maximize customer purchase exposures without making the layout so inefficient or confusing that it creates ill will. The balance between efficiency of movement and customer exposure will vary from store to store, depending on the types of products sold and the customer population. For example, in up-scale department stores where customers are in less of a hurry, stores can design more for exposure and less for efficiency of flow. These stores will often use a maze design with narrow aisles, as shown in Figure 8.23, rather than long, wide aisles. The maze configuration forces customers to weave their way through many display racks rather than walking quickly in a straight line without noticing adjacent products.

In contrast, customers at large discount stores such as Wal-Mart would be aggravated if they had to weave their way through a maze. They want to move through the store quickly and not have the feeling that they are being exploited. These stores use

FIGURE 8.23 Retail store maze.

Wide aisles such as these at Toys-R-Us can make shopping more convenient for retail customers.

long, wide aisles, which also makes it easier to restock the shelves. Similarly, if a grocery store used a maze configuration, it would create traffic jams and make customers irate as they tried to maneuver their way through the store with shopping carts.

Product Location

One way to increase product exposure without creating a maze is to allocate products to locations using an approach *opposite* to that described for warehouses. A store can determine which products tend to be purchased together, but rather than locating them close together for ease of retrieval, the store can place them as far apart in the store as possible so that customers have to traverse the entire store to buy them, which automatically exposes them to many product displays. As long as the store has long, wide aisles, customers will normally not view this practice as objectionable. This is the reason most grocery stores put bread at one end of the store and milk at the other.

This strategy has to be balanced by other considerations, though. For example, complementary products that are often used together, such as flour and sugar, will often be put next to each other so that the customer who needs one of them will see the other and perhaps buy it.

This brief discussion provides only a flavor of the complex issues surrounding the layout and allocation of products and service areas within a retail facility. As retail stores expand the number and type of products sold and the auxiliary services they provide, such as video rental or banking services in grocery stores, this complexity will continue to grow. It is an area where good operations management can produce significant benefits.

Summary

- A **product layout** is a physical configuration of the production process that is designed around the flow of a product through the production process. Product layouts are used for flow processes.
- The major issue in designing repetitive flow processes is allocating work among work stations to obtain an efficient balance and flow of product.
- Parallel work stations can be used to increase the production rate and to expand the variety of tasks assigned to a work station.
- Parallel production lines provide greater flexibility and productivity than one higher-volume production line.
- Random variations in work station times reduce the effective capacity of the production process.
- The two most common spatial arrangements for flow processes are straight-line and U-shaped layouts.
- A **functional (process) layout** is a spatial configuration of functional work areas intended to minimize flow costs while maintaining flexibility of movement. This layout is used for job-shop and cellular processes, as well as at the facility level to configure several departments or subsystems.
- The functional layout procedure can be assisted by computer-based heuristics that construct and improve on possible layouts.

- There are two types of production work cells: **Flow cells** which have a fixed sequencing of tasks; and **group cells** which allow flexible sequencing.
- The primary issues in cellular process design are to determine how many cells to have, what types to have, and what operations to perform at each cell.
- The **process flow diagram, process chart**, and **service blueprint** are tools that help identify opportunities for eliminating or combining tasks and reorganizing work to provide faster service.
- By storing items that are frequently retrieved (ordered) together, companies can improve the operating efficiency of warehouses.
- In retail sales facilities, layout plays a significant role in promoting product sales. By forcing customers to walk past many product displays, by separating noncomplementary products that are frequently purchased together, and by having complementary products stored together, retailers expose customers to many purchasing cues that encourage them to buy products.

KEY TERMS

ALDEP (automated layout design program) **396**
bottleneck work station **373**
construction heuristics **372**
CORELAP (computerized relationship layout planning) **396**
CRAFT (computerized reallocation of facilities technique) **394**
efficiency (% balance) **373**
flow cell **397**
flow-cost matrix **390**
flow matrix **390**
functional (process) layout **387**
group cell **397**
group technology **397**
improvement heuristics **378**
line balancing **372**
maximum cycle time **374**
operations analysis **404**
pack **399**
positional weight **375**
precedence requirements **372**
predecessors **374**
process chart **404**
process flow diagram **404**
product layout **371**
production cycle time **373**
production flow analysis (PFA) **398**
production line (line process) **384**
production rate **373**
proximity charts (relationship or REL charts) **390**
ranked positional weight technique (RPWT) **375**
relationship (REL) diagram **388**
service blueprint **406**
task times **372**
theoretical minimum number of work stations **375**

KEY FORMULAS

Maximum cycle time = $c_{\max}$

= 1/(minimum desired production rate)

Theoretical minimum number of work stations = $\lceil T/c_{\max} \rceil$,

where $\lceil\ \rceil$ means round *up* any fractional value

Production rate P = 1/(actual cycle time) = $1/c$

Efficiency (% balance) of the line = 100% × $[T/(N \times c)]$,

where T = total amount of work time required to make a unit of product

N = the number of work stations on the production line

SOLVED PROBLEMS

Problem 1. Sauter Manufacturing wants to design a repetitive production line to produce one of its products. The production process requires 14 tasks, which are listed in Table 8.9, along with estimated task times and predecessors for each task. Sauter wants to produce at least 270 units of product per day. It expects the production line to operate 450 minutes per day.

(a) Draw a precedence diagram for the tasks.

(b) Compute the maximum cycle time the line can have and still produce at least 270 units per day.

(c) Compute the theoretical minimum number of work stations needed.

TABLE 8.9 TASK INFORMATION FOR SAUTER MANUFACTURING

Task	Task Time (sec)	Predecessor Tasks
A	10	—
B	25	—
C	10	—
D	35	A
E	65	B, C
F	35	A, E
G	30	—
H	20	D, G
I	45	A
J	50	—
K	20	—
L	40	J, K
M	30	A, L
N	70	F, H, I, M
	Total time T = 485	

(d) Use the RPWT to construct a production line, clearly showing which tasks are assigned to each work station.

(e) Compute the actual output per day that would occur with the design from part (d).

(f) Compute the efficiency of the production line.

Solution

(a) The precedence diagram is given in Figure 8.24.

(b) $c_{max} = 1/P_{min} = 1/(270 \text{ units/day}) = (1/270) \text{ day/unit}$

$(1/270) \text{ day/unit} \times 27{,}000 \text{ sec/day} = 100 \text{ sec/unit}$

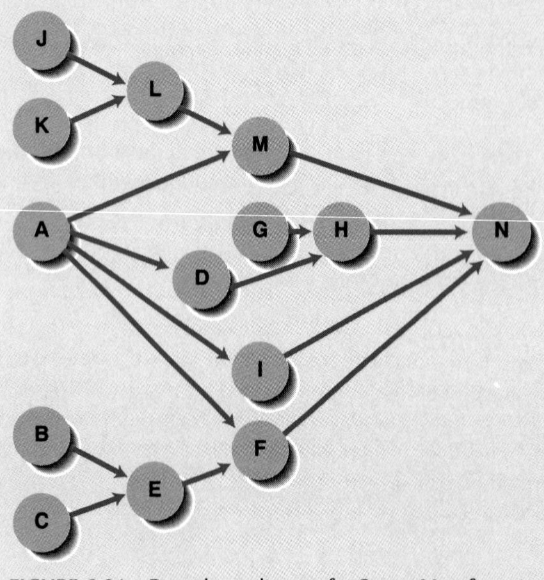

FIGURE 8.24 Precedence diagram for Sauter Manufacturing.

(c) No work station can perform more than 100 seconds of work on any unit, so the theoretical minimum number of work stations is

$$\lceil T/c_{max} \rceil = \lceil 485/100 \rceil = \lceil 4.85 \rceil = 5$$

(d) We now compute the positional weights of each task using the precedence diagram in Figure 8.24:

Task	Task Time (sec)	Positional Weight
A	10	245
B	25	195
C	10	180
D	35	125
E	65	170
F	35	105
G	30	120
H	20	90
I	45	115
J	50	190
K	20	160
L	40	140
M	30	100
N	70	70

Using the ranked positional weight technique, we make the following assignments in order:

A → WS 1
B → WS 1
J → WS 1
C → WS 1
E → WS 2
K → WS 2
L → WS 3
D → WS 3
G → WS 4
I → WS 4
F → WS 5
M → WS 5
H → WS 4
N → WS 6

The resulting production line is given in Figure 8.25.

(e) The *actual* cycle time, c = 95 seconds; so 1 unit of product will be made every 95 seconds and the production rate, P = 1/(95 sec/unit) = (1/95 unit)/sec = 284.2 units/day.

(f) The efficiency of this line design is

$$\text{efficiency} = [485 \text{ sec}/(6 \text{ WSs} \times 95 \text{ sec})] \times 100\% = 85.1\%$$

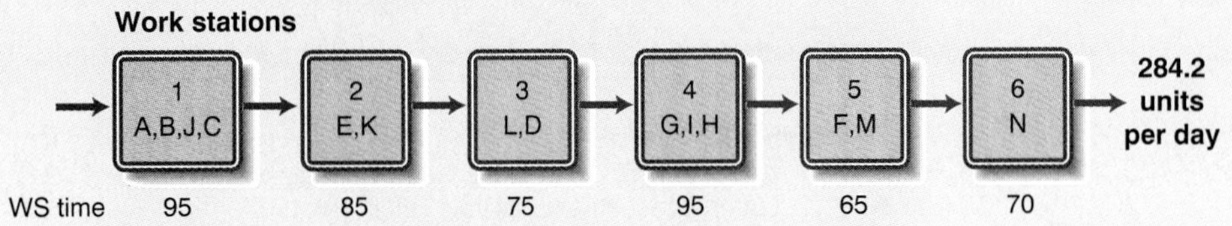

FIGURE 8.25 Production line design for Sauter Manufacturing.

Problem 2. Shortroad Industries has six departments, which are assigned to locations in its facility as shown in Figure 8.26. The estimated daily movements among departments are given in Table 8.10. There are no walls between departments, but there is a network of horizontal and vertical aisles throughout the facility, so travel distance is approximately rectilinear (movement can only be horizontal or vertical, not diagonal).

(a) Assuming all flows are equally costly per unit distance, and using the middle of each department as the location of the department, compute the daily flow cost (in person-feet) for the current layout.

(b) Construct a flow diagram showing the magnitude of flows among departments.

(c) Construct an improved layout and compute the daily flow cost for the layout.

Solution

(a) The distances between the department locations are as follows:

1–2, 2–3, 4–5, 5–6:	80 feet
1–4, 2–5, 3–6:	60 feet
1–5, 2–4, 2–6, 3–5:	140 feet
1–3, 4–6:	160 feet
1–6, 3–4:	220 feet

Summing the products of the flows and distances:

$$f_{AB}d_{AB} + f_{AC}d_{AC} + \ldots + f_{DF}d_{DF} + f_{EF}d_{EF} =$$
$$20(80 \text{ ft}) + 40(160 \text{ ft}) + \ldots + 90(160 \text{ ft}) + 20(80 \text{ ft}) = 57{,}200 \text{ person-ft}$$

(b) Figure 8.27 is an REL diagram showing interdepartmental flows.

TABLE 8.10 INTER-DEPARTMENT FLOWS FOR SHORTROAD INDUSTRIES

	Department					
	A	B	C	D	E	F
A	—	20	40	10	0	10
B	—	—	20	20	40	60
C	—	—	—	50	10	40
D	—	—	—	—	30	90
E	—	—	—	—	—	20
F	—	—	—	—	—	—

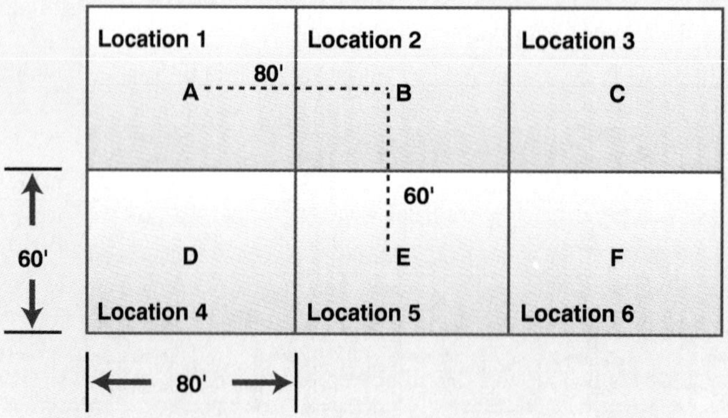

FIGURE 8.26 Shortroad Industries facility: initial layout.

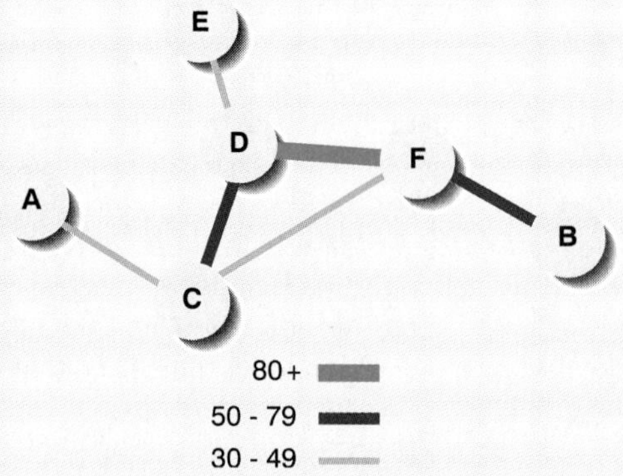

FIGURE 8.27 REL flow diagram for Shortroad Industries.

(c) Departments D and F have the largest flows between them and other departments, so we put those two in the two central locations, 2 and 5. Department B has a large flow with F, so we put it next to F; C has a large flow with D, so we put it next to D. Departments B and E have moderate flows between them, so we put E across from B. Departments A and C have moderate flows, so we put A across from C. The resulting layout of 1-C, 2-D, 3-E, 4-A, 5-F, and 6-B has a flow cost of 44,000 person-ft.

Problem 3. Somerton Corporation has devised the following PFA chart for its product packs and operations:

	Product Pack								
	1	2	3	4	5	6	7	8	9
A				X				X	X
B	X	X		X				X	
C		X			X	X			X
D		X	X		X		X		X
E		X	X		X	X		X	
F	X			X		X	X		X
G	X		X		X	X	X		

(a) Rearrange the columns to make it easier to see the similarities among product packs.

(b) Identify some possible cells (the operations to put in a cell).

Solution

(a) The following rearrangement forms several visible "blocks":

	Product Pack								
	8	4	5	2	9	3	1	6	7
A	X	X			X				
B	X	X		X			X		
C			X	X	X			X	
D			X	X	X	X			X
E	X		X	X		X		X	
F		X			X		X	X	X
G			X			X	X	X	X

(b) In this rearrangement, some likely cells are A,B for packs 4 and 8; C,D,E for packs 2 and 5 (and possibly 3, 6, and 9 as well); and F,G for packs 1, 6, and 7.

Discussion and Review Questions

1. What factors most influence the effective output rate of a flow process?
2. Once initial task assignments are made to work stations in a flow process (e.g., by using a heuristic), what other actions could one take to improve the balance of the process and increase the output rate?
3. What are the advantages of using parallel work stations as part of a production line?
4. What are the advantages and disadvantages of using parallel production lines rather than a single line with higher capacity?
5. What are the advantages and disadvantages of arranging a flow process in a straight line?
6. What are the advantages and disadvantages of arranging a flow process in a U shape?
7. How does randomness in the processing times of tasks affect the operation and effective output of a flow process?
8. What are the primary causes of variation in processing times? What actions can be taken to reduce this variation and its effects on the output rate?
9. What are the advantages and disadvantages of using computer heuristics in functional layouts (e.g., for a job-shop process)?
10. If a company had a facility that contained six separate flow processes, what layout would it use for the facility as a whole? Why?
11. What is the principle difference between a flow cell and a group cell?
12. What are the advantages and disadvantages of a flow cell? A group cell?
13. What considerations make the layout of material storage facilities different from that of other production facilities?
14. What is the significant difference between the layout of retail facilities and that of other production facilities?
15. Give a specific example, not mentioned in the chapter, of a retail store that designs its facility primarily for ease and efficiency of movement, with little or no attempt to increase the number of product exposures to customers. Explain why or why not this emphasis makes sense for that store.
16. Give a specific example of a retail store that designs its facilities primarily to maximize the number of product exposures to customers, with little consideration to efficiency of movement. Explain why or why not this arrangement makes sense for this store, and explain why or why not customers do not get angry.
17. Explain the major considerations and trade-offs when deciding where to store or display products in a retail facility.
18. What factors may make the design of a service process different from that of a manufacturing process?

Problems

1. Synchro Manufacturing Company (SMC) is developing a new repetitive process. The process will involve 12 tasks; the task times and precedence relationships are as follows:

Task	Task Time (sec)	Predecessors
A	12	—
B	8	A
C	10	—
D	16	C
E	20	B, D
F	9	—
G	15	—
H	11	E, F, G
I	8	H
J	15	I
K	8	I
L	13	J, K

(a) Compute the maximum cycle time SMC can have if it wants to produce 1100 units of product per eight-hour day. (b) Compute the theoretical minimum number of work stations needed. (c) Use the RPWT heuristic to construct a production line that minimizes the number of work stations. (d) For your solution in (c), compute the cycle time and actual production rate. (e) Compute the efficiency (% balance) of the production line.

2. Laslo Enterprises PLC assembles toys on an assembly line. The company wishes to produce 480 units per eight-hour day. The tasks, task times, and precedence requirements necessary to produce the toys are given below. (a) Compute the maximum allowable cycle time for Laslo's assembly line. (b) Compute the theoretical minimum number of work stations that Laslo will need to achieve this. (c) Use the RPWT heuristic to construct a production line that attempts to minimize the number of work stations

while producing at least 480 units per day. (d) For your solution in (c), compute the actual cycle time and the actual production rate that would result. (e) Compute the efficiency (% balance) of the line designed in (c).

Task	Time (sec)	Predecessors
A	23	—
B	28	A
C	14	B, D
D	20	A
E	15	A
F	17	D, E
G	24	C, F
H	15	G

3. Dr. Wu, operations manager at Nesa Electronics, prides herself on excellent assembly line balancing. She has been told that the firm needs to produce 1400 electric relays per work day. Due to breaks and lunch, there are 420 working minutes in a work day. The following table lists the tasks, precedence relationships, and average task time required to produce a relay.

Task	Time (sec)	Must Follow Task
A	13	—
B	4	A
C	10	B
D	10	—
E	6	D
F	12	E
G	5	E
H	6	F, G
I	7	H
J	5	H
K	4	I, J
L	15	C, K

(a) Compute the maximum cycle time Nesa can have and still produce 1400 relays per day. (b) Compute the theoretical minimum number of work stations required. (c) Use the RPWT heuristic to construct a production line that attempts to minimize the number of work stations while producing at least 1400 units per day. (d) For your solution in (c), compute the actual cycle time and the actual production rate that would result. (e) Compute the efficiency (% balance) of the line designed in (c).

4. Midwest Concepts assembles televisions on an assembly line. The process requires 12 separate tasks; the tasks, the average time for each task, and the predecessor tasks are as follows:

Task	Time (min)	Predecessors
A	4	—
B	6	A
C	5	—
D	1	A
E	8	C
F	7	A, E
G	5	D
H	10	F, G
I	3	A, C
J	2	B, C
K	5	D
L	4	F, G, J, K

The firm wishes to design an assembly line so as to produce at least five units per hour while minimizing the number of work stations. (a) Compute the maximum cycle time. (b) Compute the theoretical minimum number of work stations needed. (c) Using the RPWT heuristic, construct an assembly line that minimizes the number of work stations. (d) For your solution in (c), compute the actual cycle time and the actual production rate that would result, (e) Compute the efficiency (% balance) of the line designed in (c).

5. Rapid Fire Restaurants (RFR) is a new fast-food restaurant chain. RFR has divided its normal drive-thru service process into the following tasks:

Task	Task Time (sec)	Predecessors
A—Take order	25	—
B—Receive payment	20	A
C—Gather drinks	35	A
D—Gather food	32	A
E—Put food, etc. in bag	25	C, D
F—Give food to customer	10	B, E

Currently, RFR has a single window, with one person who takes the order, gathers the food, collects the money, and gives the food to the customer. This takes an average of 147 seconds per customer, so only 24.5 cars per hour can be served. RFR wants to increase its drive-thru capacity to 60 cars per hour by forming a multiwindow line (there is not enough room for two or three parallel lines). (a) How many windows (work stations) will RFR need to serve 60 cars per hour? (b) Using the RPWT heuristic assign the tasks to the windows to produce the desired service rate, making sure that the precedence requirements are satisfied. (c) What other changes might make the operation faster?

6.* A company wants to design a repetitive flow process that requires seven work stations in sequence. Each work station requires a 20 ft × 20 ft square work/equipment area; work stations must be separated from each other by 5 feet; conveyers will connect each work station; each work station needs a 10 ft × 10 ft storage area next to it for materials that are to be used at the work station; there must be a 15-foot-wide unobstructed aisle for the raw material transport equipment to deliver materials to each work station. (a) Design a layout in which the work stations form a straight line. Compute the approximate square footage of the area needed for the facility. Assuming one load of materials has to be transported from the receiving area to each work station per hour, compute the total transport distance per hour that the transporter must travel. (b) Repeat part (a) using a U-shaped design. (c) Compare the two designs, and explain which would be better and why.

7. For *Solved Problem* 1, suppose we want to increase output further. By switching and shifting tasks, improve the solution in Figure 8.25.

8. A company wants to design a functional layout by assigning six departments of equal size to the locations in Figure 8.28. The estimated flows among the departments are as follows:

	Department					
	A	B	C	D	E	F
A	—	50	10	40	20	0
B	—	—	20	40	25	90
C	—	—	—	15	30	40
D	—	—	—	—	0	60
E	—	—	—	—	—	30
F	—	—	—	—	—	—

(a) Construct an interdepartment flow diagram to indicate the magnitudes of flow among the departments. (b) Assign the tasks to the locations in Figure 8.28 to minimize flow cost (use rectilinear distance and assume that all flows are equally costly per unit distance).

9. A company wants to design a functional layout by assigning nine departments of equal size to the locations in Figure 8.29. The estimated flows among the departments are as follows:

	Department								
	A	B	C	D	E	F	G	H	I
A	—	50	10	40	20	0	25	100	10
B	—	—	20	40	25	90	0	40	20
C	—	—	—	15	30	40	50	10	0
D	—	—	—	—	0	60	10	15	75
E	—	—	—	—	—	30	30	10	20
F	—	—	—	—	—	—	0	40	20
G	—	—	—	—	—	—	—	25	40
H	—	—	—	—	—	—	—	—	20
I	—	—	—	—	—	—	—	—	—

(a) Construct an interdepartment flow diagram to indicate the magnitudes of flow among the departments. (b) Assign the tasks to the locations in Figure 8.29 to minimize flow cost (use rectilinear distance from the center of each department and assume that all flows are equally costly per unit distance).

10. Using the data in Figure 8.10, construct a layout for the nine work centers in that chart. Assume that the work centers are of equal size, and that the facility and possible locations of the work centers are the same as in Figure 8.29. Assign the work centers to the nine possible locations.

11.* Using the flow data in problem 9, assume that departments A and C require 20,000 square feet of

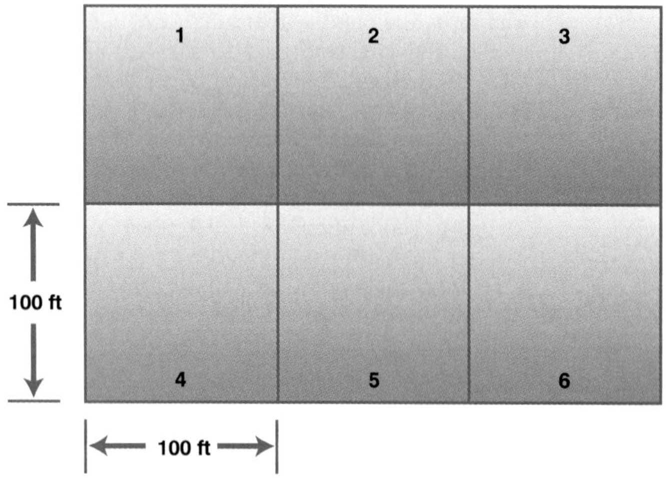

FIGURE 8.28 Possible department locations in problem 8.

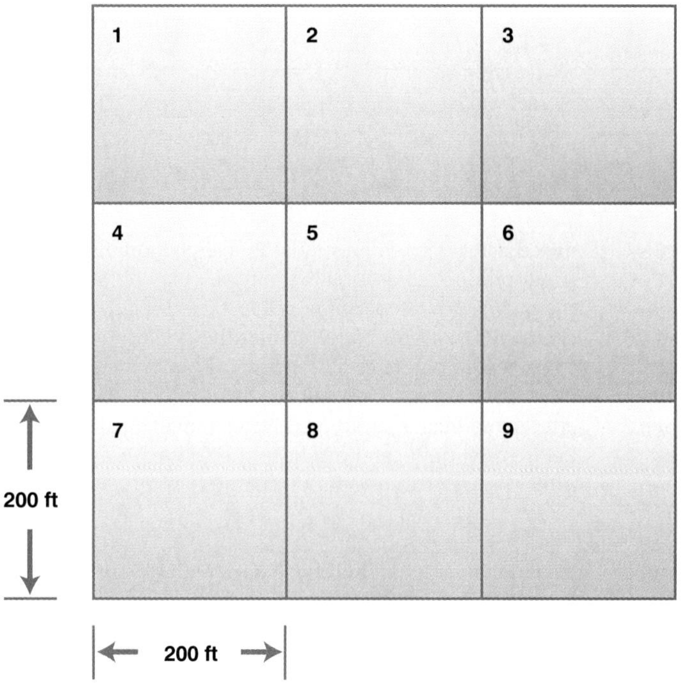

FIGURE 8.29 Possible department locations in problems 9 and 10.

space, D and F require 5,000 square feet, and all other departments require 10,000 square feet. Assume the facility is a 500 × 200 foot rectangle (100,000 square feet). (a) Use a flow diagram to construct an initial layout (hint: divide the facility into 50 × 50 foot blocks). (b) (Computer) Use CRAFT (if it is available on computer) to find an improved solution.

12.* Using the data in problem 8, assume that department A requires 9600 square feet of space, B requires 6400 square feet, and C, D, E, and F each require 16,000 square feet. Assume the facility is a 400 × 200 foot rectangle (80,000 square feet). (a) Use a flow diagram to construct an initial layout (hint: divide the facility into 40 × 40 foot blocks). (b) (Computer) Use CRAFT (if it is available on computer) to find an improved solution.

13. Brad Allen Corporation has developed the following PFA chart for its products:

	Product Pack								
	1	2	3	4	5	6	7	8	9
A			X		X			X	X
B	X	X		X			X	X	
C		X	X		X	X		X	
D	X	X		X		X	X		X
E		X	X		X			X	X
F	X			X	X		X		X
G	X		X		X	X	X		X

(a) Rearrange the columns to make it easier to see similarities among product packs. (b) Identify some possible cells (i.e., the operations to put in a cell).

14. Austin Metal Industries has divided its products into seven primary families and its operations into five, A–E. The operations sequence for the products in the families are listed below, along with each family's percentage share of the company's total sales volume.

Product Family	Sequence of Activities	% of Company Sales
1	A → B → D	10
2	A → C → B → E	15
3	B → C → D → E	25
4	C → A → B → D	10
5	A → C → D → E	20
6	B → A → B → C → D → E	15
7	D → E → A → C → B → C → D → E	5

Identify at least two possible cells that would be appropriate for Austin to use. State whether they should be flow cells or group cells and explain why.

CASE

Pesti-Chemical: A Process Design and Capacity Expansion Case

Pesti-Chemical, Ltd. (PCL), produces customized agricultural pesticides. By designing its products to treat specific crops in specific geographic regions, PCL is able to produce pesticides that are more environmentally friendly than general-purpose pesticides. However, PCL's products are produced in much smaller quantities and cost significantly more than general-purpose pesticides. Although the company produces hundreds of different products, they are all made using essentially the same production process, in which active chemicals are added to an inert chemical base and then mixed. Most chemicals can be added and mixed at the same time, but some products require sequential addition and separate mixing to avoid undesired chemical reactions, and for some products the chemicals must be heated to a certain temperature for the appropriate mixing or reactions to occur. PCL also makes some of its own input chemicals by blending or executing chemical reactions among basic chemicals. Pesticides and input chemicals are made in batches of 100–1000 gallons (the current capacity of the main mixing vessel).

Figure 8.30 illustrates the main components of the original production process, and Table 8.11 gives the range of processing times for each major step in the process. A vessel is filled with an inert liquid. The vessel is then transported to a mixing area, where one or more chemicals are added. The liquids in the vessel are then mixed using a machine similar to a large food blender. For some products, additional chemicals may be added and the mixing repeated. Some products, especially the input chemicals that are made, require the liquid in the vessel to be heated before or after chemicals are added and mixing occurs. For a few chemicals, the liquid must be cooled after some mixing, before additional mixing can occur, or before the liquid can be sent to the container-filling area. After the pesticide or input chemical is produced, it is

TABLE 8.11 PROCESSING TIMES PER BATCH FOR TYPICAL PRODUCTS

Processing	Time (min)
Clean vessel	10–12
Fill vessel with inert liquid	3–5
Transport from filling unit to mixing	1–2
Transport between mixing and heating	2
Mixing	5–15
Heating	5–20
Settling/cooling	5–15
Fill containers	4–15

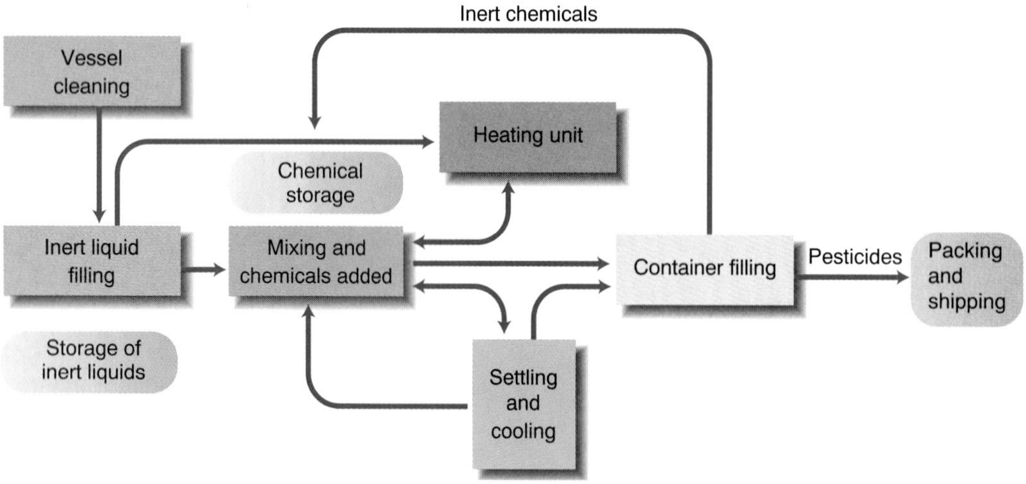

FIGURE 8.30 Original production system for PCL.

sent to an area where the liquid is put into 5-gallon containers (for final products) or 40-gallon barrels (for input chemicals). The input chemicals are then sent to the storage area near the mixing unit; the final pesticides are sent to a packaging area, where the 5-gallon containers are put into boxes. The final pesticides are then grouped into shipments and prepared for loading onto trucks or railcars.

PCL sells pesticides throughout North America and Europe. It has one plant in Canada that serves the North American market and one in Belgium that serves Europe. North American sales have been increasing rapidly, and the Canadian plant is nearing capacity even with three shifts a day, seven days a week. Despite the similarities, there are enough differences among the production processes of each product for the production system to operate more like a job-shop process than a flow process, and the process does not have the efficiency we would normally expect from a chemical production process for several reasons:

1. The time required to mix products varies considerably by type of pesticide and batch size. As a result, if one of the batches takes especially long at some step, it can cause other activities to stop.
2. Some pesticides require heating, which can cause other activities to stop.
3. The vessels have to be cleaned after every batch is produced.
4. PCL makes some of its input chemicals itself. Production of the input chemicals and mixing of pesticides occur within the same system.
5. PCL uses only two primary mixing vessels. While one vessel is involved in mixing, the second vessel is being cleaned and filled with inert liquid. Because it takes approximately 15 minutes to clean and fill a vessel but 10–60 minutes to produce a product, one vessel and some workers are idle much of the time. Two vessels are not processed concurrently within the mixing/heating/cooling areas because when a vessel has been heated to the correct temperature, it must be immediately mixed. In the past, PCL had problems because the mixing unit was occupied by the second vessel when the first one was heated and ready for mixing.

Redesign

PCL decided to redesign its production process and expand capacity in the following way. First, the company reviewed its product history and the production data for each product. It found that only 5% of the pesticides required the heating unit during final blending but 90% of the chemical inputs made by PCL required it during their production. This was because production of the pesticide inputs often required chemical reactions, whereas final pesticide manufacture was simply a mixing process with no additional chemical reactions; the chemicals were heated only to accelerate the mixing or increase the uniformity of the mixture. In addition, PCL determined that because one vessel could not be in the heating unit while another was in the mixing unit, the heating and mixing units alternated as bottlenecks in the system. As a result, not only were the vessel-cleaning, inert liquid-filling, and container-filling units idle much of the time, the two bottlenecks, mixing and heating, also had substantial idle time.

From this analysis, PCL expanded and reconfigured the system as shown in Figure 8.31. The major change was that PCL created a cellular-type production process with two primary production streams. Products that required mixing but no heating would follow the top stream, while those that required heating would follow the bottom stream. (If needed, products that require only mixing could also use the mixing/heating stream.) The major

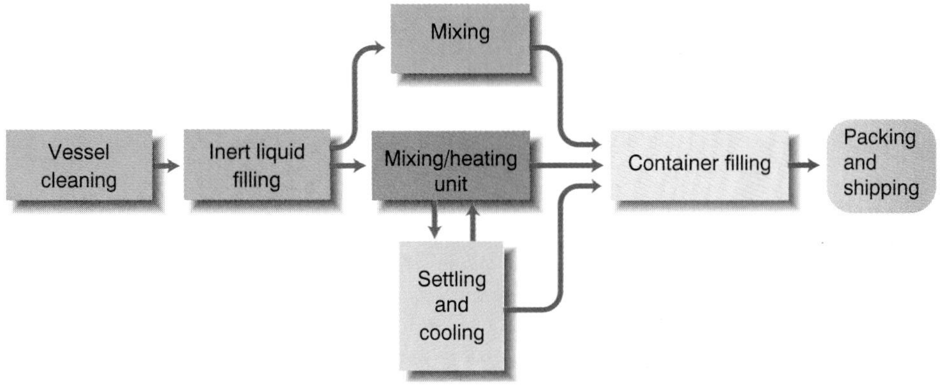

FIGURE 8.31 New production system for PCL.

capital expenditures involved (1) replacing the old heating unit with a new combination mixing/heating unit and (2) purchasing two more primary vessels.

Under the new configuration, the two streams share the vessel-cleaning, vessel-filling, and container-filling units because these had considerable unused capacity under the old system. By adding two more vessels (raising the number to four) and by keeping the products in each stream similar, two products could be mixed concurrently and the mixing units had less idle time. The operation of the new system generally followed this pattern: Approximately every 12–15 minutes a vessel was sent to the cleaning unit, from which it was sent to the inert filling unit. The vessel was then sent either to the mixing unit, if only mixing was to occur, or to the mixing/heating unit if heating was needed. Because products that required heating took approximately twice as long to produce, PCL normally sent two out of every three vessels to the top (mixing) stream.

The new system almost tripled the effective production capacity (far more than the doubling that was expected). In addition, the cost per unit decreased by 30%, the quality of some products improved, and late deliveries were cut in half. The reasons for these benefits were as follows:

1. Two batches could be mixed simultaneously with the two streams, which automatically doubled capacity.
2. By running a narrow mix of similar products on each stream, it was possible to sequence products so as to utilize the vessel-cleaning, vessel-filling, and container-filling units more efficiently.
3. The new heating/mixing unit eliminated the transporting between the heating and mixing units, which saved two to eight minutes per batch; furthermore, the temperature could be controlled better, which contributed greatly to improved quality.
4. PCL was able to lower its price, which dramatically increased sales, so it was able to make more large batches, which require proportionately less mixing time and fewer cleanings per gallon.
5. Because almost all final products were made using the top stream and input chemicals were made using the bottom stream, PCL was able to store and track materials better. Basic chemicals used to make input chemicals were stored near the heating/mixing unit, and inputs to the pesticides were stored near the mixing unit. This arrangement reduced the time that was previously lost trying to find the right chemicals for mixing.

The cost, capacity, quality, and delivery benefits were due primarily to homogenizing the products in each stream and creating two more specialized production streams. Notice, however, that PCL was able to retain considerable production flexibility because the lower stream could produce products that did not require heating as well. This capability made it possible to expedite some orders on that stream or to sequence jobs on the streams to maintain a balanced flow through the system. With the new system, PCL tripled its production and sales within two years.

QUESTIONS

1. Despite the improvements, suppose that the mixing and mixing/heating units were still idle 25% of the time, due mainly to the wait for the container-filling operation. (Liquid is drained from the vessels directly into the containers.) This was especially troublesome when both production streams finished a product at about the same time. What could PCL do to reduce this idleness and increase production?
2. If you were assigned to schedule production of chemicals at PCL, what specific rules of thumb or guiding principles would you use to sequence the production of products?
3. Suppose output increased so much that vessel cleaning became a bottleneck. What steps could be taken to reduce cleaning time?

SELECTED READINGS

ARMOUR, G. C., and E. S. BUFFA. "A Heuristic Algorithm and Simulation Approach to Relative Location of Facilities," *Management Science,*, Vol. 9, 1963, pp. 294–309.

ASKIN, RONALD G., and S. P. SUBRAMANIAN. "A Cost-Based Heuristic for Group Technology Configuration," *International Journal of Production Research*, Vol. 25, 1987, pp. 101–113.

BUFFA, E. S., and R. K. SARIN. *Modern Production/Operations Management* (8th ed.), Wiley, New York, 1987.

BUZACOTT, JOHN A., and J. GEORGE SHANTHIKUMAR. *Stochastic*

Models of Manufacturing Systems, Prentice-Hall, Englewood Cliffs, NJ, 1993.

CHOOBINEH, F. "A Framework for the Design of Cellular Manufacturing Systems," *International Journal of Production Research*, Vol. 26, 1988, pp. 1161–1172.

DAR-EL, E. M. "MALB—a Heuristic Technique for Balancing Large Scale Single-Model Assembly Lines," AIIE *Transactions*, Vol. 5, 1973, pp. 343–356.

FRANCIS, R. L., L. MCGINNIS, and J. A. WHITE. *Facility Layout and Location: An Analytical Approach* (2nd ed.), Prentice-Hall, Englewood Cliffs, NJ, 1992.

GHOSH, SOUMEN, and ROGER GAGNON. "A Comprehensive Literature Review and Analysis of the Design, Balancing, and Scheduling of Assembly Lines," *International Journal of Production Research*, Vol. 27, 1989, pp. 637–670.

GROOVER, M. P. *Automation, Production Systems, and Computer-Aided Manufacturing*, Prentice-Hall, Englewood Cliffs, NJ, 1980.

HELGESON, W. B., and D. P. BIRNIE. "Assembly Line Balancing Using Ranked Positional Weight Technique," *Journal of Industrial Engineering*, Vol. 12, 1961, pp. 292–298.

JOHNSON, ROGER. "Optimally Balancing Large Assembly Lines with FABLE," *Management Science*, Vol. 34, 1988, pp. 240–253.

MUTHER, RICHARD, and JOHN D. WHEELER, *Simplified Systematic Layout Planning* (3rd ed.), Management and Industrial Publications, Kansas City, MO, 1994.

STEUDEL, HAROLD J., and PAUL DESRUELLE. *Manufacturing in the Nineties*, Von Nostrand Reinhold, New York, 1992.

WILLIAMS, MICHAEL. "Some Plants Tear Out Long Assembly Lines, Switch to Craft Work," *Wall Street Journal*, Oct. 24, 1994.

CHAPTER 9

WAITING LINES

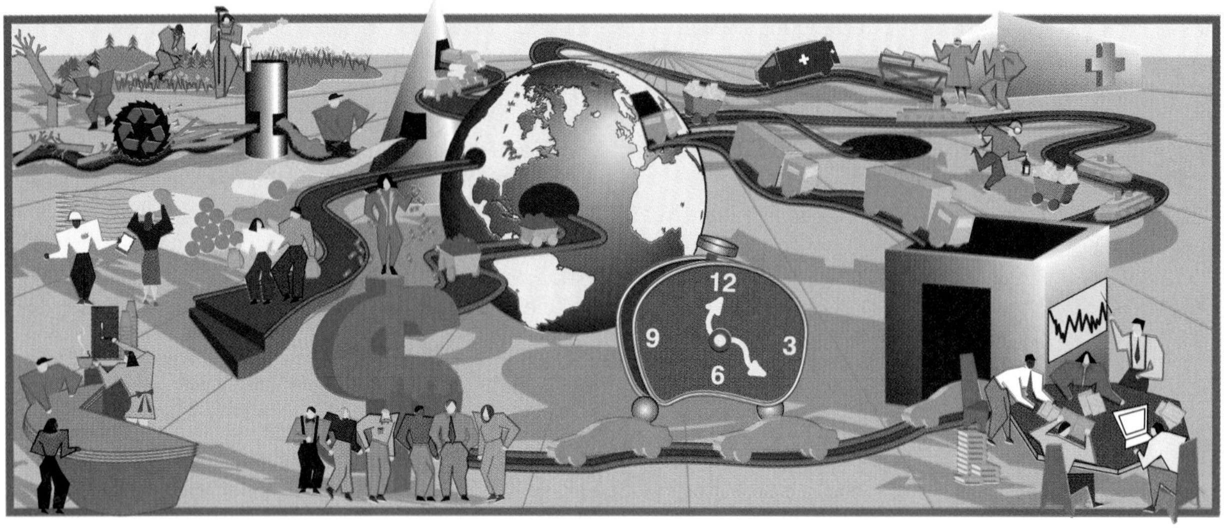

9.1 QUEUEING THEORY
On the Job: Deb Holler, Great Western Bank

9.2 CHARACTERISTICS OF QUEUEING SYSTEMS
Customer Characteristics
Service Characteristics
System Configuration

9.3 NOTATION, TERMINOLOGY, AND THE EXPLODING QUEUE PROPERTY
Measures of System Performance
Capacity Utilization and the Exploding Queue Property
The Kendall-Lee Notation for Queueing Systems

9.4 SINGLE-SERVER SYSTEMS WITH EXPONENTIAL SERVICE TIMES (M/M/1 SYSTEMS)

9.5 MULTISERVER SYSTEMS WITH EXPONENTIAL SERVICE TIMES (M/M/s SYSTEMS)
Benefits of Pooling Servers Into One System
The Number of Queues for Multiserver Systems

9.6 SINGLE-SERVER SYSTEMS WITH GENERAL OR CONSTANT SERVICE TIMES (M/G/1 AND M/D/1 SYSTEMS)

9.7 THE ROLE OF VARIANCE IN QUEUEING SYSTEMS
Slower Servers Are Sometimes More Efficient
Pacing of Customer Arrivals Reduces Waiting
Exploiting Customer Heterogeneity to Improve Service
Other Issues Regarding Designated Servers

9.8 M/M/s SYSTEMS WITH A FINITE CUSTOMER POPULATION

9.9 SERIAL AND NETWORK QUEUEING SYSTEMS
Queueing Networks

9.10 BEHAVIORAL AND OTHER CONSIDERATIONS IN QUEUEING
In Good Company: L. L. Bean Lines It Up
Nonlinear Waiting Costs and the Psychology of Waiting
Additional Suggestions for Improving Queueing Systems

Interstate Rail and Trucking Company: A Case Study in Applying Queueing Theory

9.1 Queueing Theory

We often find ourselves waiting: to make bank transactions, to talk with someone on a telephone, to renew our driving license, to get our car or television repaired, or to enroll in a class. In fact, one study found that during a lifetime the average person spends five years waiting in line. Considerable research has been done to identify and measure the causes and consequences of waiting. This field is referred to as **queueing theory**; the term **queue** is simply another name for a waiting line. Systems that contain waiting lines are often called **queueing systems**.

There are good reasons to study queueing theory. First, *queueing* is the only word in the English language with five consecutive vowels;[1] this fact can come in handy at parties. More important, waiting lines are a common and important component of most service and manufacturing systems. In many operations the design and management of queueing subsystems are critical to the success, or even survival, of the organization. For example, if customers at a fast-food restaurant have to wait too long for service, the customer base will disappear; if catalog retailers such as L. L. Bean make customers wait too long on the phone, they will lose their main source of orders; and if the number of production jobs waiting between work stations is too large, loss of efficiency, wasted space for storage, and late delivery of orders can result. The number of examples is endless, but in each case the fundamental aspects of the queueing systems are the same, and they can be studied in a unified fashion.

On the Job

Deb Holler, Great Western Bank

"Nobody likes to wait," says Deb Holler, branch vice-president at Great Western Bank in Encino, California. "We try to keep people from actually despising it." Part of Deb's responsibility is to plan staffing each month in response to a computerized report that tracks how many banking transactions each teller completes in an hour. The report helps Deb measure the average time of each transaction and the average wait time against the bank's customer service standards. The criteria she uses are the same as those of many banks: five minutes of wait time or less and two to three minutes of transaction time.

When the queue slows down or customers begin to look impatient, the branch's floor managers step in. Their goal is to counter customers' perceptions of a lengthy wait and help maintain the bank's image as a speedy, friendly place to visit. Floor managers will work the line, offering to help waiting customers fill out forms, greeting them by name, and apologizing for the delay. Always attuned to the speed of the queue, Deb finds that knowing how to manage her customers' wait times has become second nature.

Although "Nobody likes to wait," as Deb Holler, the subject of this chapter's "On the Job" segment says, waiting lines are sometimes unavoidable. Queueing theory studies how queues or waiting lines develop and behave as a function of their primary charac-

[1]The spelling *queueing* is considered archaic, and most computerized spell checkers recommend using *queuing*. But why miss a chance to use a word with such a unique feature?

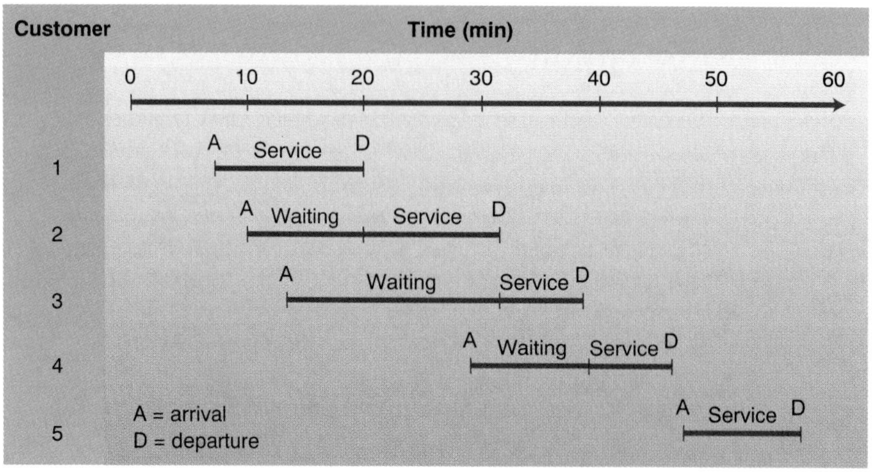

FIGURE 9.1 Arrival and service pattern for a typical one-server queue.

We spend a large part of our lives waiting in lines. Reducing customer waiting not only can increase profits, but it also makes customers' lives more productive and less stressful.

teristics. Queues form when the *short-term* demand for a service exceeds the capacity of the system to serve. Normally service systems are designed so that *on average* the service capacity is greater than the long-term expected demand. What makes queueing systems both difficult and interesting to study, however, is that the exact moment that customers will demand service and the amount of time it will take to serve them can both be random. Thus, although the average service capability may exceed the average demand rate, over a short time interval the demand rate may exceed the service capacity. (This relationship can be further confounded if the actual demand rate fluctuates over time as well, so that the average demand rate may exceed the service capacity for short periods.) Figure 9.1 illustrates this situation for a one-server queueing system. Suppose that *on average* the number of customers requesting service is six per hour, and *on average* the server can serve eight per hour. Figure 9.1 shows the arrival, service, and waiting times for the first five customers. Notice that the first three customers arrive close together (at times 8, 10, and 13) and the service times for customers 1 and 2 are longer than average, so customers 2, 3, and 4 must wait (in a queue) before receiving service.

Queueing theory is used primarily to assist in the design and operation of queueing systems. Mathematical models provide the primary form of analysis in queueing theory, but the models used are fundamentally different from the constrained optimization models presented in Tutorial 1. Constrained optimization models are *normative*; they can be solved so that the best values of specific variables (and the best action) can be determined. Queueing models are *descriptive*; they do not provide optimal solutions directly. Rather, they describe how a system would behave under various assumed designs or operating conditions. This analysis provides a mechanism for measuring the consequences of different system designs or operating procedures. The costs and benefits of these consequences can then be combined with the cost of each design or operating policy to determine the best solution.

This chapter begins by defining and explaining the primary components of queueing systems. Section 9.3 defines notation and summarizes an important qualitative property of queueing systems. Sections 9.4–9.8 present detailed analytical descriptions of four common queueing systems, which are also used to illustrate other general properties of queueing systems, such as the effects of randomness. Section 9.9 is devoted specifically to serial queueing systems because they are an integral part of multistage manufacturing systems. This section shows how variations in processing times lead to large in-process inventories, long throughput times, and decreased production capacity; this fact forms the foundation for many of the just-in-time and lean production principles presented in Chapter 15. Section 9.10 discusses other factors that should be considered when designing queueing systems, including the psychological aspects of waiting, and it provides suggestions for improving the operation of queueing systems.

9.2 CHARACTERISTICS OF QUEUEING SYSTEMS

The two principal components of queueing systems are customers and servers. **Customers** are entities (human or otherwise) that desire some form of service. The service is provided by other entities, called **servers**. The time a customer spends in the service system depends not only on the characteristics of the customer and the service process, but also on the configuration of the system and the operating policies. Table 9.1 lists some familiar examples of queueing systems and their components.

Customers do not have to be people. For example, at a tollgate, vehicles are considered to be the customers, not the people in them. The service consists of passing through the tollgate; this is not a function of who or how many people are in the car. Customers can even be electrical impulses, as in a telephone call in a telephone system or a computer job requiring access to a computer system. Clearly defining the **customer population** for a system sometimes requires great care. For example, at a restaurant, individual persons are not necessarily the customers in a queueing sense; more likely the customers are groups of people who wish to sit together. So, four people who want to dine together constitute one customer, not four customers.

Defining exactly what constitutes a server in a system requires equal care. Servers need not be human beings. The server is the entity that controls whether a customer is being served, and usually the server is dedicated to serving only one customer at a time (although it may interrupt service to serve other customers).[2] In the examples in Table 9.1, computers, tables, airport runways, or electronic equipment could all be servers. Servers can also be a combination of people and equipment. For example, a loading dock together with the workers on the dock form one server that loads and unloads trucks (the customers); the workers on the dock are *part* of the server or service mecha-

TABLE 9.1 EXAMPLES OF QUEUEING SYSTEMS

Queueing System	Customers	Servers
1. Bank	Bank customers	Tellers with computers
2. Grocery store	Grocery customers	Checkout clerks and registers
3. Telephone system	Phone calls	Switching equipment to route calls
4. Airport	Airplanes	Runways or gates
5. Highway tollgate	Vehicles	Tollgate/fee collector
6. Machine repair	Machines	Repair crew
7. Computer system	Programs to be run	Computer
8. Restaurant	Parties of people	Tables and waiters/waitresses
9. Factory	Manufacturing jobs	Machines/workers
10. Customer service department	Phone calls/customers	Service rep. and a phone

[2]There are systems, such as buses or airplanes, where one server can serve several customers at once. These are called *bulk queues*.

nism that controls the speed of service, but the individual workers are not servers in a queueing sense.

Queueing analysis specifies the conditions or characteristics of the queueing system and then uses appropriate mathematical methods to estimate or predict how the system would behave. The outputs from a queueing analysis are usually numerical measures of customer waiting times, average queue sizes, or number of customers desiring service who actually receive service. The queueing analysis measures the effects of these different designs on the system's performance. Two general methods are used to perform this evaluation:

1. ***Steady-State Equations.*** When the characteristics of the queueing system are sufficiently simple and do not change over time, equations called **steady-state equations** can be developed that describe system performance as a function of the system's characteristics; this is sometimes referred to as the **analytic approach**.
2. ***Simulation.*** When the design or operational characteristics of the queueing system are more complex, as they often are in practice, equations cannot be derived to relate performance to system characteristics. Instead we use a method called **simulation**, in which we attempt to mimic how the system would behave in practice. This method is normally implemented in the form of a computer program. The program is then run to observe the system's performance over a long period of *simulated* time in a short amount of *real* time. Simulation is discussed in detail in Tutorial 3.

No matter which approach is used to evaluate a queueing system, it is essential to specify clearly the important characteristics of the system. An obvious question is: What characteristics are important, and how do they affect customer waiting and service in a queueing system? The characteristics can be broken down into three general categories: those dealing with the customers, those dealing with the servers, and those dealing with system configuration. We will look at each.

CUSTOMER CHARACTERISTICS

1. ***Size of the Customer Population.*** The population supplying customers for the system can be either infinite or finite in size. In a purely mathematical sense, almost all populations are finite in size. However, mathematically, it is easier to work with an infinite population in queueing analysis,[3] so from a modeling perspective we are interested in knowing when a finite population can be treated as if it were infinite. The answer is that when the number of customers in the system (being served or waiting to be served) is unlikely to affect the rate at which additional customers will request service, the population can be treated as if it were infinite. For example, the potential number of customers (vehicles) that might want to pass through a toll booth on the Tri-State Tollway in Chicago is in the millions but still finite. However, at any given time it is unlikely that more than a few hundred vehicles will be in line waiting for service, and the fact that 100 vehicles are in line will not significantly affect the rate at which the remaining millions of cars arrive at the toll booth, so this population can be treated as infinite.

In contrast, consider a factory with two identical machines that occasionally break. The machines are customers that are served by repair crews. If one machine is already broken, the rate at which breakdowns are likely to occur is cut in half. In

[3]Infinite populations are easier to work with because the rate at which additional customers will request service is not affected by the number who are currently being served or are waiting to be served.

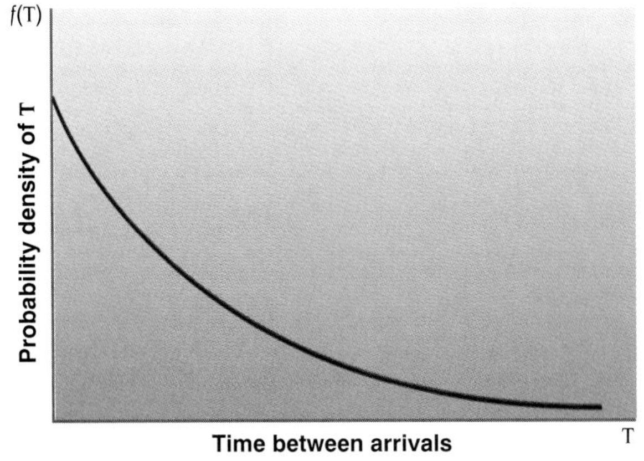

FIGURE 9.2 Probability density function for exponential distribution.

the extreme case, when both machines are broken, the rate of additional breakdowns (customer arrivals) drops to zero. In this case, the customer population must be explicitly treated as finite because the queue size affects the customer arrival rate. As a conservative rule of thumb, if no more than 1% of the customer population are ever likely to be in the queueing system (being served or waiting to be served), the population can be treated as infinite.

2. ***Composition of the Customer Population.*** An important characteristic of customers that is often overlooked is their homogeneity or heterogeneity. Most queueing models assume that all customers have the same service requirements (i.e., the same probability distribution for service times). If, in fact, customers are different in their service requirements *and* the differences can be identified in advance, it is sometimes possible to design the queueing system to exploit customer heterogeneity. For example, in a grocery store customers purchasing 10 or fewer items require much less checkout service than other customers. By assigning these customers to express checkout lines, the average waiting time for customers can be reduced without increasing the number of servers.

3. ***The Customer Arrival Process.*** In general, we do not know in advance when customers will arrive (i.e., request service). However, to evaluate the expected behavior of the system, we must be able to describe the arrival pattern. This pattern is normally expressed as a probability distribution for the **interarrival times**—the times between successive customer arrivals. In theory any distribution is possible, but a large majority of the arrival patterns in real queueing systems appear to be generated by what is called a **Poisson process**,[4] in which the time between successive arrivals is *exponentially distributed*.[5] The probability density function for an exponential random variable is illustrated in Figure 9.2. Notice that there is a large probability that the time between arrivals will be small and an exponentially

[4]The process is named after a French mathematician, Poisson, not after the French word for fish.

[5]Suppose T is a random variable that represents the time between successive arrivals. If T is exponentially distributed, its cumulative probability distribution is

$$P(T \le t) = 1 - e^{-\lambda t} \quad \text{for } t \ge 0$$

where $P(T \le t)$ is the probability that the time between arrivals is t or less. In this expression $1/\lambda$ is the average time between arrivals, so

$$\lambda = \text{average rate of arrivals in customers/unit time}$$

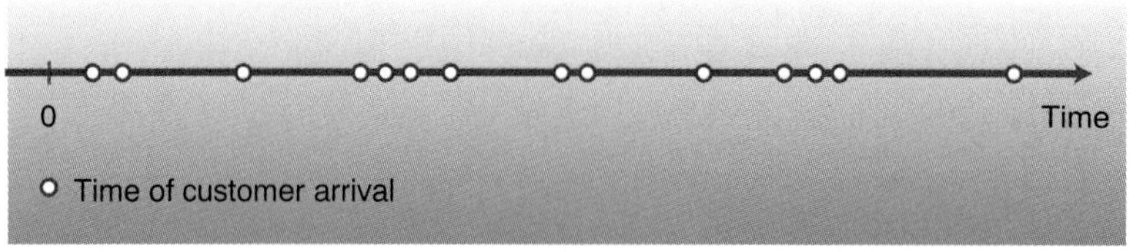

FIGURE 9.3 Typical Poisson arrival pattern.

decreasing probability of larger interarrival times. This property results in arrival patterns similar to the one shown in Figure 9.3. The distinguishing characteristic is that most customers appear to arrive in groups (short interarrival times), but there are also occasional large gaps between arrivals.

Most natural arrival processes are approximately Poisson, including arrivals of customers at banks, phone calls at switching equipment, or vehicles at toll booths. Even customers supposedly following an appointment schedule, such as patients at doctors' offices, frequently appear to follow a Poisson process. In spite of this, in practice it is a good idea to collect data on the relevant arrival process to verify that it can be approximated by a Poisson process and to determine the average arrival rate. We will designate the **average arrival rate**, expressed in customers per unit time, as λ. Notice that $1/\lambda$ is the average time *between* arrivals (interarrival time). The larger the value of λ, the more rapidly customers arrive (the larger the demand).

4. ***Attitude of the Customers.*** When customers desire service but all servers are busy, the customers are assigned to a waiting line (queue). Their attitude or behavior regarding waiting can affect how the overall system performs. There are at least three common types of customer behavior.
   (a) A customer is said to be **well behaved** if he or she joins the queue and remains there until he or she is served.
   (b) A customer is said to **balk** if, when the servers are busy, the customer leaves the system without joining the queue. Normally, balking is a probabilistic response based on the length of the queue. That is, the probability that a customer will balk changes with queue length. For example, 10% of the customers might balk when there is one customer in the queue, but 25% might balk when there are three.
   (c) A customer is said to **renege** if he or she36 joins the queue when all servers are busy but leaves before being served if the wait is too long. Reneging behavior is also usually probabilistic; some customers are willing to wait only five minutes before giving up, whereas others are willing to wait an hour.

Each type of behavior must be captured or represented accurately for a queueing analysis to be valid. If we assume that all customers are well behaved when in fact many of them balk or renege, our analysis will indicate much longer waits on average than actually occur. Balking and reneging reduce the effective demand, which reduces the amount of waiting, but this occurs at the expense of losing some customers.

SERVICE CHARACTERISTICS

1. ***Service Mechanism or Process.*** For each category of customer it is necessary to describe the service process. This is usually expressed as a probability distribution for service times; for example, service times might be normally distributed or uniformly distributed. At the least, we need to state the average time it takes for a

server to serve a customer and the variance or standard deviation of the service time. We define

$$\mu = \textbf{average service rate} \text{ possible per server in customers/unit time}$$

so $1/\mu$ is the **average service time**.

Unlike arrival processes, there is no standard probability distribution for service processes. In fact, many service processes must be described using a discrete probability distribution based on actual service data because no theoretical distribution matches the data well. When service times are exponentially distributed, the models simplify considerably.

2. ***Queue Discipline.*** When customers are in the queue, the system must have operating rules that determine which customer to serve next; these rules are called the **queue discipline**. Frequently, we assume that the queue discipline is **first-come-first-served (FCFS)**; that is, customers are served in the order in which they arrive. Although this is a reasonable rule for some systems, it is not the only possible rule or the best rule in many situations. For example, in a hospital emergency room a FCFS rule might cause the medical personnel to treat person A, with a hangnail, before person B, who has severe gunshot wounds. Other queue disciplines, such as shortest processing time, earliest due date, or highest-profit customer first are often used in manufacturing queueing systems.

   The queue discipline is an operational variable over which the system manager often has control. Queueing analysis is commonly used to evaluate the effects of different queue disciplines on system performance to determine which discipline is best.

SYSTEM CONFIGURATION

1. ***Number, Type, and Configuration of Servers.*** One of the primary design variables we study in queueing analysis is the number of servers in the system. Everything else being equal, the more servers available, the less waiting time. Thus we are often interested in determining whether savings made in reduced customer waiting or fewer customers lost justify the cost of additional servers.

   We sometimes also control the type of servers used. For example, we may choose between two types of machines, or combinations of people and machines, that have different average service rates and different variances in service times. Queueing analysis can help us determine whether a faster or less variable server is worth the extra cost.

   The configuration of servers can also influence system performance. For example, should the system have dedicated servers—only certain customers can use certain servers (express checkout, commercial bank windows)—or will all customers have access to all servers? We can also arrange a given number of servers in parallel or in series, as illustrated in Figure 9.4. In this figure configuration (a) assumes that each server can handle all customers' needs, whereas in configuration (b) first-level servers provide only some services; certain customers must be passed on to another server for the remaining service (e.g., approving loans above a certain amount or raising a credit card limit).

2. ***Queue Capacity.*** Another design variable is the maximum number of customers that can be put in the queue before additional customers must be turned away. For example, a normal telephone has a queue capacity of zero. When the phone is being used (a caller is being served), additional incoming calls cannot enter the queue; they receive a busy signal and are turned away. Phone systems can, how-

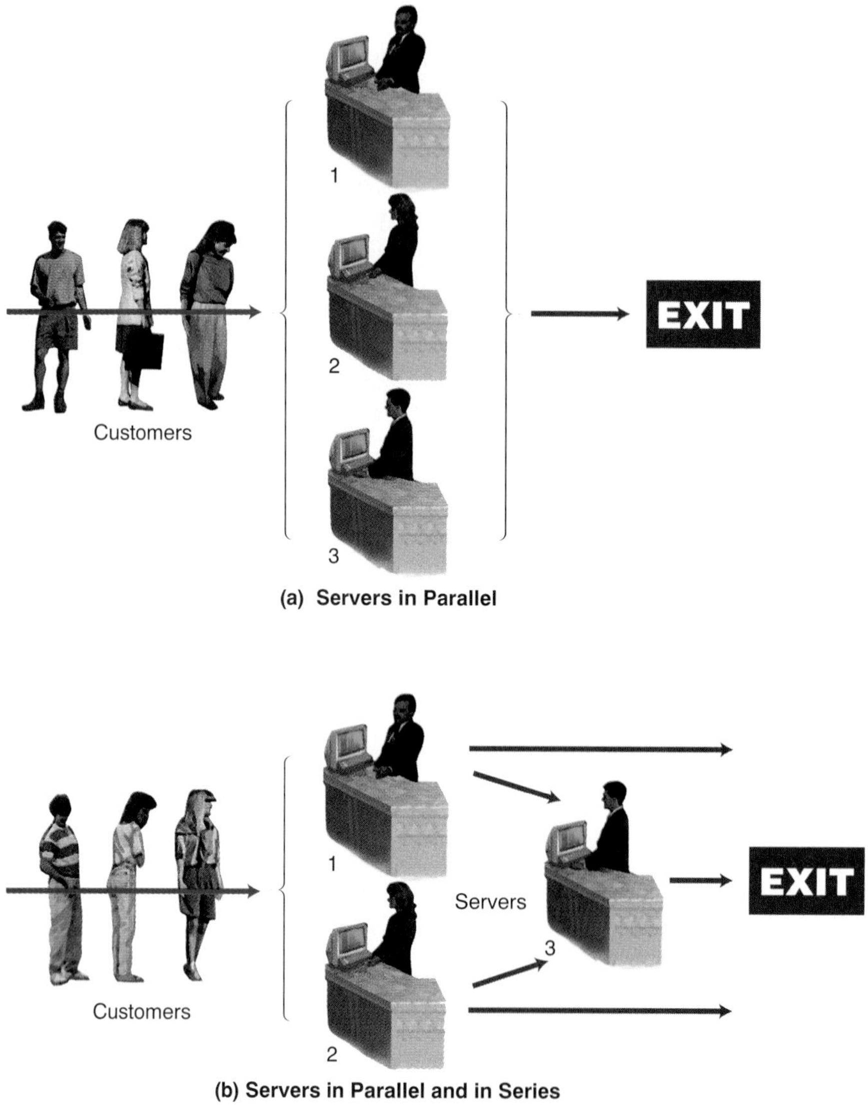

FIGURE 9.4 Two configurations of multiserver systems.

ever, be designed so that incoming calls are put "on hold" in a queue. The amount of queue capacity will affect how many callers are ultimately served.

3. ***Number of Queues.*** Whether each server has its own queue or all servers share a single queue can affect not only the average waiting time, but also the distribution and equity of waiting times as will be shown later.

9.3 NOTATION, TERMINOLOGY, AND THE EXPLODING QUEUE PROPERTY

The mathematical nature of queueing analysis makes it important to define our terminology, notation, and performance measures precisely.

MEASURES OF SYSTEM PERFORMANCE

When studying queueing systems, we are concerned with the waiting that customers experience. We will differentiate between time in the *queue* and time in the *system*. The time in the *queue* is the time a customer spends waiting until service begins; the time in the *system* is the time the customer spends in the *queue* plus the time being served (see Figure 9.5). Similarly, the *number* of customers in the system is the number in the queue plus the number being served. The four primary measures of waiting are as follows:

W_q = average time customers spend waiting in the queue
W_s = average time customers spend in the system
L_q = average number of customers waiting in the queue
L_s = average number of customers in the system

Each of these measures is a long-term average. An individual customer may experience no waiting in the queue, but the average for all customers may be substantial. Normally, these measures are assumed to be steady-state averages. The queueing system is in **steady state** when the rate of departures from the system equals the rate of arrivals. This implies that any start-up or shut-down (called **transient**) effects are eliminated. For example, when a bank opens in the morning all servers are available, so the amount of waiting in the queue is reduced, but there will also be some time lag until customers begin to leave the system. In the analytical models presented later, these transient effects are ignored; the system is assumed to be operating in a steady state. When transient effects are important, they are normally evaluated using simulation.

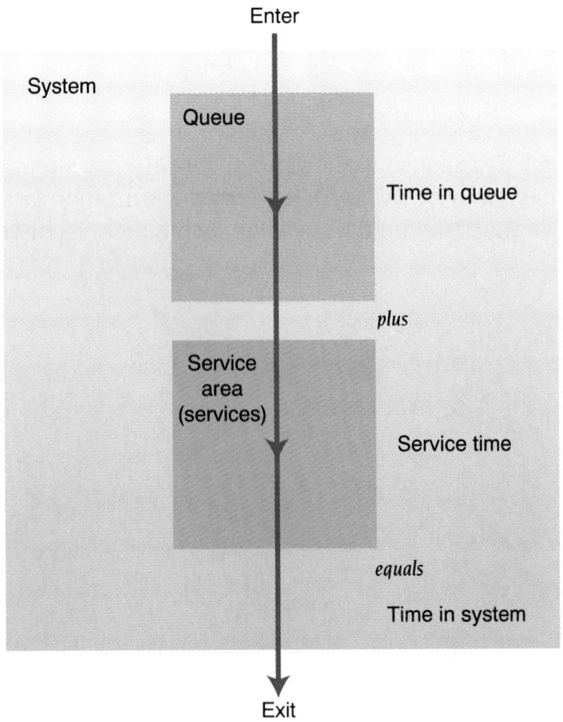

FIGURE 9.5 Distinction between the queue and the system.

The performance measures W_q, W_s, L_q, and L_s, are affected by the numerical parameters:

λ = average rate of arrivals in customers/unit time

μ = average rate at which a server can serve customers in customers/unit time

s = number of servers (sometimes called *channels*) in the system

We also define the following notation:

ρ = utilization factor (customer arrivals/unit time divided by total service capacity)

P_n = the probability or fraction of time that *exactly n* customers are in the *system*

$P_{\geq n}$ = the probability or fraction of time that *at least n* customers are in the system

$P_W = P_{\geq s}$ = the probability that a customer must wait for service (or the fraction of customers who must wait at least some time in the queue)

The **utilization factor** measures how much of the queueing system capacity is actually utilized serving customers. Thus, ρ is the fraction of time the servers are busy, and $1 - \rho$ is the fraction of time the servers are idle. In well-behaved systems (infinite queue capacity, no balking or reneging), ρ = (average arrival rate)/(average service capacity) = $\lambda/s\mu$. When the queue capacity is limited and/or balking and reneging occur, the actual or effective utilization is less than $\lambda/s\mu$ because some customers leave the system without being served.

CAPACITY UTILIZATION AND THE EXPLODING QUEUE PROPERTY

The primary property of queueing systems is that average waiting time and queue size increase slowly with utilization until utilization reaches approximately 0.70–0.80. At this point, average waiting time and queue length increase rapidly; the queue is said to *explode*. It is clear that if $\rho > 1$, then infinite queues develop and average waiting time approaches infinity. (In fact, even if $\rho = 1$ this will occur.) A fact that is not widely recognized is that queue sizes and waiting time can become extremely large even when the utilization factor is only 0.90 or 0.95. Figure 9.6 shows the relationship between server utilization and waiting times or queue sizes (the vertical axis can measure W_q, W_s, L_q, or L_s; the shape is essentially the same).

Figure 9.6 illustrates why small increases in demand can cause well-functioning queueing systems to collapse. For example, consider an interactive computer system. At 8:30 A.M. demand may be relatively light, so the utilization factor might be 0.40 (40%) and the response time (the time from when a command is entered until the computer

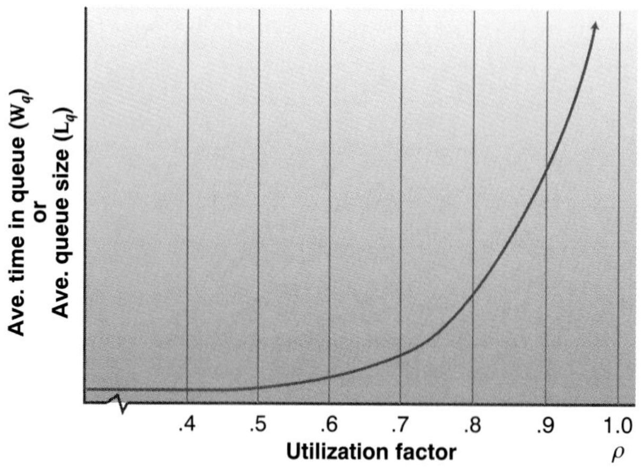

FIGURE 9.6 Waiting time and queue length as a function of server utilization.

responds to the user) is nearly instantaneous. By 9:00 A.M. demand increases, raising utilization to 0.70, and average response time may increase to one or two seconds. An additional increase in demand of 15–20% can now cause the response time to increase to 20–30 seconds, and another 10% increase in demand can cause it to become several minutes, bringing productive work to a halt.

Many people are surprised by the fact that a 10–20% increase in demand can cause average waiting time in a queueing system to go from a few seconds or minutes to several hours. But this is one of the key features of queueing systems. As long as utilization is below approximately 0.65–0.70, the queues are generally short. As soon as utilization increases to 0.80–0.85, queue lengths become long on average. Managers who are used to a manufacturing environment where 95–98% utilization of workers is normal (on a well-balanced, low-variance production line) can often wreak havoc in a service system if they attempt to achieve the same utilization of workers (with respect to the primary service).

THE KENDALL-LEE NOTATION FOR QUEUEING SYSTEMS

The following sections present four types of queueing systems. These systems are named using an abbreviated version of the Kendall-Lee convention, which specifies system characteristics in the shorthand form: a/b/s. The first characteristic, a, specifies the assumed arrival process, and the second, b, specifies the assumed service process. When the arrival process is Poisson (interarrival times are exponentially distributed), we let a = M; M comes from the name of the mathematician A. A. Markov, who did fundamental research on random processes. If a = G, then the results apply to any (*general*) arrival process; that is, the Poisson assumption is not required. If arrivals are evenly spaced with no randomness, then a = D (for *deterministic*). Similarly, if b = M, the service times are assumed to be exponentially distributed; if b = G, then the results apply to any *general* service distribution; and if b = D, the service times are assumed to be constant. M/M-type systems are the ones most commonly studied because it is easiest to derive steady-state descriptions of system behavior when the interarrival and service times are exponentially distributed.

The third characteristic, s, is the number of parallel servers in the system. So an M/M/5 system has Poisson arrivals, exponential service times, and five parallel servers. By contrast, an M/G/1 system has Poisson arrivals and one server, but any service distribution could be used, not just an exponential one.

An extended version of the Kendall-Lee notation specifies other characteristics, such as the size of the customer population, the system (or queue) capacity, and the queue discipline. However, unless specified otherwise, in the following models we will assume that the queue capacity and customer population are infinite, so these will not be designated explicitly in the model name.

We now consider specific queueing systems.

9.4 SINGLE-SERVER SYSTEMS WITH EXPONENTIAL SERVICE TIMES (M/M/1 SYSTEMS)

The simplest queueing system that includes randomness is the M/M/1 system. It is based on the following assumptions:

1. Arrivals are generated by a Poisson process.
2. Service times are exponentially distributed.
3. There is one server.

4. Any queue discipline can be used.
5. Queue capacity is infinite.
6. The customer population is homogeneous and infinite in size.
7. Customers are well behaved; no balking or reneging occurs.

Under these conditions, it is possible to derive the following steady-state formulas (derivations can be found in any queueing theory textbook):

$$\rho = \lambda/\mu \tag{9.1}$$

$$L_q = \lambda^2/[\mu(\mu - \lambda)] \tag{9.2}$$

$$L_s = \lambda/(\mu - \lambda) \tag{9.3}$$

$$W_q = \lambda/[\mu(\mu - \lambda)] \tag{9.4}$$

$$W_s = 1/(\mu - \lambda) \tag{9.5}$$

$$P_n = (1 - \lambda/\mu)(\lambda/\mu)^n \quad \text{for } n = 0, 1, 2, \ldots \tag{9.6}$$

$$P_{\geq n} = (\lambda/\mu)^n \quad \text{for } n = 0, 1, 2, \ldots \tag{9.7}$$

$$P_W = P_{\geq 1} = \lambda/\mu \tag{9.8}$$

Notice that the probability that the system is empty, $P_0 = 1 - \lambda/\mu = 1 - \rho = 1 -$ the fraction of time the server is busy. Also it follows that

$$L_s = L_q + \rho$$

(average number of customers in the system = average number in the queue plus the average number being served) and

$$W_s = W_q + 1/\mu$$

(average time customers spend in the system = average time spent in the queue plus average time being served).

The following example illustrates how these queueing formulas can be used to evaluate alternative system designs.

EXAMPLE 1

Multi-Machine Corporation (MMC) has a one-truck loading dock. Company trucks arrive at the dock according to a Poisson process at the rate of three trucks per eight-hour day. Regardless of crew size, the time it takes to load and unload trucks is exponentially distributed. Currently, the company uses two workers to load and unload trucks; two workers can load/unload trucks at the average rate of four trucks per eight-hour day. The company has estimated that each additional worker it adds to the crew would increase the loading rate by one truck per day. (Notice that additional workers are not very efficient: a 50% increase in crew size increases loading capacity by only 25%; a 100% increase in crew size increases loading capacity by only 50%.) The company pays each worker on the loading dock \$12 per hour, and the company has determined that each hour a truck is off the road (being loaded/unloaded or waiting to be loaded/unloaded) costs the company \$30.[6] MMC would like to determine how large the crew size should be to minimize its long-run cost.

The design variable (what can be controlled) is the number of workers on the dock. For any crew size, there is only one server (the dock and the loading crew) that can serve only one customer (the truck) at a time. That is, MMC must choose the *type* of server, *not* the *number* of servers, to minimize the average long-run cost. Although the relationship between crew size and loading cost is straightforward, the relationship between crew size and idle truck costs cannot be determined without the assistance of queueing theory. The simplest approach is to construct a table that relates crew size to average total cost on, say, a daily basis.

To begin, we decompose average total daily cost into its components:

Average total cost/day = ave. crew cost/day + average idle truck cost/day

The crew cost per day is not random; it is equal to \$12/hour × 8 hours/day × number of workers = \$96/day × crew size. In contrast, the cost of idle trucks varies every day, depending on how many trucks arrive, how long it takes to serve them, and how many trucks are in the system to begin with.

Average idle truck cost/day
= average no. of idle truck-hours/day × \$30/hr
= (ave. no. of idle hours/truck) × (ave. no. of trucks arriving/day) × \$30/hr
= W_s × (3 trucks/day) × \$30/hr
= \$90 W_s

But W_s can be obtained from queueing analysis. The loading dock can be considered an M/M/1 queue. For each crew size there is a different value for μ and thus a different value for W_s. For example, if the crew size is 2, then μ = 4 trucks/day and

$\rho = \lambda/\mu$ = [3 trucks/day]/[4 trucks/day] = 0.75
$W_s = 1/(\mu - \lambda)$ = 1/[(4 − 3) trucks/day] = 1 day/truck = 8 hr/truck

Figure 9.7, which shows the relevant information for possible crew sizes, indicates that the best crew size is four. This produces an average daily savings of \$288 (\$912 −

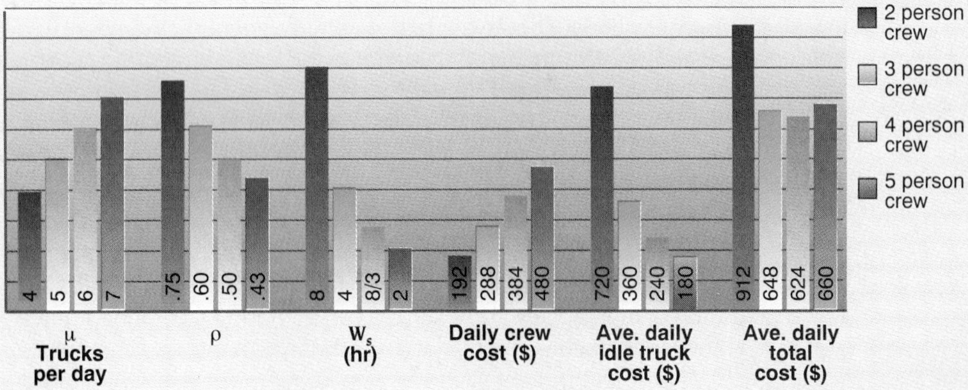

FIGURE 9.7 Comparison of different crew sizes for MMC.

[6]The idle truck cost may be due to truck drivers waiting until the truck is loaded plus the opportunity cost of the truck; for example, additional truck capacity may have to be leased if too many trucks are off the road being loaded or unloaded.

$624) compared to the current system. To the casual observer this is a surprising result for two reasons. First, the third and fourth workers are not incrementally very efficient compared to the first two. Second, a two-person crew would be idle 25% of the time; yet, it is advantageous to add more workers so that four workers could be idle 50% of the time. The savings in reduced idle truck time more than make up for the extra crew cost.

It is important to consider the psychological and organizational aspects of the situation in Example 1 as well. Many organizations have incentive or reward systems that would discourage the loading dock manager from using additional workers. Usually the manager of the loading dock is rewarded based only on a measure of the costs or worker efficiency on the loading dock (probably on a truckload per person basis), whereas the manager of transportation is rewarded based only on the activities of the trucks (cost per ton-mile delivered). Even though the company as a whole would benefit from adding two additional workers, the manager of the loading dock would be penalized because the loading cost per truck and the number of workers per truck loaded would increase. All the benefits of this action would accrue to the manager of transportation, who has no control over the situation. In order to encourage actions that are in the best interests of the organization, the company should establish a reward system that recognizes the *combined* performance of the loading dock and transportation managers or one that has a mechanism to share benefits and costs across departments when an action influences more than one unit of the company.

The idle time that is suggested by the queueing model does not necessarily imply that the workers must actually be idle. The utilization factor and idle time refer only to the service tasks around which the model is constructed; this service usually requires *real-time* attention (the customers are served when they want service). In many service systems, servers perform other tasks that do not require real-time attention, and these activities can be performed during the so-called idle periods. For example, the primary responsibility of bank tellers is to serve customers who come into the bank (or up to a drive-up window); however, they are often assigned other work to do when no customers are waiting, such as handling mail transactions or updating accounts, that does not have to be done immediately. Similarly, repair crews (servers) perform emergency repairs on a real-time basis and then use their idle time for preventive maintenance. Thus, when queueing theorists say that servers should not be busy more than 75% or 80% of the time, they are referring to real-time service tasks; however, in many systems, servers can be kept busy doing useful work 95% of the time or more if there is sufficient work that does not have to be done in real time. Of course, if the number of servers can easily be changed to adapt to the size of waiting lines, higher utilization factors are possible. For example, in a grocery store servers can sometimes be added quickly for short periods to relieve long queues when an unusually large number of customers are waiting.

The probabilities of n customers being in the system, P_n, and at least n customers, $P_{\geq n}$, are sometimes used in planning. For example, if the number of customers in the queue reaches a certain value, customers may begin to balk (we would have to change our model to account for this situation, but we need to know if it is likely to occur). Alternatively, an extra cost might be incurred if the number of customers in the queue becomes too large, as illustrated below.

EXAMPLE 2

Suppose that in Example 1 MMC had parking available on its lot for only two trucks to wait in the queue. If more than two trucks are waiting to enter the dock, additional trucks have to park in a lot across the street and MMC pays the owner of the lot $20 for each truck that parks there, regardless of how long it stays. We can use equation (9.7) to compute how this situation changes the solution.

A truck would have to use the alternate lot if there were three or more trucks in the system (two or more in the queue) *when it arrived*. The fraction of time this would happen is $P_{\geq 3}$. For a two-person loading crew

$$P_{\geq 3} = (3/4)^3 = 27/64 = 0.42$$

So 42% of the trucks that arrive would find two or more trucks already in the queue, and they would have to park in the alternate lot for at least some amount of time. The cost per day for alternate parking is then

$20/truck × (average number of trucks/day sent to the alternate lot)
= $20/truck × [(average no. of trucks arriving per day) × (fraction of trucks sent to the alternate parking lot)]
= $20/truck × [(3 trucks/day) × (27/64)]
= $25.31/day

For a four-person loading crew, $P_{\geq 3} = (3/6)^3 = 1/8$, and the extra cost for alternate parking is $7.50 per day. With additional loaders, the fraction of trucks that would have to use the alternate parking would be lower, so the cost per day for alternate parking decreases as crew size increases. The additional savings could not exceed $7.50 per day, so the optimal crew size will still be four in this case. However, in a different situation these cost savings could be large enough to change the optimum number of workers.

9.5 MULTISERVER SYSTEMS WITH EXPONENTIAL SERVICE TIMES (M/M/S SYSTEMS)

Most service systems have more than one server available at a time. An M/M/s queueing system has the same assumptions as the M/M/1 system except that there are s parallel servers (but only one queue for waiting customers). The service time distributions are assumed to be the same for each server, with μ being the mean service rate *for each server*. The following steady-state formulas can be derived.

$$\rho = \lambda/(s\mu) \tag{9.9}$$

$$P_0 = 1/\{ \sum_{n=0}^{s-1} [(\lambda/\mu)^n/n!] + [(\lambda/\mu)^s/s!] [1 - (\lambda/s\mu)]^{-1} \tag{9.10}$$

$$P_n = \begin{cases} \dfrac{[(\lambda/\mu)^n]P_0}{n!} & \text{for } 0 \le n \le s \\[2ex] \dfrac{[(\lambda/\mu)^n]P_0}{s!\,(n-s)!} & \text{for } n \ge s \end{cases} \tag{9.11}$$

$$P_W = \frac{[(\lambda/\mu)^s]P_0}{s!\,[1-\rho]} \tag{9.12}$$

$$L_q = [(\lambda/\mu)^s \rho P_0]/[s!(1-\rho)^2] \tag{9.13}$$

$$L_s = L_q + \lambda/\mu \tag{9.14}$$

$$W_q = L_q/\lambda \tag{9.15}$$

$$W_s = W_q + 1/\mu \tag{9.16}$$

All the performance measures depend on the value of P_0 in their calculation. P_0 can be cumbersome to compute for large values of s, so it is common to use tables such as Table 9.2, which give the value of P_0 for various values of s and ρ.

The following example illustrates the use of the M/M/s equations and shows the benefits of pooling servers.

EXAMPLE 3

The Acme Advertising Company has decided to purchase two facsimile transmission (fax) machines. Two departments will be the primary users of the machines: Design and Sales. These departments share the same floor of the company's building (each has half of the floor). Each department expects to generate 36 documents per eight-hour day that need to be transmitted;[7] the timing of these transmissions follows a Poisson process. The time it takes to transmit each document is exponentially distributed, with an average transmission time of 10 minutes. Each department wants to have its own machine to use exclusively (no other department can use it). The manager of Purchasing wants the two machines to be in a common area that both departments can use. What would be the consequences of each configuration, which are illustrated in Figure 9.8?

(a) *Each department has its own machine.* In this case, Acme has two separate but identical, M/M/1 queueing systems. For each machine

$\lambda = 36/\text{day}$

$\mu = 48/\text{day}$ (average service time, $1/\mu = 1/6$ hr/item $\rightarrow \mu = 6$ items/hr)

$\rho = \lambda/\mu = 36/48 = 0.75$

[7]Fax receipts are ignored in the example for simplicity, but they could easily be included in an actual analysis.

TABLE 9.2 P_0 FOR M/M/S QUEUEING SYSTEMS

$\rho =$	Number of Servers									
$\lambda/s\mu$	1	2	3	4	5	6	7	8	9	10
.10	.90000	.81818	.74074	.67031	.60653	.54881	.49659	.44933	.40657	.36788
.12	.88000	.78571	.69753	.61876	.54881	.48675	.43171	.38289	.33960	.30119
.14	.86000	.75439	.65679	.57116	.49657	.43171	.37531	.32628	.28365	.24660
.16	.84000	.72414	.61837	.52720	.44931	.38289	.32628	.27804	.23693	.20190
.18	.82000	.69492	.58214	.48660	.40653	.33959	.28365	.23693	.19790	.16530
.20	.80000	.66667	.54795	.44910	.36782	.30118	.24659	.20189	.16530	.13534
.22	.78000	.63934	.51567	.41445	.33277	.26711	.21437	.17204	.13807	.11080
.24	.76000	.61290	.48519	.38244	.30105	.23688	.18636	.14660	.11532	.09072
.26	.74000	.58730	.45640	.35284	.27233	.21007	.16200	.12492	.09632	.07427
.28	.72000	.56250	.42918	.32548	.24633	.18628	.14082	.10645	.08045	.06081
.30	.70000	.53846	.40346	.30017	.22277	.16517	.12241	.09070	.06720	.04978
.32	.68000	.51515	.37913	.27676	.20144	.14644	.10639	.07728	.05612	.04076
.34	.66000	.49254	.35610	.25510	.18211	.12981	.09247	.06584	.04687	.03337
.36	.64000	.47059	.33431	.23505	.16460	.11505	.08035	.05609	.03915	.02732
.38	.62000	.44928	.31367	.21649	.14872	.10195	.06981	.04778	.03269	.02236
.40	.60000	.42857	.29412	.19929	.13433	.09032	.06064	.04069	.02729	.01830
.42	.58000	.40845	.27559	.18336	.12128	.07998	.05267	.03465	.02279	.01498
.44	.56000	.38889	.25802	.16860	.10944	.07080	.04573	.02950	.01902	.01226
.46	.54000	.36986	.24135	.15491	.09870	.06265	.03968	.02511	.01587	.01003
.48	.52000	.35135	.22554	.14221	.08895	.05540	.03442	.02136	.01324	.00820
.50	.50000	.33333	.21053	.13043	.08010	.04896	.02984	.01816	.01104	.00671
.52	.48000	.31579	.19627	.11951	.07207	.04323	.02586	.01544	.00920	.00548
.54	.46000	.29870	.18273	.10936	.06477	.03814	.02239	.01311	.00767	.00448
.56	.44000	.28205	.16986	.09994	.05814	.03362	.01936	.01113	.00638	.00366
.58	.42000	.26582	.15762	.09119	.05212	.02959	.01673	.00943	.00531	.00298
.60	.40000	.25000	.14599	.08306	.04665	.02601	.01443	.00799	.00441	.00243
.62	.38000	.23457	.13491	.07750	.04167	.02282	.01243	.00675	.00366	.00198
.64	.36000	.21951	.12438	.06847	.03715	.01999	.01069	.00570	.00303	.00161
.66	.34000	.20482	.11435	.06194	.03304	.01746	.00918	.00480	.00251	.00131
.68	.32000	.19048	.10479	.05587	.02930	.01522	.00786	.00404	.00207	.00106
.70	.30000	.17647	.09569	.05021	.02590	.01322	.00670	.00338	.00170	.00085
.72	.28000	.16279	.08702	.04495	.02280	.01144	.00570	.00283	.00140	.00069
.74	.26000	.14943	.07875	.04006	.01999	.00986	.00483	.00235	.00114	.00055
.76	.24000	.13636	.07087	.03550	.01743	.00846	.00407	.00195	.00093	.00044
.78	.22000	.12360	.06335	.03125	.01510	.00721	.00341	.00160	.00075	.00035
.80	.20000	.11111	.05618	.02730	.01299	.00610	.00284	.00131	.00060	.00028
.82	.18000	.09890	.04933	.02362	.01106	.00511	.00234	.00106	.00048	.00022
.84	.16000	.08696	.04280	.02019	.00931	.00423	.00190	.00085	.00038	.00017
.86	.14000	.07527	.03656	.01700	.00772	.00345	.00153	.00067	.00029	.00013
.88	.12000	.06383	.03060	.01403	.00627	.00276	.00120	.00052	.00022	.00010
.90	.10000	.05263	.02491	.01126	.00496	.00215	.00092	.00039	.00017	.00007
.92	.08000	.04167	.01947	.00867	.00377	.00161	.00068	.00028	.00012	.00005
.94	.06000	.03093	.01427	.00627	.00268	.00113	.00047	.00019	.00008	.00003
.95	.05000	.02564	.01175	.00513	.00218	.00091	.00037	.00015	.00006	.00003
.96	.04000	.02041	.00930	.00403	.00170	.00070	.00029	.00012	.00005	.00002
.98	.02000	.01010	.00454	.00194	.00081	.00033	.00013	.00005	.00002	.00001

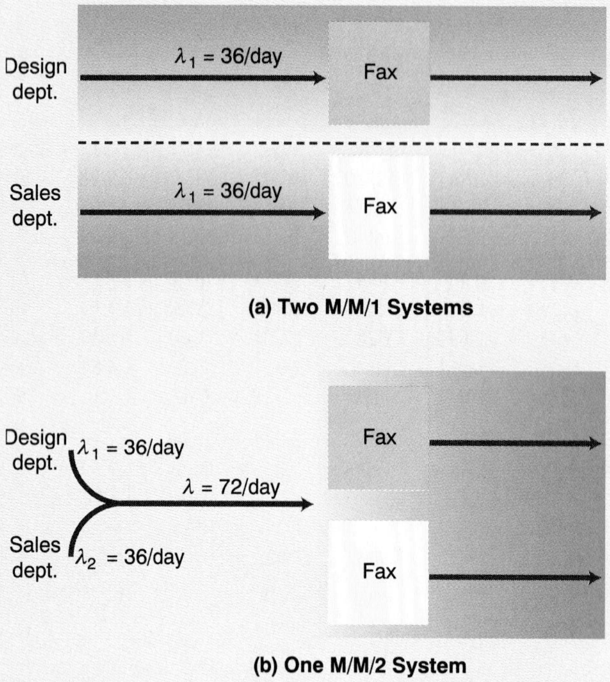

FIGURE 9.8 Alternative configurations for Acme Advertising.

Using the M/M/1 formulas, the average time an item spends waiting to begin transmission is

$$W_q = \lambda/[\mu(\mu - \lambda)] = 36/[48(48 - 36)] \text{ day} = 1/16 \text{ day} = 1/2 \text{ hr} = 30 \text{ min}$$

The total time until transmission is completed is

$$W_s = 1/(\mu - \lambda) = 1/(48 - 36 \text{ items/day}) = 1/12 \text{ day} = 2/3 \text{ hr} = 40 \text{ min}$$

Also, on average there are

$$L_q = [36^2/48(48 - 36)] = 9/4 = 2.25 \text{ items}$$

waiting to be transmitted *at each machine*. Thus, on average there are 4.5 documents (and people holding the documents) waiting for transmission at the two machines combined.

(b) *Two machines in a common pool*. In this case the documents generated by the two departments enter a common queue, so Acme has one 2-server queueing system. The average generation rate of items is the sum of the rates from each department: 36/day from Design + 36/day from Sales = 72 items/day = λ. A not so obvious question is whether or not the resulting combined (composed) process is Poisson. In fact it is, although this is not the case for all arrival processes. A desirable feature of Poisson processes is that their composition is itself a Poisson process. Furthermore, because the items from each department are homogeneous, in the sense that transmission times are exponentially distributed with a mean of 10 minutes, the resulting queueing system is an M/M/2 system with $\lambda = 72$ items per day and $\mu = 48$ items per day.

Although we are most interested in W_q, W_s, and L_q, we must first obtain P_0 either from Table 9.2 or from equation (9.10). In either case we need the value of ρ:

$$\rho = \lambda/s\mu = (72)/[(2)(48)] = 0.75$$

Using equation (9.10) we get

$$P_0 = \frac{1}{(72/48)^0/0! + (72/48)^1/1! + [(72/48)^2/2!][1 - (72/(2)(48)]^{-1}}$$

$$= \frac{1}{1 + 1.5 + [2.25/2]\,[4]} = 1/7 = 0.143 \quad \text{(the same as in Table 9.2)}$$

Then

$$L_q = [(72/48)^2(3/4)(0.143)]/[2!\,(1 - 3/4)^2] = 1.93 \text{ items}$$

$$W_q = [1.93 \text{ items}]/[72 \text{ items/day}] = 0.268 \text{ day} = 0.214 \text{ hr} = 12.86 \text{ min}$$

$$W_s = 12.86 \text{ min} + 10 \text{ min} = 22.86 \text{ min.}$$

These results show that on average the number of items waiting to be transmitted with the two-machine pool is *less than half* the number that would occur if each department had its own machine (1.93 versus 4.5 items). More important, the average time from when a person wants to transmit a document until transmission is completed is 22.86 minutes for the two-machine configuration versus 40 minutes for the departmental configuration. Even if it took an extra five minutes to walk to a fax-pool location, the two-machine pool would be more efficient. There could also be other practical benefits to pooling the machines, such as having to store paper and instruction manuals at only one location. Therefore, unless there are other overriding reasons to do otherwise, the two-machine pool is preferable.

BENEFITS OF POOLING SERVERS INTO ONE SYSTEM

The result for Example 3 holds in general: *if customers are homogeneous* (with respect to their service time distributions), then there will be less customer waiting on average if servers are pooled into one queueing system, rather than having a separate one-server system for each population of customers. With s distinct one-server systems, it is common to have customers waiting for service in one system while servers in the other systems are idle; thus, available service capacity goes unused. With a pooled system this will not happen. Notice that in both systems the utilization rates are the same, so the servers do not work any harder or longer in one configuration versus the other. Instead, they work more *effectively* in a pooled system by coordinating their idle time so that a server is never idle while other servers have queues. In general, for a fixed number of servers, average waiting time increases with the number of distinct systems. For example, suppose we have 10 customer sources with $\lambda = 40$/hour for each, and we have a total of 10 servers to serve them with $\mu = 50$/hour. If each customer source has its own M/M/1 system (a total of 10 M/M/1 systems), then $W_q = 4.8$ minutes. If the servers were combined into two M/M/5 systems (each serving five sources), $W_q = 0.665$ minutes; and if the servers were pooled into a single M/M/10 system, $W_q = 0.246$ minutes. We will see later, however, that when the customer population is heterogeneous, using separate queueing systems or separate servers for each category of customer can sometimes be beneficial.

THE NUMBER OF QUEUES FOR MULTISERVER SYSTEMS

A closely related question is, how many queues (waiting lines) should a multiserver queueing system have? Should there be one queue serving all the servers? One queue for each server? If customers are homogeneous in their service needs, having a single queue is usually superior to having a separate queue for each server for two reasons: (1) waiting time is more equitably distributed among customers, and (2) in some cases there is less average waiting time.

Using a single waiting line for several servers is usually more efficient, and it is perceived by customers as being more equitable than having separate waiting lines for each server.

On the surface, it may seem that as long as customers can choose which queue to enter and can switch among queues, a system with s queues (one for each server) should behave no differently than a system with one queue. In fact, this is not the case. Most of us have had the following unfortunate experience. We go into a bank where each window has its own line, and we join a line that looks short but moves slowly. To avoid the wait, we switch to another line. While waiting in the second line, we watch dozens of customers who came into the bank after we did leave before we do. When each server has its own waiting line, it is common for some unfortunate customers to be stuck in slow lines while more fortunate customers get in fast lines. In contrast, if one waiting line is used for a group of servers, a slow customer ties up one server, but customers continue to be served by the other servers. All the customers are slowed somewhat by a slow customer, but no one customer absorbs all of the waiting.

Figure 9.9 illustrates how the probability distribution for waiting times varies with the number of waiting lines, all other things being equal. When each server has its own waiting line, there is considerable dispersion in customer waiting times; many customers wait very little, and some wait a long time. When the number of waiting lines decreases, fewer customers have abnormally short or long waiting times; most of them wait approximately the same amount of time.

Not only is a single queue more equitable, but in many cases it can provide shorter or less costly average waits as well. In some queueing systems, customers may not know in advance which servers are idle and which are busy. For example, if a company has several phone numbers, each for a separate server, a person could enter the queue of a busy server by calling one number rather than that of an available server with another number. In this case, the queueing system behaves like s separate queueing sys-

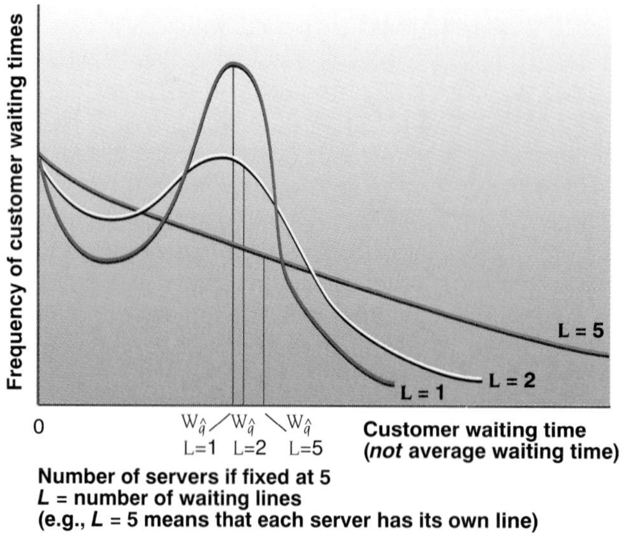

FIGURE 9.9 Waiting time distributions as a function of the number of queues.

tems. Even if the customers can choose, or are always assigned to, an idle server when one is available, it may be impossible or costly to switch to another queue after joining one. For example, if a production job is assigned to be processed by one of several identical work stations, it may be costly to revise production schedules when one work station progresses more quickly or more slowly than others. Similarly, once a customer joins a bank drive-through line, switching lines can be difficult or impossible.

Despite the advantages of using a single queue in a multiserver system, sometimes this may not be convenient or desirable for other reasons. First, it may be physically impractical to have a single queue feed all the servers. For example, in a grocery store with 10 servers, if one queue is used for all 10 servers, the line might wrap around the store, causing congestion and fights among customers. An alternative used by some retail stores, such as Venture Stores, is to have two servers share a queue. This avoids excessively long queues and also achieves some of the benefits of combining queues.

Even when a single queue is practical, it may not be most efficient, especially when the customers and servers are people. There are at least four factors that *in some cases* may make separate waiting lines for each server preferable to a single queue.

1. With separate queues, servers are sometimes able to serve two customers at once. For example, while waiting for a computer to register a transaction for one customer, the server may be able to prepare paperwork for the next customer. With a single queue, this type of coprocessing is rarely possible.
2. The time it takes for a customer to move from a common queue to the server may be longer than with individual queues for each server. For example, in a bank with separate queues, when one customer is finished the next customer can step up to the teller window. With a common queue, the customer must recognize that a server is available and then walk to that window. Leaving a server idle for even a few extra seconds (effectively increasing the service time) can have a large effect on customer waiting in a heavily utilized queueing system.
3. Servers sometimes work faster when they have their own queue; the customers in their queue are *their* customers and they are sensitive to the waiting incurred, whereas with a single queue the customer–server relationship is depersonalized until service begins and there is less sense of an obligation to serve customers quickly.
4. With separate queues, customers can choose their server. In some situations, servers can provide both faster and better-quality service to customers they have served before on a regular basis. Some customers prefer using the same server for this reason, and customer satisfaction should certainly be of primary importance in service systems.

Separate queues also make it possible to implement certain delay avoidance tactics. For example, requiring customers to use only cash in an express line at the grocery store means that the customers can obtain the benefits of a shorter wait only if they do something that also saves service time, which can translate into better service for everyone.

Finally, separate queues are sometimes necessary to implement other service improvement tactics. For example, when the population of customers is heterogeneous (customers require different types or amounts of service with substantially different average service times), it can be advantageous to have separate servers and queues for each type of customer. The circumstances under which this is advantageous, and the trade-offs that must be made, are discussed in section 9.7.

This discussion does not imply that combining queues is not beneficial; usually it is. Rather, the point is that we must look at the real aspects of any particular queueing system before making a final design decision. There are times when combining queues is beneficial, and there are times when two, three, or s separate queues are better.

9.6 SINGLE-SERVER SYSTEMS WITH GENERAL OR CONSTANT SERVICE TIMES (M/G/1 AND M/D/1 SYSTEMS)

In most queueing systems the service times are not exponentially distributed. However, if all the assumptions of the M/M/1 model are satisfied, except that the service times can have any probability distribution,[8] we have what is called an M/G/1 system, for which it is still possible to derive equations for the standard measures of customer waiting and queue length. In addition to knowing the average arrival rate, λ, and the average service rate, μ, to use the following M/G/1 formulas we also need to know the variance of the service times, σ^2 (σ is the standard deviation of the service times). By definition, the utilization factor $\rho = \lambda/\mu$, and $P_0 = 1 - \rho$. (General expressions for the probabilities P_n or $P_{\geq n}$ are not presented here; they can be found in specialized queueing theory texts.) The primary result is the formula for L_q; the formulas for L_s, W_q, and W_s are the same as for the M/M/s system.

$$L_q = [\lambda^2\sigma^2 + \rho^2]/[2(1 - \rho)] \quad (9.17)$$

$$L_s = L_q + \lambda/\mu \quad (9.14)$$

$$W_q = L_q/\lambda \quad (9.15)$$

$$W_s = W_q + 1/\mu \quad (9.16)$$

The average queue length, L_q, forms the basis for computing the other performance measures. The key fact to notice is that L_q, and thus the other performance measures, are a direct function of σ^2, the variance in service times. Everything else being equal, the more variation in service times, the longer queues will be on average and the longer customers will wait on average—*even with the same average arrival rate and average service rate.*

When the service times are a constant, so that $\sigma^2 = 0$, we say that the service distribution is **deterministic**. Then the M/G/1 system reduces to a special case called an M/D/1 system. The steady-state equations for this situation are the same as for general M/G/1 queues, except that equation (9.17) simplifies to

$$L_q = \rho^2/[2(1 - \rho)] \quad (9.17a)$$

The dependence of waiting times on service time variance has important implications for system design, some of which are illustrated by the following example.

EXAMPLE 4

Parts-to-Go (PTG) is a store that stocks and sells automobile and truck parts. PTG has over 20,000 different parts stored in a large warehouse. The store sells parts mainly to

[8] Service times do need to be independent of each other and come from the same probability distribution.

auto repair shops, gasoline stations, and individuals doing their own auto repair work. Most customers come in with a list of parts they require. The clerk knows from experience where many of the parts are stored, but sometimes he has to look them up in a book. Historically it has taken an average of three minutes per customer to find the parts and ring up the sale, but there is considerable variation in service times, depending on how many parts are requested, whether or not the clerk remembers their storage locations, and whether or not the clerk collects multiple parts efficiently. The standard deviation of service time is also three minutes.

Leonard Strauss, the owner of PTG, has observed that when there are more than two or three customers in line, many customers complain and a few leave the store without buying parts (competing stores are available). This seems to be happening too frequently, so he has decided that the average queue size (and customer wait) has to be reduced. Leonard has considered adding a second clerk, but he does not like the idea of spending \$20,000 a year in wages and benefits, especially since the current sales clerk is idle about 30% of the time. Before making a final decision, Leonard has decided to consult with a friend of his, Maria Escalia, who has a degree in operations management.

Maria suggests that he buy a computer system that would tell the clerk whether a part is in inventory and would help the clerk find parts and check out customers faster. Leonard says he has already considered this possibility, and he tested the two most popular computer systems on a trial basis. One is only an inventory control and item locator system. In this system, the clerk types in the part description or code, and the computer tells whether or not the item is in inventory and in which row and storage bin it is located. The second system does the same things, but in addition, it prints out a map and route through the warehouse, making it easier for the clerk to find all the parts in one trip, and it prints out a bill. Leonard likes the idea of buying one of the computer systems because of their inventory control and management features, but he does not see how they will reduce customer waiting. When he tested the two systems for a few days, he found that it still took an average of three minutes to serve a customer with the first computer system, and the second system was even slower. Because of the extra computer time for the routing and billing routine, it took an average of 3.1 minutes per customer for service.

Maria decided to investigate these two systems further. She went back to the data sheets Leonard used to track service times during the test. She found that his computations of average service times were correct, but she noticed that there was a big difference in service time variation between the two computer systems and the current method. The standard deviation in service time using the first computer system was 2.12 minutes, whereas for the second computer system it was only 1 minute. (The relevant data are given in Table 9.3.) Maria knew that the variation in service times can affect queue size and waiting times, so she decided to evaluate each of the options using queueing analysis.

Based on historical data, customers arrive at PTG according to a Poisson process at an average rate of 14 per hour. Thus, the current and computerized checkout processes are each M/G/1 systems, and for each $\lambda = 14$ customers per hour = 0.233 customers per minute. For the current and first computer system $1/\mu = 3.0$ minutes per customer, so $\mu = 1/3$ customers per minute and the utilization factor $\rho = (0.233)/(0.333) = 0.70$. The second computer system has an average service rate of $\mu = (1/3.1 \text{ minute}) = 0.323$ customers per minute and $\rho = (0.233)/(0.323) = 0.721$.

TABLE 9.3 SERVICE OPTIONS FOR PARTS-TO-GO

		System	
	Current	Comp 1	Comp 2
Mean service time, $1/\mu$ (min)	3.0	3.0	3.1
Service time std. deviation, σ (min)	3.0	2.12	1.0
Cost ($ 000/year)	—	2	4

The average queue lengths and waiting times for each system are as follows:

Current System

$L_q = [(0.233)^2(3)^2 + (0.70)^2]/[2(1 - 0.70)] = 1.631$ cust
$W_q = (1.631 \text{ cust})/(0.233 \text{ cust/min}) = 7.00$ min
$W_s = (7 \text{ min} + 3 \text{ min}) = 10.00$ min

Computer System 1

$L_q = [(0.233)^2(2.12)^2 + (0.70)^2]/[2(1 - 0.70)] = 1.223$ cust
$W_q = (1.223 \text{ cust})/(0.233 \text{ cust/min}) = 5.25$ min
$W_s = (5.25 \text{ min} + 3 \text{ min}) = 8.25$ min

Computer System 2

$L_q = [(0.233)^2(1.0)^2 + (0.721)^2]/[2(1 - 0.721)] = 1.029$ cust
$W_q = (1.029 \text{ cust})/(0.233 \text{ cust/min}) = 4.416$ min
$W_s = (4.416 \text{ min} + 3.10 \text{ min}) = 7.516$ min

Both computerized systems reduce the average queue size and average waiting times substantially, *even though the average service times for the computerized systems are at least as large as for the current systems*. Especially striking is the performance of the second computer system. Even though the average service time is *greater* than with the other two systems, the lower variance causes L_q, W_q, and W_s to be smaller.

Mr. Strauss has to determine whether the reductions in queue size and waiting time are sufficient for his purposes. Adding a second person (creating a two-server queueing system) instead of buying a computer system would reduce L_q to approximately 0.10 customer and W_q to approximately 0.43 minute. However, he may decide that this additional reduction is not worth the cost of an additional worker. (In addition, this system would not provide real-time inventory control and record keeping.) The computer systems are likely to pay for themselves if the improved service translates into more customers using PTG.

9.7 THE ROLE OF VARIANCE IN QUEUEING SYSTEMS

Example 4 illustrates one of the most important properties of queueing systems: everything else being equal, the greater the randomness in arrival times and/or services times, the larger the average queue lengths and waiting times. Therefore, anything we can do to reduce variation will help to reduce customer waiting. There are three practical implications of this fact.

SLOWER SERVERS ARE SOMETIMES MORE EFFICIENT

The designers of queueing systems often control the specific service mechanism used. Each service mechanism has its own probability distribution for service times. Commonly, designers measure the capacity or performance of a service mechanism by the average service rate: the number of customers that can be served or units produced per unit time. However, in a queueing environment, the service mechanism with the highest average service rate is not necessarily the most efficient. In Example 4 the second computerized service system had the slowest average service rate but produced less customer waiting on average than the other two "faster" systems. This fact is especially important in multistage production processes, called *serial queueing systems*. The harmful effects of variation in such systems were briefly illustrated in Chapter 8 for a repetitive process (a production line) and will be explained in more detail in Section 9.10, in Tutorial 3, and in Chapter 15. These effects are at the foundation of just-in-time and lean production.

PACING OF CUSTOMER ARRIVALS REDUCES WAITING

The M/G/1 queueing system illustrates the effects of variability in service times on waiting times and queue sizes, but the same effects hold with respect to arrival patterns. The more randomness there is in interarrival times, the longer the average waiting times and queue lengths, all other things being equal. This can be seen by simply comparing an M/D/1 queueing system with a D/D/1 system (no randomness in interarrival or service times). Assuming λ and μ are the same for both systems and $\lambda < \mu$, for the M/D/1 case $L_q = \rho^2/[2(1 - \rho)] > 0$ and $W_q = L_q/\lambda > 0$. In contrast, if customers arrive at equal intervals with $1/\lambda$ units of time between them, for the D/D/1 case $L_q = 0$ and $W_q = 0$, as shown in Figure 9.10. In fact, the less variation in interarrival times, the more highly utilized the system can be before long queues form, so larger values of λ can be accommodated with the same average queue length. This is the major reason for using a strict appointment schedule. For example, in a doctor's office, if patients arrive at equal time intervals the doctor has less idle time, and there should be less waiting by patients and shorter queues on average compared to the case of a random arrival pattern.

The big problem with appointment schedules and trying to control arrival patterns is that customers do not always behave the way we would like. Some customers arrive late, some arrive too early, and some simply do not show up. There has been research on alternative scheduling approaches that better utilize server capacity and still reduce waiting time. For example, one approach is the *modified wave*, which schedules several

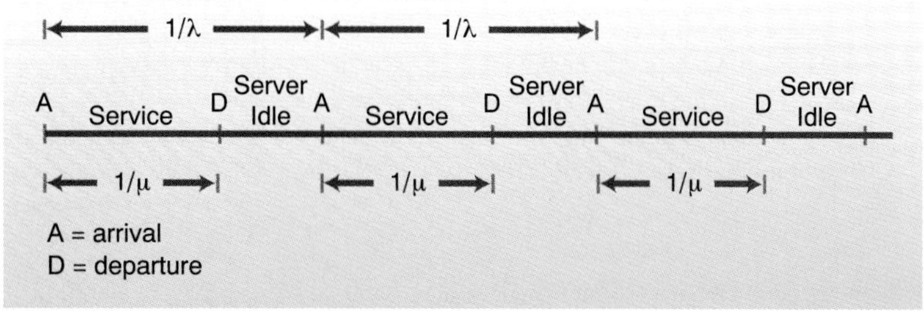

FIGURE 9.10 A D/D/1 queueing system.

customers close together at the beginning of a time period. This system creates short queues early in the period to make sure the server is never idle, but lightens the arrival rate over time until a new "wave" of customers is allowed to arrive.[9]

EXPLOITING CUSTOMER HETEROGENEITY TO IMPROVE SERVICE

Frequently, the variability in service times is not due to inherent randomness in serving homogeneous customers; rather, the customers' service requirements are heterogeneous. The customer population may contain different categories of customers who desire services with different service time distributions. For example, in a grocery store, a customer buying only a few items will require much less service time on average to check out than a customer with a full shopping cart. If we can identify this customer heterogeneity, we might exploit it by assigning different categories of customers to designated servers or by having designated time periods reserved for different categories of customers.

Segregating customers by category can produce the following benefits.

1. The variance in service times for each server can be reduced, decreasing average waiting times.
2. Servers can become more efficient at providing more homogeneous services, reducing average service time and average waiting.
3. The level of service provided to different categories of customers can be controlled by the service organization.

Variance Reduction

Suppose we collected service time data for a group of customers that use a queueing system, and the frequency distribution looked like Figure 9.11. This distribution, which has a very large variance, appears to represent customers requiring two distinct types of service: one group requires substantially longer service than the other. If all customers were treated as being from a homogeneous population and funneled into one queueing system, the service time variance would cause longer queues and more waiting than if the variance were smaller. However, if we could somehow identify the category to which a customer belongs before the customer is served, we could create two separate queueing systems: one for one category of customer and one for the other category. *Within* each queueing system, the service time variance would be much smaller than if we had pooled the customers (see Figure 9.12), thereby reducing customer waiting. If enough variance reduction occurred the overall average waiting time for customers can be reduced.

When customers require substantially different levels of service, express check-out lines, such as this one at Dierbergs Markets, can be beneficial to both the customers and the store. "Cash Only" express lines reward customers for helping to reduce service time (by not using checks or credit cards).

[9]See Stephen R. Smith, Bernard J. Schroer, and Robert E. Shannon, "Scheduling of Patients and Resources for Ambulatory Health Care," *Winter Simulation Conference Proceedings*, Institute of Electrical and Electronic Engineers, New York, 1979, pp. 553–562.

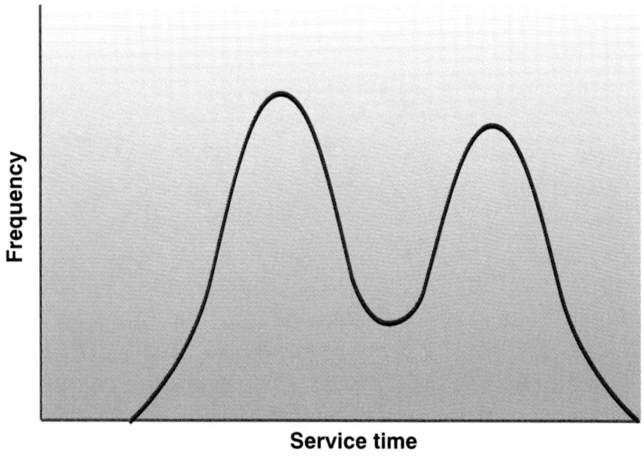

FIGURE 9.11 Service distribution when two categories of customers are pooled into one population.

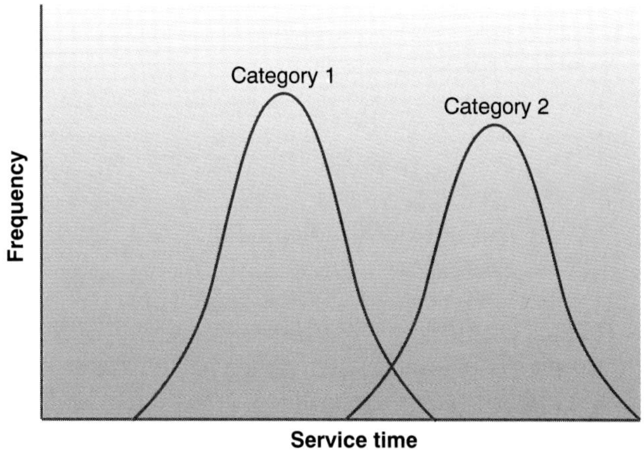

FIGURE 9.12 Service distribution for the two categories of customers in Figure 9.11 separated.

Improved Server Efficiency

Assigning different customer groups to designated servers makes it easier for servers to specialize in providing services to each category of customer. Furthermore, supporting equipment, such as computers or machinery, can be designed to serve a more limited set of customers more efficiently. For example, one reason cellular production improves efficiency is that machines in a cell can be specialized to process a narrow set of similar products rather than having to undergo frequent, large changeovers for a wide variety of products. This specialization allows *average* service time to be reduced, which, together with the variance reduction, often results in *all* categories of customers receiving better service. In some cases, the reduction in average service time alone can reduce the average wait for all customers, even when there is little reduction in service time variation.

Controlling Service Levels

There is no inherent reason why different categories of customers should receive the same level of service. For example, one category of customer may be more profitable for the company, and therefore the company may want to provide better service with less waiting. Customers in different categories may also have different expectations and tolerances for waiting in queues. For example, a person's expectation and tolerance for waiting is often related to the expected service time. A person requesting a service that should take 1 minute to perform will not be happy waiting 10 minutes to receive the service. In contrast, many people requesting service that will take 15 minutes to perform would not be bothered by a 10-minute wait. (Of course, everyone has a different tolerance level, and some people get angry if they have to wait five seconds.)

These differences in customer expectations and tolerance suggest that if we want customers of different categories to experience approximately the same level of **disutility** (aggravation, lost income) from waiting, we should design the system so that different customer categories have different average waits.

Sometimes even when customers require the same service, we may want to allow *them* to choose their level of service based on pricing. For example, some companies have two levels of telephone support. Customers can call an 800 number at no charge to receive answers to their questions, but they may have to wait in a queue for 20 minutes or more. Alternatively, they can call a 900 number and pay some charge in order to get into a different (higher-priority) queue that has little or no wait. This way customers can decide how valuable their time is. In theory this type of system could improve service for everyone. For example, if there were only one queue for all customers, the serving company might only be able to provide five servers in total. By having two separate types of servers and charging priority customers extra, the company might have enough money to provide six servers, and both categories of customers may have shorter waits.

OTHER ISSUES REGARDING DESIGNATED SERVERS

An important practical issue when servers are designated to serve different categories of customers is the loss of efficiency that pooling servers provides, as described in Section 9.5. If the separate server groups are treated as separate queueing systems, whereby customers in one category can be helped only by a server assigned to their category, this efficiency loss can be substantial. However, by simply incorporating a little flexibility into the system and designing server utilization carefully, almost all of the pooling benefits can be maintained while gaining the other benefits listed above.

First, the large benefits from pooling servers come from combining separate systems into one system, so that a server is never idle when a customer is in the queue of another server. By simply establishing an operating procedure whereby idle servers assigned to one category of customer will temporarily serve waiting customers of any category, the system will behave almost as a single system and obtain the benefits of pooling. However, if servers give first priority to customers in their assigned category, the customers served by individual servers will be relatively homogeneous.

Second, in many designated server systems it is usually advantageous not to design the system to have the same server utilization for each type of server. For example, if some customers require very brief service and others require much longer service, the system might have one or two designated "express" servers providing brief service (and the remainder serving customers of any type). The system may be designed so that the express servers cannot handle all of the demand for that category. What tends to happen is that the express customers use the express servers when those lines are relatively short but use the "general purpose" servers when their lines appear to be faster. When there are fewer express servers than needed to serve all express customers, the express servers are used almost continuously and operate at nearly 100% utilization. Utilization of the general-purpose servers is thereby lowered, so the average customer wait there may decrease. But because the express customers have a choice of queues, the express queue does not get overloaded. In many cases, the express customers wait less than with one pooled queue without causing the other customers to incur additional waiting.

Although this section has emphasized the benefits of homogenizing the customer population and using designated servers, keep in mind that it may not always be easy to categorize customers accurately even when there are substantial differences among them. Second, the differences in services required and in service time distributions among categories should be substantial to warrant the use of designated servers.

9.8 M/M/S SYSTEMS WITH A FINITE CUSTOMER POPULATION

In most queueing systems the population of potential customers is sufficiently large so that the average arrival rate, λ, is independent of the number of customers in the queueing system. In some situations, however, the pool of potential customers is small, so the rate at which they require service varies with the number of customers currently in the system. For example, if a company has five machines that break randomly at approximately the same rate, the machines can be considered customers and the repair crew(s) can be considered the server. As more machines enter the queueing system being repaired or waiting for repair, the rate at which additional machines will break decreases proportionately.

When the arrival process is Poisson and the service times are exponential, steady-state equations can be derived. Let N denote the number of customers in the population, and let n be the number of customers in the queueing system (being served or waiting for service); so $n = 0, 1, \ldots, N$. For each customer, suppose that the time between requests for service (arrivals) is exponentially distributed, with a mean time of $1/\lambda$ (so the arrival process is Poisson).[10] Let λ_n denote the average arrival rate when there are n customers already in the system, so

$$\lambda_n = \begin{cases} (N-n)\lambda & \text{for } n = 0, 1, \ldots, N \\ 0 & \text{for } n \geq N \end{cases} \tag{9.18}$$

The steady-state conditions, which are all based on the formula for P_0, are as follows:

$$P_0 = 1/\{ \sum_{n=0}^{s-1} [N!/(N-n)!n!][\lambda/\mu]^n + \sum_{n=s}^{N} [N!/(N-n)!s!s^{n-s}]\,[\lambda/\mu]^n\} \tag{9.19}$$

$$P_n = \begin{cases} P_0\,\{[N!/(N-n)!n!]\,[\lambda/\mu]^n\} & \text{if } 0 \leq n \leq s \\ P_0\,\{[N!/(N-n)!s!s^{n-s}]\,[\lambda/\mu]^n\} & \text{if } s \leq n \leq N \\ 0 & \text{if } n > N \end{cases} \tag{9.20}$$

$$L_q = \sum_{n=s}^{N} (n-s)P_n \tag{9.21}$$

$$L_s = L_q + \sum_{n=0}^{s-1} nP_n + s[1 - \sum_{n=0}^{s-1} P_n] \tag{9.22}$$

---

[10]The time between requests is the time from completion of service for a customer until the next time that customer requests service; this interval does not include time spent in the queueing system being served or waiting for service.

TABLE 9.4 P_0 FOR AN M/M/S SYSTEM WITH FINITE POPULATION N

	$N = 3$		$N = 4$	
λ/μ	$s = 1$	$s = 2$	$s = 1$	$s = 2$
0.05	0.858	0.864	0.811	0.823
0.10	0.732	0.751	0.647	0.682
0.15	0.623	0.657	0.512	0.569
0.20	0.530	0.577	0.398	0.478
0.25	0.451	0.510	0.311	0.403
0.30	0.384	0.452	0.243	0.342
0.35	0.329	0.403	0.190	0.291
0.40	0.282	0.360	0.150	0.249
0.45	0.243	0.323	0.119	0.213
0.50	0.211	0.291	0.095	0.184

When there is only one server ($s = 1$), these equations simplify to

$$P_0 = 1/\{\sum_{n=0}^{N} [N!/(N-n)!]\,[\lambda/\mu]^n\} \tag{9.19a}$$

$$P_n = \begin{cases} P_0\,\{[N!/(N-n)!]\,[\lambda/\mu]^n\} & \text{if } 1 \le n \le N \\ 0 & \text{if } n > N \end{cases} \tag{9.20a}$$

$$L_q = N - [(\lambda + \mu)/\lambda](1 - P_0) \tag{9.21a}$$

$$L_s = L_q + [1 - P_0] \tag{9.22a}$$

In either case

$$W_q = L_q/\bar{\lambda} \tag{9.23}$$

$$W_s = L_s/\bar{\lambda} = W_q + 1/\mu \tag{9.24}$$

where

$$\bar{\lambda} = \lambda(N - L_s) \tag{9.25}$$

is the *effective* average arrival rate.

Because equation (9.19) is rather complex, Table 9.4 provides the values of P_0 for selected values of N and λ/μ. The following example illustrates how a finite population model can be used for personnel planning.

EXAMPLE 5

Bursto Box Company (BBC) has four identical box-making machines. The machines break randomly according to a Poisson process, with the mean operating time between breakdowns being 100 hours. The repair time for each machine is exponentially distributed, with a mean of 25 hours. The company estimates that it loses \$500 for each hour a machine is not available for production. The company can add a second repair crew at a cost of \$60 per hour. BBC wishes to evaluate the performance and cost of an M/M/1 versus an M/M/2 queueing system with a customer population of $N = 4$.

We first note that $1/\lambda = 100$ hours per machine, so $\lambda = 0.01$ machine per hour, and $1/\mu = 25$ hours per machine, so $\mu = 0.04$ machines per hour. We can then compute the following:

With one repair crew (s = 1)

$$P_0 = 1/[(4!/4!)(1/4)^0 + (4!/3!)(1/4)^1 + (4!/2!)(1/4)^2 + (4!/1!)(1/4)^3 + (4!/0!)(1/4)^4]$$
$$= 1/[1 + 1 + 3/4 + 3/8 + 3/32]$$
$$= 0.31$$

$$L_q = 4 - [(0.04 + 0.01)/0.01]\ (1 - 0.31) = 0.55 \text{ cust}$$
$$L_s = 0.55 + (1 - 0.31) = 1.24 \text{ cust}$$
$$\bar{\lambda} = 0.01(4 - 1.24) = 0.0276 \text{ cust/hr}$$
$$W_q = (0.55 \text{ cust})/(0.0276 \text{ cust/hr}) = 19.9 \text{ hr}$$
$$W_s = (1.24 \text{ cust})/(0.0276 \text{ cust/hr}) = 44.9 \text{ hr}$$

ave. machine downtime/hr
= (ave. number of breakdowns/hr) × (ave. downtime/machine)
$= \bar{\lambda} \times W_s$
= (0.0276 breakdowns/hr) × (44.9 downtime-hr/machine)
= 1.239 downtime-hr/hr

ave. cost/hr due to downtime
= (ave. downtime-hr/hr) × (\$500 per downtime-hr)
= (1.239 downtime-hr/hr) × \$500 per downtime-hr = \$619.50/hr

With two repair crews (s = 2)

$$P_0 = 1/[(4!/4!0!)(1/4)^0 + (4!/3!1!)(1/4)^1 + (4!/2!2!2^{2-2})(1/4)^2 + (4!/1!2!2^{3-2})(1/4)^3 + (4!/0!2!2^{4-2})(1/4)^4]$$
$$= 1/[1 + 1 + 3/8 + 6/64 + 3/256]$$
$$= 0.403$$

$$P_1 = 0.403\ [(4!/3!1!)(1/4)^1] = 0.403$$
$$P_2 = 0.403\ [(4!/2!2!2^{2-2})(1/4)^2] = 0.151$$
$$P_3 = 0.403\ [(4!/1!3!2^{3-2})(1/4)^3] = 0.038$$
$$P_4 = 0.403\ [(4!/0!4!2^{4-2})(1/4)^4] = 0.005$$
$$L_q = (2 - 2)0.151 + (3 - 2)0.038 + (4 - 2)0.005 = 0.048 \text{ cust}$$
$$L_s = 1(0.403) + 0.048 + 2(1 - 0.806) = 0.839 \text{ cust}$$
$$\bar{\lambda} = 0.01(4 - 0.839) = 0.03161 \text{ cust/hr}$$
$$W_q = (0.048 \text{ cust})/(0.03161 \text{ cust/hr}) = 1.5 \text{ hr}$$
$$W_s = (0.839 \text{ cust})/(0.03161 \text{ cust/hr}) = 26.5 \text{ hr}$$

ave. machine downtime/hr
$= \bar{\lambda} \times W_s$
= (0.03161 breakdowns/hr) × (26.5 downtime-hr/machine)
= 0.838 downtime-hr/hr

ave. cost/hr due to downtime

= (0.838 downtime-hr/hr) × ($500 per downtime-hr) = $419.00/hr

The savings in reduced downtime by adding a second repair crew is ($619.50 – $419.00)/hour = $200.50/hour. This savings more than justifies the additional $60 per hour in wages. In addition, the two repair crews will have substantial idle time available to perform preventive maintenance work. This should reduce the machine failure rate and provide further benefits.

When the arrival rate is a function of the number of customers already in the system, the effective average arrival rate, $\bar{\lambda}$, will depend on the design of the system, such as the number of servers. In Example 5, $\bar{\lambda} = 0.0276$ customers per hour (a machine breaks every 36.23 hours on average) when $s = 1$, versus $\bar{\lambda} = 0.03161$ customers per hour (a machine breaks every 31.64 hours) when $s = 2$. On the surface, it may appear that machines are not as well maintained when there are two repair crews as when there is one crew because the breakdown rate is higher. This conclusion is incorrect. With only one repair crew, broken machines stay out of service longer, and therefore they cannot break as frequently. It is important to recognize these subtleties in order to make good decisions; a more informative performance measure would be the fraction of time the machines are operable rather than their frequency of failure.

9.9 SERIAL AND NETWORK QUEUEING SYSTEMS

For years, queueing theory research and applications focused primarily on service systems. However, we now recognize that queueing is an important aspect of almost all manufacturing systems, and queueing concepts form the basis of many modern principles of manufacturing, such as just-in-time production, lean production, and synchronized manufacturing. All the queueing systems we have considered so far were one-stage systems: a customer was served by a server and then left the system. Almost all manufacturing systems (and many service systems) are far more complicated than this. Production of the good or service requires products or customers to move through a series of servers, with some processing performed by each server. When servers are arranged in series, we refer to these systems as **serial** (or **tandem**) **queueing systems.** When some servers are arranged in parallel and some in series, we call the arrangement a **queueing network.**[11] A repetitive flow process is a serial queueing system in which each work station is a server and the items being processed are the customers. Cellular and job-shop systems are queueing networks in which the work cells or work stations are the servers and the products being produced are the customers. Figure 9.13 illustrates a serial queue and a queueing network.

Queueing networks can be extremely complicated to analyze, so we will focus on serial queues. In Chapter 8 the production line example associated with Table 8.4 illustrated how random variation in work station processing times reduces the effective production capacity. The following example expands on that concept by showing how random variations affect in-process inventories and production throughput time.

[11]These are also called *Jackson queues* in honor of J. R. Jackson, who derived many of the important results for queueing networks.

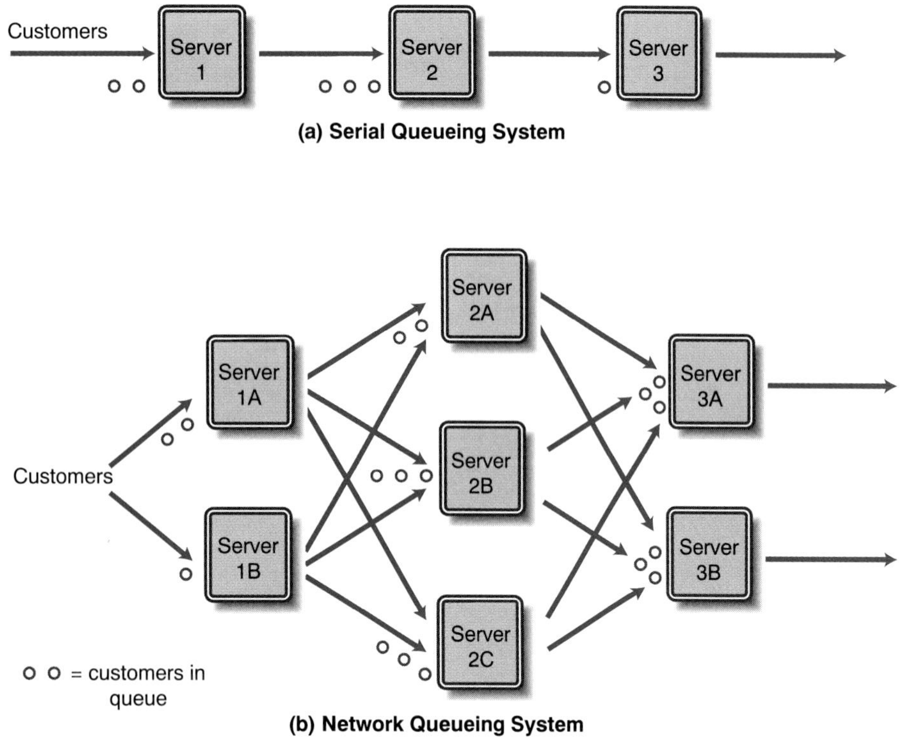

FIGURE 9.13 Serial and network queueing systems.

EXAMPLE 6

(a) Suppose a company produces a variety of similar but customized products using a three-stage batch flow process, as shown in Figure 9.14. Customer orders are received randomly during the day according to a Poisson process at the rate of five orders per day (so the number of orders received in a day is random). Because of differences in order (batch) sizes, machine setup times, and operating speeds, and because of machine breakdowns, quality problems, and worker fatigue, the time to process a customer order at each production stage is exponentially distributed, with an average processing time of 1/6 day.

The first stage of the production system is then an M/M/1 queue where the customer orders are the customers and the first stage is the server, $\lambda = 5$ orders/day and $\mu = 6$ orders/day. It can be proved that in steady state, the pattern of served customers *leaving* an M/M/1 queueing system will approximate a Poisson process with an average rate of λ. So the serial queueing system in Figure 9.14a can be treated as a series of three identical M/M/1 queues. Using the M/M/1 formulas for the first stage,

$\rho = \lambda/\mu = 5/6 = 0.83$

$L_q = \lambda^2[\mu(\mu - \lambda)] = [(5/\text{day})^2]/[6(6 - 5)] = 4.17$ orders

$W_s = 1/(\mu - \lambda) = 1/[(6 - 5)$ orders/day$] = 1$ day.

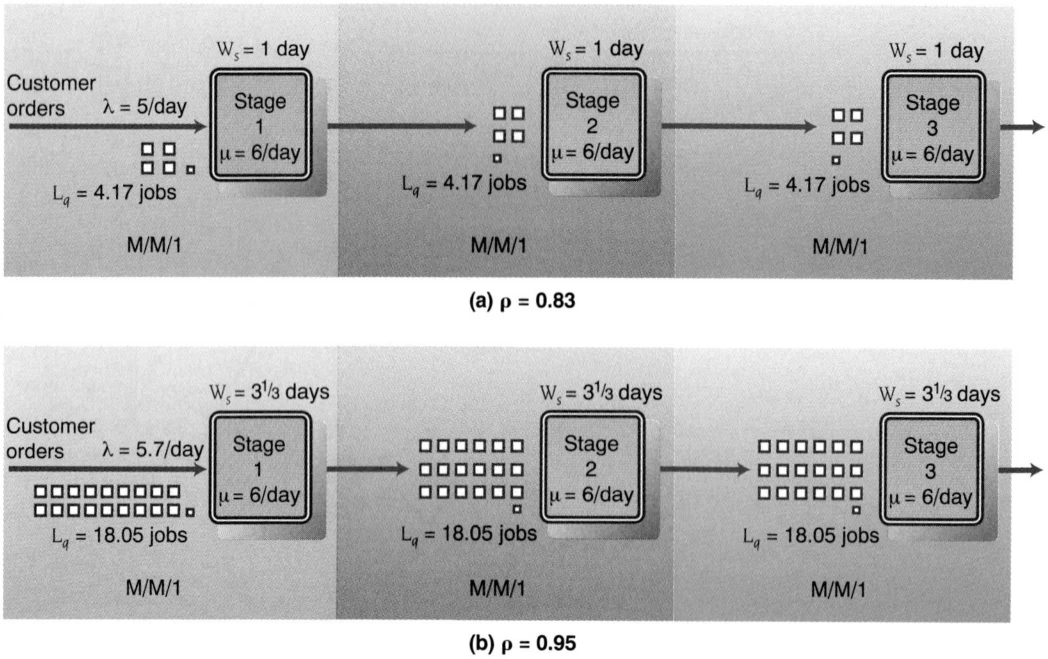

FIGURE 9.14 Batch flow Process as a series of M/M/l queues.

In front of the first stage there will be an average of 4.17 orders waiting in the queue to be processed, and it will take an order an average of one day to make its way through the first stage (from receipt of the order until processing is completed at stage 1). The other two stages are identical, so in front of each stage there will be an average of 4.17 orders in inventory (in queue), and it will take one day to get through each stage. So, on average, there will be a total of 12.51 jobs in inventory in front of the three processing stages, and the average throughput time for orders (from the time an order is received until production is completed) is three days, even though the average amount of time actually spent processing an order is one-half of a day (one-sixth of a day at each stage). This inventory buildup and extensive waiting in the queue occur even though the production stages are operating at only 83% of capacity; this is due entirely to the randomness in the arrival of customer orders and the randomness in processing times.

(b) One of the most striking features of a multistage production system with randomness is that even small increases in demand (server utilization) can cause dramatic increases in work-in-process inventories and throughput times. For example, suppose the demand rate in part (a) increased to 5.7 orders per day (see Figure 9.14b). Recomputing the M/M/1 formulas shows that at each stage L_q = 18.05 orders and W_s = 3.33 days. So a 14% increase in demand causes total in-process inventories between stages to increase by 433% to 54.15 orders and throughput time to increase 333% to 10 days (with the average order spending 9.5 of these 10 days waiting in a queue).

(c) One solution to this problem, which is at the heart of just-in-time and lean production (see Chapter 15), is to reduce the variation in processing times, such as by re-

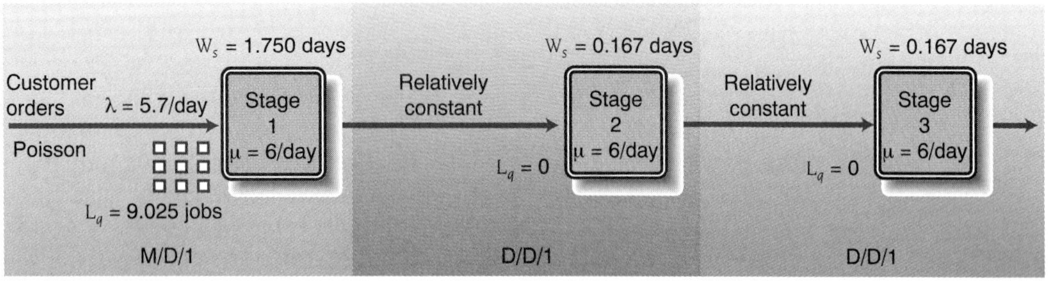

FIGURE 9.15 Batch flow process as a series of M/M/1 and D/D/1 queues.

ducing machine failures and quality defects. To demonstrate the impact of reducing processing time variation, reconsider the production process in part (b), but assume that there is *no* randomness in processing times: all orders take *exactly* one-sixth of a day to process at each stage. The three-stage process is then a serial queueing system in which the first stage is an M/D/1 system and the second and third stages are G/D/1 systems. However, the constant processing times at the first stage make departures from that stage relatively evenly spaced, so we will approximate the second-stage queue by a D/D/1 system. The departures from the second stage are even more evenly spaced than those from the first stage, so the third stage can also be approximated by a D/D/1 system. Using the M/D/1 formulas for the first stage,

$$L_q = [\rho^2/[2(1-\rho)]] = [(0.95)^2/[2(1-0.95)]] = 9.025 \text{ orders}$$
$$W_q = L_q/\lambda = (9.025 \text{ orders})/(5.7 \text{ orders/day}) = 1.583 \text{ days}$$
$$W_s = W_q + 1/\mu = 1.583 \text{ days} + 0.167 \text{ days} = 1.75 \text{ days}$$

For the D/D/1 systems at stages 2 and 3, no queues develop and the average time in the stage is just the processing time of 0.167 days. So the total in-process inventory for the system is 9.025 orders and the average throughput time is 2.08 days, as illustrated in Figure 9.15. So by eliminating the processing time randomness, in-process inventories automatically decrease by 83% and throughput time decreases by nearly 80%. Now in practice all processing time variation cannot be eliminated, but if the variance in processing times were cut in half (a very achievable target in practice), simulation studies indicate that in-process inventories and throughput time are approximately halved as well simply because of the reduced waiting in queues.

Queueing Networks

The clear implication of the preceding example and of the random production line example in Chapter 8 is that actions that reduce variation in the production process will have beneficial results. This fact is even more true in job-shop and cellular production systems where there is greater variation in lot sizes, setup times, processing speeds, and transport times, as well as greater variety of product routings through the system. In Chapter 15 we will explain how these variations can be reduced and how multistage production systems can approach a serial or network system of D/D/1 queues rather than M/M/1 queues.

9.10 BEHAVIORAL AND OTHER CONSIDERATIONS IN QUEUEING

Most research and textbooks on queueing are devoted to its mathematical aspects.[12] One consequence is that the criteria most often used for evaluating different system designs and operating procedures have been average waiting time in the queue or time in the system. However, we know from our own experiences as customers that waiting time alone does not measure the disutility of waiting in terms of aggravation or lost income. Many other factors influence the effects or perceived cost of waiting, and these should be incorporated into design and operational decisions as much as possible. This section begins by explaining how standard queueing analysis can lead to poor decisions when the costs or consequences of waiting are not proportional to waiting time. Next, it discusses important psychological factors that should be considered in queueing systems where the customers are humans. It concludes by providing practical suggestions for improving the operation of queueing systems.

NONLINEAR WAITING COSTS AND THE PSYCHOLOGY OF WAITING

When we use average customer waiting time or average queue length to compare the performance of alternative queueing system designs, we are implicitly assuming that the cost or disutility of waiting is proportional to the waiting time; in other words, the cost of a 10-minute wait is twice that of a 5-minute wait. Although this is true in many cases, both scientific research and casual empiricism suggest that the disutility customers experience depends on more than waiting time and is often nonlinear with waiting time. This implies that W_q and W_s are not necessarily the best measures for comparing queueing system designs.

Nonlinear Disutility

For many services the customer disutility function looks like that in Figure 9.16. In some cases, this is due primarily to psychological reasons. Customers have some threshold of waiting for service; for waiting times below this threshold, disutility is small and in-

[12]Much of this subsection is based on the excellent articles by Richard C. Larsen: "Perspectives on Queues: Social Justice and the Psychology of Queueing," *Operations Research*, Vol. 35, 1987, pp. 895–905, and "There's More to a Line Than Its Wait," *Technology Review*, Vol. 91, July 1988, pp. 60–67.

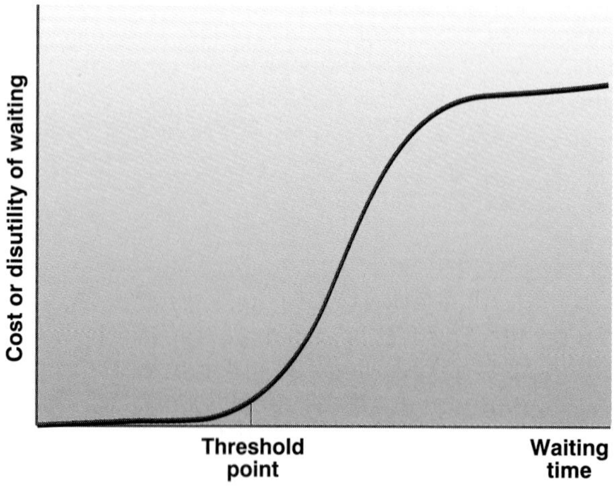

FIGURE 9.16 Typical nonlinear disutility function.

IN GOOD COMPANY

L. L. Bean

The well-known catalog retailer L. L. Bean receives a large percentage of its orders by phone, so keeping customer waiting to a minimum without overstaffing is important. Traditionally, L. L. Bean established its staffing rules based on average service factor goals (such as having at least 85% of customer calls answered by a telephone agent within 20 seconds). The schedules, however, caused the company to be understaffed during some periods, thereby costing it sales, and overstaffed during other periods, thereby inflating costs. Using a queueing analysis that explicitly considered variations in call loads over time, as well as customer balking and reneging behavior, L. L. Bean devised new staffing procedures based on economic optimization rather than trying to achieve service goals. The resulting schedules, which modify staffing more frequently over time, saved the company over $500,000 per year while reducing customer waiting during peak periods.

Source: Bruce Andrews and Henry Parsons, "Establishing Telephone-Agent Staffing Levels Through Economic Optimization," *Interfaces*, March–April 1993, pp. 14–20.

creases slowly with waiting time; above the threshold, disutility increases rapidly. (Beyond some larger waiting time, disutility is maximized and cannot increase further.) Suppose that for a given service the waiting threshold is five minutes. Then a queueing system in which everyone waits 4 minutes (so W_q = 4 minutes) may be much better than one in which 70% of the people have no wait and 30% have a 10-minute wait, even though W_q = 3 minutes. The first system causes little customer disutility, whereas the second may cause 30% of the customers to quit doing business with the company. For a company such as L. L. Bean, the subject of this chapter's "In Good Company" feature, keeping customer waiting times below this threshold is critical.

The exact shape of the disutility function and the location of the threshold point will vary from person to person, and even for the same person it will vary from situation to situation. One factor that affects disutility is the customer's expectation for waiting. For example, a person may be patient when waiting for a time-consuming service, such as receiving assistance in completing tax forms, but may be very impatient waiting to get gasoline for a car. (Steve Pryor, vice-president of fuels marketing at Mobil Oil, has observed that gasoline customers are some of the most impatient. "People get aggravated at anything that slows them down.")[13]

In addition to psychological reasons, there are often scientific and physical reasons for nonlinear disutility. For example, for building and house fires, the dollar damage as a function of fire department response time has a shape similar to the function in Figure 9.16. A 10-minute response time to a fire may result in five times more damage than a 5-minute response time; a 30-minute response time may result in almost no addi-

[13]From Caleb Solomon, "Self-Service at Gas Stations Includes Paying," *Wall Street Journal*, Aug. 4, 1993.

tional damage compared to a 15-minute response time—the structure cannot be saved in either case. Similarly, the probability of catching the perpetrator of a crime drops dramatically after the first few minutes or hours, and the probability of death from a severe heart attack increases rapidly after a few minutes without medical intervention. In each of these cases, it would be ridiculous to compare response systems by looking only at average response (waiting) time. A response system that averaged two minutes of waiting time but allowed 100 people per year to die is probably worse than one that averaged four minutes of waiting time but resulted in only 10 deaths per year.

Social Justice

One of the most annoying aspects of waiting in lines is the feeling that one is being treated unfairly relative to other customers. Waiting 10 minutes to be served is more tolerable when we know that others are waiting their turn. But to see people come in after we did and receive service first is infuriating. This is one reason most people prefer using a single queue in a multiserver system. This prevents later-arriving customers from being served before earlier-arriving ones. In fact, consultants have reported that customers sometimes prefer longer average waits in a single queue to shorter average waits in multiple queues because of the greater perceived social justice.

Queueing systems that provide social justice can also have tangible economic benefits. For example, tow boats that pull or push barges on inland waterways have nonlinear fuel consumption functions. The amount of fuel consumed is approximately proportional to the square of speed. So a change in speed, say from 4 to 6 mph, more than doubles fuel consumption. As tow boats go up or down some rivers, such as the Mississippi, they must pass through locks. It can take as much as a few hours for a boat to pass through a lock, so if the lock is congested, each position in line can be worth hundreds or thousands of dollars in time. As a result, tow boat operators often race between locks on the river to pass boats in front or to prevent being passed by those behind, consuming excessive fuel in the process. When a lock is highly congested, one solution is for boats leaving adjacent locks to receive tickets that assign them positions in the queue at the next lock. They could then travel at a more fuel-efficient speed while being assured their place in line at the next lock, and the lock would be less congested. One consultant has estimated the savings from such a plan to be in excess of $1 million per year for some locks.

A second aspect of social justice is how long one must wait relative to what is perceived to be reasonable, especially vis-à-vis other customers. When customers require different types of service, their willingness to wait is usually different. Someone who only wants to buy a carton of milk at the grocery store does not expect to wait as long as someone with a full shopping cart. And usually people with a full shopping cart also do not expect to be served as rapidly as someone with a few items. Therefore, the average level of disutility for the customer population can be reduced by having a system that creates differential waiting times based on reasonable customer expectations. As mentioned in Section 9.7, this is one reason for having queueing systems that segregate customers according to service requirements.

Environment

Our perception of waiting time and our attitude toward waiting are affected by the environment in which we wait. If customers are asked to stand in a line or sit in a chair with nothing to do except contemplate the passage of time, or if the waiting environment is unpleasant, they will be very aware that they are waiting. Each second will be excruciating. In contrast, if customers are kept busy doing other things (especially if these are perceived as useful, necessary, or entertaining) and if the environment is pleasant, then waiting may not be perceived as wasted time.

Some organizations have tried to make waiting a pleasant and enjoyable experience. One New York bank has entertainment, such as music or magicians, in its lobby from 10 A.M. to 2 P.M. each day. It even has animal shows and art exhibits, and at Christmas time it has an ice show. Customer interviews have shown that customers now consider their time spent waiting in the bank as a positive experience rather than wasted time.

Sometimes customer aggravation is primarily a perceptual problem that can be remedied by giving waiting customers special attention, as Deb Holler and Great Western Bank attempt to do by greeting waiting customers by name and helping them prepare transactions. In some cases, customer aggravation can even be reduced by putting delays in the service system to distract customers and to fill their time. For example, an airline received a large number of customer complaints about the slowness of baggage handling for specific flights, even though baggage was almost always delivered within eight minutes of the plane's arrival at the gate (a good record by industry standards). The problem was that passengers picking up luggage could get to the baggage carousel in one minute, where they then waited for seven minutes. They were further aggravated by seeing passengers from the same flight who were not claiming luggage getting into taxis and leaving the airport (social injustice on top of waiting). When the company instead had these flights arrive at more remote gates, so that it took six to seven minutes to get to the baggage area, complaints dropped to almost zero. However, although this action may reduce complaints, it does not reduce waiting; actions that reduce waiting would be preferable.

The Walt Disney Company is a world leader in managing queues and perceptions of waiting. Most Disneyland and Walt Disney World rides load and unload continuously rather than in large batches. This way the line is always moving, so people not only are kept busy walking, but they perceive that they are "making progress." Continually walking for 30 minutes in a queue is perceived by most people as being less painful than standing in the same spot for 30 minutes, especially when there is entertainment and scenery to distract them.

Waiting in line can be turned into a positive experience when customers are entertained by Mickey Mouse.

Feedback and Accurate Information

Customers are generally more patient about waiting when they receive accurate information about the expected waiting time. If people know they will have to wait 15 minutes for service, they can plan an activity appropriate for that wait. Walt Disney World and Disneyland have signs that list the expected waiting time at the queue for most rides. This allows parents to select rides that will fit their schedules and the current mood of their children better. Accurate information on expected waiting time allows customers to adjust their expectations and reduce the disutility of waiting. However, inaccurate information can make matters worse. A customer who has been told to expect a 10-minute wait will become much more aggravated once this threshold has been passed than he or she might have been otherwise. Of course, overestimating the wait can be just as bad by chasing away customers. One useful form of feedback for telephone queues is to tell waiting customers periodically their location in the queue. This allows the customers to perceive their progress through the system and to estimate the likely waiting time.

In addition to providing information on expected waits, service systems can reduce customer aggravation by explaining the cause of abnormally long waits. For example, one patient who was initially aggravated by a long wait for her gynecologist later interpreted the wait positively when she was told that the doctor had spent extra time with a patient who had suffered a miscarriage: "That meant he would do the same for me."[14]

ADDITIONAL SUGGESTIONS FOR IMPROVING QUEUEING SYSTEMS

In addition to the ideas already presented, there are a number of other ways to design service systems to improve service and reduce customer dissatisfaction. We present four of them here.

1. ***Allow Customers to Serve Themselves.*** Few things are more annoying than to wait for someone to provide services that customers can easily provide for themselves. Therefore, to the extent possible, a service system should allow customers to perform simple tasks themselves if they wish. For example, many people prefer pumping their own gas to speed up service, even if there is no price discount for doing so. Many gasoline stations have even transferred the paying function to customers by installing pumps where customers can pay for their gasoline with credit cards without dealing with a cashier.

   Many organizations, such as the IRS, insurance companies, banks, and mutual funds, provide telephone systems whereby customers perform some services themselves using a touch-tone phone. For example, if you want to check the balance in your mutual fund account, you can dial the company's phone number and receive a taped voice that says: "If you wish to receive a prospectus and other information concerning a fund in the mutual fund family, press 1; if you are inquiring about a specific account, press 2; if you want to know the current share price for a fund, press 3; if you need some other service, press 4 or stay on the line and a service agent will help you." After pressing a number, you may get another taped voice asking other questions, such as "What is your account number?" This allows customers to perform part of the service themselves by choosing the type of service they need (and in some cases they can provide all of the service themselves). This saves the service agent time because figuring out what a customer wants is time-consuming. In addition, this system homogenizes the customers so that

[14] From Marilyn Chase, "Health Journal," *Wall Street Journal*, Oct. 24, 1994.

FIGURE 9.17 Configuration with two queues per server.

when they do talk to a service agent, the agent can be a specialist with respect to the desired service.

In each of these cases, customers get faster service and the serving company saves money by needing fewer servers. Even when the system requires some investment in equipment or technology, such as automatic pumps or phone transaction systems, transferring service tasks to the customers is often worth doing.

2. ***Shorten Service Times by Performing Tasks in Advance.*** Bill Marriott, president of Marriott Corporation, has said, "Waiting in line to check in is one of life's least productive activities."[15] What makes it worse is that most of the activities required to check into or out of a hotel could be done in the customer's absence. For example, 90% of the time involved in hotel check-in consists of obtaining the name, address, and financial information from the customer. If the person is a regular customer of the hotel chain, this information could be stored in a computer in advance, with no need to reacquire it unless there is a change. Many auto rental and hotel chains now provide express check-in and check-out, so that the customer has to spend little or no time in line.

3. ***Use Two Queues for Each Server.*** For some services, such as sales transactions, a surprisingly large amount of the service time does not involve service at all, but is time wasted by customers placing goods on a counter or removing goods from the counter, putting away their money, and organizing themselves to leave. During this time, the server is unable to serve another customer. A simple but effective solution to this problem is to have two queues for each server, as shown in Figure 9.17. While the server is serving a customer in line A, the next customer in line B can position the products she is purchasing and get her money ready. When the server finishes with the customer in A, he can immediately turn to serve the customer in line B. While the customer in line B is being served, the customer in line A can put away his money, gather up his purchases, and leave, and the next customer in line A can get prepared for the next transaction. This system has been used successfully in many cafeterias, such as at the Smithsonian Institute, and by convenience stores, such as QuikTrip, Inc.

[15]From Marriott advertisement, *Wall Street Journal*, Oct. 20, 1993.

4. ***Reward Customers for Being Patient.*** Sometimes making customers wait for service is unavoidable. To the serving company, two major concerns are that (a) the customer will leave the system (balk or renege) because of the anticipated wait and the sale will be lost, and (b) even if the customer is ultimately served, goodwill and future sales may be lost because the customer was displeased with the wait. One way to address these concerns is to reward customers for their patience if they do not leave the queue. A good example of how this can be done in practice is provided by Dierbergs Florist. When a customer calls Dierbergs to place an order, if the phones are busy the customer is put in a queue and a voice tells her that if her call is not answered within two minutes she will hear the "flower of the day" announced, and if she tells the server who handles the call the name of this flower, she will receive a 5% discount. This policy accomplishes several things: (a) it tells customers that Dierbergs values their time and is willing to pay them for it if the wait is too long; (b) it tells customers that Dierbergs has an incentive to answer their calls quickly, so the wait is likely to be less than two minutes; (c) the customer is less likely to hang up and try another florist; and (d) if the customer does wait more than two minutes and obtains the discount (which is normally $2 to $5 in value), the customer may actually view the wait as a positive experience, creating goodwill. (In all my calls to Dierbergs I have never hung up, and yet have never had to wait the full two minutes.)

Queueing systems are an important part of our lives, but there is no reason for us to spend five years of our lives waiting. All too often the problem is due to poor queueing system design or operation. This chapter has explained the major causes of queue formation and has provided many suggestions on how to reduce waiting. We should all take this information as a manifesto to improve the queueing systems over which we have control.

SUMMARY

- Even when the average service capacity exceeds the average demand put on the system, waiting lines can develop because of the randomness of the arrival pattern and service times.
- Average queue size and average waiting time increase rapidly when the utilization rate of the **servers** exceeds approximately 0.70–0.80.
- The most common customer arrival pattern is a **Poisson process**, whereby the times between arrivals are exponentially distributed.
- For simple queueing systems, **steady-state equations** that compute measures of performance can be derived; in more complex cases, **simulation** must be used.
- Pooling servers from separate systems into fewer systems will reduce the average waiting time and queue sizes.
- Everything else being equal, the more variation that exists in the arrival pattern and/or service times, the longer customers will wait on average.
- Having a single waiting line for a multiserver system provides more equitable waiting for customers and can reduce average waiting time.
- When the **customer population** is made up of two or more types of customers requiring different amounts of service, establishing designated servers for each class can improve overall service.
- Multistage production systems are examples of **serial (tandem) queueing systems** (servers arranged in series) and **queueing networks** (servers arranged in parallel and in series). In multistage production processes, in-process inventories and throughput times increase as randomness in processing times increases.
- Good queueing analysis should take into account the possibility that the cost or disutility of customer waiting may not be proportional to the waiting time.

Key Terms

analytic approach **430**
average arrival rate **432**
average service rate **433**
average service time **433**
balk **432**
customers **429**
customer population **429**
deterministic **448**
disutility **454**
first-come-first-served (FCFS) **433**
interarrival times **431**
Poisson process **431**
queue **427**
queue discipline **433**
queueing network **458**
queueing systems **427**
queueing theory **427**
renege **432**
serial (tandem) queueing systems **458**
servers **429**
simulation **430**
steady state **435**
steady-state equations **430**
transient **435**
utilization factor **436**
well behaved **432**

Key Formulas

M/M/1 Model

$\rho = \lambda/\mu$ (9.1)

$L_q = \lambda^2/[\mu(\mu - \lambda)]$ (9.2)

$L_s = \lambda/(\mu - \lambda)$ (9.3)

$W_q = \lambda/[\mu(\mu - \lambda)]$ (9.4)

$W_s = 1/(\mu - \lambda)$ (9.5)

$P_n = (1 - \lambda/\mu)(\lambda/\mu)^n$ for $n = 0, 1, 2, \ldots$ (9.6)

$P_{\geq n} = (\lambda/\mu)^n$ for $n = 0, 1, 2, \ldots$ (9.7)

$P_W = P_{\geq 1} = \lambda/\mu$ (9.8)

M/M/s Model

$\rho = \lambda/(s\mu)$ (9.9)

$$P_0 = 1/\{\sum_{n=0}^{s-1} [(\lambda/\mu)^n/n!] + [(\lambda/\mu)^s/s!]\,[1 - (\lambda/s\mu)]^{-1} \quad (9.10)$$

$$P_n = \begin{cases} \dfrac{[(\lambda/\mu)^n]P_0}{n!} & \text{for } 0 \leq n \leq s \\ \dfrac{[(\lambda/\mu)^n]P_0}{s!\,(n-s)!} & \text{for } n \geq s \end{cases} \quad (9.11)$$

$$P_W = \frac{[(\lambda/\mu)^s]P_0]}{s!\,[1 - \rho]} \quad (9.12)$$

$L_q = [(\lambda/\mu)^s \rho P_0]/[s!(1 - \rho)^2]$ (9.13)

$L_s = L_q + \lambda/\mu$ (9.14)

$W_q = L_q/\lambda$ (9.15)

$W_s = W_q + 1/\mu$ (9.16)

M/G/1 Model

$L_q = [\lambda^2\sigma^2 + \rho^2]/[2(1 - \rho)]$ (9.17)

$L_s = L_q + \lambda/\mu$ (9.14)

$W_q = L_q/\lambda$ (9.15)

$W_s = W_q + 1/\mu$ (9.16)

M/M/s Model with a Finite Population

$$P_0 = 1/\{\sum_{n=0}^{s-1} [N!/(N-n)!n!][\lambda/\mu]^n + \sum_{n=s}^{N} [N!/(N-n)!\,s!s^{n-s}]\,[\lambda/\mu]^n\} \quad (9.19)$$

$$P_n = \begin{cases} P_0\,\{[N!/(N-n)!n!]\,[\lambda/\mu]^n\} & \text{if } 0 \leq n \leq s \\ P_0\,\{[N!/(N-n)!s!s^{n-s}]\,[\lambda/\mu]^n\} & \text{if } s \leq n \leq N \\ 0 & \text{if } n > N \end{cases} \quad (9.20)$$

$$L_q = \sum_{n=s}^{N} (n-s)P_n \quad (9.21)$$

$$L_s = L_q + \sum_{n=0}^{s-1} nP_n + s[1 - \sum_{n=0}^{s-1} P_n] \quad (9.22)$$

$W_q = L_q/\bar{\lambda}$, where $\bar{\lambda} = \lambda\,(N - L_s)$ (9.23)

$W_s = L_s/\bar{\lambda} = W_q + 1/\mu$ (9.24)

When there is only one server ($s = 1$) these equations simplify to

$$P_0 = 1/\{\sum_{n=0}^{N} [N!/(N-n)!]\,[\lambda/\mu]^n\} \quad (9.19a)$$

$$P_n = \begin{cases} P_0\,\{[N!/(N-n)!]\,[\lambda/\mu]^n\} & \text{if } 1 \leq n \leq N \\ 0 & \text{if } n > N \end{cases} \quad (9.20a)$$

$L_q = N - [(\lambda + \mu)/\lambda](1 - P_0)$ (9.21a)

$L_s = L_q + [1 - P_0]$ (9.22a)

SOLVED PROBLEMS

Problem 1. People's Health Clinic has one physician on duty at most times. On average it takes five minutes to examine and meet with a patient, but there is tremendous variation in actual service times; the service distribution is approximately exponential. Patients arrive randomly according to a Poisson process at an average rate of 9.6 per hour. Compute

(a) the fraction of time the physician is not seeing patients,

(b) the average number of patients waiting in line,

(c) the average time a patient spends waiting in line before being examined, and

(d) the average time a patient spends in the clinic.

Solution

The clinic is an M/M/1 queueing system with $\lambda = 9.6$ patients/hr and $1/\mu = 5$ min, so $\mu = 1/5$ patients/min= 12 patients/hr.

(a) The fraction of time the physician is busy is $\rho = \lambda/\mu = 9.6/12 = 0.80$, so the fraction of time the physician is not seeing patients is $1 - 0.80 = 0.20$

(b) The average number of patients waiting to see the physician is

$$L_q = \lambda^2/[\mu(\mu - \lambda)] = [9.6^2/12(12 - 9.6)] = 3.2 \text{ patients}$$

(c) The average time a patient waits to see the physician is

$$W_q = \lambda/[\mu(\mu - \lambda)] = 9.6/[12(12 - 9.6)] = 0.333 \text{ hrs.} = 20 \text{ min}$$

(d) The average time patients spend in the system is

$$W_s = 1/(\mu - \lambda) = 1/(12 - 9.6) = 0.417 \text{ hr} = 25 \text{ min}$$

Problem 2. American National Bank has two automatic tellers (with one waiting line). Customers arrive according to a Poisson process at an average rate of one every 2.5 minutes. The time a customer spends using an automatic teller is approximately exponentially distributed, with an average time of four minutes. Compute

(a) the average number of customers waiting in line to use an automatic teller (not counting the person using the teller),

(b) the average amount of time a customer spends waiting for *and* using an automatic teller, and

(c) the probability that a customer must wait to use an automatic teller.

(d) Suppose the bank added a third automatic teller; compute the average time a customer would spend waiting in line.

Solution

The current situation is an M/M/2 queueing system with $1/\lambda = 2.5$ min $\rightarrow \lambda = (1/2.5) = 0.40$ cust/min = 24 cust/hr, and $1/\mu = 4$ min $\rightarrow \mu = (1/4)$ cust/min = 15 cust/hr.

(a) The utilization factor is $\rho = \lambda/s\mu = 24/[(2)(15)] = 0.80$. From Table 9.2, $P_0 = 0.111$. Then using equation (9.13) the average number of customers in line is

$$L_q = [(24/15)^2(0.80)(0.111)]/[2!(1 - 0.80)^2] = 2.84$$

(b) $W_q = L_q/\lambda = (2.84 \text{ cust})/(24 \text{ cust/hr}) = 0.118 \text{ hr} = 7.10 \text{ min}$

So the average time in the system is

$$W_s = W_q + 1/\mu = 7.10 + 4.00 = 11.10 \text{ min}$$

(c) The probability that a customer must wait in line is

$$P_W = [(24/15)^2(0.111)]/[2!(1 - 0.80)] = 0.710$$

(d) With three servers, we have an M/M/3 system, so $\rho = 24/[(3)(15)] = 0.533$. From Table 9.2 (using interpolation), $P_0 = 0.187$.

$$L_q = [(24/15)^3(0.533)(0.187)]/[3!(1 - 0.533)^2] = 0.31.$$

$$W_q = L_q/\lambda = 0.31/(24 \text{ cust/hr}) = 0.013 \text{ hr.} = 0.78 \text{ min}$$

Problem 3: The Business School at Big-State University has a student advisory office with one adviser on duty at most times. Currently, students simply drop-in for advice; there are no scheduled appointments. Students arrive according to a Poisson process at an average rate of five per hour. The Business School has determined that almost all students requesting advice fall into two categories: those who have a simple question concerning a single course or degree requirement and those who need degree planning and development of a semester schedule. Students in the first category require 5 minutes for advice, with little variation, and students in the second category require 30 minutes for advice with little variation. Approximately 80% of the students are in the first category and 20% are in the second category. Compute

(a) the fraction of time the adviser is not advising students,
(b) the average number of students waiting in line to see the adviser,
(c) the average time a student spends waiting in line before seeing the adviser, and
(d) the average time a student spends in the system.

Solution

The current advising system is an M/G/1 queue with $\lambda = 5/\text{hr}$, $1/\mu = 0.8(5 \text{ min}) + 0.2(30 \text{ min}) = 10$ min $\rightarrow \mu = 0.1$ cust/min = 6/hr, and

$$\sigma = \sqrt{\Sigma p_i[x_i - E(X)]^2}$$ [16]

$$\sqrt{[0.8(5 - 10 \text{ min})^2 + 0.2(30 - 10 \text{ min})^2]} = 10 \text{ min} = 0.167 \text{ hr}$$

(a) The fraction of time the adviser is advising students is $\rho = \lambda/\mu = 5/6 = 0.83$. So the fraction of time the the adviser is not advising students is $(1 - 0.83) = 0.17$.

(b) Using equation (9.17), the average number of students waiting for an adviser is

$$L_q = [\lambda^2\sigma^2 + \rho^2]/[2(1 - \rho)]$$
$$= \{[(5^2 \times (0.167)^2) + (5/6)^2]/[2(1 - (5/6))]\} = 4.17 \text{ students}$$

(c) The average time students wait in line is

$$W_q = L_q/\lambda = (4.17 \text{ students})/(5 \text{ students/hr}) = 0.833 \text{ hr} = 50.0 \text{ min}$$

(d) The average time a student spends in the system is

$$W_s = W_q + 1/\mu = 50 \text{ min} + 10 \text{ min} = 60 \text{ min}$$

---

[16] The average value for a random variable, X, that has a probability p_i of taking on the value x_i, is

$$E(X) = \sum_i p_i x_i$$

The variance of the random variable X is

$$\sigma^2 = \sum_i p_i[x_i - E(X)]^2$$

Problem 4. Suppose that in problem 3 the advising office is currently open 10 hours per day (from 8 A.M. to 6 P.M.), so approximately 40 students in the first category (5 minute advisory) and 10 students in the second category (30 minute advising) are advised each day. The associate dean has decided to set aside certain times of the day for each type of advising on Mondays and Tuesdays. On Mondays only students in the first category can be advised from 8:00 A.M. to 12:00 noon, and only students in the second category can be advised the rest of the day. On Tuesdays only students in the first category can be advised from 2:00 to 6:00 p.m., and only students in the second category can be advised the rest of the day. Assume that the same number of students in each category will seek advice on these days as before the change, but their arrival times will be compressed into the assigned intervals. Therefore, during the four hours when the first category of students are being advised the advising office is an M/D/1 queueing system with $\lambda = 10$ students/hr and $\mu = 12$ students/hr, and during the six hours when the second category is being advised the office is an M/D/1 queueing system with $\lambda = 1.67$ students/hr and $\mu = 2$ students/hr. For each category of student, compute

(a) the average time students spend waiting in line before seeing the adviser and

(b) the average time students spend in the system.

Solution

Using equation (9.17a) for the four hours when the first category of students are being advised

$$L_q = [10/12]^2/[2(1 - (10/12))] = 2.08 \text{ students}$$

So

$$W_q = L_q/\lambda = (2.08 \text{ students})/(10 \text{ students/hr}) = 0.208 \text{ hr} = 12.5 \text{ min}$$

$$W_s = W_q + 1/\mu = 12.5 \text{ min} + 5 \text{ min} = 17.5 \text{ min}$$

During the six hours when the second category of students is being advised

$$L_q = [1.67/2.0]^2/[2(1 - (1.67/2.0))] = 2.08 \text{ students}$$

$$W_q = 2.08 \text{ students}/1.67 \text{ students/hr} = 1.25 \text{ hr} = 75 \text{ min}$$

$$W_s = 75 \text{ min} + 30 \text{ min} = 105 \text{ min}$$

Notice that with this scheduling plan the average wait in the queue *for all students* is 0.8(12.5 min) + 0.2(75 min) = 25 min. Thus, the average wait in the queue is half that of the system in which students can come in for advice at any time. This saving is due to elimination of service time variation (homogenizing customers) during each part of the day. However, the students in the first category save an average of 37.5 minutes of waiting time, while those in the second category spend 25 extra minutes in the queue on average.

Problem 5. Price Anderson is a statistical consultant to three small law firms that specialize in handling major lawsuits. The law firms never handle more than one case at a time. For each firm the times between requests for Price's services are random, with approximately an exponential distribution and an average time between requests of 60 days. The time required for Price to perform the requested statistical analysis is exponentially distributed, with an average of 12 days. Compute

(a) the average number of clients waiting for Price to provide statistical analysis for them (customers in the system) and

(b) the average amount of time it takes for a client to receive the analysis requested (time in the system).

Solution

Price Anderson's consulting business is an M/M/1 system with a finite customer population of $N = 3$, $1/\lambda = 60$ days $\rightarrow \lambda = (1/60) = 0.0167$ cust/day, and $1/\mu = 12$ days $\rightarrow \mu = (1/12) = 0.0833$ cust/day.

(a) Using equation (9.19a) we get

$$P_0 = 1/[(3!/3!)(0.2)^0 + (3!/2!)(0.2)^1 + (3!/1!)(0.2)^2 + (3!/0!)(0.2)^3]$$

$$= 1/[1 + 0.6 + 0.24 + 0.048] = 0.530$$

$$L_q = N - [(\lambda + \mu)/\lambda][1 - P_0] = 3 - [(0.0167 + 0.0833)/0.0167][1 - 0.530]$$

$$= 0.19 \text{ cust}$$

$$L_s = L_q + [1 - P_0] = 0.19 + [1 - 0.53] = 0.66 \text{ cust}$$

(b) $\bar{\lambda} = \lambda(N - L_s) = (0.0167 \text{ clients/day})(3 - 0.66) = 0.039$ cust/day

$$W_s = L_s / \bar{\lambda} = (0.66 \text{ cust})/(0.039 \text{ cust/day}) = 16.92 \text{ days}$$

DISCUSSION AND REVIEW QUESTIONS

1. If 10 customers per hour on average arrive at a store and it takes an average of five minutes to serve each one, why would a waiting line ever develop?
2. (a) Identify two production systems not mentioned in the chapter in which queueing is an important aspect of the system. (b) What can be done to improve the operation of these two systems? Explain.
3. When studying a queueing system, why does it matter whether customers balk or renege?
4. Under what conditions could one use steady-state queueing equations to evaluate a queueing system rather than simulation?
5. How would one determine whether or not the arrival process for a system is Poisson?
6. For most queueing systems the optimal server utilization factor is less than 80%. Doesn't this mean that substantial amounts of labor are automatically wasted in queueing systems? Explain.
7. In a multiserver queueing system with a heterogeneous population, what are the advantages and disadvantages of segregating servers (assigning some servers to one type of customer and other servers to any or another type of customer)?
8. Identify a queueing system not mentioned in the chapter in which there is considerable randomness in service times. Explain one way in which the variation in service times could be reduced without increasing the average service time.
9. Identify a queueing system not mentioned in the chapter for which it would be reasonable to provide different levels of service (waiting time) to different categories of customers. Explain.
10. Identify a queueing system not mentioned in the chapter for which average customer waiting time would not be a good measure of system performance. What would be a good measure?
11. Give an example not mentioned in the chapter of how the environment would influence the disutility of waiting. Explain.
12. Give an example of a queueing system not mentioned in the chapter in which giving accurate information to the customers would affect the disutility of waiting.
13. How do retail stores such as grocery stores adapt their system to account for the variations in customer arrival *rates* over time (changes in average demand during the day, not randomness between arrivals)?
14. In a serial queueing system, suppose that all service times at each server (stage) are identical and constant. Explain why the pattern of customers leaving the last server will have little variation (relatively equal spacing between departures) even if the arrival pattern at the first stage (server) is a Poisson process.

PROBLEMS

1. At Milton State University the School of Business has one photocopier that is used by the faculty and staff. Faculty and staff arrive at the copier according to a Poisson process at the rate of 12 per hour. The time it takes to use the copier is approximately exponentially distributed, with an average time of three minutes. Compute the following: (a) the system utilization, (b) the average number of people waiting to use the photocopier, (c) the average time a person spends waiting plus copying materials per visit, and (d) the probability that two or more people are waiting in line to photocopy (not counting the one using the photocopier).

2. Suppose customers arrive at a car rental office according to a Poisson process at the rate of 10 per hour. Currently, one clerk is assigned to the counter to serve them. Suppose the service time is exponentially distributed, with a mean service time of four minutes. Compute (a) the utilization factor, (b) the average number of customers waiting in line, (c) the average length of time a customer spends in the office (waiting and being served), and (d) the probability that two or more customers are in the office at the same time (i.e., at least one customer is waiting for service).

3. A small city has one ambulance that responds to emergency medical calls. The time between requests for ambulance service is exponentially distributed, with a mean of 90 minutes. The time it takes for the ambulance to serve a request (go to a house or accident site, treat a person, and take the person to a hospital, if necessary) is exponentially distributed, with a mean of 54 minutes. Compute (a) the fraction of requests for which the ambulance cannot be sent immediately, (b) the average time a person must wait until the ambulance is dispatched to the call, and (c) the probability that two or more requests are waiting for the ambulance to be dispatched (i.e., three or more customers are in the system).

4. In problem 2, suppose the company changed the information required to rent a car so that customer service times were always *exactly* four minutes. Compute (a) the average number of customers waiting in line (in the queue) and (b) the average time customers spend in the office

5. Robert Travis has a one-work-bay auto repair shop that specializes in quick repairs. Although Mr. Travis primarily handles quick repair and maintenance work, occasionally a few customers request more time-consuming work. Customers arrive at an average rate of one per hour according to a Poisson process. The repair times are approximately exponentially distributed, with a mean of 45 minutes. In order to keep customers happy, Mr. Travis has a policy of reducing the repair cost by \$5 for each hour a customer waits for a car (and the shop is open), not including the time it is being repaired (fractional hours receive a *pro rata* discount). The repair shop is open eight hours each day. (a) On average, how much does Mr. Travis reduce the repair costs for each customer? (b) Mr. Travis has room for the car he is fixing plus two more on his property. Whenever there are more than two vehicles in the queue, he must park the car in a lot next door owned by Burger Palace. He must pay Burger Palace \$2 for each car he parks there, regardless of how long it is parked . On average, how much does he have to pay Burger Palace per day for parking the cars? (Assume cars in the Burger Palace lot are moved to the repair shop as soon as room is available.) (c) Suppose Mr. Travis added a second work bay and mechanic so that he can repair two cars are once. On average, how much would Mr. Travis reduce his charges per customer for waiting time?

6. Phone calls arrive at the customer service office of the Dominion Mutual Fund Group according to a Poisson process at the rate of 30 per hour. The calls are currently handled by two service representatives. If a call arrives at the office and both service reps are busy, the call is put in a queue until one of the reps is available. Very little balking or reneging occurs, and the queue has essentially an infinite capacity. The time required to service calls is approximately exponentially distributed, with an average time of 144 seconds. Compute (a) the average number of calls waiting to be answered by a customer rep and (b) the average time a customer spends waiting and being served.

7. Customers arrive at a McDonald's drive-through window according to a Poisson process at the rate of 40 per hour. The time it takes to serve them is exponentially distributed, with an average of 72 seconds. Compute (a) the average number of cars in the drive-through line, including the car being served, and (b) the probability that four or more cars are in the line (including the one being served) at any given time. (c) Suppose McDonald's added a second *parallel* drive-through window (but with one queue serving customers). Assuming this does not affect the arrival pattern or the service times, compute the average number of cars in the system, including those being served. (d) With two windows, compute the probability that there are one or more cars in line that are *not* being served.

8. Cleveland Hopkins Airport has opened two new gate concourses that come together in the shape of a V. The airport authority is considering two proposals for security checks. The first option is to have a separate metal detector line for each concourse. The second option is to have one security area (and essentially one waiting line) at the point of the "V" with two metal detectors that serve both concourses. Passengers wishing to enter each concourse arrive according to a Poisson process at an average rate of 240 per hour (480 passengers per hour total). The time it takes to clear a person through the security area is exponentially distributed, with an average time of 12 seconds. (a) For the first option, compute (i) the average number of customers in the two security lines combined, and (ii) the average time it takes a passenger to get through the security area (waiting in line and passing through the detectors). (b) For the second option, compute (i) the average number of customers in the one security line and (ii) the average time it takes a passenger to get through the security area (waiting in line and passing through the detectors).

9. The village of Northlake provides ambulance service to its residents. Calls arrive at the dispatching office according to a Poisson process at an average rate of two per hour. The village has one ambulance on duty. The time it takes the ambulance to complete its services (the time required to drive to a house and take a person to the hospital) is exponentially distributed, with an average time of 12 minutes. (Once the patient is delivered to the hospital, the ambulance can respond to a new call without being at the dispatch site.) (a) On average, how many customers are waiting for the ambulance to be dispatched to their houses? (b) On average, how long does it take from the time a person calls the ambulance dispatcher until he or she is delivered to the hospital? (c) Compute the probability that at least one customer is waiting for the ambulance to be dispatched. (d) Northlake is adjacent to the village of Eastfork. Eastfork is identical to Northlake in the sense that it provides ambulance service using one ambulance, calls arrive according to a Poisson process at the rate of two per hour, and the average service times have the same distribution as those of Northlake. Northlake and Eastfork are considering a cooperative arrangement whereby all calls from both villages will come to one central dispatch site with two ambulances. Because the site will be on the border between the two villages, the average service time will increase to 13.8 minutes, but the service times will still be exponentially distributed. Compute the average time it takes from the moment a person calls the dispatch office until the person arrives at the hospital.

10. The Nuts-and-Bolts Auto Repair Shop must decide how many work bays and mechanics to hire. Customers arrive during a 12-hour day according to a Poisson process at an average rate of 24 per day. The time it takes to repair an automobile is exponentially distributed, with an average time of two hours. Nuts-and-Bolts charges customers \$50 per hour for each hour of actual repair time. The company claims to provide the best and fastest service in town. To support this claim, Nuts-and-Bolts reduces its charges by \$10 for every hour a customer waits before repair begins (on a pro rate basis, so a \$2.50 discount would be given for a 15-minute wait). It costs the company \$20 per hour for each mechanic and work bay. Assume there is an infinite queue capacity. (a) If Nuts-and-Bolts uses five mechanics and work bays, compute the probability that a customer has to wait in the queue. (b) If Nuts-and-Bolts uses five mechanics and work bays, compute its average daily profit. (c) Compute the average daily profit that would result if Nuts-and-Bolts added a sixth mechanic and work bay.

11. Billy Stamp operates a machine in a job shop. Jobs arrive at his machine (from an earlier work station) according to a Poisson process at the rate of two per day. The time it takes to set up the machine and run a job is exponentially distributed, with an average time of 3.5 hours. Billy normally works an eight-hour day. Compute (a) the average time it takes from the moment a job arrives at Billy's machine until it is completed by Billy, and (b) the average number of jobs that are waiting for Billy. (c) Billy has room to store only three jobs near his machine. Anytime a job is sent to him and three or more jobs are waiting (in the queue), the new job must be sent to a separate waiting area, which costs an extra \$12 for material handling. Compute the average extra material-handling cost per day. (d) The company has purchased Billy a new machine. With this machine, setups are performed by changing tool modules instead of individual tools. This system is expected to reduce the average time to setup and run a job to 3.25 hours, and it should significantly reduce the variation in set up and run times. The estimated standard deviation is two hours. Compute (i) the average number of jobs that will be in the queue (waiting to be processed) and (ii) the average time from when a job arrives at Billy's machine until it is completed by Billy.

12. Customers arrive at the checkout counter of Flash Video Store according to a Poisson process at an average rate of 75 per hour. The checkout process is fairly standardized, so there is little variation in service times. The average service time is 40 seconds, with a standard deviation of 10 seconds. The counter

is staffed by only one employee. Compute (a) the average number of customers waiting in line to be served and (b) the average time a customer spends waiting in line.

13. In problem 5, suppose Mr. Travis (with one work bay) decided to do only oil changes and tune-ups. The service times are now uniformly distributed from 30 minutes to 60 minutes. Compute (a) the average amount of time customers spend in the queue and (b) the average amount of money Mr. Travis would have to reduce each customer's bill for waiting. [Note: the variance of a uniform distribution between two values, a and b, is $\sigma^2 = [(b - a)^2/12]$.]

14.* In problem 6, suppose Dominion is considering going to a new system whereby incoming calls will be sent through a computer with a synthesized voice so that the customer can either handle the transaction entirely by computer using a touch-tone phone or talk to a human customer service rep. It is estimated that 60% of the calls will be handled by the customer on a touch-tone basis and 40% will use the customer service rep. With the new system, all calls will spend 10 seconds going through initial screening with the computer. The calls sent to the customer service rep (there will be only one rep) are expected to take an average of 150 seconds, in addition to the initial 10 seconds of screening, and the *standard deviation* for the service times will be 10 seconds. The calls that are handled entirely by the customer are expected to take only 30 seconds, in addition to the initial 10 seconds for screening, with a standard deviation of 5 seconds. (a) Compute the average number of calls of each type that are in the queues for each system. (Note: After a call is screened, it is sent either to another computer or to the human customer service rep; each of these has a queue for calls if they are busy. Assume that several calls can be handled concurrently at the screening step, so no queue is maintained there.) (Hints: this system is made up of two M/G/1 queues after the screening phase. Also, the screening time should be treated separately from the service times in the M/G/1 queues.) (b) Compute the average time each type of customer spends waiting for and receiving service (including screening time).

15. Which change in an M/M/1 system would be more effective in reducing waiting time in the queue: doubling the speed of the single server or adding a second server with the same speed?

16. (Finite Customer Population) Boilermaker Industries has four large welding units that break down on occasion. The operating time between failures for each unit is exponentially distributed, with an average time of 20 days. Boilermaker has one repair crew that can repair the units. The time required to repair the units is exponentially distributed, with an average of three days. Compute (a) the probability that a welding unit is in the queue (broken but not being repaired), (b) the average number of welding units broken at any given time, and (c) the average time a welding unit is out of service when it does break. (d)* Suppose Boilermaker added a second repair crew; recompute the values in (a)–(c) for this case.

17. (Finite Customer Population) In the noncritical care unit of General Hospital, a nurse is assigned to a group of three patients. For each patient, the time between requests for nursing services (not counting the time the patient spends waiting for service or being treated by the nurse) is exponentially distributed, with an average time of 90 minutes. The time it takes for a nurse to serve a patient is exponentially distributed, with an average time of 18 minutes. Compute (a) the probability that a patient has called for service but does not receive it immediately (is in the queue), (b) the average number of patients waiting in the queue for care, and (c) the average time a patient must wait to receive treatment.

CASE

Interstate Rail and Trucking Company: A Case Study in Applying Queueing Theory

The models and examples in this chapter are based on some strict assumptions: customers do not balk or renege, changing the number or configuration of servers does not change the service time distribution, and the systems are in steady state. In real applications these assumptions may be violated. In fact, in many cases we are especially interested in knowing what happens when the arrival rate changes or when servers are reconfigured. The following case shows how simulation and queueing analysis can be used to improve the design and operation of a service system.

A Customer Service Telephone System

Interstate Rail and Trucking Company (IRTC) is a major commercial transportation company. The IRTC Railroad network serves 38 states, and its trucking business serves the 48 continental U.S. states. IRTC has a broad mix of customers, both in terms of the products it ships and the size of the companies it serves. For example, it ships chemicals, gasoline, steel, cars, furniture, grain, livestock, milk, paper, and waste materials. Some customers own their own rail cars and truck trailers and just pay IRTC to move them between locations, while other customers lease cars and trailers from IRTC for a single trip or for a specified period of time. Large commercial customers may place several shipping orders each day involving dozens of rail cars and trucks and several routes, whereas a farmer may order a single rail car two or three times a year.

In 1989 almost all the interactions between IRTC and its customers were by telephone. Customers called IRTC to place orders, to check the status of existing orders, to change orders, to cancel orders, and so forth. All these transactions were handled by customer service reps using computer terminals. For many years IRTC divided its customers into groups and assigned a work cell of three to five people to act as the customer service reps for that group. The customer groups were constructed in two ways: some by industry and some by geographic location. There was a separate phone number for each work cell so that customers could call their assigned cell directly.

By 1989 the customer service department had grown to the point where, during the day shift, there were 110 customer service reps divided into 29 work cells, and 5–10 reps were being added each year. Even with all these service reps, customers sometimes had to wait on hold for 5–10 minutes before talking to someone. Robert Morris, the Vice-President of Customer Service, decided to hire Phonecom, a telephone network consulting firm, to determine how to give customers better service and at the same time reduce the number of customer reps needed.

For each work cell Phonecom collected data on the number of calls arriving, the types of transactions, how long each transaction required, and how long each customer had to wait. Figure 9.18 gives the aggregated service time distribution for all the work cells; the average service time per customer was 2.75 minutes, with a standard deviation of approximately 2.05 minutes. With this system, approximately 30% of the customers had to wait at least 5 seconds to speak to a service rep, and the average wait for these customers was 4.5 minutes (so the overall average wait in the queue for all customers was 1.35 minutes because 70% of them had no wait). Phonecom constructed a computer simulation model of the existing operation, and compared the waiting times and distribution predicted by the model to those that ac-

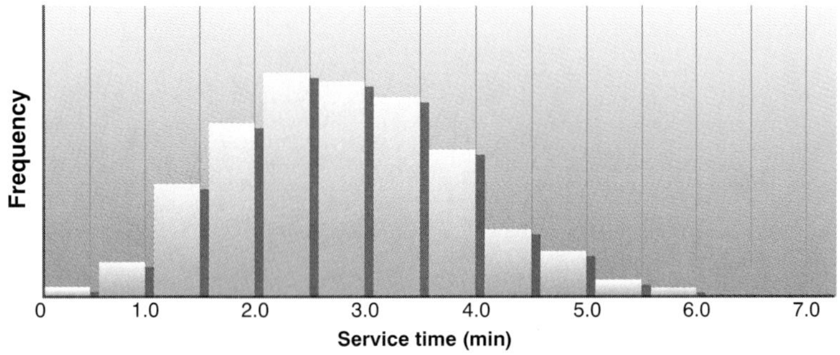

FIGURE 9.18 Original service time distribution for IRTC.

tually occurred. The model results seemed to represent the current system accurately, so Phonecom decided to use the model as its basis for evaluating modifications to the system.

One observation made by Phonecom was that customers were often on hold for one work cell while service reps in other cells were idle. This was the result of having 29 separate queueing systems for the 110 service reps rather than a single system with one queue. Another observation was that many customers hung up after being put on hold. The data on number of calls received and average waiting time were thus not totally accurate.

First Revision to the System

After extensive study, Phonecom recommended that IRTC change its system as follows: (1) All customer reps would be part of the same pool, with only one queue; there would be no individual cells. An incoming call would be forwarded to any available service rep; if all reps were busy, the call would be put in a queue (and the caller informed of this), and then the call would be forwarded to the next available rep. (2) An electronic sign would be hung on the wall where all reps could see it, listing the current number of customers in the queue and the time the next one in line had waited. Phonecom believed that the first change, pooling the reps and using a single queue, would dramatically reduce customer waiting times. The simulation showed that with 110 reps in the pool, fewer than 5% of the customers would have to wait more than 5 seconds, and the average wait for these customers would be approximately 30 seconds. In fact, Phonecom suggested reducing the number of service reps to 105. With this number, approximately 10% of the customers would have to wait at least five seconds and the average wait for these customers would be one minute, still better than the original system. The second change, putting the electronic sign on the wall, was believed to provide feedback to service reps. When a queue of customers was building, the service reps would try to speed up their service and keep their discussions to a minimum; if there were no queue, they could talk with the customers longer and try to project greater concern for them.

IRTC implemented these changes but kept all 110 reps. After four months, IRTC reviewed the performance of the system. The most significant outcomes IRTC could determine were these: (1) The number of customer complaints rose by over 500%; most complaints involved perceived errors in handling orders, and the others were general dissatisfaction with the customer reps with whom customers dealt. (2) The morale of the customer service reps was very low, and there were many complaints about a loss of personal satisfaction in dealing with customers and a recognition that they no longer felt competent in doing their jobs. (3) Waiting time performance was not as good as had been predicted. Almost 25% of the customers were still experiencing a wait, and their average wait was almost four minutes. This was better than before but not sufficiently improved to justify the other problems that were occurring.

Phonecom sent its consultants back to IRTC to collect the same data used in their original study. Phonecom identified some peculiar information. First, the service time distribution now looked like that in Figure 9.19. The average service time had increased to 3.25 minutes, and the distribution had become strongly skewed to the right (the standard deviation was over three minutes). Second, the rate of customer calls had increased by 3% even though the number of orders did not increase at all. These two factors alone explained why the number of customers waiting and the average waiting time were greater than predicted. In fact, because the average service time had increased, the average total time in the system was almost the same as it was before the system was changed.

The Phonecom consultants could not explain why this had happened, so they interviewed some of the service reps and customers. They also went back and studied the operations of the service reps more closely. This investigation uncovered the following facts:

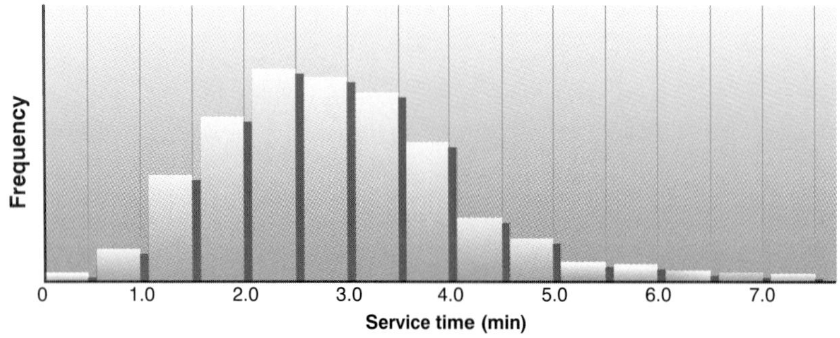

FIGURE 9.19 Service time distribution for IRTC after the first change in the system.

1. Historically, customers always talked to the same three or four service reps. These reps got to know the customers' order requirements and requests so well that they were able to fill in much of the order information without asking the customer. Many customers also had special requests about the handling of their orders (e.g., Never pick up the rail car from our loading docks until after 9 A.M." or "We prefer a 'double-door' car when it is available"), which the service reps knew from experience and put on all orders unless told otherwise. When the system was changed, customers always talked to a different service rep, so the reps could not learn the specific needs of each customer. The result was that service reps had to ask more questions each time, and they made many mistakes because the customers assumed that special services they had always received without asking, were no longer marked on the order (because the customer service rep did not know to ask). As a result, customer transactions took longer and contained more errors, and customers did not like the impersonal nature of the process.
2. Some customers refused to talk with different service reps each time, so when they called, no matter who answered, they demanded to speak with Buddy or Laura. The rep who answered the phone then had to interrupt Buddy or Laura, who were talking to other customers, and tell them that a customer wanted to talk to them. When Buddy or Laura finished their call, they had to walk to the other service rep's phone and handle the transaction there, tying up that the service rep's desk and phone so that the service rep could not serve other customers. These calls are the ones at the far right of Figure 9.19.
3. Some customers called again and again until they got someone they knew; this was the cause of the 3% increase in customer calls.
4. The service reps lost their high morale because they felt that they were not performing their jobs well. They no longer knew the customers well, so they made more mistakes, and customers were often angry with them. They also missed the personal touch gained by knowing their customers.
5. The customer service reps had to use eight different computer screens, depending on the customer's request (e.g., in placing an order versus tracking an order). In the original system, the service reps knew their customers so well that as soon as they learned who was calling, they brought up the screen most likely to be used, which saved service time.

Second Revision to the System

After studying this information, Phonecom's researchers recommended revising the system again. They determined that there was no way to give the personalized service customers desired and get quality service from the reps without having work cells that served a limited number of customers. However, they did not want to return to the original system, which was too costly. Instead, they decided to assign customers to work cells in a better way. Some customers had very similar request patterns, such as calling to place an order or calling frequently to track orders. In addition, large companies behaved differently than small companies. (Small companies had more fixed patterns, had more special features they wanted in their orders, and were more insistent on talking to the same three or four reps each time; large companies needed less of a "personal touch"). Therefore, Phonecom designed 25 cells with three to six customer service reps in each, and the customers assigned to each cell had very similar service request patterns. The service reps could become proficient at handling these requests, and computer screens could be designed to exploit the characteristics of the customers in that cell. For example, if the customers almost always wanted to place an order involving both rail and truck shipment, then the computer would always go first to a screen designed to handle this type of order. The result was that both average service time and variance in service times decreased. Customers who had very different requests each time were assigned to larger (six-server) general-purpose work cells so that the benefits of pooling servers could be obtained. Phonecom estimated the effects of these changes on service times, and then modified and reran their simulation model. The model predicted that 10% of the customers would have a wait of 5 seconds or more, and the average wait for these customers would be 0.50 minute.

IRTC implemented these changes using all 110 reps again, and the predicted results occurred. More important, customer complaints dropped below their original level and service rep morale rebounded. In fact, the predicted shorter waits occurred in spite of the fact that order volume increased by 4%. IRTC, however, was expecting more growth in customer orders and did not want to hire more service reps. The only way to handle the increased business without a loss of service was to reduce the number of service calls per order executed and/or to reduce the service times required to handle customer requests.

Phonecom was once again called in to study the system. After considerable study it made two recommendations, one addressing each issue.

1. At this time, fax machines were becoming a viable form of telecommunication. Phonecom identified those customer transactions, primarily order placement, that took a long time to handle by phone but could be transferred to fax transmission. Phonecom set up a prototype system for 10 customers whereby customers would fill out order forms and send them

by fax to IRTC. A customer service rep could then enter the order in the computer in half the time it would take over the phone. Customers liked the idea of using faxes because they could send the order whenever they wanted. They could also fax it to IRTC in a fraction of the time of a phone call.

2. The second change was to allow customers direct access to IRTC's computer order system. IRTC provided its largest customers with computer access to its order placement and tracking system. Customers could place or track orders using electronic data interchange (EDI) without talking to a service rep. This reduced the number of calls per order substantially.

The net effect of these changes was that even though the volume of orders increased by 10% during the next 2 years, the number of service reps was reduced to 100 and average customer waiting decreased.

A major conclusion we can draw from this case is that behavioral aspects should be considered carefully when designing queueing systems. When one aspect of a queueing system is changed, we should not automatically assume that everything else will stay the same. Some queueing analysts focus too much on issues such as the number of queues and the appropriate queue discipline. Although these are important, one of the best ways to improve the efficiency of a queueing system is to focus on improving the service mechanism. Better support equipment, a more homogeneous mix of customers, or a more pleasant work environment can often improve the service rate in a cost-effective manner. Finally, perceptions of customers are important. By being sensitive to customer needs, we can often obtain greater system efficiency; unhappy customers can undermine any queueing system.

QUESTIONS

1. If some customers always want to use the same three or four sales reps and other customers do not care about whom they talk to, how would you design the cells and route incoming calls to take advantage of these customer differences?
2. The use of fax machines to receive orders creates an additional queueing system. How can the customer rep and fax queueing systems be integrated for maximum efficiency of workers?

SELECTED READINGS

BEUTLER, FREDERICK, and BENJAMIN MELAMED. "Decomposition and Customer Streams of Feedback Networks of Queues in Equilibrium," *Operations Research*, Vol. 26, 1978, pp. 1059–1072.

BUZACOTT, JOHN A., and J. GEORGE SHANTHIKUMAR. *Stochastic Models of Manufacturing Systems*, Prentice-Hall, Englewood Cliffs, NJ, 1993.

DAVIS, MARK. "How Long Should a Customer Wait for Service?" *Decision Sciences*, Vol. 22, 1991, pp. 421–434.

GREENWOOD, ALLEN. "Plots of Conditional Wait-Time Intervals Provide Better Information to Queueing System Arrivals," *Decision Sciences*, Vol. 22, 1991, pp. 473–483.

GROSS, DONALD, and CARL HARRIS. *Fundamentals of Queueing Theory* (2nd ed.), Wiley, New York, 1985.

HALL, RANDOLPH. *Queueing Methods*, Prentice-Hall, Englewood Cliffs, NJ, 1991.

HILLIER, FREDERICK S., and OLIVER S. YU. *Queueing Tables and Graphs*, North Holland, New York, 1981.

JACKSON, J. R. "Networks of Waiting Lines," *Operations Research*, Vol. 5, 1957, pp. 518–521.

LARSEN, RICHARD C. "Perspectives on Queues: Social Justice and the Psychology of Queueing," *Operations Research*, Vol. 35, 1987, pp. 895–905

LARSEN, RICHARD C. "There's More to a Line Than Its Wait," *Technology Review*, Vol. 91 July 1988, pp. 60–67.

MAISTER, D. H. "The Psychology of Waiting Lines," in J. A. Czepiel, M. R. Solomon, and C. F. Surprenant, eds., *The Service Encounter, Managing Employee/Customer Interaction in Service Businesses*, Lexington Books, Lexington, MA, 1985, pp. 113–123.

MARTIN, G. E., J. L. GRAHN, L. D. PANKOFF, and L. A. MADEO. "A Mechanism for Reducing Small-Business Customer Waiting-Line Dissatisfaction," *Managerial and Decision Economics*, Vol. 13, 1992, pp. 353–361.

NEWELL, GORDON. *Applications of Queueing Theory*, Chapman and Hall, London, 1982.

ROTHKOPF, M. H., and P. RECH. "Perspectives on Queues: Combining Queues Is Not Always Beneficial," *Operations Research*, Vol. 35, 1987, pp. 906–909.

TUTORIAL 3

SIMULATION ANALYSIS FOR OPERATIONS MANAGEMENT

T3.1 A FLEXIBLE AND WIDELY USED TOOL

T3.2 TYPES OF SIMULATION MODELS
- Continuous versus Discrete Event Models
- Stochastic versus Deterministic Models
- Examples

T3.3 STEPS IN SIMULATION MODELING AND ANALYSIS

T3.4 METHODS FOR SIMULATING TIME
- Fixed-Time Incrementing
- Next-Event Incrementing

T3.5 GENERATING RANDOM PHENOMENA
- Generating Random Observations from a Discrete Probability Distribution
- Generating Random Observations from a Continuous Probability Distribution
- Generating Observations from a Continuous Uniform [*a*,*b*] Distribution
- Generating Observations from an Exponential Distribution
- Generating Observations from a Normal Distribution

T3.6 SAMPLE SIMULATIONS
- A Random Production Line Simulation
- A Queueing Simulation

T3.7 EVALUATING SIMULATION OUTPUT

T3.8 SIMULATION AND COMPUTER SOFTWARE

T3.1 A FLEXIBLE AND WIDELY USED TOOL

Simulation analysis was introduced in Chapters 8 and 9 as a way to study the design of production and queueing systems. But simulation has also been used in many other facets of operations, such as capacity planning, machine and personnel scheduling, project scheduling, inventory control, lot sizing, job scheduling and routing, facility location, and facility layout. For example, Hewlett-Packard used simulation to design its North American distribution center, which improved efficiency 60–80%, and Pacific Northwest Laboratory used simulation to evaluate the impact of work-flow automation.[1]

A **simulation model** is a set of mathematical functions, probability distributions, and decision rules that mimic the way a system behaves under specified conditions. This makes it a *descriptive* model and differentiates it from the optimization models presented in Tutorial 1, which compute the best values for variables so as to optimize some measure of system performance. Simulation models provide a convenient way to evaluate alternative system designs and operating procedures when optimization models are not practical. Testing alternatives on a real production system is usually too expensive, time-consuming, and possibly dangerous. In some cases, it may even be impossible because we may be interested in designing a system that does not yet exist. Simulation analysis allows us to do this testing and evaluation in a fast, inexpensive, and safe manner.

In operations management we often are interested in how a production system (like a production line, warehouse, or grocery store) would behave over time using various designs or operating policies, so the models discussed here are inherently dynamic. Systems are made up of interrelated components called **entities**. We describe the condition or **state of the system** using what are called **system attributes** (or **state variables**). For example, the state of a queueing system may be described by the number of customers in the system, or the state of an inventory system may be described by the number of items in inventory and the number on order. We define an **event** as a measurable change in the system; that is, the value of one or more of the attributes of the system has changed (see Figure T3.1). In a queueing system an event may be the arrival of a customer or the completion of service for a customer.

[1]See M. E. Johnson and T. Lofgren, "Model Decomposition Speeds Distribution Center Design," *Interfaces*, Vol. 24, September–October 1994, pp. 95–106, and L. O. Levine and S. S. Aurand, "Evaluating Automated Work-Flow Systems for Administrative Processes," *Interfaces*, ibid., pp. 141–151.

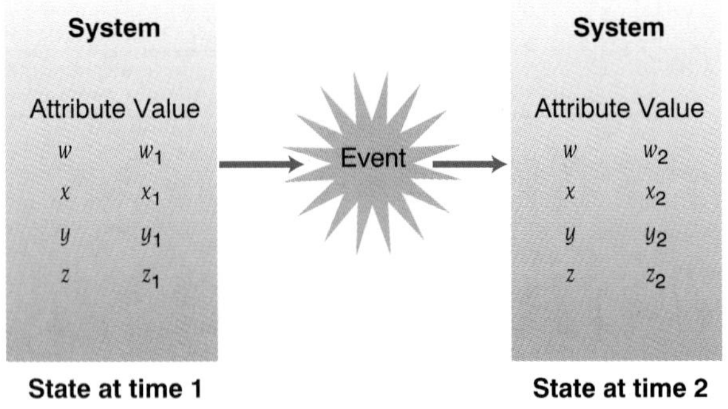

FIGURE T3.1 Simulation event.

T3.2 TYPES OF SIMULATION MODELS

Simulation models use different features and conventions, depending on the type of system they are intended to represent and the types of questions being studied.

CONTINUOUS VERSUS DISCRETE EVENT MODELS

If the state of the system changes over time in a relatively continuous fashion, the simulation model is said to be a **continuous-event model**. For example, a simulation of a missile in flight would normally be a continuous-event simulation. The attributes describing the state of the missile would be its location in space, velocity, acceleration, and rotation. These attributes change in value continuously over time; that is, speed does not jump from 1000 mph to 2000 mph; it must pass through every speed between 1000 and 2000 mph to get to 2000 mph.

If the system's state is assumed to change in a discontinuous fashion at identifiably discrete points in time, the simulation model is called a **discrete-event model.** For example, a simulation of a machine shop would be a discrete simulation. Whenever a new job entered the system or one was completed and left the system, the attribute "number of jobs in the system" or "number of jobs at machine *j*" would change by a discrete amount. Another way of thinking about discrete simulations is to imagine that the system stays in the same state for a measurable period of time and then jumps or makes a transition to a new state.

STOCHASTIC VERSUS DETERMINISTIC MODELS

In many production systems, one or more system entities are inherently random—for example, the time an order will be received, the time a customer will arrive, or the time it will take to perform a task. In these cases, we are often interested in the effects of uncertainty on system performance. We are especially interested in how the sys-

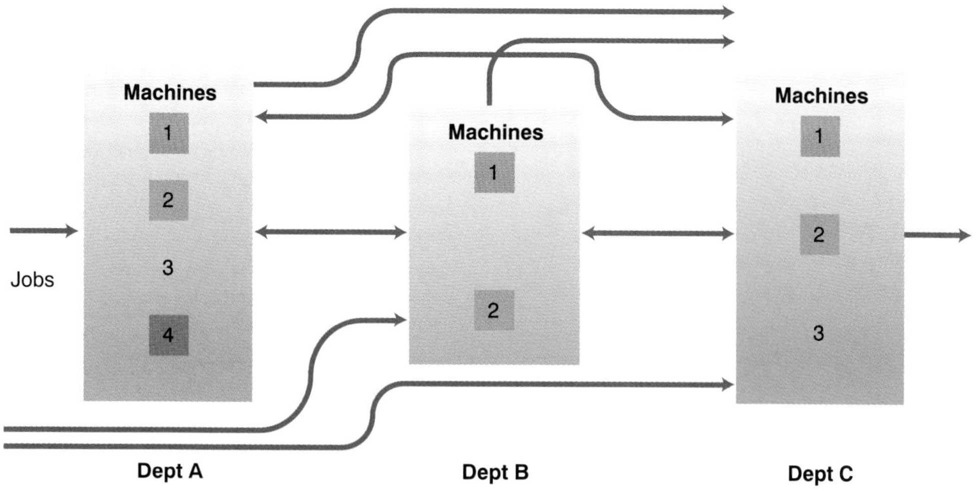

FIGURE T3.2 Job shop.

tem can be designed or the operating rules constructed to reduce this randomness or to make the system work better in spite of it. System models that explicitly include random phenomena are called **stochastic models**.[2] System models in which no randomness is assumed are called **deterministic models**. Although nearly every real system has some randomness, deterministic models are generally used when either the amount of randomness or its perceived impact is small. For example, many models used in economics, engineering, and the physical sciences are deterministic. The simulation models most used in operations management are discrete-event, stochastic models.

EXAMPLES

Simulation has been used in many ways. The following are just a few examples of the types of questions we can answer using simulation. Each of these applications involves one or more of the following characteristics: (1) large operations, (2) complex operating or decision rules, or (3) some inherent randomness in the environment or system.

Job-Shop Analysis

Figure T3.2 depicts the configuration of a manufacturing job shop containing three departments (A, B, and C), with several machines in each department. The system produces many different products, each of which is processed in one or more of the departments, and the routing of the jobs through the departments can be different. Customer orders are received on an ongoing basis. The orders specify an order quantity and a due date for delivery. This system can harbor many sources of uncertainty: the time when orders are received, the actual processing time of each order in each department (in contrast to the estimated processing time), and the actual lead time for raw material or component suppliers.

Simulation models can be used to answer the following questions:

1. How many machines of each type should be in each department? Should capacity be expanded or contracted? In which departments?
2. Should the facility be redesigned to consist of work cells based on group technology? (See Chapters 7 and 8 for discussions of work cells and group technology.)
3. How should a job be routed and sequenced through the work centers? What decision rules should be used to assign jobs to machines based on expected setup times, run times, and due dates (called *machine loading*)?
4. Where are the bottlenecks in the system? Where should overtime work be used?
5. At a given point in time, what are the best estimates for delivery dates for each job awaiting processing?

Service Facility Design, Layout, and Staffing

Simulation has been used to evaluate capacity, design, layout, and staffing alternatives for many service facilities, such as restaurants, financial institutions, hospitals, and

[2]A stochastic simulation in which the same random situation is repeated over and over, with no dependence among trials, is called a *Monte Carlo* simulation, named after the gambling haven. This is essentially a static model, and time is not a relevant parameter.

retail facilities. Typical issues that have been evaluated using simulation include the following:

1. How many personnel with different skills should be scheduled each day and shift?
2. How many machines, tables, and servers should there be, and how should they be spatially configured for maximum efficiency?

Inventory Analysis

The acquisition and management of materials, especially for organizations that use thousands of different items,

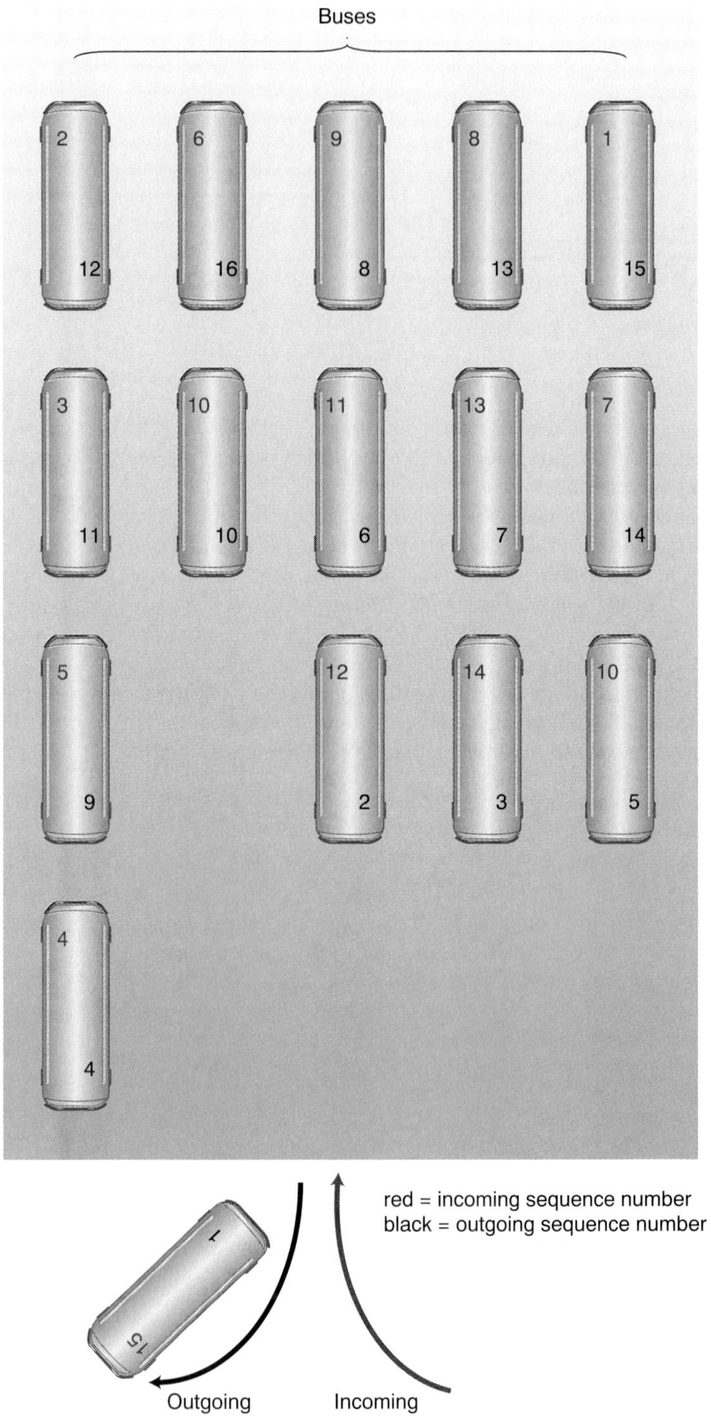

FIGURE T3.3 Bus garage parking problem.

can present many difficult problems that can be studied using simulation. Some commonly studied inventory questions are the following:

1. How much of a product should be ordered and when?
2. What is the best level of safety stock to hold for critical materials?
3. In multilocation systems, where should inventories be maintained and how much should be kept at each location (e.g., spare parts for military aircraft)?
4. How much in-process (buffer) inventory is needed to keep a process operating efficiently?

Transportation and Logistics
Simulation analysis has been used to answer the following questions for complex transportation systems:

1. What factors affect train delays? Where should single-line tracks be expanded to double tracks?
2. How can buses that return randomly to a garage at night be parked so that they can leave the garage in the morning in a set sequence and each driver can always use the same bus? (See Figure T3.3)
3. How many railcars need to be leased to make the desired shipments?
4. How should deliveries be combined in trucks and routed to customers?

T3.3 STEPS IN SIMULATION MODELING AND ANALYSIS

Simulation modeling and analysis can be divided into five steps.

1. ***Get to Know the System Being Modeled.*** For any kind of modeling, it is important to know as much about the system as possible. But it is especially important with simulation because simulation models tend to be relatively complex. Some questions the modeler should be able to answer are the following:
   (a) What is the purpose of the simulation? What questions are going to be studied? (For example, will the simulation be used to evaluate capacity decisions or scheduling?) The same system may be modeled in different ways, depending on the types of questions and the variety of questions to be addressed.
   (b) What entities and relationships are important? Some systems have hundreds or thousands of separate entities. But in a simulation model we want to capture the influence of only the most important ones without missing anything significant. For example, in a job shop does each machine or worker have to be treated as a separate entity?
   It is especially helpful at this stage to construct some type of interaction diagram, such as the one in Figure T3.4 of an inventory system, which shows which entities are important and how they interact. No fixed format needs to be used; simply constructing a visual representation can help to identify the important entities and relationships of a system.
   (c) What attributes should be used to describe the state of the system? How will we know when the state of the system has changed (what events can occur)?
   (d) Are any aspects of the environment or system random? Should this randomness be included in the model? It is important not to overlook subtle or rare events. For example, in a production system mechanical breakdowns may occur infrequently, but precisely these rare events

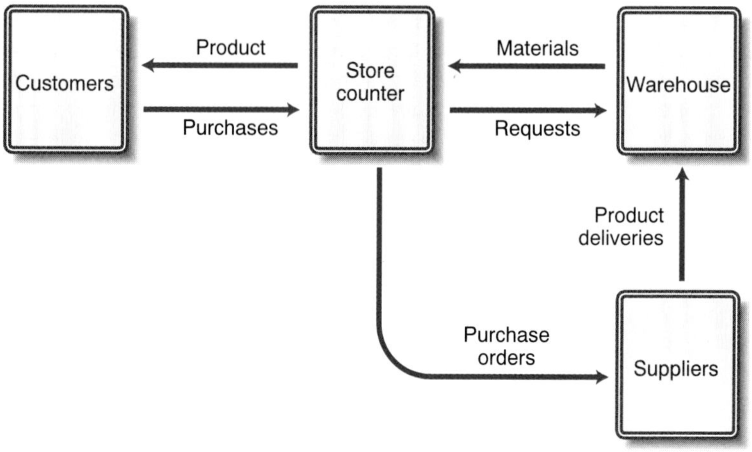

FIGURE T3.4 Interaction diagram.

may be causing or amplifying the problems under study, such as excessive in-process inventory or poor machine utilization.

(e) Which aspects of the system are controllable and can be treated as design variables, and which aspects are fixed? Sometimes existing system configurations and procedures can deceive the average observer. If an existing structure or procedure could be changed, the analysis should consider this possibility.

(f) What measures of system performance will be used to evaluate alternatives (e.g., average profit, average cost, variation of waiting times in a queue, average job lateness, fraction of time a machine is operable)?

2. ***Construct a Model of the System.*** Initially, the system should be divided into components that can be modeled as separate pieces. For example, a simulation model of a sit-down restaurant might be divided into (a) a customer arrival module that specifies when parties of people arrive and the size of the parties; (b) a queue discipline and table service module that determines when a customer is seated, what services waiters/waitresses provide, and how long they take; and possibly (c) a kitchen operations module that keeps track of cooking equipment loading, order scheduling, and staffing.

If the module contains random phenomena, we must specify the probability distributions, using actual data or scientific principles and experimentation whenever possible. For example, if we are simulating an inventory system and a random variable is the number of items demanded by customers each day, we could collect actual data. The probability distribution for the daily demand could then be either a reproduction of the data or a common theoretical distribution, such as a binomial or Poisson distribution, that approximates the data. In the latter case, a chi-square goodness-of-fit test would be used to determine whether the theoretical distribution was a good approximation for the actual data.

Once all components have been modeled, they can be tied together based on the identified relationships. Individual modules and the interfaces connecting them should contain the necessary operating or decision rules. For example, when simulating a restaurant, an operating rule is needed to determine when a waiting customer is seated at a table. A decision rule would also be necessary to determine whether a waiting customer leaves the restaurant before being seated (reneges). These rules will control when an event has occurred: when and how the system has changed.

For most simulations, the final step of model construction is to convert the model into a computer program. This can be done using general-purpose languages such as FORTRAN, BASIC, or C, or using structured simulation languages such as SLAM, Q-GERT or GPSS. These are discussed later.

3. ***Test the Model.*** The model is usually tested in two phases. First, the individual modules are tested for their accuracy. Then the entire system is tested to see whether it accurately reflects reality. If the simulation model is intended to replicate an existing system, this is relatively easy to do. The simulation model is run with the parameters of the model set to those of the existing system. The simulated behavior of the system should be similar to that of the actual system. If it is not, the reasons must be found and any errors corrected.

4. ***Plan the Experimental Design.*** Simulation analysis is an experimental rather than an optimization method whereby one alternative is evaluated at a time. Each configuration of the simulation model (i.e., each set of values for the design or operating variables) is called an **experiment** or **alternative**. A **run** is one sampling of the experiment. This will normally consist of running a computer simulation of the model for some period of simulated time. Because stochastic simulation models tend to be complex, runs of the model for a given alternative are both time-consuming and expensive. By planning runs in advance, we can be more efficient in two ways: (a) fewer alternatives will need to be simulated and evaluated and (b) fewer runs (or less total simulated time) will be needed to evaluate the alternatives fairly.

Rather than evaluating every alternative explicitly, we can categorize groups of alternatives. We then compare representative alternatives from each category. For those categories of alternatives that appear superior, we then evaluate individual alternatives within each category in more depth. When comparing alternatives, an important question is, how much simulated time is necessary to obtain an accurate measurement of the system's behavior, that is, how many runs are necessary and how long should a run be? For example, if we want to evaluate different rules for scheduling jobs in a job shop, should we simulate the equivalent of 100 work days? 1000 work days? We certainly do not want to simulate extra time that provides little additional information, but we need to differentiate the performances of different alternatives. A strategy that addresses both of these goals is to use shorter or fewer runs for some initial alternatives as a way of screening out clearly inferior alternatives, and then use longer or more runs on the good alternatives that require closer comparison.

5. ***Execute Model Runs and Analyze the Output.*** After running the simulation for various alternative designs or operating rules, we can compare the alternatives to determine which is best. For example, suppose we are comparing two rules for assigning production jobs to machines, and the performance criterion is the average percentage of jobs that are delivered after the due date. When orders are received, their due dates and the actual processing times on machines may be random (but from known distributions). Suppose we simulated 100 work days of operations and found that with rule A, 3.5% of the jobs were completed late and with rule B, 3.2% were completed late. Does this mean that rule B is better than rule A with respect to this criterion? The answer is, "not necessarily." The difference may be due to random sampling error, in the sense that the random phenomena generated for these 100 simulated days just happened to favor rule B; over the longer run, rule A might actually be better. To determine whether or not this 0.3% difference in performance is large enough to allow us to conclude that B is better than A, we can use the same statistical methods used to compare the sample means of two populations. Similarly, we can use statistical methods to determine the number of runs needed to achieve a desired level of significance in the difference.

T3.4 METHODS FOR SIMULATING TIME

A dynamic simulation model mimics how a real system would behave over time. Therefore, the model must contain a mechanism for keeping track of **simulated time (clock time)**. There are two common conventions for handling simulated time: fixed-time incrementing and next-event incrementing.

FIXED-TIME INCREMENTING

With **fixed-time incrementing** we begin with an initial time and state of the system, and then we advance the simulated clock by a fixed amount of time (e.g., 10 minutes or one day). We then update the system by determining how the system changed during the elapsed time and what the current state of the system is, and we compute any performance statistics. The time increment is normally a natural unit of time, such as a second, an hour, or a day. It should be long enough for the simulation to be computationally efficient but small enough so that changes in the system are recorded and simulated actions are allowed to occur frequently enough to represent reality. Fixed-time incrementing is especially applicable for continuous-event simulations in which the system state is changing continuously over time. It is also useful for discrete-event simulations when there are natural decision points or events that occur on a regular basis. For example, if we were simulating an inventory system, we may not be interested in whether items were bought or used at 10:02 A.M., then at 10:07 A.M., and so on. Instead we would be interested in how many items were purchased each day, what the inventory level was at the end of each day, and whether an order should be placed that day to replenish the inventory. In this case, fixed-time incrementing with a time increment of one day is appropriate.

NEXT-EVENT INCREMENTING

Some systems remain in the same state for extended periods of time, and then they change states in a discrete fashion at identifiable but random points in time. In this case, fixed-time incrementing may be inappropriate for two reasons: (1) it can be inefficient to keep checking the system at short intervals when the system may stay in the same state for a long period; (2) if the system's state changes rapidly within a short time, the simulation could miss these changes if they occurred between the moments when the system is checked. Both problems are eliminated by **next-event incrementing**, in which the time of the next event is determined and the clock advanced to that point in time. The simulation then adjusts the state of the system, computes any performance statistics, determines when the next event will occur, and repeats the process. This way, no event is missed and the simulation does not waste time checking the system during periods when the system's state is not changing. For example, in queueing the state of the system is usually described by the number of customers in the system. The system remains in the same state until a customer arrives or departs. In a simulation model the timing of these events can be determined and the clock advanced to the time of the next event, instead of checking the system every five seconds (for example) to see whether anything has happened.

T3.5 GENERATING RANDOM PHENOMENA

An important aspect of many production simulations is the ability to generate random phenomena that approximate the randomness of real systems and then to study the effects of these phenomena on the system. This section describes how to generate random values that appear to come from specified probability distributions. The

TABLE T3.1 RANDOM NUMBERS

Obs.	1	2	3	4	5	6	7	8	9	10
1	8008	7709	0096	4985	4421	6460	5004	7315	5580	5006
2	2273	4308	9831	9094	7706	4791	5816	5029	3280	5501
3	2212	3178	3382	6413	5553	1145	9283	7958	1499	5198
4	5624	9901	2988	9278	7811	7266	3441	0635	9681	1633
5	4937	8555	7117	3074	5443	9214	2268	4954	1807	3040
6	9508	3879	2002	9854	0775	7853	3149	9405	3798	3891
7	0280	2649	8117	2790	8494	5718	5213	6886	9454	7771
8	4254	6151	5726	8441	5435	7481	6567	9894	2433	4542
9	6019	0032	0223	4803	1460	6339	1375	2197	6400	2040
10	5553	8960	4323	1110	9062	3117	2235	1525	1456	9834
11	1648	4161	5781	1874	2831	9368	0302	2066	4597	6377
12	8163	4713	9221	3102	5080	2633	8562	7409	3489	7164
13	7528	8518	6767	4978	2073	4316	9537	2816	8244	8275
14	4531	2108	1374	4851	0107	4209	9302	9226	4232	5162
15	9998	8153	8056	6939	5350	0233	8512	4964	2519	2114
16	2305	3406	3347	9449	9129	0359	5858	9614	4768	3056
17	7180	0283	4676	8698	1920	2727	1628	8501	6816	6134
18	5646	2764	1845	5046	9125	5542	3646	4912	0646	1348
19	2640	0445	4717	1668	9895	7773	9334	5082	6002	0282
20	3457	5316	2940	1407	1903	8306	4691	1607	6801	7177

process is based on the ability to generate what are called *pseudorandom numbers*.

Random numbers are numbers generated in sequence from a continuous uniform distribution between 0 and 1, with successive values probabilistically independent of each other. (So the values should be evenly distributed between 0 and 1, and the value of one random number does not affect the probability distribution of subsequent random numbers).[3] For example, the numbers 0.4867, 0.1984, 0.3440, 0.9024, 0.2987, 0.7019, and 0.0063 appear to be random numbers from a [0,1] uniform distribution. With a real random number generator we could not predict what the next random number will be, nor could we regenerate the same set of random numbers on demand. In simulation models we would like a mechanism that produces a sequence of numbers that *appear* to be random numbers, but we would like to be able to reproduce the same stream of numbers easily. (This allows us to compare alternatives using exactly the same random phenomena for each alternative). This is normally done using an iterative mathematical formula. The numbers obtained from these methods are called **pseudorandom numbers** because future values are not really random (they can be predicted perfectly using the formula) and the same stream of random numbers can be generated by simply using the same formula and starting value.

We will not discuss the mathematical methods for generating pseudorandom numbers here because in practice we normally do not create our own pseudorandom number generator.[4] (For simplicity, in the remainder of the chapter we will use the term *random number* to mean pseudorandom number.) In practice, random numbers are obtained in one of two ways. (1) For small simulations, random number tables such as Table T3.1 can be used. These tables are usually in the form of four- or five-digit integers. To obtain random numbers between 0 and 1, we simply put a decimal point at the front. (2) Many computer systems have a library function that generates random numbers. The user calls up the function and specifies a "seed" value, and every time the function is called, a new random number is generated.[5]

[3]A continuous uniform [*a*,*b*] distribution means that only values between *a* and *b* can occur, and the probability of the number falling within subintervals of the same length is the same. A square bracket [,] indicates that the interval includes the endpoint; a round bracket (,) indicates that the endpoint is not included.

[4]Methods for generating pseudorandom numbers can be found in any simulation textbook.

[5]The seed value is used to start the mathematical function that creates the pseudorandom numbers. If we want to re-create the same stream of random numbers (to compare two alternatives), we use the same seed value. If we want a different stream of random numbers (for different simulation runs for the same alternative), we use a different seed value.

Once we have random numbers, we can convert them to simulated observations of random phenomena, such as random processing times or customer demands, that appear to be coming from a specified probability distribution. In theory the method for doing this is the same for all random phenomena, but in practice the details are quite different for different probability distributions. We will show how to generate simulated random observations for any discrete probability distribution and for three common continuous distributions.

GENERATING RANDOM OBSERVATIONS FROM A DISCRETE PROBABILITY DISTRIBUTION

For our purposes, a discrete phenomenon (random variable) is one that can take on a finite number of possible values or has a finite number of outcomes.[6] For example, the number of automobiles purchased from a dealer in a week or the possible outcomes of a football game (win, lose, tie) would be a discrete phenomenon. Suppose n possible values can occur and the probability of value (outcome) x_i occurring is p_i. A simple way to generate simulated observations of the phenomenon is to divide the interval [0,1] into n subintervals and to assign to each value x_i a subinterval with a width of p_i. If a random number falls within the limits of some subinterval j, then x_j is the simulated value of the phenomenon, and the probability of this occurring is p_j.

[6]Actually a discrete random variable is one that can take on only a finite or a countably infinite number of possible values (e.g., the integers). In practice we almost always simulate only a finite subset of the possible values.

EXAMPLE 1

Suppose that as part of an inventory system simulation for a store we needed to generate random daily demands for a product that approximates the actual daily demand pattern. Table T3.2 contains 500 days of historical data on the number of units of the product that were demanded each day from the store. If we let

$$X = \text{number of units of the product bought in a day}$$

X is a *discrete* random variable that can take on the values 0, 1, 2, . . . , 8. We can treat the frequency values in Table T3.2 as the probability, p_i, of each value occurring.

We can now divide the interval [0,1] into nine subintervals. For example, we would assign the subinterval [0,0.002) to a demand of 0, the subinterval [0.002, 0.096) to a demand of 1, and so on, as shown in Table T3.3.[7] Using the random numbers in Table T3.1, the first random number is

TABLE T3.2 DAILY DEMANDS FOR 500 DAYS

No. of Units Demanded	No. of Days	Frequency	Cumulative Frequency*
0	1	.002	.002
1	47	.094	.096
2	103	.206	.302
3	168	.336	.638
4	89	.178	.816
5	55	.110	.926
6	29	.058	.984
7	6	.012	.996
8	2	.004	1.000

*The cumulative frequency is the proportion of days with demand less than or equal to this amount; it is the sum of the frequency values for demand levels up to this amount.

[7]The convention for creating subintervals is to have them closed on the left and open on the right [,) because random number generators can generate the random number 0 but not the number 1.

TABLE T3.3 SUBINTERVALS FOR SIMULATING DAILY DEMAND

No. of Units Bought, x_i	Probability, p_i	Subinterval
0	.002	[0, 0.002)
1	.094	[0.002, 0.096)
2	.206	[0.096, 0.302)
3	.336	[0.302, 0.638)
4	.178	[0.638, 0.816)
5	.110	[0.816, 0.926)
6	.058	[0.926, 0.984)
7	.012	[0.984, 0.996)
8	.004	[0.996, 1.000)

$r = 0.8008$, which falls within the subinterval for $X = 4$. Therefore, the simulation model would treat the demand for that day as being four units. The next random number is 0.2273, so the simulated demand would be two units. After enough repetitions of this process, the proportion of days that X takes on a value equal to x_i will be approximately p_i.

This procedure can be generalized for simulating any discrete random phenomena.

Generating Discrete Random Phenomena

1. For each possible value, x_i, compute the cumulative probability, C_i. (C_i is the probability of X taking on a value less than or equal to x_i.)
2. Construct the subintervals $[C_0 = 0, C_1)$, $[C_1, C_2)$, . . . $[C_{n-1}, C_n = 1)$. Subinterval i corresponds to value x_i occurring, and the width of the subinterval is $p_i = C_i - C_{i-1}$.
3. Generate a random number, r. If r falls within the subinterval $[C_{i-1}, C_i)$, then the simulated value of the random variable X is x_i.

GENERATING RANDOM OBSERVATIONS FROM A CONTINUOUS PROBABILITY DISTRIBUTION

If a random variable is continuous, it can take on any real value over some range (possibly from $-\infty$ to $+\infty$). For the random variable there exists a **cumulative distribution function**, $F(x) = \text{Prob}(X \le x)$. A typical cumulative distribu-

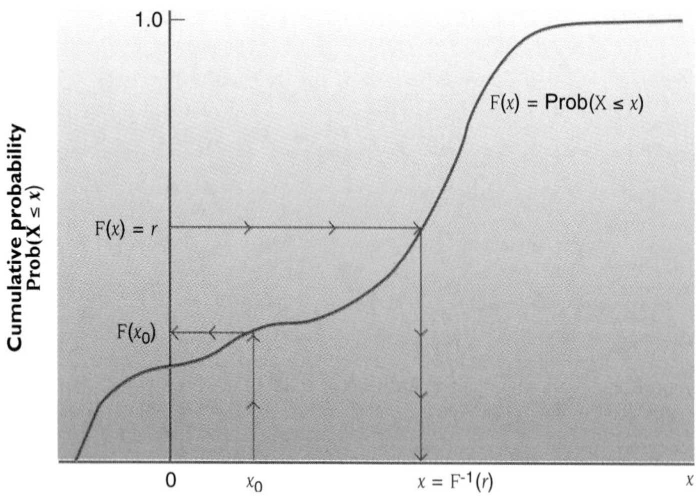

FIGURE T3.5 Generating simulated random phenomena from a cumulative distribution function.

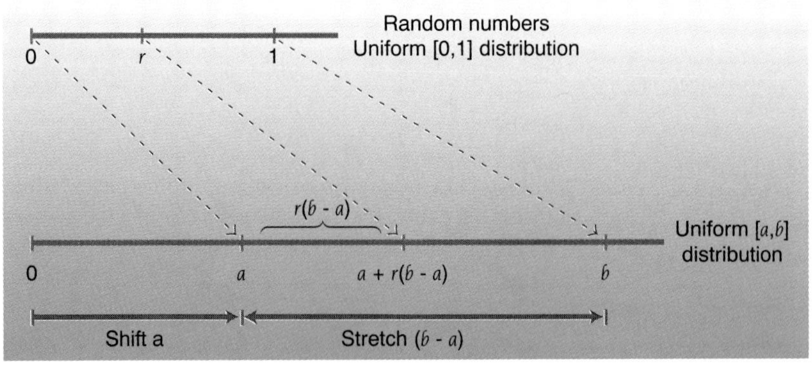

FIGURE T3.6 Simulating random phenomena from a continuous uniform [a,b] distribution.

tion function for a continuous random variable is given in Figure T3.5. Assuming $F(x)$ is available, we can generate random observations from a continuous distribution using the following procedure.

Generating Continuous Random Phenomena

1. Generate a random number, r.
2. Set r equal to $F(x)$ and solve for x; the value of x is the random observation.

This process means that in Figure T3.5 we begin at the value r on the vertical axis and move horizontally until we reach the cumulative distribution function, F. We then move down vertically to the horizontal axis to obtain the value x.[8] If this process were repeated thousands of times, the cumulative frequency distribution for the simulated observations would have a shape approximating that of F.

This procedure will work in theory for any continuous random variable, but for it to work practically, we must be able to write the cumulative distribution function, F, in a closed mathematical form (an equation). This is not possible for all continuous distributions, including some very common ones such as the normal distribution. We now show how to generate random observations from three continuous distributions.

[8]Mathematically, we are using the inverse function of F, F^{-1}, which for any value r on the vertical axis will compute the value x on the horizontal axis such that $F(x) = r$; that is, $x = F^{-1}(r)$.

GENERATING OBSERVATIONS FROM A CONTINUOUS UNIFORM [A,B] DISTRIBUTION

By definition random numbers come from a continuous uniform [0,1] distribution. We can generate random observations from a continuous uniform distribution between any two values, a and b, using the procedure described above. For values within the interval $[a,b]$ the cumulative distribution function for a continuous uniform random variable is

$$F(x) = (x - a)/(b - a) \quad \text{for } a \le x \le b$$

To obtain simulated values of x we generate a random number r, set it equal to $F(x)$, and solve for x:

$$r = (x - a)/(b - a) \rightarrow r(b - a) = x - a$$

$$\rightarrow x = a + r(b - a) \qquad \text{(T3.1)}$$

In other words, we shift the lower bound of the [0,1] uniform distribution from 0 to a and stretch (or compress) the distribution from a length of one unit to $(b - a)$ units, as illustrated in Figure T3.6.

EXAMPLE 2

Suppose the processing time at a work station has a continuous uniform distribution of 2.5 to 6.0 minutes. To simulate a random observation from this distribution, we generate a random number, say $r = 0.2212$, and then compute $x = 2.5 + 0.2212(6.0 - 2.5) = 3.2742$.

GENERATING RANDOM OBSERVATIONS FROM AN EXPONENTIAL DISTRIBUTION

In Chapter 9 we saw that the exponential distribution is very important in queueing theory because the times between customer arrivals in a Poisson process are exponentially distributed. Let X be an exponentially distributed random variable with a mean of $1/\alpha$. If X represents the time between successive arrivals in a Poisson process, then $1/\alpha$ is the average time between arrivals and α is the average customer arrival rate. (Using the notation of Chapter 9, $\alpha = \lambda$.) The cumulative distribution function, which is illustrated in Figure T3.7, is

$$F(x) = \begin{cases} 1 - e^{-\alpha x} & \text{for } x \geq 0 \\ 0 & \text{for } x < 0 \end{cases}$$

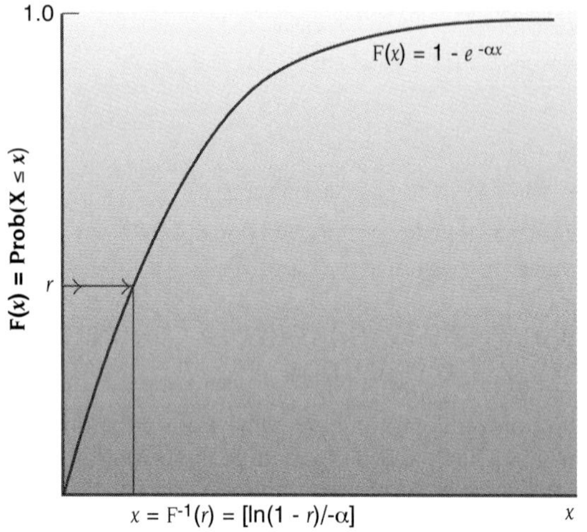

FIGURE T3.7 Cumulative distribution function for an exponential random variable.

To obtain random observations from this distribution, we first generate a random number, r. We then set $r = F(x)$ and solve for x:

$$r = F(x) = 1 - e^{-\alpha x}$$

so

$$e^{-\alpha x} = 1 - r$$

Taking the natural logarithm of both sides and dividing throughout by $-\alpha$ gives

$$x = ln(1 - r)]/-\alpha$$

If r is a random number from a uniform [0,1] distribution, then $1 - r$ is a random number from a uniform [0,1] distribution. We can save a subtraction by replacing $1 - r$ with r to get[9]

$$x = (ln\ r)/-\alpha \tag{T3.2}$$

[9]Although individual random observations will obviously be different for $x = [\ln(1-r)]/-\alpha$ and $x = [\ln r]/-\alpha$, they give equally good random observations for the desired exponential distribution. Equation (T3.2) is more commonly used.

EXAMPLE 3

Suppose we want to simulate the arrival of customers at a hairstyling shop, and suppose they arrive according to a Poisson process at an average rate of five per hour. If X = the time between successive arrivals, then by the definition of a Poisson process, X is exponentially distributed, with a mean of 1/5 hour = $1/\alpha$. So α = five customers per hour. Using equation (T3.2), random times between arrivals can be derived from the expression

$$x = (\ln r)/-5$$

Table T3.4 lists the first four random numbers from Table T3.1, the corresponding simulated interarrival times, and the times of the first four customer arrivals.

TABLE T3.4 SIMULATED ARRIVAL TIMES FOR A POISSON PROCESS

Random Number r	Interarrival Time x	Arrival Time
.8008	ln(.8008)/–5 = 0.044 hr	0.044
.2273	ln(.2273)/–5 = 0.296 hr	0.340
.2212	ln(.2212)/–5 = 0.302 hr	0.642
.5624	ln(.5624)/–5 = 0.115 hr	0.757

TABLE T3.5 RANDOM NORMAL DEVIATES

Obs.	1	2	3	4	5	6	7	8	9	10
1	0.0874	−3.0480	−0.7764	−0.1357	−1.0801	−1.5614	0.1553	−0.7156	−1.0409	−1.4195
2	−0.7187	−0.9291	0.8157	0.1094	−1.9329	1.0708	1.3974	−0.1026	1.3455	0.1317
3	0.7315	−0.2915	0.9713	−1.7219	−0.6157	−0.2420	1.7858	0.4988	1.4152	−1.0671
4	−0.2500	−0.1172	−0.5141	−0.4291	0.0568	−0.9801	0.5889	−0.0126	0.9150	−1.6123
5	1.0073	−2.7364	−1.3067	0.3768	0.2690	0.8612	0.9924	−0.1679	0.9951	1.9521
6	−1.6416	0.4008	1.4653	0.7112	−0.8084	−0.6268	−0.1488	−0.0976	−0.0317	−0.3037
7	0.4500	−0.8837	−1.6127	−0.0607	0.6121	0.3064	−1.9836	−2.6466	0.3362	−1.3045
8	0.0069	−0.2267	1.1063	−0.5674	0.3982	−0.9239	1.3919	0.4159	1.0040	−0.4167
9	0.8010	0.8433	−0.2592	1.1215	−0.6622	−0.1766	−1.8376	−0.4031	−1.4183	1.5494
10	1.5683	0.6116	0.0248	−0.3707	0.9946	−1.4287	0.9916	0.8836	0.6544	−0.1765
11	−1.1095	−0.9979	−0.9950	−1.2095	2.0402	0.5206	−0.2205	−0.5301	−1.1120	0.2345
12	−1.2327	0.2703	−0.6202	−0.2525	−0.3900	0.2285	−0.4443	−0.2165	1.3760	−0.5246
13	0.1821	0.4949	0.3480	0.1330	−0.8176	2.0228	−0.5846	−0.8661	1.3199	0.1793
14	−0.5518	0.0621	−1.1904	1.1456	0.2644	0.0199	−0.1306	1.8218	0.0584	0.5519
15	1.4770	−0.2012	0.5897	−2.0077	0.1088	−0.2868	0.5058	1.9901	−0.2224	−0.1495
16	−1.7357	−0.6896	−1.4277	2.2867	0.7201	1.1763	1.7477	−0.3816	2.5167	−0.5953
17	−1.5193	−0.3395	0.9146	−2.1025	1.1117	1.0280	−0.3912	−0.0357	0.2803	0.0225
18	1.1604	−0.1009	−0.0300	−0.4379	0.2429	−0.2679	2.4677	1.6484	−0.9752	0.6135
19	−0.1768	−2.4539	1.4081	−0.5853	−1.6130	−0.3815	−0.1926	−0.2455	−0.7595	1.4596
20	−0.5450	−1.7932	−0.4748	−0.2431	−0.0157	−0.5300	0.3161	−0.0987	1.5302	−0.2878

GENERATING OBSERVATIONS FROM A NORMAL DISTRIBUTION

Unlike the exponential and uniform distributions, the cumulative distribution function for normally distributed random variables cannot be written in closed mathematical form. Instead, the cumulative probabilities for any value, x, must be approximated using numerical methods.[10] Various methods are used to generate observations from a normal distribution with a mean of μ and a variance of σ^2 (designated an $N(\mu,\sigma^2)$ distribution). To make things simple, Table T3.5 contains what are called **random normal deviates**, random observations from the standard normal distribution ($\mu = 0$, $\sigma = 1$). (Notice that these are not restricted to values between 0 and 1.) Simulated observations, x, for any $N(\mu,\sigma^2)$ can be obtained by taking a random normal deviate, rd, and computing

$$x = \mu + (rd)\sigma \tag{T3.3}$$

[10]This is the reason z-tables are used instead of using a formula to obtain the cumulative probabilities for the z-distribution.

EXAMPLE 4

Suppose we wanted to generate random driving times between two locations, where driving times are normally distributed, with an average of 25 minutes and a standard deviation of 5 minutes. From Table T3.5 the first random normal deviate in column 1 is $rd = 0.0874$, so $x = 25 + (0.0874)5 = 25.437$; for the second random normal deviate, $rd = -0.7187$, the random driving time would be $x = 25 + (-0.7187)5 = 21.406$.

T3.6 SAMPLE SIMULATIONS

Generating simulated random phenomena is only one aspect of simulation analysis. These phenomena must be integrated with other aspects of the model in order to mimic the system being studied. This section presents two sample simulations that demonstrate the use of the different time-incrementing conventions, probability distributions, and simulation mechanics.

A RANDOM PRODUCTION LINE SIMULATION

Chapter 8 briefly explained how randomness in work station processing times could reduce the effective capacity of a production process. The results of a simulation were provided there to illustrate the effects. Here we discuss in detail the simulation model used.

Consider the three-work-station production line in Figure T3.8. Suppose the time required to process a unit of product at each work station is random, with a 0.5 probability that the time is two minutes and a 0.5 probability that it is four minutes, and the processing times at the work stations are independent of each other. We will not allow between-stage (buffer) inventories, so if work station k is busy and work station $k - 1$ finishes processing a unit, $k - 1$ must stop production until k is ready to accept the unit.[11]

1. ***Generating the Random Work Station Times.*** To generate a random processing time at a work station, we divide the interval [0,1) into two subintervals: [0,0.5) and [0.5,1.0). If the random number we select falls within the first subinterval, we will treat the processing time at that work station as being two minutes; if it falls into the second subinterval, the processing time will be four minutes. The random numbers in Table T3.1 will be used to generate the work station times: columns 1 and 4 will be used for work station 1, columns 2 and 5 for work station 2, and columns 3 and 6 for work station 3.

2. ***Time-Incrementing Convention.*** Because processing times are either two minutes or four minutes, processing of units will always begin or end in two-minute intervals. So we will use fixed-time incrementing with an increment of two minutes. To simplify the simulation mechanics, whenever work station 1 finishes processing a unit, we will generate the random work station times for the next unit for all three work stations and store them until needed.

The Simulation

We will walk through the first few minutes of simulated time to show the process.

Time 0: We generate the random processing times for the first unit of product. The first random number in column 1 is 0.8008, so the processing time at work station 1 is four minutes. The first random number in column 2 is 0.7709, so the processing time at workstation 2 is four minutes. The first random number in column 3 is 0.0096, so the processing time at work station 3 is two minutes. (The simulated processing times for the first 31 units of production are listed in Table T3.6, and full simulation results for the first 31 units of production are given in Table T3.7.)

At time 0, work station 1 begins processing unit 1 while the other two work stations are idle. We then advance the clock by two minutes.

Time 2: Work station 1 continues processing unit 1, while work stations 2 and 3 are idle, awaiting material. We advance the clock two minutes.

Time 4: Work station 1 completes unit 1, so we generate processing times for unit 2. For work station 1 the second random number in column 1 of Table T3.1 is 0.2273, so the processing time will be two minutes. For work stations 2 and 3 the random numbers are 0.4308 and 0.9831, which generate processing times of two minutes and four minutes, respectively. Work station 1 begins processing unit 2 and work station 2 begins processing unit 1, while work station 3 is still idle. We advance the clock two minutes.

Time 6: Work station 1 completes unit 2, so we generate processing times for unit 3, which are two minutes for each of the three work stations (random numbers are

[11]This assumption was made in Chapter 8 to make the comparison between two production lines equivalent.

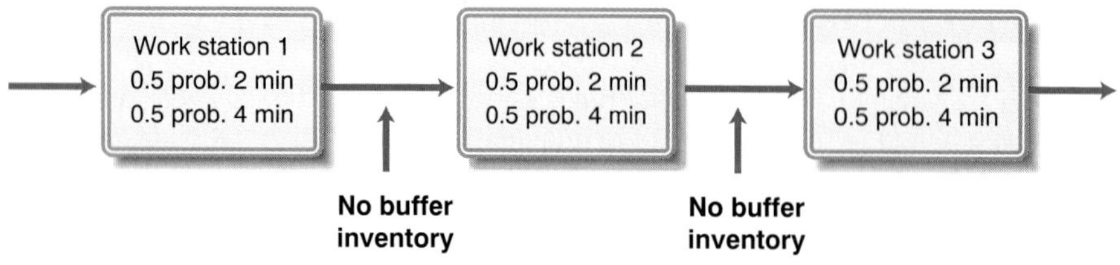

FIGURE T3.8 Production line with random processing times.

TABLE T3.6 SIMULATED PROCESSING TIMES AT EACH WORK STATION IN MINUTES

Unit	Work Station 1	Work Station 2	Work Station 3
1	4	4	2
2	2	2	4
3	2	2	2
4	4	4	2
5	2	4	4
6	4	2	2
7	2	2	4
8	2	4	4
9	4	2	2
10	4	4	2
11	2	2	4
12	4	2	4
13	4	4	4
14	2	2	2
15	4	4	4
16	2	2	2
17	4	2	2
18	4	2	2
19	2	2	2
20	2	4	2
21	2	2	4
22	4	4	2
23	4	4	2
24	4	4	4
25	2	4	4
26	4	2	4
27	2	4	4
28	4	4	4
29	2	2	4
30	2	4	2
31	2	2	4

Note: Simulated work times for work station 1 were obtained by taking the 20 random numbers of column 1 and the first 11 random numbers of column 4 of Table T3.1; if $r < 0.5$ the processing time was two minutes, and if $r \geq 0.5$ the processing time was four minutes. For work station 2 columns 2 and 5 were used, and for work station 3 columns 3 and 6 were used.

0.2212, 0.3178, and 0.3382). Work station 2 is still processing unit 1, so work station 1 must remain idle until work station 2 can accept unit 2 for processing. Work station 3 remains idle, awaiting material. We advance the clock two minutes.

Time 8: Work station 2 completes unit 1, so work station 1 begins processing unit 3; work station 2 begins processing unit 2; and work station 3 begins processing unit 1. We advance the clock two minutes.

Table T3.7 shows the simulated starting and ending times at each work station for 31 units of production. Ignoring the work station idleness during production of the first unit, from the time the first unit is completed (time 10) until the 31st unit is completed (time 120), 30 units are produced during a 110-minute period. Therefore, during this simulated time period the production line had an *effective* production rate of 1 unit per 3.67 minutes or 16.37 units per hour, *not* the 20 units per hour we might expect based on the average processing time of 3 minutes per work station. This also means that the effective line balance or work station efficiency is 81.8%, and the work stations are idle 18.2% of the time. This does not imply that the long-term efficiency is 81.8%. If we had simulated the process longer, or if we simulated it again using different random numbers, we would get a different result. But the

TABLE T3.7 SIMULATED STARTING AND ENDING TIMES AT EACH WORK STATION

Time	Work Station 1	Work Station 2	Work Station 3
0–2	Unit 1	Idle short	Idle short
2–4	Unit 1	Idle short	Idle short
4–6	Unit 2	Unit 1	Idle short
6–8	Idle 2NR	Unit 1	Idle short
8–10	Unit 3	Unit 2	Unit 1
10–12	Unit 4	Unit 3	Unit 2
12–14	Unit 4	Idle short,3NR	Unit 2
14–16	Unit 5	Unit 4	Unit 3
16–18	Idle 2NR	Unit 4	Idle short
18–20	Unit 6	Unit 5	Unit 4
20–22	Unit 6	Unit 5	Idle short
22–24	Unit 7	Unit 6	Unit 5
24–26	Unit 8	Unit 7	Unit 6
26–28	Unit 9	Unit 8	Unit 7
28–30	Unit 9	Unit 8	Unit 7
30–32	Unit 10	Unit 9	Unit 8
32–34	Unit 10	Idle short,3NR	Unit 8
34–36	Unit 11	Unit 10	Unit 9
36–38	Idle 2NR	Unit 10	Idle short
38–40	Unit 12	Unit 11	Unit 10
40–42	Unit 12	Idle short	Unit 11
42–44	Unit 13	Unit 12	Unit 11
44–46	Unit 13	Idle short	Unit 12
46–48	Unit 14	Unit 13	Unit 12
48–50	Idle 2NR	Unit 13	Idle short
50–52	Unit 15	Unit 14	Unit 13
52–54	Unit 15	Idle short, 3NR	Unit 13
54–56	Unit 16	Unit 15	Unit 14
56–58	Idle 2NR	Unit 15	Idle short
58–60	Unit 17	Unit 16	Unit 15

Notes: short = work station idle because no input material is available.
2 NR = work station idle because work station 2 is not ready for input.
3 NR = work station idle because work station 3 is not ready for input.

longer we simulate the process, the more accurate will be our estimate of the actual system performance.

A QUEUEING SIMULATION

A major application of simulation is in evaluating complex queueing systems. Although the following simple queueing system could be analyzed without simulation using the M/G/1 queueing formulas in Chapter 9, we present it to illustrate the simulation of continuous random phenomena and the logic of a queueing simulation.

The concession stand at Kane County Stadium is staffed by one worker. Customers arrive at the counter according to a Poisson process at an average rate of 80 per hour. The time required to serve a customer is normally distributed, with a mean value of 40 seconds and a standard deviation of 12 seconds. We want to simulate this one-server queueing system to estimate the amount of time customers must wait.

1. ***Customer Arrival Times.*** The time between arrivals is exponentially distributed, with an average time of $1/\alpha = 1/80$ hr, so $\alpha = 80$ per hr. We want the random arrival times and service times to be in the same units, so we convert α to a rate per second: $\alpha = (80$ cust/hr)/(3600 sec/hr) $= 0.0222$ cust/sec. We can then generate random interarrival times, x, using equation (T3.2): $x = (\ln r)/(-0.0222)$. The random numbers in column 1 of Table T3.1 will be used. The actual arrival times will be computed by adding each interarrival time to the arrival time for the previous customer.

TABLE T3.7 (continued)

Time	Work Station 1	Work Station 2	Work Station 3
60–62	Unit 17	Idle short, 3NR	Unit 15
62–64	Unit 18	Unit 17	Unit 16
64–66	Unit 18	Idle short	Unit 17
66–68	Unit 19	Unit 18	Idle short
68–70	Unit 20	Unit 19	Unit 18
70–72	Unit 21	Unit 20	Unit 19
72–74	Idle 2NR	Unit 20	Idle short
74–76	Unit 22	Unit 21	Unit 20
76–78	Unit 22	Idle short	Unit 21
78–80	Unit 23	Unit 22	Unit 21
80–82	Unit 23	Unit 22	Idle short
82–84	Unit 24	Unit 23	Unit 22
84–86	Unit 24	Unit 23	Idle short
86–88	Unit 25	Unit 24	Unit 23
88–90	Idle 2NR	Unit 24	Idle short
90–92	Unit 26	Unit 25	Unit 24
92–94	Unit 26	Unit 25	Unit 24
94–96	Unit 27	Unit 26	Unit 25
96–98	Idle 3NR	Idle 3NR	Unit 25
98–100	Unit 28	Unit 27	Unit 26
100–102	Unit 28	Unit 27	Unit 26
102–104	Unit 29	Unit 28	Unit 27
104–106	Idle 2NR	Unit 28	Unit 27
106–108	Unit 30	Unit 29	Unit 28
108–110	Idle 3NR	Idle 3 NR	Unit 28
110–112	Unit 31	Unit 30	Unit 29
112–114	Idle 2NR	Unit 30	Unit 29
114–116	Idle stop	Unit 31	Unit 30
116–118	Idle stop	Idle stop	Unit 31
118–120	Idle stop	Idle stop	Unit 31

2. ***Service Time.*** The service times, y, for each customer will be computed using equation (T3.3), $y = 40 + rd(12)$ seconds, where the random normal deviates, rd, will be chosen from the first column of Table T3.5.
3. ***Events and Time-Incrementing.*** Only two types of events can occur: the arrival of a customer and the completion of service for a customer. Between either of these events the system stays the same, so we will use next-event time incrementing.

The Simulation

The results of the simulation for the first 10 customers are summarized in Table T3.8.

Time 0: We will assume that the system begins with no customers in it.

1. We first generate the time until the first customer arrives. The first random number is $r = 0.8008$, so the first interarrival time (and the time of the first customer arrival) is $x = \ln(0.8008)/(-0.0222) = 10$ seconds.
2. There is no completion of service that can occur, so the next event must be the arrival of customer 1. Therefore, we advance the clock to time 10.

Time 10: The event is the arrival of customer 1.

1. We check to see if the server is busy or idle; he is idle, so customer 1 can be served immediately. We generate the random service time for customer 1 by selecting the first random normal deviate from Table T3.5 ($rd = 0.0874$) and then computing $y = 40 +$

TABLE T3.8 QUEUEING SIMULATION

Time	Event	Cust. in System	Service Time	Service Begins	Service Ends	Time in Queue
0	Start	0	—	—	—	—
10	C1 arr	1	41	10	51	0
51	C1 comp	0	—	—	—	—
77	C2 arr	1	31	77	108	0
108	C2 comp	0	—	—	—	—
145	C3 arr	1	49	145	194	0
171	C4 arr	2	—	—	—	—
194	C3 comp	1	—	—	—	—
	C4 begins		37	194	231	23
203	C5 arr	2	—	—	—	—
205	C6 arr	3	—	—	—	—
231	C4 comp	2	—	—	—	—
	C5 begins		52	231	283	28
283	C5 comp	1	—	—	—	—
	C6 begins		20	283	303	78
303	C6 comp	0	—	—	—	—
366	C7 arr	1	45	366	411	0
405	C8 arr	2	—	—	—	—
411	C7 comp	1	—	—	—	—
	C8 begins		40	411	451	6
428	C9 arr	2	—	—	—	—
451	C8 comp	1	—	—	—	—
	C9 begins		50	451	491	23
454	C10 arr	2	—	—	—	—
491	C9 comp	1	—	—	—	—
	C10 begins		59	491	550	37
.	.	.	.	.	.	.
.	.	.	.	.	.	.
.	.	.	.	.	.	.

arr = arrives
comp = service completed
begins = waiting customer has service begin

(0.0874)(12) = 41 seconds. So service of customer 1 will be completed at time 10 + 41 = 51.

2. We now compute the time of the next arrival. The second random number from Table T3.1 is $r = 0.2273$, so $x = (\ln 0.2273)/(-0.0222) = 67$ seconds. So the second customer will arrive at time 10 + 67 = 77.
3. The next event is the completion of service for customer 1 at time 51, so we advance the clock to time 51.

Time 51: The event is the completion of service for customer 1. No customers are waiting in line, so the next event must be the arrival of customer 2 at time 77. We advance the clock to time 77.

Time 77: The event is the arrival of customer 2.

1. We check to see if the server is busy or idle; he is idle, so customer 2 can be served immediately. We generate the random service time by selecting the second random normal deviate from Table T3.5, $rd = -0.7187$, and computing the service time for customer 2: $y = 40 + (-0.7187)(12) = 31$ seconds. So service of customer 2 will be completed at time 77 + 31 = 108.
2. We now compute the time of the next arrival. The third random number from Table T3.1 is $r = 0.2212$, so $x = (\ln 0.2212)/(-0.0222) = 68$ seconds. So the third customer will arrive at time 77 + 68 = 145.
3. The next event is the completion of service for customer 2 at time 108, so we advance the clock to time 108.

Time 108: The event is the completion of service for customer 2. No customers are waiting in line, so the next event must be the arrival of customer 3 at time 145. We advance the clock to time 145.

Time 145: The event is the arrival of customer 3.

1. We check to see if the server is busy or idle; he is idle, so customer 3 can be served immediately. We generate the random service time by selecting the third random normal deviate from Table T3.5, $rd = 0.7315$, and computing the service time for customer 3: $y = 40 + (0.7315)(12) = 49$ seconds. So service of customer 3 will be completed at time $145 + 49 = 194$.
2. We now compute the time of the next arrival. The fourth random number from Table T3.1 is $r = 0.5624$, so $x = (\ln 0.5624)/(-0.0222) = 26$ seconds. So the fourth customer will arrive at time $145 + 26 = 171$.
3. The next event is the arrival of customer 4 at time 171, so we advance the clock to time 171.

Time 171: The event is the arrival of customer 4.

1. We check to see if the server is busy or idle; he is busy, so customer 4 is put in the queue. We generate the random service time by selecting the fourth random normal deviate from Table T3.5, $rd = -0.2500$, and computing the service time for customer 4: $y = 40 + (-0.2500)(12) = 37$ seconds.
2. We now compute the time of the next arrival. The fifth random number from Table T3.1 is $r = 0.4937$, so $x = (\ln 0.4937)/(-0.0222) = 32$ seconds. So the fifth customer will arrive at time $171 + 32 = 203$.
3. The next event is the completion of service of customer 3 at time 194, so we advance the clock to time 194.

We would continue the simulation long enough to obtain accurate estimates of the system performance measures. For example, for the 10 customers in Table T3.8 the average time in the queue is the average of the 10 values in the rightmost column: $(195/10) = 19.5$ seconds.

T3.7 EVALUATING SIMULATION OUTPUT

The primary outputs from a simulation run are the values for some performance statistics of interest. For example, if we simulate a job-shop production system, we might compute the average throughput time for jobs, the average percentage of jobs delivered late, and the average in-process inventory. The simulated values of the random phenomena used in a simulation run are just one possible set out of an infinite number of possible values, so the results of the simulation run are equivalent to one data point sampled from an infinite population of possible runs. If the average throughput time during one run of a simulated job shop was 20.15 days, we cannot conclude that the long-term average is really 20.15 days. On another run with another set of random numbers the average throughput time might be 22.42 days or 11.90 days. In other words, stochastic simulation is equivalent to statistical sampling in the sense that we are only sampling a few runs (observations) from an infinite population of possible simulation runs. Consequently, if we were to make simulation runs for two alternatives (different scheduling rules) and our measure of performance was slightly better for the first alternative than for the second alternative, we should not automatically conclude that the first alternative is better in general. The difference would have to be large enough relative to the variation in the measure from run to run to justify the conclusion statistically. The type of statistical analysis that can be done is illustrated by the following example.

EXAMPLE 5

Suppose we used a computer simulation to evaluate two inventory policies. For each policy, 10 simulation runs were performed and each run simulated the equivalent of 500 days of the system. The average cost per day for each run is given in Table T3.9.

The average daily cost for the 10 runs for policy 1 is higher than for policy 2, but this is not true for each individual run. We can evaluate whether the difference is statistically significant using a t-test comparing population means. Suppose we want to test the null hypothesis that the mean daily cost for policy 1 is smaller than for policy 2 at the 95% confidence level. Then we compute the t-statistic:

$$t = |x_1 - x_2|/\sqrt{(s_1^2 + s_2^2)/10}$$

$$= +0.106/\sqrt{(0.0675 + 0.0438)/10} = 1.005 < t_{0.95}^{18} = 1.734^{12}$$

[12] The 18 degrees of freedom is an upper limit.

TABLE T3.9 SIMULATED DAILY COSTS FOR TWO ALTERNATIVE INVENTORY POLICIES

Run No.	Ave. Cost/Day ($000) Policy 1	Ave. Cost/Day ($000) Policy 2	Ave. Cost/Day ($000) Difference (1) − (2)
1	3.42	3.28	+0.14
2	3.33	3.31	+0.02
3	3.67	3.70	−0.03
4	3.93	3.68	+0.25
5	3.20	3.22	−0.02
6	3.55	3.44	+0.11
7	3.76	3.39	+0.37
8	4.01	3.87	+0.14
9	3.43	3.46	−0.03
10	3.51	3.40	+0.11
Average, $\bar{x}_i$	3.581	3.475	$+0.106 = \bar{d}$
s_i^2	0.0675	0.0438	$0.0170 = s_d^2$

s^2 = sample variance = $[\Sigma(x_i - \bar{x})^2]/(n - 1)$

With this test we *cannot* reject the null hypothesis, so we cannot conclude that policy 1 is better.

It is crucial to note that this t-test assumes that the 10 "data points" for the two policies are independent of each other, that is, each of the 20 runs used different, independent random observations for the random phenomena. So not only do the two sets of runs differ in terms of the ordering policy used, they also differ in terms of the random environment actually encountered. This introduces one additional level of randomness between the two options that is unnecessary. It is harder to determine whether any difference in performance is due to the difference in policies or to the differences in the random observations encountered. This makes the standard t-test less powerful than it could be.

Replication of Random Phenomena

An alternative approach is to *replicate* the random observations used in the policy 1 runs for the runs of policy 2. This is the advantage of using pseudorandom numbers. By using the same random number "seed," we can generate exactly the *same* random numbers and therefore the same simulated values for random phenomena for the two sets of runs. The only randomness is from run to run within the same policy, not between policies; thus, the only aspect that is different between the two sets of runs is the policy used. This allows us to use a **paired t-test**. We pair up the runs for the two policies that used the same random phenomena values. The relevant data point is the *difference* between the two runs; any difference in performance is due to the difference in policies. We then can compare the policies by testing the hypothesis that the average difference is larger than zero at a statistically significant level. The key point is that the standard deviation for the *paired differences* will usually be much smaller than the standard deviations of performance for the two policies separately.

EXAMPLE 5 (CONTINUED)

Table T3.9 shows that the sample variance for the differences, s_d^2, is 0.0170, while the variances of costs for the two policies are $s_1^2 = 0.0675$ and $s_2^2 = 0.0438$. The t-statistic for the paired t-test is then

$$t = d/\sqrt{s_d^2/n} = +0.106/\sqrt{[0.0170/10]} = 2.571 > t_{0.95}^{9} = 1.8331$$

So the difference is statistically significant at the 95% confidence level. It is important to emphasize that for a true replication, all the random phenomena values for each pair of runs must be identical.

Distribution of Performance Measures

Although alternatives are usually compared using some average performance measure, one advantage of stochastic simulation is that it is easy to obtain probability distributions of performance measures. For example, in a queueing simulation we might be interested not only in the average customer waiting time, but also in the distribution of waiting times to evaluate the equity of different designs or operating rules.

T3.8 SIMULATION AND COMPUTER SOFTWARE

Simulation models are normally implemented on computers. Three levels of computer software are relevant for simulation analysis: special-purpose simulation languages, general-purpose simulation languages, and general-purpose programming languages.

Special-purpose simulation languages are designed to simulate systems that have a special structure and application. For example, SIMFACTORY and MAP/1 are designed specifically to simulate manufacturing operations. Consequently, these languages have specific types of entities and relationships that commonly occur in manufacturing systems: work stations, methods for generating arrival times and processing times, material-handling relationships, and batch sizing. This makes it easy for someone to assemble a factory simulation by working with structured entities and relationships without having to perform more detailed modeling. The main advantages of these languages are that they provide structure and guidance for the user and require minimal programming. The disadvantage is the lack of flexibility to customize a simulation model.

General-purpose simulation languages such as SLAM, SIMSCRIPT, GPSS, and SIMAN provide some structure because they are designed to execute simulations, but they give the user more flexibility to customize the simulation model. If an organization is going to use simulation for many different applications, these languages can be used for all applications rather than buying a specialized simulation package for each one.

Even these general-purpose simulation packages, however, limit the user's flexibility. For especially complex and ill-structured simulation models, general-purpose programming languages such as FORTRAN, BASIC, or C++ are often used. With these languages there is almost no limit to the probability distributions and operating rules that can be used. In addition, if designed properly, simulations written in these languages are usually more efficient computationally than general-purpose or special-purpose simulation languages.

Deciding which type of language to use to perform a computer simulation is not easy. It depends on many factors, including:

1. The complexity of the simulations.
2. The variety of simulations that are likely to be done in the future.
3. The modeling and programming skills of the user.

When selecting among alternative general- or special-purpose simulation languages, the answers to the following questions can be important:

1. Can users incorporate their own routines to obtain more flexibility?
2. How easy is it to compute statistics on system performance?
3. What are the graphical and animation capabilities of the language? Some users find it very helpful to observe the simulation visually (e.g., seeing materials moving between machines and queues developing).
4. How easy is it to debug the program? What diagnostic aids and error messages are provided?

Simulation modeling and analysis of real systems can require substantial time and effort, so it should be used primarily when other methods, such as optimization models, cannot be used. However, its ability to incorporate randomness and its inherent flexibility make simulation analysis an invaluable tool for operations management.

SUMMARY

- A **simulation model** is a descriptive model that tries to mimic the behavior of an actual system.
- Dynamic simulation models track how the **state of the system** changes over time. An **event** is said to occur when the state of the system changes.
- The passage of time can be simulated either by repeatedly advancing the **simulated clock (clock time)** a fixed amount (called **fixed-time incrementing**) or by advancing the clock from the time of one event to the next event (called **next-event incrementing**).
- **Pseudorandom numbers** are a sequence of numbers that appear to be generated from a continuous uniform [0,1] distribution and are probabilistically independent, but they can be replicated on request, such as by using a formula. They can be used to generate

simulated observations of random phenomena that have any specified probability distribution.

- The output from stochastic simulations is similar to statistical sample information, so it must be evaluated using statistical methods. Conclusions are statistical inferences, not proven facts.

KEY TERMS

continuous-event model **482**
cumulative distribution function **490**
deterministic models **483**
discrete-event model **482**
entities **482**
event **482**
experiment (alternative) **486**
fixed-time incrementing **486**
next-event incrementing **487**
paired *t*-test **500**
pseudorandom numbers **488**
random normal deviates **493**
random numbers **488**
run **486**
simulated time (clock time) **487**
simulation model **482**
state of the system **482**
stochastic models **483**
system attributes (state variables) **482**

KEY FORMULAS

To compute a random observation, x, from a pseudorandom number, r, or a random normal deviate, rd:

Uniform $[a,b]$ Distribution

$$x = a + r(b - a)$$

Exponential Distribution with a Mean of $1/\alpha$

$$x = [\ln r]/-\alpha$$

Normal Distribution with a Mean of μ and a Variance of σ^2

$$x = \mu + (rd)\sigma$$

SOLVED PROBLEMS

Problem 1: Use the first five random numbers in column 1 of Table T3.1 to simulate the outcomes of tossing a fair coin.

Solution: There are two possible outcomes from each flip, head or tail, and each has a 0.5 probability of occurring. We divide the interval [0,1) into two subintervals, [0,0.5) and [0.5,1.0). Any random number that falls in the first subinterval will correspond to a head, and any random number that falls in the second subinterval will correspond to a tail.

Random Number	Outcome
0.8008	Tail
0.2273	Head
0.2212	Head
0.5624	Tail
0.4937	Head

Problem 2: Suppose the length of time a phone call lasts is exponentially distributed, with an average time of three minutes. Use the random numbers in column 1 of Table T3.1 to simulate the length of time of three phone calls.

Solution: The average time of a phone call is $1/\alpha = 3$ minutes, so $\alpha = 1/3$ call per minute. Using equation (T3.2), the simulated call lengths (in minutes) will be $x = (\ln r)/(-0.33)$:

Random Number	Call Length (min)
0.8008	0.666
0.2273	4.444
0.2212	4.526

Problem 3: Sumishatu Manufacturing Company produces semicustomized machine tools using a three-stage production process. The three stages will be called A, B, and C. Differences in customer orders and variations in human performance cause the processing times for each tool at each stage to be random. The production line was designed so that the average amount of work done at each stage would be five minutes, but the actual processing times at each stage approximate a *continuous uniform distribution* between three and seven minutes. In addition, the process was designed to accommodate only one unit of inventory between each stage. If more inventory develops, the preceding stage must stop until the inventory returns to one unit. Simulate this production process until the 10th unit is started. Use the random numbers in columns 1, 2, and 3 of Table T3.1 to simulate the processing times at stages A, B, and C, respectively.

Solution

1. We will use next-event time incrementing. The possible events are the beginning of processing of a unit of product at a stage or the completion of processing at a stage.
2. We will generate random processing times using equation (T3.1), so the random processing times will equal $3 + 4r$. (We will use a_i, b_i, and c_i to denote the processing time of unit i at stages A, B, and C, respectively.)

Time = 0

1. Stage A begins processing the first unit. The processing time is

$$a_1 = 3 + 4(.8008) = 6.20$$

2. The only possible event is the completion of unit 1 at stage A, so the clock is advanced to time 6.20.

Time 6.20

1. The event is the completion of unit 1 at stage A, the start of unit 1 at stage B, and the start of unit 2 at stage A.
2. Random processing times are generated for unit 1 at stage B and for unit 2 at stage A:

$$b_1 = 3 + 4(.7709) = 6.08$$
$$a_2 = 3 + 4(.2273) = 3.91$$

   So unit 1 will be done at stage B at time 6.20 + 6.08 = 12.28, and unit 2 will be done at stage A at time 6.20 + 3.91 = 10.11.
3. The next event is the completion of unit 2 at stage A, so we advance the clock to 10.11.

Time 10.11

1. The event is the completion of unit 2 at stage A. Stage B is busy, so unit 2 is put into inventory at stage B. Stage A begins processing unit 3.
2. The random processing time for unit 3 at stage A is

$$a_3 = 3 + 4(.2212) = 3.88$$

   So unit 3 is done at stage A at time 10.11 + 3.88 = 13.99.

3. The next event is the completion of unit 1 at stage B, so we advance the clock to time 12.28.

Time 12.28

1. The event is the completion of unit 1 at stage B, the start of unit 1 at stage C, and the start of unit 2 at stage B.

TABLE T3.10 SIMULATION OF SUMISHATU'S PRODUCTION PROCESS

Unit	Processing Times Stage A	Processing Times Stage B	Processing Times Stage C
1	6.20	6.08	3.04
2	3.91	4.72	6.93
3	3.88	4.27	4.35
4	5.25	6.96	4.20
5	4.97	6.42	5.85
6	6.80	4.55	3.80
7	3.11	4.06	6.25
8	4.70	5.46	5.29
9	5.41	3.01	3.09
10	5.22	6.58	4.73

Time	Unit in A	Number of Units in Inventory	Unit in B	Number of Units in Inventory	Unit in C
0	1	0	—	0	—
6.20	2	0	1	0	—
10.11	3	1	1	0	—
12.28	3	0	2	0	1
13.99	4	1	2	0	1
15.32	4	1	2	0	—
17.00	4	0	3	0	2
19.24	5	1	3	0	2
21.27	5	0	4	1	2
23.93	5	0	4	0	3
24.21	6	1	4	0	3
28.23	6	0	5	1	3
28.28	6	0	5	0	4
31.01	7	1	5	0	4
32.48	7	1	5	0	—
34.12	*	2	5	0	—
34.65	8	1	6	0	5
39.20	8	0	7	1	5
39.35	9	1	7	1	5
40.50	9	1	7	0	6
43.23	9	0	8	1	6
44.30	9	0	8	0	7
44.76	10	1	8	0	7

*means stage is idle due to inventory buildup.
— means stage is idle due to lack of material.

2. The processing times are

$$c_1 = 3 + 4(.0096) = 3.04$$
$$b_2 = 3 + 4(.4308) = 4.72$$

So unit 1 finishes at stage C at time 12.28 + 3.04 = 15.32, and unit 2 finishes at stage B at time 12.28 + 4.72 = 17.00.

Table T3.10 summarizes the simulation for the first 10 units of production.

Discussion and Review Questions

1. The first example simulation in Section T3.6 and *Solved Problem* 3 both simulate a three-stage flow process (production line). Explain why we used fixed-time incrementing in the first case and next-event incrementing in the second case.
2. What is the difference between truly random numbers and pseudorandom numbers?
3. Why do we want to use identical random phenomena (replicated runs) when we simulate two different alternatives? Why is this better than using new random values for each alternative?
4. Identify a specific system or problem not discussed in this tutorial for which simulation would be an appropriate form of analysis. What performance measures would you use in that case?

Problems

1. Suppose a basketball player makes an average of 80% of his free throws. Use the first five random numbers in column 1 of Table T3.1 to simulate the outcomes of five free throws for this player.
2. When people enter an elevator on the ground floor, the probability that they go to each of the other floors is as follows:

Floor	Probability
2	0.1
3	0.2
4	0.4
5	0.3

   Use the first five random numbers in column 1 of Table T3.1 to simulate the floors chosen by five people entering the elevator on the ground floor.
3. Use the first three random numbers in column 1 of Table T3.1 to generate three observations from the continuous uniform distribution [5,15].
4. Use the first three random numbers in column 1 of Table T3.1 to generate three observations from the continuous uniform distribution [−10,+10].
5. Suppose the times between arrivals of customers at a bank are exponentially distributed (a Poisson process), with an average time of two minutes. Use the first three random numbers in column 1 of Table T3.1 to generate the *arrival* times of the first three customers.
6. Suppose the amounts of customer purchases (in dollars) in a store are approximately exponentially distributed, with an average amount of $10. Use the first three random numbers in column 1 of Table T3.1 to simulate the purchase amounts of three customers.
7. The amount of time it takes to perform a task is random and can be approximated by a normal distribution, with a mean of 90 seconds and a standard deviation of 20 seconds. Use the first three random numbers in column 1 of Table T3.5 to simulate observations of the time it takes to do this task.
8. The number of people who attend football games at Chambersburg High can be approximated by a normal distribution, with a mean of 2000 people and a standard deviation of 400. Use the first three random numbers in column 1 of Table T3.5 to simulate the attendance at three Chambersburg football games.
9. Tele-Transmit Corporation (TTC) has designed a three–work station production line to make its products. Due to worker, machine, and material variations, as well as occasional machine breakdowns, the amount of processing time required at each work station for each unit of product is random. From historical data, TTC has determined that the processing times at each work station have approximately the following probability distribution:

Processing Time (sec)	Probability
40	0.20
60	0.50
80	0.20
120	0.10

Use the first 10 random numbers in columns 1–3 of Table T3.1 to simulate the production of 10 units of product (use column i for work station i). Assume that in front of each work station no more than one unit of product can be stored awaiting processing. Make a table that shows the beginning and ending of processing of each unit at each stage, the inventory levels over time at each stage, and the total amount of time required to finish the 10 units.

10. Golden Manufacturing Company makes a family of products using a three-stage production process (stages A, B, and C). Exactly once each hour the units processed at each stage are moved to the next stage using a fork lift. The number of units that can be processed at each stage in an hour is random, and it approximates a uniform *discrete* distribution between 6 and 10 (i.e., each integer value between 6 and 10 is equally likely). (Note: this assumes that enough units of input are available at that stage to process; if during an hour stage B has a simulated production capability of eight units but only five are available from stage A, then only five are processed.) Simulate this process for 10 simulated hours; use the random numbers in columns 1–3 of Table T3.1 to generate the random production capabilities of stages 1–3, respectively. How many units are produced? Compare this with the number that would have been produced if there were no randomness: 8 units/hour average rate times eight hours of full production (the first two hours are for start-up and are ignored) = 64 units. Explain the discrepancy.

11. A hotel has 50 rooms available. Demand for these rooms has exceeded capacity. However, frequently some people who make reservations do not show up; if the hotel has not overbooked, these rooms go empty. (Assume that the rooms cannot be filled on short notice and that customers are not forced to prepay or guarantee payment if they do not show up.) Suppose an unused room costs the hotel $40 in lost profit. Also suppose that if a customer has a reservation and no room is available, the hotel loses $60 in goodwill and the added expense of finding another room in a nearby hotel. From historical data, the hotel knows that on any given day there is a 10% chance that 95% of the customers with reservations show up, a 50% chance that 90% of the customers with reservations show up, and a 40% chance that 80% of the customers show up. The hotel is considering the reservation policy of accepting 54 reservations each day. Using the random numbers in column 1 of Table T3.1, simulate 20 days of operation using this overbooking policy. Compute the average loss per day from this policy.

12. Powerbuilders Construction Company (PCC) has agreed to build a small factory for one of its customers. The project has been divided into four phases, 1, 2, 3, and 4, which must be done in sequence. The amount of time it will take to perform each phase is uncertain. PCC has estimated that the time to perform phase 1 has a continuous uniform distribution between 5 and 10 weeks; phase 2 is exponentially distributed, with a mean of 6 weeks; phase 3 will take either 1 week or 2 weeks, each possibility being equally likely; and phase 4 has a continuous uniform distribution between 3 and 5 weeks. PCC's contract states that it will complete the building in 20 weeks or less. For each week or fraction of a week that the project is late (i.e., the project takes more than 20 weeks), PCC must pay a $5000 penalty. Simulate five completions of the project. Use the random numbers in columns 1–4 of Table T3.1 to generate the times required to perform phases 1–4, respectively.

13. A company that recharges batteries for the public is considering the purchase of new recharging equipment. The company has narrowed the choice to two options: (a) buy one high-speed recharger or (b) buy two low-speed rechargers. The time it takes to recharge a battery is random. For the high-speed recharger the recharging time is uniformly distributed between one and three minutes. For the low-speed rechargers the recharging time is uniformly distributed between two and six minutes. The purchase price and operating cost of each option are the same, so the company wants to choose the option that provides the fastest service. Suppose customers arrive randomly according to a Poisson process (i.e., interarrival times are exponentially distributed) at an average rate of 20 per hour. Perform simulation to test each alternative for 12 customers. Use the random numbers in column 1 of Table T3.1 to generate random customer arrival times and the numbers in column 2 to generate the random recharging times. Which option would you recommend? Do you have enough information to justify your recommendation?

14. A bookstore would like to stock a new income tax guide for the upcoming year. Due to the publishing lead time, the bookstore will be allowed to place an order only once (in October), and will receive the guides at the end of December. The bookstore will pay $3 per guide to the publisher and will resell the guides for $6. Any guide not sold by April 15 can be sold on sale for $1. The bookstore does not know how many guides it can sell during the tax season, but it believes that the demand will be between 201 and 300, with each value being equally likely (a discrete uniform distribution). The bookstore plans to purchase 260 tax guides in October. Use the first 20 random numbers in column 1 of Table T3.1 to simulate 20 occurrences of this situation and compute the profit the bookstore would earn each time. Then compute the expected (average) profit the bookstore would earn with this policy.

15.* Bob Smith has been hired to manage a small retail store. The store has offered him two alternative wage plans. In the first plan, Bob would receive $30 per day plus 5% commission on total sales above $200 that day. The second plan would pay Bob $50 per day plus 2% commission on any sales above $150 that day. It is known that the number of buying customers varies randomly from day to day; the following historical data describe the probabilities of each number of customers occurring in a day:

No. of Customers	Probability
0	.01
1	.05
2	.14
3	.30
4	.25
5	.15
6	.08
7	.02

The amount purchased also varies from customer to customer; from historical data, the following probability distribution of purchases per customer was derived:

Amount of Purchase	Probability
$ 50	.05
$100	.15
$150	.25
$200	.30
$250	.20
$300	.05

(a) Simulate three days of sales for Bob and compute how much he would earn under each pay plan. Use the first three random numbers in column 1 of Table T3.1 to simulate the number of customers each day, and use the random numbers in column 2 to simulate individual customer purchases. (b) Based on the simulation results, which plan would you recommend Bob choose? (c) What is wrong with simply computing the average total sales each day, computing Bob's earnings with each plan if the average sales occurred, and using the larger result as the preferred plan? Explain why this could result in an erroneous conclusion.

16.* (a) Perform the production line simulation that was done in Section T3.6, but assume that there is room to put *one unit* in inventory between each work station. Therefore, if work station 1 completes a unit and work station 2 is busy, the unit can be put into a buffer inventory between the work stations and work station 1 can begin work on another unit rather than having to wait until work station 2 completes its work on the previous unit. (If the buffer inventory is full and the preceding work station completes a unit, then the preceding work station must stop operation until the buffer is available.) (b) Compute the output rate and percent balance for this case (see Chapter 8). (c) Is the output rate higher than in Section T3.6? Why or why not?

17.* (a) Perform the production line simulation that was done in Section T3.6, but assume that the random processing times have a 0.50 probability of being 2.5 minutes and a 0.50 probability of being 3.5 minutes (instead of 2 minutes and 4 minutes, respectively). (b) Compute the effective production rate and the percent balance. (c) Did the reduction in randomness increase the output rate compared to that of the simulation in Section T3.6? Explain why or why not.

SELECTED READINGS

FISHMAN, GEORGE. *Principles of Discrete Event Simulation*, Wiley, New York, 1978.

LAW, AVERILL M., and W. DAVID KELTON. *Simulation Modeling and Analysis* (2nd ed.), McGraw-Hill, New York, 1991.

PRITSKER, A., and C. PEGDEN. *Introduction to Simulation and SLAM II* (3rd ed.), Halsted Press, New York, NY, 1986.

SHANNON, ROBERT E. *Systems Simulation: The Art and Science*, Prentice-Hall, Englewood Cliffs, NJ, 1979.

SMITH, L. D., R. M. NAUSS, and D. A. BIRD. "Decision Support for Bus Operations in a Mass Transit System," *Decision Sciences*, Vol. 21, 1990, pp. 183–203.

WATSON, HUGH. *Computer Simulation in Business*, Wiley, New York, 1981.

CHAPTER 10

JOB DESIGN, WORK METHODS, AND ORGANIZATION

10.1 People Make the Difference
On the Job: Richard Kowalewski, Roots Canada

10.2 Job Design
Job Content
Responsibility for Quality and Process Improvement
In Good Company: John Deere Overhauls Jobs . . . and Pay . . . and Productivity
Automation and the Human–Machine Interface

10.3 Methods Analysis and Improvement
Methods Analysis
Some Simple Principles of Job Design
Work Aids and Ergonomics
Training

10.4 Work Standards

10.5 Work Observation and Measurement
Motion and Time Study
Using Time-Study Data to Compute Standard Times
Elemental Standard-Time Data
Micro-Motion and Predetermined Motion-Time Data
Work Sampling

10.6 The Work Environment
Environmental Factors Affecting Worker Performance
Safety and Health

10.7 The Organization of Work
Sociotechnical Systems and Autonomous Work Groups
Job Flexibility in Time and Location
Compensation and Incentives
Unions

Ferro-Stamping, Inc.: A Job Redesign Case

10.1 People Make the Difference

We have discussed how to design products, where to locate production facilities, how to design the production process, and how to configure production facilities. The keys to the production system, however, are the workers in the system. In theory, all organizations have access to essentially the same standard equipment, materials, and facilities. It is an organization's personnel that provides the competitive advantage and makes one organization more successful than another. It is the people who create new and better products and devise better ways to make and distribute them.

Recruiting well-educated, responsible, and skilled people is a good starting point for creating a productive workforce. But, as Richard Kowalewski of Roots Canada (this chapter's "On the Job" segment) knows, how employees are trained, organized, and motivated ultimately determines the success of the company. In this chapter we focus on how jobs should be designed; how workers should be supported by and integrated with facilities, equipment, and tools; and how workers can be organized to make the production system operate most efficiently and to promote a satisfied workforce.

On the Job

Richard Kowalewski, Roots Canada

How does a successful company grow from 8 to 250 people and still have only one layer of management between owners and the shop floor? At Roots Canada, a manufacturer and retailer of high-quality leather goods, Richard Kowalewski and his two brothers have been that layer for 22 years, and the autonomy they encourage in the workforce is the answer.

In his role as general manager of leather goods manufacturing, Richard oversees a ring system that groups workers into teams of five to seven members who work together producing shoes, jackets, and handbags from start to finish. Thanks to careful cross-training and reliance on team effort, each member can handle every job in the process (there can be up to 20 different steps in assembling a piece). Workers in a ring depend on one another, help correct each other's mistakes, and learn together to become their own bosses. Richard encourages people to keep coming up with better ways to do things and uses quality to measure production instead of quotas. "If you wouldn't buy it, then don't make it," he says.

The team approach extends to management too. Richard's brothers are the head of production and the designer for Roots, and all three work together to conceptualize new products and train the staff. Although cross-training is time-consuming and requires assembling teams who can work well together over time, it has kept turnover extremely low, and the brothers are committed to extending this approach to the entire shop floor.

10.2 Job Design

A **job** can be defined as the set of tasks and responsibilities of a worker. These tasks and responsibilities, along with performance expectations, work conditions (time and place of work), general skills, and possibly methods to be used, are normally contained in a written **job description**. There is no simple formula for designing jobs that will best fit a production system. The number of variables controlled by the job designer and the number of corresponding trade-offs are enormous. However, the tasks to be done, the training provided, the tools available for use, the organization of personnel (in teams or alone), the design of the work area, and the compensation system all affect the contribution employees will make to the system. Let us begin by studying the content, responsibilities, and human–machine interface of jobs.

JOB CONTENT

A central aspect of job design is to define the tasks the employee is supposed to do—the **job content**. The extent to which tasks can or should be defined will vary from job to job. For example, for traditional repetitive jobs, such as those performed by workers on an assembly line or those collecting refuse on a garbage truck, all the required tasks of the job can be clearly listed and described in detail. Other jobs, such as that of an executive assistant or a plant engineer, encompass a much wider range of tasks, many of which are performed infrequently, and some of the tasks cannot be described ahead of time. In fact, some jobs deal with solving problems that arise unexpectedly and are not specifically assigned to anyone. In these cases, the job content has to be defined more in terms of general problem areas, skill areas, or responsibilities than in specific task descriptions.

Specialization and Task Variety

An important consideration in deciding on the task and responsibility content of a job is striking the appropriate balance between job specialization and task and skill variety. Much of the world's economic progress can be attributed to job specialization. The fewer different tasks a person must do and the narrower the range of responsibilities, the more skilled and efficient a person can become, up to a point. The major advantages and disadvantages of job specialization are summarized in Table 10.1. The primary trade-off is that as some jobs become more and more specialized, they also become less satisfying and more boring for workers, resulting in less careful work, poor quality, lower production rates, higher accident rates, and greater absenteeism and employee turnover. (Some seemingly specialized jobs, such as brain surgeon or tax attorney, actually involve a wide variety of tasks and skills, and they provide sufficient content, challenge, and fulfillment that the specialization may not lead to boredom.)

This trade-off is at the heart of the conflict between two schools of thought in job design: the scientific management school and the behavioral or psychological school. The **scientific management school**, as epitomized by Frederick Taylor's work, concentrated on making the human mechanical aspects of work as efficient as possible. This approach, in effect, treated people as little more than thinking animals. Productivity was postulated to be primarily a function of the physical work methods of employees and their motivation, which was assumed to be purely money driven. By studying work methods in a scientific manner, managers could improve them and teach them to em-

TABLE 10.1 ADVANTAGES AND DISADVANTAGES OF JOB SPECIALIZATION

Advantages

1. Workers can develop greater skill and establish a better work rhythm, resulting in high productivity.
2. A lower level of basic skills is required; wages are lower per unit of production.
3. It is easier to train and supervise workers.

Disadvantages

1. Work becomes monotonous and boring, resulting in absenteeism, poor quality, and little interest in improving the job.
2. There is no worker control and autonomy over what is done and how.
3. Scheduling flexibility is limited; workers are not easily moved to other jobs.

ployees to make them more efficient. Little more was expected of workers than to carry out the mechanical aspects of their jobs as prescribed by industrial engineers.

Subsequent study undertaken by those of the **behavioral (psychological) school** has shown that there is more to raising worker productivity than simply work methods. Both the quality and the quantity of work performed are affected by psychological and organizational factors, such as how interesting the work is, how much control the worker has over the job, and how workers interact with coworkers.

Neither school of thought fully captures the essence of job design. Successful job design requires a synthesis of both schools; we must develop efficient work methods and exploit specialization of repetitive tasks while providing workers with variety, control over their work, and a satisfying work environment. In recent years, the approaches discussed below have been used to do just that. The goal has been to reduce the layers of management, move decision making down to first-line workers, and utilize the capabilities of workers more fully, thereby making their jobs more interesting while increasing their contribution to the production process.

Job Enlargement

Job enlargement is a "horizontal" expansion of job tasks; that is, the worker is assigned more tasks at the same general skill level. In Chapter 8 we briefly considered this strategy in the construction of work stations for a flow process. In a manufacturing setting, job enlargement might mean having a worker do several tasks at a work station rather than only one or two. In a bank, it might mean training a person to write home loans, car loans, and installment loans rather than only one of these.

Job Enrichment

Job enrichment involves "vertical" expansion of a job's responsibilities and skills (see Figure 10.1). It may mean that a production worker is involved in the design of the product or production process, is responsible for her own quality testing, handles customer

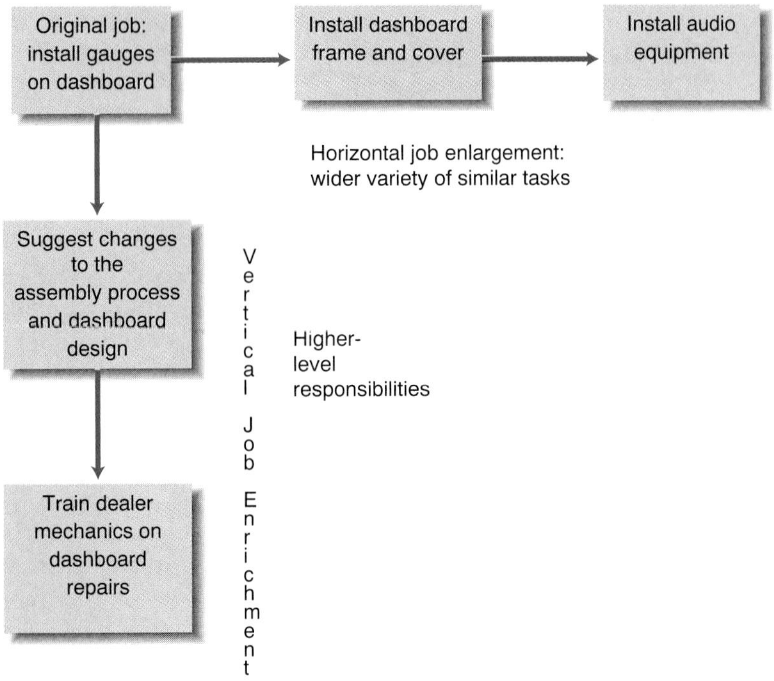

FIGURE 10.1 Job enlargement and job enrichment for an automobile assembly worker.

complaints, or deals directly with suppliers. John Deere (the subject of this chapter's "In Good Company" segment) even sends assembly line workers to visit customers and dealers to advise them on using their products and to get advice on how to improve product quality. For job enrichment to be of greatest value, at least some of the added tasks and responsibilities should involve greater use of the worker's capabilities, including creativity, pattern recognition, interpersonal communication, and problem solving. For example, some retail chains have expanded the responsibilities of sales associates to include deciding what products to stock, when and how much to order of each, and where and how to display the products, thereby expanding the job to include traditional purchasing, inventory management, and facility layout functions. Vertical expansion of the job necessitates greater training and empowerment of line workers. As we will see in later chapters, it is an integral component of so-called Japanese or lean production systems and of total quality management.

Job Rotation

An organizational step that can be used to make work more interesting while exploiting the efficiencies of narrowly defined, repetitive jobs is to have employees work in teams and exchange jobs on a periodic basis; this is called **job rotation**. Within a department or production line there may be three, four, or more different jobs, each requiring different skills, each putting different physical demands on the body, and each involving a different level of interest for the workers. If workers take turns and rotate among the jobs, no one is stuck with an extremely boring or physically demanding job all the time; the desirable and undesirable jobs are equally shared. How often rotation occurs will vary from job to job and will be affected by learning (and forgetting) rates, the time needed to switch jobs, and the relative desirability of the jobs. For example, the Cummins Engine plant in Columbus, Indiana, rotates some jobs every two hours. Job rotation is especially beneficial when workers rotate between more and less interesting jobs; simply rotating among several undesirable jobs is not always beneficial.

Cross-Training

An essential part of job rotation is **cross-training** of workers, that is, training them to do more than one job. Cross-training is a form of job enlargement and, in many cases, job enrichment as well. It puts considerable responsibility on the organization to provide the additional training needed. Although cross-training is often instituted as part of a formal job rotation policy, it can be extremely beneficial in itself. Many organizations extensively cross-train their workers to allow for greater flexibility in using staff and to improve overall worker skill. For example, Corning Inc.'s Blacksburg, Virginia, plant has 200 workers but only one job classification. Each worker is trained to handle as many as 15 different jobs, and each has the authority to sign a purchase order for up to $500 without authorization. This structure has eliminated the need for almost all supervision; there is only one supervisor for every 60 line workers. Similarly, at a Carrier Corporation plant, equipment operators are trained on several machines so that they can be moved around easily if one worker is sick, and they are trained in maintenance so that when a machine breaks down, they do not have to wait for a separate maintenance crew to repair it.[1]

Although there is evidence that job enlargement, job enrichment, and job rotation improve productivity, product quality, and worker satisfaction, it is important to recog-

[1]See Amal Naj, "Shifting Gear: Some Manufacturers Drop Efforts to Adopt Japanese Techniques," *Wall Street Journal*, May 7, 1993; and Erle Norton, "Future Factories: Small, Flexible Plants May Play Crucial Role in U.S. Manufacturing," *Wall Street Journal*, Jan. 13, 1993.

nize that some workers prefer specialized, low-responsibility jobs. In some cases this is all they are capable of handling. In other cases they obtain their satisfaction from what they do away from work, and neither expect nor want any human fulfillment or satisfaction from work; they simply work to earn a living. How or if these people should be incorporated into a production system remains an open question.

Customer Focus

An expanded view of job content takes the definition of the job beyond a listing of tasks and includes responsibility to the worker's immediate customer. Especially for jobs in service industries that involve direct contact with the organization's external customers, it is often insufficient to simply list the tasks that might or should be done. Instead, we might define the job such that the worker must decide what must be done to provide a specified level of service to the customer. In some cases, this may require performing tasks outside the normal domain of the job. For example, the job description for an admissions officer at a university includes dozens of specific administrative tasks. In addition, the officer may be expected to handle personally any unusual situations that involve applicants or new students, such as being a liaison with the campus police to waive a parking ticket for an applicant or personally escorting and assisting a disabled applicant around campus. Similarly, a sales associate in one department of a store may be expected to escort a customer to another department to help him find an item.

Defining a job's content in terms of serving a customer also applies to jobs serving customers within the organization. For example, in addition to performing specific tasks, a material transport worker may be expected to provide whatever assistance is necessary for other workers to do their jobs well, which may include helping with repairs or carrying production documents to the plant office.

RESPONSIBILITY FOR QUALITY AND PROCESS IMPROVEMENT

An increasingly important component of job design is the amount of responsibility a worker has for achieving product quality and improving the production process. A crucial element of total quality management (TQM), which we will discuss in Chapter 11, is the assignment of responsibility for product quality. The classical approach has been to place primary responsibility for quality assurance on a separate organizational unit (the quality control department). The TQM approach advocates giving most, if not all, of the responsibility for product quality to the first-line workers making the good or delivering the service. The addition of greater responsibility for product quality is a form of job enrichment and should be considered explicitly in the design and definition of a job. In fact, companies cannot successfully move toward just-in-time or lean production methods or implement TQM without devoting considerable attention to redesigning jobs and transferring greater responsibility for product quality to operations workers.

One advantage people have over machines is their ability to perceive complex patterns, learn from experience, and think. This ability makes workers a primary source of ideas for improving the production process. For example, Jerry McCoy, a worker at General Motors, has had over 75 of his suggestions for improving GM's products and processes implemented.[2] A number of organizational structures have been used to obtain and implement process improvement suggestions from workers, such as quality circles, suggestion boxes, autonomous work teams, and town hall–type meetings. The organizational structure, distribution of authority, and degree of training must, of course, be consistent with the amount of responsibility assigned to workers.

---

[2]From a General Motors advertisement, *New York Times*, May 16, 1994.

IN GOOD COMPANY

John Deere Overhauls Jobs . . . and Pay . . . and Productivity

In recent years John Deere & Company, a leading manufacturer of farm and construction equipment, has changed its image from that of a stodgy company to an innovative, cutting-edge firm. A major component of this transformation has been a complete restructuring of jobs: their content, organization, training, and compensation. First, Deere began sending its manufacturing personnel, including members of the United Auto Workers Union, on trips across the country, visiting dealers and farmers to explain their new products and to get feedback on them. This information was used to improve customer service and product quality. For example, when one worker saw that dealers had trouble unloading planting equipment from trucks without damaging them, he worked with his factory mates to change the way they were loaded so that they could be unloaded safely.

Deere has also reorganized its workers into self-directed work teams. One group at its East Moline, Illinois factory overhauled its assembly process and reduced assembly costs by 10% by bringing together at one site 12 manufacturing steps that had previously been performed at scattered sites throughout the plant. To take on these extra responsibilities, employees must be better trained and educated. John Deere has responded by teaming up with a local community college to provide two-year degrees in electromechanical technology, and by agreeing with the International Association of Machinists union to pay workers based on skill levels and courses completed rather than seniority. The results of these efforts have been increased productivity, improved quality, and record profits.

Source: Kevin Kelly, "The New Soul of John Deere," *Business Week*, Jan. 31, 1994, pp. 64–66.

AUTOMATION AND THE HUMAN–MACHINE INTERFACE

Production systems require the coordination and compatibility of people, machines, technologies, and facilities. The appropriate role of each and the best way to integrate them is a fundamental issue in overall system design, and specifically the design of jobs. As defined in Chapter 7, **automation** is the use of mechanical or electrical machinery, such as machine tools, computers, and process controls, to perform some or all activities traditionally performed by workers. Automation has played an important role in increasing productivity and improving uniformity and quality of output. In addition, it has been used to perform jobs that are repetitive, monotonous, hazardous, or physically uncomfortable for humans, and it has reduced the physical effort required by humans to perform other jobs. However, automation is not a cure-all, and it is effective only when used for the right tasks and when compatible with human workers. In fact, GE vice president Gary Reiner claims that in some cases technology and automation impede productivity.[3]

[3]From Howard Gleckman et al., "The Technology Payoff," *Business Week*, June 13, 1993, pp. 57–68.

A key aspect of job design is using machines and humans to perform the tasks for which they are each best suited. Machines are best suited for well-structured, repetitive tasks, tasks that require considerable force or speed, tasks performed in dangerous or uncomfortable conditions, and tasks that require intricate but well-defined sensing (such as temperature control). In spite of advances in artificial intelligence and expert systems, machines are not as well suited as humans for recognizing complex patterns, synthesizing information and experience, reasoning inductively, responding to new situations, communicating with other humans, and being innovative and creative. For example, humans can learn from a production process and suggest improvements, whereas machines have not yet been successful at this task.

In the ideal situation, automation should free humans to spend their time only on those tasks that fully utilize their skills. For example, partially automated work cells should be designed to use the right number and mix of machines so that one or a few workers are able to operate and monitor several machines and do other higher-level activities, such as scheduling or process improvement, while the machinery performs lower-level, repetitive tasks.

The integration of humans and machines is a far more common aspect of operations than most people realize. Many of the best-known companies have achieved competitive advantages through simple redesign of jobs and appropriate meshing of workers and machines. For example, McDonald's and other fast-food producers recognized that using a human to fill a cup with soda was very time-consuming, produced inconsistent fill levels, and underutilized human skills. With an automatic soda machine a worker can push a button, which causes the machine to fill the cup to the correct level, while the worker performs other tasks that cannot be automated easily.

In spite of its advantages, however, automation carries a few disadvantages. The most significant are cost (and consequently the large volume of product needed to justify its use), limited flexibility (most machines are designed to perform a small range of functions and are not easily converted to other uses), and lack of feedback to improve the process. Overautomating a production system (automating simply to replace workers rather than because machines are most appropriate for the task) can be very dangerous. A number of U.S. companies that tried to adopt Japanese manufacturing methods in the 1980s made the mistake of believing that automation was the key to Japanese success. As a result, they overautomated and then had to remove much of the machinery they had installed. Corning Inc.'s Blacksburg plant is an example. Originally it was highly automated and then was later redesigned to use simple machines and people in many places where robots had been installed. This system made the plant more flexible, and workers' suggestions increased productivity over 25% in the first three years.

The driving principle of job design is the same as for product and process design: keep it simple. Successful companies *do* use advanced automation for many processing tasks; however, the essence of just-in-time production and TQM is the carefully designed simplicity of the jobs, technology, and production process.

10.3 METHODS ANALYSIS AND IMPROVEMENT

Specifying the tasks and responsibilities of a job is only the first step in the job design process. The next step is to determine *how* to perform the tasks, that is, determine the best *work methods* to use when performing the job. Included in the search for the best work methods are the most efficient physical movements of the worker, the best sequence in which to perform movements or tasks, and the best way to coordinate the worker's actions with those of machines and other workers. This information must then be conveyed to the workers through training and appropriate supervision and feedback.

Identifying and implementing good work methods means doing the following:

1. Observing work and measuring its efficiency.
2. Analyzing existing work methods.
3. Applying good work methods principles.
4. Instituting and utilizing work aids and good ergonomic design.
5. Training employees.

Although work observation and measurement are an integral part of methods analysis, the specific techniques and applications are extensive, so a detailed discussion is postponed until Section 10.5. In addition, before learning the skills of work observation, it is beneficial to understand some of the information we would want to collect and how it will be used. At this point, it is sufficient to assume that we have observed workers and obtained the needed data.

METHODS ANALYSIS

An analytic approach to deciding what tasks should be done and *how* they should be done is methods analysis. **Methods analysis** utilizes structured data collection, visual aids and charts, and analytic procedures to help understand and improve work methods. The specific techniques that work best will vary, depending on the purpose and scope of the work analysis. Methods analysis relies on obtaining good observational and experimental data, which is discussed later. Here we focus on the use and analysis of these data for improving work methods.

Methods analysis focuses primarily on the activities of individual workers or groups of related workers. However, a comprehensive study should begin with a preliminary analysis at the production system or subsystem level.

System and Subsystem Analysis

Work analysis at the system or subsystem level is most appropriately performed in conjunction with, or as a part of, process design or redesign. The purpose of system or subsystem work analysis is to identify the tasks that need to be done, determine whether they are being done by the right people or in the correct location, and decide whether or not there are unnecessary movements and delays. Improving the way a worker performs a task that is unnecessary, or better performed elsewhere in the production process, provides little real benefit. The ultimate purpose is to simplify the process.

Two simple tools that can guide this analysis, the process flow diagram, and the process chart were introduced in Chapter 8. A **process flow diagram** (shown in Figure 8.19 on page 404) is an arrow diagram that shows the step-by-step sequence of the process and the corresponding movement of materials, people, or information. A **process chart** (shown in Figure 8.20 on page 405) gives a more detailed breakdown of the process into tasks. It classifies each activity as being either a processing operation, movement, inspection, delay, or storage.

These documents can be used to perform a question-based analysis whereby, for each activity or movement, we ask the following questions:

1. What is being done and why? Could the task be eliminated, and what would happen if it were? Could it be combined with another task?

2. When in the process are the task being done? Must it be done at this time or is there flexibility in its sequencing or timing?
3. Where is the task done? Could it be done elsewhere, and would there be any benefit in doing it elsewhere?
4. How is the task done? Why is it done this way? Could it be done another way or automated? Are there changes in equipment, tools, or methods that would make it easier to do?
5. Who does the task? Could someone else do it, especially as part of another job? Does the person doing it have the correct skills? Should it be done by someone of higher or lower skill?

This analysis could lead to a reorganization of work and of specific jobs. For example, Aetna Life and Casualty Company used this analysis to overhaul its process and redesign the jobs of those involved in issuing insurance policies. The original process took 15 days to issue a policy, and it required 60 people to handle the policy. The revised process has one person perform all the steps required, and it takes only five days.[4]

The difference between the process design analysis in Chapter 8 and a system-level work methods analysis is that the process analysis is normally based on following the flow of a product through the production system, whereas a work analysis concentrates initially on the activities to be performed by specific workers or group of workers. In some cases these analyses are not separable, and the job and process designs should be done together.

Worker and Task-Level Analysis

Most methods analyses and job design focus on the individual worker and the tasks he or she performs. New jobs obviously require an initial design, but most methods analyses are performed to improve or modify existing jobs. Jobs that involve primarily physical labor, such as sorting, welding, assembling, or testing, can usually be improved by simplifying the worker's motions and reducing the time and effort required. There are two strategies for accomplishing this. The first approach, promoted by Frederick Taylor, is to observe a variety of workers and identify the most productive ones. The variation in performance among workers is often due to a difference in the methods they use. By carefully studying the most productive workers, we can determine which one uses the best and simplest methods. These would then become the standard methods that would be taught to other workers and used as the basis for establishing time standards.

A second approach, developed by Frank and Lillian Gilbreth, is also based on observing a variety of workers. But in this method, each fundamental motion and action is carefully analyzed to identify the best way to perform it. This analysis is called *micromotion analysis* (discussed in Section 10.5). It is often done by filming workers and then analyzing and timing the motions frame by frame.

The best basic movements can then be synthesized into an overall work method or procedure. This process is usually aided by using a **simo (simultaneous motion) chart**. The simo chart, illustrated in Figure 10.2 for an assembly operation, tracks the motions of each hand simultaneously, so it is possible to determine whether one hand is left idle unnecessarily and whether both hands are coordinated appropriately. Frank Gilbreth characterized the work method resulting from the synthesis of the best basic movements as the "one best way" to do a job.

[4] Ibid.

SIMULTANEOUS MOTION
ANALYSIS SHEET

PART Bolt and washer assembly - Old Method DEPARTMENT AY16 FILM NO. B21

OPERATION Assemble 3 washers on bolt OP. NO. A32

OPERATOR M.Smith 1C634 DATE ANALYSED BY M.C.R. SHEET NO. 1 OF 1

CLOCK READING	SUBTRACTED TIME	THERBLIG SYMBOL	DESCRIPTION LEFT HAND	CLOCK READING	SUBTRACTED TIME	THERBLIG SYMBOL	DESCRIPTION RIGHT HAND
595	7	TL	Carries assembly to bin	595	26	TL	Reaches for lock washer
602	2	RL	Releases assembly	621	6	SL+G	Selects and grasps washer
604	4	TE	Reaches for bolt	627	7	TL	Carries washer to bolt
608	2	SL+G	Selects and grasps bolt	634	6	P	Positions washer
610	17	TL	Carries bolt to washing machine	640	12	A+RL	Assembles washer onto bolt and releases
627	5	P	Positions bolt	652	8	TE	Reaches for steel washer
632	104	H	Holds bolt	660	8	SL+G	Selects and grasps washer
736	7	TL	Carries assembly to bin	668	9	TL	Carries washer to bolt
743	2	TL	Releases assembly	677	3	P	Positions washer
745				680	10	A+RL	Assembles steel washer and releases
				690	6	TE	Reaches for rubber washer
				696	10	SL+G	Selects and grasps washer
				706	9	TL	Carries washer to bolt
				715	5	P	Positions washer
				720	16	A+RL	Assembles washer and releases
				736			

FIGURE 10.2 Simultaneous motion (simo) chart. From Ralph M. Barnes, Motion and Time Study: Design and Measurement (7th ed.), Wiley, New York, 1980, p. 146.

Worker–Machine Coordination

Most jobs, from fork-lift driver to accountant, involve interaction with machines. The worker may be called on to load and unload, control, monitor, or even repair one or more machines as part of the job. Many of these interactions require the worker to be actively involved with the machine for a small amount of time (e.g., initiate printing by a computer and printer). Then the machine may operate on its own without human involvement (printing), during which time the worker can do other things. Considerable improvement in productivity can often result from improving human–machine coordination. A **worker-machine chart**, which simultaneously tracks the activity of the worker and any relevant machines, is one tool for helping to utilize worker and machine time better. For example, Figure 10.3 is a worker-machine chart for an operator of an automatic metal stamping press. The press cuts rectangular metal blanks into various patterns by stamping a cutting die down on the blank. Once a stack of metal blanks is loaded into the feeder, the machine will automatically feed the blanks onto the stamping table, stamp the metal, remove the completed sheet to a stacking table, and clear the trim metal into a scrap hopper. The chart represents some average production cycles based on observations of actual practice. Notice that when the press is running (times 35–50, 60–80, etc.), the worker is semi-idle (monitoring the process) until he removes the finished sheets. He is also occasionally idle while waiting for metal blanks to be brought to his machine feed area.

By analyzing this chart, we can identify several improvements. First, during the worker's idle time, he could prepare the die change so that the final change of dies

Product: Stamped metal forms

Machine operator	Time	Stamping press	Time
Set up machine Die change for product 642A	20 min	Idle-being set up	20 min
Load metal blanks in feeder	5 min	Idle	5 min
Startup, checking initial quality	10 min	Stamping product 642A	10 min
Semi-idle (Monitor machine)	15 min	Stamping product 642A	15 min
Remove finished sheets	5 min	Idle	10 min
Load metal blanks in feeder	5 min		
Semi-idle (Monitor machine)	20 min	Stamping product 642A (total run = 400)	20 min
Remove finished sheets	5 min	Idle	15 min
Remove scrap from hopper and transport to scrap area	10 min		
Set up machine Die change for product 811E	15 min	Idle—being set up	15 min
Idle—waiting for blanks to be delivered	4 min	Idle	8 min
Load metal blanks in feeder	4 min		
Startup; check initial quality	9 min	Stamping product 811E	9 min
Semi-idle (Monitor machine)	18 min	Stamping product 811E (total run = 225)	18 min
Remove finished sheets	5 min	Idle	12 min
Remove and transport scrap	7 min		
Set up machine Die change for product 125A	20 min	Idle—being set up	20 min
Idle—waiting for blanks to be delivered	4 min	Idle	4 min

Summary

Operator		Machine	
Idle/semi-idle time	61 min	Idle time	109 min
Working	120 min	Working	72 min
Utilization	$\frac{120}{181} = 66.3\%$	Utilization	39.8%
Elapsed time to complete 642A	95 min		
Elapsed time to complete 811E	62 min		

FIGURE 10.3 Worker-machine chart for a metal-stamping operation.

Product: Stamped metal forms

Machine operator	Time	Stamping press	Time
Set up machine Die change for product 642A (partially prepared during previous run	12 min	Idle-being set up	12 min
Load metal blanks in feeder	5 min	Idle	5 min
Startup, initial quality check	10 min	Stamping product 642A	25 min
Find and transport metal blanks for next product—811 E	8 min		
Semi-idle (Monitor machine)	7 min		
Remove finished sheets	5 min	Idle	10 min
Load metal blanks in feeder	5 min		
Prepare machine for next setup (product 811 E)	10 min	Stamping product 642A (total run = 400)	20 min
Remove scrap from hopper and transport to scrap area	10 min		
Remove finished sheets	5 min	Idle	5 min
Complete setup for product 811 E	7 min	Idle—being set up	7 min
Load metal blanks into feeder	4 min	Idle	4 min
Startup; check initial quality	9 min	Stamping product 811E (Total run = 225)	27 min
Find and transport blanks for next run	6 min		
Prepare machine for next setup (product 125A)	9 min		
Remove scrap— will transport during next run	3 min		
Remove finished sheets	5 min	Idle	5 min
Complete setup for product 125A	12 min	Idle—being set up	12 min
Load metal blanks into feeder			

Summary

Operator		Machine	
Idle/semi-idle time	7 min	Idle time	60 min
Working	125 min	Working	72 min
Utilization	94.7%	Utilization	54.5%
Elapsed time to complete 642A	77 min		
Elapsed time to complete 811E	43 min		

FIGURE 10.4 Worker-machine chart for a revised metal-stamping operation.

would take less time (a structured method for doing this is presented in Chapter 15 and is discussed in the case at the end of this chapter). Second, he could empty the scrap bin containing scrap cuttings during the idle time rather than waiting until the end of the production run. Third, during his idle time he could transport his own metal blanks from the previous processing station, thereby eliminating the need for separate workers for transporting the product and reducing the idleness caused by waiting for a transporter to bring the blanks to him. Figure 10.4 is a revised worker-machine chart that in-

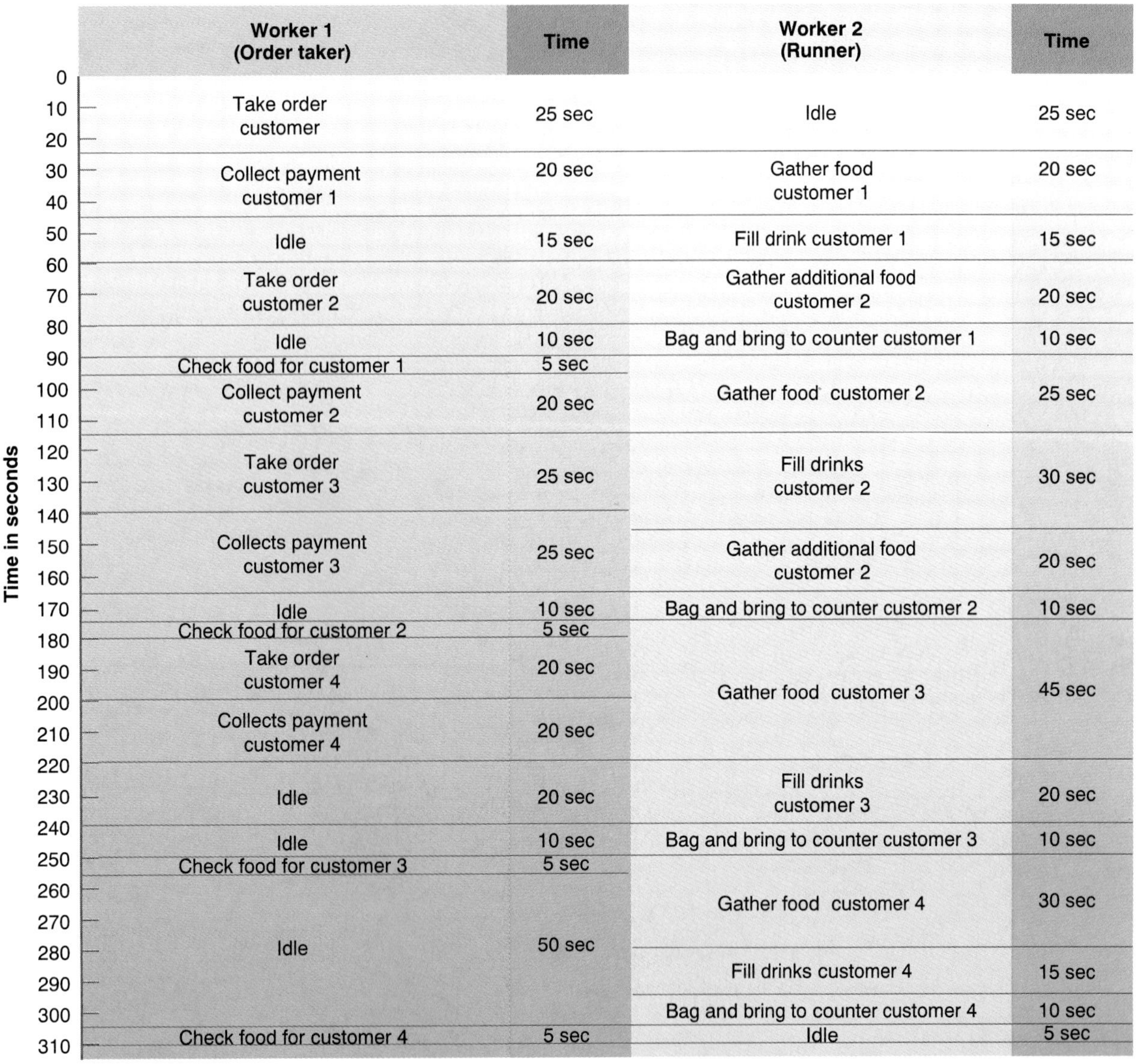

Worker 1 (Order taker)
Time
Worker 2 (Runner)
Time
Time in seconds
0
10
20
30
40
50
60
70
80
90
100
110
120
130
140
150
160
170
180
190
200
210
220
230
240
250
260
270
280
290
300
310
Take order customer
25 sec
Collect payment customer 1
20 sec
Idle
15 sec
Take order customer 2
20 sec
Idle
10 sec
Check food for customer 1
5 sec
Collect payment customer 2
20 sec
Take order customer 3
25 sec
Collects payment customer 3
25 sec
Idle
10 sec
Check food for customer 2
5 sec
Take order customer 4
20 sec
Collects payment customer 4
20 sec
Idle
20 sec
Idle
10 sec
Check food for customer 3
5 sec
Idle
50 sec
Check food for customer 4
5 sec
Idle
25 sec
Gather food customer 1
20 sec
Fill drink customer 1
15 sec
Gather additional food customer 2
20 sec
Bag and bring to counter customer 1
10 sec
Gather food customer 2
25 sec
Fill drinks customer 2
30 sec
Gather additional food customer 2
20 sec
Bag and bring to counter customer 2
10 sec
Gather food customer 3
45 sec
Fill drinks customer 3
20 sec
Bag and bring to counter customer 3
10 sec
Gather food customer 4
30 sec
Fill drinks customer 4
15 sec
Bag and bring to counter customer 4
10 sec
Idle
5 sec

FIGURE 10.5 Team-activity chart for a fast-food restaurant.

corporates these methods changes. Machine utilization increases by over 35%, and by having all machine operators transport their own products or inputs, several transport work positions could be eliminated.[5]

Group Coordination

Additional improvements in efficiency can sometimes be obtained by improving the coordination of workers with other workers. For example, Figure 10.5 is a **team-activity chart** for a two-person team that fills orders at a fast-food restaurant. The current operation has one worker take the order, collect payment, give change, and verify that all the

[5] This example is taken from the Ferro-Stamping case at the end of the chapter, where it is discussed in more detail.

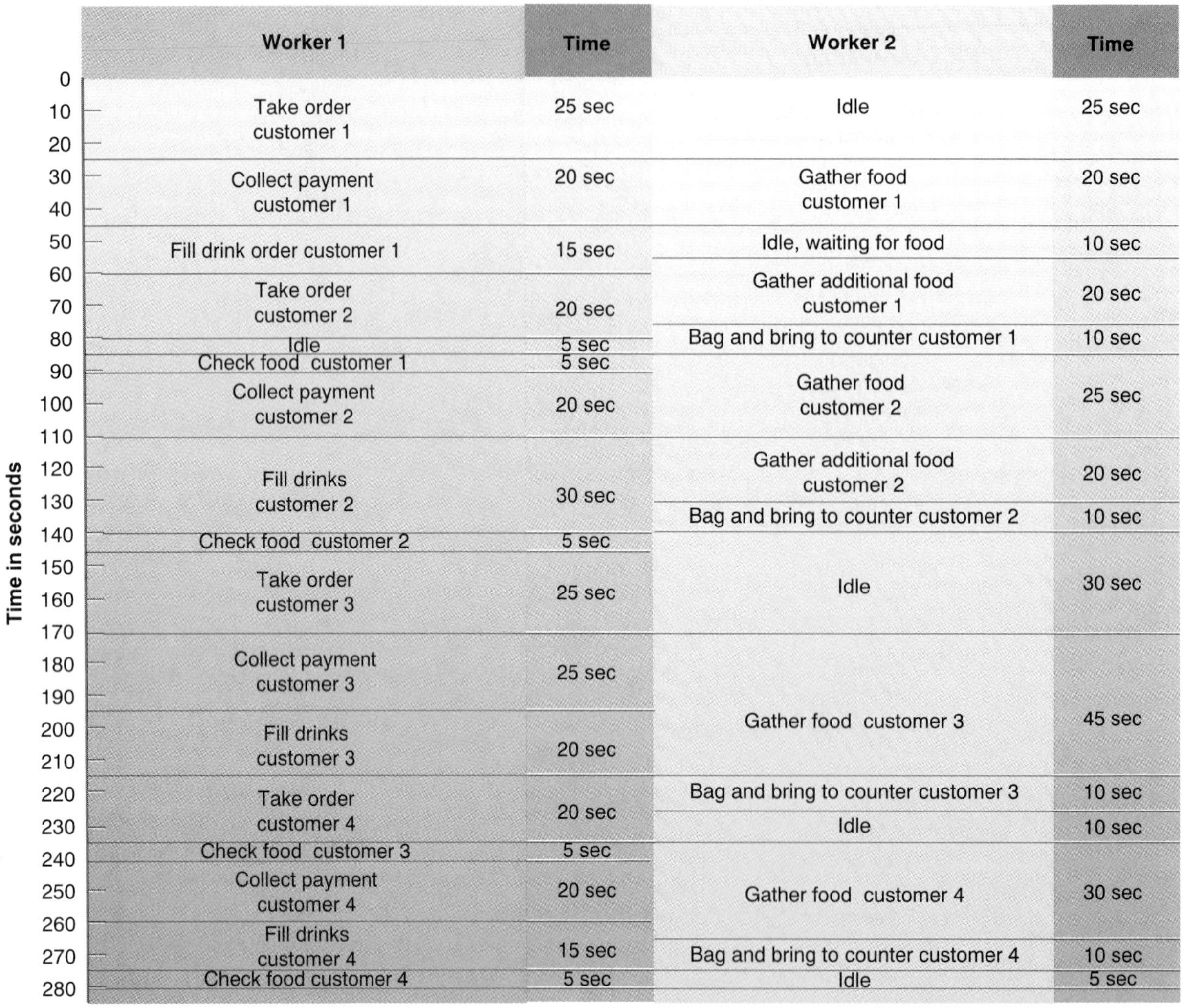
Worker 1
Time
Worker 2
Time
Time in seconds
0
10
20
30
40
50
60
70
80
90
100
110
120
130
140
150
160
170
180
190
200
210
220
230
240
250
260
270
280
Take order customer 1
25 sec
Collect payment customer 1
20 sec
Fill drink order customer 1
15 sec
Take order customer 2
20 sec
Idle
5 sec
Check food customer 1
5 sec
Collect payment customer 2
20 sec
Fill drinks customer 2
30 sec
Check food customer 2
5 sec
Take order customer 3
25 sec
Collect payment customer 3
25 sec
Fill drinks customer 3
20 sec
Take order customer 4
20 sec
Check food customer 3
5 sec
Collect payment customer 4
20 sec
Fill drinks customer 4
15 sec
Check food customer 4
5 sec
Idle
25 sec
Gather food customer 1
20 sec
Idle, waiting for food
10 sec
Gather additional food customer 1
20 sec
Bag and bring to counter customer 1
10 sec
Gather food customer 2
25 sec
Gather additional food customer 2
20 sec
Bag and bring to counter customer 2
10 sec
Idle
30 sec
Gather food customer 3
45 sec
Bag and bring to counter customer 3
10 sec
Idle
10 sec
Gather food customer 4
30 sec
Bag and bring to counter customer 4
10 sec
Idle
5 sec

FIGURE 10.6 Revised team-activity chart for a fast-food restaurant.

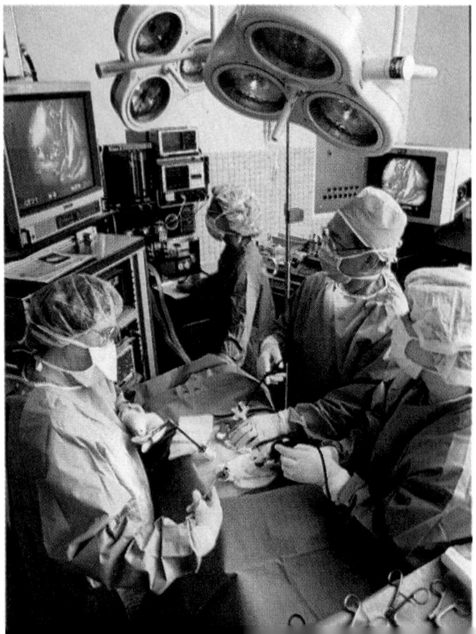

Team-activity analysis can help team members coordinate their tasks more efficiently. This analysis has been used to improve surgical procedures as well as manufacturing methods.

requested food is delivered to the customer. The second worker gathers the food from storage areas and fills beverage containers. This chart shows that the first worker has some idle time, while the second worker is almost constantly busy. If the first worker is made responsible for helping to gather food for an order, as in Figure 10.6, customers can be served faster and workers would have less wasted time. Southwest, United, USAir, and other airlines have used this type of analysis to coordinate the tasks of airplane turnaround crews. For example, USAir used this analysis to reduce deplaning and boarding times from 15 to 5 minutes.[6]

SOME SIMPLE PRINCIPLES OF JOB DESIGN

Even though observation and measurement are valuable aspects of job design, the quality of a job design can be significantly enhanced simply by following established design principles. Some of the most important and widely applicable principles are summarized below.

Coprocessing

In many jobs, from household chores to complicated manufacturing work, workers perform tasks with two levels of involvement, which we will call *active* and *passive phases*. During the **active phase** the worker must be actively involved with the task, such as cutting someone's hair, and cannot be doing any other active work. During the **passive phase** something necessary to complete the job is occurring, such as a machine running or hair drying, but the worker is not actively involved with the task and is available to do other things. If the active and passive phases of tasks are matched appropriately, a worker can be engaged in two or more tasks, or serve two or more customers, at one time. This is called **coprocessing** or **parallel processing**.

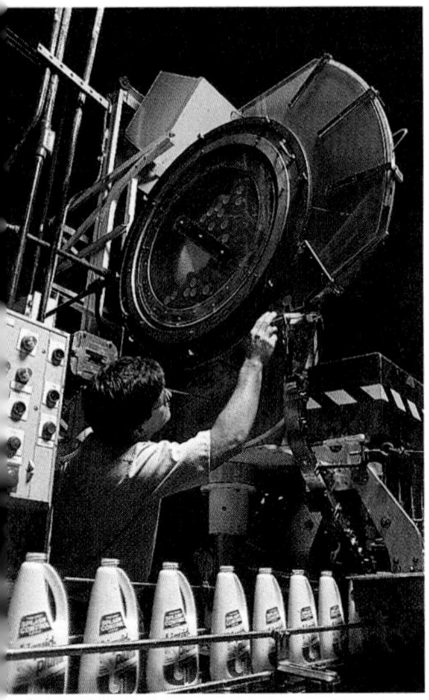

Jobs can be made more efficient by using the principle of coprocessing. Here a machine operator is able to adjust the cap dispenser while monitoring the bottle filling line.

In the examples above, many of the methods improvements were based on identifying a worker's idle time during the passive phase of a task (e.g., monitoring a machine) and having the worker perform the active phase of another task concurrently (e.g., prepare a die for a die change). Most of us utilize this principle in our everyday activities. For example, when we put food in a microwave oven, turn it on, and then do other chores while the food warms, we are coprocessing. Possibly no principle of work is more important than coprocessing, and it should be one of the first aspects of a job that we look at when we try to improve work methods. It is simply a matter of taking the time to think through the set of tasks we need to perform, identify when active involvement is necessary, and coordinate the active and passive phases of the work.

In some cases supporting equipment can facilitate coprocessing, such as the new beverage dispensers described in Section 10.2. Traditional soda dispensers require a worker to stay with a cup while it is being filled in order to hold the dispenser lever and to make sure it does not overflow, so the task of filling a cup is made up entirely of an active phase. New soda dispensers allow a person to push a button that will automatically fill the cup to a specified level without human monitoring. This changes the task into one with a short active phase (position the cup and push a button), a long passive phase during which the worker can do other tasks, and a short active phase (remove the cup). This reduces idle time and increases productivity.

The coprocessing principle plays an important role in the design and operation of work cells, as well as other modern production methods such as single-minute exchange of dies (SMED), which is a structured method of performing quick machine setups and changeovers. (SMED is discussed in detail in Chapter 15.)

[6]See Carl Quintanilla, "New Airline Fad: Faster Airport Turnarounds," *Wall Street Journal*, Aug. 4, 1994.

Back-Hauling

When my mother told me never to go up or down the stairs empty-handed, I did not realize that she was advocating an important production (and transportation) principle. Many jobs require a worker to move or carry items from place to place. **Back-hauling** means that when you carry something from location A to location B, you carry something from B back to A on the same trip rather than returning empty-handed and then later making a special trip to carry the item from B to A. This reduces movement and effort and saves time. For example, in Figure 10.4, suppose the stamping press operator had to move the metal scraps from the stamping press to a disposal cart near the storage area for metal blanks. He could then dispose of the scrap and pick up the next load of metal blanks in one trip if he coordinated his work.

Designing Human Activities to Be Compatible with the Human Body

During the past century, scientists have derived a number of physical work principles dealing with human motion. For example, humans work better if they can establish a natural work rhythm, so movements and tasks should be arranged to promote a constant rhythm. Other principles of work and motion, such as distributing work among different muscles to minimize fatigue and fully utilizing both hands, are listed in Table 10.2 and explained in greater detail in the references at the end of the chapter. Adherence to these principles not only improves productivity but also normally produces less fatigue.

Continuous Improvement and Worker Consultation

The process of job design is never complete. Jobs and work methods should constantly be reviewed and improved. In fact, job redesign is an integral part of the continuous improvement philosophy. The best sources of ideas for making jobs easier and more productive are the workers doing the work. They have the opportunity to experiment with different methods and to confront problems and try alternative solutions that a staff observer or manager often cannot use. In fact, Gary Reiner, a vice president of GE, claims that "All of the good ideas—all of them—come from the hourly workers."[7]

It is beneficial for organizations to have institutional mechanisms for encouraging and using input from workers to improve work methods. In addition, regardless of the source of a methods change, workers should be consulted and involved with methods and job content changes as much as possible so that they cooperate with changes rather than fight them.

WORK AIDS AND ERGONOMICS

Good job design principles can be enhanced by the way we configure the work area, select and design tools, and utilize work aids to reduce effort.

Using Tools and Equipment to Reduce Human Effort

Many simple, inexpensive tools and equipment called **work aids** can improve human performance greatly. For example, holding an item while drilling or cutting it can be exhausting, and it is often difficult to perform precise work this way. A vise can hold materials precisely, and it allows the operator to concentrate on the cutting, drilling, or other activity. Other simple devices, such as stop bars and guide bars, rotating work tables, and hand power tools can significantly improve performance at little cost.

Ergonomics

The benefit of a powerful microcomputer is greatly diminished if the visual display terminal makes the user's eyes hurt so much that he does not use it or if the table, chair,

[7]Gleckman, op. cit.

TABLE 10.2 PRINCIPLES OF MOTION ECONOMY

Using the Human Body the Way It Works Best

1. The work should be arranged to provide a natural rhythm which can become automatic.
2. The symmetrical nature of the body should be considered:
   a. The motions of the arms should be simultaneous, beginning and completing their motions at the same time.
   b. Motions of the arms should be opposite and symmetrical.
3. The human body is an ultimate machine, and its full capabilities should be employed:
   a. Neither hand should ever be idle.
   b. Work should be distributed to other parts of the body in line with their ability.
   c. The safe design limits of the body should be observed.
   d. The human should be employed at its "highest" use.
4. The arms and hands as weights are subject to the physical laws, and energy should be conserved:
   a. Momentum should work for the person and not against him or her.
   b. The smooth continuous arc of the ballistic is more efficient.
   c. The distance of movements should be minimized.
   d. Tasks should be turned over to machines.
5. The tasks should be simplified:
   a. Eye contacts should be few and grouped together.
   b. Unnecessary actions, delays, and idle time should be eliminated.
   c. The degree of required precision and control should be reduced.
   d. The number of individual motions should be minimized along with the number of muscle groups involved.

Arranging the Workplace to Assist Performance

1. There should be a definite place for all tools and materials.
2. Tools, materials, and controls should be located close to the point of use.
3. Tools, materials, and controls should be located to permit the best sequence and path of motions.
4. Gravity feed bins and containers can deliver material close to the point of use.
5. The workplace should be fitted to the task and to the human.

Using Mechanical Devices to Reduce Human Effort

1. Vises and clamps can hold the work precisely where needed.
2. Guides can assist in positioning the work without close operator attention.
3. Controls and foot-operated devices can relieve the hands of work.
4. Mechanical devices can multiply human abilities.
5. Mechanical systems should be fitted to human use.

Source: Frank C. Barnes, "Principles of Motion Economy: Revisited, Reviewed, and Restored," Proceedings of the Southern Management Association, Atlanta, 1983. Reproduced by permission.

By using a power lift to tilt the automobile, this Mercedes Benz worker is able to install engine components more easily with less physical stress and fatigue.

and keyboard arrangements are uncomfortable and produce carpal tunnel syndrome (a permanent injury to the nerves in the wrists). **Ergonomics** is a discipline concerned with designing tools and equipment and arranging the work area in a way that makes human work most productive while minimizing stress, injury, and fatigue. That is, the focus of ergonomics is the human–machine interface.

The range of applicability for ergonomics is large and varied. One function of ergonomics is designing work furniture and tools so that they are compatible with the physical characteristics of the workers using them. Traditionally, ergonomic researchers used physiologic data from large populations of workers to design furniture and tools to be most comfortable for a large segment of potential workers. In recent years, more attention has been devoted to designing furniture and tools that are adjustable or adaptable to individual workers. For example, tables and work benches may be adjustable

Many companies have ergonomic research laboratories to test the effects on workers of different tools and work methods. Here, Brian Peacock, Head of General Motors' Manufacturing Ergonomics Lab, uses a lumbar motion monitor to measure forces on the spine resulting from lifting activities.

to conform to different heights or dexterities (left-handed versus right-handed). The amount of lifting, moving, and stretching can be minimized, and machines and tools can be more accessible and easier to manipulate. Similarly, well-designed chairs can minimize stress on the back or reduce glare from visual displays.

One area of ergonomic study is the design of instruments and gauges to make them easier to read and monitor. Figure 10.7 illustrates how ergonomic principles can be used to reduce the time it takes to check the condition of a system while lessening the chance of an error. The figure displays five gauges that measure the condition of a power plant system. The desired levels are a temperature of 260°F, a pressure of 800 psi, a flow rate of 225 gallons per minute, a fuel recharging rate of 50 pounds per minute, and a cooling temperature differential of 35°F. Figure 10.7a contains standard gauges as normally produced by the suppliers. The desired level of each gauge is at a different "clock position," so the worker monitoring them has to be very careful when reading them. A reading that is not at the desired level does not readily stand out. Figure 10.7b is a set of gauges revised so that the desired level for each gauge is at the vertical (12 o'clock) position. If a gauge is not at the desired level, this is readily apparent from a quick glance. Gauges can be made even easier to monitor by using color coding and light and sound alarms. In Figure 10.7b the green area of the gauge signifies a safe reading, whereas an arrow in the red region clearly indicates a hazardous condition. When the arrow moves into the red zone, a flashing light or buzzer could be activated to get a worker's attention. Owens-Corning Fiberglas instituted such an alarm system so that workers could monitor equipment from afar while performing other duties.[8]

An area of current concern is redesigning tools and tasks to minimize the occurrence of **carpal tunnel (repetitive motion) syndrome**. This permanent injury, which occurs frequently among workers using computers, doing assembly work, and operating grocery checkout scanners, can often be reduced by changing the design of equipment, as well as the work methods used and the scheduling of rest periods.

Good ergonomic design has reduced the strength requirements for many jobs and has helped expand job opportunities for women and partially disabled workers. For example, the jobs at the Arkadelphia Carrier Corporation's plant have been designed so that no one has to lift more than 12 pounds, removing some physical barriers for many workers.[9]

Arrange the Workplace for Convenience

In addition to the design of equipment, the spatial arrangement of the work area affects productivity. Studies have shown that much production inefficiency results from workers spending too much time finding and acquiring tools and materials, waiting for repairs to be performed, moving to operate or check controls, and dealing with machine failures, product defects, and accidents due to cluttered and neglected facilities. One characteristic of world-class production systems is that the workplace is kept neat and clean, and tools and materials are located conveniently so that workers do not have to search for them. In addition, controls are located so that workers can check them with a minimum of movement. By diagramming every movement of assembly workers and then rearranging the workplace for convenience, companies such as Toyota and Chrysler have reduced wasted movements and idleness substantially.

Poka-Yoke: Mistake-Proofing

We are not only interested in using methods and tools that help workers perform their jobs *faster*; we also want them to work *better*: with fewer or no mistakes. **Poka-yoke** is a

[8]See Fred Bleakley,"How an Outdated Plant Was Made New," *Wall Street Journal*, Oct. 2, 1994.

[9]Norton, op. cit.

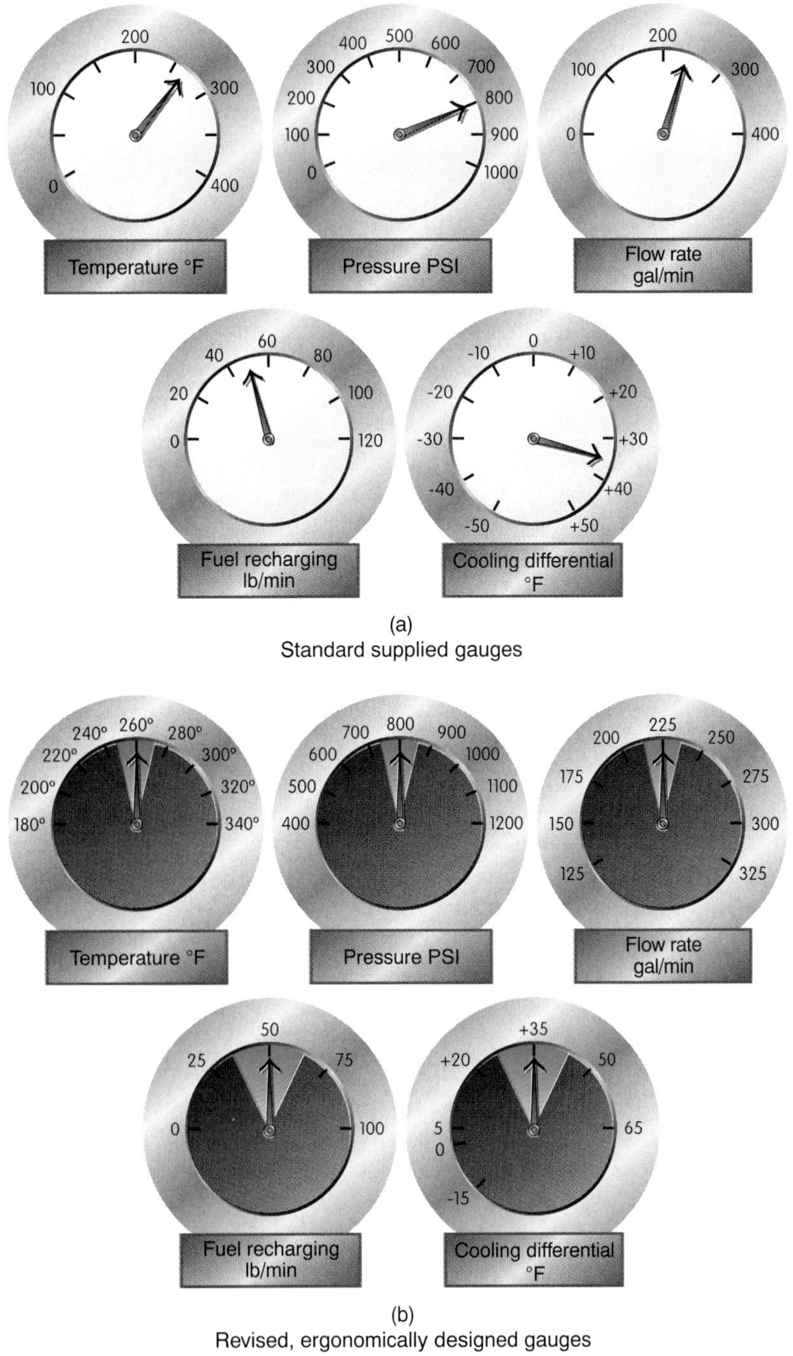

FIGURE 10.7 Ergonomic design of gauges.

Japanese term that means to "mistake-proof" a process. The idea of making mistake-proofing a systematic part of job design is due primarily to the work of Shigeo Shingo (he used the term *mistake-proofing* rather than the old term *fool-proofing* because workers thought they were fools if their process had to be *fool-proofed*). Mistake-proofing involves setting up procedures or work aids that eliminate mistakes.

One common mistake *poka-yoke* has been successful in eliminating is the omission of a component in an assembly or a container. Shingo shows how a simple change in job tasks can eliminate this mistake.[10] Yamada Electric made a switch that required workers to insert two springs. The workers would withdraw one spring from a large box, insert it into the switch, perform some other assembly tasks, then withdraw a second spring from the box and insert it, and then finish the assembly. The springs were small, and once inserted they were not visible. Sometimes the workers forgot whether they had put both springs in the switch. The result was that sometimes they opened a switch to check whether both springs were installed, and at other times they did not notice that a spring was missing and the switch went out defective. After observing the process, Shingo suggested that an extra task be added to the job. The worker would first withdraw two springs from the box, put them on a small plate, and then insert them into the switch when needed. If a spring remained on the plate at the end of assembly, the worker would know he had forgotten to insert it. Notice that this added a task to the job and increased assembly time slightly, but even more time was saved because workers no longer had to disassemble switches when they thought a spring might be missing. Moreover, the defect rate dropped to zero.

More extensive discussions of *poka-yoke* can be found in Shingo's books. Other *poka-yoke* techniques that have been applied successfully are weighing boxes to make sure all the pieces that are supposed to be in them are enclosed, placing sensors on components so that an alarm sounds if the sensor is not in the correct position when assembled, and using sensors that will stop the production line if a worker's hand does not withdraw a component from each box of parts.

TRAINING

All the effort put into selecting job content, designing work methods, and utilizing appropriate tools and ergonomic design is wasted if employees are not trained well to utilize this work. The philosophies and techniques of employee training are the subject of entire books and will not be addressed here. But it is interesting to note that the companies most widely recognized for their worker productivity invest a much higher percentage of their revenues in employee training than the average company.

Employee training is an investment, not an operating expense like raw materials. When an employee's skills are improved and broadened, the benefits accrue to the organization for years; they are not consumed by the production of a single product. Employee training should not be a one-time investment. Given the rapidly changing world in which we must live and work, continuous training and education are both necessary and financially rewarding for both the employee and the employer. For example, in 1991 when demand for autos decreased dramatically, AAP St. Mary's Corporation, an automobile wheel supplier, did not lay off its workers. Instead it shut down its plant for seven weeks and taught them analytical and statistical techniques. The payoff was that after work resumed, productivity increased by over 50% and material costs per wheel decreased by 55%.[11]

---

[10] See Shigeo Shingo and Alan Robinson (eds.), *Modern Approaches to Manufacturing Improvement: The Shingo System*, Productivity Press, Cambridge, MA, 1990, p. 217.

[11] Thomas O'Boyle, "Two Worlds: Under Japanese Bosses, Americans Find Work Both Better and Worse," *Wall Street Journal*, Nov. 27, 1991.

10.4 WORK STANDARDS

Once a job has been designed or redesigned, a company needs to know how much work it can expect from the people holding that job. **Work standards**, which specify how much output a worker should be able to produce or how much time should be spent on certain activities, play an important role in the planning and operation of organizations. For example, a standard time may be established for an employee to open envelopes, sort enclosed items, and record transactions. The **standard time** (or a corresponding standard output rate) would represent how long it should take an average but trained worker to perform the task, taking into account allowances for rest, restroom breaks, machine breakdowns, and other unavoidable delays.

Many people associate work standards, and the methods used to establish them (such as motion and time study), with piece-rate wages and production line speed-ups. Unfortunately, for many years this was, in fact, the major use of work measurement data and work standards, and there were many abuses. However, time standards have many important uses other than compensation, and most companies now use them primarily for planning.

There are at least four uses for standard time data and work standards: (1) employee performance evaluation and compensation, (2) production and personnel scheduling, (3) product costing and pricing, and (4) process design and capacity planning.

1. ***Employee Evaluation and Compensation.*** Not all workers perform at the same level of quality and productivity, but work standards can help managers determine whether or not workers are performing their jobs at a satisfactory level and highlight those cases that are out of the ordinary. Especially for newly designed jobs, work standards can be used to set target production rates, which can then be used for performance evaluation. In some industries this performance evaluation is tied directly to monetary compensation. That is, workers' pay is a direct function of how much they produce above or below some standard production rate.
2. ***Personnel and Production Scheduling.*** Even when work standards are not used for personnel evaluation or compensation, accurate work standards are important for production and personnel scheduling. To schedule production jobs and machines efficiently, there must be accurate estimates of how long the processing will take. Time standards are a primary source of data for these estimates, which form the basis for the production scheduling methods described in Chapter 16. Similarly, suppose a company has a backlog of products it must make to fill customer orders. To know how many workers must be scheduled, whether they need to work overtime, and when the orders can be delivered, the company must be able to estimate how much time will be required for each job. These estimates are often based on standard time data. Major errors in these data can lead to poor scheduling, over- or understaffing of operations, and late delivery of orders.
3. ***Product Costing and Pricing.*** For a variety of reasons, companies want to know how much it costs to produce each product. For example, if a company is asked to bid on supplying a new product for a customer, the company must have some way to estimate the amount of work required and its approximate production cost in order to set a competitive yet profitable price. Standard time information is an important component of this cost-estimating process.
4. ***Process Design and Capacity Planning.*** Two strategic uses of standard time infor-

mation are for process design and capacity planning. The task times used to design repetitive production processes in Chapter 8 and the estimated service times used to design queueing systems in Chapter 9 may be derived from standard time data. In addition, as companies project future demand for their products, they must be able to determine whether or not they will able to satisfy this demand with their current facilities. Standard time information is often used to estimate capacity, especially in cases, such as job shops, where the production capacity of a facility is affected by the product mix.

Methods for developing work standards are discussed in the following section.

10.5 WORK OBSERVATION AND MEASUREMENT

To perform the methods analysis described in Section 10.3 and to establish work standards requires observation and measurement of work methods to determine what a person is currently doing and how well he or she is doing it. Work observation and measurement were important aspects of early scientific management. Frederick Taylor and the Gilbreths closely observed how workers performed various tasks, timed them, and measured their productivity as a function of their work methods.

The usefulness and popularity of work measurement methods have fluctuated over time. Some highly regarded organizations, such as UPS, have used work measurement and time-based performance standards extensively, while many other organizations have eschewed such approaches. To understand better the controversy and potential benefits, we discuss the more common forms of work measurement here.

MOTION AND TIME STUDY

Motion and time study is a formalized procedure for observing and timing worker movements to determine the time required for each movement or task. In some cases, information can be timed and recorded as the work is being done. In other cases, it is better to videotape the worker and record the times of movements afterward. If the number of distinct movements or activities is small enough and the amount of time spent doing each one is long enough, then real-time recording of the data is feasible. This approach has the advantages of low cost, flexibility, and adaptability. For example, if a worker moves away from his normal work area or repositions his body to make it difficult to see exactly what is being done, a human observer can often move accordingly to identify and time the action. Real-time motion studies do not work well, however, if several tasks are being performed, with little time spent on each. The observer/recorder simply cannot watch and time rapid movements quickly enough. In addition, workers may change their behavior when observed; they may intentionally slow down or misrepresent the difficulty of the work to discourage establishment of excessively fast work standards, or they may simply be distracted.

Videotaped motion studies are usually performed using a stationary camera (having someone walking around with a camera can be even more distracting and intimidating to a worker than having a human observer). Videotaped time studies are more accurate because the timing and recording can be done after the fact and checked. By slowing the videotape and retiming the activities, it is possible to measure more rapid and refined movements. However, this is a more expensive process and is less well suited for jobs that require workers to move around.

EXAMPLE 1

Figure 10.8 is a typical time-study data collection form. Normally the anticipated actions or tasks are listed in advance with room to add other tasks that occur unexpectedly. The observer will record the "running times" (labeled R in Figure 10.8) when tasks begin and end, that is, the time since some starting time, 0.00. The actual task or movement times (labeled T) can be computed later from the running times. Beginning times do not have to be recorded separately because the beginning time of one task is often the ending time of the previous task. For example, in Figure 10.8 the observer begins the time study at 7:45. The worker being observed has a job that involves performing five tasks in sequence: a, b, c, d, and e. Employee 27 begins task a at time 0:00 (7:45:00) and ends it at time 0:16 (16 seconds later). He then begins task b at time 0:16 and ends at time 0:40, and then begins c at time 0:40 and ends at time 1:02. So task a took 16 seconds, b took 24 seconds, and c took 22 seconds. The time study continues long enough to get several observations of each task, so an average value can be estimated. Notice that in the fifth cycle there was a delay between tasks c and d, which was recorded on the bottom line.[12]

[12]Sometimes tasks are timed in increments of 1/100 minute or 1/1000 minute rather than in seconds.

Performance will vary with the skill and effort of the worker, so the observer must also estimate the worker's performance relative to some hypothetical average worker working at a normal level of effort. This estimated performance is called the **performance rating**, with values above 100% indicating greater than normal performance and

Operation: Fabrication of flange # 50 **Operator: T. Dewey # 27**

Date: 6/10/93 **Starting time: 7:45** **Ending time: 8:05** **Observer: V. Sauter**

Allowance rate: 12%

Activity description		Work cycles										Summary				
		1	2	3	4	5	6	7	8	9	10	Total	Mean	Perf.R	Normal time.	Std. time
a. Load flange	R	0:16	2:00	3:50	5:40	7:20	10:15	12:07	14:51*	16:38	18:20					
	T	16	15	19	22	15	16	17	15	18	16	169	16.9	110	18.59	20.82
b. Machine flange	R	0:40	2:22	4:15	6:02	7:45	10:40	12:30	15:21	16:59	18:42					
	T	24	22	25	22	25	25	23	30	21	22	239	23.9	105	23.9	26.77
c. Rotate and lubricate	R	1:02	2:46	4:36	6:25	8:06	11:09	12:55	15:40	17:22	19:11					
	T	22	24	21	23	21	29	25	19	23	29	236	23.6	105	24.8	27.78
d. Polish	R	1:30	3:15	5:02	6:50	9:41*	11:32	13:20	16:03	17:50	19:38					
	T	28	29	26	25	31	23	25	23	28	27	265	26.5	100	26.5	29.68
e. Remove and clean	R	1:45	3:31	5:18	7:05	9:59	11:50	13:36	16:20	18:04	19:54					
	T	15	16	16	15	18	18	16	17	14	16	161	16.1	110	17.7	19.82
Delay *	R					9:10			14:36							
	T					1:04			1:00							

FIGURE 10.8 Time study data sheet.

values less than 100% indicating less than normal performance. Performance ratings can be used to adjust the observed task times when establishing work standards, as shown below.

USING TIME STUDY DATA TO COMPUTE STANDARD TIMES

Although the details of establishing time/work standards vary from organization to organization, the standard time for a task can be expressed as

$$\text{standard time} = \text{normal time} \times (1 + \text{allowances})$$

where

$$\text{normal time} = [\text{average observed task time}] \times [\text{performance rating}]$$

or

normal time = total elemental task time or total predetermined task time (e.g., from MTM analysis, as discussed below)

and

allowances = time allowances for unavoidable delays (e.g., breakdowns), personal needs (restroom breaks), and worker fatigue, expressed as a fraction of total work time

EXAMPLE 1 (CONTINUED)

In Figure 10.8 the average observed time for task a is 16.9 seconds. The estimated performance rating (PR) is 110%, so the normal time for the task is 16.9 seconds × 1.10 = 18.59 seconds. The company has estimated the work allowances to be 12% of normal working time, so the standard time = 18.59 seconds × (1 + 0.12) = 20.82 seconds.

ELEMENTAL STANDARD-TIME DATA

If an organization has collected time study data over a period of time for a variety of workers, it can be advantageous to organize and codify these data. Time standards derived from a large collection of observations for common (elemental) tasks or movements are called **elemental standard times**. Standard times derived this way tend to be more accurate because they are based on different workers at different times; individual idiosyncrasies or data outliers are reduced in their effect. The database may include task times for the same tasks but performed by workers in different jobs. For example, two workers in different departments or even different facilities, making different products, may each perform a drilling task on the same general material using the same equipment. Information on their tasks times could be merged to obtain more robust time standards.

Elemental time standards make it easier to establish time standards for new jobs. We simply decompose the new job into its specific tasks or movements, match the tasks to existing elemental standard times, and add them up to get the overall standard time for the task or unit of production. This approach eliminates the cost and disruption of an actual time study, and it is often more accurate thanks to the broad set of data underlying the standards. Of course, some time study activities should be done on a continuing basis to keep the elemental time data current.

MICRO-MOTION AND PREDETERMINED MOTION-TIME DATA

In their attempts to optimize work performance, Frank and Lillian Gilbreth initiated micro-motion analysis. **Micro-motion analysis** decomposes tasks into their most basic movements and activities, such as reaching, grasping, turning, or comparing. The Gilbreths recorded work activities using motion pictures and then evaluated the films frame by frame. From this scrutiny they identified the most basic motions that made up almost all jobs, which they named **therbligs** (*Gilbreth* spelled backward, reversing the *t* and *h* to make it pronounceable). They could then measure the time and effort required for each therblig, construct a task or job motion by motion using the most efficient movements, and estimate the resulting normal task time.[13]

This type of analysis is too expensive and time-consuming for most organizations to do themselves. Consequently, a number of independent organizations have used laboratory experiments to measure a wide variety of micro-motions accurately. The resulting data are contained in tables that group different types of movements by their key characteristics and the normal time it takes to perform the movement. The most widely used predetermined motion-time system is **methods time measurement (MTM)**, which is a proprietary product of the MTM Association for Standards and Research.

Predetermined motion-time data systems have the advantages of elemental standard-time systems in the sense that they can be used to develop standards and methods before a job exists. They have the added benefit of being based on laboratory data and therefore are not biased by company-specific differences; that is, they provide an objective performance benchmark, which includes performance rating. Their use does, however, require considerable training and cost, and they are applicable only to very structured, repetitive jobs.

WORK SAMPLING

The three work measurement methods described above are used primarily to study jobs that are repetitive or to study specific tasks of a job that are performed frequently. Many jobs, such as doctor, store manager, police officer, stock broker, and accountant, involve a wide variety of activities, many of which are not standard and are not performed in any fixed sequence or with a specific frequency. For these jobs the most important issue is what fraction of time is spent doing each type of activity, or what fraction of time is spent on productive work versus idle time or relatively unproductive work. Because of the large number of different activities these people perform and the irregular pattern of tasks, it might take weeks or months of constant observation to answer such questions using a time-study approach. For example, a police officer may spend 10% of her time testifying in court, but court appearances may occur once per month for two full days. A time study for a three-week period might never observe this activity, so it would miss an important part of the officer's job.

Work sampling consists of sample observations of a worker's activities made over some extended period of time. Rather than observing the worker constantly for a week or two, the data collector may observe the worker at 25 instances during each day for one or two months. These observations are simply "snapshots" of what the worker is doing at that moment, such as "filling out patient record" or "walking to loan department," and they require only a few seconds of work by the observer. If enough observations are made over a sufficiently long and representative period of time, the fraction of time the worker spends on various activities can be estimated statistically.

---

[13]An interesting application of micro-motion analysis has been in the area of athletic performance. It is now common practice for coaches to film athletes and study their micro-motion movements, as well as those of competitors, to identify the best mechanical methods. These videos can then be used to train athletes, just as industrial micro-motion videos are used to train workers.

Work sampling studies are easy and inexpensive to perform. One observer can monitor and sample the behavior of several workers during the same period; the observer usually only needs to make a quick observation and write a few words or check a box.

Although work sampling can be used to establish work standards, the standards, and their use, tend to be different from those developed using the other three methods for repetitive work. The standards derived from work sampling might specify the proportion of time that should be devoted to specific activities rather than the amount of time required to perform a task. For example, a securities company may study 20 stock brokers using work sampling to see what percentage of time they spend calling potential new customers. The company may then relate this information to the amount and type of new business generated by these brokers and establish a standard: "brokers should spend between 10% and 15% of their time calling potential new customers." Those who are spending significantly more or less of their time on this activity may be encouraged to adjust their behavior, especially if their performance (measured by revenue generation) has been subpar. In 1994 U.S. President Bill Clinton's staff even used work sampling to determine that he was spending too little time working on economic and domestic policy.[14]

The Work Sampling Procedure

Although work sampling is relatively easy to perform, there are a few important aspects of the procedure to note. The first step is to identify the purpose of the study and what activities are of primary interest. For example, a retail store that believes its sales associates spend too little time waiting on customers and too much time doing other things might specify four types of activity: waiting on customers, interacting with customers in other ways (e.g., handling complaints or returns), doing other work (e.g., straightening products), and spending idle time. A work sampling study could help to answer the key question of how much time is being spent waiting on customers and identify where time is being spent instead.

Once this issue has been resolved, the next step is to plan the technical aspects of the work sampling study: how many observations to take and when to take them. Normally we would specify the desired level of accuracy and the desired level of statistical confidence in advance, such as "the observed (estimated) percentage of time spent waiting on customers should be within 3% of the actual value with 95% confidence." The minimum number of observations necessary to achieve this accuracy and confidence can be computed by equation (10.1).

$$\text{number of observations required} = N = [z^2\bar{p}(1-\bar{p})]/e^2 \tag{10.1}$$

where $\bar{p}$ is the proportion of observations during which the target activity (e.g., waiting on customers) is performed, e is the maximum absolute error desired, and $z = 1.65$ for a 90% confidence level, 1.96 for a 95% confidence level, and 2.33 for a 99% confidence level (these are the critical z-values for a two-tailed test of significance).

Notice that the required sample size is affected by the actual proportion of time, $\bar{p}$, that the target activity is performed. Because this is not known in advance, the sample size may be determined iteratively. An initial estimate of the proportion of time spent on the target activity is made, and then a preliminary sample size is derived.

[14]See Rick Wartzman, "Why President Clinton Spends 62.5% More Time on Policy," *Wall Street Journal*, Mar. 14, 1995.

EXAMPLE 2

Suppose we want our estimate of the proportion of time spent waiting on customers to be within 0.03 of the actual proportion of time with 95% confidence. If we believe the actual proportion of time spent waiting on customers is around 0.40, then the minimum sample size required to verify this would be

$$N = [1.96^2(0.40)(1 - 0.40)]/(0.03)^2 = 1024 \text{ observations}$$

After obtaining 100–200 observations, we would check the proportion of observations during which the target activity was performed, and if it deviated much from 0.40 we would recompute a new sample size to finish the study. An alternative to this iterative approach is to use $\bar{p} = 0.50$ because this will maximize the value of N in equation (10.1); this would ensure that the sample size is always at least as large as the amount needed for statistical accuracy.

In addition to sample size, we need to determine when and how often to observe. Suppose we decide to take 1100 observations over the course of 22 days; this means we will take 50 observations per day. Within each day we do not usually take the observations at uniform increments of time for at least two reasons: (1) There may be some cyclic pattern of work, so that the worker may do one activity for 10 minutes, then change to another for 10 minutes, and then change back to the original activity for 10 minutes. If the observations are timed to be done every 20 minutes, the observer would always see the same activity being done and conclude that 100% of the worker's time was spent on that activity. (2) A random observation pattern makes it more difficult for workers to mislead the observer. For example, if a worker has deduced that he is being observed every 20 minutes, he may change what he is doing just before he expects an observation, so the observer will see what the worker wants the observer to see (e.g., changing idleness to work).

One possible scheme to generate random observation times is given in the following example.

EXAMPLE 3

Suppose we decide to make 50 observations during each eight-hour day. We could select 50 random numbers from a random number table, such as Table T3.1 (on page 488), or generate random numbers from a computer (remember, random numbers have values between 0 and 1), multiply them by 480 (there are 480 minutes in eight hours), and use the results as the observation times. For example, suppose the first random number was 0.2946; then 0.2946 × 480 minutes = 141.4 minutes, so we would take an observation at 141 minutes after the shift begins. Obviously all 50 observation times would be determined in advance and arranged to form an observation schedule for the observer collecting the data.

10.6 THE WORK ENVIRONMENT

Since the beginning of the twentieth century, it has been recognized that the productivity and quality of work, as well as the safety and health of workers, are affected by the physical environment in which they work.

ENVIRONMENTAL FACTORS AFFECTING WORKER PERFORMANCE

Even highly skilled and motivated workers do not perform at their best in noisy, dirty, and poorly configured facilities. Extensive research has determined which aspects of the physical environment most influence work performance and what physical conditions are best for work. The following are some of the factors that matter most.

1. ***Cleanliness.*** One of the outstanding characteristics of showcase production facilities is their cleanliness. Dirty, cluttered facilities degrade production performance in several ways: (a) airborne dust, dirt, and chemicals can cause physical discomfort or illness for workers; (b) dirt and oils can impair vision and cause components and tools to become slippery and difficult to handle; (c) debris can harm tools and machinery and prevent them from working correctly; (d) impurities in the air or in work areas can contaminate chemical reactions or products, such as integrated circuits; (e) cluttered work areas make it difficult to find parts and tools, to move freely, and to maintain safety. Finally, neat, clean facilities tend to create a more positive attitude among workers, which can be especially important for those who interact directly with customers.
2. ***Illumination.*** The best amount and type of illumination, and the best location of the lighting source, depends on the type of work performed. For example, workers performing detailed work normally need more illumination than those monitoring chemical process controls. Similarly, the best location and type of light for people working at computer screens is different than for those doing other types of work. The importance of lighting has been demonstrated by the Reno, Nevada, post office, where improved lighting increased mail-sorting productivity by 8%.[15]
3. ***Temperature and Humidity.*** Clearly, the temperature and humidity of a work environment will affect worker performance. The best temperature depends primarily on the amount and type of work performed. Workers performing normal office work and other jobs with little physical activity are often most comfortable at temperatures in the 65°–70°F range. The more strenuous the work, the lower the preferred temperature. For example, brick masons and others who perform very strenuous work may prefer temperatures around 60°F. Temperature and humidity are not only important for workers' comfort, but can also influence their attention and concentration, ultimately affecting the quality of the product and the safety of the job.
4. ***Noise and Sound.*** *Noise*, which can be defined as any unwanted sound, is troublesome primarily because it distracts workers. This can cause productivity and quality losses and can be a potential safety hazard. In some cases noise can be physically harmful, causing pain or hearing loss. Ideally, we would like to reduce the amount of noise generated, such as by using less noisy machines, putting machines on a cushioned base, or having fewer people in a confined area. When this is not sufficient or possible, three other options exist: (a) separate workers from

[15]From Rochelle Sharpe, the "Work Week" column, *Wall Street Journal*, Nov. 22, 1994.

the noise more effectively, such as by building walls between workers and the source of noise; (b) use muffling materials, such as acoustical walls and ceilings that absorb or deflect sound; (c) use protective equipment such as ear protectors. For example, the percussionist for a major orchestra has a low Plexiglas wall around the timpani to protect other musicians from the loud volume, and the percussionist wears earplugs while playing certain musical pieces.

Although noise, by definition, is undesirable, other sounds can be beneficial. Music can create a more relaxed and comfortable work environment. Alarms and other sound signals can draw a worker's attention to a machine stopping or a customer entering a store.

SAFETY AND HEALTH

Employee safety and health should be central considerations when designing jobs and the workplace. In addition to reducing productivity, dangerous and unhealthy work environments are costly to the company, due to accidents, work disruptions, illness and absenteeism, disability insurance premiums, safety violations, and lawsuits. Workers suffer directly from physical pain and discomfort, mental and emotional anguish, loss of income, shortening of life, and, in extreme cases, death.

Accidents

Unsafe work environments manifest themselves in two forms: accidents and chronic occupational disabilities or diseases. **Accidents** are discrete events that result in worker injury, machine damage, or work stoppage, such as a person being run into by a fork lift, a hand being caught in a machine, or a back or arm being injured by lifting an object. There are two primary causes of accidents: unsafe acts and unsafe conditions. Unsafe acts include not using protective equipment, driving vehicles too fast, being impaired by alcohol or drugs, using improper tools, and disregarding safety procedures or overriding safety equipment. Unsafe conditions include poor lighting, cluttered floors and aisles, exposed chemicals, improper ventilation, equipment with obstructed views, poorly maintained equipment (e.g., badly worn truck brakes or tires), exposed wires, and slippery stairs and walkways.

The first steps in improving safety are to collect and analyze existing data, specifically the file of accident reports. By law most companies are required to fill out a report on any accident that results in worker injury, and most companies go beyond this to include reports on any accident that results in serious downtime or machine damage. By evaluating past accidents, we can often identify their most common locations and causes. This information provides a good starting point for the next step; observation of the operations. By walking around a facility and closely observing the operations, especially those places and activities where accidents have occurred, we can often identify unsafe behaviors or conditions that could contribute to accidents.

To reduce accidents, an organization should address both employee behavior and unsafe conditions. One of the most difficult steps in improving safety is to convince people that their actions or facilities are in fact unsafe. Accidents usually are not the result of a single unsafe act or condition, but rather of two unsafe acts or an unsafe act and an unsafe condition occurring together. Frequently, an unsafe condition will exist for a long time, or an employee will repeatedly perform an unsafe act, without an accident. Consequently, many employees do not perceive their actions or work conditions as unsafe. Only when the two are put together, or when a series of unsafe acts occurs simultaneously, does an accident occur.

Once the hazards have been identified, actions to eliminate or reduce them are often straightforward. For example, better lighting, guardrails, protective clothing and devices, emergency exits, good housekeeping, proper ventilation, and wide aisles can solve many safety problems. Eliminating unsafe acts is more difficult. Accident prevention certainly requires good training. Workers need to know not only how to do their work efficiently, but also how to do it safely and how to react in emergencies. Even workers who receive good training require constant reminders of how to work safely. For example, posting signs that remind employees of *specific* safe *behaviors*, such as "Wear your ear protectors," "Wash your hands," or "Keep safety protector in place," is effective; however, general statements such as "Be alert" or "Be safe" have little benefit. Employee safety can also be a responsibility of quality circles (these are discussed more fully in Chapter 11). In quality circles employees can discuss ways to improve safety, as well as quality and productivity. Finally, whether safety is achieved through quality circles or by having a labor–management safety team, labor and management must work together to make a safety program effective.

Employee Health

Steele's Markets has reduced the frequency of repetitive motion injuries substantially by using both right-hand and left-hand scanners and rotating workers among them. This reduces physical stress by distributing the work across both hands rather than concentrating it on one.

Although we most commonly think of accidents as the major focus of safety, employee health has become an even greater, if less obvious, problem. Some job-related health problems, such as black lung in the coal industry, hearing loss from exposure to loud noises, and chemical, radiation, and asbestos exposure have been recognized for a long time. But other health problems, such as carpal tunnel (repetitive motion) syndrome from working at keyboards or assembly operations, respiratory damage from offices with high levels of pollutants and other irritants, and general work-related stress are becoming widespread. The potential costs and human suffering from occupational health problems are at least as great as those from work accidents, and eliminating them requires the same level and type of investigation and analysis. Health damage has been reduced by redesigning equipment, restructuring tasks, changing lighting, and increasing work breaks. For example, Sara Lee Corporation reduced its carpal tunnel syndrome disabilities by 95% through simple changes in equipment and work methods, and Steele's Markets, a grocery chain in Colorado, reduced such injuries by 35% by installing both left-hand and right-hand scanners for its checkers and rotating workers between them.[16]

Worker safety and health has become an important aspect of business in the United States because of the Occupational Safety and Health Act (OSHA) passed by Congress in 1970. This act enables the U.S. Labor Department to set working condition standards and regulations, to inspect the working conditions of organizations to make sure that they are safe and healthy, to cite companies, to fine them, and even to shut them down for repeated safety violations.

10.7 THE ORGANIZATION OF WORK

Our discussion up to this point has focused primarily on the physical aspects of work mechanics and the work environment. An equally important aspect of job design is the organization and structure of the work system. Even good mechanical work methods will not produce maximum performance if the organizational structure, human–machine integration of the work system, and incentives of the workers are flawed. Let us briefly consider these factors.

[16]See Joan Rigdon, "The Wrist Watch," *Wall Street Journal*, Sept. 28, 1992; and Lourdes Lee Valeriano, "Busines Bulletin" column, the *Wall Street Journal*," Apr. 28, 1994.

SOCIOTECHNICAL SYSTEMS AND AUTONOMOUS WORK GROUPS

In the traditional view of job design, workers had an assigned set of tasks that could, and should, be performed by individual workers in most cases or by small teams when required by the difficulty of the job. There was also a strict organizational hierarchy whereby line workers were assigned to perform specific physical or clerical tasks, and any creative or decision-making work was done by supervisors or staff. This classical organization has created problems for many industries because it lacks job variety, slows decision making, and leaves unclear the responsibility for quality.

In response to these problems, many organizations have implemented an alternative work organization based on the sociotechnical systems approach. The **sociotechnical systems** approach recognizes that by creating compatibility among equipment, technology, and workers and by recognizing the social community formed by workers, more productive systems with greater job satisfaction will result.

The sociotechnical systems approach is organized around **autonomous work groups** (also called **self-directed teams**). Although the scope of work and degree of autonomy vary from situation to situation, these teams often control the design of specific jobs, hiring of personnel, staffing and scheduling of jobs, planning and scheduling of production, quality control, process improvement, and even purchasing and materials management. By their very nature, autonomous work groups embody the principles of worker empowerment, decentralized decision making, job enlargement, job enrichment, and job rotation. Several benefits can result from the use of autonomous work groups.

1. ***Job Satisfaction.*** Members of autonomous work teams perform a wider variety of tasks and utilize a wider variety of skills. In many cases, they are also collectively responsible for the production of an entire product, including the design of the system. For most workers this wider variety of work, the increased responsibility, and the opportunity to see and be part of the production of an entire product all improve job satisfaction.
2. ***Process Improvement.*** Because of their involvement in and responsibility for an entire work unit, work groups more readily suggest and implement improvements in the production process. This is especially true if the compensation system is designed to reward the group for productivity and quality improvements.
3. ***Product Quality.*** Because the group has sole responsibility for an identifiable product, poor quality reflects directly on the group. As a matter of pride, as well as financial compensation, the group will have a strong incentive to maintain or improve product quality. A key element, however, is that the group must have the authority as well as the responsibility to take the actions necessary to solve quality problems.
4. ***Productivity Improvement and Cost Reduction.*** All the above factors contribute to greater productivity. Workers with pride, who are continually improving the production process and are focused on quality, will increase productivity over time. Peer pressure becomes an important force in the system. Anyone not doing the job well or not showing up for work puts an added burden on the other members of the group. Peer pressure keeps team members from performing below par. The reduction in absenteeism alone will often give an immediate boost to productivity. In addition, the group structure greatly reduces and simplifies the managerial structure and decreases the staff needed to run the operations.
5. ***Flexibility and Responsiveness.*** The cross-training inherent in autonomous work groups makes it easier for the group to function when someone is absent. In addi-

Autonomous work teams promote process improvement, while improving productivity, product quality, and production flexibility.

tion, the decision-making autonomy and distribution of skills among workers help the group to respond to production changes and emergencies because an entire group of workers can focus on one problem or activity without the need for several levels of authorization.

The use of autonomous work groups is spreading throughout industry. Companies such as John Deere, General Motors, Owens-Corning Fiberglas, Levi Strauss, and Lakeland Regional Hospital have reported substantial cost reductions and quality improvements by using such teams. The sociotechnical approach, however, requires considerable care and resources to be devoted to employee selection and training. It also mandates a cultural change that transfers authority from management to workers (so-called **empowerment** of workers), and in many cases it eliminates the need for many middle managers. (For example, as mentioned earlier, Corning's Blacksburg plant now has only one supervisor for every 60 workers.)

Not all workers want or can handle the greater demands that autonomous work groups require. Hiring and assigning reluctant workers to autonomous work groups is like trying to force a square peg into a round hole. In addition, the managers of many companies want the benefits of the sociotechnical approach, so they create the work team form, but they are unwilling to transfer the authority and responsibility the teams need. They then blame the concept rather than their implementation. Finally, the sociotechnical systems approach is training intensive. It requires not only substantial initial training and indoctrination but also substantial ongoing training. Without this ongoing training the system will eventually deteriorate.

Despite the attractive features and successes of the sociotechnical systems approach, it is not universally beneficial. Both management and line workers must be prepared to accept this change, and in some instances they simply are not. In other cases, the type of work may not lend itself to a team approach—for example, in some individualized, craftsman-type systems.

JOB FLEXIBILITY IN TIME AND LOCATION

Normally, we envision a worker performing his or her job in the company's factory or office. With improvements in telecommunications and the fundamental changes in the nature of many jobs, the location and timing of a job have become new job design features. Many jobs, such as sales, software development, insurance underwriting, and even word processing, can be done at an employee's home and according to an employee's personal schedule without interfering with the company's other operations. Having employees work at home has several advantages:

1. There can be significant savings in office and work space. For example, Compaq Computer cut its administrative expenses nearly in half, and Perkin-Elmer eliminated 35 branch sales offices, by having their sales forces work from home.[17]
2. Employees save commuting time and spend more time on productive work. IBM reported that its "mobile" sales offices have increased the time spent with customers by 15–20%. (They also produce less pollution by eliminating the drive to work, and they reduce traffic congestion, which saves other people time as well.)
3. Employees who would not be able to work on a fixed schedule at another location (because they take care of children or an infirm family member) may be very productive working on a flexible schedule at home.

Just as workers must have certain skills and training to do any job, people who are assigned or allowed to work at home on a flexible schedule should be assessed to determine whether or not they have the discipline and mental disposition to work in that environment. Some people produce very well, but others miss the social aspects of a company work site or lack the discipline or time-management skills to work productively at home. Even for those with a desire and disposition to work at home, some training for that environment can be very helpful.

Managers who supervise home-based workers also have an added burden of maintaining communication and employee morale. Some workers feel isolated, and some work too much when they do not have the structure of a fixed workday at an office.

When employees *do* work primarily on company sites, their performance and satisfaction can sometimes be improved by allowing flexibility in timing. Many companies have adopted "flex-time" policies, which allow workers some degree of flexibility with respect to when they start and finish their work days and when they take breaks. For example, a typical flex-time system may allow workers to begin work anytime between 7:30 A.M. and 10:00 A.M. and finish work between 4:00 P.M. and 6:30 P.M. This flexibility has several benefits:

1. It makes it easier for employees to bring children to and from school or to run errands that cannot be done at night, thereby reducing employee stress. The benefits of this arrangement are clearly stated by Robert Lambert, executive vice president of Carter Hawley Hale Stores, Inc.: "If you can help employees meet their outside responsibilities, you're going to have a more productive, more turned-on and more energized work force."[18]
2. Employees can schedule commuting time to avoid traffic jams, which not only saves them time but reduces the stress they bring to work.
3. Some people simply feel better and work better at different times during the day, and flex-time allows them to take advantage of this fact.

Of course, there are some jobs in which flex-time is not practical. Some production processes must operate with full crews on a fixed schedule; retail stores must have em-

[17]See Sue Shellenbarger,"Overwork, Low Morale Vex the Mobile Office," *Wall Street Journal*, Aug. 17, 1994.

[18]From Sue Shellenbarger, "More Companies Experiment with Workers' Schedules," *Wall Street Journal*, Jan. 13, 1994.

ployees available when the store opens and closes. But anytime a job is designed or redesigned, one should ask whether it must occur at a specific location and/or a specific time. When spatial or temporal flexibility is a viable option, these issues should at least be considered on their merits and not be dismissed out of hand.

COMPENSATION AND INCENTIVES

Regardless of how workers are organized and how specific jobs are designed, the compensation system should be constructed to promote the behavior the organization desires rather than obstruct or discourage it. There are two general compensation systems: time based and output based. **Time-based compensation systems** pay workers for the time they spend on the job, regardless of the quality and quantity of output produced. Some workers are paid on a per-hour basis, so if they work extra hours they receive extra compensation. Time-based compensation for managerial, administrative, and professional workers more often is defined in terms of a monthly salary with an implied amount of work time, such as 40 hours per week, but additional time spent on the job is not specifically compensated. **Output-based compensation systems** tie pay directly to performance by paying employees according to the amount and quality of output produced. In some cases, an employee's entire compensation may be output based (such as traditional piece-rate systems in which a worker is paid for each piece of output produced). But more commonly, output-based systems are used in conjunction with time-based or guaranteed minimum pay, which rewards performance above some standard.

Time-based compensation systems tend to be more widely used. Their principal advantages are these: (1) they are easy for an employer to use; (2) many employees prefer the security of knowing what their pay will be; and (3) in many cases the type of work, such as that of an executive secretary or plant engineer, does not lend itself easily to an output-based system. The disadvantage, of course, is that time-based systems do not create an explicit financial incentive for employees to perform at their highest level. These systems are viewed as promoting adequate but not outstanding performance.

It is for this reason that output-based or **incentive compensation systems** are normally implemented. For jobs whose output can be easily measured, and where the contribution of an employee or group of employees to that output is identifiable, output-based compensation provides a good incentive for workers to do their best. In some cases, such as delivering telephone books or selling furniture, **individual incentive systems** can be designed based on the performance of each individual.

In other cases, such as a production line, a work cell, or a maintenance team, the contribution of an individual worker cannot be separated and is, in fact dependent on the performance of the other workers in the unit. In these cases, **group incentive systems** can be designed based on the performance of the entire work unit. Such systems are especially appropriate for organizations that use autonomous work groups. A number of group incentive plans have been used successfully, such as the **Scanlon plan**, developed by Joseph Scanlon in the 1930s, and the **Lincoln plan**, which has been used at Lincoln Electric Company for over 75 years. These group incentive plans have several features in common: they share the financial gains resulting from cost reductions and productivity improvements with the workers (called **gain-sharing**), and they provide official mechanisms such as suggestion systems and worker committees to improve production methods. The important thing is that the measures of performance on which the incentive is based should promote the desired behavior. So, for example, an incentive scheme based only on the *number* of widgets processed will encourage workers to handle as many widgets as possible, but if there is no component that takes into account product quality or coordination with the production schedule or with other workers, the incentive system may produce a large volume of poor-quality products and produce them at the wrong time, so overall company performance will be worse than without the system. Output-based compensation systems often fail because they reward only output volume, neglecting quality, customer service, and cooperation with other work units.

A more recent development in group incentive systems involves basing compensation, at least partially, on unit or companywide profitability rather than on cost or output measures. As work teams are given more autonomy, they can influence the revenue side of the profit equation, not just the cost side. For example, suppose that with a small additional cost a team is able to provide a better product (e.g., customize it or make it more durable) or produce and deliver it more quickly. An incentive system based on production cost would discourage the team from achieving such results. However, a scheme based on profit generation might encourage the improvement in quality or service because additional revenues might far exceed the additional cost. Wabash National, which has gone from a start-up to a market leader in manufacturing truck trailers in just 10 years, attributes part of its success to a profit-sharing program that distributes 10% of its after-tax profits to workers. More generally, economist Douglas Kruse has found that companies that use profit sharing achieve greater gains in productivity than those that do not.[19]

UNIONS

A discussion of job design and worker organization would not be complete without some mention of the role of labor unions. Despite the decrease in union membership, tens of millions of U.S. workers are still represented by unions. In addition to compensation, labor unions are actively involved in job design, work rules, work organization, and safety and health.

For many years, some of the major labor unions in the United States, Canada, and the United Kingdom actively obstructed the redesign and reorganization of work that has been discussed here. Rather than allowing companies to enlarge and enrich jobs, unions fought to keep jobs narrowly defined and specialized. Even small changes in job tasks or work methods were contested, with higher wages or newly defined jobs being the price of approval. Rather than allowing workers to take on some traditional responsibilities of management, such as process improvement, decision making, and even purchasing authority, many unions insisted on strict separation of traditional management and staff functions from those of line workers. Fortunately, in the past decade this antichange, antimanagement attitude has disappeared from most unions. Often the need to create a more cooperative atmosphere was recognized first by union members rather than union leaders. As unemployment increased, workers realized that they needed to change the way things were being done to protect their jobs. They also recognized that these changes could make their jobs more enjoyable and fulfilling rather than burdensome.

Although unions still sometimes interfere with the redesign and reorganization of jobs, partnerships between unions and management are becoming the norm. Many of the companies that enlarged jobs, instituted autonomous work groups, cross-trained workers, and actively involved workers in quality assurance and process improvement

[19]See Robert Rose, "A Productivity Push at Wabash National Puts Firm on a Roll," *Wall Street Journal*, Sept. 7, 1995; and Neela Bannerjee, "Rebounding Earnings Stir Old Debate On Productivity's Tie to Profit-Sharing," *Wall Street Journal*, Apr. 12, 1994.

did so with the cooperation of labor unions. Surprisingly, some of the greatest successes occurred in companies with a history of militant unions, such as the company highlighted in this chapter's "On the Job" section, John Deere. Many consultants involved in major job reorganizations found that if the unions were treated as partners, they tended to cooperate. Where there was union resistance, it usually resulted from management's unwillingness to accept the union's role in the change or from a history of labor–management animosity so great that it could not be overcome.

The bottom line is that in many industries and companies labor unions are part of the environment in which organizations must operate. Their existence is neither inherently good nor bad, but they must be included in the change process from the beginning, and the anticipated benefits to the workers must be made clear and be shared with them if success is to be achieved.

SUMMARY

- The **job content** is the set of tasks or responsibilities comprising the job. An important issue in establishing job content is the degree of specialization.
- **Job enlargement** is the horizontal expansion of job responsibilities: having more tasks of a similar skill level.
- **Job enrichment** is the vertical expansion of a job to include tasks of higher (and possibly lower) skill level.
- **Cross-training** is the practice of training workers to perform several different jobs so that they can be moved among jobs as needed for greater productivity and flexibility or as part of a **job rotation** program.
- **Jobs** should be designed so that humans are assigned to do those tasks for which they are most suited, such as problem solving, responding to new situations, and improving processes, while machines are used to perform simple, structured tasks requiring speed, repetition, and strength.
- **Methods analysis** is a structured procedure for observing, measuring, and improving work methods.
- The **process flow diagram, process chart, worker-machine chart,** and **team-activity chart** are tools for collecting and organizing work data to simplify work methods.
- Good job design should utilize **coprocessing (parallel processing)** of tasks and **back-hauling** of materials.
- **Work aids**, such as guide bars and power tools, and good **ergonomics** in tools and work areas can improve productivity, reduce worker fatigue and accidents, and improve worker health.
- **Work standards** can play an important role in scheduling, product costing and pricing, and process design, as well as performance evaluation and compensation.
- **Motion and time study, elemental standard times,** and **micro-motion analysis** are used to evaluate structured, repetitive jobs. **Work sampling** is most appropriate for evaluating less-structured, multitask jobs.
- The work environment influences both the productivity and quality of work and directly affects safety and worker health.
- **Autonomous work groups (self-directed teams)**, when combined with appropriate financial incentives, have improved productivity and profitability.
- Allowing flexibility in the location and time of work can improve productivity and employee morale and make more jobs accessible to qualified people.

KEY TERMS

accidents **537**
active phase **523**
automation **514**
autonomous work groups (self-directed teams) **539**
back-hauling **524**
behavioral (psychological) school **511**
carpal tunnel (repetitive motion) syndrome **526**
coprocessing (parallel processing) **523**
cross-training **512**
elemental standard times **532**
empowerment **540**

ergonomics **525**
gain-sharing **542**
group incentive systems **542**
incentive compensation systems **542**
individual incentive systems **542**
job **509**
job content **510**
job description **509**
job enlargement **511**
job enrichment **511**
job rotation **512**
Lincoln plan **542**
methods analysis **516**
methods time measurement (MTM) **533**
micro-motion analysis **533**
motion and time study **530**
output-based compensation systems **542**
passive phase **523**
performance rating **531**
poka-yoke **526**
process chart **516**
process flow diagram **516**
Scanlon plan **542**
scientific management school **510**
simo (simultaneous motion) chart **517**
sociotechnical systems **539**
standard time **529**
team-activity chart **521**
therbligs **533**
time-based compensation systems **542**
work aids **524**
work sampling **533**
work standards **529**
worker-machine chart **518**

KEY FORMULA

Number of observations, N, needed in work sampling to achieve a maximum absolute error of e:

$$N = [z^2\bar{p}(1-\bar{p})]/e^2$$

where $\bar{p}$ is the proportion of observations during which the target activity occurred and $z = 1.65$ for a 90% confidence level, 1.96 for a 95% confidence level, and 2.33 for a 99% confidence level.

SOLVED PROBLEMS

Problem 1: Using the data in Figure 10.8 (p. 531), compute the standard time required to perform activity c (rotate and lubricate).

Solution: The average task time is 23.6 seconds and the performance rating is 105%, so the normal task time is 23.6 seconds × 1.05 = 24.8 seconds. With a 12% allowance, the standard time is 24.8 seconds × 1.12 = 27.8 seconds.

Problem 2: Suppose a company wanted to estimate the proportion of time a worker spends on the phone, using a work sampling study. If the company wants its estimate, $\bar{p}$, to be within 0.04 of the actual proportion with 99% confidence, compute the minimum number of observations needed in the study. (Assume the company wants to be conservative and uses $\bar{p} = 0.50$ to compute the sample size.)

Solution: From equation (10.1) the minimum number of observations required is

$$N = [2.33^2(0.50)(1-0.50)]/(0.04)^2 = 848 \text{ observations}$$

where 2.33 is the z value for a 99% confidence estimate and $e = 0.04$ is the maximum error desired in the estimate.

Problem 3: A company has decided to observe a worker six times each hour as part of a work sampling study. Use the first six random numbers in Table T3.1 (p. 488) to compute random observation times for an hour and arrange them in order.

Solution: We will express observation times in terms of minutes. So we will multiply each random number times 60 minutes to obtain the observation times. The first random number is

0.8008, so the random observation time is 0.8008 × 60 minutes = 48 minutes. The other observation times will be:

$$0.2273 \times 60 \text{ min} = 14 \text{ min}$$
$$0.2212 \times 60 \text{ min} = 13 \text{ min}$$
$$0.5624 \times 60 \text{ min} = 34 \text{ min}$$
$$0.4937 \times 60 \text{ min} = 30 \text{ min}$$
$$0.9508 \times 60 \text{ min} = 57 \text{ min}$$

So the observer would make observations at 13, 14, 30, 34, 48, and 57 minutes after the start of the hour.

Discussion and Review Questions

1. What are the primary advantages and disadvantages of job specialization (i.e., assigning individual workers to perform a narrow range of tasks)?
2. What is the difference between job enlargement and job enrichment?
3. Think of a job you or someone you know have had. Give specific examples showing how that job could have been enlarged and explain the benefits of doing so.
4. Think of a job you or someone you know have had. Give specific examples of how that job could have been enriched and explain the benefits of doing so.
5. What is job rotation, and what supporting actions must an organization take to implement it successfully?
6. What is cross-training, and what are its main benefits?
7. Give a specific example, not mentioned in the book, of how the addition of automation made a worker more productive. How did the job have to be redesigned to benefit from the automation?
8. What is the purpose of methods analysis? How is it related to process design?
9.* Based on your experience, give a specific example, not mentioned in the chapter, of how a group of workers could be coordinated better to accomplish some job. Draw two team activity charts, one of the original procedure and the other of the improved procedure, to illustrate your point.
10. What is coprocessing? Give a specific example from your own work experience showing where coprocessing could have been used to improve job efficiency.
11. What is back-hauling? Give a specific example from your own work experience showing where back-hauling could be used to improve job efficiency.
12. Based on personal experience, show how the addition of a specific simple tool could make a job or task (including a household task) more productive and less fatiguing.
13. From your own experience, cite a job (or product) that had a bad ergonomic design. Suggest how its design could have been changed to alleviate the ergonomic problems.
14. Give a specific example, not mentioned in the book, of how *poka-yoke* could be used to eliminate a mistake in a *service job*. First, describe the mistake. Then describe your proposed *poka-yoke* technique and explain how it would prevent the mistake from occurring.
15. What are the primary purposes of motion and time study?
16. Why and when would someone use elemental standard-time data instead of motion and time study?
17. When should work sampling be used instead of motion and time study? Give a specific example of a job that could be improved by performing a work sampling analysis; what types of information would the study identify, and how could this help improve the job?
18. Why would an organization want work standards? How could these standards be used to improve operations?
19. From your own experience, give an example of how the physical environment harmed your work. What could have been done to improve the situation?
20. Identify a specific unsafe condition or unsafe act on campus that is likely to lead to an accident. State specifically how you would eliminate the condition or cause people to not perform the unsafe act (simply telling them not to do it is insufficient).
21. How would you respond to the question "If autonomous work groups are so productive a work structure, why were they not discovered and used earlier?"

22. Give an example of a job, not mentioned in the book, that might be done better or as well at home instead of in an office or factory. Justify your answer.

23. What characteristics of a job would make it difficult to use an output-based compensation system? How might these characteristics be changed when implementing a compensation system?

PROBLEMS

1. Use the data in Figure 10.8 (p. 531) to compute (a) the normal task time and (b) the standard task time for activity e (remove and clean). In part (b), assume the allowance rate is 8% rather than the 12% given in the figure.

2. Suppose a job involving three tasks was observed for eight cycles. The observed times and performance ratings for each task are as follows:

	Observed Time (min)								Performance
Task	1	2	3	4	5	6	7	8	Rating
A	1.22	1.01	1.52	1.30	1.04	1.26	1.17	1.28	105%
B	2.45	2.06	2.43	2.29	2.97	2.38	2.42	2.09	100%
C	1.13	0.89	0.96	1.04	0.92	1.23	1.05	1.02	110%

(a) Compute the average time required for each task. (b) Compute the normal time required for each task. (c) Compute the standard time required for each task, assuming an allowance rate of 11%.

3. Suppose a job involving four tasks was observed for seven cycles. The observed times and performance ratings for each task are as follows:

	Observed Time (min)							Performance
Task	1	2	3	4	5	6	7	Rating
A	0.79	0.83	0.90	1.01	0.89	0.79	1.00	115%
B	1.24	1.60	1.43	1.34	1.51	1.37	1.43	105%
C	0.45	0.61	0.59	0.70	0.81	0.68	0.59	110%
D	0.90	0.79	0.77	0.78	0.86	0.81	0.77	100%

(a) Compute the average time required for each task. (b) Compute the normal time required for each task. (c) Compute the standard time required for each task, assuming an allowance rate of 10%.

4. Suppose a company wants to perform a work sampling study to determine the proportion of time a worker spends meeting with clients. The company wants the estimated proportion to be within 0.05 of the actual proportion with 95% confidence. Compute the minimum number of observations necessary in the study, assuming the company initially believes the proportion is approximately 0.30.

5. Suppose a university wants to use work sampling to determine the proportion of time a professor spends working on campus committees and other service activities. If the university wants its estimate to be within 0.04 of the actual proportion with 90% confidence, what is the minimum number of observations required? (The university's preliminary estimate of the proportion is 0.20.)

6. A retail store manager wants to use work sampling to study the activities of her workers in the sports equipment department. The manager wants to randomize both the days selected for observation and the times during the days when observations occur. (a) During the next 50 days the manager would like to select 10 days for observation. Use the random numbers in column 1 of Table T3.1 (page 488) to determine which 10 of the 50 days (numbered 1–50) should be selected for observation. (b) On days when observation is performed, the manager would like to take 12 observations of the department during each two-hour period. Use the random numbers in column 2 of Table T3.1 to determine when the observations should occur for one of these periods. Express the randomized observation times in terms of minutes after the beginning of the period. In each part, arrange the observation days and times in increasing order.

7. A hospital wants to use work sampling to study the conditions of its emergency room (how crowded, loud, or chaotic it is). Each day it will observe one of the three operating shifts. (a) Use the random numbers in column 1 of Table T3.1 (p. 488) to determine which shift should be observed each day during the first 10 days of observation. (Hint: if a random number has a value between 0 and 1/3, assign it the first shift, 1/3 to 2/3 the second shift, and 2/3 to 1 the third shift). (b) During the first day of observation, compute 10 random observation times using the random numbers in column 2 of Table T3.1. Assume that a shift lasts 480 minutes, and express the observation times in terms of minutes after the shift begins. Arrange the observation times in increasing order.

8.* Select a job (such as cashier at the university cafeteria) and observe the worker performing that job for one hour. Construct a worker-machine chart that tracks the activities of the worker and any supporting machine.

9.* Select a group of workers that work together or coordinate their work. Observe them for one hour and construct a team-activity chart showing what each worker is doing over time.

CASE

Ferro-Stamping, Inc.: A Job Redesign Case

Ferro-Stamping, Inc. (FSI), is a medium-sized metals machining company. FSI has several multipurpose machine tools, such as drills, stamping presses, grinders, and other metal-processing tools. FSI is a job-shop operator that produces customized components for several hundred customers in order sizes ranging from 50 to 5000 (although smaller and larger order sizes occasionally occur). A typical product may undergo five or more separate operations on different machines. Every time there is a product change on a machine, the operator spends from 15 minutes to 3 hours setting up the machine, which may involve changing dies, changing drill settings, lubricating the machine, cleaning the machine, loading input materials, and checking startup quality.

Even when working at full capacity, FSI found it difficult to make a profit and was beginning to have trouble delivering products on time. Roger Hendrick, the vice president of marketing, believed that prices could not be raised significantly without a loss of customers. So the company looked to Michael Jones, the vice president of operations, to reduce costs and improve delivery. Jones had been vice president for only eight months, but he had come to believe that the plant was not operating as efficiently as possible. He decided to hire an experienced operations consultant, Ann Dolay, to be his chief of staff, with primary responsibility for studying current operations and recommending improvements.

After a few days of intensive study, Ms. Dolay decided that the stamping department was one of the biggest problem areas. It had low machine utilization, yet products seemed to take longer to make it through that department than any other.

Department-level Analysis

Ms. Dolay developed the flow diagram presented in Figure 10.9, which shows the activities that interact with the stamping department. Metal is cut into blanks in the cutting department. A material handler then moves the blanks by handlift truck from the cutting department to the stamping department. The stamping department has two stamping presses with changeable dies that cut the blanks into metal sheets with a customer-specified pat-

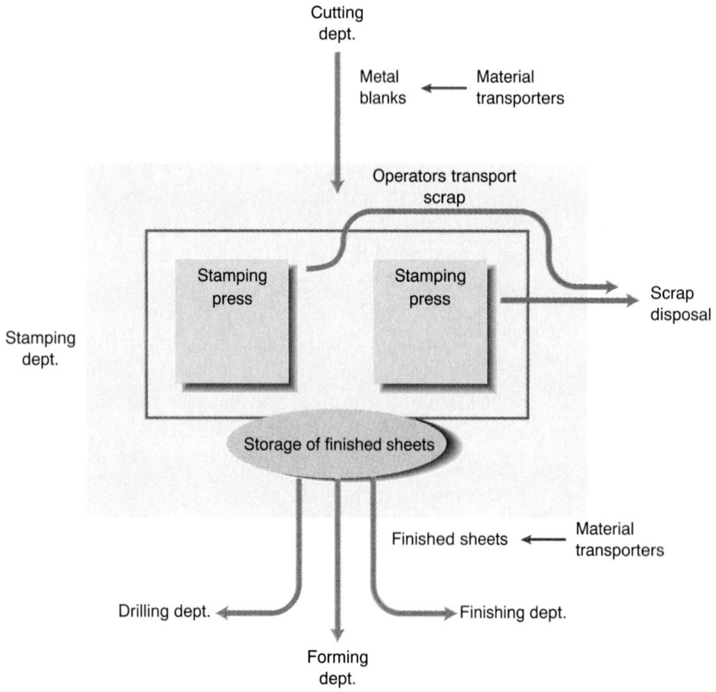

FIGURE 10.9 Flow diagram of FSI's stamping operation.

tern. The stamped sheets are removed from the press by its operator and left on the floor until they are moved by a material handler to the next department for processing, which could be either the drilling department, the forming department, or the finishing department.

Ms. Dolay's initial analysis indicated that material in the system was being handled too often. It was handled by an operator who loaded it on or removed it from the machine; then it sat until it was moved to another department by a material handler. In some cases, it had to be handled another time because it was initially moved to an inconvenient storage area, since no area near the stamping press (or other machine) was available when it was originally moved. Ms. Dolay also felt that there was always a large amount of work-in-process inventory on the floor. When she asked some workers about this, they said that the large inventory was intentional: this way there was always product to run when needed.

Stamping Press Operator Analysis

Ann Dolay's next step was to study the stamping press operators. She performed a time and motion study of an operator and then converted it into several worker-machine charts, one of which is given in Figure 10.3 (on page 519). Her analysis indicated that the stamping press operators were fully utilized only 66% of the time; 29% of the time they were semi-idle while monitoring the machine's operator, and 5% of the time they were completely idle while waiting for materials to be delivered or waiting for maintenance workers when the machine broke. In addition, the stamping presses were idle over 60% of the time, yet this operation was a bottleneck in the production system.

Redesigning the Press Operators' Job

Based on this research, Ms. Dolay focused on redesigning the jobs of the press operators. First, she applied the principle of coprocessing to reduce idle and semi-idle time. The first major improvement was to get the operators to perform some of the machine setup work for the next job while the current job was running, thereby converting semi-idle time into active work time. Any additional semi-idle time was then used to remove scrap from the press and transport it to the scrap collection area instead of waiting until after a production run was completed. These two changes reduced the amount of semi-idle time from 29% to less than 10%.

This change still did not address the idle time spent waiting for material deliveries and for repair crews to fix broken presses. So the next step was to change the material transport process itself. Ms. Dolay recommended that the material handler jobs be eliminated and that machine operators in each department do their own material handling. Her original idea was to have the stamping press operators find and transport their input materials from the cutting department. After stamping them, they would leave the finished sheets near the end of the press for workers from the next department (drilling, forming, or finishing) to find and transport them. This transport work could normally be done during semi-idle time, and it would eliminate idle time now spent waiting for materials. With this change, operator utilization was projected to increase to over 90% and press utilization to approximately 55%, as illustrated in Figure 10.4.

After testing this new job design for a few days, Ann Dolay decided that having machine operators in each department find and transport their input materials, and simply unload their output products near their machines, was not working as well as anticipated. Finding the materials in the cutting department often took longer than expected. The press operators then had to run back to their presses, turn them off at the completion of a load, and go back to the cutting department to finish their search. Not only did this running back and forth reduce efficiency, it was creating a safety hazard; operators were in such a hurry and were so distracted that two minor accidents occurred. Even when they did find the next order quickly there seemed to be extra material handling, as the operators were using the same hand trucks to move the input for the current job while trying to prepare the input for the next job.

Ms. Dolay's solution was to reverse the material-handling responsibility. The operators in each department would be responsible for transporting their *output* to the next production department. The input loads would then be more accessible to the operators in the next department, who could easily search for the next input load while monitoring their equipment. In addition, Ms. Dolay devised large labels that could be put on the loads to make them easier to find. Finally, each operator was provided with two hand trucks instead of one. One truck was used to position input materials, and the second was kept at the output side to transport output to the next department. When this new procedure was tested, Ms. Dolay found that material-handling time was lower than when designated material handlers were used; in other words, the job was being done faster with fewer workers. The net results of these changes were that worker utilization increased to over 90%, operators were no longer pressed for time, their unsafe behavior vanished, and the two transport workers were moved to other jobs in the plant.

Micro-Motion, Methods and Ergonomic Analysis

Although there was significant improvement in worker productivity and an effective increase in stamping capacity of over 30%, Ms. Dolay was still troubled by the low press utilization rate of 50–55%. The primary causes of the low utilization were machine setup time between production jobs, machine idle time while the operator was removing scrap or loading input blanks, and machine breakdowns. Ms. Dolay attacked these problems in the following ways.

Setup Improvements

With the above job revisions, the press operators were now using their (previously semi-idle) time during press operation more efficiently, preparing the setups for the next job. But Ms. Dolay was convinced that the time required to finish the setups could be reduced. With the operators' approval, she videotaped their setups for several days. Together with the operators, she then reviewed the setups and found several improvements that could be made. The study indicated that one of the most time-consuming and exhausting parts of the setup involved changing the dies in the press. The original method had the operators use a lift containing a set of arms that would stick out under the die. The lift would be raised under the die, the bolts holding the die unscrewed, and the die lowered onto the arms. The lift would then be lowered, the old die removed, and the new die put on the lift. The lift was then raised to the press, the die bolted onto the press, and then the lift lowered and moved away.

Ms. Dolay, the operators, and the plant engineer worked together to modify the press and the lift. First, the press was changed so that the dies could be slid into and out of channels that held them instead of having to lift and lower the dies vertically. The bolts, which were time-consuming to tighten and loosen, were replaced with simpler fasteners that required only one turn of a wrench to lock and unlock. The new lift (shown in Figure 10.10) had two sets of arms, one above the other. While the previous job was running on the press, the new die could be put on the lift and raised to the correct level. At the end of the run, the old die would be released and slid onto the top set of arms, the lift raised slightly and the new die slid into the press and locked into place, and the lift lowered.

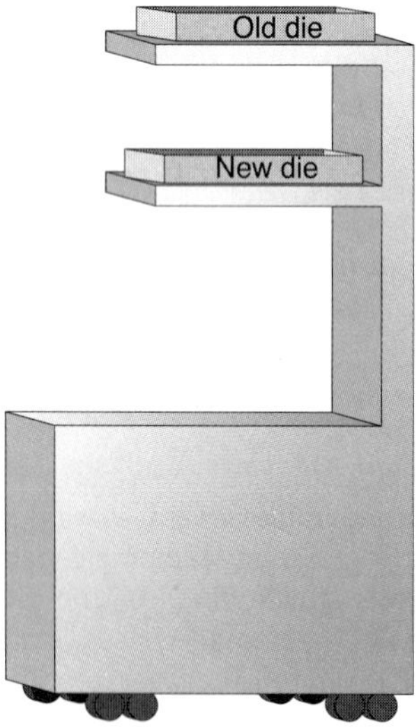

FIGURE 10.10 Revised lift design for FSI.

The second major problem was that the operators had to spend several minutes positioning guide arms and braces on the stamping table so that the metal blanks would be in the correct position when the die stamped them. This was a trial-and-error process: position the guides and braces, stamp a blank, and then correct the position. The operators and Ms. Dolay decided that they could put two-dimensional markings (similar to those on graph paper) on the stamping table. For products that were run repeatedly, they could record the precise settings of a table setup, so when that product was produced again, they could position the guides and braces correctly the first time. Although some further adjustment of the settings was usually needed because of slight variations in dies and their installation, much of the trial-and-error time was eliminated. In addition, the time required for startup and quality checks was reduced because setups were more consistent.

Scrap Removal

In the original stamping press design, after each blank was stamped, the scrap (metal trimmed off) was swept by a mechanical arm into a bin. The location of the bin below the press limited the size of the bin, so scrap had to be removed every 30 minutes of running time, making removal and replacement of the scrap bin slow and difficult. At the suggestion of the operators, the plant engineer made a simple and inexpensive modification to the scrap collection system. The engineer added a slanted chute under the scrap opening so that the scrap slid sideways to the scrap bin that was now located to the side of the press. The new scrap bin was larger, so that it had to be emptied only every 45 minutes of run time, and it reduced the time needed to remove the full bin and replace it with an empty bin from 65 to 25 seconds (it still had to be transported to the scrap area and unloaded). The biggest benefit of this change was that it freed up time for setup preparations, which were occurring more frequently with the previous improvements.

Maintenance

Although press breakdowns were uncommon, Ms. Dolay met with the maintenance crew and together they studied the maintenance records for the machines. The maintenance personnel believed that many of the breakdowns could have been eliminated, or at least the time between failures extended, if the machines had been lubricated and cleaned more often. After discussions among the press operators, the maintenance crew, and Ms. Dolay, they decided to experiment by having the press operators lubricate and clean key parts of the press when they had time. The job changes already implemented had all but eliminated idle and even semi-idle time; the press operators were either preparing setups or moving materials. However, they did find that every two to three hours they had a few minutes for extra lubrication and cleaning of the presses. Although the benefits of maintenance changes are usually long term, within a few months FSI did perceive a slight reduction in press breakdowns, which they attributed to the regular lubrication and cleaning.

Final Result

In addition to the major job changes described above, further study of the videotapes allowed the operators to improve the sequencing and physical movements of some of their setup activities, as well as their input-loading activities. The net effect of all of these changes was that worker utilization rose to nearly 97%. There was always something productive for the workers to do; press utilization increased to 65%, which increased effective stamping capacity by over 50%; in-process inventories in the department decreased; the two transport workers were moved to other jobs; and the press operators felt that their jobs were more interesting without their being overworked.

An unanticipated outcome of these improvements was that the press operators, who in the past had operated almost independently, began to view themselves as a team. When one operator had time, he would help the other operator with scrap removal or lubrication. This teamwork was made formal when Ms. Dolay recommended that the department compensation plan be revised so that workers would be evaluated and rewarded based on department performance. This became the first step in a move toward autonomous work teams. The success in the stamping department provided motivation for the same in-depth study of other departments. The framework for the improvement process was established: work closely with the employees in the department, use observational methods to understand better what is actually being done, use simple mechanical aids to improve work, and apply the principle of coprocessing whenever possible.

QUESTIONS

1. After these changes, the two press operators were busy nearly 100% of the time, while the presses were still idle approximately 35% of the time. Explain how you could increase production capacity further without buying another press.
2. Suppose you added another employee to the stamping department who would be primarily a helper. What tasks would you have this person do to increase the total output of the department, not simply give the two operators more free time?

SELECTED READINGS

BARNES, FRANK. "Principles of Motion Economy: Reviewed, Revisited, and Restored," *Proceedings of the Southern Management Association*, Atlanta, 1983, pp. 297–299.

BARNES, RALPH M. *Motion and Time Study: Design and Measurement of Work* (7th ed.), Wiley, New York, 1980.

BLEAKLEY, FRED R. "How an Outdated Plant Was Made New," *Wall Street Journal*, Oct. 21, 1994.

BOWERS, BRENT. "Businesses Fall in Love with Workplace Safety Teams," *Wall Street Journal*, Mar. 16, 1994.

GALEN, MICHELE, ET. AL. "Work and Family," *Business Week*, June 28, 1993, pp. 80–88.

GLECKMAN, HOWARD, ET AL. "The Technology Payoff," *Business Week*, June 14, 1993, pp. 57–68.

GLECKMAN, HOWARD, ET AL. "Bonus Pay: Buzzword or Bonanza," *Business Week*, Nov. 14, 1994, pp. 62–64.

GLOBERSON, S., and R. PARSONS. "Multi-Factor Incentive Systems: Current Practices," *Operations Management Review*, Vol. 3, Winter 1985, pp. 33–36.

KELLY, KEVIN, and PETER BURROWS. "Motorola: Training for the Millennium," *Business Week*, Mar. 28, 1994, pp. 158–163.

KONZ, STEPHAN. *Work Design: Industrial Ergonomics* (3rd ed.), Wiley, New York, 1990.

KRUSE, DOUGLAS L. *Profit-Sharing: Does It Make a Difference? The Productivity and Stability Effects of Employee Profit-Sharing Plans*, W. E. Upjohn, Kalamazoo, MI, 1993.

MCCORMICK, E. J., and MARK SANDERS. *Human Factors in Engineering and Design* (7th ed.), McGraw-Hill, New York, 1992.

RIGDON, JOAN E. "The Wrist Watch: How a Plant Handles Occupational Hazard with Common Sense," *Wall Street Journal*, Sept. 28, 1992.

SHELLENBARGER, SUE. "More Companies Experiment with Workers' Schedules," *Wall Street Journal*, Jan. 13, 1994.

SHINGO, SHIGEO. *Modern Approaches to Manufacturing Improvement*, Alan Robinson, ed., Productivity Press, Cambridge, MA, 1990.

WOODSON, WESLEY E., and PEGGY TILLMAN. *Human Factor Design Handbook* (2nd ed.), McGraw-Hill, New York, 1992.

CHAPTER 10 SUPPLEMENT

LEARNING AND EXPERIENCE CURVES

10s.1 LEARNING EFFECTS

10s.2 THE RATE OF LEARNING AND LEARNING CURVES

10s.3 DERIVING A LEARNING CURVE
Choice of Production Units
Forgetting

10s.4 EXPERIENCE CURVES

10s.1 LEARNING EFFECTS

From our everyday experiences, we know that the first time we perform a skilled job, such as changing a faucet, installing a CD-ROM in a computer, or making a shirt by hand, it takes much longer to do than an experienced worker would take. But the next time we perform the same job, we can perform it faster and often with better quality (assuming the time interval has not been so large that we have forgotten how to do the job). Each additional time we do the job, we become faster and better at it, although the incremental gains are usually less each time as we become more skilled and experienced. This improvement in productivity and quality of work as a job is repeated is called the **learning effect**.

When designing jobs, establishing work standards, scheduling production, and planning capacity, it is important to know at what rate worker productivity will increase through learning. For example, if it takes a worker 10 hours to make the first 50 units of a product, we do not want to plan on it taking 10 hours for every additional 50 units; otherwise, we will underestimate our true production capacity and overstaff our operations. The role of worker learning in production, its effect on production costs, and ways to measure it were first popularized 60 years ago by T. P. Wright.[1]

10s.2 THE RATE OF LEARNING AND LEARNING CURVES

The labor content (in person-hours per unit) required to make a product, expressed as a function of the cumulative number of units made, is called a **learning curve**. As illustrated in Figure 10S.1, as the cumulative number of units of the product made increases, the per unit labor requirement decreases but at a decreasing rate.[2] We normally express the rate of learning in terms of how quickly the labor requirements decrease as we double the cumulative amount of output. Specifically, we say that an activity exhibits an x % **learning rate** or has an x % **learning curve** if the amount of labor required to make the $2n$th unit of the product is x % of that required to make the nth unit.

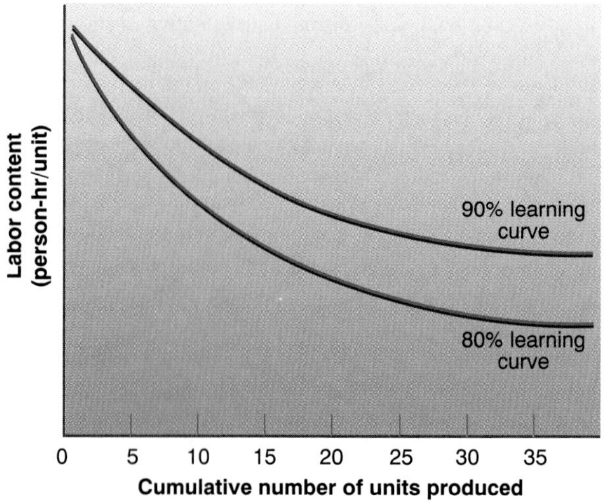

FIGURE 10S.1 Learning curves.

[1] T. P. Wright, "Factors Affecting the Cost of Airplanes," *Journal of the Aeronautical Sciences*, Vol. 3, 1936.

[2] The learning curve is sometimes plotted using logarithmic scales. In that case, the curve becomes a straight line.

EXAMPLE 1

Suppose it took 20 hours to make the first unit of a product, 16 hours to make the second unit, and 12.8 hours to make the fourth (the third unit requiring some amount between 12.8 and 16) hours. We would say that this activity has an 80% learning curve because the amount of labor required to make the second unit was 80% of the first, and the amount of labor to make the fourth unit was 80% of the second. (Notice that the smaller the value of x, the greater the learning and the more rapidly the labor content decreases.)

More generally, the amount of time required to make the nth unit of the product will be

$$T_n = T_1 \cdot n^a \qquad (10S.1)$$

where

T_n = time to make the nth unit (in person-hours)

T_1 = time to make the first unit

$a = (\ln x)/(\ln 2)$

x = learning rate (expressed as a decimal; so an 80% rate = 0.80)

EXAMPLE 1 (CONTINUED)

For Example 1 the amount of time required to make the third unit should be approximately

$$T_3 = 20\,[3^{(\ln 0.8)/(\ln 2)}] = 14.04 \text{ person-hr}$$

Although equation (10S.1) is easy to use for computing the approximate labor content to make a unit of product, frequently we would like to know the cumulative amount of work required to make the first n units or the second n units. Rather than computing the labor content for each unit and adding them together, we have constructed tables to simplify the process. For some common learning rates, Table 10S.1 lists the time required to make the nth unit of a product and the cumulative time required to make the first n units of a product, expressed as a fraction or multiple of T_1. For example, if the learning rate is 75%, Table 10S.1 tells us that the time required to make the sixth unit is 0.475 of T_1 and the cumulative amount of time required to make the first six units is 3.934 T_1.

10s.3 DERIVING A LEARNING CURVE

Equation (10S.1) and Table 10S.1 are useful in predicting how much time will be required for future production of the product. However, to use them, we must know the learning rate for that product. Therefore, the first step in using learning curves is to collect historical data on the amount of labor required to make the first n units of the

TABLE 10S.1 LEARNING AND EXPERIENCE CURVE FACTORS

	Learning Rate									
	70%		75%		80%		85%		90%	
Unit Number	Unit Time	Total Time	Unit Time	Total Time	Unit Time	Total Time	Unit Time	Total Time	Unit Time	Total Time
1	1.000	1.000	1.000	1.000	1.000	1.000	1.000	1.000	1.000	1.000
2	.700	1.700	.750	1.750	.800	1.800	.850	1.850	.900	1.900
3	.568	2.268	.634	2.384	.702	2.502	.773	2.623	.846	2.746
4	.490	2.758	.562	2.946	.640	3.142	.723	3.345	.810	3.556
5	.437	3.195	.513	3.459	.596	3.738	.686	4.031	.783	4.339
6	.398	3.593	.475	3.934	.562	4.299	.657	4.688	.762	5.101
7	.367	3.960	.446	4.380	.534	4.834	.634	5.322	.744	5.845
8	.343	4.303	.422	4.802	.512	5.346	.614	5.936	.729	6.574
9	.323	4.626	.402	5.204	.493	5.839	.597	6.533	.716	7.290
10	.306	4.932	.385	5.589	.477	6.315	.583	7.116	.705	7.994
11	.291	5.223	.370	5.958	.462	6.777	.570	7.686	.695	8.689
12	.278	5.501	.357	6.315	.449	7.227	.558	8.244	.685	9.374
13	.267	5.769	.345	6.660	.438	7.665	.548	8.792	.677	10.052
14	.257	6.026	.334	6.994	.428	8.092	.539	9.331	.670	10.721
15	.248	6.274	.325	7.319	.418	8.511	.530	9.861	.663	11.384
16	.240	6.514	.316	7.635	.410	8.920	.522	10.383	.656	12.040
17	.233	6.747	.309	7.944	.402	9.322	.515	10.898	.650	12.690
18	.226	6.973	.301	8.245	.394	9.716	.508	11.405	.644	13.334
19	.220	7.192	.295	8.540	.388	10.104	.501	11.907	.639	13.974
20	.214	7.407	.288	8.828	.381	10.485	.495	12.402	.634	14.608
21	.209	7.615	.283	9.111	.375	10.860	.490	12.892	.630	15.237
22	.204	7.819	.277	9.388	.370	11.230	.484	13.376	.625	15.862
23	.199	8.018	.272	9.660	.364	11.594	.479	13.856	.621	16.483
24	.195	8.213	.267	9.928	.359	11.954	.475	14.331	.617	17.100
25	.191	8.404	.263	10.191	.355	12.309	.470	14.801	.613	17.713
26	.187	8.591	.259	10.449	.350	12.659	.466	15.267	.609	18.323
27	.183	8.774	.255	10.704	.346	13.005	.462	15.728	.606	18.929
28	.180	8.954	.251	10.955	.342	13.347	.458	16.186	.603	19.531
29	.177	9.131	.247	11.202	.338	13.685	.454	16.640	.599	20.131
30	.174	9.305	.244	11.446	.335	14.020	.450	17.091	.596	20.727
31	.171	9.476	.240	11.686	.331	14.351	.447	17.538	.593	21.320
32	.168	9.644	.237	11.924	.328	14.679	.444	17.981	.590	21.911
33	.165	9.809	.234	12.158	.324	15.003	.441	18.422	.588	22.498
34	.163	9.972	.231	12.389	.321	15.324	.437	18.859	.585	23.084
35	.160	10.133	.229	12.618	.318	15.643	.434	19.294	.583	23.666
36	.158	10.291	.226	12.844	.315	15.958	.432	19.725	.580	24.246
37	.156	10.447	.223	13.067	.313	16.271	.429	20.154	.578	24.824
38	.154	10.601	.221	13.288	.310	16.581	.426	20.580	.575	25.399
39	.152	10.753	.219	13.507	.307	16.888	.424	21.004	.573	25.972
40	.150	10.902	.216	13.723	.305	17.193	.421	21.425	.571	26.543

product. From these data we can use curve-fitting procedures similar to nonlinear regression to derive a learning curve that describes the learning process and to estimate the learning rate. In Figure 10S.2 we see that the actual labor content from unit to unit will hop around and not form a steadily decreasing function. But the overall trend is approximately that of the learning curve shown in Figure 10S.2.

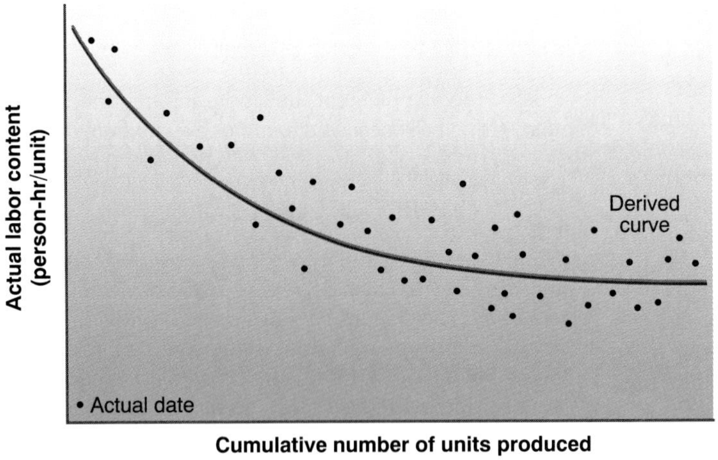

FIGURE 10S.2 Actual labor content.

In practice, we would use sophisticated methods to estimate the actual learning rate, but a crude estimate of it can be obtained easily using the following method.

EXAMPLE 2

Suppose we have the labor content for the first eight units of production.

Unit No.	Labor Content (person-hr)
1	41
2	34
3	29
4	26
5	24
6	24
7	23
8	21

For each pair of units, n and $2n$, we can compute the ratio of labor content. The average of these ratios would then be an approximation of the learning rate. For example, the ratio of labor content for items 2 and 1 is 34/41 = .829. The other relevant ratios would be:

n	$2n$	Ratio of Labor Content For Items $2n$ and n
2	4	26/34 = 0.765
3	6	24/29 = 0.828
4	8	21/26 = 0.808

The average of these four ratios is 0.807, or approximately 80%. So we might use the 80% learning curve column in Table 10S.1 to predict future labor requirements.

CHOICE OF PRODUCTION UNITS

An important issue in deriving and using learning curves is the definition of a unit of production. The unit of production in learning curve analysis need not be one actual unit of the product, such as one bolt, one baseball glove, or one automobile. For many items, the labor content in a single item is so small that it is difficult to measure and may not be meaningful. Furthermore, the rate of learning from item to item, if you produce 10,000 items per day, may be so small that the learning rate may be 99.999% and difficult to work with. Therefore, the unit of production used in expressing a learning curve may be 1000 or even 1,000,000 actual units of the product. The definition of the production unit is important because the rate of learning will be different if the learning curve is defined in terms of a single unit of the product versus 1000 units of the product. Knowing how many actual units of the product should constitute a unit of production for expressing the learning curve must be gained through experience, but a unit of production used in learning curves will normally represent at least a few hours of production, and possibly the equivalent of a month or several months of production.

FORGETTING

On an individual worker basis, the amount of time needed to perform a job will not decrease uniformly and without interruption. In fact, an area of recent research is the degree to which workers forget or lose skills and the causes of this forgetting. Forgetting is generally the result of an interruption in the production process. The degree to which a worker forgets or loses skill, and how quickly he or she will regain the previous level of skill, is primarily a function of how long the interruption is and what activities the worker performs in the meantime. A detailed discussion of forgetting and learning curves is beyond the scope of this supplement, but more information can be found in the references at the end of the supplement.

10s.4 EXPERIENCE CURVES

For most products, the per-unit real cost of production (ignoring inflation) also decreases in line with cumulative production. This cannot be due simply to worker learning and skill improvement, because that would only decrease the cost of labor, not the total cost by a comparable amount. Moreover, these cost decreases continue even though workers are replaced over time, so new workers must learn the job. Research suggests that many factors other than worker learning contribute to this cost reduction. Some of these factors are process improvements, improved equipment, better management and information flows, and exploitation of scale economies (as product volume increases, new production facilities or processes are created). The term **experience curve** (or **progress curve**), drawn from the concept of the learning curve, is used to describe these combined effects.

An experience curve looks, behaves, and can be used exactly like a learning curve, except that it expresses the *cost per unit* as a function of cumulative output rather than labor content per unit. Equation (10S.1) and Table 10S.1 can be used to predict per-unit production costs, with the understanding that T_1 is the *cost* to produce the first unit, T_n is the *cost* to produce the *n*th unit, and *x* % is the **experience rate** rather than the learning rate. For example, if it cost a company $500 to make the first unit of a product, $400 to make the second, $320 to make the fourth, and

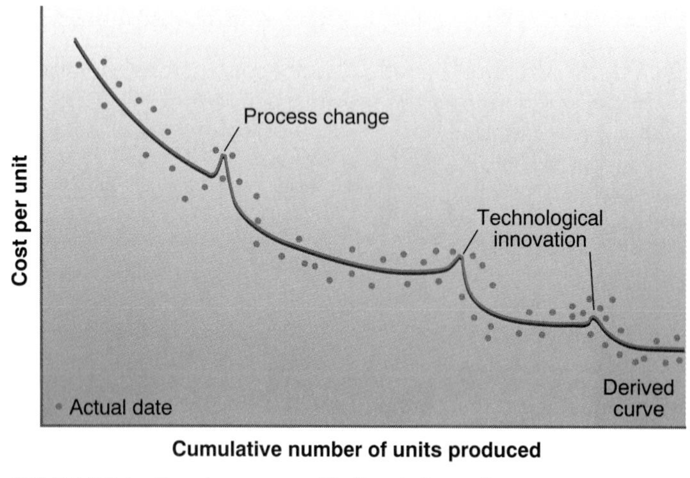

FIGURE 10S.3 Experience curve with discrete innovations.

$256 to make the eighth, we would say that the process exhibits an 80% experience curve and the experience rate would be 0.80 or 80%.

Note that the experience rate, the rate at which cost decreases, is not necessarily equal to the learning rate for the same product, and it should be derived separately. Figure 10S.3 shows that the actual per-unit cost is not smooth and constantly decreasing, and actually jumps around quite a bit. In fact, when major process or technological changes occur, the cost per unit may initially increase and then decrease rapidly, as in Figure 10S.3.

In addition to using learning curves and experience curves to schedule production and plan capacity, experience effects can be used strategically to undercut the prices of competitors while earning a good profit (see Chapter 2). Companies that have steeper experience curves and/or larger volume sales will move down the experience curve more quickly, and be able to produce at lower cost, than competitors.

SUMMARY

- The **learning curve (experience curve)** measures how the labor content (cost) per unit decreases as the cumulative number of units produced of a product increases.
- An *x* % **learning (experience) rate** means that as the cumulative number of units produced doubles, the labor content (cost) per unit decreases to *x* % of its previous value.

KEY TERMS

experience curve (progress) curve **556**
experience rate **556**
learning curve **552**
learning effect **552**
x % learning rate (*x* % learning curve) **552**

SOLVED PROBLEMS

Problem 1. A company has made 6000 units of a product. The labor content to make each thousand units is as follows:

Unit No. (000)	Labor Content (person-hr.)
1	385
2	344
3	325
4	310
5	301
6	292

(a) Estimate the learning rate for this product using 1000 units of the product as the unit of production. (b) Predict the labor requirements to make the next 2000 units.

Solution

(a) The ratio of the labor content to make the second thousand items versus the first thousand is 344/385 = 0.894. The ratios for the fourth and second thousands and the sixth and third thousands are 310/344 = 0.901, and 292/325 = 0.898. The average is 0.898 or approximately 90%.

(b) From equation (10S.1) (or using Table 10S.1), the labor required to make the seventh and eighth thousand items will be approximately

$$T_7 = 385 \times 7^{[(\ln 0.9)/(\ln 2)]} = 286$$
$$T_8 = 385 \times 8^{[(\ln 0.9)/(\ln 2)]} = 281$$

Problem 2. McNally-Bolling is an aircraft manufacturer that has introduced a new airplane model. It expects the first plane to cost \$150,000,000 to manufacture (not including development costs), but its products have historically exhibited an 85% experience curve. Assuming the same experience rate will apply to this product,

(a) compute the cost of producing each of the first 5 planes, and

(b) compute the average cost per plane to produce the first 25 planes.

Solution

(a) Using the 85% column from Table 10S.1, the costs for the first five planes should be approximately

$$T_1 = \$150,000,000 \times 1.000 = \$150,000,000$$
$$T_2 = \$150,000,000 \times 0.850 = \$127,500,000$$
$$T_3 = \$150,000,000 \times 0.773 = \$115,950,000$$
$$T_4 = \$150,000,000 \times 0.723 = \$108,450,000$$
$$T_5 = \$150,000,000 \times 0.686 = \$102,900,000$$

(b) From the 85% column in Table 10S.1, the "total time" factor for 25 units is 14.801, so the total cost for the 25 planes will be \$150,000,000 × 14.801 = \$2,220,150,000. Dividing this by 25 gives an average cost of \$88,806,000 per plane.

PROBLEMS

1. A mobile home manufacturer has collected the following data on the labor requirements for the first 600 mobile homes it made.

Unit No. (00)	Labor Content (person-hr)
1	1250
2	1070
3	1010
4	920
5	890
6	850

(a) Estimate the learning rate for this product. (b) Use this learning rate to predict the amount of labor that will be required to make the next 300 mobile homes.

2. A title insurance company has hired two new people to perform title searches for property. The workers are new and had to be taught how to perform a title search. The times required to perform the first four title searches are given for each worker.

Search No.	Time (hr.) Person 1	Time (hr.) Person 2
1	3.4	3.7
2	2.8	3.2
3	2.4	2.8
4	2.1	2.3

(a) Use the data for both workers to estimate the learning rate. (b) Using this rate for both workers, predict how long it will take to do the fifth and sixth title searches.

3. Gateway General Insurance has found that whenever it accepts a new corporate client for its medical insurance program, it takes approximately 500 person-hours to process the first 1000 medical claims; afterward, the company exhibits approximately a 75% learning rate. Use this information to predict how many person-hours it will take to process the first 10,000 claims a client files.

4. Woody Harold designs and manufactures wooden furniture in a small shop. From historical records he

has determined that when he designs and manufactures a new style of furniture, he exhibits approximately an 80% learning rate (using one unit of furniture as the production unit). It took him 6.5 hours to make the first unit of a new style of table. Compute how long it should take him to make the next three units of the table.

5. Parallel Piping collected the following data on the cost of making a new model of plastic pipe:

Unit No. (thousand ft)	Cost ($)
1	270
2	249
3	235
4	225
5	219
6	212
7	207
8	202

(a) Determine the approximate experience rate reflecting the decrease in cost for this product. (b) Use this rate to predict how much it will cost to make the next 10,000 feet of pipe.

6. Wind Dynamics Corporation estimates that its experience rate for making power-generating windmills is approximately 85%. If it cost $12,000 to make the first windmill of a new model, predict how much it will cost to make the first 30 windmills.

7.* Dynamo Manufacturing Company manufactures optical scanning and sorting equipment. This year Dynamo introduced a new product, the Dyno V scanner. It manufactured and sold 400 of these scanners during the year. Dynamo collected data on the production hours for each 100 scanners made (Dynamo uses 100 scanners as its unit of measure); this information is given in the table below. It costs Dynamo $250,000 per year to keep the production line operating (fixed cost), plus $2250 per scanner for materials and $20 per person-hour for variable labor expenses.

	Person-Hr of Labor
First 100 scanners	71,000
Second 100 scanners	60,200
Third 100 scanners	54,950
Fourth 100 scanners	51,900

(a) Estimate the approximate learning rate based on 100 scanners as one unit of production. (b) Dynamo sold the 400 scanners this year at a price of $12,500 per scanner. Compute Dynamo's total net profit (or loss) on the Dyno V scanner this year. (c) Dynamo must decide whether or not to keep producing the Dyno V. Because of competitive pressures, Dynamo does not believe it can raise its price for the scanner, but believes that it can sell 600 scanners next year at $12,500 each. Compute Dynamo's expected profit next year, assuming that it can sell 600 scanners and assuming that the material cost per scanner, labor cost per person-hour, and fixed cost per year stay the same as they are this year. Should Dynamo keep producing Dyno V scanners next year?

SELECTED READINGS

AQUILANO, NICHOLAS, and RICHARD CHASE. *Production and Operations Management* (7th ed.), Richard D. Irwin, Burr Ridge, IL, 1995.

ARGOTTE, LINDA, and DENNIS EPPLE. "Learning Curves in Manufacturing," *Science*, Vol. 247, 1990, pp. 920–924.

BAILEY, CHARLES D. "Forgetting and the Learning Curve: A Laboratory Study," *Management Science*, Vol. 35, 1989, pp. 340–352.

SMITH, DAVID B., and JAN L. LARSSON. "The Impact of Learning on Cost: The Case of Heart Transplantation," *Hospital and Health Sciences Administration*, Vol. 34, Spring 1989, pp. 85–97.

SMUNT, TIMOTHY. "A Comparison of Learning Curve Analysis and Moving Average Ratio Analysis for Detailed Operational Planning," *Decision Sciences*, Vol. 17, 1986, pp. 475–495.

YELLE, Y. E. "Learning Curves: Historical Review and Comprehensive Survey," *Decision Sciences*, Vol. 10, 1979, pp. 302–328.

CHAPTER 11

THE QUALITY MANAGEMENT SYSTEM

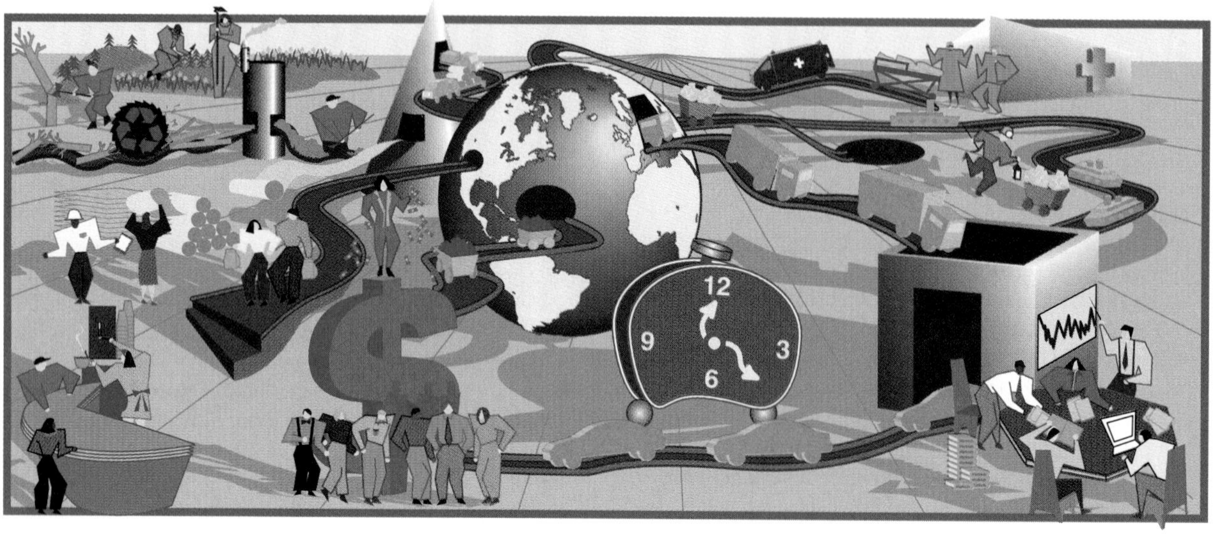

11.1 THE NEW PHILOSOPHY OF QUALITY
On the Job: Valerie Mayer, ADT

11.2 WHAT IS PRODUCT QUALITY?
The Dimensions of Quality
In Good Company: UPS Delivers Relationships

11.3 THE QUALITY COST AUDIT
Quality Cost Categories
Typical and Desirable Cost Distributions
Obtaining Quality Cost Data
Two Examples of Quality Cost Audits and Scorecards

11.4 ACHIEVING AND ENHANCING PRODUCT QUALITY

11.5 DESIGN QUALITY
Identifying Customer Preferences
Incorporating Customer Preferences Into the Product

11.6 QUALITY CONFORMANCE
Product Design and Quality Conformance
Process Design and Quality Conformance
Production Operations and Quality Conformance

11.7 STATISTICAL QUALITY CONTROL
Statistical Process Control
SPC by Variables
SPC by Attributes
Defect Tracking and Cause–Effect Analysis

11.8 SERVICE QUALITY

11.9 TOTAL QUALITY MANAGEMENT
History of TQM
Principles of TQM
Why TQM Programs Fail and Succeed

11.10 PROSPECTS FOR PRODUCT QUALITY
The Baldrige Awards
ISO 9000 Standards and Certification

Digicomp Computer: A Quality Management Case

11.1 The New Philosophy of Quality

The strategies of companies such as Motorola, Harley-Davidson, Intel, and L. L. Bean reflect a general trend in business during the past two decades: product quality has become a primary order-winning dimension for organizations. Companies perceived as producing products of poor quality have either failed or are struggling for survival, while those recognized for quality have generally flourished. For example, Valerie Mayer, the subject of this chapter's "On the Job" segment, points out that home security companies "can't . . . expect people to put their homes in our hands" if the quality of work is poor. Much of the credit for creating this greater attention to product quality and customer service can be given to Japanese manufacturers in the automotive, electronics, and machinery industries, who have made product quality a key element of their strategies. During the 1970s and 1980s, some Japanese products had defect rates 10–100 times lower than those of competing products, and customers expressed greater satisfaction with them. However, in recent years, by devoting greater attention to quality and customer service, many U.S., Canadian, and other Western companies have eliminated this gap and have even exceeded their Japanese competitors in quality. For example, Motorola reduced the defect rates on its cellular phones from 6000 per million in 1985 to 30 per million in 1992, with a goal of 3 per million in 1995; Solectron, a producer of circuit boards, cut its defect rate from 100 per million to 2 per million; and in 1992 L. L. Bean, which correctly fills over 99.9% of its orders, correctly shipped over 500,000 packages consecutively without a mistake.[1]

On the Job

Valerie Mayer, ADT

As residential sales manager for ADT, one of the country's largest home security installers, Valerie Mayer sees quality control as an integral part of her job. ADT sells customized home security and fire systems that operate with 24-hour-a-day monitoring, automatically dispatching fire department or police personnel to customers' homes when their signals are tripped.

After the salesperson writes the order, installers reassess the job at the site. Any changes they recommend must be cleared with the office, offering Valerie her first checkpoint for quality control. Installers also go through a quality checklist before leaving the job, and the customer signs it. Random surveys are sent from the office to customers to gauge their satisfaction, and throughout the operation of the service, the home security system continually checks itself. If power is cut off, for example, the central station's backup system provides emergency power, and the local office contacts the homeowner before sending the police.

"It's very important to people that the job is complete," says Valerie. "We can't be sloppy and expect people to put their homes in our hands."

[1]See G. Christian Hill and Ken Yamada, "Motorola Illustrates How an Aged Giant Can Remain Vibrant," *Wall Street Journal*, Dec. 9, 1992, and Otis Port et al., "Quality: Small and Midsize Companies Seize the Challenge—Not a Moment Too Soon," *Business Week*, Nov. 30, 1992, pp. 66–75.

Catalogue retailer L. L. Bean has excelled as a service quality leader by correctly filling over 99.9% of its orders. During one period it shipped over 500,000 packages consecutively without a mistake.

Products with superior quality obviously are more attractive to customers and therefore will experience greater sales. But product quality has become increasingly important for three other reasons. First, customers who purchase a product based on quality have greater product loyalty than those who purchase based on price. Normally, a customer who is pleased with a product's quality will continue to purchase that product until dissatisfied or until another product can demonstrably be proved superior, which is quite difficult for competitors to do. In contrast, customers who buy based on price readily change to competing products that sell at a lower price.

The second reason, which is contrary to traditional business thinking, is that poor quality is more expensive than good quality. Many companies have discovered that higher product quality does *not* have to cost more. In fact, in many cases the methods used to improve quality simultaneously increase productivity, reduce material usage, and reduce cost. For example, changes in the assembly of steering columns at General Motors tripled worker productivity and substantially reduced costs while at the same time improving quality by a factor of 7.[2] This fact was the basis for Philip Crosby's best-selling book *Quality Is Free*. Finally, organizations can be exposed to considerable financial liability when defective products cause injuries or death to users or simply do not perform adequately. Improved product quality reduces the exposure to such financial and moral risks.

These important benefits lead to some obvious questions: What is quality? What level or form of quality is best for our products? How can we achieve our quality goals? A number of so-called quality gurus, such as W. Edwards Deming, Joseph Juran, Philip Crosby, Kaoru Ishikawa, Genichi Taguchi, and Shigeo Shingo, have addressed these issues. They have developed, and successfully demonstrated, a variety of philosophies and techniques that improve product quality and make it an integral part of an organization's strategy and operations.

Although this work has been successfully adopted by thousands of organizations worldwide, there have also been many cases of companies failing in their attempts to adopt quality management philosophies and techniques. An unfortunate consequence of these failures has been the proliferation of doomsayers who have condemned the quality movement as nothing more than a series of fads without substance. They are wrong. These failures, for the most part, have been the result of poor application and implementation rather than of fundamental flaws in the philosophies and techniques. Many companies have lacked the top management commitment or the patience required by these programs, while others have either become caught up in individual techniques with catchy names, such as *quality function deployment*, *quality circles*, *fish-bone charts*, and *statistical process control*, or have treated the various philosophies and techniques as mutually exclusive substitutes for each other.

The quality philosophies and techniques that have appeared over the past few decades contain several common principles, and these principles make sense. No single approach or technique will solve an organization's quality problems. In fact, quality can and should be improved in a variety of ways. Product quality is affected by organizational structure, by worker training and job design, by the product design process, by the production process and its operation, and by purchasing and materials management. So opportunities exist in each of these areas to improve quality (and productivity).

The approaches of Deming, Juran, Shingo, and others actually complement each other, so this chapter synthesizes their contributions to the many aspects of quality

[2]See Neal Templin and Joseph White, "GM Drive to Step Up Efficiency Is Colliding with UAW Job Fears," *Wall Street Journal*, June 23, 1993.

management. In fact, the success of the quality revolution among Japanese manufacturers has been due to their willingness to synthesize, enhance, and expand the ideas of many individuals over time rather than to adopt one view.

Most notable about the new quality philosophies is their explicit departure from classical quality control ideas. Traditionally, quality criteria were set inside the organization, the responsibility for quality was assigned to a separate functional unit (the quality control department), and the methodological focus was on final product inspection and using statistical methods to keep the percentage of defective products shipped to an "acceptable" level. In contrast, the new philosophies of quality management are customer focused, they recognize quality management as an organizationwide responsibility, and they concentrate on ways to make products correctly the first time rather than catching defects after the fact. There is also greater recognition of the role of product and process design in quality and of the need for continuous improvement.

This chapter begins by defining product quality and describing some of the characteristics and components essential to good product quality. Poor product quality is far more expensive than most companies recognize. Section 11.3 proposes developing a "quality cost scorecard" as part of a "quality cost audit" to identify the full costs of poor quality and to highlight the trade-offs that exist when making quality-related decisions. The quality scorecard also helps to identify the most cost-effective areas for quality improvement. The remainder of the chapter is devoted to specific suggestions for achieving the type and level of quality desired. Section 11.9 synthesizes these suggestions and the new quality philosophies to form an approach called *total quality management* (TQM).

11.2 WHAT IS PRODUCT QUALITY?

Good product quality does not occur by accident. To achieve it, an organization must know what constitutes good quality and must be able to measure and monitor it in some way. Many definitions of quality have been proposed, but J. M. Juran's statement that quality is the product's "fitness for use" captures the essential feature that applies to all products: *quality is customer oriented*. Products, whether goods or services, are of good quality only if customers say they are, that is, only if they meet customers' needs and expectations in terms of their expected use. Products that do not satisfy those needs and expectations, whether due to poor design or poor production, are of poor quality.

For example, a company that produces flat-head screwdrivers may assume that customers will use them to turn screws. However, many customers also use them (regardless of warnings) as chisels, levers, and scrapers. Thus, even if the screwdrivers are designed and made well to turn screws, customers may consider them to be of low quality, and may not purchase them, if they cannot withstand the extra punishment and wear of these other uses. The ultimate sales of the product depend on the customers' perceptions of its fitness for use, not the producer's.

THE DIMENSIONS OF QUALITY

The quality characteristics of a typical product are multidimensional because products provide satisfaction and value to customers in many ways. Some product characteristics are quantitative and easily measurable, such as a product's weight or the time required to complete a service. But other characteristics, such as attractiveness or friendliness, are qualitative, without any natural scale of measure. The specific quality dimensions that are relevant to the customer vary from product to product, but we can categorize them into the following groups.

1. ***Performance.*** Of primary importance to the customer is whether the good does what it is supposed to do or the service is provided correctly. If the customer provides product specifications, such as the weight, viscosity, or strength of a good or the timeliness or correctness of a service (e.g., filing a correct income tax return), adherence to these specifications is an important dimension of quality. (Measurable performance characteristics that are embedded in a product are sometimes called *structural* characteristics.)
2. ***Range and Type of Features.*** In addition to the primary product functions or services, customers are often interested in other features or capabilities. For example, a television may have stereo sound or high resolution, or a bank may offer electronic banking at home.
3. ***Reliability and Durability.*** **Reliability** measures how *consistently* the product performs at an acceptable level under normal maintenance, while **durability** measures how *long* the product performs acceptably until repair is needed and the overall usable life of the product. For a service, durability may measure how current or up-to-date the service is.
4. ***Maintainability and Serviceability.*** These dimensions measure the frequency, expense, and difficulty of actions required to keep the product operating at the desired level of performance. Important aspects of these dimensions may be the training provided to customers, the assistance available (such as a telephone hotline), and the availability of replacement parts.
5. ***Sensory Characteristics.*** For many products, sensory characteristics such as appearance, feel, smell, taste, or sound may be important aspects of quality. Healthy food that is not tasty is not usually considered to be of high quality.
6. ***Ethical Profile and Image.*** Quality is largely a matter of customer perception, so *how* customers are treated is very important. Especially for service products, customers' perceptions of the courtesy, honesty, and responsiveness of the producer are relevant quality dimensions. For example, UPS (the subject of this chapter's "In Good Company" segment) found that the courtesy and helpfulness of its drivers was one of its greatest quality assets.

Table 11.1 gives examples of these quality dimensions for a typical good and service.

TABLE 11.1 EXAMPLES OF QUALITY DIMENSIONS FOR A GOOD AND A SERVICE

Quality Characteristic	Good	Service
	Portable Computer	Consumer Banking
Performance	Processing speed	Accuracy of transactions
Range of features	Modem/networking	Foreign funds handling
Reliability/durability	Time until failure	Up-to-date services
Maintainability/serviceability	Number of repair outlets	Telephone hotline
Sensory	Readability of screen	Ambience of facilities
Ethics/image	Warranty adherence	Fair advertising of fees

IN GOOD COMPANY

UPS Delivers Relationships

UPS had always been sensitive to its customers' needs. After all, it had spent a lot of time and money surveying customers about how pleased they were (or weren't) with UPS's delivery time and whether they thought packages could be handled faster, and wasn't that what mattered most? It turned out that UPS was asking the wrong questions. When it started asking customers more open-ended questions in its quest for quality, UPS learned that customers really wanted more interaction with drivers, the company's most visible representatives. "We've discovered that the highest-rated element we have is our drivers," says UPS service quality manager Lawrence E. Farrel. As a result, the company now encourages drivers to spend time answering customers' questions, offering advice, and establishing good relationships that will eventually generate sales. While quotas are still important, more drivers have been added so that UPS personnel can spend up to 30 minutes of discretionary time every day working with customers on their routes.

Source: David Greising, "Quality: How to Make It Pay," *Business Week*, Aug. 8, 1994, pp. 54–59.

11.3 THE QUALITY COST AUDIT

Many organizations require compelling evidence to be convinced that they need to design and implement an organizationwide quality management system. The marketing and revenue advantages of good product quality may be evident to top managers, but frequently they will view the additional cost of achieving higher quality as not being worth the expense. An enlightening and effective exercise to encourage improvements in quality management is to perform a **quality cost audit**, which involves identifying all costs related to achieving good quality or resulting from bad quality. These costs are then organized and reported on a **quality cost scorecard**.

Most companies have little idea how much they are actually spending on quality related activities, especially the cost of poor quality. Some will estimate their quality costs by adding up the costs of their quality control department and the costs associated with defective items returned by customers. An in-depth quality cost audit will often demonstrate to a company that it is actually spending several times this amount on quality-related activities. More important, the audit can identify specific problem areas and ways in which total spending on quality can be reduced and product quality enhanced by reallocating expenditures and effort.

QUALITY COST CATEGORIES

Any expenditures or revenue losses that are associated with preventing production of defective products, and with making, finding, repairing, or replacing defective products, can be considered quality costs. J. M. Juran, a leading proponent of quality cost audits, classifies quality costs into four categories: external failure costs, internal failure costs, appraisal costs, and prevention costs. **Failure costs** are those costs that result from producing defective products. The failure cost is considered an **external failure cost** if it is discovered outside the organization—that is, by the customer. It is considered to be an **internal failure cost** if it is discovered within the organization before shipment to a customer. **Appraisal costs** are the costs of discovering the condition of materials and products and identifying defective ones. **Prevention costs** are those incurred to minimize appraisal and failure costs. Each of these categories contains a variety of costs; some of the more important ones are listed below.[3]

External Failure Costs

1. ***Complaint Investigation and Adjustment.*** Cost incurred to investigate and resolve complaints attributable to defective products, installation, or service.
2. ***Return, Replacement, or Allowances.*** Cost of replacing a defective product, including shipping and handling, or any price reduction or allowance to compensate for a defective product.
3. ***Warranty Expenses.*** Cost of resolving complaints under warranty other than replacement, such as repair costs and costs of renting a replacement product.
4. ***Liability.*** Cost of defending lawsuits and compensating customers for injury, death, and business losses, including possible punitive damages.
5. ***Goodwill.*** Loss of future profits due to perceived poor quality. This is difficult to measure, but it can be very large.

Internal Failure Costs

1. ***Disposition.*** Cost of determining what action to take when defective items are found: rework the item, scrap it, or correct the process.
2. ***Scrap.*** Net loss in labor and material when an item must be discarded due to poor quality.
3. ***Rework.*** Cost of correcting defective items to make them usable, including any extra activities added to the production process to alleviate or compensate for an ongoing quality problem.
4. ***Retest.*** Cost of reinspecting and retesting reworked items and additional testing added to the production process to compensate for recurring quality problems.
5. ***Yield Losses.*** Cost of wasted materials above that which is technically necessary to make the product, such as overfilling packages sent to customers.
6. ***Downtime.*** Cost of idle personnel and facilities when production is stopped to correct a quality problem, such as adjusting a machine, as well as stoppages due to defects in materials, such as paper breaking in a printing press or paint not covering a material correctly.
7. ***Inventory Safety Stocks.*** Cost of extra safety stocks held specifically to guard against shortages and breakdowns due to making defective components or products.

---

[3]See J. M. Juran and Frank M. Gryna, Jr., *Quality Planning and Analysis* (3rd ed.), McGraw-Hill, New York, 1993, for more details on quality cost audits and quality cost categories.

8. ***Defect-Generated Overtime Costs.*** Incremental costs of having employees work overtime to meet delivery deadlines for orders that were late because defective items had to be reworked or remade.
9. ***Excess Capacity Costs.*** Cost of excess capacity that must be maintained to make up for capacity lost from making defective products. This includes the cost of extra facilities and equipment above those that would be needed if production were defect free. This can be one of the largest yet most hidden quality costs.

Appraisal Costs

1. ***Incoming Material Inspection.*** Cost of inspecting and testing items received from suppliers.
2. ***In-Process Inspection and Testing.*** Cost of inspecting and testing the product throughout the production process to ensure conformance, including testing performed by customers or by third-party laboratories.
3. ***Maintaining Testing Equipment.*** Cost of keeping testing equipment in good working condition, including calibration, to ensure accurate testing.
4. ***Evaluation of Stock.*** Cost of evaluating the condition of materials and final products in stock.

Prevention Costs

1. ***Quality Planning.*** All costs related to developing and planning the quality assurance system, such as the costs of setting up design and operational policies and procedures related to quality, the development of an inspection plan, and the costs of communicating quality plans to workers.
2. ***Product Design and Review.*** Any incremental costs of product design incurred to review and improve the quality of the product. (This would not include the basic costs of product design but would, for example, include the Taguchi design tests discussed in Chapter 5.)
3. ***Process Design and Review.*** Any incremental costs of process design incurred to review and improve quality conformance of the product, including equipment enhancements intended primarily to improve quality.
4. ***Job Design and Training.*** Cost of developing work methods (e.g., mistake-proofing) to eliminate production mistakes, and the cost of developing and implementing training programs related to quality, including the preparation of training manuals.
5. ***Process Control.*** Process control costs intended primarily to achieve quality conformance rather than productivity or safety.
6. ***Data Collection, Analysis, and Reporting.*** Cost of collecting data related to quality, such as defects, quality problems, downtime, and so on, and the cost of analyzing and reporting the data to monitor and improve quality.
7. ***Quality Improvement Programs.*** Costs related to special activities or projects designed to monitor and improve quality, such as quality circles and defect reduction programs.

TYPICAL AND DESIRABLE COST DISTRIBUTIONS

The two most striking results of quality cost audits are the *magnitude* of the total quality costs and the *distribution* of the costs among the four categories.

The Magnitude of Quality Costs

Those companies that do not explicitly perform a quality cost audit, and do not seek out the costs listed above, will significantly underestimate their quality costs. Many organizations' accounting and information systems have difficulty separating quality costs from other costs, and managers often fail to recognize all the costs that are, in fact, attributable to the quality system and its failures.

Many of the quality costs listed above are incurred by departments other than the quality control department. For example, the costs of inspection and testing done by production personnel are often mistakenly omitted. Similarly, rework, downtime, extra production activities added to ensure quality, and yield losses are often hidden and treated as normal costs of production. In some cases, even scrapped items are treated as normal material and labor costs. Although allowances and the cost of replacing a defective item may be recognized as quality costs, the personnel costs incurred to investigate and resolve complaints, the extra cost of shipping, and especially the liability and goodwill costs often show up in the marketing, sales, transportation, or legal department budgets or in lost sales and are not recognized as actual quality costs.

When all of these hidden costs are included, it is not unusual for the actual quality costs to be over 20% of the company's revenues, several times as large as the company originally believed. Even quality leaders, such as Motorola, have quality costs equivalent to 10% of revenues. The quality cost scorecard, which identifies these hidden costs, creates greater recognition of the importance of quality and the pervasiveness of its effects throughout the organization. Thus it shows that quality must be addressed throughout the organization, not simply within the quality control department. For example, when Tenneco found that its quality costs were over 20% of its revenues, it undertook a companywide program that reduced quality costs and increased operating income by $461 million over two years.[4]

Quality Cost Distribution Among Categories

When the quality costs are tallied up by category, it is normal to find that failure costs account for 50–80% of the total quality costs, appraisal costs for 15–40%, and prevention for only 5–10%, as shown in Figure 11.1. This distribution information focuses attention on reducing the failure costs, and it identifies a successful strategy for doing so. Specifically, most organizations devote far too little money to preventing defects through product design, process design, planning, training, and process control, and consequently pay too large a price in failure costs. For most organizations, total quality costs would probably be minimized if 25–50% of their quality costs were invested in prevention and 50–80% in prevention and appraisal combined. These proportions are almost obligatory for an organization that adopts the principles of total quality management and tries to make products right the first time rather than relying heavily on final product inspection.

Quality Cost Distribution Among Products and Divisions

An organization's quality cost scorecard is normally the accumulation of separate scorecards that are developed for each product, facility, or division. The magnitude of quality costs and their distribution among cost categories will vary among products, facilities, and divisions. This distribution information is helpful because it identifies where the most opportunity exists for quality improvement and cost reduction. In addition, during the quality cost audit we can begin to identify the primary causes of defects and the highest quality costs. First, we want to focus our efforts on the "important few"

---

[4]From John A. Byrne, "The Craze for Consultants," *Business Week*, July 25, 1994, pp. 60–66.

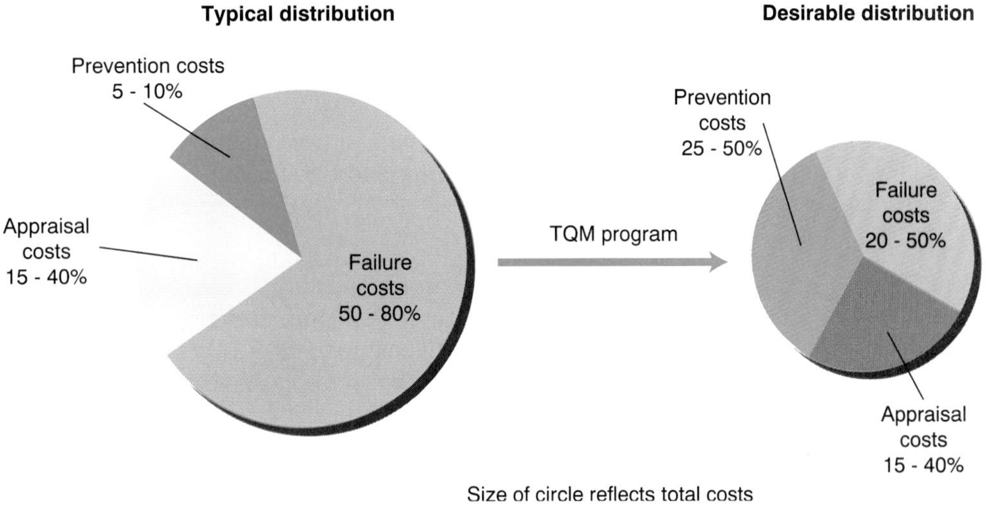

FIGURE 11.1 Quality cost distributions.

products, divisions, or causes that will have the most impact, rather than the "unimportant many" that will have little impact (this is called the **Pareto principle**).

OBTAINING QUALITY COST DATA

The most direct and obvious quality costs, such as those incurred by the quality control department, are often reported in existing accounting records. However, most quality cost information is not reported separately by the accounting system. Quality costs such as the time a production worker spends performing quality checks, material lost due to scrapping defective products, the cost of inventories held as protection against defect-generated shortages or work stoppages, and overtime wages incurred due to defects are rarely calculated and recorded in separate accounts. Therefore, the people performing the quality cost audit must estimate many of the cost components in one of three other ways: (1) by reviewing and analyzing basic production documents and employee work records, (2) by creating and maintaining temporary or new direct records, or (3) by directly observing operations.

The task of collecting this information from scratch can appear overwhelming. The magnitude of the job can be greatly reduced, however, by recognizing the purpose and information needs of the audit: specifically, well-founded estimates are sufficient; exact cost numbers are not needed. For example, if the actual cost of machine downtime due to quality problems is $84,682 in a year, it does not matter much if the derived estimate is $60,000 or $100,000; the amount of attention this problem will receive and the likely actions taken will be the same in either case.

Although conventional accounting systems are not set up to identify and separate quality costs into the components identified above, it is beneficial to try to institutionalize the collection of these data so that the results of quality improvements can be tracked and assessed over time. In many cases the necessary primary data are already being collected on work reports, but they are not organized and reported to the right people. For example, machine work reports often record the amount and cause of downtime, but these data remain in department files and may never be used for quality management purposes. In other cases, it will be necessary to create or modify forms and procedures to collect and transmit the necessary quality cost data so that they can be recorded properly.

TWO EXAMPLES OF QUALITY COST AUDITS AND SCORECARDS

This section provides the results of two quality cost audits: one for a division of a personal computer manufacturer and one for a medical claims processing division of an insurance company.

Personal Computer Manufacturer

Table 11.2 is the quality cost scorecard that resulted from the audit of Digicomp, a personal computer manufacturer. Digicomp designs, assembles, and sells its own models of computers, but almost all components are purchased from outside vendors. To guide its quality cost audit, the company used a standard quality cost scorecard form containing the cost categories defined earlier. For those categories where costs could not be reliably estimated, an * was entered.

The audit used quality cost data from existing financial reports wherever possible. However, in few cases were the desired costs normally collected and reported in the categories desired; therefore, accounting, production, payroll, customer service, and other reports had to be studied carefully and original data forms reviewed to separate the quality costs from other costs. For example, some of the costs of returned and replaced products and some allowances were due to factors other than quality defects, so it was necessary to use the original customer records to identify the reason for and costs of returns. Liability and legal costs due to defects had to be determined from legal department work records and case documents. The goodwill losses of $200,000, which were obtained from the sales department, represented the marginal profit from the estimated sales the company lost due to poor quality.

Internal failure costs were even more difficult to obtain than external costs. The company aggregated its material costs in its reports, so the costs of scrapped material had to be estimated based on production records that reported the number of items scrapped, and yield losses had to be estimated from observational and engineering studies of how much material was being wasted on average in the production process. The cost of downtime was estimated by looking at original production records. Whenever an operation stopped production, the operator had to explain the reason. Some of the causes of the downtime were not always clear, so some informed guessing was required. The cost of overtime production due to defects was obtained by going back to production and payroll records to see when overtime occurred, comparing it with the production schedule and records, and then asking the supervisor to what extent the overtime was necessitated by lost production from quality defects or other reasons.

The company did not maintain excess facilities and equipment to compensate for the lost production from defects. It did, however, have to overstaff and sometimes work overtime to make up for this lost production, but these costs were believed to be captured in other categories. The company's production was nearing the capacity of its facilities, though, and unless defects could be reduced or efficiency increased, additional facilities and equipment would soon be needed. So although the excess capacity cost was currently zero, it could become significant in the near future.

Two employees were permanently assigned to inspecting incoming materials and the quality control department kept good records on other appraisal costs, so these could be obtained easily from its reports.

The $135,000 quality planning cost was primarily the cost of the quality control department manager and her assistant, who developed and monitored quality control

TABLE 11.2 QUALITY COST SCORECARD FOR DIGICOMP COMPUTER CORPORATION (IN $000)

External Failure Costs		
Complaint investigation and adjustment	43	
Returns, replacements and allowances	610	
Warranty expenses (rentals and repairs)	24	
Liability and related legal	38	
Goodwill losses	200	
Total external failure costs (% of total)	915	(14%)
Internal Failure Costs		
Disposition	105	
Scrap (components and labor)	290	
Rework	2150	
Retest	120	
Yield losses	65	
Downtime	910	
Extra safety stock (carrying cost)	50	
Defect-generated overtime	340	
Excess capacity	*	
Total internal failure costs (% of total)	4030	(64%)
Appraisal Costs		
Incoming material inspection	60	
In-process inspection and testing	630	
Maintenance of test equipment	120	
Evaluation of stocks	*	
Total appraisal costs (% of total)	810	(13%)
Prevention Costs		
Quality planning	135	
Product design review teams	90	
Process design and review for quality	100	
Training (quality related)	75	
Process control	15	
Data collection, analysis, and reporting	95	
Quality improvement programs	70	
Total prevention costs (% of total)	580	(9% of total)
Total Quality Costs	6335	

*Costs in these categories could not be reliably estimated.

policies and procedures. The company began to use multidisciplinary teams to review product designs for quality and producibility. The $90,000 cost was estimated by computing the total cost of the time spent by team members reviewing the designs and assigning half of this cost as a quality cost, because it was believed that approximately half of the time and suggestions of these teams were aimed at quality improvements. The process design costs were the costs of reviewing and modifying the process specifically to improve product quality. Training costs were estimated by taking the total training cost and allocating one-third of it to quality, because it was believed that approximately one-third of the training was devoted to quality-related issues and skills. The process control costs were based on engineering estimates of additional equipment installed primarily for quality monitoring. The data collection and reporting costs were primarily the costs of two employees who gathered quality information and prepared reports (including their computer costs and other support costs). The company did have in place a suggestion program, and some departments were experimenting with quality circles to improve productivity and quality. The quality-related portion of these costs was estimated to be $70,000.

The total quality cost was estimated at $6,335,000 annually, which was 11.5% of the division's sales of $55 million and more than its yearly profit of $5 million. Of this quality cost, 9% was incurred in prevention and only 13% in appraisal. The overwhelming majority of the cost was the consequence of making defective product. In addition, from the audit it became apparent that 10–20% of the division's production capacity was wasted on producing and reworking defective product. If this cost could be dramatically reduced, future expansion costs could be postponed or curtailed. The audit indicated that there was considerable room for improvement, with a substantial potential payoff. Possible actions are discussed in the end-of-chapter case, which is based on the information presented in Table 11.2.

Medical Insurance Company

For various reasons, quality cost audits are not generally performed by service organizations, even though they are just as applicable and useful as for manufacturers. Table 11.3 is the quality cost scorecard for the medical claims processing division of an insurance company. The scorecard is customized for the costs of a claims processing operation, but the cost categories are equivalent to those defined earlier.

The claims processing operation is relatively straightforward. A claim form is submitted either by the insured patient or directly by the health care provider (physician, hospital, etc.), along with supporting documentation. A claims processor checks the forms to make sure that all the necessary information is provided and that the claimed care is covered by the insurance (e.g., is a surgical procedure cosmetic rather than medically necessary?). If the procedure is not covered or if information is missing, the claims processor prepares a standard explanatory letter to the submitter of the claim. If the claim appears to be covered the information is input into a computer, which calculates the amount of reimbursement due and records the information in a master file for the customer. A report for the customer is prepared and a check is printed. The file then goes to a review officer, who checks the claim processor's work. The report and check are then either sent to the claimant or returned to the claims processor if an error is found or a question arises.

If a claimant is dissatisfied with the disposition of a claim, he or she contacts the insurer. Most complaints are handled by the original claims processor, but a claimant who is still dissatisfied can file a formal appeal, which goes to a supervisor for evaluation and a hearing panel, if requested.

In this operation, "defective" products can take many forms: underpayment or overpayment of claims, incorrect letters of explanation, and claims returned unnecessarily for more information.

As with the computer manufacturer, almost all the quality costs had to be obtained by going to original payroll or work documents and sometimes by making estimates. The complaint investigation and reprocessing costs were derived by determining how many complaints were received and reprocessed. Then using work measurement studies, the amount of time needed to investigate and resolve typical complaints was estimated and used to estimate the cost. The cost of overpayments was estimated by taking a sample of claims and then reviewing them in detail, including asking for detailed documentation from health providers, talking with patients to verify that claimed services were really received (especially charges for hospital services and tests), and

TABLE 11.3 QUALITY COST SCORECARD: MEDICAL INSURANCE CLAIMS PROCESSING DIVISION (IN $000)

External Failure Costs	
Complaint investigation	310
Reprocessing claims to correct valid complaints	760
Overpayment errors (estimated)	410
Appeals to hearing board	90
Goodwill loss (risk of losing client accts.)	*
Total external failure costs (% of total)	1570+ (55%)
Internal Failure Costs	
Reprocessing claims with errors caught internally	375
Rechecking reprocessed claims	40
Forms and worksheets for reprocessed claims	5
Excess capacity (facilities only)	100+
Total internal failure costs (% of total)	520 (18%)
Appraisal Costs	
Review of processed claims	390
Review of standard data for processing claims	90
Total appraisal costs (% of total)	480 (17%)
Prevention Costs	
Quality planning	70
Training (quality related)	120
Data collection, analysis, and reporting	110
Total prevention costs (% of total)	300 (10%)
Total Quality Costs	2870+

* Cost could not be reliably estimated.

closely checking whether the reimbursed procedures were really covered or reimbursed at the correct amount for the customer's policy. Estimated net overpayments for the sample were then projected for the company as a whole. The appeals costs were already a separate accounting item and were readily available.

The costs of reprocessing and rechecking claims with internally identified errors were estimated similarly to the complaint investigation and reprocessing costs. Approximately 15% of all claims had to be reprocessed for some reason. Therefore, the company had approximately 25 more employees than it would have needed if there were no mistakes. (Note that even if no mistakes were made, complaints and appeals would come from customers who thought differently. The estimated number of extra employees was based on how many complaints would be eliminated if the company made no mistakes.) The personnel costs of this "wasted capacity" were captured elsewhere, but the company was renting additional office space to support these people. The additional cost of space, furniture, utilities, and so on was at least $100,000, but a more precise estimate was not attempted.

The cost of reviewing processed claims was an available accounting item because designated personnel performed this work. An important aspect of the system is using "medical procedure" cost data, which are updated quarterly, entered into the computer system, and printed on "help sheets" for the claims processors. Two employees were primarily responsible for preparing this information, entering it into the computer, and checking its accuracy. The estimated cost of revising the data was the sum of their salaries and supporting expenses.

The prevention costs were all incurred in a quality tracking department, which made them easy to estimate. These included the cost of the department head, who was in charge of setting policies, tracking quality performance, and reporting on it to his supervisor, and the cost of three employees who did the actual data collection and analysis and computer processing. In addition, it was believed that two-thirds of the training provided was related to service quality; the $110,000 cost reflects that portion of total training.

The total quality costs for the company were estimated at $2,870,000, which was over 13% of the division's total expenditures of $22 million. Once again the failure costs made up the overwhelming majority of the costs, with over half of these being external failure costs.

11.4 ACHIEVING AND ENHANCING PRODUCT QUALITY

A good with an excellent design (functional, attractive, and with a wide range of features) that is manufactured poorly (does not adhere to specifications, uses poor materials) will be a poor-quality product. Similarly, a perfectly manufactured good that has fundamental design flaws will be a poor-quality product. Achieving good product quality requires two distinct activities: designing products well and conforming to the design in the production process. These aspects of product quality are referred to as the **design quality** and the **conformance quality**, respectively.

The traditional approach to quality management has been to devote extensive resources to conformance quality—making sure final products satisfy design specifications. Even more narrowly, attention was primarily devoted to inspecting samples of products to determine whether or not the products had so many defects that they should be reworked or scrapped rather than shipped to the customer. Although conformance to product specifications is important and necessary to achieve good product quality, it is far from sufficient, and in many cases it is the less important of the two aspects. Furthermore, we have now come to realize that we cannot "inspect quality into a product." Rather than focusing on catching defects before products are shipped to customers, the more cost-effective approach is usually to focus on preventing defects from occurring or at least identifying them as early in the production process as possible. All the quality experts mentioned earlier advocate the general principles of improving quality through better product design and then making the product right the first time rather than catching errors later.

The following sections look specifically at what can be done to improve design quality and conformance quality.

11.5 DESIGN QUALITY

The finest operations system cannot produce a high-quality product if its fundamental design is deficient. Many quality problems of the U.S. automobile industry in the 1970s and 1980s were not the result of sloppy or incompetent production line workers; rather, they were due to poor product design. There are two requirements for good design quality.

1. *The product design and features must appropriately address customer wants and expectations.* Many organizations have devoted considerable resources to making products exactly according to their own specifications. But if the product does not adequately

satisfy the desires and expectations of customers, perfect conformance to specifications is of little value. One failure of companies has been a form of hubris, the feeling that they know better than their customers which features the product should contain and in what form. Firms have been very surprised when products they believed to be of top quality have been rejected by customers.

2. Even if the producer determines the correct features or characteristics of the product, *these features must be designed into the product correctly to achieve the intended purpose.* For example, when an automobile is designed to have a reliable and fuel-efficient engine but the engine components are not readily accessible for repair, even the best production conformance will not make that a good automobile.

IDENTIFYING CUSTOMER PREFERENCES

Some obvious questions for product designers are how to identify customer preferences and expectations and how to incorporate these preferences into products in the best way possible. For years, companies have sought direct contact with customers to determine and assess their desires and preferences, often using focus groups and customer surveys. More recently, many companies have invited customers to participate in design teams and have adopted quality function deployment.

Intel Corp. has become the market leader in personal computer processors and system boards because of its product innovation and quality. Intel quality is so highly regarded that most personal computer manufacturers that use Intel components advertise this fact to promote their own product quality.

1. **Customer Participation in Design Teams.** Chapter 5 discussed the increasing use of multidisciplinary teams to design products. An important aspect of this team approach is to include customers in the design process. The use of customers in designing the Marriott Courtyard Hotels and their services has become almost legendary. Potential customers were asked what features they most liked or disliked about current hotels and what features they would like hotels to offer. Hotel prototypes were then constructed and tested by actual customers, and their feedback was used to refine the product. Speculation and conventional wisdom were replaced by customer-based data and standards.

2. **Quality Function Deployment.** **Quality function deployment (QFD)**, which was discussed in detail in Chapter 5, is a structured system for obtaining customer preference information and converting it into product design attributes. Customers are asked to specify the relative importance of various product features or requirements in their purchase decision. They are also asked to rate the performance of competitors' products with respect to these requirements. Product designers then determine which technical product attributes will affect product performance with respect to these customer requirements. This information is expressed in a relationship matrix or an expanded set of matrices called the *house of quality* (see Figs. 5.7 and 5.8 in Chapter 5). The information in these matrices can help designers to focus their attention on the most important technical product attributes, and to select features that satisfy customers better than do competing products.

INCORPORATING CUSTOMER PREFERENCES INTO THE PRODUCT

Identifying customers' preferences and product requirements is a crucial step in achieving design quality, but it is not sufficient. These preferences must be incorporated into the product in an effective manner. QFD is specifically designed to achieve this. But even when considerable effort has been made to incorporate customers' requirements into products, designers do not really know whether the effort was successful until customers can see or use the product.

One of the most cost-effective methods for determining this before full-scale production is to create and test product prototypes as early in the design process as possible.

For example, suppose a company using QFD to guide its design of a new laptop computer found that customers wanted long operating times before battery recharging was necessary. This could be achieved with a special type of battery, but it might cause the computer to have a somewhat odd shape, such as a bulge at one point, making it difficult to put into a standard briefcase. Another possibility is that the screen used is readable in the laboratory but exhibits severe glare or becomes blurry when used in the lighting conditions of airplanes, hotel rooms, or outdoors. By testing prototypes under realistic conditions, these problems can be identified before large-scale production begins.

Prototypes are especially helpful in testing the spatial configuration of products. For example, a product may contain all the technical attributes at the desired level, but the arrangement of its components may make the product less user friendly than it should be.

Prototyping meshes well with the use of customers on design teams. Initial product designs normally must undergo several modifications before production anyway, so it makes sense to let those who are most knowledgeable about customers' preferences—the customers themselves—test the prototypes as part of the evaluation process.

11.6 QUALITY CONFORMANCE

Once a company has a product design that incorporates customer preferences and requirements effectively, it must turn that design into a product. The production system must be designed and operated to ensure that the product is produced in a way that *conforms* to the design; that is, it must have a high level of conformance quality. Historically, quality conformance was believed to be determined primarily by the operational aspects of the production process, especially the statistical quality control methods used. But, in fact, quality conformance is determined by the product design and the production process design, as well as the operational procedures of the production system, of which statistical quality control is only one part.

PRODUCT DESIGN AND QUALITY CONFORMANCE

Product design dictates more than the design quality of a product. Design features can be adjusted to make *conformance* to the design specifications easier to achieve. By keeping the design as simple as possible and by designing the product with the production process in mind, quality conformance can be made easier. These two ideas were captured in the product design principles presented in Chapter 5, with special emphasis on their cost-saving benefits. Here we will summarize how some of these principles can reduce errors in the production process, thereby enhancing product quality.

1. ***Minimize the Number of Parts Used.*** Besides the obvious cost savings, the fewer parts a product contains, the fewer assembly tasks that have to be performed and the less complicated assembly will be, and therefore the less chance of an assembly error. For example, when Motorola redesigned one of its cellular phones using 70% fewer components, it not only reduced assembly time by 90%, but it also reduced defects by 90% and the phone was smaller and lighter.[5] In addition, the fewer the components the less chance of a component failure, and the easier it is to test products and correct defects.

---

[5]Hill and Yamada, op. cit.

2. **Use Common Components.** Using common components across a variety of products reduces the chance of using the wrong components in making the product. The range of performance across companies of using common components is illustrated by a 1993 comparison between General Motors and Ford (done by GM!). GM used 139 different hood hinges in its cars, whereas Ford used only 1. The potential for errors at GM is evident.[6]
3. **Use Standard Components.** Standard components are made in larger quantities than specially made components, so producers can afford to use equipment and methods designed specifically for the standard components. Also, the use of standard components allows producers to benefit from learning and experience to a greater extent than it can by using specially made components.
4. **Simplify and Foolproof the Assembly Process.** The more attention devoted to the assembly process during product design, the more likely it is that assembly will be simpler and more error free. We certainly want to avoid the situation General Motors plant manager Barry Herr described concerning a car his plant had to assemble: "There are things in that instrument panel that Superman couldn't put together."[7] Design tools such as "design for assembly," described in Chapter 5, can help product designers evaluate the difficulty of assembly during product design. Furthermore, prototyping can be helpful in evaluating the difficulty of production.
5. **Make Product Specifications Reasonable.** It is usually not advantageous to specify tolerances more stringent than those needed for the product to work well. This simply increases the cost of production without providing customers with a better product. Of course, if the small tolerance is necessary for product performance, that is a different matter. An important consideration in establishing specifications is the risk of **tolerance stack-up**. When several components must be combined or several operations performed to make a product, one component or operation can be near its quality specification limit without creating a defective product if the other components or operations are safely within their own limits. But when several components are near their limits, these deviations from the target can "stack up" and create a defective final product even though no one component is outside its specification limits.

PROCESS DESIGN AND QUALITY CONFORMANCE

It is much easier to incorporate the principles discussed above when the production process can be designed and tested in conjunction with the product design. This is one of the major benefits of using multidisciplinary teams and concurrent design methods (see Chapter 5). The following methods and principles, which are discussed in more detail in other chapters, can be used to design or redesign production processes to enhance quality conformance.

1. **Poka-Yoke.** **Poka-yoke** is the principle of setting up procedures and/or using equipment that prevent mistakes or, more correctly, prevent mistakes from turning into defects.[8] For example, suppose that in an assembly process a worker is responsible for adding five components to a product moving along an assembly

[6]Templin and White, op.cit.

[7]Ibid.

[8]See Shigeo Shingo, *Modern Approaches to Manufacturing Improvement* (Alan Robinson, ed.), Productivity Press, Cambridge, MA, 1990, for a detailed discussion of *poka yoke*.

line. One *poka yoke* technique is to prepare a container that holds the five components. Thus, if any items are not installed they would remain in the container, and this would be obvious to the assembler. Other forms of *poka-yoke* include making components so that they cannot physically fit in the wrong place and making product housings that cannot close if the product is assembled incorrectly. Such techniques played an important role in reducing steering column assembly errors in GM's Pontiac Grand Am.

2. ***Robust Processes and Taguchi Methods.*** The **Taguchi method** for testing the effects of alternative product design options on the quality of a product can be used in the same way to evaluate alternative methods for *producing* products (see Chapter 5). For example, if a product needs to undergo some combination of heating, fabricating, and cooling, there are many combinations of temperatures, processing times, and methods that can produce the same average product characteristics. However, the amount of production variation around this average may differ considerably, depending on the combination of temperatures and methods used. Taguchi analysis can identify the methods that minimize variation, thereby improving the level of quality conformance.

3. ***Job Design and Ergonomics.*** Many conformance defects are the result of poor job design, a poor work environment, or inadequate tools for workers. All jobs should be analyzed regularly to make sure workers are not expected to perform tasks that are unnecessarily difficult, and therefore prone to mistakes, and that they have the appropriate tools. In some cases, work complexity can be reduced through better product design. In others, job tasks can be improved and made less mistake-prone by using the job analysis and design techniques discussed in Chapter 10, or by providing workers with better tools. For example, Savin Corporation, which supplies and services photocopiers, found that a major service quality problem was due to service technicians dropping screws into the machines. By simply providing technicians with magnetic screwdrivers, they virtually eliminated the problem.[9]

4. ***Organization and Responsibility of Workers.*** One of the more widely publicized quality enhancement techniques is the use of **quality circles**. Quality circles are small groups of workers (usually 5–10) who meet regularly to discuss ways to improve productivity and product quality. Most members of the circle participate directly in the production process, so they have firsthand experience with current work methods and ideas on how to make them better. Quality circles provide a formal mechanism to solicit and evaluate ideas, transmit them to management, and implement them quickly on approval. However, although quality circles have been used successfully, they are not easy to implement and operate. They require good training, good selection of circle members, and support of management so that circle recommendations are evaluated, approved, and implemented quickly and members can see the benefit of their work. There must also be an incentive system that rewards serious participation in the quality circles.

   A more ongoing organizational structure is the use of *work teams*, which was discussed in Chapter 10. In addition to their flexibility, teams bring together the skills of several workers to solve quality problems and improve methods on a constant basis, rather than once a month at special meetings.

5. ***Setups and Startups.*** Many quality conformance problems are due to poor ma-

[9]From Robert Williams, "Putting Deming's Principles to Work," *Wall Street Journal*, Nov. 4, 1991.

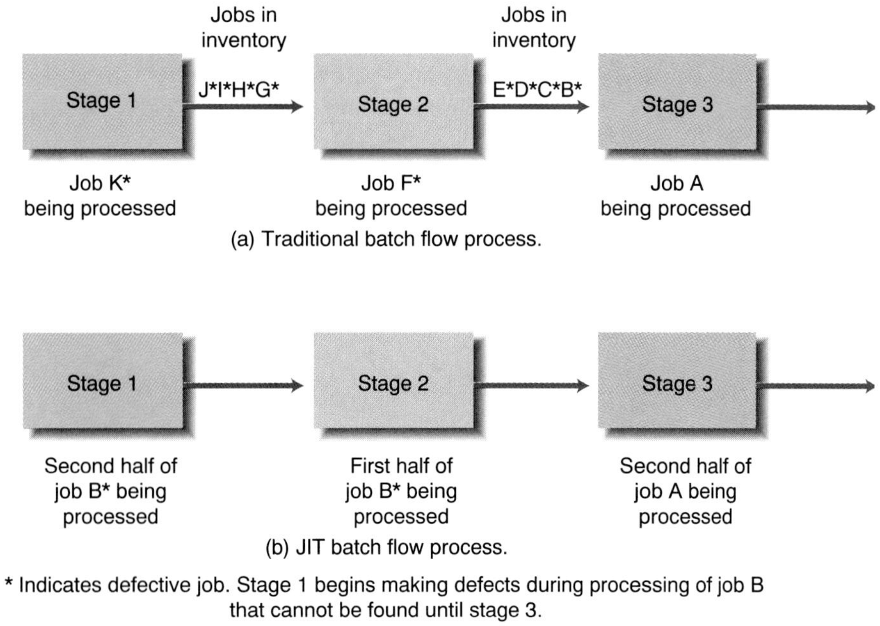

FIGURE 11.2 Identifying quality problems.

chine setups, and defects are most likely to occur during the startup of a production run as the operators are trying to calibrate the process. In the past, workers were often expected to devise their own procedures for setting up a machine and then testing it. We now know that setups can be done more efficiently and consistently, and produce better-quality products more quickly, by using structured methods. (Procedures for doing so are discussed in Chapter 15.) The key idea is to replace trial-and-error setups with structured and tested ones.

6. ***Just-in-Time Systems.*** **Just-in-time (JIT) production systems** have been touted not only for their productivity, but especially for the quality of the products they produce. Chapter 15 is devoted entirely to the characteristics of these systems; here, we briefly sketch some of their features that promote good conformance quality.

   In traditional batch flow processes, significant in-process inventories are maintained between work stages, as shown in Figure 11.2a, so production stages can operate more independently. If one stage shuts down because of a production setup or machine breakdown, other stages of the process will not be delayed. Although there is some validity to this approach, one implication of it is that the time a product waits between stages and the cycle time (the interval between the start and completion of product processing) can be long. Fred Wenninger, CEO of Iomega Corporation, summarizes the consequences: "When your cycle time is 28 days and you spot a defect at the end of the line, you can imagine how hard it is to isolate the problem."[10] In addition, a substantial number of defective items may be produced before the defect is found.

[10]Port et al., op. cit.

In contrast, key features of JIT production systems are a tight linkage between production stages, small lot sizes, small in-process inventories between stages, and short cycle times. The effect on quality can be seen by comparing Figures 11.2a and 11.2b. Suppose that in Figure 11.2a, while stage 1 was processing job B, it began making defects that could not be identified until the product reached stage 3. Then jobs B through K might all be defective before corrective action could be taken. However, in the JIT system in Figure 11.2b, if the same defect occurred at stage 1 while processing job B, it would be identified at stage 3 before product C began processing at stage 1, thereby making the problem easier to diagnose and reducing the number of defective items produced.

PRODUCTION OPERATIONS AND QUALITY CONFORMANCE

The final component of quality conformance is the operation of the production system itself. We will look at three aspects of the operations: (1) the quality of input materials, (2) the quality and training of personnel, and (3) the quality monitoring, testing, and feedback system.

1. ***Quality of Inputs.*** The quality of materials and components purchased from outside vendors can be improved by making suppliers partners in the production process. Supplier–customer partnerships have been an important part of the Japanese manufacturing infrastructure. Suppliers, who often have special expertise and experience, can improve the quality of their customers' products by helping them design and select components that will best suit the products they are making. In addition, suppliers make a big contribution by delivering products of good quality in a timely fashion. Poor-quality components cause work stoppages, machine shutdowns, and the production of defective products. A producer that can rely on timely deliveries of high-quality components can forgo quality inspections and schedule production more efficiently.
2. ***Quality and Training of Personnel.*** In spite of the benefits of automation, the simple fact is that product quality ultimately depends on how skilled workers are, how well they are trained to do their jobs, and how well they work. Job training that focuses on speed and ignores product quality will eventually lead to a production system that has product quality problems. Employee training should emphasize the quality of the products being made, the work techniques that will most likely ensure good product quality, and methods for evaluating and testing product quality.

These automated milling machines and lathes can produce superior quality products only if their operators are well-trained.

Training should help workers develop a sensitivity and a mind set that views everything the worker does with respect to its impact on the immediate and ultimate customers. The immediate customer for a production line worker may be the worker at the next work station. An accountant who prepares reports late or designs reports that do not provide useful information to others in the company is creating a quality problem for her internal customers. The ultimate customers are, of course, those who will eventually purchase the good or service.

3. ***Quality Monitoring, Testing, and Feedback.*** Even the best production processes will experience problems. The secret of maintaining good quality conformance in spite of such failures is to have a monitoring and feedback system that identifies quality problems and initiates corrective action as soon as possible. The quickest way to identify quality problems is to make individual workers responsible for monitoring and testing the quality of their own work. To accomplish this, workers must first be given the responsibility for monitoring their own quality and the authority to stop production and correct problems. Next, quality testing procedures must be established and workers trained to use them. These procedures may be as simple as visual inspection, or they may use chemical tests or electronic test equipment. In addition, some quality testing may be statistically based, such as the procedures discussed in Section 11.7, so appropriate mathematical training may be required.

   When defects are not caught at the source, the sooner the product can be processed at the next stage, where the defect may be caught, the better. We saw above that this is one of the advantages of a JIT production system with minimal inventories between production stages. In addition, some defects cannot be identified easily or inexpensively until the product is completed or nearly completed. For example, it is time-consuming to test every component in a radio when it is installed. However, once the receiver and amplifier are installed, it is easy to perform a crude quality test: just turn the radio on.

   The "final line of defense" against defective products is a final inspection stage. In some cases, it may be worthwhile to inspect every item produced, such as automobiles and television sets. In others, a random sample can be checked and the quality of the batch inferred to make sure a prohibitively large number of items are not defective within any shipment, such as toy figurines or other high-volume, low-value items. Methods for doing this are presented in the supplement to this chapter.

11.7 STATISTICAL QUALITY CONTROL

In recent years there has been a backlash against statistical quality control techniques, but statistical methods can play a useful role in some aspects of quality conformance. Statistical quality control was first introduced in 1924 by W. Shewhart, who devised the first control charts for monitoring production quality. These charts are used to identify when a production process has gone out of control and needs corrective action. A few years later, H. F. Dodge and H. G. Romig developed acceptance sampling procedures and tables. In acceptance sampling, the quality of a large quantity of items (e.g., a shipment or production lot) is estimated based on the quality of a small sample of items.

Statistical quality control spread rapidly after World War II. At first it produced many positive results, and it was an integral part of W. Edwards Deming's initial program for improving production quality in Japan. However, there was an excessive emphasis on acceptance sampling techniques. One problem with acceptance sampling is that it is based on the assumption that some proportion of defects is acceptable to the customer and that as long as the defect rate is below that level, everything is fine. Even if this assumption is true, which it is in some cases, it led to three unfortunate consequences: (1) companies started designing their production processes and methods to achieve this acceptable level of defects rather than to obtain the best quality that was reasonable (or even most profitable); (2) as long as the process was achieving the acceptable quality level, there was little incentive to improve the process to attain higher quality; and (3) quality management focused on inspecting incoming materials and final products to make sure that the level of defects was not above the acceptable level, rather than on preventing defects from occurring or catching them early. Rather than being a minimum threshold of quality that companies tried to improve on continuously, the acceptable quality level became an invisible barrier to improvement.

Modern quality management approaches now recognize the potential dangers of the assumption underlying acceptance sampling, and it has become less widely used. However, there are still situations where acceptance sampling can be helpful, especially for inspecting incoming goods. But because of its decreasing use, we discuss acceptance sampling techniques in the supplement to this chapter.

While acceptance sampling has become less popular, two other forms of statistical analysis have become more popular in quality management: statistical process control and defect cause–effect analysis.

STATISTICAL PROCESS CONTROL

Production processes, especially those involving machining or processing of materials, face two quality conformance problems. First, all processes exhibit some natural or normal variation in quality conformance, whether it be the precision of cuts or welds, the exactness of a chemical mixture, or the tightness of an assembly. This variation can be due to several factors, such as machine vibration, temperature and humidity variations, and normal randomness in human actions.

Second, almost all production processes will at some time experience abnormal variations in performance when the process goes out of control, causing defective products to be produced. This abnormal variation is sometimes called **assignable variation** because its cause, such as poor equipment setup, tool or die wear, equipment needing adjustment, or worker fatigue, can usually be assigned to some specific cause and corrected.

The challenge facing the process operators is to distinguish between these two situations. The company does not want to shut down a process that is operating in control, nor does it want to continue operating a process that goes out of control.[11] The purpose of **statistical process control (SPC)** is to provide a cost- and time-effective method for determining whether variations from a target level of quality are due to normal randomness or to the process being out of control, and to identify an out-of-control condition *before* defective items are actually produced.

SPC begins with the recognition that some normal level of quality variation is inherent in the production process. (The amount of normal variation can often be reduced through good product and process design, but once these designs are completed the natural variation of the process is somewhat fixed; it is this residual variation that we call *normal variation*.) Although the general notion of SPC is the same for most situations, the specific methods and charts used differ according to whether the quality di-

[11]In statistical hypothesis testing, concluding that the process is out of control when it is really in control is called a *type I error*, and concluding that the process is in control when it is not is called a *type II error*.

mension is measurable over some range of numerical values, such as the product's weight, or whether items can only be categorized as defective or nondefective, such as the quality of a weld. In the former case, we utilize **process control by variables**; in the latter, **process control by attributes**.

SPC BY VARIABLES

Processes can be out of control in at least two important ways, as shown in Figure 11.3: (1) the average value of the product characteristic (the amount of soda in a bottle) may wander away from the target value (12 fluid ounces), and (2) the amount of variation from item to item may be greater than normal, whether or not the average value is near the target value. Identifying these two situations requires different forms of analysis. The methods presented here are based on statistical sampling theory, but to make their use easier most of the statistical analysis has been converted to simple charts called **control charts**.

The $\overline{X}$-Chart

Suppose an important dimension of quality for a product, say a metal shaft, is its diameter. The product design would specify some *target* diameter for the shaft, such as 2.500 cm, and a tolerance range, such as ± 0.020 cm. Ideally, we would like to make every shaft with exactly a 2.500 cm diameter, but in practice this is probably impossible. In-

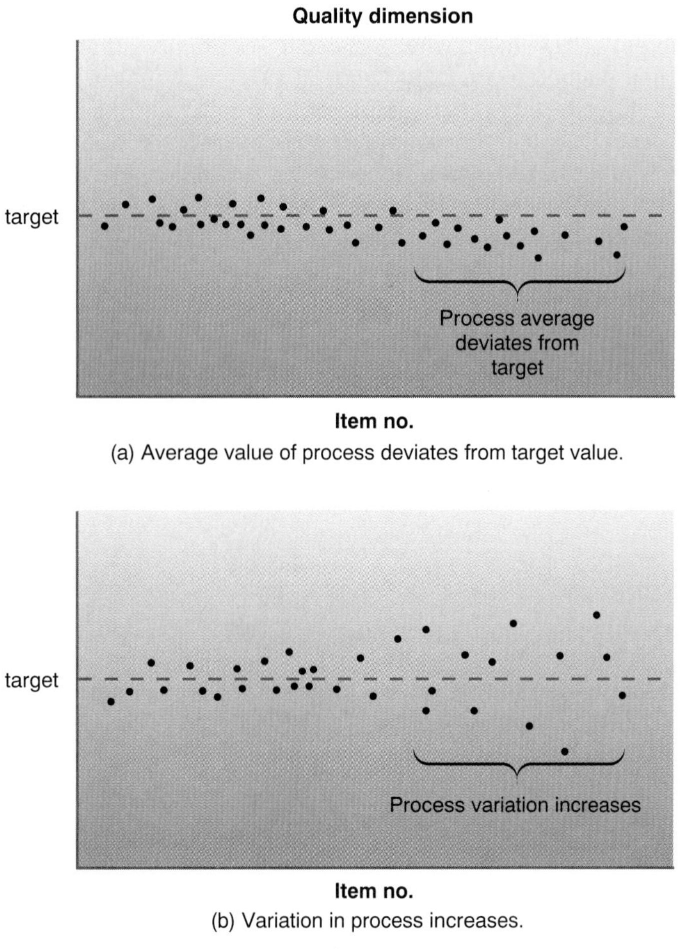

FIGURE 11.3 Out-of-control processes.

stead, we say that the shaft is of acceptable quality (is usable) if the diameter is within the range of 2.480–2.520 cm; these are called the **design** or **tolerance limits**. Even when the machining process is operating as planned, there will be random variations in the shaft diameters, so that a typical sequence of shafts produced may have diameters of 2.502, 2.503, 2.499, and 2.505 cm. None of the shafts has exactly the target diameter, but all of them are within the design limits. Does this imply that the process is in control? The answer is, "not necessarily." Processes can be out of control and still be producing product that is within specification; in other, though much rarer cases, the process could produce a defective item while still being in control.

To get an understanding of the theory underlying SPC, suppose μ is the target value for the product characteristic of interest, say shaft diameter, and σ is the **process standard deviation**—the standard deviation of the product characteristic values *when the process is operating in control*. If we were to measure the relevant characteristic, say shaft diameter, for each item produced and plot these values, we would get a **process distribution**, which is shown in Figure 11.4. This distribution is often approximately normally distributed, although it need not be.

With statistical process control, we use data from random samples of units made to infer whether or not the process is in control. Suppose we randomly select n items produced by the production process during a short period of time and compute the sample mean, $\bar{X}$, for some characteristic of this sample. Remember that the sample mean statistic is itself a random variable; depending on which units are in the sample, a different sample mean value will occur. For example, if we take a sample of four shafts and their diameters are 2.504, 2.501, 2.497, and 2.504 cm, the sample mean, $\bar{X}$, equals 2.5015. If we take another sample of four units and their diameters are 2.494, 2.502, 2,499, and 2.495 cm, the sample mean equals 2.4975. If $\bar{X}$ differs from the target value, μ, we would like to know whether or not this difference was due to the process being out of control—specifically, whether its mean value has shifted—or whether it was the result of normal variation for a process that is in control.

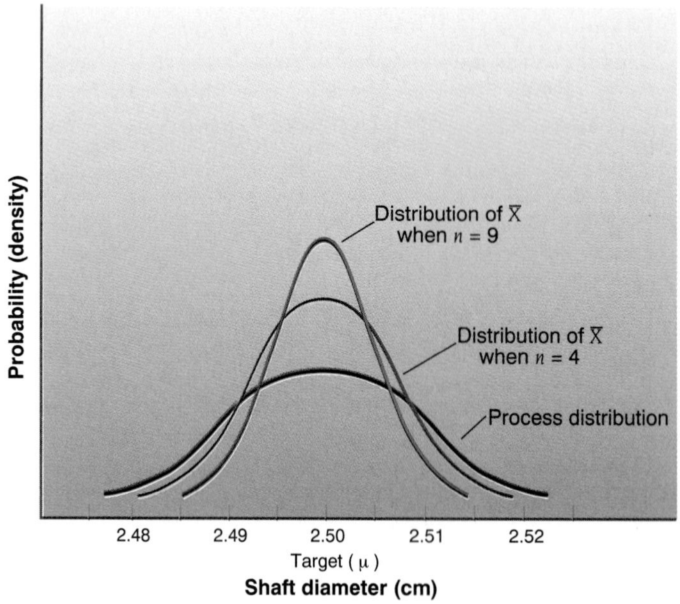

FIGURE 11.4 Process distribution and distributions of sample means for shaft diameters.

Statistical process control can identify small changes in this baking process before defective items are actually produced.

The Central Limit Theorem states that for sufficiently large random samples of size n, the sample mean, $\bar{X}$, is approximately normally distributed, with a mean of μ and a standard deviation of $\sigma_{\bar{X}} = \sigma/\sqrt{n}$.[12] In other words, the mean of the sample means should be the same as the mean for the process distribution, but the standard deviation of the sample means is smaller than σ and decreases with the square root of n. (This is so because the average of several data points should have less variation than the individual items being produced.) Figure 11.4 illustrates how the sampling distribution of the sample mean is related to the distribution of the underlying process and how it is affected by the size of the sample.

Based on the normal distribution for $\bar{X}$, if the process is in control the probability of the sample mean, $\bar{X}$, differing from the target value, μ, by as much as $|\bar{X} - \mu|$ is equal to $2 \times \text{Prob}\{z > |\bar{X} - \mu|/\sigma_{\bar{X}}\}$, where z is the standard normal random variable. This probability can be determined using the z-table in Appendix A. For example, we would expect the sample mean to take on a value more than $3\sigma_{\bar{X}}$ away from the target value only 0.26% of the time:

$$\text{Prob}\{|\bar{X} - \mu| > 3\sigma_{\bar{X}}\} = 2 \times \text{Prob}\{z > 3\sigma_{\bar{X}}/\sigma_{\bar{X}}\} = 2 \times \text{Prob}\{z > 3\} = 2(0.0013) = 0.0026$$

If, on the other hand, the process were out of control, so that the true mean value of the process differed from the target value, then it would be more likely for $\bar{X}$ to deviate significantly from the target value. Therefore, if we were to take a sample and $\bar{X}$ were more than $3\sigma_{\bar{X}}$ away from the target value, we could conclude that there is less than a 0.26% chance that such a large deviation was due to the normal variation of a process that is actually in control. It is more likely, though not certain, that the process is out of control and action may need to be taken.

To make it easier to use this analysis, we can construct what is called an **$\bar{X}$-control chart**, or simply an **$\bar{X}$-chart**, which is illustrated in Figure 11.5. A worker who is tracking the quality of units produced by some operation would regularly take random samples and record the mean of the sample (for some product characteristic) on the $\bar{X}$-chart. On the vertical axis the target value specified for the product is marked, along with an **upper control limit ($UCL_{\bar{X}}$)** and a **lower control limit ($LCL_{\bar{X}}$)**. If the sample mean falls between the $LCL_{\bar{X}}$ and the $UCL_{\bar{X}}$, the deviation from the target value is considered small enough to allow us to conclude that the process is not out of control. On the other hand, if a sample mean value is greater than the upper control limit or less than

[12]This assumes that the items being sampled are normally distributed or that n is sufficiently large; $n = 4$ or 5 is often enough if the deviations around the target value are not too skewed.

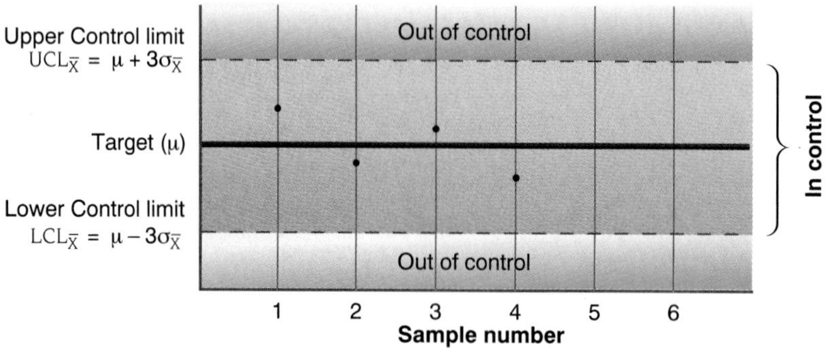

FIGURE 11.5 Three-sigma $\bar{X}$-chart.

the lower control limit, we would conclude that this is probably not due to normal randomness; instead, the process is probably out of control. We would then either seek additional information to verify this or we would take action to identify the cause of the problem and correct it, which may involve stopping the production process.

The $UCL_{\bar{X}}$ and $LCL_{\bar{X}}$ values on the control chart are determined by how large a sample we are willing to take and how much risk of mistakenly stopping an in-control process we are willing to incur. The upper and lower control limits can be stated as

$$UCL_{\bar{X}} = \mu + z\,\sigma_{\bar{X}} \qquad (11.1)$$
$$LCL_{\bar{X}} = \mu - z\,\sigma_{\bar{X}}$$

where z is the number of standard deviations of the sample mean required to achieve the desired level of confidence. The value of z can be determined based on some specified level of confidence; for example, for a 95% level of confidence $z = 1.96$, and for a 99% level of confidence $z = 2.58$. In other words, with $z = 2.58$ there is less than a 1% chance of the sample mean taking a value outside the control limits (above $UCL_{\bar{X}}$ or below $LCL_{\bar{X}}$) if the process is actually in control. Rather than setting a confidence level in advance and computing z, it has become more common to use some safe round

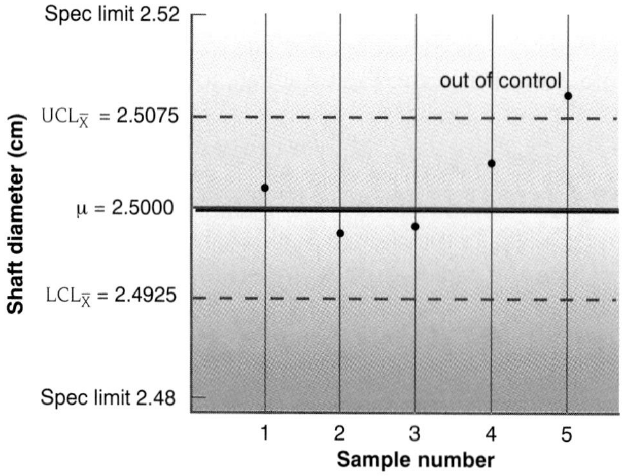

FIGURE 11.6 Three-sigma $\bar{X}$-chart for shaft diameters.

number for z, such as $z = 3$, which is equivalent to a 99.7% confidence level. Control charts using $z = 3$, such as Figure 11.5, are called *three-sigma* control charts.

In addition to the confidence level (the value of z), the width of the control range is determined by the sample size, n, because

$$\sigma_{\overline{X}} = \sigma/\sqrt{n}.$$

Usually we try to keep the sample size small to save time and money, especially if the testing is at all destructive to the product. But the smaller the sample size, the more $\overline{X}$ has to deviate from the target value for us to conclude that the process is out of control for some specified confidence level. The drawback is that the chance of not recognizing a process that is out of control is larger with a smaller sample size. Most commonly, samples of 4–10 items are used.

The use and properties of $\overline{X}$-charts are shown in the following example.

EXAMPLE 1

Suppose we produce metal shafts that are supposed to have a diameter of 2.500 ± 0.020 cm. The process standard deviation, σ, is estimated to be approximately 0.005. If we plan to take samples of size 4, then $\sigma_{\overline{X}} = 0.005/\sqrt{4} = 0.0025$, and the three-sigma $\overline{X}$-chart (shown in Figure 11.6) would have control limits of

$$UCL_{\overline{X}} = 2.500 + 3(0.0025) = 2.5075$$
$$LCL_{\overline{X}} = 2.500 - 3(0.0025) = 2.4925$$

Suppose we now begin to sample units that are produced. The shafts in the first sample have diameters of 2.502, 2.504, 2.501, and 2.503, cm, with a sample mean of $\overline{X} =$ 2.5025. This is within the control limits, so the process would be considered in control. Suppose that later a sample had diameters of 2.505, 2.509, 2.508, and 2.510 cm. The sample mean is 2.508, which is above the upper control limit, so this suggests that the mean or central tendency of the process is out of control. (For example, machine vibration may have caused the setting on some tool to move away from its original location.)

Notice that from the second sample it was concluded that the process was out of control, *even though no unit in the sample was defective*, that is, outside the design specification limits of 2.480–2.520 cm. Ideally, we would like this to occur, that is, to find a process that is out of control *before* it produces defective items. In reality, the rule for deciding what action to take when the value of $\overline{X}$ falls outside the control limits may be more complex than "Shut down the process if $\overline{X}$ is outside of the control range and do nothing if it is within the control range." If $\overline{X}$ is only slightly outside the control limits, we might instead take another sample immediately to verify the condition before taking more serious action, because if we take enough samples even a process that is in control will occasionally produce sample means outside the control range by random chance.

Now suppose the process has, in fact, gone out of control so that the mean value of the process has shifted to 2.510 cm. Suppose we select a sample of four shafts and the diameters are 2.512, 2.514, 2.511, and 2.513 cm (notice that the deviations from the actual process mean are the same as in the first sample). The sample mean is 2.5125, which is outside the control limits. In this case, we would conclude that the process is

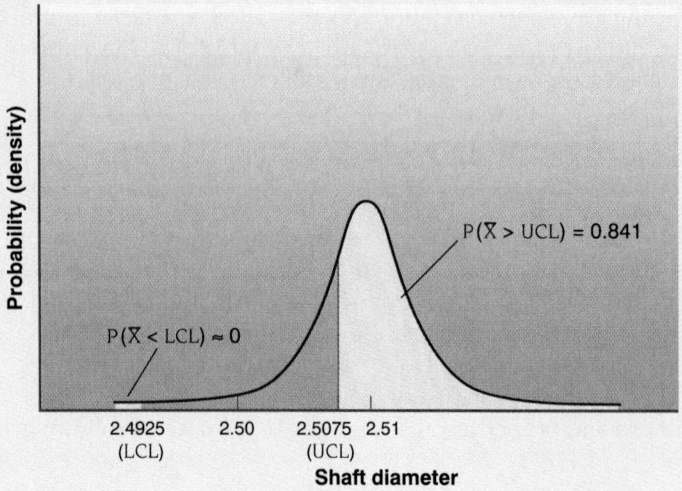

FIGURE 11.7 Distribution of $\bar{X}$ when the process mean shifts to 2.51 cm.

out of control, which it is, but again, no individual shaft in the sample is defective; we identified a true out-of-control condition before defectives occurred.

More generally, if the mean shaft diameter for the process shifted to 2.510 cm, Figure 11.7 shows that the probability that the sample mean would fall outside the control limits is

$$\begin{aligned}&\text{Prob}\{\bar{X} > 2.5075\} + \text{Prob}\{\bar{X} < 2.4925\}\\&= \text{Prob}\{z > (2.5075 - 2.510)/0.0025\} + \text{Prob}\{z < (2.4925 - 2.510)/0.0025\}\\&= \text{Prob}\{z > -1.0\} + \text{Prob}\{z < -7.0\}\\&= 0.841 + 0.000 = 0.841\end{aligned}$$

In other words, if the process is in control, there is only a 0.3% chance that $\bar{X}$ would be outside the control limits and mistakenly signal an out-of-control condition. But if this process shifts out of control by 2σ (0.01 cm), the chance of $\bar{X}$ falling outside the control limits for any given sample is 84.1%. Therefore, the chance of the out-of-control condition existing for long is relatively small as long as sampling is done frequently enough.

Process Capability and Design Limits

An important concept in quality conformance is process capability. The **process capability** is the probability or rate at which product will be produced within design limits (tolerances). If the design tolerance is large relative to the process standard deviation, σ, the process capability will be good and very few units will be produced with characteristic values outside the design limits when the process is in control. More important, a large process capability implies that even when the process mean moves out of control by 1–2 σ, few defective items will be produced. On the other hand, if the design tolerances are small relative to σ, the process capability is poor and even when the process is in control, defective items will be produced frequently. Further, even slight out-of-control conditions will dramatically increase the defect rate. In general, the greater the process capability, the more the process can be allowed to move from the

TABLE 11.4 THREE-SIGMA $\bar{R}$-CHART CONSTANTS

Sample Size	d_2	LCL_R Constant d_3	UCL_R Constant d_4
2	1.13	0	3.27
3	1.69	0	2.57
4	2.06	0	2.28
5	2.33	0	2.11
6	2.53	0	2.00
7	2.70	0.08	1.92
8	2.85	0.14	1.86
9	2.97	0.18	1.82
10	3.08	0.22	1.78
11	3.17	0.26	1.74
12	3.26	0.28	1.72
13	3.34	0.31	1.69
14	3.41	0.33	1.67
15	3.47	0.35	1.65
16	3.53	0.36	1.64
17	3.59	0.38	1.62
18	3.64	0.39	1.61
19	3.69	0.40	1.60
20	3.74	0.41	1.59

Source: E. L. Grant and R. Leavenworth, Statistical Quality Control (6th ed.), McGraw-Hill, New York, 1988.

target without causing defects. If the design limits are set at $\pm 6\sigma$ (the so-called Motorola standard), then when the process is in control only 2 parts per *billion* would be defective, and the process could be out of control (shifted from the target value) by as much as 1.5σ and still only 3.4 parts per million would be defective.

Estimating σ

Unless the process standard deviation is known through controlled experiments, σ is usually estimated using the average range for an initial set of samples. This estimation procedure is easier than computing the sample standard deviation, yet it is very accurate and stable. Using a minimum of 20 samples, we first compute the **range,** R, for each sample, where R is the difference between the largest and smallest values in the sample. We then compute the average, $\bar{R}$, of these ranges. The process standard deviation can be estimated by

$$\sigma = \bar{R}/d_2, \tag{11.2}$$

where the values of d_2 are given in Table 11.4.[13] The values of d_2 are based on the relationship between the standard deviation of a normal distribution and the range that would be expected from a sample of size n.

[13]The notation d_2, d_3, and d_4 is widely used in the quality control literature for the constants in Table 11.4, so that notation is used here even though no d_1 is discussed.

R-Charts

Suppose in the previous example we took a sample of shafts and their diameters were 2.530, 2.468, 2.525, and 2.477 cm. The sample mean is exactly 2.500 cm, so the $\bar{X}$-chart would tell us that the process appears to be in control. Yet every one of the shafts sampled is defective. Does this mean that the $\bar{X}$-chart is useless? Or is the process really in control, but by pure chance we sampled four defective shafts?

The answer to both questions is "no." The $\bar{X}$-chart is intended to identify only one type of out-of-control condition: when the mean of the process shifts away from the target value. Another way in which a process can go out of control occurs when the magnitude of variation increases above its normal level; this can occur even when the mean value of the process stays near or at the target value. This problem can be caused by a variety of things. For example, vibration and wear can cause machine tools or dies to shift back and forth, so that the dimension of one unit may be above the target value and the next one may be below it. If the sample takes a few items from each group, the sample mean may be near the target value but the variation may be very large. Worker fatigue and inattention can also increase production variation.

One way to identify this out-of-control condition is to use a statistical test on the *range* of the sample rather than the sample mean. If the range is larger than expected, given the process standard deviation, we can conclude that the process is probably out of control (i.e., there is excessive variation). The decision rule is captured by the **range control chart** or ***R*-chart**. The general idea of an R-chart is the same as that of an $\bar{X}$-chart. We can compute an upper control limit (UCL_R) and a lower control limit (LCL_R). If the range from a sample is outside the control limits, this signals that the process appears to be behaving abnormally.

The upper and lower control limits for the R-chart are as follows:

$$UCL_R = d_4\bar{R}$$
$$LCL_R = d_3\bar{R} \qquad (11.3)$$

where $\bar{R}$ is the average sample range and d_3 and d_4 are constants that can be obtained from Table 11.4. The upper and lower control limit constants are based on the relationship between the standard deviation of a normal distribution and the expected range for a sample of a given size. (If σ is known, then from equation (11.2)

$$UCL_R = d_4d_2\sigma \text{ and } LCL_R = d_3d_2\sigma.)$$

The following example illustrates how to develop and use an $\bar{X}$-chart and an *R*-chart.

EXAMPLE 2

A beverage company would like to use SPC to monitor how much liquid beverage it puts into each 350 ml bottle. To be safe, it wants the filling machine to fill bottles with an average of 351 ml of liquid, and any bottle with less than 349.5 ml or more than 352.5 ml of liquid is considered defective. To establish its $\bar{X}$-chart and *R*-chart, the com-

TABLE 11.5 DATA FOR 21 SAMPLES OF FILLED BOTTLES

Sample No.	Ml. in Each Bottle				Sample Mean X	Range R
1	351.2	350.9	350.6	350.7	350.850	0.6
2	350.3	351.0	351.1	350.8	350.800	0.8
3	351.4	350.9	351.3	351.2	351.200	0.5
4	350.8	350.5	351.1	350.1	350.625	1.0
5	350.6	350.9	351.4	351.1	351.000	0.8
6	351.2	351.3	350.8	351.5	351.200	0.7
7	351.2	351.6	350.9	350.9	351.150	0.7
9	351.4	351.1	350.8	351.4	351.175	0.6
10	350.4	350.8	350.7	350.6	350.625	0.4
11	350.8	351.1	350.9	351.1	350.975	0.3
12	351.3	351.1	351.0	351.5	351.225	0.5
13	351.6	351.2	351.1	351.2	351.275	0.5
14	350.8	351.0	351.1	351.6	351.125	0.8
15	350.9	350.7	350.6	350.9	350.775	0.3
16	351.3	350.8	351.1	350.6	350.950	0.7
17	350.8	350.5	351.0	350.9	350.800	0.5
18	351.1	351.2	350.7	351.1	351.025	0.5
19	351.7	351.4	351.2	350.8	351.275	0.9
20	350.9	351.2	350.8	350.9	350.950	0.4
21	350.7	350.6	351.0	351.1	350.850	0.5
					$\bar{X}$ = 350.945	
					$\bar{R}$ =	0.571

pany operated its bottle-filling line under careful supervision for 7 hours. Every 20 minutes it sampled four bottles and carefully measured the amount of liquid in each bottle. The data are given in Table 11.5.

The average range is 0.571 ml, so using equation (11.2) and $d_2 = 2.06$ from Table 11.4, we can estimate the process standard deviation to be $\sigma = 0.571/2.06 = 0.277$ and $\sigma_{\bar{X}} = 0.277/\sqrt{4} = 0.139$. From equations (11.1) the control limits for the $\bar{X}$-chart are

$$UCL_{\bar{X}} = 351.000 + 3(0.139) = 351.417$$

$$LCL_{\bar{X}} = 351.000 - 3(0.139) = 350.583$$ [14]

Using equations (11.3), we can compute UCL_R and LCL_R for the R-chart:

$$UCL_R = d_4\bar{R} = 2.28(0.571) = 1.302$$

$$LCL_R = d_3\bar{R} = 0.00(0.571) = 0.000$$

We would now regularly take samples of four bottles, compute the sample mean and range, and plot them on the control charts. If the values were outside the control limits we would initiate some action, such as taking another sample immediately or stopping the operation to identify the cause of the problem.

[14]Some books compute UCL $= \bar{\bar{X}} + 3\sigma_{\bar{X}}$ and LCL $= \bar{\bar{X}} - 3\sigma_{\bar{X}}$, where $\bar{\bar{X}}$ is the average of many sample means taken when the process is in control. When the characteristic of interest does not have some specified value in the product design, such as the average time required to provide some service, it is reasonable to center the chart on $\bar{\bar{X}}$, but when there is a target value, μ, this value should be used; otherwise, the process would automatically be biased by the original samples.

Notice that in Table 11.4 the lower control limit for the R-chart can be greater than zero. A reasonable question is, why should there be *any* lower control limit for the R-chart, and if there is one, why would we care if the range were unusually small? Certainly we would not want to change the process to make the variation larger. The answer is that from a statistical viewpoint, a very low range for a sample is probabilistically unusual and might indicate that the process is behaving abnormally—abnormally well! We would not consider this to be a problem, as we would for a range above the upper control limit, but we would be interested in finding out why it was so low. For example, we might find that the operator has made some change in the process or that we are using components from a new supplier. In this case, we would want to incorporate these changes into the process on a regular basis.

Other SPC Methods: Run Patterns and Cycles

Occasionally, the average value of a process remains close to the target value and the variation in values does not increase above its normal level, yet the process is out of control. Suppose that for the process in Example 1 the diameters of eight shafts from two consecutive samples were 2.502, 2.501, 2.505, 2.504 and 2.505, 2.508, 2.503, and 2.504 cm. The sample means are 2.503 and 2.505 cm, both within the control limits on the $\overline{X}$-chart, and the sample ranges of 0.4. and 0.5 are within the control limits on the R-chart. Yet the fact that every one of the eight shafts has a diameter *greater than* the target value appears odd. Assuming that when the process is in control deviations above and below the target value are equally likely, the probability of eight randomly chosen shafts all being above the target value is $(1/2)^8 = 1/256$. Similarly, the probability that all eight would be below the target value if the process were under control is 1/256. So the probability of having a "run" of eight sample items all being above or all below the target value by a process that is under control is $1/256 + 1/256 = 1/128$.[15]

Such a run pattern may indicate that the process mean has shifted away from the target value but that the shift has been too subtle for the $\overline{X}$-chart to detect. Therefore, it is reasonable to provide an additional control check after each sample: if x consecutive items are all above or all below the target value, take action A. The action may be to take an additional sample before the scheduled time, or it may involve stopping the process.

Another out-of-control condition that is even more difficult to detect occurs when the process is *cycling* around the target value. For example, suppose the diameters for 10 consecutive shafts (not a sample) were 2.493, 2.498, 2.501, 2.507, 2.511, 2.506, 2.502, 2.497, 2.490, and 2.494 cm. None of the items is defective, and the average diameter is 2.500. Neither an $\overline{X}$-chart nor an R-chart will indicate any problem, but Figure 11.8, which is a plot of these values, suggests that these deviations from the target value are not random; instead, they appear to be cycling below the target, then above the target, then below it, and so on. This type of out-of-control condition can occur in several ways; for example, a machine setting or die that is loose will vibrate to some barrier and then vibrate back to another barrier. Cyclic variations are also sometimes the result of worker fatigue when someone consistently deviates from a target and then realizes it and overcompensates for a while.

Cyclic out-of-control conditions are difficult to detect for two reasons: (1) the patterns are rarely as clear as in Figure 11.8 and (2) normal sample sizes are too small and samples are taken too infrequently to detect such patterns. If, by the nature of the pro-

---

[15] In general, the probability that all n items in a sample have values above the target value is $(1/2)^n$, and the probability that the values of all items in a sample are on the same side of the target is $2 \times (1/2)^n = (1/2)^{n-1}$.

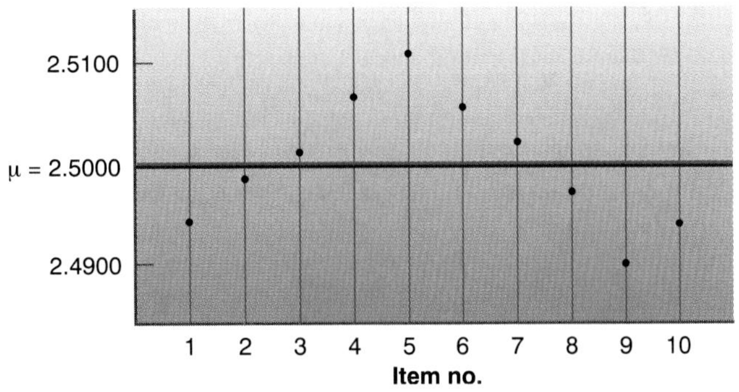

FIGURE 11.8 A process that is cycling.

duction process, cyclic out-of-control conditions are likely to occur, then the SPC sampling needs to be designed specially to detect this problem. This usually means using larger sample sizes, more frequent samples, and graphs of individual items to help identify patterns.

SPC BY ATTRIBUTES

The quality of many products is not determined by any measurable variable. Instead, the product is judged to be either acceptable or defective; for example, an electronic product either operates correctly or it does not. SPC can be applied to this situation using a $\overline{p}$-chart, which is similar to an $\overline{X}$-chart. The **$\overline{p}$-chart** tracks the *proportion* of defective items in random samples and compares this to the normal proportion of defective items that occur when the process is in control.

Let p be the normal proportion of items that are defective when the process is in control. This value may be obtained through controlled production experiments, or it could be the average proportion for all samples that were taken when the process was believed to be in control. Using the properties of the Bernoulli distribution, the control limits are

$$\begin{aligned} UCL_{\overline{p}} &= p + z\sigma_{\overline{p}} \\ LCL_{\overline{p}} &= \max\{p - z\sigma_{\overline{p}}, 0\} \end{aligned} \tag{11.4}$$

where $\sigma_{\overline{p}} = \sqrt{p(1-p)/n}$ is the standard deviation of the sample proportion and z is the number of standard deviations away from the mean to achieve a desired confidence level. As with the $\overline{X}$-chart it is common to use $z = 3$, that is, a three-sigma $\overline{p}$-chart.

We take regular samples of n items produced by the process, compute the sample proportion defective, $\overline{p}$, and plot these values on the $\overline{p}$-chart. If the sample proportion is above $UCL_{\overline{p}}$, this would signal that the process may be out of control and is producing an abnormally large number of defective items. As with the R-chart, a sample proportion *below* $LCL_{\overline{p}}$ is not a cause for concern but rather a signal to try to find out why the defect rate is so low. Has there been a change in the process that should be adopted permanently?

Because of the statistical properties of the sample proportion, the sample sizes required for the $\overline{p}$-chart to be effective are much larger than for the $\overline{X}$-chart and the R-

chart (in the 25–100 range). The following example illustrates the development and use of the $\bar{p}$-chart in a service operation.

EXAMPLE 3

A hardware distributor stocks thousands of different plumbing and electrical products. It receives hundreds of orders every day from its customers. The company has always been known for the quality of its service in filling orders correctly within 24 hours, and it wants to maintain this reputation. From historical audits of purchase orders, the company has estimated that when it is operating well only 0.25% of the orders are filled incorrectly or shipped late. Because personnel, computer hardware and software, suppliers, and the customer population are changing constantly, processing errors can quickly increase above this level without warning. The company wants to identify any degradation in service quality immediately, so it has decided to institute SPC by attributes. Each day the customer service manager will select 25 customer orders randomly and investigate whether they were filled correctly and on time. The normal defect proportion is $p = 0.0025$, so $\sigma_{\bar{p}} = \sqrt{[(0.0025)(1 - 0.0025)]/25} = 0.010$. From equations (11.4) the upper and lower control limits for a three-sigma $\bar{p}$-chart are

$$UCL_{\bar{p}} = 0.0025 + 3(0.010) = 0.0325$$
$$LCL_{\bar{p}} = 0.0025 - 3(0.010) = -0.0275 = \rightarrow LCL_{\bar{p}} = 0$$

These control limits imply a simple decision rule. If the manager finds one or more order-processing "defects" in a sample, the sample proportion is 0.04 or larger, which is above $UCL_{\bar{p}}$. This suggests that the process may be going out of control. However, the company does not want to invest much time or money in investigating what might be one randomly chosen, normal mistake. So it developed the following rule: If there are two or more "defects" in a sample or two consecutive samples have at least one defect each, then the manager will investigate the cause of the errors and determine whether corrective actions are necessary.

DEFECT TRACKING AND CAUSE–EFFECT ANALYSIS

One of the simplest and most valuable things an organization can do to improve quality is to collect data on the frequency and causes of defects. Accurate data on quality help the organization evaluate its performance by comparing itself with competitors and other benchmarks. Further, the organization can track its performance over time to determine whether or not it is improving. In addition, collecting data on all defects is an essential element in identifying and solving quality problems and improving the production process. For example, Promus Company, a major hotel company, found that an important customer complaint was the amount of time customers had to wait to get irons and ironing boards delivered to their rooms. Rather than having employees shuttle these items among rooms, Promus found that it could provide each room with its own iron and board at minimal cost; this action completely eliminated this complaint.[16]

SPC can be very helpful in identifying failures in the production system quickly, but it cannot identify the *cause* of the problem or suggest a solution. For example, it is rela-

[16]From David Greising, "Quality: How to Make It Pay," *Business Week*, Aug. 8, 1994, pp. 54–59.

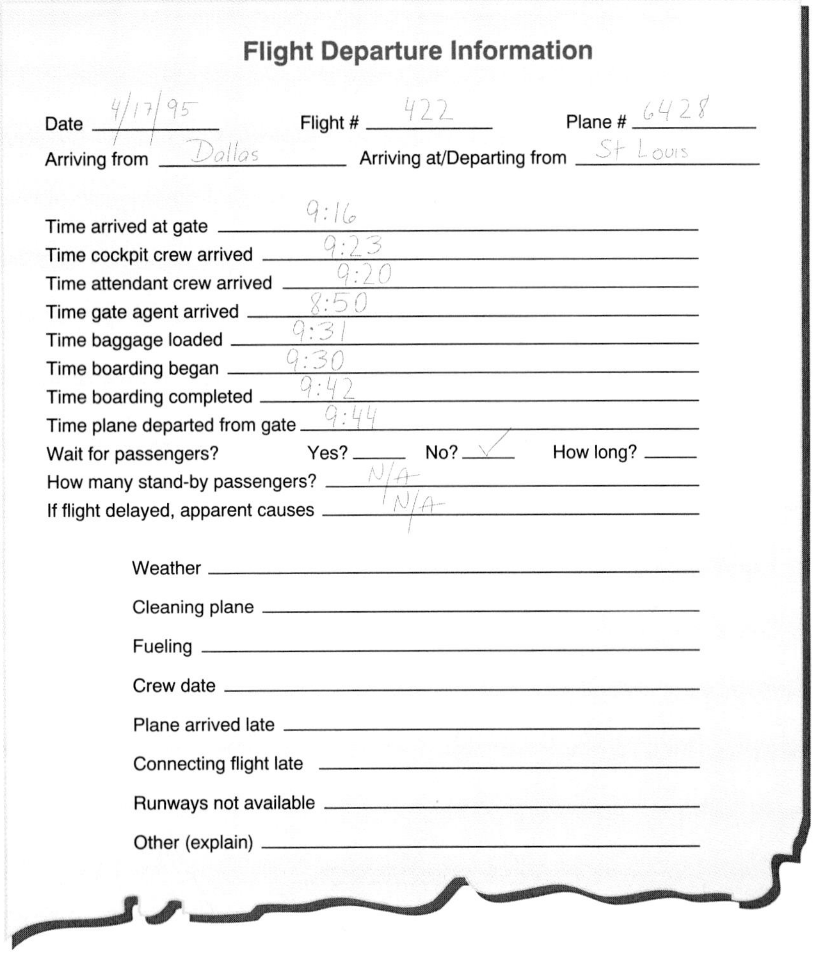

Flight Departure Information

Date 4/17/95 Flight # 422 Plane # 6428

Arriving from Dallas Arriving at/Departing from St Louis

Time arrived at gate 9:16

Time cockpit crew arrived 9:23

Time attendant crew arrived 9:20

Time gate agent arrived 8:50

Time baggage loaded 9:31

Time boarding began 9:30

Time boarding completed 9:42

Time plane departed from gate 9:44

Wait for passengers? Yes? ___ No? ✓ How long? ___

How many stand-by passengers? N/A

If flight delayed, apparent causes N/A

Weather

Cleaning plane

Fueling

Crew date

Plane arrived late

Connecting flight late

Runways not available

Other (explain)

FIGURE 11.9 Data collection instrument for defect-tracking analysis

tively easy for an airline to determine if too many of its flights are taking off and arriving late; in the United States this information is, in fact, made public by the government. The important issue is *why* so many flights are late; what are the primary causes? To answer this question, the airline should have a mechanism for collecting data on the possible causes. For example, gate attendants can record on prepared forms, such as the one in Figure 11.9, the times crews arrive, whether or not the flight is intentionally held for passengers from connecting flights, or whether or not standby passengers had to be processed for the flight.

Cause–Effect/ Fishbone Charts

Defect data are often most useful when used in conjunction with a **cause–effect chart**, commonly referred to as a **fishbone chart** because the network of causes looks like the skeleton of a fish, such as the one in Figure 11.10. A fishbone chart is constructed to identify the causes of a specific quality defect, such as late departure. To construct a fishbone chart, general types of causes are identified (the main bones of the skeleton); then, within each general category, specific causes are listed (the smaller bones). This chart is best developed by someone who is knowledgeable about the overall operation,

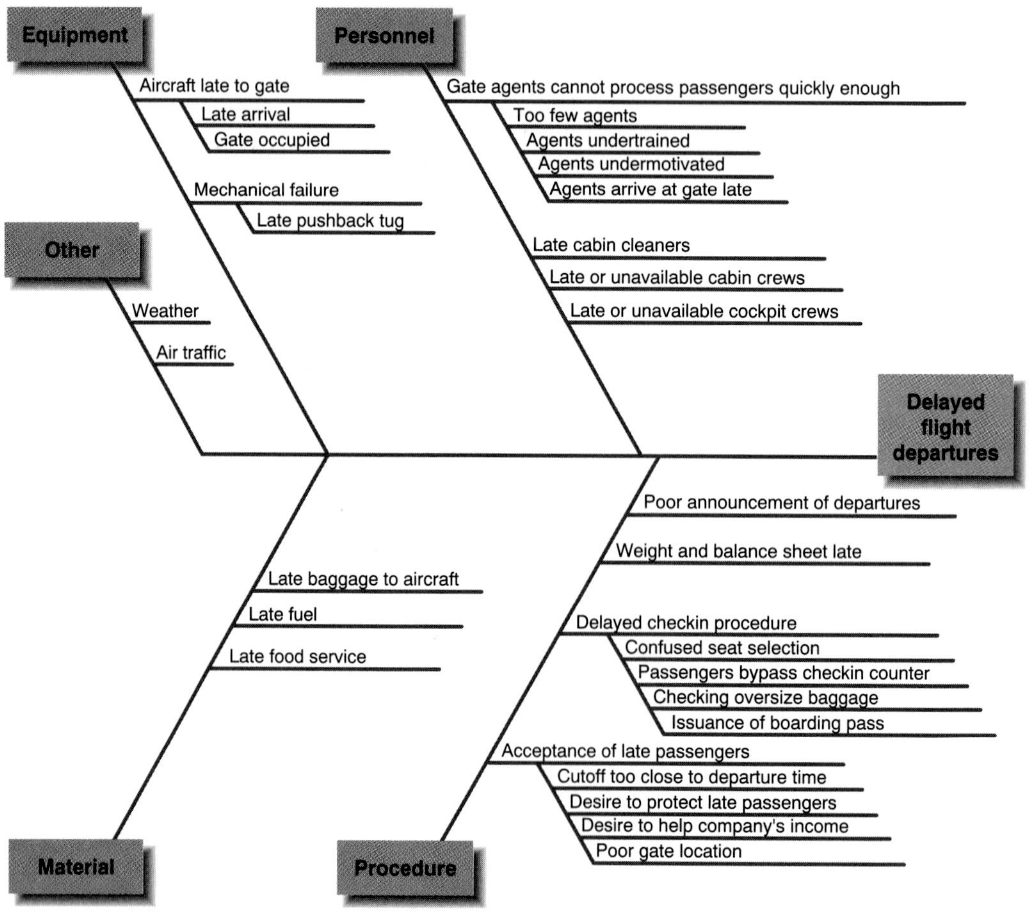

FIGURE 11.10 Fishbone Chart for Airline
Source: D. Daryl Wyckoff, "New Tools for Achieving Service Quality," The Cornell Hotel and Restaurant Administration Quarterly, November 1984, pp. 78–91. Copyright Cornell University. All rights reserved. Used by permission.

using input from those involved in the operation itself. It also requires hard data such as those discussed above. Defect tracking data and cause–effect data collection support each other and are often developed initially as part of the quality cost audit. As one collects detailed data on the location and magnitude of quality costs, the primary causes of defects become apparent and motivate an in-depth study of these causes. Figure 11.10 shows a fishbone chart used by a passenger airline to reduce the number of late flights. From the chart and analysis the airline determined that the primary causes of late flights were late-arriving customers and slow boarding rather than mechanical or weather problems. This helped the airline focus on getting customers to the gates early and speeding up plane turnaround and boarding.

11.8 SERVICE QUALITY

Although much of the theory and many of the techniques of quality management discussed in this chapter were developed by and for manufacturing companies, almost all of them are equally applicable to service organizations and service operations within manufacturing companies. The quality of service depends on the design of the service product and the service system at least as much as the quality of a manufactured good does, and in many cases the link between customer requirements and service product attributes is clearer than for goods. Furthermore, Example 3 demonstrated that SPC can be used to monitor and improve service quality.

Service quality has been discussed in other places throughout this book. Here we simply emphasize a few of the quality dimensions that are especially important for most service systems.

1. ***Performance.*** Whether the service is getting a haircut, processing a bank loan, completing a tax return, or performing a medical procedure, service customers are usually most concerned with whether or not the service is performed correctly. Some organizations have tried to improve the quality of their services by increasing the range or amenities of the services. This can help, but Frank Vitek of the Coin Laundry Association warns that the core business has to be done right: "If you don't get their clothes clean, it won't matter if you put a beer in their hand."[17]

2. ***Timeliness and Speed of Service.*** The value obtained from a service often depends on its timeliness. A home loan approval that is not received until weeks after the contracted closing date may be of no value to a house buyer; an illness diagnosed and a medical procedure performed one week later than it should have been could be fatal. For most services, speed of delivery should be treated as an important quality dimension and should be monitored regularly.

   For real-time services that the customer wants as soon as possible (in contrast to scheduled service), waiting may be unavoidable. However, Chapter 9 provided a number of suggestions on how to reduce customer waiting, and how to make waiting as equitable and tolerable as possible. Even a little attention to queueing and customer waiting, such as the use of single lines, express servers, self-service facilities, and enhancements of the waiting environment, can significantly increase customer satisfaction. For example, at very little cost, the "We'll Clean Auto Spa" increased the number and satisfaction of customers by installing a rabbit-petting pen, an aquarium, a TV, and other amenities for kids.

[17]From Melissa Lee, "Service Providers Try to Make the Mundane Bearable," *Wall Street Journal*, July 13, 1993.

3. **Honesty and Courtesy.** Perceptual attributes are usually more important for service products than for goods. For services such as retailing, there is little difference among companies in terms of the products sold or the prices charged. Instead, they compete in terms of honesty, courtesy, helpfulness, and other perceptual dimensions that in some cases are almost inseparable from performance itself.

11.9 TOTAL QUALITY MANAGEMENT

Given the many aspects of quality discussed above and the large number of quality experts espousing their own approaches, it is easy to be overwhelmed by the magnitude and complexity of the problem. One might ask: (1) which actions are best for improving quality? and (2) whose quality program and philosophy should be adopted? The answer is that there are many ways to improve product quality. And in spite of the disagreements among recognized quality experts on specific issues, several common themes are shared by most or all of the successful quality management programs. An overriding theme of these experts is that good product quality requires a coherent program of activities and policies that combines people, technology, and processes within an institutional infrastructure that provides the correct vision, organization, incentives, and support.

This section presents a wide-reaching, integrated quality program and philosophy, called **total quality management (TQM)**, that synthesizes the most important quality principles and practices proposed by quality gurus, such as Deming, Juran, Ishikawa, Shingo, and others. TQM addresses both the design and conformance aspects of quality, and it provides a coherent approach that readily encompasses all the quality management principles and tools discussed above.

HISTORY OF TQM

TQM has evolved over the past five decades to incorporate and synthesize ideas from many sources. Many of the basic ideas underlying TQM originated in the United States and then were organized and presented to Japanese companies following World War II as part of the Civil Communication Section seminars and Training Within Industry program. The two people most closely associated with the development of comprehensive quality management programs in Japan, and subsequently in the United States, are W. Edwards Deming and Joseph M. Juran.

Deming was most widely noted for teaching the need for management to take responsibility for the quality system and for having organizationwide participation. He especially emphasized the need for a total quality system to make products right the first time rather than inspecting away defects. Although Deming supported the use of statistical methods, he advocated using them primarily as a quality monitoring and improvement device rather than as a defect-catching mechanism. This quality management philosophy is summarized by **Deming's 14-point program**, which is paraphrased in Table 11.6.

Juran similarly lays the blame for poor quality on management, and he insists that good product quality requires an organizationwide approach and management involvement. Juran characterizes his quality program as a **quality trilogy** made up of quality planning, quality monitoring and control, and quality improvement. Some of his distinctive contributions include (1) attention to the customer as the determiner of quality, (2) an emphasis on identifying the true costs of quality, (3) making trade-offs that

TABLE 11.6 DEMING'S 14-POINT PROGRAM FOR QUALITY

1. Create constancy of purpose to improve products and service.
2. Adopt the new philosophy of quality. We can no longer accept delays, mistakes, defective materials, and poor workmanship.
3. Cease dependence on mass inspection. Instead, require quality that is built in. Prevent defects rather than detect them.
4. Buy components based on quality as well as price. Eliminate suppliers whose quality is not acceptable.
5. Search for problems and continually improve the production system.
6. Institute and improve training; teach workers to do the job right.
7. Institute leadership so that supervisors help workers improve rather than simply ordering and punishing workers.
8. Drive out fear so that everyone may work effectively for the company.
9. Break down barriers between departments so that people in different departments will work as a team.
10. Eliminate numerical goals, posters, and slogans, which ask for new levels of productivity without providing improved methods.
11. Eliminate work standards based on numerical quotas.
12. Remove barriers that stand between workers and their pride of workmanship.
13. Institute a vigorous program of education and retraining.
14. Top management must take action to institute the new program.

Source: Adapted from Mary Walton, Deming Management at Work, Perigee Books, New York, 1991, pp. 17–19.

W. Edwards Deming was one of the founders of total quality management. The Deming Prize, established in his honor, is the most prestigious quality award in Japan.

promote the use of more quality planning rather than corrective action after poor products are made, and (4) striving for continuous improvements.

Under the direction of Deming and Juran, many Japanese companies implemented companywide quality management systems that focused on and expanded the responsibilities of individual employees. In addition, several Japanese became serious students of quality management and made significant new contributions themselves, most notably Shigeo Shingo, Kaoru Ishikawa, Yoji Akao, and Genichi Taguchi. Shigeo Shingo was a codeveloper of the Toyota production system, which has become a model for many manufacturers worldwide. Shingo focused especially on designing the production process and work methods to ensure perfect quality conformance. He was a primary developer of *poka-yoke* (mistake-proofing) techniques and a leading advocate of zero-defect systems that include 100% inspection, either by the workers performing the operation or by workers at the next stage. Ishikawa contributed much to the methods of continuous improvement. For example, he was instrumental in the development of cause–effect diagrams and the use of quality circles. Akao was the developer of quality function deployment for obtaining customer preferences and incorporating them into product design, and Taguchi developed his now famous method for robust product and process design.

Philip Crosby made a major contribution to American business by bringing quality management to public attention through his books and consulting. He has argued very persuasively that good quality pays, and that the assumed trade-off between higher quality and higher cost is generally false; better quality can often be obtained while lowering costs.

THE PRINCIPLES OF TQM

TQM is based on the following principles:

1. ***Primary Responsibility for Product Quality Rests with Top Management.*** Management must create an organizational structure, product design process, produc-

tion process, and incentives that encourage and reward good quality. Juran has stated clearly that "The critical variable in Japanese quality leadership is the extent of active participation by senior managers."[18]

2. ***Quality Should Be Customer Focused and Evaluated Using Customer-Based Standards.*** A product is not easy to use, and a service is not courteous and prompt unless customers say they are. This fact requires organizations to work closely with their customers to determine what the customers want in the products and how they receive value from the products.
3. ***The Production Process and Work Methods Must Be Designed Consciously to Achieve Quality Conformance.*** Using the right tools and equipment, mistake-proofing processes, training workers in the best methods, and providing a good work environment help to prevent defects rather than catching them. In addition, tightly synchronized production systems with quick communication among workers promote quick identification and solution of quality problems when they do occur.
4. ***Every Employee Is Responsible for Achieving Good Product Quality.*** This translates into self-inspection by workers rather than by separate quality control personnel, and it requires workers to cooperate in identifying and solving quality problems.
5. ***Quality Cannot Be Inspected into a Product, So Make It Right the First Time.*** Making it right or doing it right the first time should be the goal of every worker. Methods such as *poka-yoke* and structured machine setups, which increase the chance of doing it right the first time, should be utilized as much as possible.
6. ***Quality Must Be Monitored to Identify Problems Quickly and Correct Quality Problems Immediately.*** The statistical methods discussed in Section 11.7 can play a useful role in monitoring quality and identifying problems quickly. But self-inspection and assessment of work by employees and customer assessments of quality are important components of the quality monitoring mechanism.
7. ***The Organization Must Strive for Continuous Improvement.*** Excellent product quality is the result of workers striving to improve product quality and productivity on an ongoing basis using experience and experimentation. However, continuous improvement does not happen on its own. Organizational structures, work procedures, and policies should be established that promote and accelerate continuous improvement.

   A variety of organizational mechanisms have been used to promote continuous improvement, such as work teams, quality circles, and suggestion systems. Each of these methods utilizes workers who are directly involved in the production process as a primary source for improvement ideas. Some experts, however, believe that separate improvement teams should be used to initiate and guide improvement projects. A valuable technique that can be used in either case to promote continuous improvement is the **plan-do-check-act cycle** (also called the **Shewhart cycle** or the **Deming wheel**), shown in Figure 11.11. The first step of the technique (plan) is to study the process, collect data to identify problems, analyze the data, and develop a plan for improvement. We then implement the plan (do) on a small-scale, trial basis and collect data on its performance. Third, we evaluate the data (check) to see whether the planned improvements really im-

---

[18]From Joseph Juran, "Made in U.S.A.: A Renaissance in Quality," *Harvard Business Review*, Vol. 71, No. 4, 1993, p. 50.

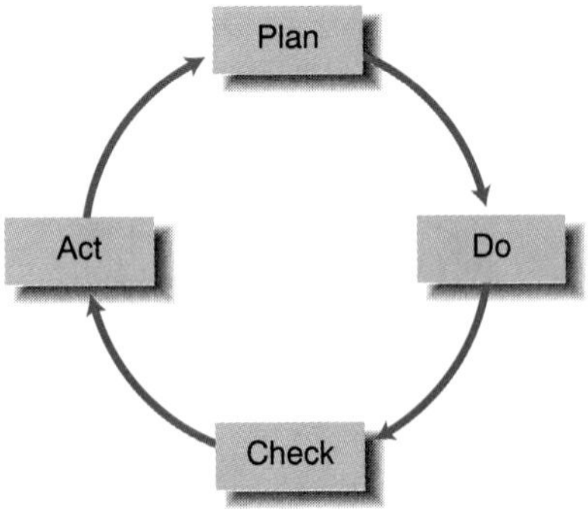

FIGURE 11.11 Plan-do-check-act cycle.

prove the process. Finally, if the proposed changes do improve the process, we standardize the methods, communicate them to the workers, and implement the new methods in the training process (act).

8. ***Companies Must Work with, and Extend TQM Programs to Their Suppliers to Ensure Quality Inputs.*** For many manufacturing companies, purchased components and materials account for well over 50% of their production costs. Similarly, over 80% of the costs of many wholesalers and retailers are the costs of goods intended for resale. If suppliers are providing low-quality components, materials, or goods, then the purchasing company will find it impossible to achieve a high level of quality in the goods and services it produces. In fact, many companies now require suppliers to have quality management programs that have been certified by the customer or by a recognized certification organization, such as the International Organization for Standardization. (ISO 9000 certification is discussed in the next section.)

Disagreements among quality experts have received considerable publicity, but the differences have been over minor issues, not the central themes of their programs. One need not agree with a person's entire philosophy or all of the program's details in order to adopt the program in part. In fact, the success of the Japanese in producing quality products can be attributed to their willingness to borrow and synthesize ideas from many sources and to the effort of each organization to customize the quality system to its own character. Some companies use quality circles, while others do not; some have extensive suggestion systems, while others do not; some use statistical methods, while others do not; and some strive for zero defects, while others simply seek continual improvement or more achievable goals such as one defect per 100,000 units. The success of these companies seems to be unrelated to which program they follow or which technique they use. Rather, success depends on whether they have a TQM program in place with policies and structures that fit their own organizational culture and personnel.

WHY TQM PROGRAMS FAIL AND SUCCEED

The popular business press has published hundreds of articles describing the resounding successes of TQM and an increasing number of articles discussing some major failures of companies trying to use it. How can TQM be a tremendous success in some cases and a terrible failure in others? Is it because some companies used statistical quality control, while others did not? Is it because some companies used concurrent design and others did not? Is it because some used quality circles and others did not?

When we look at the principles of TQM, it is clear that they make eminent sense, and a quality system that embodies these principles should be successful. Failures attributed to TQM are not due to a deficiency in the program's philosophy or its basic principles. Certainly no one would claim that top management should *not* take responsibility and be involved in quality, or that the company should *not* strive to improve or *not* consider customer preferences and standards. Nor is TQM too new or conceptually complicated. Many of the principles of TQM have been used for several decades, and the basic features of TQM are quite simple.

The primary cause of failure is in the *implementation* of TQM. Many business and military leaders and sports coaches claim that the secret of success is not necessarily to have the best strategy (which may not exist), but rather to *have* a strategy that is well thought out and fits the culture and personnel of the organization (exploits its strengths), and to have everyone in the organization committed to the strategy and its underlying goals. By reading the comments of the managers who failed in their implementations of TQM, we can see that failure was almost guaranteed. They lacked a real strategy and commitment from management and the employees.

The most common causes for TQM failures appear to be the following.

1. ***Lack of Commitment by Top Management.*** Top management cannot simply proclaim that the organization will now use TQM. Management must itself learn what TQM is, establish the organizational structure and reward system to support it, and be willing to devote the significant up-front resources and effort required to implement and monitor it.
2. ***Focusing on Specific Techniques Rather Than on the System.*** A surprising number of managers read an article about the success another company has had with some quality management technique, such as SPC or quality circles, and assume the technique will work for them as well. In most cases, the technique worked for the first company because it was part of a larger quality management system that supported its use, and it evolved and was implemented over time. No simple recipe of techniques ensures high quality (take two cups of SPC amd one cup of quality circles and sprinkle the mixture with Deming's 14 points). TQM is an entire system with reinforcing and synergistic components. Although TQM can and maybe should be implemented on a small scale initially, the focus needs to be on the system as a whole and the achievement and improvement of quality as a process, not a slogan, formula, or technique.
3. ***Not Obtaining Employee Buy-In and Participation.*** The success of TQM depends on employee buy-in and commitment to its principles and their increased responsibility for quality. This commitment cannot be achieved by edict. It requires informing employees about the reasons for and goals of a TQM system, and involving them in setting up the training and implementation of the system. They must also see clearly why it is in their best interest to participate.

   Middle managers especially must be sold on TQM or they must be taken out of the process. TQM transfers some job responsibilities and authority to the lowest levels in the organization, which usually reduces the number of middle managers needed and changes the functions of those managers who remain. Unless this issue is addressed, middle managers can sabotage the entire implementation.
4. ***Program Stops with Training.*** Some organizations obtain management and employee commitment and provide training but then expect that the rest will happen on its own; it won't. The next step is crucial: turning the training into action. This can take several forms, such as specific quality improvement projects or the cre-

ation and operation of a suggestion system. These steps must produce clear improvements in the system. Nothing ignites a TQM, or any production improvement system, more than initial visible successes.

5. ***Expecting Immediate Results, Not a Long-Term Payoff.*** For most companies TQM involves a complete organizational and cultural change. Such changes do not occur quickly, and significant tangible results may take one or two years to achieve. Certainly it is helpful to achieve some tangible, quick successes. But realistically, these quick successes are likely to be small at first. Too many companies gave up on TQM after six months because they did not see large benefits. To accelerate benefits, some companies try to do too much too fast. Terrence Ozan of Ernst and Young, who has studied TQM implementation, found this to be a prescription for failure: "A lot of companies . . . tried to implement 9,000 new practices simultaneously. But you don't get results that way. It's just too much."[19]
6. ***Forcing the Organization to Adopt Methods That Are Not Productive or Compatible with It's Production System and Personnel.*** Not all quality management techniques are suitable for every organization. For example, in some production processes, such as one that makes customized goods, SPC is not practical or does not provide sufficient benefit to justify the effort. When companies try to force the use of techniques and organizational structures in situations where they do not fit, not only do those techniques fail, they undermine confidence in the entire TQM system. Anger and frustration are then directed to the entire system rather than to the real cause. Companies need to be flexible in how they implement specific aspects of TQM, and they must be willing to backtrack quickly when some aspect of it clearly is not appropriate for their situation.

We have described reasons why TQM sometimes fails, but why does TQM succeed and what factors contribute to success? The necessary ingredients for TQM to succeed are implicit in the causes of failure. Successful TQM systems are the result of a committed top management that takes the steps necessary to educate all employees about the reasons for adopting TQM, sharing a vision, getting them to buy into and participate in designing and implementing the system, providing the necessary training, following up with action, and then having the patience to wait for benefits that may take years to be fully realized.

One crucial question is, where should we start? Clearly, we want to start where we believe we have the best chance of producing substantial benefits quickly. A large percentage of quality costs and defects involve a relatively small number of products, production activities, or departments (the *Pareto principle*). By collecting good data on where quality problems and costs occur, we can locate those areas with the greatest *potential* for improvement. Second, once we identify the major problem areas, we have to determine what actions are necessary to solve the problems—quickly and easily, if possible. Frequently, there is no simple or easy solution, and we may be better off initially attacking problems that have fewer potential payoffs but can be solved more quickly and easily. Third, changes can be implemented more successfully by cooperative people. So a major consideration in deciding where to implement the first changes is the personnel and performance history of the units. Those departments or facilities with enthusiastic, cooperative personnel should be prime candidates for the initial implementation.

When a quality management program is implemented successfully in one part of a company by enthusiastic employees, that program can become a model and a rallying

[19]From Gilbert Fuchsberg, "Quality Programs Show Shoddy Results," *Wall Street Journal*, May 14, 1992.

point for other divisions and provide a talent pool that can be tapped to help other units design and implement their quality management programs. These successes can create momentum that carries the program throughout the organization.

11.10 PROSPECTS FOR PRODUCT QUALITY

Just a decade ago, many U.S., Canadian, and European companies were losing the competitive battle with Pacific rim companies, most notably the Japanese. This situation has changed rapidly. Many companies have awakened to the methods used by Japanese companies and the work of Deming, Juran, and others. The popular press has made almost all businesspersons aware of their own product quality deficiencies, and has provided hope with reports of companies, such as Motorola or Xerox, that have reduced defects by a factor of 100 or more and regained world competitiveness in quality. This enlightenment and sensitivity to quality has been exhibited in many ways, including national and international efforts by governments and professional organizations to encourage and recognize outstanding efforts in product quality, and to provide role models and mechanisms to organizations that wish to improve their quality.

THE BALDRIGE AWARDS

In 1987 the U.S Congress passed legislation that created the **Malcolm Baldrige National Quality Improvement Awards**, named after former secretary of commerce, Malcolm Baldrige. This act grew out of the belief that the United States needed to make quality a national priority and to have a national award comparable to that of the Deming Prize, Japan's highest award for product quality.

The goals of the Baldrige Award are to recognize outstanding achievements in product quality, to publicize these achievements, and thereby to promote efforts to improve product quality in U.S. companies. Awards are given annually to companies in three categories: large manufacturers, large service organizations, and small businesses (500 or fewer employees). (In 1996 new categories for not-for-profit educational and health service organizations were created.) The criteria for the Baldrige Award are far-reaching, and the application process is very time-consuming and requires considerable documentation. The award puts considerable weight on customer satisfaction, employee training and participation, senior management leadership, continuous improvement, and the quality assurance process and results—the principles embodied in TQM. In addition to their use for evaluating applicants, the criteria are intended "to help elevate quality standards and expectations; to facilitate communication and sharing among and within organizations of all types based upon common understanding of key quality requirements; and to serve as a working tool for planning, training, assessment, and other uses."[20] The past winners of this award include some of the best-known companies in the United States, such as Motorola, Westinghouse, Xerox, and Federal Express, as well as some less well-known companies, such as Solectron, Zytec, and Globe Metallurgical.

The Baldrige Award seems to have accomplished its goals well. It has helped to bring quality management to the national spotlight and has motivated many organizations to take a serious, detailed look at their own quality assurance systems. Some tangible improvements in quality have resulted from this self-evaluation exercise. Some people, however, have begun to question the continued need for the award, or the need

---

[20] U.S. Department of Commerce, 1992 *Award Criteria—Malcolm Baldrige Award*, Gathersburg, MD, 1992.

for such a complex and costly application and evaluation process. Companies spend tens or hundreds of thousands of dollars and a tremendous amount of work time simply documenting or formalizing existing activities. In some cases, winners of the award have even admitted that the application and review process directed them away from their main work and hurt their companies financially! Others have contended that winning the award can cause companies to feel that they have achieved near-perfection or have solved their problems, and they tend to relax their efforts. Also, there is the legitimate question, which occurs in any subjective competition, of whether or not the best companies win. Many companies with outstanding product quality have applied and not won in recent years. Although the critics have made some valid points, the benefits to this award suggest that the solution is to streamline the process, and possibly increase the number of awards given, rather than to eliminate the award altogether.

ISO 9000 STANDARDS AND CERTIFICATION

Another method to encourage better product quality is the establishment of international quality standards for vendor certification. The International Organization for Standardization (ISO), which now includes the standards bodies of almost 100 countries, is an international body that works toward standardization of products, technical requirements, and regulations to promote industrial efficiency and quality. The Quality Management and Assurance Committee of ISO has established a series of standards for quality management systems. The standards, referred to as the **ISO 9000 series**, are guidelines related to the design, development, production, testing, and servicing of products. ISO 9004 specifically addresses the application of TQM systems.

The importance of ISO 9000 standards is that companies that wish to be primary suppliers to companies in the European Union must be certified as meeting the ISO 9000 standards, and an increasing number of U.S. companies are requiring suppliers to be ISO certified. The certification process takes one to two years and involves on-site visits by members of the national member organization. A set of procedures leads the company through the steps that must be taken to seek and receive certification. On certification, companies are registered in an international directory of ISO-certified companies, which can open new markets for them. By 1994 7% of all mid-sized U.S. manufacturers had received ISO 9000 certification; twice that number were certified in 1995, and by 1996 over half plan to be certified.[21] Clearly, the drive to implement TQM programs and to improve product quality is not likely to slow in the near future.

SUMMARY

- Quality has become a major order-winning dimension for companies.
- Customers who buy products based on quality rather than price tend to be more loyal.
- The methods used to improve product quality often reduce costs as well.
- Quality can be defined as a product's fitness for use.
- Quality is often measured in several dimensions, including performance, range of features, reliability, maintainability, and image.
- A **quality cost audit** identifies the amount and types of quality-related costs a company incurs. Most companies can achieve higher quality at lower cost by devoting more resources to quality planning and appraisal, thereby reducing the number of defects produced.
- Good quality is the result of good product design and conformance to design specifications in the production process.
- Good product design requires that customer prefer-

[21]From Pamela Sebastian, "Business Bulletin," *Wall Street Week*, Sept. 1, 1994.

ences be incorporated into the product and that the product be easy to produce, use, and maintain.

- Simplifying the product design by reducing the number of parts, using standard and common parts, and foolproofing assembly will improve quality conformance.
- **Statistical process control (SPC)** can help identify quality problems quickly, often before the process makes defective items.
- SPC uses simple charts to track and evaluate samples of items produced to determine whether the process appears to be out of control.
- Defect cause–effect analysis helps determine the causes of quality problems and illuminates possible solutions.
- **Total quality management (TQM)** is a synthesis of many approaches to quality improvement. Its major components include customer-focused quality, involvement of top management, organizationwide responsibility for quality, making products right the first time, identifying and correcting problems quickly, and continuous improvement.
- The **Malcolm Baldrige National Quality Improvement Awards** were created to promote improved product quality by U.S. companies.
- The **ISO 9000 series** certification is an international certification of the quality management processes used by companies. It can open new markets, such as the European Union, to certified companies.

KEY TERMS

appraisal costs **566**
assignable variation **582**
cause-effect chart **595**
conformance quality **574**
control charts **583**
Deming's 14-point program **598**
Deming wheel (Shewart cycle or plan-do-check-act cycle) **598**
design (tolerance) limits **584**
design quality **574**
durability **564**
external failure cost **566**
failure costs **566**
fishbone chart (cause–effect chart) **595**
internal failure cost **566**
ISO 9000 series **605**
just-in-time (JIT) production systems **579**
lower control limit ($LCL_{\bar{X}}$) **585**
Malcolm Baldrige National Quality Improvement Awards **604**
$\bar{p}$-chart **593**
Pareto principle **569**
poka-yoke **577**
prevention costs **566**
process capability **588**
process control by attributes **583**
process control by variables **583**
process distribution **584**
process standard deviation **584**
quality circles **578**
quality cost audit **565**
quality cost scorecard **565**
quality function deployment (QFD) **575**
quality trilogy **598**
range control chart (R-chart) **590**
range **589**
reliability **564**
statistical process control (SPC) **582**
Taguchi method **578**
tolerance stack-up **577**
total quality management (TQM) **598**
upper control limit ($UCL_{\bar{X}}$) **585**
$\bar{X}$-control chart ($\bar{X}$-chart) **585**

KEY FORMULAS

Standard deviation of the sample mean

$$\sigma_{\bar{X}} = \sigma/\sqrt{n}$$

where σ is the process standard deviation.

Estimator for the Process Standard Deviation

$$\sigma = \bar{R}/d_2 \qquad (11.2)$$

where $\bar{R}$ is the average of the ranges for several samples.

3–σ Control Limits

$\bar{X}$-Chart

$$UCL_{\bar{X}} = \mu + 3\,\sigma_{\bar{X}} \qquad LCL_{\bar{X}} = \mu - 3\,\sigma_{\bar{X}} \qquad (11.1)$$

R-Chart

$$UCL_R = d_4\bar{R} = d_4 d_2 \sigma \qquad LCL_R = d_3\bar{R} = d_3 d_2 \sigma \qquad (11.3)$$

$\bar{p}$-Chart

$$UCL_{\bar{p}} = p + 3\sigma_{\bar{p}} \qquad LCL_{\bar{p}} = \max\{p - 3\sigma_{\bar{p}}, 0\} \qquad (11.4)$$

DISCUSSION AND REVIEW QUESTIONS

1. Define product quality.
2. How does the definition of product quality differ for a good and a service?
3. What does it mean to say that product quality is multidimensional?
4. How would you describe the main differences between the traditional quality management philosophy and the new philosophies of quality management?
5. Select a product with which you are familiar and list examples of its features for the six groups of quality characteristics; that is, make a table equivalent to Table 11.1 for the product.
6. Some experts have said that a quality cost audit is a waste of time because it simply shows an organization where it stands. Explain why or why not a quality cost audit should be done as part of a quality management review.
7. Why does it matter where quality costs are incurred? Why isn't the total cost alone important?
8. If you were asked to do a quality cost audit for a university, state which specific costs would be most important and explain how you would acquire the needed data.
9. Can a company ever be operating at its lowest possible cost if it is still producing some defective units of its products? Explain.
10. What is the purpose of quality function deployment (QFD)? How can it help improve the quality of products?
11. Reducing the number of components in a product should reduce costs, but why would it improve product quality?
12. Give a specific example of how you would apply one of the product design principles (e.g., use common components) to improve the design and delivery of a service provided by your bank.
13. What is the difference between the $\bar{X}$-chart and the R-chart? Why would someone want to use both?
14. Why would a run test be necessary? If a product characteristic is consistently above or below the target value, wouldn't an $\bar{X}$-chart identify this? Explain.
15. How is TQM different from Deming's 14 points?
16. What do you consider to be the two most important aspects of TQM for improving product quality? Explain why.
17. What types of problems would a service producer have in implementing TQM that a manufacturer would be less likely to have?

SOLVED PROBLEMS

Problem 1: International Pickle Company (IPC) makes 16-ounce jars of pickles (net weight) for sale. As company policy, a jar is considered unacceptable if the net weight is more than 0.1 ounce greater or less than this amount. IPC took 20 samples of five jars each (100 in total) from the production line when the process was known to be in control. The average weight for the 100 jars was 16.003 ounces, and the average *range* for the 20 samples was 0.093 ounce.

(a) Compute the upper and lower limits for a three-sigma $\bar{X}$-chart.

(b) Compute the upper and lower limits for a three-sigma *R*-chart.

(c) Based on (a) and (b), suppose IPC now samples five jars from the production line. The net weights of these jars are 16.018, 15.870, 16.115, 16.002, and 16.005 ounces. Determine whether or not the process is under control. If not, specify what the problem is and how you determined this.

Solution:

(a) First, we note that the target amount of pickles IPC wants to put in a jar is 16.000 ounces, not 16.003; 16.003 just happens to be the average value of the sampled jars. The process standard deviation, σ, is not given, so we must use equation (11.2) to derive it from $\bar{R}$, the average of the 20 sample ranges: $\sigma = \bar{R}/d_2 = 0.093/2.33 = 0.040$. Then $\sigma_{\bar{X}} = \sigma/\sqrt{n} = (0.040)/\sqrt{5} = 0.018$. Using equations (11.1), the control limits are

$$UCL_{\bar{X}} = 16.000 + 3(0.018) = 16.054$$
$$LCL_{\bar{X}} = 16.000 - 3(0.018) = 15.946$$

(b) Using equations (11.3) and Table 11.4, the control limits for the R-chart are

$$UCL_R = d_4\overline{R} = 2.11(0.093) = 0.196$$
$$LCL_R = d_3\overline{R} = 0(0.093) = 0$$

(c) For the sample, $\overline{X} = 16.002$ and $R = 0.245$. The value of $\overline{X}$ is within the control limits of the $\overline{X}$-chart, but the range exceeds the control limits of the R-chart. So the process appears to be out of control in terms of its process variation.

Problem 2: Chrysler Corporation has just installed new robotic welders to weld automobile parts together. Welds are inspected regularly and judged to be either acceptable or defective; if they are judged defective, the components must be cleaned and rewelded. During controlled tests Chrysler determined that when the welders are operating properly, the proportion of defective welds is only $p = 0.0002$.

(a) Suppose Chrysler is going to sample 36 welds every hour. Construct the control limits for a three-sigma $\overline{p}$-chart.

(b) Suppose a sample of 36 items is taken and one weld is defective. What should Chrysler conclude?

Solution:

(a) The standard deviation of $\overline{p}$ is $\sigma_{\overline{p}} = \sqrt{p(1-p)/n} = \sqrt{(0.0002)(0.9998)/36} = 0.0024$. Then from equation (11.4)

$$UCL_{\overline{p}} = 0.0002 + 3(0.0024) = 0.0074$$
$$LCL_{\overline{p}} = 0.0002 - 3(0.0024) = -0.0070 \rightarrow LCL_{\overline{p}} = 0$$

(b) If one item in the sample is defective, then the sample proportion defective is $\overline{p} = 1/36 = 0.0278$. This is greater than the upper control limit, which indicates that the process is out of control. However, this may be just a random occurrence, so Chrysler might take another sample to verify the conclusion.

PROBLEMS

1. Waterbury Soap Ltd. (WSL) manufactures laundry detergent. One of its products is packaged in a 5-pound carton. When the carton-filling operation is working correctly, the cartons are filled with an average of 5 pounds of detergent, with a process standard deviation of 0.058 pound. (a) Calculate the upper and lower control limits for a three-sigma $\overline{X}$-chart for WSL, assuming a sample size of nine boxes. (b) Calculate the upper and lower control limits for a three-sigma R-chart, assuming a sample size of nine boxes. (Hint: use equation (11.2) to estimate $\overline{R}$.)

2. Tele-Survey Corporation performs telephone surveys for clients. Preliminary testing of a new market survey indicated that survey phone calls (for which someone agrees to answer the survey) should take an average of 3.25 minutes to administer, with a standard deviation of 0.42 minutes. Tele-Survey would like to monitor the length of the phone calls to make sure that the employees administering the survey are not rushing through it too fast or having problems that cause them to be too slow. (a) Compute the upper and lower control limits for a three-sigma $\overline{X}$-chart for Tele-Survey, assuming a sample size of five calls. (b) Compute the upper and lower control limits for a three-sigma R-chart, assuming a sample size of five calls. (Hint: use equation 11.2 to estimate $\overline{R}$.)

3. A metal stamping operation for an automobile manufacturer makes door panels. A crucial feature in how well the door panel fits (and how quietly the car rides) is the angle of one of its corners. The angle is supposed to be exactly 90° During controlled tests, 12 samples of five panels each were checked for their angle; the data are given in Table 11.7. (a) Compute the upper and lower control limits for a three-sigma $\overline{X}$-chart, assuming a sample size of 5 panels. (b) Compute the upper and lower control limits for a three-sigma R-chart, assuming a sample size of 5 panels. (c) Suppose the following sample angle measure-

TABLE 11.7 SAMPLE DATA FOR DOOR ANGLES

Sample No.	Angle in Degrees					$\bar{X}$	R
1	90.01	90.01	90.00	90.00	90.02	90.008	0.02
2	90.00	89.98	89.99	89.99	90.03	89.998	0.05
3	89.99	89.98	90.00	90.00	89.99	89.992	0.02
4	90.01	90.02	90.00	90.01	90.02	90.012	0.02
5	90.00	89.99	90.00	89.99	90.01	89.998	0.02
6	89.97	89.98	89.99	89.98	89.99	89.982	0.02
7	89.99	90.00	90.00	89.98	90.00	89.994	0.02
8	90.01	90.00	90.01	89.98	90.00	90.000	0.03
9	90.02	90.01	90.01	89.99	89.98	90.002	0.04
10	90.01	89.99	90.00	89.99	89.98	89.994	0.03
11	89.97	89.96	90.01	90.00	90.02	89.992	0.06
12	90.02	90.02	90.00	89.97	90.01	90.004	0.05

ments were taken: 89.99, 89.98, 89.97, 90.01, 90.00. Do the control charts indicate that the process is in control or out of control? Explain.

4. The manager of the cafeteria at North-By-Northwest University wants to monitor the service quality of the checkout process. Students have complained that some cashiers take too long to add up the cost of their food, collect the money, and give change. This has led to unnecessarily long lines during busy periods. To monitor performance, the manager observed and timed how long it took his best cashiers to check out customers. The data for 15 samples of five customers each are given in Table 11.8. The manager wants to use the average of his best cashiers as the target value for checkout time. (a) Compute the upper and lower control limits for a three-sigma $\bar{X}$-chart, assuming a sample size of 5 customers. (b) Compute the upper and lower control limits for a three-sigma R-chart, assuming a sample size of 5 customers. (c) Suppose the following checkout times were taken for a cashier: 29, 38, 34, 35, 32. Do the control charts indicate that the process is in control or out of control? Explain. (d) Suppose the following checkout times were taken: 21, 19, 11, 10, 50. Do the control charts indicate that the process is in control or out of control? Explain. (e) If the process is identified as being out of control, what should the manager do? (Please do not say "fire the cashier.")

5. Geo-Bit Corporation manufactures drilling bits for the oil industry. For a given type of bit the diameter is

TABLE 11.8 SAMPLE CHECKOUT TIMES FOR CASHIERS

Sample No.	Checkout Time in Seconds					$\bar{X}$	R
1	24	21	36	30	13	24.8	23
2	16	23	11	32	19	20.2	21
3	19	34	12	20	27	22.4	22
4	41	16	15	22	13	21.4	28
5	19	20	23	29	10	18.2	19
6	27	14	26	18	21	21.2	13
7	9	32	17	15	23	19.2	23
8	14	23	25	28	11	20.2	17
9	25	21	48	27	16	27.4	32
10	21	18	11	10	34	18.8	24
11	23	8	27	19	15	18.4	19
12	15	21	22	27	13	19.6	14
13	24	20	27	21	15	21.4	12
14	29	15	19	23	30	23.2	15
15	25	41	30	28	17	28.2	24

supposed to be 5.200 inches, plus or minus 0.010 inch. When the manufacturing process is in control, the deviations from 5.200 inches are normally distributed, with a natural (process) standard deviation of $\sigma = 0.005$ inch. Suppose the company regularly takes a sample of six bits from the production line to determine whether the process is in control. (a) Compute the control limits for a three-sigma $\bar{X}$-chart to monitor this process. (b) Compute the control limits for a three-sigma R-chart to monitor this process. (c) Suppose the following sample of bit diameters was obtained: 5.206, 5.212, 5.199, 5.215, 5.188, 5.197. Using the control charts from (a) and (b), is the process in control? Explain. (d) What is the probability that all six bits in a sample will have a diameter of more than 5.200 inches?

6. Electrolamp Corporation manufactures light bulbs. When the production process is operating correctly, approximately 0.4% of the bulbs do not light at all. Electrolamp plans to implement SPC by attributes. Compute the upper and lower control limits for Electrolamp's three-sigma p-chart, assuming a sample size of 30.

7. The U.S. Internal Revenue Service (IRS) provides customer information telephone lines to answer questions from people filing income tax forms. Based on experiments with trained representatives, the IRS believes that the representatives can be expected to give an incorrect answer to a tax question 20% of the time. The IRS plans to monitor the quality of each of its offices by having quality control staff call and ask prepared questions to see whether correct answers are provided. The IRS plans to place 40 calls each week to each IRS office. (a) Compute the upper and lower control limits for a three-sigma $\bar{p}$-chart to determine whether or not the question-answering operation is out of control. (b) What action do you think IRS should take if an out-of-control condition is suspected?

8. Bertlab Company performs medical lab tests for doctors. Industry standards indicate that no more than 0.1% of these tests should be performed incorrectly. Bertlab plans to sample 25 tests per day to determine whether or not they were performed correctly. Compute the upper and lower control limits for a three-sigma $\bar{p}$-chart.

9. Rapid-Fire Delivery (RFD) is an express local delivery service that guarantees pickup and delivery of packages in one hour. When the system is operating well, RFD fails to deliver a package within an hour only 0.1% of the time. To monitor its service, RFD is going to sample 20 deliveries per day to determine if its system is operating well. Construct the upper and lower control limits for RFD's three-sigma $\bar{p}$-chart.

10.* Select a service product with which you are familiar, and feel that the quality of the service is inadequate. Construct a fishbone (cause–effect) chart that will identify the possible causes of the quality problems.

CASE

Digicomp Computer: A Quality Management Case

Digicomp Computer Corporation designs, assembles, and sells a variety of personal computers. Although its prices are competitive, Digicomp competes primarily by assembling and shipping within 48 hours computers that are customized to customers' specifications. Almost all components for the computers, from the chips, boards, and disk drives to the cases and keyboards, are purchased from vendors. In the early 1990s, feverish price competition within the industry made it crucial for Digicomp not only to reduce its operating costs but also to distinguish itself in terms of product quality. Florence Ross, the CEO of Digicomp, decided to perform a strategic reevaluation of the company, especially of its quality management system.

Evaluating Current Performance

The first two phases of this evaluation involved (1) meeting with customers to determine their perceptions of Digicomp's quality and getting customers' input on what quality dimensions needed attention, and (2) performing a quality cost audit of Digicomp to identify the primary sources and magnitudes of quality costs.

Customer Assessments

Digicomp formed two three-person teams to meet with randomly selected customers and potential customers of Digicomp. Each team included one representative from the marketing/sales division, the manufacturing division, and the product design group. After meeting with nearly 500 customers, the teams were able to agree on several common themes they were hearing:

1. Digicomp handled complaints quickly and courteously, frequently replacing computers at no charge. But the frequency of complaints was too large, with over 20% of customers reporting some quality problem within the first year of ownership.
2. Customers perceived most of the quality defects as being due to carelessness or poor assembly, such as installing the wrong disk drives or putting them in the wrong slots, or forgetting to install a modem, rather than component failure.
3. Purchasers of Digicomp's laptop computers were pleased with the performance, but they felt that the computers were too heavy and big and that recharging the battery took too long.
4. Although Digicomp was good at customizing well-established computer technology, it was often behind its competitors in introducing and making available state-of-the-art technology.

Quality Cost Audit

A team of three people, one each from marketing, manufacturing, and quality control, performed a quality cost audit. The audit took over a month to complete because most of the data had to be gathered from basic production or personnel reports or special studies. Table 11.2 (on page 571) is the quality scorecard for Digicomp. The quality costs were estimated aι $6,335,000 per year, which was equivalent to 11.5% of the division's annual sales of $55 million and more than its profits of $5 million. With such a large amount spent on quality, one would expect fewer quality problems than those reported by the customers. But the general problem is apparent from the cost distribution: costs of over $4.9 million were incurred due to failures (making defective products), and only 9% of the quality costs were devoted to prevention.

As the audit team studied some primary production and material management documents, they identifed the main causes of quality defects. The customers' perceptions were generally correct: most defects were due to assembly errors at Digicomp facilities. However, the audit team also found some quality problems with the hard disks, disk drives, and cases.

Revising the System

After reviewing the reports on the customer assessments and the quality cost audit, Florence Ross met with the division vice-presidents and group directors. They decided that an organizationwide effort was necessary to make Digicomp a recognized quality leader. They also felt that some major improvements could be made quickly, and that a long-term quality program could be introduced within six months of the time the initial steps were taken. Revision of the quality management system was to concentrate initially on three areas:

1. Improve product design to make it more responsive to customer preferences and introduce new technologies faster.
2. Improve the assembly process to reduce the number of assembly-related errors by a factor of 5.
3. Work with vendors to improve the quality of components, especially the hard disks, disc drives, and cases.

Product Design

Digicomp's product design group does not design computers from scratch. Its primary job is to decide which standard components to include as options for customized computers. Because the designers saw their job primarily as one of selecting from among available options, they never consulted customers directly for their preferences.

After a meeting to discuss the results of the customer assessments, the design group decided to consult customers regularly on a formal basis. They agreed to develop a QFD relationship matrix for each product line and revise it every six months.

From the very beginning, use of the QFD relationship matrix was successful. First, customers were pleased to be asked for their opinions, and noncustomers were impressed with Digicomp's efforts; many of them said that they would consider Digicomp's products more carefully in the future. Second, the results led the design group to revise several of their products. For example, they made the laptop computer smaller so that it could fit in a briefcase and still leave room for papers and files. Third, the competitive benchmarking awakened the design group to the fact that their products were not as competitive as they had thought. This led to the idea of using multidisciplinary teams consisting of representatives from marketing/sales, manufacturing, and purchasing to review all new and existing products quarterly.

Process Design and Operations

Wilson Sanders, the vice president of manufacturing, was shocked at the magnitude of quality costs. He quickly organized a task force to investigate their causes. The team identified the following problems:

1. Some components, especially the microprocessors, were being installed backward or upside down.
2. Some components were missing, especially internal modems and graphics cards.
3. Hard drive and disk drive failures accounted for the overwhelming majority of component defects, and these were often not discovered until the computer was completely assembled and tested.
4. The computer cases (housing the computers) tended to crack. This cracking normally did not occur until the computer was completely assembled, and in many cases not until after it was shipped.

Special teams were formed to address each of these problem areas.

1. ***Misinstallation of Components.*** The team found that there were three distinct types of misinstallation. The first was *installing the correct part incorrectly*. Several components were symmetrical, so it was easy to have a chip facing the wrong direction or installed upside down. The manufacturing team met with the designers and arranged to have some components redesigned; for example, one chip supplier suggested that the top of some components be marked in red. Other components were redesigned to have notches so that they could be installed only in the correct way.

   The second misinstallation was *installing the correct part in the wrong location*. The most common situation involved two disc drives of different sizes (3.5 and 5.25 inches). Some customers wanted the smaller drive on the bottom rather than on the top. The team determined that a large part of the problem was that special customer requests were not highlighted on the production documents. The system was changed so that work orders with components requested in special locations had a colored sticker attached to them to get the workers' attention.

   The final misinstallation problem was *installing the wrong components*, such as the wrong disc drive. Many components looked almost identical, so it was easy for them to get mixed up. Digicomp's solution was a complete revision of the assembly process. Because of the customized assembly, each computer was assembled by one person (in contrast to using a repetitive flow process if all the computers were essentially identical). In the original process at each work bench, a supply of the most common components was maintained; if the assembler needed any special components, he would go to the material storeroom and get them. Frequently the assembler would not notice a request for a less common version or would accidentally use the wrong component. In addition to the assembly errors, each work area looked sloppy and required considerable extra space for storage and maneuvering.

   Digicomp decided to stop storing components at each work bench, except for the computer cases and hard drives. Instead, two people were assigned to work with customer service representatives preparing assembly kits for each computer ordered. As soon as an order was received, the order form was handed to one of the kit preparers, who would gather all of the components from the material storeroom (which was adjacent to the kit preparation area) and put them into a kit box, with a copy of the order form attached to it. Every few hours the kit boxes would be taken to the assembly area and distributed to the assemblers. Because the assemblers did not have to gather components, which disrupted their work, their efficiency increased and the number of installation errors dropped to almost zero. In addition, work benches were reorganized so that there was one storage area for cases and hard drives for every four work benches and several hundred square feet of work space were freed up for other uses.

2. ***Missing Components.*** The use of kits essentially eliminated the problem of missing components. Kit preparers checked off parts on the order form as they

were put in the kit, and the assembler installed every component in the kit; a component left in the kit would be obvious (a form of *poka yoke*).

3. ***Hard Drive and Disk Drive Failures.*** The team found that there was little it could do alone to eliminate defective hard drives and disc drives. This was something that the company had to work on with the suppliers of these components. However, in the short term, the team did change the testing procedure so that simple tests of the drives, which could identify some of the defects, were performed immediately before installation. If a drive had an identifiable defect, it was not installed.

4. ***Cracked Computer Cases.*** Digicomp identified three causes of cracked computer cases. The first was the design of the cases. The cases were designed to have uniform strength in all directions. However, most impacts (e.g., dropping) occurred at corners, so Digicomp redesigned the cases with reinforced corners. Second, Digicomp bought its cases from three suppliers. It found that cases from one of the suppliers failed at a rate five times that of the other two. Digicomp informed the supplier of this fact. Digicomp agreed to work with the supplier to solve the problem, but if quality did not improve to equal that of the other two suppliers, Digicomp would stop buying from it. Third, some of the cracked cases were due to assemblers dropping and bumping the computers as they removed them from the work tables and loaded them for transport to the packaging department. These problems were reduced by using padded transport carts. If the computer was dropped on the cart there was less concentrated impact.

5. ***Relations with Suppliers.*** Digicomp made a concerted effort to work more closely with suppliers in three ways. First, anytime a supplier-related defect was identified, the vendor was contacted and a meeting with its representatives was held to find a solution. The immediate problems involved improving the reliability of the hard drives and disk drives and the durability of the cases from one supplier. Second, suppliers were helpful in finding ways to reduce assembly errors (e.g., painting the tops of components or notching components to reduce the chance of misinstallation). Third, vendors were involved in the product design process on an ongoing basis. The purposes were to improve the design of the computers by using more common and standard components and to incorporate the newest technologies into Digicomp's computers more quickly.

Outcome of the Redesign and Reorganization

Redesign and reorganization of the quality management system was successful. Many of the changes were instituted within the first six months and began producing benefits soon thereafter. The number of defects was reduced by a factor of 10; defects caused by forgetting to install parts became very rare, and misinstallation of parts was reduced by a factor of 5. By eliminating the need to rework or replace defective computers, and by gaining efficiency by having assemblers work from kits rather than gathering their own components, effective productivity increased by 25%. Total quality costs were cut in half, even though little additional costs were incurred for prevention.

Relationships with suppliers improved considerably. New technologies became usable in Digicomp computers one to two months earlier than before, and several product redesigns were made that simplified assembly. The product development cycle was also reduced by one to two months by using design review teams and working more closely with suppliers. More important, Digicomp was producing computers that were more responsive to the desires of customers, and sales began to rise at twice their previous rate.

These initial successes led Florence Ross to conclude that a significant redesign of the quality management system was feasible, necessary, and cost effective. Despite the substantial improvements in quality, reduction in production costs, and increase in effective capacity, Ms. Ross decided that further incremental improvements would be too small and slow to realize. So she decided to implement a full-scale TQM system that would be phased in over two years, during which time incremental improvements would still be encouraged.

QUESTIONS

1. What other short-term actions should Digicomp consider implementing to improve product quality?
2. When Digicomp implements its TQM system, what actions would you recommend it take first? Why?

SELECTED READINGS

CROSBY, PHILIP. *Quality Is Free: The Art of Making Quality Certain*, NAL-Dutton, New York, 1980.

———. *Quality Without Tears: The Art of Hassle Free Management*, McGraw-Hill, New York, 1984.

DEMING, W. EDWARDS. *Quality Productivity and Competitive Position*, MIT Center for Advanced Engineering Study, Cambridge, MA, 1982.

FLYNN, BARBARA B. "Managing for Quality in the U.S. and in Japan," *Interfaces*, Vol. 22, 1992, pp. 69–80.

GRANT, E. L., and R. LEAVENWORTH. *Statistical Quality Control* (6th ed.), McGraw-Hill, New York, 1988.

GREISING, DAVID. "Quality: How to Make It Pay," *Business Week*, Aug. 8, 1994, pp. 54–59.

HARMON, ROY. *Reinventing the Factory II*, Free Press, New York, 1991.

HARRIS, C. RUTH, and WALTER YIT. "Successfully Implementing Statistical Process Control in Integrated Steel Companies," *Interfaces*, Vol. 24, 1994, pp. 49–58.

HILL, G. CHRISTIAN, and KEN YAMADA. "Motorola Illustrates How an Aged Giant Can Remain Vibrant," *Wall Street Journal*, Dec. 9, 1992.

The International Quality Study: Best Practices Report, American Quality Foundation and Ernst & Young, New York, 1992.

JURAN, J. M. "The Quality Trilogy," *Quality Progress*, Vol. 19, No. 8, 1986, pp. 19–24.

———. "Made in U.S.A.: A Renaissance in Quality," *Harvard Business Review*, Vol. 71, No. 4, 1993, pp. 42–50.

——— and Frank M. Gryna. *Quality Planning and Analysis (3rd ed.)*, McGraw-Hill, New York, 1993.

PORT, OTIS, ET AL. "Quality: Small and Midsize Companies Seize the Challenge—Not a Moment Too Soon," *Business Week*, Nov. 30, 1992, pp. 66–75.

The Quality Imperative. Special issue of Business Week, Oct. 25, 1991.

ROBINSON, ALAN (ed.). *Continuous Improvement in Operations*, Productivity Press, Cambridge, MA, 1991.

SANCHEZ, S. M., J. S. RAMBERG, J. FIERO, and J. J. PIGNATIELLO, JR. "Quality by Design," in Andrew Kusiak (ed.), *Concurrent Engineering: Automation, Tools, and Techniques*, Wiley, New York, 1993.

SHINGO, SHIGEO. *Modern Approaches to Manufacturing Improvement*, Alan Robinson (ed.), Productivity Press, Cambridge, MA, 1990.

WALTON, MARY. *Deming Management at Work*, Perigee Books, New York, 1991.

WYCKOFF, D. DARYLL. "New Tool for Achieving Service Quality," in, C. H. Lovelock, (ed.), *Managing Services: Marketing, Operations, and Human Resources*, Prentice-Hall, Englewood Cliffs, NJ, 1988, pp. 226–239.

CHAPTER 11 SUPPLEMENT

ACCEPTANCE SAMPLING

11s.1 THE PURPOSE OF ACCEPTANCE SAMPLING

11s.2 TYPES OF ACCEPTANCE SAMPLING PLANS
Selecting a Plan

11s.3 OPERATING CURVES
Computing α and β for a Typical Sampling Plan

11s.4 DERIVING A SAMPLING PLAN

11s.5 THE ROLE OF ACCEPTANCE SAMPLING

11s.1 THE PURPOSE OF ACCEPTANCE SAMPLING

Acceptance sampling is the process of inferring the quality of a large number of items (a **batch** or **lot**) based on the quality of a small sample of the items. Acceptance sampling might be used by a customer to evaluate the quality of incoming materials or by a producer to evaluate the quality of outgoing product. With simple acceptance sampling we select n items from a batch and test their quality. If the number of defective items in the sample is greater than some specified level, we conclude that the batch probably has an unacceptable number of defective items, and we *reject* it and take some action (e.g., inspect all items in the batch or return it to the supplier). If the number of defective items in the sample is less than or equal to the specified number, the batch is deemed to be of acceptable quality. The purpose is to determine with reasonable accuracy whether the proportion of defects in a batch is greater than some acceptable proportion of defects without having to test every item in the batch.

11s.2 TYPES OF ACCEPTANCE SAMPLING PLANS

Many different sampling plans are used in practice. The differences among them are primarily in the number of samples taken to evaluate a batch of items. In general, sampling plans specify the batch size, N, the sample size, n, the number of samples to be taken, and the criteria for accepting or rejecting a batch.

1. ***Single-Sampling Plans.*** With these plans, we draw a single random sample of n items from the batch and evaluate each item as being acceptable or defective. If the number of defective items in the sample is more than some value, c, we reject the batch.
2. ***Double-Sampling Plans.*** Double-sampling plans have the form (n_1, c_1, c_2; n_2, c_3). We first take a sample of n_1 items. If the number of defective items is c_1 or less, we accept the batch; if the number of defectives is more than c_2, we reject the batch; if the number of defectives is more than c_1 but not more than c_2, we take a second sample of n_2 items. If the total number of defectives from the two samples combined is c_3 or less, we accept the batch; otherwise, we reject it.
3. ***Sequential or Multiple-Sampling Plans.*** These are similar to double-sampling plans except that we keep sampling items until the cumulative proportion of defectives either exceeds some value (in which case we reject the batch) or the cumulative proportion of defectives falls below some value (in which case we accept the batch).

SELECTING A PLAN

The cost and time required to evaluate a batch of items are primarily determined by the number of samples taken and the total number of items tested. The primary advantage of double- and multiple-sampling methods is that on average the total number of items sampled is less than with single sampling. So if the per unit cost of evaluating items is high, such as when testing is destructive, these methods may be advantageous. However, if the cost of obtaining and testing a sample (regardless of the number of items in the sample) is high, such as when test equipment must be cleaned or recalibrated after taking every sample, it may be more efficient to take a single large sample. We will only present single-sampling plans here; double- and multiple-sampling procedures are discussed in any quality control textbook.

11s.3 OPERATING CURVES

Acceptance sampling procedures are based on two parameters. First, the **acceptance quality level (AQL)** is the acceptable proportion of defective items in a batch. A crucial assumption underlying this parameter is that the customer and producer have agreed that if the proportion of defective items in a batch is AQL or less, the batch is of acceptable quality to the customer. Second, the **lot tolerance proportion defective (LTPD)**[1] is the proportion of defectives in a lot (batch) that defines a clearly unacceptable batch. It would seem that any batch with a defect rate greater than AQL would be unacceptable, but because we cannot perfectly determine the proportion defective using a sample, a separate rate specifying unacceptable batches must be defined and LTPD must be larger than AQL (often three or four times larger).

If we inspected (tested) every item in a batch, we could perfectly differentiate between good batches (defect rates of AQL or less) and bad batches (defective rates above AQL), as illustrated in Figure 11S.1. However, if we inspect less than 100% of the items and simply base our decision on a sample, there is always some chance that we will make a mistake and reject a good batch or accept a bad one. For a sampling plan, the probability of mistakenly rejecting a good batch (one with a defect rate below AQL) is called the **producer's risk** and is designated as α. The probability of mistakenly accepting a bad batch (one with a defect rate above LTPD) is called the **consumer's risk** and is designated as β.[2]

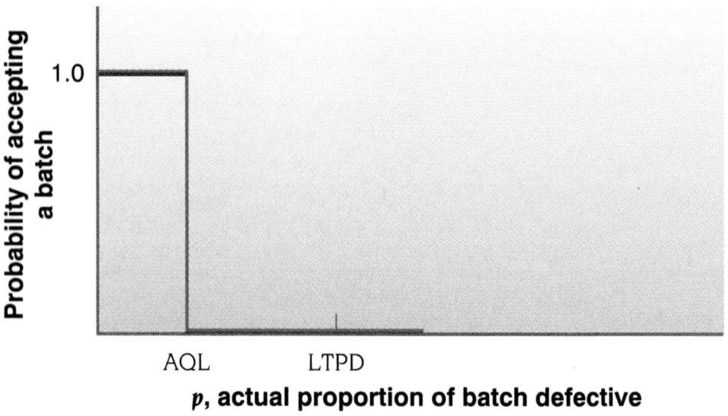

FIGURE 11S.1 Operating characteristic curve with 100% inspection.

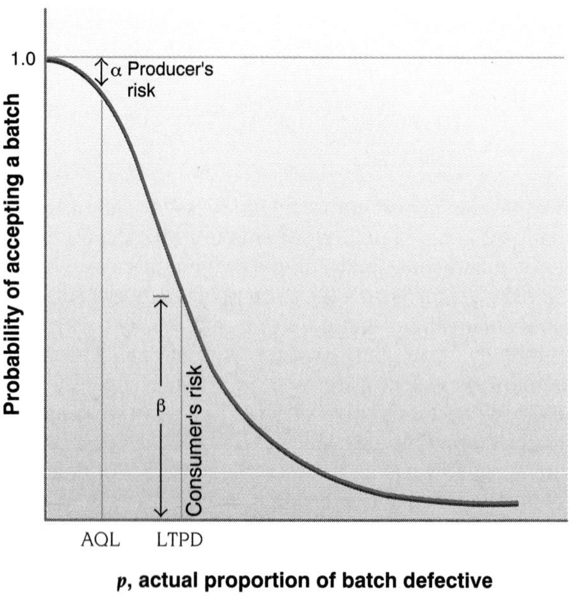

FIGURE 11S.2 OC curve for a typical sampling plan (n,c).

COMPUTING α AND β FOR A GIVEN SAMPLING PLAN

For any sampling plan (n,c) we can construct an **operating characteristic curve (OC curve)**, which gives the probability of accepting a batch (the number of defectives in the sample is c or less) as a function of the *actual* proportion of defective items in the batch. Obviously, the larger the proportion defective in the batch, the smaller the probability that the number of defects in the sample will be c or less and the batch accepted, as illustrated in Figure 11S.2.[3] The goal of acceptance sampling is to design a sampling procedure (n,c) with as small a sample size as possible that will keep the producer's and consumer's risks below some specified levels. The values of α and β used are typically less than 0.05 and 0.10, respectively.

To derive the OC curve, we need to compute the probability of accepting a batch for a given sampling plan as a function of the *actual* proportion defective in the batch. Let p be the actual proportion of defective items in the batch, and let X be the number of items in the sample that are defective. X is a random variable that has a hypergeometric distribution, but as long as $p < 0.10$ (which we would hope is true) and the sample size is less than 1/10th the size of a batch, we can approximate the probability distribution of X using the Poisson distribution:

$$\text{Prob}(X = k) = [(np)^k e^{-np}]/k! \quad \text{for } k = 0, 1, 2, \ldots \qquad (11S.1)$$

[1] LTPD is normally defined as the lot tolerance *percent* defective, but to be consistent with AQL and because we usually work in terms of proportions rather than percentages, the word *proportion* is used here instead.

[2] α and β are actually defined in terms of *marginally* good and bad batches. α is the probability of rejecting a batch that has an actual proportion defective of *exactly* AQL, and β is the probability of accepting a batch with a defect rate of *exactly* LTPD. In hypothesis testing, α is the type I error and β is the type II error.

[3] Note that the OC curve is the complement of the *power curve* in hypothesis testing.

EXAMPLE 1

Suppose we receive a shipment of 3000 items. If our AQL = 0.02, LTPD = 0.06, and our sampling plan is ($n = 60$, $c = 3$), then

$$\begin{aligned}\alpha &= \text{probability of rejecting a batch that has a defective rate of } p = 0.02\\ &= \text{probability that four or more items in the sample are defective given } p = 0.02\\ &= \text{Prob}(X \geq 4|\ p = 0.02) = 1 - \text{Prob}(X \leq 3|\ p = 0.02)\end{aligned}$$

Noting that $np = (60)(0.02) = 1.2$, we use equation 11S.1 to compute

$$\text{Prob}(X = 0|\ p = 0.02) = [(1.2)^0 e^{-1.2}]/0! = 0.3012$$
$$\text{Prob}(X = 1|\ p = 0.02) = [(1.2)^1 e^{-1.2}]/1! = 0.3614$$
$$\text{Prob}(X = 2|\ p = 0.02) = [(1.2)^2 e^{-1.2}]/2! = 0.2169$$
$$\text{Prob}(X = 3|\ p = 0.02) = [(1.2)^3 e^{-1.2}]/3! = 0.0867$$

So $\text{Prob}(X \leq 3|\ p = 0.02) = 0.3012 + 0.3614 + 0.2169 + 0.0867 = 0.9662$ and

$$\alpha = \text{Prob}(X \geq 4|\ p = 0.02) = 1 - 0.9662 = 0.0338$$

So if a batch has an actual defective rate of p = AQL = 0.02, an acceptable proportion of defectives, there is a 0.0338 probability of rejecting it by mistake.

The entire OC curve for this test can be derived by computing $\text{Prob}(X \leq 3)$ for values of p from 0 to 1. For example, repeating the computations done above for $p = 0.04$, 0.06, 0.08, and 0.10, the probabilities of accepting the batches are

p	0.02	0.04	0.06	0.08	0.10
$\text{Prob}(X \leq 3)$	0.9662	0.7787	0.5153	0.2942	0.1512

These values were used to derive Figure 11S.2.

Notice that

$$\begin{aligned}\beta &= \text{probability of accepting a batch with } p = \text{LTPD} = 0.06\\ &= \text{Prob}(X \leq 3|\ p = 0.06) = 0.5153\end{aligned}$$

So even though there is only a 0.0338 chance of mistakenly rejecting a good batch, there is over a 0.50 chance of accepting a bad batch. This illustrates one of the problems with acceptance sampling. Graphically, a sampling plan that distinguishes between good and bad batches well is one that has a very steep OC curve. But the steepness of the OC curve is primarily a function of the sample size, so in order to keep both α and β at reasonably low levels, the sample size must usually be large. For example, if we doubled our sample size to 120 and raised c to 6:

$$\alpha = \text{Prob}(X \geq 7|\ p = 0.02) = 1 - P(X \leq 6) = 1 - 0.9884 = 0.0116$$

and

$$\beta = \text{Prob}(X \leq 6|\ p = 0.06) = 0.420$$

11s.4 DERIVING A SAMPLING PLAN

The strategy for deriving a sampling plan is straightforward. For given values of AQL and LTPD, we can use tables that are available in most quality control texts to identify the sampling plan with the smallest sample size that guarantees that α and β will be less than any specified limits. Even without tables we can develop reasonably good sampling plans by trial and error. We would select a sample size, n, and then an acceptance value, c, such that AQL < c/n < LTPD. We could then construct an OC curve and compute α and β. If the values for α or β are unacceptably large, we would adjust the values of n or c using the following facts:

1. For any fixed ratio c/n, the larger n is, the better the differentiation between good and bad batches (the lower α and β will be).
2. For a fixed n, the larger c is, the larger the acceptance rate, which decreases α but increases β.
3. For a fixed n, the smaller c is, the smaller the acceptance rate, which increases α but decreases β.

In Example 1, we found that with $n = 60$ and $p = 3$, β was much too large. Simply doubling n and c did not help; β was still greater than 0.40. Instead, we might double n but increase c to only 4 or 5. (The effect of this is shown in solved problem 1.)

11s.5 THE ROLE OF ACCEPTANCE SAMPLING

The previous example highlighted some of the reasons acceptance sampling has been decreasing in popularity. First, the values historically used for AQL and LTPD, such as 0.01–0.10, are rarely acceptable levels of quality today. When companies such as Motorola have defect rates of 0.00003, customers are often unwilling to accept batches with defect rates of 0.01 or more. The only way to achieve these lower defect rates is by using the TQM methods discussed in Chapter 11, especially by making products right the first time. When this is done, acceptance sampling often becomes unneccesary. Second, acceptance sampling requires relatively large sample sizes to obtain fine levels of distinction between good and bad batches.

Although acceptance sampling has lost popularity, there are still instances where it is used as an additional level of protection. Suppliers to the U.S. military are often required to perform standard acceptance sampling on all shipments. For these reasons, some basic knowledge of acceptance sampling is of value.

KEY TERMS

acceptance quality level (AQL) **616**
acceptance sampling **615**
batch (lot) **615**
consumer's risk **616**
lot tolerance proportion defective (LTPD) **616**
operating characteristic curve (OC curve) **616**
producer's risk **616**

SOLVED PROBLEMS

Problem 1: Compute the producer's risk and the consumer's risk for the sampling plan ($n = 120$, $c = 5$) when AQL = 0.02, LTPD = 0.06, and the batch size is $N = 3000$.

Solution:

α = probability of rejecting a batch with $p = 0.02$
= probability that six or more items in the sample are defective
= $\text{Prob}(X \geq 6 \mid p = 0.02) = 1 - \text{Prob}(X \leq 5 \mid p = 0.02)$

Noting that $np = (120)(0.02) = 2.4$, we use equation 11S.1 to compute

$$\text{Prob}(X = 0 \mid p = 0.02) = [(2.4)^0 e^{-2.4}]/0! = 0.0907$$
$$\text{Prob}(X = 1 \mid p = 0.02) = [(2.4)^1 e^{-2.4}]/1! = 0.2177$$
$$\text{Prob}(X = 2 \mid p = 0.02) = [(2.4)^2 e^{-2.4}]/2! = 0.2613$$
$$\text{Prob}(X = 3 \mid p = 0.02) = [(2.4)^3 e^{-2.4}]/3! = 0.2090$$
$$\text{Prob}(X = 4 \mid p = 0.02) = [(2.4)^4 e^{-2.4}]/4! = 0.1254$$
$$\text{Prob}(X = 5 \mid p = 0.02) = [(2.4)^5 e^{-2.4}]/5! = 0.0602$$

So $\text{Prob}(X \leq 5 \mid p = 0.02) = 0.0907 + \ldots + 0.0602 = 0.9643$, and

$\alpha = \text{Prob}(X \geq 6 \mid p = 0.02) = 1 - 0.9643 = 0.0357$

β = probability of accepting a batch with $p = 0.06$
= probability that five or fewer items in the sample are defective
= $\text{Prob}(X \leq 5 \mid p = 0.06)$

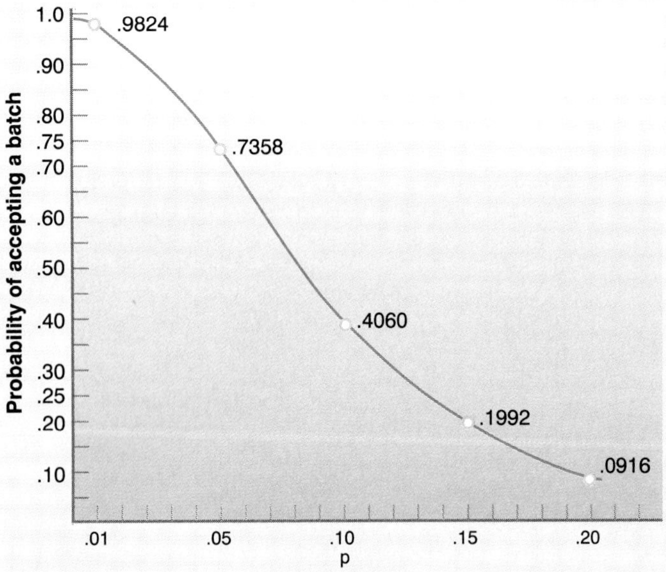

FIGURE 11S.3 OC curve for solved problem 2.

Repeating the same process, but with $np = (120)(0.06) = 7.2$, we get

$$\beta = \text{Prob}(X \le 5) = 0.2760$$

Problem 2: Suppose $N = 1000$, AQL = 0.01, and LTPD = 0.05. Compute the OC curve for the sampling plan ($n = 20$, $c = 1$).

Solution:

For a variety of values for p, we compute $\text{Prob}(X \le 1|\ p)$, the probability of accepting the batch. These are listed below and graphed in Figure 11S.3.

p	0.01	0.05	0.10	0.15	0.20
$\text{Prob}(X \le 1)$	0.9824	0.7358	0.4060	0.1992	0.0916

Notice that $\alpha = 1 - 0.9824 = 0.0176$ and $\beta = 0.7358$.

PROBLEMS

1. A company has decided to use an acceptance sampling plan with $n = 25$, $c = 2$, to evaluate incoming shipments. Suppose that AQL = 0.01 and LTPD = 0.06. Compute the producer's risk, α, and the consumer's risk, β.
2. A company supplies toys to a customer in lots of 10,000. The company and customer have agreed on an AQL of 0.01 and an LTPD of 0.03. The customer has suggested that the following procedure be used to determine whether or not it will accept a shipment: 20 toys will be sampled; if 1 or fewer toys are defective, it will accept the shipment; if 2 or more are defective, it will reject the shipment. Compute the producer's risk (α) and the consumer's risk (β) for this sampling plan.
3. For the sampling plan in problem 1, derive the OC curve.
4. For the sampling plan in problem 2, derive the OC curve.
5. Suppose that in problem 1 we doubled the sample size to $n = 50$. Compute the producer's and consumer's risks for the cases: $c = 2, 3, 4$. Which one would you recommend using? Why?

PART 3

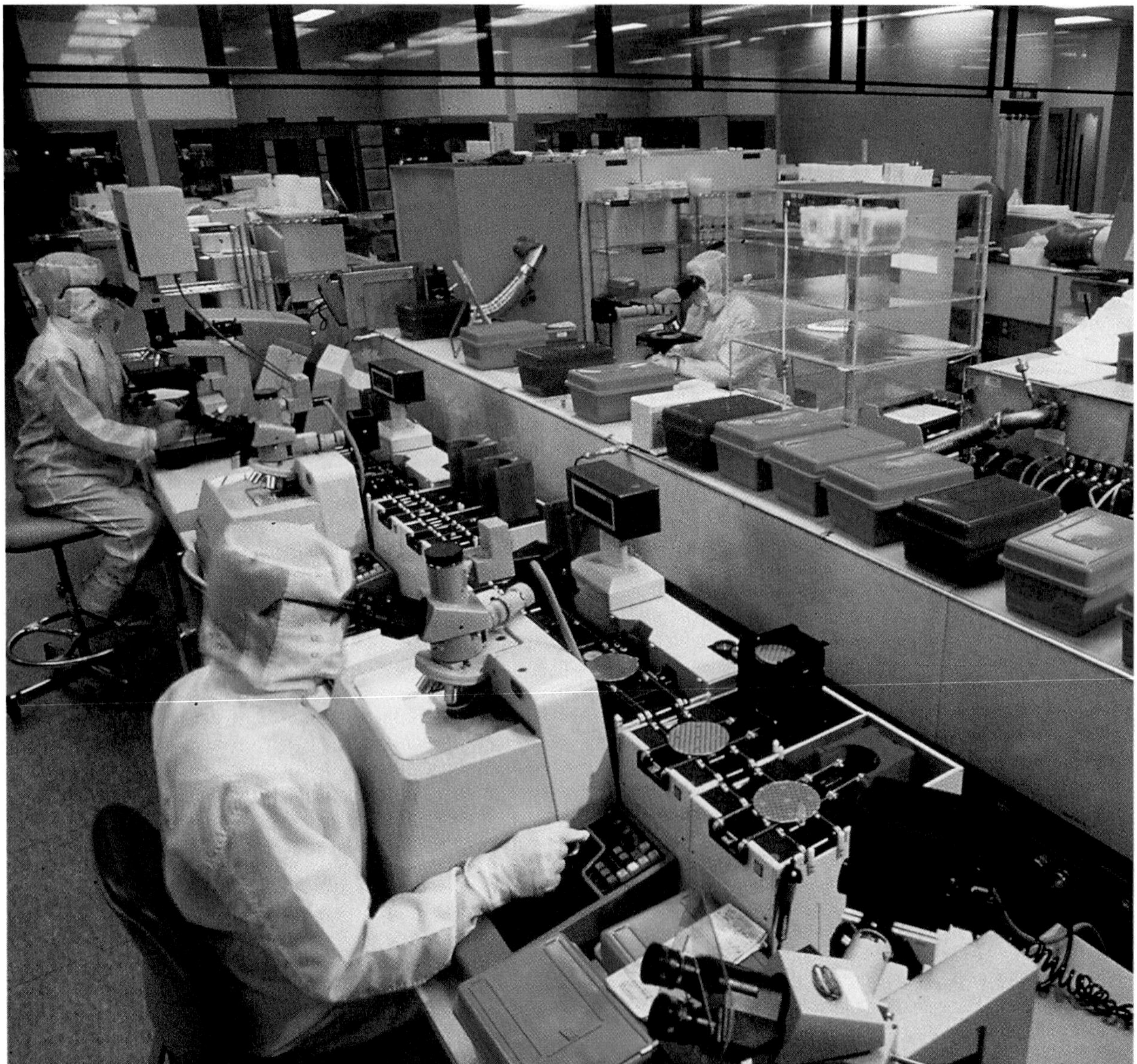

Scheduling, Operating, and Controlling the Production System

Chapter 12: Aggregate Planning
Chapter 13: Inventory Planning and Managing Materials with Independent Demands
Chapter 14: Managing Materials with Dependent Demands
Chapter 15: Just-in-Time, Lean, and Synchronous Production Systems
Chapter 16: Operations and Personnel Scheduling
Chapter 17: Project Planning and Scheduling

Rather than spending all their time putting out fires, managers can prevent many fires, such as material shortages and late deliveries, through good short-term planning. This frees their time for more strategic design issues, such as improving the production process or quality management system.

Part 3 begins with aggregate (or intermediate-term) planning, which acts as the link between long-term design decisions and short-term operational decisions. Next, we discuss an important aspect of most companies: the acquisition of materials and the management of inventories.

Just-in-time and Lean production systems represent comprehensive and evolutionary changes in classical production management. In covering them, Chapter 15 brings together the various design and operational aspects of operations management. The last two chapters on scheduling discuss ways to coordinate personnel, machines, and other resources to perform work in a timely manner.

CHAPTER 12

AGGREGATE PLANNING

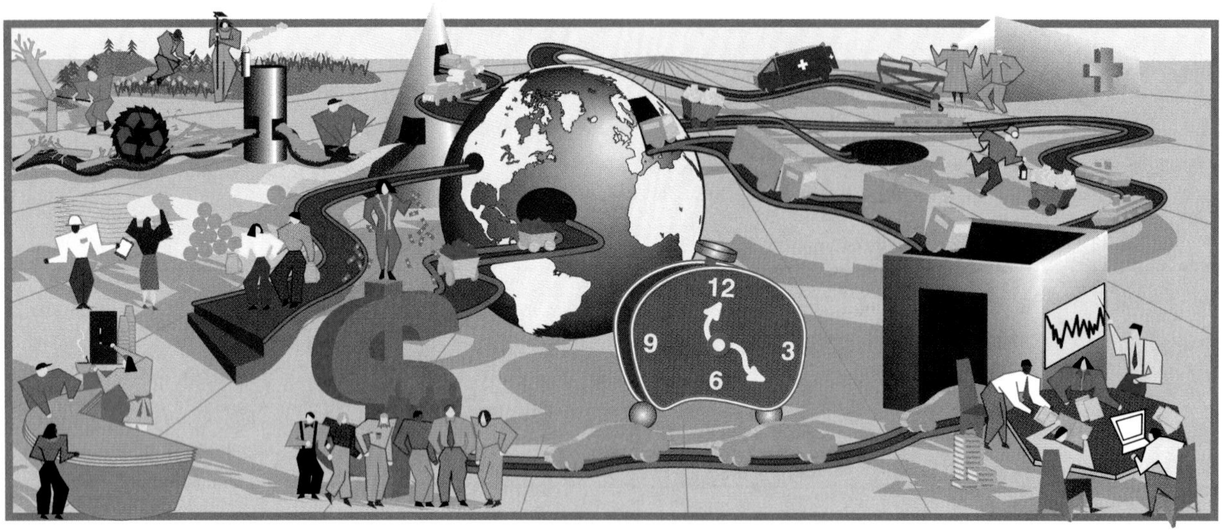

12.1 LINKING LONG-TERM AND SHORT-TERM PLANNING
On the Job: Randy Sanderson, Famous-Barr Stores

12.2 AGGREGATE UNITS OF PRODUCTION AND RESOURCES

12.3 THE AGGREGATE PLANNING PROCESS AND VARIABLES: CONTROLLING SUPPLY
Forecasting
Identifying the Planning Variables
Implementing an Aggregate Plan: The Rolling Horizon

12.4 SIMPLE PLANNING HEURISTICS
The Chase Demand Strategy
The Level Workforce Strategy

12.5 USING LINEAR PROGRAMMING FOR AGGREGATE PLANNING
A Linear Programming Model
Refinements and Variations of the Model
Dynamic Planning and Implementing the Linear Program

12.6 DISAGGREGATING THE AGGREGATE PLAN
Factors in Disaggregation
The Master Production Schedule

12.7 DEMAND INFLUENCING TACTICS TO REDUCE COST
Advertising, Pricing, and Product Promotion
Countercyclic but Similar Products
In Good Company: Polaris Industries Has All Seasons Covered
Reservation Systems

Force-Master: An Aggregate Planning Case

12.1 Linking Long-Term and Short-Term Planning

Ford Motor's decisions to manufacture a sport utility vehicle (the Explorer), to produce it in Louisville, Kentucky, and to have a production capacity of 300,000 vehicles per year were key strategic decisions. Decisions such as these, involving the design and mix of products, the location and capacity of facilities, and the design of production processes, are long-term decisions that fix the environment within which the production system must operate. **Aggregate** or **intermediate-term planning**, on the other hand, is the process of determining the company's production, inventory, and personnel levels for 3–12 months ahead. Aggregate plans act as an interface (as shown in Figure 12.1) between strategic decisions, which fix the operating environment, and short-term scheduling and control decisions, which guide the firm's day-to-day operations. Although aggregate planning is commonly considered to be mainly a concern of manufacturers, Randy Sanderson (the subject of this chapter's "On the Job" segment) finds that intermediate-term planning of personnel levels is an important part of his job as head of a staff function for a major retailer.

Aggregate planning typically focuses on manipulating several aspects of operations—aggregate production, inventory, and personnel levels—to minimize costs over some planning horizon while satisfying demand and policy requirements. Intermediate-term planning is normally performed in terms of *aggregate* production units and resources (hence the term *aggregate planning*) rather than for individual products. Although in the intermediate term major facility and process changes usually cannot be made, intermediate-term capacity can usually be expanded by using overtime work, subcontracting production, hiring additional workers, or even adding entire work shifts. This approach takes the demand pattern as given (using forecasts) and focuses on minimizing costs. More recently, some organizations have expanded their view of aggregate planning to include coordinating supply and demand over time, using marketing tactics to create demand patterns that can be served more profitably.

On the Job

Randy Sanderson, Famous-Barr Stores

It is a fact of the retail business that sales are highly concentrated in a few short periods of the year, such as Christmas, summer, and back-to-school time. With such seasonal fluctuations on the selling floor, it's no wonder that support systems experience peaks and valleys in their workloads too.

Randy Sanderson, vice president–controller for the Famous-Barr division of May Department Stores, has developed work measures and standards to forecast his fluctuating staffing needs throughout the year. He uses these forecasts to plan hiring, and to schedule permanent and seasonal employees who accommodate the high seasonal variations in the accounting and financial operations for which he is responsible. Because his unit's operations are very labor intensive, Randy encourages his staff to "work smarter, not harder." This means he sometimes redesigns jobs and processes both to eliminate unproductive tasks and to improve the way productive tasks are performed.

Along with his management responsibilities and the need to provide other senior managers with data and analyses for key decisions, Randy must be constantly aware of the need to train and develop his staff to handle the varying flow of work.

FIGURE 12.1 Planning hierarchy.

Aggregate planning is based on establishing appropriate units of aggregate production, so Section 12.2 explains how products might be aggregated. Section 12.3 then describes the aggregate planning process and the supply choices available to firms. Section 12.4 compares some simple heuristics for establishing aggregate production plans that focus on minimizing only one component of cost, rather than total cost. However, frequently aggregate production planning fits the structure of linear programming well, in which case it makes sense to utilize linear programming models to develop optimal or near-optimal aggregate plans rather than using crude heuristics; Section 12.5 illustrates how this can be done. Section 12.6 describes how the aggregate plan is disaggregated to prepare efficient and consistent master production and short-term schedules. The chapter concludes by suggesting several ways to modify the de-

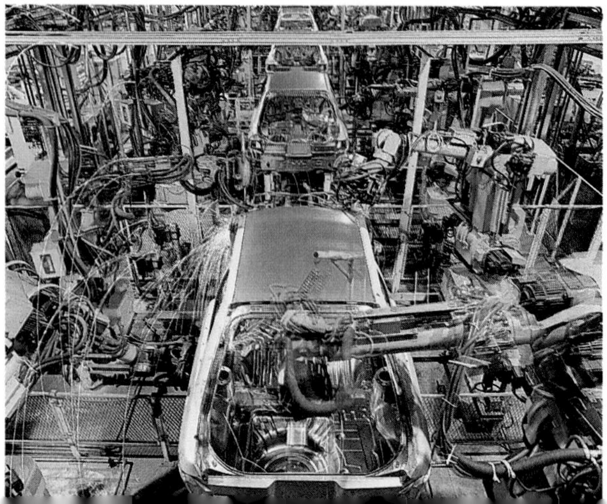

The large production capacity and highly automated process at its Louisville Explorer plant establish the parameters within which Ford Motor Co. can operate in the short-to-intermediate term. The large fixed equipment and personnel costs and seasonal nature of auto sales make aggregate planning especially important for Ford Motor Co.

mand pattern to make it less costly to serve customers and to utilize capacity better. The end-of-chapter case illustrates how production and demand influencing tactics can be synthesized to create a successful aggregate plan.

12.2 AGGREGATE UNITS OF PRODUCTION AND RESOURCES

Suppose a large appliance manufacturer makes refrigerators, washing machines, dish washers, and clothes dryers. Each general product is made in different sizes and colors with different features. Some or all of the appliances may be produced in the same facilities and may utilize the same production equipment and workers. There is very little difference in the production processes for refrigerators of the same size and style but of different color; there is slightly more difference in the production of various styles and sizes, and much difference in the production of dishwashers as opposed to clothes dryers.

When we are trying to plan 3–12 months ahead, it is usually not practical or useful to think in terms of the smallest production units, such as a specific model and color of refrigerator. Forecasting the demand for individual products tends to be inaccurate, and the number of forecasts required (one for each product) can be large. Instead, it is better to develop forecasts for aggregate groups of products. Fewer forecasts are needed, and they tend to be more stable and accurate than those for individual products. For example, we can usually forecast quite accurately how many refrigerators will be purchased from a company during the next three months because we can determine the general consumer need for new refrigerators and the company's historical market share. This value does not change substantially except when general economic conditions change. However, predicting the demand for a 10-cubic-foot model or yellow refrigerators is more difficult. There can be substantial swings in consumer preferences at this level, even though the total demand for the company's refrigerators may be predictable.

One convention for aggregating products, proposed by Arnoldo Hax and H. C. Meal,[1] uses the following definitions:

Items are the end products sold to customers.

Families are groups of items that are processed on the same equipment and share the same general machine setup.

Product types are groups of product families that have similar cost structures, holding costs per unit, productivities, and seasonal demand patterns.

Aggregate planning is normally done at the product type level of aggregation and at the facility level, rather than at the corporate level. Once aggregate plans have been developed, they must be disaggregated into family and item production plans with shorter time horizons. Disaggregating the aggregate plan is discussed in Section 12.6.

Assigning items to families and product types is easier than it may at first appear. One of the tricks to making these assignments is somewhat counterintuitive. Product types, families, and items form a hierarchy, with product types being the highest level of the three, as shown in Figure 12.2. Intuitively it may seem that we would want to build up the hierarchy from the bottom; that is, we first group items into families and then group the families into product types. Although this works well in many cases, sometimes it is easier to group the items into product types first, based on similarities in seasonal demand patterns and cost structures. Then the product types can be decom-

[1]See Arnoldo Hax and H. C. Meal, "Hierarchical Integration of Production Planning and Scheduling," in M. A. Geisler (ed.), *Studies in Management Sciences*, Vol. 1, *Logistics*, North Holland–American Elsevier, New York, 1975, for a discussion of product aggregation.

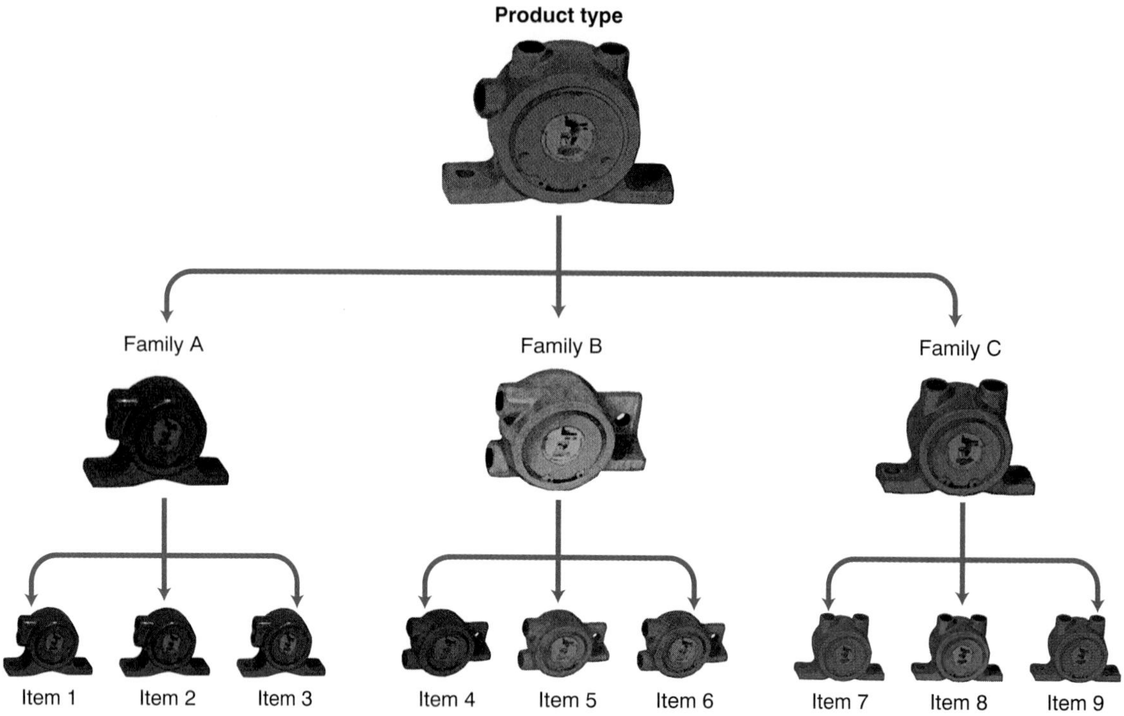

FIGURE 12.2 Product classification hierarchy.

These three Sony camcorder models are all of the same product type so their production is planned together at the same facilities.

posed into families according to which items share the same general machine setups. (The three-level hierarchy is not strict; in some cases, items and families are essentially identical, so aggregate products can be decomposed directly into items.) One factor that simplifies the aggregation process is that frequently all the products made at a facility belong to only one or two product types.

Selecting the aggregate measures of production and inventory is normally straightforward because items within the same product type should be very similar physically. For example, the units may be expressed in terms of the number of appliances, number of refrigerators, thousands of motors, or tons of Fiberglas produced and stored. Production resources and capacity should be expressed in aggregate form as well. For example, one of the variables to be determined by the plan is the amount of direct labor (workforce level) needed, including the amount of overtime labor to use in each time period. The measure of workforce or overtime would be expressed in labor-hours or person-equivalents rather than in terms of specific individuals. Similarly, the amount of resources consumed in production, such as gallons of paint or hours of machine time, should be expressed in terms of the aggregate amount of each resource consumed to produce one unit of the *aggregate* product.

12.3 THE AGGREGATE PLANNING PROCESS AND VARIABLES: CONTROLLING SUPPLY

If the demands for a company's products were absolutely stable, there would be no need for aggregate planning. For example, if the company made three products, A, B, and C, and the demand for each was a constant 1000 units per month, then the company could develop a production process and a workforce level that would produce exactly this amount of product every month in a repeating cycle while maintaining almost no inventories. However, in practice the total demand for a company's products, and the demand mix among the products, fluctuate over time. For some products this is due to normal seasonal patterns, such as the demand for lawnmowers, which is very high in the spring and summer and very low in the winter and fall. Other products may simply have irregular, lumpy demand patterns, such as specialized products supplied to a few major customers (e.g., specialized navigational systems for military aircraft). In these cases, demand may exceed the company's normal production capacity in some periods and fall well below it in others.

The problem facing the company is to create production, inventory, and workforce plans far enough in advance to satisfy the anticipated demand at minimum total cost without harming the company's long-term strategy and viability. The output of the planning process should be a period-by-period (say, month-by-month) plan of how much of each product type to produce; how much to add to or remove from inventory; how much the workforce should be increased or decreased; how much overtime work should be planned; and, if applicable, how much production should be subcontracted. In addition to the preliminary step of aggregating items into product types, the following steps are necessary to create a good aggregate plan.

FORECASTING

The aggregate plan is based on satisfying expected intermediate-term demands, so accurate forecasts of these demands are necessary. Because seasonal patterns are usually important in aggregate planning, time series models that include a seasonal component are frequently used to make these forecasts.

In addition to demand, over the intermediate term wage rates, material prices, and holding costs can change enough to affect the optimal plans. So forecasts of these quantities should be included in the plan. Frequently, these forecasts are relatively easy to obtain because they are specified in contractual agreements. For example, a wage increase may be scheduled to go into effect in three months, or a raw material supplier may have already announced a price increase that becomes effective in two months.

IDENTIFYING THE PLANNING VARIABLES

The two most obvious aggregate planning variables are the amount of the aggregate product to produce during each time period and the amount of direct labor needed. Two indirect variables that naturally result from planning these other quantities are the amount of product to add to or remove from inventory and the amount the workforce should be increased or decreased in each period. The company may also have the option of scheduling overtime work, subcontracting production with another company, or transferring production to another facility within the company.

Identifying the planning variables includes determining any restrictions on them. For example, there may be a limit on the number of additional workers that can be hired during some period of time, and a training period may be required before they can be fully productive. Similarly, there may be limits on the amount of overtime that can be scheduled, production subcontracted, inventory stored, or personnel laid off.

IMPLEMENTING AN AGGREGATE PLAN: THE ROLLING HORIZON

Aggregate plans are normally generated using analytical heuristics or optimization methods. They act as guides to decision making, but rarely are they fully realized in practice. During a planning period, employees may produce more or less than expected; actual demands may not be the same as predicted; more employees may leave the company voluntarily than expected; more or fewer may be hired than expected; some items in inventory may be found to be damaged and unusable; and so on. Each of

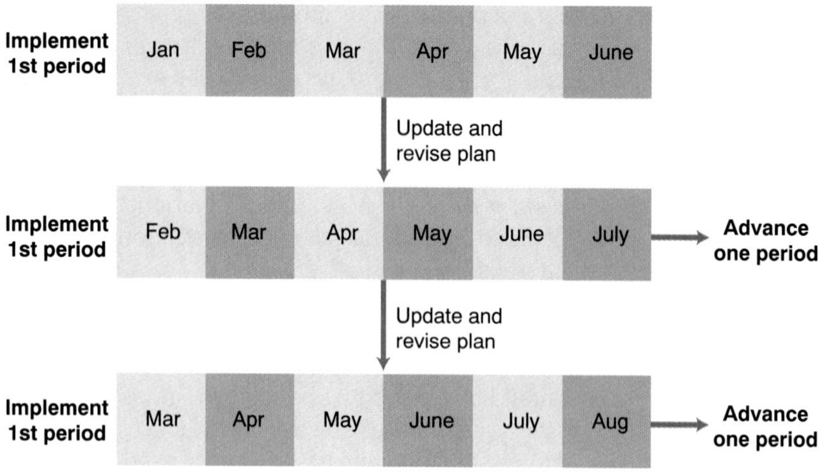

FIGURE 12.3 A rolling horizon for a six-month aggregate plan.

these variations means that at the end of the first period of the plan, the company is not likely to have the same workforce and inventory levels it expected. In addition, after a month or a quarter has passed, the predicted product demands, material prices, and even inventory holding costs may have changed. Therefore, the 6- or 12-month aggregate plan devised one period earlier may no longer be optimal for the next several months.

We do not simply generate one plan for the next 12 months and then keep that plan until it has been completely implemented. Aggregate planning is a dynamic process that requires constant updating. In practice, we first develop an aggregate plan that identifies the best thing to do during each period of the planning horizon to optimize the long-term goals of the organization. We then implement only the first period of the plan; as more information becomes available, we update and revise the plan. Then we implement actions in the first period of the revised plan, gather information, and update again, as shown in Figure 12.3. This is called using a **rolling horizon**.

If we are only going to implement the first period of the plan, why not simply treat the problem as a one-period planning model and optimize over that one period? The reason is that the actions that optimize performance for one period may leave the organization in a poor condition for future periods, so that the long-term performance will be suboptimal. For example, suppose product demand is expected to be low during the next two months and then to surge well above normal capacity for a few months. A short-term plan that optimizes only with respect to the next month may recommend that the company use up its product inventories, produce below its capacity, and keep its workforce low to maximize profits next month. But these actions would lead to catastrophic consequences and high costs later when demand surges. Developing a multiperiod plan takes into account these demand changes and allows us to take cost-effective preparatory actions well before major demand changes occur.

12.4 SIMPLE PLANNING HEURISTICS

Suppose the demand for a company's product type follows the pattern shown in Figure 12.4. During periods of low demand the company's normal production capacity exceeds demand, while during periods of high demand capacity is less than demand. Two sim-

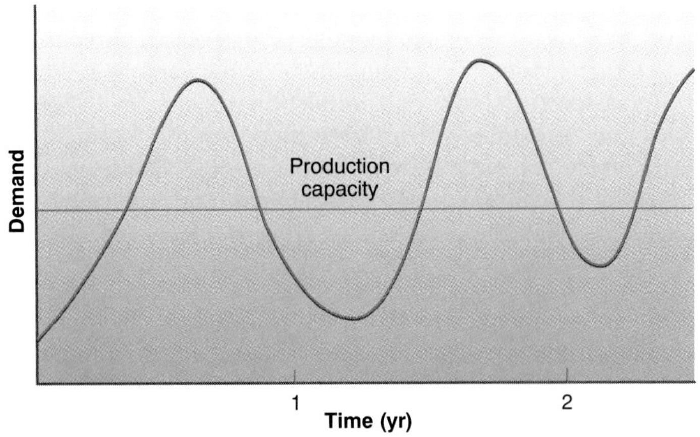

FIGURE 12.4 Typical demand pattern.

ple strategies are obvious: (1) adjust production level and staffing to match demand, thereby keeping product inventories low (called a **chase demand strategy**), and (2) maintain a relatively constant level of production and staffing, building inventories during periods of low demand and depleting them during periods of high demand (called a **level production/workforce strategy**). After briefly explaining these strategies, we illustrate the economic implications of each using the following example.

EXAMPLE 1

Starlight Corporation makes several models of compact disc players (CDPs), which form a product type, at its New York facility. The predicted sales for these products for the next six months are as follows:

Month	Sales	Work Days
October	200,000	23
November	220,000	21
December	310,000	19
January	300,000	21
February	240,000	20
March	230,000	23

Each unit of product requires approximately 1.5 person-hours of labor to make. Workers work an eight-hour day, and they receive an average of \$2000 per month in wages and fringe benefits. It costs approximately \$2500 to lay off or terminate an employee and approximately \$3000 to recruit and train a new employee. CDPs produced in one month can be held in inventory and shipped in subsequent months, but it costs \$10 per month to hold the item in inventory.

For simplicity we assume that at the beginning of each month a decision to hire/dismiss workers is made. Then production occurs during the month and all shipments are made at the end of the month. Any item on hand at the end of a month that is not shipped incurs the \$10 holding cost. The decisions facing Starlight are to select the number of production employees to have on staff for each of the next six months (and therefore the number to hire/dismiss), the number of CDPs to produce each month, and then indirectly how many to have in inventory at the end of each month.

Starlight expects to have 1850 production workers on staff during September, and it expects to end September with 5000 units of inventory available for use. In addition, Starlight wants to complete March with between 1800 and 1900 production workers on staff and with between 2000 and 2150 units of product in inventory.

THE CHASE DEMAND STRATEGY

The first strategy mentioned above was to adjust production levels to match demand as much as possible, thereby keeping inventory costs to a minimum. Although this strategy of "chasing" demand can minimize inventory costs, the consequence is often substantial costs associated with increasing and decreasing staffing, such as the costs of hiring and training new employees, unemployment insurance, separation or severance pay, possibly a wage premium because of the lack of job security for workers, and productivity losses from poor employee morale and reduced loyalty.

To determine the production levels that would minimize inventory costs over the planning horizon, we begin by setting the production level in each time period (month, quarter) equal to the net requirements for that period. **Net requirements** are the predicted demand minus any product inventories at the beginning of the time period that are available for use (i.e., not held as safety stock). If in any period the net requirements are greater than the maximum production capacity, we increase production in the preceding periods to stay within limits.

EXAMPLE 1 (CONTINUED)

Starlight's net requirements for October are 200,000 − 5,000 (in inventory) = 195,000; the net requirements for later months equal the demand, except for March, which requires an additional 2000 units for ending inventory. Table 12.1 lists the number of workers needed each month to produce the net requirements. (The number of units that can be produced by an employee each month equals [8 hr/day × number of work days/month]/[1.5 person-hr/unit].) This information is then used to derive the production and staffing plan in Table 12.2, which minimizes inventory costs during the next six months. (For simplicity, we will assume that all workers produce the maximum number

TABLE 12.1 EMPLOYEES NEEDED TO MAKE NET REQUIREMENTS EACH MONTH

Month	(A) Net Requirements (units)	(B) Maximum Production per Employee (units/month)	(C) = (A)/(B) No. of Employees Needed to Make (A)*
October	195,000	122.67	1590
November	220,000	112.00	1965
December	310,000	101.33	3060
January	300,000	112.00	2679
February	240,000	106.67	2250
March	232,000	122.67	1892

*The number of workers is rounded up to the next integer.

TABLE 12.2 STARLIGHT'S AGGREGATE PLAN USING THE CHASE DEMAND STRATEGY

Month	No. of Workers	No. Hired	No. Dismissed	Production	Ending Inventory
September	1,850				5,000
October	1,590	0	260	195,045	45
November	1,964*	374	0	219,968	13
December	3,060	1,096	0	310,070	83
January	2,678*	0	382	299,936	19
February	2,250	0	428	240,007	26
March	1,892	0	358	232,092	2,118
April	1,892				
Totals (Oct.–Mar.)	13,434	1,470	1,428		2,304

*This number is less than the minimum needed from Table 12.1 because of available inventory from the preceding month.

of units possible each month. In reality, we could allow underproduction to control inventories.)

The total production-related costs for this strategy (October–March) will be as follows:

Wages costs	= 13434 pers-months × \$2000	= \$26,868,000
Hiring costs	= 1470 workers × \$3000	= \$ 4,410,000
Dismissal costs	= 1428 workers × \$2500	= \$ 3,570,000
Inventory costs	= 2304 items × \$10	= \$ 23,040
Total cost		\$34,871,040

THE LEVEL WORKFORCE STRATEGY

Rather than increasing production and employment during periods of high demand and then decreasing them when demand drops, the firm can maintain a steady output that builds inventory during periods of low demand that can be used during periods of high demand, thereby avoiding dramatic and costly changes in production and staffing.

EXAMPLE 1 (CONTINUED)

A simple way to construct an aggregate plan that keeps personnel adjustment to a minimum is to first compute the net *cumulative* requirements for each period; these are simply the net requirements summed for all periods in the planning horizon up to that period. Column A of Table 12.3 gives the net cumulative requirements for the data in Table 12.1.

Now for each month we compute the minimum stable workforce that would be required to produce the net cumulative requirements *up to that point*. For example, Table 12.3 shows that during the first two months the net cumulative requirements are

TABLE 12.3 EMPLOYEES NEEDED TO MAKE NET CUMULATIVE REQUIREMENTS

Month	(A) Net Cumulative Requirements (units)	(B) Cumulative Production per Worker (units)	(C) = A/B No. of Workers Needed to Make (A)*
October	195,000	122.67	1590
November	415,000	234.67	1769
December	725,000	336.00	2158
January	1,025,000	448.00	2288
February	1,265,000	554.67	2281
March	1,497,000	677.33	2211

*The number of workers is rounded up to the next integer.

415,000 units. An employee working during these two months has a cumulative production capability of 234.67 units (122.67 in October and 112 in November), so if Starlight were to maintain a stable workforce during this two-month period, it would need at least [415,000 units]/[234.67 units/worker] = 1769 workers. With this workforce Starlight would produce 217,003 units in October, 22,003 more than needed in that month. These could be put into inventory and used in November. The workforce in November could be maintained at 1769 rather than increased to 1965, which would be needed to produce all the November net requirements during November. However, a stable workforce of 1769 would not be sufficient to produce all the units needed by December, January, or February. So we select the largest value in column C of Table 12.3, which is 2288, to be our initial target personnel level. We would increase employment to 2288 in October and keep it at that level until the end of January, at which point we could reduce it to meet the lower production and personnel requirements. During October and November inventories would be built, and then they would be used in December and January. With this strategy the workforce would never have to exceed 2288, whereas the chase demand strategy reaches a maximum of 3060 employees.

Converting the information in Table 12.3 into a stable employment strategy produces the aggregate plan in Table 12.4.

TABLE 12.4 STARLIGHT'S AGGREGATE PLAN USING THE LEVEL STAFFING STRATEGY

Month	No. of Workers	No. Hired	No. Dismissed	Production	Ending Inventory
September	1,850				5,000
October	2,288	438	0	280,669	85,669
November	2,288	0	0	256,256	121,925
December	2,288	0	0	231,843	43,768
January	2,288	0	0	256,256	24
February	2,250	0	38	240,007	31
March	1,892	0	358	232,092	2,123
April	1,892				
Totals (Oct.–Mar.)	13,294	438	496		253,540

The total production-related costs (October–March) for this level-workforce strategy will be as follows:

Wages costs	= 13294 pers-months × $2000	= $26,588,000
Hiring costs	= 438 workers × $3000	= $ 1,314,000
Dismissal costs	= 496 workers × $2500	= $ 1,240,000
Inventory costs	= 253,540 items × $10	= $ 2,535,400
Total cost		$31,677,400

Although this level strategy incurs $2.5 million more in inventory costs, hiring and dismissal costs are $5.5 million less than with the chase demand plan and total costs are $3.2 million less.

12.5 USING LINEAR PROGRAMMING FOR AGGREGATE PLANNING

The total cost for the aggregate plans above is made up of two components: inventory costs and personnel-related costs. The chase and level strategies are two extreme or "pure" strategies; they focus on minimizing one cost component while ignoring the other. Not surprisingly, the best aggregate plan is usually one that strikes a balance between the two. We usually do not want to build up enormous inventories simply to keep the workforce size completely stable, nor do we want to whipsaw the workforce in order to keep inventories low.

For many years, planners tried to incorporate these trade-offs into their aggregate plans using simple cost–trade-off analyses. For example, in a period in which demand will exceed current production capacity, one can compute the marginal cost of adding workers to produce the required output, and then compare it with the cost of producing product in an earlier, low-demand period and holding the items in inventory. Although for simple situations (e.g., with one product type and only a few time periods) this analysis is satisfactory, for more realistic and complex aggregate planning situations it soon becomes cumbersome and less reliable. Especially when the production resources are shared by two or more product types, and when overtime production and subcontracting of production are available options, a better method for devising the aggregate plan is necessary.

Fortunately, most aggregate planning problems fit very well into a linear programming structure. The objective function of the plan is to minimize costs over a planning horizon, and each of the relevant cost components is relatively proportional to the number of units produced and stored and the number of employees hired, laid off, and on staff. The constraints of the problem are primarily "bookkeeping" constraints that ensure that materials and employees do not simply appear or vanish from period to period without relevant costs being tabulated, and the constraints specify how the amount of materials, production, and personnel are related to each other between periods.

A LINEAR PROGRAMMING MODEL

Starlight Corporation's aggregate planning problem can easily be formulated as a linear program and then solved to obtain an optimal aggregate plan. The first step is to identify those quantities over which the planner or decision maker has control; these will be the decision variables for the problem.

EXAMPLE 2

In Example 1, Starlight is trying to determine (1) how much product to make each month, (2) how many people to employ each month, (3) how many employees to hire at the beginning of each month, (4) how many employees to lay off or terminate at the beginning of each month, and (5) how many units of finished product to have in inventory at the end of each month. We therefore define the following variables for the problem:

P_t = number of units of product to produce during month t, $t = 1, \ldots, 6$
L_t = number of production workers on staff during month t, $t = 1, \ldots, 7$
H_t = number of workers to hire at the beginning of month t, $t = 1, \ldots, 7$
D_t = number of workers to dismiss at the beginning of month t, $t = 1, \ldots, 7$
I_t = number of units of product in inventory at the end of month t, $t = 1, \ldots 6$

where $t = 1$ corresponds to October, $t = 6$ corresponds to March, and $t = 7$ corresponds to April.

There are a total of 33 variables in this formulation. Notice that there is an L_7, an H_7, and a D_7, so that if the workforce level in March is not between 1800 and 1900, the hiring or dismissing necessary at the beginning of April to get within these limits can be computed and the cost charged to the plan. The number of variables could, in fact, be reduced by eliminating the production and inventory variables because these quantities can be deduced using the other variables, but it is easier to formulate the problem and interpret the solution by including these quantities as explicit variables (and problem size is not a severe limitation).

The objective function is to minimize the relevant personnel and inventory costs during the next six months, including any personnel adjustment costs needed in April to keep the workforce within the 1800–1900 employee range. It can be written in terms of the decision variables as follows:

$$\text{minimize TC} = \$2000 \sum_{t=1}^{6} L_t + \$3000 \sum_{t=1}^{7} H_t + \$2500 \sum_{t=1}^{7} D_t + \$10 \sum_{t=1}^{6} I_t \qquad (12.1)$$

The problem requires three sets of constraints. The first set performs double duty; it ensures that the required number of units of product are available for shipment each month, and it defines the inventory variables. For each month we need a constraint that states:

production + beginning inventory = amount shipped + ending inventory

Subtracting the ending inventory from both sides and substituting the variables into this identity for each month gives the following constraints:

$$P_1 + 5000 - I_1 = 200{,}000 \quad \text{or} \quad P_1 - I_1 = 195{,}000$$
$$P_2 + I_1 - I_2 = 220{,}000$$
$$P_3 + I_2 - I_3 = 310{,}000$$
$$P_4 + I_3 - I_4 = 300{,}000$$
$$P_5 + I_4 - I_5 = 240{,}000$$
$$P_6 + I_5 - I_6 = 230{,}000$$

$I_6 > 2000$
$I_6 \leq 2150$

Notice that if beginning inventory plus production in a month is greater than the amount shipped, the ending inventory is forced to equal the difference; for example, in the second constraint, if $I_1 = 20{,}000$ and $P_2 = 240{,}000$, then I_2 must equal 40,000 because 220,000 units will be sold. The last two constraints simply guarantee that the ending inventory requirements are satisfied.

The amount of production that occurs in a month is determined by the size of the workforce. As in the previous section, we will assume that all workers produce the maximum amount of product possible, so the relationship between production and workforce is given by the following constraints:

$$P_1 = 122.67\,L_1;\quad P_2 = 112\,L_2;\quad P_3 = 101.33\,L_3$$
$$P_4 = 112\,L_4;\quad P_5 = 106.67\,L_5;\quad P_6 = 122.67\,L_6$$

The final set of constraints maintains the conservation of personnel; that is, in each month, t, the number of workers is equal to the number of workers during month $t-1$ plus the number hired at the beginning of month t minus the number dismissed at the beginning of month t:

$$L_1 = 1850 + H_1 - D_1 \quad \text{or} \quad L_1 - H_1 + D_1 = 1850$$
$$L_2 - L_1 - H_2 + D_2 = 0$$
$$L_3 - L_2 - H_3 + D_3 = 0$$
$$L_4 - L_3 - H_4 + D_4 = 0$$
$$L_5 - L_4 - H_5 + D_5 = 0$$
$$L_6 - L_5 - H_6 + D_6 = 0$$
$$L_7 - L_6 - H_7 + D_7 = 0$$
$$L_7 \geq 1800$$
$$L_7 \leq 1900$$

Finally, all the variables should be nonnegative.

This formulation has 33 variables and 23 constraints (not counting the nonnegativity of the variables). Its optimal solution (obtained using a computer package) is given in Table 12.5.

If fractional values for the variables are problematic, we can round off, truncate, and "adjust" the linear programming solution to obtain the aggregate plan given in

TABLE 12.5 LINEAR PROGRAMMING SOLUTION FOR STARLIGHT

Var.	Value	Var.	Value	Var.	Value	Var.	Value	Var.	Value
P_1	226,939.50	L_1	1850.00	H_1	0	D_1	0	I_1	31,939.50
P_2	274,744.97	L_2	2453.08	H_2	603.08	D_2	0	I_2	86,684.43
P_3	248,570.63	L_3	2453.08	H_3	0	D_3	0	I_3	25,255.05
P_4	274,744.97	L_4	2453.08	H_4	0	D_4	0	I_4	0
P_5	240,000.02	L_5	2249.93	H_5	0	D_5	203.15	I_5	0
P_6	232,000.02	L_6	1891.25	H_6	0	D_6	358.68	I_6	2,000.00
		L_7	1891.25	H_7	0	D_7	0		

Total cost = 31,373,440

TABLE 12.6 STARLIGHT'S AGGREGATE PLAN USING LINEAR PROGRAMMING

Month	No. of Workers	No. Hired	No. Dismissed	Production	Ending Inventory
September	1,850				5,000
October	1,850	0	0	226,939	31,939
November	2,453	603	0	274,736	86,675
December	2,453	0	0	248,562	25,237
January	2,454	1	0	274,848	85
February	2,250	0	204	240,000	85
March	1,891	0	359	231,969	2,065
April	1,891				
Totals (Oct.–Mar.)	13,351	604	563		146,075

Table 12.6. The total production-related costs for this linear programming generated plan will be as follows:

Wages costs	= 13351 pers-months × \$2000	= \$26,702,000
Hiring costs	= 604 workers × \$3000	= \$ 1,812,000
Dismissal costs	= 563 workers × \$2500	= \$ 1,407,500
Inventory costs	= 146,075 items × \$10	= \$ 1,460,750
Total cost		\$31,382,250

This plan represents a balance between the chase demand and level production plans. It incurs higher personnel-related costs than the level plan, but its lower inventory costs more than make up for this, and it results in a total cost that is approximately \$300,000 less.

REFINEMENTS AND VARIATIONS OF THE MODEL

Each of the three aggregate production plans derived above recommends substantial workforce changes between some months. For example, the linear programming–based plan in Table 12.6 requires hiring 603 workers at the beginning of November and laying off 204 in February and 359 in March. Even the so-called level production and employment plan involves hiring 438 workers in October and laying off 358 at the beginning of March. Although such large changes may be possible in some instances, such as when the "dismissing" and "hiring" of workers really represent temporary layoffs and recalls of experienced workers, in many cases such large changes are not possible. Especially when hiring means recruiting, hiring, and training, most companies do not have the resources to increase their workforce by 20–40% in one month. In reality there may be some physical limit or company policy on workforce changes, such as: "employment should not increase or decrease by more than 10% in any one month." One advantage of using linear programming is that such refinements can easily be incorporated into the model. For example, a 10% monthly limit on personnel changes could be incorporated into Starlight's linear programming model by adding constraints of the form $L_t \leq 1.1\, L_{t-1}$ and $L_t \geq 0.9\, L_{t-1}$ for each month.

Many other refinements are commonly added to improve the accuracy of the aggregate plan. The more common ones are described briefly below, and some are illustrated in the case at the end of the chapter and in the end-of-chapter problems.

Overtime Work, Adding Shifts, Subcontracting

During temporary periods of high demand, most organizations are able to ask their employees to work longer hours than normal, usually in exchange for a pay premium. This factor can be included in a linear programming model by adding variables that allow and track overtime work. Normally, the cost coefficients in the objective function for this work would be larger than those for regular-time work, and constraints would limit the overtime to some proportion of regular-time work. In some cases, an entire work shift can be added by hiring additional workers. For example, deciding whether and when to add or eliminate shifts at their manufacturing plants are key variables in the aggregate plans of the major auto manufacturers. (Modeling the addition of entire shifts would require the use of an integer programming model, not simply a linear program; see Tutorial 1.)

Similarly, some companies are able to have production work performed by subcontractors. Variables can be defined as the number of units produced by subcontractors, with an associated cost included in the objective function.

Back-Ordering

In some situations, demand does not have to be satisfied in the period in which it occurs. Instead, temporary shortages (called *back-orders*) can be allowed as long as delivery eventually occurs. Back-order variables can be defined to track these shortages, but just as carrying inventories incurs a cost, back orders incur a cost that would be included in the objective function.

Multiple Product Types and Sharing Resources

The Starlight example illustrated aggregate planning with only one product type in the plan. Frequently, a company is interested in planning the production of two or more product types that share production resources, such as machine time or labor. The case at the end of this chapter illustrates how additional product types can be included by defining new variables for production of the additional products and by modifying constraints on labor and other resources; additional resource constraints are often not needed.

Different Labor Skills and Training

An important component of most aggregate plans is the scheduling of workforce changes: hiring and laying off workers and using part-time instead of full-time workers. When new workers are hired, and even when experienced workers are recalled from extended layoffs, initially they are not as productive as continuing employees. During periods of training, the effective output of new workers may be only a fraction of that of experienced workers, and net output may even be negative because an experienced worker may have to be removed from production to instruct the new worker. This differential in production capability between new and experienced workers should be included explicitly in the aggregate planning model. Separate variables for new workers and experienced workers would be defined, different coefficients would be used for their respective production capabilities, and constraints would be needed to track and transform workers as they gain experience and move from being trainees to being experienced workers.

There also may be differences in the types of production skills utilized. For example, production may involve processing in four different departments, with each department having its own labor force requiring its own special skills. In this case, separate labor variables for each department and separate constraints for labor changes and capacities would be needed.

Natural Attrition

In any large organization, employees will leave on a regular basis due to retirements, deaths, and job changes. The model used above ignored these changes, but the natural rate of attrition can be included in the plan, with hiring and dismissals planned to take this factor into account.

Although we want to keep our planning model as simple as possible, a realistic representation of the planning problem and options may require some complex modeling. Surprisingly, fewer options can often make planning more difficult and important. For example, in the United States, United Parcel Service has relied heavily on part-time and temporary workers to adjust to fluctuations in demand, but when it expanded to Europe, it found that many European countries prohibit this practice, requiring UPS to use only full-time workers with large penalties for layoffs. Terry Gantt, the company's U.K. operations director, summarizes the required response: "It's a lot more planning at longer range."[2] What is clear is that linear (or integer) programming can accommodate almost any reasonable level of complexity that is likely to occur in aggregate planning. With advances in solution algorithms and computer capabilities, linear programming models with even thousands of variables and constraints can be solved in minutes.

DYNAMIC PLANNING AND IMPLEMENTING THE LINEAR PROGRAM

One advantage of using linear programming is that aggregate plans can be revised easily and quickly as part of a rolling horizon plan. Suppose the aggregate plan in Table 12.6 was implemented by Starlight Corporation. For October, the following are the planned and actual outcomes:

	Planned	Actual
Workforce	1,850	1,849
Hired	0	0
Fired	0	0
Production	226,939	228,450
Sales	200,000	200,900
Ending inventory	31,939	32,550

In October one more employee than planned left voluntarily, so the workforce was one person below the planned level, but production, sales, and inventory were all larger than planned. According to the plan made at the end of September (from Table 12.6), Starlight should hire 603 workers at the beginning of November. But at the end of October the actual workforce and inventory positions are slightly different from those planned; more important, Starlight has updated its sales estimates for the next six months, which are given in Table 12.7.

If we put these new forecasts and the actual workforce and inventory levels at the end of October into the linear programming model (again assuming an ending inventory between 2000 and 2150 and an April workforce between 1800 and 1900), the aggregate plan obtained from linear programming, adjusting the optimum to obtain integer solutions, is given in Table 12.8.

[2]Dana Milbank, "Can Europe Deliver?" *Wall Street Journal*, Sept. 30, 1994.

TABLE 12.7 STARLIGHT'S REVISED SALES FORECASTS

Month	Previous Sales Forecast	Updated Sales Forecast
November	220,000	225,000
December	310,000	300,000
January	300,000	295,000
February	240,000	245,000
March	230,000	235,000
April	—	240,000

TABLE 12.8 STARLIGHT'S LP-BASED AGGREGATE PLAN UPDATED FOR OCTOBER

Month	No. of Workers	No. Hired	No. Dismissed	Production	Ending Inventory
October	1,849				32,550
November	2,420	571	0	271,040	78,590
December	2,421	1	0	245,327	23,917
January	2,421	0	0	271,152	69
February	2,297	0	124	245,014	83
March	1,988	0	309	243,862	8,944
April	1,987	0	1	233,140	2,084
May	1900		87		

So instead of hiring 603 workers at the beginning of November, as originally planned, Starlight would hire only 571, and 130 fewer layoffs would be planned for February and March. At the end of November the actual workforce and inventory levels, along with the updated sales forecasts, would be used to devise a new aggregate plan for December through May.

12.6 DISAGGREGATING THE AGGREGATE PLAN

For the aggregate production plan to be useful in short-term production scheduling, it must undergo **disaggregation** into individual product families and items. For example, suppose the aggregate product (product type) used in Starlight Corporation's aggregate plan is made up of three families (A, B, and C) of CDPs, and each family has various models. The aggregate plan in Table 12.6 says that Starlight should plan on producing 226,939 CDPs in October. This planned production must now be allocated among the three families of CDPs. This disaggregation must then be repeated as we decompose the plan for each family into production plans for individual items, as shown in Figure 12.5.

The disaggregation process is not a simple procedure because there are several steps in the process and a variety of trade-offs that must be made before a final item-by-item production schedule is obtained. When we allocate Starlight's planned production of 226,939 CDPs in October to the three product families, should it make 50,000 units of family A? 100,000? If we allocate too much production to family A, Starlight may not be able to meet the demand for items in families B or C during October. If we

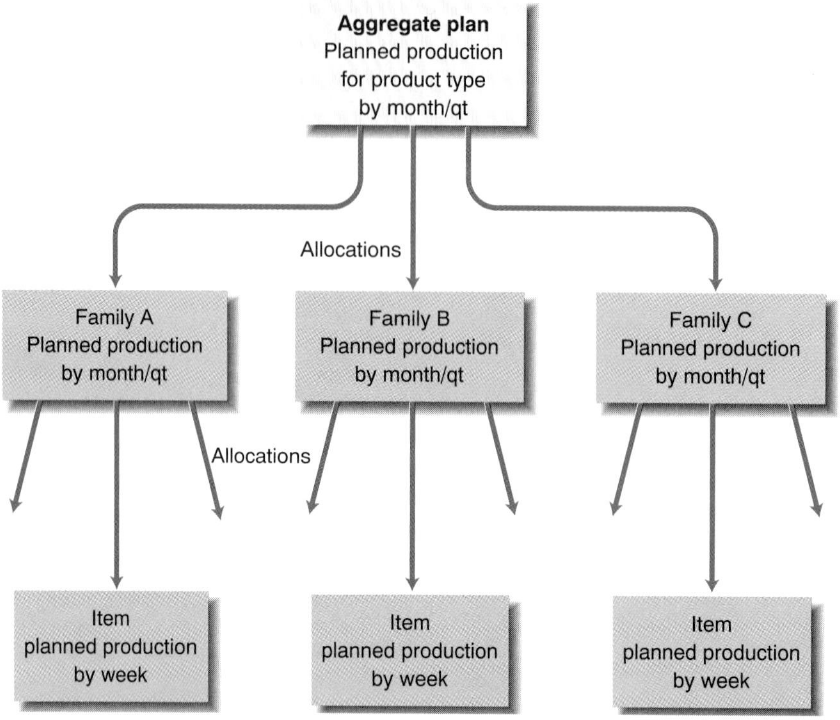

FIGURE 12.5 Disaggregating the aggregate plan.

allocate 100,000 units of production to family A, we must still decide whether to produce all 100,000 units at one time or divide this production into two or three separate runs (i.e., run family A, then B, then A, then C, etc.). Finally, for a run of each family, we must allocate production to each item within the family and sequence production of individual items.

FACTORS IN DISAGGREGATION

Researchers have developed various procedures to disaggregate production among families and items. The most successful schemes use a hierarchical planning model that explicitly ties together decisions at each level of planning in order to be internally consistent. Companies such as Owens-Corning Fiberglas have used these methods to reduce total production costs by over 5% in some cases while increasing equipment utilization.[3] We will not discuss specific disaggregation methods, which can get quite complicated, but we will briefly discuss some of the considerations and general principles of these methods. (See the work of Bitran et al. or that of Leong et al. in the Selected Readings for specific disaggregation methods.) We will, however, discuss the development of the master production schedule (MPS), which is used in Chapter 14. In Chapter 16 we discuss converting the MPS into item lot sizes and run sequences.

Because, by definition, products in one family have quite different setups than those in other families, the cost of switching production among families can be expensive, so we want to keep switching to a reasonable level. Everything else being equal, we want to

[3]E. E. Burch, M. D. Oliff, and R. T. Sumichrast. "Linking Level Requirements in Production Planning and Scheduling," *Production and Inventory Management*, 2nd Quarter 1987, pp. 123–131.

run those families that are expensive or time-consuming to set up less often than those that are inexpensive to set up. In addition, aggregate planning combines the starting inventories and demands of all families, some of which may have large inventories relative to demand and some of which may have little or no inventories. Therefore, it is not wise to simply allocate production to the families based on the *gross* forecast demand; instead, the net requirements (demand minus available inventories) are the relevant quantities. For these reasons, some disaggregation schemes allocate production among families approximately in proportion to their setup costs and net requirements.

Because items within families use essentially the same setup, the goal is to run all or as many items as possible in the family together. To do this efficiently, we would like all of the items in the family to be running low of inventories at approximately the time their family is scheduled for its next production run. Therefore, a guiding principle used in disaggregating family production is to allocate production to the items so that all items have approximately the same run-out time, taking into account the fact that items run later in the sequence must have enough inventories to sustain sales until the item is run.

THE MASTER PRODUCTION SCHEDULE

The disaggregated production levels are used as input in developing a **master production schedule (MPS)** for each item. The MPS specifies the amount and timing of production for each item. Because the MPS is a more detailed and shorter-term production plan, often only the first two or three periods of the aggregate plan are used, and the time periods are more refined. For example, Starlight might disaggregate only the first two months of its aggregate plan into specific item plans, and the monthly aggregate plans might be converted to weekly plans in the MPS (with a six- to eight-week planning horizon).

The MPS is developed in steps by making tentative allocations of production to each item in each time period. A **rough-cut capacity analysis** is then performed to determine whether the planned allocation of production is feasible in terms of production, warehouse, and labor capacity and whether necessary materials are available. The MPSs for the items in a family must match, so that the total production allocated to the family is not exceeded during the planning period. If an inconsistency occurs, one or more of the item MPSs must be modified to obtain a feasible plan. The master production schedules then form the basis for short-term production scheduling and materials management.

EXAMPLE 3

To illustrate the process, suppose that in Example 2 we decided that of the 226,939 units of production planned for October, 90,000 would be allocated to family A. To make things simple, suppose the items in family A are so homogeneous that they can be treated as one item for planning purposes. We will develop a four-week master production schedule for item (family) A using weeks as the time interval and assume that the forecast demand for each week is 22,000 units. We will also assume that the company has established a preferred production lot size for this item of 40,000–60,000 units.

TABLE 12.9 TENTATIVE MPS FOR STARLIGHT'S ITEM A

	Week			
	1	2	3	4
Beginning inventory	3,000	21,000	39,000	17,000
Forecast demand	22,000	22,000	22,000	22,000
Projected inv./needs(−)	−19,000	−1,000	17,000	−5,000
MPS (production)	40,000	40,000	0	40,000

TABLE 12.10 REVISED MPS FOR STARLIGHT'S ITEM A

	Week			
	1	2	3	4
Beginning inventory	3,000	26,000	4,000	27,000
Forecast demand	22,000	22,000	22,000	22,000
Projected inv./needs(−)	−19,000	4,000	−18,000	5,000
MPS (production)	45,000	0	45,000	0

Table 12.9 provides a *tentative* master production schedule for item A. The beginning inventory for week 1 is assumed to be 3000 and demand is 22,000, so we initially schedule a production run of 40,000 units during week 1. The expected beginning inventory for week 2 is 21,000 units (40,000 units produced minus 19,000 needed in week 1), which is less than demand, so we schedule another run of 40,000 units, which leaves a starting inventory in week 3 of 39,000. This is greater than the demand in week 3, so we do not schedule a production run. But in week 4 another run is required. We now check the MPS to make sure we are within the allocated production limit; we are not. We have scheduled 120,000 units of production, but only 90,000 units have been allocated to family A from the aggregate plan. We can revise the MPS by increasing the lot size in week 1 to 45,000 units. Then production is not needed in week 2. The revised MPS given in Table 12.10 is not only feasible, it also saves one production run (and setup) during the planning horizon.

The revised schedule in Table 12.10 would then be evaluated with the MPSs for the other families to make sure their combined weekly production plans are compatible. Clearly, the development of the MPSs is an iterative process that involves constant updating, just like aggregate planning.

12.7 DEMAND INFLUENCING TACTICS TO REDUCE COST

Intermediate-term planning has traditionally focused on manipulating resources related to supply so as to satisfy a predicted demand at minimum cost. That is, planners began the process assuming that a given demand pattern must be satisfied; then, by modifying production resources such as workforce size, overtime production, and subcontracting, the company attempted to minimize costs. The starting assumption—that the demand pattern was unalterable—was not questioned. Actions affecting the quantity and pattern of demand were considered to be outside the domain of the operations function.

We now recognize that aggregate planning should be viewed as a way to coordinate and match demand and supply over the intermediate term to maximize profits or achieve other organizational goals. This viewpoint expands the focus of aggregate planning from simply manipulating production resources to include marketing tactics that create a demand pattern that can be served more efficiently and profitably.

Consider the demand pattern in Figure 12.6a. Demand regularly fluctuates above and below production capacity. During periods of high demand the company must either incur extra overtime production costs, raise hiring costs, or use inventories, while during periods of low demand it must either carry workers that produce at less than maximum capacity, lay off workers, or produce above the rate of demand and build inventories. If, however, the same total demand were spread more evenly over time, as in Figure 12.6b, total cost could be reduced and responsiveness to customers increased. For example, it has been estimated that for the U.S. food processing industry alone, over $3 billion a year in extra costs are incurred by trying to adjust to fluctuations in demand.[4]

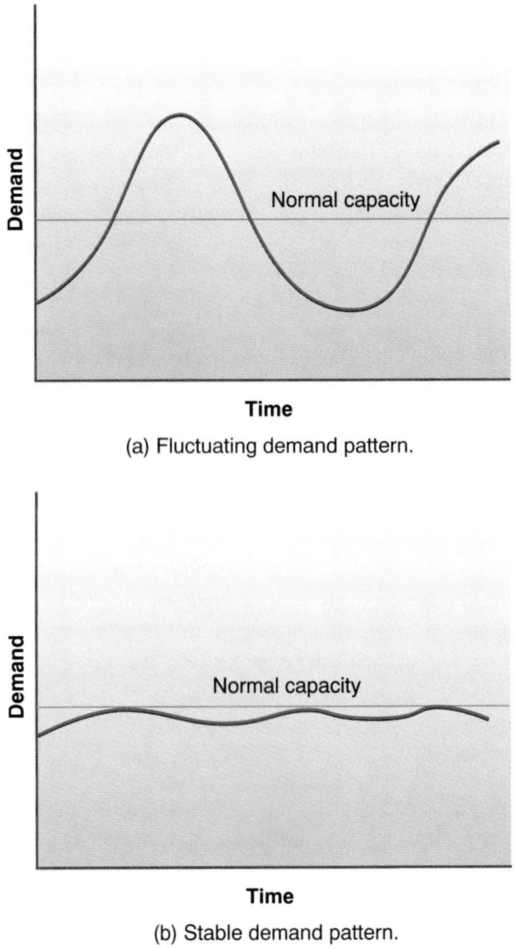

FIGURE 12.6 Demand with different time patterns.

[4]See Zachary Shiller, "Not Everyone Loves a Supermarket Special," *Business Week*, Feb. 17, 1992, pp. 64–68.

In general, maintaining relatively constant workforce and production levels is less costly than regularly increasing and decreasing production, unless maintaining a constant production level results in large average inventories. Especially for services, which cannot be stored in inventory, highly fluctuating demand patterns can be very expensive to serve. The more time a company has to adjust to a demand change, the more efficiently it can be done, such as by changing the workforce or inventory levels gradually or by devising better work schedules. Therefore, whenever possible, a company would prefer demand to occur in a steady rather than a fluctuating pattern and demand changes to be predictable rather than unexpected. In fact, various marketing tactics can be used to obtain a demand pattern that is more profitable to satisfy without hurting overall demand. The following simple, yet effective, tactics can improve both short-term and intermediate-term demand patterns.

ADVERTISING, PRICING, AND PRODUCT PROMOTION

Many products, both goods and services, have demand patterns that fluctuate in a regular pattern. For example, many beverages display a highly seasonal pattern, with summer demand perhaps 20–30% higher than winter demand. The production cost structure for this and similar products is such that the costs of overtime production and inventory are relatively high. If the company could convince customers to move even 5% or 10% of their peak period purchases up by one month and store the inventories themselves, the manufacturer could reduce costs substantially. The company can do this by advertising heavily, offering price discounts, and using other product promotions (e.g., coupons and contests) during periods of low demand while reducing advertising, charging price premiums, and not using promotions during periods of high demand. For example, a company may offer a $1-off coupon for a case of soda, but with an expiration date of March 31 to encourage customers to buy the product earlier than needed and store it themselves.

Service industries such as airlines and hotels have been especially large users of differential pricing among seasons, and even days of the week, to encourage people to move discretionary travel from peak summer periods and holidays to less busy times. For example, a round-trip airline ticket between New York and London may be twice as expensive during the summer months as during February. Airlines and hotels can usually fill all of their capacity during peak periods and often cannot expand capacity. Their cost structures tend to have large fixed costs for planes or facilities and relatively low variable costs, so they can afford to offer off-peak services at very low prices and still more than cover their variable costs. Not only does differential pricing smooth the demand, but it can actually increase total demand. It increases demand in off-peak periods, while the firm is still operating at capacity during peaks; and during peak periods, fewer customers must be turned away due to a shortage of capacity, which increases goodwill.

COUNTERCYCLIC BUT SIMILAR PRODUCTS

One of the best strategies for smoothing demand and production is to produce products that can share the same parts, facilities, and workers yet have countercyclic demand patterns, so that the peak demand periods for one product are the low demand periods for another product. A classic example involves producers of lawn mowers and snow blowers. The machining operations and components of a lawn mower are very similar to those of a snow blower, and they can easily be made in the same production system by the same workers. The sales patterns for the two, however, are almost exactly mirror opposites, (see Figure 6.4, p. 261). The manufacturer can then maintain a stable workforce while making both products at the same facility by simply changing the product mix during the year.

A number of other companies have diversified their product lines to benefit from a mix of countercyclic products. For example, Polaris Industries (the subject of this chapter's "In Good Company" segment) began as a manufacturer of snowmobiles, but it added all-terrain vehicles and jet skis to its product line because they use many of the same parts and are sold through the same dealers. Service companies have been especially effective in developing countercyclic services, such as ski resorts that become golf and tennis camps during the summer and retail stores that specialize in garden supplies from January to October and become holiday stores during November and December.

RESERVATION SYSTEMS

When the timing of demand cannot be influenced, a company may still be able to develop more cost-effective production plans if it has more lead time on demand changes. One way to achieve this for services is to institute a reservation system so that customers can inform the supplier of their intentions well in advance. In some cases, if a supplier knows one or two months in advance that demand will be unusually large, it can make capacity modifications that it could not make with only a few days' notice. For example, if an airline receives 1000 reservation requests for a given route rather than the normal 500, it may be able to switch planes of different sizes between two routes for a few days, or it may be able to add extra flights (assuming airport capacity allows it). Similarly, other service providers can schedule extra workers or reposition resources (e.g., automobiles for an auto rental company) during unusual demand surges if they have sufficient notice, but they may not be able to do so on shorter notice.

Of course, for this method to be useful to the company, customers must be aware of the reservation system and have an incentive to use it. One incentive is to be assured

IN GOOD COMPANY

Polaris Industries Has All Seasons Covered

When sales of noisy, gas-guzzling snowmobiles began to slump more than 20 years ago, one manufacturer, Polaris, switched to quieter and more efficient models that helped it hang on to about 30% of the shrinking market. In the mid-1980s, Polaris expanded its production to include all-terrain vehicles. These use some of the same parts as snowmobiles, such as engines and clutches, and they are sold by many of the same dealers who sell the snowmobiles. Best of all, they can be manufactured (to order) in the fall and winter, after the preceding spring's and summer's orders for snowmobiles have been filled.

When Polaris diversified again in the early 1990s, it was into the production of jet skis—expensive, powered water skis that fly across the water at up to 40 miles an hour. "It's a natural fit to what we already do," says Polaris executive W. Hall Wendel, Jr. "It uses a similar engine, and it can go through our existing distribution channels."

of the desired service; another incentive can be financial. Having advance information does, in fact, save the supplier money by achieving better capacity utilization and production scheduling. These savings can be shared with customers in the form of price discounts. For example, most airlines, car rental companies, and hotels provide discounts for reservations made well in advance of the service date. By combining differential pricing and reservations, a company can smooth customer demand and be better prepared for those variations that still exist.

SUMMARY

- **Aggregate (intermediate-term) planning** acts as an interface between long-term strategic planning and short-term scheduling decisions.
- Aggregate planning is performed using aggregate production units that contain several distinct items that share facilities and have similar cost structures and demand patterns.
- Aggregate planning uses an intermediate-term planning horizon of 3–12 months.
- An aggregate plan determines the planned aggregate production, inventories, subcontracting, staffing, and overtime during each of the planning periods to minimize total costs or maximize profits.
- Only the results for the first period of the aggregate plan are implemented. After the first period, the plans are revised using updated information; the first period of the new aggregate plan is then implemented. This is called a **rolling horizon** plan.
- Linear programming is useful for aggregate planning because the linearity assumptions are generally satisfied.
- To be useful in developing short-term plans, the aggregate plan must be disaggregated into a **master production schedule (MPS)** for each item in the aggregate product.
- Differential pricing, product promotion, and other marketing tactics can be used to smooth demand patterns, which can be served more economically.

KEY TERMS

aggregate (intermediate-ierm) planning **623**
chase demand strategy **629**
disaggregation **639**
families **625**
items **625**
level production/workforce strategy **629**
master production schedule (MPS) **641**
net requirements **630**
product types **625**
rolling horizon **628**
rough-cut capacity analysis **641**

SOLVED PROBLEMS

Problem 1: A General Motors Buick plant manufactures several Buick models. The company has forecast its quarterly demands during the next four quarters, which are listed below. The plant can produce approximately 25 autos per quarter for each worker on staff. Workers receive an average of $15,000 per quarter in wages and benefits, and it costs $7000 to hire and train a new worker and $10,000 to lay off a worker. Workers can be hired or laid off at the beginning of any quarter. GM expects to have 480 workers on staff and 2000 autos in inventory at the end of the current quarter. Any auto held in inventory at the end of a quarter incurs a holding cost of $1000.

(a) Construct an aggregate plan for the next four quarters using the chase demand strategy and compute its total cost.

(b) Construct an aggregate plan for the next four quarters using a level production strategy and compute its total cost.

(c) Construct an aggregate plan for the next four quarters using linear programming and compute its total cost.

Quarter	Aggregate Demand
1	10,000
2	12,000
3	9,000
4	11,000

Solution:

(a) *Chase Demand Strategy*: For each quarter we determine the number of workers needed to meet the demand in that quarter exactly. Then we adjust the workforce accordingly.

Qt	Aggregate Demand (units)	Planned Output (units)	Workers on Staff	Workers Hired	Workers Laid Off	Inventory (units)
0			480			2000
1	10,000	8,000	320	0	160	0
2	12,000	12,000	480	160	0	0
3	9,000	9,000	360	0	120	0
4	11,000	11,000	440	80	0	0
Totals	(qts. 1–4)		1600	240	280	0

Salaries	1600 workers × $15,000/qt	= $24,000,000
Hiring cost	240 workers × $7,000	= $ 1,680,000
Layoff cost	280 workers × $10,000	= $ 2,800,000
Inventory cost	0 units × $1,000/unit =	0
Total cost		$28,480,000

(b) *Level Strategy*: For each quarter we compute the net cumulative requirements and the number of workers needed to make the cumulative requirements.

Qt	Net Cumulative Requirements	Workers Needed to Make Cum. Req.
1	8,000	320.00
2	20,000	400.00
3	29,000	386.67
4	40,000	400.00

The largest number of workers ever needed is 400, so we will reduce the workforce to 400 and keep it there.

Qt	Aggregate Demand (units)	Planned Output (units)	Workers on Staff	Workers Hired	Workers Laid Off	Inventory (units)
0			480			2000
1	10,000	10,000	400	0	80	2000
2	12,000	10,000	400	0	0	0
3	9,000	10,000	400	0	0	1000
4	11,000	10,000	400	0	0	0
Totals	(qts 1–4)		1600	0	80	3000

Salaries	1600 workers × $15,000/qt	= $24,000,000
Hiring cost	0 workers × $7,000	= $ 0
Layoff cost	80 workers × $10,000	= $ 800,000
Inventory cost	3000 units × $1,000/unit =	$ 3,000,000
Total cost		$27,800,000

(c) *Linear Programming Strategy*: We define our decision variables as follows:

P_t = number of autos to make during quarter t
W_t = number of workers on staff during quarter t
H_t = number of workers to hire at the beginning of quarter t
L_t = number of workers to lay off at the beginning of quarter t
I_t = number of autos in inventory at the end of quarter t

The problem is as follows:

$$\text{minimize TC} = 15{,}000\ \Sigma\ W_t + 7{,}000\ \Sigma\ H_t + 10{,}000\ \Sigma\ L_t + 1000\ \Sigma\ I_t$$

subject to

constraints to ensure demand satisfaction and inventory definition:

$$P_1 = 8{,}000 + I_1$$
$$P_2 + I_1 = 12{,}000 + I_2$$
$$P_3 + I_2 = 9{,}000 + I_3$$
$$P_4 + I_3 = 11{,}000 + I_4$$

constraints for the relationship between output and workforce:

$$P_t = 25\ W_t \quad \text{for } t = 1, 2, 3, 4$$

constraints defining workforce size:

$$W_t = W_{t-1} + H_t - L_t \quad \text{for } t = 1, 2, 3, 4$$

The optimal solution to this problem (using a linear programming computer package) is as follows:

Qt	Aggregate Demand (units)	Planned Output (units)	Workers on Staff	Workers Hired	Workers Laid Off	Inventory (units)
0			480			2000
1	10,000	10,000	400	0	80	2000
2	12,000	10,000	400	0	0	0
3	9,000	9,000	360	0	40	0
4	11,000	11,000	440	80	0	0
Totals	(qts 1–4)		1600	80	120	2000

Salaries	1600 workers × \$15,000/qt	= \$24,000,000
Hiring cost	80 workers × \$7,000	= \$ 560,000
Layoff cost	120 workers × \$10,000	= \$ 1,200,000
Inventory cost	2000 units × \$1,000/unit	= \$ 2,000,000
Total cost		\$27,760,000

Problem 2: Zap Corporation manufactures fax machines. It has developed an aggregate plan for the next several months, and has tentatively allocated 220 units of production to its Model 330 machines during the next five weeks. Zap wants to produce this model in lot sizes of between 100 and 120 units at a time. Zap expects to begin week 1 with 40 machines on hand, and the forecast demands for the Model 330 for the next five weeks are given below. Construct an MPS (planned weekly production) for this item.

Week	1	2	3	4	5
Forecast demand	60	30	40	40	45

Solution: In each week we will compare the forecast demand with the beginning inventory. If the demand exceeds the inventory, we will perform a production run of 100 units; otherwise, we will simply supply demand from inventory. We will then inspect the schedule and modify the sizes of the production runs if a change would improve the schedule. The resulting MPS is as follows:

	Week				
Fax Machines	1	2	3	4	5
Beginning inventory	40	80	50	10	70
Forecast demand	60	30	40	40	45
Expected inventory/needs (−)	−20	50	10	−30	25
Planned production (MPS)	100	0	0	100	0

We have 20 units of unused but allocated production available with this MPS. We could increase our lot sizes or use the excess for another product.

Discussion and Review Questions

1. What is the difference between product types, product families, and items?
2. Why do we perform intermediate-term (aggregate) planning using aggregate products rather than individual items?
3. What are the advantages and disadvantages of using a chase demand strategy for developing an aggregate plan?
4. What are the advantages and disadvantages of using a level production and workforce strategy for developing an aggregate plan?
5. Why do we use a rolling horizon approach in implementing aggregate plans? Why don't we just implement the entire plan?
6.* Suppose a company could not increase production simply by adding individual workers or by requiring overtime, but rather had to add an entire shift of 200 people. Why could we not use a pure linear programming model to represent this case? How would the model have to be changed?
7. How could actions that modify the timing of demand reduce total cost if the total demand remains the same or increases?
8. What is the difference between an aggregate plan and a master production schedule?
9. Suppose we took the planned production for a period from our aggregate plan and simply allocated it to each family (or item) in the product type in proportion to that family's forecast demand for the period. What potential problems could occur?

Problems

1. Compaq Computer would like to develop an aggregate plan for one of its product types. The monthly demands for the next six months are given below. Compaq can produce approximately 120 computers each month for each production worker. Compaq expects to end March with 15,000 computers on hand and 1000 workers on staff. It costs $6000 to hire and train a worker and $4000 to lay off one. Workers receive $3000 per month in salary and benefits. Any computer held in inventory at the end of a month costs $50 in holding costs. Compaq would like to end September with at least 10,000 computers on hand and between 1100 and 1200 workers on staff. (a) Develop an aggregate plan for Compaq using the chase demand strategy. (b) Compute the total six-month cost using this plan.

Month	Demand
April	140,000
May	125,000
June	120,000
July	150,000
August	155,000
September	130,000

2. Using the same data as in problem 1, (a) develop an aggregate plan for Compaq Computer, using a level workforce strategy, and (b) compute the total six-month cost using this plan.

3. Using the data in problem 1, (a) formulate a linear program that can be used to develop an aggregate plan for Compaq Computer. (b) (Computer required.) Solve the problem formulated in part (a) and construct an aggregate plan from it. (c) Compare the cost of this plan to the costs in problems 1 and 2.

4. The demand for a company's product during the next four months is given below. It costs the company $9 per unit to produce the product using regular-time labor and $12 per unit to produce it using overtime. A limit of 500 units can be made each month using regular-time production and a limit of 100 units per month using overtime production. Excess units produced can be stored at a cost of $2 per unit per month. There are no initial inventories. (a) Formulate this company's problem as a linear program to minimize its total production and storage costs during the next four months and to satisfy demand. (b) (Requires Computer) Solve the linear program formulated in part (a) and convert it into an aggregate plan.

Month	Demand
1	450
2	575
3	490
4	530

5. Basel Tool and Die Company (BTD) makes a special type of pipe wrench in one of its factories. The marketing department has estimated the demand for this product during the next six months to be as follows:

Month	Demand
January	370
February	430
March	380
April	450
May	520
June	440

With its current labor force, BTD believes it can make approximately 420 pipe wrenches per month at a cost of $40 per wrench using regular-time production. An additional 80 wrenches per month can be made using overtime production, but then the cost per wrench is $45. Wrenches can be made in one month and held in inventory for later shipment at a cost of $3 per month per wrench. The monthly demand for wrenches must be satisfied every month. At the end of December BTD has 10 wrenches in inventory. BTD wants to plan its production, including overtime, and inventory for the next six months so as to minimize cost while satisfying demand. (a) Formulate BTD's aggregate planning problem as a linear program. (b) (Requires computer.) Solve the linear program in part (a) and use the solution to develop an aggregate plan for the next six months.

6. Taneytown Hotel wants to plan its workforce for the next four quarters using the projected room demands given below. For cleaning, food service, and so on, the hotel needs approximately one person for every 500 room-nights (one room used for one night) utilized during a quarter. Because services cannot be stored, the hotel can only use overtime and changes in workforce to adapt to demand changes. The hotel currently has 12 workers on staff who receive an average of $4000 per quarter in pay and benefits. To hire an additional worker costs $3000 and to lay off a worker costs $1500. Each room-night above 500 per worker can be served using overtime at an extra cost of $12. Assuming the hotel wants to have 12–14 workers on staff at the end of next year, (a) derive an aggregate plan using the chase demand strategy and compute the resulting cost. (b) Derive an aggregate plan using a level workforce strategy and compute the resulting cost. (c) (Requires computer.) Develop an aggregate plan by formulating and solving a linear programming model of the hotel's problem and compare the cost with the the costs of plans in parts (a) and (b).

Quarter	1	2	3	4
Forecast demand (room-nights)	6200	4900	6800	6900

7.* The demand for Acme Inc.'s product during the next four months is given below. The product is made up of two components, A and B. Acme can either manufacture components itself or it can subcontract with another company. If Acme manufactures the components, each component must go through two production departments: fabricating and finishing. Component A requires two hours of fabricating time and four hours of finishing time; component B requires three hours of fabricating and two hours of finishing. Each department has 550 hours of time available each month for production. Acme has determined that it costs $200 per unit to make A and $240 per unit to make B. Acme believes that its production capacity is insufficient to satisfy demand, so it has arranged to buy units of A and B from a subcontractor, if needed, for $220 per unit of A and $255 per unit of B. Any units of the components can be held in inventory at a cost of $8 per month. (a) Formulate Acme's aggregate planning problem as a linear program to minimize its cost during the next four months while delivering the amount demanded each month. (b) (Requires computer.) Solve the problem formulated in part (a) and use the solution to construct an aggregate plan.

Month	Demand
1	90
2	85
3	95
4	100

8. Scratch Corporation manufactures videotape for video recorders. Based on disaggregation of its aggregate plan, Scratch has allocated to one of its products 3800 units of production capacity during the next five weeks. The weekly demands for the product are given below. Assuming the starting inventory in week 1 is 1000 units, the safety stock (minimum inventory during any week) is 200 units, and the desired lot size for the product is 1200 units, develop an MPS for this product during the next five weeks.

	Week				
	1	2	3	4	5
Beginning inventory	1000				
Forecast demand	1300	700	600	600	750

9. Ace Audio Company manufactures answering machines. The weekly forecast demands for the next six weeks are given below. Suppose Ace expects to begin week 1 with 300 units in inventory; it has a desired safety stock of 100 units (inventory cannot be below this level in any week), and it has a desired lot size of 600 units. Construct an MPS for Ace.

	Week					
	1	2	3	4	5	6
Beginning inventory	300					
Forecast demand	400	500	400	300	380	430

10. The Mavis Furniture Company wants to perform a rough-cut analysis of the MPSs for the two bookcase models it makes. Each Model 100 bookcase requires 2.5 person-hours of labor, and each Model 200 require 2 person-hours of labor. The MPSs for each model are listed below, along with the total labor available for bookcase manufacturing during the next six weeks. (a) Does Mavis have enough labor available in each week to execute the MPSs? (b) If not, how could the MPSs be changed to satisfy the labor capacities?

	Week					
	1	2	3	4	5	6
MPS (production) for Model 100	500	200	0	700	0	400
MPS (production) for Model 200	200	0	500	0	0	600
Available labor (person-hours)	1700	1500	1400	1500	1200	1500

11.* Linear programs for aggregate planning can sometimes be formulated and solved more easily as transportation problems (see the Chapter 6 supplement). (a) Reformulate the aggregate planning problem for Basel Tool and Die Company (problem 5) as a transportation problem. (Hint: treat each combination of month and production type, regular or overtime, as a source of supply for wrenches and each month as a demand point. The variables are then R_{ij} = number of wrenches made in month i using regular-time production and shipped in month j, and O_{ij} = number of wrenches made in month i using overtime production and shipped in month j). (b) Solve the problem in part (a) using a transportation problem computer program.

CASE

Force-Master: An Aggregate Planning Case

Force-Master Corporation is a medium-sized manufacturer specializing in large gasoline-powered home and yard tools. During its first 10 years of business, Force-Master produced only lawn mowers. Approximately eight years ago it expanded its product line by making snow blowers, and later it expanded further to include roto-tillers and shredders. Similarities in production make it possible to manufacture these products in the same plant.

Production workers at Force-Master are cross-trained and relatively interchangeable among jobs. Based on experimentation and measurement, Force-Master has determined that approximately 1.8 person-hours of direct labor are required to make a lawn mower and 2.5 person-hours are required to make a snow blower.

Lawn mowers and snow blowers are treated as two distinct product types because of their differential use of resources and their different demand patterns. Force-Master uses a 12-month aggregate plan divided into six 2-month periods, where January and February are combined for one period (JF), March and April for another (MA), and so on. During a planning period, a worker can perform approximately 300 hours of productive work and receives an average of $6000 per period (including fringe benefits). Employees can work up to 60 hours of overtime each period at the rate of $28 per hour (this accounts for overtime wages, but there are no additional costs for medical and life insurance and retirement benefits).

Force-Master has a normal worker attrition rate of approximately 2% per planning period. According to state laws and the union contract, any worker who is laid off must receive two months' worth of pay and benefits ($6000). When the company hires a new worker or recalls a laid-off worker, it costs approximately $2000 to find and retrain the worker. In addition, during the first two months of work, a "new" worker is only half as productive as an experienced worker (even if the worker is a former worker recalled from layoff). So an experienced worker would spend 1.8 hours on a lawn mower, but a new worker would require 3.6 hours.

It is estimated that during the next year, the cost of materials and components will be $95 for each lawn mower and $110 for each snow blower. The company also estimates that the cost to hold a lawn mower in inventory for two months is $8 and the cost to hold a snow blower is $10.

Based on planned selling prices of $210 per lawn mower and $250 per snow blower, Force-Master's sales department has predicted the following period-by-period demands during the next 12 months:

Period	Lawn Mower Demands	Snow Blower Demands
JF	12,000	16,000
MA	85,000	4,000
MJ	80,000	0
JA	32,000	5,000
SO	8,000	35,000
ND	3,000	45,000

During the current period (November–December) Force-Master would like to develop an aggregate plan for the following year. Its current workforce is composed of 350 experienced and no new workers. Force-Master expects to end December with 4500 snow blowers and 500 lawn mowers in inventory.

Force-Master's Current Planning Approach

Historically, Force-Master tried to maintain a relatively stable workforce, and it has used overtime work extensively to satisfy demand during peak periods. This strategy proved to be a problem because Force-Master incurred extremely high inventory and overtime costs, and often it held off hiring workers during peaks until too late and shortages occurred that resulted in lost sales. By the time the new workers were hired and gained experience, sales had dropped. Using this classical planning approach, Force-Master's chief production scheduler, Ira M. Laust, has devised the plan in Table 12.11 for the next 12 months. Laust was instructed to devise the plan so that Force-Master would end next year with between 335 and 365 workers, and with at least 4000 snow blowers and 500 lawn mowers in inventory.

The projected costs for the next year using this plan are as follows:

Wages:	2088 workers × $6000/period	= $ 12,528,000
Overtime:	42,712 hours × $28/hour	= $ 1,195,936
Hiring:	27 workers × $2000/worker	= $ 54,000
Materials:	220,000 mowers × $95/mower	= $20,900,000
	104,500 snow blowers × $110	= $ 11,495,000*
Inventory:	39,232 lawn mowers × $8/mower	= $ 313,856
	31,960 snow blowers × $10	= $ 319,600*
Total cost:		$46,806,392

*Material and inventory costs for the excess 2800 snowblowers in inventory at the end of the year are not included.

TABLE 12.11 IRA LAUST'S AGGREGATE PLAN

	Workers			Overtime	Lawn Mowers		Snow Blowers	
Period	Experienced	Hired	Fired	Hours	Made	Invent.	Made	Invent.
ND	350	0				500		4,500
JF	343	0	0	0	41,194	29,694	11,500	0
MA	336	27	0	21,780	64,344	9,038	4,000	0
MJ	356	0	0	20,932	70,962	0	0	0
JA	349	0	0	0	32,000	0	18,840	13,840
SO	342	0	0	0	8,000	0	35,280	14,120
ND	335	0	0	0	3,500	500	37,680	6,800
Total	2061	27	0	42,712	220,000	39,232	107,300	34,760

*Note: The number of workers on staff decreases by 2% (approximately seven workers) in each period due to normal attrition.

Notice that during the second period all workers are working the maximum amount of overtime allowed. With this plan, Force-Master's predicted net contribution to overhead will be as follows:

Revenue: [(220,000 lawn mowers × $210) + (105,000 snow blowers × $250)]	$72,450,000
– Cost:	$46,806,392
Contribution to overhead and profit:	$25,643,608

Force-Master's total fixed costs for facilities, personnel, and so on were expected to be $20,500,000, so the net before-tax profit would be $5,143,608 with this aggregate plan if the sales and other assumptions are accurate.

A Linear Programming–Based Aggregate Planning Model

Although overtime, hiring, and inventory costs with this plan are small relative to total costs, Force-Master decided to use a linear programming model to develop its aggregate plan. Oliver Robertson, the head of industrial engineering, created the following linear programming model.

Variables

W_t = number of experienced workers on staff during period t

N_t = number of new workers hired at the beginning of period t

F_t = number of workers fired at the beginning of period t

OW_t = number of overtime hours worked by experienced workers in period t

ON_t = number of overtime hours worked by new workers in period t

L_t = number of lawn mowers produced during period t

S_t = number of snow blowers produced during period t

LI_t = number of lawn mowers in inventory at the end of period t

SI_t = number of snow blowers in inventory at the end of period t

Objective Function

$$\text{minimize TC} = \$6000\,\Sigma\, W_t + \$8000\,\Sigma\, N_t + \$6000\,\Sigma\, F_t + \$28\,\Sigma\, OW_t + \$28\,\Sigma\, ON_t + \$8\,\Sigma\, LI_t + \$10\,\Sigma\, SI_t$$

where all summations are for $t = 1, \ldots, 6$.

Constraints

Conservation of Employees

$$W_t = 0.98\, W_{t-1} + 0.98\, N_{t-1} - F_t \quad \text{for } t = 1, \ldots 6$$
$$\text{and } W_0 = 350 \text{ and } N_0 = 0$$

These constraints state that the number of experienced workers in a period is equal to 98% of the total number of workers in the previous period (2% attrition) minus any involuntary dismissals.

Limiting Production to Available Labor

$$1.8\, L_t + 2.5\, S_t \le 300\, W_t + 150\, N_t + OW_t + 0.5\, ON_t \quad \text{for } t = 1, \ldots 6$$

These constraints state that the number of direct labor hours consumed in production cannot be more than the number of productive labor hours available. The coefficient of 150 for new workers indicates that 300 hours of work during a period by a new worker are equivalent to 150 hours of work by an experienced worker (similarly for overtime). Note that these constraints allow Force-Master to produce less than the maximum possible in a period.

Limit on Overtime Hours

$$OW_t \le 60\, W_t \quad \text{for } t = 1, \ldots, 6$$
$$ON_t \le 60\, N_t \quad \text{for } t = 1, \ldots, 6$$

These limit the amount of overtime per person to 60 hours per worker.

Satisfying Demand and Defining Inventories

$LI_{t-1} + L_t = LS_t + LI_t$ for $t = 1, \ldots, 6$ and LS_t is the estimated lawn mower sales in period t (a parameter, not a variable)

$SI_{t-1} + S_t = SS_t + SI_t$, for $t = 1, \ldots, 6$ and SS_t is the estimated snow blower sales in period t (a parameter, not a variable)

These equations state that the starting inventory plus units produced in a period must equal the number sold plus the ending inventory.

Ending Conditions

$$LI_6 \ge 500$$
$$SI_6 \ge 4000$$
$$W_6 + N_6 \ge 335$$
$$W_6 + N_6 \le 365$$

The first two constraints ensure adequate ending inventories, and the second two ensure that the workforce finishes within the desired limits.

The optimal solution for this problem was converted to the aggregate plan given in Table 12.12. The projected total cost for the next year using this plan is as follows:

Wages:	2070 workers × \$6000/period	= \$ 12,420,000
Overtime:	40,552 hours × \$28/hour	= \$ 1,135,456
Hiring:	27 workers × \$2000/worker	= \$ 54,000
Materials:	220,000 mowers × \$95/mower	= \$20,900,000
	104,500 snow blowers × \$110	= \$ 11,495,000*
Inventory:	36,738 lawn mowers × \$8/mower	= \$ 293,904
	32,720 snow blowers × \$10	= \$ 327,200*
Total cost:		\$ 46,625,560

*Material and inventory costs for the extra 100 snow blowers in inventory at the end of the year are not included.

The total projected cost for this plan is \$180,832 less than that of Mr. Laust's plan, so Force-Master's net profit will be \$180,832 higher—an increase of over 3% simply through better aggregate planning.

Differences Between the Plans

The primary differences between the two plans are as follows:

1. Both plans require hiring 27 workers, but the linear programming (LP)–based plan hires 18 of these immediately and the remaining 9 in November, whereas Laust postpones hiring new workers until March and must then hire more workers to satisfy the peak in demand.
2. The LP-based plan uses the extra workers in the first period to create larger inventories of snow blowers at the end of the first period, but then no workers need to be hired in the second period and less overtime has to be worked in the second and third periods to handle the large demand in these periods.
3. The LP-based plan never has new workers work overtime because they are very inefficient and expensive, whereas Laust's plan uses considerable overtime work by new workers.

Implementation of the Aggregate Plan

Rather than plunge into the new LP-based plan, the vice president of operations decided that the company would implement a "compromise plan." This would involve hiring nine new workers at the beginning of January and producing 13,500 snow blowers in the first period, then adding more workers at the beginning of March as needed.

Fortunately for Force-Master, at least part of the LP-based plan was implemented, because during January and February total sales of lawn mowers and snow blowers were slightly larger than predicted: 12,200 and 16,500, respectively. In addition, nine workers rather than the expected seven left the company involuntarily. These factors created a shortfall in planned inventories and a shortage of workers. Near the end of February, updated inventory and personnel levels and demand forecasts were used to develop an updated aggregate plan. Once again, the LP-based plan recommended hiring 18 workers at the beginning of March and having only experienced workers work overtime, whereas Laust's plan recommended hiring only 12 workers immediately and having everyone work maximum overtime, but then hiring more workers in the next period (beginning of May) and using more overtime than that required by the LP-based plan.

After receiving the two aggregate plans, the vice president of operations decided to implement the LP-based plan for March and April. However, he instructed his assistant to prepare a report at the end of April estimating the actual cost during March and April, future costs, and the personnel and inventory positions resulting from the LP-based plan, and to do the same for Laust's plan, assuming it had been implemented. At the end of April, based on this report, the vice president decided that the LP-based approach did, in fact, lower costs and leave the company in a consistently better position to respond to

TABLE 12.12 LP-BASED AGGREGATE PLAN

	Workers			Overtime	Lawn Mowers		Snow Blowers	
Period	Experienced	Hired	Fired	Hours	Made	Invent.	Made	Invent.
ND	350	0				500		4,500
JF	343	18	0	0	37,138	25,638	15,500	4,000
MA	354	0	0	19,732	69,962	10,600	0	0
MJ	347	0	0	20,820	69,400	0	0	0
JA	340	0	0	0	32,000	0	17,760	12,760
SO	333	0	0	0	8,000	0	34,200	11,960
ND	326	9	0	0	3,500	500	37,140	4,100
Total	2043	27	0	40,552	220,000	36,738	104,600	32,820

future conditions. Mr. Laust was trained to use linear programming for devising future aggregate plans.

Demand Strategies

After using LP-based aggregate planning for a few months, Mr. Laust and Mr. Robertson began studying the computer outputs carefully. They decided that the large variation in demand between the peak months of March–June and the trough months of July, August, January, and February were causing substantial overtime and inventory costs. Using simple analysis, they determined that lawn mower production during January and February cost approximately \$131: \$95 for materials + 1.8 person-hours × \$20 per hour (\$6000 per period per worker ÷ 300 effective hours per period). During the March–June period, however, lawn mower production using overtime labor cost \$145.40: \$95 for materials + 1.8 person-hours × \$28 per hour for overtime pay (using experienced workers; new workers are twice as expensive). In addition, to avoid hiring large numbers of employees during the peak months, Force-Master had to produce excess lawn mowers in the trough months and store them, at a cost of \$8 per period, until they were shipped. If Force-Master could ship them when produced, it would save this cost as well.

Laust and Robertson discussed this issue with the vice president of operations, who called a meeting with the vice president of marketing and her product sales managers. Laust suggested that Force-Master offer a price discount on lawn mowers for any customer who purchased and took delivery of a mower during January or February to encourage customers to purchase in these months. The marketing personnel pointed out that any discount given would probably have to apply to those lawn mowers already being purchased during those months, and the revenue loss might be substantial. For example, if Force-Master lowered the price in these months by \$10 to \$200, causing customers to move purchases of 5000 lawn mowers from March and April to January and February, Force-Master would reduce its revenues by \$170,000 a year (17,000 lawn mowers sold × \$10 reduction per mower). Unless Force-Master could reduce its costs by a larger amount, the company would make less profit.

Beth Adams, the vice president of marketing, was intrigued by the general idea, however. She pointed out that the company needed market research and fine-tuning of the right prices to use and when to offer the discounts, but she pointed out two factors supporting the idea.

1. Lowering the price of the mowers even for a limited period would likely increase the *total* number of mowers sold at least slightly, in addition to affecting the timing of sales. Since the variable costs of production were about half the selling price, even a 1% increase in annual unit volume could result in a profit increase.
2. Force-Master might not have to offer the discount on all purchases. Instead, it could use a quantity discount in those two months that applied *only* to lawn mowers bought above some minimum threshold amount. For example, a typical customer (a retail store) might normally buy 5 mowers in February, 20 in March, 25 in April, 20 in May, and 20 in June. If Force-Master offered a \$10 discount on each mower purchased in January or February *after the 10th one bought*, then the normal price would be paid for the first 10. If the threshold were set at the right level, Force-Master would limit the revenue loss, the discount would still be appealing, and it would encourage customers to make larger shifts in the purchases than if they received the discount for every mower.

Everyone agreed that the discount strategy suggested by Ms. Adams was a good idea and worth an experiment. The market research staff evaluated historical purchasing patterns to determine a reasonable threshold level above which the discount would apply. They also performed market surveys to estimate the effect of different discount sizes on the amount of purchases shifted and additional total purchases that would result.

Simulation and Implementation

In October, Force-Master decided to implement the following pricing policy. Any dealer who accepted delivery of more than 12 lawn mowers during the January–February period would receive a 5% ($10.50) discount on each mower purchased in this period after the 12th mower. Based on their research, the marketing department estimated that had this pricing policy been in effect during the current year, total sales would have have increased by 2000 mowers and sales would have had the following pattern:

Period	Lawn Mower Sales	Snow Blower Sales
JF	24,000	16,000
MA	78,000	4,000
MJ	77,000	0
JA	32,000	5,000
SO	8,000	35,000
ND	3,000	45,000

Of the 24,000 mowers sold in the first period, Force-Master estimated that 9000 would *not* have been subject to the discount and 15,000 would have been. To determine the effect on total costs and profitability, Laust and Robertson reran the LP-based aggregate production plan for the year, which is given in Table 12.13, and compared it with the plan in Table 12.12 and with the corresponding costs.

The projected costs for the next year using this plan are as follows:

Wages:	2070 workers × $6000/period	= $12,420,000
Overtime:	44,151 hours × $28/hour	= $ 1,236,228
Hiring:	27 workers × $2000/worker	= $ 54,000
Materials:	222,000 mowers × $95/mower	= $21,090,000
	104,500 snow blowers × $110	= $ 11,495,000
Inventory:	23,248 lawn mowers × $8/mower	= $ 185,984
	32,720 snow blowers × $10	= $ 327,200
Total cost:		$46,808,412

A number of interesting results occur. First, the aggregate plan for the new demand pattern had exactly the same hiring and workforce plans as the original situation. The extra 2000 lawn mowers would be produced by using more overtime production, which costs approximately $101,000 more. However, by shipping more lawn mowers in the first period, much smaller inventories would be carried at the end of the first two periods, resulting in an inventory savings of approximately $108,000! Ignoring the cost of *materials*, the total cost of production and inventory is actually $7148 *less* to produce the 222,000 mowers with the new pattern than to produce the original 220,000! More important, net profit would increase by approximately $80,000 if the assumed customer behavior occurred:

Revenue: (15,000 mowers × $199.50) + (207,000 mowers × $210) + (105,000 snow blowers × $250) = $72,712,500

Costs: $46,808,412 direct costs + $20,500,000 fixed costs = $67,308,412

Profit = $5,404,088.

The plan was implemented. During the following year, lawn mower sales increased by over 2000 units and the shift in sales from March–June to January–February occurred almost exactly as predicted. The estimated net gain in profit was ultimately $100,000. The success of this experiment caused Force-Master to review its pricing and production strategies in detail. The company found that additional fine-tuning of its pricing and promotions could further increase sales, reduce costs, and increase profit.

QUESTIONS

1. What other demand-smoothing actions should Force-Master consider taking other than the discount for lawn mowers purchased in January and February?

TABLE 12.13 LP-BASED PLAN USING DEMAND STRATEGY

	Workers			Overtime	Lawn Mowers		Snow Blowers	
Period	Experienced	Hired	Fired	Hours	Made	Invent.	Made	Invent.
ND	350	0				500		4,500
JF	343	18	0	2,499	38,527	15,027	15,500	4,000
MA	354	0	0	21,050	70,694	7,721	0	0
MJ	347	0	0	20,602	69,279	0	0	0
JA	340	0	0	0	32,000	0	17,760	12,760
SO	333	0	0	0	8,000	0	34,200	11,960
ND	326	9	0	0	3,500	500	37,140	4,100
Total	2043	27	0	44,151	222,000	23,248	104,600	32,820

How would you expect these actions to affect the aggregate production plan?

2. Suppose Force-Master wanted to end the year with at least 350 workers rather than 335. Solve the problem (use a computer program), and explain the differences between the aggregate plan in Table 12.12 and your revised aggregate plan.

SELECTED READINGS

BITRAN, GABRIEL R., ELIZABETH A. HAAS, and ARNOLDO C. HAX. "Hierarchical Production Planning: A Single-Stage System," *Operations Research*, Vol. 29, 1981, pp. 717–743.

BUFFA, E. S., and J. G. MILLER. *Production-Inventory Systems: Planning and Control* (*3rd ed.*), Richard D. Irwin, Homewood, IL, 1979.

BURCH, E. E., M. D. OLIFF, and R. T. SUMICHRAST. "Linking Level Requirements in Production Planning and Scheduling," *Production and Inventory Management*, 2nd Quarter 1987, pp. 123–131.

DUBOIS, FRANK L., and MICHAEL D. OLIFF. "Aggregate Planning in Practice," *Production and Inventory Management Journal*, 3rd Quarter, 1991, pp. 26–30.

FISHER, M. L., J. H. HAMMAND, W. R. OBERMEYER, and A. RAMAN. "Making Supply Meet Demand in an Uncertain World," *Harvard Business Review*, Vol. 72. No. 3, 1994, pp. 83–93.

JOHNSON, L. A., and D. C. MONTGOMERY. *Operations Research in Production Planning, Scheduling and Inventory Control*, Wiley, New York, 1974.

LEONG, G. K., M. D. OLIFF, and R. MARKLAND. "Improved Hierarchical Production Planning," *Journal of Operations Management*, Vol. 8, 1989, pp. 90–114.

PETERSON, R., and E. A. SILVER. *Decision Systems for Inventory Management and Production Planning*, Wiley, New York, 1979.

VOLLMAN, T. E., W. L. BERRY, and D. C. WHYBARK. *Manufacturing Planning and Control Systems*, (3rd ed.), Richard D. Irwin, Homewood, IL, 1992.

CHAPTER 13

INVENTORY PLANNING AND MANAGING MATERIALS WITH INDEPENDENT DEMANDS

13.1 CLASSICAL INVENTORY ANALYSIS IN A JUST-IN-TIME WORLD
On The Job: Gil Burford, Chrysler Corporation

13.2 REASONS FOR HOLDING INVENTORIES
Economic Efficiency
Quick Customer Response
Risk Reduction and Safety
Exploiting or Protecting Against Unusual Events
Types of Inventories

13.3 INVENTORY-RELATED COSTS
Holding Costs
Ordering or Setup Costs
Shortage or Stockout Costs
Hidden Costs

13.4 CHARACTERISTICS OF INVENTORY MODELS
Independent versus Dependent Demand
Inventory Review Policies
Continuous versus One-Period Decisions

13.5 THE BASIC ECONOMIC ORDER QUANTITY MODEL
Computing the Reorder Point
Computing the Optimal Order Quantity
Validity of the Assumptions and Model Robustness

13.6 THE EOQ MODEL WITH QUANTITY DISCOUNTS

13.7 THE ECONOMIC PRODUCTION LOT-SIZE MODEL

13.8 SAFETY STOCK POLICIES
Selecting the Reorder Point Based On Service Level
Selecting the Reorder Point Using Cost Analysis
In Good Company: Fine-Tuning Inventory Control at Syntex Agribusiness

13.9 PERIODIC REVIEW POLICIES

13.10 ONE-PERIOD MODELS
Optimal Order Quantity: Continuous Demand Distribution
Optimal Order Quantity: Discrete Demand Distribution
Computing the Expected Profit
The Evaluation Criterion
Flexible Spending Accounts: A Personal Financial Application

13.11 IMPLEMENTING INVENTORY MANAGEMENT SYSTEMS
ABC Classification of Items and the Pareto Principle
Data Requirements
The Two-Bin System
Purchasing Policies and Sole versus Multiple Sourcing
Materials and the Environment

Mediserve, Inc.: An Inventory Management Case

13.1 CLASSICAL INVENTORY ANALYSIS IN A JUST-IN-TIME WORLD

In recent years, companies have devoted considerable attention to reducing material inventories. For example, despite the large scope and numerous benefits of just-in-time (JIT) production systems, it is the resultant inventory reduction that has captured the greatest public attention. Attention to inventory reduction is well founded. First, inventories are expensive; they tie up financial resources that could be used for other purposes and they incur ongoing costs of storage, handling, taxes, and spoilage. Second, and more important, excessive inventories are frequently a symptom of more fundamental problems with the production system, such as poor quality, slow setups, poor scheduling, and poor process design.

The many successes in inventory reduction, especially using JIT systems, have led some people to adopt the mistaken notion that inventories are of *no* value and should be completely eliminated. However, well-designed, well-run production systems, including JIT systems, require some inventories of raw materials, supplies, in-process goods, and final products to operate efficiently. Well-planned inventories can also provide great strategic advantages by allowing companies to respond quickly to surges in demand. For example, Compaq Computer increased its finished goods inventory substantially in the fall of 1994 to be ready for the expected high demand in December. This strategy was extremely successful and led it to first place in personal computer market share. (The strategy was adopted in direct response to its large number of lost sales in December 1993 due to inadequate inventories.[1] Finally, some businesses and industries, such as wholesale and retail supply companies, depend on having inventories of products readily available for customers. For example, a major challenge facing Gil Burford, the subject of this chapter's "On the Job" segment, is providing replacement auto parts to dealers quickly without overstocking his own inventories.

Some advocates of zero-inventory systems claim that classical inventory analysis is of little value because it focuses on determining the most economical amount of inventory to carry rather than eliminating all inventory—mainly through the use of JIT production. But this ignores the fact that inventories can have value (as we will see in the next section), so our goal should not be to eliminate all inventories but rather to eliminate all *unnecessary* inventories: those that are not cost effective. In addition, zero-inven-

[1]From Peter Burrows, "Yes, Compaq, There Is a Santa Claus," *Business Week*, Jan. 30, 1995, p. 6.

ON THE JOB

GIL BURFORD, CHRYSLER CORPORATION

Gil Burford is purchasing agent for power train and chassis parts at Chrysler Corporation. He supervises six buyers who order service parts and components, such as axles, doors, and steering columns for Chrysler vehicles, which are then supplied to dealers. With every purchase, Gil must determine the right quantity of parts to buy.

The more parts ordered, the lower the price. For cars still in production, he can "lunch off" the production department's parts orders, but for past-model cars it's harder to make an economical purchase in the relatively small quantities he usually needs. Inventory control may not want to stock as many parts as Gil would like to order, but sometimes he is able to hold part of the larger order at the supplier's warehouse and still obtain a better purchase price. Many of his suppliers rely on JIT purchasing, just as Gil does.

Adding to the complexity of the task is the purchasing department's focus on customer service. When a car owner brings a Chrysler car in for repair, the dealer needs the parts. Chrysler's purchasing department is committed to supplying them, even if the car is several years old.

tory advocates ignore several other facts: (1) JIT systems still require inventories to function under real circumstances; (2) most businesses currently do not (or cannot) operate in a JIT environment; (3) even those companies that use a JIT system for the primary materials of their production system find it more efficient to purchase or produce less frequently used materials in large quantities rather than daily; and (4) inventory management involves much more than the primary materials used in manufacturing processes; it also applies to the purchase of supplies by every department throughout every organization, as well as the purchase of goods by wholesalers and retailers for resale. Classical inventory analysis has a large role to play in these cases (as demonstrated later by Syntex Agribusiness, the subject of this chapter's "In Good Company" segment). Therefore, the focus of this chapter is on classical inventory analysis and models.

The first part of this chapter provides a general introduction to inventory management: the reasons for holding inventories, the costs associated with doing so, and ways to classify inventory systems. The next part of the chapter is devoted to what are called **independent demand** models. These are applicable to items, such as tools sold by a hardware store or common components used by a manufacturer, whose demand or usage rate can be treated in isolation from the demand for other items. Inventory management methods for items with **dependent demand**, such as tires or transmissions used by an auto manufacturer, which depend directly on production of finished automobiles, are the focus of Chapter 14. The chapter concludes with a discussion of implementation issues that are applicable to all material management systems: the ABC classification for prioritizing inventory management efforts, data requirements, supplier relations and sourcing policies, and environmental aspects of purchasing.

JIT production *has* changed our way of looking at materials management and inventory policies. Operating flaws in the production system such as defective items, long setup times, long lead times, and frequent machine failures cause unnecessary inventories. Rather than accepting these flaws as laws of nature, as we did in the past, we now realize that they can be eliminated. Chapter 15, which describes the principles and operation of JIT production systems, will explain how eliminating these problems through better production system design and operating procedures can reduce inventories significantly.

13.2 REASONS FOR HOLDING INVENTORIES

Any materials that are held for future use can be considered **inventories**.[2] There are at least four reasons to hold inventories: (1) to increase operating efficiency, (2) to provide a quick response to customers, (3) to provide safety against normal business uncertainties, and (4) to take advantage of unusual price opportunities or to protect against irregular business risks.

ECONOMIC EFFICIENCY

Inventories can improve operating efficiency in several ways.

1. ***Spreading the Fixed Costs of Procurement or Setups.*** Some costs of acquiring materials, such as processing and transmitting orders and possibly shipping, are fixed and independent of the order quantity. Therefore, the larger the quantity purchased per order, the smaller the fixed cost *per unit*. Quantities purchased above immediate needs, however, must be held in inventory and incur holding costs. The same idea can apply to outputs. If there is a fixed setup cost to produce a product, then the more units produced per production run (the larger the production lot size), the lower the setup cost *per unit*. But any units produced above those needed for immediate shipment must be held in inventory and incur a holding cost.
2. ***Decoupling of Production.*** Most goods pass through a series of production stages (work stations, cells, or departments) during the manufacturing process. If production is halted or slowed at one stage due to product changeovers, machine adjustments, personnel training, or machine failure, subsequent stages will soon have to stop operation unless they have in-process inventories available to process. In-process inventories make it possible to decouple one production stage from another, allowing greater scheduling and staffing flexibility. For example, in Figure 13.1, if in-process inventories exist between stages, production at

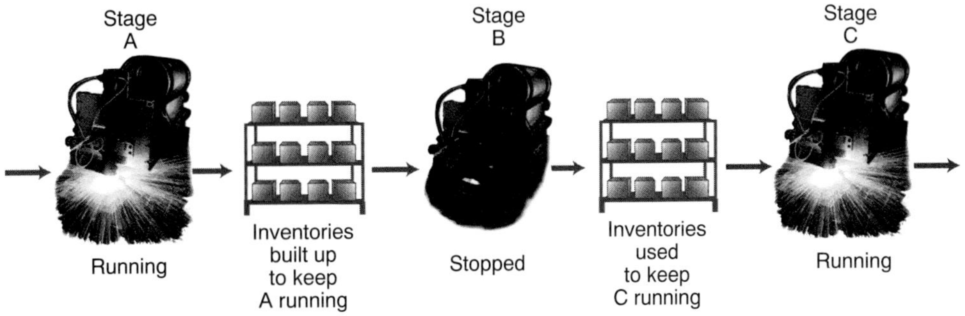

FIGURE 13.1 In-process inventories decoupling production stages.

[2] Although here we are interested only in material inventories, an argument can be made that other resources, such as cash or human resources, can be inventoried for future use as well. In fact, the EOQ inventory model has been used to explain financial behavior concerning individuals' decisions to hold cash.

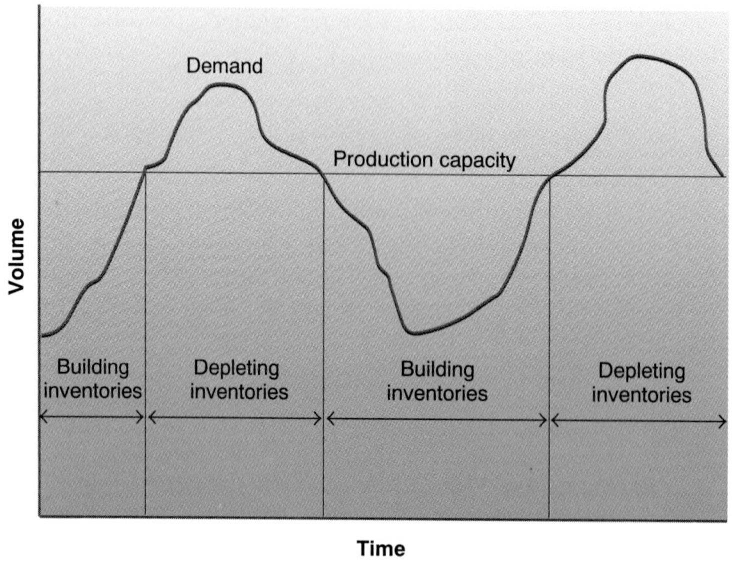

FIGURE 13.2 Smoothing production of seasonal product.

stage B could be stopped for a while without forcing stages A and C to stop. Although it is desirable to keep inventories of semifinished goods as low as possible, even JIT production systems allow for minimal amounts of inventories between stages.

3. ***Smoothing and Stabilizing Production.*** As we saw in Chapter 12, if demand for a product is seasonal, it is often less expensive to maintain a constant level of production and employment throughout the year than to alter production and employment levels to match demand. During periods of low demand, production exceeds demand and inventories of the product increase; then, during periods of high demand, these inventories are depleted, as illustrated in Figure 13.2.

QUICK CUSTOMER RESPONSE

1. By maintaining inventories of its final products, a company can respond immediately to customer demands (rather than having to produce the products or acquire them from another supplier), thereby providing more competitive service. In fact, some companies maintain inventories at regional warehouses specifically so that they can deliver products to customers more quickly than they could by shipping from the production site.
2. Raw material and in-process inventories can also be used to shorten the response time to customers. If raw materials or partially finished products are already available, a company can begin production to fill an order faster than if it had to acquire the raw materials.

RISK REDUCTION AND SAFETY

Inventories play a major role in risk reduction for organizations.

1. ***Uncertainties in the Supply System.*** Inventories of raw materials can protect a company against late inventories, allowing the production process to operate until inventories are replenished.

Office Depot competes by carrying a wide variety of office products and by maintaining sufficient inventories so it can satisfy customer demands immediately.

2. **Decoupling Production Stages.** As mentioned earlier, inventories of semifinished products allow firms to decouple production stages. This not only allows production of other stages to continue while one stage stops for a product changeover or planned maintenance, it also protects against *unplanned* stoppages such as machine failures or employee absences.
3. **Unexpected Surges in Demand.** Inventories of final products can satisfy unexpected surges in demand. Inventories also put the company in a better competitive position, allowing it to supply new customers quickly when competitors are out of stock.

EXPLOITING OR PROTECTING AGAINST UNUSUAL EVENTS

Inventories called **speculative inventories** are sometimes held to protect against unusual events or to take advantage of unusual opportunities. For example, if a company expects the workers at a supplier firm to go on strike, the company may increase its inventories temporarily so that it will have adequate supplies to last during the strike. Similarly, a company that expects the price of a raw material to increase in the near future may purchase large amounts of the material now at the lower cost to avoid the price increase, causing a temporary increase in inventories.

TYPES OF INVENTORY

Inventories of the same product may look the same physically, but they may be held for different reasons. Inventories held primarily to achieve economic efficiency normally increase and decrease in a planned cycle and are called **cycling inventories** (not to be confused with cycle counting of inventories, which is discussed later). In contrast, inventories that are held to protect the organization against normal business uncertainties and risks are called **safety stocks**. Firms try to maintain a set level of safety stock, which they use only when random variations in demand, lead time, or production require it.

Any attempt to achieve optimal inventory levels must look explicitly at the amount of each type of inventory being held and the policies that determine these levels. In many cases, a company can reduce its total average inventory levels while increasing its protection against business risks by changing the relative mix of safety stock and cycling inventories. The case at the end of the chapter illustrates such a situation.

A final type of inventories is speculative inventories. These inventories, as mentioned above, do not grow or shrink in a regular fashion, nor are they held perpetually for protection; rather, they are held for short periods on an irregular basis to take advantage of special opportunities or to protect against unusual risks.

13.3 INVENTORY-RELATED COSTS

When developing inventory control policies and systems, we want to make sure that we can supply our customers in a timely fashion but at low cost. Three primary costs influence the inventory policy: holding costs, ordering or setup costs, and stockout or shortage costs.

HOLDING COSTS

The **holding cost** is the cost of actually keeping items in inventory. The primary components of this cost are (1) the opportunity cost of capital, (2) taxes and insurance, (3) breakage, spoilage, pilferage, and obsolescence, and (4) handling and storing.

The opportunity cost of capital is usually the largest component of holding cost. Money invested in inventories could instead be used for some other productive purpose, such as purchasing equipment or reducing debt. The cost of this foregone return from other uses is typically about 10–25% of the inventory's value. Taxes and insurance are also a direct function of the monetary value of inventories, as are the costs of deterioration, pilferage, and obsolescence. The cost of handling and storage is the only cost that is usually not directly proportional to the monetary value of the item, but we can allocate such costs on a proportional basis without seriously distorting the total holding cost. We will designate the *holding cost per unit of product per unit time* as c_h.

Per unit holding costs are usually computed using a companywide **holding cost rate**, i (this generally assumes that the handling, storage, deterioration, and pilferage rates are either relatively small or similar for most products). The rate i represents the holding cost per unit time as a fraction of the item's value. For example, suppose i = 0.24 per year (or 24% per year). The holding cost per unit for an item that was purchased at the price p = \$20 (the value of the inventory) would then be

$$c_h = p \times i = \$20/\text{unit} \times 0.24/\text{year} = \$4.80/\text{unit/year}$$

In other words, we are incurring a cost of 24% of the value of each item for each year it is in inventory. Over time the inventory levels fluctuate considerably, so the holding cost is based on the average inventory level.

ORDERING OR SETUP COSTS

For many items the cost of purchasing or making Q units of an item, $C(Q)$, has the form

$$C(Q) = c_o + pQ$$

where c_o is the fixed cost to execute an order or to start a production run and p is the per unit price of purchase or variable cost of production. If we purchase the product from a supplier, c_o includes the cost of processing an order and possibly a fixed component of transportation cost (e.g., within some range of values for Q the same size truck may be used for shipping, and the cost is the same whether 1 unit or 500 units are shipped). If the item is produced within the organization, c_o would include any fixed machine setup or changeover costs directly attributable to the product. It is important to note that c_o should include only fixed costs (independent of order size) that are *directly* attributable to ordering or producing the product; general overhead costs such as corporate office expenses or maintenance should not be included.

We consider fixed ordering costs because the best number of units to order or produce at a time is a function of the fixed cost of acquisition. The larger the order size or production lot size, the lower the fixed ordering or setup cost per unit because the fixed cost is spread over a larger number of units.

SHORTAGE OR STOCKOUT COSTS

When customers wish to buy a product and it is not available, the supplier incurs a cost, which might include not only lost profit but also lost future profits if the customer changes suppliers. Likewise, if a company runs out of a raw material, it may have to stop its production system, idling workers and possibly causing shortages of the final product. These costs are called **stockout** or **shortage costs**. Sometimes it is accepted practice in an industry to accept orders for future rather than immediate delivery. This is called **backordering** Backordering is similar to having a negative inventory level and may involve a cost per unit time, usually due to loss of goodwill.

The amount of shortage, stockout, and backordering costs actually incurred depends on the inventory strategy followed. Sometimes firms consciously plan a certain amount of backordering or shortages to keep from building excessive inventories. In Sections 13.8 and 13.10 stockout costs will be explicitly incorporated into inventory planning.

HIDDEN COSTS

The three previous costs are the ones most commonly associated with inventory management, and they are frequently included explicitly in inventory decision making. However, inventories also carry many hidden costs. Companies keep extra raw materials on hand to protect themselves against unreliable deliveries by suppliers. They maintain substantial in-process inventories to keep some activities operating when machines break or workers fail to show up for work. They overproduce products in the expectation that some will be defective. And substantial final product inventories are maintained because of long production lead times and poor demand forecasting. In each of these cases, inventories are used to compensate for and effectively hide the real problems. All the extra costs incurred by not identifying and solving the underlying production problems are inventory-induced costs, but they are not easy to measure.

Not only do excessive inventories hide production problems, they often amplify them. As inventories grow, facilities become more cluttered, material handling becomes less efficient, accidents become more likely, and "lost" materials destroy schedules and leave workers and machines idle. Therefore, it is crucial for a company to recognize these problems and work to keep inventories to a minimum. Chapter 15 will focus on eliminating these hidden costs; here we will address ways to minimize the most visible costs.

13.4 CHARACTERISTICS OF INVENTORY MODELS

The appropriate method to use when developing inventory policies depends on the characteristics of the environment. We can categorize inventory situations and models according to our assumptions regarding demand or usage patterns, review policies, time horizons, and product perishability.

INDEPENDENT VERSUS DEPENDENT DEMAND

A fundamental issue in managing inventories is whether or not the demand for an item is directly associated with the demand for another item, which is assumed to be known. If the demand for the item, such as an axle, *is* directly associated with (dependent on) that of another item, especially a higher-level product such as assembled automobiles, we can utilize a dependent demand model. Assuming the manufacturer had a final assembly schedule, automobile components would be prime candidates to have their purchases, production, and inventories managed by a dependent demand system. Dependent demand systems focus primarily on coordinating the timing of production and purchases for related products and managing their inventories as a group. During the 1970s and early 1980s, considerable attention was devoted to items with dependent demands. An approach called *material requirements planning* (*MRP*), which is discussed in Chapter 14, was widely adopted. The overall success of MRP has been modest, and in many cases it has been superseded by or integrated with JIT production systems.

More commonly, the demand for or usage of items cannot be tied to that of another product and must be treated as having an independent demand. Inventory management policies for independent demand items are developed in isolation from policies for other independent demand items (unless we order them from the same supplier, in which case we may want to combine orders). Typical situations where independent demand models would be applicable involve purchases of products by a retailer for resale to customers, or supplies, such as paper, packaging materials, or fuel, used by a company to support its operations. Even items that are components of end products, and therefore have a dependent demand, are often better managed as independent demand items if the demand is relatively constant. In contrast to dependent demand items, which occur almost exclusively in manufacturing systems, independent demand items occur extensively in both manufacturing and service systems. The models in this chapter are devoted exclusively to independent demand items.

INVENTORY REVIEW POLICIES

A fundamental aspect of an inventory policy is deciding whether the **inventory position** (the number of units in inventory plus those on order) will be reviewed on a continuous or periodic basis. Traditionally, the cost of maintaining a continuous knowledge of the inventory position of thousands of items was prohibitive, so most organizations used **periodic review policies**. In this case, the organization reviews (counts) the inventory for the product and places orders at fixed time intervals. The amount ordered each time may vary according to the inventory position and the expected demand. A major disadvantage of this system is that between reviews the inventory can become dangerously low without the company's knowledge until the next review occurs.

With advances in computer technology, maintaining real-time information on the inventory position of thousands of products has become simple so **continuous** (or **perpetual**) **review policies** have become widespread. Continuous review systems involve less risk (and require less inventory) because the company always knows its current inventory position; as soon as inventories drop to a predetermined level, called the **reorder point (RP)**, the company can place an order for some fixed amount. One way of differentiating the two systems is that periodic review systems typically have variable order quantities but fixed time intervals between orders, whereas continuous review systems have fixed order quantities but variable time intervals between orders. This chapter concentrates on continuous review systems, but periodic review is discussed in Section 13.9.

CONTINUOUS VERSUS ONE-PERIOD DECISIONS

In most cases, ordering policies are established for use on a continuous basis. Products are assumed to be nonperishable within reasonable time limits. However, acquisition policies for highly perishable products, such as deciding the number of copies of a weekly magazine to print, are often most appropriately analyzed as one-time decisions (possibly a series of one-time decisions). Uncertainty of demand is the fundamental component of these problems. Discussion of one-period decisions is postponed until Section 13.10.

13.5 THE BASIC ECONOMIC ORDER QUANTITY MODEL

Two of the most important decisions related to controlling the inventories of raw materials or supplies is *when* to place an order and *how much* to order. In 1913 F. W. Harris[3] developed a rule for determining the optimal number of units of an item to purchase if several fundamental assumptions are satisfied. This model, which is referred to as the **basic economic order quantity (EOQ) model**, has broad applicability; it can be used in planning the purchases of raw materials and supplies and in planning purchases for wholesalers and retailers who resell products. This model and the generalizations that follow in later sections are all independent demand, continuous review models.

The assumptions of the basic EOQ model are as follows:

1. The demand for or usage of the item is relatively constant over time at a rate of D units per unit time.
2. The item's cost (price), p, is independent of the quantity ordered; that is, there are no quantity discounts.
3. There is a fixed cost, $c_{o,}$ for executing an order that is independent of the quantity ordered, Q.
4. The holding cost for inventories is proportional to the quantity stored; that is, the holding cost per unit per unit time, c_h, is independent of the inventory level.
5. No shortages are allowed; all demand must be satisfied when requested.
6. The **lead time (LT)** for deliveries, which is the time from when an order is placed until it is delivered, is known with certainty and is constant.
7. All items ordered are delivered at the same time; there are no split deliveries.

Based on these assumptions, the inventory level over time can be graphed as in Figure 13.3. We assume that at time zero a delivery of Q units arrives that replenishes inventories to a level of Q. The inventory level then decreases linearly at a rate D. When the inventory position reaches some predetermined level, RP, the reorder point, an order is placed. If RP is chosen correctly, the new order of Q units will be delivered just as the last unit of inventory is used. Over time the inventory level forms the sawtooth pattern shown in Figure 13.3.[4]

The issue facing the firm is, what should be the values for RP and Q that will minimize the long-term cost to the firm? In this situation, these values can be determined separately.

COMPUTING THE REORDER POINT

It is straightforward to show that, regardless of the order quantity, the reorder point should be chosen so that the inventory level reaches zero at the end of each reordering cycle. (If RP is set higher than this level, the average inventory level and associated cost

[3]See Donald Erlenkotter, "Fred Whitman Harris and the Economic Order Quantity Model," *Operations Research*, Vol. 38, 1990, pp. 937–946.

[4]For clarity we will assume in our illustrations, such as Figure 13.3, that no units are already on order when an order is placed, so the inventory *position* is equal to the inventory *level*.

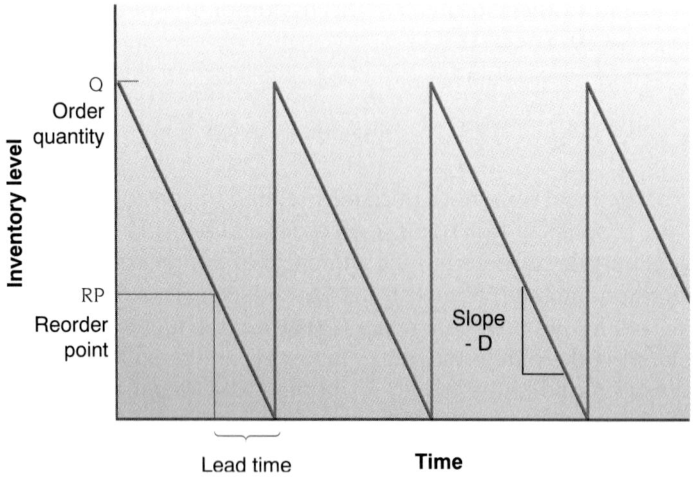

FIGURE 13.3 Inventory pattern for the basic EOQ model.

increases without any benefit.) Thus, RP should be set equal to the number of units used during the lead time, called the **demand during lead time (DDLT)**. This is simply

$$RP = DDLT = D \times LT \tag{13.1}$$

The units of time used to express D and LT must be the same: if D is expressed in units per month, then LT must be expressed in months.

COMPUTING THE OPTIMAL ORDER QUANTITY

To determine the optimal order quantity, we begin by expressing the firm's **total material cost (TMC)** for the product during a unit of time (e.g., a year) as a function of the order quantity, Q. Because shortages are not allowed, there *appear* to be three components to the material cost function: ordering costs, holding costs, and variable item costs (the amount paid to the supplier, or the variable production cost). The ordering cost per unit time is equal to the fixed cost per order, c_o, times the number of orders placed per unit time. The number of orders placed per unit time is equal to the demand per unit time divided by the order quantity, D/Q. For example, if the firm uses 100,000 units per year and orders 25,000 units per order, then four orders are placed per year. So

$$\text{ordering cost per unit time} = c_o[D/Q]$$

The holding cost per unit time is equal to the holding cost per unit per unit time, c_h. times the average inventory level. Because D is constant, the inventory level decreases linearly over time during any order cycle (as shown in Figure 13.3), and it can be proved that the average inventory level equals the maximum inventory level plus the minimum level divided by two. So

$$\text{holding cost per unit time} = c_h[Q/2]$$

The third cost component is the variable item cost per unit time. This will equal the cost per unit, p, times the number purchased or used per unit time, D. So the total material cost per unit time has the form

$$\text{TMC} = C_o[D/Q] + C_h[Q/2] + pD \tag{13.2}$$

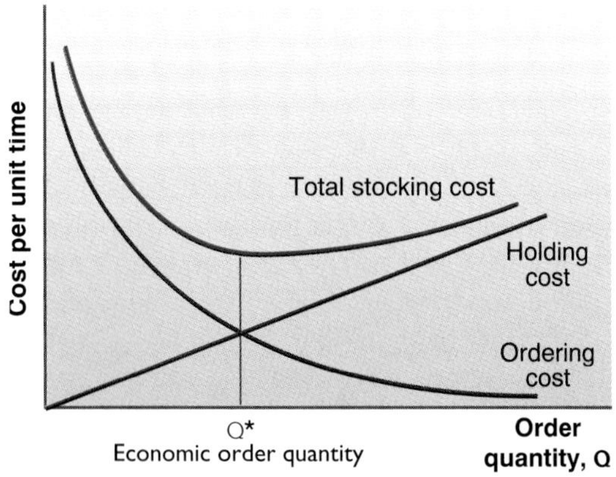

FIGURE 13.4 Holding, ordering, and total stocking costs.

But *the item cost is not a function of the order quantity*—there are no quantity discounts—so the amount spent on the items per unit time, pD, is a constant. Therefore, the value of Q that minimizes equation (13.2) is the value that minimizes the sum of the ordering and holding costs, called the **total stocking cost (TSC)**. The problem then reduces to finding the value of Q that minimizes

$$\text{TSC} = \text{ordering cost} + \text{holding cost} = c_o[D/Q] + c_h[Q/2] \qquad (13.3)$$

Figure 13.4 illustrates the ordering cost, the holding cost, and the total stocking cost per unit time as a function of the order quantity, Q. The ordering cost per unit time decreases as Q increases because fewer orders are placed per unit time and the fixed ordering costs are spread over more units. The holding cost increases linearly with Q because the average inventory, $Q/2$, increases proportionally with Q and the holding cost per unit is assumed to be constant. Using calculus[5] we can determine that the value of Q that minimizes equation (13.3) and therefore equation (13.2) is

$$EOQ = \sqrt{2c_o D/c_h} \qquad (13.4)$$

Expression (13.4) is referred to as the *economic order quantity formula*, and EOQ is the **economic order quantity**. The following example illustrates its use.

[5] TSC is a convex function that reaches its minimum at some nonnegative value of Q. So we can obtain the value of Q that minimizes equation (13.3) by computing its derivative with respect to Q, setting this equal to zero, and solving for Q:

$$\text{TSC}'(Q) = dTSC(Q)/dQ = -[c_o D/Q^2] + c_h/2 = 0$$
$$\rightarrow c_h/2 = c_o D/Q^2$$
$$\rightarrow Q^2 = 2c_o D/c_h$$
$$\rightarrow EOQ = Q^* = \sqrt{2c_o D/c_h}$$

EXAMPLE 1

Fastcomp is a Japanese electronics firm that buys computer chips from a supplier in the United States. The cost of a chip is \$80 per unit, regardless of the order quantity. In addition, the company incurs a fixed cost of approximately \$1000 per order to process the order and obtain import licenses. Fastcomp has determined that it costs approximately 12% per year of an item's cost to hold the item in inventory. The lead time for delivery is 1.5 month. The company uses 10,000 computer chips per month at a relatively constant rate. Historically, Fastcomp has followed a policy of buying a one-month supply of chips (10,000) every month. We want to determine the optimal order quantity and reorder point for Fastcomp, the annual cost resulting from the optimal policy, and compare it with the current policy.

Using equation (13.1), the optimal reorder point is

$$RP = (10{,}000 \text{ units/month}) \times (1.5 \text{ months}) = 15{,}000 \text{ units}$$

To calculate the optimal order quantity, we need the following information: D = 10,000 units per month, c_o = \$1000 per order. The only information not provided directly is the holding cost, c_h. This is computed using the price of the item and the company's holding cost rate:

$$\begin{aligned} c_h &= p \times i \\ &= \$80/\text{unit} \times 0.12/\text{year} = \$9.60/\text{unit/year} \end{aligned}$$

Notice that the time unit for c_h is different from that for D. Therefore, either c_h has to be converted to a cost per month or demand converted to demand per year. *Monetary units and time units must be the same for all quantities.* Converting D to demand per year gives D = 120,000 units per year.

From equation (13.4) the optimal order quantity is then

$$\begin{aligned} EOQ &= \sqrt{[2(120{,}000 \text{ units/year})(\$1000/\text{order})]/[\$9.60/\text{unit/year}]} \\ &= 5{,}000 \text{ units/order} \end{aligned}$$

Putting $Q = 5000$ into equation (13.3) gives a total stocking cost per year of

$$\begin{aligned} TSC_{5000} &= (\$1000/\text{order})[(120{,}000 \text{ units/year})/(5{,}000 \text{ units/order})] + \\ &\quad (\$9.60/\text{unit/year})(5{,}000 \text{ units}/2) \\ &= \$24{,}000 + \$24{,}000 = \$48{,}000/\text{year} \end{aligned}$$

In contrast, using the current policy of ordering 10,000 units once per month, the company's total stocking cost per year is

$$\begin{aligned} TSC_{10{,}000} &= (\$1000/\text{order})[(120{,}000 \text{ units/year})/(10{,}000 \text{ units/order})] + \\ &\quad [(\$9.60/\text{unit/year})(10{,}000 \text{ units}/2)] \\ &= \$12{,}000 + \$48{,}000 = \$60{,}000/\text{year} \end{aligned}$$

So Fastcomp would save \$12,000 per year by using its optimal order quantity rather than its current policy of ording once a month. When multiplied by the hundreds or thousands of different components the company may use, the total annual savings from using an optimal policy can be substantial.

Notice that Fastcomp's inventory *on hand* will cycle between 0 and 5000 units, but its inventory *position* will vary between 15,000 and 20,000 units because it will always have 3 shipments on order. (It is ordering 5000 units twice a month, but a shipment requires 1.5 months to be delivered.) When the inventory *position* hits 15,000 the actual inventory will be 5,000 and an order will be placed. Notice also that for the optimal value, *EOQ*, the annual ordering cost and annual holding cost are equal. This is not a coincidence for this specific example; it will always be true for the *basic* EOQ model because of the form of the function in equation (13.3). This equality of costs provides a good way to verify the optimal value of Q.

VALIDITY OF THE ASSUMPTIONS AND MODEL ROBUSTNESS

Although the assumptions underlying the EOQ model appear to be highly restrictive, one of the most appealing aspects of the model is that it is quite robust. Some of the assumptions, such as no quantity discounts, no uncertainty in demand or lead times, and no stockouts, will be dropped in later sections. Others, such as a constant demand rate and a constant holding cost per unit, can be violated somewhat without substantially reducing the accuracy of the solution. If demand has predictable seasonal patterns, the model can be modified to accommodate this fact as well.

An especially important characteristic of the EOQ model is that the total stocking cost function is relatively flat around the optimal order quantity (see Figure 13.4). This is important because estimates for c_o and c_h are not always extremely accurate, so the value computed for *EOQ* may not equal the true optimum value. However, because of the flatness of the TSC function, even if the computed *EOQ* is 20–30% different from the true optimum, the cost penalty is relatively small. Notice that if both c_o and c_h are overestimated or underestimated by approximately the same proportion, there is no error in the computed value of *EOQ*. (A problem occurs when one of the cost estimates is far from the correct value or when one of them is substantially overestimated and the other is substantially underestimated.)

As a practical matter, we are not as interested in obtaining the true optimal order quantity as we are in *not* using order quantities that are substantially different from the true optimum. For as obvious as this seems, field studies indicate that it is common for organizations to use order quantities that are 100% or more in error. There are many reasons for this, but two common ones are that (1) organizations use the same simple rules of thumb to purchase all products (e.g., buy once per month) and (2) ordering rules that were initially established based on certain data have not been updated even though the environment has changed.

If an organization uses hundreds of different products and each product has its own usage rate and holding cost, the optimal ordering quantities and frequencies can easily differ by a factor of 10. Obviously, any ordering rule that is common to all products will be incorrect for almost any product. The end-of-chapter case illustrates this point clearly.

The flatness of the TSC function also addresses one final issue: If $Q^* = 8942$, should the company order exactly this many? The answer is, "probably not." The cost penalty for ordering 9000 (or even 10,000) units at a time rather than 8942 is likely to be small (unless the item is being used to fill a specific order of 8942 units for another customer, in which case the firm probably should not be using an EOQ approach). For example, as long as the order quantity in Example 1 is between 4000 and 6000, the annual material cost is no more than \$1200 above the optimum. The goal is to avoid substantially incorrect order quantities such as 2000 or 10,000.

13.6 THE EOQ MODEL WITH QUANTITY DISCOUNTS

Suppliers commonly offer a **quantity discount** to customers that purchase a sufficiently large number of units at once. The most common form of quantity discount is given in Table 13.1. In this case, when a customer purchases more than some quantity, such as Q_1, it pays a lower price, p_2, on *all* the units purchased. The number of different prices offered will vary from case to case, but two to five price levels are common. A less common form of quantity discount awards the lower price only for those units above the price-break level. This section only considers the former case; the latter case is similar, but the solution method requires some modification.

The inclusion of quantity discounts does not affect the optimal reorder point; RP still equals $LT \times D$. The optimal order quantity may be affected, however, because the second assumption of the basic EOQ model is eliminated. To illustrate the impact of this change, we begin by considering the components of the total material cost that can be affected by the value of Q.

total material cost/year = ordering cost/year + holding cost/year + item cost/year

Without quantity discounts, the item cost per year was a constant, pD, so the total material cost was equal to the total stocking cost plus a constant. But with quantity discounts the price paid is itself a function of Q, $p(Q)$. So the item's cost per year must be included in the analysis. In addition, the per unit holding cost, c_h, may be affected by Q because, if a lower price is paid for the item, then less money is tied up in each unit of inventory: $c_h(Q) = p(Q) \times i$. The problem is to select the value of Q to

$$\text{minimize TMC/year} = c_o[D/Q] + [c_h(Q)]\,[Q/2] + [p(Q)]D \qquad (13.5)$$

Figure 13.5 shows each component cost and the total material cost as functions of the order quantity, Q. Two characteristics are worth noting:

1. Between any two price-break quantities (quantities at which a lower price becomes effective), the annual item cost is constant because the price is constant within that range. But at a price-break quantity, the variable item cost drops to a lower level.
2. The annual holding cost function is no longer a straight line. Between any two price-break quantities the function is linear. But at each price-break quantity two things occur: (a) the total holding cost drops discontinuously because a lower value of c_h applies to *all* units of product in inventory, and (b) the slope of the holding cost function decreases because c_h decreases as Q increases.

TABLE 13.1 QUANTITY DISCOUNT STRUCTURE

No. of Units Purchased	Price per Unit
$0 < Q < Q_1$	p_1
$Q_1 \le Q < Q_2$	p_2
$Q_2 \le Q < Q_3$	p_3
$Q_3 \le Q$	p_4

where $p_1 > p_2 > p_3 > p_4$

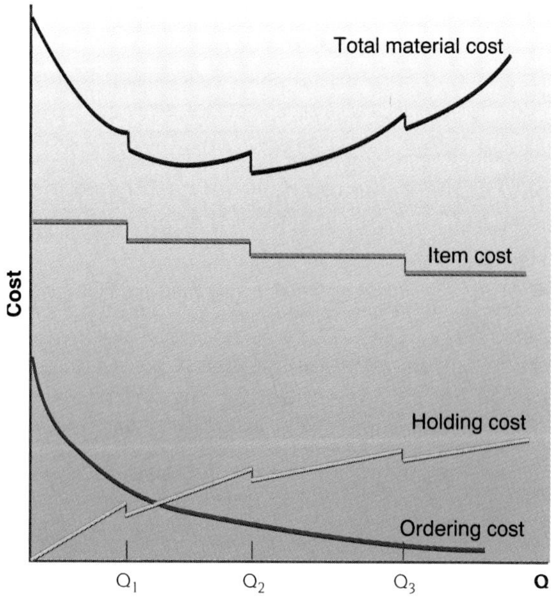

FIGURE 13.5 Inventory-related costs with quantity discounts.

Because the total cost curve is not smooth over all values of Q, the differential calculus method used to derive the basic EOQ formula cannot be used to find the optimum value of Q. Instead, a solution method has been developed using the fact that the total cost function can be derived in the following way. Suppose four different prices are possible. For each price we can derive the total material cost function that would result *if that price applied over all values of* Q. These functions will always form the pattern illustrated in Figure 13.6: the function corresponding to a higher price will always lie totally

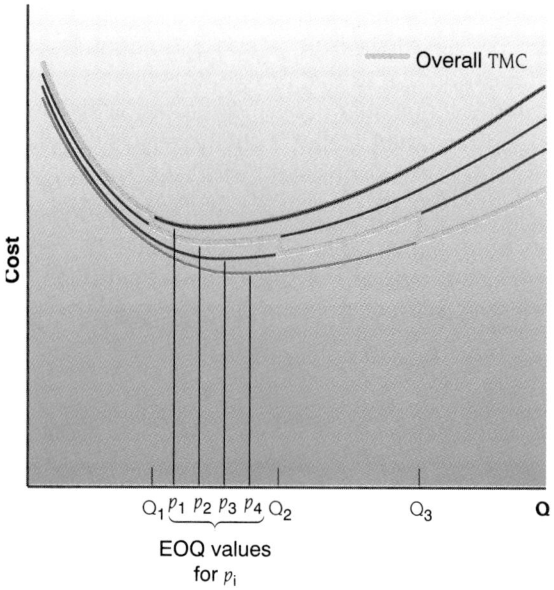

FIGURE 13.6 Total material cost for each price.

above the curve for a lower price, and for each successively lower price the minimum point for the cost function occurs at a larger value of Q (i.e., farther to the right). The total material cost curve in Figure 13.5 can be obtained by taking the part of each cost curve in Figure 13.6 that applies to each price range.

The solution algorithm is then based on the following observations of Figure 13.6:

1. The value of Q at the minimum point for each curve in Figure 13.6 can be found using the basic EOQ formula (13.4) for that price. We will call these points *smooth minimum points*.
2. The value of Q that minimizes TMC must either be a smooth minimum point or a price-break quantity.
3. If the smooth minimum point on the lowest price curve in Figure 13.6 occurs at a value of Q large enough to entitle the customer to the lowest price, then this quantity *must* be the optimal order quantity (it is the lowest point on the lowest curve).
4. The total material cost for a smooth minimum point on any curve will be less than the total material cost of *any* point on that curve or *any* higher price curve.

A Solution Algorithm

From observations 1 and 2 we could solve the order quantity problem as follows. We first use equation (13.4) to find the smooth minimum point for each price (each function in Figure 13.6). Then we compute the TMC per year using equation (13.5) for each of these quantities *and* for each price-break quantity. Whichever quantity produces the lowest TMC per year is the optimum. But in some cases this involves more work than necessary.

Observations 3 and 4 allow us to streamline the algorithm as follows:

Step 1: Using the lowest possible price, solve equation (13.4) to compute the smooth minimum point, $\hat{Q}$, that minimizes the cost curve for this price. If $\hat{Q}$ is *consistent* with this price—that is, if $\hat{Q}$ is large enough to merit the lowest possible price—then the optimal order quantity $Q^* = \hat{Q}$; stop.

Step 2: If $\hat{Q}$ is *inconsistent* with the price used ($\hat{Q}$ is too small to merit the lowest price), then select the next lowest price and use equation (13.4) to find the smooth minimum point corresponding to that price. If this quantity is consistent with the price used, then go to step 3. If this quantity is inconsistent with the price (too small to merit the price), then keep repeating step 2 with successively higher prices until a smooth minimum point is found that is consistent with its price.

Step 3: Using equation (13.5), compute the TMC per year that would result from using the quantity obtained in step 2 as the order quantity, and compute the TMC that would result from using *each* of the price-break quantities that are *larger* than this amount (corresponding to a lower price). The order quantity with the lowest TMC is optimal.

EXAMPLE 2

Capital National Bank (CNB) uses laser printer cartridges at the rate of 10 per week. The price charged by the supplier of the cartridges varies with order quantity as follows:

Order Quantity	Price
0–99	$40.00
100–249	$39.60
250–499	$39.00
500+	$38.00

CNB estimates that it pays $100 per order for delivery and for execution of the purchase order. In addition, CNB believes that it costs 18% per year of a cartridges's price to hold it in inventory. CNB would like to determine the optimal number of cartridges to order at a time.

Step 1: We select the lowest price, $38.00, and compute the economic order quantity (smooth minimum point) *for this price*. Note that c_h = $38.00 × 0.18/year = $6.84/cartridge/year; D = 10 units/week × 52 weeks/year = 520 units/year; and c_o = $100/order. From equation (13.4)

$$\hat{Q} = \sqrt{[2(\$100)(520/\text{year})]/(\$6.84/\text{cartridge/year})]}$$
$$= 123 \text{ cartridges/order}$$

This quantity is *inconsistent* with the $38.00 price.

Step 2: We select the next lowest price, $39.00, and recompute equation (13.4); notice that in this case c_h = $39.00 × 0.18/year = $7.02/cartridge/year.

$$\hat{Q} = \sqrt{[2(\$100)(520/\text{year})]/(\$7.02/\text{cartridge/year})]}$$
$$= 122 \text{ cartridges/order}$$

This is also inconsistent with the price. (Notice that we could have skipped this computation and gone directly to the $39.60 price because, as the price gets larger, the value of equation (13.4) must get smaller; the numerator of the expression stays constant, while the denominator increases with price. So we know the value of equation (13.4) for a price of $39.00 will be less than 123 and is clearly inconsistent.)

We now recompute equation (13.4) using a price of $39.60 and c_h = $39.60 × 0.18/year = $7.128/cartridge/year.

$$\hat{Q} = \sqrt{[2(\$100)(520/\text{year})]/(\$7.128/\text{cartridge/year})]}$$
$$= 121 \text{ cartridges/order}$$

This quantity is consistent with the price; if CNB orders 121 cartridges at a time, it will pay a price of $39.60 per cartridge.

Step 3: We now use equation (13.5) to compute the TMC per year that would result if we ordered 121, 250, or 500 cartridges at a time. (From observation 4 we know that the price-break quantity Q = 100 cannot be optimal.)

$$TMC_{121} = (\$100)[(520 \text{ units/year})/121 \text{ units/order})] + [(\$7.128/\text{unit/year})(121 \text{ units}/2)] + [(\$39.60/\text{unit})(520 \text{ units/year})]$$
$$= \$429.75 + \$431.24 + \$20{,}592.00 = \$21{,}452.99/\text{year}$$ [6]

[6] The annual ordering cost and holding cost are not equal because the EOQ for a price of $39.60 is actually 120.79; rounding off to 121 creates the discrepancy.

$$TMC_{250} = (\$100)[(520 \text{ units/year})/250 \text{ units/order})] + [(\$7.02/\text{unit/year})(250 \text{ units}/2)] + [(\$39.00/\text{unit})(520 \text{ units/year})] = \$208.00 + \$877.54 + \$20{,}280.00 = \$21{,}365.54/\text{year}$$

$$TMC_{500} = (\$100)[(520 \text{ units/year})/500 \text{ units/order})] + [(\$6.848/\text{unit/year})(500 \text{ units}/2)] + [(\$38.00/\text{unit})(520 \text{ units/year})] = \$104.00 + \$1710.00 + \$19{,}760.00 = \$21{,}574.00/\text{year}$$

The optimal number of cartridges to order is 250, and CNB will place D/Q = 520/250 = 2.08 orders per year, or approximately one every 6 months. The reason CNB should not order 500 at a time is that the extra holding costs more than outweigh the savings in ordering and item costs combined.[7]

[7]Printer technology is changing rapidly, so we would also make sure that we intended to keep the current printers for the next six months before ordering a six-month supply of cartridges.

Although the algorithm involves more work than the basic EOQ formula, it does save effort in Example 2 relative to solving equation (13.4) for each price and then computing equation (13.5) for every smooth minimum and price-break quantity. The smooth minimum for the \$40.00 price and the TMC for this quantity and the 100 unit price-break did not have to be computed.

13.7 THE ECONOMIC PRODUCTION LOT-SIZE MODEL

A problem frequently encountered by manufacturers is to determine how many units of a product or component to produce during a production run. This quantity is called the **production lot size**. The problem of determining the optimal lot size, called the **economic lot size (ELS),** is similar to the economic order quantity problems, with only minor differences.

A typical company may produce dozens or hundreds of different products. Each time a different product is processed, some fixed costs of setup/changeover, c_o, are incurred. For simplicity, suppose the demand for or usage of this product is relatively constant at some rate D units per unit time. This demand may be from an outside customer or from a department elsewhere in the production process. During production, suppose the product is produced at a rate of P units per unit time. Notice that P must be greater than D; otherwise, we have a capacity shortage problem, not a lot-sizing problem.

Figure 13.7 shows that during production, items are sent to the customer (or next production stage) continuously at rate D, and the excess production goes into inventory at the rate $(P - D)$ until Q units have been produced. Production then stops until some later time (and other products are probably produced on the machine). When the inventory level reaches some specified amount, RP, setup begins and production starts just as inventories reach zero. If there is no uncertainty, the reorder point should again equal $D \times LT$.

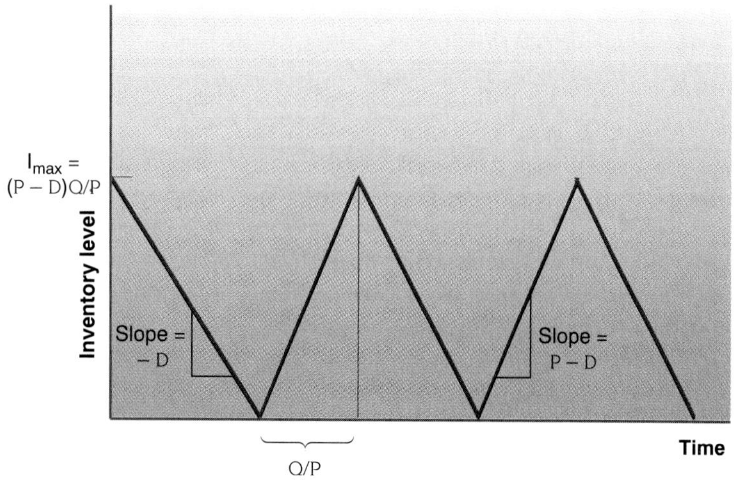

FIGURE 13.7 Inventory pattern for a production lot-size model.

Assuming the cost of producing Q units of product is $c_o + pQ$, where p is a constant marginal production cost, the economic lot size is the value of Q that minimizes total annual stocking costs:

$$TSC = \text{setup costs/year} + \text{holding costs/year}$$

The setup costs per year will be the number of setups per year, D/Q, times the fixed setup cost, c_o (where D is the demand per year). The holding costs per year will be c_h times the average inventory level, which is $(I_{\text{max}} + I_{\text{min}})/2$. The minimum inventory will be zero, but the maximum inventory is *not* Q because while Q units are being produced during a production run, some of them are being sold or used at the rate D. To determine the maximum inventory, notice that in Figure 13.7 the inventory begins to grow at the beginning of a production run at the rate of $(P - D)$ units per unit time. The amount of time a production run lasts is Q/P; for example, if we make 50,000 units per production run and the production rate is $P = 10{,}000$ units/day, then a production run would last five days. So $I_{max} = [(P - D)(Q/P)]$, and the average inventory is $[(P - D)(Q/2P)]$. Then the total stocking cost is

$$TSC = c_o(D/Q) + c_h[(P - D)(Q/2P)] \tag{13.6}$$

The value of Q that minimizes equation (13.6), which can be found using calculus as with the basic EOQ model,[8] is given by:

$$ELS = Q^* = \sqrt{[2c_oD/c_h][P/(P - D)]} \tag{13.7}$$

[8] $TSC(Q)' = dTSC(Q)/dQ = -[c_oD/Q^2] + [(c_h/2)(P - D)/P] = 0$

$\rightarrow [(c_h/2)(P - D)/P] = c_oD/Q^2$

$\rightarrow Q^2 = \{[(2c_oD/c_h)][P/(P - D)]\}$

$\rightarrow ELS = Q^* = \sqrt{[(2c_oD/c_h)][P/(P - D)]}$

EXAMPLE 3

Dominion Soap Ltd. (DSL) manufactures several types of powdered laundry detergent. The demand for one of its products, Wave Detergent, is approximately 1,000,000 cartons per month. DSL estimates that it costs approximately \$800 to set up the production line to produce Wave. DSL's production facilities operate 24 hours a day, seven days a week, and it estimates that it can produce Wave at the rate of 100,000 cartons per 24-hour day. DSL estimates that it invests \$2.00 in each carton of Wave Detergent, and the holding cost rate is estimated to be 0.24 per year of the item's value.

Summarizing the information available, $c_o = \$800$; $c_h = p \times i = \$2.00\text{/unit} \times 0.24\text{/year} = \$0.48\text{/unit/year} = \$0.04\text{/unit/month}$; $D = 1{,}000{,}000$ units/month; and $P = 100{,}000$ units/day × 30 days/month = 3,000,000 units/month (assuming 30 days/month). From equation (13.7) the economic lot size is then

$$\text{ELS} = \sqrt{[2(\$800)(1{,}000{,}000/\text{month})/\$0.04/\text{month}][3{,}000{,}000/(3{,}000{,}000 - 1{,}000{,}000)]}$$
$$= 244{,}949 \text{ cartons}$$

DSL should produce 244,949 cartons of Wave each production run, which would take approximately 2.45 days of running time (actually, we would probably round the ELS to 250,000 cartons). Converting D to a daily basis, DSL sells 33,333 cartons of Wave each day, so a production run of Wave would supply customers for Q/D = [244,949 cartons/33,333 cartons/day] = 7.39 days. Figure 13.8 shows the timing of production runs for Wave alone. In practice, the lot sizes and timing of production runs would have to be coordinated among many products that share the same production resources. The ELS for each product would be used as input for a separate heuristic, to be discussed in Chapter 16, that adjusts the lot sizes and coordinates the production schedule.

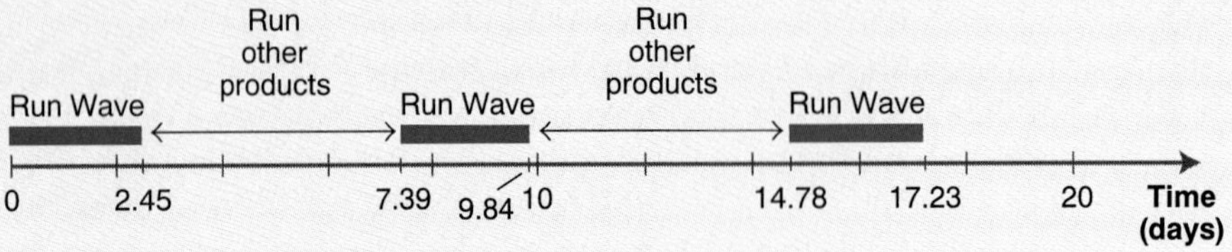

FIGURE 13.8 Timing of production runs for Dominion Soap.

13.8 SAFETY STOCK POLICIES

In Sections 13.5–13.7 a basic assumption was that there was no uncertainty concerning lead times and demand rates, so we could set our reorder point at $RP = D \times LT$ and receive deliveries exactly as our inventories reached zero. In reality, there can be substantial variation and uncertainty in both lead times and demand. The consequence of this uncertainty is illustrated in Figure 13.9. Suppose demand is random, with an average rate of $\overline{D}$, and lead time is random, with an average value of $\overline{LT}$. The **average** or **expected demand during lead time (DDLT)** is then equal to $\overline{D} \times \overline{LT}$. Suppose we set our reorder point, RP, equal to $\overline{DDLT}$. When our inventory position hits RP, we place an

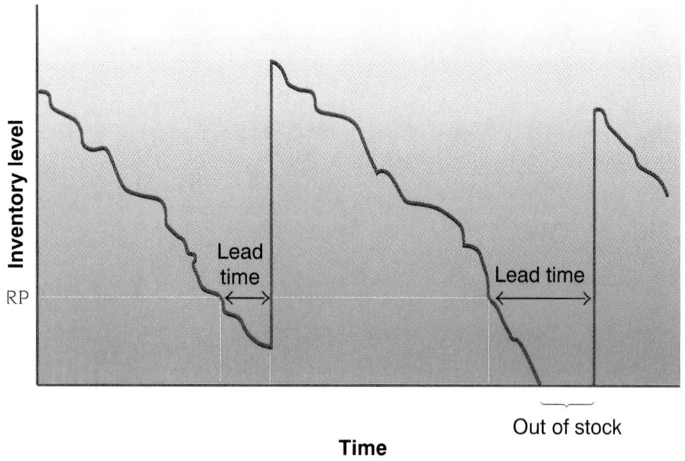

FIGURE 13.9 Inventory pattern with random demand and lead times.

order. The *actual* demand during lead time may be more than $\overline{DDLT}$, either because the lead time is longer than average, the demand rate is higher than average, or both. In this case, we are out of stock (called a **stockout**) for some period of time and cannot satisfy demand. On the other hand, there will be order cycles when the actual demand during lead time is less than average, so product will still be in inventory when delivery occurs.

We can control both the likelihood and the magnitude of stockouts through wise selection of our reorder point. By setting RP greater than $\overline{DDLT}$, *on average* we will have some inventories on hand when an order is delivered. These extra inventories are called *safety stocks*, and they incur a cost of c_h per unit time. Formally, we define the safety stock level as

$$\text{safety stock } (SS) = \text{reorder point } (RP) - \text{average demand during lead time } (\overline{DDLT})$$

so

$$RP = \overline{DDLT} + SS = \bar{D} \times \overline{LT} + SS$$

Two analytical approaches are commonly used to determine the appropriate reorder point and thus the level of safety stock: a service level/cost trade-off method and an explicit cost minimization method.

SELECTING THE REORDER POINT BASED ON SERVICE LEVEL

Stockout costs are difficult to measure precisely, especially when the stockout is for a product sold to an external customer (in contrast to running out of a raw material for a production process). Consequently, it is common to treat the problem as a two-dimensional trade-off between the cost of holding safety stock and the level of service provided to customers. An important issue is how to define or measure customer service level.

One measure is the **order cycle service level**, the percentage of order cycles during which a stockout does *not* occur. Although commonly discussed in books, and even used in practice, this is not a good measure of customer service because it does not

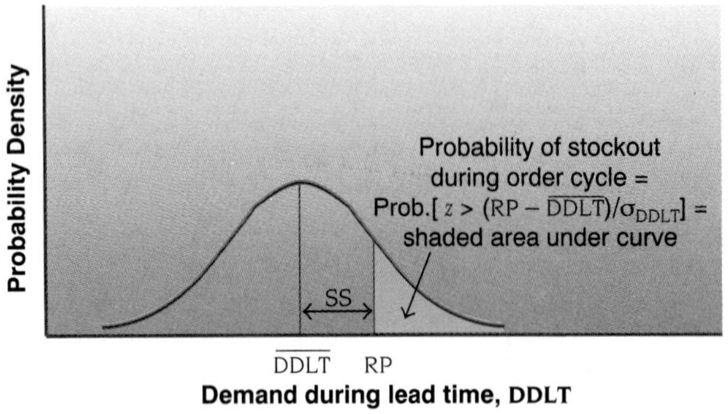

FIGURE 13.10 Probability of a stockout during an order cycle.

consider the frequency of order cycles or the magnitude of the stockouts: a 1-unit stockout and a 1000-unit stockout are treated the same way. Therefore, we will not discuss it explicitly here. A much better measure is the **demand service level**, SL_d, (also called the **fill rate**), which is the percentage of units that are supplied when demanded:

$$SL_d = [(\text{annual demand} - \text{ave. number of units short per year})/\text{annual demand}] \times 100\%$$

or

$$SL_d = [1 - (\text{ave. number of units short per order cycle}/Q)] \times 100\%$$

To compute SL_d we need an approximate probability distribution for the demand during lead time, $DDLT$, in order to determine the probability and magnitude of stockouts. Whenever possible, it is best to derive the distribution for $DDLT$ directly from historical data. When this is not possible, we often assume $DDLT$ is normally distributed.

To compute SL_d we need to determine the average number of units short per order cycle. This will equal the probability of a stockout occurring during an order cycle times the average size of a stockout. If $DDLT$ is normally distributed, the probability of a stockout on any order cycle for a given reorder point can be obtained using a z-table,[9] (see Figure 13.10). But computing the average size of a stockout when lead time demand is normally distributed is difficult. In effect, for a given reorder point we must multiply every possible stockout quantity—an infinite number of them—by the probability (density) of a stockout occurring and then sum these products; this requires integral calculus. R. G. Brown has done this for the case where demand during lead time approximates a standard normal distribution (the z-distribution).[10] Brown has converted these results to tables that *combine* the probability of a stockout and the average size of a stockout to give the *expected number of units short per order cycle*; this quantity is designated $E(z)$. (Table 13.2 lists the values of $E(z)$ for a range of values of z.) If $DDLT$ is normally distributed, with a mean of $\overline{DDLT}$ and a standard deviation of σ_{DDLT}:

$$\text{ave. number of units short per order cycle} = E(z)\sigma_{\text{DDLT}}$$

where $z = (RP - \overline{DDLT})/\sigma_{DDLT}$. In other words, z is the number of standard deviations of demand during lead time that the reorder point is set above $\overline{DDLT}$.

[9]The probability of a stockout on any reorder cycle is

$\text{Prob}(z > (RP - \overline{DDLT})/\sigma_{DDLT})$, where z is the standard normal random variable.

[10]Robert G. Brown, *Decision Rules for Inventory Management*, Holt, Rinehart & Winston, New York 1967).

TABLE 13.2 EXPECTED SHORTAGES PER ORDER CYCLE WHEN DDLT HAS A Z-DISTRIBUTION

z	$E(z)$	z	$E(z)$	z	$E(z)$
0.0	0.3989	1.0	0.0833	2.0	0.0085
0.1	0.3509	1.1	0.0686	2.1	0.0065
0.2	0.3069	1.2	0.0561	2.2	0.0049
0.3	0.2668	1.3	0.0455	2.3	0.0037
0.4	0.2304	1.4	0.0367	2.4	0.0027
0.5	0.1978	1.5	0.0293	2.5	0.0020
0.6	0.1687	1.6	0.0232	2.6	0.0015
0.7	0.1429	1.7	0.0183	2.7	0.0011
0.8	0.1202	1.8	0.0143	2.8	0.0008
0.9	0.1004	1.9	0.0110	2.9	0.0005

We illustrate how to use this in the following example.

EXAMPLE 4

In Example 1 we determined that Fastcomp's best order quantity was 5000 chips. In that example we assumed that the demand of 120,000 chips per year and the lead time of 1.5 months were known and constant (also, remember that c_h = \$9.60/chip/year). Now suppose that both demand and lead time are random. From historical data, Fastcomp believes the demand during lead time is normally distributed, with a mean of 15,000 and a standard deviation of 2000.

To illustrate how to compute the demand service level for a reorder point, consider the case where $RP = 18{,}000$ (so $SS = RP - \overline{DDLT} = 18000 - 15{,}000 = 3000$). Then

$$z = (RP - \overline{DDLT})/\sigma_{DDLT} = (18{,}000 - 15{,}000)/2{,}000 = 1.5$$

Using Table 13.2 for $E(z)$, the average number of units short per order cycle is $E(z)\sigma_{DDLT} = E(1.5) \times 2000 = 0.0293 \times 2000 = 58.6$. The average number of units short per year will be (58.6 units short/cycle) × (24 order cycles/year) = 1406 units short/year. So

$$SL_d = [(120{,}000 - 1406)/120{,}000] \times 100\% = 98.83\%$$

(Alternatively, SL_d = [1 − (58.6 units short/cycle/5000 units ordered per cycle)] × 100% = 98.83%]. The annual cost of holding the 3000 units of safety stock will be $c_h \times SS$ = \$9.60/year × 3000 = \$28,800. The service level values and safety stock costs for various reorder points are given in Table 13.3.

TABLE 13.3 SERVICE LEVELS FOR VARIOUS REORDER POINTS

RP	SS	SS Cost per Year	z	$E(z)$	Ave. No. Short per Cycle	Ave No. Short per Year	SL_d
15,000	0	\$ 0	0	0.3989	797.8	19,147	84.04%
16,000	1000	\$ 9,600	0.5	0.1978	395.6	9,494	92.09%
17,000	2000	\$19,200	1.0	0.0833	166.6	3,998	96.66%
18,000	3000	\$28,800	1.5	0.0293	58.6	1,406	98.83%
19,000	4000	\$38,400	2.0	0.0085	17.0	408	99.66%
20,000	5000	\$48,000	2.5	0.0020	4.0	96	99.92%

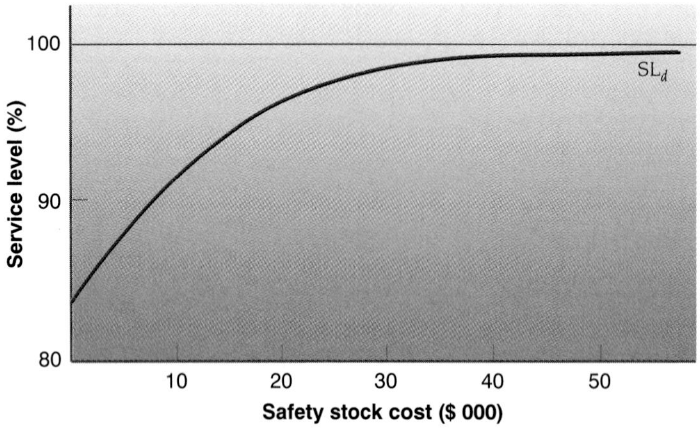

FIGURE 13.11 Demand service level as a function of safety stock cost.

What Is the Best Service Level?

This information allows us to make trade-offs between customer service level and cost without having to assign an explicit cost to shortages. For example, Table 13.3 tells us that for Fastcomp to increase SL_d by 12.62%, from 84.04% to 96.66%, would require 2000 units of safety stock, which would cost $19,200. An additional 3000 units of safety stock, at an additional cost of $28,800, would increase the service level by only 3.26% to 99.92%. Without assigning an explicit cost to stockouts or shortages, we might decide that the extra 12.62% service level is worth $19,200 per year, whereas the additional 3.26% increase is not worth another $28,800. Figure 13.11 illustrates these trade-offs. The concave shape of the curve indicates that there are diminishing marginal benefits to service level from incremental investments in safety stock.

Calculating *DDLT* from *LT* and *D* Distributions

The preceding analysis was based on having a probability distribution for the demand during lead time. In practice, empirical data are sometimes available only for demand and lead time separately. In this case, these two probability distributions must be combined to obtain a distribution for *DDLT*. If the rate of demand, *D*, is normally distributed, with a mean of $\bar{D}$ and a standard deviation of σ_D, and lead time, *LT*, is normally distributed, with a mean of $\overline{LT}$ and a standard deviation of σ_{LT}, and lead time and demand rate *are independent of each other*, then *DDLT* will be normally distributed, with a mean of

$$\overline{DDLT} = \bar{D} \times \overline{LT}$$

and a standard deviation of

$$\sigma_{DDLT} = \sqrt{\overline{LT}\sigma_D^2 + \bar{D}^2\sigma_{LT}^2}$$

where lead time, demand rate, and the corresponding standard deviations must all be in the same time units.

Example 5

Suppose a company's use of a product is normally distributed, with an average rate of 5000 units per month and a standard deviation of 1500 units per month, and the lead time for replenishing its supplies is normally distributed, with an average of 0.8 month and a standard deviation of 0.2 month. Then the demand during lead time for the product is normally distributed, with

$$\overline{DDLT} = 5000 \text{ units/month} \times 0.8 \text{ month} = 4000 \text{ units}$$

$$\sigma_{DDLT} = \sqrt{(0.8 \text{ month}) \times (1500 \text{ units/month})^2 + (5000 \text{ units/month})^2 \times (0.2 \text{ month})^2}$$
$$= 1673.32 \text{ units}$$

SELECTING THE REORDER POINT USING COST ANALYSIS

In those cases where we can accurately estimate the cost of a stockout, we can perform an explicit cost minimization analysis to determine the optimal reorder point and safety stock level. In this section, we will assume that for each unit of product we cannot supply on demand, we incur a stockout cost of c_s. This cost may represent lost profit from a sale, an allowance to the customer for the inconvenience of a delayed delivery, a premium incurred from obtaining the product from an alternative source, or the long-term costs of aggravating or turning away customers.[11]

The following example illustrates a simple analysis we can perform to determine the cost-minimizing reorder point.

Example 6

Consider Example 4 but assume that if Fastcomp runs out of computer chips, it will buy replacement chips from an alternative source for \$85 each. In other words, c_s = \$5 per unit.

We can perform the same analysis as shown in Table 13.3, except that instead of computing the service level for each reorder point, we compute the *average stockout cost per year,* which is simply the average number of units short per year times c_s. The total average cost associated with a safety stock policy is then

total safety stock policy cost/year = average safety stock cost/year + average stockout cost/year

Table 13.4 provides this information for selected reorder points and safety stock levels.

The optimum reorder point is approximately 17,800, with a total cost of \$35,690 per year. (Notice in Table 13.4 that we first searched possible reorder points in increments of 1000. Then, when we saw that the minimum-cost *RP* value was between 17,000 and 19,000, we searched that interval in smaller increments of 200.)

[11] If the cost structure for shortages is different—for example, if orders can be delivered late (backordering) but the cost is a function of the lateness of delivery—explicit cost analyses can still be performed, but these cases are not considered here.

TABLE 13.4 AVERAGE ANNUAL COST FOR VARIOUS REORDER POINTS

RP	*SS*	*SS* Cost/Yr	*z*	*E(z)*	Ave. No. Short/Cycle	Ave. No. Short/Yr.	Ave. SO Cost/Yr	Total Cost/Yr
15,000	0	$ 0	0.0	0.3989	797.8	19,147	$ 95,735	$ 95,735
16,000	1000	$ 9,600	0.5	0.1978	395.6	9,494	$47,470	$57,070
17,000	2000	$ 19,200	1.0	0.0833	166.6	3,998	$ 19,990	$ 39,190
18,000	3000	$28,800	1.5	0.0293	58.6	1,406	$ 7,030	$ 35,830
19,000	4000	$38,400	2.0	0.0085	17.0	408	$ 2,040	$40,440
17,200	2200	$ 21,120	1.1	0.0686	137.2	3,293	$ 16,465	$ 37,585
17,400	2400	$23,040	1.2	0.0561	112.2	2,693	$ 13,465	$ 36,505
17,600	2600	$24,960	1.3	0.0455	91.0	2,184	$ 10,920	$35,880
17,800	2800	$26,880	1.4	0.0367	73.4	1,762	$ 8,810	$ 35,690*
18,000	3000	$28,800	1.5	0.0293	58.6	1,406	$ 7,030	$ 35,830

SO = stockout
* = optimum reorder point (approximate).

These models do not require sophisticated computer systems. This chapter's "In Good Company" profile of Syntex Agribusiness illustrates how significant cost savings can result from developing appropriate but simple safety stock and order quantity policies.

13.9 PERIODIC REVIEW POLICIES

In the previous four sections we developed inventory policies in which the order quantity, Q, was the same for each order cycle, but the *time* when we placed an order could vary according to how quickly our inventory position reached RP; that is, variations in demand and lead time were reflected by *when* we ordered. That analysis was based on the assumption of continuous review of our inventory position. In some cases, such continuous review is not practical or cost effective. Instead, we check the inventory position at regular intervals; that is, we use periodic review. In this case the time between orders is fixed, but the *quantity* ordered in each cycle changes according to the inventory position at the time of review.

Although the cost of reviewing inventory periodically may be less than the cost of reviewing it continuously, a major disadvantage is that it introduces more stockout risk. With a continuous review system, as soon as the inventory position reaches the reorder point, an order is placed. However, with a periodic review system, soon after an order is placed a large surge in demand could deplete inventories dangerously low (or to zero), and the company would not know this until the next review time or until a stockout was reported. Even if an order were placed immediately, the company would be out of stock until a delivery occurred. That is, the company would be vulnerable to a stockout for a period of $T + LT$, where T is the time between reviews. (This is shown in Figure 13.12.) For this reason, a periodic review (fixed order interval) system requires larger safety stocks than a continuous review system in order to achieve the same service level.

To make things simpler, we will assume that only the demand is random, with a normal distribution, and that lead time is constant. In this case, the safety stock required to achieve a given demand service level is

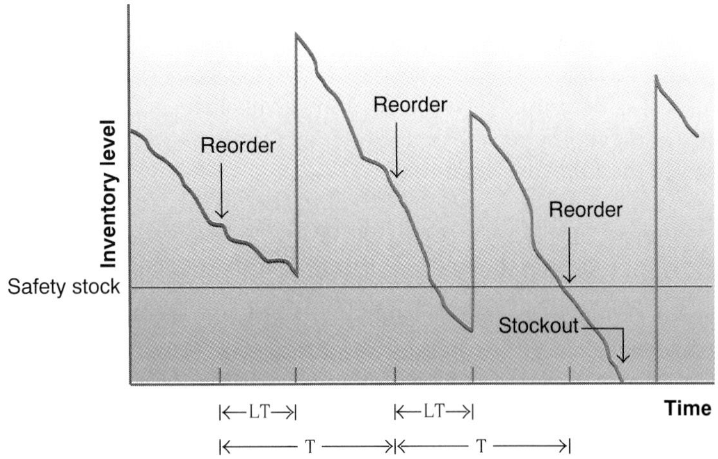

FIGURE 13.12 Inventory pattern for a periodic review policy.

IN GOOD COMPANY

Fine-Tuning Inventory Control at Syntex Agribusiness, Inc.

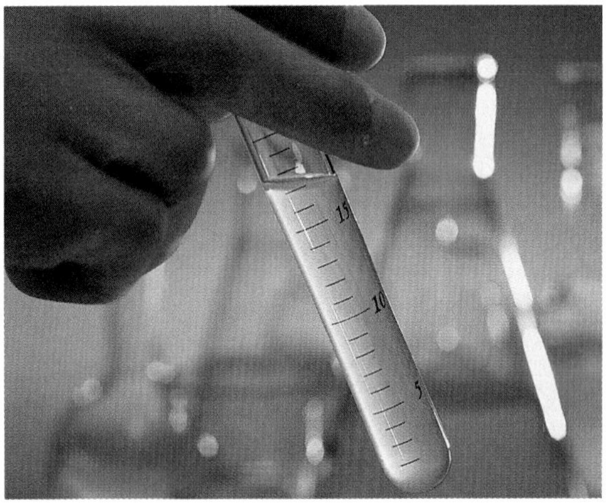

Without using high-priced consultants or complex computerized inventory management systems, the Nutrition and Chemical Division (NCD) of Syntex Agribusiness reduced its raw material inventories by over 65% and total inventories by over 45%. Pharmaceutical companies are especially reluctant to reduce inventories because customers are quick to change suppliers when a shortage occurs. But NCD was able to reduce inventories without jeopardizing its supply reliability by carefully analyzing its sales and establishing systematic ordering, production, and safety stock policies. For each item, minimum and maximum inventory levels were established and monitored regularly. When demand and usage patterns changed, the inventory policies were revised and "dead inventories" of slow-moving items were quickly liquidated.

NCD's success was due to upper management's involvement in and commitment to inventory reduction. Inventory reduction was considered during salary review and job performance evaluation for managers in all departments. For example, the personnel manager was expected to develop training programs that help employees reduce inventories. In addition, Earl Barkley, NCD's vice president and general manager, felt that openness and candor with employees about the need for inventory reduction and the financial facts of the company created the cooperation needed for success.

Source: D. Keith Denton, "Top Management's Role in Inventory Control," *Industrial Engineering*, August 1994, pp. 26–27.

$$\text{safety stock} = z\sigma_{T+LT} \tag{13.8}$$

where z is determined by the desired service level and σ_{T+LT} is the standard deviation of demand over the review period and lead time. The appropriate value of z is the one that solves the following equation:

$$E(z) = [\bar{D}T(1 - SL_d)/\sigma_{T+LT}] \tag{13.9}$$

where $E(z)$ is obtained from Table 13.2, $\bar{D}$ is the average demand rate, and the demand service level, SL_d, is expressed as a proportion rather than a percentage.

At each review point we then place an order for Q units where

$$\begin{aligned} Q &= \text{ave. demand during period } (T + LT) + \text{safety stock} - \text{inventory position} \\ &= \bar{D} \times (T + LT) + z\sigma_{T+LT} - I \end{aligned} \tag{13.10}$$

Notice that the amount we order each time will vary, depending on the inventory position at the time the order is placed.

EXAMPLE 7

Suppose the weekly demand for a company's product is normally distributed, with a mean of $\bar{D} = 20$ units and a standard deviation of $\sigma_D = 5$ units; the lead time for acquiring the product is two weeks, and the company would like to achieve a 96% demand service level. The company reviews its inventory every four weeks, and at its most recent review the inventory position was 50 units. How much should the company order?

To answer this question, we first need to compute the necessary safety stock. The standard deviation of demand during the time $T + LT$, σ_{T+LT}, is the square root of the sum of the *variances* for each week:

$$\sigma_{T+LT} = \sqrt{(T + LT)\sigma_D^2} = \sqrt{(4 + 2)(5^2)} = 12.25 \text{ units}$$

We can now solve equation (13.9) to obtain z.

$$E(z) = [\bar{D}T(1 - SL_d)/\sigma_{T+LT}] = [(20)(4)(1 - 0.96)]/[12.25] = 0.261$$

We now find the value of z in Table 13.2 with $E(z)$ approximately 0.261; using interpolation, the value for z is approximately $z = 0.32$. Putting this value into Equation (13.10), the order quantity is

$$Q = \bar{D}(T + LT) + z\sigma_{T+LT} - I = (20)(4 + 2) + (0.32)(12.25) - 50 = 73.92 \text{ units}$$

By ordering 74 units, we can expect to satisfy 96% of the anticipated demand on time during the next order cycle. (Notice that the safety stock is (0.32)(12.25) = 3.92 units.)

Although periodic review policies are still used, they are becoming less common because the proliferation of optical scanning and computer capabilities makes continuous review of inventories affordable. However, even companies that maintain continuous review of their inventories sometimes use a fixed-interval ordering policy (ordering different amounts of product but at regular time intervals) in order to combine orders with the same vendor. Combining orders produces tremendous cost savings. Methods for doing this in a nearly optimal manner can be found in many advanced inventory management books.

13.10 ONE-PERIOD MODELS

Some products are extremely perishable. For example, a newspaper has value the day it is issued, but its value drops to nearly zero the next day; old news is not worth much. Similarly, calendars for the next year are valuable in December but their value drops considerably by the end of January, and fashionable lines of clothing are valuable when they are first introduced but go out of style quickly. In these cases, the problem of deciding how much of a perishable product to order or make can be modeled as a one-period inventory problem because we usually make a single purchase (or production run) of the product to last throughout its sales life.

The primary characteristics of a one-period inventory problem are as follows:

One-period inventory models can be very helpful to producers, wholesalers, and retailers of highly perishable products such as flowers.

1. The company must acquire units of the product at some cost, c, at some point in time. After this time, additional items cannot be acquired during the relevant planning period.
2. During the period that begins with the time of ordering, customers purchase the product at some price, $p > c$. The number of units demanded by customers during the period, D, is a random variable with a cumulative probability distribution, $F(d)$; that is, $F(d)$ = probability (demand $\leq d$) for any value of d.
3. At the end of the period, unsold units of the product have a salvage value of $s < c$; s may be equal to zero or even negative in some cases.

The company must determine how many units, Q, of the product to acquire at the beginning of the period. Every unit of the product that the company acquires and successfully resells produces a profit of $p - c$. However, any unit that the company acquires and is unable to sell during the period must be liquidated at a loss of $c - s$. As the company increases the value of Q, the chance of having customer demands unsatisfied goes down; that is, a profit of $p - c$ is likely to occur from more customers on average. On the other hand, a larger value of Q also increases the average number of units that are likely to be unsold (called the **overage**) at a loss of $c - s$. (Notice that in one-period models the quantity Q directly determines the service level provided to customers.)

To determine which value of Q is best, we have to identify the criterion to be used to evaluate alternatives. The most common one is to *maximize the expected value of profit* (*average long-term profit*). (This is not the only criterion possible, however, as will be discussed later.) With expected profit maximization as our objective, we can determine the best value of Q using the following intuitive process. We begin with Q set equal to the lowest demand possible. Then we iteratively increase the value of Q by a unit; each time, we compute the additional expected profit that would result from the higher expected sales and the higher expected loss that would result from the higher expected overage. We keep increasing Q as long as the additional expected profit gain exceeds the additional expected overage loss. We stop increasing Q further if these two values are equal or if the additional expected loss would exceed the additional expected gain.

OPTIMAL ORDER QUANTITY: CONTINUOUS DEMAND DISTRIBUTION

The only technical issue in finding the optimal order quantity, Q^*, is calculating the expected gains and losses from increasing Q. Suppose Q is set at some value $\hat{Q}$, and suppose that the probability distribution for D is a continuous distribution. If we increase Q by an incrementally small amount, the probability that the additional amount will be sold is

$$\text{probability (demand} > \hat{Q}) = 1 - \text{probability (demand} \leq \hat{Q}) = 1 - F(\hat{Q})$$

and a profit of $p - c$ per unit will be earned on the additional sales. Thus, the additional expected or average gain from ordering a little more is $(p - c)(1 - F(\hat{Q}))$ per unit. The probability that the additional amount ordered is *not* sold is

$$\text{probability (demand} \leq \hat{Q}) = F(\hat{Q})$$

and a loss of $c - s$ per unit will be incurred for the additional amount ordered. The expected loss from the additional amount is $(c - s)F(\hat{Q})$ per unit. As long as

$$(p - c)(1 - F(\hat{Q})) \geq (c - s)F(\hat{Q}) \qquad (13.11)$$

we should increase Q incrementally, and if inequality (13.11) does not hold, we should stop increasing Q. The optimal order quantity, Q^*, is the value that makes (13.11) hold as an equality:

$$(p - c)(1 - F(Q^*) = (c - s)F(Q^*)$$
$$\rightarrow \quad p - c - pF(Q^*) + cF(Q^*) = cF(Q^*) - sF(Q^*)$$
$$\rightarrow \quad p - c = (p - s)F(Q^*)$$

then Q^* is the quantity such that

$$F(Q^*) = (p - c)/(p - s) \qquad (13.12)$$

The expression $(p - c)/(p - s)$ is referred to as the **critical probability**. Because $F(Q^*)$ is the probability that demand will be less than or equal to Q^*, $F(Q^*)$ is the probability that no shortage will occur; in this sense, $F(Q^*)$ can be thought of as the *optimal service level*. Equation (13.12) implies that the order quantity should be selected so that there is a $1 - [(p - c)/(p - s)]$ probability of having a shortage during the period.

EXAMPLE 8

Thirst Quencher, Inc. (TQI), sells lemonade in city parks during the summer. TQI mixes a new batch of lemonade each morning. Once the TQI truck goes to the park, it is not feasible for it to return to its mixing facility to pick up more lemonade. TQI has determined that it costs $2.50 per gallon to make lemonade; it sells the lemonade in variously sized cups at an average price of $6 per gallon. Any lemonade that is not sold by the end of the day loses its fresh taste and is sold to a canned juice producer at a price of $1 per gallon. The demand for juice is approximately a continuous uniform distribution between 30 and 80 gallons per day (its probability density function is given in Figure 13.13). TQI wants to determine the amount of lemonade to produce each morning to maximize long-term profit.

The *cumulative* distribution for lemonade is given by

$$F(d) = \begin{cases} 0 & \text{for } d < 30 \text{ gallons} \\ 0.02(d - 30) & \text{for } 30 \leq d \leq 80 \\ 1 & \text{for } d > 80 \end{cases}$$

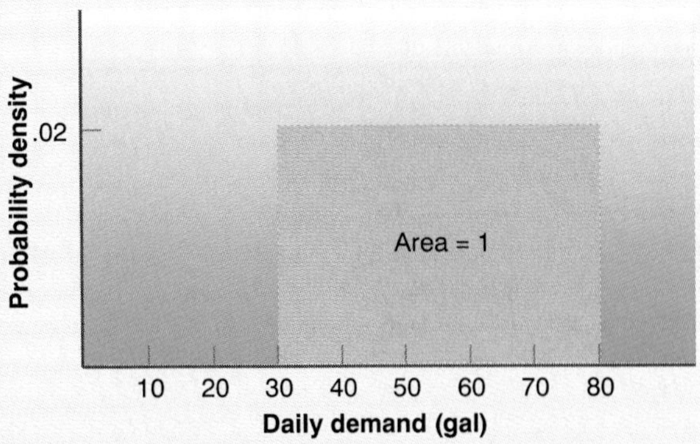

FIGURE 13.13 Continuous uniform demand function for TQI.

The critical probability is

$$(p - c)/(p - s) = (6.0 - 2.50)/(6.0 - 1.0) = 0.70$$

So the optimal value of Q is the one that satisfies equation (13.12):

$$F(Q^*) = 0.02(Q^* - 30) = 0.70$$

or

$$0.02Q^* - 0.60 = 0.70 \rightarrow Q^* = 65$$

TQI will maximize its daily expected profit, which will be computed later, by producing 65 gallons of lemonade each morning. Notice that on 30% of the days, TQI will run out of lemonade before the end of the day.

OPTIMAL ORDER QUANTITY: DISCRETE DEMAND DISTRIBUTION

More commonly, the probability distribution for demand is expressed as a discrete distribution with a finite number of possible demand levels; this distribution is usually based on historical data. Let p_i be the probability that demand during the period is d_i, where $d_1 < d_2 < \ldots < d_n$. Then the cumulative probability can be computed for any demand level d_j by

$$F(d_j) = \text{probability (demand} \le d_j) = \sum_{i=1}^{j} p_i$$

The same strategy can be used to find Q^* that was used for a continuous demand distribution. The only complication is that with a discrete demand distribution there may be no value of Q such that inequality (13.11) holds as an equality. This is the case in the following example.

EXAMPLE 9

A bookstore sells a type of artistic calendar each year. Because these calendars are specially printed by the publisher, the bookstore must order them in September. After this date, additional calendars cannot be obtained. The calendars cost $5 each from the

TABLE 13.5 DEMAND FOR CALENDARS, NOVEMBER–JANUARY

Demand	Prob (d)	F(d)
100	0.10	0.10
110	0.10	0.20
120	0.20	0.40
130	0.10	0.50
140	0.10	0.60
150	0.15	0.75
160	0.10	0.85
170	0.10	0.95
180	0.05	1.00

publisher. The bookstore resells them from November through January at \$10 each. Any calendars not sold by January 31 are sold at a clearance price of \$2 each. From historical data, the bookstore estimates that the demand for these calendars from November 1 to January 31 is given by Table 13.5.

The critical probability for this problem is

$$(p-c)/(p-s) = (10-5)/(10-2) = 0.625$$

Notice that no level of demand has a cumulative probability exactly equal to 0.625.

It can be proved that it would never be advantageous to order an amount other than some d_i amount; that is, Q^* should always equal some level of demand that has a positive probability of occurring. The previous incremental analysis indicates that it is clearly advantageous to make Q at least 140. The question is whether it is worthwhile to increase Q to 150. If we purchase an additional 10 calendars, the expected gain from selling the additional units is

(profit from selling an additional 10 units) × (probability of selling an additional 10 units)

$$= 10(p-c) \times (1 - F(140) = 10(10-5)\ (1-0.60) = \$20$$

Similarly, the expected loss from additional overage is

$$10\ (c-s)\ F(140) = 10(5-2)\ (0.60) = \$18$$

So there is a net expected gain of \$2 by purchasing the additional 10 units. The optimal order quantity is $Q^* = 150$. (It can be proved that the additional expected gain from increasing Q beyond 150 is less than the additional expected loss.)

The result in Example 9 can be generalized to any one-period problem by the following rule, which holds for both continuous and discrete demand distributions.

Rule for Finding Q^*: Q^* equals the *smallest* value of d (level of demand) such that $F(Q^*) \geq (p-c)/(p-s)$.

When the distribution for demand is continuous, this rule reduces to satisfying equation (13.12). Notice that for a discrete demand distribution, we should not simply select the demand level with the cumulative probability that is closest to the critical value. Had we done this in the previous example, Q would have equaled 140, which we showed was not optimal.

COMPUTING THE EXPECTED PROFIT

In addition to determining the optimal number of units to make or purchase, a company wants to know the amount of profit it could expect to earn using the optimal policy. Because demand is random, the amount of profit the company will earn during *any given period* is random. In the preceding example, if the bookstore ordered 150 calendars, the profit that would occur depends on the actual demand. If the demand were only 100, then the bookstore would sell 100 calendars at a profit of \$5 each and would have 50 calendars left over, on which it would lose \$3 each, for a net profit of

$$(\$5/\text{calendar} \times 100 \text{ calendars}) - (\$3/\text{calendar} \times 50 \text{ calendars}) = \$350$$

If instead the demand were 180 calendars, the bookstore would sell only 150 (it can sell only as many as it bought) at a profit of \$5 each, and it would have none left over; this produces a profit of \$750. The expected (average) profit from the calendars is simply the sum of the profits that would occur at each possible level of demand times the probability of that demand level occurring:

$$\text{Expected profit} = \sum_i [\text{prob}(\text{demand} = d_i) \times (\text{profit if demand} = d_i)] \qquad (13.13)$$

$$\begin{aligned} &= 0.1[(\$5)(100) - (\$3)(50)] + 0.1[(\$5)(110) - (\$3)(40)] + \\ &\quad 0.2[(\$5)(120) - (\$3)(30)] + 0.1[(\$5)(130) - (\$3)(20)] + \\ &\quad 0.1[(\$5)(140) - (\$3)(10)] + 0.4[(\$5)(150)] = \$606 \end{aligned}$$

Notice that we combined the demand outcomes of 150, 160, 170, and 180 because in each case 150 calendars will be sold and the same profit produced.

When the demand distribution is continuous, as it was in Example 8, the expected profit is harder to compute because an infinite number of demand levels are possible (any real number between 30 and 80 gallons). If TQI makes 65 gallons of lemonade each day and if the demand level, d, occurs, the profit will be

$$[\$3.50/\text{gal} \times d] - [\$1.50/\text{gal} \times (65 - d)] = 5d - \$97.50 \qquad \text{if } d \le 65$$

and

$$\$3.50/\text{gal} \times 65 \text{ gal} = \$227.50 \qquad \text{if } d \ge 65$$

The expected profit can be approximated by converting the continuous distribution into a discrete one and using the previous method; for example, we might assume that daily demand can be 30.5, 31.5, . . . , 79.5 gallons. To obtain an exact answer, integral calculus must be used, which is beyond the scope of this book; however, as a matter of interest, the optimal profit for the TQI example is \$166.25.[12]

---

[12]For a continuous distribution we need to weight the profit from each demand level by the *density function* value rather than the probability and then sum across an uncountably infinite number of demand levels; this latter operation means performing mathematical integration. For the demand distribution in the TQI example, the density function is

$$\begin{aligned} f(d) &= 0.02 \quad \text{for } 30 \le d \le 80 \\ &= 0 \quad \text{otherwise} \end{aligned}$$

For TQI the expected daily profit is

$$\int_{30}^{65} [(\$5\,d - \$97.50)\,0.02] + \int_{65}^{80} \$227.50\,(0.02)$$

$$\begin{aligned} &= (0.02)[2.5d^2 - 97.50d]_{30}^{65} + (0.02)[227.50d]_{65}^{80} \\ &= (0.02)[4900] + (0.02)[3412.5] \\ &= \$166.25 \end{aligned}$$

THE EVALUATION CRITERION

The preceding discussion was based on the assumption that the company wanted to *maximize expected profit*. In most cases this is a reasonable assumption. For example, if a company such as TQI in Example 8 faces the same type of risk repeatedly, then days of small demand and small profit will be balanced out by days of large demand and large profit, so that the expected profit represents a long-run average.

However, in some cases maximizing expected profit is not appropriate; the form and extent of risk are important. For example, suppose an aircraft leasing company must decide how many airplanes to buy for later lease. If it buys 100 planes, it believes there is a 60% chance that it will earn $500 million and a 40% chance that it will lose $200 million, for an expected profit of (0.6)($500 million) + (0.4)(–$200 million) = $220 million. If it buys only 60 airplanes, it believes there is a 95% chance that it will earn $200 million, and a 5% chance that it will lose $20 million for an expected profit of $189 million. Although the first option has a higher expected profit, the company might prefer the second one because it has a smaller probability of a loss and a smaller maximum possible loss. This would be especially true if the company would be forced into bankruptcy if a large loss (say, more than $50 million) occurred. When maximizing expected profit is not an appropriate objective, decision analysis methods that incorporate risk preferences should be used.

FLEXIBLE SPENDING ACCOUNTS: A PERSONAL FINANCIAL APPLICATION

The one-period inventory model has many obvious applications in business. However, it can also be of great value on a personal basis for many people working in the United States. Under current U.S. tax laws (as of 1995), companies are allowed to establish **flexible spending accounts** to allow employees to pay child-care and medical expenses. If a company establishes such a plan, the plan must follow these rules: by December 31 an employee must state whether he or she wishes to create a flexible spending account for child-care expenses, medical expenses, or both, and if so, how much money is to be taken from the employee's paycheck and put into each account (medical and child-care accounts are separate) the following year. This declaration is irreversible; the amount of withholding cannot be changed until the following year. The employer deducts the appropriate amount of money from the employee's paycheck and holds it in these accounts. Salary and wages placed in these accounts *are not subject to federal income and Social Security taxes or to state incomes taxes in most states*. Whenever an eligible child-care or medical expense occurs, the employee can be reimbursed from these accounts for the amount spent.

If, at the end of the year, unused funds in the accounts were returned to the employee, deciding how much to put in the accounts would be easy: withhold the maximum amount allowed, because this would maximize after-tax income. The problem, however, is that any unused funds in the accounts are forfeited. Because of this risk of losing unused funds, most brochures advising employees on how much to withhold each year typically recommend the overly conservative strategy of withholding only the amount that the employee feels certain he or she will use. This strategy is suboptimal with respect to maximizing long-term after-tax income.

Rosenfield recognized that this problem is essentially a one-period inventory problem with the following equivalences:[13]

Q = the amount of pay to have withheld in the flexible spending account

d = the random amount of eligible expenses incurred during the year

---

[13] D. B. Rosenfield, "Optimal Management of Tax-Sheltered Employee Reimbursement Programs," *Interfaces*, Vol. 16., No. 3, 1986, pp. 68–72.

$F(d)$ = the cumulative probability distribution for eligible expenses (this would be estimated by the employee)

Using the same incremental analysis used to derive the optimal order quantity, the optimal amount of pay to have withheld, Q^*, to maximize long-term after-tax income is the following:

Q^* is the smallest value of d such that $F(Q^*) \geq t$

where t is the total effective marginal tax rate.[14]

So, if the effective marginal tax rate is 30% ($t = 0.30$), the employee should withhold enough money so that there is a 30% chance of not using it all. Psychologically this may be difficult to accept, but it does indeed maximize expected after-tax income. Because one can often control the timing of some medical expenses (e.g., when to buy new eyeglasses), an employee can even be more aggressive by moving some expenses ahead into the current year or back to the following year, depending on whether any money is left in the medical benefits account in the current year. For a typical employee, the optimal approach could produce hundreds of dollars per year of additional after-tax income compared to the conservative approach.

13.11 IMPLEMENTING INVENTORY MANAGEMENT SYSTEMS

Each of the models presented so far carries the implicit assumption that the necessary data are available and the implicit suggestion that we should use as sophisticated a model as necessary to minimize material and inventory-related costs. In reality the data are not always available, and we must weigh the time and costs of data gathering and model development against the potential benefits to be gained from more precise data and more sophisticated models. In addition, for a company such as Air Canada, which stocks 140,000 different parts, it may be cost effective to develop sophisticated inventory systems to manage some materials, but not all 140,000. Finally, it is often impractical to implement an improved inventory control system for all materials used by a company at one time; we must prioritize our efforts.

[14]This rate would combine federal, state, and local taxes that are avoided through the flexible plan. This would *not* be simply the sum of the marginal tax rates because state and local taxes are deductible from federal taxes and federal taxes are often deductible from state and local taxes. The formula combining these rates can be obtained from the author.

Air Canada uses sophisticated computer-based systems to manage the most important items (typically the "A" and "B" category items) in its 140,000-parts inventory.

ABC CLASSIFICATION OF ITEMS AND THE PARETO PRINCIPLE

In the nineteenth century, the Italian economist Vilfredo Pareto discovered empirically that wealth is maldistributed; for example, 80% of a nation's wealth is typically owned by less than 20% of the population (and therefore, less than 20% of the nation's wealth is owned by 80% of the population). This concept of maldistribution, called the **Pareto principle**, has been applied in several aspects of management. Specifically, the management version of this principle states that a few large problems or issues an organization encounters have a large effect on its performance, whereas a large number of small problems or issues have a small impact. Therefore, managers should categorize problem areas so that they spend most of their time working on the important few problems and only minimal time on the unimportant many. With respect to inventory management, we should focus on those items that have the largest impact on total inventory-related costs; normally, these are the ones on which we spend the most money annually.[15]

Suppose we computed the total amount we spend each year on each item used by the company (or the total sales of each good the company sells). Table 13.6 lists the annual monetary usage (defined as the number of units used times the item's price) of 11 items used by a typical firm. The items are listed in decreasing order of monetary value usage.

Two of the 11 items (18%) account for 66% of the material costs, whereas the remaining 9 items (C–K) account for only 34% of these costs. Also, six of the items (55%) account for less than 5% of the material costs. This pattern is typical for most organizations. In Figure 13.14 we have plotted the cumulative *monetary value* as a percentage of the total monetary value of all items used versus the *cumulative number of item types* as a percentage of the total number of item types.

The data in Table 13.6 and Figure 13.14 can be used to classify items using an **ABC classification** system. Items are divided into three categories according to their impact on the organization, as illustrated in Figure 13.14. Items in category A account for a small number of the item *types* but have a large cumulative *monetary* impact. Normally, category A items account for 10–20% of the item types and 60–80% of the total value of

[15]The Pareto principle is used extensively in quality management; most quality problems occur in a few departments or processes, or have a few causes, so we focus our attention on these.

TABLE 13.6 ANNUAL $ USAGE OF ITEMS FOR A TYPICAL FIRM

Item Name	No. Used/Yr	$ Cost/Unit	$ Usage/Yr	$ Usage/Total	Cum. $ Usage/ Total $ Usage
A	500,000	20.00	10,000,000	.413	.413
B	40,000	150.00	6,000,000	.248	.661
C	120,000	30.00	3,600,000	.149	.810
D	50,000	50.00	2,500,000	.103	.913
E	70,000	15.00	1,050,000	.043	.956
F	20,000	25.00	500,000	.021	.977
G	40,000	7.50	300,000	.012	.989
H	5,000	35.00	175,000	.007	.996
I	6,000	12.00	72,000	.003	.999
J	2,000	9.00	18,000	.001	1.000
K	200	60.00	12,000	.000	1.000
Total			24,227,000	1.000	

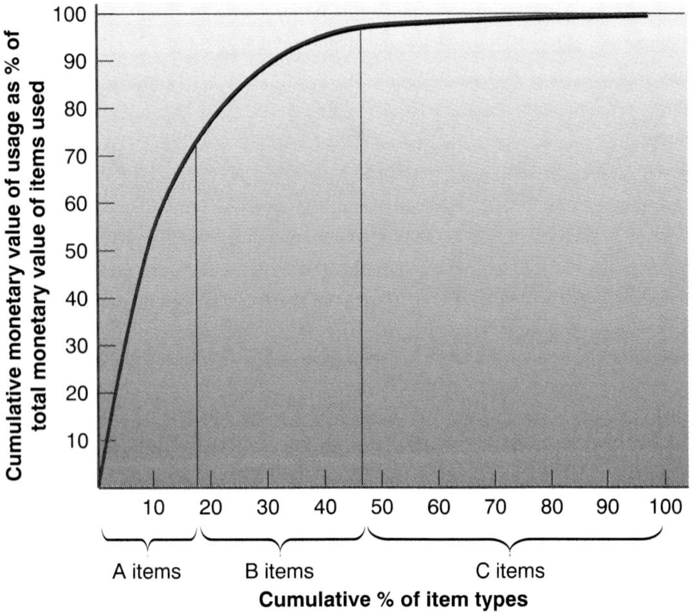

FIGURE 13.14 ABC classification of inventory items.

all items used. Category C items are those that have a small impact on the firm's material costs. Normally, these account for 50–60% of the item *types* but only 5–10% of the *material costs*. The remaining items are classified as type B items, which constitute 20–40% of the items and 15–30% of the total cost.

It is usually most cost effective to devote our initial effort and our greatest attention to the few items in category A; a small percentage reduction in their inventory costs has a large impact on the organization. Inventory management systems for category A items may include a demand forecasting module, a real-time inventory tracking module, and sophisticated ordering rules. In contrast, we often use simpler, lower-cost methods (such as the two-bin system discussed below) to control the inventories of category C items because even substantial reductions in inventory costs for these items will produce only small overall savings. Category B items receive an intermediate amount of attention once the inventories of type A items are under control.

DATA REQUIREMENTS

An essential component of any materials management system is accurate, timely inventory records. Often the number of units reported in inventory by the inventory records differs from the actual number. When this difference is very small relative to the expected number in inventory, the harm done may be minimal. But for many items, errors of even 1% or 2% can cause costly stockouts of critical components. Consequently, the American Production and Inventory Control Society (APICS) recommends accuracy levels for inventories of ±0.2% for A items, ±1% for B items, and ±5% for C items.

Causes of Inaccuracy

Although advances in computerized inventory systems have eliminated some of the clerical mistakes that reduce inventory accuracy, discrepancies can still occur in many ways. Obviously, an open stockroom makes it easy for people to remove items from inventory without recording the withdrawal; even when the item is used for legitimate purposes, a discrepancy results. Other causes include the following: (1) orders are recorded as received when they have not been or vice versa; (2) the number or type of items received in a delivery do not match what was ordered, and the difference is not recognized; (3) items withdrawn from inventory may later be returned but not recorded (e.g., a mechanic may withdraw two sizes of a part to fix a machine and then return the one that does not fit); (4) items may be stored in the wrong place—even though they exist, they are not of use because they cannot be found.

These and other types of errors can be costly, and they present opportunities for improvement. For example, Leviton Manufacturing estimated that it saves $300,000 a year from improvements it has made in inventory accuracy.[16] But how can inventory accuracy be improved?

Maintaining Inventory Accuracy

To achieve inventory accuracy, several steps are necessary. First, access to inventories must be controlled, and deliveries to and withdrawals from inventory must be recorded accurately. This may require using closed storerooms. With this system, only storeroom workers can accept or disperse materials, and they are responsible for inventory record accuracy. In this case, it is essential that storeroom employees be trained and motivated to record all transactions accurately. In fact, a major cause of inventory inaccuracy is the failure of storeroom workers to record, or to physically count the number of units in, an order received or a withdrawal of items.

Closed storerooms can be effective for controlling expensive spare parts inventories or for raw materials that can be stored in a separate location until needed by the production process. However, work-in-process inventories and final products usually cannot be locked up after every stage of production; to keep the production process operating smoothly, these usually must be kept in open areas. One way to maintain an accurate record of the amount and location of inventories is to use bar coding and optical scanning technology. When materials enter the production system a bar-coded sticker can be attached to them (e.g., a sticker placed on each box or pallet load) indicating the type and number of items. The bar code is scanned at each work station or department as it moves through the production process, and the information is relayed to a central computer. Changes in the information would be recorded as well. For example, 20,000 cardboard cartons might enter a folding and gluing machine, but only 19,721 may be successfully processed, the rest being scrapped for quality problems or after being damaged during production. This way, accurate information on the amount and location of materials is available on a continuous basis. (This information can also be helpful in determining the true costs and required time to produce various products.)

Even with the best monitoring systems, it is still necessary to make a physical count of inventories on a regular basis to reconcile differences between inventory records and actual inventory amounts. The traditional approach has been to devote a few days (or longer) each year to counting all items in inventory at one time. Even though this is often done on weekends to reduce disruption of operations, disruption still often occurs because the process puts a large strain on employees, who work long hours under pressure doing a job they are not trained to do.

An alternative approach is to use **cycle counting** of inventories. With this method, all items are counted on a rotating basis. For example, each month 1/12th of the company's items may be physically counted. This reduces disruptions and even makes it

---

[16] Harry Meyer, "Inventory Accuracy—Is It Worth It? A Case Study," *Production and Inventory Management Journal*, 2nd Quarter 1990, pp. 15–17.

possible (and in many cases more efficient) to have permanent staff devoted to physical counting and reconciliation of inventory records. Cycle counting also makes it easier to develop counting strategies that give differential attention to items according to their importance. For example, counting cycles can be designed so that A items are counted more often (say, two or four times per year) than C items. Cycle counting can also be made more efficient by selecting items to count during a cycle using the following guidelines:

1. Count items when inventory records show a small quantity in stock, thereby reducing the number of objects to count.
2. Count items when inventory records show a positive level but a stockout is reported.
3. Count items after an unusually large amount of inventory activity (receipts and withdrawals) for that item.

Modern computerized inventory management systems can be designed to signal when these conditions exist and to prepare cycle counting plans. Air Canada found that computer-generated cycle counting plans provided more efficient and disciplined counts and improved its inventory accuracy.[17]

Usage, Lead Time, and Cost Data

Most companies maintain accurate quarterly and annual sales and usage data because these are necessary for basic financial reports. However, for inventory management purposes, accurate information about monthly and even daily rates of demand and usage may be needed. Especially important for determining the correct reorder point and amount of safety stock is to know the amount of variation in the demand pattern. Similarly, accurate lead-time data, both averages and variances, are needed to establish good safety stock policies. This requires that the purchasing and accounting system be designed to record accurately the time an order is placed and the time it is received. This can be much more difficult than it appears. For example, we might think that we can simply compare the dates on the purchase order and the receiving document indicating that the material was received. Unfortunately, it is not uncommon for purchase orders to be prepared and dated but held for a few days before being sent, or for a phone order to be placed and a written purchase order prepared and sent several days later with a different date; each case can cause inaccurate lead times. Electronic transmission of purchase orders can help reduce these discrepancies, but training and motivation are still essential. Employees must be convinced of the importance of recording accurate data.

Estimating the fixed ordering cost and the per unit holding cost for items requires detailed accounting analysis beyond the scope of this book. But it is important to separate fixed and variable costs of product shipments, processing purchase orders, and checking the accuracy of shipments. In addition, less visible costs of storing inventories, such as damage, obsolescence, material handling, and space that is shared with other business functions, should be included in estimating the holding cost. As mentioned in Section 13.5, cost estimates only have to be within 20–30% of the actual values for the EOQ models to be useful, but in some cases obtaining even this degree of accuracy may be a challenge.

---

[17]See Reg Rees, "Smooth Landing at Air Canada for 140,000 Aircraft Parts," *Industrial Engineering*, June 1994, pp. 28–29.

THE TWO-BIN SYSTEM

Inventory accuracy is especially important for continuous review systems so that orders are placed when the reorder point is reached. For small items, a simple way of identifying when the reorder point has been reached is to use a **two-bin system** for storage. In this system, units of a product are literally stored in two bins; the first bin holds a number of units equal to the reorder point quantity, and the second bin holds the remainder. Items are withdrawn from the second bin until it is empty. When the last item is withdrawn from the second bin, this is a signal to place an order; until delivery is received, items are drawn from the first bin.

Distinct storage bins are not necessary to make this system work. For example, retail stores sometimes stock the "first bin" items upside down and the "second bin" items in front of them right side up. This way an employee can simply walk down the aisle and see if the right-side-up items are all gone, signaling that an order should be placed.

PURCHASING POLICIES AND SOLE VERSUS MULTIPLE SOURCING

Chapter 5 discussed in detail how suppliers can assist customers in designing products that use the most cost-effective components. Chapter 15 will discuss in detail the importance of the link between suppliers and customers needed to operate JIT production systems. In this subsection, we focus specifically on the number of suppliers to use.

For years many U.S. companies have followed the policy of using several different suppliers for the major components they purchase. Companies regularly ask for new price bids from suppliers. Then they allocate purchases to them based on their prices and on historical service and quality performance. This approach supposedly utilizes competition to keep prices down and service up. Because those companies with the lowest price and best quality will receive more business, they will work hard to be more efficient.

In some cases this system works as intended, but frequently more harm than good results. First, this purchasing approach often becomes one in which purchasing decisions are based almost entirely on price. The result is that suppliers devote little effort to improving product quality as long as the quality is adequate enough to keep the contract. In addition, there is little incentive to make product or process innovations. Because demand is not guaranteed for the long term and because the supplier may be receiving only a fraction of the customer's business, the supplier has little incentive (or financial resources) to enhance or customize its production for that customer. In many cases, a significant investment in specialized equipment or rearranged production facilities could reduce the cost or improve the quality of a supplier's product, but the supplier will not take that risk if there is a chance that a few months later some other supplier will undercut its price and steal the business.

In recent years, companies have found that there are substantial benefits from establishing a long-term **sole-supplier (sole-sourcing)** relationship with vendors. By offering a supplier all of the customer's purchases of an item for the next three to five years, the customer can insist on guarantees of reliable delivery, high quality, stable or decreasing prices, and a share in productivity improvements. Because of the high guaranteed volume and long-term commitment, the supplier can undertake production changes, invest in improvements, participate with the customer in product design and production process enhancements, and in general devote special attention to that customer. In fact, a supplier may even recommend that the customer *not* buy a product when the supplier is confident that it will receive future purchases. For example, Bailey Controls persuaded a major customer not to buy one of its control consoles because a better one would soon be available. Bailey's senior vice president, Gabe Rosica, says, "If

Xerox has reduced its costs and simplified its purchasing system by reducing the number of suppliers it uses by more than 50%.

this was a competitive bid, I would never have raised the issue and jeopardized getting the order, but because this was a partnership alliance, there was no risk."[18]

Not only can a company benefit from making all purchases of an item from one or two suppliers, it can also benefit from buying several different items from one supplier rather than using a separate supplier for each item. This reduces the total number of suppliers with whom the company must interact, which can substantially reduce the administrative costs of purchasing. Furthermore, by combining orders of different items from the same supplier, the company can obtain economies of scale in purchasing and shipping, and often suppliers will provide greater quantity discounts. A number of companies, such as Xerox, Motorola, Ford, and General Motors, have reduced the number of suppliers they use by 50–90% or more.

Although long-term sole sourcing has many benefits, this should not be viewed as a universally superior approach. Sometimes a company may benefit from having two or three suppliers of a component. For example, a supply disruption caused by a strike or natural disaster (such as the 1995 Kobe, Japan, earthquake) can shut down a company if it has no other ready supplier. A company must consider carefully the use of sole sourcing for each of its items as well as the long-term effects, not just the short-term price.

MATERIALS AND THE ENVIRONMENT

Decisions regarding the materials a company purchases, as well as the materials it disposes, can have a significant impact on the environment and on the company's profits. Recycling of materials such as paper, aluminum, and glass has received considerable attention in recent years. But simply increasing the supply of recycled materials does not solve the environmental problem; we must also be willing to purchase recycled and recyclable materials. In the past, buying recycled materials such as paper often meant paying a price premium for a lower-quality product. But recycling technology has improved to the point where many recycled materials are no more expensive, and often less so, than original materials. When companies buy recycled materials, they not only provide an outlet for the supply, but the larger volume promotes even more cost-effective recycling technologies. For example, the cost of making tissue paper, newsprint, and many forms of cardboard using recycled paper is now essentially the same as that using virgin wood fibers. So McDonald's decision to buy over $200 million a year of paper products made from recycled paper is a sound economic as well as environmental decision.

Companies can contribute to improving the environment by purchasing products made from recycled materials. Because of improvements in technology, many recycled products are now of equal quality and price as products made from virgin materials.

An entire industry has started in recycling computer components. Until the late 1980s, old computers (especially mainframes) were simply dumped in landfills. But, says Michael Filandro, president of Texas Recycling and Refining, Inc., "After a million years or so and a couple nuclear blasts, old computers are biodegradable in landfills—but not before then."[19] Therefore, several companies now buy used computers, salvage the parts, and sell them for use either as replacement parts or in the assembly of new computers. One computer recycler claims that once it has dismantled a computer, as little as 3% of it goes to a landfill. Part of the success of computer component recycling involves finding the right markets for reused components. Many components are used to manufacture low-priced computers that are sold in less developed countries, where a computer with a recycled 386 chip is quite valuable.

Finally, purchasing *reusable* materials eliminates the entire recycling process. For example, Chrysler saved $9 million a year by switching from using cardboard boxes to

[18]From Myron Magnet, "The New Golden Rule of Business," *Fortune*, Feb. 21, 1994, pp. 60–64.

[19]From Timothy Aeppel, "For Recycler, Old Computers Offer New Niche," *Wall Street Journal*, Aug. 24, 1994.

hold parts to reusable containers.[20] Clearly, materials management involves much more than simply deciding how much to buy and when to buy; the initial question should be what to buy.

SUMMARY

- **Inventories** are any materials held for future use.
- Inventories are held (1) to increase operating efficiency, (2) to provide quick response to customers, (3) to protect against normal business risks, and (4) to take advantage of or protect against unusual events.
- **Cycling inventories** are those that increase and decrease in a planned way to achieve economic efficiency. **Safety stocks** are inventories held as protection against normal variations in demand, usage, or lead time.
- The more **safety stock** a company holds, the less chance of a stockout occurring, the higher the service level, and the lower the stockout costs but the higher the costs of holding the safety stocks.
- In addition to explicit costs of inventories, such as the opportunity costs of capital, spoilage, and insurance, inventories create other costs by hiding fundamental operating problems.
- **Continuous (perpetual) review policies** for inventory are normally based on ordering the same quantity in each reorder cycle whenever the inventory position reaches a preestablished reorder point. **Periodic review policies** are designed to place orders at fixed time periods, but the quantity ordered varies according to the inventory position.
- **Economic order quantity (EOQ) models** compute the optimal number of units to order with a continuous review system.
- One-period inventory models can be used for managing inventories of highly perishable products for which the company must select an amount to buy or produce that cannot be revised later.
- The **ABC classification** scheme is a way to set priorities on the amount of attention to devote to the inventories of various items.
- Accurate inventory records are essential for managing materials.
- In many situations, using a **sole-supplier (sole-sourcing)** method can reduce costs and enhance product innovation; the main problem is the risk of a supply interruption.
- Buying recycled and recyclable materials can be profitable as well as environmentally sound.

KEY TERMS

ABC classification **694**
average (expected) demand during lead time ($\overline{DDLT}$) **678**
backordering **665**
basic economic order quantity (EOQ) model **667**
continuous (perpetual) review policies **666**
critical probability **688**
cycle counting **696**
cycling inventories **663**
demand during lead time (*DDLT*) **668**
demand service level (fill rate) **680**
dependent demand **660**
economic lot size (ELS) **676**
economic order quantity (EOQ) **669**
flexible spending accounts **692**
holding cost **664**
holding cost rate **664**
independent demand **660**
inventories **661**
inventory position **666**
lead time **667**
order cycle service level **679**
overage **687**
Pareto principle **694**
periodic review policies **666**
production lot size **676**
quantity discount **672**
reorder point (RP) **666**
safety stocks **663**
sole-supplier (sole-sourcing) **698**
speculative inventories **663**
stockout **679**
stockout (shortage) costs **665**
total material cost (TMC) **668**
total stocking costs (TSC) **669**
two-bin system **698**

[20]See Bradley Stertz, "Driving Back: Chrysler Is Making Solid Progress in Spite of Executive Turmoil," *Wall Street Journal*, Mar. 3, 1992.

KEY FORMULAS

Continuous Review Models

Total Stocking Cost

TSC = ordering cost + holding cost

Total Material Cost

TMC = ordering cost + holding cost + item cost

Economic Order Quantity, Basic Model

$$EOQ = \sqrt{2c_o D/c_h}$$

Economic Production Lot Size

$$ELS = Q^* = \sqrt{[2c_o D/c_h][P/(P - D)]}$$

Reorder Point When There Is No Uncertainty

$$RP = DDLT = D \times LT$$

Definition of Safety Stock

$$SS = RP - \overline{DDLT} = RP - \bar{D} \times \overline{LT}$$

Demand Service Level

$$SL_d = [(\text{annual demand} - \text{ave. number of units short/year})/\text{annual demand}] \times 100\%$$
$$= [1 - (\text{ave. number of units short/order cycle}/Q)] \times 100\%$$

Ave. number of units short/order cycle = $E(z)\sigma_{DDLT}$

where $z = (RP - \overline{DDLT})/\sigma_{DDLT}$, $E(z)$ is obtained from Table 13.2, and $DDLT$ is normally distributed, with a mean of $\overline{DDLT}$ and a standard deviation of σ_{DDLT}.

The distribution for $DDLT$, when the rate of demand, D, and lead time, LT, are normally distributed and independent of each other:

$DDLT$ will be normally distributed, with a mean of

$$\overline{DDLT} = \bar{D} \times \overline{LT}$$

and a standard deviation of

$$\sigma_{DDLT} = \sqrt{\overline{LT}\sigma_D^2 + \bar{D}^2\sigma_{LT}^2}$$

Periodic Review Model

safety stock = $z\sigma_{T+LT}$

where σ_{T+LT} is the standard deviation of demand over the review period and lead time and z is the value that solves the following equation:

$$E(z) = [\bar{D}T(1 - SL_d)/\sigma_{T+LT}]$$

where $E(z)$ is given in Table 13.2, $\bar{D}$ is the average demand rate, and SL_d is the desired demand service level expressed as a proportion.

The order quantity at each review point should be

$$Q = \text{ave. demand during period } (T + LT) + \text{safety stock} - \text{inventory position}$$
$$= \bar{D} \times (T + LT) + z\sigma_{T+LT} - I$$

One-Period Model

critical probability = $(p - c)/(p - s)$

$$\text{expected profit} = \sum_i [\text{prob(demand} = d_i) \times (\text{profit if demand} = d_i)]$$

SOLVED PROBLEMS

Problem 1: Suppose a hospital is considering its inventory and ordering policy for surgical trays. The hospital uses 200 trays per month at a relatively constant rate. Each tray costs $8.00, regardless of the quantity ordered. The hospital has determined that it costs approximately $48 to place an order and approximately 18% per year of an item's value to hold it in inventory.

(a) Compute the hospital's optimal order quantity.

(b) Suppose the supplier is willing to sell the surgical trays for $7.90 each if the hospital will buy 1000 trays at a time and $7.80 each if the hospital will buy 1600 or more at a time. Under these conditions, what is the optimal order quantity for the hospital?

Solution:

(a) The holding cost per tray per year is $c_h = p \times i = \$8.00 \times 0.18$ per year = \$1.44 per unit per year; demand is $D = 200$ trays per month = 2400 trays per year; the ordering cost is $c_o = \$48$ per order. Then, using equation (13.4),

$$Q^* = \sqrt{2c_oD/c_h} = \sqrt{2(\$48)(2400/\text{year})/(\$1.44/\text{tray/year})} = 400 \text{ trays}$$

So the hospital should order 400 trays every two months.

(b) We first solve equation (13.4) using the lowest price possible, \$7.80. For this case, $c_h = \$7.80 \times 0.18 = \$1.404$ per tray per year; so

$$EOQ = \sqrt{2(\$48)(2400/\text{year})/(\$1.404/\text{tray/year})} = 405.1 \text{ trays}$$

This quantity is inconsistent with a price of \$7.80, so we would recompute equation (13.4) using the next highest price, \$7.90. We can see that this will be less than 405.1, which is too small to obtain this price. So we recompute equation (13.4) using a price of \$8.00. We have already done this in part (a); the quantity is 400, which is consistent with the price. We must now compute the total material cost for order quantities of the consistent smooth minimum point 400, and the price break quantities greater than this, 1000 and 1600, using equation (13.5):

$$TMC_{400}/\text{year} = (\$48)(2400/400) + (\$1.44)(400/2) + (\$8.00)(2400)$$
$$= \$288 + \$288 + \$19{,}200 = \$19{,}776$$

$$TMC_{1000}/\text{year} = (\$48)(2400/1000) + (\$1.422)(1000/2) + (\$7.90)(2400)$$
$$= \$115.20 + \$711 + \$18{,}960 = \$19{,}786.20$$

$$TMC_{1600}/\text{year} = (\$48)(2400/1600) + (\$1.404)(1600/2) + (\$7.80)(2400)$$
$$= \$72 + \$1123.20 + \$18{,}720 = \$19{,}915.20$$

In this case, it is not worthwhile to increase the order quantity to receive the price breaks. The optimal order quantity is still 400.

Problem 2: In problem 1, suppose the average lead time to receive trays after ordering them is 1/2 month. Although the supplier is relatively reliable, there is some random variation in lead time and in the usage rate for surgical trays. Suppose that the hospital has determined from historical records that the amount of demand during lead time is normally distributed, with a mean of 100 trays and a standard deviation of 20.

(a) Compute the demand service level for a reorder point of 110.

(b) Compute the minimum amount of safety stock required to produce a 99.5% demand service level.

(c) Suppose that anytime the hospital needs a surgical tray but cannot get one from inventory, it must purchase one on an emergency basis from a supply store at a price of \$10 (\$2 above the normal price). Assuming the hospital uses the order quantity computed in problem 1, compute the average total annual cost (safety stock cost plus shortage cost) that would result from the following three reorder points: $RP = 120$, $RP = 124$, and $RP = 130$. Which is better?

Solution:

(a) The average number of units short per order cycle will be $E(z)\sigma_{DDLT}$. So we first compute z for a reorder point of 110:

$$z = (RP - \overline{DDLT})/\sigma_{DDLT} = (110 - 100)/20 = 0.50$$

From Table 13.2, $E(0.50) = 0.1978$, so the average number of units short per cycle will be $0.1978(20) = 3.96$ trays. Because 400 units are ordered in each cycle, the demand service level is

$SL_d = [1 - (\text{ave. no. short/cycle}/Q)] \times 100\% = [1 - (3.96/400) \times 100\%] = 99.01\%$

(b) A 99.5% demand service level means that the average number of units short in each cycle cannot be more than $0.005 \times 400 = 2$ trays. So we want to find z such that $E(z)\sigma_{DDLT} = 2$ or $E(z) = 2/\sigma_{DDLT} = 2/20 = 0.10$. From Table 13.2 we see that $E(0.9)$ equals 0.1004, so we want to choose a reorder point so that $z = 0.9$. But $z = (RP - \overline{DDLT})/\sigma_{DDLT}$, so $RP = \overline{DDLT}) + z\sigma_{DDLT}$ $= 100 + (0.9)(20) = 118$. So SS = 118 – 100 = 18.

(c) The per unit holding and shortage costs are $c_h = \$1.44$ per year and $c_s = \$2.00$, respectively. For $RP = 120$ the safety stocks are 20 units ($RP - \overline{DDLT}$), and the annual safety stock cost will be 20($1.44) = $28.80. The average number of units short during an order cycle will be $E(z)\sigma_{DDLT}$, where

$$z = (RP - \overline{DDLT})/\sigma_{DDLT} = (120 - 100)/20 = 1.00.$$

Using Table 13.2, $E(z)\sigma_{DDLT} = E(1.0)20 = (0.0833)(20) = 1.666$ units short per order cycle. There are six order cycles per year (2400 per year/400 per order), so the average annual shortage is $6 \times 1.666 = 10.00$ units. The average annual shortage cost is then 10 units × $2 = $20, and the total annual cost is $28.80 + $20.00 = $48.80. Repeating the process for the other reorder point values gives the following:

RP	*SS*	*SS* cost/Yr	*z*	*E(z)*	Ave. No. Short/Cycle	Ave. No. Short/Year	Ave. Shortage Cost/Year	Ave. Total Cost/Yr
120	20	$28.80	1.0	0.0833	1.666	10.00	$20.00	$48.80
124	24	$34.56	1.2	0.0561	1.122	6.73	$13.46	$48.02
130	30	$43.20	1.5	0.0293	0.586	3.52	$7.04	$50.24

The least-cost reorder point among these three is $RP = 124$.

Problem 3: The daily sales of a brand of cereal at Robertson's Grocery are normally distributed, with a mean of 12 boxes and a standard deviation of 4 boxes. The manager checks the inventories on shelves and places an order every three days, and the delivery lead time is two days.

(a) Compute the safety stock the store must maintain to achieve a 99% service level.

(b) If the inventory position at the time of an order is four boxes, how much should the store order?

Solution:

(a) The standard deviation of demand during the period $T + LT$ is

$$\sigma_{T+LT} = \sqrt{(T + LT)\sigma_D^2} = \sqrt{(3 \text{ days} + 2 \text{ days})(4 \text{ boxes}^2)} = 8.94 \text{ boxes}$$

We now solve equation (13.9) to find the value of z corresponding to $SL_d = 99\%$:

$$E(z) = [(12 \text{ boxes/day})(3 \text{ days})(1 - 0.99)/(8.94 \text{ boxes})] = 0.040$$

From Table 13.2 the value of z such that $E(z) = 0.040$ (using linear interpolation) is $z = 1.37$. Then the safety stock required, using equation (13.8), is

$$SS = z\sigma_{T+LT} = (1.37)(8.94 \text{ boxes}) = 12.25 \text{ boxes}$$

(b) From equation (13.10) the order quantity should be

$$Q = \bar{D} \times (T + LT) + z\sigma_{T+LT} - I$$
$$= (12 \text{ boxes/day})(3 + 2 \text{ days}) + 12.25 \text{ boxes} - 4 \text{ boxes} = 68.25 \text{ boxes}$$

Problem 4: A florist buys roses each morning from a supplier at \$6 per dozen and resells them to the public the same day at \$15 per dozen. If the roses are not sold the same day, they are sold the next day at \$3 per dozen (all roses offered at this price sell out). The demand for fresh roses at the florist shop is given by the following distribution:

Demand (doz)	Probability	Cumulative Probability
6	.1	.1
8	.2	.3
10	.2	.5
12	.2	.7
14	.1	.8
16	.1	.9
18	.1	1.0

(a) Compute the optimal number of dozens of roses the florist should buy to maximize expected daily profit.

(b) Compute the expected daily profit that would result from your answer in part (a).

Solution:

(a) In this problem p = \$15, c = \$6, and s = \$3, so the critical probability is

$$(p - c)/(p - s) = (15 - 6)/(15 - 3) = 0.75$$

The optimal order quantity is the smallest level of demand that has a cumulative probability of at least 0.75; this is $Q = 14$ dozen.

(b) Using equation (13.13), the expected daily profit will be

$$\begin{aligned} &0.1[(\$9)(6 \text{ doz}) - (\$3)(8 \text{ doz})] + 0.2[(\$9)(8 \text{ doz}) - (\$3)(6 \text{ doz})] \\ &+ 0.2[(\$9)(10 \text{ doz}) - (\$3)(4 \text{ doz})] + 0.2[(\$9)(12 \text{ doz}) - (\$3)(2 \text{ doz})] \\ &+ 0.3[(\$9)(14 \text{ doz})] = \$87.60 \end{aligned}$$

DISCUSSION AND REVIEW QUESTIONS

1. Give two reasons for holding inventories and explain the benefits.
2. If the fixed cost of ordering or setting up equipment is reduced by a factor of 4, what happens to the optimal order quantity or production lot size?
3. Safety stocks cost money, so why would we ever hold them?
4. What is the most important component of the holding cost? Why is it proportional to the monetary value of the inventories?
5. In the basic EOQ model, why will minimizing the total stocking cost also minimize the total material cost?
6. Suppose the optimal order quantity for an item a company uses is 3571. Would it be all right for the company to order 3500 or 4000 units at a time instead? Under what conditions should you *not* do this?
7. Why should suppliers of a product provide quantity discounts? What is the economic rationale or justification for doing so?
8. Why would a company want to provide its customers with only a 95% demand service level rather than a 100% level?
9. Why do we need more safety stock with a periodic review inventory policy than with a continuous review policy to achieve the same service level?
10. Some newspapers use the one-period inventory model to determine the number of newspapers to print each day. Because they are making the same decision day after day, why is it not more appropriate for them to use an EOQ model rather than a one-period model?

11. What is the purpose of classifying items using the ABC classification scheme? Should we not try to minimize the inventory-related costs for all items?
12. List two major causes of inventory record inaccuracy. Describe how the inaccuracy resulting from these causes can be reduced.
13. What are the advantages of using a sole supplier for an item? What is the primary disadvantage of using sole suppliers?
14. Give a specific example of how a company could help the environment through good purchasing methods without increasing costs.

PROBLEMS

1. Electronic Computer Services (ECS) uses paper at the rate of 1500 boxes per month. It costs ECS $75 to place an order, and the holding cost for paper is $3.75 per box per year. (a) Compute the optimal order quantity for ECS. (b) How many orders will ECS place per year with this order quantity?
2. Wilson Grocery would like to develop an optimal ordering/inventory policy for one of its soda products. The grocery sells soda at the rate of 200 cases per week. The soda costs $6 per case from the supplier, and the lead time for delivery is half a week. Wilson estimates that it costs $80 per order to execute the order and receive delivery. Wilson also estimates that it costs approximately 26% of an item's price to hold it in inventory for a year. (a) Compute the optimal number of cases Wilson should order at a time. (b) How many orders per year will Wilson place? (c) What should be Wilson's reorder point if there is no randomness in lead time or demand?
3. The Plugger Plumbing Supply Company stocks a particular type of brass valve. Plugger operates 250 days per year and sells approximately 1000 valves per year at a constant rate. The valve costs $4 from the supplier, and the lead time for delivery is five work days. It costs Plugger $20 in fixed costs to place an order, and the annual holding cost is 25% of the item's cost. (a) Compute the economic order quantity for Plugger. (b) Calculate the total annual stocking cost for Plugger. (c) Compare this with the total annual stocking cost that would result from a policy of ordering once a month. (d) Compute the reorder point assuming that there is no randomness.
4. Pilot University uses 100 packages of paper towels every week, 52 weeks a year. The towels cost $1.20 per package and Pilot pays $20 per order in transaction and delivery costs, regardless of quantity. Pilot estimates that its holding cost rate is 20% per year of an item's value. (a) Compute Pilot's economic order quantity for paper towels. (b) Calculate Pilot's total annual stocking cost. (c) Compare this with the total annual stocking cost that would result from a policy of ordering once a month.
5. Titan Industries uses approximately 5000 compressors per month in a product it manufactures. Titan purchases the compressors from an outside supplier that offers the following quantity discounts for large purchases.

Quantity Purchased	Price/Unit
0–999	$200
1000–2499	$198
2500 or more	$197

The fixed cost of executing an order is estimated to be $350, and the estimated holding cost rate is 18% per year of the item's value. (a) Compute the optimal number of compressors that Titan should buy at a time. (b) Compute the total annual material cost with this order quantity.

6. Zonk Corporation uses 20,000 pounds of chemical dye a year. The annual holding cost is 20% per year of the purchase price, and it costs Zonk $80 to place an order and receive delivery. Zonk's supplier offers quantity discounts on the dye as follows:

Quantity Bought	Price per Pound
1–999	$1.10
1000–4999	$1.00
5000	$0.90

(a) Determine the optimal amount of dye Zonk should buy each time it orders. (b) Compute its total material costs per year.

7. A toy manufacturer uses 400 wheels per day to manufacture a dump truck it sells. The firm makes its own wheels at the rate of 1600 per day. It costs $180 to set up the equipment to manufacture wheels, and the variable manufacturing cost for each wheel is $0.25. The annual holding cost is 24% of the variable manufacturing cost, and the company operates 240 days per year. (a) Compute the optimal number of wheels to make during each production run. (b) How long will it take to complete a production run (in days)? (c) How many days will there be between the start of production runs for these wheels? (d) Suppose the company is able to reduce the setup cost to $45 per

production run. What would be the optimal number of wheels to make in each run?

8. Athena Fixtures Corporation can manufacture a type of faucet at the rate of 1000 per day, but it sells the faucet at the rate of 125 per day. It costs Athena approximately $120 to set up its equipment to produce the faucets, and the holding cost is approximately $2 per faucet per year. (a) Assuming Athena operates approximately 300 days per year, compute the optimal number of faucets it should produce in a production run. (b) How many days will it take to complete a production run? (c) Compute the total annual setup and holding costs for this product.

9. A school uses photocopying paper at a relatively constant rate of 100 packages per week. The fixed ordering cost is $32 per order, and the holding cost is $0.52 per package per year. (a) Compute the optimal number of packages to buy per order. (b) On average, how frequently will the school order paper? (c) The lead time to receive deliveries from its supplier is random. From historical data, the school knows that the demand (usage) during lead time is normally distributed, with a mean of 200 and a standard deviation of 50. Compute the demand service level that would result if the school used a reorder point of 250. (d) Compute the smallest reorder point and safety stock level that would be required to achieve a demand service level of 98%.

10. Microcircuits, Inc. (MI), makes solid state switches for the electronics industry. One of the inputs for the production process is glass tubing, which MI buys from a supplier. MI uses 1000 three-foot rods of tubing each day in the production process, and the process operates approximately 250 days per year. The fixed cost to process an order is $25, and the supplier charges $75 to deliver an order, regardless of its size. MI estimates that its holding cost is $2 per rod per year. (a) Compute the optimal number of rods MI should order at a time. (b) Compute the total annual cost MI incurs for ordering, delivery, and inventories. (c) Suppose the lead time and demand rate are random and the demand during lead time has a normal distribution, with a mean of 10,000 and a standard deviation of 2500. Compute the demand service level that would result from a reorder point of 12,000, assuming MI uses the ordering quantity computed in part (a). (d) Using the information in part (c), compute the minimum amount of safety stock that would be required to achieve a 98% demand service level.

11. Amazing Corporation is a wholesale distributor. It sells 50,000 units per year of one of its products. It buys the product from the manufacturer five time per year (10,000 units per order). The daily demand for the product is normally distributed, with a mean of 200 units and a standard deviation of 40 units. The lead time from the supplier is also normally distributed, with a mean of eight days and a standard deviation of two days. (Amazing operates 250 days per year.) (a) Compute the probability distribution for *DDLT*. (b) Compute the demand service level that would result if Amazing used a reorder point of 2200 units. (c) Compute the minimum amount of safety stock required for Amazing to achieve a 99% demand service level. (d) If the annual holding cost was $1.50 per unit and the stockout cost was $9.00 per unit, compute the total annual cost (holding plus stockout) that would result from reorder points of 1800 and 2000. Which produces a lower total cost?

12. Super Circuits Electronics (SCE) is an electronics retailer. Weekly demand for a type of VCR player it sells is normally distributed, with a mean of 12 and a standard deviation of 4. SCE purchases 39 VCR players at a time from its supplier whenever it places an order. The lead time for delivery is normally distributed, with a mean of 1 week and a standard deviation of 0.4 week. (a) Compute the demand service level that would result if SCE used a reorder point of 18 units. (b) Compute the minimum amount of safety stock required for SCE to achieve a 96% demand service level. (c) If SCE's holding cost for VCRs was $0.75 per unit per week and the cost of a stockout was $10 per unit, compute the combined safety stock and stockouts costs for the two reorder points: $RP = 16$ and $RP = 20$. Which is better?

13. The daily usage of caulking by a construction company is normally distributed, with a mean of 60 tubes and a standard deviation of 15. The materials supervisor checks the material inventories and places orders every seven days. The lead time for delivery of caulking is three days. (a) Compute the safety stock required to achieve a 98% service level. (b) If the inventory position at the time of an order is 190 tubes, how many tubes should be ordered?

14. The office manager of an investment brokerage house is responsible for managing office supplies. She checks the supplies of forms every week, and it takes two weeks for new forms to be printed and delivered. The weekly usage of trade confirmation forms by the brokerage house is normally distributed, with a mean of 6000 and a standard deviation of 1800. (a) Compute the safety stock required to achieve a 99.5% service level. (b) If the inventory position at the time of an order is 14,000, how many forms should be ordered?

15. Compute the expected profit that would result in *Solved Problem* 4 if 12 dozen and 16 dozen roses were ordered.

16. The *World Tribune Times* newspaper spends $0.28 per copy printing the newspaper and distributing it. It sells the paper for $0.50 per copy, and any copy not sold has a salvage value of zero. The company's historical data indicate that the number of newspapers requested on Mondays is given by the following probability distribution. (a) Determine the number of newspapers the company should print on Mondays to maximize expected profit. (b) Compute the average daily profit for Mondays resulting from the answer in part (a).

Demand	Probability
75,000	0.05
76,000	0.10
77,000	0.20
78,000	0.25
79,000	0.20
80,000	0.10
81,000	0.10

17. A bookstore would like to stock a new income tax guide for the upcoming year. Due to the publishing lead time, the bookstore will be allowed to place an order only once (in October) and will receive delivery of the guides at the end of December. The bookstore will pay $3 per guide to the publisher and will resell them for $6. Any guide not sold by April 15 can be sold on sale for $1. The bookstore does not know how many guides it can sell during the tax season, but it believes that the demand has a discrete uniform distribution between 201 and 300 guides (each integer value between 201 and 300 has a 0.01 probability of occurring). (a) Compute the optimal number of guides the bookstore should order to maximize its expected profit. (b)* Using the order quantity in part (a), compute the bookstore's expected profit. (Hint: do not add up the profit for each demand level explicitly; look for a pattern that can simplify the summation.)

18. Natural Patterns, Inc. (NPI), manufactures and dyes a wide variety of fabrics used in making clothes. Many of its products are produced in a single batch and used to make only one batch of clothes (dresses, blouses) by a clothing manufacturer. NPI believes that the likely demand for one of its new patterns can be described by a continuous uniform distribution between 2000 and 4000 yards. It costs NPI $3 a yard to make the cloth, which will be sold for $7 a yard. Any cloth that is unsold initially will be donated to a charity. Determine the optimal number of yards of cloth NPI should make to maximize its expected profit, assuming it will make only one production run. (Hint: The cumulative distribution function is $F(d) = 0.0005\,(d - 2000)$ for $2000 \leq d \leq 4000$.)

19. The University Alumni Association (UAA) is sponsoring a European tour in August. The UAA has arranged a deal with an airline whereby the airline provides transportation and lodging for the tour at a cost of $800 per person to UAA. UAA will then sell spaces on the tour to its members for $1500 per person. UAA must make a firm commitment to the airline immediately on the number of seats it will reserve and must pay in advance. Alumni will be able to buy seats for the tour until August 1. UAA will sell any remaining seats to a discount travel agent for $400. The president of UAA believes that the demand for seats on the tour (at $1500 per seat) has the following distribution:

Demand	Probability
50	0.1
60	0.2
70	0.2
80	0.2
90	0.2
100	0.1

(a) Compute the number of seats that UAA should reserve to maximize its expected profit. (b) Compute the expected profit that would result from the policy found in part (a). (c)* Suppose that on July 20 UAA had 25 seats remaining. The airline has offered to repurchase any remaining seats for $550, but UAA must decide immediately. Based on previous sales and other factors, the president of UAA has estimated that the demand by alumni for tickets between July 20 and August 1 has the following distribution.

Demand	Probability
5	0.2
10	0.2
15	0.3
20	0.2
25	0.1

On August 1 UAA still can sell the remaining tickets to the travel agent for $400. Determine how many seats (if any) it should resell to the airline. (d)* Compute the expected revenue obtained for the 25 seats if the answer in part (c) is used, and compare it with the revenue obtained if all 25 seats are sold back to the airline.

20. A company uses 10 items in its operations. The annual usage and item costs are given below. (a) Compute the annual monetary usage of each item. (b)

Classify each item as being either an A, B, or C item.

Item	Annual Usage (units)	Item Cost per unit
A	8,500	$ 10.00
B	125,000	$ 3.00
C	20,000	$ 1.50
D	5,000	$120.00
E	30,000	$ 15.00
F	1,500	$ 4.00
G	50,000	$ 2.00
H	4,000	$ 30.00
I	3,000	$ 5.00
J	10,000	$ 7.50

21. Electric Service Corporation is an electronics reconditioner. The annual usage and item costs for the 12 items it uses are given below. (a) Compute the annual monetary usage of each item. (b) Classify each item as being either an A, B, or C item.

Item	Annual Usage (units)	Item Cost per Unit
A	800	$ 40.00
B	500	$ 12.00
C	1,600	$ 15.00
D	200	$200.00
E	150	$ 25.00
F	2,250	$ 6.00
G	5,000	$ 9.00
H	10,000	$ 1.50
I	1,500	$ 45.00
J	6,000	$ 2.50
K	1,000	$ 5.00
L	750	$ 4.00

CASE

Mediserve, Inc.: An Inventory Management Case

Mediserve, Inc., is a hospital management company that manages over 20 hospitals on a contract basis for a variety of not-for-profit organizations. Mediserve's contracts normally include performance incentives for efficiency of operations, mortality rates, and general quality of care, especially improvements relative to some baseline measures.

Mediserve recently signed a five-year contract to manage Westgrove Memorial Hospital (WMH), where it believes it can substantially improve purchasing and materials management. During a year, Westgrove spends over $25,000,000 on operating materials and supplies such as surgical instruments, linens, building maintenance parts, paper, uniforms, and pharmaceuticals. During the past year, WMH purchased nearly 21,000 different products from 1302 different vendors and executed nearly 27,000 separate purchase orders.

Purchasing responsibilities are divided among three units. All material purchases by the Hospital Pharmacy (both prescription and nonprescription drugs) are made directly by a purchasing administrator in the Pharmacy Department. Materials needed by the Maintenance and Engineering (M&E) Department are ordered directly by supervisors in that department. All other hospital materials and supplies, which are primarily those needed to perform medical and administrative functions, such as linens and gowns, x-ray plates and materials for laboratory tests, and paper forms and computer supplies, are purchased by the Hospital Purchasing Department, which has 10 employees.

Each of the three units has its own purchasing procedures and inventory management policies. Furthermore, each purchasing agent specializes in certain types of materials and vendors, and each has developed his or her own purchasing policies in terms of number of suppliers, order quantities, utilization of quantity discounts, safety stock levels, and use of expedited deliveries.

Data Collection and Observations

Robert Sanchez is the inventory and materials management expert of Mediserve's in-house consulting team, which helps develop new systems for hospitals. Robert's first step was to obtain historical data on material spending, including volume and distribution of purchases, average amount of inventory on hand, amount spent on special shipping and expediting, and number of stockouts. Table 13.7 summarizes some of the findings. The Pharmacy Department has the highest inventory turnover of any department, maintaining only 11% of its annual purchases in inventory.

Data on the distribution of purchases by products and vendors (Table 13.8a) shows that 5% of the products purchased by the Purchasing, Pharmacy, and M&E departments accounted for 27%, 35%, and 22% of the total value of purchases by those departments, respectively. Furthermore, 50% of the products accounted for only 3–4% of the total purchases by the Purchasing and Pharmacy departments.

Table 13.8b shows that the five largest vendors accounted for 9% of the purchases by the Purchasing Department, 32% by the Pharmacy, and 29% by the M&E Department. Even more striking is the fact that well over half of the vendors used by the Purchasing and M&E departments supplied only one or two products. However, only 3% of the Pharmacy vendors supplied two or fewer products. This is further reflected in the number of products purchased by each purchase order, which ranges from 1.9 for M&E to 4.6 for Purchasing to 82.3 for the Pharmacy.

TABLE 13.7 INVENTORY COST COSTS UNDER THE OLD SYSTEM

	Purchasing Dept.	Pharmacy	Maint./Eng.
Total purchases (199x)	$14,872,395	$7,698,211	$2,459,611
Ave. inventory level ($)	$4,600,000	$850,000	$700,000
Cost for normal deliveries*	$14,825	$19,610	$1,058†
Extra cost to expedite delivery	$20,502	$9,560	$4,845†
Number of stockouts	208	32	75

*Delivery cost for most orders is included as part of the price and does not appear here.

†The cost of M&E department personnel and vehicles used to pick up products from vendors is not included here.

TABLE 13.8 DISTRIBUTION OF COSTS BY PRODUCT AND VENDOR

(a) Pareto Distribution of Item Usage Under the Old System

% of Products	% of $ Value Purchases: Purchasing Dept.	Pharmacy	Maint./Eng.
Top 5%	27%	35%	22%
Top 20%	45%	56%	41%
Top 50%	96%	97%	89%

(b) Distribution of Vendor Purchases Under the Old System

	Purchasing Dept.	Pharmacy	Maint./Eng.
% of purch. from 5 largest vendors	9%	32%	29%
No. of vendors used*	1,132	104	157
No. of products purchased	14,472	4283	1970
No. of purchase order transactions	17,429	7890	1631
Ave. no. of products/P.O.	4.6	82.3	1.9
No. of vend. supplying 20+ products	129	77	20
No. of vend. supplying 1–2 products	697	3	95

*Some vendors supply more than one department (e.g., purchasing and pharmacy); the total number of suppliers is 1302, which is less than the sum for the three units.

Data Analysis

Based on the data in Tables 13.7 and 13.8, as well as interviews, observation, and comparisons with other hospitals managed by Mediserve, Robert Sanchez identified the following patterns and potential areas for improvement.

1. The Purchasing and M&E departments used an abnormally large number of vendors and purchased a relatively small number of products with each purchase order. However, the number of vendors used by the Pharmacy was about the same as that of similar hospitals.
2. The average inventory values of items purchased by the Purchasing and M&E departments were quite high relative to usage (equivalently, the inventory turnover—usage/inventories—is low) compared to other hospitals. The Pharmacy inventory is only slightly higher than that of comparable hospitals.
3. Considering the large inventory levels, the number of stockouts and expedited orders (and costs) are abnormally high for Purchasing and M&E. For the latter department especially, the reported costs do not fully represent the real costs. Further investigation indicated that Westgrove personnel made nearly 200 trips each year to pick up items needed quickly.
4. The safety stock levels and normal order quantities relative to the usage rate varied considerably from product to product in Purchasing and M&E. Robert found that some of the safety stock and order quantities had been established years ago and were never changed, and many were based on rules of thumb. In the Pharmacy, consistent rules were used because most products were purchased on a regular basis (once or twice per week) as part of a joint purchase order of several products from the same vendor.
5. Except in the Pharmacy, there were deficiencies in the inventory records system. M&E maintained a storeroom with a bin system. Inventory records were kept on index cards attached to the product bins, and when inventories were perceived to be low, an item was ordered. A computerized system had been implemented but only for more frequently used items, and it did not contain any decision aids, such as a usage tracking system or an automated reorder mechanism.

A big problem for the Purchasing Department was that its inventories were distributed throughout the hospital. Items used hospitalwide were kept in a central storeroom that had a computerized recordkeeping system. But many items were used by only one or two departments, which maintained their own inventories and notified the Purchasing Department when they needed more. Some departments did a good job of tracking inventories and making purchase requests, but others did not.

Methods Analysis and Policy Recommendations

Robert Sanchez identified the following improvements, which addressed the major deficiencies.

Reduce the Number of Vendors

In over 90% of the purchases from vendors who supplied only one or two products, the same or equivalent products were available from other Westgrove vendors. Robert found two main reasons that purchases were being made from these "special" vendors: (1) the purchaser did not know that the item was available elsewhere or (2) the purchaser knew of alternative vendors but believed the price or quality of the vendor chosen was better.

Robert set out to reduce substantially the number of vendors Westgrove used. He first established a short training program to make employees familiar with alternative vendors. In addition, he created a simple computer file for ready access that listed alternative vendors according to the types of products sold.

He then selected 100 items purchased from unique vendors (suppliers of two or fewer products) and asked the purchaser to explain the choice of vendor. In 30 cases the purchaser believed the vendor provided a lower price. But when Robert used the new computer program to identify alternative suppliers, for 19 of the 30 products he found an alternative supplier with prices that were the same or lower.

When these results were presented to the purchasing agents, they were surprised. Robert determined that purchasing agents normally checked the prices of alternative suppliers to find a lower-cost source, but the catalog prices were inaccurate. Westgrove's major suppliers normally gave a discount from the catalog price because the hospital was a big customer, especially if the item was part of a multiproduct purchase; however, the purchasing agents were not always aware of these agreements with vendors. Robert then went to the major suppliers and negotiated additional 1–10% price reductions in exchange for more purchases. The negotiated prices were then marked in all the hospital's price catalogs.

For the M&E Department, Robert noticed one additional problem. The department was ordering a large number of parts either directly from manufacturers whose deliveries were slow or from several different retailers. So he negotiated deals with four major wholesale distributors and retailers to be the primary suppliers for most of the department's supplies. This meant that the purchasers could find almost everything they needed from a handful of suppliers instead of having to track down manufacturers and retailers. In exchange for the guaranteed volume, Robert negotiated price concessions and service guarantees superior to those currently received.

Robert then met with all of the persons responsible for purchasing in all three departments, and they established a list of 125 preferred vendors who provided both superior prices and service. The purchasers were asked to go through all the products they normally purchased and, using the computerized vendor data system and the new price list, to transfer as many purchases to preferred vendors as possible. A vendor other than a preferred vendor could be used only if the vendor was the sole supplier of the item, the vendor's quality and service were clearly superior to those of other vendors, or the price was at least 3% below that of a preferred vendor. Robert estimated that the number of vendors could easily be reduced to approximately 300 in Purchasing, 100 in the Pharmacy, and 30 in M&E.

Improving the Order Quantities and Reorder Policies

Robert believed that many of the inventory problems could be solved by establishing consistent and systematic ordering policies. The economic order quantity models presented in Sections 13.5–13.7 assume that only one product is ordered at a time; that is, we do not order several different products from one vendor at the same time. Clearly, this is not true for Westgrove; Table 13.8 shows that the average number of products purchased per order ranged from 1.9 for the M&E Department to 82.3 for the Pharmacy. For jointly ordered items, which share some of the fixed purchase costs, alternative versions of the EOQ model exist; they can be found in more advanced inventory books. However, as a first step in determining approximate order quantities and order frequencies, Robert computed the basic EOQ values for each product. (This allowed him to identify the products that might be ordered jointly, which is helpful in using the joint-purchase EOQ models.) The per unit holding costs for products were then estimated, taking into account any special storage needs or perishability conditions. The fixed ordering cost varied, depending on whether the supplier charged a separate delivery charge, whether there were special expenses in dealing with certain vendors, and whether there were extra costs for regulatory reporting of purchases (e.g., purchases of chemicals that require special disposal must be reported to government agencies). Although one could argue that the cost of a purchaser's time to execute the order is zero because that person would be paid anyway, some time cost was allocated to c_0 because, if the number of purchase orders could be reduced enough, the number of employees could be reduced and/or the time of supervisors could be freed up for other productive uses.

Table 13.9 gives the relevant data and the economic order quantities for 10 selected products (none that were considered critical). In a separate analysis (using the methods discussed in Section 13.8), reorder points and safety stock levels were computed. Table 13.10 compares the cost and service level consequences of the economic order quantities in Table 13.9 and the new ordering policies to those previously used. (The costs are approximate because the effects of joint ordering are not included.) In the past, orders were not necessarily placed when inventories reached a reorder point. Many orders occurred because the purchaser decided to check the inventory levels of some products and place an order. There were frequent stockouts, expedited orders, and purchase orders for one product rather than combining it in a joint order. Because of this lack of commonality, the old safety stock levels in Table 13.10 are estimates.

TABLE 13.9 EOQ VALUES FOR 10 SELECTED PRODUCTS

Product	Usage/Month	c_h/Month	c_o	*EOQ*	*TSC/yr.*
A	52	$ 0.90	$25	54	$ 580
B	208	$ 4.75	$40	59	$3,374
C	36	$ 1.50	$25	35	$ 624
D	85	$ 8.00	$50	33	$3,129
E	830	$ 2.10	$25	141	$3,542
F	13	$45.00	$50	5	$2,902
G	2168	$ 0.75	$40	481	$4,328
H	30	$ 1.25	$75	60	$ 900
I	451	$ 0.60	$25	194	$1,396
J	22	$ 2.40	$50	30	$ 872
				Total	$21,647

TABLE 13.10 COMPARISON OF NEW AND OLD INVENTORYPOLICIES FOR 10 SELECTED PRODUCTS

Prod.	Usage/ Month	Old Q	Old TSC/yr	New EOQ	New TSC/yr	Old SS	Old SL_d	Old Ave Inv	New SS	New SL_d	New Ave Inv
A	52	60	$ 584	54	$ 580	25	99%	55	20	99%	47
B	208	400	11,650	59	3374	50	98%	250	60	99%	89
C	36	50	666	35	624	0	96%	25	10	99%	27
D	85	100	5,310	33	3129	30	97%	80	50	99%	66
E	830	1000	12,849	141	3542	200	99%	700	300	99%	370
F	13	25	7,062	5	2902	5	96%	17	10	99%	12
G	2168	2000	9,520	481	4328	800	100%	1800	600	99%	840
H	30	25	1,267	60	900	0	95%	12	15	99%	45
I	451	500	2,071	194	1396	200	99%	450	250	99%	347
J	22	50	984	30	872	20	99%	45	25	99%	40

Cost	Old	New
Stocking cost (ordering + cycling inventory)	$51,963	$21,647
Safety stock cost	22,956	29,721
Total cost	74,919	51,368

The EOQ values in Tables 13.9 and 13.10 were later modified to take into account joint ordering opportunities, quantity discounts, and natural order sizes (e.g., ordering in multiples of 10, 12, 24, 100, or 144 rather than, say, 33). The increased cost of adjusting order quantities to natural sizes was more than compensated for by reduced ordering costs. So the total stocking cost reported in Table 13.10 actually overstates the true costs that resulted from the new policies.

Although the new policies in Table 13.10 are only approximate and were subsequently modified, a few patterns in that table held generally: (1) most order quantities were reduced by 50% or more, so orders were placed more frequently, and cycling inventory was cut substantially; (2) safety stocks for most products were increased slightly. The overall effects were as follows:

1. A 35–40% reduction in the physical inventories maintained.
2. A 25–30% reduction in combined stocking and safety stock costs.
3. A consistent and higher service level of 99% for all products compared to approximately 97.5% with the old policies.

Creating a Computerized Inventory Management System

To support and implement the new inventory policies, Robert had Mediserve's information systems staff install a new computerized inventory records and decision support system for the Purchasing and M&E departments at Westgrove. The system in the Pharmacy appeared to be functioning well, especially in tracking restricted narcotics and maintaining appropriate safety stocks, so that system was not changed. The "new" system was actually the same system Mediserve was using at several of the other hospitals it managed, so the installation and conversion cost was low. The system kept real-time information on current inventories, outstanding orders, and historical usage data. The system also automatically signaled when the inventory position reached the reorder point established for the product, suggested optimal order quantities, and identified the most recent vendor and alternative preferred vendors that might be consulted when new purchases were made.

All employees who would use the inventory system were given a short training course in its use. Within a few weeks all inventory information had been input to the system, optimal order quantities and reorder points established, and vendors established.

Results

Tables 13.11 and 13.12 report information comparable to that in Tables 13.7 and 13.8 but two years later; the year in between was the period of study and transition. Even a casual comparison of the tables indicates significant improvements. First, note that the reported improvements are not the result of a reduction in business activity or a change of activity in the hospital. The first line of Tables 13.7 and 13.11 shows that the general volumes of purchases for the two years are comparable, and Tables 13.8a and 13.12a show that the relative mix of products and their usage is almost identical; there was no significant reduction in the number of products purchased.

The major benefits that resulted from the new system are as follows:

1. ***The Cost of Materials Decreased in Real Terms.*** Although the nominal amount spent by the Purchasing and Pharmacy departments increased over the two-year period, due to an increase in patient volume it rose at only half the rate of price increases. This saved an estimated $500,000, mostly from price concessions negotiated by concentrating purchases among preferred vendors. The amount of purchases from the five largest vendors in each department increased significantly, and the number of vendors who supplied two or fewer products was cut by almost 90% (from 795 to 86; see Tables 13.8b and 13.12b).

TABLE 13.11 INVENTORY COSTS UNDER THE NEW SYSTEM

	Purchasing Dept.	Pharmacy	Maint./Eng.
Total purchases (199y)	$15,166,734	$8,545,417	$2,371,607
Ave. inventory level ($)	$3,350,000	$870,000	$510,000
Cost for normal deliveries	$6,825	$15,610	$610
Extra cost to expedite delivery	$7,301	$ 8,750	$530
Number of stockouts	79	29	12

TABLE 13.12 NEW DISTRIBUTION OF COSTS BY PRODUCT AND VENDOR

(a) Pareto Distribution of Item Usage Under the New System

	% of $ Value Purchases		
% of Products	Purchasing Dept.	Pharmacy	Maint./Eng.
Top 5%	28%	34%	21%
Top 20%	44%	56%	40%
Top 50%	97%	97%	91%

(b) Distribution of Vendor Purchases Under the New System

	Purchasing Dept.	Pharmacy	Maint./Eng.
% of purch. from 5 largest vendors	11%	31%	51%
No. of vendors used	342	101	37
No. of products purchased	13,931	4,410	1,648
No. of purchase order transactions	13,609	7,724	917
Ave. no. of products/P.O.	11.2	83.1	8.3
No. of vend. supplying 20+ products	132	82	18
No. of vend. supplying 1–2 products	68	5	13

2. ***The Amount of Material in Inventory Decreased by Over 25% in Real Terms.*** Although safety stocks were increased for most products, total inventory decreased because more frequent, smaller orders kept the cycling inventory much lower than previously. This not only freed up over $1,500,000 in cash and saved the corresponding holding costs, it also freed 25% of the space used for storage.
3. ***The Number of Stockouts Was Reduced By Two-Thirds, with Only Modest Increases in Safety Stock.*** This reduced direct stockout costs for expediting orders, but more important, it reduced indirect stockout costs related to inconvenience and operational stoppages. In the M&E Department employees almost never had to make special pickups of orders, which freed several hundred hours of work time for other purposes.
4. ***Fewer Vendors Had to Be Monitored and Fewer Purchase Orders Processed.*** Although most individual products were being ordered more frequently, these orders were being combined. Table 13.12b shows that the number of products per purchase order almost tripled in the Purchasing Department and more than quadrupled in the M&E Department. This gave the hospital more opportunities to take advantage of quantity discounts (those based on the total size of the order) and reduced the delivery charges that were often imposed on small orders. The reduction in the number of purchase orders and vendors made it possible to eliminate two purchasing positions (one employee who retired and another one who moved to another department were not replaced), yet the remaining agents reported that they were less overworked than before. Supervisors and engineers in the M&E Department also reported that they had more time for other activities because they were spending less time trying to find vendors, process orders, and track orders. The reduction in purchase orders and vendors also reduced the amount of work in the Accounts Payable Department enough that one employee position was eliminated there as well.

When all the benefits were combined, Westgrove was saving approximately $1 million per year. In addition, $1.5 million in inventory was freed, stockouts were reduced, and general functioning of the material management system improved considerably. An interesting side effect of this exercise was that even the Pharmacy Department, which had been operating efficiently to begin with, became more attuned to the opportunities for improvement and was able to reduce many of its costs modestly.

QUESTIONS

1. What other techniques discussed in this chapter might be beneficial at Westgrove Memorial?
2. What special factors should a hospital consider that a typical manufacturer would not have to consider when it establishes its safety stock policies?
3. The hospital needs to track inventories of each item to place orders at the correct time and for the correct amounts. Why else is it even more important for the Pharmacy than for the other departments to have extremely accurate inventory information? (In fact, why is that accuracy required by law?)

SELECTED READINGS

BLEAKLEY, FRED. "Some Companies Let Suppliers Work on Site and Even Place Orders," *Wall Street Journal*, Jan. 13, 1995.

BROWN, ROBERT G. *Decision Rules for Inventory Management*, Holt, Rinehart & Winston, New York 1967.

ERLENKOTTER, DONALD. "Fred Whitman Harris and the Economic Order Quantity Model," *Operations Research*, Vol. 38, 1990, pp. 937–946.

JOHNSON, LYNWOOD, and DOUGLAS MONTGOMERY. *Operations Research in Production Planning, Scheduling, and Inventory Control*, Wiley, New York, 1974.

MAGNET, MYRON. "The New Golden Rule of Business," *Fortune*, Feb. 21, 1994, pp. 60–64.

MEYER, HARRY. "Inventory Accuracy—Is It Worth It? A Case Study," *Production and Inventory Management Journal*, 2nd Quarter 1990, pp. 15–17.

PETERSON, REIN, and EDWARD SILVER. *Decision Systems for Inventory Management and Production Planning* (2nd ed.), Wiley, New York, 1985.

REID, RICHARD. "The ABC Method in Hospital Inventory Management: A Practical Approach," *Production and Inventory Management Journal*, Fourth Quarter 1987, pp. 67–70.

ROSENFIELD, D. B. "Optimal Management of Tax-Sheltered Employee Reimbursement Programs," *Interfaces*, Vol. 16., No. 3, 1986, pp. 68–72.

CHAPTER 14

MANAGING MATERIALS WITH DEPENDENT DEMANDS

14.1 DEPENDENT DEMAND AND IRREGULAR PRODUCTION PATTERNS
On the Job: Satish C. Nayak, Union Electric Company

14.2 STRUCTURE AND PRINCIPLES OF MRP

14.3 MRP INPUTS
The Master Schedule File
The Bill-of-Materials File
The Inventory Records File

14.4 MRP LOGIC AND MECHANICS
Exploding the Product
Developing the Material Requirements Plans
Consolidating Requirements

14.5 MRP OUTPUTS

14.6 LOT SIZING IN MRP
Economic Order Quantity
Part-Period Balancing
The Wagner-Whitin Optimization Algorithm

14.7 CAPACITY REQUIREMENTS PLANNING

14.8 UPDATING THE MRP SYSTEM AND SYSTEM NERVOUSNESS
Net-Change Systems
Regenerative Systems
Time Fences
Rolling Horizon

14.9 UNCERTAINTY AND SAFETY STOCK

14.10 MRP II: MANUFACTURING RESOURCES PLANNING

14.11 BENEFITS, LIMITATIONS, AND IMPLEMENTATION OF MRP
Benefits
Limitations and Implementation Problems
Computer-Based Systems
In Good Company: Tubetronics

Waste Overhaul, Inc.: An MRP Case

14.1 Dependent Demand and Irregular Production Patterns

The economic order quantity models in Chapter 13 assume that the demand for or usage of an item is relatively constant and independent of any other item. But demand for many items, especially components and raw materials, can be irregular and directly determined by the production plans for other products. In this case we say the component items have a **dependent demand** pattern. If production of the end product, and thus demand for its components, is constant, we can often treat the component demands *as if* they were independent and use the economic order/production quantity models to determine the timing and amount of purchases or production runs. However, there are at least three situations in which item demands are likely to be irregular and lumpy, as in Figure 14.1, in which case the dependent demand pattern must be considered explicitly.

First, in some cases the actual purchase pattern is irregular and lumpy. For example, Falcon Products, which makes furniture for the fast-food industry, sells a large portion of its products to a small number of large customers. Customers such as McDonalds' or Wendy's may order new tables and chairs for 200 restaurants one month and then not order again for 6 or 12 months, depending on their construction and remodeling plans. Second, even when end product demand is constant, it may be more economical to produce infrequently in larger batches rather than producing in small amounts on a continuous basis. For example, Sigma Chemical Company manufactures thousands of specialty chemicals, some using unique materials such as cabbages and fireflies. The demand for many of its end products is relatively constant but small (an entire year's sales might be produced in a day), so Sigma finds it more economical to produce one type of chemical at a work center one day and another type the next day. The time between production runs of a given chemical may be several months or more, and the size of a run may vary, depending on demand and inventory at the time of the run. Once Sigma has established a production schedule, it can plan acquisition of its raw materials, such as cabbage, exactly when they are needed. Third, dependent demand patterns occur in the maintenance and replacement of multicomponent modules. For example, replacing a boiler pump triggers a need for many component parts. This is one of the inventory situations Satish Nayak, featured in this chapter's "On the Job" segment, encounters in his work at Union Electric.

In dependent demand situations, the problem facing the manufacturer is to schedule the purchase of externally obtained components and raw materials and the production of internally manufactured components or subassemblies and final assembly in a timely and cost-effective manner. This situation is fundamentally different from that de-

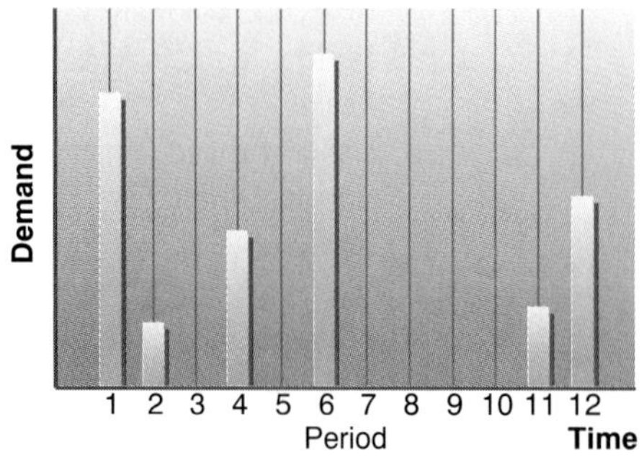

FIGURE 14.1 "Lumpy" dependent demand.

ON THE JOB

SATISH C. NAYAK, UNION ELECTRIC COMPANY

Electric utility companies use a vast array of materials to keep the electric system operating: from nuts and bolts to electric poles, transformer parts, and power turbine parts (generators, pumps), to name a few. Evaluating and improving the systems that manage these items is a difficult task, but that is one of the responsibilities of the Management Services group under Dr. Satish Nayak, a supervising engineer for Union Electric Company. Satish is a troubleshooter who performs operational reviews and supervises special productivity projects for Union Electric, especially in the area of materials management.

Because of the differences among items in terms of size, cost, and usage pattern, Satish must be able to develop and work with a variety of inventory strategies and purchasing procedures. For example, some items, such as the components of a boiler feeder pump, have a dependent demand structure. When a boiler feeder pump is scheduled for replacement, a bill-of-materials can be used to determine which components will be needed, how many, and when.

A recent project in which Satish has been involved concerns the purchasing procedures for inexpensive and infrequently used items. Rather than stocking the items or purchasing them through a formal procurement process, which is expensive and time-consuming, Satish helped to implement and monitor a procurement card system. Procurement cards are credit cards employees use to buy inexpensive items when needed. The issuing bank provides a monthly statement of the purchases, including which budgets to charge for purchases. This system has eliminated all the paperwork in the purchasing process and has provided Union Electric with better information on purchases.

scribed in Chapter 13, and using independent demand analysis for dependent demand items is like using a Phillips-head screwdriver to screw in a flathead screw: the tool is in the same general family (inventory analysis), but it is the wrong tool and the results will be poor. As shown in the following example, deriving the time and size of component orders and production runs using independent demand models may lead to the worst of all worlds: carrying substantial inventories during periods when the end product is not being produced, while incurring component shortages during planned final production.

EXAMPLE 1

Falcon Products manufactures furniture for the fast-food restaurant industry. One of its products, a swivel seat (which connects to a table support and is installed at the restaurant site), is made up of two components, a seat unit and a swivel arm unit, which the company manufactures itself and then assembles. The company can manufacture up to 1500 units of each component in a week and can assemble up to 2000 units of the end product in a week.[1] The average annual sales for the swivel seat are 5200 units, but demand and production are irregular. Falcon has developed a master production schedule whereby it plans to produce 1000 swivel seats in week 2, 1500 in week 14, and 1000 in week 26.

The company estimates that it costs \$50 to set up the equipment that produces seat units and \$100 to set up the equipment that produces swivel arms. The holding costs for the components are \$8 per unit per year for seat units and \$4 per unit per year

[1]The production rates, demands, and costs do not represent actual values for Falcon Products; they were selected for illustration purposes.

for swivel arms. Using equation (13.7) to estimate the optimal production lot sizes, we get:

$$\text{lot size}_{seats} = \sqrt{[2(\$50)(5200)/\$8][(78{,}000)/(78{,}000 - 5200)]} = 264$$

$$\text{lot size}_{arms} = \sqrt{[2(\$100)(5200)/\$4][(78{,}000)/(78{,}000 - 5200)]} = 528$$

Based on an average demand of 100 units per week, production runs of seat units would occur every 2.64 weeks and runs of swivel arms would occur every 5.28 weeks. A production and inventory pattern resulting from these lot sizes and production schedules is given in Table 14.1.

Notice that the company is carrying substantial component inventories from weeks 3–12 and 19–25 when they are not needed, yet it has insufficient components to execute final assembly of 1500 units during week 14 as planned. Instead it can only assemble 1156 units (assuming it can use 50 of the seats produced during week 14), leaving a shortage of 344 units. The company can produce the additional 344 units during week 17, but this may disrupt production for other products Falcon makes.

TABLE 14.1 PRODUCTION SCHEDULE FOR SWIVEL SEATS

Week	Planned Final Assembly	Actual Final Assembly	Production Seat Units	Ending Invent. Seat Units	Production Swivel Arms	Ending Invent. Swiv. Arms
0	—	—	—	1050	—	1100
1	0	0	0	1050	0	1100
2	1000	1000	0	50	0	100
3	0	0	264	314	0	100
4	0	0	0	314	0	100
5	0	0	0	314	528	628
6	0	0	264	578	0	628
7	0	0	0	578	0	628
8	0	0	264	842	0	628
9	0	0	0	842	0	628
10	0	0	0	842	0	628
11	0	0	264	1106	528	1156
12	0	0	0	1106	0	1156
13	0	0	0	1106	0	1156
14	1500	1156*	264	214	0	0*
15	0	0	0	214	0	0
16	0	0	264	478	528	528
17	0	344	0	134	0	184
18	0	0	0	134	0	184
19	0	0	264	398	0	184
20	0	0	0	398	0	184
21	0	0	264	662	528	712
22	0	0	0	662	0	712
23	0	0	0	662	0	712
24	0	0	264	926	0	712
25	0	0	0	926	0	712
26	1000	1000	264	190	528	240

*Shortage of material.

For dependent demand components, once the production schedule for the end product is established, the *amounts* of each type of component needed and *when* they are needed can be determined. This information can be used to develop a more effective production and inventory plan for the components that recognizes the irregular, lumpy pattern of final assembly. In Example 1, such a schedule would result in carrying little or no inventories until week 1; then 1000 seats and swivel arms would be produced in week 1 in order to be available for assembly in week 2; little or no inventories would be carried from weeks 2 through 12; then 1500 units of each component would be produced in week 13 in order to be available for assembly in week 14; and so on. The result of this approach is much lower inventory carrying costs and a simultaneous reduction in the chance of a component stockout. A popular method that uses this approach to schedule production and purchasing of dependent demand items is **material requirements planning (MRP).**

This chapter describes the logic and mechanics of MRP and how it can assist in managing production schedules and ordering purchased items so that materials will be available in a cost-effective, timely manner. It is a valuable tool not only for manufacturing scheduling but also for maintenance operations, as will be demonstrated in the end-of-chapter case.

14.2 STRUCTURE AND PRINCIPLES OF MRP

MRP is a computer-based information system for scheduling production and purchases of dependent demand items. It uses information about end product demands, product structure and component requirements, production and purchase lead times, and current inventory levels to develop cost-effective production and purchasing schedules.

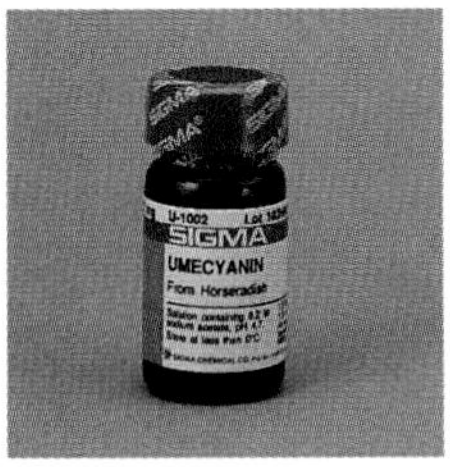

Sigma Chemical Company makes umecyanin by isolating it from horseradish root, which is only available during a short period each year. Although demand is relatively uniform throughout the year, Sigma must make enough during its one production run each year to meet demand for the entire year. So the receipt of horseradish root and production of umecyanin must be well-coordinated.

The basic philosophy and mechanics of MRP are simple and straightforward. The system assumes that the end product is made up of a hierarchy of assemblies, subassemblies, components, and raw materials, as illustrated in Figure 14.2. A schedule of end product requirements, based on demand forecasts or actual customer orders, is developed outside the MRP system. Using these end product requirements, product structure data, and historical lead time information, the MRP system traces back when assemblies, subassemblies, and components must be produced or ordered in order to have the materials when needed for subsequent production steps, but no earlier than necessary to avoid excessive inventory costs.

As long as production and procurement lead times are reasonably reliable, this process, which is illustrated in detail in Section 14.4, is quite simple. However, if a company makes dozens or hundreds of products, the number of components that must be produced and scheduled can be in the thousands, many of which may be common to several products. This is where the power of a computer system becomes essential. The computer is able to maintain current inventory information on all components, integrate component needs over time, and schedule and coordinate production and purchasing activities quickly, so that they can be updated on a regular basis.

The primary outputs of an MRP system are production and purchasing schedules and order releases for each required item, that is, a schedule of *how much* of each component item to produce or order and *when*. In addition, the MRP system may produce resource utilization reports, inventory reports, exception reports, performance reports, and other planning and control documents. The following three sections describe in greater detail the inputs required, the system logic and processing performed, and the primary outputs produced by a typical MRP system.

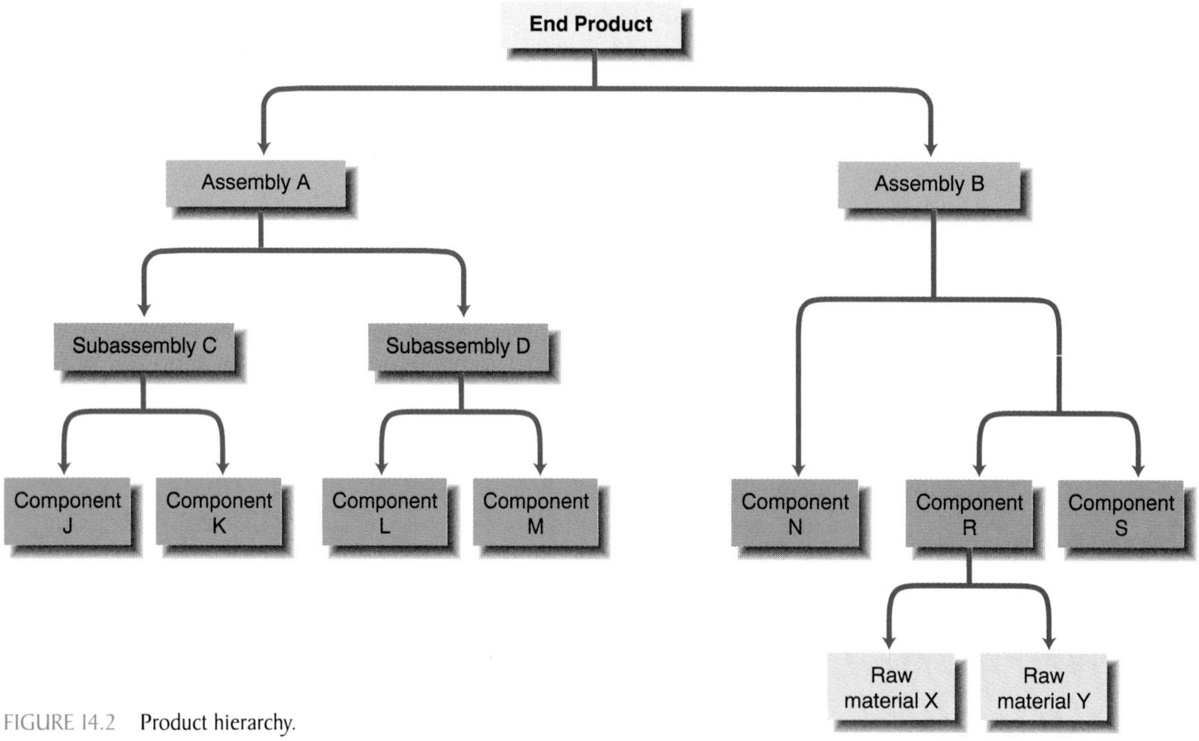

FIGURE 14.2 Product hierarchy.

14.3 MRP INPUTS

An MRP system requires four specific types of information: a schedule of requirements (or planned production) for each end product, a list of all components of the product according to the product's hierarchical structure, expected lead times for producing or purchasing all components and materials, and information about current inventory levels, as shown in Figure 14.3. This information is maintained in three standard data files: the master schedule file, the bill-of-materials file, and the inventory records file. These files are used not only by the MRP system but also for product design, personnel scheduling, purchasing, shipping, and accounting activities.

THE MASTER SCHEDULE FILE

The **master schedule file** contains the master production schedule for each product. The **master production schedule (MPS)** for a product specifies how much of the end product is needed or is to be produced and when. The MPS is derived from the aggregate production plan based on demand forecasts, customer orders, and capacity limitations, as shown in Chapter 12. The MPS is divided into time periods called **time buckets**. These time buckets are usually conventional units of time, most frequently weeks, although one-day, two-week, and one-month time buckets are not uncommon. The time buckets need not be the same for the entire schedule. For example, it is common to use shorter time buckets, such as a day or week, to plan short-term requirements and longer time buckets, such as two weeks or a month, to plan requirements several months ahead. Figure 14.4 illustrates an MPS for a climbing toy made by PCA Indus-

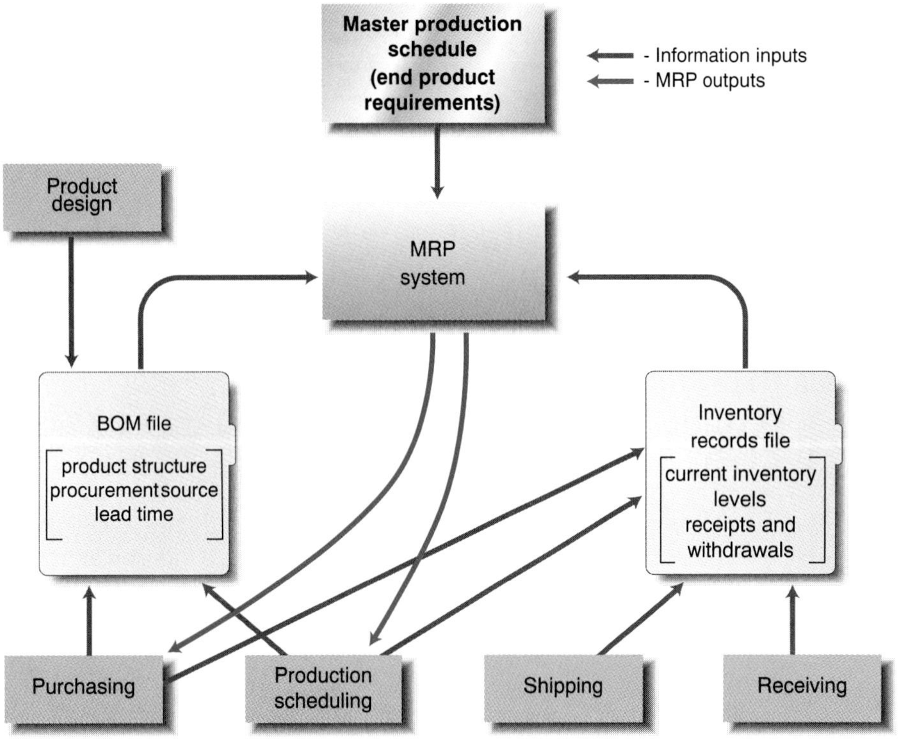

FIGURE 14.3 MRP information flows.

	Days										5 days			
Time period	1	2	3	4	5	6	7	8	9	10	10–15	16–20	21–25	26–30
Product requirements	0	40	0	0	10	0	0	0	20	0	30	10	50	40

FIGURE 14.4 MPS for the "Charlotte the Spider" climbing toy.

tries. Each product has its own MPS, and there is also an *overall* master schedule that synthesizes the requirements for all products or a group of products that share facilities.

The planning horizon for an MPS should be at least as large as the cumulative lead time for the product. The **cumulative lead time** is the amount of time required from when the first procurement or production activity must occur until the end product is produced (see Figure 14.7).

THE BILL-OF-MATERIALS FILE

Chapter 5 introduced the need for a bill-of-materials file as part of product and process design. The **bill-of-material (BOM) file** lists for each end product all assemblies, subassemblies, components, and raw materials necessary to produce the product. A BOM file, shown in Figure 14.5, includes information about how many units of each item are needed for each higher-level item in the product hierarchy (and possibly for the end product itself), whether the item is produced internally or purchased, and the produc-

Level No.	Item No.	Item Description	No. Required	Make/Buy	Lead Time
00		Spider climber		Make	1 day
01	M231	Curved ladder	4	Make	2 days
02	M110	Ladder leg	2	Make	2 days
03	B324	10 ft aluminum pipe	1	Buy	3 days
02	B278	Ladder step	7	Buy	3 days
01	M386	Leg support	4	Make	1 day
02	B324	10 ft aluminum pipe	1/4	Buy	3 days
01	M486	Shell	1	Make	3 days
02	M190	Shell quad	4	Make	3 days
03	B752	Aluminum ingots	3	Buy	In stock
01	B278	Bolt/nut set	32	Buy	In stock

FIGURE 14.5 BOM for the spider climber.

tion or purchase lead time necessary to acquire the item. The items appear in order according to the product structure hierarchy. A good way to visualize the hierarchical structure of the product is to use a **product structure tree**, as shown in Figure 14.6, which is a variation of an assembly chart (see Chapter 5).[2] We will illustrate the devel-

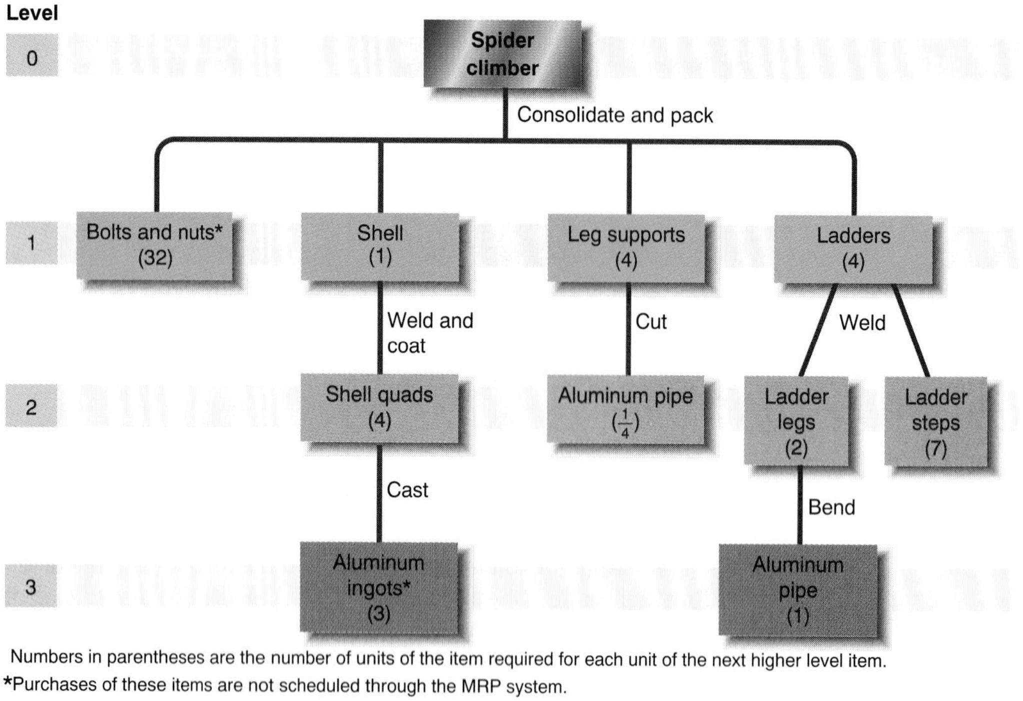

FIGURE 14.6 Product structure tree for the spider climber.

[2]An item can occur at more than one level of the BOM and the product structure tree, such as aluminum pipe in Figures 14.5 and 14.6. For computational ease, the BOM is often restructured so that a common component appears at the same level throughout. This procedure is often called *low-level coding* because the component will be incorporated into the BOM at the lowest level at which it appears in the original product structure tree.

"Charlotte the Spider," made by PCA Industries, has a hierarchical, dependent demand product structure. Acquisition of the components must be coordinated with the periodic production runs of the product.

opment of a product structure tree and a BOM using a climbing toy made by PCA Industries, called Charlotte the Spider (see the accompanying photo). This product will also be used to illustrate the logic and mechanics of an MRP system.

PCA Industries manufactures the climber using a combination of purchased parts and materials and several manufacturing operations.[3] The climber is assembled by the customer from four main components: a shell (or body), four ladders, four support legs, and 32 bolts and nuts. The climber is made as follows:

1. Aluminum ingots are melted in a furnace, and the molten metal is used to cast shell quads (the shell is divided into four shell quads).
2. Four shell quads are welded together to make a shell. The shell is then coated with a colored polyester coating.
3. One length of aluminum pipe is cut into four support legs and holes are tapped into the legs (for connection with the shell).
4. Eight lengths of aluminum pipe are bent into curved ladder legs and the ends prepared for attachment to the shell.
5. Seven ladder steps are welded to each pair of ladder legs to form ladders.
6. A shell, four ladders, four leg supports, and the necessary bolts and nuts are collected, packed in a box, and prepared for shipment.

The BOM and product structure tree for this product are given in Figures 14.5 and 14.6. The BOM is then used to construct a **materials list**, which combines and summarizes all the material needs for one spider climber. For example, the total number of shell quads and aluminum pipes required to make one climber can be computed as follows:

total number of shell quads =
  [(4 quads/shell) × (1 shell/climber)] = 4 quads/climber

[3]The actual production process, component information, and lead times have been modified to make illustration of the MRP system simpler.

total number of aluminum pipes =
[(1/4 pipe/leg support) × (4 leg supports/climber)] +
[(1 pipe/ladder leg) × (2 ladder legs/ladder) ×
(4 ladders/climber)] = 9 pipes/climber

This helps us to determine the total component needs and to schedule purchases and production appropriately.

THE INVENTORY RECORDS FILE

In a typical production system that uses MRP, every day hundreds or thousands of different items are being purchased, manufactured, withdrawn from stock, moved to other operations, assembled, and shipped to customers. Deliveries are early or late, production levels are not exactly as planned, and throughout the system defective items are found and possibly discarded. All these factors make it crucial that the current inventories and status of requirements, orders, and production activities be maintained accurately. The **inventory records file** is a file listing the current inventories and outstanding purchase and production orders for each item.

Although accuracy is important throughout the MRP system, the file whose accuracy is most crucial, and is most prone to error, is the inventory records file. For example, if components are removed from stock and used in an operation, but this action is not recorded in the inventory records file, the company may believe it has components that are really not available. This can cause it to schedule subsequent production using nonexistent components. Ultimately, the scheduled production will not occur because of the shortage, and ordering of the needed components will have been delayed.

14.4 MRP LOGIC AND MECHANICS

The logic underlying MRP is to use the product structure and lead time information to determine when purchase and production orders should be released so that materials are obtained just when they are needed.

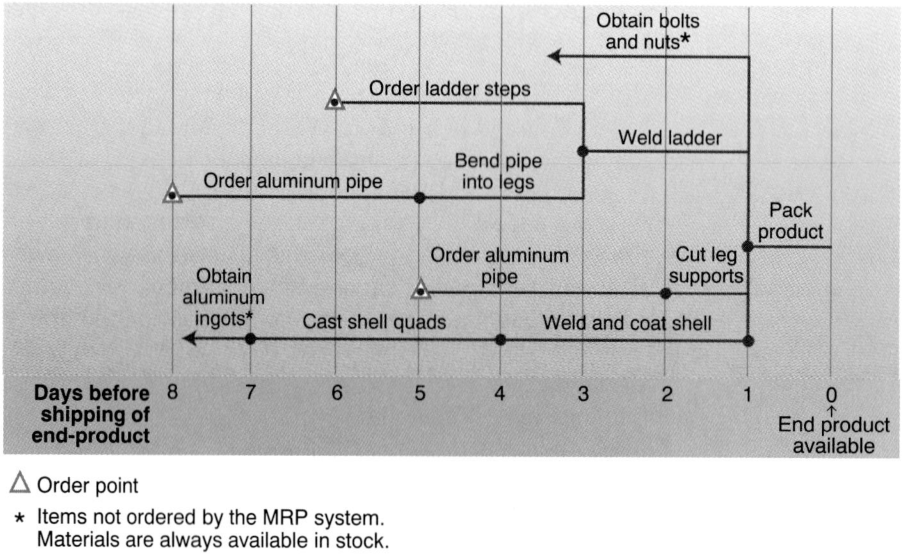

FIGURE 14.7 Production time chart for the spider climber.

EXPLODING THE PRODUCT

The first step is to use the BOM to "explode" the product into a **production** (or **assembly**) **time chart.** Figure 14.7 is a production time chart for PCA's spider climber. The explosion begins with the time the end product is needed and then works backward through each production or purchasing activity that must be done to make each succeeding item. For example, consolidating and packing a spider climber requires one day of lead time, so if a supply of climbers is required at time T, shells, leg supports, ladders, and bolts and nuts must be available one day earlier, at time $T - 1$. Welding and coating a shell requires three days of lead time, so an order to begin welding shell quads must be released three days earlier, or at time $T - 4$. Casting and demolding shell quads also has a three-day lead time, so an order to cast shell quads must be issued and aluminum ingots must be available at time $T - 7$. Figure 14.7 shows that the cumulative lead time for producing a spider climber is eight days, so the company would have to initiate production or purchase activities at least eight days before climbers are required.

DEVELOPING THE MATERIAL REQUIREMENTS PLAN

The next step is to construct a material requirements plan for each item in the BOM, as illustrated in Figure 14.8. A **material requirements plan** is a production or purchase schedule for an item that makes up the end product. The procedure begins by converting the gross product requirements in the MPS into net product requirements. The *gross requirements* are the number of units actually required (desired) at the beginning of each time period. The *net requirements* are the gross requirements less any available inventories, where the available inventories are total inventories for the item at the beginning of the period less any desired safety stock (in the MRP, available inventories are normally labeled as *projected on hand*):

$$(\text{net requirements})_t = (\text{gross requirements})_t - (\text{projected on hand})_t$$
$$(\text{projected on hand})_t = (\text{total expected inventory})_t - (\text{safety stock})_t$$

Gross product requirements are transferred from the MPS to the material requirements plan for the end product, and the net requirements are computed, as in Figure 14.8. The next line in the material requirements plan is the amount of product or material planned to be received through production or from a vendor at the *beginning* of the time period; this is called the *planned order receipts*. Under **lot-for-lot ordering (production)** we order or produce exactly what is needed in a time period so that the planned order receipts will equal the net requirements. (In Section 14.6 we will consider placing orders or producing items in more economical lot sizes, in which case the planned order receipts may exceed the net requirements.)

The final line in the material requirements plan for an item is the *planned order releases*. This is the amount that must be ordered (internally through production or externally from a vendor) at the beginning of a time period so that the planned order receipts occur when needed. Therefore, the planned order releases equal the planned order receipts, except that they are offset by the lead time. For example, in Figure 14.8 the net requirements and planned order receipts for the spider climber are 20 units on day 9 and 30 units on day 11. The lead time for final consolidation and packing is one day, so the planned order releases for the climber must be 20 on day 8 and 30 on day 10.

The planned order releases for the end product or component item directly determine the gross requirements for the items at the next lower level of production (which make up the higher-level product). For example, the planned order release of 20 climbers on day 8 means that on day 8 the gross requirements for shells, leg supports,

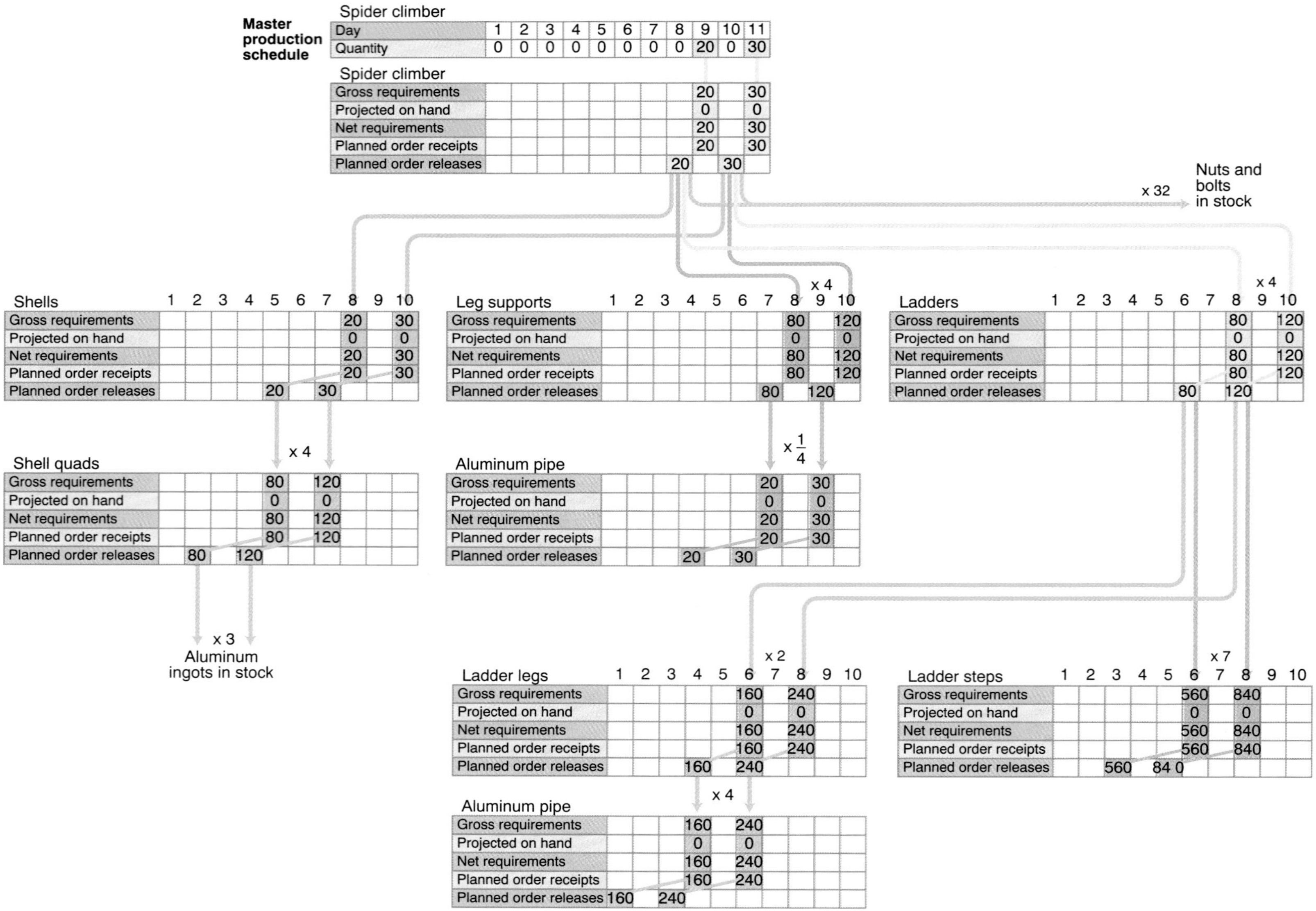

Spider climber (Master production schedule)

Day	1	2	3	4	5	6	7	8	9	10	11
Quantity	0	0	0	0	0	0	0	0	20	0	30

Spider climber

	1	2	3	4	5	6	7	8	9	10	11
Gross requirements									20		30
Projected on hand									0		0
Net requirements									20		30
Planned order receipts									20		30
Planned order releases								20		30	

Shells

	1	2	3	4	5	6	7	8	9	10
Gross requirements								20		30
Projected on hand								0		0
Net requirements								20		30
Planned order receipts								20		30
Planned order releases					20		30			

Leg supports

	1	2	3	4	5	6	7	8	9	10
Gross requirements								80		120
Projected on hand								0		0
Net requirements								80		120
Planned order receipts								80		120
Planned order releases							80		120	

Ladders

	1	2	3	4	5	6	7	8	9	10
Gross requirements								80		120
Projected on hand								0		0
Net requirements								80		120
Planned order receipts								80		120
Planned order releases						80		120		

Shell quads

	1	2	3	4	5	6	7	8	9	10
Gross requirements					80		120			
Projected on hand					0		0			
Net requirements					80		120			
Planned order receipts					80		120			
Planned order releases		80		120						

Aluminum pipe

	1	2	3	4	5	6	7	8	9	10
Gross requirements							20		30	
Projected on hand							0		0	
Net requirements							20		30	
Planned order receipts							20		30	
Planned order releases				20		30				

Ladder legs

	1	2	3	4	5	6	7	8	9	10
Gross requirements						160		240		
Projected on hand						0		0		
Net requirements						160		240		
Planned order receipts						160		240		
Planned order releases				160		240				

Ladder steps

	1	2	3	4	5	6	7	8	9	10
Gross requirements						560		840		
Projected on hand						0		0		
Net requirements						560		840		
Planned order receipts						560		840		
Planned order releases			560		84 0					

Aluminum pipe

	1	2	3	4	5	6	7	8	9	10
Gross requirements				160		240				
Projected on hand				0		0				
Net requirements				160		240				
Planned order receipts				160		240				
Planned order releases	160		240							

FIGURE 14.8 Material requirements plans for the spider climber.

ladders, and bolt/nut pairs are 20, 80, 80, and 640, respectively. Following shells through Figure 14.8, as an example, no inventories are expected at the beginning of day 8, so the net requirements at the beginning of day 8 are 20 and the planned order receipts *must* be 20. Because there is a three-day lead time to weld and coat shells, the planned order releases on day 5 must be 20. The planned order releases of 20 shells on day 5 then dictate that on day 5 the gross requirement for shell quads is 80 (4 quads for every shell). No shell quads are expected to be on hand on day 5, so the net requirements and planned order receipts will be 80. The lead time for casting quads is three days, so the planned order releases for quads on day 2 will be 80. Because the raw material needed for casting, aluminum ingots, is maintained in stock rather than ordered through the MRP system, no material requirements plan for ingots is derived. The same logic was used to derive the material requirements plans in Figure 14.8 for the other items used to make the climbers.

Notice that materials requirements plans are not derived for aluminum ingots and bolt/nut pairs because these are maintained in stock. Because these are used for almost every product and are consumed at a steady rate, their purchases are planned using an independent demand analysis rather than the MRP system

CONSOLIDATING REQUIREMENTS

In Figure 14.8 two separate material requirements plans were developed for aluminum pipe because it appeared twice in the product structure tree. In practice, these two plans for pipe would be merged so that there would be a single plan, as shown in Figure 14.9. The gross requirements for pipe would then be the sum of the requirements for leg supports and ladder legs.

More generally, many items may be common to several end products. Rather than ordering or producing an item separately for each end product in which it is used, the material requirements plans for the item for all the end products in which it occurs should be merged into one master material requirements plan. This way a more coherent and efficient production or procurement plan can be devised. For example, if shell quads were used in 10 different end products, the material requirements plans for shell quads for all of the end products would be combined into a single material requirements plan. Figure 14.10 illustrates this merging of requirements across end products.

Aluminum pipe for leg supports	1	2	3	4	5	6	7	8	9	10
Gross requirements							20		30	
Projected on hand							0		0	
Net requirements							20		30	
Planned order receipts							20		30	
Planned order releases				20		30				

Aluminum pipe for ladder legs	1	2	3	4	5	6	7	8	9	10
Gross requirements				160		240				
Projected on hand				0		0				
Net requirements				160		240				
Planned order receipts				160		240				
Planned order releases	160		240							

Total aluminum pipe	1	2	3	4	5	6	7	8	9	10
Gross requirements				160		240	20		30	
Projected on hand				0		0	0		0	
Net requirements				160		240	20		30	
Planned order receipts				160		240	20		30	
Planned order releases	160		240	20		30				

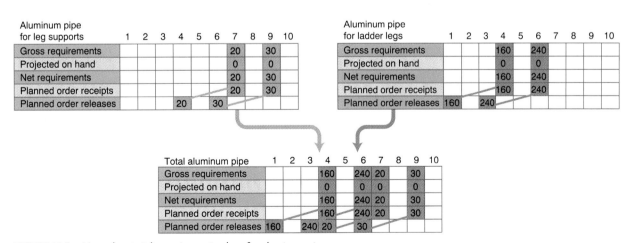

FIGURE 14.9 Merged materials requirements plans for aluminum pipe.

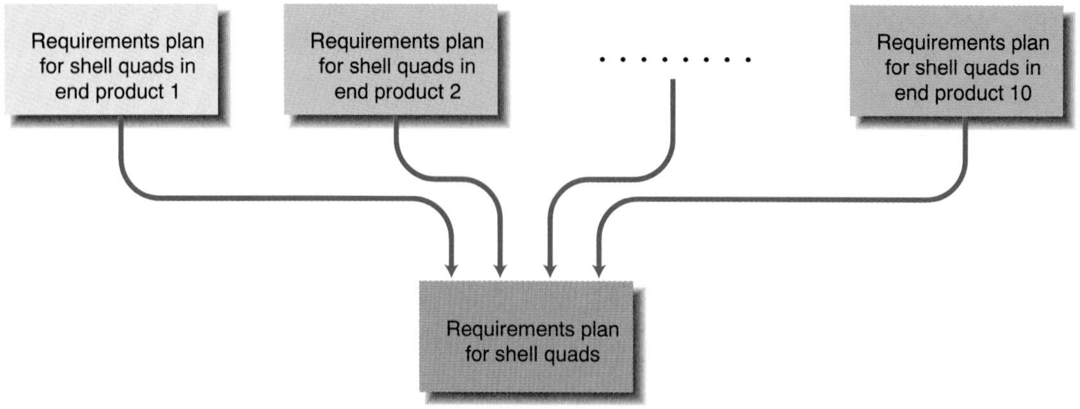

FIGURE 14.10 Merging material requirements plans for shell quads from several end products.

It is interesting to note that in a complex, multiproduct production system the end products may have independent demands; product-specific components and assemblies may have dependent demands that are best managed using MRP; and some widely used common components (such as the aluminum ingots and bolts and nuts) might best be managed as independent demand items. Understanding the variety of inventory and scheduling procedures available, and having the capability to experiment with or simulate various material management options, can enhance the efficiency and effectiveness of a company's operations.

14.5 MRP OUTPUTS

The primary outputs of an MRP system are the material requirements plans for each item, such as those in Figures 14.8 and 14.9, and master material requirements plans that aggregate requirements for all products, as shown in Figure 14.10. These would be used to generate the following other reports and documents:

1. **Order and production release schedules**, which specify the amount and timing of future orders and production runs for each item.
2. **Order releases**, which authorize the purchase or production of items.
3. **Change reports**, which highlight changes to the previous production and purchase plans.
4. **Load reports**, which indicate the amount of each major production resource or department capacity that is to be utilized with the plan.

The load reports are used for more than production planning and personnel scheduling; preliminary load reports play an important role in developing feasible material requirements plans, as will be shown in Section 14.7.

The information produced by the MRP system can be combined with other company data to produce various financial, production, and delivery performance reports, as well as exception reports that highlight deviations from plans. In general, companies customize the types, content, and format of reports produced from their MRP system to meet their specific needs.

14.6 LOT SIZING IN MRP

In the PCA example we assumed a lot-for-lot procurement policy whereby we either ordered or produced exactly the number of units required to be available exactly when needed. When final products are unique, such as customer-specified products, and the possibility or timing of repeat orders is unclear, then lot-for-lot procurement is the most prudent approach. Acquiring larger quantities than the known requirements for items could result in substantial inventory holding costs or scrapping of unused items.

However, when an item is needed on an ongoing though possibly irregular basis, and when there is a substantial fixed cost for procurement or production setup, it may be more economical to purchase or produce the item in lot sizes other than those matching immediate net requirements. We will consider three additional approaches for lot sizing. The first two (EOQ and part-period balancing) are approximation methods; the third (the Wagner-Whitin method) is more complicated but minimizes costs.

ECONOMIC ORDER QUANTITY

Example 1 showed how using an independent demand model for lot sizing and scheduling within a dependent demand environment can lead to inefficiencies and shortages. In that example, economic lot sizes were computed and production runs of those sizes were made on a regular basis for two components, without regard to the timing and magnitude of actual product requirements. Although the EOQ and lot-sizing models of Chapter 13 are most appropriate for independent demand situations, they *can* be used in MRP if (1) the EOQ (or lot size) is greater than the gross requirements in a typical period and (2) the *timing* of the production runs or orders is scheduled more in synch with product requirements. This is illustrated in the following example.

EXAMPLE 2

A company's gross requirements for an item during the next 10 weeks are given in Table 14.2. There is a two-week lead time for acquiring the item from an outside vendor, and the company has no available inventories at time 0. Using a lot-for-lot purchasing plan, the net requirements, planned order releases, and receipts are given in Table 14.2.

Suppose the fixed ordering cost is \$160 per order and the cost to carry the product in inventory is \$1 per unit per week. With the lot-for-lot approach, the **total stocking cost (TSC)** (ordering cost plus holding cost) during the planning horizon is

TSC = (6 orders × \$160/order) + zero holding cost = \$960

Now instead of a lot-for-lot approach, suppose we use equation (13.4) to compute the EOQ, but we schedule the order releases so that net requirements are always satis-

TABLE 14.2 MATERIAL REQUIREMENTS PLAN USING LOT-FOR-LOT PROCUREMENT

Week	1	2	3	4	5	6	7	8	9	10
Gross requirements	—	—	50	0	40	90	110	0	30	40
On hand	—	—	0	0	0	0	0	0	0	0
Net requirements	—	—	50	0	40	90	110	0	30	40
Planned order receipts	—	—	50	0	40	90	110	0	30	40
Planned order releases	50	0	40	90	110	0	30	40	—	—

TABLE 14.3 MATERIAL REQUIREMENTS PLAN USING EOQ LOT SIZING

Week	1	2	3	4	5	6	7	8	9	10
Gross requirements	—	—	50	0	40	90	110	0	30	40
On hand	—	—	0	70	70	30	60	70	70	40
Net requirements	—	—	50	0	0	60	50	0	0	0
Planned order receipts	—	—	120	0	0	120	120	0	0	0
Planned order releases	120	0	0	120	120	0	0	0	—	—

fied while holding no more inventory than necessary. To use the EOQ model, we treat the demand during the 8-week period (weeks 3–10) as if it were constant. The total demand is 360 units so the average weekly demand is 45. Then

$$EOQ = \sqrt{(2 \times 45 \text{ units/week} \times \$160\text{/order})/(\$1\text{/unit/week})} = 120$$

The resulting material requirements plan is given in Table 14.3. With this plan, only three orders are placed and a total of 410 units will be held in inventory for a week, so the total stocking cost during the planning horizon will be

$$TSC = [(3 \text{ orders} \times \$160\text{/order}) + (410 \text{ units in inv.} \times \$1\text{/unit/week})] = \$890$$

In this case, using an EOQ model reduces total stocking cost. Notice that if the EOQ is less than the gross requirements in a typical period, the resulting plan tends to place too many orders and order material too soon.

PART-PERIOD BALANCING

A problem with using a pure EOQ approach to determine lot size is that it does not take into account the variations in requirements over *time*. The EOQ approach smoothes out the different gross requirements to compute an assumed constant demand rate and then uses this rate to compute a single order quantity or lot size, which is utilized throughout the planning horizon. Because of the significant variations in gross requirements from period to period, an intuitively superior approach would be to modify the lot sizes according to near-term requirements while still taking into account the economies of smoothing fixed costs over a larger procurement quantity. A simple heuristic method that does this is the **part-period balancing (PPB)** method developed by DeMatteis.[4]

We first define a **part period** as a unit of measure that is equivalent to carrying one unit of an item (a part) in inventory for one period. The PPB heuristic is based on the observation that in the basic EOQ model the optimal order quantity or lot size occurs when the total ordering or setup cost equals the total holding cost. Using this idea, the PPB algorithm first computes the **economic part period (EPP)**:

$$EPP = [\text{setup or ordering cost}]/[\text{holding cost/unit/period}]$$

In Example 2 $EPP = \$160/\$1 = 160$, so holding the equivalent of 160 units in inventory for one week would cost the same as placing one order. Therefore, an ordering policy that results in holding the equivalent of 160 units in inventory for one week for every

[4] J. J. DeMatteis, "An Economic Lot-Sizing Technique: The Part-Period Algorithm," IBM *Systems Journal*, Vol. 7, No. 1, 1968, pp. 30–38.

order placed would balance the holding cost and the cost of placing an order. The heuristic finds this policy by adding cumulative requirements for successive periods and computing the number of part-periods that would result if an order or production run were made equal to the requirements for those cumulative periods. This is done until the part-period value equals or exceeds EPP. The lot size chosen is the cumulative requirement that has a part-periods value closest to *EPP*. We now illustrate this algorithm for Example 2.

EXAMPLE 2 (CONTINUED)

We first compute EPP = (ordering cost)/(holding cost) = \$160/\$1 = 160. We then begin with the net requirements in week 3, which are 50. We act as if we order just enough units to satisfy these requirements just when they are needed; that is, we tentatively assume that we order 50 units in week 1. The part-period value for this option (see Table 14.4) is the number of units that would be carried in inventory until they are used up, which is zero because they are used in week 3 when they arrive. We then combine the requirements for weeks 3 and 4, which are also 50. We act as if in week 1 we order just enough units to satisfy these cumulative requirements, which are still 50, and no units would be held in inventory during weeks 3 and 4. We then combine requirements for weeks 3, 4, and 5. The cumulative requirements are 90. So we act as if we order 90 units in week 1 to satisfy the cumulative requirements for weeks 3–5. In this case 90 units would be received at the beginning of week 3, 50 would be used immediately, and 40 would go into inventory. The 40 units would be in inventory at the beginning of week 4 and remain there until the beginning of week 5, so the part-period value of this strategy would be 40 + 40 = 80. We now combine the requirements for weeks 3–6, which are 180. If we ordered 180 units in week 1 to satisfy the requirements in weeks 3–6, we would use 50 units in week 3 and have 130 units in inventory to start week 4, 130 in inventory to start week 5, and 90 in inventory at the beginning of week 6. So the part-period value would be 130 + 130 + 90 = 350. The part-period value of 80 from ordering 90 units (demand for weeks 3–5) is closer to the EPP value of 160 than the part-period value of 350 from ordering 180 units (demand for weeks 3–6), so we would order 90 units in week 1 to satisfy the requirements in weeks 3–5.

We now determine the amount to buy in week 4 to satisfy the requirements for week 6 and beyond. Table 14.5 computes the part-period values for various lot sizes for purchases in week 4. It shows that we should order 230 units in week 4 to satisfy the requirements in weeks 6–9.

TABLE 14.4 PART-PERIOD VALUES FOR REQUIREMENTS IN WEEK 3 AND BEYOND (ORDER PLACED IN WEEK 1 AND RECEIVED IN WEEK 3)

Periods Combined	Trial Lot Size (Cumulative Net Requirements)	Part Periods
3	50	0
3, 4	50	0
3, 4, 5	90*	80 = 40 + 40
3, 4, 5, 6	180	350 = 130 + 130 + 90

*Lot size with a part-period value closest to an EPP of 160.

TABLE 14.5 PART-PERIOD VALUES FOR REQUIREMENTS IN WEEK 6 AND BEYOND (ORDER PLACED IN WEEK 4 AND RECEIVED IN WEEK 6)

Periods Combined	Trial Lot Size (Cumulative Net Requirements)	Part Periods
6	90	0
6, 7	200	110
6, 7, 8	200	110
6, 7, 8, 9	230*	200 = 140 + 30 + 30

*Lot size with part-period value closest to an EPP of 160.

TABLE 14.6 MATERIAL REQUIREMENTS PLAN USING THE PPB METHOD

Week	1	2	3	4	5	6	7	8	9	10
Gross requirements	—	—	50	0	40	90	110	0	30	40
On hand	—	—	0	40	40	0	140	30	30	0
Net requirements	—	—	50	0	0	90	0	0	0	40
Planned order receipts	—	—	90	0	0	230	0	0	0	40
Planned order releases	90	0	0	230	0	0	0	40	—	—

The requirements for week 10 would then be satisfied by an order placed in week 8. (This might subsequently be revised as information about weeks 11 and 12 become available.) The resulting material requirements plan is given in Table 14.6.

The total stocking cost for the PPB lot-sizing plan would be

$$TSC = [(3 \text{ orders} \times \$160/\text{order}) + (280 \text{ units in inv.} \times \$1/\text{unit/week})] = \$760$$

So the solution from the PPB heuristic is superior to the solution from the other two methods used in this case.

THE WAGNER-WHITIN OPTIMIZATION ALGORITHM

The lot-sizing methods mentioned above are all heuristics, which do not guarantee a total cost-minimizing solution. The lot-for-lot approach minimizes holding cost because it acquires materials only when needed and only in the quantities needed; however, this can result in high setup or ordering costs. The EOQ and PPB approaches try to reduce total stocking costs by approximately balancing the holding and procurement costs. Although the resulting procurement schedules and lot sizes are often superior to those resulting from a lot-for-lot approach, they do not guarantee that the resulting stocking cost is minimized. An approach that does guarantee an optimal solution is the **Wagner-Whitin algorithm**.

Without describing this solution method in detail, we can say that Wagner and Whitin formulated the lot-size and scheduling problem as a dynamic program that can be solved to find the *optimal* lot sizes over time.[5] A **dynamic program** is a constrained optimization problem (see Tutorial 1) formulated in such a way that it can be solved using a special recursive (repetitive) technique. Specifically, the problem is broken into decision *stages* that correspond to time periods. The algorithm sequentially determines

[5]For a simple explanation of the algorithm, see James M. Fordyce and Francis M. Webster, "The Wagner-Whitin Algorithm Made Simple," *Production and Inventory Management*, 2nd Quarter 1984, pp. 21–27.

TABLE 14.7 MATERIAL REQUIREMENTS PLAN USING THE WAGNER-WHITIN ALGORITHM

Week	1	2	3	4	5	6	7	8	9	10
Gross requirements	0	0	50	0	40	90	110	0	30	40
On hand	0	0	0	40	40	0	110	0	0	40
Net requirements	0	0	50	0	0	90	0	0	30	0
Planned order receipts	0	0	90	0	0	200	0	0	70	0
Planned order releases	90	0	0	200	0	0	70	0	—	—

the best action to take in the last (first) time period (in this case, whether an order should be released and, if so, the lot size to use), then the best action to take in the last (first) two periods combined, the last (first) three periods, and so forth. The solutions at each stage are *optimal*, and the method used to solve the problem at each stage is moderately efficient, although much less efficient than linear programming. Because of the nature of dynamic programming, multiperiod problems such as the MRP lot-sizing problem are especially suitable for solution in this manner.

Although Wagner and Whitin first proposed their method in 1958, and although it provides an optimal solution for the given parameter values, it has not been widely used in practice. There may be two reasons. First, dynamic programming is far less widely known by managers, engineers, and computer scientists than other operations management modeling and solution methods. Second, for even moderate-sized problems, obtaining the optimal solution is computationally slow and cumbersome compared to other optimization models and algorithms. If the MRP system is tracking thousands of items, the solution time could be prohibitive. However, the constantly improving speed and processing capabilities of computers, as well as improved algorithms and software, have now made the Wagner-Whitin algorithm far more computationally feasible. The optimal material requirements plan for Example 2 that results from the Wagner-Whitin algorithm is given in Table 14.7.

The total stocking cost for the Wagner-Whitin lot-sizing plan is

$$TSC = [(3 \text{ orders} \times \$160/\text{order}) + (230 \text{ units in inv.} \times \$1/\text{unit/week})] = \$710$$

14.7 CAPACITY REQUIREMENTS PLANNING

So far, we have assumed that the company can produce or order any number of units of an item in any time period. In practice this is usually not the case; capacity limitations exist throughout the production system. An important benefit of MRP is that it can identify potential bottlenecks and capacity problems far enough in advance to adapt the schedule to them.

Developing material requirements plans is an iterative process. Using the available data, we first derive a tentative production schedule and a corresponding material requirements plan for each item, with no production or procurement limitations imposed. The MRP system uses these to generate load reports for each production department and/or work center. The load reports convert the material requirements into resource (personnel, machinery) requirements.[6] If the loads are within capacity limitations, the material requirements plans are feasible and can be used. However, as shown

[6]Because of this explicit consideration of production resources in planning, many people have redefined MRP to mean "manufacturing resources planning."

in Figure 14.11, the load assigned to a department, work center, or machine may exceed its capacity in a given period. In that case, either some of the planned production must be shifted to other time periods to smooth production or short-term production capacity must be added (e.g., by working overtime). Production can be shifted to other time periods by moving item requirements forward or back in time, by modifying lot sizes, or by splitting planned production lots over two periods. After these modifications are made, the MRP system is run again and new load reports are generated to determine the feasibility of the plan. This process is repeated until feasible material requirements plans are obtained.

As long as the overloads are not too large and capacity is available in surrounding time periods, making these adjustments is relatively easy. For example, in Figure 14.11a the production planned for periods 3 and 8 exceeds capacity. We would move production of the highest-priority jobs or items produced in the department from period 3 to period 2 and from period 8 to period 7. The MRP system would then be rerun. If the resulting material requirements plans satisfied the capacity limitations, as in Figure 14.11b, then the new plan could be finalized. If not, other adjustments could be made. One complication of production shifting, however, is that the sequential nature of production often means that when we change the production schedule for one item in one department, it can cause changes in the timing of production for other items, possibly in several departments.

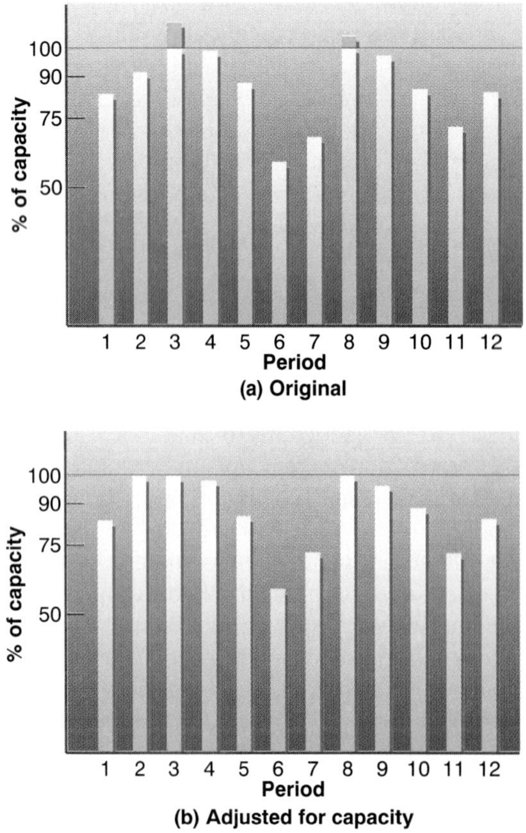

FIGURE 14.11 Load reports.

It is important to note that load reports should be generated for every important resource and work unit in the production system. For example, the labor requirements in a department for a given production schedule may not exceed the amount available, but the schedule may require more machine capacity than is available. Similarly, a given schedule may be within the capacity of all the machines in a department except for one, but that one machine can postpone production unless the schedule is modified.

14.8 UPDATING THE MRP SYSTEM AND SYSTEM NERVOUSNESS

The material requirements plans and production schedules produced by an MRP system are intended to be dynamic and adaptable to changes in the operating environment. The material requirements plans may have a 10- or 20-week time horizon, but the plans and schedules are not fixed for the entire time horizon. As soon as the plans for the first period are implemented, deviations from the plans will occur: (1) new orders may be received and existing orders may be canceled, postponed, or accelerated, changing the requirements in the master schedule; (2) the number of units of an item actually produced or received from a supplier may differ from the planned number due to production variations, quality problems, machine breakdowns, and lead-time variations.

These changes can affect a company's production and purchasing plans. The important questions are *how* and *when* deviations should be incorporated into the MRP system. Two common approaches are used to update MRP systems: a net-change system and a regenerative system.

NET-CHANGE SYSTEMS

A **net-change system** is one in which production and ordering plans are continually revised whenever new information on orders, production levels, and receipts is available. For example, if a customer asks to postpone delivery of a product by one week, the production and material requirements plans would be immediately revised to reflect this change. Rather than reproducing all the plans, however, we would identify only the *changes* to the plan and disseminate them through a change report.

The main advantage of the net-change system is that it keeps the plans current. However, there are at least two major disadvantages. First, it is costly to update the system continually, even though only changes are identified. Second, and more important, the system may become more "nervous" than it need be and never be stable. For example, one day the actual production of an item may be only 150 units instead of the planned 160. The net-change system would then change plans for all items affected by this deficiency. The next day actual production may be 170 units instead of the originally planned 160, so that the system again changes the plan back to its original values. By simply waiting for a while, we may see many of the deviations in orders, production levels, and receipts cancel each other and balance out, so that a stable production plan would, in fact, be appropriate over the longer term.

REGENERATIVE SYSTEMS

With a **regenerative system** information about order changes, material receipts, and actual production levels is gathered for a time period (say, a week). Then the MRP system is rerun, incorporating this new information, and new material requirements plans and production schedules are generated. This type of updating is easier to manage because it can be done at the same time in every period. It is also less costly and creates a more stable operating atmosphere. The only risk is that if *major* changes occur (e.g., a large order is canceled), the delay in updating the production plans can be harmful. One way to handle this potential problem is to allow for emergency updates of the regenerative MRP system.

TIME FENCES

Even regenerative updating can lead to frequent changes in production and procurement plans. In a firm's attempt to stay current, these frequent changes can become disruptive and inefficient, especially if they call for substantial changes in short-term plans. Consequently, it is advisable to put some restrictions on the amount of change in production and procurement plans that are allowed between regeneration periods. A common approach is to use time fences. **Time fences** are periods of time during which changes to production and procurement plans are restricted. For example, a company may use two time fences: three weeks and six weeks. During the three-week time fence the production schedule is essentially frozen, with only minor changes allowed; from three to six weeks into the future, larger changes in production and possibly resequencing of production runs may be allowed; beyond six weeks, unlimited changes may be allowed.

ROLLING HORIZON

The multiperiod nature of material requirements plans and production plans derived from MRP is similar to that for the aggregate production plans discussed in Chapter 12. Like aggregate production planning, MRP uses a **rolling horizon** approach. That is, although a 15-week plan may be derived, only the first 1 or 2 weeks are implemented as planned. The plans for subsequent periods are revised and updated over time, but taking into account what is best over the entire time horizon.

14.9 UNCERTAINTY AND SAFETY STOCK

If there were no randomness in lead times and production rates and no variation in defect or scrap rates, production and purchasing could be scheduled to meet all requirements exactly as needed without safety stocks. However, as we know, this is rarely the case. Because a shortage of *any* component in a hierarchically constructed product can stop production, some mechanism must be incorporated into the system to accommodate variations and uncertainties. The traditional approach is to maintain safety stocks. But we may not want to maintain safety stocks of every item used to make a product. This is especially true if the end product is a customer-specific product that may not be purchased again for a long time, if at all, because any unused safety stocks would become obsolete.

The key to adapting to these uncertainties efficiently is to determine which items and processes are most subject to randomness, as well as the type and cause of the variation. The most effective approach, which is at the heart of JIT production systems and is discussed extensively in Chapter 15, is to reduce or eliminate the variations and uncertainty. For example, if the lead times for items purchased from a vendor are highly variable, the company might work with the vendor to reduce this variation; or if large, variable defect rates are a problem, the company should directly address the quality issue. If these direct actions have been taken and randomness still remains, two accommodations might be made.

For those items in which variations are prevalent, we want to determine whether the variation is in *time* or in *quantity*. If the variations are in the quantity produced, safety stocks can make up for small production shortfalls and keep the process operating. But variations in time (when items are delivered or produced) are *not* effectively remedied by maintaining safety stock. For example, in Figure 14.8 PCA Industries wants to consolidate and ship 20 spider climbers on day 9. To do this, it orders 560 ladder *steps* from its supplier on day 3, to be received on day 6, so that they can be welded into ladders. Suppose delivery of the steps is two days late (arriving on day 8). Unless PCA maintained 560 ladder steps as safety stock, welding of the ladders and final shipment of the climbers would be delayed. But maintaining such a large level of safety stock would almost certainly not be profitable.

A far more efficient way to address variations in lead times (including production lead times) is to use **safety time**, that is, to place orders or schedule production earlier than necessary so that if there is a delay the items will still arrive when needed. Notice that if delivery occurs on time the items are held only a short period of time before they are used in production, so the holding cost is relatively small compared to that of maintaining continual safety stocks.

For regularly produced items, small amounts of safety stock of the end product and/or strategically selected components can compensate for minor production or procurement shortages and possibly for short time delays. It is important to emphasize, however, that safety stocks should not be maintained for all items—only for those with the greatest risk or variation in supply. For custom-made products that may not be produced again, safety stocks should be avoided.

14.10 MRP II: MANUFACTURING RESOURCES PLANNING

Because the production planning aspects of MRP are related to most other functions of a company, the scope of MRP has been expanded in recent years to integrate MRP with the order processing, billing, shop floor scheduling, and personnel and machine utilization activities of the company. These newer systems, called **manufacturing resources planning** or **MRP II**, contain the classical MRP scheduling function as their centerpiece. However, MRP II systems may include a module that collects sales and customer order data and generates an MPS for future end product requirements (e.g., using a forecasting model). In addition, an MRP II system may convert information from the material requirements plans into specific work schedules for departments and machines, evaluate department workloads and capacity conditions, generate shipping documents and customer invoices, and produce management reports on production and financial performance. Typically, these systems have a feedback mechanism (and are therefore called *closed-loop* MRP systems) so that if department, machine, or personnel capacity limits are exceeded, the material requirements plans and corresponding production schedules are revised to stay within capacity limits.

MRP II systems are an expansion of MRP to interconnect with and support other activities better, but the basic method used to generate material requirements plans is the same.

14.11 BENEFITS, LIMITATIONS, AND IMPLEMENTATION OF MRP

When used in the correct environments, MRP can provide many benefits. Of course, as with most computer information systems, the degree of success depends crucially on how it is implemented.

BENEFITS

The benefits of using an MRP system, summarized here, were all in evidence in the preceding discussion.

1. **Low Inventory Levels, Especially for In-Process Materials.** Because materials are acquired or produced only when needed and in the quantities required, inventories are kept to a minimum.
2. ***Good Material Tracking and Production Scheduling.*** The material requirements plans for each item provide a quick summary of the status of each item used in production: how much is on hand, the status of outstanding orders, and the schedule for production.
3. **A Method to Evaluate and Allocate Production Capacity.** Tentative material requirements plans identify possible production bottlenecks and capacity problems. These plans can be used to decide whether to expand short-term capacity or reschedule production and how to reallocate production among time periods to stay within capacity limits.

Many companies have reported success with MRP systems. For example, Publishers Equipment Corporation reported that in a single year its savings from the use of its MRP II system exceeded the $260,000 initial cost of equipment, software, and installation.[7]

LIMITATIONS AND IMPLEMENTATION PROBLEMS

Despite the potential benefits of MRP, the record of successful implementations is not good. Some researchers have characterized as many as 50–90% of MRP implementations as being either "failures" or "disappointments."[8] Although a more recent study[9] has found much lower failure and disappointment rates, one has to wonder why there have been so many unsuccessful implementations when the underlying logic of MRP is so simple. There are at least three major reasons why MRP systems do not yield the benefits expected: (1) poor file maintenance and data inaccuracy, (2) inadequate employee training and participation in implementation, and (3) inappropriate business and product environments.

File Maintenance and Data Accuracy

An MRP system relies on having accurate, up-to-date information. Surprisingly many companies have tried to implement MRP systems with gross deficiencies in their BOM and inventory files. For example, some companies have BOM records that are out of date and do not include recent design changes, supplier information, or lead times. As a result, the MRP system does not create the necessary material requirements plans for some components, creates them for nonexistent components, and times order releases incorrectly. The BOM file must be kept current; any changes in product design, vendor, method of production, or lead times should be incorporated immediately.

An even more common data problem is maintaining accurate inventory records. One problem that needs to be resolved before an MRP system is implemented is to identify common parts that are used in several products but carried in inventory

---

[7]From J. G. Ormsby, S. Y. Ormsby, and C. R. Ruthstrom, "MRP II Implementation: A Case Study," *Production and Inventory Management Journal*, Fourth Quarter 1990, pp. 77–81).

[8]See S. C. Aggarwal, "MRP, JIT, OPT, FMA," *Harvard Business Review*, Vol. 63, No. 5, 1985, pp. 8–16, and R. J. Shaw and M. O. Regentz, "How to Prepare for a New System," *Management Focus*, (Mar–Apr) 1980, pp. 33–36.

[9]See R. P. Cerveny and L. W. Scott, "A Survey of MRP Implementation," *Production and Inventory Management Journal*, Third Quarter 1989, pp. 31–34.

Accurate inventory information is essential to operate an MRP system successfully. Bar coding and optical scanning technology have made it much easier to obtain accurate and timely data on the arrival, movement, and shipment of materials.

records under different descriptions and part numbers. These items need to be combined into a single identifier. Similarly, outdated parts need to be purged from the records. An ongoing data management task is to make sure that material receipts from suppliers, completion of production runs by the company, withdrawals from inventory, scrapped items due to defects, and returns to suppliers are all entered into the inventory records in a timely and accurate fashion. An MRP system can bring production to a screeching halt if the system believes that inventories of a component are available (and therefore does not release an order for more) when, in fact, the inventories do not exist. This can easily happen if someone withdraws materials from inventory or returns defectives to a supplier but fails to record it in the inventory files. Companies that have reported successful implementations, such as Publishers Equipment Corporation, consistently mention achieving data accuracy as a crucial element in their success.

Employee Training and Involvement

Many of the problems attributable to inaccurate and untimely data occur because employees are not trained to use the system or are not involved in its design and implementation. Timely and accurate data will not get into the MRP system and the supporting data files automatically. Procedures must be developed and employees trained to use them. The best way to accomplish both is to involve employees in the development of the MRP system and the supporting procedures as early as possible. The employees responsible for receiving materials, maintaining and transporting inventories, and supervising production are in an excellent position to help decide who should be responsible for updating which files, how this should be done, and when it should be done. Employee involvement will not only create better systems, but employees will have a sense of ownership of and commitment to the success of the system. Furthermore, participation in developing the system is one aspect of training employees to use the system. Many MRP implementation failures occurred when companies developed a system with no input from the employees most affected by it and then imposed it on them with minimal training. The employees did not understand the system, the system was not as well designed as it could have been, and no one was committed to it or had an incentive to make it work.

Product Environment

MRP systems can be beneficial when the product environment is appropriate, but they are not appropriate for all situations. Specifically, MRP is most useful when (1) a company must manage the production and purchase of a large number of items (several hundred or more); (2) the items are primarily components and assemblies of end products, with a dependent demand pattern; (3) the demand for the items is irregular in timing and lumpy in quantity; and (4) lead times are reasonably consistent and reliable. When these conditions are not reasonably satisfied, MRP may not be beneficial, and in some cases it can be far inferior to alternative material management methods. For example, in recent years one common mistake has been to use MRP in situations where JIT systems would have been better, such as when the demand for products is relatively constant. In Chapter 15 we will discuss when JIT systems should be used instead of MRP and when both systems are best used together.

COMPUTER-BASED SYSTEMS

A final issue in implementation is the actual development and installation of the computer system. When MRP was relatively new in the 1960s and 1970s, a majority of systems were developed in house by the user companies. Since 1980, however, an ever-increasing majority of new MRP installations are off-the-shelf systems purchased from commercial suppliers. Not only has this become a less expensive option for most companies, but the implementation time is approximately half as long.

IN GOOD COMPANY

Tubetronics Cures Its Growing Pains

How does a small manufacturer solve its first big inventory problem? For Tubetronics, a San Diego tube- and pipe-bending supplier to the aerospace industry, the answer was a sophisticated software program called E-Z-MRP.

Tubetronics manufactures over 1500 different tube configurations using 100 or more different types of tubes. Its products, destined for airplanes' air-conditioning, hydraulic, brake, and oxygen lines, can have as many as three part numbers—one each for the customer, the fittings supplier, and Tubetronics itself. The company turned to its computerized MRP system after its first year of operation, when it began to experience such typical growing pains as late deliveries, erratic purchases, lost receivables, cash flow problems, and missing parts. The new system has imposed a welcome order on the firm's database of 3200 parts, 1000 BOMs, and 600 sales orders.

"Small as it is, [the system] has provided us with the ability to control our overhead, meet our deadlines, and keep down our costs," says Olivier Conler, cost accounting manager at Tubetronics' parent firm.

Source: Marsha Sutton, "Multi-User E-Z-MRP Runs on Network of Micros," *Industrial Engineering*, April 1994, pp. 34–35.

Dozens of commercial systems are now available, which run on a full spectrum of computer systems.[10] The advent of personal computers and client/server systems has dramatically reduced the prices of MRP systems, and has made them financially accessible to small and medium-sized companies. In the mid-1980s, when MRP systems were almost exclusively mainframe based, the average MRP system required an investment of over $600,000. Recently, companies such as Tubetronics, the subject of this chapter's "In Good Company" segment, have reported successful implementations of microcomputer-based MRP systems costing less than $10,000. Regardless of the system selected, it is important for users to obtain the technical assistance needed. Cerveny and Scott (see note 9) found that the chance of a successful MRP implementation increased with the amount of outside technical assistance and training utilized.

Summary

- Items with demands that are directly determined by the demand or use of another product are called **dependent demand** items. This is most common for items used to make end-products.
- **Material requirements planning (MRP)** is a computer-based system for scheduling production and purchases of items with dependent demands. MRP uses product structure and lead time information to determine when purchase and production orders should be released to obtain items exactly when they are needed and in the quantities needed.
- The **bill of materials (BOM)** is a list of all the components and subassemblies necessary to make an end-product.
- A **material requirements plan** is a purchase or production schedule for an item; these plans are the primary outputs of an MRP system. Other outputs of an MRP system can include **order releases, change reports, load reports,** and performance reports.
- It is not always most cost effective to order or produce exactly the amount of an item needed. A variety of methods, such as the **part-period balancing (PPB)** method and the **Wagner-Whitin algorithm**, can be used to determine more economical lot sizes or order quantities for dependent demand items.
- Randomness in procurement lead-times are better accommodated using **safety time** (releasing orders early) rather than safety stock.
- Successful implementation of MRP requires considerable employee involvement and training, data accuracy, appropriate demand patterns, and reliable lead times.

Key Terms

bill-of-material (BOM) file **721**
change reports **728**
cumulative lead time **721**
dependent demand **716**
dynamic program **732**
economic part-period (EPP) **730**
inventory records file **724**
load reports **728**
lot-for-lot ordering (production) **725**
manufacturing resources planning (MRP II) **737**
master production schedule (MPS) **720**
master schedule file **720**
material requirements plan **725**
material requirements planning (MRP) **719**
materials list **723**
net-change system **735**
order releases **728**
order (and production) release schedule **728**
part period **730**
part-period balancing (PPB) **730**
product structure tree **722**
production (assembly) time chart **725**
regenerative system **735**
rolling horizon **736**
safety time **737**
time buckets **720**
time fences **736**
total stocking cost (TSC) **729**
Wagner-Whitin algorithm **732**

[10] J. Haddock and D. E. Hubicki, "Which Lot-Sizing Techniques Are Used in Material Requirements Planning?" *Production and Inventory Management Journal*, Third Quarter 1989, pp. 53–56, provides a list of over 60 commercial MRP packages.

SOLVED PROBLEMS

Problem 1: A company manufactures product Z, using four basic components and performing two additional machining operations and three assembly operations. Components A and C are made by the company, and components B and D are purchased from vendors. (The BOM for product Z is given in Figure 14.12.) The product is made as follows:

1. A unit of component A is machined and converted into component E.
2. A unit of E is then assembled with two units of B to make F.
3. A unit of C is machined and converted into G.
4. A unit of A and three units of D are assembled into H.
5. One unit of F, two units of G, two units of H, and four units of B are then assembled into product Z.

(a) Construct a product structure tree for product Z.

Level No.	Item No.	Item Description	No. Required	Make/Buy	Lead Time
00		Product Z		Make	1 week
01	A231	Assembly F	1	Make	1 week
02	M110	Machined E	1	Make	2 weeks
03	C324	Component A	1	Make	2 weeks
02	C278	Fastener B	2	Buy	2 weeks
01	M386	Machined G	2	Make	1 week
02	C190	Component C	1	Make	3 weeks
01	A486	Assembly H	2	Make	1 week
02	C324	Component A	1	Make	2 weeks
02	C752	Component D	3	Buy	4 weeks
01	C278	Fastener B	4	Buy	2 weeks

FIGURE 14.12 BOM for product Z.

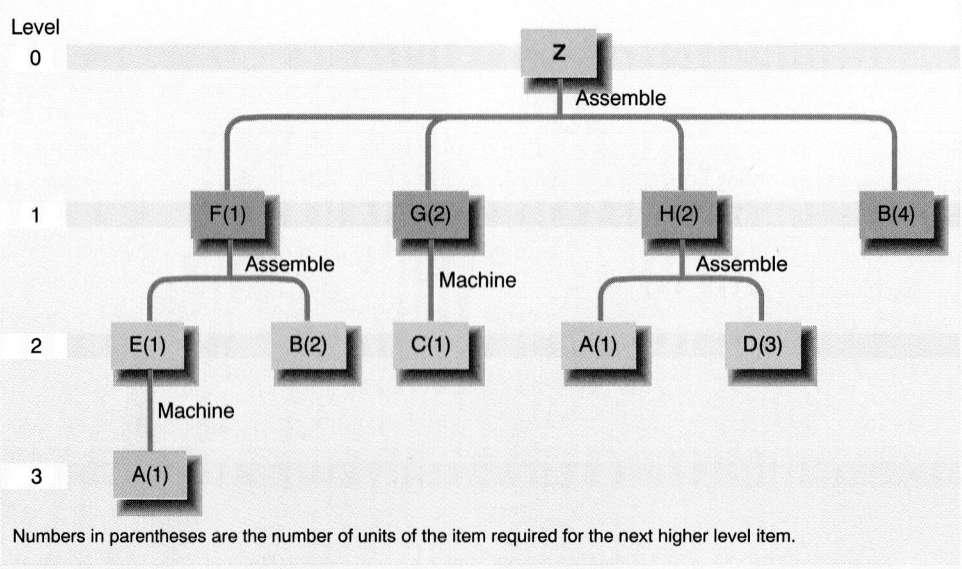

FIGURE 14.13 Product structure tree for product Z.

(b) Construct a production time chart for product Z.

(c) Derive the material requirements plans for product Z and components F and E using lot-for-lot procurement, assuming the requirements for product Z (from the master production schedule) are as follows:

Week	1	2	3	4	5	6	7	8	9	10
Requirements	0	0	0	0	0	0	200	0	0	300

Solution: The solution is given in Figures 14.13–14.15.

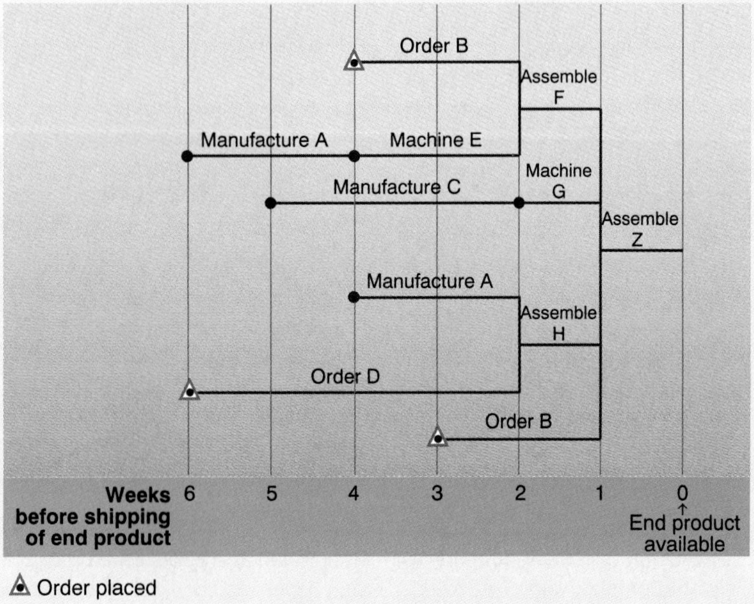

FIGURE 14.14 Production time chart for product Z.

Master production schedule

Week	1	2	3	4	5	6	7	8	9	10
Quantity	0	0	0	0	0	0	200	0	0	300

		1	2	3	4	5	6	7	8	9	10
Z	Gross requirements							200			300
	Projected on hand							0			0
	Net requirements							200			300
	Planned order receipts							200			300
	Planned order releases						200			300	
F	Gross requirements						200			300	
	Projected on hand						0			0	
	Net requirements						200			300	
	Planned order receipts						200			300	
	Planned order releases					200			300		
E	Gross requirements					200			300		
	Projected on hand					0			0		
	Net requirements					200			300		
	Planned order receipts					200			300		
	Planned order releases			200			300				

FIGURE 14.15 Material requirements plans for prducts Z, F, and E.

Problem 2: Suppose a company uses a product at an average rate of 50 units per week, but the requirements during the next 12 weeks are as follows:

Week	1	2	3	4	5	6	7	8	9	10	11	12
Requirements	0	0	200	0	100	0	175	0	0	0	125	0

If it costs $200 to place an order and $0.50 per unit per week to hold the item in inventory,

(a) Compute the EOQ using equation (13.4).

(b) Derive a purchasing plan for this company using the EOQ in part (a) and assuming there is a one-week lead time to procure the product.

(c) Derive a purchasing plan for the company using the PPB heuristic.

(d) Compute the total stocking cost over the planning horizon for the plans in parts (b) and (c).

Solution:

(a) From equation (13.4):

$$EOQ = \sqrt{(2 \times 50 \text{ units/week} \times \$200/\text{order})/\$0.50/\text{week}} = 200$$

(b)

Week	1	2	3	4	5	6	7	8	9	10	11	12
Gross requirements	0	0	200	0	100	0	175	0	0	0	125	0
Project on hand	0	0	0	0	0	100	100	125	125	125	125	0
Net requirements	0	0	200	0	100	0	75	0	0	0	0	0
Order receipts	0	0	200	0	200	0	200	0	0	0	0	0
Order releases	0	200	0	200	0	200	0	0	0	0	0	0

(c) The economic part period in this case is

EPP = |ordering cost|/|holding cost| = $200/$0.50 = 400

We begin with the requirements in week 3, which are 200. If we order 200 units in week 2, all units would be used in week 3 with no inventories, so the part-period value is 0. The cumulative requirements in weeks 3–4 are 200 and the part-period value would also be 0. The cumulative requirements in weeks 3–5 are 300. If the company ordered 300 units in week 2, received them in week 3, and used 200 in week 3, there would be 100 in inventory at the end of weeks 3 and 4 until they were used in week 5. So the part-period value would be 100 units × 2 weeks = 200. For weeks 3–6 the part-period value would also be 200. For weeks 3–7 the cumulative demand would be 475. If 475 units were ordered in week 2, the inventories would be 275 at the end of weeks 3 and 4 and 175 at the end of weeks 5 and 6, for a part-period value of 275 + 275 + 175 + 175 = 900. The part-period value closest to the EPP of 400 is 200 for weeks 3–6, so we would order 300 units in week 2, which would satisfy requirements for weeks 3–6. We would repeat this process beginning with the requirements for week 7. The resulting material requirements plan is as follows:

Week	1	2	3	4	5	6	7	8	9	10	11	12
Gross requirements	0	0	200	0	100	0	175	0	0	0	125	0
Project on hand	0	0	0	100	100	0	0	125	125	125	125	0
Net requirements	0	0	200	0	0	0	175	0	0	0	0	0
Order receipts	0	0	300	0	0	0	300	0	0	0	0	0
Order releases	0	300	0	0	0	300	0	0	0	0	0	0

(d) The *TSC* for the plan in part (b) is

TSC = (3 orders × $200/order) + (700 units in inventory × $0.50/unit) = $950

The *TSC* for the plan in part (c) is

TSC = (2 orders × $200/order) + (700 units in inventory × $0.50/unit) = $750

DISCUSSION AND REVIEW QUESTIONS

1. What four specific types of information are needed by an MRP system to develop accurate material requirements plans?
2. What information is contained in the BOM file?
3. In the PCA Industries example, we found that the company should order aluminum pipe eight days before spider climbers are needed. Why should PCA not order *all* of its purchased components, rather than just pipe, eight days before climbers are needed?
4. If a common component is used in several different end products, what should the MRP system do with this component?
5. How can load reports be used to develop material requirements plans?
6. Why would lot-for-lot procurement not always be optimal given that it minimizes the amount of inventories carried?
7. What does it mean for an MRP system to be nervous?
8. What is the difference between a net-change and a regenerative updating system?
9. What is the difference between safety stock and safety time? Under what conditions would safety time be more advantageous than safety stock?
10. What is the difference between MRP II (material resources planning) and simple MRP?
11. Explain two of the main reasons why MRP systems sometimes do not produce the expected improvements.
12. Why is it sometimes better to use independent demand models to manage the procurement of dependent demand items with constant usage than to use MRP with lot-for-lot ordering?

PROBLEMS

1. Suppose a company produces an electric controller. The controller is made by assembling two circuit modules into a subassembly and then assembling the subassembly, a sensor, and a housing. The BOM is as follows:

Level No.	Item No.	Item Description	No. Required	Make/ Buy	Lead Time (days)
00	A 100	Controller		Make	1
01	S 200	Sensor	1	Buy	5
01	H 10	Housing	1	Buy	3
01	SA50	Subassembly	1	Make	1
02	C 05	Response circuit	1	Buy	3
02	C 55	Detection circuit	1	Buy	2

(a) Construct a product structure tree for the controller. (b) Construct a production time chart. (c) For the following end product requirements, construct the material requirements plans for the controller and each of its components using lot-for-lot procurement (assume no starting inventories).

Days	1	2	3	4	5	6	7	8	9	10	11	12
Requirements	—	—	—	—	—	—	100	0	300	0	0	250

2. Suppose a company produces a type of desk that has the BOM given below. The desk is made by assembling two drawers, two handles (one for each drawer), one drawer frame, and two legs into a drawer module. Then two drawer modules, a desk back, and a desk top are assembled into a desk. (a) Construct a product structure tree. (b) Construct a production time chart. (c) For the following desk requirements, construct the material requirements plans for the desk and each of its components using lot-for-lot procurement (assume no starting inventories).

Week	1	2	3	4	5	6	7	8	9	10
Requirements	—	—	—	—	20	0	50	0	0	30

Level No.	Item No.	Item Description	No. Required	Make/ Buy	Lead Time (weeks)
00	MD 20	Desk		Make	1
01	T 25	Desk top	1	Buy	2
01	B 10	Desk back	1	Buy	1
01	D 50	Leg/drawer module	2	Make	1
02	F100	Drawer frame	1	Buy	1
02	L 75	Desk legs	2	Buy	1
02	D100	Drawers	2	Buy	2
02	H 20	Handles	2	Buy	2

3. For *Solved Problem* 1 construct the material requirements plans for product Z and components G and C.
4. For *Solved Problem* 1 (a) Construct the material requirements plan for fastener B as a level 01 item (for assembling Z) and as a level 02 item (for assembling F). (b) Combine the two material requirements plans in part (a) to form a single material requirements plan for fastener B.

5. One unit of product Z is made from one unit of A and two units of B. A is made from two units of C and one unit of D. B is made from three units of E, one unit of F, and two units of G. Items Z, A, D, E, F, and G have lead times of one week; items B and C have lead times of two weeks. Items Z, A, B, D, and F are made by the company, and items C, E, and G are purchased. (a) Construct a BOM for product Z. (b) Construct a product structure tree for Z. (c) Construct a production time chart for Z.

6. One unit of product Y is made from four units of A, one unit of B, and one unit of C. B is made from one unit of D and two units of E. C is made from one unit of F and three units of G. Items Y, B, F, and G have lead times of one week; items C, D, and E have lead times of two weeks, and item A has a lead time of three weeks. Items Y, B, C, and G are made by the company, and the other items are purchased. (a) Construct a BOM for product Y. (b) Construct a product structure tree for Y. (c) Construct a production time chart for Y.

7. In problem 5 suppose the gross requirements for product Z during the next 10 weeks are 100 units in week 5, 200 in week 7, 400 in week 8, and 150 in week 10. Also suppose the company expects to have 20 units of A, 60 units of E, and 50 units of G on hand at the beginning of week 1 and no units of the other items on hand. Construct the material requirements plans for product Z and each of its component items using lot-for-lot procurement.

8. In problem 6 suppose the gross requirements for product Y during the next 12 weeks are 40 in week 6, 60 in week 9, 20 in week 10, and 50 in week 12. Also suppose the company expects to have 50 units of A, 20 units of B, 40 units of E, and 90 units of G on hand at the beginning of week 1. Construct the material requirements plans for product Y and each of its components using lot-for-lot procurement for all items except E, which is to be purchased in lots of 100 units.

9. Suppose the gross requirements during the next 12 weeks for an item used in production are the following:

Week	1	2	3	4	5	6	7	8	9	10	11	12
Requirements	0	60	10	90	50	0	0	30	0	80	40	0

If it costs \$150 to place an order and \$0.75 per week per unit to hold an item in inventory: (a) Compute the EOQ for the item using equation (13.4). (b) Derive a purchasing (material requirements) plan for this item using the order quantity in part (a) and assuming there is a one-week lead time to procure the product. (c) Derive a purchasing (material requirements) plan using the PPB heuristic. (d) Compute the total stocking costs over the planning horizon for the plans in parts (b) and (c), and compare them with the total stocking cost of a lot-for-lot plan.

10. Suppose the gross requirements during the next eight weeks for an item used in production are the following:

Week	1	2	3	4	5	6	7	8
Requirements	0	0	220	0	280	200	0	100

If it costs \$75 to place an order and \$0.25 per week per unit to hold an item in inventory, (a) compute the EOQ for the item using equation (13.4). (b) Derive a purchasing plan for this item using the order quantity in part (a) and assuming there is a one-week lead time to procure the product. (c) Derive a purchasing plan using the PPB heuristic. (d) Compute the total stocking costs over the planning horizon for the plans in parts (b) and (c), and compare them with the total stocking cost using a lot-for-lot purchasing plan.

11. Suppose in *Solved Problem* 2 the ordering cost was \$50 rather than \$200. (a) Compute the EOQ for the product. (b) Derive a purchasing plan for the item that only makes purchases during a week equal to the amount computed in part (a). (c) Compute the total stocking cost resulting from the policy in part (b), and compare it with the total stocking cost of using lot-for-lot purchasing. (d) Why is the cost of the EOQ plan in part (b) so much higher than that of the lot-for-lot plan? What can we conclude concerning when an EOQ-based plan would be better than a lot-for-lot plan and when it would be worse in MRP?

12.* Suppose product W is made up of one unit of A and two units of B, and product X is made up of two units of A, one unit of B, and one unit of E. Item B is made up of one unit of C and two units of D, and item E is made up of one unit of D and one unit of F. Items W, X, B, and D have lead times of one week, and A, C, E, and F have lead times of two weeks. Items A, D, and F are purchased; the others are made by the company. Suppose the gross requirements for product W during the next 10 weeks are 50 units in week 5, 80 units in week 8, and 40 units in week 10. The gross requirements for X are 30 units in week 6, 40 in week 7, 20 in week 9, and 20 in week 10. Finally, suppose there are 20 units of A, 50 units of C, 10 units of E, and 20 units of F on hand at the beginning of week 1. Construct material requirements plans for each product and each item. Remember that these products share parts, so their requirements plans must be merged.

CASE

Waste Overhaul, Inc.: An MRP Case

Waste collection vehicles, more commonly known as garbage trucks, are subjected to considerable stress: motors operate 8–12 hours a day, with large amounts of idling and slow-speed driving, carrying heavy loads, and constantly using their lifting and/or compacting equipment. Because of these conditions, garbage trucks wear out quickly even when they are reasonably well maintained, which they often are not. However, these trucks are quite expensive, so waste collection companies try to use them as long as possible before replacement. Many companies have found it cost effective to overhaul badly worn trucks at least once before replacing them: a \$10,000–\$20,000 overhaul might add two to three years to the life of a \$100,000 truck.

Waste Overhaul, Inc. (WOI), specializes in overhauling waste collection vehicles. It serves several companies in a major metropolitan area, overhauling 200–500 trucks per year. Although each overhaul is slightly different, trucks are usually sent to WOI to overhaul one or more of the following: the motor, transmission, lifting unit, or compacting unit. Other smaller repairs, such as replacing brakes, fluids, hoses, belts, handles, and mirrors and repainting the trucks, are often performed in conjunction with these major repairs.

Background

The normal procedure is for customers to send a work order to WOI explaining in general terms what needs to be overhauled. A team of WOI workers then evaluates the truck, which may take one or two days. The team makes a detailed list of what has to be done and provides an estimate of the overhaul cost, which is sent to the customer for approval. When a subsystem of the truck is to be overhauled, a large set of material requirements is generated. For example, overhauling a motor may require new valves, a new water pump, and a new distributor. A major problem for WOI's repair personnel is to determine which components can be repaired or refurbished and which need to be replaced. Typically, initial judgments made in developing the price estimate are revised when the overhaul is actually being performed.

A major expense for WOI is the cost of parts and materials used in the overhauls. During the course of a year, WOI uses over 1000 different items, and each one has its own usage pattern. Some of them, such as spark plugs, transmission fluid, and wiper blades, are used at a relatively constant rate in relatively large volumes. Others, such as compactor motors or hydraulic controls, are used in modest quantities but are required only periodically. (For example, WOI may overhaul the compactors on 20 trucks for a company and then may not overhaul the same type of compactor for several months.) Still others are special items, such as a drive arm for a rare power lift model, that may be used once a year.

A major competitive issue for WOI is the ability to perform overhauls quickly; each day a truck is off the road costs the customer money. In the late 1980s, WOI found that it was losing market share because it was not only slower on average than its competitors in overhauling trucks, it was also unreliable in delivering on promises: trucks that it initially thought it could overhaul in six to eight days might not be ready for three weeks. The primary reason for the delays was the unavailability of parts. Items WOI thought were in inventory were not there, and many parts needed for an overhaul were not ordered until the day the mechanic wanted to replace the part.

Because of these delays, and because materials and inventories are a major expense for WOI, in 1989 Wayne Reed, the president of WOI, decided to hire a consulting firm and purchase inventory management software to improve the company's materials management. After two years of work and at a cost of \$200,000, the new system was instituted in 1991. After three years of operation, however, WOI found no improvement in its inventory situation: average inventory levels had increased by 10% (to \$675,000), shortages and resulting late orders were just as frequent, and the value of "dead" parts in inventory that had not been used for one year or more had increased (to over \$50,000). As a result, Wayne Reed asked WOI's purchasing manager, Brian Langer, to review the system and recommend improvements.

Analysis

With the help of WOI's information systems specialist, Brian began by studying the logic and algorithms used by the current computerized inventory system. He found that the system was based entirely on EOQ models, implicitly assuming that all items had independent demands. Item usage information was entered into the system daily. Using data for the past year, a forecasting module in the system estimated the annual usage rate and used this rate to compute an EOQ for the item. So if WOI used 12 units of an item one week and did not use that item again for a year, the computer system treated the usage as if it were constant, at the rate of one unit per month. The system also estimated the average lead time and standard deviation of lead time based on when orders were placed and received. From this information, reorder points were

TABLE 14.8 WOI'S USAGE AND PURCHASE PATTERN FOR A HYDRAULIC JOINT

	1991			1992		
Month	Usage	Inventory	Purchases	Usage	Inventory	Purchases
Jan	0	2	3	0	1	3
Feb	0	5	0	0	4	0
Mar	0	5	0	0	4	0
Apr	0	5	0	0	4	0
May	0	5	0	0	4	0
Jun	0	5	0	1	3	0
Jul	0	5	0	0	3	0
Aug	2	3	0	6*	3	3
Sep	0	3	0	2*	0	3
Oct	0	3	0	0	1	3
Nov	0	3	0	0	4	0
Dec	5*	3	3	0	4	0

Note: inventory values are on the first day of the month.
*A stockout occurred that delayed work.

computed for each item (using the method presented in Chapter 13), with the goal of achieving a 99% demand service level.

Brian reviewed the purchasing and usage records for several products during the past two years and found some strange and inefficient behavior. For example, one type of hydraulic joint for a compactor, which had an EOQ value of 3 and a reorder point of 2, had the usage and ordering pattern shown in Table 14.8.

Table 14.8 shows that the intended goal of keeping inventories low to minimize holding costs while protecting against stockouts was not being achieved. Inventories were high, averaging over 40% of annual demand (fewer than 2.5 inventory turns per year), yet stockouts occurred in three of the five months in which the item was needed. Unfortunately, this situation was the norm, not the exception.

However, Brian also found other items, such as oil filters and belts, for which the inventory system seemed to be working extremely well. For these products, average inventory levels were less than 10% of annual usage and stockouts were almost nonexistent. The obvious feature of these products was that their usage was steady, at approximately the same rate every week.

Recommendations

Brian concluded that most of the parts WOI used, especially the most expensive ones and the ones with the longest and most variable lead times, had dependent demand patterns. Therefore, their purchases should be determined using an MRP system, not one developed for independent demand items. Working from historical records, Brian divided the parts into three categories: (1) those with relatively constant demands; (2) those that were used at least twice per year, but in variable amounts and on an irregular basis;[11] and (3) those that were used less than twice per year.

Brian recommended that purchases for the three types of items be handled separately. Category 1 items, which essentially have an independent demand structure, would continue to be managed using the current EOQ-based system. The second and third categories would be managed using a new MRP-based system that contained some front-end features specifically designed for WOI. Whenever a type of overhaul, such as a compactor overhaul, was requested, a list of all the parts typically needed to perform the overhaul would be generated by the computer. The inspector would then check off those parts that actually had to be replaced, and this information was entered into the computer. Using lead-time information, the MRP system would generate material requirements plans for that overhaul and merge them with the requirements for other planned overhauls. Purchase orders would then be generated. For category 2 items, the amount to buy would be determined using the PPB method because it was expected that any items left in inventory would be used within the year. Items in category 3 would be ordered on a lot-for-lot basis to avoid their becoming dead parts because their future use was highly uncertain.

To make the system more effective, WOI began working with its major customers to obtain information about their overhaul plans as early as possible. So if a customer planned to have the transmissions of eight trucks overhauled beginning in two weeks, this information would be conveyed to WOI. WOI would then develop preliminary

[11]These items had to be used on at least two separate occasions during each of the last two years. Simply using two or more units per year for the same overhaul was not enough to allow them to be classified this way.

material requirements plans for transmission overhauls using historical probabilities that certain parts would have to be replaced. When the trucks were brought in for overhaul and evaluated, the actual replacement requirements would be put into the system and the material requirements plans updated.

WOI was able to install and implement this system within 18 months at a total cost of $100,000, including training. The results were better than hoped. Average inventories declined to $450,000, saving an estimated $33,000 per year in carrying costs, and dead parts inventories dropped to $30,000 as approximately $20,000 worth of dead parts were eventually used and few new ones added. More important, WOI became more competitive. Stockouts decreased dramatically so that average overhaul time was reduced to 25% less than that of its competitors, and the percentage of overhauls completed after the promised date was cut to one-third of the previous value.

QUESTIONS

1. WOI found that lead times still presented a problem for category 2 and 3 items. Rarely used parts had especially long and variable lead times. What actions might WOI take to reduce the overhaul delays caused by this problem?
2. The replacement parts ultimately required for an overhaul were often different from those in the material requirements plans derived from customers' original overhaul plans. The deviations, however, seemed random; parts expected to be needed were not, and parts not expected to be needed were required. Should WOI use a net-change or a regenerative updating system? Explain why one might be better than the other in this case.

SELECTED READINGS

AGGARWAL, S. C. "MRP, JIT, OPT, FMA," *Harvard Business Review*, Vol. 63, No. 5, 1985, pp. 8–16.

CERVENY, R. P., and L. W. SCOTT. "A Survey of MRP Implementation," *Production and Inventory Management Journal*, 3rd Quarter 1989, pp. 31–34.

DEMATTEIS, J. J. "An Economic Lot-Sizing Technique: The Part-Period Algorithm," IBM *Systems Journal*, Vol. 7, No. 1, 1968, pp. 30–38.

FORDYCE, JAMES M., and FRANCIS M. WEBSTER. "The Wagner-Whitin Algorithm Made Simple," *Production and Inventory Management*, 2nd Quarter, 1984, pp. 21–27.

HADDOCK, J., and D. E. HUBICKI. "Which Lot-Sizing Techniques Are Used in Material Requirements Planning?" *Production and Inventory Management Journal*, Third Quarter 1989, pp. 53–56.

LAFORGE, R. C. "MRP and the Part-Period Algorithm," *Journal of Purchasing Management*, Winter 1982, pp. 21–26.

ORLICKY, JOSEPH. *Orlicky's Material Requirements Planning* (2nd ed.), McGraw-Hill, New York, 1994.

ORMSBY, J. G., S. Y. ORMSBY, and C. R. RUTHSTROM. "MRP II Implementation: A Case Study," *Production and Inventory Management Journal*, Fourth Quarter 1990, pp. 77–81.

PRIMROSE, P. L. "Selecting and Evaluating Cost-Effective MRP and MRP II," *International Journal of Operations and Production Management*, Vol. 10, No. 1, 1990, pp. 51–66.

WAGNER, H., and T. M. WHITIN. "Dynamic Version of the Economic Lot Size Model," *Management Science*, Vol. 5, No. 1, 1958, pp. 89–96.

CHAPTER 15

JUST-IN-TIME, LEAN, AND SYNCHRONOUS PRODUCTION SYSTEMS

15.1 THE JUST-IN-TIME REVOLUTION
On the Job: Bruce Hamilton, United Electric Controls

15.2 AN IDEAL PRODUCTION SYSTEM AND JIT PRODUCTION
An Ideal World for Production

15.3 THE PRINCIPLES OF LITTLE JIT: JIT SCHEDULING
Speculative versus Assured Production: Push versus Pull Systems
Large versus Small Lot Sizes
Comparing JIT and Classical Scheduling
Quick Response as a Substitute for Inventories

15.4 THE MECHANICS OF JIT PRODUCTION
The Number and Size of Kanbans

15.5 THE INGREDIENTS OF BIG JIT: APPROACHING THE IDEAL SYSTEM
Quick Setups: Single-Minute Exchange of Dies
Reliable Delivery of Materials
Reducing Machine Breakdowns: Total Productive Maintenance
Quality and JIT Production
Continuous Improvement
JIT and Employee Morale

15.6 IMPLEMENTING JIT PRODUCTION
When to Use JIT Scheduling
When Not to Use JIT Scheduling: JIT versus MRP
Guidelines for JIT Implementation
In Good Company: Federal-Mogul Corporation Gives JIT a Second Chance
JIT in Service and Hybrid Industries

15.7 SYNCHRONOUS PRODUCTION AND THE THEORY OF CONSTRAINTS
Some Principles of Synchronous Production
The Drum-Buffer-Rope Mechanism
JIT, Synchronous Production, and MRP

UKAX: A Case of Lean Production

15.1 The Just-in-Time Revolution

During the 1970s and 1980s, Japan became an international economic power. Its manufacturing companies, especially in the automotive and electronics industries, became the leaders in world markets, and they set the standards for product quality and cost against which firms of other countries were compared. This success is often attributed to the Japanese development and use of just-in-time (JIT) production systems.

What exactly does JIT mean? Some people apply the term to a form of production scheduling and inventory management whereby products are produced only to meet actual demand, and materials for each stage of production are received or produced "just in time" for use in the next stage of production or for delivery to a customer. This limited definition of JIT has been called **Little JIT**. However, the Japanese manufacturing revolution was really the result of a more extensive change. The entire way products were designed, work was organized, and responsibilities were assigned was transformed, and a constant striving for improvement and elimination of waste was instilled. This **Big JIT** encompasses the full range of organizational and operational improvements practiced by many Japanese companies and is called Japanese or **lean production**. Many aspects of big JIT have now been adopted by leading companies throughout the world, from manufacturers such as Chrysler, Ford, General Motors, Xerox, Black and Decker, Honeywell, and Intel to retailers such as Wal-Mart, Home Depot, and Toys-R-Us.

Hundreds of successful implementations of JIT methods have been reported, and they have become so common that they are no longer newsworthy.[1] Companies such as Dover Corporation, Hewlett-Packard, 3M, General Electric, Harley-Davidson, and John Deere have reported reductions in inventories and throughput times of up to 90% and substantial improvements in productivity and on-time delivery. Bruce Hamilton, the subject of this chapter's "On the Job" feature, reduced his company's in-process inventories by over 95% and space requirements by a third when he reinvented his company's production system using lean production methods on the job.

With all these successes, it is surprising that some individuals have dismissed JIT as nothing more than a fad, citing companies that found JIT did not improve their operations. But in almost every case of failure the problem was poor implementation or a complete misunderstanding of JIT.[2] For example, some companies interpreted JIT to mean making the production process more automated and inflexible. This, in fact, is almost the antithesis of JIT, which tries to simplify the process and make it more flexible. Other companies implemented isolated methods, such as quality circles or JIT scheduling, where they were not appropriate or without establishing the appropriate infrastructure first. For example, a company that produced 40,000 different products with highly erratic demand tried to use JIT scheduling; as we will see later, this is completely counter to the conditions required for JIT scheduling. In these cases, failure was almost guaranteed. In fact, JIT production is based on sound production principles, and it has

[1]Richard Schonberger, in his book *World Class Manufacturing*, Free Press, New York, 1986, lists 84 successful implementations of JIT in the United States by 1985. He also gives brief descriptions of the improvements that resulted. Since that time, many more successes have been reported.

[2]For example, the failures cited in Amal Naj, "Some Manufacturers Drop Efforts to Adopt Japanese Techniques," *Wall Street Journal*, May 7, 1993, are clearly cases of poor implementation that included installing too much automation, installing inflexible automation, using large batch sizes, and forcing inventories onto suppliers rather than changing their own production process.

ON THE JOB

BRUCE HAMILTON, UNITED ELECTRIC CONTROLS

In 1987 Bruce Hamilton, vice president of operations of the Massachusetts electronic instrument manufacturer United Electric Controls, took the company on a 180-degree turn and never looked back. Under the production-driven thinking of its first 50 years, United Electric, like most other firms, had set up its production processes to maximize utilization of its high-speed machines—producing, for instance, 1000 lead wires at a time for a few pennies apiece. It looked efficient, and accounting called the inventory an asset; the problem, as Bruce realized, was that this "asset" was a four-year supply of the product that was costing the company thousands of dollars to store.

Firmly convinced of the value of lean production methods, Bruce undertook to eliminate waste, trim inventory, and at the same time do a better job of getting customers "what they want when they want it." Thanks to the introduction of kanban (JIT) production systems, United Electric has cut its work-in-process from 30,000 to 1000 units, reduced the space needed for manufacturing by a third, confined inventory to a manageable area, and—not least—reduced defects and waste by producing in smaller batches whereby problems are identified and corrected quickly. Most customer orders are now filled in a day.

Bruce takes the principles of lean production to heart. His stripped-down office is a cubicle in the factory furnished with a file cabinet, a table, and a telephone that he answers himself. Seeing the firm save millions of dollars still thrills him. "This is exciting stuff!" he says.

been supplemented with numerous operational techniques that can dramatically improve the quality and cost effectiveness of almost any production system. But the implementation is crucial. JIT is not a fad; in some cases, it is a company's lifeblood. Don Bowker of Fireplace Manufacturers, Inc., credits JIT for his firm's survival: "I don't think we'd be here today if it wasn't for JIT."[3]

The JIT system we see today, however, is the result of over 40 years of work by many people and many companies to improve the design and operation of production systems. We also need to recognize that many features of JIT cannot be applied effectively to all production systems; in some situations they are simply not suitable.

Despite its association with Japanese companies, the basis for JIT production is universal, and many of the methods used to implement it are culturally neutral. The basic idea of JIT scheduling and minimal inventories was at the heart of Ford Motors' production system over 75 years ago, in which iron ore received at the docks was converted into a Model T car and shipped to the customer in two days! Similarly, process simplification and employee involvement programs have been used in some U.S. companies since the nineteenth century.

This chapter presents both the scheduling aspects of Little JIT production and the wide array of enhancements encompassed by Big JIT. Section 15.2 presents a paradigm that describes an ideal production system, which in practice does not exist. But rather than accepting deviations from the ideal as unchangeable facts of life, as classical production management does, the philosophy underlying Big JIT is to reduce or eliminate the deviations, thereby bringing the system closer to the ideal. Section 15.3 describes the scheduling principles of Little JIT and the expected benefits that should result. Section 15.4 illustrates the basic mechanics of a production system using JIT scheduling.

[3]From Steven P. Galante, "Small Manufacturers Shifting to Just-in-Time Techniques," *Wall Street Journal*, Dec. 21, 1987.

Section 15.5 describes many of the operational enhancements associated with Big JIT. Most of these enhancements, such as mistake-proofing, faster machine setups, and better maintenance, are beneficial independent of JIT scheduling. Section 15.6 describes the conditions under which JIT is most suitable for use and where it may be unsuitable. It also provides guidance on implementation problems and solutions. Section 15.7 introduces synchronous production and explains its relationship to JIT production. The case at the end of the chapter illustrates how successful implementation of JIT production is multifaceted and must address job design, process design, quality control, scheduling, and organizational issues together.

15.2 AN IDEAL PRODUCTION SYSTEM AND JIT PRODUCTION

Throughout this book, a central theme has been that production and operations management focuses on avoiding and solving problems in the production system. Why focus on problems? Because the actual environment in which organizations operate is not the one we would ideally want.

So what *is* the ideal production system? For a manager, it might be described by the following.

AN IDEAL WORLD FOR PRODUCTION

1. Only one type of product is produced.[4]
2. Demand for the product is constant at the rate of one unit every t units of time.
3. Customers purchase the product at the production facility.
4. All resources needed to produce the product (materials and labor) are available at the production site.
5. All materials are without defect and will be delivered exactly when needed, and only the amount needed will be provided (every t units of time, the materials to make one unit of product are delivered).
6. The amount of processing time required to make one unit of the product is Nt, where N is a positive integer. In other words, the processing time is a multiple of the time between purchases.
7. The work or processing required to make one unit of product is sequential and can be infinitesimally decomposed, so exactly t amount of work can be assigned to each of N sequential work stations.
8. There is no randomness in processing times.
9. No defects are produced.
10. Machines never wear out or break down.
11. Employees always show up for work and never make mistakes.

Designing and operating an efficient production system in this ideal world would be easy. Under these conditions we could construct a repetitive flow process with N work stations, such as the one in Figure 15.1 for assembling one type of automobile. At each work station t units of processing time are spent on each auto. Every t units of time, one automobile is produced and provided to a customer exactly when demanded.

[4]A good argument can be made that an ideal world would be one where the production system can make many products or *any* product with no changeover cost or time.

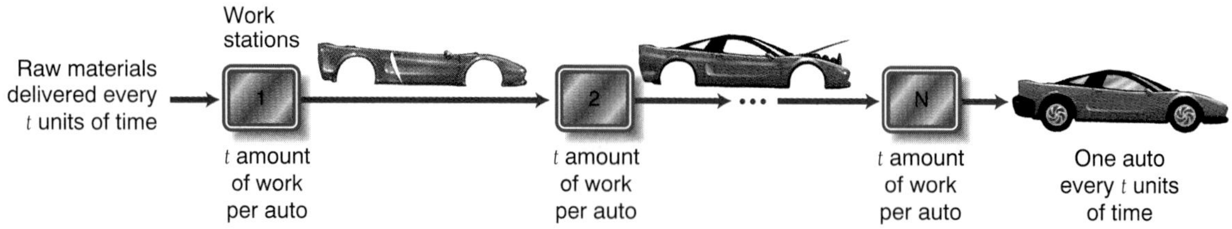

FIGURE 15.1 An ideal production system for auto assembly.

There are no raw material, final product, or in-process inventories, except for the autos actually being processed at the N work stations. There is no need for safety stocks of any kind because we know when demand will occur, and there are no unexpected production shortages due to quality defects, machine breakdowns, or employee absences. Because only one product is made, no time is lost on changing over or setting up machines, and no scheduling or coordinating of different products or jobs is necessary. This system would indeed be easy to manage.

Unfortunately (or maybe fortunately for those of us who enjoy a challenge), real life is not like this. Most companies produce a variety of products that share equipment and personnel in their production; demand is not uniform and totally predictable; final products must be transported to spatially dispersed customers; resources must be gathered from various locations; deliveries are not always reliable; and there are economies of scale in acquisition. The tasks performed in the production process are often lumpy (not totally decomposable) in terms of their processing times, processing times are variable, mistakes are made, defects occur, machines break down, and employees are absent. Companies normally accommodate these deviations from the ideal environment by changing the design and operation of the system in ways that result in higher cost, lower quality, and less timely product delivery than occur in the ideal system.

For example, two ways in which companies adapt to uncertainties in product demand are to (1) improve their demand forecasting and (2) produce in anticipation of demand, that is, maintain final product inventories. The first solution is never perfect and can still result in stockouts or late deliveries, and the second solution increases costs. Other deviations from the ideal world are accommodated by doing the following:

1. Increasing inventories of raw materials to accommodate variations in delivery times and to take advantage of economies of scale in purchasing.
2. Increasing raw material, in-process, and final product inventories, as well as overpurchasing materials and overproducing products, to make up for lost production due to defective raw materials and processing.
3. Scheduling large production runs, and consequently holding large cycling inventories, to spread the fixed costs of machine setups over a larger number of units.
4. Maintaining large in-process inventories between production stages to keep operations running during product changeovers at other production stages and to protect against delays resulting from machine breakdowns and employee absences.

The one consistent symptom of deviations from the ideal production system is excessive inventories. In addition, excessive amounts of materials and products have to be scrapped due to poor quality and to overproduction in anticipation of demand that does not materialize. In spite of carrying large inventories and overproducing, companies may still suffer from poor product quality and late deliveries to customers.

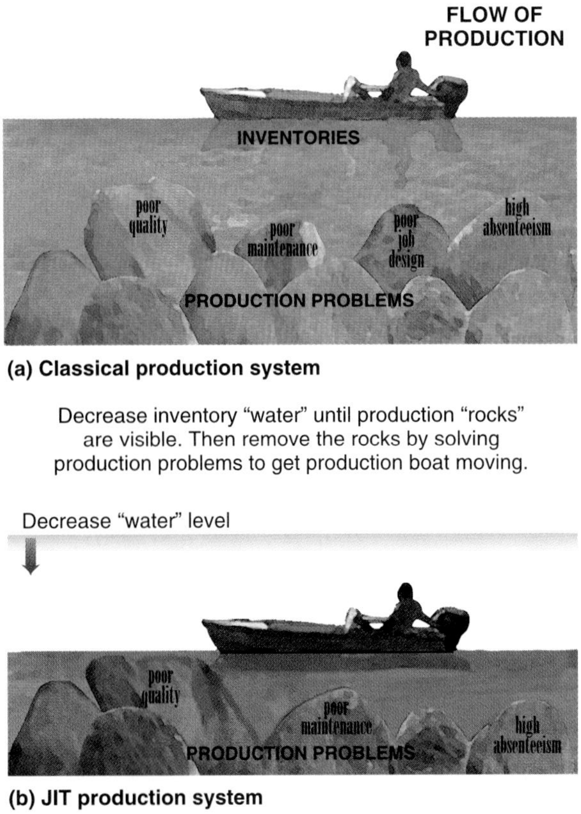

FIGURE 15.2 Production as a boat in a stream.

The JIT philosophy and system has been successful not simply because it reduces inventories and scrap but, more important, because it recognizes that excessive inventories are symptomatic of more fundamental problems. Big JIT focuses on *eliminating* problems of demand variations, unreliable deliveries of raw materials, defects, machine breakdowns, processing time variations, and excessive setup times. Reduction of inventories is then a natural consequence of the improvements in the production system.

An analogy that has been used to explain the strategy underlying JIT production is illustrated in Figure 15.2. Operating a production system is like trying to float a boat down a stream. The normal production system contains flaws, just as a stream has rocks. The rocks inhibit the boat from moving, just as production flaws prevent efficient, high-quality production from occurring. The classical solution to the existence of these production "rocks" is to increase the level of water in the stream, where the water represents inventories. High enough water levels will let the boat float over the rocks, just as high inventories will protect the company from shortages and work stoppages due to poor quality, machine breakdowns, long setup times, and other production problems. But these inventories are expensive, and they hide the real problems. The JIT approach is to reduce inventories slowly, that is, to lower the water level in the stream until the production problems (rocks) become visible. We then solve the problem, thereby removing the rocks, and then lower the inventories further. A production system with low inventory levels cannot have any serious problems left; otherwise, the production "boat" would get caught on the "rocks."

15.3 THE PRINCIPLES OF LITTLE JIT: JIT SCHEDULING

If we restrict our attention to the scheduling of production, JIT systems differ from classical production systems in two important ways: (1) the scheduling of production relative to demand and (2) the size of production batches.

SPECULATIVE VERSUS ASSURED PRODUCTION: PUSH VERSUS PULL SYSTEMS

Production in classical systems is normally based on **speculative demand**. That is, the company forecasts the demand that is likely to occur in the future. This demand forecast is then "folded back" based on the procurement or production lead times for each step in the production process to determine when production would have to begin to satisfy demand. (This is the approach used in Chapter 14 for materials requirements planning systems.) Materials are then ordered, and the first step in the production process is scheduled. Subsequent steps in the production process are also scheduled, but their execution will depend on when earlier production stages are completed. In other words, production is initiated by scheduling the *first* production stage, and then output is "pushed" through the production system, as shown in Figure 15.3a. This approach is commonly characterized as a **push production system**.

JIT scheduling differs from this system in a fundamental way. Short-term production is not based on demand forecasts (although demand forecasting is done for other planning purposes); rather, it is based on replenishing stocks that are depleted by actual sales (as shown in Figure 15.3b). Specifically, when the inventory of a product drops to a certain level, the final stage of the production process signals that more of that product is needed soon. The final stage of the process then begins production of that product as soon as possible; this requires that some inventory of inputs to the final stage be maintained (or be far enough along in the production pipeline). As the final stage produces units of product, it consumes its inputs, which are outputs from preceding operations. When the inputs needed to make the product are withdrawn from stock, the operator of the final production stage signals the preceding stage(s) of production that more input is needed for that product. This signal initiates production for the preceding stage. This process continues all the way back to the first production stage and the materials acquisition process; that is, suppliers are signaled that raw materials are needed. With this approach, production of a specific product is initiated by the *final* stage of production in response to *actual* or **assured demand**, and production is "pulled" through the system; the final stage pulls the needed materials from the pre-

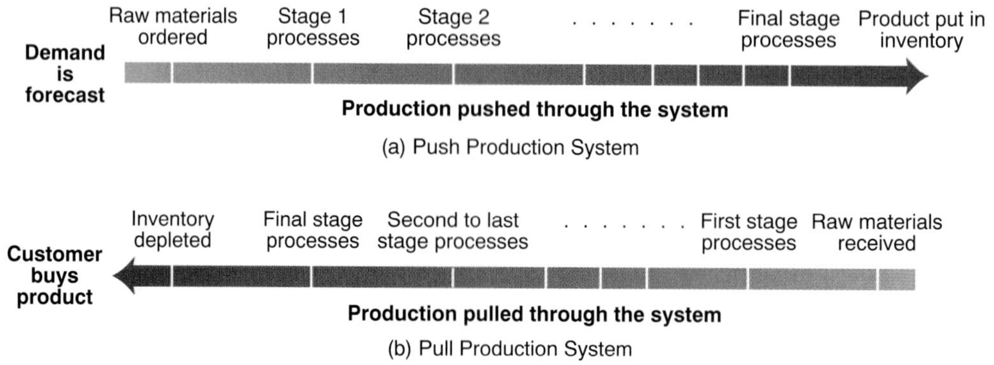

FIGURE 15.3 Push versus pull production systems.

ceding stage, which pulls from its preceding stage, and so on. As a result, JIT scheduling has been characterized as a **pull production system**, in contrast to the classical push system. Bruce Hamilton summarizes the underlying idea of an assured demand, pull system as follows: "Anything not produced for a customer is overproduction. That's the mindset we have to have."[5]

LARGE VERSUS SMALL LOT SIZES

A second feature that distinguishes JIT from classical production systems is the production lot sizes used. Classical production systems normally produce products using larger lot sizes (longer production runs) than do JIT systems. In many cases, the lot sizes for classical systems are selected based on the economic order quantity or economic lot size models discussed in Chapter 13. The large fixed costs and time of production setups and product changeovers make large lot sizes more economical by spreading these costs over a larger number of units produced, retaining more time for production. But it also leads to large quantities of cycling inventory and long periods of time between replenishment of stock for each product.

In contrast, JIT production systems reduce cost and increase system responsiveness to demand changes by using small production lot sizes (and, when appropriate, using even smaller "transfer" lot sizes so that part of a production lot from one stage can be transferred to another stage for processing before the entire production run is completed at the first stage). The comparative benefits of this lot-sizing approach, when combined with those of a pull production system, can best be seen by looking at a simple example.

COMPARING JIT AND CLASSICAL SCHEDULING

The following example compares the inventory levels that result from using a JIT pull system based on assured demand and small lot sizes with those resulting from a classical push system and large lot sizes.

EXAMPLE 1

Alpha, Inc., makes four models of valves, designated A, B, C, and D, using a batch (disconnected) flow process. Each product passes through three production departments—1, 2, and 3—in that order, but the specific processing for each product at a stage is different (so the stages of the process cannot be connected tightly). The weekly demand for each product is random, but the averages for the past year have been 600, 800, 400, and 1000 units for the four products, respectively.

The Classical System:

Because of the large equipment setup times when products are changed, the company has devised a lot-size policy of producing the average of one week's demand for each product before a product changeover; that is, the company runs each product once every week with lot sizes of 600, 800, 400, and 1000 units, respectively. Because demand is random and because production delays and shortages occur due to machine breakdowns, quality problems, and delays in receiving raw materials from suppliers, the company maintains two days' average product demand as safety stock. Figure 15.4 rep-

[5]From Michael Verespej, "The Self-Education of Bruce Hamilton," *Industry Week*, Apr. 1, 1991, pp. 16–22.

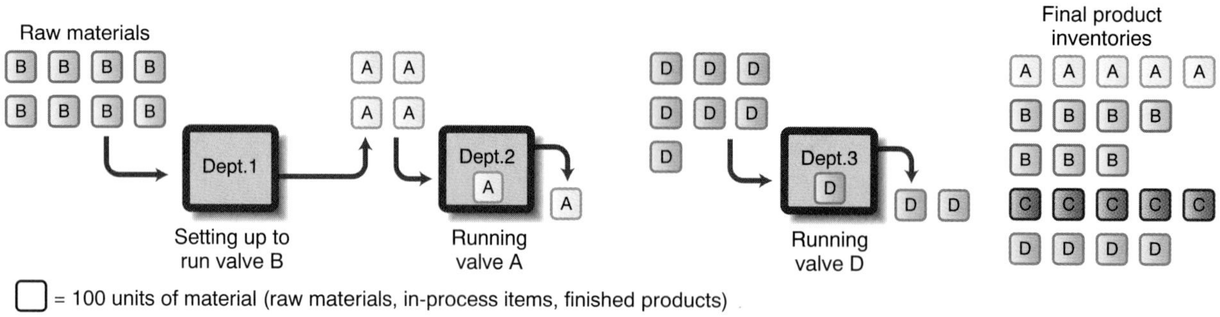

FIGURE 15.4 Snapshot of Alpha's classical push production system.

resents a "snapshot" of this system at one point in time (taken from a simulation) that shows typical inventory levels of final products, units in process, and raw materials.

On average the company would hold *final product* inventories of approximately 400 units of product A, 500 units of B, 250 units of C, and 700 units of D.[6] Approximately 40% of this is cycling inventory due to the production lot sizes, and 60% is safety stock. Also, if a significant change in demand for some product occurs (say, demand for B surges), it could take up to one week to adjust the production schedule and respond to this change, depending on the production status of product B in the production scheduling cycle. Inventories of *raw materials* and *in-process materials* (between departments) are even larger, averaging approximately 550, 750, 325, and 850 units of the four products, respectively.

A JIT *Alternative*:

Figure 15.5 illustrates one possible JIT version of the same situation. The company has decided to produce products in lot sizes of 100 units. Whenever 100 units of a product are sold, department 3 receives a signal to produce 100 units to replace those units sold; in JIT jargon the signal is given by issuing a ***kanban*** (the Japanese word for "card" or "ticket") to department 3. Department 3 puts that ticket in line for production and begins production on it within hours of receipt. Whenever department 3 uses the amount of materials (from department 2) required to make 100 units of product, it signals department 2 to produce replacement units. This process continues all the way back to department 1 and the company's vendors.

[6]The inventory estimates for Example 1 are based on simulations of the system. Some of the assumptions underlying the simulations are described in subsequent sections.

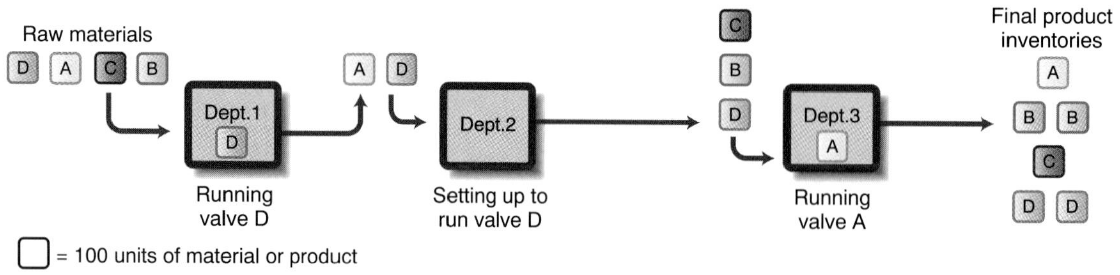

FIGURE 15.5 Snapshot of the JIT System for Alpha.

Figure 15.5 illustrates the JIT system at a typical point in time. The inventories of the final products average between 80 and 150 units: one-quarter of those of the classical system! Of these inventories, approximately 60% act as safety stock and 40% are cycling inventory due to lot sizing. Furthermore, despite maintaining at least the equivalent of 200 units of raw materials or in-process materials for each product at all times (to accommodate a quick response), the average inventories of raw materials and in-process products average between 200 and 350 units: less than half those of the classical system shown in Figure 15.4.

Despite the common perception that JIT systems have almost no interstage inventories, many of them *do* need regular inventories between production stages to maintain smooth operations and responsiveness. JIT systems that are highly connected flow processes, such as the Toyota Motors assembly line, can operate with minimal interstage inventories, but less tightly connected systems, especially those that must produce a variety of products, normally have to maintain some interstage inventories to keep the system functioning smoothly. However, as shown in Example 1, the overall level of inventory is much lower than with the classical system due to the smaller cycling inventories resulting from smaller lot sizes and less safety stocks needed because the system is more responsive to changes in demand.

QUICK RESPONSE AS A SUBSTITUTE FOR INVENTORIES

Shigeo Shingo has pointed out that a company can satisfy customer demands quickly, especially when the timing and magnitude of demands vary, in two ways: (1) by carrying large inventories or (2) by having a highly responsive production system, that is, one that can produce needed quantities of products soon after receiving orders.[7] In Example 1 the JIT system operates with less inventory than the classical system because the small lot sizes and pull mechanism make it more responsive than the classical system. A surge in demand for a product will automatically put in motion additional production of that product. Within a few hours or a day of receiving a *kanban*, production of the product is initiated at the final stage, and the entire system is replenished soon thereafter. Similarly, if demand slackens, there is an automatic delay in issuing *kanbans* for that product. These features also reduce the risk of overproduction because only small amounts of product are ever held in inventory and production is based only on actual demand.

In the past, many companies confused large-volume production with large-lot production. There are many cost and quality benefits to producing a large *volume* of a product, such as enhancing learning effects and spreading the costs of product development and facilities over more units of product. However, the only benefits of producing units in large *lot sizes* are that the time and cost of setups are spread over more units, and fewer startup losses or inefficiencies occur because there are fewer product changeovers. But if the setup time can be reduced and if the changeover process is structured to eliminate startup losses, the benefits of large lot sizes vanish and only the disadvantages remain: excessive inventories, slow responsiveness to demand, and slow detection of quality problems. Dramatically reducing the setup time and production

[7]For a clear explanation of Shingo's suggestions regarding JIT production, see Alan Robinson (ed.), *Modern Approaches to Manufacturing Improvement: The Shingo System*, Productivity Press, Cambridge, MA, 1990.

losses of product changeovers, which are described in Section 15.5, therefore are major goals of Big JIT.

15.4 THE MECHANICS OF JIT PRODUCTION

Figure 15.5 provided a snapshot of a simple JIT system. To understand fully the philosophical foundations, the operation, and the benefits of JIT scheduling, it is helpful to look at the flow of activities in a dynamic sense. Table 15.1 and Figure 15.6 illustrate how the JIT system in Figure 15.5 would operate during a four-hour period.

The success of JIT is primarily due to the simplicity of the information and the production flow structure. This creates a tight linkage and coordination of the production activities. In Table 15.1, whenever 100 units of a final product are purchased (i.e., inventory of final products crosses a 100 unit multiple) a *kanban* is sent to department 3 requesting production of 100 units of that product. The *kanban* is placed in the schedule rack (in the "kanb" column of each department in Table 15.1) in the order in which it was received. When department 3 completes a production run, it selects the next *kanban* in the schedule to run *if it has the materials needed*. If the materials are not available, the next job in the *kanban* list with material available would be run; the first job would remain the highest-priority job in the schedule and would be run as soon as materials are available. For example, at time 3.0 job A was first in line in department 3, but job B was set up and run because the materials for A had not yet arrived from department 2.

Whenever department 3 uses 100 units of material for a product, it issues a *kanban* to department 2 instructing it to make more materials for the product. Department 2 puts the *kanban* in its schedule rack and proceeds in the same way as department 3. This process continues back to department 1. Whenever department 1 uses 100 units of its raw materials for a product, it issues a release of goods from its suppliers and its inventory is replenished. Although some JIT systems use *kanban* cards that recirculate between pairs of departments or machines, the exact medium used to communicate between departments is irrelevant, as long as the communication is timely and accurate.

TABLE 15.1 DYNAMICS OF A JIT SYSTEM FOR FOUR HOURS

		Dept 1			Dept 2			Dept 3			Prod. Inv.				Sales			
Hour	SUPPLIER	Raw Matl	Activ	Kanb	Inv.	Activ	Kanb	Inv.	Activ	Kanb	A	B	C	D	A	B	C	D
											70	220	130	150				
0–0.5		ADCB	SU D	BC	AD	Run C	DB	BDA	SU A	DA					15	20	10	25
0.5–1		ACB	Run D	BC	AD	Run C	DBA	BD	Run A	DA	55	200	120	125				
1–1.5		DACB	Run D	BC	AD	SU D	BA	CBD	Run A	DAB					15	20	10	25
1.5–2		DACB	SU B	CD	DA	Run D	BA	CBD	SU D	AB	140	180	110	100				
2–2.5		DAC	Run B	CD	DA	Run D	BAD	CB	Run D	ABD					15	20	10	25
2.5–3		BDAC	Run B	CD	DA	SU A*	BD	DCB	Run D	ABD	125	160	100	75				
3–3.5		BDAC	SU C	DA	BD	Run A	BD	DCB	SU B*	ADC				175	15	20	10	25
3.5–4		BDA	Run C	DA	BD	Run A	BDB	DC	Run B	ADC	110	140	90	150				

Notes: Letters A–D represent 100 units of materials for products A–D or kanbans requesting 100 units of production for that product.
→, material movements; ←--, information movements (kanban issued).
SU stands for "setting-up" product run.
Run means product is being processed.
*Materials for the next product scheduled are not available; the following product is run.
Setup time for each product is 0.5 hour in each department. Running time for each product is 0.01 hour per unit in each department.

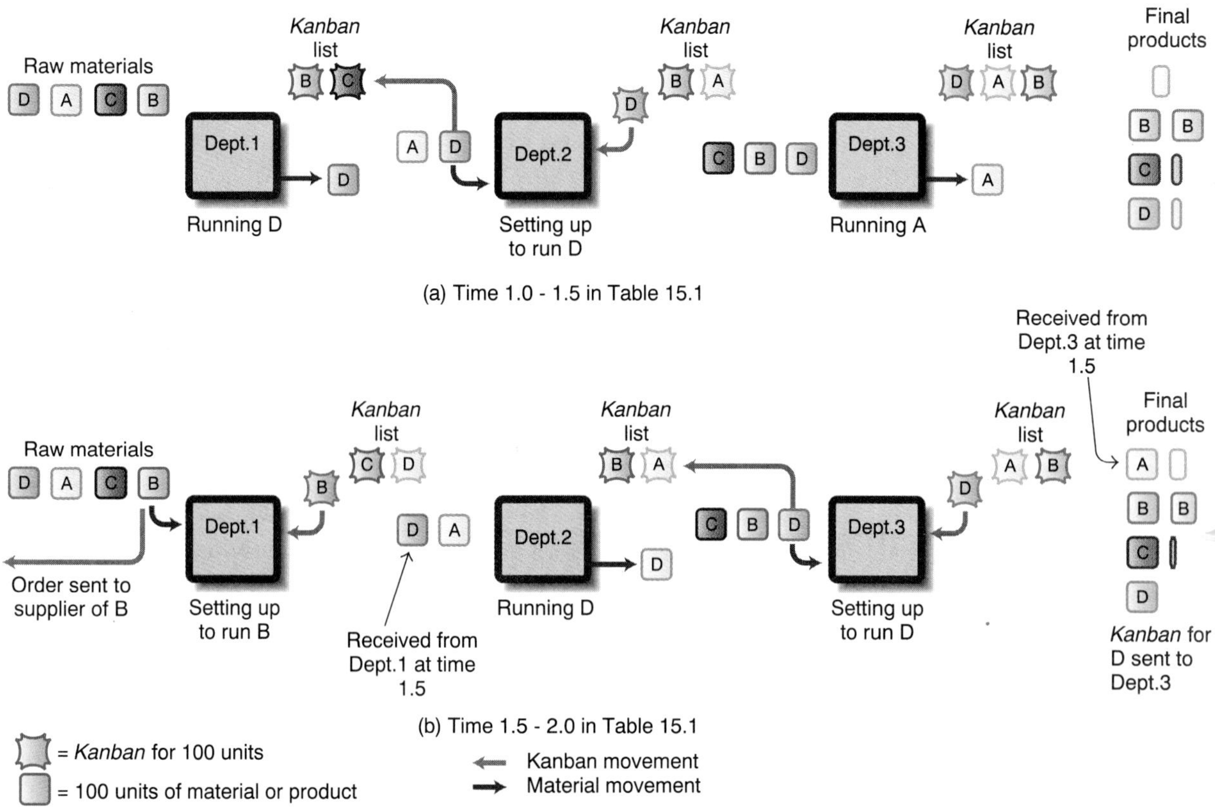

FIGURE 15.6 JIT Dynamics for one hour.

Table 15.1 demonstrates how the JIT system can operate with such low inventories while providing greater customer responsiveness and greater protection against sudden changes in demand than the classical system. For each product, the equivalent of 200–400 units of material or partially processed product is always available within the system, so if more of a product is needed, it can be pulled through the system and turned into final product within one day. Any surge in demand automatically puts more *kanbans* for *that product* into the system, which accelerates replenishment of in-process supplies for that product and increases the frequency of its production runs. Similarly, slowdowns in demand for a product quickly translate into wider spacing of production runs for that product.

THE NUMBER AND SIZE OF KANBANS

Several methods have been proposed for determining the best lot sizes (also called *kanban sizes*) and number of *kanbans* to use in a JIT system.[8] In practice, the size of a *kanban* is determined by the time and cost of a setup, the demand rate, and the number of units that can be conveniently stored and transported. Despite some criticism of economic lot-size models, the longer the setup time required to change over, the more economical it is to use larger lot sizes even in JIT systems. This is one reason Big JIT devotes so much effort to decreasing setup time; reductions in setup time automatically translate into smaller economic lot sizes.

[8]See Yasuhiro Monden, *Toyota Production System*, Industrial Engineering and Management Press, Atlanta, GA, 1983.

The number of *kanbans* to use is best determined by initially putting enough *kanbans* in the system to produce enough product to satisfy daily demand plus a reasonable amount of safety stock. The more randomness in the system (and there may be much when JIT is first implemented), the more *kanbans* and safety stock required for each product. As the system improves and variations decrease, the number of *kanbans* and the amount of inventory in the system can be systematically reduced without disrupting production flow or risking stockouts.

15.5 THE INGREDIENTS OF BIG JIT: APPROACHING THE IDEAL SYSTEM

The classical production system illustrated in Figure 15.4 was a somewhat idealized situation. We assumed that demand was relatively constant in volume and product mix; raw materials were delivered as needed; production times were constant; defects did not occur, so products did not have to be rerun or lot sizes increased to account for discarded defects; machines did not break down; and so on. In practice, these idealized conditions do not hold, and the company would probably respond by holding even more inventories of each raw material and each product between production stages. The resulting inventories might be two or three times as large as those reported for Example 1.

The pull mechanism and small lot sizes of JIT systems directly address only one type of deviation from the ideal production environment—randomness in customer demand—and indirectly address a few others. But the developers of JIT scheduling recognized that its benefits would be limited, and that JIT itself might be infeasible, if the other deviations from the ideal production world were not corrected. For example, using small lot sizes, which is essential for effective JIT scheduling, would be infeasible if production setups took a long time. Comparing the classical and JIT systems in Example 1, the classical system involves 4 setups each week, whereas the JIT system requires 28. If the setup time were not reduced in the JIT system, there would not be sufficient production capacity to meet the demand.[9] Similarly, if machines regularly broke down or deliveries of raw materials were unreliable, the JIT system would be forced to maintain larger inventories of materials and work-in-process than those shown in Example 1 to meet demands. Therefore, over the course of about 40 years, the developers of JIT devoted considerable attention to reducing or eliminating these other deviations from the ideal world. It is this total system improvement, known as *lean production* or *Big* JIT, to which we now turn.

QUICK SETUPS: SINGLE-MINUTE EXCHANGE OF DIES

As soon as the notion of using small production lot sizes was developed, it became obvious that setup times would have to be reduced.

Internal versus External Setup Activities

In 1950, while working for Toyo Kogyo's Mazda plant, Shigeo Shingo began his systematic study of production setups.[10] Shingo was asked to study a stamping operation, which was a major production bottleneck, to determine whether additional stamping

[9]The simulations for Example 1 were based on an assumed setup time of two hours for the classical system but only half an hour for the JIT system. (The processing rate was assumed to be 100 units per hour.) With a two-hour setup time the company could not even perform all its setups during a 40-hour week, much less produce product if it used the JIT System.

[10]From Robinson, op. cit., pp. 307–316. An excellent source for SMED is Robinson, pp. 291–369.

By executing the external set-up tasks, such as collecting all the necessary parts, before shutting down the bottling line, this worker is able to execute a product change-over more quickly.

presses were needed. As he studied and collected data on the operation, Shingo noticed that the presses were actually operating only a small part of the time. The rest of the time they were either idle while being set up or operating at low efficiency while being adjusted after setup. The key event occurred while Shingo was observing a die change for one of the presses. During the setup, he noticed everyone running around frantically. One of the workers he questioned told him that a bolt needed for the setup was missing. After an hour, the worker finally returned to the machine with a bolt. On seeing him Shingo said, "Ah, you've found it." The worker responded, "No, I didn't actually find it. I borrowed a long die bolt from the next machine over there. I cut it to make it shorter and then threaded it. That's what took so long. It wasn't easy, I can tell you."

Shingo found that similar problems occurred frequently during setups. At that point he made the key discovery that would lead to faster setups: setup operations actually consisted of two different activities: what Shingo calls *internal* and *external*. **Internal setup** activities, such as mounting a die or changing the ink cartridge on a photocopier, are those that can be performed only while the equipment is stopped. **External setup** activities, such as collecting all bolts needed to mount a die or unpacking an ink cartridge from its carton, are those that can be done while the equipment is operating.

Shingo put this dichotomy of setup activities into action by preparing a structured plan for the external setup activities of the die change. For example, before the stamping press was stopped for setup, all bolts were collected and put into a box, all tools were arranged for easy access, the new die was transported to the machine, and all preparatory activities were performed. Simply by doing external activities while the press was still operating and doing only internal setup activities while it was stopped, the setup time was cut in half.

Changing Internal to External Setup

A second major discovery occurred while Shingo was observing the setup of a large side planer used to machine diesel engine beds. Much time was spent "centering and dimensioning the engine bed . . . on the planer table itself." This was done while the planar was shut down, so it was treated as an internal setup activity. Shingo recognized that this work could be done on a second table while the planar was operating. Then when the planar stopped, the table in the planar could be switched with the second table, on which the engine was already aligned. This approach converted an internal to an external setup activity and resulted in a 40% increase in productivity.

Procedure for Reducing Setup Times

Shingo's two observations formed the foundation of a procedure for reducing setup times that he called **single-minute exchange of dies (SMED)** (named for consulting projects in which he reduced the time for die changes on large presses from several hours down to less than 10 minutes). Despite its name, SMED is applicable to almost any type of machine setup or changeover. Shingo's most striking successes with the method involved reducing the setup time for a bolt-making machine at Toyota from 8 hours to one minute and reducing the setup time for a boring machine at Mitsubishi Heavy Industries from 24 hours to less than three minutes!

SMED uses the following four-step procedure:

1. ***Observe and Analyze How the Setup Is Currently Performed.*** Setups should be observed carefully, and *activity charts* and *worker-machine charts* such as those described in Chapter 10 should be constructed. Whenever possible, one should videotape the setups. This is not only helpful in constructing the necessary data and charts, it is invaluable in showing workers what they are currently doing and how the setup can be improved. For example, when 3M Corporation videotaped its changeover process, it was noticed that workers often did not have the correct tools when needed. Putting tool boxes near the changeover sites eliminated wasted time getting tools and reduced the changeover time.[11]
2. ***Separate Internal from External Setup Activities.*** One of the most effective ways to reduce setup times is to separate internal from external activities and then to make a written setup plan that ensures that external setup activities are performed while the process is operating. Some of the most common external setup activities are preparing and testing parts and tools, transporting these to the machine, bringing materials to be processed to the machine, and transporting materials away from the machine, such as finished products to storage or waste to disposal bins. The following suggestions can help workers perform these as external setup activities.

   (a) Make a checklist of the items needed for each setup/changeover. Then create a "part-holder" box (kit) that will hold the parts, with the list attached, so that the worker can check off parts while gathering them before the setup. As part of the gathering process, the worker may also test the items collected, such as making sure that bolt threads are not damaged. One of the biggest wastes of setup time results from not discovering until internal setup is being performed that a required part is defective; checking and testing parts during the external phase eliminates these delays.

   (b) Provide machine operators with their own material-handling equipment, such as hand trucks, so that they can perform most or all of the material transport themselves. This makes it easier for them to transport materials as an external activity rather than waiting for separate transport workers to be available (it may also reduce the need for transport workers).

   Simply performing external activities while production continues will normally reduce setup times by 30–50%.
3. ***Convert Internal to External Setup Activities.*** As Shingo found with setting up the engine-bed side planer, activities that *appear* to be internal setup activities can sometimes be converted to external activities. Changing work methods, adding work aids, or buying duplicate sets of tools or equipment can assist in this conversion. The following general examples show how this can be done.

[11]From Kevin Kelly, "3M Run Scared? Forget About It," *Business Week*, Sept. 16, 1991, pp. 59–62.

(a) Many operations require the heating of molds or materials to be processed. Rather than doing all the heating as part of the internal setup, workers can often preheat outside of the setup so that final heating during internal setup requires less time. This may require the purchase of a second mold or holding vessel. For example, rather than heating a fluid in the main production vessel, which requires the production process to be stopped, one can preheat in a second vessel during production of the previous batch, and then the second vessel can be switched with the main vessel when the process is stopped. The time the process is stopped is considerably reduced. The same idea applies to cooling or mixing of materials.

(b) Cleaning activities can often be transferred from internal to external setup. For example, by having two sets of tools or two processing vessels, one can replace the dirty or contaminated one with a clean one quickly during internal setup, and then the dirty one can be cleaned after production has restarted. For fluid vessel cleaning, rather than having two separate vessels, a lower-cost solution is often to use plastic vessel liners that can be exchanged quickly.

4. ***Simplify and Streamline Activities.*** Once as many activities as possible have been assigned to external setup, setup time can be reduced further by simplifying and streamlining work and by concentrating work more effectively. Although reducing the time needed to perform any activity is likely to have some benefit, the primary focus should be on reducing the time for internal setup activities because this will reduce production system idleness.

The best way to reduce setup activity times is by task simplification using the methods described in Chapter 10. In addition, Shingo advocates the following techniques and principles.

(a) Provide each work station with its own tools and store the tools conveniently. For example, several technicians at a medical laboratory were required to recalibrate their scales before each batch of tests they performed. This was done by weighing three standard weights. When each technician was given her own set of standard weights, she did not have to wait between batches to use a set of standard weights shared with others.

(b) Standardize the size and shape of dies and other parts that must be changed during setups. Even though the working area of the dies is different—for example, one job may require stamping 10-inch-diameter circles and another requires stamping 24-inch squares—the external dimensions of the dies can be the same, as shown in Figure 15.7. This way the dies or tools can be inserted and removed like cassettes in a cassette player without having to calibrate and align the die or tool.

(c) Use the same fasteners, such as bolts, for each setup. The fasteners can stay with the machine; they simply have to be loosened and retightened for each setup, rather than removed, replaced, transported, and stored.

(d) Use fasteners that can be loosened and tightened with a single turn rather than those that require turning the fastener several revolutions.

(e) Reduce or eliminate adjustments by using fixed settings and markings on dies, tables, and guide bars. Every setup can be premarked so that tools and dies do not have to be measured each time. For example, the printer in our department at the university is used to print on paper and envelopes of different sizes. Originally, a trial-and-error approach was used to adjust the width of guide bars and the printer settings to print each item correctly. Now set-

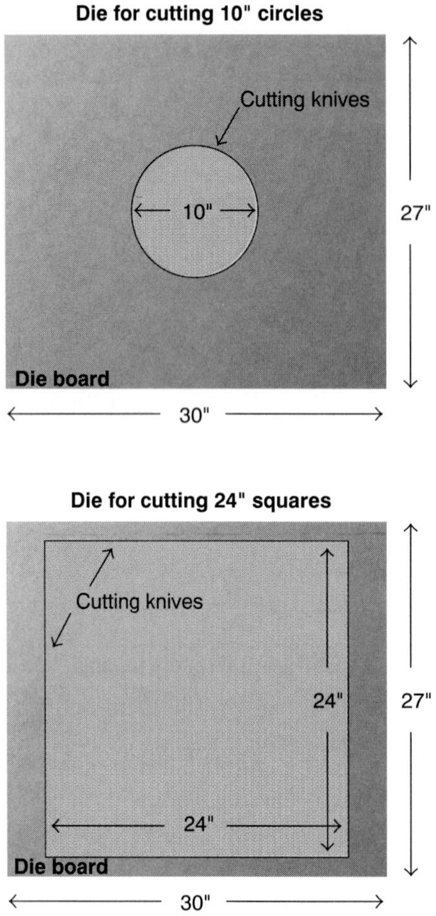

FIGURE 15.7 Standardized die size: same external dimensions.

tings are marked on the print feeder for the most common items printed, reducing changeover time from several minutes to just a few seconds.

Generalization of SMED Techniques

The use of SMED procedures has become widespread in manufacturing, with hundreds of success stories reported. For example, Ford Motor Company reduced the time for a die change on one of its presses from 5 hours to 5 minutes, and Packaging Corporation of America cut its changeover time for its carton-making machines from 21 hours to under 8 hours.[12] The principles of SMED have been applied to many situations other than setups for different products. They can be used to minimize downtime while replacing parts or tools, such as drill bits in a drill, or while performing maintenance and repair jobs. For example, steel, aluminum, and paper manufacturers regularly change the rolls on their rolling mills or paper machines as part of their preventive maintenance. Many roll-changing activities, such as prepositioning new rollers and gathering

[12]See Robert Manor, "Will Modular Assembly Lines Be Next?" *St. Louis Post-Dispatch*, Nov. 18, 1991, and Michael Selz, "Small Manufacturers Display the Nimbleness the Times Require," *Wall Street Journal*, Dec. 29, 1993.

SMED techniques can be used to reduce the set-up time of operating rooms between surgical procedures. This increases the utilization of scarce surgical facilities and personnel.

tools and replacement parts, can be done as external setup, thereby minimizing the time the mills are shut down.

Although originally developed in heavy manufacturing industries for die changes and other large machine setups, the principles of SMED apply readily to many activities in service production. For example, they have been used to change over medical operating rooms between surgeries and to turn around airplanes between flights. They can even be used in our everyday lives, such as in changing a cartridge in a printer or preparing meals (unpackaging one food to be microwaved while another is cooking).

RELIABLE DELIVERY OF MATERIALS

For companies that use JIT production, it is common to have vendors make deliveries once or twice a day (or even hourly) rather than once or twice a month. For example, Spartan Manufacturing, which makes chassis for fire trucks, buses, and other customized vehicles, receives daily deliveries from its suppliers.

The potential benefits of such a tightly coordinated system are evident, but it is also a high-risk system. Late deliveries of supplies or delivery of poor-quality components will quickly bring the JIT system to a halt. So suppliers must be able to make reliable, on-time delivery of consistently good-quality products and still remain flexible. To accomplish this, customers and suppliers must work closely together so that suppliers can produce as if they were coordinated parts of the customer's production system. This requires the customer and supplier to form a new business relationship that differs from the classical arms-length dealings of the past. Lawrence Milligan of Procter & Gamble summed up the need for this close relationship as follows: "We saw a potential savings of $1 billion annually in the U.S. for P&G and just as much, if not more, for our customers. But the elephants have to dance together to get there."[13]

There are at least four ways in which customers and suppliers can work together to provide reliable delivery to the customer at lower cost to both.

1. ***Share Production Scheduling Plans Quickly.*** The customer and supplier must share production plans in real time. It is especially important for the customer to notify suppliers immediately of any change in its scheduled production volume and product mix. This information gives the supplier greater flexibility in adjust-

[13]Barnaby Feder, "Moving the Pampers Faster Cuts Everyone's Cost," *New York Times*, July 14, 1991.

ing its production schedule to maintain reliable deliveries at the lowest possible cost. Similarly, problems in the supplier's production system that could affect deliveries, such as a machine breakdown or a quality problem, should be communicated to the customer immediately so that the customer has maximum flexibility to modify its own production plans.

2. ***Include Suppliers in Product Design.*** Suppliers that participate in the design of their customers' products can often modify the designs so that components will be easier to produce, with more consistent quality and lower cost. For example, by involving suppliers in its product design, Chrysler cut its late engineering design changes for one model from 1000 to 300, and it reported that suppliers' suggestions saved it $156 million.[14] The more "vendor friendly" the components are, the less likely quality problems will occur and production and delivery will be interrupted.

3. ***Help Suppliers Improve Their Production Methods.*** Users of JIT production are likely to have more advanced production methods, in terms of quality, continuous improvement, and production coordination and flexibility, than many of their suppliers. It is in the customer's best interest to share its production expertise and help suppliers to improve their production systems. Many users of JIT systems make such cooperation and technology transfer an explicit part of their contracts with suppliers. The suppliers, with the assistance of the customer, are required to adopt production methods that improve product quality, reduce cost, and increase flexibility. Financial benefits are split between the suppliers and customer. For the customer, these benefits are reflected in price reductions and more consistent quality of the products they are supplied. The suppliers keep some of the cost savings as additional profit and receive the benefits of using the new methods in all their other sales.

4. ***Have Spatially Close Facilities.*** The farther supplies have to be shipped to a customer, the more uncertain the delivery due to traffic congestion, bad weather, and so on. In addition, the longer it takes to ship products, the more inventory that is needed in the transportation pipeline to keep the customer's system operating smoothly and the less responsive the supplier can be to changes in the customer's needs. One way to reduce delivery randomness and inventories is for suppliers to locate near their major customer(s). For example, four hours before General Motors assembles an automobile at its Eisenach, Germany, plant, Lear Seating Company makes the seats at a plant just 600 yards away and trucks them directly to the GM assembly line.[15] Because of changes in production technology, many products can be made in small plants by 100–500 workers as efficiently as in large plants. Therefore, the agglomeration of supplier facilities around one or two major customers is becoming more common and financially advantageous.

   In some cases, suppliers actually lease space in their customer's production facilities. The supplier can stay in close contact with the customer regarding production schedules; shipping cost, shipping time, and inventories can be greatly reduced; and cooperation in product design and quality assurance are facilitated.

---

[14]Bradley Stertz, "Detroit's New Strategy to Beat Back Japanese Is to Copy Their Ideas," *Wall Street Journal*, Oct. 1, 1992.

[15]Karen Lowry Miller and Kathleen Kerwin,"GM's German Lessons," *Business Week*, Dec. 20, 1993, pp. 67–68.

Customer–Supplier Cooperation, Sole Sourcing, and Long-Term Commitments

To motivate a supplier to participate in the four ways discussed above, the customer must provide a guaranteed long-term commitment. A supplier will not change its production system, open new facilities near a customer, or even upgrade its information exchange system or assign its personnel to help design a customer's products unless it anticipates a profitable, long-term relationship. Many of the improvements the customer will suggest require a significant financial investment that can be recouped only if a large volume of product is produced.

These issues strongly suggest that, whenever possible, companies should use long-term agreements with suppliers that guarantee sole sourcing or nearly sole sourcing of purchases. These agreements, which were discussed in Chapter 13, provide the supplier with stability and a guaranteed volume of production that can justify enhancements to its production system. In return, the customer can insist on guarantees of reliable delivery, high quality, stable or decreasing prices, and a share of productivity improvements. These agreements also promote closer ties between the companies in the areas of product design and information exchange. Companies that have used this approach, such as Xerox, Motorola, and Ford, have realized substantial financial benefits by dealing with fewer suppliers, by simplifying logistics and scheduling, and by achieving lower component prices resulting from improvements made by their suppliers.

Sole sourcing is not without risks. The primary risk is that of a supply disruption. A natural disaster or a strike or major accident at a supplier's production facility can bring the customer's production process to a screeching halt. In several instances, U.S auto manufacturers have found that a strike at a supplier's plant quickly stopped assembly of an entire product line. It is easy to see from our earlier example that if automobile seats are being assembled into finished autos within hours of their production, even a short disruption at the supplying plant will stop final assembly within hours.

REDUCING MACHINE BREAKDOWNS: TOTAL PRODUCTIVE MAINTENANCE

Work stoppages and product defects are often the result of poor equipment maintenance. Therefore, a major aspect of Big JIT production is a system for improving maintenance and reducing machine breakdowns. Poor maintenance is harmful in several ways. First, it is expensive. Fixing catastrophic machine failures is usually far more expensive than preventive maintenance, and while machines are being repaired, production workers are idled. Second, breakdowns make production unreliable, which results in product shortages and late deliveries. Third, breakdowns waste capacity in two ways: (1) production is lost during unplanned shutdowns caused by machine failures, and (2) improperly operating machines can produce defective products that have to be remade.

Causes of Machine Failures

Any attempt to create a systematic maintenance policy should identify the primary causes of machine failures. The following are some of the most common causes of machine breakdowns:

1. Inadequate preventive maintenance.
2. Overusing and operating machines at excessive speeds.
3. Dirt, oil, and chemical damage.
4. Collisions (e.g., a fork lift hitting a machine).
5. Incorrect machine setup for operation.
6. Materials fed into machine or processed incorrectly.

The cost of machine breakdowns can be substantial, yet eliminating these six causes can be relatively inexpensive. That is the focus of the following maintenance strategy, which is sometimes called **total productive maintenance (TPM)**.

Preventive Maintenance, Job Design and Operator Training

One of the primary causes of inadequate preventive maintenance is the fact that preventive maintenance is assigned to specialized maintenance crews. Because such personnel are expensive, most companies keep their number small and give the repair of breakdowns the highest priority. What time is left for preventive maintenance is usually devoted to "major" work, such as overhauls, which the maintenance personnel consider to be most important, while routine preventive maintenance goes undone, ultimately leading to more frequent breakdowns.

This wire machine operator is able to make minor repairs, such as replacing a pulley, himself. This eliminates time wasted waiting for maintenance workers to do it, and frees up maintenance workers to focus on more serious maintenance tasks.

A solution to this problem is to train machine operators to perform some of their own maintenance, especially preventive maintenance. A study by Tennessee Eastman Chemical Company found that 40% of a traditional maintenance worker's job could be done by machine operators with minimal training, and another 40% could be done by operators with additional training but below the level of a certified mechanic.[16] Many preventive maintenance tasks are actually quite simple, such as lubricating bearings and rollers, tightening loose fasteners, replacing worn parts, and cleaning components. When these are a normal part of the operator's job, preventive maintenance is performed more reliably, and much of it can be done while the machine is running or while it is idle for other reasons, so the maintenance is essentially costless.

With additional training, operators can even repair their own machines when failures do occur, or they can at least prepare the machines for repair while waiting for the maintenance personnel to arrive and then assist them in repairing it. In fact, as operators gain experience and familiarity, they can often become more skilled at repairing their own machines than a maintenance crew, which may have to maintain 30 or 40 different machines. This strategy also reduces the scheduling and coordination problems that cause machine idleness when specialized crews perform the maintenance.

Tennessee Eastman found that training its machine operators better and transferring maintenance tasks to them resulted in substantial cost savings and productivity improvements: 90% fewer breakdowns occurred for some machines; repair times for some repairs were cut by over 75%; and machine availability increased by up to 6% for some machines, with a companywide average increase of 1–2%. Machine operators now perform approximately 80% of all maintenance tasks, and the annual net savings resulting from the TPM program is estimated at $8 million.

This strategy reduces the number of specialized maintenance personnel needed, but it does not mean that companies should eliminate all their maintenance personnel. Rather, it implies a change in their focus and duties. Specialized maintenance crews would still repair machines that cannot be repaired by operators, and they would perform major overhauls and rebuild badly worn machines. However, a large part of their job would be to develop better machine designs, maintenance practices, and work aids to make the machines more reliable and easier to maintain, as well as to train operators to perform maintenance. This actually expands the job of maintenance personnel and raises their level of responsibility.

Maintaining Excess Capacity

For many machines the amount of wear the machine incurs and the number of failures per unit time, are not proportional to their operating speeds. Instead the relationship

[16]Bill Maggard and David Rhyne, "Total Productive Maintenance: A Timely Integration of Production and Maintenance," *Production and Inventory Management Journal*, 4th Quarter 1992, pp. 6–10.

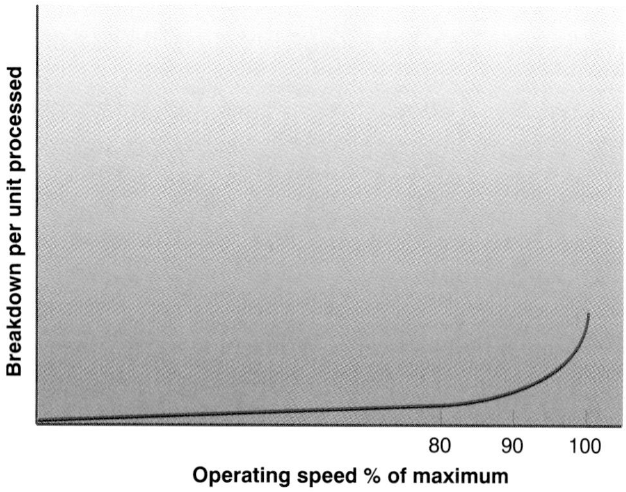

FIGURE 15.8 Machine wear as a function of operating speed.

looks more like that in Figure 15.8. At low to moderate operating rates the wear on the machine is relatively low, but at utilization near its *nameplate capacity* (the maximum speed at which the manufacturer claims the machine can be operated), wear and failure rates increase rapidly with higher speed of operation and increased time of use.

Operating at 80–90% of the nameplate level makes failures much less frequent than operating above this level, which over the long run can actually result in higher effective capacity. The output of machines operated near their nameplate capacity will alternate between 100% of capacity and 0% (i.e., broken). Over the long term this may produce less output than a steady 80–90% operating rate.

For many production processes, as operating speed reaches some limit, the precision and quality of work decrease. This may be due to machine vibration or to workers' inability to feed materials into and align them in the machine correctly fast enough. Again, maintaining a more moderate but steady pace is often better than a faster speed with erratic quality.

Finally, JIT systems produce for actual demand rather than anticipated demand. When moderate increases in demand occur, the production system must be capable of increasing production rapidly. One feature of JIT systems is that they are designed to operate normally at 80–90% of capacity so that they can increase production rapidly when necessary. As long as these increases in production are of short duration or are accompanied by additional preventive maintenance, the wear on machines and failures are not excessive.

Cleanliness and Housekeeping

One thing you will immediately notice if you visit a world-class manufacturing facility is its cleanliness. A major cause of machine failures and poor product quality is the buildup of dirt, oil, and chemicals in machines or on materials. Cleaning machines should be a normal part of the preventive maintenance done by machine operators. Maintaining general cleanliness and orderliness should also be a responsibility of production operators, and this can usually be done during idle times. Tools should be stored neatly in a designated place, materials arranged neatly, and aisles kept clear of clutter. This not only creates a more attractive and pleasant work atmosphere, but also improves visibility and sight lines and reduces accidents that can injure employees and damage machines.

Structured Setups

One of the extra benefits of SMED is that fewer mistakes occur in the setup. Incorrect machine setup can lead to material jamming in the machine or other processing problems that can damage the machine. The structured nature of SMED-driven setups almost guarantees that no setup task is omitted by accident. In addition, the work aids and calibration of tools and machines make it more likely that the setup will be done accurately.

Work Aids

Human errors are a frequent cause of machine failure. Many can be reduced or eliminated by employing the job design principles and work aids discussed in Chapter 10. For example, guide bars, stop bars, and various *poka yoke* (mistake-proofing) devices can (1) prevent materials from being fed into or removed from machines incorrectly, (2) prevent the wrong materials from being fed into a machine, (3) ensure that every required operational task is performed, and (4) guarantee that the machine is operated at the correct speed. Emergency cutoff switches should be readily accessible, both as a safety device and to keep small malfunctions from turning into major machine failures. In addition, human errors can be reduced by painting lubrication points with bright colors to make them easy to find or marking fasteners and calibration points with bright colors that will not line up when a fastener is loose.

More Maintenance Principles

Several other principles and actions can enhance equipment maintenance.

1. As in product and process design, the secret of better machine maintenance is *simplicity*. Machines should be kept as simple as possible while still accomplishing their required functions. Firms should standardize replacement parts and reduce the variety of machines for maintenance personnel. For example, Southwest Airlines simplifies its maintenance by using only Boeing 737 airplanes.
2. To solve maintenance problems and to allocate maintenance resources efficiently, it is important to collect useful data on the frequency and causes of machine failures. Roy Harmon, founding partner of Anderson Consulting's factory productivity practice, suggests posting a sticker on each machine when it breaks down. It will quickly become apparent which machines need special attention—those with the most stickers attached.[17]
3. When some parts of a machine start to wear out, many other components are wearing out as well. It is better to rebuild the machine by replacing all worn parts at once instead of replacing them one by one, as is sometimes done. If a company maintains good records, it can make this a cost-effective approach by repairing machines only as needed and scheduling the rebuilding during off-peak periods.
4. It is surprising how much time is wasted when a machine is shut down for overhaul and key components are not available when needed. Procurement should be carefully planned so that all parts are on hand when needed.

QUALITY AND JIT PRODUCTION

JIT production systems cannot tolerate stoppages due to poor quality any more than those due to machine failures. For this reason, development of total quality manage-

[17]Roy Harmon's book *Reinventing the Factory*: II, Free Press, New York, 1992, Chapter 9, is an excellent source for maintenance management.

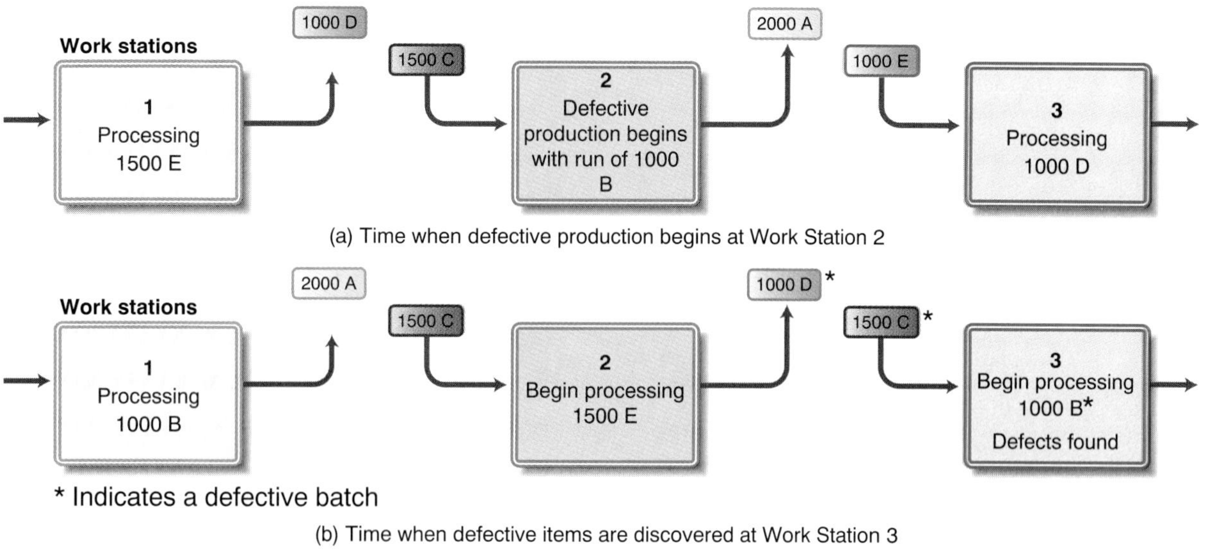

FIGURE 15.9 Identifying defective operation in a classical production system.

ment (TQM), which was discussed in Chapter 11, has been an important aspect of JIT production. Good product quality depends on at least four things: (1) the product should be designed so that it is easy to make, (2) materials from suppliers should not be defective, (3) the production process should not introduce defects, and (4) if defective items are produced, they need to be found quickly and the cause of the problem eliminated. In Chapters 5 and 11 we discussed in detail how to improve product quality through good product design and how to prevent and detect defects. Also, in this chapter, we have discussed the role of suppliers in providing high-quality components.

JIT scheduling can actually help achieve the fourth factor: identifying defects and correcting quality problems quickly. Because items are processed in small lot sizes and not kept between processing stages for long, defects occurring at one stage of production are often found quickly at the next stage. For example, consider a company that makes five types of metal containers, designated as models A, B, C, D, and E, in lot sizes of 1000–2000 units using a classical push production system. Suppose, as illustrated in Figure 15.9a, a subtle quality problem occurs at work station 2 during a production run of product B that the workers at work station 2 do not recognize but that will become evident during processing at work station 3. However, work station 3 will not begin processing B until work station 2 has already produced 1000 units of B, 1500 units of C, and 1000 units of D, all of which are defective, as shown in Figure 15.9b.

In contrast, suppose the company used a JIT pull system with a lot size of 100 units. Figure 15.10 shows that when a similar problem occurs in the production of B at work station 2, the quality problem is discovered at work station 3 after only 100 units of B, 100 units of C, and 100 units of D have been made. Work station 3 can notify work station 2 quickly, which saves 3200 units of wasted material and the production capacity needed to remake the defective items.

In addition to recognizing quality problems promptly, TQM and JIT can correct quality problems quickly. Although JIT systems do not tolerate stoppages well, an essential part of JIT is that production will be stopped to find and solve the causes of quality problems whenever they occur, rather than continuing to produce defective items and then trying either to rework them or work around them. Because JIT systems

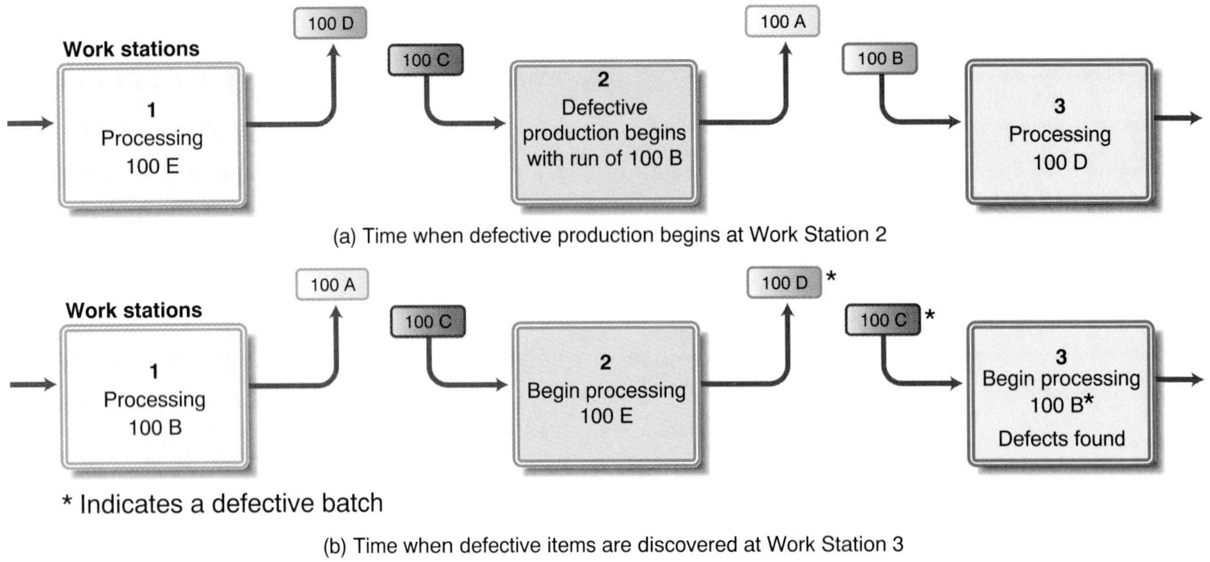

FIGURE 15.10 Identifying defective operation in a JIT production system.

operate with low safety stock levels, safety stocks cannot be used to make up for, or buffer the company from, production shortages due to defects. Quality problems are rocks in the production stream, and if the JIT system is to lower the inventory "water level," those rocks must be removed for the "production boat" to float. This is one reason why it is good to design excess capacity into the production system so that stoppages can be made without disrupting delivery.

CONTINUOUS IMPROVEMENT

A basic principle underlying Big JIT is that regardless of how efficient the production system is, it can always be made better. Some people characterize this principle by saying that the goal of Big JIT is to eliminate all forms of waste, especially activities that do not add value to the company's products. Institutionalizing this principle of **continuous improvement** (or ***kaizen*** in Japanese) is an integral part of any Big JIT production system. We have already seen several specific ways to do this; SMED, TPM, and TQM are all ways to generate continuous process improvement. The most successful continuous improvement systems are those that encourage employees themselves to find ways to improve production methods and to improve products. Three ways to promote this process are to use employee suggestion systems, quality circles, or autonomous work teams. These were discussed in Chapters 10 and 11, but they are briefly repeated here because of their importance.

Employee suggestion systems have been used for over a century, and some companies have reported astounding success with them. For example, in a single year Canon, Inc., received nearly 1 million suggestions (78 per employee) and paid $2.2 million in prizes for them, but these suggestions produced over $200 million in savings![18] Although Canon is an extreme case, hundreds of companies, such as Whirlpool and General Electric, have reported significant success with suggestion systems, and the conclusion is clear: It would be hard to find a better business investment than a well-implemented suggestion system.

[18]Robinson, op. cit., p. 13.

Quality circles are small groups of employees who meet regularly to discuss and evaluate ways to improve productivity, quality, and safety. **Autonomous work teams** are groups of employees who work together as a team to perform some aspect of production. They are often evaluated and rewarded as a team, and one aspect of the evaluation is improvement in performance. The development of both quality circles and autonomous work teams was motivated by the continuous improvement philosophy.

JIT AND EMPLOYEE MORALE

Most people like to do their jobs well. They want to make a contribution to the organizations for which they work, and they want job security and some control over their work environment. Big JIT exploits and supports these natural human desires. JIT production systems normally require greater worker training, responsibility, skill, and empowerment. Workers are encouraged to suggest improvements in the production system and working conditions and are allowed to participate in decision making. When they can control how products are made and the way work is organized and performed, there is greater enthusiasm, creativity, and dedication. The resulting reductions in inventory, machine failures, and quality defects and the increases in productivity provide tangible evidence that employee efforts have an impact. This success further enhances dedication and effort, which are exhibited in other tangible ways, such as reduced absenteeism and accidents.

15.6 IMPLEMENTING JIT PRODUCTION

The productivity-enhancing methods of Big JIT, such as quick setups, TPM, and continuous improvement, are applicable to almost any organization, regardless of its products and production processes. JIT *scheduling*, however, is *not* universally applicable, and in some cases using a pure pull mechanism to control production can be damaging. Before presenting suggestions on how to implement Big JIT, we begin with a discussion of when and when not to use JIT scheduling.

WHEN TO USE JIT SCHEDULING

It is a universally sound principle not to produce products or acquire materials until they are needed, but it is not always possible to postpone production until customers request a product. JIT scheduling is not suitable for every situation, and even when it is appropriate, there are several implementation issues that should be addressed for the system to realize its maximum potential. The factors that most significantly affect the desirability of using JIT scheduling are the demand pattern, the product mix, and the structure of the production process.

Demand Pattern

JIT scheduling works best when the demand for products is relatively stable over time and production capacity is large enough to handle short-term surges in demand. In industries where weekly demand may vary by only 10–20% during the year, a pure pull system based on assured demand is practical. However, in industries where the demand pattern is highly seasonal and unpredictable, such as those that produce toys or garden tools, an assured demand scheduling system is not practical. In these cases, the company must forecast future demands and produce in anticipation of demand; otherwise, shortages during peak demand periods are almost guaranteed. Howard Davidowitz, a retail consultant, describes it this way: "Just-in-time is great for Crest toothpaste, not toys. With toys, you've got to make a forecast because so much of your business is done in the last three months of the year."[19]

There are some actions that companies can take to create a steadier demand pattern. For example, consolidating their product line by making fewer models and options will normally reduce short-term variations. In addition, pricing and promotion strategies, such as those discussed in Chapters 6 and 12, can be used to shift demand from high- to low-demand periods. This highlights the fact that JIT scheduling and a quick response not only enhance marketing efforts but also rely on the marketing strategy to keep the demand pattern stable.

Product Mix

JIT scheduling works best when the system produces a limited number of stock items. Because production is pulled through the system, the materials needed at a production stage should be stock items that are produced on a routine basis by that stage. If the product being made at some stage is truly unique, the materials for that product could not have been pulled through the earlier stages with *kanbans*.

Systems using JIT scheduling can accommodate minor customization of products. The world-famous Toyota production system offers customers a limited set of options that require only minor modifications to a very structured production process, such as installing one type of audio system versus another, installing automatic versus manual transmission, or adding extra components that the standard models do not contain. In addition, most of Toyota's options come in "packages"; that is, individual options cannot be modified. If a customer wants a tilt steering wheel, he can only get it as part of a "deluxe" package that might include tinted glass, fold-down seats, and a higher-quality audio system as well. This arrangement limits the variations of products made by the production system.

One great benefit of JIT production is that it responds quickly to changes in the *mix* of products demanded. For example, Procter & Gamble's JIT production system can easily change its mix of detergent products on a packaging line from 70% Tide and 30% Bold to 60% Tide and 40% Bold simply by changing the mix and sequence of *kanbans*. However, there should still be a steady flow of demand for each product. If the demand is highly irregular, as is assumed in Chapter 14, JIT scheduling will be much less successful. Similarly, low-volume producers of a wide variety of customized products should probably not use pure JIT scheduling because they cannot pull customized products through the system; components must be obtained and prepositioned at work centers and production pushed through the system.

Production Process Structure

JIT production works best when materials and production move from work area to work area in a consistent, steady sequence. But the steady demand for a narrow set of products required above is exactly the condition in which flow production processes are most efficient. Therefore, it is not surprising that JIT scheduling is most suitable for, and has been most successfully utilized with, flow production processes.

When the stages of the flow process are tightly connected, such as on an automobile or electronics assembly line, interstage inventories will normally be very small even without JIT scheduling. In this case, JIT scheduling makes its greatest contributions in two areas: (1) it matches the speed of production and the mix of products to actual demand, so that excess finished product inventories do not develop, and (2) it coordi-

---

[19]Joseph Pereira, "Toy Industry Finds It's Harder and Harder to Pick the Winners," *Wall Street Journal*, Dec. 21, 1993.

nates delivery of raw materials to production to keep raw materials inventory at a minimum.

JIT production has even greater potential benefit in *disconnected* flow processes, such as the one illustrated in Example 1. Disconnected flow systems are most common when there is a greater variety of products and a greater variety of processing at each work station, such as in book publishing or lock manufacturing. In these cases, even using quick setup methods, it is more efficient to process and transfer products between work stations in batches rather than to make and transfer one item at a time, as with a repetitive flow process. Without JIT scheduling, disconnected systems tend to develop substantial interstage inventories; by contrast, JIT scheduling greatly reduces such inventories, along with raw material and final product inventories, as shown in Example 1.

WHEN NOT TO USE JIT SCHEDULING: JIT VERSUS MRP

In some circumstances, JIT scheduling may not be beneficial and may even be detrimental. The most obvious one is a production system that produces a wide variety of products, especially customer-specified products that may never be repeated. In this case, it is impossible for the JIT system to pull items through the system. When a *kanban* is issued to the final production stage, no production materials have been pulled through the system up to that stage, so production cannot occur. For unique products such as a printed paper form, it is normally preferable to use a well-coordinated push system, such as MRP, to control production. Even for stock items that are sold on an ongoing basis, if the purchase pattern is such that a few customers make large purchases on an irregular basis, MRP may be preferable to JIT. With MRP the acquisition of raw materials and components and the sequencing of production activities can be scheduled so that just the right amount of materials is acquired and processed to fill the order when needed. The initiation of production can still be based on assured demand, but the production signal is sent to the first stage of production (and raw materials purchased) rather than the last stage.

When the type and sequencing of production tasks vary among the products so that a job-shop production system is used, JIT scheduling can create havoc rather than improve scheduling. In these cases, the mix of products is so large and variable and the load on individual work centers can vary so much that a pull mechanism may be impractical. This does not mean that companies using job-shop production systems should not investigate JIT scheduling. One study reported that grouping products into families and converting operations to cellular production was the most important factor in successful implementation of JIT production.[20] This way production was converted to a series of mini-flow processes of narrow product families, which were quite suitable for JIT scheduling. It is also important to note that JIT scheduling can be used for those parts of the production system that satisfy the necessary conditions, and push scheduling can be used to schedule operations requiring a push approach.

GUIDELINES FOR JIT IMPLEMENTATION

The ultimate success or failure of JIT production will depend on how it is implemented. Implementation is not always a smooth process, however. Mistakes will be made, and a company must be willing to backtrack and revise its plans. It was this willingness to change its approach that turned Federal-Mogul's initial failure into a successful implementation of lean production (see this chapter's "In Good Company" segment). Follow-

[20]Thomas J. Billesbach, "A Study of the Implementation of Just-in-Time in the United States," *Production and Inventory Management Journal*, 3rd Quarter 1991, pp. 1–4.

ing are some proven suggestions for increasing the likelihood of success and the magnitude of the benefits.

Be Patient

Toyota's Lean Production system took over 20 years to develop. Companies that implement lean production must be patient and should not expect to see substantial benefits within months.

The Toyota production system took over 20 years to develop, and it is foolish to think that it can be completely copied by another organization in 5 years. Both JIT scheduling and the production enhancements of Big JIT require substantial changes not only to the mechanics of the system and the work of its employees, but also to the corporate philosophy and work culture. Such changes cannot occur quickly. They require considerable restructuring of work and both initial and ongoing training. Although some changes, such as rapid setup methods, can sometimes produce tangible benefits quickly, most will take time to produce visible results, and in the short term productivity may actually decrease until workers gain proficiency. Patience is required.

Shigeo Shingo, one of the codevelopers of JIT, recommends reducing inventories slowly while making gradual reductions in setup time, batch sizes, defects, and machine breakdowns. He warns that "Stock reduction should not become an end in itself, . . . cutting stock blindly may cause delivery delays or a drop in machine operating rates."[21] As the system drains the "inventory water" out of the stream, the production problem "rocks" will become visible and cause temporary problems. But once the problems are solved, they will be solved for good and then more draining can occur. For example, suppose a company adopts JIT scheduling and small lot sizes. At first the reduction in setup times may be insufficient to make up for all the extra setups occurring, so production begins to fall behind. Perhaps stockouts will occur or overtime production will be required. As workers keep finding ways to reduce setup time, this problem will disappear and lot sizes may even be reduced further. Similarly, quality and maintenance problems will disappear over time. Although substantial reductions in inventory and improvements in productivity usually occur slowly, inventory reductions of 20–40% and productivity improvements of 5–10% per year for each of the first two to three years are not uncommon.

Customize Implementation

JIT scheduling cannot be successful without adopting other production improvements. The small inventories and small batch sizes make it essential that setup times be reduced and anything that might cause production delays, such as quality or maintenance problems, be eliminated. However, this does not imply that all implementations must include the same changes or that they progress in the same sequence. Not all companies are at the same level in terms of quality management, setup methods, job design, or maintenance methods. As the company implements JIT scheduling and begins to drain the inventory "water" from its system, the problems that become visible and must be addressed first will vary from case to case. Therefore, rather than setting improvement programs in advance, such as declaring that the company will adopt TQM or TPM immediately on implementation of JIT scheduling, it may be better to wait for the most pressing problems to appear and then to respond quickly.

Even companies that do not adopt JIT scheduling can benefit from the production enhancements of Big JIT. Implementing Big JIT does not have to be an all-or-nothing undertaking. Each situation is unique, and the organization should choose those aspects of JIT that apply, as well as the sequence in which to implement them. For some compa-

[21]Paul Zipkin, "Does Manufacturing Need a JIT Revolution?" *Harvard Business Review*, Vol. 69, No. 1, 1991, p. 44.

nies, quick setup methods produce substantial improvements very quickly, whereas other companies may find that improving product quality is their highest priority.

Be Flexible and Adaptive

JIT systems do not, and frequently should not, operate with minimal inventories. A mistaken notion has developed that once a JIT system is adopted, especially JIT purchasing and scheduling, it is somehow wrong to increase inventories. This idea is foolish. JIT scheduling and purchasing are based on the assumption that product demands do not vary greatly over time and that production capacity is sufficient to satisfy peak demands. When these conditions are violated, JIT systems may have to respond, at least temporarily, by increasing inventories. Several so-called JIT failures have occurred in cases where the demand pattern was highly erratic and unpredictable, such as clothing and toys, or demand increased substantially over previous levels. Even with JIT systems, the more variation and uncertainty that exist in the demand pattern, the more inventories must be held. Even if JIT scheduling can be used during part of the year, before a seasonal surge in demand JIT production has to be abandoned temporarily and inventories have to be built up during periods of low demand in anticipation of peak demand.

The optimal number of *kanbans* and therefore inventories in a JIT system is directly related to the output rate; if output increases for a sustained period inventories should increase naturally, but the increases are less than proportional to the demand increase. Those companies that have successfully used JIT scheduling have been flexible enough to make these inventory changes when needed in order to avoid stockouts. Ronald Smith, of Purchasing Support Services, Inc., describes it by saying, "JIT has to be tweaked regularly."[22]

Maintain Excess Capacity

JIT systems work best when they are designed to operate most of the time at 80–90% of capacity. This allows production to accelerate when demand surges. Shigeo Shingo has pointed out that companies that try to operate near capacity are forced to carry larger inventories to protect against surges in demand or other production problems; otherwise, they will run out of stock. In addition, operating at 80–90% of capacity makes it possible to stop production immediately to correct quality problems when they occur. This lower utilization rate also gives employees time to experiment with and test improvements to the production process. Over time these improvements will lead to greater productivity and raise the production capacity. A system that is operating near capacity for extended periods of time cannot be stopped for such experimentation.

JIT IN SERVICE AND HYBRID INDUSTRIES

Although JIT production is most effective in manufacturing systems, it has also been applied effectively in the service sector. JIT principles are being used widely in the retail industry by companies such as Wal-Mart, Home Depot, and Kmart. In the past, retail stores had to forecast the demand for the products they sold, place their own orders with suppliers, buy goods in efficient (usually large) quantities, and wait several days or weeks for delivery. They ran the risk of having unsold merchandise if demand for the products dropped dramatically, but they had to maintain large inventories to avoid being out of stock if demand did not decrease.

---

[22]Fred Bleakley, "Just-in-Time Inventories Fade in Appeal as the Recovery Leads to Rising Demand," *Wall Street Journal*, Oct. 25, 1994.

IN GOOD COMPANY

Federal-Mogul Corporation Gives JIT a Second Chance

In 1987 Federal-Mogul Corporation mistakenly thought that Japanese companies obtained their cost advantages through greater automation, so it installed robots, production computers, and other state-of-the-art automation at its Lancaster, Pennsylvania, auto parts plant. Although the plant was able to produce parts faster than before, it lost its flexibility because product changeovers were much slower and more costly than before. Federal-Mogul could not respond quickly enough to changes in the parts needs of its customers, who were introducing and revising auto models more quickly. In addition, the automation did not lower costs due to the slow changeovers and the extensive maintenance required for the complex machinery.

In 1992 Federal-Mogul removed most of the robots, computers, and automated material-handling equipment, and the production line was redesigned and simplified. Using modular equipment and quick setup methods, Federal-Mogul can quickly change over from one product to another product by wheeling away a section of the production line and replacing it with another section already prepared for the next product. The plant, which makes 1800 different parts, can now produce three times as many different parts as before. The ease of changeovers has allowed it to reduce typical batch sizes by a factor of 20 (from 5000–10,000 to only 250–500), so it now produces only the parts customers want when they want them, rather than anticipating demand.

Federal-Mogul has improved its competitive position by learning from its mistakes. Rather than labeling JIT a fad and discarding it, Federal-Mogul learned more about it and implemented it correctly the second time.

Source: Amal Naj, "Some Manufacturers Drop Efforts to Adopt Japanese Techniques," *Wall Street Journal*, May 7, 1993.

Today many retailers are using optical scanning and electronic data interchange (EDI) technologies to maintain real-time information on their product inventories and to allow suppliers to track the retailers' sales and inventories. The suppliers can then ship products to the retailer as soon as inventories get low without waiting for the retailer to process a purchase order. By knowing the daily status of customer inventories, the supplier is also better able to plan its own production to deliver merchandise to the retailer just in time. These two factors reduce the effective lead time needed to restock the retailer and the variation in lead time. The net result is that retailers are able to maintain much smaller inventories while reducing the risks of both stockouts and unsold goods. This linking of retailers and manufacturers has been given various names, but a formal program called the *Quick Response Program* (QRP) was initiated in the United

Retailers such as Office Depot use just-in-time replenishment systems to keep their inventories low while supplying customers' needs. Electronic data interchange (EDI) systems allow suppliers to execute deliveries as soon as retailers' inventories drop to specified levels.

States in the 1980s to help U.S. manufacturers supply retailers more competitively than foreign suppliers.

Another example of JIT in a service system concerns an internal consulting division of Eastman Kodak Company. By instituting JIT production, the division, which provides testing, engineering, and information services to other units of Kodak, has decreased lead times from days or weeks to minutes or hours and has reduced its costs by over $2 million a year.[23]

McDonald's Corporation has been using JIT scheduling for years in food preparation at its restaurants. Hamburgers, cheeseburgers, and other products are prepared in small batches, and *kanbans* (usually plastic markers) are issued to the kitchen whenever inventories reach a certain point. This approach has increased McDonald's ability to serve customers quickly with freshly cooked food.

15.7 SYNCHRONOUS PRODUCTION AND THE THEORY OF CONSTRAINTS

Another approach to production scheduling and inventory management that is especially useful in job-shop environments is **synchronous** (or **synchronized**) **production**. Synchronous production has some similarities to JIT production, such as recognizing the harm resulting from production variations, trying to coordinate and pace production so all production stages are producing at the same rate, and using small batch sizes. However, synchronous production differs from JIT in two ways: (1) It focuses more on adapting efficiently to variations and imbalances in the system, rather than eliminating them, and (2) Production scheduling is a hybrid of classical push and JIT pull approaches.

[23] W. C. Wasco, R. E. Stonehocker, and L. H. Feldman, "Success with JIT and MRP II in a Service Organization," *Production and Inventory Management Journal*, 4th Quarter 1991, pp. 15–21.

SOME PRINCIPLES OF SYNCHRONOUS PRODUCTION

Synchronous production, developed by Eliyahu Goldratt, is based on the **theory of constraints**.[24] This theory was developed from three empirical observations: (1) In multistage production systems not all stages have the same production capacity; (2) Variations and randomness in production systems reduce effective capacity and output; and (3) The procedures used in classical production systems generally amplify rather than solve the problems created by capacity imbalance and production variations.

We saw in Chapter 8 that in a multistage production process the maximum rate of production (the **throughput**) is dictated by the stage with the smallest production capacity. A **bottleneck resource** is any resource that limits the flow of production through the system. Alternatively, a bottleneck resource is one that has a capacity less than or equal to the demand put on it. A **nonbottleneck resource** is one that has a capacity greater than demand and therefore does not restrict the system throughput. For example, in Figure 15.11 work station 3 would be a bottleneck resource, and work stations 1, 2, and 4 would be nonbottleneck resources. A third category, a **capacity-constrained resource**, is not a bottleneck but is operating close to capacity and could become a bottleneck if not operated efficiently.

An important consequence of having capacity imbalances among the stages is that an hour of production lost at a bottleneck resource will decrease the throughput of the *entire* system by the equivalent of one hour of production. In addition, an improvement that saves an hour of time at a nonbottleneck resource simply increases the amount of idleness at that resource by an hour without increasing system throughput. These facts lead to the key principle of the theory of constraints: *to manage production effectively, one must focus on the constraining resources—the bottlenecks.*

Goldratt's second observation is one we saw in Chapters 8 and 9: variations in processing times due to machine breakdowns, defects, material shortages, or worker fatigue can reduce the effective capacity of a production system and increase inventories and throughput time. These variations can turn nonbottleneck resources into bottlenecks and vice versa.

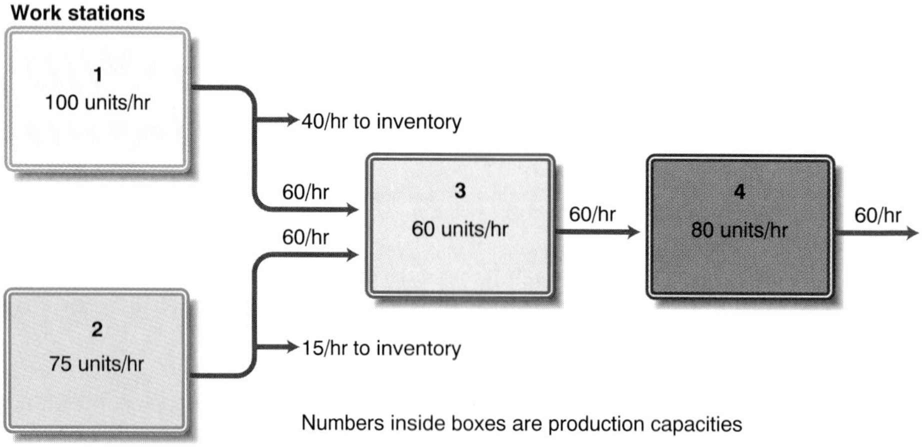

FIGURE 15.11 Overproduction by nonbottleneck resources.

[24]An enjoyable and readable description of the underlying principles of the theory of constraints is Eliyahu Goldratt and Jeff Cox, *The Goal*, North River Press, Croton-on-Hudson, NY, 1984. For a more rigorous treatment see Eliyahu Goldratt, "Computerized Shop Floor Scheduling," *International Journal of Production Research*, No. 26, 1988, pp. 443–455.

Finally, production systems are often operated in ways that amplify problems. For example, consider the production system in Figure 15.11. Because of the measures of productivity normally used to evaluate operations, such as machine utilization, the managers of work stations 1 and 2 will try to keep their work stations operating all the time. As long as materials are available, such as for stock items, work stations 1 and 2 will keep processing items that may not be sold for months. But work station 3 cannot handle all the production from work stations 1 and 2, so large inventories develop in front of work station 3. These large inventories begin to create material-handling problems and misplaced inventories. Work station 4, on the other hand, is starved for material to process. Synchronous production is designed to prevent these problems.

THE DRUM-BUFFER-ROPE MECHANISM

The solutions recommended by Goldratt are wide-ranging and include many aspects of Big JIT: better maintenance, more efficient setups, and smaller lot sizes. However, his key recommendation is a mechanism for coordinating production so that the *flow of production* (rather than the nameplate capacities) among the stages is balanced, and inventories are kept to a minimum except where they are really needed. This scheduling method is called the **drum-buffer-rope** method, as illustrated in Figure 15.12.

The Drum

The *drum* is the mechanism that controls the pace of production; that is, the drum "beats" the rhythm of production. In a JIT pull system the drum is the final product demand; production occurs only at the pace of actual demand. In a push production system such as MRP, the drum is the master production schedule, which tells all the production stages what to produce and when. In synchronous production the drum is the bottleneck resource(s). The production schedule is developed around the bottleneck, which *pulls* production from earlier stages and *pushes* it to the subsequent stages. In this sense, synchronous production is a hybrid of the push and pull systems. The demand pattern driving the bottleneck could be either an assured demand system, as in JIT, or a speculative demand system.

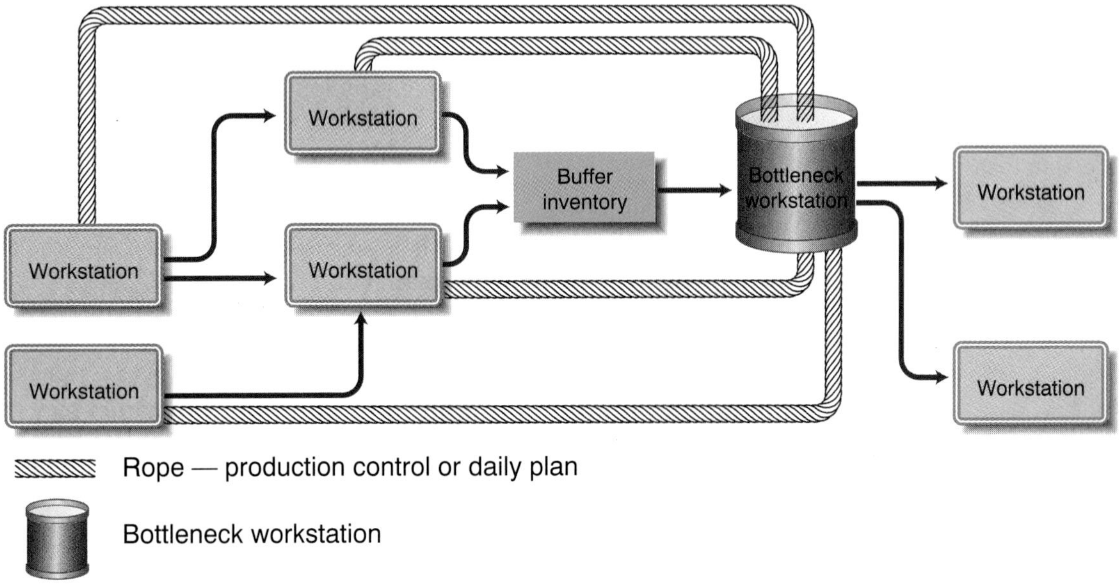

FIGURE 15.12 Drum-buffer-rope production control.

Buffer

Regardless of how carefully production is planned, there will be variations in the production system, and the units scheduled to be produced at some work center will not be available on time. If a nonbottleneck resource stops because of a material shortage, production will not normally be lost because the nonbottleneck resource has idle time available and can quickly catch up. However, if a bottleneck operation must stop because of a shortage of material to process, then the entire system will lose production, which cannot be regained. Therefore, in synchronous production we normally keep inventories in front of nonbottleneck operations very low, but in front of bottleneck operations a supply of safety stock is maintained to *buffer* or protect the bottleneck operation from material shortages; *the bottlenecks must be kept operating.*

Synchronous manufacturing also encourages the use of inventories in front of assembly operations because a shortage of a single item can stop the entire process. Final product inventories, however, can be kept to a minimum if an assured demand approach is used to drive the bottleneck.

The Rope

Although the drum is supposed to set a production rhythm that everyone follows, a communication link is needed to ensure that all stages are working at the same pace. The rate of production for operations that follow the bottleneck will be controlled directly by the amount of material made available to them by the bottleneck for processing. But nonbottleneck operations *preceding* the bottleneck are frequently evaluated using measures that encourage them to overproduce, so they must be controlled. We do not want nonbottleneck operations running simply to keep workers busy. The *rope* is the link between the bottleneck and preceding work stations that keeps them from running ahead of the bottleneck. In JIT scheduling the rope is the *kanban* pull mechanism. In synchronous production the rope can also be *kanbans* pulling production, or flow can be controlled by using a daily production schedule based on the production of the bottleneck.

JIT, SYNCHRONOUS PRODUCTION, AND MRP

In addition to developing the drum-buffer-rope concept of synchronous production, Goldratt has been an advocate of many methods that are commonly associated with Big JIT, especially the need for ongoing improvement. Synchronous production, JIT, and MRP are not mutually exclusive approaches. All three can be integrated to varying degrees, depending on the situation. Synchronous production fits well with a JIT production system that has some imbalances and variations, which most do. The drum-buffer-rope method of controlling production flow is especially helpful in job-shop processes, where JIT scheduling may be impractical due to the variety of products and product routings. Furthermore, complex production systems are made up of subsystems that may be quite different in the demand patterns for their outputs and the organization and form of production. One subsystem may best be driven with a JIT mechanism, while another may be better suited to MRP. In fact, these three philosophies use different approaches to accomplish the same goals: maintain low inventories, deliver products on time, and avoid stockouts.

One company that has successfully integrated these methods is Valmont Industries, a job-shop steel fabricator in Texas. By using an integrated drum-buffer-rope and MRP system, Valmont increased its rate of on-time deliveries from less than 80% to approximately 95% while eliminating the end-of-month overtime production that previously had been routine.[25]

---

[25]Glenn Reimer, "Material Requirements Planning and the Theory of Constraints: Can They Coexist? A Case Study," *Production and Inventory Management Journal*, 4th Quarter 1991, pp. 48–52.

Summary

- There are many forms of just-in-time (JIT) production, and not everyone agrees on its definition. Often we differentiate between Little JIT and Big JIT production.
- **Little JIT** is a form of production scheduling and control whereby (1) items are produced only to satisfy actual demand; (2) production is performed in small lot sizes; and (3) production is "pulled" through the production system by the last production stage rather than "pushed" through by the first production stage. The consequences of Little JIT are smaller inventories and shorter throughput times.
- **Big JIT** (or **lean production**) is a complete reengineering of the production process that emphasizes continuous improvement, quality management, reduced setup times, improved maintenance procedures, and cooperation with suppliers.
- **Single-minute exchange of dies (SMED)** is a structured procedure for performing machine setups more quickly. It is based on distinguishing between setup activities that can be performed while the process is operating **(external setup)** and those that can only be performed while the process is stopped **(internal setup)**.
- **Total productive maintenance (TPM)** emphasizes preventive maintenance and transfers routine maintenance activities from specialized maintenance personnel to machine operators.
- The principles of Big JIT are applicable to almost any production system, but JIT scheduling is primarily applicable to processes that make a limited range of stock items using flow or cellular production processes.
- Both Little and Big JIT are applicable to service systems, such as retailing, and to hybrid production systems that provide a combination of goods and services, such as restaurants.
- **Synchronous (synchronized) production** is a procedure for balancing the *flow* of production. It focuses on keeping the bottleneck stages fully utilized and forcing the other stages to produce in synch with the bottleneck. The mechanism for forcing the stages to produce at the same pace is called the **drum-buffer-rope** procedure.
- Synchronous production is especially useful for job-shop processes, where JIT scheduling is least applicable.

Key Terms

assured demand **756**
autonomous work teams **775**
Big JIT (lean production) **751**
bottleneck resource **782**
capacity-constrained resource **782**
continuous improvement (*kaizen*) **774**
drum-buffer-rope **783**
employee suggestion systems **774**
external setup **763**
internal setup **763**
kanban **758**
lean production **751**
Little JIT **751**
nonbottleneck resource **782**
pull production system **757**
push production system **756**
quality circles **775**
single-minute exchange of dies (SMED) **764**
speculative demand **756**
synchronous (synchronized) production **781**
theory of constraints **782**
throughput **782**
total productive maintenance (TPM) **770**

Solved Problems

Problem 1: Lexigraph Corporation makes three models of chemical analyzers—called models A, B, and C—using a three-stage batch flow process. The company uses a JIT production system that produces each model in lots of 50 units at a time. At each stage, changing from one model to another requires a one-hour setup, and the company can process 10 units per hour at each stage when the stage is operating. Below is a table showing the operation of the factory during the past day (eight-hour days). For the demands listed for the next day, fill in the table, indicating what is being done at each production stage, where and when *kanbans* are issued, how materials flow between stages, and what the inventory levels are at each stage and for the final products. Assume that materials completed at one stage are available at the next stage in the next hour. Raw materials requested one day are received from the supplier at the beginning of the next day (regardless of when they were requested during the previous day).

Day-Hour	Raw Matl	Stage 1 Activ	Stage 1 Kanb	Stage 1 Inv.	Stage 2 Activ	Stage 2 Kanb	Stage 2 Inv.	Stage 3 Activ	Stage 3 Kanb	Beginning Prod. Inv. A	Beginning Prod. Inv. B	Beginning Prod. Inv. C	Demands A	Demands B	Demands C
1–1	BAC	Run B	CA	ABC	SU C	BA	BC	Run A	CB	60	80	90	5	10	0
1–2	BAC	Run B	CAC	AB	Run C	BA	BC	Run A	CB	55	70	90	10	5	10
1–3	BAC	Run B	CAC	AB	Run C	BA	BC	Run A	CB	45	65	80	5	5	5
1–4	BAC	SU C	AC	BAB	Run C	BA	BC	Run A	CBA	40	60	75	5	10	10
1–5	BA	Run C	AC	BAB	Run C	BA	BC	SU C	BA	85	50	65	5	0	0
1–6	BA	Run C	AC	BAB	Run C	BAC	B	Run C	BAB	80	50	65	5	5	5
1–7	BA	Run C	AC	BAB	SU B	AC	CB	Run C	BAB	75	45	60	0	0	5
1–8	BA	Run C	ACB	BA	Run B	AC	CB	Run C	BAB	75	45	55	5	5	0
2–1	—	—	—	—	—	—	—	—	—	—	—	—	0	5	5
2–2	—	—	—	—	—	—	—	—	—	—	—	—	5	0	5
2–3	—	—	—	—	—	—	—	—	—	—	—	—	5	5	0
2–4	—	—	—	—	—	—	—	—	—	—	—	—	5	0	5
2–5	—	—	—	—	—	—	—	—	—	—	—	—	5	5	5
2–6	—	—	—	—	—	—	—	—	—	—	—	—	0	0	5
2–7	—	—	—	—	—	—	—	—	—	—	—	—	5	5	0
2–8	—	—	—	—	—	—	—	—	—	—	—	—	5	0	5

Solution

Day-Hour	Raw Matl	Stage 1 Activ	Stage 1 Kanb	Stage 1 Inv.	Stage 2 Activ	Stage 2 Kanb	Stage 2 Inv.	Stage 3 Activ	Stage 3 Kanb	Prod. Inv. A	Prod. Inv. B	Prod. Inv. C	Demands A	Demands B	Demands C
1–1	BAC	Run B	CA	ABC	SU C	BA	BC	Run A	CB	60	80	90	5	10	0
1–2	BAC	Run B	CAC	AB	Run C	BA	BC	Run A	CB	55	70	90	10	5	10
1–3	BAC	Run B	CAC	AB	Run C	BA	BC	Run A	CB	45	65	80	5	5	5
1–4	BAC	SU C	AC	BAB	Run C	BA	BC	Run A	CBA	40	60	75	5	10	10
1–5	BA	Run C	AC	BAB	Run C	BA	BC	SU C	BA	85	50	65	5	0	0
1–6	BA	Run C	AC	BAB	Run C	BAC	B	Run C	BAB	80	50	65	5	5	5
1–7	BA	Run C	AC	BAB	SU B	AC	CB	Run C	BAB	75	45	60	0	0	5
1–8	BA	Run C	ACB	BA	Run B	AC	CB	Run C	BAB	75	45	55	5	5	0
2–1	CBA	Run C	ACB	BA	Run B	AC	CB	Run C	BAB	70	40	55	0	5	5
2–2	CBA	SU A	CB	CBA	Run B	AC	CB	Run C	BAB	70	35	50	5	0	5
2–3	CB	Run A	CB	CBA	Run B	AC	CB	SU B	ABC	65	35	95	5	5	0
2–4	CB	Run A	CB	CBA	Run B	ACB	C	Run B	ABC	60	30	95	5	0	5
2–5	CB	Run A	CB	CBA	SU A	CB	BC	Run B	ABC	55	30	90	5	5	5
2–6	CB	Run A	CBA	CB	Run A	CB	BC	Run B	ABC	50	25	85	0	0	5
2–7	CB	Run A	CBA	CB	Run A	CB	BC	Run B	ABCA	50	25	80	5	5	0
2–8	CB	SU C	BA	ACB	Run A	CB	BC	Run B	ABCA	45	20	80	5	0	5

DISCUSSION AND REVIEW QUESTIONS

1. What are the two main structural differences between classical push production scheduling and Little JIT production scheduling (i.e., what are the two main features of Little JIT)?

2. JIT systems have generally been implemented by companies in the automobile and electronics industries. Why do those industries make the structural aspects of JIT scheduling work so effectively?

3. What is the difference between Little JIT and Big JIT?
4. In what types of production systems is Little JIT most beneficial?
5. In what types of production environments is JIT (pull) scheduling not likely to be beneficial?
6. Having a good quality management system is crucial to using JIT scheduling because any quality problems can bring the system to a stop. However, JIT scheduling can also help improve product quality. Explain how JIT scheduling with small batch sizes can improve product quality.
7. Why do small batch sizes make JIT production systems more responsive to changes in demand than systems with large batch sizes?
8. If a JIT production system is based on assured demand, why is there any need for final product inventories?
9. "Quick setup procedures (SMED) are important only for companies using Little JIT." Is this statement true or false? Justify your answer.
10. Give an example of how a seemingly internal setup activity could be converted to an external setup activity.
11. What is the primary change in job responsibilities advocated by TPM?
12. Explain two advantages of operating machinery at 80–90% rather than at 98% of capacity. How can it be more cost effective to operate at these lower rates?
13. Is it possible to implement Big JIT principles without using Little JIT scheduling? Is Little JIT simply a subset of Big JIT?
14. What is the primary difference between production scheduling based on materials requirements planning (MRP) and Little JIT?
15. What is the primary difference between synchronous production (based on the drum-buffer-rope system) and Little JIT?
16. Why does synchronous production scheduling frequently work better in job shops than Little JIT scheduling?

Problems

1. Rapid-Roll makes three types of conveyer sections (A, B, and C) using a three-stage batch flow process. The company uses a Little JIT production system that produces each product in lots of 300 units at a time. At each stage, changing from one product to another requires a one-hour setup, and the company can process 100 units per hour at each stage when the stage is operating. The following table shows the operation of the factory during the past 10 hours. The table also lists the actual demands for the three products during the next six hours. Fill in the table for the next six hours, indicating what is being done at each production stage, where and when *kanbans* are issued, how materials flow between stages, and what the inventory levels are at each stage and for the final products. Assume that materials completed at one stage are available at the next stage in the next hour (as shown below). Raw materials requested are received one hour later from the supplier. (Note: the letters A, B, and C in the Inv and Kanb columns represent 300 units of product.)

Day-	Raw	Stage 1		Stage 2			Stage 3			Prod. Inv.			Demands		
Hour	Matl	Activ	Kanb	Inv.	Activ	Kanb	Inv.	Activ	Kanb	A	B	C	A	B	C
1–1	BCA	Run B	AC	CBA	SU A	BC	BA	Run C	ABCA	250	400	125	25	20	20
1–2	BCA	Run B	ACA	CB	Run A	BC	BA	SU A	BCA	225	380	405	15	25	20
1–3	BCA	SU A	CA	BCB	Run A	BCA	B	Run A	BCA	210	355	385	25	30	15
1–4	BC	Run A	CA	BCB	Run A	BCA	B	Run A	BCA	185	325	370	20	25	20
1–5	ABC	Run A	CA	BCB	SU B	CA	AB	Run A	BCA	165	300	350	30	20	20
1–6	ABC	Run A	CAB	BC	Run B	CA	AB	SU B	CAB	435	280	330	20	35	25
1–7	ABC	SU C	AB	ABC	Run B	CAB	A	Run B	CAB	415	245	305	25	20	35
1–8	AB	Run C	AB	ABC	Run B	CAB	A	Run B	CAB	390	225	270	35	25	30
2–1	CAB	Run C	AB	ABC	SU C	AB	BA	Run B	CABC	355	200	240	20	15	35
2–2	CAB	Run C	ABC	AB	Run C	AB	BA	SU A	CBC	335	485	205	25	20	25
2–3	—	—	—	—	—	—	—	—	—	—	—	—	25	30	30
2–4	—	—	—	—	—	—	—	—	—	—	—	—	35	20	25
2–5	—	—	—	—	—	—	—	—	—	—	—	—	20	25	35
2–6	—	—	—	—	—	—	—	—	—	—	—	—	35	20	15
2–7	—	—	—	—	—	—	—	—	—	—	—	—	25	25	20
2–8	—	—	—	—	—	—	—	—	—	—	—	—	30	20	25

2. Texas Gear makes four types of gears for the heavy machinery industry. The gears, designated models A, B, C, and D, are made using a three-stage batch flow process. The company uses a Little JIT production system that produces each product in lots of 100 units at a time. At each stage, changing from one product to another requires a 0.5-hour setup, and the company can process 100 units per hour at each stage when the stage is operating. Below is a table showing the operation of the factory during the past three hours. The table also lists the actual demands for the three products during the next three hours. (a) Fill in the table for the next three hours, indicating what is being done at each production stage, where and when *kanbans* are issued, how materials flow between stages, and what the inventory levels are at each stage and for the final products. Assume that materials completed at one stage are available at the next stage in the next hour (as shown below). Raw materials requested are received one hour later from the supplier. (b) At the end of time 5.5 stage 2 should have just completed a run of D; B and A should be on its *kanban* board, but only materials for C and D should be available in its inventory. What activity should stage 2 undertake during the period 5.5–6? (Hint: Consider what is being run at stage 1.)

	Raw	Stage 1			Stage 2			Stage 3		Prod. Inv.				Demands			
Hour	Matl	Activ	Kanb	Inv.	Activ	Kanb	Inv.	Activ	Kanb	A	B	C	D	A	B	C	D
0–0.5	ADBC	SU B	CD	AD	Run D	AB	CBD	Run B	DBADC	165	60	95	55	10	5	5	10
0.5–1	ADC	Run B	CD	AD	Run D	AB	CBD	SU D	BADC	155	155	90	45	5	5	5	15
1–1.5	BADC	Run B	CD	AD	SU A	BD	DCB	Run D	BADC	150	150	85	30	10	0	10	15
1.5-2	BADC	SU C	DA	BD	Run A	BD	DCB	Run D	BADC	140	150	75	15	0	10	5	10
2–2.5	BAD	Run C	DA	BD	Run A	BD	DCB	SU B	ADC	140	140	70	105	10	5	0	5
2.5–3	CBAD	Run C	DA	BD	SU B	DB	ADC	Run B	ADC	130	135	70	100	0	15	5	10
3–3.5	—	—	—	—		—	—	—	—	—	—	—	—	15	0	0	15
3.5–4	—	—	—	—	—	—	—	—	—	—	—	—	—	0	10	5	15
4–4.5	—	—	—	—	—	—	—	—	—	—	—	—	—	5	10	10	5
4.5–5	—	—	—	—	—	—	—	—	—	—	—	—	—	10	15	5	10
5–5.5	—	—	—	—	—	—	—	—	—	—	—	—	—	5	10	0	15
5.5–6	—	—	—	—	—	—	—	—	—	—	—	—	—	10	5	5	15

CASE

UKAN: A Case of Lean Production

UKAN, Ltd., is a multinational manufacturer that makes hundreds of products ranging from auto parts to electrical products and computer components. Once a very successful company, UKAN found itself becoming less and less competitive in worldwide markets. A study of its competitors found that in most markets UKAN had higher production costs, carried higher inventories per unit sales, had more quality complaints, required longer lead times for delivery of its products, and still had more late deliveries and stockouts than its competitors. It was clear that unless something was done soon, the company would not stay in business for long.

UKAN's president, John Billingsworth, called a week-long retreat of his top executives along with a small group of consultants. After analyzing the products made by UKAN and their markets, the group decided that the main problem appeared to be a production system that had not adapted to changes in the environment. The consultants proposed implementing a companywide TQM program and a plant-by-plant reconstruction of its manufacturing operations. After developing an outline of their plan, the consultants and UKAN executives selected the Electric Motor and Components Division to be the prototype or test case.

The Electric Motor and Components Division

The Electric Motor and Components (EMC) Division had six manufacturing facilities focused on specific product types. Although different products were made at each plant, the production processes were similar in terms of the number of different products, the complexity and sequencing of flows, and the numbers of components made internally and purchased from vendors. The London, Ontario, plant, illustrated in Figure 15.13, is typical of the facilities.

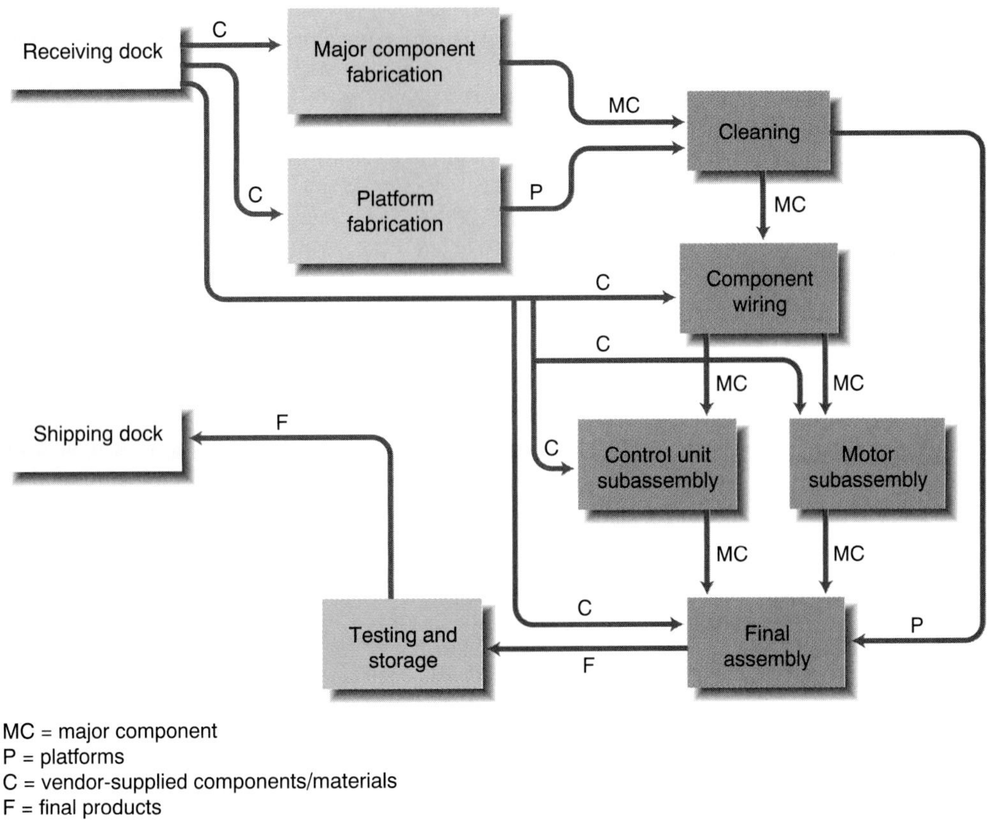

FIGURE 15.13 Production process at UKAN's London, Ontario, plant.

TABLE 15.2 PRODUCT MIX AT UKAN'S LONDON, ONTARIO, PLANT

Products	Annual Sales	Reported Defect Rate*	Demand Service Level†
Model 20 motor	400,000	1.3%	98.6%
Model 30 motor	350,000	1.0%	98.7%
Model 40 motor	200,000	1.6%	97.5%
Other motors	50,000	2.5%	91.4%
Model 400 control unit	600,000	2.2%	98.3%
Model 500 control unit	400,000	2.1%	97.9%
Model 550 control unit	300,000	2.3%	97.7%
Model 560 control unit	150,000	1.8%	96.4%
Other control units	65,000	3.4%	87.1%
Total		1.85%	97.7%

*Defect rate is the rate for products shipped to customers.
†Demand service level is the percentage of units delivered on time.

Over 90% of the production at the London plant was devoted to just seven products: the model 20, 30, and 40 electric motors and the model 400, 500, 550, and 560 control units. Table 15.2 lists the product mix data for the plant.

Each product is made up of a metal "platform" or housing, the container that holds the motor or control unit. These platforms are fabricated by UKAN as the first step in the production process. Each unit also consists of three major components made by UKAN in its Component Fabrication and Component Wiring departments, as well as dozens of simple, low-cost components purchased from vendors. The components are assembled into subassemblies and then assembled further into the final products. Some of the products share common major components, as specified in Table 15.3.

Original Conditions

UKAN decided to form several consulting teams made up of one outside consultant and two or three UKAN employees. The teams were coordinated by a central coordinating committee made up of an outside consultant and one employee from each team. The first step was to study the current operation and collect data on its performance and problems. Table 15.2 provides the data the teams collected on sales, defect rates, and delivery service levels for the products. In addition, one team collected data on the estimated cost of making each product, broken out by cost categories (direct variable labor, indirect labor, overhead, materials, etc.), lot size and throughput patterns, defect rates, and inventory levels by product and department. Each team also spent considerable time walking through the plant and observing operations in order to put the data into a meaningful context. To evaluate its efforts, the coordinating committee formed its own profit and loss statement for the plant, which is given in Table 15.4

All information was brought to the coordinating committee, which tried to reach a consensus on the main problem areas. The coordinating committee then assigned each team responsibility for studying and proposing solutions to specific problems.

The most noticeable symptoms were the following:

1. Every department in the plant had the capacity to produce at least 2.5 million units of product per year in a two-shift, five-day-per-week operation. (The department capacities, which are shown in Table 15.5, actually ran from 2.5 million to 3.5 million units per year.) Yet, to meet the demand, UKAN was regularly

TABLE 15.3 COMPONENTS OF UKAN'S PRODUCTS

	Motors			Control Units			
Model	20	30	40	400	500	550	560
Platforms	X1	X2	X3	Y1	Y2	Y2	Y2
Major components	A1 B1 C1	A1 B2 C2	A2 B1 C3	D1 E1 F1	D2 E2 F2	D3 E3 F2	D3 E3 F3

TABLE 15.4 PROFIT/LOSS FOR UKAN'S LONDON, ONTARIO, PLANT (ALL VALUES IN THOUSANDS OF CANADIAN DOLLARS)

Sales revenue		$247,521
Direct labor	73,846	
Indirect labor	39,490	
Materials	42,138	
Utilities, waste disposal, etc.	7,365	
Plant & equip deprec	32,182	
Direct inventory Expenses (financing, taxes, etc.)	4,912	
Total operating costs		199,933
Operating profit*		47,588
Corporate and division overhead and selling expenses		46,004
Net plant profit		1,584

*Operating profit is not exactly the same as the normal accounting definition; this form was used for the coordinating committee's purposes.

paying for overtime—$11,890,000 in 1994 alone, with the largest share paid to the Cleaning and Wiring departments.

2. Average inventories were approximately $56 million, which were distributed as $9 million in unprocessed materials and components, $27 million in in-process inventories, and $20 million in finished products. The direct costs of maintaining these inventories were estimated at $4.912 million per year (during a period of very low interest rates).

3. Nearly $15 million of the in-process inventories and $3 million of the unprocessed materials were in front of the Component Wiring Department, which appeared to be the main bottleneck. Another $8 million

TABLE 15.5 UNITS PROCESSED BY DEPARTMENTS

Department	No. of Units Processed	Number Discarded After Process	Estimated Capacity
Platform Fabrication	2,800,000	1,000*	3,500,000
Component Fabrication	10,000,000	6,000*	8,500,000†
Cleaning	12,793,000	0*	11,000,000
Component Wiring	9,994,000	11,000*	7,500,000†
Control Unit Subassembly	6,039,000	1,025,000	5,200,000†
Motor Subassembly	3,944,000	642,000	3,500,000†
Final Assembly	2,772,000	219,000	2,800,000

2,553,000 units were approved for shipment; of these, 2,515,000 were shipped to customers on original orders, and the remainder were shipped to customers as replacements for defective products or put into inventory.

*No formal quality check was performed; these units were discarded because of obvious defects or were damaged during production.

†There are three major components per product and three subassemblies per product. So capacities in terms of finished products are one-third of these values.

of in-process inventories and \$3.5 million of unprocessed materials were in front of the Final Assembly Department.

4. Defect rates for items shipped to customers were twice those of the leading competitors and were especially high for lower-volume special products.
5. The demand service levels were slightly below those of competitors.
6. *Internal* defect rates based on samples were very high:
   (a) Approximately 4% of the platforms and 10% of the major components coming out of the fabrication departments had defects.
   (b) Of the items leaving the Component Wiring Department, 15% were defective: two-thirds due to defective component fabrication and one-third due to errors made in the Wiring Department.
   (c) Of the items leaving the subassembly departments, 17% were defective, with most defects due to fabrication or wiring errors.

Items were generally not inspected until they left the subassembly departments, at which point almost all defective subassemblies were found. Items leaving final assembly had a defect rate of 8%. Approximately one-half of these were due to defective platforms, one-fourth were mistakes in assembly, and one-fourth were due to defective components from vendors.

Because of these internal defect rates, most departments had to process far more than the equivalent of 2.5 million final units per year (7.5 million major components), the amount demanded. The number of units actually passing through each department per year, along with the capacities and number discarded due to quality defects, are listed in Table 15.5.

Analysis and Recommended Changes

Overtime and Quality Control

Overtime production costs were given first priority because they were so high. Time and motion studies were performed to estimate setup and processing times in order to determine each department's true production capacities, assuming a two-shift, five-day-per-week operation. Except for the Component Wiring Department, every department had a capacity equivalent to the production of 2.7 million units of end products per year or more. Only the Wiring Department's capacity of 7.5 million components (2.5 million end products) was below the amount needed to meet the 2,515,000-unit annual demand. Yet every department except Platform Fabrication and Final Assembly exceeded its regular-time capacity and had to work moderate or large amounts of overtime to meet product demand. The obvious question was, why?

The answer was that early in the production process, departments had to process far more units of product than would ultimately be shipped because of the high defect rates. For example, theoretically only 7,545,000 components should have been processed by the Component Wiring Department to produce the 2,515,000 motors and control units demanded, but actual production was almost 10 million. Therefore, it was clear that the capacity and overtime problems were, to a large extent, quality problems.

The team approached this problem in two ways. As a short-term solution, they decided to institute component inspection *before* major components went to the Cleaning Department. This way, approximately 1 million defective component fabrications would not have to be cleaned or wired, nor would they become part of a subassembly. The extra inspection was estimated to cost approximately \$120,000 per year, but within days dramatic effects appeared. Overtime in the Cleaning and Component Wiring departments was cut by more than half, and overtime in the subassembly departments was almost completely eliminated. Based on data for the first month after implementation, it was estimated that annual overtime costs would drop by almost \$7 million to approximately \$5 million. In addition, over \$1 million in material costs would be saved by not assembling small components with defective major components in the subassemblies.

The long-term solution involved the development of a TQM system at the plant. The initial efforts focused on job redesign, training, and mistake-proofing of operations. In addition, an employee suggestion system was established and many employee suggestions were implemented, such as buying relatively inexpensive tools that produced cleaner, more accurate soldering of wires and connectors.

Special attention was devoted to the two fabrication departments because of their high defect rates. The three most important problems were identified as incorrect machine setups, using worn tools, and failure to catch quickly systematic defects that occurred when a tool wore out or a machine setting or fastener slipped or loosened. These problems were solved by standardizing setups and marking calibrations clearly on machines, changing tools more frequently, and instituting a simple inspection system by machine operators to catch tool wear or machine slippage quickly. These changes reduced the platform and component fabrication defect rates from 4% and 10%, respectively, to less than 1%. At this point, the inspection activities that had been instituted between the fabrication and cleaning steps were eliminated and these resources were moved elsewhere.

Similar programs in other departments reduced defects generated in those departments by at least half. In the subassembly and assembly departments, mistake-proofing techniques helped to eliminate defects due to using the wrong components or forgetting to install components.

After all of these changes were instituted, the major cause of the remaining defects was found to be defective components from suppliers. This problem was transferred to another team that was to deal with supplier issues.

Process Reorganization and Job Design

In addition to reducing costs and eliminating almost all the capacity problems, the teams' efforts resulted in a dramatic improvement in the quality of products sent to customers. Within 18 months the defect rates for the three large-volume motors and the four large-volume control units declined by a factor of 10 to approximately 0.1% and 0.2%, respectively. Although the quality of the smaller-volume motors and control units also improved considerably, a large proportion of defective units were being made and found at final inspection. To achieve defect rates for shipped units of below 0.2%, considerable resources had to be expended for final inspection.

Close observation suggested that the main cause of the defects was errors made in component wiring. Because the same workers did the wiring for all components, they were constantly changing what they were working on and every worker had to be familiar with the wiring for several dozen major components for the several low-volume products. The improvement team found that this system resulted in errors because employees forgot all the differences in wiring requirements (even though production documents were available). The improvement team was worried about specializing the work because the original situation provided greater task variety, but after interviewing the workers the team found that they actually hated the wide variety of products. Once they had more than 5–10 different components to work on, additional variety made the job too complex and frustrating.

The improvement team decided to reorganize the Wiring Department so that most of the workers were devoted entirely to making the 16 major components contained in the model 20, 30, and 40 motors and the model 400, 500, 550, and 560 control units. The workers were further divided into those who worked primarily on the seven major motor components and those who worked primarily on the nine major control unit components. A small number of workers in the department were put into a separate work cell that handled only the low-volume motors and control units. The workers chosen for this group were those who liked the large variety and viewed themselves as creator/craftsmen.

As a result of the reorganization, productivity increased 30% because workers were not slowed by many product changes and relearning, wiring defects were reduced to 0.05%, and job satisfaction surveys indicated a substantial improvement in morale and employee self-esteem.

JIT Scheduling and Lot Sizing

A second team focused on reducing inventories and improving the delivery service level. This team made several observations:

1. At times when UKAN ran short of needed products, it frequently had large inventories of other product models on hand, and the final assembly department was often assembling models that already had ample inventories rather than models that were in short supply.
2. Typical production lot sizes for the seven large-volume products were in the range of 10,000–50,000 (one to five days of production), and the lot sizes for the other products were 100–1000. Purchased components were normally delivered by suppliers once a month or once every two weeks, and the lot sizes were in the range of 50,000–250,000 units, depending on the item.
3. Inventories were not evenly spread throughout the plant but were concentrated in front of the Wiring and Assembly departments.
4. Although the subassembly and assembly departments were producing at less than capacity, they worked overtime to avoid stockouts. Assembly sometimes stopped during normal hours because needed components were missing, either because of poor scheduling or an unusually high defect rate in a production run. When the components became available an emergency run would be made, often during overtime.

The team determined that the cause of the first problem was the classical push scheduling UKAN was using, based on speculative demand. Although total demand volume was relatively constant, the mix of products fluctuated randomly. A long production run of one product might be scheduled for wiring and assembly while demand for a different product may have surged, creating a shortage. The team decided to implement a JIT pull system wherever possible and reduce production lot sizes.

Approximately three months into its study, the team instituted a *kanban* scheduling system for production and reduced the lot sizes for all products by half. The plan was to institute the changes slowly so that a dramatic increase in production setup time would not choke the system. Furthermore, the safety stock levels and number of *kanbans* in the system were chosen to be very conservative to avoid serious shocks. The team's expectation was that inventories would slowly drop to approximately 50–60% of their previous level and that stockouts might show some small improvement. The team was not ready for the actual consequences.

Within a week after the institution of these changes, in-process inventories in front of the Cleaning Department and component inventories from vendors increased dramatically. In-process inventories in front of the other departments dropped substantially. Total inventories seemed to be increasing, but no improvement in the delivery service level was apparent.

The team quickly went into emergency mode to determine the cause of these unexpected events. The cause was initially difficult to identify because these events were the result of two conflicting forces occurring simultaneously. First, the scheduling and lot-size changes were made soon after the quality improvements had been made in the fabrication operations. Since the defects from early production stages were eliminated, fewer components from suppliers were needed to make the same number of acceptable end products. However, orders to suppliers had not been changed, so the excess components began to pile up in inventory.

Second, the reduction in lot sizes caused more setups to be performed. This did not create a problem in the Platform Fabrication and Final Assembly departments because they already had excess capacity, and the Wiring, Subassembly, and Assembly departments saved enough production time by not having to process defective items to make up for the extra time required for the added changeovers. So material flowed through these departments smoothly, and inventories did not build up in front of them. Changeovers for the cleaning operation, however, were very time-consuming, so the increase in their number overwhelmed the savings from the quality improvements. Further, the cleaning operation could not keep up with fabrication, causing the inventory in front of the Cleaning Department to increase.

The team instituted two actions to solve these problems. First, it contacted suppliers and adjusted the delivery quantities and delivery schedule for components. Although there were problems with a few suppliers, most had no trouble increasing the frequency of deliveries with smaller quantities, thereby better matching UKAN's production rate. The second problem was how to increase the cleaning capacity. The quality improvements in fabrication had effectively shifted the production bottleneck from the wiring operation to cleaning. The cleaning operation involved connecting the platforms and components to a dipping tray, submerging the tray in cleaning solvents, shaking it, and then removing and drying the items. Each type of component and platform was cleaned with a different solvent, and it took two to three hours to drain the solvent, clean the solvent tub and the material-handling equipment, and refill the tub with the new solvent.

Utilizing SMED principles, the team redesigned the cleaning facilities by adding a second tub and a second set of dipping trays. Before a changeover occurred, the next set of items would be attached to the clean set of trays and the new solvent would be put in the clean tub. When the cleaning operation stopped, the tub containing the current solvent and the contaminated trays were re-

TABLE 15.6 PROFIT/LOSS FOR UKAN'S LONDON, ONTARIO, PLANT THIRD YEAR AFTER PROJECT STARTED (ALL VALUES IN THOUSANDS OF CANADIAN DOLLARS)

Sales revenue		$302,850
Direct labor	70,042	
Indirect labor	36,118	
Materials	45,890	
Utilities, waste disposal, etc.	7,723	
Plant & equip deprec	33,506	
Direct inventory expenses (financing, taxes, etc.)	1,037	
Total operating costs		194,316
Operating profit		108,534
Corporate and division overhead and selling expenses		44,550
Net plant profit		63,984

TABLE 15.7 UNITS PROCESSED BY DEPARTMENTS AFTER PROCESS CHANGES

Department	No. of Units Processed	No. Discarded After Process	Estimated Capacity
Platform Fabrication	3,150,000	25,000	3,850,000
Component Fabrication	9,450,000	70,000	10,000,000
Cleaning	12,505,000	0	12,500,000
Component Wiring	9,380,000	5,000	9,500,000
Control Unit Subassembly	5,675,000	55,000	6,300,000
Motor Subassembly	3,700,000	30,000	4,000,000
Final Assembly	3,097,000	42,000	3,250,000

3,055,000 units were approved for shipment.

placed by the clean tub and trays. The contaminated tub and trays could then be cleaned as an external setup activity while the next job was running. With this change, the internal setup time (the time the process was stopped) was reduced to 12 minutes. The cleaning operation not only was no longer a bottleneck, but also its capacity increased because the number of setups had only been doubled, while the internal time required to perform a setup was reduced to 1/15th of its previous value.

Results

After these changes were made and the changes made by the other teams began to settle in, the system began to function well, with some minor fine-tuning. All inventories began to diminish and stockouts decreased. Lot sizes were made progressively smaller, and the number of *kanbans* in the system for each product was adjusted to balance the system better. As lot sizes were reduced, UKAN made a special effort to work with suppliers to provide frequent JIT deliveries of high-quality components. This was such a substantial effort that it required a separate team.

Other teams were assigned to work on maintenance, product design and customer relations, and reducing overhead and indirect costs. The result of these efforts was a dramatic improvement in quality, a large reduction in the cost per unit, and improved delivery performance. Although the improvements in quality and delivery helped to increase sales by 10%, the process improvements increased effective capacity so much that none of the departments were working at capacity. So the vice president of production approached the vice president of marketing and explained that the production cost had decreased so much that the company could afford to cut prices and still make a healthy profit. Because of the competitive nature of the markets, the marketing vice president believed that a 3–5% reduction in price, combined with the fact that UKAN now had the best quality and delivery performance of any company in their markets, would result in a large increase in market share. This strategy was implemented, and unit sales increased by 15%. At this point, UKAN was at its production capacity and decided not to cut prices further until it could create an updated long-term strategy for the division.

To evaluate its success, the coordinating committee created updated versions of Tables 15.4 and 15.5 for the third year after the project began. They are given in Tables 15.6 and 15.7.

The large increase in profits is even more impressive than it appears because the labor costs in Table 15.6 include large wage increases (18% over three years), which were justified by the large productivity gains. The large reduction in labor cost was due almost entirely to elimination of overtime production, not personnel; net employment in the plant decreased only 1% during the three-year period, all of it through normal attrition.

After the successes of the London plant were clear, similar changes were instituted at the five other plants in the division and ultimately at the other divisions of UKAN. Although some plants did not achieve as much improvement as the London plant, most had substantial improvements and some even exceeded London. UKAN has left in place at each plant a group of improvement teams responsible for promoting improvement projects, employee training, and quality enhancements.

QUESTIONS

1. Identify the specific JIT concepts and techniques utilized by UKAN.
2. When UKAN first instituted its quality improvement methods and reduced lot sizes, inventories increased. What lesson can be learned from this fact and from UKAN's response to it?
3. Of all the changes UKAN made, which two do you believe were the most important? Why?

Selected Readings

Billesbach, Thomas J. "A Study of the Implementation of Just-in-Time in the United States," *Production and Inventory Management Journal*, 3rd Quarter 1991, pp. 1–4.

Farwell, C. R., S. Brady, and B. A. Rosencrans. "MRP II in a JIT Environment," *Journal of Manufacturing*, Winter 1990, pp. 5–12.

Galante, Steven P. "Small Manufacturers Shifting to Just-in-Time Techniques," *Wall Street Journal*, Dec. 21, 1987.

Goldratt, Eliyahu. "Computerized Shop Floor Scheduling," *International Journal of Production Research*, No. 26, 1988, pp. 443–455.

Goldratt, Eliyahu, and Jeff Cox. *The Goal*, North River Press, Croton-on-Hudson, NY, 1984.

Hammer, Michael, and James Champy. *Reengineering the Corporation*, HarperBusiness, New York, 1993.

Harmon, Roy L. *Reinventing the Factory*: II, Free Press, New York, 1992.

Hay, Edward J. *The Just-in-Time Breakthrough*, Wiley, New York, 1988.

Karmarkar, Uday. "Getting Control of JIT," *Harvard Business Review*,Vol. 67, No. 5, 1989, pp. 122–131.

Maggard, Bill, and David Rhyne. "Total Productive Maintenance: A Timely Integration of Production and Maintenance," *Production and Inventory Management Journal*, 4th Quarter 1992, pp. 6–10.

Monden, Yasuhiro. *Toyota Production System*, Industrial Engineering and Management Press, Atlanta, GA, 1983.

Ohno, Taiichi. *Toyota Production System: Beyond Large-Scale Production*, Productivity Press, Cambridge, MA, 1988.

Robinson, Alan (ed.). *Modern Approaches to Manufacturing Improvement: The Shingo System*, Productivity Press, Cambridge, MA, 1990.

Robinson, Alan (ed.). *Continuous Improvement in Operations*, Productivity Press, Cambridge, MA, 1991.

Schonberger, Richard. *World Class Manufacturing*, Free Press, New York, 1986.

Schragenheim, Eli, and Boaz Ronen. "Drum-Buffer-Rope Shop Floor Control," *Journal of Production and Inventory Management Journal*, 3rd Quarter 1990, pp. 18–23.

Selz, Michael. "Small Manufacturers Display the Nimbleness the Times Require," *Wall Street Journal*, Dec. 29, 1993.

Stertz, Bradley. "Detroit's New Strategy to Beat Back Japanese Is to Copy Their Ideas," *Wall Street Journal*, Oct. 1, 1992.

Steudel, Harold J., and Paul Desrulle. *Manufacturing in the Nineties*, Van Nostrand Reinhold, New York, 1992.

Verespej, Michael. "The Self-Education of Bruce Hamilton," *Industry Week*, Apr. 1, 1991, pp. 16–22.

Wasco, W. C., R. E. Stonehocker, and L. H. Feldman. "Success with JIT and MRP II in a Service Organization," *Production and Inventory Management Journal*, Vol. 32, No. 4, 4th Quarter 1991, pp. 15–21.

Womack, J. P., D. T. Jones, and D. Roos. *The Machine That Changed the World: The Story of Lean Production*, Harper Perennial, 1991.

Zipkin, Paul. "Does Manufacturing Need a JIT Revolution?" *Harvard Business Review*, Vol. 69, No. 1, 1991, pp. 40–50.

CHAPTER 16

OPERATIONS AND PERSONNEL SCHEDULING

16.1 EVERY MANAGER'S CHALLENGE
On the Job: Diane Conboy, Brigham-Women's Hospital

16.2 SCHEDULING PRODUCTION FOR CONTINUOUS AND REPETITIVE FLOW PROCESSES
Coordinating Production Lot Sizes with Cyclic Production Schedules

16.3 SCHEDULING BATCH PRODUCTION SYSTEMS
Approaches to Job Sequencing
Criteria for Evaluating Schedules
Sequencing Rules for the One-Stage Problem
Two-Stage and Three-Stage Flow Processes
Dynamic Dispatching Rules and Multistage Systems

16.4 OPTIMIZED PRODUCTION TECHNOLOGY

16.5 ASSIGNMENT PROBLEMS
Hungarian Method
Unbalanced Assignment Problems

16.6 SCHEDULING SERVICE OPERATIONS
Pricing and Promotion
Appointment and Reservation Systems

16.7 PERSONNEL SCHEDULING
In Good Company: Smooth Sailing in Hampton Roads

16.8 IMPLEMENTING PRODUCTION AND PERSONNEL SCHEDULING

Home Helper Discount: A Scheduling Case

16.1 Every Manager's Challenge

Although few managers will encounter all the issues we have considered so far, the one operational responsibility almost all managers continually face is the need to schedule resources. **Scheduling** can be defined as the assignment and timing of the use of resources—such as personnel, equipment, and facilities—for production activities or jobs. The range of scheduling problems that must be solved by organizations is vast. For example, manufacturers must determine the sequence in which products or jobs will be processed at each work cell or work center, and accounting and consulting firms must decide which employees will work on each project. Repair, installation, and delivery companies such as cable TV, heating and air-conditioning service firms, and furniture stores must schedule service calls so that workers are utilized efficiently, driving is kept to a minimum, and service is performed when customers want it. Hospitals must decide how many physicians, nurses, and technicians must work each day, when they must start and end their work, and possibly the floor or ward where they will work. For example, Diane Conboy, the subject of this chapter's "On the Job" segment, must carefully schedule the personnel in her intensive care unit so that they can handle any emergency.

On the Job

Diane Conboy, Brigham-Women's Hospital

What would you do if you had only 20 minutes to respond to a critical emergency? In the Burn/Trauma Unit at Brigham-Women's Hospital in Boston, Diane Conboy and her staff face this situation routinely.

Diane's 10-bed intensive care unit is one of only two burn units in the New England area. When critically injured patients arrive, Diane, who is charge nurse for her unit, must quickly evaluate existing resources, determine whether additional staff is needed, and decide which of her existing patients, if any, can be moved out of intensive care to accommodate new arrivals. Thanks to her careful advance scheduling, Diane usually has the right mix of nursing staff on hand to deal with almost any emergency. But catastrophic incidents with a larger number of patients sometimes create an overflow that must be directed to other facilities. "The most difficult thing," says Diane, "is getting people to realize the need to keep things moving."

To schedule in advance for emergency care, Diane has to know her people as individuals. After 14 years in the Burn/Trauma Unit, she has learned that "you really have to know your staff's limitations. You have to know what kind of stresses they can handle and what kinds they can't."

Scheduling is an especially important aspect of management because it normally must be done repeatedly. Many companies establish daily production and work schedules, but as problems occur and customer demands change, the schedules may be revised one or more times during the day. For example, as flights are delayed, canceled, or rerouted, airlines must reschedule aircraft and crews on an ongoing basis.

Despite the short-term nature of most schedules, scheduling can be of strategic importance. Time-based competition is becoming more widespread. Companies such as UPS and Federal Express compete primarily on the speed and reliability of their shipping services; for them the scheduling of personnel, package pickup and delivery sequencing, and scheduling of truck and aircraft movements are crucial to on-time de-

Delta Airlines saved approximately $300 million over a three year period by using an improved fleet assignment and scheduling model.

livery. In Chapter 3 we saw that UPS must collect packages from customers and deliver them to sorting facilities early enough each day to have them sorted and transferred to long-distance feeder trucks the same day. The arrival, loading, and departure of the feeder trucks must be perfectly coordinated for deliveries to occur on time.

Scheduling clearly has a direct impact on the profitability of organizations. The more efficiently workers, jobs, and equipment are scheduled, the lower the cost and the greater the profit a company will achieve. For example, Delta Airlines estimated that it saved approximately $300 million over a three-year period by using an improved fleet assignment and scheduling model.[1] In addition, good production scheduling increases work flow and reduces inventories, which directly increase cash flow to the company.

Each organization has unique constraints, objectives, and business conditions. Entire books have been devoted to a single type of scheduling, such as personnel or job-shop scheduling, so we can barely scratch the surface of the topic here. The purpose of this chapter is to provide a small sampling of some common scheduling problems and solution methods.

The next three sections are devoted to production sequencing problems. Section 16.5 presents the assignment problem, which occurs in various scheduling situations, and provides a solution method for it. Although many of the solution methods discussed in Sections 16.2–16.5 are applicable to service as well as manufacturing systems, Section 16.6 is devoted to issues that are especially important in scheduling service operations. Section 16.7 discusses common personnel scheduling problems and shows how some of them can be solved using linear programming. The chapter ends with some comments on the implementation of scheduling procedures, including the information needed to schedule effectively and simple suggestions for improving production and personnel scheduling.

16.2 SCHEDULING PRODUCTION FOR CONTINUOUS AND REPETITIVE FLOW PROCESSES

Most organizations produce several products using the same production resources and system. So a common production scheduling problem is determining the sequence in which products or jobs should be processed and the amount of each product to produce (for stock items). In this section we will discuss a problem that is especially common in tightly connected flow production systems or subsystems. In these systems every product passes through the same work stations in the same order, and the products move almost continuously from one work station to another, so the entire system acts and can be scheduled as a unit. The products made by these types of systems are normally stock items, which we will assume throughout this section.

COORDINATING PRODUCTION LOT SIZES WITH CYCLIC PRODUCTION SCHEDULES

When several products are made using the same production system, a major consideration in production scheduling is the setup cost and time required to change from producing one product to another. In Chapter 13 we derived the following formula for the economic lot size (ELS) for stock items with independent demands:

$$ELS = Q^* = \sqrt{[2c_oD/c_h][P/(P - D)]} \qquad (13.7)$$

[1]Radhika Subramanian et al., "Coldstart: Fleet Assignment at Delta Air Lines," *Interfaces*, Vol. 24, No. 1, 1994, pp. 104–120.

where

Q^* = optimal amount to produce in a production run

D = rate of demand or usage of the product

P = rate at which items can be produced by the production process

c_o = setup cost to produce the product

c_h = holding cost per unit per unit time for the product

This derivation implied that several products would be produced using the same equipment and that the resulting ELSs for the products were somehow consistent; runs of the products could be sequenced so that the desired lot sizes could be produced without running out of stock.

In reality, this implication may be false unless there is considerable excess production capacity. If we ran the products sequentially using these lot sizes, we might run out of stock of some products unless we maintained substantial safety stock inventories, as shown in the following example.

EXAMPLE 1

Dominion Soap PLC makes three laundry detergents—Wave, Bright, and Power—using the same production process. Dominion can produce 100,000 cartons of detergent each day, regardless of the brand. The daily demand for the three detergents is 40,000, 35,000, and 20,000 boxes, respectively. Suppose the holding cost for each product is \$0.01 per carton per day, and the setup cost is \$800 for Wave and \$1600 for the other two products. The ELSs for the three products (using equation (13.7)) are approximately 103,000 for Wave, 131,000 for Bright, and 89,000 for Power. The amount of time needed to run each lot and the maximum times between runs (the time a lot will last until inventories are depleted) are given in Table 16.1.

We can see that it will take Dominion 1.03 days to produce 103,000 cartons of Wave, and this will satisfy the demand for (103,000)/(40,000) = 2.58 days until another run of Wave must be started. However, if Dominion makes one run of each product during each production cycle, as illustrated in Figure 16.1a, a full cycle would last 3.23 days. So if Dominion began with no inventories of Wave at time 0, inventories would increase at the rate of 60,000 cartons per day while production occurred, reaching a max-

TABLE 16.1 RUN TIMES AND MAXIMUM TIME BETWEEN RUNS

Product	ELS	Run Time (days)	Max. Time Between Runs (days)
Wave	103,000	1.03	2.58
Bright	131,000	1.31	3.74
Power	89,000	0.89	4.45
Total	323,000	3.23	

Run time = *ELS/P*

Maximum time between runs = *ELS/D*

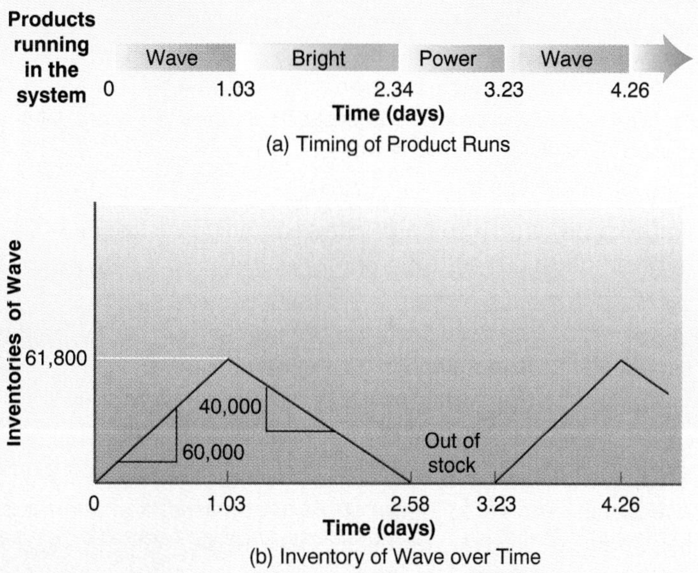

FIGURE 16.1 Production cycle for Dominion Soap using ELSs.

imum of 61,800 cartons at time 1.03, when production of Wave ended. The inventories of Wave would then decrease at the rate of 40,000 per day until they were depleted at time 2.58, as shown in Figure 16.1b. The next run of Wave would not begin until at least time 3.23.[2] On the other hand, production of Bright and Power would occur before their inventories were depleted (assuming they began at time 0 with just enough inventories to carry them until their first production run began). So average inventories of these two products would increase over time.

These problems occur because the maximum times between runs for the products are different; that is, their lot sizes are *incompatible*. This situation could be corrected in various ways, such as by holding extra inventories of Wave, and making an extra run of Wave every few cycles and omitting runs of the other two products to equalize inventories. But this would result in unnecessary inventories and would eliminate the simplicity of a **cyclic schedule**, whereby the same sequence of production runs is repeated in every cycle.

An alternative approach is to modify the lot sizes of the products so that the maximum time between production runs is the same for all products. For example, suppose Dominion changed the lot sizes for the products to 136,000, 119,000, and 68,000 for Wave, Bright, and Power, respectively. The maximum time between runs would then be 3.40 days for each product, and Dominion could run each product once every 3.40 days. During the 3.40-day cycle the production process would be running 3.23 days to make 323,000 units of product, the same as using the ELSs, and would be idle (possibly for setup) the other 0.17 day. No product would ever run out of stock; just as the inventories of a product reached zero, a production run of that product would begin.

[2]It would actually be later because Figure 16.1 assumes that there is no set up *time*, which in fact there would be.

Running each product exactly once in a cycle sometimes requires substantial modifications in the ELSs, which can increase costs unnecessarily. When the maximum times between runs resulting from the ELSs differ by a factor of 1.5 or more, it can be more economical to use a production schedule in which one or more products are run multiple times during a production cycle. The following is one of several heuristics that can be used to devise such a schedule.

Heuristic for Constructing Efficient Cyclic Schedules

1. For each product, i, compute the economic lot size, ELS_i, and the required time between runs, T_i, where $T_i = ELS_i/D_i$ and D_i is the demand or usage rate for i.
2. Let T_{max} be the largest of the T_i values. For each i, compute T_{max}/T_i and round to the nearest integer. This will be the number of runs of product i to make during each production cycle and will be denoted as R_i.
3. Compute the total number of units of product i that will be made during a cycle, $Q_i = T_{max}D_i$, and compute the total amount of production time to be allocated to product i during a cycle, $t_i = Q_i/P_i$, where P_i is the production rate for product i.
4. Use a chart similar to Figure 16.1a to construct a sequence of product runs that has R_i runs of product i during a cycle and the total run time for product i during a cycle is t_i.

EXAMPLE 2

Using the data for Example 1, the heuristic produces the following schedule:

1. $T_1 = 103{,}000/40{,}000 = 2.58$; $T_2 = 131{,}000/35{,}000 = 3.74$; $T_3 = 89{,}000/20{,}000 = 4.45$.
2. $T_{max} = 4.45$, so $R_1 = 4.45/2.58 = 1.72 \rightarrow 2$; $R_2 = 4.45/3.74 = 1.19 \rightarrow 1$; $R_3 = 4.45/4.45 = 1$.
3. $Q_1 = 4.45(40{,}000) = 178{,}000$; $Q_2 = 4.45(35{,}000) = 156{,}000$; $Q_3 = 4.45(20{,}000) = 89{,}000$. $t_1 = 178{,}000/100{,}000 = 1.78$ days; $t_2 = 156{,}000/100{,}000 = 1.56$ days; $t_3 = 89{,}000/100{,}000 = 0.89$ days. During every 4.45-day cycle the production process will be busy 4.23 days and idle 0.22 day.
4. If we divide Q_1 into two equal lot sizes of 89,000 each, we get the schedule in Figure 16.2. At the end of the run of Power, enough inventory of Wave remains to last until time 2.22, so we use the allotted idle time of 0.22 during this part of the cycle to minimize inventory costs.

By splitting the production of Wave into two runs in each cycle, we get a total annual stocking cost for the schedule in Figure 16.2 of approximately $11,000 a year less than the "consistent" schedule derived in Example 1, which has only one run of Wave in each cycle.

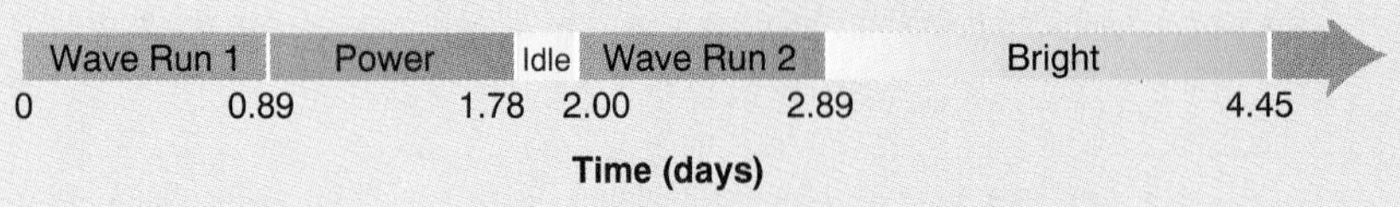

FIGURE 16.2 Consistent production cycle generated by heuristic.

Although we have discussed cyclic schedules in terms of scheduling entire production systems, the same procedures can be used to schedule individual work units that produce the same set of stock items on a regular basis.

16.3 SCHEDULING BATCH PRODUCTION SYSTEMS

In terms of production scheduling, batch production systems (batch flow, job shops, and cellular processes) have much in common. In each case, a variety of products is normally made, many of which are made to order. The time required to process each job or product at each work station, work center, or work cell varies from job to job because of differences in setup and processing requirements and in customer order sizes. Because the products are made in batches and the stages of production are disconnected, each stage has to be scheduled separately but coordinated with the other stages. Batch production environments are especially dynamic because customer orders arrive continuously and products are being processed and shipped all the time. At any given time, dozens of jobs may be awaiting processing, so the key issue is to determine the best sequence in which to process jobs at the production stages.

APPROACHES TO JOB SEQUENCING

We can choose one of two general approaches to sequence batch jobs. The first is to use a series of static but rolling schedules. Daily or weekly, we make a static schedule that sequences those jobs currently in the system (jobs for which there are firm orders). The schedule specifies the sequence in which jobs are to be run at each stage. After a period of time (a day or a week), a new static schedule is made that takes into account the receipt of any new orders, the completion of jobs, and the production status of jobs in the system.

The second approach is an explicitly dynamic method that uses dispatching rules. With this approach, every time a job finishes processing at a production stage, a **dispatching** or **priority rule** is used to select the next job for processing at that stage (e.g., the job with the earliest due date). Any new jobs entering the queue of waiting jobs at that stage would be included in the analysis.[3]

CRITERIA FOR EVALUATING SCHEDULES

Whether a company decides to generate and revise job sequences periodically using rolling static schedules or to select the sequence dynamically using dispatching rules, the best job sequence (and scheduling procedure) will depend on what we want to achieve. Do we want to maximize the number of jobs delivered by their due dates, or do we want to minimize the average throughput time for jobs (the time jobs spend in the production system)? Some common criteria used to guide and evaluate schedules are the following:

1. ***Minimize Average Job Flow Time.*** The **flow time** for a job is the time from some starting point (usually the time processing begins on the first job of some set) until that job is completed.
2. ***Minimize the Make Span Time.*** The **make span** for a *set of jobs* is the longest flow time for the jobs in that set. Alternatively, it is the time from when processing begins on the *first job* in the set until the *last job* is *completed*.

[3]Remember from Chapter 9 that multistage production systems are actually queueing networks, so the dispatching rules are identical to the queue disciplines discussed in that chapter.

3. ***Minimize the Average Number of Jobs in the System (or at the Work Station).*** For a fixed set of jobs, this will be the total flow time for all the jobs divided by the make span. This criterion corresponds closely with, and is used as a proxy for, minimizing work-in-process.
4. ***Minimize Average Tardiness.*** The **tardiness** of a job is the amount of time after its due date that the job is completed; if a job is completed before the due date, the tardiness is zero.[4]
5. ***Minimize the Number or Fraction of Tardy Jobs.***

SEQUENCING RULES FOR THE ONE-STAGE PROBLEM

Although we are ultimately interested in multistage production systems, we will first assume jobs are run through a single work station; this is often called the *one-stage* or *one-machine sequencing problem*. Although processing jobs on a first-come-first-served basis is equitable, it is not usually a very effective job sequencing method in terms of the criteria listed above because it takes into account neither the processing time required nor the due dates of the jobs. Here are some of the simpler and more common job sequencing rules.

1. The **shortest processing time (SPT) rule** sequences jobs in increasing order of their processing times (including setup).
2. The **earliest due date (EDD) rule** sequences the jobs in order of their due dates, earliest first.
3. The **critical ratio (CR) rule** sequences jobs in increasing order of their critical ratio, where the critical ratio for a job is the amount of time until the due date divided by the remaining amount of processing time required.
4. The **slack time remaining (STR) rule** for a job is the due date minus the remaining processing time. We sequence jobs in increasing order of their STRs.

The following example illustrates the job sequences that would result from each of these rules and computes common measures of performance.

EXAMPLE 3

Andy Arthurson is an independent computer software consultant. After completing his most recent project, he had five jobs awaiting completion. Following are the estimated work times required to complete each job and the due dates requested by customers.

Job	Processing Time (days)	Due Date (days from present)
A	12	52
B	16	37
C	8	28
D	20	57
E	6	31

[4]Sometimes the *lateness* of a job, defined as the completion time minus the due date, is used. A job completed early would have a negative lateness.

SPT: Sequencing jobs in increasing order of processing times produces the sequence ECABD; the flow times and tardiness for each job are given in Table 16.2.

TABLE 16.2 SEQUENCE USING THE SPT RULE

Sequence	Job	Completion (Flow) Time	Time Until Due Date	Tardiness
1	E	6	31	0
2	C	14	28	0
3	A	26	52	0
4	B	42	37	5
5	D	62	57	5
Total		150		10

Average flow time per job = 150/5 = 30.0
Make span = 62
Average no. of jobs in the system = 150/62 = 2.42
Average tardiness per job = 10/5 = 2.0
Number of jobs tardy = 2

EDD: Sequencing jobs according to their due dates produces the sequence CEBAD; the results for this case are given in Table 16.3.

TABLE 16.3 SEQUENCE USING THE EDD RULE

Sequence	Job	Completion (Flow) Time	Time Until Due Date	Tardiness
1	C	8	28	0
2	E	14	31	0
3	B	30	37	0
4	A	42	52	0
5	D	62	57	5
Total		156		5

Average flow time per job = 156/5 = 31.2
Make span = 62
Average no. of jobs in the system = 156/62 = 2.52
Average tardiness per job = 5/5 = 1.0
Number of jobs tardy = 1

CR: Sequencing jobs according to their critical ratios produces the sequence BDCAE, as shown in Table 16.4.

STR: Sequencing jobs according to slack time remaining produces the sequence CBEDA, as shown in Table 16.5.

Table 16.4 SEQUENCE USING THE CR RULE

Sequence	Job	Critical Ratio	Completion (Flow) Time	Time Until Due Date	Tardiness
1	B	37/16 = 2.31	16	37	0
2	D	57/20 = 2.87	36	57	0
3	C	28/8 = 3.50	44	28	16
4	A	52/12 = 4.33	56	52	4
5	E	31/6 = 5.17	62	31	31
Total			214		51

Average flow time per job = 214/5 = 42.8
Make span = 62
Average no. of jobs in the system = 214/62 = 3.45
Average tardiness per job = 51/5 = 10.2
Number of jobs tardy = 3

Table 16.5 SEQUENCE USING THE STR RULE

Sequence	Job	Slack Time Remaining	Completion (Flow) Time	Time Until Due Date	Tardiness
1	C	28 − 8 = 20	8	28	0
2	B	37 − 16 = 21	24	37	0
3	E	31 − 6 = 25	30	31	0
4	D	57 − 20 = 37	50	57	0
5	A	52 − 12 = 40	62	52	10
Total			174		10

Average flow time per job = 174/5 = 34.8
Make span = 62
Average no. of jobs in the system = 174/62 = 2.81
Average tardiness per job = 10/5 = 2.0
Number of jobs tardy = 1

We can make several observations from Example 3. First, the make span is the same for every sequence. For a one-machine problem the make span will *always* be equal to the sum of the processing times, so it is independent of the job sequence. This will *not* be the case when jobs must be processed on two or more machines in sequence. Second, the SPT rule produced the sequence with the smallest average flow time and the smallest average number of jobs in the system. Will this always be true? Although we should not reach such a general conclusion from one simple example, it can be proved that *for the one-machine problem* the SPT rule will *always* produce the sequence that has the smallest average flow time and smallest average number of jobs in the system.[5] For these reasons, the SPT rule is popular in practice.

[5]It can also be proved easily that this means it will also be the sequence with the smallest average job *lateness* (but not tardiness).

Unfortunately, no other strong conclusions can be drawn. Although the EDD rule resulted in the sequence with the fewest tardy jobs and the smallest average job tardiness, this is not always the case. Normally, EDD does a good job of keeping tardiness low, but sometimes it results in large average flow times. The STR rule performs reasonably well with respect to tardiness, but it can also perform poorly in terms of average flow time and average number of jobs in the system. A surprising result is that the CR rule does not do well in minimizing the two measures of tardiness, even though it explicitly includes due dates in its ratios. This result is quite common. The static CR rule, which constructs the sequence based on ratios *at time 0*, frequently performs poorly. However, a dynamic version of the critical ratio (DCR), which recomputes the ratios after each job is assigned, works reasonably well, especially in a dynamic dispatching mode, which we will discuss later, and when processing times are random.

The sequencing rules discussed here are just a small subset of the many that have been proposed. Some methods, such as the SPT rule, produce the best sequence with respect to one or two of the criteria. (Similarly, Moore has presented a method that constructs the sequence that minimizes the number of tardy jobs.[6]) However, in practice, scheduling usually involves trade-offs among several criteria, so one method will rarely produce a universally perfect schedule. In practice we test different sequencing rules, often using computer simulation with actual order arrival, due date, and processing time data, to see which rule produces the sequences that best balance the relevant criteria for our situation.

TWO-STAGE AND THREE-STAGE FLOW PROCESSES

Many production systems are two-stage batch flow processes whereby all products are made in batches (possibly of size one) and must pass through two consecutive work stations (machines) in the same sequence. For example, a print shop may have 10 jobs that have to be completed using a two-stage process. Each job requires making multiple copies of a document on a photocopier (stage 1); then inserts must be added, and each copy straightened and stapled (stage 2).

Some multistage processes can be decomposed into smaller subsystems for scheduling purposes. For example, Empresa Nacional Siderurgica (a Spanish steel company) treated its steel conversion and casting stages as a two-stage flow process and separated these stages from the remainder of its steel production process for scheduling purposes. The key issue in these cases is whether there is one sequence in which the jobs should be run that is better than others. Again, this depends on our evaluation criteria.

In some situations we have a fixed number of jobs, and our goal is to complete them all as soon as possible—in other words, minimize the make span. This would certainly be a reasonable criterion for someone with a set of jobs to do for a fixed amount of pay (or someone who cannot go home until they are all completed). It would also be good for a company that must keep its facility open and pay its workers until the last job is completed.

Johnson's Rule

The following algorithm, called **Johnson's rule**, constructs the sequence that minimizes the *make span* for a two-stage problem.[7] The algorithm "builds" the sequence from the front and back toward the middle.

---

[6] J. M. Moore, "An *n*-job, One-Machine Sequencing Algorithm for Minimizing the Number of Late Jobs," *Management Science*, Vol. 15, 1968, pp. 102–109.

[7] S. M. Johnson, "Optimal Two and Three Stage Production Schedules with Set-up Time Included," *Naval Research Logistics Quarterly*, Vol. 1, 1954, pp. 61–68.

1. For a given set of jobs, let i_1 and i_2 be the estimated times to set up and run job i at stages 1 and 2, respectively.
2. Select the remaining job with the smallest estimated time on either of the machines. If the smallest time occurs at stage 1, schedule that job at the front of the sequence but *after* any other job already assigned to the front of the sequence. If the smallest time occurs at stage 2, schedule that job at the end of the sequence but *before* any other jobs already assigned to the end of the sequence.
3. Delete the jobs as they are scheduled and stop when none remain.[8]

EXAMPLE 4

Standard Metals is a small manufacturer of simple, customized metal products. Standard has six orders that must be completed and shipped today. Each product (order) is made using a two-stage process. In the first stage, items are cut to the appropriate shape and size: in the second stage, they are ground and polished. Each stage is staffed by one person. The workers at each stage can go home when their work is complete, but Standard realizes that it will require more than eight hours to complete the six jobs. The firm wishes to minimize its overtime expense; this is equivalent to minimizing the make span for the jobs.[9] The estimated setup and processing times (in hours) for each job at each stage are as follows:

Job	Stage 1	Stage 2
A	1.5	0.6
B	3.2	1.9
C	0.8	1.3
D	2.7	2.0
E	1.1	1.4
F	1.6	0.7

1. We first select the job with the smallest stage time, which is 0.6 hour for job A. This time occurs at the second stage, so we make job A *last* in the sequence and delete A from our list.
2. Next, we select job F because it has a stage time of 0.7 hour. This time also occurs at the second stage, so we put F at the end of the sequence but *before* job A. So our sequence is now – – – – FA. We then delete F from the list.
3. We now select job C, with a stage time of 0.8 hour. This time occurs at stage 1, so we put job C at the front of our sequence, giving the sequence C – – – FA, and delete C from our list.
4. We select E, with a stage time of 1.1 hours at stage 1. We assign this to the front of the sequence *but behind* C, so the sequence is now CE – – FA. We then delete E.

[8]The formal statement of the algorithm is that if i_1 and i_2 are the stage times for job i, then job i precedes job $i + 1$ if $\min(i_1, (i+1)_2) < \min((i+1)_1, i_2)$.

[9]Suppose the worker at each stage can leave as soon as she finishes processing at her stage. The time when the worker at stage 1 can leave is independent of the job sequence (prove this to yourself). The amount of time the worker at stage 2 must stay is the make span, so minimizing the make span will minimize overtime costs.

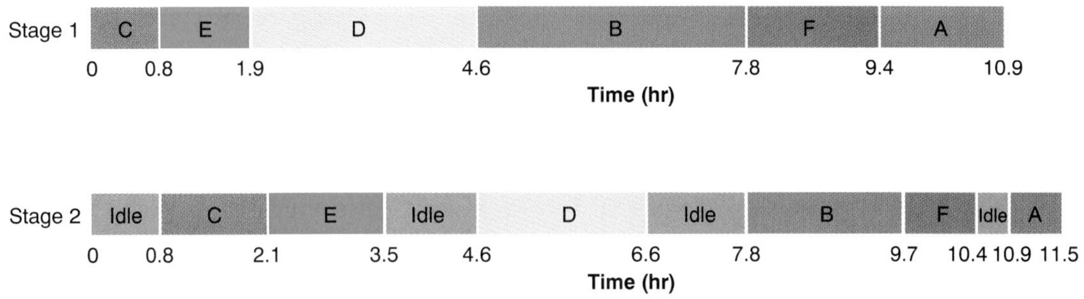

FIGURE 16.3 Job sequence using Johnson's rule.

5. We now select job B, with a stage time of 1.9 hours at stage 2. We assign this to the end of the sequence but in front of F, so the sequence is now CE–BFA. We then delete job B.
6. The only job remaining is D, which fills the position between E and B. The final sequence is CEDBFA.

The make span can be computed and the operation of the two stages visualized by making the chart in Figure 16.3. The last job, A, will be completed at stage 1 after 10.9 hours (this will be true regardless of the sequencing, assuming jobs are started without delay). The last job is completed at stage 2 at time 11.5, so the make span is 11.5 hours. Notice that stage 2 is idle for 3.6 hours. It may appear that idle time at stage 2 could be reduced by rearranging the jobs, but in fact it cannot. Rearranging jobs can postpone the second period of idleness (stage 2 will always be idle at time 0), but it will not reduce the total idleness. For example, the sequence CEADBF postpones the idle period that occurred at time 3.5 at stage 2 until time 4.1, but it results in more total idleness later and the make span increases to 11.9 hours.

Johnson's rule puts jobs with the shortest times at stage 1 early in the sequence so that stage 2 can be brought into production quickly. Once stage 1 has finished processing all the jobs, the jobs awaiting processing at stage 2 have the smallest stage 2 times, so completion time for these jobs is minimized.

Johnson's rule constructs the sequence that minimizes make span time, but it does not necessarily minimize the average flow time or the average number of jobs in the system (see problem 7 at the end of the chapter), and it does not consider differential due dates for the jobs. Although in practice the make span–minimizing sequences tend to perform well with respect to average flow time and number of jobs in the system, Johnson's rule should be used mainly to complete a fixed set of jobs as soon as possible, as in Example 4.

Johnson's Rule for Three-Stage Problems

When the production process has three or more stages, a general algorithm for finding the make span–minimizing sequence does not exist, so heuristics are normally used. However, if the stage times for a three-stage problem have a special form, the three-stage problem can be simplified to a two-stage problem and solved using Johnson's rule. The requirement is as follows: Suppose i_1, i_2, and i_3 are the stage times for job i at the three stages, respectively. If

$$\min i_1 \geq \max i_2 \quad \text{or} \quad \min i_3 \geq \max i_2$$

we can define $i_1^* = i_1 + i_2$ and $i_2^* = i_2 + i_3$ and solve the problem with Johnson's rule using i_1^* and i_2^* as the stage times for a two-stage problem. In other words, if the *smallest* time at stage 1 for any job is at least as large as the *largest* time at stage 2, *or* if the *smallest* time at stage 3 is at least as large as the *largest* time at stage 2, we can treat the problem as a two-stage problem. Notice that only one of the two conditions must be satisfied. In the resulting two-stage problem, the revised stage 1 times will be the sum of the original stage 1 and 2 times, and the revised stage 2 times will be the sum of the original stage 2 and 3 times. This revised problem is used *only* to obtain the optimal sequence; the make span time must be computed using the original three-stage data.

EXAMPLE 5

Suppose Clayton Printing had six jobs awaiting processing. Their estimated processing times on Clayton's three-stage process are given below. The company wishes to minimize the make span for the jobs.

Job	Stage Times (hr) Stage 1	Stage 2	Stage 3
A	6	5	9
B	10	4	7
C	8	3	5
D	11	6	4
E	9	6	3
F	7	5	5

In this case, min $i_1 = 6$ and max $i_2 = 6$, so min $i_1 \geq$ max i_2 and the problem can be reduced to a two-stage problem where the stage times are as follows:

Job	Stage 1	Stage 2
A	11	14
B	14	11
C	11	8
D	17	10
E	15	9
F	12	10

An optimal sequence using Johnson's rule is then ABFDEC (notice that because of the tie between D and F at the second stage, an alternative optimum is the sequence ABDFEC). The resulting make span, which is determined by making a three-stage diagram similar to that in Figure 16.3, is 59.

DYNAMIC DISPATCHING RULES AND MULTISTAGE SYSTEMS

When jobs need not be processed in the same sequence at every stage, and especially when products are made in a job-shop or cellular production system, so that each product may have a unique routing through the system, determining an optimal sequence (with respect to some objective) for all jobs through all stages is usually an intractable problem. Instead we commonly treat the scheduling of each production stage as a one-

Dispatching rules are used in job-shop systems to sequence work among work-centers.

stage problem, and we use *dynamic* dispatching rules to determine which of the jobs waiting *at that stage* to run next.

These dispatching rules are based on the one-stage rules we considered earlier. They are inherently dynamic because the job sequence can be revised after each job is completed at a stage, during which time new jobs may have arrived at the work station and due dates approach. The following example illustrates how jobs might be sequenced at a given work station using dynamic versions of each of the four one-stage dispatching rules. The CR and STR rules have been modified as follows: The critical ratio for the CR rule will be the time until the due date divided by the expected amount of processing required for *all* remaining stages, and the slack time remaining for the STR rule will be the time until the due date minus the expected amount of processing required for *all* remaining stages.

EXAMPLE 6

Suppose three jobs—A, B, and C—are awaiting processing at a company's testing department at time 0. Additional jobs—D, E, and so on—arrive at the department over time. Table 16.6 lists the times at which jobs arrive, the expected time required for testing, the remaining processing time required for all stages (including testing) until shipment, and the shipment due date.

Shortest Processing Time

1. At time 0 three jobs are awaiting processing: A, B, and C. Job C has the shortest expected testing time, so it would be run first, and the run would last until time 3.

TABLE 16.6 JOBS TO BE PROCESSED BY THE TESTING DEPARTMENT

Job	Arival Time	Expected Testing Time	Remaining Processing Time*	Due Date
A	0	4	13	23
B	0	6	11	18
C	0	3	15	20
D	5	8	16	32
E	8	2	9	34
F	14	6	12	38
—	—	—	—	—
—	—	—	—	—

*Includes testing time.

2. At time 3 only jobs A and B would be waiting, so A would be run next because it has the shorter testing time.
3. A would be completed at time 7, by which time D would have arrived, so B and D would be awaiting testing. B has the shorter testing time, so it would be run next and finish at time 13.
4. At time 13 D and E would be waiting, so E would be run next. The resulting sequence for the first four jobs would be CABE.

Earliest Due Date

1. Of the three jobs waiting at time 0, B has the earliest due date so it would be run first and finish at time 6.
2. At time 6 jobs A, C, and D would be waiting, and C would be chosen because it has the earliest due date.
3. C would finish testing at time 9, and A, D, and E would be waiting. A, with the earliest due date, would be processed next, and it would finish testing at time 13.
4. At time 13 D and E are waiting and D would be run next, so the resulting sequence for the first four jobs would be BCAD.

Critical Ratio

1. The CRs for the three jobs waiting at time 0 are 23/13 = 1.77 for A, 18/11 = 1.64 for B, and 20/15 = 1.33 for C, so C is processed first.
2. When C finishes running at time 3, jobs A and B are waiting. Their new CRs are (23 – 3)/13 = 1.54 for A and (18 – 3)/11 = 1.36 for B, so B is run next.
3. When B finishes at time 9, three jobs are waiting. Their CRs are (23 – 9)/13 = 1.08 for A, (32 – 9)/16 = 1.44 for D, and (34 – 9)/9 = 2.78 for E, so A is run next.
4. When A finishes at time 13, the CRs for the two waiting jobs are (32 – 13)/16 = 1.19 for D and (34 – 13)/9 = 2.33 for E, so D is run next. The resulting sequence up to this point is then CBAD.

Slack Time Remaining

1. At time 0 the slack times remaining for the three jobs are (23 – 13) = 10 for A, (18 – 11) = 7 for B, and (20 – 15) = 5 for C, so C is processed first.

2. When C is finished at time 3, the remaining slack times are (23 – 3) – 13 = 7 for A and (18 – 3) – 11 = 4 for B, so B is processed next.
3. When B is finished at time 9, the remaining slack times for the three waiting jobs are (23 – 9) – 13 = 1 for A, (32 – 9) – 16 = 7 for D, and (34 – 9) – 9 = 16 for E, so A is processed next.
4. When A is finished at time 13, the remaining slack times are (32 – 13) – 16 = 3 for D and (34 – 13) – 9 = 12 for E, so D is run next. The resulting sequence for the first four jobs run is then CBAD.

To determine which of these dispatching rules is best for our specific situation, we would have to test each of them using realistic data for job arrivals, due dates, and processing times. This would normally be done using computer simulation. For each set of data we would use the rules to sequence the jobs and then compute the measures of performance that are important to us, such as percentage of jobs tardy or average number of jobs awaiting processing (in-process inventories). Although the specific rule that will be best varies from case to case according to job characteristics, the rules that have been found to be most effective over a variety of situations are those that explicitly consider the amount of time before the due date and the number of operations and amount of operation time remaining to be performed.

Gantt Charts and Visual Scheduling

One complication of scheduling jobs on machines is that the expected stage time for a job may not be a constant; frequently the setup time will depend on which job preceded it. For a given job, the setup time may be as short as a few minutes if the preceding job is very similar and as long as several hours if the preceding job is very dissimilar. This is one reason why we may want to schedule a set of jobs together rather than one at a time. Scheduling similar products and jobs together (those using the same inks, flip hooks, or guide bars) can save considerable setup time, thereby increasing the effective capacity of the system and reducing throughput time.

A discussion of scheduling algorithms and heuristics that explicitly consider different setup times based on job sequencing is beyond the scope of this book. However, a century-old visual tool, called a **Gantt chart** (named after its developer, Henry Gantt), is commonly used to accomplish the same thing through experimentation. A Gantt chart has a time line for each machine or work center to be scheduled (Figure 16.4). Each job assigned to be processed on a machine is then allocated part of that machine's time line. This way we can track the scheduled movement of a job through the production system, see when it should be at each machine, and predict when it will be completed. The chart also makes it easy to avoid scheduling conflicts, so that two jobs are not assigned to the same machine at the same time, and a job is not assigned to a machine later in the process until its processing has been completed at earlier stages.

Traditionally, Gantt charts had tracks to hold cardboard strips on each time line. For each stage of processing, a strip of cardboard was cut, with its length corresponding to the amount of setup and processing time required for the job, depending on the preceding job at the stage. Alternative job sequences could then be tested to determine their consequences.

Many companies now maintain and modify their Gantt charts using computers. Setup times can easily be modified by computer when job sequences are changed, and the Gantt

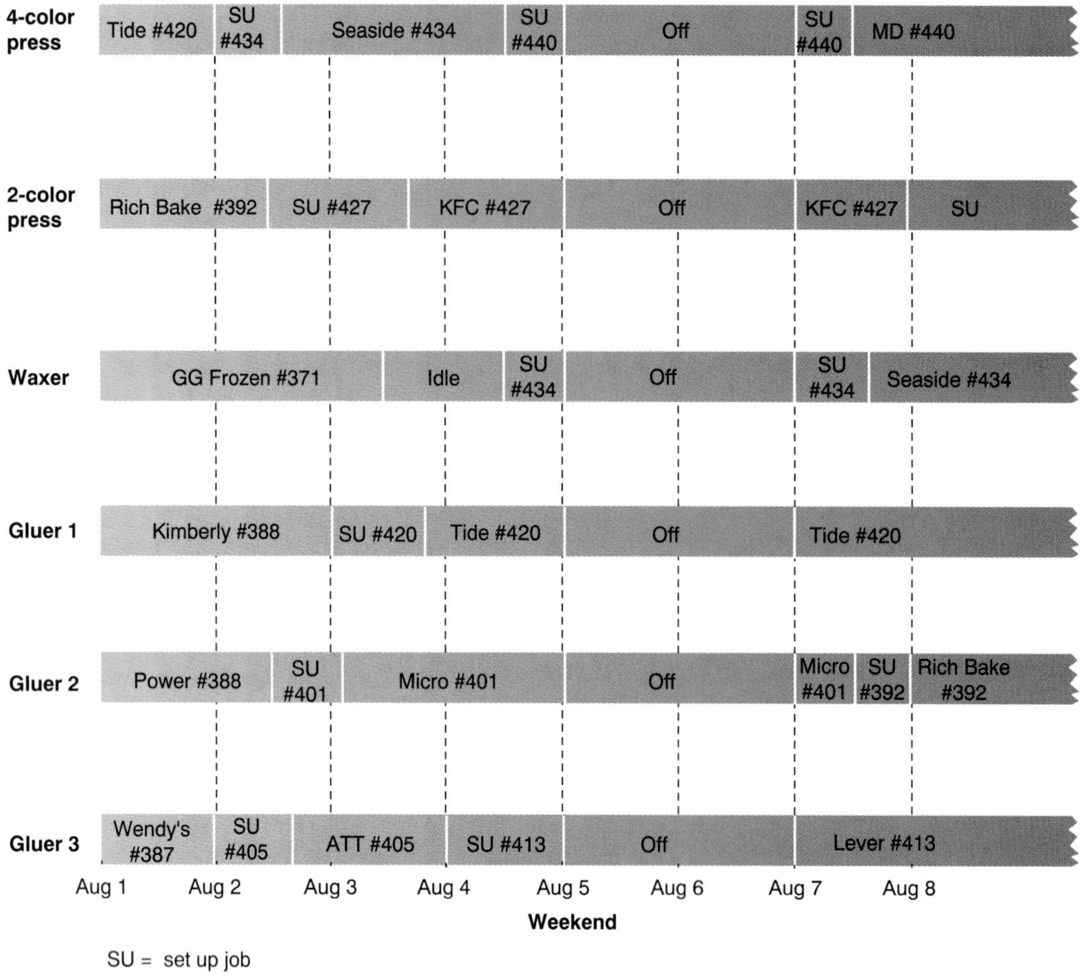

FIGURE 16.4 Typical Gantt chart for a carton manufacturer.

chart can easily be updated. One other feature of Gantt charts is that they can track the progress of jobs over time. So as jobs are completed they are pulled "off the board," and new jobs are added. Computerized Gantt charts make it especially easy to evaluate and display the consequences of production delays and changes to the schedule.

16.4 OPTIMIZED PRODUCTION TECHNOLOGY

In Chapter 15 we introduced synchronous production and, more specifically, the drum-buffer-rope scheduling procedure. The principal idea underlying synchronous production is that the flow of product through a production system is controlled by the bottleneck operation(s), so production scheduling should begin with the bottleneck and be constructed around it. The drum-buffer-rope method (1) establishes the pace of production at the bottleneck (the drum, which beats the pace); (2) maintains buffer inventories in front of the bottleneck operation to ensure that it never stops due to a material shortage; and (3) uses an informational mechanism (the rope) to keep nonbottleneck operations working at the same pace as the bottleneck to prevent them from operating too fast and creating unneeded inventories.

Optimized Production Technology (OPT) is a computer software package designed to implement the synchronous production principles and the drum-buffer-rope mechanism. Because it is a proprietary product of Creative Output, Inc., the details and algorithms of the program are not fully known, but OPT is based on network flow algorithms and computer simulation. As we mentioned in Chapter 9, a multistage production system such as a job shop can be represented as a *network* of activities. A network can be thought of as a set of circles, called *nodes*, and lines connecting them, called *arcs*. In a production system the arcs could represent work stations or machines that have (production) capacities. Algorithms exist to determine the maximum flow through such a network (between the first and last nodes in the production process), and the bottlenecks can be identified. Algorithms are then used to schedule work at each work station based on the bottleneck capacities. Because of the randomness of production systems (which we saw in Chapters 8 and 9), computer simulations are used to verify the bottleneck locations and to evaluate various schedules.

Many companies have used OPT to schedule their operations, but because of its proprietary nature and the fact that it is based on the drum-buffer-rope technique, it should be used with care. We saw in Chapter 15 that this approach can be quite useful, especially in job-shop systems, but other scheduling methods such as JIT pull systems can be superior in other cases.

16.5 ASSIGNMENT PROBLEMS

The previous sections focused on how to sequence jobs that pass through a single machine (production stage) or series of machines. A different problem occurs when several jobs can be performed by any one of several machines (or workers or production systems), and the key issue is deciding how best to assign the jobs to the various machines. (For simplicity, throughout this section we will use the word *machines* even though the work may be assigned to teams of workers, production departments, or some other production entities, rather than to actual machines.) The problem is made more complex by the fact that the machines often have different capabilities, so the processing time for a given job will differ from machine to machine. For example, a typical commercial printing plant may have 10 different printing presses. It may be possible to print a given job on any one of the presses based on print quality and the size of the job. But because of differences in the age, size, and technology of the presses, it may require 10 hours to print the job on one press but only 5 hours to print it on a different press.

HUNGARIAN METHOD

One scheduling approach is to formulate the problem as an **assignment problem**, in which we want to assign N jobs to N machines so as to minimize some measure of cost. Each job will be assigned to exactly one machine, and each machine is assigned to process exactly one job. We assume that for every job, i, and machine, j, we can estimate the cost, c_{ij}, of processing job i on machine j. If job i cannot be processed on machine j (machine j does not have the capability), we assign c_{ij} an extremely large value. Assignment problems are a type of integer programming problem (see Tutorial 1), but because of their structure they can be treated as a special type of linear program for which a simple and efficient solution method has been devised. The method, called the **Hungarian method**,[10] is best explained using a numerical example.

EXAMPLE 7

Universal Systems provides consulting and software development services to industry. The company has divided its workers into five teams, each with its own mix of skills and experience. Universal has received five consulting jobs that must be done within the next few weeks, and the managing partner has made the following cost estimates for each team to complete each project based on each team's skills and salaries.

		Costs ($000) Team				
		1	2	3	4	5
Jobs	A	9	5	13	12	17
	B	13	19	9	17	16
	C	11	5	4	7	13
	D	9	2	7	13	5
	E	3	7	9	5	17

Algorithm

1. For each row in the cost matrix, subtract the smallest cost in that row from every element in that row. For the resulting costs, subtract the smallest cost in each column from all the elements in the column. This step is shown in Table 16.7.
2. Using only horizontal and vertical straight lines, cover all the zero elements with the minimum number of lines possible. (This can usually be done by inspection, but if it cannot, a formal procedure exists for doing it.[11]) If the minimum number of lines equals N (the number of rows), an optimal assignment can be made; go to step 4. If the minimum number of lines is less than N, more cost matrix reduction must be performed according to step 3. Table 16.8a shows that the zeros in Table 16.7b can all be covered using only four lines, so we go to step 3.
3. Select the smallest cost element in the table that was not covered by a line in step 2; in Table 16.8a this value is 1. Subtract this value from all cost elements that *were not covered by lines*. Add this value to all cost elements that are at the *intersection* of two lines in step 2. (The result of this operation is given in Table 16.8b.) Then go to step 2 and construct new lines to cover the zeroes.

   The zeroes in Table 16.8b cannot be covered with fewer than five lines, so we go to step 4.
4. As soon as a matrix has been constructed such that the minimum number of lines required to cover all the zeros equals N, an optimal assignment is identifiable. The assignment is made as follows. Select the row or column with the *fewest* zeroes in it.[12] Select an element in that row or column that is zero. Assign the job in that

[10]The algorithm is named after D. Konig, a Hungarian mathematician, who first proved a theorem on which the algorithm is based.

[11]See Robert Markland, *Topics in Management Science* (3rd ed.), Wiley, New York, 1989, p. 221.

[12]If the selected row or column has more than one zero remaining in it, there is more than one optimal assignment. Select any zero in the row or column for the assignment and proceed with the process.

TABLE 16.7 ROW- AND COLUMN-REDUCED COSTS

(a)
After Subtracting Lowest-Cost Element in Each Row from All Row Costs

		Team				
		1	2	3	4	5
Jobs	A	4	0	8	7	12
	B	4	10	0	8	7
	C	7	1	0	3	9
	D	7	0	5	11	3
	E	0	4	6	2	14

(b)
After Subtracting Lowest-Cost Element in Each Column of (a) from All Column Elements

		Team				
		1	2	3	4	5
Jobs	A	4	0	8	5	9
	B	4	10	0	6	4
	C	7	1	0	1	6
	D	7	0	5	9	0
	E	0	4	6	0	11

row to the team (machine) in that column. For example, in Table 16.8b, row A has only one zero, so we can select that row. The zero occurs in column 2, so we assign job A to team 2. We then delete the assigned row and column (row A and column 2 in this case). Of the remaining rows and columns, select the one with the fewest zeros and repeat the preceding procedure. In this example row B has only one zero, so we assign job B to team 3. Repeating this procedure should produce a

TABLE 16.8 FIRST ITERATION OF STEPS 2 AND 3

(a)
Crossing Out of Zeroes Using Straight lines

		Team					
		1	2	3	4	5	
Jobs	A	4	0	8	5	9	
	B	4	10	0	6	4	Smallest
	C	7	1	0	1	6	Uncovered
	D	7	0	5	9	0	Element is 1
	E	0	4	6	0	11	

(b)
Revised Costs After Step 3

		Team				
		1	2	3	4	5
Jobs	A	4	0	9	5	9
	B	3	9	0	5	3
	C	6	0	0	0	5
	D	7	0	6	9	0
	E	0	4	7	0	11

TABLE 16.9 OPTIMAL ASSIGNMENT

		Team				
		1	2	3	4	5
Jobs	A	4	[0]	9	5	9
	B	3	9	[0]	5	3
	C	6	0	0	[0]	5
	D	7	0	6	9	[0]
	E	[0]	4	7	0	11

Total cost equals $c_{A2} + c_{B3} + c_{C4} + c_{D5} + c_{E1}$ = $29,000, where c_{ij} are the original costs.

complete assignment, with each row assigned to one and only one column and vice versa. The optimal assignment, given in Table 16.9, is A–2, B–3, C–4, D–5, E–1, and it has a total cost of $29,000.

Notice that simple heuristics do not guarantee an optimal solution. For example, suppose we first match the job and team with the lowest cost, delete that row and column, then match the remaining row and column with the lowest-cost element, and so on (this is called the *greedy* or *myopic* heuristic). In Example 7, the greedy heuristic would produce the assignment A–4, B–5, C–3, D–2, E–1, which has a total cost of $37,000. This approach does not work because, if one job is assigned to the lowest-cost team, the company may be forced to assign another job to a very-high-cost team; the greedy heuristic does not consider these trade-offs.

UNBALANCED ASSIGNMENT PROBLEMS

If the assignment method could be used only when the number of jobs and number of machines were identical, it would be of very limited value. However, the method can easily accommodate those cases where the number of jobs to be assigned either exceeds or is less than the number of machines. The only restriction is that no job can be assigned to more than one machine and vice versa. Imbalance between the number of jobs and machines can be handled by creating "dummy" jobs (when the number of machines exceeds the number of jobs) or "dummy" machines (when jobs exceed machines). For example, suppose we wanted to assign six jobs to eight possible machines. We would create two dummy jobs (rows in the cost matrix), and the assignment costs in the dummy rows would all be zero. The Hungarian algorithm would be applied as above. Any machine assigned a dummy job is actually assigned no job. Solved problem 4 at the end of the chapter illustrates this case.

The logic and algorithms for the basic assignment problem often play a role in solving more complicated assignment and scheduling problems. The potential benefits of good assignment solution methods can be substantial. For example, every day Delta Airlines solves its fleet assignment problem, assigning 450 planes to its 2500 daily domestic flights. Delta estimates that it saves approximately $100 million a year by using an improved solution method. Mobil Oil estimates that it saves $1 million a year in transportation costs for just one product line by using an improved method for assigning trucks to delivery routes. The schedules must consider product consolidation, timing of deliveries, and assignment of trucks to routes. Some universities, such as the

University of Montreal and Sherbrooke University, even use assignment-type algorithms to schedule their courses to minimize course conflicts for students and faculty.[13]

16.6 SCHEDULING SERVICE OPERATIONS

Service operations present unique scheduling problems because service products such as a haircut, an allergy shot, or a property title search cannot be produced and stored in inventory until customers need them; they must be produced when customers request them. Therefore, short-term service scheduling must accommodate peaks in demand without leaving people and facilities idle during low-demand periods.

PRICING AND PROMOTION

Good short-term service scheduling begins with good long-term and intermediate-term capacity planning. Chapters 6 and 12 presented ways in which customer demand during peak periods could be displaced to periods of low demand, where it could be served more efficiently. The two most common approaches are differential pricing and promotion. For example, demand for airline travel is highest during the summer and lowest during the winter, so most airlines offer much lower airfares during the winter months to encourage people to move discretionary travel to this period. They also offer special promotions, such as extra frequent-flier miles or free auto rentals, during low-demand periods.

The same incentives can be used to improve short-term scheduling and service operations. For example, golf courses charge lower fees on weekdays, movie theaters have lower prices for matinee and "rush hour" shows when most people are at work or school, and many restaurants charge lower "early bird" prices for exactly the same meal if a party arrives before 5:30 or 6:00 P.M. With differential pricing, these firms can more fully use facilities and personnel that would otherwise be underutilized during low-demand periods. The marginal cost of providing services during these times is extremely low and more than compensated for by the price. This tactic also reduces the customer load during peak periods, lowering the number of dissatisfied customers who must be turned away or must wait longer for service. Finally, this makes personnel scheduling (discussed in Section 16.7) much easier. Workers can be scheduled for longer shifts, such as eight hours, rather than short periods, such as four or five hours, to accommodate peak periods.

APPOINTMENT AND RESERVATION SYSTEMS

Even with differential pricing and promotion, the demand pattern for most services will not only have peaks and valleys but will also exhibit considerable randomness in terms of *when* customers want service. Certain times of the day and days of the week are more convenient or desirable for customers than others, but if all customers wanted to play golf or have their teeth cleaned at the same time, most of them would have to wait a long time for service or not be served at all that day. By requiring customers to have an appointment or a reservation that specifies when they should arrive for service, firms can offer more efficient service at lower cost.

---

[13]See Subramanian, op. cit.; D. Bausch, G. Brown, and D. Ronen, "Consolidating and Dispatching Truck Shipments of Mobil Heavy Petroleum Products," *Interfaces*, Vol. 25, No. 2 1995, pp. 1–24; and J. A. Ferland and C. Fleurent, "SAPHIR: A Decision Support System for Course Scheduling," *Interfaces*, Vol. 24, No. 1, 1994, pp. 105–115.

Improving Appointment Systems

In theory, appointments should keep providers busy and prevent long customer waits. But in practice, this is not always the case for at least three reasons: (1) some customers with appointments fail to show up; (2) other customers arrive early or late; and (3) the time required to serve customers can be highly variable. The following are some approaches for alleviating these problems.

1. ***Provide Economic Incentives for Showing Up***. An increasing number of physicians, dentists, and golf courses charge customers a fee if they fail to show up for an appointment.
2. ***Remind People of Their Appointments.*** Many firms call customers the day before an appointment to remind them of it. If the customer can no longer make the appointment, the firm is better able to fill the time with another customer.
3. ***Penalize Customers Who Arrive Late, and Do Not Reward Customers for Arriving Early.*** Customers who arrive late should not be served before customers who arrived on time and are waiting. Similarly, customers who arrive very early should not be served before customers with earlier appointments who arrive on time (unless a server, such as a physician, is available and no other on-time customers are waiting).
4. ***Use Wave Schedules Where Appropriate.*** Typically, customers are assigned appointments at equally spaced intervals; for example, a physician may schedule a patient every 10 minutes. If a customer arrives late or does not show up at all, the physician can be left idle for a while and then have to work later than scheduled. A **wave schedule** can partially compensate as follows. If we schedule two customers at the beginning of each hour, the chances are high that at least one will be on time, so the server(s) can begin. A third customer can be scheduled a short time afterward, such as five minutes past the hour. The next three customers are scheduled at 15, 30, and 50 minutes past the hour, as shown in Figure 16.5. This way, a small queue of customers is always in the system so that the servers can be kept fully utilized, but the increased spacing of appointment times later in the hour keeps the queue from getting large. If all customers do arrive approximately on time, none of them should have an unreasonable wait. Each hour the wave can start again.

   Wave schedules have been used successfully in medical settings such as clinics.[14] Obviously, the general principle can easily be modified to accommodate other situations.

Improving Reservation Systems

Appointments specify *when* customers will be served; **reservations**, on the other hand, allocate a fixed portion of capacity for a service provided at a given time, such as seats on an airplane or rooms in a hotel. The main problem is determining the number of reservations to offer. Because some customers with reservations do not show up, if the firm offers only as many reservations as it has capacity, some capacity will go unused even when demand exceeds capacity. For example, suppose an auto rental company had 100 autos available in Pittsburgh on a given day, and 120 customers called up asking to reserve an auto for that day. The company made 100 reservations and turned away the other 20 customers. If only 90 of the customers with reservations showed up, 10 autos would go unrented (assuming no walk-ins). By contrast, if the company had

[14]Stephen Smith, Bernard Schoer, and Robert Shannon, "Scheduling of Patients and Resources for Ambulatory Health Care, *Winter Simulation Conference Proceedings*, 1979, pp. 552–561.

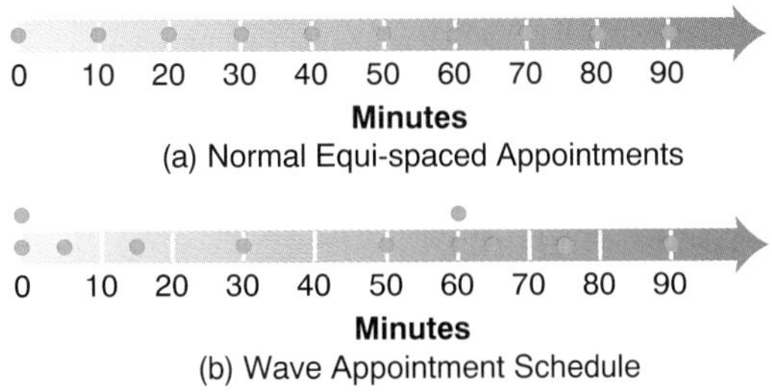

FIGURE 16.5 Normal and wave appointment schedules.

Effective reservation systems make it easier for auto rental companies to schedule the availability and location of their cars to meet their customer demands.

made 120 reservations and 108 customers showed up, it would have had 8 angry customers who thought an auto was waiting for them.

Companies can improve their reservation systems by using the first two suggestions for appointment systems: create incentives for showing up and remind people of their reservations. An increasing number of airlines, hotels, and auto rental companies are charging a no-show penalty.

The question still remains of how many reservations to make. The optimal amount of overbooking can be determined using an analysis similar to that for the one-period inventory problem described in Chapter 13. However, the overbooking problem is more difficult because demand (number of customers who show up) is affected by the number of reservations offered. Using computer simulation, it is relatively simple to compute the effect on net expected profit of different reservation limits. In fact, most airlines and hotel chains carefully analyze the probability that customers with reservations will show up, the cost of turning away a customer who has a reservation (including lost goodwill and harm to a company's reputation), and the probability of walk-in customers to fill open spots left by no-shows. From this analysis, they can determine the best number of reservations to offer. A detailed analysis of the problem is beyond the scope of this book, but a simplified version of such a simulation analysis is given in problem 11 at the end of Tutorial 3.

16.7 PERSONNEL SCHEDULING

Personnel scheduling is an ever-present operations management problem. For many service providers, such as police departments, retail stores, financial institutions, hair salons, and hospitals, production scheduling is almost inseparable from personnel scheduling. When production is steady over time, such as for a paper mill operating near capacity, personnel scheduling is relatively easy because fixed schedules can be established for workers and maintained for extended periods of time, possibly for years. However, when there are substantial variations in demand and production from day to day and during the course of the day, such as at retail stores or hospitals, efficient scheduling becomes more difficult. Yet in these types of service operations, where direct personnel costs are a large proportion of total costs, efficient personnel scheduling is also the key factor in profitability.

The goal of personnel scheduling is to schedule enough workers to meet the demand at any given time at minimum cost. A typical problem is the following.

EXAMPLE 8

Floor-Mart is a home furnishings retail store that is open from 10 A.M. to 10 P.M., seven days a week. The manager of Floor-Mart has divided each 12-hour workday into three 4-hour intervals and has estimated the number of employees needed during each interval for each day of the week as follows:

	Time		
Day	10–2	2–6	6–10
Sunday	12	15	6
Monday	4	6	8
Tuesday	4	7	9
Wednesday	5	7	10
Thursday	5	6	10
Friday	6	8	9
Saturday	14	16	11

The manager wants to devise a weekly schedule that minimizes his employee costs, but employees must (1) work exactly five consecutive days with two days off; (2) work eight consecutive hours per day, beginning at either 10 A.M. or 2 P.M.; and (3) begin work at the same time each day they work. Floor-Mart pays $300 per week per employee, but because it is more difficult to find employees willing to work on Sundays, any employee scheduled to work on Sunday receives a $25 weekly premium.

Various methods have been proposed to construct schedules for these types of problems. A simple method, and one that will provide an optimal solution, is to formulate and solve the problem as a linear programming problem. The trick to using linear programming in this case is the definition of the decision variables. For each possible schedule an employee can work (time of day and days of the week), a corresponding decision variable will represent the *number of employees* assigned to *that* work schedule. So we start by identifying all possible schedules. For example, one possible work schedule here is from 10 A.M. to 6 P.M. Monday through Friday; another is 2 P.M. to 10 P.M. Wednesday through Sunday. In total there are 14 possible schedules (variables) in this case (2 possible starting times × 7 possible starting days of a five-day schedule).

Suppose we define the variables as follows:

x_{ij} = the number of workers scheduled to begin work at time i, and day j is the first day of their five consecutive workdays.

So the variable $x_{2,Tu}$ is the number of people scheduled to work from 2 to 10 P.M. Tuesday to Saturday.

The next step is to formulate the objective function, which is to minimize the weekly labor cost:

$$\text{minimize } z = 325x_{10,Su} + 325x_{2,Su} + 300x_{10,M} + \ldots + 325x_{2,Sa}$$

Notice that each variable corresponding to an employee working on Sunday is multiplied by 325, while those variables that do not include a Sunday are multiplied by 300. (If all workers received the same pay regardless of the schedule, such as no weekend or night pay premium, the objective function could be simplified to minimizing the total number of workers scheduled.)

The only constraints in the problem are those that guarantee that at least the minimum number of workers required during each time period are actually scheduled. In this example there will be 21 constraints, one for each of the three four-hour. periods for each of the seven days. For example, the constraint guaranteeing that at least 12 employees will be scheduled to work from 10 A.M. to 2 P.M. on Sundays will be

$$x_{10,Su} + x_{10,W} + x_{10,Th} + x_{10,F} + x_{10,Sa} \geq 12$$

The left-hand side of the constraint adds up all workers who have Sunday as part of their schedules and who begin work at 10 A.M.; they will all work from 10 A.M. to 2 P.M. on Sunday. Similar constraints will exist for the 10-2 period for Monday through Saturday. The constraints for the 2 P.M. to 6 P.M. period are a bit more complicated because anyone who begins work at 10 A.M. or at 2 P.M. will be working from 2 to 6 P.M. that day. So, for example, the constraint that requires at least eight people to work from 2 to 6 P.M. on Friday will be

$$x_{10,M} + x_{2,M} + x_{10,Tu} + x_{2,Tu} + x_{10,W} + x_{2,W} + x_{10,Th} + x_{2,Th} + x_{10,F} + x_{2,F} \geq 8$$

Solving this problem using a linear programming computer package gives the following solution:

$$\begin{array}{ll} x_{10,Su} = 0 & x_{2,Su} = 0 \\ x_{10,M} = 0 & x_{2,M} = 2 \\ x_{10,Tu} = 2 & x_{2,Tu} = 5 \\ x_{10,W} = 4 & x_{2,W} = 0 \\ x_{10,Th} = 0 & x_{2,Th} = 3 \\ x_{10,F} = 0 & x_{2,F} = 0 \\ x_{10,Sa} = 8 & x_{2,Sa} = 3 \end{array}$$

A total of 27 people are scheduled, and the total weekly cost will be $8550. (This is not the only optimal solution; alternative ones exist.) Notice that no one is scheduled to work a Sunday–Thursday or Friday–Tuesday schedule. Also, notice that even though we did not explicitly require that the variables take on integer values (which would have made the problem an integer program and more difficult to solve; see Tutorial 1), this often occurs with scheduling problems, but it is not guaranteed. However, if the optimal variable values are fractional, we can often modify them through rounding and obtain a near-optimal solution.

As the number of scheduling options increases and the scheduling problems grow more complex, linear programming becomes an even more valuable tool. For example, suppose in Example 8 that split days off (e.g., having Monday and Thursday off) were allowed or that a certain percentage of part-time workers could be used. These cases can be handled readily by defining additional variables corresponding to these options and modifying the constraints. Similarly, 14-day or 28-day schedules can be accommodated. Linear programming is especially beneficial in developing schedules that integrate employees working four-day (10 hours per day) and five-day per week schedules.

Linear programming–based personnel scheduling methods have been used extensively in a variety of industries, including publishing, airlines, retail, and health care. With appropriate constraints and differential costs, personnel schedules can often be

The scheduling of police, paramedics, and firefighters is an important aspect of effective emergency service operations. Linear programming can help to develop schedules such that there are enough personnel on duty when needed, without leaving too many workers idle.

derived that not only minimize employer costs but also better suit employees, such as by eliminating or minimizing the number of workers with split shifts or split days off. For example, in this chapter's "In Good Company" feature, the objective in scheduling harbor pilots at Hampton Roads, Virginia, was to obtain fair and equitable schedules that satisfied the pilots' preferences for off-duty time.

IN GOOD COMPANY

Smooth Sailing in Hampton Roads

A small group of harbor pilots in the port of Hampton Roads, Virginia, wanted help in scheduling their on-duty, off-duty, and standby tours to provide them with both equitable working hours and a lot of free time. Since the harbor pilots' job is to guide larger ships through the crowded harbor 24 hours a day, year round, their schedule had to accommodate their customers' growing needs, as well as adhere to government regulations limiting the maximum number of consecutive duty hours.

The solution was a flexible rotation in which two-day units of time are distributed to give each pilot alternating on-duty/standby cycles interspersed with 6-day and 10-day off-duty periods. No two pilots are on the same schedule, so harbor coverage is assured.

Source: Marek Wermus and James Pope, "Scheduling Harbor Pilots," *Interfaces*, April–May 1994, pp. 44–52.

16.8 IMPLEMENTING PRODUCTION AND PERSONNEL SCHEDULING

Production and personnel scheduling can be highly complex and frequently is best accomplished using analytical heuristics or mathematical optimization techniques. In addition, we can improve scheduling using good information and the following commonsense principles:

1. ***Keep Work Standards Up to Date.*** All the analytical methods proposed in this chapter assume that the company can accurately estimate the times to set up and process jobs. This information is normally derived from work standards (see Chapter 10 for a discussion of methods for deriving work standards). Accurate, and up-to-date work standards form the foundation of most production and personnel scheduling procedures. If the standards are inaccurate, the resulting schedules may incur extra costs or delay deliveries.
2. ***Exploit the Power of Decision Support Systems.*** Analytical scheduling methods are normally part of a computer-based decision support system (DSS). The DSS contains a database module that can access various forms of data, such as historical demands, work standards, and production capacities. The DSS itself may contain various decision models and algorithms that forecast future requirements and construct production or personnel schedules. Many of the most successful scheduling DSSs allow human interaction with and modification of the model-generated schedules. User-friendly computer interface tools make it possible to visualize the model-generated schedules, to modify them easily and see the resulting effects, and to add or remove schedule requirements. The ease with which workers can use a scheduling system is a key determinant of the ultimate success of the system.[15]
3. ***Coordinate Short-Term and Aggregate Plans.*** The short-term scheduling options of a firm are dictated by the number and type of personnel, inventories, and equipment available. These are normally determined months in advance as part of the aggregate (intermediate-term) planning process (see Chapter 12). However, aggregate plans, by their nature, deal with *aggregate* units of production, such as the amount of each product family to produce during a given week or month. Short-term schedules must convert these aggregate plans into detailed day-by-day and hour-by-hour production plans for individual products that are consistent across products. For example, suppose a company makes 30 different products that are divided into three families of 10 products each. The aggregate plan may call for the company to produce 10,000 units of family A products and 5000 units of family B products during the next week, and then to produce another 10,000 units of family B products and 5000 units of family C products the following week. Within each week, production must be allocated to individual products within the families to be consistent with these plans. These short-term plans must take into consideration the expected *run-out time* (the time until current inventories are depleted) for each product, the costs and time required to change production runs among products and families, the economic lot sizes for individual products, and the total production time allocated to each product family by the aggregate plan. Analytical methods for doing this are complex and beyond the scope of this book, but they can be found in more advanced scheduling books.

[15]See V. L. Sauter, *Decision Support Systems*, Wiley, New York, 1997, for a detailed discussion of these systems.

SUMMARY

- Economic production lot sizes must normally be modified to achieve a consistent cyclic production schedule without product shortages.
- Common goals of batch production scheduling are to minimize average flow time, average inventories, and average job tardiness.
- Two batch production scheduling methods are static rules, which sequence the production of a given set of jobs, and dynamic dispatching rules, which at the completion of each job select the next production job to be run.
- For one-stage production systems, the **shortest processing time (SPT) rule** will always minimize average flow time and the average number of jobs in the system.
- For two-stage and some three-stage production systems, **Johnson's rule** will construct a sequence of jobs that minimizes the **make span** for a set of jobs.
- In multistage production systems where jobs are arriving over time (especially job shops and cellular systems), dynamic dispatching rules are commonly used.
- **Gantt charts** are a visual representation of start times for jobs to be processed at each production work station.
- **Optimized Production Technology (OPT)** is a scheduling system based on synchronous production that develops a schedule around the bottlenecks of the production system.
- The **assignment problem** can be used to assign a given set of jobs to a given set of machines, people, or teams.
- Because their products cannot be stored in inventory, service operations must be scheduled to accommodate peaks and valleys in demand. Differential pricing and promotion can smooth the peaks and valleys, and appointments and **reservations** can reduce customer waiting and turn-aways.
- Many personnel scheduling problems can be formulated and solved as linear programming problems. The key feature is that each decision variable corresponds to a possible employee schedule.

KEY TERMS

assignment problem **815**
critical ratio (CR) rule **804**
cyclic schedule **801**
dispatching (priority) rule **803**
earliest due date (EDD) rule **804**
flow time **803**
Gantt chart **813**
Hungarian method **816**
Johnson's rule **807**
make span **803**
Optimized Production Technology (OPT) **815**
reservations **820**
scheduling **798**
shortest processing time (SPT) rule **804**
slack time remaining (STR) rule **804**
tardiness **804**
wave schedule **820**

SOLVED PROBLEMS

Problem 1: A tile manufacturer makes four styles of tile, designated A–D. The annual demands, production rates, setup costs, holding costs, and ELSs (using equation (13.7)) are given below. Use the heuristic presented in Section 16.2 to construct a consistent cyclic schedule.

Tile	Demand (lb/yr)	Production Rate (lb/yr)	Setup Cost	Holding Cost (per lb/yr)	Economic Lot Size
A	60,000	900,000	$800	$0.10	32,071
B	300,000	1,200,000	$800	$0.12	73,030
C	250,000	1,100,000	$600	$0.09	65,679
D	350,000	1,100,000	$900	$0.14	81,240

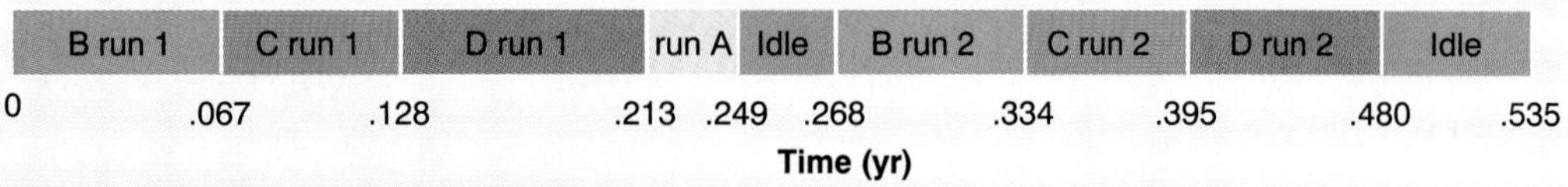

FIGURE 16.6 Production cycle for solved problem 1.

Solution:

1. For each product, we first compute the required time between runs: $T_i = ELS_i / D_i$: T_A = (32,071/60,000) = 0.535 yr; T_B = (73,030/300,000) = 0.243 yr; T_C = (65,679/250,000) = 0.263 yr; T_D = (81,240/350,000) = 0.232 yr. So T_{max} = 0.535 yr.
2. Dividing T_{max} by each T_i and rounding off gives $R_A = 1$, $R_B = R_C = R_D = 2$. These are the number of runs of each product in each production cycle.
3. The total production in each cycle for each product will be Q_A = 0.535 yr × 60,000 = 32,100; Q_B = 0.535 × 300,000 = 160,500; Q_C = 0.535 × 250,000 = 133,750; Q_D = 0.535 × 350,000 = 187,250. Each product will then be allocated the following amount of production time in each cycle: t_A = (32,100/900,000) = 0.036 yr; t_B = (160,500/1,200,000) = 0.133 yr; t_C = (133,750/1,100,000) = 0.122 yr; t_D = (187,250)/(1,100,000) = 0.170 yr.
4. Dividing the production of B, C, and D into two runs in each cycle gives the cycle shown in Figure 16.6.

Problem: 2: At an electronics repair shop all items are first diagnosed by an expert technician. He estimates the amount of repair work required and assigns it to a second technician for completion. The second technician has five jobs awaiting work, with the expected work time required and due date listed below. Construct job sequences using the SPT, EDD, STR, and CR rules, and compute the average flow time, average number of jobs in the system, average tardiness per job, and number of jobs tardy for each sequence.

Job	Expected Repair Time	Due Date
A	5.5	8
B	6.0	16
C	3.5	16
D	5.0	20
E	4.0	24

Solution: The schedules and performance measures for each rule are presented in Table 16.10.

Problem 3: Marine Electro-Plating has six customized electroplating jobs to process through its two-stage production system. The estimated processing times for the jobs at each stage are given below. Use Johnson's rule to construct a production sequence that minimizes the make span time.

Job	Stage 1	Stage 2
A	12	9
B	21	13
C	10	17
D	8	15
E	16	11
F	19	14

TABLE 16.10 SOLUTIONS FOR FOUR SEQUENCING RULES

	SPT		EDD		STR		CR	
Sequence	Job	Ends	Job	Ends	Job	Ends	Job	Ends
1	C	3.5	A	5.5	A	5.5	A	5.5
2	E	7.5	B	11.5	B	11.5	B	11.5
3	D	12.5	C	15.0	C	15.0	D	16.5
4	A*	18.0	D	20.0	D	20.0	C*	20.0
5	B*	24.0	E	24.0	E	24.0	E	24.0
Total flow time		65.5		76.0		76.0		77.5
Ave. flow time		13.1		15.2		15.2		15.5
Ave. no. of jobs in system		2.73		3.17		3.17		3.23
Ave. tardiness per job		3.6		0		0		0.8
Number of jobs tardy		2		0		0		1

*Indicates a tardy job. The make span is 24 for each sequence.

Solution:

1. We first select the job with the smallest stage time, which is 8 for job D. This time occurs at the first stage, so we make job D *first* in the sequence, and we delete D from our list.
2. We next select job A because it has a stage time of 9. This time occurs at the second stage, so we put A last in the sequence. The sequence is now D----A.
3. We now select job C, with a stage time of 10 hours. This time occurs at stage 1, so we put job C at the front of our sequence but after D. The sequence is now DC---A.
4. Continuing this process gives the sequence DCFBEA. The last job will finish at stage 2 at time 95, so the make span is 95.

Problem 4: The track and field coach of Chesterfield High School must assemble a medley relay team for a track meet. The relay race requires four runners to run "legs" of 200, 400, 800, and 1600 meters. The coach has five runners from whom to form the team and has estimated the likely running times for each runner for each distance as follows:

	Distance (m)				
Runner	200	400	800	1600	
Nancy	26	54	140	295	
Sue	27	59	147	325	
Jennifer	27	58	144	298	Times
Alex	25	53	139	300	in Seconds
Beth	29	60	142	305	

The coach must decide which four runners will be on the relay team and which race each will run.

Solution: Because we have more runners (jobs) to assign than races (machines), we create a dummy race to balance the assignment problem. For each runner, we assign a time of 0 seconds for the dummy race. So we obtain the cost (time) matrix presented in Table 16.11.

1. We begin by subtracting the smallest element in each row from each element in that row. (Because of the dummy race, this step does not change the matrix.) We then repeat this for each column, obtaining the matrix in Table 16.12a.
2. We now cover all the zeroes with as few straight lines as possible. We can do this with the three lines shown in Table 16.12a. We now subtract the smallest uncovered element "2" from

TABLE 16.11 INITIAL COST MATRIX

Runner	Distance 200	400	800	1600	Dummy
Nancy	26	54	140	295	0
Sue	27	59	147	325	0
Jennifer	27	58	144	298	0
Alex	25	53	139	300	0
Beth	29	60	142	305	0

TABLE 16.12

(a)
Reduced-Cost Matrix

Runner	Distance 200	400	800	1600	Dummy
Nancy	1	1	1	0	0
Sue	2	6	8	30	0
Jennifer	2	5	5	3	0
Alex	0	0	0	5	0
Beth	4	7	3	10	0

(b)
Second Cost Matrix

Runner	Distance 200	400	800	1600	Dummy
Nancy	1	1	1	0	2
Sue	0	4	6	28	0
Jennifer	0	3	3	1	0
Alex	0	0	0	5	2
Beth	2	5	1	8	0

(c)
Third Cost Matrix

Runner	Distance 200	400	800	1600	Dummy
Nancy	2	1	1	[0]	3
Sue	[0]	3	5	27	0
Jennifer	0	2	2	0	[0]
Alex	1	[0]	0	5	3
Beth	2	4	[0]	7	0

all other uncovered elements and add this amount to all elements at the intersection of two lines. The resulting matrix is given in Table 16.12b.

3. The zeroes in Table 16.12b can all be covered with only four lines, as shown. So we repeat the process of subtracting the smallest uncovered element (1) from all uncovered elements and adding this value to all elements at the intersection of lines, giving the matrix in Table 16.12c.
4. The zeroes in Table 16.12c cannot be covered with fewer than five lines, so the optimum assignment can be found. To obtain the optimum, we look for any row or column with only one

zero; the 400 column has only one zero, in the "Alex" row, so we assign Alex to the 400-meter race. We now delete the "400" column and the "Alex" row. The "Nancy" row has only one zero, in the "1600" column, so we assign Nancy to the 1600-meter run and delete this row and column. The "800" column now has only one zero, which is in the "Beth" row, so we assign Beth to the 800-meter race and delete that row and column. Each of the remaining rows and columns have two zeroes, indicating that there is more than one optimal assignment. We could assign either Sue or Jennifer to the 200-meter leg and have the other one sit out. The minimum expected time for the relay would then be 517 seconds.

Problem 5: Backyard Hotels maintains a nationwide reservation service 24 hours a day. Based on historical data, the reservations manager has *estimated staffing requirements as* follows:

Period	No. of Reservation Agents Needed
midnight to 4 A.M.	3
4 A.M. to 8 A.M.	6
8 A.M. to noon	13
noon to 4 P.M.	15
4 P.M. to 8 P.M.	12
8 P.M. to midnight	9

Employees work shifts of eight consecutive hours, and shifts can start at the beginning of any of the six periods shown. The manager has complete freedom in deciding the *number* of days each employee works each week, so she is interested only in knowing how many employees should start work at the beginning of each time period in order to minimize the total number of employees needed each day. (a) Formulate her problem as a linear program. (b) Solve the problem on a computer using a linear programming package.

Solution:

(a) Let x_j = the number of employees who begin work at the beginning of period j.
The objective function is then to

$$\text{minimize } z = x_1 + x_2 + \ldots + x_6$$

For each of the six time periods there will be a constraint:

$$x_1 + x_6 \geq 3$$
$$x_1 + x_2 \geq 6$$
$$x_2 + x_3 \geq 13$$
$$x_3 + x_4 \geq 15$$
$$x_4 + x_5 \geq 12$$
$$x_5 + x_6 \geq 9$$

and all the variables must be nonnegative.

(b) The optimal solution is x_1 = (number of employees working from midnight to 8 A.M.) = 5; x_2 = (number working from 4 A.M. to noon) = 1; $x_3 = 12$; $x_4 = 3$; $x_5 = 9$; x_6 (number working from 8 P.M. to 4 A.M.) = 0; $z = 30$ employees.

DISCUSSION AND REVIEW QUESTIONS

1. Why can a tightly connected flow production system, such as an assembly line, be treated as a one-machine system for scheduling purposes, even though the system may have 20 work stations in series?
2. What makes scheduling batch production systems more complex than scheduling tightly connected flow processes?
3. What is the difference between flow time and make span time?
4. Using an example, explain why a company may want to schedule jobs so as to minimize the make span time rather than some other criterion.
5. What is the difference between using rolling static schedules and using dynamic dispatching rules? What are the advantages of each method?
6. "Johnson's rule will produce the optimal sequence for a two-stage batch processing system." Is this statement true or false? Explain why or why not.
7. What makes scheduling a job-shop production system more difficult than scheduling a batch flow production system?
8. List the benefits of using Gantt charts for scheduling. Can Gantt charts be used with other scheduling methods, or must they be used alone?
9. Identify a problem, not mentioned in this chapter, for which the assignment method can be used to obtain an optimal solution.
10. Suppose a company had to schedule 10 jobs on four machines, and all jobs had to be assigned to one of the machines. Can this problem be solved using the Hungarian algorithm? Why or why not?
11. Suggest two ways in which companies can make their reservation systems function more effectively.
12. What should the decision variables be if we use linear programming to obtain personnel schedules?

PROBLEMS

1. Modern Fabrics manufacturers three types of cloth—denim, twill, and gabardine—on its new computer-controlled weaving system. The system can produce denim and twill at the rate of 240,000 square yards per year and gabardine at the rate of 280,000 square yards per year. Modern estimates the annual demand for its three products to be 30,000, 120,000, and 90,000 square yards, respectively. It costs \$2000 in setup costs to change products, and it costs \$1 per square yard per year to hold each cloth in inventory. (a) Compute the ELSs for the three products using equation (13.7). (b) Use the heuristic in Section 16.2 to construct a cyclic schedule for the three products; clearly identify the number of times each product will be run during a cycle and the lot sizes to use.
2. Plexi-Flex Glass Company (PFG) makes four types of shatterproof glass: 0.75-, 0.60-, 0.50-, and 0.25 inch thick. It can make only one type at a time and produces at the rate of 50,000, 60,000, 75,000, and 125,000 square feet per week, respectively. PFG estimates weekly demand for its four products to be 20,000, 10,000, 15,000, and 25,000 square feet, respectively. It costs \$1500 to set up production runs of the 0.75-, 0.60-, and 0.50-inch glasses and \$1000 to set up the 0.25-inch glass. The weekly holding costs per square foot for the glasses are \$0.20, \$0.15, \$0.12, and \$0.10, respectively. (a) Compute the ELSs for the four products using equation (13.7). (b) Use the heuristic in Section 16.2 to construct a cyclic schedule for the four products; clearly identify the number of times each product will be run during a cycle and the lot sizes to use.
3. Bright Expressions, a house painting contractor, has five houses to paint. Following are the estimated times required to paint each house and the due date for completion.

House	Estimated Time (days)	Due Date
Adams	2.5	8
Bradley	4.0	10
Chin	3.0	7
Dalton	5.0	14
Evans	2.0	16

(a) Use the SPT rule to sequence the five jobs. Compute the average flow time and average tardiness per job using this sequence. (b) Use the EDD rule to sequence the five jobs. Compute the average flow time and average tardiness per job using this sequence. (c) Use the CR rule to sequence the five jobs. Compute the average flow time and average tardiness per job using this sequence. (d) Use the STR rule to sequence the five jobs. Compute the average flow time and average tardiness per job using this sequence.

4. Robert Crump is a student at Pomville University. Robert has five term papers due soon, and he must decide in what order to complete them. Below are

the estimated number of days required to complete each paper and the due dates. Because all the instructors deduct 5 points per day for any term paper that is tardy, Robert wants to minimize tardiness. (a) Use the SPT, EDD, CR, and STR rules to sequence the jobs. Which one(s) results in the least average tardiness? (b) Which result(s) in the fewest tardy papers?

Course	Estimated Time (days)	Due Date
History	3.5	7
Finance	3.0	8
P/OM	6.0	12
Accounting	4.5	17
Math	2.5	16

5. Suppose a plastic parts manufacturer makes its products using two machines, 1 and 2. All jobs must be processed on machine 1 first and then on machine 2. The company currently has six jobs to run. The estimated processing times and due dates for these jobs are given below. (a) Determine the optimal sequence in which the jobs should be run to minimize the make span (i.e., minimize the completion time of the last job run). (b) Compute the make span time. (c) Compute the average job tardiness that results from the sequence in part (a).

	Processing Time (days)		
Job	Mach 1	Mach 2	Due Date from Now
A	5	9	41
B	4	6	38
C	7	10	37
D	8	8	52
E	12	9	47
F	9	6	41

6. Joe has five loads of laundry to do before he can go to the beach. Based on the colors and fabrics, he has estimated the washing and drying times for each load. All loads must first be washed and then dried. (Clothes that have been washed can sit in a basket waiting to go into the dryer so that the washer can be used.) (a) Use Johnson's rule to determine the sequence of loads to minimize the make span time. (b) When will Joe complete all the laundry?

	Processing Time		
Load	Washer	Dryer	
A	30	40	
B	25	35	
C	38	50	Times
D	40	20	(minutes)
E	32	45	

7. Suppose a company must process three jobs through a two-stage production process. The estimated processing times at each stage are as follows:

Job	Stage 1	Stage 2
A	10	5
B	2	20
C	6	6

(a) Use Johnson's rule to determine the sequence that minimizes the make span time. (b) Compute the make span and average flow time per job for the sequence in part (a). (c) Compute the make span and average flow time per job that results from the sequence CBA. Compare these values with the results in parts (a) and (b). What can we conclude from this result?

8. Suppose a company wanted to complete six jobs using a three-stage flow process with the stage times given below. Construct the sequence in which the jobs should be run to minimize the make span time.

	Stage Times (hr.)		
Job	Stage 1	Stage 2	Stage 3
A	9	12	17
B	13	7	14
C	14	10	15
D	10	9	20
E	15	11	13
F	8	5	15

9. The procedure used in problem 5 ignores due dates. Therefore, the company has decided to use a heuristic to schedule the jobs at each stage based on the remaining processing time for the job and the due date. Specifically, each machine is scheduled separately. At each machine, each time a machine becomes available (i.e., a job has finished on that machine) the jobs to be processed are sequenced based on which one has the smallest ratio of (time until due date)/(remaining total processing time for that job). (a) Compute the sequence that results from this heuristic (specify the sequence for each machine; it may not be the same on each machine). (b) Compute the tardiness for each job and the average tardiness for all the jobs using this critical ratio heuristic.

10. Suppose six jobs arrive at the packing department of a company at the times listed below. The packing department is the last stage before shipment. Assume that the estimated packing times and due dates are accurate.

Job	Arrival Time	Expected Packing Time	Due Date
A	0	14	23
B	0	17	28
C	13	23	50
D	26	18	82
E	48	12	64
F	51	15	92

(a) Use the dynamic versions of the SPT, EDD, CR, and STR rules to determine the sequence in which the jobs should be run (i.e., revise the sequence after the completion of each job, taking into account arrivals of new jobs). (b) Compute the average tardiness per job using each of the four dispatching rules. Which rule produces the least tardiness?

11. A company has five repair crews. Each crew has different skills and experience, and therefore their costs for service calls differ from job to job. The company has received calls from five customers requiring service. The service department manager has made the following estimates of how much it will cost to provide service for each customer with each service crew:

		Customer				
		A	B	C	D	E
	1	9	7	5	4	11
	2	6	8	7	8	10
Service	3	10	5	7	9	12
Crew	4	11	10	10	11	13
	5	6	8	8	6	11

Each crew can serve only one customer. The company wants to minimize the total service cost, and each customer must be serviced. Solve this problem using the Hungarian algorithm (or use a computer package). Clearly identify the optimal solution (i.e., which crew should serve which customer and what the total cost will be).

12. The operations management department of a university is moving into a new building. The chair of the department must assign her six faculty members to the six offices available. The chair has estimated the amount of criticism she will receive from each faculty member based on the office assigned to that member. (We will make the extreme assumption that a faculty member's satisfaction/dissatisfaction depends only on the office received, not on what offices other faculty members receive, i.e., no jealousy.) Use the Hungarian method (or a computer package) to determine the assignments that minimize total criticism for the department chair.

	Office					
Faculty	1	2	3	4	5	6
Anderson	10	20	0	15	40	30
Boyd	25	40	5	37	50	48
Ronen	5	4	0	2	15	10
Thomas	12	30	0	5	35	37
Oliver	40	50	10	30	60	70
Smith	22	24	0	16	13	40

13. The supervisor of orderlies at Metro Hospital must schedule orderlies during the day shift. Based on forecasts of patient admissions, the supervisor estimated that he will need the following number of orderlies each day of the week:

Day	No. of Orderlies Needed
Sunday	12
Monday	26
Tuesday	24
Wednesday	23
Thursday	23
Friday	26
Saturday	19

Orderlies receive \$350 per week plus a \$25 bonus for each Saturday or Sunday worked. The supervisor wants to determine the number of orderlies to work each schedule, but all orderlies must work five consecutive days and have two days off (assume weekly schedules will repeat, so an employee who begins work on Thursday will work Thursday, Friday, Saturday, Sunday, and Monday). (a) Formulate the supervisor's problem as a linear program to minimize total costs. (b) (Computer exercise) Solve the problem formulated in part (a) using a computer package, and clearly indicate the optimal number of orderlies who should work each schedule.

CASE

Home Helper Discount: A Scheduling Case

Home Helper Discount (HHD) is a family-owned retailer that specializes in home repair and garden products. Since its inception, HHD has been known for its enlightened personnel and work policies. Almost all employees are cross-trained and receive above-average salaries and annual bonuses based on company profits. In addition, the company has maintained a no-layoff policy. As part of its continuous improvement program, the company uses an employee suggestion system, and it regularly polls its employees regarding various work-related issues.

In 1994 the Suggestion Evaluation Committee received several notes recommending that the company convert from a 5-day per week, 8-hour per day work schedule to a 4-day per week, 10-hour per day schedule. The committee decided to poll employees to see whether they would prefer this change. Over 70% were in favor. Among those against it, the two most common reasons were concerns that it might cost the company more money by reducing scheduling flexibility, and that it would be difficult to coordinate work schedules with spouses and arrange for child care.

The proposal was brought to the company's management, with a summary of perceived advantages and disadvantages. The primary advantage was improved employee morale, with possibly higher productivity resulting from giving employees a schedule they preferred. The two main disadvantages were the concerns expressed above. HHD's management agreed to create a five-person team to study the issue.

Original Schedule

The team first met with the store manager and associate managers to determine how they currently scheduled employees. Chris Templeton, the store manager and part owner, was primarily in charge of employee scheduling. Chris explained that he collected extensive data on the number of customers entering the store and making purchases, the number of deliveries received from suppliers, and the subsequent shelf stocking required on an hourly and a daily basis. From this information, he estimated the number of employees needed during each two-hour period the store was open. Because employees were cross-trained, Chris scheduled only the times employees worked; then during the day the associate managers assigned specific workers to jobs (checking, stocking, loading dock, etc.) according to the immediate needs.

The store's operating hours are 9 A.M. to 9 P.M. Monday through Saturday and 11 A.M. to 9 P.M. Sunday. Although employee schedules vary during the year, HHD keeps them as stable as possible. Based on employee requests, each employee is scheduled to work five consecutive days and then take two days off, and employees start and end work at the same time each day unless they are asked to work overtime. Employees start work at either 9 A.M., 11 A.M., or 1 P.M., and they work eight consecutive hours.

Chris Templeton provided the team with the data in Table 16.13, giving his estimates of the number of employees needed in each two-hour period during a typical week. Chris also provided the schedule in Table 16.14, which is the one he used most often to satisfy these requirements. After a year of refining the schedule, Chris reduced the total number of scheduled employees to approximately 80 each week; an additional 5 employees were normally on vacation or not working due to requested days off.

Employees earn approximately \$400 per week including fringe benefits, and they receive a bonus of \$25 for each Saturday or Sunday worked (so someone working a Thursday–Monday schedule would earn \$450 per week). Consequently, the weekly payroll cost for the 80 employees scheduled in Table 16.14 is \$34,975. In addition, even though this schedule results in periods when more employees are scheduled than necessary (because of the wide variations in requirements among periods and days), there are times when employees are asked to work

TABLE 16.13 EMPLOYEE REQUIREMENTS FOR HOME HELPER DISCOUNT

Hours	Sunday	Monday	Tuesday	Wednesday	Thursday	Friday	Saturday
9-11	12*	14	13	16	16	18	24
11–1	27	22	19	23	22	24	39
1–3	38	13	14	24	20	25	43
3–5	36	21	20	25	26	28	41
5–7	21	23	21	25	27	24	29
7–9	19	25	22	26	28	26	33

*The store is not open, but employees are used to stock and clean the store.

TABLE 16.14 NORMAL SCHEDULE FOR HHD

Sun9 = 0	Sun11 = 0	Sun1 = 0	
Mon9 = 3	Mon11 = 0	Mon1 = 5	
Tue9 = 12	Tue11 = 0	Tue1 = 13	
Wed9 = 8	Wed11 = 0	Wed1 = 0	Total employees scheduled = 80
Thu9 = 7	Thu11 = 8	Thu1 = 12	
Fri9 = 4	Fri11 = 0	Fri1 = 0	Weekly payroll cost = $34,975
Sat9 = 0	Sat11 = 0	Sat1 = 8	

Notes:
The first three letters identify the first day of five consecutive days worked.
The number identifies the starting time for an eight-hour shift.
The number after the = sign is the number of employees assigned to that schedule.

overtime due to employee absences, sales, holidays, or demand changes; as a result, HHD has spent an average of $2000 per week on overtime pay.

Devising and Evaluating Alternative Schedules

The team's first step was to determine whether it was possible to devise four-day per week schedules that would satisfy the requirements in Table 16.13 without incurring higher labor costs. The team also wanted to develop a method for changing schedules easily. Chris Templeton claimed that modifying his normal schedule in Table 16.14 took so long, and was so difficult, that he often ended up simply making "seat of the pants" changes and then using overtime work to fill in any shortages. Two team members were familiar with linear programming, and they suggested that a linear programming model be used to devise employee schedules. Before developing four-day per week schedules, they considered the current policy of having employees work five days per week, eight hours per day.

Under the original policies, there were 21 possible schedules an employee could work: three different starting times (9 A.M., 11 A.M., and 1 P.M.) times seven possible starting days for a five-day sequence. The objective function was to minimize the payroll costs for scheduled employees. Finally, every two-hour period each day of the week required a constraint to ensure that at least the minimum number of employees needed were scheduled; this resulted in 42 constraints. The linear programming formulation of this problem was as follows:

Variables

xxxy = number of employees scheduled to work five consecutive days beginning with day *xxx*, beginning work at time *y*, and working eight hours

Objective Function

minimize $z = 425$ Sun9 + 425 Sun11 + 425 Sun1 + 400 Mon9 + . . . + 450 Sat1

Constraints

Sun9 + Wed9 + Thu9 + Fri9 + Sat9 ≥ 10 (Sunday 9–11 requirement)

Sun9 + Sun11 + Wed9 + Wed11 + . . . + Sat9 + Sat11 ≥ 27 (Sunday 11–1)

. . . . . .

Tue11 + Tue1 + Wed11 + Wed1 + . . . + Sat11 + Sat1 ≥ 29 (Saturday 5–7)

Tue1 + Wed1 + Thu1 + Fri1 + Sat1 ≥ 33 (Saturday 7–9)

The optimal solution to this problem had fractional values for some of the variables. Therefore, it was resolved as an integer program (variables were forced to take on integer values). The optimal solution is given in Table 16.15. This solution required only 77 employees to be scheduled rather than 80, and the payroll cost for the scheduled employees was $1200 a week less. So even if HHD did not change to four-day per week scheduling, the project team had identified a more cost-effective schedule and, more important, a scheduling method.

The next step, however, was to evaluate the consequences for employees of moving to a four-day schedule. The same linear programming model was formulated, with only minor modifications. Notice, however, that with the longer days there are only 14 variables because employees can begin work only at 9 or 11 A.M.

Variables

xxxy = number of employees scheduled to work four consecutive days beginning with day *xxx*, beginning work at time *y*, and working 10 hours

TABLE 16.15 OPTIMAL FIVE-DAY WORK WEEK SCHEDULE FOR HHD

Sun9 = 0	Sun11 = 0	Sun1 = 0	
Mon9 = 0	Mon11 = 0	Mon1 = 5	
Tue9 = 12	Tue11 = 0	Tue1 = 13	
Wed9 = 5	Wed11 = 0	Wed1 = 0	Total employees scheduled = 77
Thu9 = 7	Thu11 = 8	Thu1 = 12	
Fri9 = 1	Fri11 = 0	Fri1 = 0	Weekly payroll cost = $33,775
Sat9 = 6	Sat11 = 0	Sat1 = 8	

Objective Function

minimize $z = 425\ \text{Sun9} + 425\ \text{Sun11} + 400\ \text{Mon9} + \ldots + 450\ \text{Sat11}$

Constraints[16]

$\text{Sun9} + \text{Thu9} + \text{Fri9} + \text{Sat9} \geq 10$ (Sunday 9-11 requirement)

$\text{Sun9} + \text{Sun11} + \text{Thu9} + \text{Thu11} + \ldots \text{Sat9} + \text{Sat11} \geq 27$ (Sunday 11–1)

. . . . . .

$\text{Wed9} + \text{Wed11} + \text{Thur9} + \text{Thur11} + \ldots + \text{Sat9} + \text{Sat11} \geq 29$ (Saturday 5–7)

$\text{Wed11} + \text{Thu11} + \text{Fri11} + \text{Sat11} \geq 33$ (Saturday 7–9)

The optimal solution for this model also had fractional values for the variables, so it was re-solved as an integer program; the optimal solution is given in Table 16.16.

The optimal solution for the four-day schedule actually required fewer employees than the optimal five-day schedule, and the weekly payroll cost was $1400 less ($2600 less than Chris Templeton's original schedule). On studying the solutions, the team found that even though the 10-hour day reduced scheduling flexibility somewhat (there were two rather than three starting times each day), the four-day week increased the day-to-day flexibility enough to more than compensate for this change. HHD's original assumption that the four-day schedule would increase payroll costs and require more workers was wrong. This result eliminated one of the two major concerns about the four-day schedule.

The second issue, possible child-care problems, was next. After polling the employees, the team found that 20–25 of them regularly used child-care services but only 8–10 felt they might have occasional child-care problems with the four-day schedule—mainly the cost of covering child-care for an extra hour or two until the employee or spouse arrived home from work. This cost could be up to $40 per week, depending on the time of day. On the other hand, the employees noted that they would be home an additional day each week, which could eliminate an entire day's worth of child-care expense. Some employees suggested that if HHD helped with the extra expense of child care, they would be happy to change to a four-day work-week. The team agreed to take this issue to HHD's top management.

Implemented Solution

The team met with HHD's top management, demonstrated the linear (integer) programming model, and showed how four-day schedules would reduce the number of employees needed to staff the store and lower payroll costs. The team had set up a simple system on a microcomputer so that Chris Templeton or anyone else could simply enter the period-by-period personnel requirements and the weekly costs for each employee schedule, and the computer (using a $100 computer package) would solve the problem in less than a minute. The team pointed out, however, that the $2600 per week cost savings over the original schedule occurred because five fewer employees were needed. HHD's management said this was actually a timely blessing, because HHD had decided to open another store and wanted some experienced employees to work there. So HHD could painlessly reduce the staff at the original store by five people and hire additional workers as well.

As for the child-care issue, rather than trying to determine which employees would incur additional child-care costs due to the schedule change, the president offered an across-the-board benefit for all employees: HHD would reimburse each employee up to $40 per week for child-care expenses (if receipts were provided). Assuming no more than 25 employees would file for this benefit, it

[16]There are 42 constraints, but they can be reduced to 21. On any given day, the constraints for the periods 11–1, 1–3, 3–5, and 5–7 are identical on the left-hand side; only the right-hand-side constants differ. So these four constraints can be replaced by one constraint, with the right-hand side being the largest personnel requirement of these four periods on that day. This simplification cut HHD's solution time for the model by more than half.

TABLE 16.16 OPTIMAL FOUR-DAY WORK WEEK SCHEDULE FOR HHD

Sun9 = 2	Sun11 = 4	
Mon9 = 1	Mon11 = 7	
Tue9 = 2	Tue11 = 2	
Wed9 = 12	Wed11 = 13	Total employees scheduled = 75
Thu9 = 1	Thu11 = 6	
Fri9 = 3	Fri11 = 5	Weekly payroll cost = $32,375
Sat9 = 8	Sat11 = 9	

would cost HHD no more than $1000 per week, well below the anticipated savings from the new schedules.

After implementing the four-day schedule and the new child-care benefit, HHD tracked its costs and monitored employee opinion. Surveys found that the employees were extremely happy with the change, and productivity seemed to improve. Weekly payroll costs not only decreased by the $2600 anticipated, but because revising the schedules was so easy, Chris Templeton was more willing to make changes during the year as customer traffic changed. The more efficient scheduling resulted in $1000 per week less overtime pay at the store. Finally, the actual child-care reimbursement program was costing approximately $700 per week.

The bottom line was that HHD was saving nearly $150,000 per year after the changes. Employees were happier not only with their jobs, but also with the additional profit-sharing bonuses.

QUESTIONS

1. Suppose HHD could assign employees to work any set of hours and days of the week (e.g., an employee could be scheduled to work two hours on Monday, six hours on Wednesday, etc.). Compute (or approximate) the absolute minimum weekly payroll cost that could be achieved with this complete flexibility. How much would HHD save compared to the schedule in Table 16.16?
2. Even with the cost savings computed in question 1, why would HHD probably not schedule employees this way?
3. Suppose employees had to work the same eight consecutive hours, five days per week, but HHD could give split days off (say, Monday and Thursday). Describe how this would change the linear programming model.

SELECTED READINGS

AKINC, U. "A Practical Approach to Lot and Setup Scheduling at a Textile Firm," IIE *Transaction*, Vol. 25, No. 2, 1993, pp. 54–64.

BAKER, K. R. *Introduction to Sequencing and Scheduling*, Wiley, New York, 1974.

———. "The Effects of Input Control in Simple Scheduling Problem," *Journal of Operations Management*, Vol. 4, 1984, pp. 99–112.

BAUSCH, D., G. BROWN, and D. RONEN. "Consolidating and Dispatching Truck Shipments of Mobil Heavy Petroleum Products," *Interfaces*, Vol. 25, No. 2, 1995, pp. 1–24.

DIAZ, ADENSO, ET AL. "A Dynamic Scheduling and Control System in an NSIDEA Steel Plant," *Interfaces*, Vol. 21, No. 5, 1991, pp 53–62.

FOX, R. E., "OPT—an Answer for America, Part II," *Inventories and Production Magazine*, Vol. 2, No. 6, 1982, pp. 10–19.

GERSHKOFF, I. "Optimizing Flight Crew Schedules," *Interfaces*, Vol 19, No. 4, 1989, pp. 29–43.

GRAVES, S. "A Review of Production Scheduling," *Operations Research*, Vol. 29, 1981, pp. 646–675.

JOHNSON, S. M. "Optimal Two and Three Stage Production Schedules with Set-up Time Included," *Naval Research Logistics Quarterly*, Vol. 1, 1954, pp. 61–68.

MORTON, THOMAS, and DAVID PENTICO. *Heuristic Scheduling Systems*, Wiley, New York, 1993.

NANDA, RAVINDER, and JIM BROWNE. *Introduction to Employee Scheduling*, Van Nostrand Reinhold, New York, 1992.

RICHTER, H. "Thirty Years of Airline Operations Research," *Interfaces*, Vol. 19, No. 4, 1989, pp. 3–9.

SMITH, L. D., R. M. NAUSS, and D. A. BIRD, "Decision Support for Bus Operations in a Mass Transit System," *Decision Sciences*, Vol. 21, 1990, pp. 183–203.

SUBRAMANIAN, RADHIKA, ET AL. "Coldstart: Fleet Assignment at Delta Air Lines," *Interfaces*, Vol. 24, No. 1, 1994, pp. 104–120.

VOLLMANN, THOMAS, WILLIAM BERRY, and D. CLAY WHYBARK. *Manufacturing Planning and Control Systems*, (3rd ed.), Homewood, IL, Richard D. Irwin, 1992.

WERMUS, M., and J. A. POPE. "Scheduling Harbor Pilots," *Interfaces*, Vol. 24, No. 2, 1994, pp. 44–52.

CHAPTER 17

PROJECT PLANNING AND SCHEDULING

17.1 PRODUCING UNIQUE PRODUCTS
On the Job: Mike Sargenti, Service Construction Company

17.2 THE CHARACTERISTICS OF A PROJECT AND THE ROLE OF THE PROJECT MANAGER
Project Environments
Challenges of the Project Manager
Benefits of Project Work

17.3 DATA COLLECTION AND ANALYSIS
Dividing the Project Into Tasks
Identifying Precedence Relationships
Estimating Task Times
Data Collection as an Iterative Process

17.4 PROJECT SCHEDULING: GANTT CHARTS

17.5 NETWORK-BASED PROJECT SCHEDULING METHODS: PERT/CPM
In Good Company: Software Charms the Viper at Chrysler Corporation
Activity-on-Arc Convention
Activity-on-Node Convention
Which Convention to Use

17.6 COMPUTING THE PROJECT COMPLETION TIME AND CRITICAL PATH
The Two-Pass Method
Finding the Critical Path

17.7 IMPROVING THE PROJECT SCHEDULE: TIME–COST TRADE-OFFS
Crashing
Optimizing the Time–Cost Trade-offs

17.8 PROBABILISTIC TASK TIME ESTIMATES
Probability Distribution For Task Times
Deriving the Probability Distribution for Project Completion Time
Answering Probabilistic Questions
Validity of Assumptions and Simulation

17.9 MONITORING PROJECTS USING PERT/CPM

17.10 IMPLEMENTATION AND USE OF PROJECT SCHEDULING METHODS

Flood Relief Concert: A Project Planning Case

17.1 PRODUCING UNIQUE PRODUCTS

Most operations are repetitive and routine. Even job-shop production systems, which may produce hundreds of different products, normally make hundreds or thousands of units of each product at a time. The preceding chapters have focused on the design and operation of such systems. In this chapter we turn to production systems that make one-of-a-kind products called **projects**. Project processes are used to construct buildings, to develop computer software, to introduce new products, or to perform consulting studies. Projects normally utilize an inherently different production system than other types of products. Although they can range in magnitude from small consulting studies to multi-billion-dollar construction projects involving thousands of people, projects have several characteristics in common:

1. They require a wide variety of tasks or activities (possibly thousands), some of which can be performed concurrently and others consecutively.
2. There are usually tight time and budget limits.
3. Resources can be reallocated among tasks to affect performance time.

Successful completion of large-scale projects requires the management of personnel with a wide variety of skills, such as engineers, designers, lawyers, laborers, and skilled craft workers. How to select, supervise, motivate, and communicate with this array of workers is not the subject of this chapter, but several books listed in this chapter's Selected Readings address these issues. This chapter deals with the planning, scheduling, and monitoring of projects.

One of the most difficult challenges facing a project manager, such as Mike Sargenti, the subject of this chapter's "On the Job" segment, is coordinating the various tasks and resources so that the project can be completed on time and within budget. The methods presented in this chapter were initially developed to manage large-scale projects, but they are equally applicable and widely used for small-scale projects as well.

ON THE JOB

MIKE SARGENTI, SERVICE CONSTRUCTION CO.

Hard hats are common on construction sites, but wearing them is only one aspect of Mike Sargenti's job. "We wear a lot of hats," says Mike, a project manager for Service Construction Company. Mike, who has a degree in finance from Lemoyne College, is responsible first of all for getting new clients for Service, a nationwide construction company that provides everything from design and construction to repair and maintenance of retail stores and office buildings. From the inception of a new project to its completion, Mike also manages the activities of Service's network of subcontractors, including electricians, plumbers, drywall workers, and other crews, providing "one-stop shopping" for his clients. A constant stream of reports from the client and the subcontractors keeps Mike up-to-date on the progress and quality of each project.

Mike coordinates all the construction activities necessary to meet the client's needs, including cost estimating, quality assurance checks, scheduling of labor and resources, billing, and following up to ensure customer satisfaction. With activities of this depth and breadth, Mike is able to serve companies with locations across the country, providing everything from routine filter replacements to construction of new stores.

We begin this chapter by briefly discussing the role of the project manager, as well as some of the difficulties the manager and other workers may face. The remainder of the chapter is devoted to scheduling the project and coordinating activities. Section 17.3 describes the data required to plan projects well. Sections 17.4–17.8 describe analytical tools, such as Gantt charts and network-based methods, used to schedule projects. Section 17.9 describes how these methods can be used to monitor, as well as plan, projects. Section 17.10 is concerned with the implementation of project-scheduling tools.

17.2 THE CHARACTERISTICS OF A PROJECT AND THE ROLE OF THE PROJECT MANAGER

During the early stages of the project life cycle a project manager must be appointed, resources gathered, and commitment of workers obtained. At this point, the project goals and desired final product must be clearly specified. The final product may be a building, a functioning piece of computer software with written documentation, a consultant's or auditor's report, the successful startup of a production process, or the introduction of a new product. Not clearly specifying the deliverable product will almost surely lead to problems later on. The availability of resources, the project deadline, and the authority of and restrictions on the project manager must be established. Once these are known, the project manager must plan, coordinate, and monitor the project's activities.

PROJECT ENVIRONMENTS

Companies in construction, consulting, book publishing, and software development perform most of their work in the form of projects. Personnel are organized around project production processes: Projects are managed by full-time project managers (such as Mike Sargenti), workers are evaluated by project managers, and they work with the expectation that when one project is done there will be additional projects to do.

In organizations where the primary products are made using other types of production structures, projects may occur as special events. For example, converting to a new accounting system represents a distinct project involving dozens or hundreds of tasks and the coordination of many people. Similarly, the design and introduction of a new automobile model is a project that requires a production process distinct from the manufacturing process that will eventually produce the automobiles.

CHALLENGES OF THE PROJECT MANAGER

Every project should be assigned a project manager who is responsible for obtaining and managing the needed resources, coordinating activities and personnel, scheduling and monitoring progress, and ultimately bearing the responsibility for the success or failure of the project. Even under the best conditions this is not an easy job. Coordinating people and tasks on a dynamic basis, however, can be made much easier with analytical planning tools; these tools are the focus of subsequent sections of this chapter.

Although managing projects is always a challenge, in an organization that is already project oriented it is less difficult than in other organizations. In project-oriented organizations, workers recognize that their work will focus mainly on projects and that they will move from project to project. Workers with specific expertise, such as mechanical engineering, may officially be part of the mechanical engineering department of the company, but because they are always working on projects, they have few ties to that department. Rather, they receive job satisfaction and are evaluated primarily on their project work. The project manager therefore has less need to motivate, coax, or coerce workers to participate in the project.

In contrast, managing special projects in a company that is not project focused, such as a hospital, furniture manufacturer, or bank, requires the project manager to obtain workers on loan from other departments and to motivate them to devote their best efforts to the project. This presents several challenges and possible conflicts between the project manager and the heads of functional departments. The project manager would like to have the best possible workers for the project. But of course, the department heads do not want to give up the services of their best people.

Workers themselves are often reluctant to participate in projects for two reasons. First, working on a project creates two bosses—the project manager and the supervisor of the worker's home department, who still controls performance evaluation, pay, and future promotions. Therefore, workers borrowed for a project will often have limited commitment to it. Second, workers appointed full-time to long-term projects are concerned about having a job to return to when the project ends. Few workers want to take this risk unless the project promises compensating rewards.

These factors make the job of a project manager difficult. Normally, the manager has little authority to decide who will work on the project and only limited authority and control over project personnel. He or she must persuade supervisors to lend some of their best workers to the project, as well as persuade and motivate project workers to join the project and commit themselves to it.

BENEFITS OF PROJECT WORK

Despite these drawbacks, project managers can make the work attractive in many ways. First, projects provide a change of environment. Because they involve unique products, they take employees away from the repetitive, mundane aspects of their regular work. The interdisciplinary nature of projects also allows employees to learn about other people and other areas of the company. For a person interested in making an intracompany job change, working on a project can be an excellent way of learning about other opportunities within the company and making personal contacts that can help land a position.

Project work can also be intrinsically exciting. Many projects are initiated to accomplish some important goal of the organization: introduce a new product, reorganize some aspect of the company, or investigate a new area of growth. A successful project can show project workers that their efforts have had a strategic impact on the organization. It can also open up employment opportunities in growth areas of the organization. For example, if the project is to evaluate where the company should open a new division in a foreign country, members of the project team are often in the best position to be appointed to jobs in the new division.

Once the goals and resources have been established and the personnel selected, the project manager must move to the next phases of the project: (1) data collection and analysis, (2) planning and scheduling, and (3) executing and monitoring project tasks and delivering the final product.

17.3 DATA COLLECTION AND ANALYSIS

To complete the project on time and within budget, a project manager must have the right people, materials, and equipment available in the right place at the right time. For example, if we are constructing a house, we do not want the roofers to show up at the construction site to put on the shingles before the roof has been constructed. The manager must have an accurate schedule of when each task is expected to begin and end. To develop that schedule, the manager must first obtain information about the project.

DIVIDING THE PROJECT INTO TASKS

A crucial first step is to decompose the project into individual tasks or activities (we will use these words interchangeably). A **task** or **activity** represents an identifiable unit of work that is performed by a single individual or group of workers, with a clear beginning and end. For example, in constructing a house, a task might be to paint the exterior. This would be done by a team of painters, and it would be clear when painting begins and ends. For a maintenance project, such as overhauling a piece of machinery, a task might be to replace the bearings on the drive shaft.

IDENTIFYING PRECEDENCE RELATIONSHIPS

A project manager must determine which tasks must be completed before other tasks can begin and, implicitly, which tasks can be done concurrently. For example, in preparing this textbook, the task of reviewing and editing Chapters 1–5 could be performed concurrently with writing Chapters 6–10. The first task was performed by one set of workers (professors and an editor) while the second task was being done by the author. However, the task of typesetting the final version of Chapter 1 could not be started until the task of writing it was completed by the author. If all the tasks in preparing this book had to be done consecutively, it would have taken 20 years to complete it. Instead, with many people working concurrently on different tasks, it was completed much more quickly.

Determining precedence relationships is best done in conjunction with defining the project tasks. The reason is that sometimes it may seem that task B cannot begin until task A is complete when B could actually begin once A is half complete. In this case we would decompose A into two tasks, A1 and A2. Then B could begin when A1 is completed, and A2 and B could be done concurrently. For example, a team developing a factory simulation model may be able to begin constructing a prototype system once some preliminary data are collected without waiting for all the data to be obtained. In this case, data collection can be divided into two subtasks.

ESTIMATING TASK TIMES

Frequently, the amount of time required to perform a task depends on the amount of money and other resources that are devoted to it. By using more workers or equipment or by working overtime, we can complete many tasks more quickly. It is therefore common to make a range of estimates. Typically, a normal task time is estimated assuming

Tasks must be well-planned and coordinated using accurate task time estimates in order to complete construction projects on time.

some normal level of resource commitment. Estimates of the cost to reduce the task time, called the *crash cost*, and the minimum task time possible, called the *crash time*, may also be made to evaluate the desirability of reallocating resources among tasks. Task times can also be highly uncertain (even with a fixed set of resources), so in some cases we estimate probability distributions for the task times rather than single numbers. Methods to incorporate task costs and random task times into project scheduling are discussed in Sections 17.7 and 17.8.

DATA COLLECTION AS AN ITERATIVE PROCESS

Defining tasks and gathering task information is an iterative process, and if done correctly, it can be instructive for those who will be supervising or working on the various tasks. One approach is to have task supervisors complete simple forms, such as the one in Figure 17.1, concerning their proposed tasks. The task supervisors can determine which tasks must be complete or partially complete before they can begin their tasks.

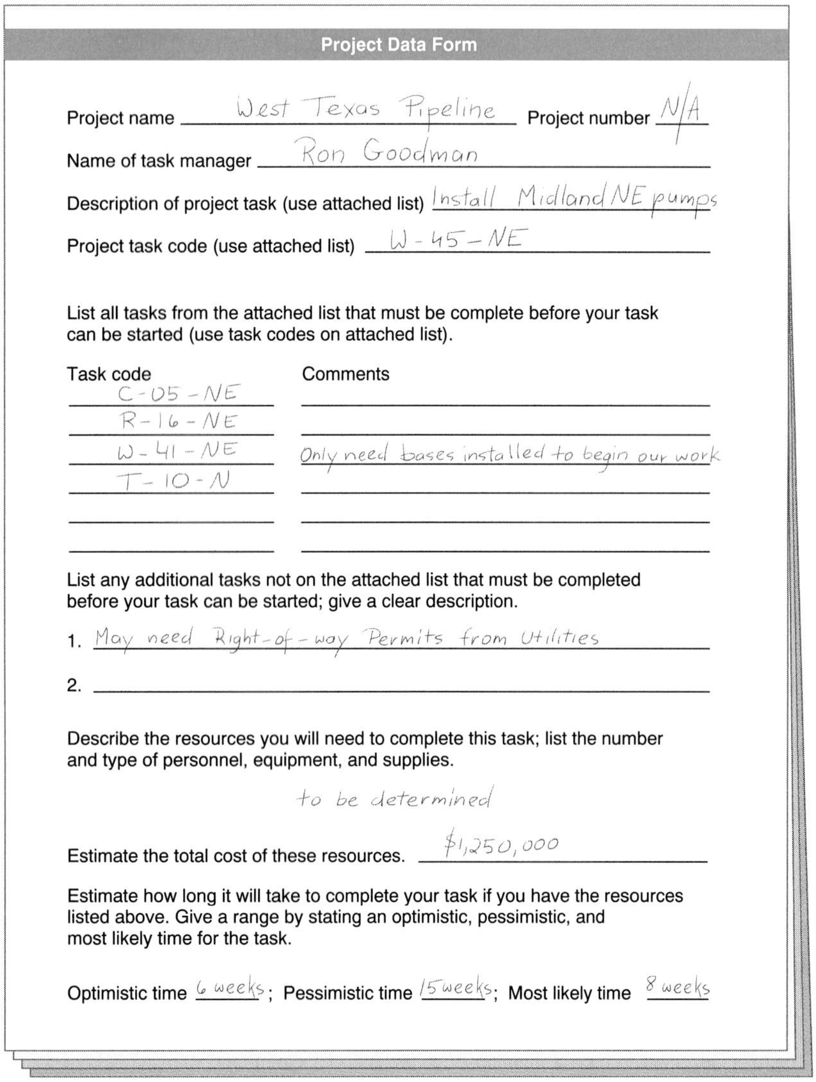

Project Data Form

Project name West Texas Pipeline Project number N/A

Name of task manager Ron Goodman

Description of project task (use attached list) Install Midland NE pumps

Project task code (use attached list) W-45-NE

List all tasks from the attached list that must be complete before your task can be started (use task codes on attached list).

Task code	Comments
C-05-NE	
R-16-NE	
W-41-NE	Only need bases installed to begin our work
T-10-N	

List any additional tasks not on the attached list that must be completed before your task can be started; give a clear description.

1. May need Right-of-way Permits from Utilities
2.

Describe the resources you will need to complete this task; list the number and type of personnel, equipment, and supplies.

to be determined

Estimate the total cost of these resources. $1,250,000

Estimate how long it will take to complete your task if you have the resources listed above. Give a range by stating an optimistic, pessimistic, and most likely time for the task.

Optimistic time 6 weeks; Pessimistic time 15 weeks; Most likely time 8 weeks

FIGURE 17.1 Project data form.

They can also specify the resources they need and estimate the task times. This exercise, when combined with the critical path scheduling methods discussed later, can be enlightening—and sometimes hair-raising.

For example, this process was used to plan a major pipeline project. After each task supervisor returned his data form, the minimum project completion time and cost estimates were computed. The resulting completion time was over 200 years, quite a bit more than the hoped-for 4 years, and the cost was several times higher than originally anticipated. These large disparities quickly got everyone's attention, and the data forms and schedule were carefully reviewed. One fact that became clear was that many task supervisors wanted almost every other related aspect of the project completed before they began their tasks. Needless to say, this would delay the project. Supervisors also were padding their resource requests to guarantee that they would not run over budget. After these issues were discussed and management identified clear problem areas, the supervisors were asked to repeat the process.

The second iteration reduced the project completion time to 40 years and lowered the projected cost substantially, but both were still unacceptably large. After several more iterations of the process, a cost-effective four-year schedule was achieved. One result of this process was that the supervisors gained a much better understanding of the importance of keeping their tasks on schedule because they could see how their tasks affected the time when other tasks could begin.[1]

17.4 PROJECT SCHEDULING: GANTT CHARTS

Once the project tasks, precedence relationships, and time estimates are known, the next step is to use them to devise a schedule. For simple projects Gantt charts, similar to those discussed in the previous chapter, can be useful. A **Gantt chart** is a bar chart along a time axis that illustrates the planned starting and completion times for each task. For example, Figure 17.2 is a Gantt chart for the project described in Table 17.1, which is to reorganize and move a credit operation to a new location. The primary advantage of Gantt charts is their visual appeal. We can easily see when a task is supposed to begin and end and whether or not it is on schedule.

However, Gantt charts have several disadvantages. First, they do not show the precedence relationships among the tasks. For example, in Figure 17.2 tasks D (design office layout) and F (select personnel to move) are both scheduled to begin at time 8. It is not clear whether this is so because predecessor tasks must be completed first or whether there is some other reason. If there are predecessor tasks, it is not clear whether these two tasks have the same predecessors. In fact, they do not. Task F can begin as soon as task C is complete, but task D cannot begin until C and A are *both* complete. Similarly, it appears that F and I are immediate predecessors of G, because they are both scheduled to finish at week 10 and G begins at time 10, but actually only F is an immediate predecessor of G. For this reason, there is no way of knowing from the chart what effect the early or late completion of a task will have on the starting times of subsequent tasks. Therefore, the chart can show whether or not individual tasks are on schedule, but it cannot show whether the entire project is on schedule as actual task times vary from the scheduled times.

A second disadvantage is that Gantt charts do not help determine which tasks can or cannot take more time than planned without slowing the project as a whole. Third, Gantt charts provide no help in reallocating resources among tasks to stay on schedule, mainly

[1]This is based on a project in which the author was involved.

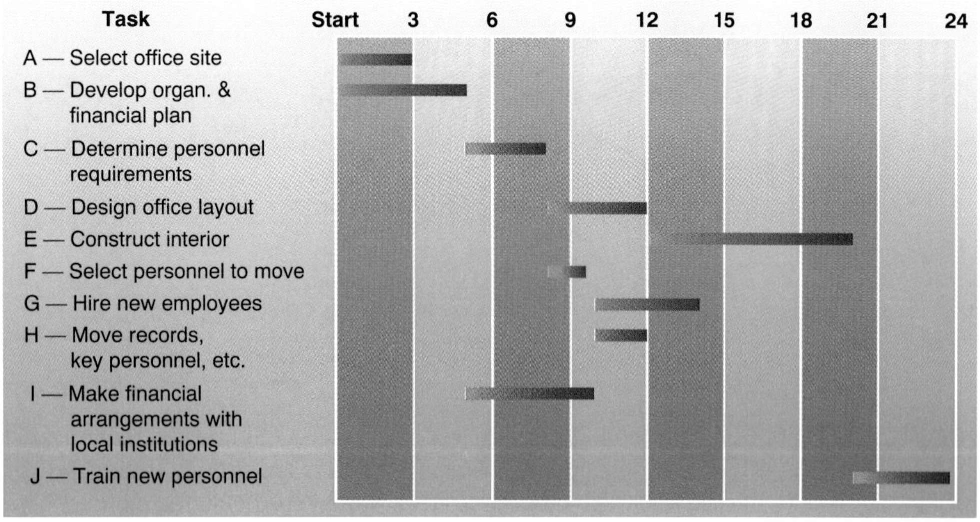

FIGURE 17.2 Gantt chart for credit operation relocation project.

TABLE 17.1 PROJECT: REORGANIZE AND MOVE CREDIT OPERATION TO A NEW OFFICE LOCATION

Task	Immediate Predecessors	Expected Task Time (wk)
A—Select office site	—	3
B—Develop organization and financial plan	—	5
C—Determine personnel requirements	B	3
D—Design office layout	A, C	4
E— Construct office interior	D	8
F— Select personnel to move	C	2
G—Hire new employees	F	4
H—Move records, current personnel, etc.	F	2
I— Make financial arrangements with local institutions	B	5
J— Train new personnel	H, E, G	3

because they cannot differentiate between critical and noncritical tasks. Finally, for complex projects with hundreds or thousands of tasks, constructing and updating a Gantt chart that is consistent, with precedence relationships satisfied, is extremely difficult.

For these reasons, Gantt charts are rarely used alone in planning complex projects. More commonly, they are used in conjunction with network-based methods, which are discussed below. In these cases, the network-based method is used to establish and update the schedule for the tasks. Then the individual task schedules are transferred to Gantt charts for visual clarity.

17.5 NETWORK-BASED PROJECT SCHEDULING METHODS: PERT/CPM

Because projects can require completion of hundreds or thousands of interrelated tasks over long periods of time, it is extremely helpful to have a method for visualizing these interrelationships. Networks provide a natural form in which to represent both

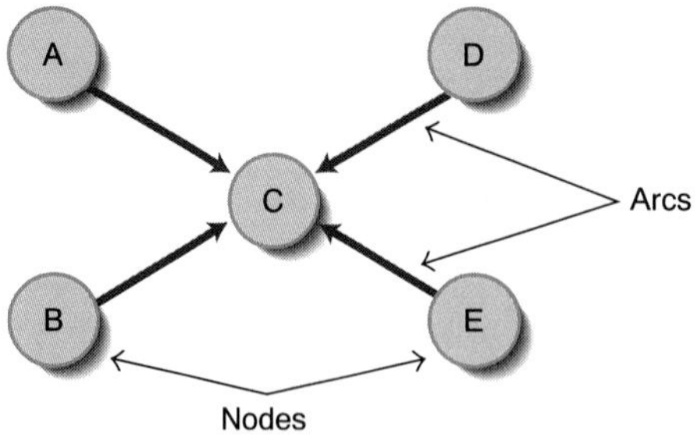

FIGURE 17.3 A network.

concurrent and consecutive tasks. **Networks** are mathematical structures made up of two entities: nodes and arcs. The *nodes* are usually designated by circles and are connected to each other by arrows, which represent *arcs* (Figure 17.3).

The value of using a network representation for project planning and scheduling was discovered simultaneously by two independent groups during the late 1950s. During the development of the Polaris missile system, Lockheed Aircraft, the U.S. Navy, and the consulting firm of Booz, Allen & Hamilton developed a network-based scheduling method called **PERT (program evaluation and review technique)**. The project involved billions of dollars, over 3000 contractors, and several thousand tasks. PERT was credited with reducing the system development time by over two years. At approximately the same time, J. E. Kelly of Remington Rand Corporation and M. R. Walker of DuPont developed a network-based procedure, called **CPM (critical path method)**, for scheduling and coordinating maintenance projects. Because of the different purposes and projects for which each method was developed there were some differences in the methods, but over time the two methods have merged, and network-based project scheduling is now commonly referred to as **PERT/CPM**; we will use that designation here.

PERT/CPM has been used for a wide variety of projects, such as constructing buildings and highways, developing military hardware systems, planning corporate mergers and legal cases, developing computer software systems, planning audits, executing facility relocations, and developing new products. Almost every major construction company, such as Fluor Corporation and Bechtel Corporation, and many consulting companies, such as Anderson Consulting and Booz, Allen, and Hamilton, use PERT/CPM to plan projects. In addition, the U.S. Department of Defense and many other government agencies require contractors to use PERT/CPM analysis in all major projects. An increasing number of manufacturers have found PERT/CPM especially helpful in concurrent product and process design. For example, the subject of this chapter's "In Good Company" feature, Chrysler Corporation, used this project planning tool to develop its Viper model automobile in only three years.

The popularity of network-based scheduling can be attributed to its many benefits, especially its ease of use. Other benefits include the following:

1. It provides a visual display of the needed tasks and their temporal ordering, which makes it easy to see how tasks should be sequenced. This assists communication and cooperation among task teams because each team can see how its work affects that of other teams.
2. It provides a relatively accurate estimate of the time required to complete the project at the proposed resource level.

IN GOOD COMPANY

Software Charms the Viper at Chrysler Corporation

Among the many challenges facing the design and production teams assigned to the Viper, Chrysler Corporation's 1992 entry in the high-performance sports car market, were tight deadlines and finite resources—plus the mandate to set a new precedent for all of Chrysler's future vehicle development projects. All this had to be done while the new model was brought from concept to production in three years instead of the usual five.

Critical to the ultimate success of the effort were hand-picked personnel and strong project management, aided by a computerized project management system known as Artemis Prestige. This network-based software package contributed a "what if" capability that allowed Viper's designers and engineers to judge the effect of any changes in their plans before committing their resources. It also helped them troubleshoot by projecting the impact of potential bottlenecks or problems in time for corrective actions to be taken.

The project team brought the Viper out on time, and its first shipment was sold out before it reached the dealerships.

Source: Stephen W. T. O'Keeffe, "Chrysler and Artemis: Striking Back with the Viper," *Industrial Engineering*, December 1994, pp. 15–17.

3. It identifies and highlights the tasks that are critical to keeping the project on schedule.
4. It provides a method for evaluating the time–cost trade-offs resulting from reallocating resources among tasks.
5. It provides a method for monitoring the project throughout its life cycle. As the project progresses, PERT/CPM easily identifies changes in which tasks are critical and how the expected completion date is affected.
6. It provides a convenient method for incorporating uncertainty regarding task times into the schedule, and it helps to evaluate the effect of this uncertainty on project completion time.

There are two standard conventions for representing a project using a network: activity-on-arc and activity-on-node. Life being what it is, the developers of PERT and CPM chose different conventions, so both conventions are still used.

ACTIVITY-ON-ARC CONVENTION

The **activity-on-arc (A-O-A)** convention represents each task (activity) as a directed arc (arrow). The nodes are called **events**, and they represent points in time at which one or more tasks start or finish. For example, Figure 17.4 is an A-O-A network for the following project:

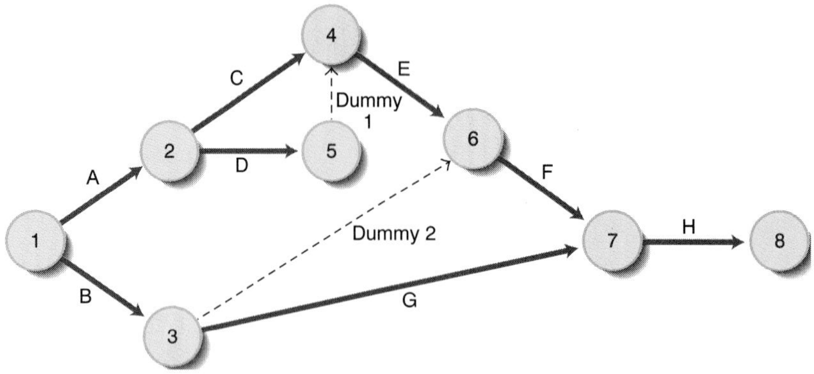

FIGURE 17.4 A-O-A representation of a project.

Task	Immediate Predecessors
A	None
B	None
C	A
D	A
E	C, D
F	B, E
G	B
H	F, G

Good project planning is just as important for software development and consulting projects as it is for construction projects.

Event (node) 1 represents the beginning of the project. Because tasks A and B have no predecessors, event 1 identifies the start of both. Event 2 represents the completion of task A; tasks C and D can begin as soon as event 2 has occurred, so the arcs corresponding to C and D emanate from event node 2. Similarly, event 3 designates the completion of task B, and because task G can begin as soon as event 3 has occurred, the arc corresponding to G emanates from event node 3. Notice that two "dummy" tasks are used in the network. **Dummy tasks** are artificial tasks with zero task time that are required (or are at least convenient to use) to clarify sequencing. Dummy tasks are used with the A-O-A convention in the following situations:

1. If two or more tasks have the same starting and ending events (the same predecessors and successors), a dummy task is created to differentiate the two. For example, dummy task 1 in Figure 17.4 is required because tasks C and D have the same immediate predecessor and successor tasks.
2. If a task is a predecessor for two or more successor tasks and the set of predecessor tasks is not identical for the successor tasks, then a dummy task must be created. For example, in Figure 17.4, task G can begin as soon as B is completed, but F cannot begin until *both* B and E are completed. So event 3 represents the completion of task B, and event 6 represents the completion of both tasks B and E; to show this, dummy task 2 is required from event 3 to event 6.

Dummy tasks can also be added in other situations to clarify task sequencing. There is no restriction on the number of dummy tasks that can be used for clarity.

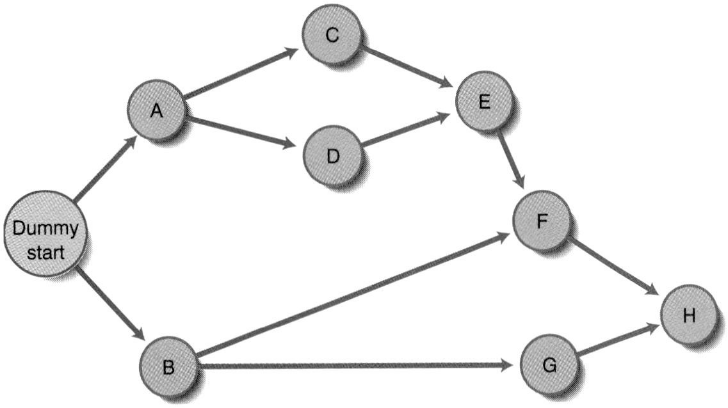

FIGURE 17.5 A-O-N representation of a project.

ACTIVITY-ON-NODE CONVENTION

The **activity-on-node (A-O-N)** convention represents each task as a node and then uses directed arcs to designate precedence relationships. This convention is identical to the one used in Chapter 8 for constructing networks to represent the sequencing of tasks in designing flow processes (line balancing). An A-O-N representation of the project corresponding to Figure 17.4 is given in Figure 17.5. There is no unique starting task, so a dummy task is created. Once the project begins, tasks A and B can begin because they have no real predecessor tasks. Task G can begin as soon as B is completed, so there is a single arc leading from B to G. Task F, however, cannot begin until tasks B *and* E are completed, so there are arcs from both B and E leading to task F. In general, there will be an arc leading to a task node from each of its immediate predecessors.

WHICH CONVENTION TO USE

Which convention to use is really a matter of choice; some people find A-O-N more natural and others prefer A-O-A. An advantage of A-O-N is that it requires fewer dummy tasks, which are necessary only at the beginning or end of a project when there are concurrent starting or ending tasks. In contrast, for complex projects A-O-A often requires the use of many dummy tasks. On the other hand, it has an advantage in that the lengths of the arcs can represent the lengths of the task times (although in some cases this does not work well). For brevity, in subsequent sections we will only use the A-O-N convention, but the conversion to the A-O-A convention is straightforward, and some of the subsequent material is repeated using the A-O-A convention in solved problem 2 at the end of the chapter.

17.6 COMPUTING THE PROJECT COMPLETION TIME AND CRITICAL PATH

The main purposes of PERT/CPM are to determine the amount of time required to complete the project and to identify those tasks whose on-time completion is critical to on-time completion of the entire project. The method used to accomplish both purposes is called the **two-pass method**.

THE TWO-PASS METHOD

We will illustrate the two-pass method using the project given in Table 17.1. We begin by constructing an A-O-N PERT/CPM network for the project, which is shown in Figure 17.6.

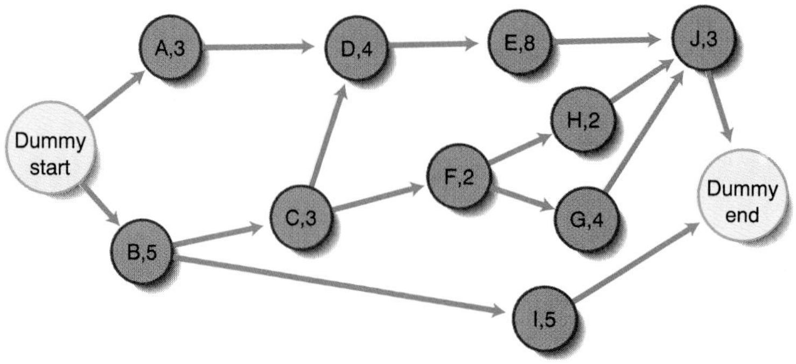

FIGURE 17.6 PERT/CPM diagram for the credit operation relocation project.

For each task we will eventually compute four quantities:

1. The **earliest starting (ES) time** for a task, which is the earliest time work can start on the task, assuming all tasks take their estimated times to accomplish.
2. The **earliest finishing (EF) time** for a task, which is the earliest time the task can be finished assuming all tasks take their estimated times to accomplish.
3. The **latest starting (LS) time**, which is the latest time work can start on a task without postponing completion of the project, assuming tasks take their expected times to complete.
4. The **latest finishing (LF) time**, which is the latest time a task can be finished without postponing completion of the project, assuming tasks take their expected times to complete.

Forward Pass

During the first or **forward pass** phase of the two-pass method, we move from left to right (forward) through the PERT/CPM network and compute the ES and EF times for each task using the following rules:

ES = largest EF time of the task's immediate predecessors; for those tasks with no predecessors, $ES = 0$[2]

$EF = ES + t$ where t is the time required for that task

EXAMPLE 1

For the project in Table 17.1 and Figure 17.6 we have a dummy starting task for convenience; it has no predecessor, so $ES = 0$, and because its task time is 0, $EF = 0$ as well. The ES time for task A equals the EF time of its only predecessor, the dummy starting task, so its $ES = 0$. Then the earliest time that task A can be finished is $EF = ES + t = 0 + 3 = 3$ weeks. Similarly, for task B, $ES = 0$ and $EF = 0 + 5 = 5$ weeks. Task C has only one predecessor, task B. So task C can begin as soon as task B has been finished:

ES for task C = EF for task B = 5

[2]In practice we would convert time 0 into a calendar date, such as midnight on August 29. August 29 would then be day 1 and a task scheduled to begin on day 11 would correspond to starting on September 8.

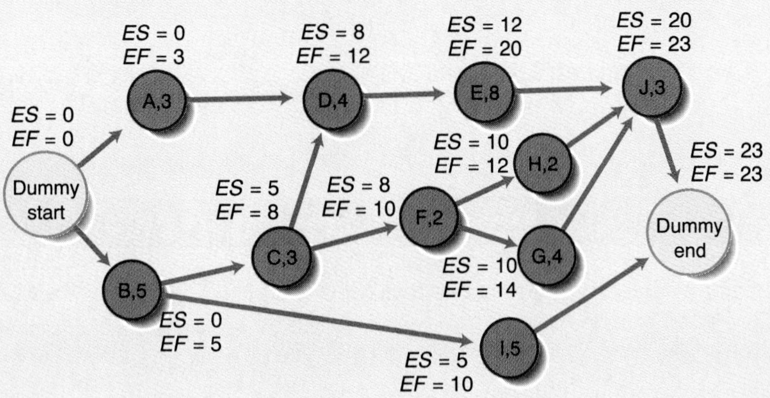

FIGURE 17.7 PERT/CPM diagram for the credit operation relocation project with forward pass results.

If C begins at time 5 and requires three weeks to complete, then

$$EF \text{ for task C} = ES \text{ for task C} + \text{task time for C} = 5 + 3 = 8$$

Task D has two predecessors, A and C, so D cannot begin until *both* A and C are finished. Task A can be finished as early as time 3, but task C cannot be finished until time 8, so the earliest D can be started is at time 8:

$$ES \text{ for task D} = \max(EF \text{ for task A}, EF \text{ for task C}) = \max(3,8) = 8$$

where "max" means choosing the largest value within the parentheses. Then the earliest time task D can be finished is $EF = ES + 4 = 12$. Continuing this procedure for all tasks gives the *ES* and *EF* values listed in Figure 17.7 and Table 17.2. At the completion of the forward pass we have determined that if all tasks take their expected times, the project will require 23 weeks to complete, which is the *EF* time for the last task (the dummy end task).

TABLE 17.2 CRITICAL PATH COMPUTATIONS FOR THE CREDIT OFFICE RELOCATION PROJECT

Task	*ES*	*EF*	*LS*	*LF*	Slack	Critical Path
Start	0	0	0	0	0	—
A	0	3	5	8	5	No
B	0	5	0	5	0	Yes
C	5	8	5	8	0	Yes
D	8	12	8	12	0	Yes
E	12	20	12	20	0	Yes
F	8	10	14	16	6	No
G	10	14	16	20	6	No
H	10	12	18	20	8	No
J	20	23	20	23	0	Yes
I	5	10	18	23	13	No
End	23	23	23	23	0	—

Backward Pass

The second phase or **backward pass** moves from right to left through the network, computing *LF* and *LS* times for each task as follows:

LF = smallest *LS* time of all immediate *successor* tasks; if the task has no successors, *LF* = the project completion time computed in the forward pass

LS = *LF* – *t*, where t is the task time

EXAMPLE 1 (CONTINUED)

Beginning with the dummy end task, we set *LF* = 23 weeks, and then *LS* = 23 – 0 = 23. In Figures 17.6 and 17.7 the only successor for task J is the end task, so *LF* for task J = *LS* for the end task = 23. Then *LS* = 23 – 3 = 20 weeks. In other words, task J cannot be started any later than time 20; otherwise, the project will be delayed. For example, if J were not started until time 21 and took three weeks to perform, then J would not be finished until time 24, which would postpone completion of the project by one week. Similarly, *LF* for task I = *LS* for the end task = 23, and *LS* = 23 – 5 = 18. Continuing this procedure, we have

LF for task E = *LS* for task J = 20, and *LS* for E = 20 – 8 = 12
LF for task G = *LS* for task J = 20, and *LS* for G = 20 – 4 = 16
LF for task H = *LS* for task J = 20, and *LS* for H = 20 – 2 = 18

Computing *LF* for task F is a bit more complicated because it has two successor tasks, G and H. Although H can be started as late as time 18 without postponing the project, G cannot be started any later than time 16. Therefore, F must be finished no later than time 16; otherwise, G would have to be started later than time 16 and the project would be postponed. In other words,

LF for task F = min(*LS* for task G, *LS* for task H) = min(16,18) = 16

where "min" means to select the smallest value within the parentheses. The LF and LS times resulting from the backward pass are given in Table 17.2 and Figure 17.8.

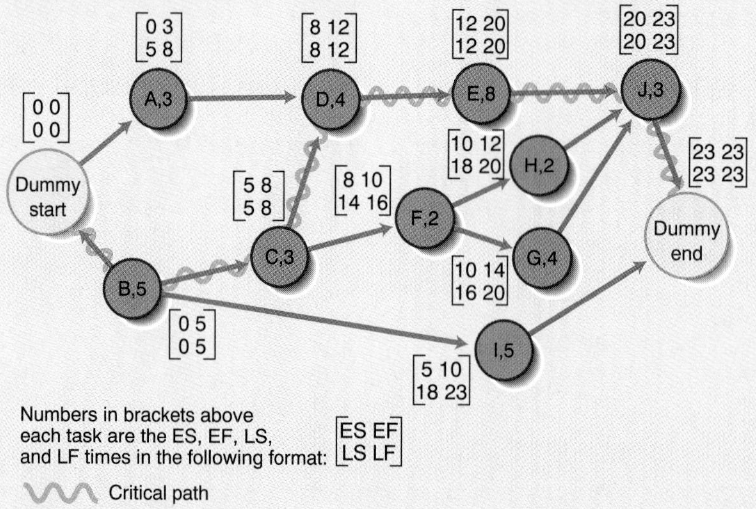

FIGURE 17.8 PERT/CPM diagram for the credit operation relocation project with forward and backward pass results.

With all the numbers that must be computed for each task, the PERT/CPM diagram can get very cluttered. One way to simplify it is shown in Figure 17.8, where we have created a box near each task node. In the upper left corner of the box we enter ES, in the upper right corner EF, in the lower left corner LS, and in the lower right corner LF. This way, we can identify each of the values without having to write the identifying letters ES, EF, LS, and LF everywhere.

FINDING THE CRITICAL PATH

In Figure 17.8 we see that if all tasks take as long as expected, then task I could be started as early as time 5 and finished as early as time 10. Suppose for some reason task I was not begun until time 15 and was not finished until time 20. Will this 10-week delay postpone completion of the project? The answer is "no." Because $LF = 23$ for this task, as long as task I is finished by time 23, it will not postpone completion of the project. Specifically, task I can be completed $LF - EF = 23 - 10 = 13$ weeks later than its earliest finish time; equivalently, we can delay the start of task I by $LS - ES = 18 - 5 = 13$ weeks without delaying completion of the project. We therefore say there are 13 weeks of **slack** or **float** in the scheduling of this task. More generally, for each task we define its slack as follows:

$$\text{slack (float)} = LF - EF = LS - ES$$

If a task has zero slack, then any delay in starting the task later than its ES time will cause a delay in the entire project unless the time is made up later. Tasks that have zero slack are called **critical tasks**, and a set of critical tasks that form a continuous path from the beginning to the end of the project is called a **critical path**. Every project will have at least one critical path.

The slacks for every task are listed in Table 17.2, and the critical tasks are identified. Tasks B-C-D-E-J form a critical path (excluding the dummy tasks). These tasks need to be closely monitored as the project progresses. In fact, the project completion time is the sum of the task times for the tasks on the critical path; that is, the completion time of the project depends *only* on the critical tasks. If any task on the critical path is started later than its ES time or finished later than its EF time, time will have to be saved somewhere else *on the critical path* to get the project back on schedule.

Correspondingly, noncritical tasks (those with positive slack) do not need to be monitored as closely. If a task with a slack of six weeks falls two weeks behind its "earliest start" schedule, the project completion date is not affected. In Section 17.7 we will see that by transferring resources from noncritical tasks (thereby slowing their completion) to critical ones, we may simultaneously be able to reduce the project completion time and lower the project cost.

17.7 IMPROVING THE PROJECT SCHEDULE: TIME–COST TRADE-OFFS

Suppose we wanted to complete the credit operation relocation project in Table 17.1 in 20 weeks rather than the 23 weeks we computed. To do this we need to reduce some tasks times, but which ones? Because we want to reduce the project time by 14% (3 weeks/23 weeks), we could add enough resources to reduce each of the task times by 14%. But this strategy is quite wasteful. Reducing the task times of noncritical tasks, such as task I, will not reduce the project completion time. On the other hand, reducing the task time of a single task on the critical path by one week will reduce the completion time of the entire project by one week, so we can focus our resources on only a few tasks. For example, if we reduced the task times for D by 1 week and for E by 2 weeks, the project would be completed in 20 weeks. Adding resources to a task to reduce its task time is called **crashing** the task.

CRASHING

The amount of time required to complete a task can vary considerably, depending on the resources used. We will refer to our original task time estimates as the **normal times (NT)** and the cost of completing the task in those times as the **normal cost (NC)**. The *shortest possible* time in which a task can be completed will be called the **crash time (CT)** and its corresponding cost the **crash cost (CC)**. The relationship between task times and costs looks like that in Figure 17.9, but for simplicity we will act as if it is linear, so the per time unit cost of reducing a task time, which we will call the *per unit crash cost*, will be

$$\text{per unit crash cost} = (CC - NC)/(NT - CT)$$

Our problem is to determine which tasks to crash and by how much. A simple method for doing this is the following.

Rules for Crashing

1. Select the task on the critical path that has the smallest per unit crash cost and is not already at its minimum possible time. Crash the task as much as possible until either (a) the task time is at its lowest possible value, (b) the amount of the reduction equals the smallest slack value of tasks not on the critical path, or (c) the desired project completion time is achieved. If (c) occurs, stop.
2. If (a) or (b) in step 1 occurs, recompute the slack values and critical path and repeat step 1.

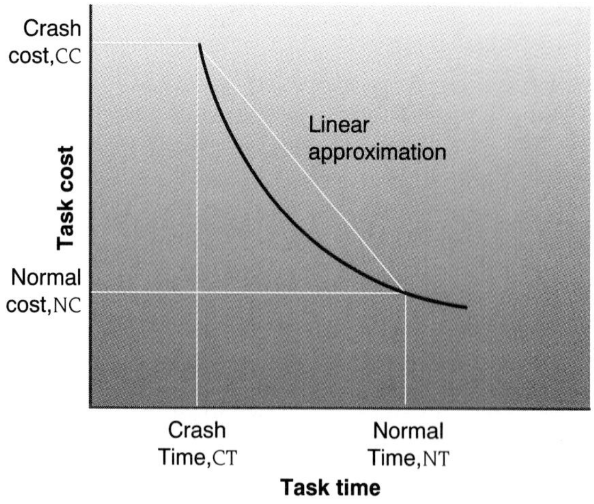

FIGURE 17.9 Relationship between time and cost for a given task.

Step 2 is necessary because if a task time on the critical path is reduced by more than the smallest slack value of tasks not on the critical path, the critical path can change. If it changes, the new critical path activities are the ones to use at the next iteration.

EXAMPLE 2

Suppose we want to reduce the completion time for the project in Table 17.1 from 23 to 20 weeks, and the normal times, normal costs, crash times, and crash costs for the tasks are given in Table 17.3.

From our earlier analysis we know that the critical path tasks are B, C, D, E, and J, and among the noncritical tasks the smallest slack time is 5 weeks (see Table 17.2).

1. The critical task with the smallest per unit crash cost is B, with a cost of $400 per week saved. So we crash B from five weeks to its minimum of four weeks. A quick inspection of Figure 17.8 shows that the project can now be completed in 22 weeks, the critical path will not change, and the smallest slack for a noncritical task (task A) is 4.
2. The critical task with the smallest per unit crash cost that is not at its minimum time is now J. We crash J from three weeks to its minimum of two weeks. The project completion time decreases to 21 weeks, and again the critical path does not change.
3. Next, we select task D and crash it only one week, from four weeks to three. We do not crash it all the way to its minimum because we need to save only one additional week to reach our project completion target of 20 weeks. By reducing the project completion time by three weeks, we have increased our cost by $1500, from $37,000 to $38,500. This is the minimum-cost strategy. Figure 17.10 shows that as we continue to crash tasks to reduce project completion time, the incremental project cost will increase.

TABLE 17.3 NORMAL AND CRASH DATA FOR THE CREDIT OFFICE RELOCATION PROJECT

Task	Normal Time (wk)	Crash Time (wk)	Normal Cost	Crash Cost	Crash Cost per Week
A	3	2	$ 1,500	$ 1,900	$ 400
B*	5	4	$ 2,200	$ 2,600	$ 400*
C*	3	3	$ 1,200	$ 1,200	—*
D*	4	2	$ 2,600	$ 3,800	$ 600*
E*	8	5	$ 12,000	$15,000	$1000*
F	2	2	$ 1,500	$ 1,500	—
G	4	3	$ 3,000	$ 3,500	$ 500
H	2	2	$ 6,000	$ 6,000	—
I	5	4	$ 3,000	$ 3,400	$ 400
J*	3	2	$ 4,000	$ 4,500	$ 500*
		Total	$37,000		

*Task is on the original critical path.

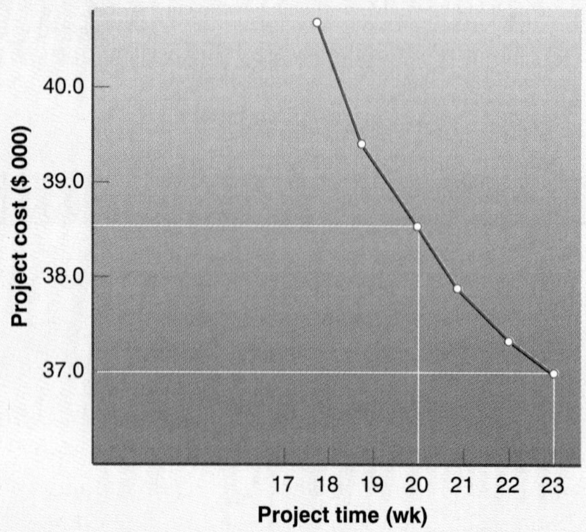

FIGURE 17.10 Project cost as a function of completion time for the credit operation relocation project.

OPTIMIZING THE TIME–COST TRADE-OFFS

To keep the discussion simple, we considered only *additions* of resources to tasks and corresponding reductions in task times. In reality, a complete analysis would also consider the possibility of *removing* resources from noncritical tasks, thereby increasing their task times. For example, suppose that by using one fewer person to interview potential employees, we could reduce the cost of task G (hire new employees) from $3000 to $2400, but the task time would increase from three weeks to five weeks. Because G had 6 weeks of slack originally and still had 5 weeks of slack after reducing the project to 20 weeks, we could increase the activity time of G by 2 weeks without delaying the project.

In fact, if each task has a range of possible task times and we know the cost per unit to reduce these times from their practical maximum values, we can determine the optimal task time for each task to minimize total project cost while completing the project by some due date. In other words, we could determine how to allocate our resources among tasks to minimize project cost. This optimization, which is beyond the scope of our discussion, can be done quite readily using linear programming (see Tutorial 1).

17.8 PROBABILISTIC TASK TIME ESTIMATES

So far, we have treated the estimated task times as being certain. In reality, the task times of projects are highly uncertain. Many of the tasks in a project may have never been performed by the project team members, or by anyone at all, so estimates of the task times may be quite speculative. For example, if developing a new product requires creating a new technology, this may occur within weeks or it may take years. Even for well-structured, commonly performed tasks such as painting a house, the time required to paint a specific house cannot be predicted exactly due to variations in human performance, weather, and unforeseen factors. The need to incorporate such uncertainty into the project planning process was one reason underlying the development of PERT. Many of the tasks in developing the Polaris missile system were totally new tasks that had never been done before, and no one knew how long they would take.

PROBABILITY DISTRIBUTION FOR TASK TIMES

From our own experiences, we know that some tasks take more time than expected and others take less. The pattern or probability distribution of completion times for typical activities often approximates a **beta distribution**, which is illustrated in Figure 17.11. Notice that the beta distribution is skewed to the right. The obvious explanation is that even if everything goes well, the amount of time saved relative to the most likely task time is limited. By contrast, when things go poorly, there is almost no limit on how much the activity can be delayed, so the tail of the distribution stretches far to the right.

We typically characterize the probability distribution for project tasks by specifying three time estimates: the most likely task time (m), the optimistic task time (a), and the pessimistic task time (b). The optimistic time implies that almost everything will go well, so that the probability of the activity's taking less time than a is approximately 0.01. Similarly, the pessimistic time, which assumes that almost everything will go wrong, is estimated, so there is approximately a 0.01 probability that the activity will take more than this amount of time. The most likely time is exactly that: the task time that has the largest probability of occurring. Notice that this is *not* the average or expected task time. For a beta distribution with (parameter) estimates m, a, and b, the average or expected task time for task j, $\bar{t}_j$, is approximately

$$\bar{t}_j = (a + 4m + b)/6 \tag{17.1}$$

and the variance of the distribution, σ_j^2, is approximately

$$\sigma_j^2 = [(b - a)/6]^2 \tag{17.2}$$

Notice that because the distribution is skewed, with $b - m > m - a$, the expected task time will be greater than the most likely time: $\bar{t}_j > m$.

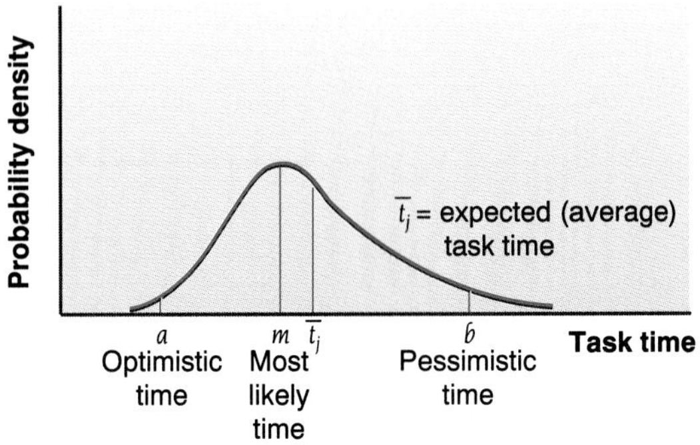

FIGURE 17.11 Beta distribution for task times.

DERIVING THE PROBABILITY DISTRIBUTION FOR PROJECT COMPLETION TIME

If we make the following two assumptions, the validity of which we will discuss later, the approximate probability distribution for the *project* completion time, T, can be derived easily.

1. The task times are probabilistically independent of each other. In other words, whether or not one task takes more time to complete than expected is unrelated to the probability of any other task taking more or less time than expected.
2. Variations in actual task times are never large enough to cause the critical path to change from the one that would result if all tasks took their expected times.

Project task times are not always independent of each other. Bad weather can delay an entire set of tasks.

With these two assumptions the following can be proved, using the central limit theorem (although we will not do so here):[3]

1. The project completion time, T, is approximately normally distributed.
2. The expected project completion time, $\bar{T}$, will equal the sum of the expected task times of those tasks *on the critical path*:

$$\bar{T} = \sum_{j \varepsilon CP} \bar{t}_j \tag{17.3}$$

3. The variance of the project completion time, σ_T^2, will equal the sum of the variances of the activities *on the critical path*:

$$\sigma_T^2 = \sum_{j \varepsilon CP} \sigma_j^2 \tag{17.4}$$

In other words, we see again that the completion time of the project is affected only by the activities on the critical path; noncritical activities are irrelevant.

The implication of these results is that the project completion time distribution can be derived in the following way.

Deriving the Project Completion Time Distribution

1. Compute the expected time and variance for each task using equations (17.1) and (17.2).
2. Construct a PERT/CPM network and use the expected task times to derive the critical path.
3. Compute the expected project completion time and the variance of project completion time using equations (17.3) and (17.4).

[3]The central limit theorem (CLT) states that as long as n is large enough, the sum of n independent random variables is approximately normally distributed, with an expected value equal to the sum of the expected values of the random variables and a variance equal to the sum of the variances of the random variables. This is true regardless of the distributions of the random variables, although the more symmetrical the random variables, the smaller n usually has to be. Because the project completion time is the sum of the task times on the critical path, and because we are assuming that these times are independent, the CLT applies in this case.

EXAMPLE 3

Consider the project described in Table 17.4. We begin by computing the expected task times and their variances using equations (17.1) and (17.2). For example, for task A

$$\bar{t}_A = [3 + 4(5) + 8]/6 = 31/6 \quad \text{and} \quad \sigma_A^2 = [(8 - 3)/6]^2 = 25/36$$

The expected task times and their variances are given in the last two columns of Table 17.4. Using the expected task times in Table 17.4, we derive the PERT/CPM network given in Figure 17.12. By comparing the ES and LS times for the activities, we can see that the critical path is A-C-E-F.

The expected completion time of the project is then

$$\bar{T} = \bar{t}_A + \bar{t}_C + \bar{t}_E + \bar{t}_F = 31/6 + 61/6 + 44/6 + 19/6 = 155/6 = 25.83$$

and the variance for the project completion time is

$$\sigma_T^2 = \sigma_A^2 + \sigma_C^2 + \sigma_E^2 + \sigma_F^2 = 25/36 + 81/36 + 36/36 + 9/36 = 151/36 = 4.19$$

TABLE 17.4 PROJECT WITH PROBABILISTIC ACTIVITY TIMES

		Task Times (days)				
		Optim.	Most Likely	Pessim.	Expected	Variance
Task	Predecessors	a	m	b	$\bar{t}_j$	σ_j^2
A	—	3	5	8	31/6	25/36
B	A	4	7	12	44/6	64/36
C	A	6	10	15	61/6	81/36
D	B	3	4	6	25/6	9/36
E	B, C	5	7	11	44/6	36/36
F	D, E	2	3	5	19/6	9/36

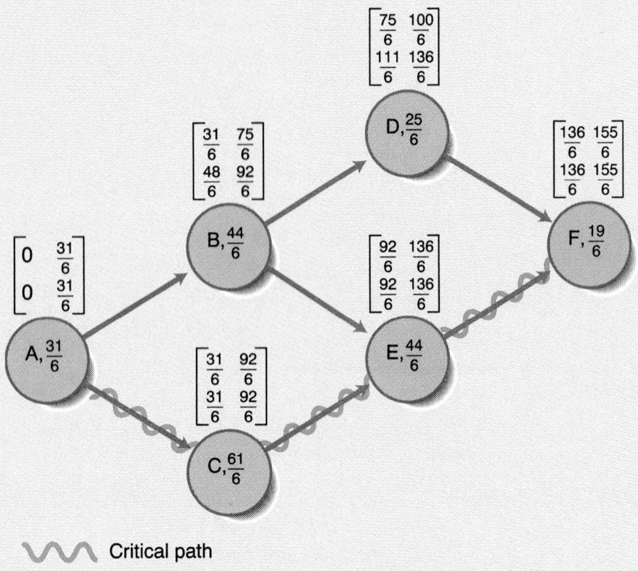

FIGURE 17.12 PERT/CPM diagram for the project described in Table 17.4 using expected task times.

The time in which the project will be completed is random, but given our assumptions, it has approximately a normal distribution, with an expected value of 25.83 days and a variance of 4.19 days-days.

ANSWERING PROBABILISTIC QUESTIONS

We can use the probability distribution for T to answer the following questions for Example 3: What is the probability that the project will take more than 27 days to complete? Less than 25 days? We know from probability theory that if we have a random variable, T, that has a normal distribution, with an expected value of $\overline{T}$ and a variance of σ_T^2, the probability that T will take on a value greater than some value t is

$$\text{prob}(T > t) = \text{prob}[z > (t - \overline{T})/\sigma_T] \quad (17.5)$$

where z is the standard normal distribution (probability tables for the standard normal distribution are given in Appendix A). Similarly,

$$\text{prob}(T < t) = \text{prob}[z < (t - \overline{T})/\sigma_T)] \quad (17.6)$$

EXAMPLE 3 (CONTINUED)

In Example 3 the project completion time, T, is normally distributed, with $\overline{T} = 25.83$ and $\sigma_T^2 = 4.19$ (so $\sigma_T = 2.05$). Therefore, the probability that the project will require more than 27 days to complete is

$$\text{prob}(T > 27.0) = \text{prob}[z > (27.0 - 25.83)/2.05] = \text{prob}(z > 0.57) = 0.2843$$

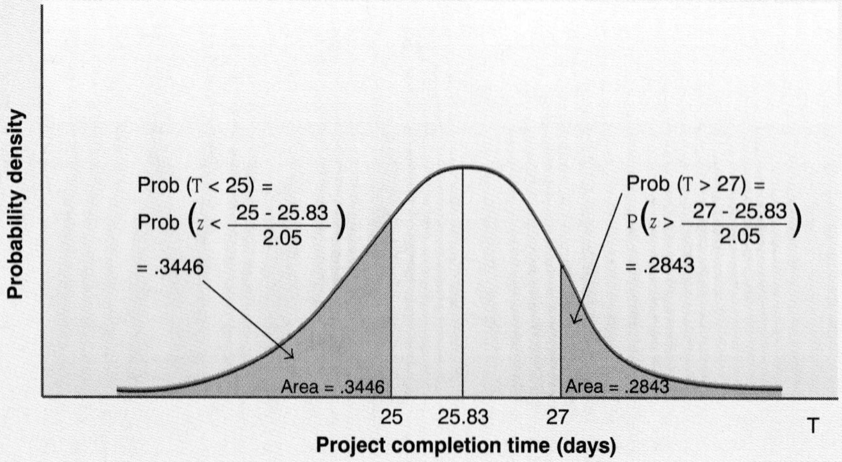

FIGURE 17.13 Probability distribution for project completion time.

as shown in Figure 17.13. Similarly, the probability that the project will be completed in less than 25 days is

$$\text{prob}(T < 25.0) = \text{prob}[z < (25.0 - 25.83)/2.05] = \text{Prob}(z < -0.40) = 0.3446$$

Answers to these types of questions are useful not only in predicting project completion times and planning contingencies, but also in negotiating performance contracts. For example, it is becoming increasingly common for construction contracts to include bonus payments if the project is completed by a given date and to assess penalties if it is completed after some other date. If we were negotiating a contract to perform the project in Table 17.4, we might be reluctant to agree to a late penalty that became effective after 27 days because there is a 0.2843 probability of this occurring. By pushing the penalty date back to 28 days, we reduce the probability of incurring the late penalty to

$$\text{prob}(T > 28.0) = \text{prob}[z > (28.0 - 25.83)/2.05] = \text{prob}(z > 1.06) = 0.1446$$

VALIDITY OF ASSUMPTIONS AND SIMULATION

The preceding analysis was based on two assumptions: that task times are independent of each other and that variations in task times are never large enough to change the critical path. In some situations these assumptions are satisfied. However, when they are violated, the preceding method would give us invalid results. Let us begin by identifying some situations in which the assumptions may not be valid. We will then discuss how these situations can be accommodated.

If tasks are sufficiently different and are performed independently by different workers, the assumption of independent task times is likely to be valid. But there are many cases in which task times may be correlated. In construction projects, weather is a major factor in determining how long activities take. Suppose the project in Table 17.4 is a construction project, and tasks B and C are both outdoor tasks. Because they are being performed at the same time, bad weather that delays task B is also likely to delay task C; their times are not independent. Even though there is no causal relationship—the slow task time for B does not *cause* C to be slow or vice versa—they are both affected by a common phenomenon. Interdependence also occurs when tasks share equipment, so an equipment failure can slow several tasks, not just one.

The assumption that the critical path is not affected by task time variations is even more likely to be violated. Suppose the project in Table 17.4 were performed and the *actual* task times (in days) were A = 6, B = 11, C = 9, D = 6, E = 5, and F = 3. Our analysis above assumed that A-C-E-F was the critical path, so the project completion time would be the sum of the task times for these activities: 6 + 9 + 5 + 3 = 23 days. In fact, with these task times the project would not be completed for 26 days because the critical path is actually A-B-D-F. Therefore, our derivation of the probability distribution for the project completion time, which is based on A-C-E-F always being the critical path, will lead to a distorted result that is biased downward; that is, the method above will tend to predict that the project will finish earlier than it really will. This partially explains why, when activities are delayed, project completion is often delayed more than our PERT/CPM analysis estimates; the critical path may change, further lengthening the project.

We can accommodate these situations by using computer simulation (see Tutorial 3) rather than the procedure discussed above. With simulation we can simulate random

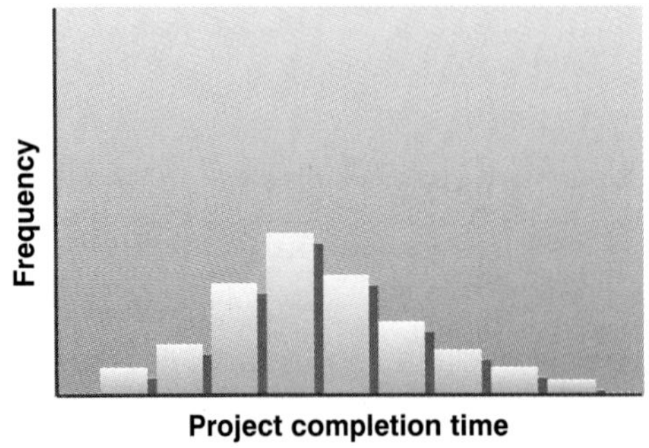

FIGURE 17.14 Histogram of project completion times from computer simulation.

task times that come from any specified probability distribution. These times can then be used to determine how long the project would actually take if those task times occurred. This procedure can be repeated thousands of times, using new simulated task times for each simulation run. The project completion times can then be plotted in a histogram, such as that in Figure 17.14, and then a probability distribution can be fit to those data.

There are several advantages to this method. First, for every combination of simulated task times, we can identify and use the real critical path in computing the project completion time rather than assuming that the same critical path will occur. Second, we can sometimes simulate correlated activity times to represent reality better. For example, suppose the times for several activities are all affected by the weather that occurs at some time. The model could simulate daily weather conditions, and then the simulated weather conditions could be converted to simulated task times. Simulating correlated activity times is a rather sophisticated and time-consuming enhancement. However, simulating independent random activity times, with resulting changes in the critical path, is quite easy and is a feature in some project management computer packages.

17.9 MONITORING PROJECTS USING PERT/CPM

Few projects progress exactly as planned, so critical path analysis does not end when an initial project schedule is established. By updating our PERT/CPM diagram as the project progresses, we can update our estimate of the project completion date, spot any changes in the critical path, and identify those tasks that might have to be expedited to finish the project on time.

EXAMPLE 4

For the project in Table 17.1, suppose we decided to begin each task as soon as possible. With this plan the project could be scheduled for completion in 23 weeks, with a critical path of B-C-D-E-J. Now suppose that 12 weeks have passed. During that time the following have been accomplished:

1. Task A took four weeks to complete (three weeks planned).
2. Task B took five weeks to complete (five weeks planned).

3. Task C took two weeks to complete (three weeks planned).
4. Task D took three weeks to complete (four weeks planned).
5. Task E is progressing faster than planned; it took two weeks to complete half the task, and it is estimated that only three weeks more will be needed (a total of eight had been planned).
6. Task F has run into trouble; it has taken five weeks to complete half of this task, and we estimate that another two weeks will be required to complete it (a total of six had been planned).
7. Task I is also troublesome; it has taken seven weeks to complete 80% of this task, and it is estimated that another two weeks will be required to complete it (five had been planned).

At the end of 12 weeks, the remaining project is made up of the following tasks and estimated times:

Task	Time
E	3
F	2
G	4
H	2
I	2
J	3

The PERT/CPM network for the remainder of the project is given in Figure 17.15, with the forward and backward pass analysis.

The estimated project completion time is now 21 weeks rather than the original 23, and activity E is no longer on the critical path. Instead, the critical path for the remainder of the project is now F-G-J. Suppose the company decides that now that it is ahead of schedule, it would like to push to finish the project in 20 weeks; that is, it wants to save 1 more week. The critical path analysis indicates that to achieve this, the company must focus its efforts on activities F, G, and J, not on E.

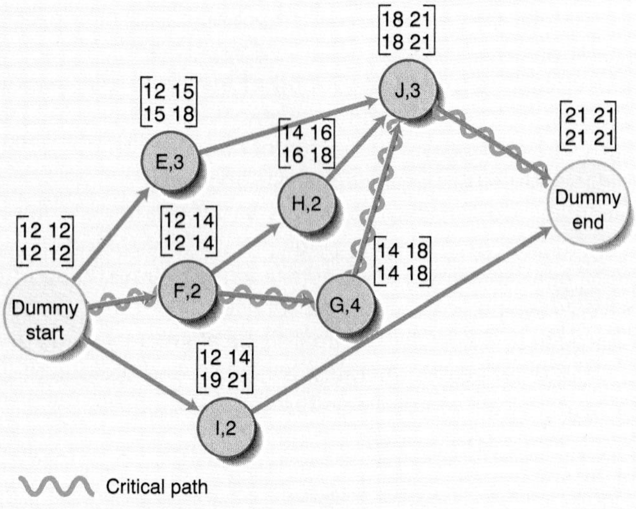

FIGURE 17.15 Updated PERT/CPM diagram for the credit operation relocation project after 12 weeks.

17.10 IMPLEMENTATION AND USE OF PROJECT SCHEDULING METHODS

Although the mechanics of PERT/CPM analysis are quite simple, for large projects it can be cumbersome and time-consuming to do by hand. Fortunately, there are dozens of commercial computer programs for personal computers that will perform this analysis quickly and make it easy to answer "what if" questions. For example, we can quickly see the effect on project completion time of adding an extra task to the project after it begins or reducing a task time by two days.

Another advantage of project planning software packages is that they often provide good graphical representations of the project, such as converting the PERT/CPM network into a Gantt chart to facilitate management and monitoring of individual tasks. As the project progresses, data can be updated and revised project schedules derived. In addition, some computer packages contain modules that simulate the project task times and derive the resulting probability distribution for the project completion time. More sophisticated packages even allow the management and coordination of several subprojects, and they can keep track of resources used on the project and their corresponding costs.

The large number of software packages available makes it difficult to select one. Reviews of project management software appear every few years in relevant professional journals, such as PMNET*work*, *Industrial Engineering*, and OR/MS *Today*.[4] In addition, producers of these packages often summarize their features and capabilities in advertisements appearing in these journals.

Although it may appear that we always try to finish projects as quickly as possible, this is not necessarily the case. Barry Naft of AWT Technologies, a subsidiary of Dow Chemical that does environmental project work, states that although his company often has to complete projects on a "fast-track" basis, "Not every project requires such an approach. Contractual, operational, or cash management [considerations] may in fact dictate a longer-term path to project completion. Time should be managed according to your specific needs."[5] A key advantage of PERT/CPM and its time–cost trade-off capabilities is that we can easily determine the time and financial implications of various levels of resources and effort. Speeding up and slowing down projects to suit our needs or those of a client can have substantial financial benefits.

Finally, the principles and tools of project management have been applied in other areas of operations, including routine and repetitive activities. For example, airline companies have analyzed the turnaround of an airplane between flights as a project and have determined how to allocate workers and sequence tasks to reduce turnaround time. Similarly, the changeover and setup of machines to run different products can be made more efficient using a project analysis approach.

The conclusion we can draw from this and the other chapters in this book is that operations management concepts, principles, and decision-making tools are readily transferable to new situations. Managers working in a manufacturing setting may actually be involved in managing projects or service subsystems. No one knows which of the topics presented in this book will ultimately be of greatest value to an individual, so understanding a wide range of principles, concepts, and tools is the best preparation for what awaits us in our lives and our professions.

---

[4]See P. Peterson, "Project Management Software Survey," PMNET*work*, Vol. 8, No. 5, 1994, pp. 33–41.

[5]Barry Naft, "Tailoring the Pace of Project Completion to Clients' Needs," *Environment Today*, January–February 1992, pp. 53–54.

SUMMARY

- **Projects** are distinguished by the fact that they produce unique products; they require the completion of a variety of tasks using a variety of resources and human skills; and task performance must be well coordinated to complete the project on time and within budget.
- To be scheduled accurately, a project must first be decomposed into each fundamental **task** or **activity**. Precedence relationships among the tasks and estimates of the time required to complete each task must then be obtained.
- A **Gantt chart** displays the planned starting and finishing times of each task on a time scale. Although visually informative for monitoring individual tasks, the Gantt chart does not show the interrelationships among the tasks.
- **PERT/CPM** is a scheduling method that uses networks to represent the sequencing of tasks in a project. By using a **two-pass method**, PERT/CPM diagrams can be evaluated to determine when a project is likely to be completed and which task(s) is (are) critical in keeping the project on schedule.
- The set of tasks that determine when a project will be finished form the **critical path**.
- PERT/CPM analysis can be modified to evaluate trade-offs between the time and cost required to complete tasks and the effect on project completion time. It can also be modified to evaluate explicitly the effects of uncertainty in task time estimates.
- PERT/CPM is typically implemented using computer software packages.

KEY TERMS

activity-on-arc (A-O-A) **847**
activity-on-node (A-O-N) **849**
backward pass **852**
beta distribution **857**
CPM (critical path method) **846**
crash cost (CC) **854**
crash time (CT) **854**
crashing **854**
critical path **853**
critical tasks **853**
dummy tasks **848**
earliest finishing (EF) time **850**
earliest starting (ES) time **850**
events **847**
forward pass **850**
Gantt chart **844**
latest finishing (LS) time **850**
latest starting (LS) time **850**
networks **846**
normal cost (NC) **854**
normal time (NT) **854**
PERT (program evaluation and review technique) **846**
PERT/CPM **846**
projects **839**
slack (float) **853**
task (activity) **842**
two-pass method **849**

KEY FORMULAS

Slack (float) = $LF - EF = LS - ES$

For task j with random task times having a beta distribution:

average task time: $\bar{t}_j = (a + 4m + b)/6$

variance: $\sigma_j^2 = [(b - a)/6]^2$

where a, b, and m are the optimistic, pessimistic, and most likely task times for task j.

For a project with random task times:

expected project completion time:

$$\bar{T} = \sum_{j \varepsilon CP} \bar{t}_j$$

variance of the project completion time:

$$\sigma_T^2 = \sum_{j \varepsilon CP} \sigma_j^2$$

where $j\varepsilon CP$ are the tasks on the critical path.

The probability that the project completion time, T, will be greater (less) than some value t is as follows:

$$\text{prob}(T > t) = \text{prob}[z > (t - \bar{T})/\sigma_T]$$

$$\text{prob}(T < t) = \text{prob}[z < (t - \bar{T})/\sigma_T]$$

where $\bar{T}$ is the expected value of T and σ_T is the standard deviation.

Discussion and Review Questions

1. "A company that manufactures automobiles would never use a project process." Give an example illustrating why this statement is false.
2. What makes a project process different from a metal-processing job shop that makes customized metal parts? Is it different?
3. What are some of the benefits of working on special projects? What are two of the major disadvantages?
4. What is the primary advantage of using Gantt charts? What are the disadvantages of using Gantt charts to schedule complicated projects?
5. What does it mean to crash an activity in project scheduling?
6. Why are the probability distributions of activity times skewed to the right?
7. How could we reduce the time required to complete a project without increasing the project cost?
8. Suppose there is considerable uncertainty with respect to activity times and relatively small slack for activities off the critical path. If we wanted to estimate the probability distribution for the project completion time, what should we do?
9. Suppose we developed a project schedule using PERT/CPM and then constructed a Gantt chart to represent the project visually. Why can we not simply monitor the progress of the project and update our estimated completion time using the Gantt chart? Why would we need to update the PERT/CPM diagram as well?

Solved Problems

Problem 1: Peterson Pipeline Company wanted to schedule a pipeline construction project that it divided into the 13 activities listed in Table 17.5. Peterson also estimated the normal time and cost and the crash time and cost for each activity.

(a) Construct a PERT/CPM chart for this project.

(b) Do a two-pass analysis to determine the earliest time the project will be completed using the normal activity times, and identify the critical path activities.

(c) Suppose Peterson wanted to complete the project in two months' less time than that found in part (b); which activities should it crash and by how much?

TABLE 17.5 PETERSON PIPELINE COMPANY PROJECT

		Normal		Crash	
Activity	Predecessors	Time	Cost	Time	Cost
A	None	2	250	1.5	300
B	A	4	620	3.0	750
C	B	4	380	2.5	500
D	A	4	220	3.0	280
E	C	5	900	4.0	1150
F	E	6	750	4.5	975
G	E	3	180	3.0	180
H	F	3	340	2.0	450
I	D, F	3	200	2.5	300
J	F, G	5	700	3.5	950
K	H	2	75	1.5	125
L	J	3	160	2.5	240
M	I, K, L	1	60	1.0	60

Note: Times are in months; costs are in $000.

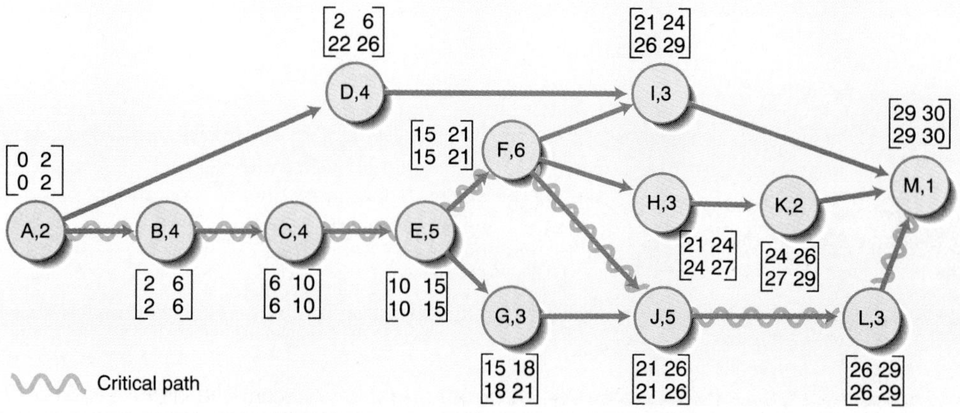

FIGURE 17.16 PERT/CPM diagram for the Peterson Pipeline project.

Solution

(a) The PERT/CPM chart using the A-O-N convention is given in Figure 17.16.

(b) To perform the forward pass, we set $ES = 0$ for the first activity, A. Then EF for A is $0 + 2 = 2$. B can start as soon as A is finished, so $ES = 2$ for activity B and $EF = 2 + 4 = 6$. Similarly, D can begin as soon as A finishes, so $ES = 2$ and $EF = 2 + 4 = 6$. The ES and EF times for all the activities are given in Table 17.6. Notice that for activities with more than one predecessor, such as I and M, the ES time equals the largest EF time of its predecessors. The earliest time the project will be completed using the normal activity times is 30 months.

To perform the backward pass, we set $LF = 30$ for the last activity, M. Then $LS = 30 - 1 = 29$. Activity L has only one successor, M, so we set LF for L = LS for $M = 29$. Then LS for L is $29 - 3 = 26$. We continue this procedure for all activities; these values are given in Table 17.6. Notice that for activity F, which has three successors, we set LF equal to the smallest LS time of its three successors: LF for F = min(LS for H, LS for I, LS for J) = min(24,26,21) = 21.

TABLE 17.6 PERT/CPM ANALYSIS RESULTS FOR PETERSON PIPELINE

Task	*ES*	*EF*	*LS*	*LF*	Slack	Per Unit Crash Cost	Normal Time	Crash Time
A*	0	2	0	2	0	100*	2	1.5
B*	2	6	2	6	0	130*	4	3.0
C*	6	10	6	10	0	80*	4	2.5
D	2	6	22	26	20	60	4	3.0
E*	10	15	10	15	0	250*	5	4.0
F*	15	21	15	21	0	150*	6	4.5
G	15	18	18	21	3	—	3	3.0
H	21	24	24	27	3	110	3	2.0
I	21	24	26	29	5	200	3	2.5
J*	21	26	21	26	0	167*	5	3.5
K	24	26	27	29	3	100	2	1.5
L*	26	29	26	29	0	120*	3	2.5
M*	29	30	29	30	0	—*	1	1.0

*Indicates a critical path task.

The slack values are then equal to $LS - ES$, and those with slack values of zero are on the critical path: A-B-C-E-F-J-L-M.

(c) To determine the best activities to crash, we first compute the per unit crash cost for each activity: (crash cost – normal cost)/(normal time – crash time). These values are given in Table 17.6. We now select the activity *on the critical path* that has the lowest per unit crash cost, which is C. (Notice that D has a lower per unit cost, but it is not on the critical path.) We crash C all the way to its minimum time of 2.5 months, thereby reducing the project time by 1.5 months. Checking the PERT/CPM diagram shows that the critical path has not changed (the smallest slack time off the critical path was originally 3). We now select the activity on the critical path with the next lowest per unit crash cost, which is A. We crash A by 0.5 month to its minimum of 1.5 months. The resulting project will be completed in 28 months.

Problem 2: For the project in Table 17.1, construct an A-O-A PERT/CPM network, and perform the two-pass analysis to determine the ES, EF, LS, LF, and slack times for each activity.

Solution. The A-O-A PERT network for the project is given in Figure 17.17. Computing the ES, EF, LS, and LF times using this convention is similar to that for the A-O-N convention. Each activity can be expressed by its beginning (leftmost) node and its ending (rightmost) node. If there is only one predecessor activity (one activity that enters the activity's beginning node), then ES for that activity equals the EF time for the predecessor. If there are two or more predecessors (arcs entering the activity's beginning node), ES equals the largest EF time for the predecessors. Similarly, in the backward pass, if an activity has only one successor (activity leaving the activity's ending node), LF equals the successor's LS time. If there are two or more successors (arcs leaving the ending node), LF equals the smallest of the successors' LS times.

Problem 3: A company wants to perform the following five-task project. For each task the company has estimated an optimistic, a most likely, and a pessimistic task time. (a) Determine the probability distribution for the project completion time, including the expected completion time and variance. (b) Determine the probability that the project will be finished in 20 weeks or less.

		Task Times (wk)		
Task	Predecessors	a	m	b
A	—	3	5	8
B	A	2	4	7
C	A	5	7	12
D	B, C	3	5	9
E	C	2	4	8

Solution:

(a) We first compute the expected task times and variance for each task using equations (17.1) and (17.2). These are as follows:

Task	t_j	σ_j^2
A	31/6	25/36
B	25/6	25/36
C	45/6	49/36
D	32/6	36/36
E	26/6	36/36

We now construct the PERT/CPM network and perform the two-pass analysis using the expected task times, as shown in Figure 17.18. The critical path is A-C-D, so the project completion time is

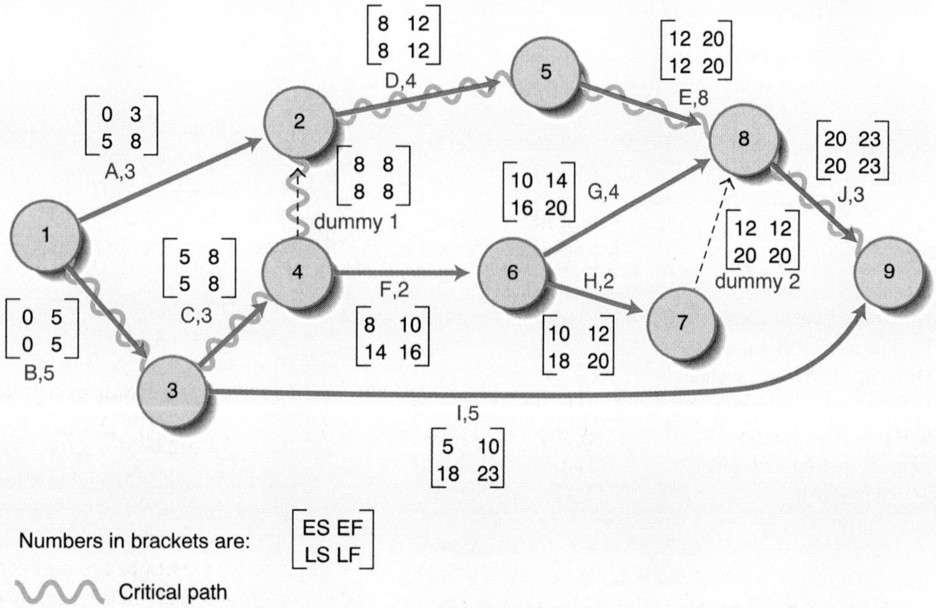

FIGURE 17.17 A-O-A PERT/CPM diagram for the credit operation relocation project.

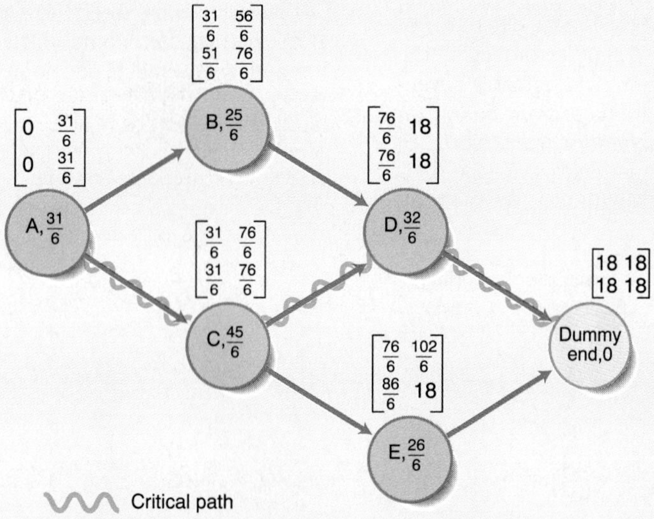

FIGURE 17.18 PERT/CPM diagram for solved problem 3.

approximately normally distributed, with an expected value equal to the sum of the expected times of the critical path tasks:

$$T = 31/6 + 45/6 + 32/6 = 108/6 = 18 \text{ weeks}$$

The variance is equal to the sum of the variances of the critical path tasks:

$$\sigma_T^2 = 25/36 + 49/36 + 36/36 = 110/36 = 3.06, \text{ so } \sigma_T = 1.75$$

(b) The probability that the project will be completed in 20 or less weeks is

$$\text{prob}(T < 20) = \text{prob}[z < (20 - 18)/1.75] = \text{prob}(z < 1.14) = 0.8504$$

PROBLEMS

1. A maintenance crew has been given the assignment of overhauling an important piece of equipment. The overhaul involves eight activities that have the following estimated activity times and precedence relationships:

Activity	Immediate Predecessors	Time (days)
A—Procure primary parts	—	21
B—Dismantle drive section	—	15
C—Procure drive section parts	B	18
D—Dismantle remainder section	—	10
E—Procure remainder parts	D	7
F—Reinstall drive section	A, C	20
G—Reinstall remainder section	A, E	14
H—Test and adjust	F, G	2

(a) Construct a PERT/CPM diagram for the project. (b) Compute the ES and EF times for every activity and the earliest time the project can be completed. (c) Compute the LS, LF, and slack times for each activity and identify the critical path activities.

2. Electra Corporation wants to contract out the production of one of its new computer products. The contracting process has been divided into a seven-task project described by the data given below. (a) Construct a PERT/CPM diagram for the project. (b) Determine the earliest completion time for the project. (c) Determine the critical path tasks for the project.

Task	Immediate Predecessors	Time (wk)
A—Prepare product specs	—	3
B—Award development contract	A	1
C—Prepare test specs	A	2
D—Contractor develops process	B	8
E—Prepare production estimates	C, D	2
F—Test	C, D	3
G—Award production contract	F	1

3. A consulting company has been assigned a contract to evaluate an appliance company's manufacturing operations. The tasks, precedence relationships, and task times for the project are given below. (a) Construct the PERT/CPM diagram for the project. (b) Determine the earliest time the project can be completed by performing a forward pass. (c) Determine the critical path tasks and the amount of slack for each noncritical task. (d) Construct a Gantt chart for the project, clearly showing the scheduled beginning and ending time for each task.

Task	Immediate Predecessors	Time (days)
A—Meet with managers	—	3
B—Collect operations data	A	20
C—Meet with opns. workers	A	15
D—Observe operations	A	10
E—Develop prel. improvements	B, C,D	15
F—Test possible improvements	E	10
G—Second meeting with workers	F	5
H—Second meeting with managers	F	3
I—Write report	G, H	12
J—Final meeting with managers	I	1

4. You are given the tasks, precedence relationships, normal task times, crashing costs, and minimum possible task times for a project shown in the following table. (a) Draw a PERT/CPM diagram for the project. (b) Compute the earliest time the project can be completed using the normal task times, and compute the corresponding cost. (c) List the tasks on the critical path. (d) Suppose the project had to be completed in three weeks' less time than you computed in part (b); determine which tasks should be crashed and by how much, and compute the resulting project cost.

Task	Predecessors	Normal Time	Crash Time	Normal Cost	Crash Cost
A	—	3	2	13	16
B	—	4	2	22	27
C	B	6	5	9	11
D	A, B	5	3	18	22
E	A	4	3	11	16
F	D, E	8	6	30	36
G	C, D	4	3	14	18
H	F, G	5	3	21	26
I	G	3	3	14	14
J	G	4	3	10	13
K	H, I, J	2	2	7	7

Note: Times are in weeks and costs are in thousands of dollars.

5. The following tasks, precedence relationships, normal task times, crash costs, and minimum possible task times are given for a software development project. (a) Draw a PERT/CPM diagram for this project. (b) Compute the earliest time the project can be completed using the normal task times, and compute the corresponding cost. (c) List the tasks that are on the critical path. (d) Suppose the project had to be completed in five days' less time than the amount computed in part (b); determine which tasks should

be crashed and how much their task times should be reduced, and compute the resulting project cost.

Task	Predecessors	Normal Time	Crash Time	Normal Cost	Crash Cost
A	—	10	8	31	34
B	A	4	3	12	17
C	A	8	5	10	18
D	B	12	11	18	21
E	C	7	6	20	22
F	D, E	15	12	40	47
G	E	7	7	14	14
H	F, G	4	3	9	12

Note: Times are in days and costs are in hundreds of dollars.

6. Suppose that in *Solved Problem* 1, after 18 months the following table describes how long it has taken to complete some tasks and the amount of time still required to complete other tasks. (a) Construct a PERT/CPM diagram for the remainder of the project (i.e., do not include completed tasks). (b) Determine how many more months will be required to complete the project. (c) List the critical tasks for the remainder of the project.

Activity	% Complete	Time Spent	Remaining Time Required
A	100%	2.5	0
B	100%	3.5	0
C	100%	4.0	0
D	100%	5.0	0
E	100%	4.0	0
F	80%	4.0	1.5
G	50%	4.0	3.0
H	0%	0	3.0
I	0%	0	3.0
J	0%	0	5.0
K	0%	0	2.0
L	0%	0	3.0
M	0%	0	1.0

7. An accounting firm has been hired to perform an audit. The audit has been divided into six activities. The firm has estimated the optimistic (a), pessimistic (b), and most likely (m) times for each task. (a) Construct a PERT/CPM diagram for this project and compute its expected completion time, assuming all tasks take their expected (not "most likely") completion times. (b) Compute the probability that the project will take more than 20 weeks to complete. (c) Compute the probability that the project will be completed in less than 16 weeks.

Task	Predecessors	Activity Times (wk) a	m	b
A	—	2	3	5
B	A	3	5	8
C	A	3	6	11
D	B	4	7	12
E	C	3	5	9
F	D, E	2	3	6

8. The following optimistic (a) pessimistic (b) and most likely (m) time estimates for each task have been given for a project. (a) Construct a PERT/CPM diagram for this project and compute its expected completion time, assuming all tasks take their expected (not their "most likely") completion times. (b) Compute the probability that the project will take more than 50 days to complete.

Task	Predecessors	Activity Times (days) a	m	b
A	—	10	12	15
B	—	6	10	16
C	A, B	3	5	10
D	C	8	12	17
E	C	4	7	12
F	C	3	4	6
G	D, E	5	8	13
H	F, G	5	7	10

9.* The U.S. Army has been ordered to airlift troops into a country for peacekeeping duty. The airlift and deployment has been divided into tasks A–I. (a) Construct a PERT/CPM diagram for this project and compute its completion time and cost, assuming all tasks take their normal times to complete. (b) Suppose the Army wanted to reduce the project time by five days. Which tasks should be crashed, and by how much, so as to minimize the cost?

Task	Predecessors	Normal Time	Crash Time	Normal Cost	Crash Cost
A	—	4	3	450	650
B	A	7	5	320	400
C	A	6	6	180	180
D	A	4	3	120	170
E	B, C	5	3	300	420
F	D, E	6	3	400	700
G	E	2	1	150	240
H	F, G	4	3	350	500
I	H	2	2	120	120

Note: Times are in days and costs are in thousands of dollars.

10. Ypres, Ltd., plans to develop and introduce a new product. The product development and introduction process has been divided into nine tasks. The optimistic (a), pessimistic (b), and most likely (m), time estimates for each task are given below. (a) Construct a PERT/CPM diagram for this project and compute its expected completion time, assuming all tasks take their expected times to complete. (b) Compute the probability that product development and introduction will take more than 26 weeks to complete.

Task	Predecessors	Task Times (wk) a	m	b
A	—	4	6	10
B	—	2	3	5
C	—	1	2	5
D	A, B	2	3	6
E	A, B, C	4	7	12
F	D, E	1	2	4
G	F	2	4	7
H	F	3	6	10
I	G, H	1	2	4

CASE

Flood Relief Concert: A Project Planning Case

In 1993 many areas of the central United States were ravaged by severe flooding. Although considerable financial assistance was provided by the federal and state governments, private charities such as the Red Cross and the Salvation Army saw their disaster relief funds depleted by the enormous burden of assisting flood victims. Recognizing that great needs still existed, a group of citizens decided to organize a benefit concert to raise money. A fund-raising goal of $200,000 was established, and in order for the effort to be of maximum value to flood victims, the group determined that the concert, named Flood Relief 93, should be held within 60 days.

No one in the group had experience organizing large-scale concerts, so they decided to approach the process methodically yet expeditiously. They held an all-day meeting to lay out each step required for a successful concert. The plan was to have a 10- to 12-hour outdoor concert with a mix of local and nationally known musical performers. Because of their lack of experience, the group members realized that they would probably have to rely on paid professional workers as well as volunteers. As they worked through the planning process, their two major concerns were making a profit and being able to schedule the concert within 60 days.

One member of the group was John Rivers, a manager for a local construction company. To determine the feasibility of holding the concert within 60 days, John decided to construct a PERT/CPM diagram for the preliminary list of tasks the group had identified. He worked with other members of the group to determine probable precedence relationships, but they made no attempt at first to estimate task times. The original set of tasks and precedence relationships are given in Table 17.7, and the resulting PERT/CPM diagram is given in Figure 17.19.

Even without task time estimates, the PERT/CPM diagram in Figure 17.19 suggested that tasks C (obtaining seed money), D (hiring and assigning personnel), H (hiring performers), and I (selecting and contracting for a site) would be crucial because so many other tasks depended on their completion. Each member of the group was instructed to find out more about how to accomplish one of these tasks and how long it would probably take. Two members knew a concert promoter and decided to meet with her to obtain as much information as possible. When the group reconvened a few days later, members used the time estimates they had obtained to schedule the tasks.

The meeting was a mixture of discouragement and excitement. Using the time estimates, some of which were very fuzzy, John did a quick PERT/CPM analysis indicating that the earliest the concert could occur was in 95–130 days. Tasks such as choosing the site and selecting and contracting with concessionaires, printers, and so on were all time-consuming, and if they could not occur until personnel were hired, seed money obtained, and so forth, there was no way the concert could be held within the desired time (which was now down to 55 days). The good news was that one group member, John Junall, had contacted a business lawyer friend who had handled other special event promotions. The lawyer agreed to provide his services for the concert at minimal cost. A second group member, Martha Ross, had begun soliciting sponsors to obtain seed money. She received a commitment for a $2500 gift from one company, and another individual had agreed to lend the group $10,000, interest free, with the assurance that it would be repaid as soon as ticket sales reached $50,000.

Though this was good news, the problem of finding some way to accelerate the project remained. The group came to several conclusions. First, they decided that based on Martha's early success, the group would act as if it would be able to obtain the necessary seed money quickly enough to pay bills as they occurred, effectively eliminating this task as a predecessor for other tasks. (Martha was then put in charge of raising the rest of the seed money as soon as possible.) This saved an estimated 5–10 days. The group then reviewed each task and determined that although final decisions could not be made or contracts signed with concessionaires, security providers, and so on until they knew who the performers were and where the concert would be held (and therefore how large an audience they would have), they could start preliminary work to identify such service providers. So they broke up these tasks into subtasks. The group also identified some tasks that originally had been considered sequential but could in fact be done concurrently, such as task R (preparing the program layout) and task S (selecting the printer), as long as they were coordinated. Also, originally the group had felt that a site could not be selected until the performers were chosen because the program would determine how large a site would be necessary. But by agreeing on a general concert format and caliber of acts and the resulting target audience size, they decided that a site could be selected and specific performers chosen concurrently.

After making these modifications, the group had reduced the projected completion time to 70–75 days, but this was still unacceptable. Of the tasks on the likely criti-

TABLE 17.7 TASKS FOR FLOOD RELIEF CONCERT

Task	Predecessors
A— Select and retain attorney	—
B— Establish accounting/organization/reporting system	—
C— Obtain seed money from investors/sponsors	A, B
D— Hire personnel	C
E— Identify/evaluate potential performers	D
F— Identify/contact potential concessionaires	D
G— Identify/evaluate potential sites	D
H— Hire performers	E
I— Select and rent site	G, H
J— Identify/hire security services	I
K— Identify/hire providers of sanitary facilities	I
L— Contract with concessionaires	F, I
M— Identify/hire medical personnel	I
N— Design layout of site	I
O— Rent stage/sound equipment	N
P— Purchase insurance	I
Q— Obtain program advertisers	I
R— Prepare program layout/content	Q
S— Select program printer	R
T— Print programs	S
U— Print tickets and arrange ticket outlets	I
V— Hire clean-up service	I
W— Set up stage	O
X— Set up concession stands	L, N
Y— Set up sanitary facilities	K, N
Z— Set up medical and other facilities	N
AA—Arrange print/radio advertising	U
BB— Performers arrive in town	H
CC—Transport performers to concert	BB
DD—Concert occurs	J, M, P, T, V, W, X, Y, Z, AA, CC,
EE— Clean up	DD

cal path, those projected to be most time-consuming were selecting and contracting with performers, selecting and contracting for a site, hiring paid workers and finding volunteers, and preparing the advertising and ticket-printing and selling system. Identifying these critical tasks illuminated a possible strategy. The group decided that one way to save time was to prioritize the hiring/volunteer recruitment process as follows: (1) hire or recruit personnel to perform the critical tasks of performer selection, site selection, advertising, and ticket system development first; and (2) unless knowledgeable volunteers existed for these tasks, hire professionals and use volunteers for noncritical tasks. Tasks were assigned to the group members; those having to do with hiring/recruitment took highest priority. John Rivers agreed to develop a new PERT/CPM diagram and a Gantt chart to show when each task was scheduled to be performed. He also adjusted the task times of the critical tasks, setting the target values necessary to complete the project on time.

The group was successful in its hiring and recruitment. The concert promoter originally consulted agreed to help in selecting and negotiating contracts with musical performers, thereby accomplishing this task in half the originally estimated time. An experienced ticket manager was hired who got the ticket preparation and distribution system functioning within two days, with tickets available at dozens of outlets. A volunteer in the advertising industry developed an advertising program within days, and was even able to obtain some free advertising time and space from radio stations and newspapers. And Martha Ross raised the necessary seed money, as had been hoped.

Although some problems occurred along the way, the concert occurred 62 days after the original idea was con-

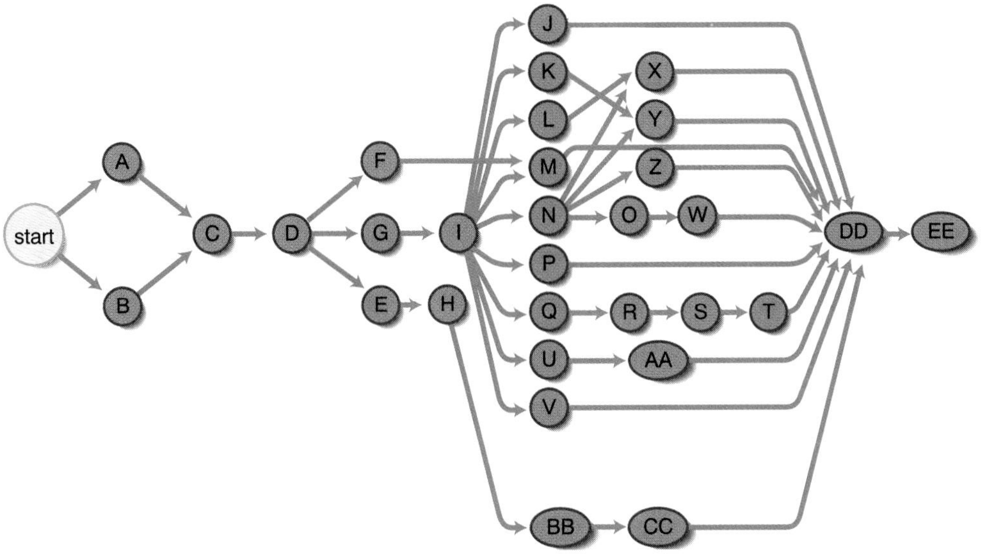

FIGURE 17.19 Preliminary PERT/CPM diagram for the Flood Relief 93 concert.

ceived. The only serious problem was that it rained all day. The rain reduced the size of the crowd, but it reminded everyone of their purpose. Although profits fell short of the goal, the concert occurred on time due to good project scheduling analysis; but not even PERT/CPM could stop the rain.

QUESTIONS

1. Even before the planning group had estimates of the task times, how did PERT/CPM analysis help in planning the project?
2. The planning group made some implicit cost-time tradeoffs and decided to "crash" some of the tasks. Which tasks were crashed and how was this accomplished?

SELECTED READINGS

HAMBURGER, D. "'On Time' Project Completion—Managing the Critical Path," *Project Management Journal*, Vol. 18, No. 4, 1987, pp. 79–85.

KERZNER, HAROLD. *Project Management: A Systems Approach to Planning, Scheduling, and Controlling* (3rd ed.), Van Nostrand Reinhold, New York, 1989.

KEZSBOM, D. "Are You Really Ready to Build a Project Team?" *Industrial Engineering*, Vol. 22, No. 10, 1990, pp. 50–55.

MEREDITH, JACK, and SAMUEL MANTEL, JR. *Project Management: A Managerial Approach* (2nd ed.), Wiley, New York, 1989.

PETERSON, P. "Project Management Software Survey," PMNET*work*, Vol. 8, No. 5, 1994, pp. 33–41.

ROGERS, TOM. "Project Management: Emerging as a Requisite for Success," *Industrial Engineering*, Vol. 25, No. 6, 1993, pp. 42–43.

SMITH-DANIELS, DWIGHT E., and NICHOLAS AQUILANO. "Constrained Resource Project Scheduling," *Journal of Operations Management*, Vol. 4, 1984, pp. 369–387.

APPENDIX A

THE STANDARD NORMAL DISTRIBUTION

This table gives the area under the standardized normal curve from 0 to z, as shown by the shaded portion of the following figure.

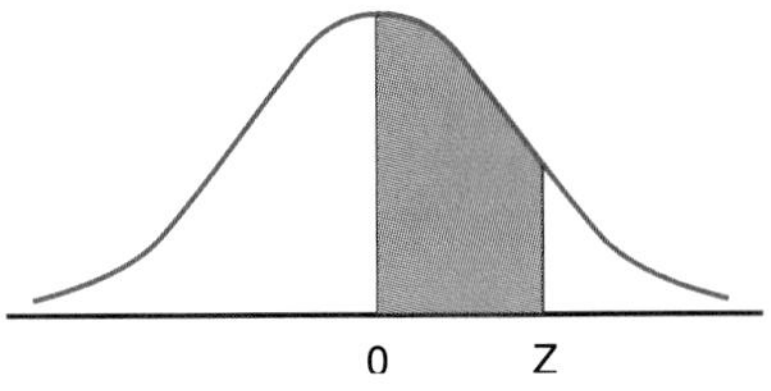

Examples: If z is the standard normal random variable, then

$\text{Prob}\ (0 \le z \le 1.32) = 0.4066$

$\text{Prob}\ (z \ge 1.32) = 0.5000 - 0.4066 = 0.0934$

$\text{Prob}\ (z \le 1.32) = \text{Prob}\ (z \le 0) + \text{Prob}\ (0 \le z \le 1.32)$

$= 0.5000 + 0.4066 = 0.9066$

$\text{Prob}\ (z \le -1.32) = \text{Prob}\ (z \ge 1.32) = 0.0934$ (by symmetry)

z	0.00	0.01	0.02	0.03	0.04	0.05	0.06	0.07	0.08	0.09
0.0	0.0000	0.0040	0.0080	0.0120	0.0160	0.0199	0.0239	0.0279	0.0319	0.0359
0.1	0.0398	0.0438	0.0478	0.0517	0.0557	0.0596	0.0636	0.0675	0.0714	0.0753
0.2	0.0793	0.0832	0.0871	0.0910	0.0948	0.0987	0.1026	0.1064	0.1103	0.1141
0.3	0.1179	0.1217	0.1255	0.1293	0.1331	0.1368	0.1406	0.1443	0.1480	0.1517
0.4	0.1554	0.1591	0.1628	0.1664	0.1700	0.1736	0.1772	0.1808	0.1844	0.1879
0.5	0.1915	0.1950	0.1985	0.2019	0.2054	0.2088	0.2123	0.2157	0.2190	0.2224
0.6	0.2257	0.2291	0.2324	0.2357	0.2389	0.2422	0.2454	0.2486	0.2518	0.2549
0.7	0.2580	0.2612	0.2642	0.2673	0.2704	0.2734	0.2764	0.2794	0.2823	0.2852
0.8	0.2881	0.2910	0.2939	0.2967	0.2995	0.3023	0.3051	0.3078	0.3106	0.3133
0.9	0.3159	0.3186	0.3212	0.3238	0.3264	0.3289	0.3315	0.3340	0.3365	0.3389
1.0	0.3413	0.3438	0.3461	0.3485	0.3508	0.3531	0.3554	0.3577	0.3599	0.3621
1.1	0.3643	0.3665	0.3686	0.3708	0.3729	0.3749	0.3770	0.3790	0.3810	0.3830
1.2	0.3849	0.3869	0.3888	0.3907	0.3925	0.3944	0.3962	0.3980	0.3997	0.4015
1.3	0.4032	0.4049	0.4066	0.4082	0.4099	0.4115	0.4131	0.4147	0.4162	0.4177
1.4	0.4192	0.4207	0.4222	0.4236	0.4251	0.4265	0.4279	0.4292	0.4306	0.4319
1.5	0.4332	0.4345	0.4357	0.4370	0.4382	0.4394	0.4406	0.4418	0.4429	0.4441
1.6	0.4452	0.4463	0.4474	0.4484	0.4495	0.4505	0.4515	0.4525	0.4535	0.4545
1.7	0.4554	0.4564	0.4573	0.4582	0.4591	0.4599	0.4608	0.4616	0.4625	0.4633
1.8	0.4641	0.4649	0.4656	0.4664	0.4671	0.4678	0.4686	0.4693	0.4699	0.4706
1.9	0.4713	0.4719	0.4726	0.4732	0.4738	0.4744	0.4750	0.4756	0.4761	0.4767
2.0	0.4772	0.4778	0.4783	0.4788	0.4793	0.4798	0.4803	0.4808	0.4812	0.4817
2.1	0.4821	0.4826	0.4830	0.4834	0.4838	0.4842	0.4846	0.4850	0.4854	0.4857
2.2	0.4861	0.4864	0.4868	0.4871	0.4875	0.4878	0.4881	0.4884	0.4887	0.4890
2.3	0.4893	0.4896	0.4898	0.4901	0.4904	0.4906	0.4909	0.4911	0.4913	0.4916
2.4	0.4918	0.4920	0.4922	0.4925	0.4927	0.4929	0.4931	0.4932	0.4934	0.4936
2.5	0.4938	0.4940	0.4941	0.4943	0.4945	0.4946	0.4948	0.4949	0.4951	0.4952
2.6	0.4953	0.4955	0.4956	0.4957	0.4959	0.4960	0.4961	0.4962	0.4963	0.4964
2.7	0.4965	0.4966	0.4967	0.4968	0.4969	0.4970	0.4971	0.4972	0.4973	0.4974
2.8	0.4974	0.4975	0.4976	0.4977	0.4977	0.4978	0.4979	0.4979	0.4980	0.4981
2.9	0.4981	0.4982	0.4982	0.4983	0.4984	0.4984	0.4985	0.4985	0.4986	0.4986
3.0	0.4986	0.4987	0.4987	0.4988	0.4988	0.4989	0.4989	0.4989	0.4990	0.4990
3.5	0.4999									

Source: Adapted from Robert Markland, Topics in Management Science (3rd Ed.) Wiley, New York 1989.

APPENDIX B

SOLUTIONS TO SELECTED ODD-NUMBERED PROBLEMS

CHAPTER 2 – OPERATIONS STRATEGY

1. (a) 2500 cans/person-hr
(b) \$68.75/person-hr.
(c) \$31.25/person-hr.

3. (a) \$12.50/per-hr.
(b) Company saves no overhead or indirect costs; Costs are independent of output level and direct labor.

5. (a) System 1: Revenue/hr. = \$70
System 2: Revenue/hr. = \$68.40
(b) System 1: Revenue/hr. = \$77.60
System 2: Revenue/hr. = \$77.70

CHAPTER 4 – FORECASTING

1. ME = +7/12 = 0.583
MAD = 49/12 = 4.08
MAPE = 72.6%/12 = 6.05%
MSE = 271/12 = 22.58

3. (a) \$255.05
(b) \$270.65
(c) Extra profit for the week = \$15.60; extra profit/day = \$2.29.

5. (a) $F_{16} = 403.4$
(b) $F_{16} = 452.2$
(c) $F_{16} = 426.0$

7. (a)&(b)

Week	SMA(3) Forecast	Error	Cum. Ave. Forecast	Error
5	8952	–1549	8301	–898
6	8207	–100	8122	–15
7	8647	+2718	8119	+3246
8	8958	–468	8583	–93

(c)

	SMA(3)	Cum. Ave.
MAD	1209	1063
MSE	2,503,987	2,837,948

9. (a)

Week	Actual	Forecast	Error	Error^2	%Error
4	1389	1257.4	+131.6	17,319	9.5%
5	1436	1290.3	+145.7	21,228	10.1%
6	1297	1326.7	– 29.7	882	2.3%

(b) MAD = 102.3; MAPE = 7.3%; MSE = 13,143
(c) $F_7 = 1319.3$.

11. (a)&(b)

Month	Forecasts α=0.3	Forecasts α=0.1
6	41.73	43.08
7	42.41	43.17
8	45.29	44.05
9	44.90	44.04

13. (a) $\text{Transactions}_t(000) = 30.33 + 2.74t$
(b) $F_{11}(000) = 60.47$
$F_{12}(000) = 63.21$

15. The 10-day moving average of deseasonalized data is 3081. So
$F_{\text{Sun}} = 3081(1.39) = 4283$
$F_{\text{Mon}} = 3081(0.87) = 2680$

17. $F_{\text{Fall}} = [8423 + 72(16)]\,[1.17] = 11{,}203$
$F_{\text{Winter}} = [8423 + 72(17)]\,[1.08] = 10{,}419$
$F_{\text{Summer}} = [8423 + 72(18)]\,[0.75] = 7289$

19. (a) $\text{Sales}_t = -0.63 + 1.54(\text{Adv}_{t-2} + \text{Adv}_{t-1})$
(b) $\text{Sales}_9 = -0.63 + 1.54(15 + 20) = 53.27$

21. $F_{10} = I_9 + S_9 = 50 + 2.5 = 52.5$
$F_{11} = 53.6 + 2.6 = 56.2.$

Tutorial 1 – Optimization Models and Linear Programming

1. (a) Let $X2$ = # 2-color lithos to make/week
$X4$ = # 4-color lithos to make/week

Maximize z = \$10000 $X2$ + \$24000 $X4$
subject to
$8\,X2 + 16\,X4 \leq 100$ (roller avail.)
$12\,X2 + 30\,X4 \leq 160$ (gear cutting cap.)
$3\,X2 + 8\,X4 \leq 40$ (polishing cap.)
$X2 \geq 2$
$X4 \geq 2$

$X2, X4 \geq 0.$

(b) Optimum is $X\,2 = 8$, $X4 = 2$, z = DM 128,000.

3. (a) x_j = # tons of grade j scrap to use to make 500 tons of paperboard, j = 1,2,3,4.

Minimize $z = 150\,x_1 + 110\,x_2 + 90\,x_3 + 50\,x_4$

subject to
$1\,x_1 - 1\,x_2 - 2\,x_3 - 4\,x_4 \geq 0$ (strength)
$4\,x_1 + 2\,x_2 - 1\,x_4 \geq 0$ (color)
$2\,x_1 - 1\,x_2 - 1\,x_4 \geq 0$ (texture)
$x_1 + x_2 + x_3 + x_4 = 500$ (demand)

(Alternatives to the first three constraints are
$8\,x_1 + 6\,x_2 + 5\,x_3 + 3\,x_4 \geq 3500$
$9\,x_1 + 7\,x_2 + 5\,x_3 + 4\,x_4 \geq 2500$
$8\,x_1 + 5\,x_2 + 6\,x_3 + 5\,x_4 \geq 3000$)
all x_j's ≥ 0.

(b) An optimum is $x_1 = 400$, $x_2 = 0$, $x_3 = 0$, $x_4 = 100$, $z = 65000$. An alternative optimum is $x_1 = 250$, $x_2 = 250$, $x_3 = x_4 = 0$.

5. (a) Let x_{ij} = # cashiers who work shift i on weekly schedule j, where $i = 1$ means 9 am - 5 p.m.; $i = 2$ means 1 p.m. - 9 p.m. $j = 1$ means the cashier works Mon-Fri, $j = 2$ means Tue-Sat, and so on.

Minimize $z = \sum_{i=1}^{2} \sum_{j=1}^{7} x_{ij}$

subject to

$x_{11} + x_{14} + x_{15} + x_{16} + x_{17} \geq 6$
$x_{11} + x_{14} + x_{15} + x_{16} + x_{17} + x_{21} + x_{24} + x_{25} + x_{26} + x_{27} \geq 5$
$x_{21} + x_{24} + x_{25} + x_{26} + x_{27} \geq 8$

$x_{13} + x_{14} + x_{15} + x_{16} + x_{17} \geq 4$
$x_{13} + x_{14} + x_{15} + x_{16} + x_{17} + x_{23} + x_{24} + x_{25} + x_{26} + x_{27} \geq 12$
$x_{23} + x_{24} + x_{25} + x_{26} + x_{27} \geq 6$

all variables ≥ 0.

(b) The optimum, which requires 20.33 employees, is

	Mon-Fri	Tue Sat	Wed-Sun	Thu-Mon	Fri-Tue	Sat-Wed	Sun-Thu
9am-5pm	0	2	2	2	2	2	1.33
1pm-9pm	2	2.33	0	2.33	0	2.33	1.33

(c) Divisibility is not satisfied. Although for personnel scheduling the optimal solution will frequently be integer-valued if the requirements in each period are integers, this is not guaranteed.

7. (a) Let A_j = # dollars in advertising spent in district j
R_j = # sales reps assigned to district j

Maximize $z = 7\,A_1 + 12\,A_2 + 10\,A_3 + 11\,A_4 + 380000\,R_1 + 250000\,R_2 + 360000\,R_3 + 410000\,R_4$

subject to
$A_1 + A_2 + A_3 + A_4 \leq 800{,}000$ (advertising)
$R_1 + R_2 + R_3 + R_4 \leq 10$ (sales reps available)
$A_1 \geq 50000$
$A_2 \geq 50000$
$A_3 \geq 50000$
$A_4 \geq 50000$
$R_1 \geq 1$
$R_2 \geq 1$
$R_3 \geq 1$
$R_4 \geq 1$

all variables ≥ 0.

(b) Optimum is $A1 = A3 = A4 = \$50000$, $A2 = \$650000$, $R1 = R2 = R3 = 1$, $R4 = 7$, $z = \$13{,}060{,}000$.

9. (a) R_t = # units produced during month t using regular-time production
O_t = # units produced during month t using overtime production
I_t = # units in inventory at the end of month t

Minimize $z = 9\,\Sigma\,R_t + 12\,\Sigma\,O_t + 2\,\Sigma\,I_t$
s.t. $R_1 + O_1 = 450 + I_1 \Rightarrow R_1 + O_1 - I_1 = 450$
$I_1 + R_2 + O_2 = 575 + I_2 \Rightarrow I_1 - I_2 + R_2 + O_2 = 575$
$I_2 + R_3 + O_3 = 490 + I_3 \Rightarrow I_2 - I_3 + R_3 + O_3 = 490$
$I_3 + R_4 + O_4 = 530 + I_4 \Rightarrow I_3 - I_4 + R_4 + O_4 = 530$
$R_t \leq 500$ for all $t = 1, \ldots, 4$
all var ≥ 0.

(b) $R_1 = R_2 = R_3 = R_4 = 500$; $O_1 = 0$, $O_2 = 25$, $O_3 = 0$, $O_4 = 20$, $I_1 = 50$, $I_2 = 0$, $I_3 = 10$, $I_4 = 0$, $z = \$18{,}660$.

11. (a) Let x_{ij} = the number of pounds of metal i used to make alloy j each day

Maximize $z = 3.0\,x_{CA} + 2.0\,x_{NA} + 3.5\,x_{AA} + 4\,x_{CB} + 3.0\,x_{NB} + 4.5\,x_{AB}$

subject to

$$0.6\,x_{CA} - 0.4\,x_{NA} - 0.4\,x_{AA} \geq 0$$
$$-0.1\,x_{CA} + 0.9\,x_{NA} - 0.1\,x_{AA} \geq 0$$
$$-0.25x_{CA} + 0.75x_{NA} - 0.25x_{AA} \leq 0$$
$$-2\,x_{NA} + x_{AA} = 0$$
$$0.65\,x_{CB} - 0.35\,x_{NB} - 0.35\,x_{AB} \leq 0$$
$$-0.4\,x_{CB} + 0.6\,x_{NB} - 0.4\,x_{AB} \geq 0$$
$$-0.3\,x_{CB} - 0.3\,x_{NB} + 0.7\,x_{AB} \leq 0$$
$$x_{CA} + x_{CB} \leq 2000$$
$$x_{NA} + x_{NB} \leq 3000$$
$$x_{AA} + x_{AB} \leq 4000$$

and all x_{ij}'s ≥ 0.

(b) Optimum solution is $x_{CA} = 0$, $x_{CB} = 2000$, $x_{NA} = 0$, $x_{NB} = 3000$, $x_{AA} = 0$, $x_{AB} = 2142.87$, z = \$26,642.86/day.

13. (a) Let x_{ij} = # units produced at plant i and sent to wholesaler j

Minimize $z = 19\,x_{A1} + 22\,x_{A2} + \ldots + 21\,x_{C3} + 20\,x_{C4}$

s.t.

$$x_{A1} + x_{A2} + x_{A3} + x_{A4} \leq 300$$
$$x_{A1} + x_{A2} + x_{A3} + x_{A4} \geq 180$$
$$x_{B1} + x_{B2} + x_{B3} + x_{B4} \leq 400$$
$$x_{B1} + x_{B2} + x_{B3} + x_{B4} \geq 240$$
$$x_{C1} + x_{C2} + x_{C3} + x_{C4} \leq 500$$
$$x_{C1} + x_{C2} + x_{C3} + x_{C4} \geq 300$$
$$x_{A1} + x_{B1} + x_{C1} = 150$$
$$x_{A2} + x_{B2} + x_{C2} = 300$$
$$x_{A3} + x_{B3} + x_{C3} = 350$$
$$x_{A4} + x_{B4} + x_{C4} = 250$$

all variables ≥ 0.

(b) The optimal solution is $X_{A1} = 50$, $X_{A2} = 0$, $X_{A3} = 0$, $X_{A4} = 250$, $X_{B1} = 0$, $X_{B2} = 300$, $X_{B3} = 100$, $X_{B4} = 0$, $X_{C1} = 100$, $X_{C2} = 0$, $X_{C3} = 250$, $X_{C4} = 0$, $z = \$18{,}650$.

15. Let x_{ij} = # tons of paper to make at mill i and to send to market j

Minimize $z = 230\,x_{A1} + 235\,x_{A2} + \ldots + 243\,x_{C4} + 251\,x_{C5}$

s.t.

$$x_{A1} + x_{A2} + x_{A3} + x_{A4} + x_{A5} \leq 1200$$
$$x_{B1} + x_{B2} + x_{B3} + x_{B4} + x_{B5} \leq 1500$$
$$x_{C1} + x_{C2} + x_{C3} + x_{C4} + x_{C5} \leq 900$$
$$x_{A1} + x_{B1} + X_{C1} = 600$$
$$x_{A2} + x_{B2} + X_{C2} = 1000$$
$$x_{A3} + x_{B3} + X_{C3} = 500$$
$$x_{A4} + x_{B4} + X_{C4} = 800$$
$$x_{A5} + x_{B5} + X_{C5} = 500$$

all variables ≥ 0.

17. (a) Hint: Let

MA_t = the number of units of A made during month t

MB_t = the number of units of B made during month t

PA_t = the number of units of A purchased during month t

PB_t = the number of units of B purchased during month t

IA_t = the number of units of A in inventory at the end of month t

IB_t = the number of units of B in inventory at the end of month t

(b) The minimum total cost = \$163,070

19. The optimal solution is $A = 2.5$, $B = 0$, $z = 25$

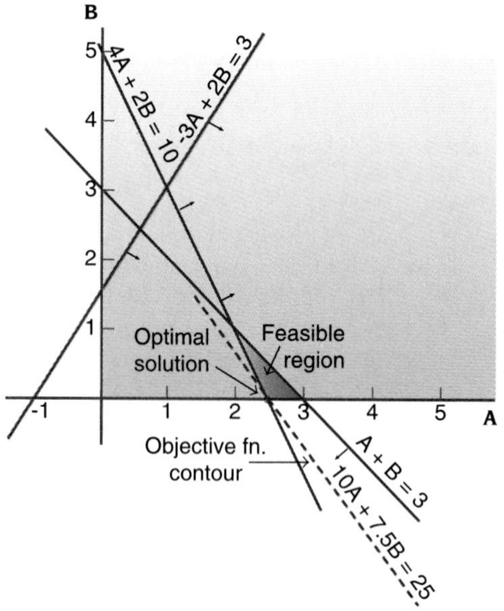

21. Optimum is $A = 0$, $B = 6$, $Z = 6$

23.

First Tableau

		X	Y	s_1	s_2	s_3		
	basic							
c_B	var.	5	8	0	0	0	b	ratio
0	s_1	2.5	5	1	0	0	50	50/5
0	s_2	2	1	0	1	0	20	20/1
0	s_3	7.5	2	0		1	60	60/2
	z_j	0	0	0	0	0	0	
	$c_j - z_j$	5	8	0	0	0		

Second Tableau

		X	Y	s_1	s_2	s_3		
	basic							
c_B	var.	5	8	0	0	0	b	ratio
8	Y	0.5	1	0.2	0	0	10	10/0.5
0	s_2	1.5	0	−0.2	1	0	10	10/1.5
0	s_3	6.5	0	−0.4	0	1	40	40/6.5
	z_j	4	8	1.6	0	0	80	
	$c_j - z_j$	1	0	−1.6	0	0		

Third and Final Tableau

		X	Y	s_1	s_2	s_3	
	basic						
c_B	var.	5	8	0	0	0	b
8	Y	0	1	.231	0	−.077	6.923
0	s_2	0	0	−.107	1	−.231	0.775
5	X	1	0	.062	0	.154	6.154
	z_j	5	8	1.538	0	.154	86.154
	$c_j - z_j$	0	0	−1.538	0	-.154	

Optimum is $X = 6.154$, $Y = 6.923$, $s_1 = 0$, $s_2 = 0.775$, $s_3 = 0$, $z = 86.154$

25. The original solution is $A_1 = 20$, $A_2 = 15$, and all other variables are 0. The entering variable is C and the leaving variable is A_2. After the pivot, the new solution is $A_1 = 17$, $C = 3$, and all other variables are 0. The entering variable is then A and the leaving variable is A_1. After the pivot the final tableau is

		A	B	C	s_1	A_1	A_2	
c_B	var.	3	4	1	0	M	M	b
3	A	1	4/9	0	−5/9	—	—	85/9
1	C	0	1/9	1	1/9	—	—	10/9
	z_j	3	13/9	1	−14/9	—	—	265/9
	c_j-z_j	0	23/9	0	14/9	—	—	

Optimum is $A = 85/9$, $B = 0$, $C = 10/9$, $s_1 = 0$, $z = 265/9$

27. Let x_{ij} = 1 if crew i is assigned to customer j
0 if crew i is not assigned to customer j

Minimize $z = 8x_{1A} + 7x_{1B} + \dots + 6x_{5D} + 11x_{5E}$

s.t. $x_{1A} + \dots + x_{1E} = 1$
$x_{2A} + \dots + x_{2E} = 1$
$x_{3A} + \dots + x_{3E} = 1$
$x_{4A} + \dots + x_{4E} = 1$
$x_{5A} + \dots + x_{5E} = 1$

$x_{1A} + \dots + x_{5A} = 1$
$x_{1B} + \dots + x_{5B} = 1$
$x_{1C} + \dots + x_{5C} = 1$
$x_{1D} + \dots + x_{5D} = 1$
$x_{1E} + \dots + x_{5E} = 1$

Chapter 5 Supplement – Product Reliability

1. (0.99)(0.95)(0.98)(0.995) = 0.917

3. (a) $(0.98)^3(0.96)^3 = 0.833$
(b) $(0.98)(0.95)(0.96)^2 = 0.858$; slightly more reliable

5. (a) (0.995)(0.99)(0.98)(0.975) = 0.941
(b) (0.995)(0.99)(0.9996)(0.975) = 0.960
(c) Have a redundant C and a redundant D. Resulting reliability is (0.995)(0.99)(0.9996)(0.9994) = 0.984.

7. Best design is *A,2B,C,D;* reliability = (0.995)(0.9999)(0.98)(0.975) = 0.951.

Chapter 6 – Capacity Planning and Facility Location

1. Total hours required/day is 36.67. Lines needed = ⌈(36.67 hr./day)/(21 hr. per line/day)⌉ = 1.75 ⇒ 2 lines.

3. (a) For 300,000 unit facility: BE = 200,000 units/yr.
For 450,000 unit plant: BE = 218,750 units/yr.
(b) MCP should build the smaller plant.

5. (a)
So. Cal.: 8.35
No. Cal.: 7.05
New Eng.: 7.00
Florida : 9.10

7. Coordinates are $x = 2.775$ and $y = 5.400$.

9. For each alternative (open at A or open at B) we solve a transportation problem with three sources (the two existing ones and the new one). We then add the fixed costs to the minimum transportation cost.
The costs for each alternative are

Alternative	Transport Cost	Fixed Cost	Total Cost
Open *A*	\$37,900	\$40,000	\$77,900
Open *B*	\$35,900	\$45,000	\$80,900

Best alternative is to open the greenhouse at A. Optimal supply pattern is to ship 600 truck-loads from Greenhouse 1 to distributor 2; 200 loads from *GH* 1 to Dist. 4; 400 loads from *GH* 2 to Dist 5; 500 loads from *A* to Dist. 1; and 300 loads from *A* to Dist. 3.

11. (a) Keep *A* open 24 hours; no pharmacy is more than 22 units away from A.
(b) Best pairs are *BE* and *DE*; no pharmacy will be more than 14 units from a 24-hour pharmacy.

Chapter 6 Supplement – Solving Transportation Problems

1. (a) Shipments for NW corner solution are

	Distribution Centers			
Plants	A	B	C	D
Norfolk	10	2		
Lexington		8	9	
Milwaukee			1	10

z = 3700

(b) Shipments for VAM solution are

	Distribution Centers			
Plants	A	B	C	D
Norfolk		2		10
Lexington		7	10	
Milwaukee	10	1		

z = 3260

3. For the VAM solution the c_{ij}-z_{ij} values for the nonbasic cells are

cell	Nor-A	Nor-C	Lex-A	Lex-D	Mil-C	Mil-D
$c_{ij}-z_{ij}$	+10	−10	+40	+20	+40	+30

So we bring the Norfolk –> C cell into the basis. The optimal shipments are

	Distribution Centers			
Plants	A	B	C	D
Norfolk			2	10
Lexington		9	8	
Milwaukee	10	1		

5. (a) VAM solution is

	Customers		
Warehouses	1	2	3
A		180	
B		50	200
C	250	70	

z = 19,090

The optimal solution is

	Customers		
Warehouses	1	2	3
A			180
B		250	
C	250	50	20

z = 18,890

All $c_{ij}-z_{ij} < 0$ so this is an optimum solution; z = 18,890. (There is an alternative optimum: $A2$ = 50, $A3$ = 130, $B2$ = 250, $C1$ = 250, $C3$ = 70.)

7. (a) Total demand and total supply are not equal, so we add a dummy source with a capacity of 100 units. The objective function coefficients are profits so we compute the VAM penalties by taking the difference between the two largest values in each row and each column. VAM solution is

	Customers			
Plants	1	2	3	4
A		100		200
B	150	300		
C	50		200	
Dummy			100	

z = 11,750

(b) All $c_{ij}-z_{ij}$'s ≤ 0, so this is optimal. There is an alternative optimum: $A4$ = 300, $B1$ = 150, $B2$ = 300, $C1$ = 50, $C3$ = 20, Dum2 = 100, Dum4 = 0 (but basic).

TUTORIAL 2 – DECISION ANALYSIS

1. (a)
(i) Maximax – best is 50% expansion
(ii) Maximin – best is no expansion.
(iii) Laplace – best is 25% expansion.
(iv) Minimax Regret – best is 25% expansion

(b) Expected payoffs are 0.18, 0.87, and 0.57. Best is 25% expansion.

3. (a) Minimin – Use no vaccine.
(b) Minimax – Use vaccines 1 and 2.
(c) Minimax Regret - use vaccines 1 and 2.
(d) Expected numbers of deaths are 750, 655, 695, 620. Use both vaccines.

5. (a)

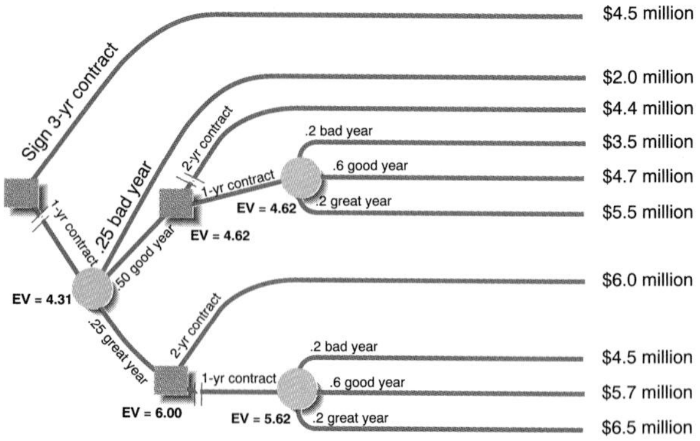

(b) Sign three-yr contract now; payoff is $4.5 million.

CHAPTER 7 – SELECTING THE PROCESS STRUCTURE AND TECHNOLOGY

1. (a) Cross-over point is 100,000. For annual output below 100,000 process A is cheaper; for annual output above 100,000 process B is cheaper.

3. (a) The cross-over points are at 35,000 and 82,500. Contract 1 is best for volumes below 35,000; contract 2 is best between 35,000 and 82,500, and contract 3 is best for volumes greater than 82,500 min/mon.
(b) Contract 2 would be best.

5. NPV = +$2838. Tartan should buy the copier.

7. NPV = +2,736,317. Mastodon should buy the FMS.

CHAPTER 8 – PROCESS DESIGN AND FACILITY LAYOUT

1. (a) c_{max} = 26.18 sec/unit
(b) Theor. min. # WS's = 6
(c)

WS 1	WS 2	WS 3	WS 4	WS 5	WS 6	WS 7
C,A	D,B	E	G,F	H,I	J,K	L

(d) c^* = 24 seconds; P = 1108 units/day
(e) % balance = 86.3%.

3. (a) c_{max} = 18 sec./unit
(b) Theor. min. # WS's = 6

(c)

WS 1	WS 2	WS	3WS 4	WS 5	WS 6
D,E	F,G	A,B	H,I,J	C,K	L

(An improved alternative can be obtained by switching tasks I and J at WS 4 with task C at WS 5; this reduces the cycle time to 17 sec.)
(d) c* = 18 seconds; P = 1400 units/day
(e) % balance = 89.8%.

5. (a) Theor. min. # WS's = 3
(b)

Window 1	Window 2	Window 3	
A,C	D,E	B,F	
60	57	30	(sec)

7. Move A to WS 3 and H to WS 5; cycle time becomes 85 sec.

9. (b) A reasonable assignment is A–>1, B–>5, C–>9, D–>2, E–>7, F–>8, G–>6, H–>4, I–>3.

11. (a) A possible starting layout (in CRAFT form) is

```
A A A A D D I I I I
A A A A B B G G G G
H H H H B B C C C C
E E E E F F C C C C
```

(b) Using CRAFT, the best layout found is

```
A A A A I I G G G G
A A A A I I E E E E
H H H H D D C C C C
B B B B F F C C C C
```

13. (a) One possible rearrangement is

	1	7	9	5	3	8	2	6	4
A		X	X	X	X	X			
B	X					X	X		X
C				X	X	X	X	X	
D	X	X	X				X	X	X
E			X	X	X	X	X		
F	X	X	X	X					X
G	X	X	X	X	X			X	

(b) Some possible cells: FG, AC, CE, and AFG.

Chapter 9 – Waiting Lines

1. (a) $\rho = 0.60$
(b) $L_q = 0.9$ customers
(c) $W_s = 7.5$ minutes.
(d) $P_{\geq 3} = 0.216$

3. (a) $P_{\geq 1} = 0.60$
(b) $W_q = 1.35$ hrs = 81 minutes.
(c) $P_{\geq 3} = 0.216$

5. (a) $11.25/cust.
(b) $6.75.
(c) $0.61 per cust

7. (a) $L_s = 4$
(b) $P_{\geq 4} = 0.4096$
(c) $L_s = 0.952$ customers
(d) $P_{\geq 3} = 0.091$

9. (a) $L_q = 0.267$ cust.
(b) $W_s = 20$ minutes.
(c) $P_{\geq 2} = 0.16$.
(d) $W_s = 17.5$ minutes

11. (a) $W_s = 3.5$ days = 28 hr.
(b) $L_q = 6.125$ jobs
(c) Ave. Cost = $14.07
(d) $L_q = 2.427$; $W_s = 12.96$ hours

13. (a) $L_q = 1.167$ customers
(b) $5.84

15. Customers spend less time in the queue but more time in the system with two slower servers than with one faster server.

17. (a) $P_{\geq 1} = 0.470$.
(b) $L_q = 0.18$
(c) $W_q = 6.89$ min

Tutorial 3 – Simulation Analysis for Operations Management

1. miss, made, made, made, made

3. 13.008; 7.273; 7.212

5. arrival times: 0.444, 3.407, 6.424 min

7. 91.7; 75.6; 104.6 sec

9. Divide the [0,1) interval as follows to generate random processing times

[0,0.2) => 40 sec
[0.2,0.7) => 60 sec
[0.7,0.9) => 80 sec
[0.9,1.0) => 120 sec

The simulated times for each stage are as follows:

	Stage 1		Stage 2		Stage 3	
Unit	r	time	r	time	r	time
1	.8008	80	.7709	80	.0096	40
2	.2273	60	.4308	60	.9831	120
3	.2212	60	.3178	60	.3382	60
4	.5624	60	.9901	120	.2988	60
5	.4937	60	.8555	80	.7117	80
6	.9508	120	.3879	60	.2002	60
7	.0280	40	.2649	60	.8117	80
8	.4254	60	.6151	60	.5726	60
9	.6019	60	.0032	40	.0223	40
10	.5553	60	.8960	80	.4323	60

Total time to make 10 units is 860 seconds.

11. Average daily loss = \$132.70.

15. Plan 2 is better, but three days of simulation are insufficient to make a general conclusion.

Chapter 10 – Job Design, Work Methods, and Organization

1. (a) 17.7 sec.
   (b) 19.1 sec.

3.

Task	(a) Average Time	(b) Normal Time	(c) Standard Time
A	0.89	1.02	1.12
B	1.42	1.49	1.64
C	0.63	0.69	0.76
D	0.81	0.81	0.89

5. $N = [1.65^2(0.2)(1-0.2)]/(0.04)^2 = 272$.

7. (a)

day	1	2	3	4	5	6	7	8	9	10
shift	3	1	1	2	2	3	1	2	2	2

   (b) Observation times (in min): 1.5, 127.2, 152.2, 186.2, 206.8, 295.2, 370.0, 410.6, 430.1, 475.2

Chapter 10 Supplement – Learning and Experience Curves

1. (a) 85%
   (b) 2306 person-hr

3. 2795 person-hr

5. (a) approximately 90%.
   (b) \$1825

7. (a) approximately 85%
   (b) \$911,000 loss
   (c) \$545,180 profit

Chapter 11 – The Quality Management System

1. (a) $UCL_{\overline{X}} = 5.057$ and $LCL_{\overline{X}} = 4.943$
   (b) $UCL_R = 0.314$ and $LCL_R = 0.031$

3. (a) $UCL_{\overline{X}} = 90.018$; $LCL_{\overline{X}} = 89.982$
   (b) $UCL_R = 0.067$; $LCL_R = 0$
   (c) $\overline{X} = 89.99$ => in control; R = 0.04 => in control

5. (a) $UCL_{\overline{X}} = 5.206$ and $LCL_{\overline{X}} = 5.194$
   (b) $UCL_R = 0.025$ and $LCL_R = 0$
   (c) $\overline{X} = 5.203$; R = 0.027. Process is out of control in terms of its variation.

7. (a) $UCL_{\overline{p}} = 0.389$; $LCL_{\overline{p}} = 0.011$

9. $UCL_{\overline{p}} = 0.022$; $LCL_{\overline{p}} = 0$

Chapter 11 Supplement – Acceptance Sampling

1. $\alpha = 0.0022$; $\beta = 0.8088$

3. We compute Prob($X \le 2|p$) for various values of p.

p	0.01	0.02	0.04	0.06	0.10	0.20
Prob($X \le 2$)	0.9978	0.9856	0.9197	0.8781	0.5438	0.1186

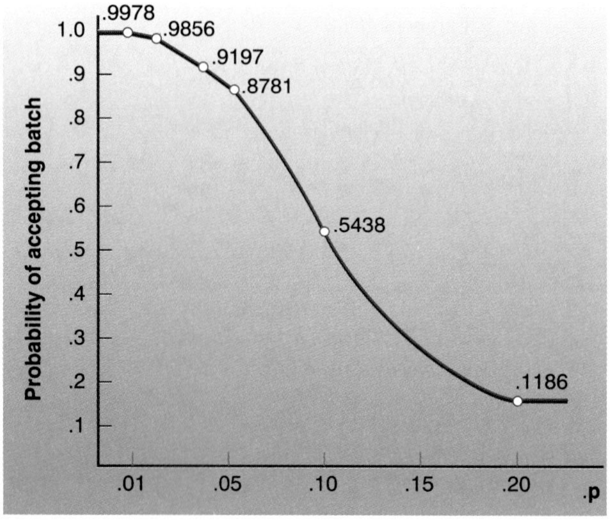

5. For $n = 50$, $c = 2$: $\alpha = 0.0128$ and $\beta = 0.4232$ For $n = 50$, $c = 3$: $\alpha = 0.0018$ and $\beta = 0.6472$ For $n = 50$, $c = 4$: $\alpha = 0.0002$ and $\beta = 0.8152$.
   The plan $n = 50$, $c = 2$ is probably best; it balances the risks better than the other two.

Chapter 12 – Aggregate Planning

1. (a)

Mon	Aggregate Demand (units)	Planned Output (units)	Workers On Staff	Workers Hired	Workers Laid Off	Inventory (units)
Mar			1000			15,000
Apr	140,000	125,040	1042	42	0	40
May	125,000	125,040	1042	0	0	80
Jun	120,000	120,000	1000	0	42	80
Jul	150,000	150,000	1250	250	0	80
Aug	155,000	154,920	1291	41	0	0
Sep	130,000	140,040	1167	0	124	10,040
Totals (Apr-Sep)			6792	333	166	10,320

(Note: inventories are carried in each month due to using whole workers rather than fractional numbers.)

   (b) \$23,554,000

3. (a) Hints: Define your decision variables to be
P_t = the number of computers made during month t
W_t = the number of workers on staff during month t
H_t = the number of workers hired at the beginning of month t
L_t = the number of workers laid off at the beginning of month t
I_t = the number of computers in inventory at the end of month t

Two of the demand/inventory constraints are
$P_1 = 125{,}000 + I_1$
$P_2 + I_1 = 125{,}000 + I_2$

(b) The optimal solution is $P_1 = 125{,}000$, $P_2 = 125{,}000$, $P_3 = 125{,}000$, $P_4 = 150{,}000$, $P_5 = 150{,}000$, $P_6 = 140{,}000$, $W_1 = 1041.67$, $W_2 = 1041.67$, $W_3 = 1041.67$, $W_4 = 1250$, $W_5 = 1250$, $W_6 = 1166.67$, $H_1 = 41.67$, $H_2 = 0$, $H_3 = 0$, $H_4 = 208.33$, $H_5 = 0$, $H_6 = 0$, $L_1 = \ldots = L_5 = 0$, $L_6 = 83.33$, $I_3 = 5000$, $I_4 = 5000$, $I_6 = 10{,}000$ and all other variables equal 0; $z = \$23{,}208{,}330$. Converting this to an aggregate plan by rounding gives the following:

Mon	Aggregate Demand (units)	Planned Output (units)	Workers On Staff	Workers Hired	Workers Laid Off	Inventory (units)
Mar			1000			15,000
Apr	140,000	125,040	1042	42	0	40
May	125,000	125,040	1042	0	0	80
Jun	120,000	125,040	1042	0	0	5,120
Jul	150,000	149,880	1249	207	0	5,000
Aug	155,000	150,000	1250	1	0	0
Sep	130,000	140,040	1167	0	83	10,040
Totals (Apr-Sep)			6792	250	83	20,280

Total Cost = $23,222,000

5. (a) Let R_t = number of wrenches made during month t using regular-time production
O_t = number of wrenches made during month t using overtime production
I_t = number of wrenches in inventory at the end of month t

$$\text{minimize } z = \sum_{t=1}^{6} (40\,R_t + 45\,O_t + 3\,I_t)$$

subject to
$R_t \leq 420$ for $t = 1,\ldots,6$
$O_t \leq 80$ for $t = 1,\ldots,6$

$I_0 + R_1 + O_1 = 370 + I_1$ or $R_1 + O_1 - I_1 = 360$
$I_1 + R_2 + O_2 = 430 + I_2$ or $R_2 + O_2 + I_1 - I_2 = 430$
$I_2 + R_3 + O_3 = 380 + I_3$ or $R_3 + O_3 + I_2 - I_3 = 380$
$I_3 + R_4 + O_4 = 450 + I_4$ or $R_4 + O_4 + I_3 - I_4 = 450$
$I_4 + R_5 + O_5 = 520 + I_5$ or $R_5 + O_5 + I_4 - I_5 = 520$
$I_5 + R_6 + O_6 = 440 + I_6$ or $R_6 + O_6 + I_5 - I_6 = 440$
all variables ≥ 0

(b) Optimal solution is $R_1 = 370$, $R_2 = \ldots = R_6 = 420$, $O_1 = O_2 = O_3 = 0$, $O_4 = 10$, $O_5 = 80$, $O_6 = 20$, $I_1 = 10$, $I_2 = 0$, $I_3 = 40$, $I_4 = 20$, $I_5 = I_6 = 0$.

The resulting aggregate plan is

Month	Units Regular	Produced Overtime	Ending Inventory
Jan	370	0	10
Feb	420	0	0
Mar	420	0	40
Apr	420	10	20
May	420	80	0
Jun	420	20	0

7. (a) Hint: Let
MA_t = the number of units of A made during month t
MB_t = the number of units of B made during month t
PA_t = the number of units of A purchased during month t
PB_t = the number of units of B purchased during month t
IA_t = the number of units of A in inventory at the end of month t
IB_t = the number of units of B in inventory at the end of month t

9.

Week	1	2	3	4	5	6	7
Beginning Inventory	300	500	600	200	500	120	290
Available Inventory	200	400	500	100	400	20	
Forecast Demand	400	500	400	300	380	430	
Expected Inv./Needs(−)	−200	−100	200	−200	120	−410	
Planned Production (MPS)	600	600	0	600	0	600	

Chapter 13 – Inventory Planning: Independent Demands

1. (a) $EOQ = 848.5$
   (b) 21.2 orders/yr
3. (a) $EOQ = 200$
   (b) TSC/yr = $200
   (c) If plugger ordered once/mon, TSC/yr = $281.65
   (d) $RP = 20$
5. (a) 2500.
   (b) annual material cost = $11,872,725.
7. (a) $ELS = 27{,}713$ wheels
   (b) 17.32 days
   (c) 69.28 days
   (d) $ELS = 13{,}856$.
9. (a) $EOQ = 800$ packages.

(b) once every 8 weeks
(c) $SL_d = 99.5\%$.
(d) $RP = 208.5$ (round up to 209); $SS = 9$

11. (a) DDLT will be normally distributed with a mean of 1600 units and a standard deviation of 415.7.
(b) $SL_d = 99.86\%$
(c) $RP = 1754$, so $SS = 154$.
(d)

RP	*SS* cost per yr.	shortage cost/yr	Total Cost/yr
1800	$300	$3825	$4125
2000	$600	$1665	$2265

RP = 2000 is better

13. (a) Safety stock = 27.2
(b) $Q = 437$

15. For $Q = 12$ and $Q = 16$, expected daily profit = $86.40

17. (a) $Q = 260$
(b) $691.50

19. (a) UAA should buy 80 seats.
(b) $46,100
(c) UAA should keep 20 of the seats and sell the other 5 to the airline.

21.

Item	Annual Usage (units)	Item Cost per unit	Annual $ Usage	Classification
A	800	$ 40.00	$ 32,000	A
B	500	$ 12.00	$ 6,000	C
C	1600	$ 15.00	$ 24,000	B
D	200	$200.00	$40,000	A
E	150	$ 25.00	$ 3,750	C
F	2250	$ 6.00	$ 13,500	B or C
G	5000	$ 9.00	$ 45,000	A
H	10000	$ 1.50	$ 15,000	B
I	1500	$ 45.00	$ 67,500	A
J	6000	$ 2.50	$ 15,000	B
K	1000	$ 5.00	$ 5,000	C
L	750	$ 4.00	$ 3,000	C
			Total $ 269,750	

Chapter 14 – Managing Materials with Dependent Demands

1. (a)

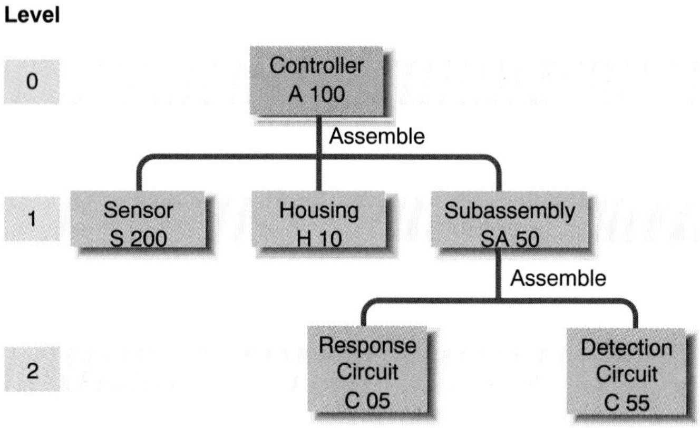

(b)

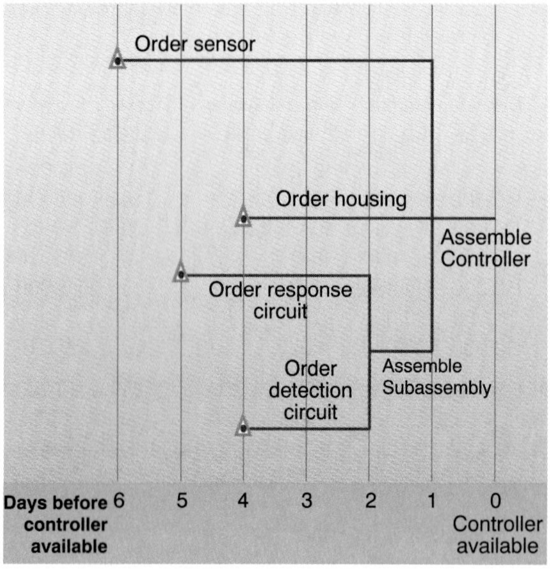

(c) Answers for the controller, subassembly, and circuits only.

Controller

day	1	2	3	4	5	6	7	8	9	10	11	12
gross requir.	-	-	-	-	-	-	100	0	300	0	0	250
on hand	0	0	0	0	0	0	0	0	0	0	0	0
net requir.	-	-	-	-	-	-	100	0	300	0	0	250
order receipts	-	-	-	-	-	-	100	0	300	0	0	250
order releases	-	-	-	-	-	100	0	300	0	0	250	-

Subassembly

day	1	2	3	4	5	6	7	8	9	10	11	12
gross requir.	-	-	-	-	-	100	0	300	0	0	250	0
on hand	0	0	0	0	0	0	0	0	0	0	0	0
net requir.	-	-	-	-	-	100	0	300	0	0	250	-
order receipts	-	-	-	-	-	100	0	300	0	0	250	-
order releases	-	-	-	-	100	0	300	0	0	250	-	-

Response Circuit

day	1	2	3	4	5	6	7	8	9	10	11	12
gross requir.	-	-	-	-	100	0	300	0	0	250	-	-
on hand	0	0	0	0	0	0	0	0	0	0	-	-
net requir.	-	-	-	-	100	0	300	0	0	250	-	-
order receipts	-	-	-	-	100	0	300	0	0	250	-	-
order releases	-	100	0	300	0	0	250	-	-	-	-	-

Detection Circuit

day	1	2	3	4	5	6	7	8	9	10	11	12
gross requir.	-	-	-	-	100	0	300	0	0	250	-	-
on hand	0	0	0	0	0	0	0	0	0	0	0	0
net requir.	-	-	-	-	100	0	300	0	0	250	-	-
order receipts	-	-	-	-	100	0	300	0	0	250	-	-
order releases	-	-	100	0	300	0	0	250	-	-	-	-

3.

Product Z

Week	1	2	3	4	5	6	7	8	9	10
gross requir.	0	0	0	0	0	0	200	0	0	300
on hand	0	0	0	0	0	0	0	0	0	0
net requir.	0	0	0	0	0	0	200	0	0	300
order receipts	0	0	0	0	0	0	200	0	0	300
order releases	0	0	0	0	0	200	0	0	300	0

Component G

Week	1	2	3	4	5	6	7	8	9	10
gross requir.	0	0	0	0	0	200	0	0	300	-
on hand	0	0	0	0	0	0	0	0	0	0
net requir.	0	0	0	0	0	200	0	0	300	-
order receipts	0	0	0	0	0	200	0	0	300	-
order releases	0	0	0	0	200	0	0	300	0	-

Component C

Week	1	2	3	4	5	6	7	8	9	10
gross requir.	0	0	0	0	200	0	0	300	-	-
on hand	0	0	0	0	0	0	0	0	0	0
net requir.	0	0	0	0	200	0	0	300	-	-
order receipts	0	0	0	0	200	0	0	300	-	-
order releases	0	200	0	0	300	0	-	-	-	-

5. (a)

Level #	Item Description	# Required	Make/Buy	Lead-time
00	Z		make	1 wk
01	A	1	make	1 wk
02	C	2	buy	2 wk
02	D	1	make	1 wk
01	B	2	make	2 wk
02	E	3	buy	1 wk
02	F	1	make	1 wk
02	G	2	buy	1 wk

7. (Answers for Z, A, C, and D only)

Product Z

Week	1	2	3	4	5	6	7	8	9	10
gross requir.	0	0	0	0	100	0	200	400	0	150
on hand	0	0	0	0	0	0	0	0	0	0
net requir.	0	0	0	0	100	0	200	400	0	150
order receipts	0	0	0	0	100	0	200	400	0	150
order releases	0	0	0	100	0	200	400	0	150	0

Component A

Week	1	2	3	4	5	6	7	8	9	10
gross requir.	0	0	0	100	0	200	400	0	150	-
on hand	20	20	20	20	0	0	0	0	0	0
net requir.	0	0	0	80	0	200	400	0	150	-
order receipts	0	0	0	80	0	200	400	0	150	-
order releases	0	0	80	0	200	400	0	150	0	-

Component C

Week	1	2	3	4	5	6	7	8	9	10
gross requir.	0	0	160	0	400	800	0	300	-	-
on hand	0	0	0	0	0	0	0	0	-	-
net requir.	0	0	160	0	400	800	0	300	-	-
order receipts	0	0	160	0	400	800	0	300	-	-
order releases	160	0	400	800	0	300	0	-	-	-

Component D

Week	1	2	3	4	5	6	7	8	9	10
gross requir.	0	0	80	0	200	400	0	150	-	-
on hand	0	0	0	0	0	0	0	0	-	-
net requir.	0	0	80	0	200	400	0	150	-	-
order receipts	0	0	80	0	200	400	0	150	-	-
order releases	0	80	0	200	400	0	150	0	-	-

9. (a) The 12-week demand was 360 units = 30/wk, so $EOQ = 63$.

(b)

Week	1	2	3	4	5	6	7	8	9	10	11	12
gross requir.	0	60	10	90	50	0	0	30	0	80	40	0
on hand	0	0	3	56	29	42	42	42	12	75	58	18
net requir.	0	60	7	34	21	0	0	0	0	5	0	0
order receipts	0	63	63	63	63	0	0	0	63	63	0	0
order releases	63	63	63	63	0	0	0	63	63	0	0	0

(c) $EPP = 200$. So material requirements plan is

Week	1	2	3	4	5	6	7	8	9	10	11	12
gross requir.	0	60	10	90	50	0	0	30	0	80	40	0
on hand	0	0	100	90	0	30	30	30	0	0	40	0
net requir.	0	60	0	0	50	0	0	0	0	80	0	0
order receipts	0	160	0	0	80	0	0	0	0	120	0	0
order releases	160	0	0	80	0	0	0	0	120	0	0	0

(d) For the *EOQ* plan $TSC = \$1182.75$

For the *PPB* plan $TSC = \$690.00$

With the lot-for-lot plan $TSC = \$1050$.
The *PPB* plan in part (c) is best.

11. (a) $EOQ = 100$.

(b) The resulting purchasing plan is

week	1	2	3	4	5	6	7	8	9	10	11	12
gross requir.	0	0	200	0	100	0	175	0	0	0	125	0
on hand	0	0	100	0	0	0	100	25	25	25	25	0
net requir.	0	0	100	0	100	0	75	0	0	0	100	0
order receipts	0	100	100	0	100	100	100	0	0	0	100	0
order releases	100	100	0	100	100	100	0	0	0	100	0	0

(c) For the plan in part (b) $TSC = \$450$

For a lot-for-lot plan $TSC = \$200$

Chapter 15 – Just-In-Time, Lean, and Synchronous Production Systems

1.

Day-Hour	Raw Matl	Stage 1 Activ	Kanb	Inv.	Stage 2 Activ	Kanb	Inv.	Stage 3 Activ	Kanb	Prod. Inv. A	B	C	Demands A	B	C
1–1	BCA	Run B	AC	CBA	SU A	BC	BA	Run C	ABCA	250	400	125	25	20	20
1–2	BCA	Run B	ACA	CB	Run A	BC	BA	SU A	BCA	225	380	405	15	25	20
1–3	BCA	SU A	CA	BCB	Run A	BCA	BC	Run A	BCA	210	355	385	25	30	15
1–4	BC	Run A	CA	BCB	Run A	BCA	B	Run A	BCA	185	325	370	20	25	20
1–5	ABC	Run A	CA	BCB	SU B	CA	AB	Run A	BCA	165	300	350	30	20	20
1–6	ABC	Run A	CAB	BC	Run B	CA	AB	SU B	CAB	435	280	330	20	35	25
1–7	ABC	SU C	AB	ABC	Run B	CAB	A	Run B	CAB	415	245	305	25	20	35
1–8	AB	Run C	AB	ABC	Run B	CAB	A	Run B	CAB	390	225	270	35	25	30
2–1	CAB	Run C	AB	ABC	SU C	AB	BA	Run B	CABC	355	200	240	20	15	35
2–2	CAB	Run C	ABC	AB	Run C	AB	BA	SU A	CBC	335	485	205	25	20	25
2–3	CAB	SU A	BC	CAB	Run C	ABA	B	Run A	CBC	310	465	180	25	30	30
2–4	CB	Run A	BC	CAB	Run C	ABA	B	Run A	CBC	285	435	150	35	20	25
2–5	ACB	Run A	BC	CAB	SU A	BA	CB	Run A	CBCA	250	415	125	20	25	35
2–6	ACB	Run A	BCA	CB	Run A	BA	CB	SU C	BCA	530	390	90	35	20	15
2–7	ACB	SU B	CA	ACB	Run A	BAC	B	Run C	BCA	495	370	75	25	25	20
2–8	AC	Run B	CA	ACB	Run A	BAC	B	Run C	BCA	470	345	55	30	20	25

Chapter 16 – Operations and Personnel Scheduling

1. (a) ELS(denim) = 11,711
ELS(twill) = 30,984
ELS(gabardine) = 23,033

(b) During each cycle Modern should run denim once and twill and gabardine twice. Total production in each cycle for each product will be $Q_d = 11{,}700$; $Q_t = 46{,}800$; $Q_g = 35{,}100$. The lot sizes will be 11,700, 23,400, and 17,550, respectively.

3. The results for the four rules are as follows:

	(a) SPT		(b) EDD		(c) CR		(d) STR	
Sequence	Job	Ends	Job	Ends	Job	Ends	Job	Ends
1	Ev	2.0	Ch	3.0	Ch	3.0	Ch	3.0
2	Ad	4.5	Ad	5.5	Br	7.0	Ad	5.5
3	Ch*	7.5	Br	9.5	Da	12.0	Br	9.5
4	Br*	11.5	Da*	14.5	Ad*	14.5	Da*	14.5
5	Da*	16.5	Ev*	16.5	Ev*	16.5	Ev	16.5
Ave flow time		8.4		9.8		10.6		9.8
Ave tardiness per job		0.9		0.2		1.4		0.2

* Indicates tardy job

5. (a) Optimal sequence is BACDEF (an alternative is BACEDF).
(b) The make span = 52.
(c) Average tardiness = 1.83

7. (a) BCA.
(b) Make span = 33; ave. flow time per job = 27.67
(c) For the sequence CBA, Make-span = 37 and average flow time per job = 27.00

9. (a) & (b)

	Stage 1		Stage 2				
Job	Start	Finish	Job	Start	Finish	Due Date	Tardiness
C	0	7	C	7	17	37	0
E	7	19	E	19	28	47	0
F	19	25	F	28	34	41	0
A	25	30	B	34	40	38	2
B	30	34	A	40	49	41	8
D	34	42	D	49	57	52	5

Average tardiness = 2.50

11. There are three optimal solutions; all have an objective function value of 35.

Crew	Customers		
1	D	D	C
2	C	E	A
3	B	B	B
4	E	C	E
5	A	A	D

13. (a)
Let x_j = the number of orderlies scheduled to work schedule j, where $j = 1$ means Sunday-Thursday, $j = 2$ means Monday-Friday, etc.

Minimize $z = 375\, x_1 + 350\, x_2 + 375\, x_3 + 400\, x_4 + 400\, x_5 + 400\, x_6 + 400\, x_7$

subject to
$$x_1 + x_4 + x_5 + x_6 + x_7 \geq 12$$
$$x_1 + x_2 + x_5 + x_6 + x_7 \geq 26$$
$$x_1 + x_2 + x_3 + x_6 + x_7 \geq 24$$
$$x_1 + x_2 + x_3 + x_4 + x_7 \geq 23$$
$$x_1 + x_2 + x_3 + x_4 + x_5 \geq 23$$
$$x_2 + x_3 + x_4 + x_5 + x_6 \geq 26$$
$$x_3 + x_4 + x_5 + x_6 + x_7 \geq 19$$
all x_j's ≥ 0

(b) Optimum is $x_1 = 0$, $x_2 = 12.33$, $x_3 = 5.33$, $x_4 = 0$, $x_5 = 7.33$, $x_6 = 1.00$, $x_7 = 5.33$, z = \$11,783.33. This is not an integer solution; it would have to either be rounded to a feasible one or the problem must be resolved as an integer program.

Chapter 17 - Project Planning and Scheduling

1. (a)

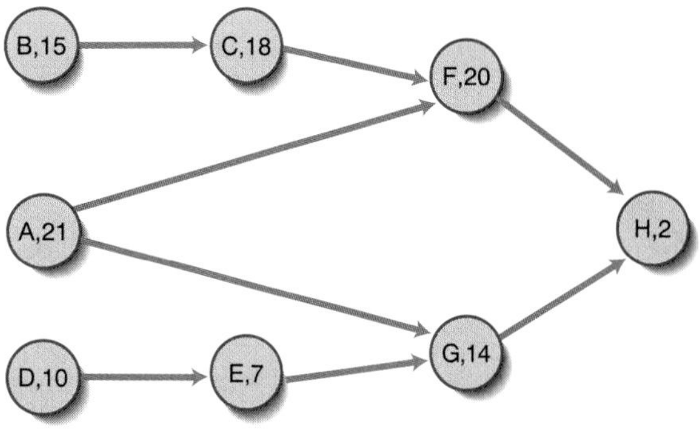

(b)&(c)The earliest time the project can be completed is 55 days.

Task	ES	EF	LS	LF	Slack	Critical Path
A	0	21	12	33	12	No
B	0	15	0	15	0	Yes
C	15	33	15	33	0	Yes
D	0	10	22	32	22	No
E	10	17	32	39	22	No
F	33	53	33	53	0	Yes
G	21	35	39	53	18	No
H	53	55	53	55	0	Yes

The critical path is BCFH

3. (a)

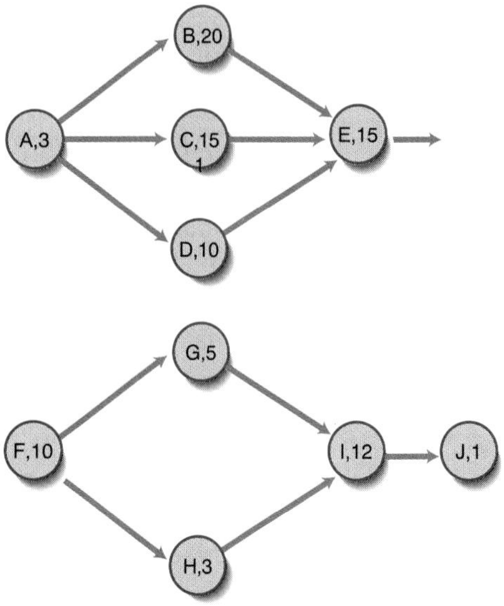

(b)&(c) Project can be completed in 66 days. The critical path is ABEFGIJ

(d)

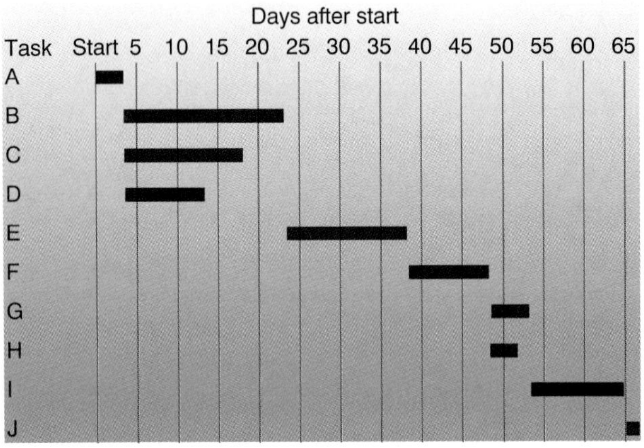

5. (b) Using normal times and costs, earliest project completion time is 45 days; cost is \$15,400.

(c) Critical path is ABDFH

(d) Crash task A by 2 days, F by 3 days; cost increases to \$16,400.

7. (a) Earliest expected completion for the project is 19 wk.

(b) $\text{Prob}(T > 20) = \text{Prob}(z > [(20-19)/1.78]) = 0.2877$.

(c) $\text{Prob}(T < 16) = \text{Prob}(z < (16-19)/1.78) = 0.0455$

9. (a)

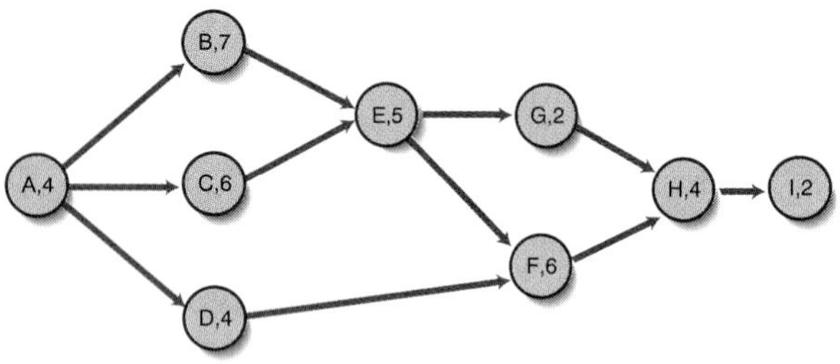

Earliest completion time using the normal task times is 28 days; cost = \$2,390,000.

(b) Crash B by 1 day, E by 2 days, and F by 2 days.

PHOTO CREDITS

Part 1 Opener: Steven Peters/Tony Stone Images/New York, Inc.

Chapter 1
Page 6: Courtesy Carol Caruthers. Page 8 (top): Lightscapes/The Stock Market. Page 8 (bottom): David Joel/Tony Stone Images/New York, Inc. Page 9: Dennis O'Clair/Tony Stone Images/New York, Inc. Page 12: © William Waldron. Page 14: Courtesy JC Penney. Page 19: Harald Sund/The Image Bank. Page 23: Courtesy Ford Motor Company. Page 25: Courtesy Saturn.

Chapter 2
Page 35: Courtesy Bob Anastasi. Page 39: Courtesy Hyatt Regency Hotel, Dearborn, Michigan. Page 41: Courtesy Barnes & Nobles, Inc. Page 47: © William Waldron. Page 61: Courtesy Hewlett Packard. Page 69: Suzanne Brookens/The Stock Market.

Chapter 3
Page 75: Courtesy Jefferson Smurfit Corporation. Pages 76-77: Courtesy Jefferson Smurfit Corporation. Pages 83-85: Courtesy Joseph Martinich. Page 89: Courtesy United Parcel Service. Page 90: Courtesy United Parcel Service. Page 95: Photo by Art Smialek, Jr.

Part 2 Opener: David Parker/Science Photo Library/Photo Researchers.

Chapter 4
Page 102: Courtesy Jayne Rosselli. Page 104: Courtesy Compaq. Page 132: Pat Lacroix/The Image Bank.

Chapter 5
Page 212: Courtesy Dee Ambrosia. Page 217: Courtesy Chrysler Corporation. Page 218: Courtesy Marriott Corporation. Page 220: Courtesy Northern Telecorn Ltd. Page 226: Courtesy PCA Industries. Page 235: Courtesy Silicon Graphics. Page 236: Courtesy The Boeing Corporation. Page 238: Courtesy Citibank.

Chapter 6
Page 251: Courtesy Sandy Boyd. Page 258: © B&G Bowater/The Image Bank. Page 268: Grant V. Faint/The Image Bank. Page 271: David Brownell/The Image Bank. Page 274: Courtesy Mercedes-Benz of North America. Page 281: George Hall/Check Six.

Chapter 7
Page 326: Courtesy Marvin Dixon. Page 327: John Olson/The Stock Market. Page 329: Courtesy U.S. Steel Corporation. Page 330: Gabriel Covian/The Image Bank. Page 331: Arthur d'Arazien/The Image Bank. Page 335: Michael Rosenfeld/Tony Stone Images/New York, Inc. Page 344 (left): Steve Dunwell/The Image Bank. Page 344 (right): Photo by Sandra Small, courtesy University of San Diego Medical Center. Page 347: Jon Feingersh/The Stock Market. Page 349: Courtesy Anheuser-Busch. Page 366: Courtesy Southwest Airlines Co.

Chapter 8
Page 370: Courtesy Chuck Wise. Page 371: Courtesy Honda of America. Page 381: Fernando Bueno/The Image Bank. Page 396: Tony Stone Images/New York, Inc. Page 403: Courtesy Sony Corporation. Page 409: Ron Sherman/Tony Stone Images/New York, Inc. Page 412: Courtesy Toys R Us.

Chapter 9
Page 427: Courtesy Deb Holler. Page 428: Bob Daemmrich/Stock, Boston. Pages 446 and 452: Courtesy Joseph Martinich. Page 463: Courtesy L. L. Bean, Inc. Page 465: Seth Resnick/Stock, Boston.

Chapter 10
Page 509: Courtesy Richard Kowalewski. Page 514: Courtesy Deere & Company. Page 522: David Joel/Tony Stone Images/New York, Inc. Page 523: Tom Tracy/FPG International. Page 525: Courtesy Mercedes-Benz of North America. Page 526: Courtesy General Motors Corporation. Page 538: Courtesy Steele's Markets. Page 540: Walter Hodges/Tony Stone Images/New York, Inc.

Chapter 11
Page 561: Courtesy Valerie Mayer. Page 562: Courtesy L. L. Bean, Inc. Page 565: Courtesy United Parcel Service. Page 575: Courtesy Intel. Page 580: Michael Rosenfeld/Tony Stone Images/New York, Inc. Page 585: Ken Whitmore/Tony Stone Images/New York, Inc. Page 599: Corbis-Bettmann.

Part 3 Opener: Steve Dunwell/The Image Bank.

Chapter 12

Page 623: Courtesy Randy Sanderson. Page 624: Courtesy Ford Motor Company. Page 626: Courtesy Sony Corporation. Page 645: Courtesy Polaris Industries.

Chapter 13

Page 660: Courtesy Gil Burford. Page 663: Courtesy Office Depot. Page 685: Leo de Wys, Inc. Page 687: Steven Peters/Tony Stone Images/New York, Inc. Page 693: Courtesy Air Canada. Page 699 (top): Courtesy Xerox Corporation. Page 699 (bottom): Dugald Bremner/Tony Stone Images/New York, Inc.

Chapter 14

Page 717: Courtesy Satish Nayak. Page 719: Courtesy Sigma Chemical Company. Page 723: Courtesy PCA Industries. Page 739: Courtesy TRW, Inc. Page 740: David Ximeno Tejada/Tony Stone Images/New York, Inc.

Chapter 15

Page 752: Courtesy Bruce Hamilton. Page 763: Michael Rosenfeld/Tony Stone Images/New York, Inc. Page 767: Charles Thatcher/Tony Stone Images/New York, Inc. Page 770: Theodore Anderson/The Image Bank. Page 778: Courtesy Toyota. Page 780: David Pollack/The Stock Market. Page 781: Courtesy Office Depot.

Chapter 16

Page 798: Courtesy Diane Conboy. Page 799: Courtesy Delta Airlines. Page 811: Bill Varie/The Image Bank. Page 821: Courtesy The Hertz Corporation. Page 824 (top): Bill Aron/PhotoEdit. Page 824 (bottom): Tommy Nixon/Courtesy Arthur Johnson.

Chapter 17

Page 839: Courtesy Mike Sargenti. Page 842: John Gray/Tony Stone Images/New York, Inc. Page 847: Courtesy Chrysler Corporation. Page 848: Tim Brown/Tony Stone Images/New York, Inc. Page 858: Jim Cummins/Tony Stone Images/New York, Inc.

COMPANY INDEX

AAP St. Mary's Corp., 528
ACME Advertising Co., 442–445
Adam Opel, 286
ADT, 561
Aetna Life and Casualty Co., 408, 517
Air Canada, 693
Allen-Bradley Corp., 216, 346, 388
Allied Signal, 346
Alpha, Inc., 757–759
American Airlines, 50, 352
American Express Corp., 39, 238
Andersen Consulting, 62
Anheuser-Busch, 256, 349
Antietam Carpet Co., 137–140
Approved Statewide Title Agency, 91–96
AST, 64
A.T. Kearney, Inc., 218–219
Au Bon Pain, 52
AWT Technologies, 864

Bailey Controls, 698–699
Barclays de Zoete, 396
Barnes and Noble, 41, 51
Basel Tool and Dye Co. , 177–179
Ben and Jerry's Ice Cream, 349
Black & Decker, 237, 751
Boeing Co., 216, 217, 218, 221, 236
Booz, Allen & Hamilton, 846
Boston Park Plaza Hotel, 348
Bowmar Instruments, 48
Brigham-Women's Hospital, 798
Burger King, 51
Bursto Box Co., 456–458

Canon, Inc., 774
Capital National Bank, 674–676
Carrier Corp., 512
Carter Hawley Hale Stores, Inc., 541
Celestica, Inc., 39
Charles Schwab, 237, 358
Chase Econometrics, 109
Chrysler Corp., 215, 217, 224, 231, 382, 526, 660, 699–700, 751, 768
Cincinnati Milacron, 212, 216, 220
Citibank, 237, 238
Clayton Printing, 810
Coin Laundry Association, 597
Compaq Computer, 63–64, 104, 220, 226, 258, 541, 659
Corning, Inc., 30, 38, 48, 218, 370, 512, 515
Creative Output, Inc., 815
CTI-Cryogenics, 35
Cummins Engine, 28, 512

Dana Corp., 221
Dell Computer, 39, 64
Delta Airlines, 50, 260, 352, 799, 818
Dierbergs Florist, 468
Digicomp Computer Corp., 570–572, 611–613
Dillard's Department Stores, 49
Dominion Soap, 678, 800–801
Dover Corp., 751
Dow Chemical, 864
DuPont, 348, 846

Eastman Kodak Co., 781
Electronic Data Systems, 62
Empresa Nacional Siderurgica, 807
Ernst and Young, 603
Espresso Roma, 251
Eurosound, 61–62

Falcon Products, 716, 717–718
Famous-Barr Stores, 623
Fastcomp, 670–671, 681–684
Feature Enterprises, 235
Federal Express, 347, 604, 798
Federal-Mogul Corp., 777, 780
Ferro-Stamping, Inc., 548–551
Fibre-Pack, Ltd., 244–245
Fireplace Manufacturers, 752
Fisher-Price, 217, 218
Floor-Mart, 822–823
Force-Master Corp., 652–657
Ford Motor Co., 23, 28, 48, 212, 221, 382, 623, 624, 699, 751, 766

GapKids, 47
The Gap, 12, 47
Garden Valley Ranch, 102
Gasoline Heaven, 237–238
Gateway 2000, 64
General Electric, 28, 57, 212, 220, 348, 514, 524, 751, 774
General Motors, 56, 220, 286, 513, 526, 540, 562, 577, 578, 699, 751, 768
Globe Metallurgical, 604
Great Western Bank, 427, 465

Harley-Davidson, 561, 751
Healthy Pet Food Co., 168–170, 175, 179–182, 185, 187, 188, 193–195
Herman Miller, Inc., 27
Hewlett-Packard, 35, 36, 39, 48, 53, 56, 63, 212, 751
Home Depot, 751, 779
Home Helper Discount, 834
Honda, 57, 219, 220, 232, 371
Honeywell, 216, 751
H&R Block Tax Services, 357
Hyatt Legal Services, 357
Hyatt Regency Hotels, 39
Hydroworks, Inc., 353–355
Hyundai, 11

IBM, 39, 53, 62, 63–64, 212, 222, 237, 344
IBM Credit Corp., 360
Ikea, 238
Imperial Commerce Bank, 133–136
Intel Corp., 561, 575, 751
International Association of Machinists, 514
International Wool Co., 173–174
Interstate Rail and Trucking Co., 477–480
Iomega Corp., 579
IRS, 466

Jefferson Smurfit Corp., 72–79, 330
John Deere & Co., 512, 514, 540, 544, 751

Kajima Corp., 343
Keithley Instruments, 220
Kinko's Copies, 251
Kmart, 237, 779

Lafayette Industries, 195–196
Lakeland (Florida) Regional Medical Center, 408
Lakeland Regional Hospital, 540
Lear Seating Co., 768
Levi Strauss, 540
Leviton Manufacturing, 696
Lincoln Electric Co., 26, 542
L.L. Bean, 463, 561, 562
Lockheed Aircraft, 846

McDonald's, 40, 51, 55, 215, 268, 388, 515, 699, 716, 781
McDonnell Douglas Corp., 220
McKinsey and Co., 39
Marriott Corp., 212, 217, 218, 467
Marriott Courtyard Hotels, 218, 575

May Department Stores, 623
Mazda, 762–763
Mediserve, Inc., 709–714
Meersburg Grocery Store, 116–117, 120, 122, 125
Mercedes-Benz, 11, 269, 274, 525
Metro Hospital, 126–129
Microsoft, 56
Mobil Oil, 463, 818
Monsanto Corp., 348
Morgan Stanley, 44
Motorola, 28, 212, 216, 235, 346, 561, 568, 576, 604, 699
MTM Association for Standards and Research, 533
Multi-Machine Corp. , 438–441

Nabisco Foods, Inc., 326
New York Air Brake, 215
Nippon Airlines, 236
Nissan, 225
Northern Telecom Ltd., 220
Nucor, 38, 39

Office Depot, 781
Otis Elevator, 52
Owens-Corning Fiberglas, 540, 640
Packaging Corporation of America, 766
Parts-to-Go , 448–450
PCA Industries, 226, 720–724, 737
Pesti-Chemical, Ltd., 422–424
Phillips NV, 53
Phonecom, 477–480
Piper Industries, 264–265
Pizza Hut, 215
Polaris Industries, 645
Port of Hampton Roads, 824
Price Waterhouse LLP, 6
Procter & Gamble, 26, 255, 256, 767, 776
Promus Co., 594
Publishers Equipment Corp., 738, 739
Purchasing Support Services, Inc., 779

Quad-Tech, 222

Rama Manufacturing, 278–280
Red Cross, 873
Remington Rand Corp., 846
Reynolds and Hill College, 162–165
Rockwell International, 219
Roots Canada, 509

Salvation Army, 873
Sara Lee Corp., 538
Saturn Division, 25, 56
Savin Corp., 578
Sealtest Dairies, 256
Service Construction Co., 839
7-Eleven, 57, 347
Sharp Corp., 39
Shenandoah Valley Trauma Centers, 295–297
Sherbrooke University, 819
Sigma Chemical Co., 716, 719
Solar Oil Co., 175–177, 195
Solectron, 561, 604
Sony, 36, 53, 237, 346, 403, 626
Southland Corp., 57
Southwest Airlines, 39, 221, 352, 357, 366–367, 408, 523
Spartan Manufacturing, 767
Standard Metals, 808–809
Standard Register Co., 79–87, 212, 342, 388, 397
Starlight Corp., 629–636
Steele's Markets, 538
Sushivox, 61–62
Suzuki, 285
Syntex Agribusiness, Inc., 685

Taco Bell, 212, 215
Tektronix, 346
Tenneco, 568
Tennessee Eastman Chemical Co., 770
Terminal Industries, 275–278
Texas Instruments, 346
Texas Recycling and Refining, Inc., 699
Thirst Quencher, Inc., 688–689
3M Corp., 212, 237, 388, 751, 764
Titan Electronic Corp., 374–377
Toshiba, 346
Toyota, 23, 26, 40, 53, 57, 221, 342, 526, 599, 759, 776, 778
Toys-R-Us, 751
Tri-State Tollway, 430
Tubetronics, 740–741

UKAN, Ltd., 789–795
Union Electric Co., 717
Union Pacific, 347
United Airlines, 50, 236, 352, 523
United Auto Workers, 514
United Electric Controls, 752
United Parcel Service (UPS), 87–91, 237, 347, 530, 565, 638, 798–799
U.S. Navy, 846
United Technologies, 52
Universal Systems, 816–818
University of Montreal, 819
UPS: See United Parcel Service (UPS)
U.S. Precision Lens, Inc., 370
USAir, 523
Valmont Industries, 784
Volkswagen, 224

The Wall Street Journal, 109
Wal-Mart, 38–39, 237, 348, 411, 751, 779
Walt Disney Co., 35, 48–49, 68–70, 388, 465, 466
Waste Overhaul, Inc., 747–749
Wendy's, 716
Western Electric Co., 23
Westinghouse, 604
Wharton Econometrics, 109
Whirlpool, 330, 774

Xerox, 28, 212, 237, 604, 699, 751

Yamada Electric, 528

Zenith, 285
Zesty Beverage Co., 299
Zytec, 604

NAME INDEX

Adams, Beth, 655
Akao, Yoji, 228, 599
Ambrosia, Dee, 212
Anastasi, Bob, 35
Arthurson, Andy, 804

Babbage, Charles, 20
Baldrige, Malcolm, 604
Barkley, Earl, 685
Billingsworth, John, 789
Birnbaum, Joel S., 48
Bitran, Gabriel R., 640
Bohren, Kevin L., 104
Boothroyd, Geoffry, 235–236
Bowker, Don, 752
Boyd, Sandy, 251
Burford, Gil, 660

Carstedt, Goran, 238
Caruthers, Carol, 6
Clinton, Bill, 534
Conboy, Diane, 798
Conler, Olivier, 740
Cooper, Marvin, 238
Crosby, Philip, 562, 599
Cutter, Peggy, 133

Dantzig, George, 182
Davidowitz, Howard, 775
DeMatteis, J.J., 730
Deming, W. Edwards, 26, 562, 581–582, 598–599
Dewhurst, Peter, 235–236
Dixon, Marvin D., 326
Dodge, H.F., 581
Dolay, Ann, 548–551

Eggert, Robert, 109
Erlang, A.K., 24
Escalia, Maria, 449

Farrel, Lawrence E., 565
Farrell, Brenda, 162–165
Filandro, Michael, 699
Ford, Henry, 23
Fulton, Robert, 19

Gantt, Henry, 22, 813
Gantt, Terry, 638
Gilbreth, Frank, 22, 517, 533
Gilbreth, Lillian, 22, 517, 533
Goldratt, Eliyahu, 782–784
Hamilton, Bruce, 752, 757
Harris, F.W., 667
Hax, Arnoldo, 625
Hayes, Robert, 12
Hendrick, Roger, 548
Herr, Barry, 577
Hill, Terry, 12, 48
Holler, Deb, 427, 465

Ishikawa, Kaoru, 562, 598, 599
Ito-Yokado, 57

Johnson, S.M., 807–810
Jones, Michael, 548
Juran, Joseph M., 26, 562, 563, 566, 598–599

Karmarkar, Narendra, 182
Kelly, J.E., 846
Kitano, Mikio, 342
Kowalewski, Richard, 509
Kruse, Douglas, 543

Lambert, Robert, 541
Langer, Brian, 747–748
Laust, Ira M., 652, 655
Leong, G.K., 640

McCoy, Jerry, 513
Markov, A.A., 437
Marriott, Bill, 467
Maudley, Henry, 20
Mayer, Valerie, 561
Meal, H.C., 625
Metcalfe, Henry, 21
Mikano, Robert, 374–377
Miles, Lawrence, 231
Milligan, Lawrence, 767
Moore, J.M., 807
Morris, Robert, 477

Naft, Barry, 864
Nayak, Satish C., 717

Ohno, Taiichi, 23
Ozan, Terrence, 603

Peacock, Brian, 526
Pryor, Steve, 463
Reed, Wayne, 747
Reimann, Curt W., 29
Reiner, Gary, 514, 524
Rivers, John, 873
Roach, Stephen, 44
Robert, Nicholas-Louis, 73
Robertson, Oliver, 653, 655
Romig, H.G., 581
Rosenfield, Donald B., 31, 692
Rosica, Gabe, 698–699
Ross, Florence, 611
Ross, Nancy, 282–283
Rosselli, Jayne, 102

Sanchez, Robert, 709–712
Sanders, Wilson, 612
Sanderson, Randy, 623
Sargenti, Mike, 839
Scanlon, Joseph, 542
Schmenner, Roger W., 270
Shewhart, Walter, 24, 581
Shingo, Shigeo, 527–528, 562, 598, 599, 759, 762–763, 778, 779
Shortroad, James, 137–140
Skinner, Wickham, 12, 17, 256
Smith, Donald, 356
Smith, Frederic, 21
Smith, Ronald, 779
Soderberg, Leif, 218
Strauss, Leonard, 449–450

Taguchi, Genichi, 227, 562, 599
Taylor, Frederick W., 21–22, 25, 510, 517
Templeton, Chris, 834
Trevithick, Richard, 19
Vitek, Frank, 597

Wagner, H., 732–733
Walton, Sam, 38–39
Watt, James, 19
Weber, Max, 24
Wendel, W. Hall, Jr., 645
Wenninger, Fred, 579
Wheelwright, Steven, 12
Whitin, T.M., 732–733
Whitney, Eli, 19
Wise, Chuck, 30, 218, 370
Woolard, Edgar, 348
Wright, T.P., 552

SUBJECT INDEX

ABC classification system, 694–695, **700**
Acceptance sampling, 582
Accessibility
  in assembly, product design and, 224–225
  service facility site location and, 271–272
Accidents, 537–538
Accounting practices, cost measures and, 44–45
Accuracy incentives, qualitative forecasting and, 108
Active phase, of work involvement, 523
Activity, 842, **865**
Activity-based costing, 45
Activity-on-arc (A-O-A) convention, 847–849
Activity-on-node (A-O-N) convention, 849
Adaptive models, 147
Additive seasonal model, 132, 149
Additivity, linear programming models and, 172
Advertising, demand patterns and, 644, 819
Agglomeration effects, 271
Aggregate planning, 177, 622–657, **646**
  case study, 652–657
  cost reduction
    demand-influencing tactics, 642–645
    reservation systems, 645–646
  defined, 623
  disaggregation: *See* **Disaggregation**
  forecasting, 627
  implementation, 627–628
  linear programming model for, 633–639
    adding shifts, 637
    back-ordering, 637
    labor skills, 637–638
    multiple product types, 637
    natural attrition, 638
    overtime work, 637
    refinements/variations, 636–638
    revision of, 638–639
    subcontracting, 637
    training workers, 637
  master production schedule (MPS) and, 641–642, **646**
  planning hierarchy, 624
  product aggregation, 625
  rolling horizon, 628, 646
  scheduling considerations, 825
  simple planning heuristics for, 628–633
    chase demand strategy, 629–631
    level production/workforce strategy, 629, 631–633
  units of production/resources, 625–626
  variables, identification of, 627
ALDEP (automated layout design program), 396
Alternative, simulation model, 486
American Production and Inventory Control Society (APICS), 695
Analytical tools, need for, 17–18
Analytic approach, 430
Appointment systems
  improving, 820
  service operations scheduling and, 819
Appraisal costs, 566, 567
Arcs, network, 846
ARIMA (autoregressive/integrated/moving average models), 145
Arm, industrial robot, 343
Artificial variables, linear programming models, 188–191
Assembly
  design for (DFA), 235–237, **242**
  mistake-proof, 225, 577
  process simplification
    product design and, 222–225
    for quality conformance, 577
    setup time reduction, 765–766
Assembly chart, 239
Assembly drawing, 222, 239
Assembly time chart, 725
Assignable variation, 582
Assignment problems, in production scheduling, 815–819, **826**
Associative forecasting: *See* **Causal forecasting/models**
Associative models, 113
Assured demand, 756
Attribute variables, 227
Automation, 342–344, **361**
  job design and, 514–515
Autonomous work groups/teams, 538–539, 544, 775
  group incentive systems for, 542–543
  quality conformance and, 578
Average arrival rate, 432
Average or expected demand during lead time (DDLT), 678–680
  calculated from lead time and demand, 682–683
Average service rate, 433
Average service time, 433

Back-hauling, 524, **544**
Backordering, 665
Backup components, 247–248
Backward pass, two-pass method, 852–853
Balance and output, line design for, 377–379
Baldrige Awards, 29, 604–605, 606
Balk, 432
Bar codes, 49, 346–347
Base, industrial robot, 343
Basic cells, 299–300, **305**
Basic feasible solution, 184
Basic solution, 184
Basic variables, 184
Basis, simplex algorithm, 184
Batch flow processes, 54, 331, **361**
  quality conformance and, 579
  repetitive process design, 383–384
  scheduling: *See* Job sequencing
Behavioral considerations, queueing systems: *See* **Queueing systems**
Behavioral (psychological) school, 511
Beta distribution, for task times, 857
Bias, in models, 122–123
Big JIT: *See* **Lean production (Big JIT)**
Big-M method, linear programming models, 189–190
Bill-of-material (BOM) file, 721–724, **741**
Bill of materials, 239
Blending problem, 78
  linear programming models, 175–177
Blue Chip Report, 109
Bottleneck resource, 782

Bottlenecks, 378
Breakdown models, for forecasting, 148
Break-even analysis, 287
  capacity planning, 263–265
Break-even point, 265
Buffer, 784
Buffer inventories, 387
Buildup models, for forecasting, 148
Business unit strategy, 38
Canonical form, simplex algorithm problems, 183
Capacity/Capacity planning, 14, 250–266
  break-even analysis, 263–265
  decision analysis, 265–266
  demand and
    forecasting, 262–263
    strategies, 260–262
  dynamic capacity and, 263
  evaluation methods, 262–266
  excess
    JIT implementation and, 779
    machine maintenance and, 770–771
    quality failure cost of, 567
  expansion and, 50, 257–260
    advantages/disadvantages, 259
    case study, 422–424
    demand leading, 257, 258, 259
    demand matching, 257, 259
    demand trailing, 257, 258–259
    steady expansion, 257, 259–260
  experience effects and, 263
  factors, determining, 253–255
  imbalances, synchronous production and, 782–783
  importance of, 251
  material requirement planning (MRP) and, 733–735
  measuring, 252–255
  rough-cut capacity analysis, 641
  sharing, 262
  strategy for, 49–51, 255–262
    economies of scale *vs.* distribution costs, 50
    facility organization and, 255–257
    facility sizing, 50–51
    lumpiness of capacity, 50–51
    market-organized facilities, 256
    process-organized facilities, 255
    product-organized facilities, 255
    product variety vs. customer service, 51
  utilization: *See* **Capacity utilization**
  work standards and, 529–530
Capacity-constrained resource, 782
Capacity efficiency, 253
Capacity utilization, 253
  production cost structure and, 58–60
  queueing systems, 436–437
Capital investment analysis, 355–356
Carpal tunnel syndrome, 526
Causal forecasting/models, 141–144, **149**
  independent variables, selecting, 141–142
  practical hints for using, 144
  quantitative, 113–115
  relationship estimation, 142–144
Cause-effect chart, 562, 595–597
Cells
  process design
    composition and type, 397–398
    detailed, 400–401
  transportation model, 299–300, 302–303
Cellular processes, 54, 335–340, **361**
  advantages/disadvantages, 338–340
  process design, and facility layout, 397–403
    cell composition and type, 397–398
    detailed design considerations, 400–402
    flow cells, 397, 401, 402–403, **413**
    group cells, 397–398, 401, 403, **413**
    number of operations in a cell, 401
    operations sequence and cell type, 400–401
    pack decomposition, 401
    production flow analysis: *See* **Production flow analysis (PFA)**
    spatial configuration, 402–403
Centered moving average (CMA), 135
Center of gravity location model, 284, **288**
Central limit theorem, 585, 858
Certainty, linear programming models and, 172
Chain-of-title, 94
Change reports, 728, **741**
Chase demand strategy, 629–631
Circuits, stepping stone method, 301–302
Civil Communication Section (CCS) seminars, 25
Clarke-Wright heuristic, 197
Classical inventory analysis, 659–660
Cleanliness, of work environment, 536
Clock time, 487, **501**
Coefficients, 172
  objective function, 192
  right-hand-side, 192–193
Collating and finishing, Standard Register Co., 83–84
Column index, 303–304
Combination products, 8
Commitment to insure, 94
Common components, product design and, 221
Community attractiveness, facility location and, 269
Compatible industry, facility location and, 269
Compensation systems, 542–543
  work standards and, 529
Competitive analysis, 37
Competitiveness, 28–29
Competitive service facilities, location of, 271–272
Competitive weapon, operations strategy as, 38–40
Complaint investigation/adjustment, 566
Complementary businesses, service facility site location and, 271
Complex problems, optimization models for, 171
Computer-aided design (CAD), 25, 234–235, **242**
Computer-aided design/computer-assisted manufacturing (CAD/CAM), 235, 344
Computer-aided engineering, 235
Computer-controlled machines, 342
Computer-integrated manufacturing (CIM), 346, **361**
Computerized layout heuristics, functional layouts, 394–397
Computerized reallocation of facilities technique (CRAFT), 394–396
Computerized relationship layout planning (CORELAP), 396
Computer numerically controlled (CNC) machines, 342
Computers/Computer software
  decision support systems (DSS), 825
  for linear programming models, 191–193
  for material requirement planning (MRP) systems, 740–741
  in operations management, 24–25
  Optimized Production Technology (OPT), 814–815, **826**
  recycling of components, 699
  simulation analysis and, 387, 501
Concurrent design, 215–216
Concurrent engineering (CE), 215–216

Consensus forecast, 109
Constant process, 115–116, 133–137
with multiplicative seasonality, 135–137
/quasi-constant seasonal processes, 133–137
Constrained optimization models, 167–170, **198**
constraints: *See* **Constraints**
decision variables, 167
dynamic programs, 732–733
objective functions, 167
Constraints, 168
additional, 194
parameters of, 183–184
relevant, 173
Construction heuristics, 197, 372–373, 396
Continuous-event model, 482
Continuous flow processes, 73, **96,** 329–330, **361**
production scheduling, 799–803
repetitive process design, 383–384
Continuous improvement, 26, 774–775
job design principles, 524
plan-do-check-act cycle, 600–601
TQM and, 600–601
Continuous probability distribution, random phenomena generation from, 490–491
Continuous review policies, for inventory, 666, **700**
Continuous uniform distribution, random phenomena generation from, 491
Contour line, 180
Control charts, 583
Convenience, as competitive advantage, 39
Coprocessing, 523, **544**
CORELAP (computerized relationship layout planning), 396
Cost accounting, cost measures and, 44–45
Cost advantages
of autonomous work groups, 539
of international facilities, 285
Cost centers, 44
Cost competitiveness, low-cost process, 39
Costing, work standards and, 529
Cost measures and accounting practices, 44–45
Cost of Manufactures, 21
Cost/risk analysis, production processes, 352–355
Cotton gin, 19
Countercyclic products, 260–261
demand patterns and, 644–645
Covering problem, 282
CPM (critical path method), 846: *See also* **PERT/CPM** analysis
CRAFT (computerized reallocation of facilities technique), 394–396
Crash cost (CC), 854
Crashing, task, 854–856
Crash time (CT), 854
Critical path, 853, **865**
computing: *See* **PERT/CPM** analysis
Critical probability, 688
Critical ratio (CR) rule, 804, 806, 812
Critical tasks, 853
Crossover analysis, 361
production processes, 352–355
Crossover points, 352–353
Cross-training, 84–85, 512–513, **544**
Cumulative average, 116, 133–134
Cumulative average forecasting model, 116–117, 133–134, 149
Cumulative distribution function, 490–491
Cumulative lead time, 721
Customer contact intensity, 358–359
Customer focus, in job design, 513
Customer population, 429, **468:** *See also* **Customers**
queueing systems and
arrival process, 431–432
attitude of, 432
composition of, 431
finite, 455–458
size of, 430–431
Customers, 429: *See also* **Customer population; Queueing systems**
Approved Statewide Title Agency (ASTA), 92–93
characteristics of: *See* **Queueing systems**
customer contact intensity, service systems structure and, 358–359
heterogeneity of, 452–454
involvement
in product design, 217–218, 575–576
in service product design, 237–238
pacing of, and reduced waiting, 451–452
patience of, rewarding, 468
preferences of, 575–576
service of, *vs.* product variety, 51
Cutting, Jefferson Smurfit Corp., 76
Cutting-stock problem, 78
Cycle counting, of inventory, 696–697
Cycle time, maximum, 374
Cyclic component, time series models, 114
Cyclic schedules
heuristic for, 802
lot size coordination with, 799–803
Cycling inventories, 663, **700**

Data collection
production flow analysis (PFA), 399
project processes, 841–844
quality cost audit, 567, 569–570
Decision analysis, 265–266, **287,** 312–324
linear programming models for, 193–195
sequential decisions and decision trees, 315–**319**
constructing a decision tree, 315–316
expected value of perfect information (EVPI), 318–**319**
folding back the tree and computing the expected payoff, 316–318
static decisions, 313–315
criteria for, 313–315
under risk, 314–315, **319**
under uncertainty, 313–314, **319**
Decision making: *See* **Decision analysis**
Decision making under risk, 313, 314–315, **319**
Decision making under uncertainty, 313–314, **319**
Decision nodes, 315–316
Decision support systems (DSS), scheduling methods, 825
Decision theory: *See* **Decision analysis**
Decision tree, 315–318, **319**
Decision variables, 167, **198**
formulation, 173
Defects
overtime costs from, 567
randomness and, 386
tracking, 594–597
Degeneracy, linear programming models, 191
Degenerate solution, 191, 305, **305**
Delivery
network and cycle, UPS, 87–89
on-time, 46
times, quick, 39
Delphi method, 110, 149
Demand
aggregate planning and, 626–627, 642–645
chase demand strategy, 629–631
level production/workforce strategy, 629, 631–633
assured, 756

Demand (*continued*)
capacity expansion strategies and
case study, 422–424
demand leading, 257, 258, 259
demand matching, 257, 259
demand trailing, 257, 258–259
capacity planning strategies and, 260–262
dependent: *See* **Dependent demand**
and forecasting, importance of, 103–104
independent: *See* **Independent demand**
patterns of
advertising and, 644
improving, 819
JIT scheduling and, 775–776
pricing and, 644
speculative, 756
Demand service level, 680
Deming's 14-point program, 598–599
Deming wheel, 600–601
Dependent demand, 660, 716, **741**
independent demand *vs.*, 665–666
and irregular production patterns, 716–719
Dependent variables, 111
Descriptive models, 428
Deseasonalizing, 133, 134
Design
product: *See* Product design
randomness, implications of, 387
Design capacity, 252, **287**
Design for assembly (DFA), 235–237, **242**
Design for manufacturability (DFM), 235–237, **242**
Design for service (DFS), 236
Design limits, 584
process capability and, 588–589
Design storage and retrieval, computer-aided design (CAD) and, 235
Deterministic models, 482–485
Deterministic service distribution, 448
Differential pricing, as capacity demand strategy, 261–262
Disaggregation, 639–642
factors in, 640–641
Disconnected flow processes, 331, **361**
Discrete-event model, 482
Discrete flow processes, 330, **361**
Discrete probability distribution, random phenomena generation from, 489–490
Diseconomies of scope, 256
Dispatching rule, 803
Disposition, of defective products, 566
Distribution costs, economies of scale *vs.*, 50
Disutility, 454
Diversification, international facilities for, 53, 286
Divisibility, linear programming models and, 172
Documents for production, 238–240
Dollar cost averaging, 259
Double exponential smoothing (DES), 130–132, 149
Downtime, 566
Drum, 783
Drum-buffer-rope mechanism, 783–784, **785**
Optimized Production Technology (OPT), 814–815, **826**
Dual price, 192
Dummy destination, 298–299, **305**
Dummy source, 298–299, **305**
Dummy tasks, 848
Durability
materials, 241
product, 564
Dynamic capacity and experience effects, 263
Dynamic dispatching rules, for job sequencing, 810–813
Dynamic expansion, facilities location and, 52
Dynamic program, 732–733

Earliest due date (EDD) rule, 804, 805, 807, 812
Earliest finishing (EF) time, task, 850
Earliest starting (ES) time, task, 850
Economic incentives, facility location and, 269
Economic lot size (ELS) model, 676–678
cyclic production schedules, coordination with, 799–803
Economic order quantity (EOQ) model, 667–676, **700**
assumptions of, 667
formula for, 669
lead time, 667
optimal quantity computation, 668–671
with quantity discounts, 672–676
reorder point computation, 667–668
robustness of, 671
total material cost (TMC), 668
Economic part period (EPP), 730–732
Economies of scale, 64
international facilities for, 285–286
production cost structure and, 60–63
vs. distribution costs, 50
Effective capacity, 252, **287**
Effectiveness, 41
Efficiency, 41
capacity, 253
energy, 349
international facilities and, 52–53
operating, holding inventories and, 661–662
production line, 373–374
server, 451, 453
Electronic data interchange (EDI), 49, 86, 347–348
systems for, 780–781
Elemental standard-times, 532
Employee evaluation, work standards and, 529
Employee suggestion systems, 774
Employee turnover, 46
Empowerment, 540
Energy efficiency, modern technologies and, 349
Engineering drawings, 239
Entering cell, 302
Entering variable, 186
Entities, 482
Environment
waiting line, 464–465
work: *See* Work environment
Environmental concerns
Jefferson Smurfit Corp., 78
materials management and, 699–700
modern technologies and, 348–349
product design, 240–241
recycling, 241, 699–700
Standard Register Co., 86
Environmental regulations, facility location and, 269
Equipment, work aids and ergonomics, 524, 578
Ergonomics, 524–526, **544,** 578
Escrow agent, 94
Ethical profile/image, of products, 564
European Union (EU), 53, 107, 286, 605
Evaluation, employee, 529
Event, 482, **501**
Event node, 316, 847
Excess capacity costs, 567
Expansion
space for, site decisions and, 270
strategy for, capacity planning and: *See* **Capacity/Capacity planning**
Expected monetary value, 314–315
Expected payoff, 314–315, 316–318, **319**

Expected value of perfect information (EVPI), 318–**319**
Experience curves, 60–62, 556–**557:** *See also* **Learning curves**
Experience effects, 60, **64,** 263
production cost structure and, 60–63
Experience rate, 556–**557**
Experiment, 486
Expertise, product/process, 39
Exploding queue property: *See* **Queueing systems**
Exponential distribution, 431–432
random phenomena generation from, 492
Exposure, service facility site location and, 272
External failure costs, 566
External setup activities, 763–766, **785**
Extreme points, 180

MFacilities
capacity of: *See* **Capacity/Capacity planning**
description of, functional layouts, 388
location and layout, 14, 51–53, 266–278
case study, 295–297
competitive service facilities, 271–272
dynamic expansion, 52
existing *vs.* new facilities, 278
importance of, 251
international, 52–53, 285–287
checklist for, 286–287
for diversification, 53
efficiency and, 52–53
for market access, 53
for risk reduction, 53
local decisions, 268–270
community attractiveness, 269
compatible industry, 269
economic incentives, 269
environmental regulations, 269–270
government policy and attitude, 269
taxes, 269
transportation network, 269
market proximity vs. production costs, 51–52
mathematical models for, 275–285
center of gravity, 284
fixed-charge location problem, 278–280
median problem, 283–284
planar location, 282–285
public service facilities, 280–282
Steiner-Weber, 283–284
process design and: See Process design, and facility layout
public service facilities, 270–271, 280–282
regional decisions, 267–268
labor supply, 268
market proximity, 267–268
raw material proximity, 268
restrictions, local, 268
taxes, 268
unionization, 268
utilities, availability of, 268
retail/competitive service facilities, 271–272
scoring rule for, 272–275
site decisions, 270
UPS, 90
size of, 40, 50–51
UPS, 89
Facilities-based services, 357
Failure costs, 566–567
Families, of items, 625–626
disaggregation and, 640–641
Fasteners, 224
Feasible region, 179
Feasible set, 179
Feasible solution, 179
basic, 184
Features, product, 564
Feedback
for quality conformance, 581
queueing systems, 466
Feeders, 88
Feed mix problem, 173–174
Field-based services, 357
Fill rate, 680
Financial function, 9
Finishing, Standard Register Co., 83–84
First-come-first-served (FCFS), 433
Fishbone charts, 562, 595–597
Fixed-charge location problem, 278–280, **288**
Fixed-time incrementing, 487, **501**
Flexibility
job, 540–542
in production, 39
autonomous work groups and, 539–540
flexible manufacturing systems (FMSs), 25
Flexible manufacturing systems (FMSs), 25, 344–346, **361**
Flexible spending accounts, 30, 692–693
Flex-time work policies, 541–542
Float, scheduling, 853
Flow cells
cellular processes, 402–403
process design, 397, 401, **413**
Flow charts, 96
Flow-cost matrix, work center interactions, 390
Flow diagrams, 96, **96**
Flow matrix, work center interactions, 390
Flow processes, 328–329, **361**
Flow time, 803
FMS module, 345
Focused facility, 256
Focus forecasting, 147
Forecasting, 101–165, **149**
accuracy of, 123–125
adaptive models, 147
advanced models, 144–145
alternative models, comparing, 122–125
forecast accuracy, 123–125
model assumptions, 122–123
Approved Statewide Title Agency (ASTA), 94–95
ARIMA (autoregressive/integrated/moving average models), 145
breakdown models, 148
buildup models, 148
case study, 162–165
causal models: *See* **Causal forecasting/models**
combining methods, 145–146
constant processes
and cumulative averages, 115–117, 133–134
with multiplicative seasonality, 135–137
defined, 102–103
demand, importance of, 103–104
of demand and capacity requirements, 262–263
focus, 147
linear trend processes, 126–132, 149
double exponential smoothing (DES), 130–132
linear regression, 127–129, 149
moving, 129–130
trend-adjusted moving average, 130–132
methods, 105–115
characteristics of, 149
intermediate-term forecasts, 105
long-term forecasts, 105
qualitative: *See* **Qualitative forecasting methods**
quantitative: *See* **Quantitative forecasting methods**

Forecasting (*continued*)
short-term forecasts, 105
time, role of, 105–106
model evaluation and testing, 145
monitoring forecasts, 107–108, 146–147
qualitative: *See* **Qualitative forecasting methods**
quantitative: *See* **Quantitative forecasting methods**
quasi-constant processes, 117–122, 133–137
moving averages, 118–120
simple exponential smoothing, 120–122, 149
simple moving average, 118–119, 149
weighted averages, 118, 149
weighted moving average, 119–120, 149
seasonal processes, 132–141, 149
additive seasonal model, 132
constant/quasi-constant, 133–137
linear trend processes with, 137–141
multiplicative seasonal model, 132–141
systems implementation, 145–148
tracking signals, 146–147
Foreign cultural preferences, international facilities and, 286
Forgetting, learning curves and, 556
Forward pass, two-pass method, 850–851
Fourdrinier machine, 75
Fourdrinier process, 73
Fourth tableau, simplex algorithm, 187–188
Function, quantitative forecasting and
general form of, 112
parameters, estimating, 112–113
Functional layouts, **387–397,** 412
computerized layout heuristics, 394–397
CRAFT, 394–396
facility description, 388
location assignment problem, 392–394
structured analytical layout tools, 391–392
work-center description, 388
work-center interactions, 388–391
Functional units, of organizations, 9–10
Fundamental theory of linear programming, 181

Gain-sharing, 542
Gantt charts
job sequencing, 813–814, **826**
project scheduling, 844–845, **865**
GATT, 285
Goals and performance measurement, 41–46
cost measures and accounting practices, 44–45
employee turnover, 46
goal-based measures of performance, 45–46
machine breakdowns, 46
on-time delivery, 46
operations management and, 11–13
of organizations, 36
output/labor ratio, 42–43
output value/labor ratio, 43
productivity measurement, 42–44
quality, 46
safety, 46
technical capability, 46
value-added/labor ratio, 43
Goods, production of, 7–9: *See also* **Products**
Goodwill, 566
Government policies
facility location and, 269
international facilities and, 286
Graphical solution, linear programming models, 180–181
Gripper, 343
Group averaging, 109, 149
Group cells
cellular processes, 403
process design, 397–398, 401, **413**
Group consensus, 109–110, 149
Group coordination, methods analysis and, 521–523
Group incentive systems, 542–543
Lincoln plan, 542
Scanlon plan, 542
Group methodologies, 108–110, 149
Group technology (GT), 341–342, 397

Harmful materials, 241
Hawthorne Studies, 23
Health problems, employee, 538
Heuristics, 197, **198**
aggregate planning, 628–633
Clarke-Wright, 197
computerized layout, 394–397
construction, 197, 372–373, 396
for cyclic schedule construction, 802
greedy, 818
improvement, 197, 378
myopic, 818
operations methods, mathematical models, 197–198
work station minimizing, 374–377
Hidden costs, of inventories, 665
Holding cost, 664
Holding cost rate, 664
Holdout data, 145
Home-based workers, 540–541
Home content laws, 53
House of quality, 228, 230–231, 575
Human body, job design principles and, 524
Human relations movement, 23
Human resources strategies, 56–57
Human variation, randomness and, 386
Humidity, of work environment, 536
Hungarian method, of scheduling, 815–818

Idea formulation, product development, 213
Illumination, of work environment, 536
Immediacy of services, service systems structure, 358
Improvement heuristics, 197, 378
Incentive compensation systems, 542–543
Incoming material inspection, 567
Independent demand, 660
dependent demand *vs.*, 665–666
Independent (predictor) variables, 111
selecting, 141–142
Individual incentive systems, 542
Industrial Engineering, 864
Industrial revolution, 18–20
Infeasible problems, linear programming models, 182, 191
Information
accurate, queueing systems and, 466
in operations strategy, 57–58
perfect, expected value of (EVPI), 318–**319**
Initial feasible solution, transportation problems, 299–300
In-process inspection/testing, 567
Integer programs, 195–197, **198**
Intended customers, service systems structure and, 357
Interarrival times, 431
Interchangeable parts, 19
Intermediate-term forecasts, 105
Intermediate-term planning: *See* **Aggregate planning**
Internal failure costs, 566–567
Internal setup activities, 763–766, **785**

International facilities, location and layout: *See* Facilities
International Organization for Standardization (ISO), 601
  ISO 9000 standards, 605, **606**
Inventories: *See also* Inventory and materials management
  aggregate measures of, 626
  buffer, 387
  cycling, 663, **700**
  defined, 661, **700**
  evaluation cost, for quality cost audit, 567
  quick response as substitute for, 759–760
  reducing, JIT production and, 755
  safety stocks, 567, 663, **700**
  speculative, 663–664
Inventory and materials management, 15, 658–714: *See also* **Inventories**
  capacity planning and, 254
  with dependent demands, 715–749
    irregular production patterns and, 716–719
    material requirements planning: *See* **Material requirements planning (MRP)**
  with independent demands, 77–78, 658–714
    case study, 709–714
    classical inventory analysis, 659–660
    continuous review policies, 666, **700**
    costs
      backordering, 665
      hidden, 665
      holding, 664
      ordering/setup, 664–665
      stockout (shortage), 665
    economic order quantity model: *See* **Economic order quantity (EOQ) model**
    economic production lot-size model, 676–678
    holding of inventories
      cost of, 664
      customer response time, 662
      and inventory types, 663–664
      operating efficiency, 661–662
      risk reduction, 662–663
      unusual events, 663
    implementation, of management system, 693–700
      ABC classification system, 694–695, **700**
      accuracy, maintaining, 696–697
      causes of inaccuracy, 695–696
      cycle counting, 696–697
      usage, lead time, and cost data, 697
    data requirements, 695
    environmental considerations, 699–700
    Pareto principle, 694
    sole-supplier relationships, **700**
    sole-supplier vendor relationships, 698–699
    two-bin system, 698
  independent vs. dependent demand, 665–666
  inventory position, 666
  materials requirements planning (MRP), 666
  one-period models, 687–693
    continuous decisions *vs.*, 666–667
    continuous demand distribution and, 688–689
    discrete demand distribution and, 689–690
    expected profit computation, 691
    flexible spending accounts and, 692–693
  order cycle service level, 679–680
  periodic review policies, 666, 684–687, **700**
  reorder point (RP), 666
  review policies, 666
  safety stock policies, 678–684
    using cost analysis, 683–684
    using customer service levels, 679–683
  Standard Register Co., 86
  zero-inventory systems, 659–660
inventory analysis
  classical, 659–661
  simulation models, 484–485
Jefferson Smurfit Corp., 77–78
Inventory position, 666
Inventory records file, 724
ISO 9000 series, 606
Items, 625–626

Japanese production system: *See* **Lean production (Big JIT)**
Job, 509, **544**
Job content, 544: *See also* Job design
Job description, 509
Job design, 14, 508–515
  automation and, 514–515
  capacity planning and, 254–255
  case study, 548–551
  cross-training, 512–513, **544**
  customer focus, 513
  human-machine interface, 514–515
  job content, 510–513
  job enlargement, 511, **544**
  job enrichment, 511–512, **544**
  job rotation, 512, **544**
  principles, 523–528
    activities compatible with the human body, 524
    back-hauling, 524, **544**
    continuous improvement, 524
    coprocessing (parallel processing), 523, **544**
    training, 528
    work aids and ergonomics: *See* **Work aids**
    worker consultation, 524
  process improvement, 513
  quality improvement, 513, 567
  repetitive process design, 378–379
  specialization, 510–511
  Standard Register Co., 84–85
  task variety, 510–511
  total quality management (TQM) and, 513
  UPS, 91
  work methods: *See* Work methods, analysis and improvement
Job enlargement, 511, **544**
Job enrichment, 511–512, **544**
Job rotation, 512, **544**
Job satisfaction, autonomous work groups and, 539
Job sequencing, 803–814
  approaches to, 803–804
  dispatching rule, 803
  dynamic dispatching rules, 810–813
  Gantt charts, 813–814, **826**
  Johnson's rule, 807–810, **826**
  one-stage problem rules, 804–807
    critical ratio (CR) rule, 804, 806, 812
    earliest due date (EDD) rule, 804, 805, 807, 812
    shortest processing time (SPT) rule, 804, 805, 807, 811–812, **826**
    slack time remaining (STR) rule, 804, 806, 812–813
  priority rule, 803
  schedule evaluation criteria, 803–804
    flow time, 803
    make span, 803, **826**
    tardiness, 804
  three-stage problems, 809–813
  two-stage problems, 807–809
  visual scheduling, 813–814

Job-shop processes, 80, **96,** 332–335, **361**
drum-buffer-rope mechanism, 783–784, **785,** 813–814
simulation models, 483
Job shops, 54
Johnson's rule, 807–810, **826**
for three-stage batch flow problems, 809–810
for two-stage batch flow problems, 807–809
Just-in-time (JIT) production systems, 15, 750–781
Big JIT: *See* **Lean production (Big JIT)**
described, 751–753
electronic data interchange (EDI) and, 780–781
employee morale and, 775
ideal systems and, 753–755
lean production: *See* **Lean production (Big JIT)**
little JIT, 751, **785**
mechanics of, 760–762
kanbans, number and size of, 761–762
and MRP, integration with, 784
quality of products and, 579–580, 772–774
scheduling, 756–760, 775–777
and classical scheduling, compared, 757–759
demand patterns and, 775–776
assured demand, 756
kanbans, 758
large *vs.* small lot sizes, 757
production process structure and, 776–777
product mix and, 776
pull *vs.* push strategies, 756–757
quick response, as inventory substitute, 759–760
unsuitable conditions for, 777
in service industries, 779–781
and synchronous production, integration with, 784

Kaizen: *See* **Continuous improvement**
Kanbans, 758, 761–762
Kendall-Lee notation, queueing systems, 437

Labor supply, regional facility location and, 268
Labor unions, 543–544
regional facility location and, 268
Laplace, 314, **319**
Latest finishing time (LF) time, task, 850
Latest starting (LS) time, task, 850
Layout tools, functional layouts, 391–392
Lead time, 667
cumulative, 721
Lean production (Big JIT), 751, 762–781, **785:** *See also* **Just-in-time (JIT) production** systems
case study, 789–795
continuous improvement, 774–775
delivery of materials, reliability of, 767–768
employee morale and, 775
implementation
customization of, 778–779
excess capacity, maintaining, 779
flexibility, 779
guidelines for, 777–778
patience, 778
quality of products and, 772–774
setup activities
internal *vs.* external, 762–764
quality conformance and, 578–579
single-minute exchange of dies (SMED), 764–767, 772, **785**
time reduction of, 764–766
total productive maintenance (TPM): *See* **Total productive maintenance (TPM)**
Learning curves, 60, **557:** *See also* **Experience curves**
deriving, 553–556
forgetting and, 556
rate of learning and, 552–553
units of production and, 556
Learning effect, 552
Learning rate, 552–553, **557**
Leaving cell, 302
Leaving variable, 186
Legals and taxes, 92
Level production/workforce strategy, 629, 631–633
Leverage, production cost structure and, 58–60
Liability, product, 566
Lincoln plan, 542
Linear program: *See* **Linear programming models**
Linear programming models, 170, **198**
for aggregate planning, 633–636
artificial variables and, 188–191
Big-M method, 189–190
blending problem, 175–177
characteristics/assumptions of, 172
computer solution of, 191–193
constraints, relevant, 173
for decision making, 193–195
additional resources, pricing, 193–194
constraints, additional, 194
product demand and, 194–195
uncertainty and, 193
decision variable formulation, 173
degeneracy, 191
feed mix problem and, 173–174
formulating, 173–179
fundamental theory of, 181
geometry of, 179–182
graphical solution, 180–181
infeasible problems, 182, 191
multiperiod planning, 177–179
multiple optima, 182, 191
objective function definition, 173
for personnel scheduling, 823–824
simplex algorithm: *See* **Simplex algorithm**
transportation: *See* **Transportation problems**
two-phase method, 190–191
unbounded problems, 182, 191
Linear regression, 127–129, 149
moving, 129–130, 149
Linear scoring rule (LSR), 273–275, **287**
Linear trend model, 127, 149
with multiplicative seasonality, 138–140, 149
Linear trend processes, 126–141: *See also* **Forecasting**
double exponential smoothing (DES), 130–132
regression for, 127–130
with seasonality, 137–141, 149
Line balancing, 372: *See also* Repetitive process design, and facility layout
Line design, for balance and output, 377–379
Line process, 384
Little JIT, 751, **785:** *See also* **Just-in-time (JIT) production** systems
Loading, UPS, 90
Load reports, 728, **741**
Location, as competitive advantage, 39
Location assignment problem, functional layouts, 392–394
Logistics, simulation models, 485
Long-term forecasts, 105
Lot-for-lot ordering, 725
Lot-for-lot production, 725
Lot-size differences, randomness and, 387
Low-cost process, 39
Lower control limit, 585–586

Luddite Rebellion of 1812, 20
Lumpiness of capacity, 50–51

Machine breakdowns, 46: *See also* **Total productive maintenance (TPM)**
Machining centers, 343
Made to order, 328
Made to stock, 328
Maintainability, product, 564
Maintenance
  capacity planning and, 254
  Jefferson Smurfit Corp., 79
  total productive: *See* **Total productive maintenance (TPM)**
Make span, 803, **826**
Malcolm Baldrige National Quality Improvement Awards, 29, 604–605, **606**
Management, interpretation of, 11
Management science, 24
Management Training Program (MTP), 25
Manipulator, industrial robot, 343
Manufacturability, design for (DFM), 235–237, **242**
Manufacturing resources planning (MRP II), 737
Manufacturing/service mix, service systems structure, 357
Manufacturing systems, 7–8, **31**
Marketing function, 9
Marketing strategy, 40
  and production cost structure
    experience effects and economies of scale, 60–63
    leverage and capacity utilization, 58–60
Market-organized facilities, 256
Markets
  access to, international facilities for, 53
  analysis of, 37
  identification and evaluation of, 213
  proximity to
    regional facility location and, 267–268
    vs. production costs, 51–52
  selection of, 37–38
Master production schedule (MPS), 646, 720–721
  aggregate planning and, 641–642
Master schedule file, for MRP, 720–721
Material requirements plan, 725–727, **741**
Material requirements planning (MRP), 666, 719–741, **741**
  benefits, 738
  capacity requirements planning, 733–735
  case study, 747–749
  change reports and, 728, **741**
  computer-based systems, 740–741
  inputs, 720–724
    bill-of-material (BOM) file, 721–724
    cumulative lead time, 721
    inventory records file, 724
    master schedule file, 720–721
    materials list, 723
    product hierarchy, 720
      product structure tree, 722–724
    time buckets, 720
  and JIT, integration with, 784
  JIT scheduling *vs.*, 777
  limitations/implementation problems
    computer system installation, 740–741
    data accuracy, 738–739
    employee training and involvement, 739
    file maintenance, 738–739
    product environment, 740
  load reports and, 728, **741**
  logic and mechanics, 724–728
    consolidation of requirements, 727–725
    lot-for-lot ordering/production, 725
    material requirements plan development, 725–727
    planned order receipts, 725
    planned order releases, 725–727
    production time chart, 725
  lot sizing in, 729–733
    economic order quantity (EOQ), 729–730
    economic part period (EPP), 730–732
    part-period balancing (PPB), 730–732, **741**
    Wagner-Whitin algorithm, 732–733, **741**
  manufacturing resources planning (MRP II) and, 737
  order releases and, 728, **741**
  outputs, 725
  production release schedules and, 728
  structure and principles, 719
  and synchronous production, integration with, 784
  uncertainty and safety stock, 736–737
  updating
    net-change system, 735
    regenerative system, 735–736
    rolling horizon approach, 736
    time fences, 736
Materials
  management of: *See* Inventory and materials management; **Material requirements planning (MRP)**
  in production, 241
  quality of, 580
  shortages, 386
  usage reduction, modern technologies and, 348
  variations, 386
Materials list, 723
Mathematical models, 166–210
  for facilities location: *See* Facilities, location and layout
  heuristic methods in operations, 197–198
    production line balancing, 197
    vehicle routing, 197
  integer and mixed integer programs, 195–197
  linear programming models: *See* **Linear programming models**
  operations decision making and, 166
  optimization models, 167–171
    advantages and disadvantages, 170–171
      for complex problems, 171
      objectivity, increasing, 170–171
      thought process structuring, 170
    constrained: *See* **Constrained optimization models**
Maximax, 314, **319**
Maximin, 314, **319**
Maximization problems, transportation, 304
Maximum cycle time, 374
Mean absolute deviation (MAD), 123–125
Mean absolute percentage error (MAPE), 123–125
Mean error (ME), 122–123
Mean squared error (MSE), 123–125
Mechanical failures, randomness and, 386
Median problem, mathematical model for, facilities location, 283–284
Methods analysis, 544: *See also* Work methods, analysis and improvement
Methods time measurement (MTM), 533

Micro-motion analysis, 517, 533, **544**
Minimax, 314, **319**
Minimax regret, 314, **319**
Minimin, 314, **319**
Mission statement, 36
Mistake-proofing, 225: *See also* **Poka-yoke (mistake-proofing)**
Mixed-integer programs, 195–197, **198**
Mixed production model, repetitive process design, 382–383
Models, 167, **198:** *See also* individual models
  assumptions, verifying, 122–123
  best, selecting, 113
  evaluation and testing, 145
  quality of, 113
  quantitative forecasting and, 111–113
Modification, product development and, 214
Modified distribution (MODI) method, 303–304, **305**
Modified wave, 451–452
Modularity, product design and, 225–226
Monitoring
  of forecasts, 107–108, 146–147
  of projects, 862–863
Motion and time study, 530–532, **544**
Motion economy principles, 525
Motion-time data, predetermined, 533
Moving averages, 118–120
Moving linear regression, 129–130, 149
Multiple optima, 182, 191
Multiplicative seasonal model, 132–141, 149
Multiserver with exponential service times (M/M/S), queueing systems: *See* **Queueing systems**

NAFTA, 53, 107, 285, 286
Naive model, 121
Nameplate capacity, 771
Net-change system, for updating MRP, 735
Net present value (NPV), 355, **361**
Net requirements, 630
Networks, 846
  for project scheduling: *See* **PERT/CPM** analysis
Next-event incrementing, 487, **501**
Nodes, network, 846
Noise, in work environment, 536–537
Nonbasic cells, 299–300, **305**
Nonbasic variables, 184
Nonbottleneck resource, 782
Nonlinear disutility, queueing systems, 462–464
Nonlinear waiting costs and waiting psychology, 462–466
Nonnegative right-hand sides, simplex algorithm, 183
Normal cost (NC), task, 854
Normal distribution, random phenomena generation from, 493
Normal times (NT), task, 854
Normative models, 428
Northwest (NW) corner method, 300, **305**
Notation, queueing systems, 437
N-period simple moving average (SMA(N)), 118, 149
N-period weighted moving average (WMA(N)), 119, 149
Numerically controlled (NC) machines, 342

Objective forecasting methods, 106
Objective function, 167, **198**
  coefficients, 192
  definition, 173
Objective function contours, 180
Objectivity, optimization models and, 170–171
Observation and measurement, work standards and, 530–535
Occupational Safety and Health Act (OSHA), 538
O/1 integer programs, 275
On the Economy of Machines and Manufactures, 21
On-time delivery, 46
Operations
  number of, in a cell, 401
  tours of, 71–97
Operations analysis, 404
Operations function, 9
Operations management, 10–**31**
  computers in, 24–25
  defined, 10–18
  environmental awareness and, 27
  for everyone, 29–31
  history of, 18–27
    industrial revolution, 18–20
    interchangeable parts, 19
    scientific management: *See* **Scientific management**
    specialization of labor, 20
  human relations movement, 23
  Japanese (lean) production system, 25–27, **31**
    continuous improvement, 26
    quality comes first, 26
    waste elimination, 26
  just-in-time production: *See* **Just-in-time (JIT) production** systems
  mathematical models and: *See* Mathematical models
  operations research/management science (OR/MS), 24
  productivity and, 11
    competitiveness with, 28–29
  quality and: See Quality, product
  reaching goals, 11–13
  responsibilities and challenges of, 13–16
  service economy and, 27
  skills and knowledge needed, 16–18
    analytical tools, 17–18
    production principles, 17
    production process knowledge, 16–17
  as strategic weapon, 11–13
  today, 27
Operations research/management science (OR/MS), 24
Operations sequence and cell type, process design, 400–401
Operations strategies, 34–70, **64:** *See also* **Operations management**
  for capacity: *See* **Capacity/Capacity planning**
  case study, 68–70
  as competitive weapon, 38–40
  developing, 40–41
  facility location: *See* Facilities
  goals and performance measurement: *See* Goals and performance measurement
  human resources, 56–57
  information in, 57–58
  of organizations, 36–38
    business unit strategy, 38
    competitive analysis, 37
    goals, 36
    market analysis, 37
    market selection, 37–38
    order-winning dimensions, 37–38
    philosophy and policies, 38
    product selection, 37–38
  processes, continuous flow, 53–54
  production cost structure and: *See* **Production**
Opportunity cost, 186
Optical scanners, 49, 346–347, 780
Optimality, stepping stone method, 301
Optimal solution, 179, **198**
Optimized production technology (OPT), 814–815, **826**
Order and production release schedules, 728

Order cycle service level, 679–680
Order receipt, Standard Register Co., 81–82
Order releases, 728, **741**
Order-winning dimensions, 37–38, **64**
Organization strategy, 64: *See also* **Operations strategies**
Orientation in assembly, product design and, 224–225
OR/MS*Today*, 864
Output, line design for, 377–379
Output-based compensation systems, 542
Output/labor ratio, 42–43
Output value/labor ratio, 43
Outsourced, 48
Overage, 687
Over-the-wall design process, 214

Packing and shipping, Standard Register Co., 84
Packs
decomposition of, 401
product categorization into, 399
Paired t-test, 500
Parallel processing, 523, **544**
Parallel production lines, 381–382
Parallel work stations, 380–381
Parameters, 113, 172, **198**
Parametric (sensitivity) analysis, 191–192, **198**
Pareto principle, 603, 694
Part period, 730
Part-period balancing (PPB) method, 730–732, **741**
Parts minimization, product design and, 220, 576
Passive phase, of work involvement, 523
Patience of customers, rewarding, 468
Payoff table, 313, **319**
P-center model, 280–282
P-chart, 593–594
Percent balance, production line, 373–374
Performance, product, 564
Performance measures, queueing systems, 434–436
Performance rating, 531–532
Periodic review policies, inventory, 666, 684–687, **700**
Permanent component, time series models, 113
Perpetual review policies, 666, **700**
Personal finance, flexible spending accounts, 692–693
Personnel management
capacity planning and, 254–255
scheduling, 821–825
implementation principles, 825
linear programming-based methods, 823–824
work standards and, 529, 825
Standard Register Co., 84–85
PERT/CPM analysis, 845–853, **865**
benefits, 846–847
computer software, 864
conventions
activity-on-arc (A-O-A), 847–848
activity-on-node (A-O-N), 849
compared, 849
implementation and use, 864
project monitoring, 862–863
two-pass method, critical path computation, 849–853, **865**
backward pass stage, 852–853
forward pass stage, 850–851
PERT (program evaluation and review technique), 846: *See also* **PERT/CPM** analysis
Philosophy and policies, 38
Pivot column, 186
Pivot element, 186–187
Pivot row, 186
Planar location, mathematical model for, 282–285
Plan-do-check-act cycle, 600–601
Plant-within-a-plant (PWP), 256–257
PMNET*work*, 864
Point-of-sale cash registers, 49
Poisson process, 431–432, **468**
Poka-yoke (mistake-proofing), 225, 526–528, 599
devices for TPM, 772
and quality conformance, 577–578
Policies, 38
Pooling servers, queueing systems, 445
Positional weight, 375–376
Precedence requirements, 372
Predecessors, 374
Present value analysis, 355
Prevention costs, quality, 566, 567
Pricing
demand patterns and, 644, 819
differential, as capacity demand strategy, 261–262
and service scheduling, 819
work standards and, 529
Printing, Standard Register Co., 82–83
Priority rule, 803
Problem preparation, transportation, 298–299
Process capability, 588–589
Process chart, 516
job design, 516–517, **544**
service system design, 404–406, **413**
Process control by attributes, 593–594
Process control by variables, 583–592
Process design
and facility layout, 369–425
case study, 422–424
cellular processes: *See* **Cellular processes**
functional layouts: *See* **Functional layouts**
repetitive process design: *See* Repetitive process design, and facility layout
service system design: *See* **Service systems**
quality improvement costs, 567
work standards and, 529–530
Process distribution, 584
Process expertise, 39
Process flow diagram, 516, **544**
service system design, 404–406, **413**
Process layouts: *See* **Functional layouts**
Process-organized facilities, 255
Process sheet, 239
Process standard deviation, 584
Product correlations, warehouse and storage layout, 409–410
Product costing and pricing, work standards and, 529
Product design, 13–14, 211–249
capacity planning and, 253
case study, 244–245
documents for production, 238–240
environmentally sensitive, 240–241
process of, 214–219
concurrent design, 215–216
concurrent engineering (CE), 215–216
customer involvement, 217–218, 575–576
over-the-wall, 214
for production: *See* **Production,** product design for supplier involvement, 218–219, 768
team design, 217
product development, 213–214
detailed product design, 213–214
idea formulation, 213
market identification and evaluation, 213
modification and redesign, 214
production ramp-up, 214
prototyping, 213–214, 237

Product design (*continued*)
quality and, 567, 574–581
revolution in, 212
for services, 237–238
tools for, 228–237
assembly, design for (DFA), 235–237
computer-aided design (CAD), 234–235
manufacturability, design for (DFM), 235–237
prototyping, 237
quality conformance and, 577
quality function deployment (QFD), 228–231
Taguchi method, 232–234
value analysis, 231–232
Product development: *See* Product design
Production, 78
aggregate measures of, 626
cost structure of
experience effects and economies of scale, 60–63
leverage and capacity utilization, 58–60
market proximity *vs.*, facilities location and layout, 51–52
operations and marketing strategies, 40, 58–63
decoupling of, 661–662
flexibility in, 39, 539–540
line balancing, 197
planning, Jefferson Smurfit Corp., 78
principles of, 17
processes: *See* Production processes
product design for, 215, 219–228
assembly
accessibility in, 224–225
process simplification, 222–225, 577
common components, 221, 577
fasteners and, 224
mistake-proof assembly, 225, 577
modularity and, 225–226
orientation in assembly, 224–225
parts minimization, 220, 576
robustness and, 227–228
specifications and, 226–227, 577
standard components, 221–222
testing, 225
tolerances and, 226–227, 577
product structure tree, 722–724
ramp-up of, 214
scheduling: *See* Production scheduling
strategic tasks, 40
systems: *See* **Production systems**
Production cost function, 58, 263–264
Production cycle time, 373–374
Production flow analysis (PFA), 398–400
cell design, detailed, 400
trade-offs and considerations, 400–402
chart analysis, 399–400
chart construction, 399
data collection, 399
packs, product categorization into, 399
Production lines, 384
parallel, 381–382
simulation, random, 494–496
Production lot size, 676
JIT systems and, 757
Production processes, 53–56: *See also* **Production; Production systems**
Approved Statewide Title Agency (ASTA), 93–94
assignable variation, 582
autonomous work groups and, 539
batch flow, 54, 331, **361**
cellular, 54, **361**
cellular processes, 335–340
advantages/disadvantages, 338–340
continuous flow, 329–330, **361,** 383–384
continuous improvement, 26
control costs, quality and, 567
design of, 14
capacity planning and, 253
Jefferson Smurfit Corp., 77
quality conformance and, 577–580
UPS, 90
disconnected flow, 331, **361**
discrete flow, 330, **361**
flow processes, 328–332, **361**
advantages/disadvantages, 331–332
job-shops, 54, 80, **96,** 332–335, **361**
knowledge of, need for, 16–17
low-cost, 39
out of control, 583, 592–593
product life cycle, 55–56
project: *See* **Project processes**
quality conformance and, 576–581
quality strategy, 56: *See also* **Statistical process control (SPC)**
repetitive, 53–54, 90, **96**
repetitive flow: *See* **Repetitive flow processes**
revising and updating, 63–64
standardization of, qualitative forecasting and, 107
steering the ship, 35
strategy of: *See* **Operations strategies**
structure and technology, selecting, 325–368
alternatives, evaluating, 349–356
capital investment analysis, 355–356
case study, 366–367
common classifications, 327–328
cost/risk analysis, 352–355
crossover analysis, 352–355
customizing, 360–361
product-process matrix, 350–352
product variety and volume, 350
service systems structure: *See* **Service systems**
technologies, modern: *See* **Technology**
substrategies, 47–57
technology and: *See* **Technology**
Total Quality Management (TQM): *See* **Total Quality Management (TQM)**
Production rate, 373–374
Production scheduling
assignment problems, 815–819, **826**
Hungarian method, 815–818
unbalanced, 818–819
for batch production systems: *See* Job sequencing
capacity planning and, 254
for continuous/repetitive flow processes, 799–803
cyclic, lot size coordination and, 799–803
implementation principles, 825
optimized production technology (OPT), 814–815, **826**
Standard Register Co., 81–82
work standards and, 529, 825
Production systems, 5–33: *See also* Production processes
functional units of the organization, 9–10
ideal, JIT and, 753–755
just-in-time: *See* **Just-in-time (JIT) production** systems
P/OM's value, 6
production of goods and services, 7–9
pull *vs.* push systems, 756–757
quality conformance and, 580–581
synchronous: *See* **Synchronous (synchronized) production**
Production time chart, 725

Productivity, 11
  autonomous work groups and, 539
  and competitiveness, 28–29
  measurement of, 42–44
  work environment and, 536–538
Product layout, 371, **412:** *See also* Repetitive process design, and facility layout
Product life cycle, 55–56
Product location, warehouse and storage layout, 412
Product mix problem, 175
Product-organized facilities, 255
Product-process matrix, 350–352, **361**
Products, 7, **31**
  aggregation of, 625
  Approved Statewide Title Agency (ASTA), 92–93
  combination, 8
  continuous improvement of, 26
  countercylic, 644–645
  demand for, linear programming models and, 194–195
  design of: *See* Product design
  differences in, randomness and, 387
  expertise on, 39
  Jefferson Smurfit Corp., 73–74
  product cycle, short, 39
  promotion of
    as capacity demand strategy, 261–262
    demand patterns and, 644, 819
  quality of: *See* Quality, product
  reliability of, 247–249
  selection of, 37–38
  unique: *See* **Project processes**
  variety of, 40, 350
    capacity planning and, 253
    vs. customer service, 51
Product similarity, warehouse and storage layout, 410
Product structure tree, 722–724
Product types, 625–626
Profit
  expected, computation, 691
  maximization of, risk and, 692
Profit centers, 44
Progress curve, 556–557
Project processes, 53, 340, **361,** 838–875
  benefits of, 841
  case study, 873–875
  data collection and analysis, 841–844
    as iterative process, 843–844
    task identification, 842
    time estimations, 842–843
  environments of, 840
  monitoring progress, 862–863
  project manager, role of, 840–841
  scheduling/planning
    computer software for, 864
    crashing, 854–856
    Gantt charts, 844–845
    network-based methods: *See* **PERT/CPM** analysis
    probabilistic task time estimates, 856–862
      answering questions with, 860–861
      assumptions, validity of, 861–862
      central limit theorem, 858
      completion time distribution, 857–860
      computer simulation, 861–862
    time-cost trade-offs, 853–856
Projects, 839, **865**
Proportionality, linear programming models and, 172
Prototyping, 213–214, 237
Proximity, to other industry, site decisions and, 270
Proximity charts, 390–391
Pseudorandom numbers, 488, **501–502**
Public service facilities, location of, 270–271, 280–282
Pull production system, 757: *See also* **Just-in-time (JIT) production** systems
Pulp preparation, Jefferson Smurfit Corp., 74
Push production system, 756

QFD relationship matrix, 228–230
Qualitative forecasting methods, 149
  improving, 107–110
    accuracy incentives, 108
    group methodologies, 108–110, 149
      averaging, 109
      consensus, 109–110
      Delphi method, 110, 149
    monitoring forecasts, 107–108
    process standardization, 107
  time to use, 107
Quality, product, 12, 14–15, 539: *See also* **Total Quality Management (TQM)**
  Approved Statewide Title Agency (ASTA), 95–96
  Baldrige Awards, 29, 604–605
  capacity planning and, 253
  case study, 611–613
  as competitive advantage, 40
  defined, 563
  design quality, 574–576
    conformance and, 576–577
  dimensions of, 563–565
  goals and performance measurement, 46
  house of quality, 228, 230–231, 575
  importance of, 562
  improving
    conformance considerations, 576–581
    cost of: *See* **Quality cost audit**
    design considerations, 574–576
  ISO 9000 series standards, 605
  Jefferson Smurfit Corp., 78–79
  lean production system, 26
  of models, 113
  new philosophy of, 561–563
  planning, cost of, 567
  Quality is Free, 562
  Standard Register Co., 85–86
  statistical control: *See* Statistical quality control
  strategy for, 56
Quality, service, 597–598
  honesty/courtesy, 598
  performance, 597
  timeliness/speed of service, 597
Quality circles, 562, 578, 775
Quality conformance, 574, 576–581
  process capability, 588–589
  process design and, 577–581
  product design and, 576–577
  production operations and, 580–581
Quality cost audit, 565–574, **605**
  case study, 611–613
  cost categories, 566–567
    appraisal costs, 566, 567
    external failure costs, 566
    internal failure costs, 566–567
    prevention costs, 566, 567
  cost distributions
    among categories, 568
    among products/divisions, 568–569
    desirable *vs.* typical, 569
  cost magnitudes, 568
  data collection, 567, 569–570
  examples
    medical insurance company, 572–574
    personal computer manufacturer, 570–572
Quality cost scorecard, 565, 571, 573: *See also* **Quality cost audit**
Quality function deployment (QFD), 242, 562, 575–576
  product design and, 228–231
Quality trilogy, 598–599

Quantitative forecasting methods, 106, 110–115, **149**
background, 110–111
causal models: *See* **Causal forecasting/models**
characteristics of, 149
modeling steps, 111–113
(1) graph the relevant data, 111–112
(2) select general form of the function, 112
(3) estimate the parameters of the function, 112–113
(4) evaluate the quality of the model, 113
(5) select and implement the best model, 113
strategy, 110–111
time series models: *See* **Time series models**
Quantity discount, 672
Quasi-constant processes: *See* **Forecasting**
Queue discipline, 433
Queueing networks, 458–461, **468**
Queueing simulation, 496–499
Queueing systems, 426–480
behavioral and other considerations, 462–468
environment, waiting, 464–465
feedback and accurate information, 466
nonlinear disutility, 462–464
nonlinear waiting costs, 462–466
social justice, 464
waiting psychology, 462–466
capacity utilization, 436–437
case study, 477–480
characteristics of, 429–434
customer characteristics, 430–432
examples of, 429
exploding queue property, 436–437
improving, 466–468
patience of customers, rewarding, 468
self-service, 466–467
service time reduction, 467
tasks performed in advance, 467
two queues for each server, 467
Kendall-Lee notation, 437
multiserver with exponential service times (M/M/S), 441–448
finite customer population, 455–458
number of queues for, 446–448
pooling servers into one system, benefits of, 445
notation, 437
queue discipline, 433
queueing theory, 427–429
serial and network, 458–461
service characteristics, 432–433
service mechanism or process, 432–433
simulation and, 430
single-server with exponential service times (M/M/1), 437–441
single-server with general or constant service times (M/G/1 and M/D/1), 448–450
steady-state equations for, 430
system configuration, 433–434
number of queues, 434
queue capacity, 433–434
servers and, 433
systems performance measures, 434–436
terminology, 434–437
variance in, 450–455
customer heterogeneity, exploiting, 452–454
server efficiency and, 453
service levels and, 453–454
customer pacing reduces waiting, 451–452
designated servers, 454–455
slower servers, 451
Queueing theory, 427–429
Queues, 427
capacity of, 433–434
number of, 434
for queueing systems, 446–448
two for each server, 467
Quick Response Program (QRP), 780–781

Random component, time series models, 115
Random event node, 316
Randomness effects, repetitive process design, 385–387
Random normal deviates, 493
Random numbers, 488
Random phenomena
generation of: See Simulation analysis
replication of, 500
Random production line simulation, 494–496
Random variables, 110
Range control chart, 590–592
Range (R), 589
Ranging, 192
Ranked positional weight technique (RPWT), 375
Raw material proximity, location decisions and, 268
R-chart, 590–592
Recycling, 241, 699–700
Redesign, product development and, 214
Redundant components, 247–248
Regenerative system, for updating MRP, 735–736
Regional facilities, location and layout, 267–268
Regret, 314
Regulations, environmental, 269
Relationship estimation, causal forecasting, 142–144
Relationship (REL) diagram, 388
Relevant data, graphs of, 111–112
Reliability, product, 247–249, 564
Renege, 432
Reorder point (RP), 666
Repetitive flow processes, 90, **96,** 330, **361**
Repetitive motion syndrome, 526
Repetitive process design, and facility layout, 371–387
batch flow processes, 383–384
continuous flow processes, 383–384
cycle time, 373–374
efficiency (% balance), 373–374
improvement heuristics, 378
job design, 378–379
line design for balance and output, 377–379
mixed production model, 382–383
parallel production lines, 381–382
production rate, 373–374
randomness effects, 385–387
skill variation, 379
spatial configuration, 384–385
staffing, 378–379
support equipment, 379
task compatibility, 379
task decomposition, 372
technological improvements, 378–379
work station design, 372–373
number minimizing heuristic, 374–377
parallel, 380–381
Repetitive processes, 53–54, 90, **96**
Replacement, product, 566
Replication of random phenomena, 500
Reservations, 820, **826**
systems for
improving, 820–821
service operations scheduling and, 819
Resources
bottleneck/nonbottleneck, 782
capacity-constrained, 782
demand coordination, 15
pricing, 193–194

Responsibilities and challenges, of operations management: *See* **Operations management**
Restrictions, local, regional facility location and, 268
Retail/competitive service facilities, location of, 271–272
Retail facilities layout, 410–412
  aisle configuration, 411–412
Retesting, quality and, 566
Returns, product, 566
Reverse engineering, 230
Rework, of defective products, 566
Right-hand-side coefficients, 192
Risk
  in decision making, 313
  and profit maximization, 692
  reduction of
    holding inventories and, 662–663
    international facilities for, 53, 286
Risk averse, 315
Risk neutral, 315
Robots, 343–344
Robust design, 227–228, **242**
Rolling horizon
  aggregate planning, 628, **646**
  material requirements planning (MRP), 736
Rope, 784
Rough-cut capacity analysis, 641
Route sheet, 239
Routing, UPS, 90–91
Row index, 303–304
Run, 486

Safety
  goals and performance measurement, 46
  of work environment, 537–538
Safety stocks, 663, **700**
  material requirements planning (MRP) and, 736–737
  policies for, 678–684
  quality failure cost and, 566
Safety time, 737, **741**
Scale economies: *See* **Economies of scale**
Scanlon plan, 542
Scheduling, 15–16
  Approved Statewide Title Agency (ASTA), 94–95
  case study, 834–837
  defined, 798
  implementation principles, 825
  Jefferson Smurfit Corp., 78
  of JIT systems: *See* **Just-in-time (JIT) production** systems
  personnel: *See* Personnel management
  production: *See* Production scheduling
  project: *See* **Project processes**
  of service operations, 819–821
  UPS, 91
  work standards and, 529
Scientific management, 20–23
Scientific management school, 510
Scoring rule, for facilities location, 272–275
Scrap, 566
Seasonal component, time series models, 113–114, 149
Seasonal factors, 133
Seasonal indices, 133
Seasonal models, 149
Self-directed teams, 544: *See also* **Autonomous work groups/teams**
Self-service, customer, 466–467
Sensitivity (parametric) analysis, 191–192, **198**
Sensory characteristics, of products, 564
Sequential decisions and decision trees: *See* **Decision analysis**
Serial (tandem) queueing systems, 451, 458–461, **468**
Servers, 429, **468**
  designated, 454–455
  efficiency of, 451, 453
  and queueing systems, 433
  slower, 451
Serviceability, product, 564
Service blueprint, 240, **413**
  service system design, 406–408
Service economy, 27
Service-process matrix, service systems structure, 359
Service region design, UPS, 90–91
Services, 8–9, **31:** *See also* **Service systems**
  characteristics of, 432–433
  immediacy of, 358
  levels of, 453–454
  mechanism or process of, 432–433
  package of and intended customers, 357–358
  product design for, 237–238
  site of, 357–358
  time reduction, 467
Service systems, 8, **31:** *See also* **Services**
  design of, 404–412
    process charts, 404–406, **413**
    process flow diagrams, 404–406, **413, 544**
    retail facilities layout, 410–412
    aisle configuration, 411–412
    service blueprint, 240, 406–408, **413**
    warehouse and storage layout, 408–410
      product correlations, 409–410
      product location, 412
      product similarity, 410
      three-dimensional analysis, 409
  JIT principles and, 779–781
  quality dimensions, 597–598
    cost audit example, 572–574
  scheduling, 819–821
    appointment and reservation systems, 819–821
    and pricing and promotion, 819
  simulation models, 483–484
  structure of, 356–360
    customer contact intensity, 358–359
    design and strategy, 360
    immediacy of services, 358
    manufacturing/service mix, 357
    service package and intended customers, 357
    service-process matrix, 359
    site of services, 357–358
Shadow price, 192
Shewhart cycle, 600–601
Shipping
  Jefferson Smurfit Corp., 76
  Standard Register Co., 84
Shortage costs, 665
Shortest processing time (SPT) rule, 804, 805, 807, 811–812, **826**
Short-term forecasts, 105
Simo chart, 517–518
Simple exponential smoothing (SES), 120–122, 149
Simple linear causal models, 141
Simple moving average, 118–119, 149
Simplex algorithm, 182–188
  algebraic foundations of, 184–185
  constraint parameters, 183–184
  fourth tableau, 187–188
  initial simplex tableau, 185–186
  nonnegative right-hand sides, 183
  problem solution, preparing for, 183
  simplex pivot and second tableau, 186–187
  third tableau, 187
  variables must be nonnegative, 183–184
Simplex pivot and second tableau, 186–187
Simplex tableaus, 185–188
Simulated clock (clock time), 501
Simulated time (clock time), 487

Simulation, 468: *See also* Simulation analysis
computer, 387
and queueing systems, 430
Simulation analysis, 481–507
computer software and, 501
flexibility of, 482
output evaluation, 499–501
queueing simulation, 496–499
random phenomena generation, 487–493
from an exponential distribution, 492
from a continuous probability distribution, 490–491
from a continuous uniform distribution, 491
from a discrete probability distribution, 489–490
from a normal distribution, 493
random production line simulation, 494–496
replication of random phenomena, 500
sample simulations, 494–499
simulation models, 482, **501**
continuous *vs.* discrete event, 482
steps for, 485–487
know the system being modeled, 485–486
construct a model of the system, 486
test the model, 486
execute model runs and analyze the output, 487
plan the experimental design, 486
stochastic *vs.* deterministic, 482–485
types of, 482–485
time, simulation of, 487
utility of, 482
Simulation models, 482, **501:** *See also* Simulation analysis
Simultaneous motion chart, 517–518
Single-minute exchange of dies (SMED), 785
generalization of techniques, 766–767
procedure for, 764–766
total productive maintenance and, 772
Single-server systems
with exponential service times (M/M/1), 437–441
with general or constant service times (M/G/1 and M/D/1), 448–450
Site decisions, facility location, 270
Skill variation, repetitive process design, 379
Slack, scheduling, 853
Slack time remaining (STR) rule, 804, 806, 812–813
Slack variable, 183
Smoothing constant, 121, 149
Social justice, queueing systems, 464
Sociotechnical systems, of work organization, 538–539
Sole-sourcing (sole-supplier) vendor relationships, 698–699, **700,** 768
Solutions, 167
Sorting, UPS, 89
Sound, in work environment, 536–537
Spatial configuration
cellular processes, 402–403
repetitive process design, 384–385
Specialization of labor, 20
and job content, 510–511
Specifications
automatic evaluation of, 235
product design and, 226–227
Speculative demand, 756
Speculative inventories, 663–664
Staffing
Approved Statewide Title Agency (ASTA), 94–95
repetitive process design, 378–379
Standard components, product design and, 221–222
Standard time, 529
State of the system, 482, **501**
State variables, 482
Static decisions: *See* **Decision analysis**
Statistical process control (SPC), 562, 582–594, **606**
by attributes, 593–594
cycles, 592–593
run patterns, 592
theory of, 584
by variables, 583–592
Statistical quality control, 581–597
acceptance sampling, 582
cause-effect analysis, 594–597
defect tracking, 594–595
fishbone charts, 595–597
process control: *See* **Statistical process control (SPC)**
Steady expansion strategy, 257, 259–260
Steady state, 435
Steady-state equations, for queueing systems, 430, **468**
Steam engine, 19
Steiner-Weber model, 283–284
Stepping stone method, 305: *See also* **Transportation problems**
Stochastic models, 482–485
Stockout costs, 665
Storage
two bin system, for inventory storage, 698
and warehouse layout, 408–410, 412
Strategic production tasks, 40
Strategic weapon, operations management as, 11–13
Strategy, 12–13, **31,** 35
Structured analytical layout tools, functional layouts, 391–392
Subjective forecasting methods, 106
Subsystems, 11
Sum-of-digits weights, 120
Suppliers
product design participation, 218–219, 768
quality conformance and, 580
reliable delivery of materials, 767–768
sole-supplier relationships with, 698–699, **700,** 769
TQM programs extended to, 601
Support equipment, repetitive process design, 379
Synchronous (synchronized) production, 781–784, **785**
drum-buffer-rope mechanism, 783–784, **785,** 813–814
and JIT, integration with, 784
and MRP, integration with, 784
principles of, 782–783
theory of constraints, 782
System configuration, queueing systems: *See* **Queueing systems**
Systems and subsystems, methods analysis of, 516–517
Systems attributes, 482

Taguchi method
conformance quality and, 578
product design and, 227, 232–234
Tardiness, 804
Task decomposition, repetitive process design and, 372
Task level analysis, methods analysis for, 517
Tasks
performed in advance, queueing systems, 467
project, 842, **865**
critical, 853
dummy, 848
repetitive process design and, 379

Tasks *(continued)*
variety, specialization and, 510–511
Task times, 372
Taxes, facility location and, 268, 269
Team-activity chart, 521–522
Team design, 217
Technical capability, 46
benefits of, 48–49
maintaining, 47–48
Technology
Approved Statewide Title Agency (ASTA), 95
improvements in, repetitive process design, 378–379
Jefferson Smurfit Corp., 77
production processes and, 47–49, 325–368, 340–349
automation, 342–344
bar coding and optical scanning, 346–347
computer-aided design/computer-assisted manufacturing (CAD/CAM), 344
computer-integrated manufacturing (CIM), 346
computer numerically controlled (CNC) machines, 342
electronic data interchange (EDI), 347–348
energy efficiency and, 349
environmental considerations, 348–349
flexible manufacturing systems (FMS), 344–346
group technology (GT), 341–342
machining centers, 343
material usage reduction and, 348
numerically controlled (NC) machines, 342
Optimized Production Technology (OPT), 814–815, **826**
organization-wide application, 49
robots, 343–344
technical capability
benefits of, 48–49
maintaining, 47–48
toxic by-product reclamation/reduction, 348–349
Standard Register Co., 86–87
strategy: *See* **Operations strategies**
Temperature, of work environment, 536
Terminology, queueing systems, 434–437
Testing, design for, 225
Testing equipment, maintaining, 567
Theoretical minimum number of work stations, 375
Theory of constraints, 782
Therbligs, 533
Third tableau, simplex algorithm, 187
Thought processes, structuring, 170
Three-dimensional analysis, warehouse and storage layout, 409
Throughput, 782
Time, simulation of, 487
Time-based compensation systems, 542
Time buckets, 720
Time-cost trade-offs, in project process scheduling, 853–856
Time fences, 736
Time lag, 144
Time series data, 111
Time series models, 149
quantitative forecasting and, 113–115
cyclic component, 114
permanent component, 113
random component, 115
seasonal component, 113–114, 149
trend component, 113
Tolerance limits, 584
Tolerances, product design and, 226–227
Tolerance stack-up, 577
Tools, work aids and ergonomics, 524
Total material cost (TMC), 668
Total productive maintenance (TPM), 769–772, **785**
cleanliness and housekeeping, 771–772
excess capacity and, 770–771
human error reduction, 772
machine failures, 769–770
operators, maintenance and repairs by, 770
poka-yoke devices, 772
SMED setups and, 772
specialized personnel, 770
Total Quality Management (TQM), 56, 85, 598–604, **606**
Baldrige Awards, 604–605
Deming's 14-point program, 598–599
failure, common causes of, 601–603
history of, 598–599
ISO 9004 standards, 605
JIT production systems and, 772–774
job design and, 513
Juran's quality trilogy, 598–599
principles of, 599–601
success factors, 603–604
Total stocking cost (TSC), 669, 729
Toxic waste
reclaiming/reusing, 348–349
reducing production of, 348
Tracking control chart, 147
Tracking signals (TS), 146–147, **149**
Training
job design principles, 528
quality conformance and, 580–581
UPS, 91
Training Within Industry (TWI), 25
Transient, 435
Transportation network, 269
Transportation problems, 276–278, 298–311, **305**
degeneracy, 305
initial feasible solution, 299–300
maximization problems, 304
modified distribution (MODI) method, 303–304, **305**
northwest (NW) corner method, 300
problem preparation, 298–299
simulation models, 485
stepping stone method, 301–303
circuits and, 301–302
improving the solution, 302–303
optimality, checking for, 301
total supply not equal to total demand, 304–305
transportation tableau, 298–299
Vogel's approximation method (VAM), 300–301
Trend-adjusted moving average, 130–132
Trend component, time series models, 113
Truck assignments, UPS, 90–91
Two bin system, for inventory storage, 698
Two-pass method, of PERT/CPM analysis, 849–853, **865**
Two-phase method, linear programming models, 190–191
Two queues for each server, 467

Unbalancing, of processes, randomness and, 387
Unbounded problems, linear programming models, 182, 191
Uncertainty
in decision making, 313–314
linear programming models and, 193
Unions, 543–544
regional facility location and, 268
Unique products: *See* **Project processes**
U.S. Labor Department, 538

Units of production, learning curves and, 556
Universal product code (UPC), 346
Upper control limit, 585–586
Utilities, facility location and, 268
Utilization factor, 436

Value-added/labor ratio, 43
Value analysis, 242
  product design and, 231–232
Value-based productivity measures, 43–44
Value engineering, 231–232
Variance, in queueing systems: *See* **Queueing systems**
Vehicle routing, heuristic methods, 197
Vendors: *See* Suppliers
Vogel's approximation method (VAM), 300–301, **305**

Wagner-Whitin algorithm, 732–733, **741**
Waiting lines: *See* **Queueing systems**
Warehouse and storage layout, service system design, 408–410
Warranty expenses, 566
Waste elimination, lean production system, 26
Wave schedule, for appointments, 820
Weighted averages, 118, 149
  moving, 119–120, 149
Well behaved, 432
Winding, cutting and shipping, Jefferson Smurfit Corp., 76
Work aids, 524–528, **544**
  ergonomics, 524–526, 578
  motion economy principles, 525
  poka-yoke (mistake proofing), 526–528, 577–578, 599
  tools and equipment, 524
  workplace convenience, 526
Work cells, 335: *See also* **Cells**
Work centers
  description, 388
  interaction estimation, 388–391
    flow-cost matrix, 390
    flow matrix, 390
    proximity charts, 390–391
Work environment, 536–538
  accidents, 537–538
  factors affecting performance, 536–537
  health of employees and, 538
  safety of, 537–538
Worker and task level analysis, methods analysis for, 517
Worker consultation, job design principles, 524
Worker-machine chart, 518–520, **544**
Worker-machine coordination, 518–521
Work methods, analysis and improvement, 515–528
  methods analysis, 516–523, **544**
    group coordination, 521–523
    process charts/flow diagrams, 516–517, **544**
    systems and subsystems, 516–517
    worker and task level analysis, 517
    worker-machine coordination, 518–521
  training, 528
  work aids and ergonomics: *See* **Work aids**
  work environment: *See* Work environment
  work standards: *See* **Work standards**
Work organization, 538–544
  autonomous work groups: *See* **Autonomous work groups/teams**
  compensation system, 542–543
  flex-time policies, 541–542
  home-based workers, 540–541
  labor unions and, 543–544
  self-directed teams, 539–540
  sociotechnical systems, 539–540
Workplace convenience, work aids and ergonomics, 526
Work sampling, 533–535, **544**
Workshop Management, 21
Work standards, 529–530, **544**
  capacity planning, 529–530
  developing, 530–535
  elemental standard-time data, 532
  employee evaluation and compensation, 529
  micro-motion, 533, **544**
  motion and time study, 530–532, **544**
  motion-time data, predetermined, 533
  observation and measurement, 530–535
  personnel and production scheduling, 529
  process design and capacity planning, 529–530
  product costing and pricing, 529
  scheduling and, 825
  work sampling, 533–535, **544**
Work stations, 329
  design of, for repetitive processes, 372–373
    number minimizing heuristic, 374–377
  parallel, 380–381
X-(control) chart, 585–586, 590–592

Yield losses, 566

Zero-inventory systems, 659–660